Dreamweaver CC

the missing manual®

The book that should have been in the box®

David Sawyer McFarland and Chris Grover

O'REILLY®

am | Köln | Sebastopol | Tokyo

Dreamweaver CC: The Missing Manual

by David Sawyer McFarland and Christopher Grover

Published by O'Reilly Media, Inc.,
1005 Gravenstein Highway North, Sebastopol, CA 95472.

O'Reilly books may be purchased for educational, business, or sales promotional use. Online editions are also available for most titles (*http://my.safaribooksonline.com*). For more information, contact our corporate/institutional sales department: (800) 998-9938 or *corporate@oreilly.com*.

December 2013:   First Edition.

Revision History for the First Edition:

2013-12-09   First release

See *http://oreilly.com/catalog/errata.csp?isbn=0636920027461* for release details.

ISBN-13: 978-1-449-34170-1

Contents

Part Two: Building a Better Web Page

Part Six: **Appendixes**

The Missing Credits

ABOUT THE AUTHORS

 David Sawyer McFarland is president of Sawyer McFarland Media, Inc., a web development and training company in Portland, Oregon. He's been building websites since 1995, when he designed his first site, an online magazine for communication professionals. He's served as the Webmaster at the University of California at Berkeley and the Berkeley Multimedia Research Center, and he has helped build, design, and program numerous websites for clients including *Macworld.com*, among others.

In addition to building websites, David is a writer, trainer, and instructor. He's taught web design at the UC Berkeley Graduate School of Journalism, the Center for Electronic Art, the Academy of Art College, and the Art Institute of Portland. He currently teaches in the Multimedia Program at Portland State University. He's written articles about web design for *Practical Web Design*, *Macworld*, and *CreativePro.com*.

David is also the author of *CSS: The Missing Manual* and *JavaScript & jQuery: The Missing Manual*.

 Chris Grover is a veteran of the San Francisco Bay Area advertising and design community. Chris is the owner of Bolinas Road Creative (*www.bolinasroad.com*), an agency that helps businesses promote their products and services. Chris has written several books in the Missing Manual series and has produced training videos for video2brain, *Educator.com*, and *Lynda.com*.

Chris welcomes feedback about this book by email at *dreamweaver@bolinasroad. com*. (If you need technical help, however, please refer to the sources listed in Appendix A: Getting Help.)

ABOUT THE CREATIVE TEAM

Peter McKie (editor) has a master's degree from Boston University's School of Journalism and lives in New York City. In his spare time, he digitizes archival photos of his summer community. Email: *pmckie@oreilly.com*.

Kara Ebrahim (production editor) lives, works, and plays in Cambridge, MA. She loves graphic design and all things outdoors. Email: *kebrahim@oreilly.com*.

Murray R. Summers (technical reviewer) is an Adobe Certified Dreamweaver Developer and Community Professional. He has co-authored and contributed chapters to several books on Dreamweaver, been the technical editor for the last eight editions of the Dreamweaver Missing Manual, and presented at multiple national conferences. His company, Great Web Sights, has been active in web development since 1998. Murray lives in southern Delaware with his wife, Suzanne. One daughter works at Clemson University and lives in Greenville, SC, and the other is a skilled web developer (*carolinawebcreations.biz*). His two sons live and work in Virginia Beach.

Danilo Celic, Jr. (technical reviewer) has been using Dreamweaver since version 1.2. In the years since, he has contributed to the Dreamweaver community in a variety of capacities. He has been a co-author, technical editor, and technical reviewer for a shelf full of Dreamweaver- and Web-related books. He loves sharing what he has learned over the years of the inner workings of Dreamweaver and various web technologies. Danilo lives in the suburbs of Chicago with his wife, Melissa, who patiently forgives the late hours he puts in in front of a glowing screen. Email: *danilo@shimmerphase.com*.

Carla Spoon (proofreader) is a freelance writer and copyeditor. An avid runner, she works and feeds her tech gadget addiction from her home office in the shadow of Mount Rainier. Email: *carla_spoon@comcast.net*.

Julie Hawks (indexer) is a teacher and eternal student. She can be found wandering about with a camera in hand. Email: *juliehawks@gmail.com*.

ACKNOWLEDGMENTS

Thanks to all those who have helped with this book (and all of my books over the years): my students, colleagues, and the wonderful people at O'Reilly. Thanks to Murray Summers and Danilo Celic for their careful scrutiny and erudite corrections to my writing; thanks also to Peter McKie for making my writing more energetic and clearer.

—Dave McFarland

I'm always amazed at the number of pros it takes to create a book like *Dreamweaver CC: The Missing Manual*. My thanks go to out to everyone who worked on this book, including the technical reviewers. I also want to thank my wife, Joyce, for her love and support.

—Chris Grover

THE MISSING MANUAL SERIES

Missing Manuals are witty, superbly written guides to computer products that don't come with printed manuals (which is just about all of them). Each book features a handcrafted index.

Recent and upcoming titles include:

Windows 8.1: The Missing Manual by David Pogue

Switching to the Mac: The Missing Manual, Mavericks Edition by David Pogue

OS X Mavericks: The Missing Manual by David Pogue

HTML5: The Missing Manual, Second Edition by Matthew MacDonald

Photoshop Elements 12: The Missing Manual by Barbara Brundage

Photoshop CC: The Missing Manual by Lesa Snider

Office 2013: The Missing Manual by Nancy Connor, Matthew MacDonald

Quickbooks 2013: The Missing Manual by Bonnie Biafore

WordPress: The Missing Manual by Matthew MacDonald

For a full list of all Missing Manuals in print, go to *www.missingmanuals.com/library. html.*

Preface

Websites evolve every year, growing in scope, capability, and complexity, making sites look and work ever better over time. Even people with personal sites use a collection of programming languages and server technologies to dish up their content.

Throughout its history, Dreamweaver has kept pace with the changing web-development landscape, and Adobe's latest offering, Dreamweaver Creative Cloud, is no exception—it does more than any previous version of the program. Whether you want to use Cascading Style Sheets (CSS) for cutting-edge site design, create JavaScript-powered dynamic web pages, incorporate HTML5, build websites for mobile devices, use content management systems like WordPress or Drupal, or simply stick to straightforward HTML, Dreamweaver has just about all the tools you need.

Any enterprising designer can create web pages, Cascading Style Sheets, and even JavaScript programs using just a simple text editor. In fact, Dreamweaver CC's powerful text editor lets you handcraft files to create any kind of web file you want, from simple HTML content to complex database-powered web pages. However, typing in HTML, CSS, and JavaScript code is not only a recipe for carpal tunnel syndrome, it's a slow and typo-prone way to build web pages. Dreamweaver provides buttons, dialog boxes, and panels that let you add HTML, CSS, and JavaScript quickly, with fewer keystrokes. For example, in a matter of seconds, a simple button lets you insert the complex HTML required to insert a video into your web page. And Dreamweaver is flexible enough to let you hand-code pages and use time-saving HTML shortcuts in tandem—the choice is yours.

NOTE   To emphasize that its Creative Suite applications (Dreamweaver, Photoshop, InDesign, and so on) now reside exclusively in the cloud, Adobe added "CC" to the creative suite product names. So, for this new version of Dreamweaver, what used to be Dreamweaver CS6 has become Dreamweaver CC. Throughout this book, and out there in the site design/developer world, the name is usually shortened to CC.

■ What Dreamweaver Is All About

Dreamweaver is a complete website development and site-management program. It works with web technologies like HTML, XHTML, CSS, JavaScript, and PHP.

Its CSS support lets you create fast-loading, easily modified pages, while its support for the popular jQuery JavaScript framework lets you create complex, interactive page elements, like tabbed panels and collapsible content panels, with a single key click.

Dreamweaver also includes plenty of tools to manage your sites once you build them. You can check for broken links, use templates to implement site-wide page changes, and reorganize your site in a flash with the program's site-management tools.

NOTE   If you're unfamiliar with the acronym CSS, it stands for Cascading Style Sheets—a set of rules you write that dictate the look of your pages. Dreamweaver includes advanced tools to create, test, and edit CSS in your pages.

If you've built one or more sites without Dreamweaver, you don't have to start over again. The program happily opens web pages and websites created in other programs without destroying any of your carefully crafted code.

■ Why Dreamweaver?

You can find dozens of web design programs on the market, but Dreamweaver is one of the leaders, thanks to key benefits like these:

- **Visual page-building**. If you've ever spent time using a text editor to punch out HTML for your web pages, you know the tedium involved in adding even a simple photograph. When your boss asks you to add her photo to the company home page, you launch your trusty text editor and type in something like *<img src="images/staff/bigcheese.jpg" width="100" height="150" alt="The Boss">*. Not only is this approach prone to typos, it separates you from what you want the page to *look* like.

  Dreamweaver, on the other hand, gives you a several ways to stay in touch with your page's visual design. If your interest is in design and not HTML, you can work in the program's Design view. Drag an image to your budding web page there, and Dreamweaver displays the picture on the page. Just as a word processor displays documents as they'll look when you print them out, so Dreamweaver gives you a close approximation of what your page will look like in a web browser.

Because Dreamweaver's Design view is only an approximation of what a page will look like in a browser, the program offers Live view, too—a real-time look at your page in a browser built right into Dreamweaver. Using it, you can see what a page looks like and how it behaves without leaving Dreamweaver!

Another approach web designers commonly use is monitoring a page's code and its appearance side-by-side. Dreamweaver's Split view handles that, giving you direct access to the HTML of a page on one half of the screen and to its visual look on the other half. For the visual half, you can use either Design view, or, for greatest accuracy, Live view. Using this technique, you can hammer out your HTML in the Code view half of the monitor and quickly see the effect in a web browser in the Live view half of your screen.

- **Complex interactivity, simply**. You've probably seen web pages where an image (on a navigation bar, for example) lights up or changes appearance when you mouse over it. Dynamic effects like these—mouse rollovers, alert boxes, and pop-up dialog boxes—usually require JavaScript programming, a language browsers understand. While JavaScript can do amazing things, it requires time and practice to learn.

  Dreamweaver CC now supports the wildly popular jQuery JavaScript framework, and its sister project, jQuery UI, which provides easy-to-use "widgets" that make adding interactive page elements like tabbed panels, pop-up date selectors, and dialog boxes a breeze.

> **NOTE** Dreamweaver CC drops the "Spry" JavaScript framework that older versions of the program supported in favor of the jQuery framework. See page 573 and the note on page 575 for details.

- **Solid code**. Every now and then, even in Dreamweaver, you may want to put aside the visual view and look at a page's underlying HTML. You may want to tweak the code that Dreamweaver produces, for example, or see how Dreamweaver writes code.

  Adobe realizes that many professional web developers do a lot of work "in the trenches," typing in HTML, CSS, and JavaScript code by hand. In Dreamweaver, you can edit a page's raw HTML to your heart's content. Switching back and forth between Design view and Code view is seamless and, best of all, nondestructive. Unlike many visual web page programs, where making a change in the visual mode stomps all over the underlying HTML, Dreamweaver respects hand-typed code and doesn't try to rewrite it (unless you ask it to). You can even use Dreamweaver's Split view to see your HTML side-by-side with a representation of your final page.

  In addition, Dreamweaver can open many other types of files commonly used on websites, such as external JavaScript files (.js files), so you don't have to switch to another program to work on them. Dreamweaver's Related Files toolbar lists all CSS, JavaScript, and server-side files the current document uses. For hand-coders, this feature means that editing a page's CSS or JavaScript is just a click away (instead of a time-draining File→Open hunt for that danged file). Chapter 7 has the scoop on how Dreamweaver handles writing and editing code.

- **Site-management tools**. Rarely will you build just a single web page. More often, you'll create and edit pages that work together to form part of a website. Or you may build an entire website from scratch.

  Either way, Dreamweaver's site-management tools make your job easier. They automate many of the routine tasks every webmaster faces, from managing links, images, pages, and other media, to working with a team of people and moving your site to a web server. Part 4 of this book looks at how Dreamweaver helps you build and maintain websites.

UP TO SPEED

Hand Coding vs. Visual Editors

At one time, creating web pages in a text editor was considered the best way to build websites. The precise control that hand-written code gave you over HTML was (and often still is) seen as the only way to assure quality web pages.

Professional site developers championed hand-coding because many early visual page-building programs added unnecessary code—code that affected how a page appeared and how long it took to download over the Internet. But hand-coding is time-consuming and error-prone. One typo can render a web page useless.

Fortunately, Dreamweaver creates solid code even in a visual environment. Since its earliest incarnation, Dreamweaver has prided itself on its ability to produce clean HTML and its tolerance for code created by other programs—including text editors. In fact, Dreamweaver includes a powerful built-in text-editing mode that lets you freely manipulate the HTML of a page—or any other code, including JavaScript, Visual Basic, XML, PHP, and ColdFusion Markup Language.

But the real story behind the code Dreamweaver produces in Design mode is that it's as solid and well-written as hand-hewn code. Knowing this, feel free to take advantage of the increased productivity that Dreamweaver's visual-editing mode brings to your day-to-day work with its one-click objects, instant JavaScript, and simplified layout tools. Doing so won't compromise your code and will certainly let you finish your website in record time.

Honestly, no web design program is really WYSIWYG ("what you see is what you get"). Because every browser renders the HTML language slightly differently, web design is more like WYSIRWYGOAGD: "what you see is roughly what you get, on a good day." That's why Dreamweaver's Live view can help you make sure your pages look the way you *really* want them to.

Finally, if you have experience hand-coding HTML and CSS, you'll be pleasantly surprised by Dreamweaver's powerful text-editing capabilities. In fact, even though Dreamweaver has a reputation as a *visual* web page editor, it's also one of the best text-editing programs on the market.

- **Have it your way**. As if Dreamweaver didn't have enough going for it, the program's engineers have created a completely customizable product, or, as they call it, an *extensible* program. Anyone can add to or change Dreamweaver's menus, commands, objects, and windows.

  Suppose, for example, that you hardly ever use any of the commands in the Edit menu. By editing one text file in the Dreamweaver Configuration folder, you can get rid of unwanted menu items—or even add commands of your own creation. This incredible flexibility lets you customize Dreamweaver to fit the way you work, and even add features that Adobe's programmers never imagined. Best of all, the Adobe Exchange website includes hundreds of free and commercial extensions for Dreamweaver. See Chapter 21 for details.

■ What's New in Dreamweaver CC

If you haven't used Dreamweaver before, see Chapter 1 for the grand tour. If you're upgrading from Dreamweaver CS6 or some other version of the program, you'll find that Dreamweaver CC offers a host of new features:

- **HTML5** is touted by everyone from AT&T to Google as the next big thing (described in more detail on page 430). It's the first major change to HTML in years, and it promises to make building powerful websites easier than ever. Dreamweaver CS6 introduced very basic support for HTML5 that simplified hand-coding the new HTML5 tags. Fortunately, Dreamweaver CC brings HTML5 to Design view, providing simple menu options that let you insert new HTML5 elements like <header>, <article>, <nav>, <section>, and so on. It also now lets you insert the many useful HTML5 form elements, such as web addresses, date, email addresses, and search fields, among others. Finally, CC makes adding the HTML5 <video> and <audio> tags easy, so you can insert video and audio that works on smartphones as well as web browsers.

- **CSS** is the heart of web design. While HTML provides the structure for content, CSS gives it color, layout, and graphical interest. Because CSS is so fundamental to web design, Adobe took a long look at how designers use CSS and completely revamped CSS creation and editing in CC. As a result, you'll use the CSS Designer panel to visually manage complex sets of styles. You'll use the CSS Transitions panel to develop engaging and useful visual effects. These new tools are covered on page 397.

- **Web Fonts.** Dreamweaver CC's typography options build off of the web fonts feature added in Dreamweaver CS6. In addition to being able to use your own set of fonts, CC lets you take advantage of free, hosted fonts from Adobe using Adobe Edge Web Fonts. This free service gives you access to dozens and dozens of fonts. You'll learn more about this new feature on page 128.

- **Mobile web design**. Dreamweaver CS6 introduced many new tools to help designers build websites that work on mobile devices like smartphones and tablets. CC improves on this "fluid grid layout" feature, which lets you create designs that re-flow content to match different devices. For example, using the same HTML, you can create designs that display a single column of content for a phone, two columns for a tablet, and three or more columns for a spacious desktop monitor. CC adds support for nested elements, and significantly improves the workflow for fluid grids.

- **jQuery UI.** Dreamweaver CC replaces Adobe's outdated Spry framework with the wildly popular jQuery library and its user-interface toolkit known as jQuery UI. Unfortunately, jQuery UI doesn't replace all the Spry widgets available in earlier versions of Dreamweaver (see page xix for more on Spry and what's missing).

Life in the Cloud

Adobe Creative applications, like Dreamweaver, no longer come from a disc in a box—they come from the cloud. That change may have a greater effect on your wallet than it does on your computer. Like many other companies, Adobe decided it is better to get a little money from you each month than it is to get big whopping sums every couple of years. In essence, you lease Creative Cloud software. You can pay $19.99 a month for the license to use Dreamweaver or $49.99 a month for the license to use Dreamweaver and a whole suite of creative apps such as Photoshop, Illustrator, InDesign, Flash, and Premiere Pro. Those are just the major tools; the complete list is really pretty impressive. See *http://www.adobe.com/products/ creativecloud.html*.

The first time you install an app, like Dreamweaver, from the Creative Cloud, you use the Download Center—a web page that you log into after you've paid the licensing fee. Click on the Download button next to the Dreamweaver icon and follow the links and instructions to download and install the application on your computer. Yes, that's right, Dreamweaver CC is an application that's installed on the hard drive of your computer, just like the previous versions. The difference is that periodically, Dreamweaver will check back with the mothership to make sure you still have a license to use the program. Depending on your agreement with Adobe, that period is either 30 days or 99 days. If you don't have a valid license, you can't use the app. The web pages that you've created in Dreamweaver won't disappear, you just can't use Dreamweaver to work on the project unless you're paid up and licensed.

When you first install Dreamweaver or any other Creative Cloud app on your computer, you also install the Creative Cloud desktop app, which keeps track of the Adobe CC apps on your computer and notifies you when there are updates. Once the CC app is installed, you can install and update Dreamweaver or any of the other apps that you are licensed to use. All it takes is a click of a button.

NOTE The Creative Cloud app is compatible with Windows 7 or later or Mac OS X 10.7 or later. If you have an earlier operating system, you use the older Adobe Application Manager to download and install CC applications.

What's Gone in Dreamweaver CC

With Dreamweaver CC, Adobe took a long, hard look at a fairly old program. They decided that it was time for some serious housecleaning:

- **Server behaviors.** Dreamweaver's innovative server behaviors were a boon to those afraid of server-side programming. They let non-programmers add basic database integration into their websites, making it easy to add forms to collect (and store) visitor information. For the last several versions of the program, however, Adobe largely ignored Dreamweaver server behaviors, and the code behind their magic wasn't up to current programming standards. In CC, Adobe finally pulled the plug on these database tools. If you want to integrate your site with a database, you either need to learn how to program the website-database interaction yourself or use an extension that adds the tools necessary to create database-driven web pages. For that, you can turn to a third party solution, such as WebAsisst (*www.webassist.com*).

- **Spry.** Adobe's Spry JavaScript Framework for AJAX was once a cutting-edge set of tools that made building forms, drop-down menus, and other interactive page features simple. However, the programming behind these elements is out of date, and a hugely popular replacement, jQuery, has arisen out of the world of open source software. jQuery is a free JavaScript framework that more than 40 percent of the world's websites use. Adobe wisely realized that they could never keep their Spry framework up to the level of jQuery and, in Dreamweaver CC, dropped support for Spry and replaced it with jQuery and the jQuery user interface library. However, while Adobe replaced many Spry widgets with jQuery counterparts, there are a few exceptions: For example, there's no longer a tool that lets you build drop-down navigation menus, nor are there any tools that let you validate forms. See the box on page 575 for more.

- **BrowserLab.** Earlier versions of Dreamweaver integrated directly with BrowserLab, Adobe's online service that displayed your web pages in a variety of browsers. BrowserLab let you see, for example, if your page looked the same in Internet Explorer 7 as it did in Google Chrome. However, Adobe closed BrowserLab in March 2013 and removed it from Dreamweaver CC. Adobe now refers developers to BrowserStack (*www.browserstack.com/*) and Sauce Labs (*https://saucelabs.com/*) for web pages. Adobe recommends using their Edge Inspect tool (*adobe.com/edge/inspect/*) for mobile web projects.

- **Assorted changes.** Dreamweaver CC boasts a number of smaller changes, too. Among them are the removal of the panel that let you manage absolutely positioned elements (see page 457 for more on absolute positioning), the link to Adobe's Bridge program so you could browse for files outside of Dreamweaver, and the File→Convert tool that translated the HTML of one type (say, XHTML) to the HTML of another type (HTML5, for example).

◼ HTML Basics

Under the hood of any web page—whether it's your uncle's "Check out this summer's fishin'" page or the front door of a billion-dollar online retailer—is nothing more than line after line of ordinary text. You embed simple commands, called tags, within this text. Web browsers know how to interpret these tags to properly display your pages.

When you create a page with tags in it, the document becomes known as an HTML page (for Hypertext Markup Language). HTML is at the heart of most of the Web.

The HTML code that creates a web page can be as simple as this:

```
<!DOCTYPE HTML PUBLIC "-//W3C//DTD HTML 4.01 Transitional//EN"
                "http://www.w3.org/TR/html4/loose.dtd">
<html>
<head>
<title>Hey, I am the title of this web page.</title>
</head>
<body>
<p>Hey, I am some body text on this web page.</p>
</body>
</html>
```

While it may not be exciting, this short bit of HTML is all you need to create an actual web page.

■ Document Types

The first line of the code above:

```
<!DOCTYPE HTML PUBLIC "-//W3C//DTD HTML 4.01 Transitional//EN"
                "http://www.w3.org/TR/html4/loose.dtd">
```

is called a "doctype," and it identifies the flavor of HTML you used to create the page. Developers have used two doctypes for years—HTML 4.01 and XHTML 1.0—and each has two versions: *strict* and *transitional*. Dreamweaver can create any type of HTML— you simply tell it which you want when you create a new web page (see page 25).

Dreamweaver even lets you use the latest, greatest, and simplest doctype, HTML5. It replaces the extraneous code of earlier doctypes with much simpler and straight-forward code:

```
<!DOCTYPE HTML>
```

Yep, that's the entire doctype declaration. HTML5 is much easier to use than plain old HTML in many ways, and Dreamweaver CC supports this new version of the web's *lingua franca*. This book uses the HTML5 doctype—it's short, simple, and supported by every major browser (even back to Internet Explorer 6). And because HTML5 is the future of the Web, there's no reason to use older doctypes.

But no matter which doctype you use, it's important that you always use one, be-cause without it, different browsers display CSS differently, and your pages will look different depending on your visitor's browser.

Different doctypes do require that you write your HTML in a particular way. For example, the line break tag looks like this in HTML 4.01:

```
<br>
```

But in XHTML, you write it this way:

```
<br />
```

HTML5 lets you write it either way. Fortunately, you won't have to worry about these subtle differences when you use Dreamweaver to insert your HTML—it automatically adjusts to the doctype you chose, inserting the appropriate HTML.

■ Of Tags and Properties

In the preceding example—and, indeed, in the HTML of any web page—you'll notice that most commands appear in *pairs* that enclose a block of text or other commands.

These bracketed commands, like the <p> command that denotes the beginning of a paragraph, constitute the "markup" part of HTML (hypertext *markup* language), and they're called *tags*. Sandwiched between greater-than and less-than signs, tags are simply instructions that tell a web browser how to display a page.

The starting tag of each pair tells a browser where the instruction begins, and the closing tag tells it where the instruction ends. A closing tag always includes a forward slash (/) after the first bracket symbol (<), so the closing tag for the paragraph command above is </p>.

Fortunately, Dreamweaver can generate all these tags *automatically*. You don't have to memorize or even type them in (although many programmers still enjoy doing so for greater control). Behind the scenes, Dreamweaver's all-consuming mission is to convert your visual design into underlying code, like this:

- The <html> tag appears once at the beginning of a web page and again (with an added closing slash) at the end. This tells a browser that the information between these two tags is written in HTML, as opposed to some other language. All the contents of the page, including any other tags, appear between these opening and closing <html> tags.

  If you were to think of a web page as a tree, the <html> tag would be its trunk. Springing from the trunk are two branches that represent the two main parts of any web page: the head of the page and the body.

- The *head* of a web page contains the title of the page ("Izzie's Mail-Order Pencils"). It may also include other, invisible information, such as a page description, that browsers and search engines use. You surround the head section with opening and closing <head> tags.

  The head section can also include information that browsers use to format a page's HTML and add interactivity. You can store CSS styles and JavaScript code in the head, for example, or you can embed links to external CSS and JavaScript files there. In fact, the interactivity you'll see in Dreamweaver's jQuery UI widgets (Chapter 13) work with the help of JavaScript code stored in separate files on a server; the link to these files resides in the page's head section.

The *body* of a web page, identified by its beginning and ending <body> tags, contains all the content that appears inside a browser window—headlines, text, pictures, and so on. When you work in Dreamweaver's Design view, the blank white portion of the document window represents the body area. It resembles the blank page of a word-processing program.

Most of your work with Dreamweaver will involve inserting and formatting text, pictures, and other objects into the body portion of a document. Many tags commonly used in web pages appear within the <body> tag. Here are a few:

- You can tell a web browser where a paragraph of text begins with a <p> (opening paragraph) tag, and where it ends with a </p> (closing paragraph) tag.

- The <strong> tag emphasizes text. The text between an opening and closing <strong> tag shows up as boldfaced. The HTML snippet <strong>Warning!</strong> tells a web browser to display the word "Warning!" in bold type on the screen.

- The <a> tag, or anchor tag, creates a link (hyperlink) on a web page. A link, of course, can lead anywhere on the Web. How do you tell a browser where the link should point? Simply give address instructions inside the <a> tags. For instance, you might type *<a href="http://www.missingmanuals.com">Click here!</a>*.

The browser knows that when your visitor clicks the words "Click here!", it should go to the Missing Manuals website. The *href* part of the tag is called, in Dreamweaver, a *property* (you may also hear it called an *attribute*), and the URL (the Uniform Resource Locator, or web address) is the *value* of that property. In this example, *http://www.missingmanuals.com* is the value of the *href* property.

Fortunately, Dreamweaver exempts you from having to type any of this code, letting you add properties to tags (and other page elements) through an easy-to-use window called the *Properties panel*. To create links the Dreamweaver way (read: the easy way), turn to Chapter 4.

NOTE For a full-fledged introduction to HTML, check out *Creating a Website: The Missing Manual, 3rd Edition*. For a primer geared to readers who want to master CSS, pick up a copy of *CSS3: The Missing Manual*. And if you want to add interactivity to your web pages (beyond the cool, ready-to-use features that Dreamweaver offers), you might be interested in *JavaScript & jQuery: The Missing Manual*. End of advertisements; now back to your regularly scheduled book.

■ XHTML in Dreamweaver

Like any technology, HTML has evolved over time. Although standard HTML has served its purpose well, it's always been a somewhat sloppy language. Among other things, it allows uppercase, lowercase, and mixed-case letters in tags (<body>, <BODY>, and <bODy> are all correct, for example) and permits unclosed tags (so you can use an opening <p> tag without a closing </p> tag to create a paragraph, for instance). While this flexibility may make page-writing easier, it also makes life more difficult for web browsers, smartphones, and other technologies that must interact with these pages. Additionally, HTML doesn't work with one still-useful Internet language, XML (Extensible Markup Language).

To keep pace with the times, an improved version of HTML, called XHTML, was introduced back in 2000, and you'll find it used frequently on many sites (in fact, XHTML is just an "XML-ified" version of HTML). Dreamweaver CC can create and work with XHTML files as well as plain old HTML pages.

NOTE XHTML was seen as the future back in 2000, but HTML5 has since supplanted it. While web browsers still understand XHTML (and probably will for a long time), you won't be using it in this book.

■ HTML5, The New Markup Standard

HTML5 isn't some radically new technology. In fact, unlike XHTML, which was intended to foster a new way to build web pages, HTML5 is about making sure the Web continues to work as it always has. Most of the basics of HTML are still in place. HTML5 adds a few new elements that support the way designers build websites today. In HTML5, for example, the <header> tag contains the content you'd usually find at the top of a page, such as a logo and site-wide navigation links; the new <nav> tag encloses the set of links used to navigate a site; and the <footer> tag houses the stuff you usually put at the bottom of a page, like legal notices, email contacts, and so on.

In addition, HTML5 adds new tags that let you insert video and audio into a page, add sophisticated form elements like drop-down date-pickers, and validate forms to make sure visitors fill them out correctly. Unfortunately, browser support for these new features isn't consistent and it's therefore difficult to use the new tags without some pretty elaborate workarounds to ensure cross-browser support.

Dreamweaver CC includes new tools that work with HTML5. Click-to-insert buttons make it easy to insert HTML5 tags like <header>, <footer>, <article>, and <section>. And CC supports the HTML5 <video> and <audio> tags that make your pages come to life with video and sound.

But new tags are just one small part of the HTML5 story. HTML5 started life as a product of the Web Hypertext Application Technology Group (WHATG), which wanted to create a version of HTML that provided the tools needed to build powerful, browser-based applications, like Google's Gmail program. So, much of HTML5 is devoted to powerful (and complicated) technologies like Canvas (for drawing pictures and diagrams on a web page), data storage (for storing information like game scores, preferences, and notes on a visitor's computer), drag and drop functionality, "web workers" for making JavaScript programs run faster and more efficiently, and "web sockets" for streaming data from a web server. All these technologies are promising, but browser support for them varies. In addition, Dreamweaver doesn't provide any easy-to-use tools to tap into these complicated technologies, so you're a few years off from being able to easily include most HTML5 functionality on your site.

Add Style with Cascading Style Sheets

In the beginning, HTML was the only language you needed to create web pages. You could build them with colorful text and graphics, and make words jump out using a limited selection of fonts, font sizes, and font colors. Today, however, you can add much more visual stimulation using Cascading Style Sheets. CSS is a formatting language that lets you design pages with sophisticated layouts and precise typographic control. For example, it gives you site-wide design consistency for headings and subheads, lets you create unique-looking sidebars, and lets you add special graphics treatment for quotations.

From now on, think of HTML as merely the scaffolding you use to organize a page. It helps identify and structure page elements. Tags like <h1> and <h2> denote headlines and reflect their relative importance. A *Heading 1* is more important than a *Heading 2*, for example (and can affect how a search engine like Google adds a page to its search listings). The <p> tag indicates a basic paragraph of information. Other tags provide further structural clues: For example, a <ul> tag identifies a bulleted list (to, say, make a list of recipe ingredients more intelligible).

Cascading Style Sheets, on the other hand, add *design flair* to that highly structured content, making it more beautiful and easier to read. Take a look at the CSS Zen Garden site (*www.csszengarden.com*). Each of the striking, very different websites profiled there use the same underlying HTML. The only difference among them—and the sole reason they look different—is that each uses a different style sheet. Essentially, a CSS style is just a rule that tells a browser how to display a particular page element—to make an <h1> tag appear orange, 36 pixels tall, and in the Verdana font, for example.

But CSS is more powerful than that. You use it to add borders, change margins, and even control the exact placement of an element on a page.

To be a successful web designer, you need to get to know Cascading Style Sheets. You'll learn more about this exciting technology throughout this book.

Add Interactivity with JavaScript

A normal web page—just regular HTML and CSS—isn't very interactive. About the only interaction visitors have with a page like that is clicking a link to load a new page. JavaScript is a programming language that lets you supercharge your HTML with animation, interactivity, and dynamic visual effects. It can also make a web page more responsive to visitors by supplying immediate feedback. For example, a JavaScript-powered shopping cart can instantly display the total cost of your purchase, tax and shipping included, the moment a visitor selects a product to buy. Or

JavaScript can produce an error message immediately after someone attempts to submit a web form that's missing information.

JavaScript's main selling point is immediacy. It lets web pages respond instantly to visitor actions: clicking a link, filling out a form, or merely moving the mouse around the screen, for instance. JavaScript doesn't suffer from the frustrating delay associated with "server-side" interactive programming languages like PHP, which require that a web browser communicate with a remote web server before the browser does anything. It doesn't rely on constantly loading and reloading pages, so your pages respond with the immediacy of a desktop program.

If you've visited Google Maps (*http://maps.google.com*), you've seen JavaScript in action. Google Maps lets you zoom in to get a detailed view of streets and zoom out to get a birds-eye view of how to get across town, the state, or the nation, all from the same web page. While there have been lots of map sites before Google, they always loaded a new page every time you changed a view (a usually slow process).

The JavaScript programs you create can range from the really simple (such as popping up a new browser window with a web page in it) to full-blown "web applications," such as Google Docs (*http://docs.google.com*), which let you edit documents, build spreadsheets, and create presentations using your web browser—all as though the program were running on your computer.

JavaScript programming can be difficult, but Dreamweaver has plenty of tools that let you add sophisticated interactivity to your sites—from animations to pop-up dialog boxes—with just a few clicks of your mouse.

■ Mobile Web Design

There's no doubt that mobile phones have changed how we live. They're also changing how we build websites. The small screens of iPhones and Android phones don't treat wide, three-column web pages kindly. Many sites shrink down to postage-stamp size when you look at them on a phone, requiring you to pinch, zoom, swipe, and scroll to find what you're looking for. Fortunately, you can have websites redraw themselves to fit the smaller sizes of mobile phones. Dreamweaver CC includes several solutions: the new fluid grid layout tool (page 544) lets you design three layouts (for phones, tablets, and desktop screens) using the same HTML. In other words, you only have a single web page, but using CSS, you can dynamically alter the page's layout depending on the width of the viewing screen. You can also craft your own "media queries" (a CSS3 feature discussed on page 506) to create CSS styles that apply only to screens at particular widths or within a particular range of widths.

Dreamweaver CC lets you create mobile-only websites, too, using jQuery Mobile (page 521), a JavaScript tool that makes traditional websites look and function more like mobile applications (and less like web pages).

■ How This Book Is Organized

Dreamweaver CC: The Missing Manual is divided into five parts, each with several chapters:

- **Part 1** explores Dreamweaver's main screens and takes you through the basic steps of page-building. It explains how to add and format text, link from one page to another, and spice up your design with graphics. It also introduces you to Cascading Style Sheets.

- **Part 2** takes you deeper into Dreamweaver and provides in-depth CSS coverage, including that for Dreamweaver's new CSS Designer and CSS Transitions tools. In addition, you'll get step-by-step instructions for creating advanced page layouts, as well as advice on how to view and work with the underlying HTML of a page.

- **Part 3** helps you add interactivity to your site. From the new jQuery UI widgets that let you add tabbed interfaces to forms that collect information from visitors, this section guides you through adding animation, multimedia, and other interactive effects with ease. The last chapter in this section explains how to add HTML5 video and audio, Flash animation, and Edge Animate compositions to your web pages.

- **Part 4** covers the big picture: managing the pages and files on your site, testing links and pages, and moving your site to a web server connected to the Internet. And since you're not always working solo, this section covers features that let you work with a team of web developers, too.

- **Part 5** shows you how to take advantage of timesaving Dreamweaver features like libraries, templates, and history-panel automation. It also covers Dreamweaver's Extension Manager, a program that can add hundreds of free and commercial features to the site-builder.

■ About This Book

Despite the many improvements in software over the years, one feature has grown consistently worse: documentation. Until version 4, Dreamweaver came with a printed manual. In MX 2004, all you got was a *Getting Started* booklet. Now, mostly likely, you're getting the entire application from the cloud. If you do get a physical disc, it arrives in an otherwise empty cardboard box. To get any real information, you need to delve into the program's online help.

But even if you have no problem reading a help screen in one window as you work in another, something's still missing. At times, the terse electronic help assumes you already understand the discussion at hand and hurriedly skips over important topics that require in-depth explanation. In addition, you don't always get an objective evaluation of the program's features. Engineers often add technically sophisticated capabilities to a program because they *can*, not because you need them. You shouldn't have to waste your time learning tools that don't help you get your work done.

The purpose of this book, then, is to serve as the Dreamweaver manual that should have been in the box. You'll find step-by-step instructions for every Dreamweaver feature, including those you may not otherwise have understood, let alone mastered, such as libraries, Design view, behaviors, and Dreamweaver's JavaScript tools. In addition, you'll find honest evaluations of each tool to help you determine which are useful to you, as well as how and when to use them.

> **NOTE** This book periodically recommends *other* books, covering topics that are too specialized or tangential for a manual on Dreamweaver. Careful readers may notice that not every one of these titles is published by *Missing Manual* parent O'Reilly Media. While we're happy to mention other Missing Manuals and books in the O'Reilly family, if there's a great book out there, we'll let you know about it.

Dreamweaver CC: The Missing Manual is designed to accommodate readers at every technical level. The primary discussions are written for advanced-beginner or intermediate computer users. But if you're new to building web pages, special sidebars called "Up To Speed" provide the introductory information you need to understand the topic at hand. If you're a web veteran, on the other hand, keep your eye out for similar boxes called "Power Users' Clinic." They offer more technical tips, tricks, and shortcuts for the experienced computer fan.

■ Windows and Macintosh Commands

Dreamweaver CC works almost precisely the same way on the Macintosh as it does in Windows. Every button in every dialog box is exactly the same, and the response to every command is identical. This book uses images that alternate between the various operating systems where Dreamweaver feels at home (Windows 8, Windows 7, Windows Vista, and Mac OS X).

One of the biggest differences between Windows and Mac software is the keystrokes, because the Ctrl key in Windows is equivalent to the Macintosh's ⌘ key. And the key labeled Alt on a Windows PC (and on non-U.S. Macs) is equivalent to the Option key on American Macs.

Whenever this book refers to a key combination, therefore, you'll see the Windows keystrokes listed first (using the + symbol for compound commands, as is customary in Windows documentation); the Macintosh keystrokes follow in parentheses (with - symbols, in time-honored Mac fashion). In other words, you might read, "The keyboard shortcut for saving a file is Ctrl+S (⌘-S)."

■ The Very Basics of Reading This Book

You'll find very little jargon or technical terminology in this book. You will, however, encounter a few terms and concepts you'll come across frequently in your computing life:

- **Clicking.** This book gives you three kinds of instructions that require you to use your computer's mouse or trackpad. To *click* means to point the arrow cursor at something on the screen and then—without moving the cursor—press and release the clicker button on the mouse (or laptop trackpad). To *double-click*, of course, means to click twice in rapid succession, again without moving your cursor. And to *drag* means to move the cursor while holding down the mouse button.

- **Keyboard shortcuts.** Every time you take your hand off the keyboard to move the mouse, you lose time and potentially disrupt your creative flow. That's why many experienced computer fans use keystroke combinations instead of menu commands wherever possible. Ctrl+B (⌘-B for Mac folks), for example, gives you boldface type in Dreamweaver documents (and most other programs).

  When you see a shortcut like Ctrl+S (⌘-S), it's telling you to hold down the Ctrl or ⌘ key and type the letter S, then release both keys. (This command, by the way, saves changes to the current document.)

- **Choice is good.** Dreamweaver frequently gives you several ways to trigger a particular command—by selecting a menu command *or* by clicking a toolbar button *or* by pressing a key combination, for example. Some people prefer the speed of keyboard shortcuts; others like the satisfaction of a visual command available in menus or toolbars. This book lists all the alternatives; use whichever you find most convenient.

◼ About→These→Arrows

Throughout this book, and throughout the Missing Manual series, you'll find sentences like this one: "Open the System→Library→Fonts folder." That's shorthand for a much longer instruction that directs you to open three nested folders in sequence, like this: "On your hard drive, you'll find a folder called System. Double-click it to open it. Inside the System folder is a folder called Library; double-click it to open it. Inside *that* folder is yet another folder called Fonts. Double-click to open that folder, too."

Similarly, this kind of arrow shorthand helps to simplify the business of choosing commands in menus, as shown in Figure P-1.

◼ Online Resources

This book is designed to get your work onto the Web fast and professionally; it's only natural, then, that part of the value of this book also lies on the Web.

The Missing CD

This book doesn't have a CD pasted inside the back cover, but you're not missing out on anything.

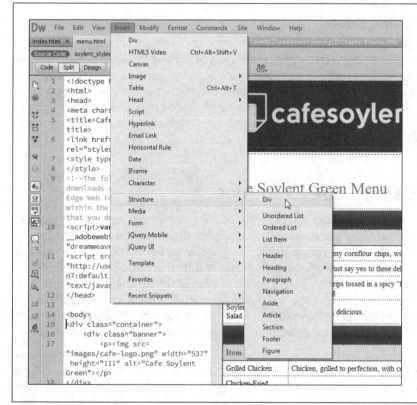

FIGURE P-1

When you read "Choose Insert→Structure→Div" in this Missing Manual, that means, "From Dreamweaver's menu bar, click the Insert command. From the drop-down menu that appears, select Structure. That opens a list of HTML tags you can add to the currently open document; select Div from that list."

As you read the book, you'll find a number of tutorials that show you how to build web pages using raw materials, like graphics and half-completed web pages. You can download these practice files from this book's Missing CD page (*http://oreilly.com/missingmanuals/cds/dreamweaverccmm13/*). If you take the time to work through the tutorials, you'll discover that they give you unprecedented insight into the way professional designers build web pages.

The download also includes the completed tutorial pages, so you can compare your Dreamweaver work with the final result. In other words, you won't just see pictures of Dreamweaver's output in the pages of the book; you'll find the actual, working pages in this download.

Finally, the Missing CD site gives you one-click access to the reference websites mentioned in this book—that'll save your fingers some typing.

Registering Your Book

If you register this book at oreilly.com (*http://oreilly.com/register*), you'll be eligible for special offers—like discounts on future editions. If you buy the ebook from oreilly.com and register your purchase, you get free lifetime updates for that edition of the ebook; we'll notify you by email when updates become available. Registering takes only a few clicks.

Reporting Errata

To keep this book as up to date and accurate as possible, each time we print more copies, we'll make any confirmed corrections you suggest. We also note such changes on the book's website, so you can mark important corrections in your own copy of the book if you like. And if you bought the ebook from us and registered your purchase, you'll get an email notifying you when you can download a free updated version of this edition of the ebook. Go to *http://tinyurl.com/dreamweaverccerrata* to report an error and view existing corrections.

■ Using Code Examples

This book is here to help you get your job done. In general, you may use the code in this book in your programs and documentation. You don't need to contact us for permission unless you're reproducing a significant portion of the code. For example, writing a program that uses several chunks of code from this book does not require permission. Selling or distributing a CD of examples from O'Reilly books does require permission. Answering a question by citing this book and quoting example code does not require permission. Incorporating a significant amount of example code from this book into your product's documentation does require permission.

We appreciate, but do not require, attribution. An attribution usually includes the source book's title, author, publisher, and ISBN. For example: "*Dreamweaver CC: The Missing Manual* by David Sawyer McFarland and Chris Grover (O'Reilly). Copyright 2014 David McFarland and O'Reilly Media, Inc., 978-1-4493-4170-1."

If you feel your use of code examples falls outside fair use or the permission given above, feel free to contact us at *permissions@oreilly.com*.

■ Safari® Books Online

Safari® Books Online is an on-demand digital library that lets you search over 7,500 technology books and videos.

With a subscription, you can read any page and watch any video from our library. Access new titles before they're available in print. Copy and paste code samples, organize your favorites, download chapters, bookmark key sections, create notes, print out pages, and benefit from tons of other time-saving features.

O'Reilly Media has uploaded this book to the Safari Books Online service. To have full digital access to this book and others on similar topics from O'Reilly and other publishers, sign up for free at *http://my.safaribooksonline.com*.

Building a Web Page

Dreamweaver CC Guided Tour

D reamweaver CC is a powerful program for designing and building websites. If you're brand-new to Dreamweaver, turn to page xiv for a quick look at what the program can do; if you're a longtime Dreamweaver fan, page xvii tells you what's new in this latest incarnation of the program.

This chapter gives you an overview of Dreamweaver—a guide to the windows, tool-bars, and menus you'll use every time you build a web page. It also shows you how to set up the program so you can begin building pages. And, because *doing* is often a better way to learn than just *reading*, you'll get a step-by-step tour of web page design—the Dreamweaver way—in the tutorial at the end of this chapter.

■ Download Dreamweaver CC

To install a Creative Cloud app like Dreamweaver, go to Adobe's Download Center (*www.adobe.com/downloads.html*). Once there, you can try out an application or go ahead and sign up for the Creative Cloud app itself—that is, pay the licensing fee for the program. To download and install Dreamweaver, click the Join button next to the Dreamweaver icon and then follow the links. In addition to adding the application, this download installs Adobe's Creative Cloud desktop app, which keeps track of all the Creative Cloud apps on your computer and notifies you when there are updates.

■ The Dreamweaver CC Interface

When you launch Dreamweaver, the program's Welcome screen greets you (Figure 1-1). This simple starting point lets you reopen the last nine most recently opened files, create a new web page, view instructional videos, and get online help.

Dreamweaver CC's interface shares its look and feel with the other programs in Adobe's Creative Cloud suite, including Photoshop, Illustrator, and Flash. The various panels that make up Dreamweaver's main screen appear as a unified whole (see Figure 1-2). That is, the edges of all the windows touch each other, and resizing one window affects the others around it. This type of interface is common on Windows computers, but Mac fans accustomed to independent floating panels might find it strange. Give it a chance. As you'll soon see, this layout has its benefits. (If you just can't stand this locked-in-place style, you can detach the various panels and place them wherever you like; see page 13 for instructions.)

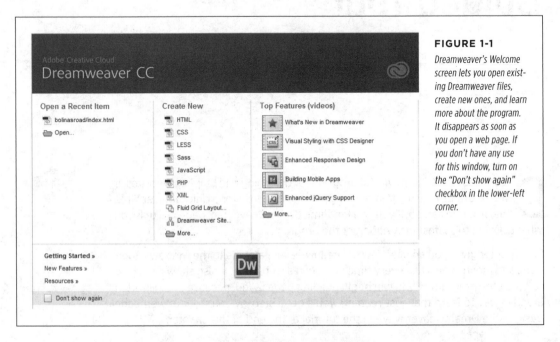

FIGURE 1-1

Dreamweaver's Welcome screen lets you open existing Dreamweaver files, create new ones, and learn more about the program. It disappears as soon as you open a web page. If you don't have any use for this window, turn on the "Don't show again" checkbox in the lower-left corner.

Many of Dreamweaver's individual windows help you handle specific tasks, like building CSS styles. You'll read about each panel in relevant chapters of this book, but you'll frequently interact with three main groups of windows: the document window, the Properties panel (below the document window), and a set of panels on the right side of the workspace.

NOTE The look of Dreamweaver's windows depends on whether you use a Windows or Mac PC, and what changes you make in the program's Preferences settings. Even so, the features and functions generally work the same way on both computers. In this book, where the program's operation differs dramatically in one operating system or the other, special boxes and illustrations (labeled "For Windows Only" or "For Macs Only") will let you know.

The Document Window

What you see on a web page is the end result of the interaction between your browser and the page's underlying code: its HTML, CSS, and (sometimes) JavaScript.

Because of this interrelationship, Dreamweaver's *document window* lets you view pages-in-progress four ways: as straight code (in Code view), in an editable, visual view (called Design view, pictured in Figure 1-3), with both views side-by-side (known as Split view, pictured in Figure 1-2), and as the page will appear in a web browser (Live view, which turns the document window into a real web browser).

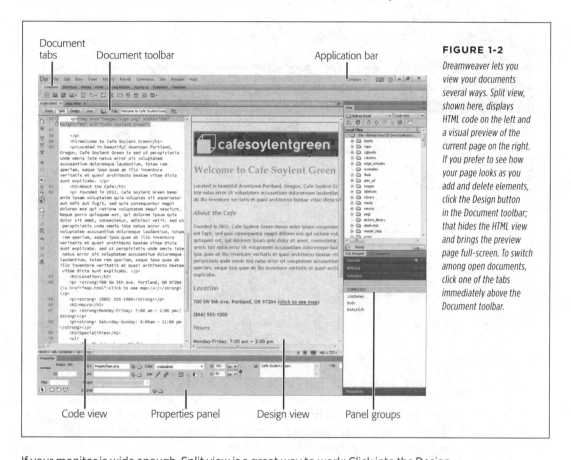

Document tabs   Document toolbar   Application bar

Code view   Properties panel   Design view   Panel groups

FIGURE 1-2

Dreamweaver lets you view your documents several ways. Split view, shown here, displays HTML code on the left and a visual preview of the current page on the right. If you prefer to see how your page looks as you add and delete elements, click the Design button in the Document toolbar; that hides the HTML view and brings the preview page full-screen. To switch among open documents, click one of the tabs immediately above the Document toolbar.

If your monitor is wide enough, Split view is a great way to work: Click into the Design view half of the document window to add HTML visually, and, when it's easier just to type HTML, click into the Code view part of the document window and type away. Split view even lets you see the code in one half, and turn on Live view in the other half so you can work on the HTML code while you see the page as it will appear in a real web browser (you can't, however, edit a page in Live view). In addition, if you're new to HTML, Split view is a great way to learn the language: Add elements like paragraphs, headlines, and tables in Design view and see the relevant HTML in Code view. (You work in the document window's Design view much as you do in a word processor: To add text to a page, for example, you simply click inside the window and start typing.)

Document Document Related
tabs   toolbar   files

Application bar

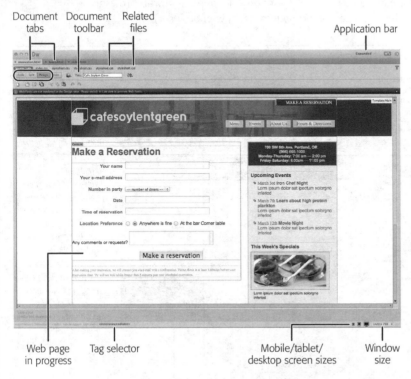

FIGURE 1-3

*A document window like
this represents a web page
in progress; here's where
you add text, graphics, and
other objects as you build
the page. Useful widgets
and document information
surround the window. For
example, you can instruct
Dreamweaver to display
the current document
at different widths
and heights so you can
simulate what the page
will look like in different
size browsers, like those
on mobile phones, tablets,
and desktop computers.
The window size setting
lets you see the page as it
would appear on different-
size monitors.*

Web page   Tag selector   Mobile/tablet/   Window
in progress   desktop screen sizes size

When you build a page, you work in the document window, and, as you add pages
to your site or edit existing ones, you open new document windows. Several screen
components provide useful information about your document. They may appear in
different locations on Windows and Mac computers (see Figure 1-2 and Figure 1-3,
respectively), but they work the same way.

For example:

- **Document tabs.** When you have more than one web document open at a time,
  small tabs appear at the top of the document window—one for each open file.
  The name of the file appears in the tab; to switch to it, just click its tab.

TIP If you mouse over a document tab and pause, the location of the file appears in a small pop-up window
called a *tooltip*.

- **Related Files bar.** The Related Files bar lists all CSS (Cascading Style Sheets), JavaScript, and server-side programming pages (like PHP pages) the current web page uses. You'll learn more about these external files later in this book, but as a quick summary, it's common in current web design to have other files supply design and interactivity to a page of HTML. Web designers frequently work on these files in addition to the basic HTML file, so the Related Files bar lets you quickly jump to and work on these "helper" files. You choose which files to display using the Filter Related Files button on the right side of the related files toolbar.

- **Document toolbar.** The Document toolbar (View→Toolbars→Document) lets you change the title of a page, switch between Design and Code views, jump to Live view (to see how the page looks and works in a web browser), preview a page in different browsers, make sure your page is free of HTML errors, and change the look of the document window. You'll read about the toolbar's various buttons and menus in the relevant chapters of this book, but you'll want to be aware of the Code, Split, and Design buttons (circled in Figure 1-3). They let you see the page you're working on in the four views described earlier.

> **NOTE** You may also find Dreamweaver's Standard toolbar useful. The Standard toolbar is common on many Windows programs and includes buttons for frequent file and editing tasks, like creating a new page, opening a page, saving one or all open documents, canceling and repeating commands, and cutting, copying, and pasting page elements. (Dreamweaver hides this toolbar until you summon it by choosing View→Toolbars→Standard.)

- **Tag Selector.** The Tag Selector is extremely useful. It provides a sneak peek at the HTML that composes your web page, behind the scenes. It indicates how Dreamweaver nests HTML tags in your document to create what you see on the page. In addition, it lets you isolate, with a single mouse click, an HTML tag and all the information inside it. That means you can cleanly remove a page element or set its properties (see page 11), and precisely control the application of styles to it (Chapter 3).

  You'll make good use of the Tag Selector in the tutorials to come. For experienced Dreamweaver fans, it's one of the program's most useful tools.

> **NOTE** In Design view, clicking the <body> tag in the Tag Selector is usually the same as pressing Ctrl+A (⌘-A) or choosing Edit→Select All. It selects everything in the document window. However, if you click inside a table (Chapter 6) or a <div> tag (see page 428), choosing Edit→Select All selects only the contents of the table cell or the <div> tag. In such a case, you need to press Ctrl+A (⌘-A) several times to select everything on the page. After you do, you can press the delete key to instantly get rid of everything in your document.
>
> Careful, though: Pressing Ctrl+A (⌘-A) or choosing Edit→Select All in Code view selects *all* the code, including the information in the head section of the page. Deleting all the code gives you an empty file—and an invalid web page.

The Insert Panel

Dreamweaver provides many windows (also referred to as panels) for working with the various technologies required to build and maintain a website. You open and close all these windows using the Window menu. For the most part, they appear in tidy groups on the right edge of your screen. The windows and their uses will come up in relevant sections of this book, and you'll learn how to organize the panels on page 14. But two are worth mentioning up front: the Insert panel and the Files panel.

If the document window is your canvas, the Insert panel holds your brushes and paints, as you can see in Figure 1-4. You can create a page simply by typing HTML in Code view, but it's often easier to work in Design view, where the Insert panel can simplify the process of adding page elements like images, video, horizontal rules, forms, and special text characters. Want to put a picture on your web page? Just click the Images icon in the Insert panel.

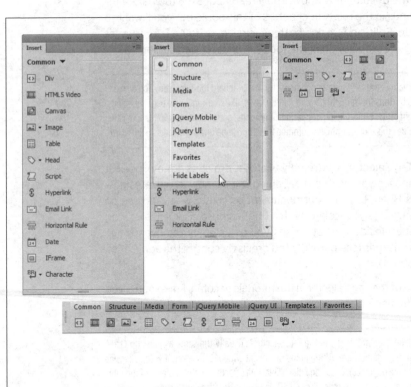

FIGURE 1-4

The Insert panel offers several drop-down menus that let you select the type of page element you want to add, in categories like Common (pictured here), Structure, Media, and so on. You can see that the list of elements—which has both icons and labels—take up a lot of real estate. Fortunately, you can display the Insert panel more compactly by hiding the labels. When you choose Hide Labels from the list of Insert categories (middle), Dreamweaver displays the icons side by side in rows, taking up a lot less space (top-right). Finally, you can turn the Insert panel into an Insert bar that appears above the document window instead of grouped with the right-hand panels; this space-saving option is a favorite among many web developers (bottom). To get the Insert toolbar, drag the Insert panel by its tab into position above the document tabs. Release the mouse button when you see a blue bar.

NOTE Adding elements to your web page using the Insert panel may feel like magic, but it's really just a quick way to add HTML to a page. Clicking the Images icon, for instance, simply inserts the <img> tag into the underlying HTML of your page. Of course, Dreamweaver's visual approach hides that code and cheerfully displays a picture on the page.

When you first start Dreamweaver, it opens in what is known as the Expanded workspace, where Dreamweaver's windows and panels are arranged in a certain layout. (For more details on workspaces, see page 14.) At first, in the expanded workspace, the Insert panel is open in the upper-right corner. If you ever close it by mistake, you can reopen the Insert panel by choosing Window→Insert or by pressing Ctrl+F2 (⌘-F2). On the other hand, if screen space is at a premium, you can close the Insert panel and use the Insert *menu* instead. The menu offers all the objects in the panel or toolbar, but they're not grouped by sets, as the panel and toolbar are. (You can turn the Insert panel into a toolbar that sits above the document window as described in Figure 1-4.)

The Insert panel offers eight sets of objects, each available from the drop-down menu at the top of the panel (see Figure 1-4, top right) or by clicking one of the tabs on the Insert toolbar (bottom image in Figure 1-4):

- **Common.** Common objects are those you'll most likely add to web pages: images, videos, hyperlinks, email links, tables, horizontal lines, heading tags, canvas tags, and the most versatile all-around utility player, the div tag.

- **Structure.** There's some overlap between Common and Structure objects. You'll find the div and heading tags here, along with paragraph, list, navigation, article, and aside tags. You use structure tags to identify elements on your web page. Then you use CSS to format those elements

- **Media.** The media insert objects include: Edge Animate compositions, HTML5 video, HTML5 audio, Flash SWF, Flash Video, and a less well-defined catchall, Plugin. For details on inserting media into web pages, see Chapter 15.

- **Form.** Want to hear back from your visitors? Forms let them make comments, order products, and answer questions. You can add form elements like radio buttons, pull-down menus, and text boxes (see Chapter 15). And because Dreamweaver includes sophisticated form validation, you can make sure visitors input the correct information *before* they submit the form.

NOTE In Web parlance, a *form* is a web page that lets visitors type in information that your web server processes. For example, you might ask a guest to type in his email address when he signs up for a newsletter.

- **jQuery Mobile.** jQuery Mobile is a JavaScript-powered toolset for building websites that work well on mobile devices, like iPhones and Android phones. The objects listed here include page elements like lists, form fields, and text areas for mobile-enhanced websites. You'll learn about these tools in Chapter 12.

- **jQuery UI.** Another part of the jQuery family, this toolset provides familiar user interface objects like buttons, checkboxes, sliders, accordion sections, and progress bars. You don't need to reinvent the wheel every time you want to add a widget to your web page.

- **Templates.** Templates let you build basic web page designs you can use over and over again, speeding up page development and facilitating easy updates. See Chapter 20 for details.

- **Favorites.** Perhaps the most useful category, Favorites can be anything you want it to be. After you discover which objects you use the most (like the Image command, if you work with a lot of graphics), you can add those objects to this set of personal tools. You may find that once you populate this category, you'll never again need the other categories in the Insert panel. For instructions on adding objects to the Favorites category, see the box below.

FREQUENTLY ASKED QUESTION

Adding Favorite Objects to the Insert Panel

Help! I'm tired of wading through so many pull-down menus to find all my favorite Dreamweaver objects. How can I see my most-used objects in one place?

Dreamweaver includes a marvelous productivity tool: the Favorites category of the Insert panel. It lets you collect your most-used objects in a single place, without any interference from the buttons for HTML tags and objects you never use. Maybe you use the Common category's Email Link object all the time but never touch the IFrame object, for example. This is the timesaving feature for you.

To add objects to the Favorites category, right-click (Control-click) anywhere in the Insert panel (or the Insert toolbar, if you made the changes described on page 8). From the pop-up menu, choose Customize Favorites to open the Customize Favorite Objects window. All the objects available in all the Insert categories appear in the left-hand list. Select an object and then click the >> button to add that object to your Favorites list. (You can view the objects for just one category by selecting the category from the "Available objects" menu.) Repeat with other objects if you like.

To rearrange the order of the toolbar buttons, click one and then click the up or down arrow. Depending on whether you display the panel buttons with or without labels, buttons you put higher in the list appear either toward the top of the panel or toward the beginning of the rows of buttons. You can even use the Add Separator button to insert a thin gray line between buttons—to separate one group of similar elements (graphics-related objects, say) from another (such as form objects). Unfortunately, you can't group Favorite objects into submenus. Each item you add becomes a single button on the Insert bar.

To delete a button or separator from the list, select it and then click the trash icon. Click OK to close the window and create your new list of Favorite objects, which are now available under the Favorites category of the Insert panel.

After you create your Favorites tab, you can always add more objects (or delete ones you no longer need) by right-clicking (Control-clicking) the Insert bar and then, from the shortcut menu, choosing Customize Favorites.

The Files Panel

The Files panel, another Dreamweaver element you'll turn to frequently (see Figure 1-5), lists all the files—web pages, graphics, CSS, and JavaScript—that make up your website. It gives you a quick way to open the files you want to work on—just double-click the file name in the panel—lets you switch among different sites you're building or maintaining, and provides some valuable tools for organizing your files. If the Files panel isn't open, summon it by choosing Window→Files or by pressing F8 (Shift-⌘-F on Macs).

To use the Files panel effectively, you need to create a local site for each website you work on—setting up a site is a specific Dreamweaver task and one of the most important steps in using Dreamweaver correctly. You'll learn how to do so starting on page 19.

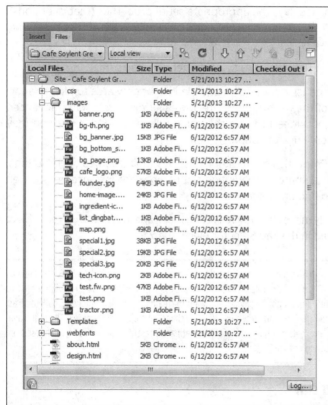

FIGURE 1-5

The Files panel gives you a bird's-eye view of your site's files. But it's more than just a list—you can quickly open files, rename and rearrange them in your site, and switch among sites. Later in this chapter, you'll learn how to organize site files using this panel.

The Properties Panel

After dropping an image, table, or anything else from the Insert panel into your web page, you can use Dreamweaver's Properties panel to fine-tune the element's appearance and attributes (see Figure 1-6). Suppose, for example, that your boss has decided she wants her picture to link to her personal blog. After highlighting her picture in the document window, you can use the Properties panel to add the link.

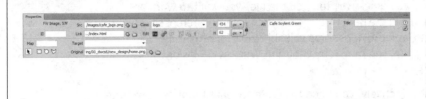

FIGURE 1-6

If you don't see the Properties panel, open it by choosing Window→Properties or pressing Ctrl+F3 (⌘-F3).

The Properties panel, sometimes referred to as the Properties Inspector, is a chameleon. It's aware of what you're working on in the document window—a table, an image, some text—and displays the appropriate set of properties (that is, options). It works whether you're in Design view or Code view. You'll use the Properties panel extensively in Dreamweaver.

For now, though, here are two essential tips to get you started:

- In the Properties panel, double-click any blank light gray area to hide or show the bottom half of the panel, where Dreamweaver displays a set of advanced options. (It's a good idea to leave the panel fully expanded, since you may otherwise miss some useful options.)

- At its heart, the Properties panel simply displays the attributes of HTML tags. The *src* (source) attribute of the image tag (<img>), for instance, tells a web browser where to find an image file.

  You can most easily make sure you're setting the properties of the correct object by selecting its tag in the Tag Selector (see page 7).

NOTE When you work with text, the Properties panel has two buttons—labeled HTML and CSS—that let you either work with the page's HTML properties related to text or create CSS styles. You'll read more about these two buttons in Chapter 3, but here's a quick pointer: When you want to create paragraphs, headlines, bulleted lists, and bold or italic text, click the HTML button. When you want to change the appearance of text (its font, color, and size), use the CSS button—or, better yet, use the CSS Designer panel, described on page 104, to choose from a much wider range of formatting options.

The Application Bar

As in most programs, the Application bar offers menus and the usual controls for expanding, shrinking, hiding, and closing the workspace window. As you can see in Figure 1-7, these controls are in their usual positions on Windows PCs (top) and Macs (bottom). The application bar gives you two other toolsets, on the right side:

- The **Workspace Switcher** lets you reorganize Dreamweaver's layout. You can choose one of Dreamweaver's stock workspaces, or, as discussed on page 14, you can design a custom layout to create the ultimate workspace. (You can access these same options from the Window→Workspace Layout menu.)

- The **Creative Cloud** tools let you sync CC files on your computer with those stored in the cloud. They also give you quick access to Adobe's Creative Cloud pages and let you log into your personal cloud using your Adobe ID.

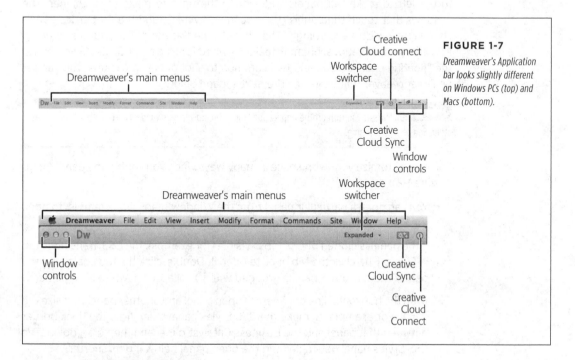

FIGURE 1-7

Dreamweaver's Application bar looks slightly different on Windows PCs (top) and Macs (bottom).

Hiding the Application Bar

On Windows PCs, the Application bar is unobtrusive—it sits just to the right of Dreamweaver's main menu items. However, if you have a particularly small monitor, the Application bar will poke up above the menu, taking up a good chunk of vertical space on the screen. In previous versions of Dreamweaver, you could hide the Application bar, but that's no longer the case.

On Macs, the Application bar always sits on its own. With just a few menu items and widgets, the Application bar is mostly a waste of space. You can hide it on Macs as well, but at a cost: You'll lose the Application Frame, which binds all the panels, toolbars, and windows into a cohesive whole. With the Application Frame turned on, changing the width of the panel groups on the right side on the screen resizes the document window and Properties panel, too. If you turn off the Application bar, however, the document window, Properties panel, and panel group act as separate windows you can resize independently of each other.

So if you're a Mac user willing to give up the unified workspace of the Application Frame, here's how to hide the Application bar: Turn off the Application Frame by choosing Window→ Application Frame, and then choose Window→Application Bar to hide the Application bar. You can always turn the Application Frame back on, but doing so automatically brings the Application bar back.

Organizing Your Workspace

Dreamweaver's basic user interface includes the document window, Application bar, Properties panel, and panel groups. All these windows act as though they were a whole; that is, if you resize one window, the other windows readjust themselves to fit the available space. For example, you can drag the left edge of the panel groups to the left to make the panels wider or to the right to make them thinner. The windows that touch the panels (the document window and the Properties panel) change their widths accordingly. This kind of joined-at-the-hip interface is common in Windows applications, but may feel a bit weird for Mac enthusiasts. (If you prefer the "floating palette" look and feel common to a lot of Mac programs, you can set up Dreamweaver that way—see the next section below.)

NOTE On Macs, if you turn off the Application Frame, Dreamweaver's windows act independently of each other. See page 13 for more.

You can customize your workspace in many ways when you control the panel group (Figure 1-8):

- You can open a particular panel from the Window menu. For example, to open the Files panel, choose Window→Files.

- If the panel is hidden but its tab is visible (for example, the CSS Transitions tab in Figure 1-11), click the tab once to open it. Double-click the tab again, and the panel (and any other panels grouped with it) collapses down to a single bar.

- Drag the horizontal line between an open panel and another panel to resize the panel. For example, to make the CSS Styles panel taller, grab the thick border between that panel and the Business Catalyst panel and then drag down. The CSS Styles panel gets taller and the open panel below it gets shorter.

- To completely close a panel so that even its tab no longer appears, right-click (Control-click) the tab and then choose Close. (Choose Close Tab Group to hide all the tabs in a group.) To get the panel back, use the Window menu or use the panel's keyboard shortcut—for example, F8 opens and closes the Files panel.

- To hide all windows *except* the document window, choose Window→Hide Panels or press F4—a useful trick when you want to maximize the amount of screen space for the web page you're working on. To bring back all the panels, press F4 again or choose Window→Show Panels

■ FLOATING PANELS

As mentioned earlier, you can drag a panel by its tab to another part of the screen. Dragging it to the edge of the screen docks the panel to that edge. However, if you drag a panel and drop it when it's not near a screen's edge, it becomes a floating panel (see Figure 1-9). Floating panels are often nuisances, since they hide whatever is beneath them, so you often end up having to move them out of the way just to see what you're doing. However, they come in handy when you have two monitors. If that's the case, you can dedicate your main monitor to the document window and

Properties panel (and maybe your most important panels), and then drag a bunch of floating panels onto your second screen.

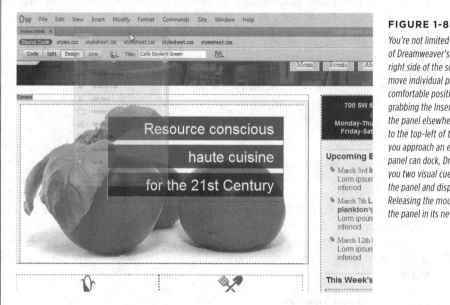

FIGURE 1-8

You're not limited to keeping all of Dreamweaver's panels on the right side of the screen—you can move individual panels to more comfortable positions. In this figure, grabbing the Insert tab lets you drag the panel elsewhere, in this case, to the top-left of the screen. When you approach an edge where the panel can dock, Dreamweaver gives you two visual cues: It ghosts out the panel and displays a blue line. Releasing the mouse button docks the panel in its new position.

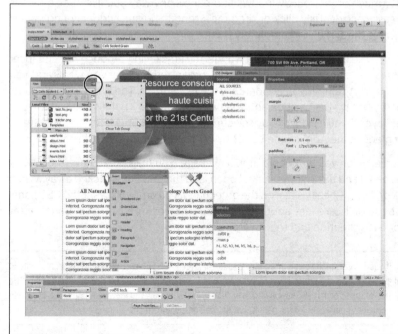

FIGURE 1-9

Here, the Files, Insert, and CSS Designer panels float. Each panel has its own Context menu icon (circled in the Files panel). Clicking the button reveals a shortcut menu that lets you work with commands specific to that panel. This menu also offers generic panel actions, such as closing the panel. If you find you've made a mess of your workspace and want to return Dreamweaver to the way it normally lays out panels, use the Workspace Switcher.

To "unfloat" a floating panel, drag it to the edge of your screen (if you have more than one monitor, drag the panel to one of the edges of your *main* monitor). If you already have panels at that edge, drag the panel to either the bottom of the panels (to dock it at the bottom of the column of panels), between the bottom edge of one panel group and the top edge of another (to insert the panel in its own group between the other panels), or next to another panel's tab to group the panels together.

> **TIP** Drag a panel to either side of a docked column of panels to create a second column. In other words, you can create two side-by-side columns of panels.

■ ICONIC PANES

As if you didn't already have enough ways to organize your panels, Dreamweaver includes yet another one. By clicking the "Collapse to Icons" button at the top right of a column of panels, you can shrink the panels to a group of much smaller icons. To reopen the controls for a panel you shrunk, click the panel name. For example, in Figure 1-10, clicking CSS Designer opens the CSS Designer panel to the left. Once you finish working with the panel, click the panel name again or click elsewhere on the screen and the pop-up panel disappears. This so-called iconic view is particularly good if you have a small monitor and need to preserve as much screen real estate as possible.

■ WORKSPACE LAYOUTS

Sometimes too much choice is a bad thing, and even though Dreamweaver lets you pretty much organize its windows and panels any way you like, it also means you can easily accidentally click or drag the wrong thing and suddenly find panels strewn across the screen or completely gone.

Fortunately, Dreamweaver includes a wonderful, timesaving productivity enhancer that ensures you always have your windows organized the way you want, and you can return to that setup if you accidentally move anything. The Workspace Layouts feature lets you save the position and size of Dreamweaver's panels and windows as a custom "layout" you can invoke by selecting the layout's name from the Workspace Switcher menu in the Application bar or by choosing Window→Workspace Layout.

For example, when you work on a mobile website, you may like to have the jQuery swatches panel and the Snippets panel open, and the CSS panel tucked away. When you work on design-heavy sites, on the other hand, you probably want the CSS panel open but couldn't care less about the Code Inspector. You can create a different layout for each situation and then switch among them.

> **NOTE** If you have a small screen or an older, squarish screen, the Compact workspace is a great way to free up real estate. It tucks the Insert, File, CSS Designer, and CSS Transitions panels into a relatively small strip on the right side of the screen. If you have a larger, or cinema-style, display, you may want to use the Expanded workspace. It provides more room for the panels, but fits well on a wide screen.

Expand Panels button

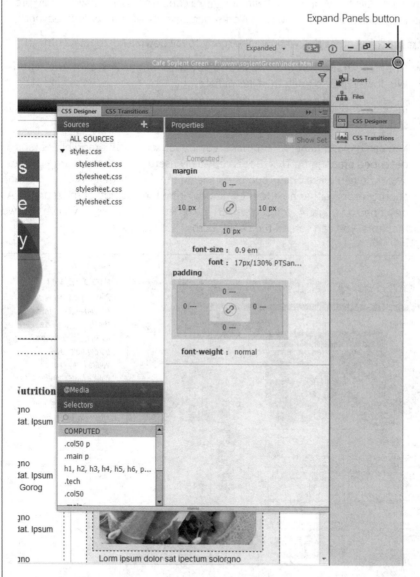

FIGURE 1-10

Iconic panes, like those for Insert and Files in the top-right here, let you preserve screen real estate. To return the panels to their normal widths, click the Expand Panels button.

After you tweak a workspace to perfection by closing, opening, and rearranging panels, you can save the result as a custom layout. Go to Window→Workspace Layout→New Workspace; when the New Workspace dialog box appears, provide a meaningful name like "Dual Monitors" and click OK. (You'll find the same New Workspace command on the Workspace Switcher menu in the Application bar.) If you type in a name that matches a workspace you already use, Dreamweaver gives you the option to replace the old layout with the new one. That's the only way to update a workspace layout you previously created. Once you save a custom workspace, you can call it up in the Workspace Switcher with a couple of mouse clicks. If you prefer menus, you can choose Window→Workspace Layout→[*Name of Your Layout*].

Here are a few other tips when you're ready to lay down a custom layout:

- Open the panels you work with most frequently. For example, choose Window→Files to open the Files panel.

- Increase or decrease the height of a panel by dragging up or down the empty space to the right of a panel or panel-group name (see Figure 1-11).

- You can move a panel to another area of your screen by dragging its tabs as described on page 14. This trick is especially useful if you have a large monitor, since you can place one group of panels on the right edge of the monitor and another group either next to the first one or on the left side of the monitor. As described on page 14, you can also create untethered panels—if you've got two monitors, you can spread the panels across both screens.

FIGURE 1-11

Resizing a panel vertically (circled at the bottom of the Insert panel) is as easy as dragging its bottom border up or down. If you're lucky enough to have a large monitor, it's often helpful to put the Files panel by itself on either the left or right side of the screen.

■ Setting Up a Site

Whenever you build a new website or want to edit a site you created outside of Dreamweaver, you have to introduce the program to the site—a process Dreamweaver calls *setting up a site*. This is *the* most important first step when you start using Dreamweaver, whether you plan to whip up a 5-page site, build a 1,000-page online store, or edit the site your sister built for you. At its most basic, defining a site lets Dreamweaver know where you store your web pages on your computer. It also helps Dreamweaver correctly insert images and add links from one page to another. In addition, if you want to take advantage of Dreamweaver's many timesaving site-management tools, such as the link checker (page 745), Library items (Chapter 19), templates (Chapter 20), and FTP feature for moving your files to a web server (Chapter 18), you *have* to set up a site.

There are a lot of ways to configure a site, depending on your needs. For example, if you're ready to move pages to the Web, you need to tell Dreamweaver how to connect to your web server. But to get started with a new site, you only need to provide a couple of pieces of information:

1. **Choose Site→New Site to open the Site Setup window (Figure 1-12).**

   You'll supply basic site info here.

2. **In the "Site name" field, name your site.**

   The name you type here is for your own reference, to help you identify the site when it appears in the Files panel; the name won't show up on the Web.

NOTE In Web argot, a *field* is simply a box where you type in information.

3. **Click the folder icon to the right of the "Local site folder" field.**

   The Choose Root Folder window opens, letting you select a folder on your hard drive to serve as your *local site* or, more specifically, your local site's *main*, or *root*, folder. You'll store all your site's files—HTML documents and graphics, CSS files, and so on—in this local root folder or in the root's subfolders (such as an Images subfolder).

NOTE Another way to think of the local site folder is as the folder on your computer in which you'll put your site's home page.

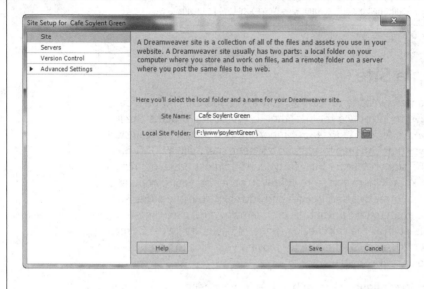

FIGURE 1-12

The Site Setup window tells Dreamweaver about your site—where you store your files, how to connect to your web server so you can upload pages to the Internet, and so on. But to get started, you only need to fill in these two fields. You'll find the other Site Setup categories, listed on the left, discussed later: The Servers category lets you point Dreamweaver to your online web server so you can upload files to your site (Chapter 18) and to a "testing server" so you can put complex, database-driven websites through their paces before going live (Chapter 22); the Version Control category is for those using the (very complex) Subversion system (most people—the author of this book included—never use this option, but if you're curious, see the box on page 788 for more). You'll find the Advanced settings discussed in step 5 below and elsewhere in this book.

4. **Browse to and select a folder for your site's files.**

   Figure 1-13 demonstrates the process. If you're editing an existing site, select the folder that contains the site's files. If you're creating a new site, create a folder for that site using the New Folder button in this window.

5. **For a few additional options, select Advanced Settings from the left-hand list of setup categories (see Figure 1-14).**

   This step is optional and you can happily skip it to begin building web pages. You'll find most of the categories listed here discussed elsewhere in the book, but you may want to visit the options in the Local Info category:

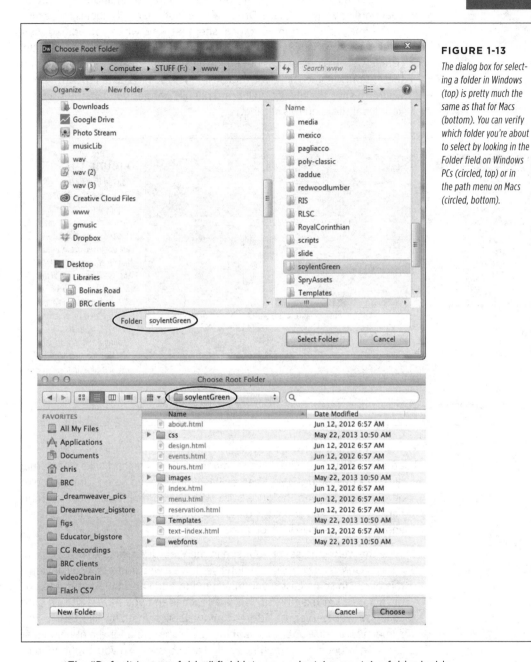

FIGURE 1-13

The dialog box for selecting a folder in Windows (top) is pretty much the same as that for Macs (bottom). You can verify which folder you're about to select by looking in the Folder field on Windows PCs (circled, top) or in the path menu on Macs (circled, bottom).

- The "Default Images folder" field lets you select (or create) a folder inside your local site folder to hold the images you'll use on your web pages. Choosing a default images folder is useful only if you tend to add images to your pages-in-progress from outside your local site folder—if, for example, you add images that are sitting on your desktop or in another folder on your hard drive. In that case, Dreamweaver automatically copies those files to the Images folder on your local site; that way, when you upload your local site to your online web server, all your images go along for the ride. (Dreamweaver copies "outside" image files to your local site without setting this option, but each time you add an image, you have to tell Dreamweaver where to save the file. If you'll primarily use images you already saved in your local site, skip this setting.)

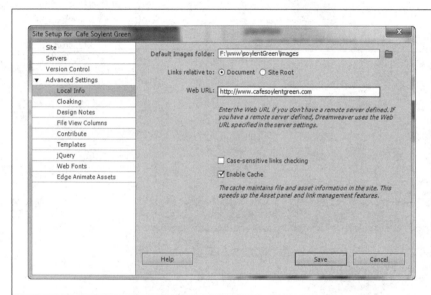

FIGURE 1-14

You can happily use Dreamweaver without ever visiting Advanced Settings in the Site Setup window. The Local Info options are discussed earlier, and the other options are discussed elsewhere in this book: cloaking on page 782, Design Notes on page 795, File View columns on page 723, templates in Chapter 20, jQuery on page 573, Web fonts on page 128, and Edge Animate assets on page 701.

- The "Links relative to" setting determines how Dreamweaver writes links to other pages in your site, links to images in your site, and links to external files, like Cascading Style Sheets, Flash movies, and so on. Unless you're an experienced web designer, stick with the normal "Document" setting here—you can read about the difference between (and uses for) document- and site root-relative links on page 166.

- Type the web address for your site in the Web URL field, like *http://www.cafesoylentgreen.com/.* If you don't yet have a web address, you can leave this blank. In some cases, you may need to add information after the domain name. For example, if you're a teacher and you have a site on your college's web server, its address might look something like this: *www.somecollege.edu/~bob.* Or you might be responsible for maintaining just part of a larger site—sometimes called a "sub-site"—so you might need to append, for example, */marketing* to the end of the URL. Regardless, just type the address you normally type into a web browser to visit your site; for example, *www.mybigcompany.com/marketing.*

- Leave the checkbox next to "Case-sensitive links checking" turned off. This is useful only when you have web pages and files on a UNIX server that allows files with the same name but different letter cases: for example, *HOME.html*, *home.html*, and *HoMe.html*. Since Windows PCs and Macs don't let you do this, you'll probably never have a site with file names like these.

- Keep the Enable Cache checkbox turned on. Dreamweaver creates a cache for each site you set up. That's a small database that tracks pages, links, images, and other site components. The cache helps Dreamweaver's site-management tools avoid breaking links, lets Dreamweaver warn you when you're about to delete important files, and lets you reorganize your site quickly. The only reason to turn off this checkbox is if you have a really large website (tens of thousands of pages and images) and you notice that Dreamweaver is really slow whenever you begin to work on the site, move a file, change a file's name, delete a file, or perform one of Dreamweaver's other site-management tasks. In that case, you may see a box saying "updating the site cache" or "checking links" that stays open and prevents you from using Dreamweaver for a minute or more—basically your site is so big that Dreamweaver has to spend a lot of time keeping track of your files and links.

6. **Click Save to finish the site setup.**

    Your site's files (if there are any yet) appear in the Files panel. Now you're ready to create and edit web pages and take advantage of Dreamweaver's powerful site-building tools.

NOTE Dreamweaver lets you set up *multiple* websites, a handy feature if you're a web designer with several clients, or if your company builds and manages more than one site. To define an additional site, choose Site→New Site and then repeat the steps on page 19. You can then switch from one site to another using the Sites menu at the top-left of the Files panel.

■ Creating a Web Page

After you define a site, you'll want to start building pages. Just choose File→New or press Ctrl+N (⌘-N on Macs) to open Dreamweaver's New Document window (see Figure 1-15). It's a little overwhelming at first—there are so many options, it's hard to know where to start. Fortunately, when you just want to create a new HTML file, you can skip most of these options.

To create a basic HTML file for a web page:

1. **From the left-hand list of document categories, choose Blank Page.**

    The Blank Page category lets you create a new empty document—maybe a web page or something a bit more esoteric, like an XML file, an external JavaScript file, or one of the several types of server-driven pages (such as a PHP file, discussed in Chapter 22).

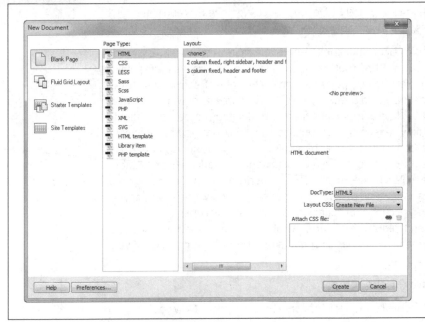

FIGURE 1-15

The New Document window lets you create nearly every type of web document under the sun. Dreamweaver CC includes a set of prepackaged CSS layouts that use the latest Web design tools, including HTML5. You'll learn more about these layouts in Chapter 10.

The Fluid Grid Layout option is relatively new in Dreamweaver. It lets you create a web page that adapts to three browser widths: one for a phone, a tablet, and a desktop browser. You'll learn how to use this feature on page 544.

The Starter Templates and Site Templates categories relate to Dreamweaver's Template feature discussed in Chapter 20. Within Starter Templates you'll find starter pages for creating mobile-only websites (page 521). The Site Templates category holds templates for sites you've created, so initially it will be empty.

2. **From the Page Type list, choose HTML.**

   You can create other types of documents, too, some of which you'll learn about later in this book, such as templates (Chapter 20), Library items (Chapter 19), and CSS files (Chapter 3).

3. **From the Layout list, choose <none>.**

   This creates a blank document. The other choices ("2 column fixed, right sidebar, header and footer," "3 column fixed, header and footer," and so on) are pre-designed page layouts (you'll learn more about using these layouts in Chapter 10). They use CSS, which you'll learn about in Chapter 3.

Terms Worth Knowing

During the tutorial in these pages—and, indeed, everywhere in Dreamweaver—you'll encounter a few terms frequently heard at web designer luncheons:

- **Root folder.** The first rule of managing a website is that every piece of the site you're working on—web pages (HTML files), images, sound files, and so on—must sit in a single master folder on your hard drive. This is the *root* folder for your website, and because it's on your computer, it's called the *local* root folder, though Dreamweaver calls it your local site folder. The *root* (a.k.a. site) folder is the master, outer, main folder. Think of it as the edge of the known universe for that site; nothing exists outside the root. Of course, to help organize your site's files, you can include any number of subfolders *within* that main folder.

  When you finish creating a site on your computer, you'll move the files in your local root folder onto a web server for the world to see. You call the folder where you place your site files on the server the *remote root folder*.

- **Local site.** The usual routine for creating web pages goes like this: Create the page on your own computer—using a program like Dreamweaver—and then upload it to a computer on the Internet called a web server, where your handiwork becomes available to the masses. So, it's very common for a website to exist in two places at once, one copy on your computer and the other on the server.

  The copy on your computer is called the *local site*, or the development site. Think of the local site as a sort of staging ground, where you build your site, test it, and modify it. Because the local site isn't on a web server, the public can't see it and you can freely edit and add to it without affecting the pages your visitors see (they're on the remote site, after all).

- **Remote site.** When you add or update a file, you move it from your local site to the remote site. The *remote*, or live, site is a mirror image of your local site. Because you create the remote site by uploading your local site, the folder on your web server has the same structure as the folder on your local site, and it contains the same files. Only polished, fully functional pages go online to the remote site; save the half-finished, typo-ridden drafts for your local site. Chapter 18 explains how to use Dreamweaver's FTP features to define and work with a remote site.

4. **Select a document type from the DocType menu.**

   Selecting a *doctype*, or document type, identifies the type of HTML you'll use to create your page. It affects how Dreamweaver writes HTML code and how a web browser understands it. Fortunately, since Dreamweaver writes all the code for you, you don't need to worry about the subtle differences between the different doctypes.

   HTML5 is the latest version of HTML, and the normal setting in Dreamweaver—it's what all the cool kids on the block are using, and you should, too. However, XHTML 1.0 Transitional, as well as HTML 4.01 Transitional, HTML 4.01 Strict, and XHTML 1.0 Strict also work just fine; so if you're working on a site whose pages use one of these older doctypes, you might want to stick with it.

   If you don't really understand or care about doctypes, just select HTML5, making sure to avoid None (which can force browsers to display pages in what's called "quirks mode" and makes perfecting designs difficult), XHTML Mobile, and XHTML 1.1 (which is not only obsolete, it also requires a special setting on your web server to work properly).

TIP If you don't want to deal with the New Document window every time you create a page using Dreamweaver's New Document keyboard shortcut (Ctrl+N in Windows, ⌘+N on Macs), choose Edit→Preferences in Windows (Dreamweaver→Preferences on Macs). In the Preferences dialog box, click the New Document category and then turn off the "Show New Document Dialog on Ctrl+N (⌘+N)" checkbox.

While you're at it, you can specify the type of file Dreamweaver creates whenever you press Ctrl+N (⌘-N). For example, if you usually create plain HTML files, choose HTML. But if you usually create dynamic pages, choose a different type of file—PHP, for example. You can also select the default doctype—choose HTML5—for all new pages.

Once you set these options, pressing Ctrl+N (⌘-N) instantly creates a new blank document using the doctype you chose previously. (Choosing File→New, however, still opens the New Document window.)

5. **Click Create.**

Dreamweaver opens a new, blank page ready for you to save and title (see Figure 1-16).

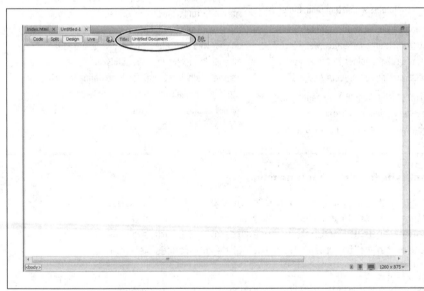

FIGURE 1-16

Here's a new blank web page. Always remember to title the page by clicking inside the Title field at the top of the document window (circled) and then entering a descriptive name.

6. **Choose File→Save.**

The Save As dialog box appears. You need to save the file somewhere inside your local site folder. You can save it inside any subfolder within the site folder as well.

TIP If you've set up a site, Dreamweaver provides a quick shortcut to the local root folder. When you save a web page, click the Site Root button in the Save As dialog box—this jumps directly to the local root folder. The Site Root button appears at the bottom-right of the Save As dialog box in Windows, and at the bottom-left of that window on Macs.

7. **Type a name for the file and then click Save.**

   Make sure the name doesn't contain spaces or any characters except letters, numbers, hyphens, and underscores, and that it ends in either .html or .htm.

   Although most operating systems let you save files with long names, spaces, and characters like #, $, and & in them, some browsers and servers have trouble interpreting anything other than letters and numbers. Furthermore, web servers rely on file extensions like .htm, .html, .gif, and .jpg to know whether a file is a web page, graphic, or some other type of file. Dreamweaver for Windows automatically adds the extension to your saved documents. But on Macs—which let you save files without extensions—make sure the file ends in the suffix .html or .htm when you save it.

8. **At the top of the document window, click inside the Title field and then type a name for the page.**

   Every new document Dreamweaver creates has the unflattering name "Untitled Document." If, at any given time, you do a quick search on Google for "Untitled Document," you'll find about 40 million pages. Dreamweaver probably created most of those pages, but obviously some people still need to pick up a Missing Manual. You should change this to a descriptive title indicating the main topic of the page, like "Directions to Cafe Soylent Green," "About Cafe Soylent Green," or "Technical Specifications for the Anodyne 3000 Indoor Lawn Mower." Not only is replacing "Untitled Document" more professional, providing a descriptive title can improve a web page's ranking among search engines.

UP TO SPEED

Naming Your Files and Folders

The rules for naming files and folders in Windows and on Macs are fairly flexible. You can use letters, numbers, spaces, and even symbols like $, #, and !.

Web servers, on the other hand, are far less accommodating. Because many symbols—such as &, ⌘, and ?—have special significance on the Web, using them in file names can confuse web servers and cause errors.

The precise list of no-nos varies from web server to web server, but you'll be safe if you stick to letters, numbers, hyphens (-), and underscore characters (_) when you name files and

folders. Stay away from spaces. File names like *company logo. gif* or *This company's president.html* may or may not work on a web server. Replace spaces with underscores or inner caps—*company_logo.gif* or *companyLogo.gif*—and remove all punctuation marks.

Sure, some operating systems and web servers permit strange naming conventions, but why take the chance? Someday you may need to move your site to another, less forgiving server. Play it safe: Keep your file names simple.

■ Managing Files and Folders with the Files Panel

Dreamweaver's Files panel provides a fast way to add blank web pages to your site. With one click, you can create a new page in any folder, saving you several steps compared to using the File menu. In addition, you can use the Files panel to add folders, rename files and folders, and move files into and out of folders on your site.

Adding Files

To create a new, blank web page, open the Files panel using one of the methods described on page 23 (for example, choose Window→Files), and then right-click (Control-click) on a file or folder in the Files panel. In the shortcut menu that appears, choose New File. Dreamweaver creates a new, empty page in the same folder as the selected page or, if you selected a folder, it creates the page there.

The type of file Dreamweaver creates depends on the type of site you're creating. For a plain HTML site, Dreamweaver produces a blank HTML page. If you're building a dynamic, database-driven site, however (like those described in Chapter 22), Dreamweaver creates a blank page based on the type of server model you select. For example, if you build a site using PHP and MySQL, Dreamweaver creates a blank PHP page (named *untitled.php*).

> **NOTE** The doctype (page xx) of a new web page created with the Files panel depends on your Dreamweaver Preferences settings: Choose Edit→Preferences (Dreamweaver→Preferences on Macs), select the New Document category, and choose HTML5 (or whichever doctype you prefer) from the Default Document Type menu. You can set other options for new documents in this window as well, such as the file extension you prefer (.html or .html, for instance).

The new file appears in the Files panel with a highlighted naming rectangle next to it; type a name for the page here. Don't forget to add the appropriate HTML extension (.htm or .html)—if you do forget, Dreamweaver creates a completely empty file, no starter HTML included (and changing the name by adding the .html extension won't fix the problem). If this happens, delete the file and create a new one. (If you're creating a PHP file, make sure the file name ends in .php.)

> **NOTE** If, immediately after creating a new file in the Files panel, you rename that file and add a new extension, Dreamweaver updates the file to reflect the new file type. For example, changing *untitled.html* to *global.css* erases all the HTML code in the file and turns it into an empty CSS file.

Adding Folders

You can add folders to your site using the Files panel, too. Right-click (Control-click) any file or folder. From the shortcut menu, choose New Folder. If you click a file name, Dreamweaver creates the new folder in the same folder as that file; if you click a folder, you get a new folder inside the existing one.

If you crave variety, you can add a folder another way. Select a file or folder in the Files panel, click the contextual menu button (at the top-right of the Files panel), and then select File→New Folder. Finally, in the naming rectangle that appears in the Files panel, type a name for the new folder.

Moving Files and Folders

Because the Dreamweaver Files panel looks and acts so much like Windows Explorer and the Mac Finder, you may think it does nothing more than let you move and rename files and folders. You may even be tempted to work with your site files directly on your Windows or Mac desktop, thinking that you're saving time. Think again. When it comes to moving site files and folders, Dreamweaver does more than your computer's desktop ever could.

In your Web travels, you've probably encountered the dreaded "404: File Not Found" error. This "broken link" message doesn't necessarily mean that the page doesn't exist; it just means that your web browser didn't find the page at the location (URL) the link specified. Someone working on the website probably moved or renamed the file without updating the link. Because website files are interrelated in such complex ways—pages link to other pages, which include paths to graphics, which in turn appear on other pages—an action as simple as moving one file can wreak havoc on an entire site. That's why you should always use the Files panel, rather than Windows Explorer or the Macintosh Finder, to rearrange your files.

Moving and reorganizing website files is so headache-ridden and error-prone that some web designers avoid it altogether, leaving their sites straining under the weight of thousands of poorly organized files. But Dreamweaver's Files panel makes organizing a site easy and error-free. When you use the panel to move files, Dreamweaver looks for actions that could break your site's links and automatically rewrites the paths of links, images, and other media (see the cautionary note below).

TIP Note to JavaScript coders: If your custom JavaScript programs include paths to web pages, images, or other files on your site, Dreamweaver can't help you. When you reorganize your site with the Files panel, the program updates *links* it created, but not any *paths* in your JavaScript programs.

Just be sure to do your file and folder moving from within Dreamweaver, like this: In the Files panel, drag the file or folder into its new folder (see Figure 1-17). To move multiple files, Ctrl-click (⌘-click) each and then drag them as a group; to deselect a file, Ctrl-click or ⌘-click it again. You can also select a file or folder and then Shift-click another file or folder to select all the content between the two.

NOTE Close *all* your web documents *before* you reorganize your files. Dreamweaver has been known to skip updating links in open files. But if you do end up with malfunctioning links, you can always use Dreamweaver's Find Broken Links tool (page 745) to ferret out and fix them.

When you release the mouse button, the Update Files dialog box appears (Figure 1-17); click Update and Dreamweaver rewrites the links.

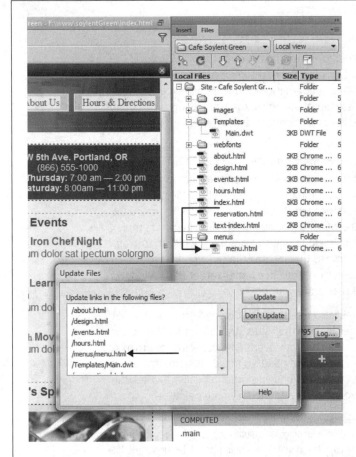

FIGURE 1-17

You can move files and folders within the Files panel just as you would in Windows Explorer or the Macintosh Finder. Simply drag the file into (or out of) a folder. Here, you're moving the menu.html file from the Webfonts folder to the Menus folder. Unlike your computer's file system, Dreamweaver monitors the links between web pages, graphics, and other files. If you move a file using Windows Explorer or the Finder, you'll most likely end up breaking the links. By contrast, Dreamweaver is smart enough to know when moving files will cause problems. The Update Files dialog box triggers Dreamweaver to update the links to and from the moved files so your site keeps working properly.

NOTE If you accidentally drag a file or folder to the wrong location, click Don't Update. Then drag the file or folder back to its original location and, if Dreamweaver asks, click Don't Update once again.

Renaming Files and Folders

Renaming files and folders poses the same problems as moving them. Because links include file and folder names, altering a name can break a link just as easily as moving or deleting a file or folder.

Say you create a new site with a home page named *home.html*. You cheerfully continue building the other pages of your site, linking them to *home.html* as you go along. But after reading this chapter and checking the default file name your web server requires (see "Setting Up a Site" on page 19), you find you need to rename your home page *index.html*. If you were to rename the file *index.html* using Windows Explorer or the Macintosh Finder, every link to *home.html* would result in a "File not found" error!

Dreamweaver handles this potential disaster effortlessly, as long as you rename the file in the Files panel. To do so, click the file or folder name in the panel, pause a moment, and then click it again. (The pause ensures that Dreamweaver won't think you just double-clicked the name to launch the file.) Dreamweaver highlights the name, ready for you to type in a new name. Be sure to include the proper extension. For example, image GIFs end with .gif and Cascading Style Sheets end with .css. Although Dreamweaver lets you name files without using an extension, extension-less files won't work when you move them to a web server, and Dreamweaver may not open the file correctly without an extension.

Finally, in the Update Files dialog box, click Update. Dreamweaver updates all the links to the newly named file or folder.

NOTE It bears repeating: Never rename or move files or folders *outside* of Dreamweaver. If you use Windows Explorer or the Macintosh Finder to reorganize your site's files, links will break, images will disappear, and the earth will open underneath your feet. (Well, that last thing won't happen, but it can *feel* that way when your boss comes in and says, "What happened to our website? Nothing works!")

If you move files outside of Dreamweaver by accident and break links, see "Finding Broken Links" on page 745 to learn how to fix them.

Deleting Files and Folders

It's a good idea to clean up your site from time to time by deleting old and unused files. Just as with moving and renaming files, you delete them from the Files panel.

To delete a file or folder, select it in the Files panel and then press Backspace or Delete. (To select multiple files or folders, Ctrl-click [⌘-click] them.) If no other page references the doomed file or folder, a simple "Are you sure you want to delete this file?" warning appears; click Yes.

If other files link to the file or to files within the folder you want to delete, Dreamweaver displays a warning message (Figure 1-18) informing you that you're about to break links on one or more pages.

The message even lists the first few pages that use the file.

If you're sure you want to delete the file or folder, click Yes. If you made a mistake, click No to leave your site untouched.

Clicking Yes breaks the links in all the pages. Repairing those links, which usually means using a new URL, requires a separate step: using the Site→Change Links Sitewide command, as described on page 751.

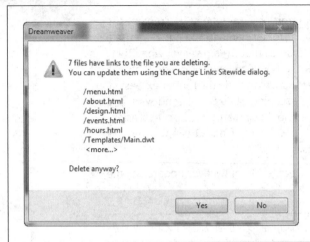

FIGURE 1-18

When you delete files in the Files panel, Dreamweaver tells you if other site pages link to that file. If they do, you need to repair the links in the relevant files. Dreamweaver makes that easy via the Change Links Sitewide command (see page 751)—and it reminds you of the feature in this dialog box.

NOTE If you move files to your site folder using Windows Explorer or the Mac Finder, Dreamweaver might not be aware of those files or links between those files and others in your site. If that's the case, when you move or delete files, Dreamweaver may not correctly update links or warn you of broken links caused by deleting a necessary file. To make Dreamweaver aware of any new files you add, choose Site→Advanced→Recreate Site Cache. Dreamweaver scans the files in the local site folder and updates the cache (its database of files and links on the site).

■ The Dreamweaver Test Drive

Although reading a book is a good way to learn the ins and outs of a program, nothing beats sitting in front of a computer and putting that program through its paces. Many of this book's chapters, therefore, conclude with hands-on training: step-by-step tutorials that show you how to create a real, working, professionally designed website for a fictional cafe, Cafe Soylent Green.

The rest of this chapter introduces Dreamweaver by taking you step by step through the process of building a web page. It shouldn't take more than an hour. When it's over, you'll have learned the basic steps for building any web page: creating and saving a new document, adding and formatting text, inserting graphics, adding links, and tapping the program's site-management features.

If you already use Dreamweaver and want to jump right into the details of the program, feel free to skip this tutorial. (And if you're the type who likes to read first and try second, read Chapters 2 through 5 and then return to this point to practice what you just learned.)

NOTE The tutorial in this chapter requires the example files from this book's website at *http://oreilly.com/ missingmanuals/cds/dreamweaverccmm13/*. Click the Download Tutorials link to save the files to your local drive. The tutorial files are in ZIP format, a technology that compresses a lot of files into one, smaller archive file.

Windows folks should download the ZIP file and then double-click it to open the archive. Click Extract All Files and then follow the instructions to store the files on your computer. Mac users can just double-click the file to decompress it.

After you download and decompress the files, you should have an *MM_DWCC* folder on your computer, containing all the tutorial files for this book.

FREQUENTLY ASKED QUESTION

Beware "Site-Less" Web Design

Why doesn't Dreamweaver update links when I move a file or warn me when I delete a file that other pages link to?

Dreamweaver's site-management tools always have your back—unless you're not working within a site. That can happen if you make the wrong choice in the Files panel.

The Files panel lets you browse all the files on your local drive, just like Windows Explorer or the Mac Finder does. If you click the Sites menu in the Files panel (where you'd normally switch between sites) and scroll to the top of the list, you'll see a list of all the hard drives and other storage devices on your home or office network.

Sometimes people accidentally select their hard drive (C: or Macintosh HD, for example) instead of the site they want to work on, and *then* they navigate to the folder holding their

site's files. They begin working, blissfully unaware that they're doing so without Dreamweaver's safety net. When you work on your files this way, Dreamweaver doesn't monitor the changes you make to your files—like moving, deleting, or renaming them. In other words, Dreamweaver normally rewrites page links when you move a file that other pages link to, and it warns you when you delete a file that other pages use. But when you're working in "site-less" mode, with your hard drive selected in the Sites menu, Dreamweaver can't help you. Similarly, all of Dreamweaver's other site-management features, like libraries (Chapter 19), templates (Chapter 20), and file transfers (Chapter 18), don't work when you're off in Unmonitored-Site Land. In other words, it's best to always set up a local site, and always make sure you select the site's name in the Files panel to work on that site.

Phase 1: Getting Dreamweaver in Shape

Before you start working in Dreamweaver, make sure the program's set up to work for you. In the following steps, you'll double-check some key Dreamweaver settings and organize your workspace using Dreamweaver's Workspace Layout feature.

First, make sure your preferences are all set:

1. **If it isn't already open, start Dreamweaver.**

   Hey, you've got to start with the basics, right?

2. **Choose Edit→Preferences (Windows) or Dreamweaver→Preferences (Macs).**

The Preferences dialog box opens, listing a dizzying array of categories and options (see Figure 1-19).

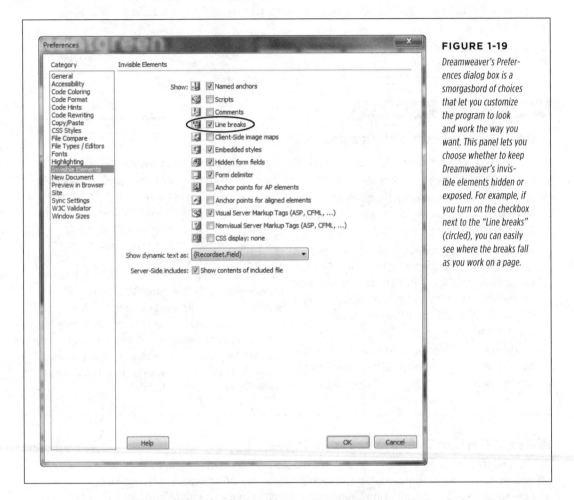

FIGURE 1-19

Dreamweaver's Preferences dialog box is a smorgasbord of choices that let you customize the program to look and work the way you want. This panel lets you choose whether to keep Dreamweaver's invisible elements hidden or exposed. For example, if you turn on the checkbox next to the "Line breaks" (circled), you can easily see where the breaks fall as you work on a page.

3. **Select the Invisible Elements category and then turn on the fourth checkbox from the top, Line Breaks (circled in Figure 1-19).**

Sometimes, when you paste text from other programs, like Microsoft Word or an email program, Dreamweaver displays what were once separate paragraphs as one long, single paragraph broken up with invisible characters called *line breaks* (for you HTML-savvy readers, this is the <br> tag). Normally, you can't see the line break character in Dreamweaver's Design view. This setting makes sure you can—it uses a little gold shield to represent breaks in the document. The shield gives you an easy way to select a line break and remove it to create a single paragraph by combing the text before and after the line break, or to create two paragraphs from one long one.

4. **Click OK.**

The Preferences dialog box closes. You're ready to get your workspace in order. As noted at the beginning of this chapter, Dreamweaver offers many windows to help you build web pages. For this tutorial, though, you need only four: the Insert panel, the document window, the Properties panel, and CSS Designer. But for good measure (and to give you a bit of practice), you'll open another panel and rearrange the workspace a little. To get started, have Dreamweaver display the space-saving Compact workspace.

5. **From the Workspace Switcher on the Application bar, select Compact (see Figure 1-20), or go to Window→Workspace Layout from the main menu and then select Compact from the drop-down list.**

If you see Compact already selected, choose Reset 'Compact,' which moves any panels that were resized, closed, or repositioned back to their original locations. The Compact workspace puts the Properties panel below the document window and displays the Insert and Files panels on the right. You choose one or the other of these panels by clicking the appropriate tab. Below that, in the panels group, you find the CSS Designer and the CSS Transitions panels.

In the next step, you'll turn the handy Insert panel into a toolbar, so you have easy access to its commands.

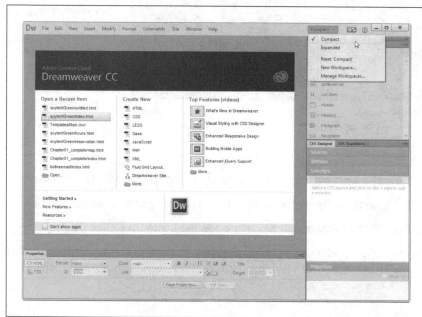

FIGURE 1-20

The Dreamweaver Welcome screen (middle) lists recently opened files in the left-hand column. Clicking a file name opens that file for editing. The middle column provides a quick way to create a new web page or define a new site. In addition, you can access introductory videos and other getting-started material from the screen's right-hand panel. Dreamweaver displays the Welcome screen when you have no documents open in the document window.

6. **Grab the Insert tab and then drag the Insert panel to just below the Application bar. When you see a blue line as shown in Figure 1-21, release the mouse button.**

When you drag the Insert panel away from the panel group, it looks like a floating palette, and that's what it would be if you let go of the mouse button. When it's near workspace edges where it can dock, you see a blue line. When you let go of the mouse to dock the panel, Dreamweaver transforms it into a toolbar with no text labels, just icons. Tabs across the top let you choose from different Insert sets like Common, Media, and Favorites. If you don't know what a button does, hold the cursor over the button and Dreamweaver displays a descriptive tooltip. That won't work now because the buttons are disabled since you don't have a document open.

Now the workspace looks great. It displays most of the tools you need for this tutorial (and for much of your web page building). Since this arrangement is so useful, you'll want to save it as a custom layout (OK, maybe you don't, but play along).

FIGURE 1-21

Customize your workspace to match the way you want to work. A key to this is positioning Dreamweaver's windows and palettes where you need them. Here, you're positioning the Insert panel under the Application bar. When you see a thick blue line, the panel is ready to dock in a new location. When you move the Insert panel to this position, it changes into a toolbar.

7. **From the Application bar's Workspace Switcher, choose New Workspace.**

The Save Workspace window appears, waiting for you to name your new layout.

8. **Type *Missing Manual* (or any name you like), and then click OK.**

You just created a new workspace layout. To see if it works, switch to another one of Dreamweaver's layouts, see how the screen changes, and then switch back to your new setup.

9. **From the Workspace Switcher, choose Expanded.**

   This moves the panels around a bit. The Insert panel jumps back over to the panels group. The whole group is wider, which gives the CSS Designer more room to display its tools. This is just a demonstration/detour, so now you'll switch back.

10. **From the Workspace Switcher, choose Missing Manual (or whatever you named your custom space in step 8).**

    Voilà! Dreamweaver resets everything the way you had it before. You can create multiple workspaces for different websites or different types of sites.

Phase 2: Creating a Website

As discussed on page 19, whenever you use Dreamweaver to create or edit a website, your first step should always be to show Dreamweaver the location of your *local site folder* (also called the local root folder)—the master folder for all your website's files. You do this by *setting up a site*, like so:

1. **Choose Site→New Site.**

   The Site Setup window appears. You only need to provide two pieces of information to get started.

2. **Type *Test Drive* in the Site Name field.**

   The name you type here is for your own reference; it lets you identify the site in Dreamweaver's Site menu. Dreamweaver also asks where you want to store the website's files. In this example, you'll use one of the folders you downloaded from this book's website (at other times, you'll choose or create a folder of your own).

3. **Click the folder icon next to the label "Local site folder."**

   The Choose Root Folder window opens so you can navigate to a folder on your hard drive to serve as your local folder. (This is where you'll store the HTML documents and graphics, CSS, and other web files that make up your site.)

4. **Browse to and select the *Chapter01* folder located inside the *MM_DWCC* folder you downloaded earlier. Click the "Select Folder (Choose)" button to set this folder as the local root folder.**

   At this point, you've given Dreamweaver all the information it needs to successfully work with the tutorial files.

NOTE   You'll find finished versions of all the tutorials in this book in the *MM_DWCC* folder; the completed files have "_complete" appended to the chapter name. The finished version of *this* tutorial is in the *Chapter01_complete* folder.

---

5. Click Save to close the Site Setup window.

After you set up a site, Dreamweaver creates a *site cache* for it (see page 23). Since there are hardly any files in the *Chapter01* folder, you may not even notice this happening—it goes by in the blink of an eye.

Phase 3: Creating and Saving a Web Page

"Enough already! I want to build a web page," you're probably saying. You'll do just that now:

1. Choose File→New.

The New Document window opens. Creating a blank web page involves a few clicks.

2. From the left-hand list of document categories, select Blank Page; in the Page Type list, highlight HTML; and from the Layout list, choose <none>. From the DocType menu in the bottom-right, select HTML5.

As discussed on page xx, HTML comes in a variety of flavors, called doctypes. HTML5 is the latest and greatest version, so use it.

3. Click Create.

Dreamweaver opens a new, blank HTML page. Even though the underlying code for an HTML page differs in slight ways depending on which document type you chose (HTML 4.01 Transitional, XHTML 1.0 Strict, HTML5, and so on), you have nothing to worry about: When you add HTML in Design view, Dreamweaver writes the correct code for your doctype.

If you see a bunch of strange text in the document window, you're looking at the underlying HTML, and you're in either Code or Split view. If your monitor is wide enough to view both the Code and Design views side by side, select the Split button at the top of the document window; if monitor is on the small side, click Design. (If you don't see these buttons, choose View→Toolbars→Document.) You'll work mainly in the visual Design view for this tutorial.

4. Choose File→Save.

The Save As dialog box opens.

Always save a newly created page right away. This good habit prevents serious headaches if the power goes out as you finish that beautiful—but unsaved— creation.

5. Save the page in the *Chapter01* folder as *index.html*.

You could also save the page as *index.htm*; both .html and .htm are valid extensions for HTML files. On most web servers, you'll name the home page *index. html* (see the box on page 713 for an explanation).

Make sure you save this page in the correct folder. In Phase 2 earlier, you told Dreamweaver to use *Chapter01* as the site's root folder—the folder that holds all the pages and files for the site. If you save the page in a folder outside of *Chapter01*, Dreamweaver gets confused and its site-management features won't work correctly.

TIP When you save a file, you can quickly jump to the current site's root folder. In the Save As dialog box, click the Site Root button—that takes you right to the root folder. This little trick also works when you link to or open a file.

---

6. **If the document window toolbar isn't already open, choose View→Toolbars →Document to display it.**

   The toolbar at the top of the document window provides easy access to a variety of tasks you'll do frequently, like titling a page, previewing it in a browser, and looking at the HTML.

7. **In the toolbar's Title field, select the text "Untitled Document," and then type in *Welcome to Cafe Soylent Green.***

   The Title field holds the page's title—the information that appears in the title bar of a web browser. The title also shows up as the name of your page when someone searches the web. In addition, a clear and descriptive title that identifies the main point of a page can also help increase a page's rank among the major search engines.

   If you have Split view turned on, you'll notice that in Code view, Dreamweaver updated the <title> tag in the HTML to read "<title>Welcome to Cafe Soylent Green</title>."

8. **In the Properties panel, click the Page Properties button, or choose Modify→ Page Properties.**

   The Page Properties dialog box opens (see Figure 1-22), letting you define the basic look of each web page you create. Six categories of settings control attributes like text color, background color, link colors, and page margins.

9. **From the "Page font" menu, select "Segoe, Segoe UI, DejaVu sans, Trebuchet MS, sans-serif."**

   This sets a basic font (and backup fonts, in case your visitor's machine lacks Segoe) that Dreamweaver automatically uses for all the text on the page. But as you'll see later in this tutorial, you can always specify a different font for selected text.

   Next, you'll set a basic text color for the page.

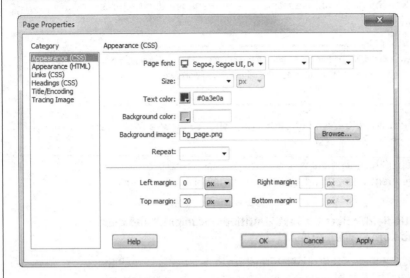

FIGURE 1-22

Dreamweaver clearly indicates which page properties use CSS and which rely on HTML. Avoid the category labeled "Appearance (HTML)," as the options there add old, out-of-date code to your pages.

10. **Click the small gray box next to "Text color." From the palette that pops up, choose a color (a dark green color works well with this site).**

    Unless you intervene, all web page text starts out black; the text on this page reflects the color you select here. In the next step, you'll add an image as a background to liven up the page.

    NOTE Alternatively, you could type a color value, like *#333333*, into the color field. That's *hexadecimal* notation, which is familiar to HTML coding gurus. Both the pop-up color palette and the hexadecimal color-specifying field appear fairly often in Dreamweaver. Dreamweaver CC even lets you specify a color using other values, such as RGB (red-green-blue) and HSL (hue-saturation-lightness) values. See page 138 for more on setting colors in Dreamweaver.

11. **To the right of "Background image," click the Browse button.**

    The Select Image Source window appears (see Figure 1-23). Use it to navigate to and then select a graphic.

12. **Click the Site Root button at the top of the window (bottom on Macs). Select the file *bg_page.png*, and then click OK (Open).**

    In Dreamweaver, you can select a file *and* close the selection window just by double-clicking the file name.

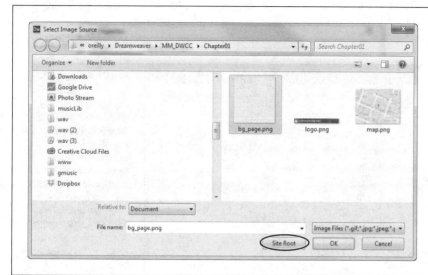

FIGURE 1-23

Use the Select Image Source window to insert graphics on a web page. The Site Root button (circled) is a shortcut to your local site's main, or root, folder—a nifty way to quickly get to your root folder when you search for a file.

NOTE Note for Windows users: Windows normally doesn't display a file's extension. So when you navigate to the images folder in step 12 previously, you might see *bg_page* instead of *bg_page.png*. Since file extensions are an important way people (and web servers) identify the types of files a website uses, you probably want Windows to display extensions. Here's how you do that: In Windows Explorer, navigate to and select the *MM_DWCC* folder. If you use Windows 7 or Vista, choose Organize→"Folder and search options." If you use Windows XP, choose Tools→Folder Options. In the Folder Options window, select the View tab, and then turn off the "Hide extensions for known file types" checkbox. To apply this setting to the tutorial files, click OK; to apply it to all the files on your computer, click the "Apply to Folders" button, and then click OK.

13. **In the Left margin field, type *0*; in the Top margin field type *20*.**

    The 0 setting for the left margin removes the little bit of space web browsers insert between the contents of your web page and the left side of the browser window. The 20 adds 20 pixels between the top of the browser window and the page contents.

    If you like, you can change this setting to make the browser add more space to the top and left side of the page, or set both values to 0 to remove any space between the page's content and the browser window edges. In fact, you can even add a little extra empty space on the *right* side of a page. (The right margin control is especially useful for languages that read from right to left, like Hebrew or Arabic.)

14. **Back in the Category menu (far left of the Page Properties window), click Links (CSS), and then add the following properties: In the "Link color" field, type *#336633*; in the "Visited links" field, type *#999999*; in the "Rollover**

links" field, type *#CC9900* ; and in the "Active links" field, type *#FF0000*
(see Figure 1-24).

These hexadecimal codes specify the colors for links on your web page (see
page 138 for more on choosing colors in Dreamweaver).

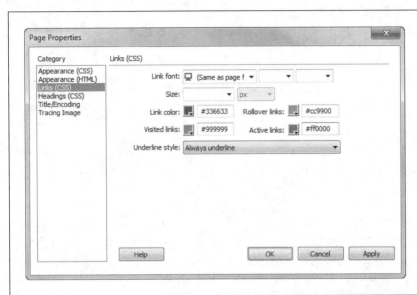

FIGURE 1-24

*You can set several hyperlink
properties using the Links
(CSS) category of the Page
Properties dialog box. For
example, you can choose
a different font and size
for links, as well as specify
colors for the four link states
(unvisited, hovered over,
clicked, and visited). Finally,
you can choose whether (or
when) a browser underlines
links. Most browsers automatically do, but you can
override that behavior with
the help of this dialog box.*

Links come in four varieties: regular, visited, active, and rollover. A *regular* link
is a plain old link, unvisited, untouched. A *visited* link is one you've already
clicked, as noted in your browser's History list. An *active* link is one you're currently clicking, so you see this color for the split second that you're pressing
the mouse button. And finally, a *rollover* link changes color as you mouse over
it without clicking. You can choose different colors for each of these states.

While it may seem like overkill to have four link colors, the regular and visited
links provide useful feedback to visitors by telling them which links they already
followed and which remain to be checked out. For its part, the rollover link gives
you instant feedback, changing color as soon as you move your cursor over it.
The active link color isn't that useful for navigating a site since its color changes
so briefly you probably won't even notice it.

NOTE   Although Dreamweaver uses the term *rollover* link, in the world of Cascading Style Sheets, this is
called a *hover* link.

15. **Click OK to close the window and apply your changes.**

If you look at the top of the document window, you'll see an asterisk next to
the file name—that's Dreamweaver's way of telling you that you haven't saved

a page you edited, a nice reminder to save your files frequently and prevent heartache if the program suddenly shuts down (see circled image in Figure 1-25).

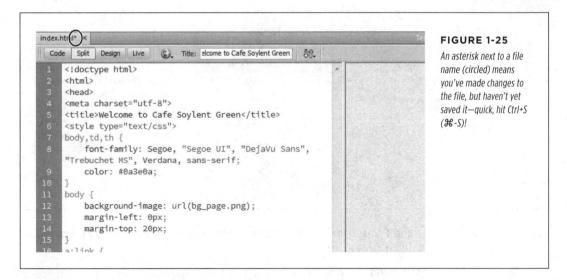

FIGURE 1-25

An asterisk next to a file name (circled) means you've made changes to the file, but haven't yet saved it—quick, hit Ctrl+S (⌘-S)!

If you've been working in Split view, you'll also notice that Dreamweaver added the HTML <style> tag along with some other code—this is called a CSS style sheet and the code dictates how a browser displays your pages (you'll learn all about this in Chapter 3).

16. **Choose File→Save (or press Ctrl+S [⌘-S]).**

    Save your work frequently. (This isn't a web technique so much as a computer-always-crashes-when-you-least-expect-it technique.)

Phase 4: Adding Images and Text

Now you'll add the real meat of your web page, words and pictures:

1. **From the Image menu on the Insert bar's Common tab, select Image (see Figure 1-26).**

    Alternatively, choose Insert→Image. Either way, the Select Image Source dialog box opens. (If you didn't make changes to your workspace as described in Phase 1 earlier, the Insert bar is really the Insert panel and it appears in the right-hand group of panels.)

2. **Make sure you're in the local root folder and double-click the *logo.png* graphics file.**

    The Cafe Soylent Green image appears in the upper-left corner of your web page. After you insert an image, it remains selected as shown in Figure 1-27. Its properties appear in the Properties panel below the document window. If you click elsewhere on the page, that deselects the image and its properties are no longer displayed.

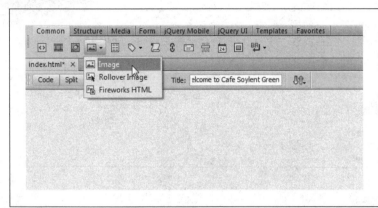

FIGURE 1-26

Some of the buttons on Dreamweaver's Insert toolbar do double duty as menus (the ones with the small, black, down-pointing arrows). Once you select an option from the menu (in this case, the Image object), it becomes the button's current setting. If you want to insert the same type of object again, you don't need to use the menu—just click the button.

3. **In the Properties panel's Alt text box (circled in Figure 1-27), type *Cafe Soylent Green*.**

"Alt" stands for Alternative, but the text you type here is really all about accessibility. It makes your pages more accessible to people who visit websites using alternative devices—for example, people with viewing disabilities who require screen readers to read the contents of a web page out loud. That's where the *alt* property comes in. This text description is useful not only for screen-reading software, but for people who deliberately *turn off* pictures in their web browser so pages load faster. (Search engines also look at *alt* properties when they index a page, so an accurate description can help your site's search-engine rankings.)

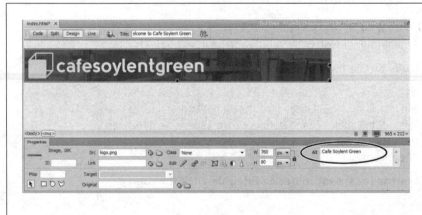

FIGURE 1-27

When you select an image in the document window, the Properties panel reveals the image's dimensions. A thumbnail of the image appears in the top-left of the panel, as does the word "Image" (to identify the type of element you selected), along with the image's file size (in this case, 16 KB). You'll learn about other image properties in Chapter 5.

4. **Deselect the image by clicking anywhere else in the document window or by pressing the right arrow key.**

Keep your keyboard's arrow keys in mind—they're a great way to deselect a page element *and* move your cursor into place to add text or more images.

5. **Press Enter (Return) to create a new paragraph. Type *Welcome to Cafe Soylent Green.***

Make sure you're in Design view here—pressing Enter (Return) in Code view simply inserts a carriage return and no paragraph tags. Notice that the text is a dark color and uses the Segoe (or, if you don't have Segoe installed, a substitute sans-serif) font; you set these options earlier, in the Page Properties dialog box. The Properties panel now displays text-formatting options.

NOTE The key called Enter on a Windows keyboard is named Return on most Macintosh keyboards and Enter on others. So on Macs, you press either Return or Enter.

6. **In the Properties panel, click the HTML button and then, from the Format menu, choose Heading 1 (see Figure 1-28).**

The text you just typed becomes big and bold—the default style for Heading 1. Right now, the text doesn't stand out enough, so you'll change its color.

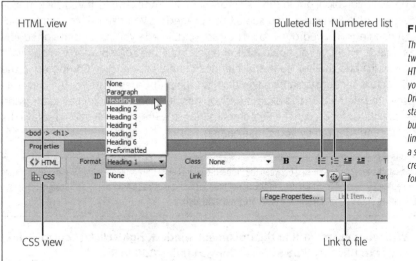

HTML view   Bulleted list   Numbered list

CSS view   Link to file

FIGURE 1-28

The Properties panel includes two views: HTML and CSS. The HTML view, shown here, lets you control the HTML tags Dreamweaver uses to create standard text elements like bulleted lists, paragraphs, and links. The CSS view provides a simple interface so you can create fancy CSS styles that format your text to look great.

7. **Select the text you just typed.**

Do so by either dragging carefully across the entire line or by triple-clicking anywhere inside the line. (Unlike the Format menu, which affects an entire *paragraph* at a time, many options in the Properties panel—like the one you'll use next—apply only to text you *select*.)

8. **In the Properties panel, click the CSS button so you can style the text. Look for New Rule under the Targeted rule drop-down menu, and then choose <New Inline Style> from the submenu. In the Color field to the right, replace the current value with #CC9900 (or select a color using the color box). Click in the document window to deselect the text so you can see its new color.**

Congratulations! You created a new CSS style in the middle of your content using what's known as an inline style. With your cursor somewhere inside this headline, the Properties panel's Targeted Rule box shows that it is an <inline style>.

9. **In the panels group on the right and part way down, you see the tab for CSS Designer. Under that is a section called Selectors. Section headers like Selectors and Properties work like an accordion—when you click a headline, the section expands to display the contents inside. If necessary, click the Selectors bar to view the contents, where you'll see a few selectors, including "<inline style>: h1."**

This is another way of explaining that the cursor is inside an h1 heading, but the heading isn't displaying the usual style because you added an inline style for it.

10. **To see the style Dreamweaver applies to a selector, look in the Properties section of CSS Designer (just below the Selectors section). Use the scroll bar to see all the properties.**

The items Dreamweaver displays in the Properties section change depending on what you highlight in the Selectors section. For example, if you click *<inline style>: h1* in Selectors, you see all the properties you can use to format your h1 headings. Grayed out properties are undefined—you haven't assigned any values to them. Scroll down a bit and you'll see the *color* property, along with a swatch and the hex code that defines the hue. If you click Computed in the Selectors section, Dreamweaver displays the properties in use for the currently selected element. In this example, if you position your cursor in the heading and highlight Computed in the Selectors section, the Properties section displays the color and font-family you chose earlier.

NOTE It's easy to get confused between the Properties panel below the document window and the properties *section* of the CSS Designer, which lives in the panel group. The Properties section of the CSS Designer displays the properties of CSS styles. Chapters 3 and 9 give you more details.

---

11. **With your cursor still in the document window, right-click (Control-click) any text. Choose "CSS Styles→Convert Inline CSS to Rule."**

The Convert Inline CSS dialog box opens.

12. **Set the "Convert to" menu to "All h1 tags," turn on the radio button labeled "The head of this document," and then click OK.**

You've successfully redefined the h1 style in your document. Now all h1 tags will sport the new color. Dreamweaver writes the CSS definition in the "head" section of your document. Want to take a peek? Change your document view to Split or Code view, and then look for h1 near the top of the code window.

In the CSS Designer panel's Selectors section, you'll see h1 listed, but it no longer displays <inline style> because you're no longer using an inline style. Dreamweaver formats the text using the new h1 style. What's more, when you create new h1 paragraphs, they'll look the same as this one.

You're not done yet. Next, you'll make more changes to h1, using the CSS Designer panel.

13. **In CSS Designer's Sources section, click <style>.**

The <style> entry represents the internal style sheet in the <head> part of your web page. When you choose <style>, CSS Designer's Selectors section displays the selectors defined in the internal style sheet.

14. **In the Selectors section of CSS Designer, click h1. In the Properties section, scroll down until you see the Text group and the font-family property within it. Click the grayed out words *default font* and then choose "Baskerville, Palatino Linotype, Palatino, Century Schoolbook L, Times New Roman, serif" from the drop-down menu.**

Once again, you're changing the definition of the h1 heading (also called the h1 tag). No extra steps are necessary when you change the definition in the CSS Designer panel. You can confirm the change by inspecting the code in the document window as you did in the previous step.

Time to add more text.

15. **Back in Design view, click to the right of the heading, and then press Enter (Return) to create a new paragraph.**

Although you may type a headline now and again, you'll probably get most of your text from word processing documents or emails from your clients, boss, or coworkers. To get that text into Dreamweaver, you simply copy it from the document and paste it into your web page.

16. **In the Files panel, double-click the file *home-page.txt* to open it.**

This file is just plain text—no formatting, just words. To get it into your document, you'll copy and paste it.

17. **Click anywhere inside the text, and then choose Edit→Select All, followed by Edit→Copy. Click the *index.html* tab to return to your web page and, finally, choose Edit→Paste.**

You should see a few gold shields sprinkled among the text (circled in Figure 1-29). If you don't, make sure you completed step 3 in Phase 1. These shields represent line breaks—spots where text drops to the next line without creating a new paragraph. You'll often see these shields in pasted text. If you find them, you need to remove them, and then create separate paragraphs.

18. **Click one of the gold shields and then press Enter (Return). Repeat this on all the other gold shields in the document window.**

This deletes the line break in the document (it actually deletes the HTML tag <br>) and creates two paragraphs out of one.

At this point, the pasted text is just a series of paragraphs. To give it some structure, you'll add headings and a bulleted list.

19. **Click in the paragraph that has the text "About the Cafe." In the Properties panel, click the HTML button, and then choose Heading 2 from the Format menu.**

That changes the paragraph to a headline, making it bigger and bolder.

FIGURE 1-29

Line breaks (circled) often crop up when you copy and paste text from other programs into Dreamweaver. Follow the steps on page 33 to make sure you can see the line breaks in Design view.

20. **Using the same technique as in step 19, assign the Heading 2 tag to the labels Location, Hours, and Specialties.**

You now have one Heading 1 and four Heading 2 headlines. The Heading 2 headlines could use a little style.

21. **Triple-click the headline "About the Cafe" to select it. In the Properties panel, click the CSS button. Make sure Targeted Rule is set to <New Inline Style>. Then, in the Size field, delete "none," and type *20*.**

Once again, you've created an inline style. This time it's within this h2 heading (About the Cafe). Notice that it is the only h2 heading affected by the size change to 20 pixels (px). Next, you'll update all the h2 headings to match.

22. **With your cursor in the "About the Cafe" heading, right-click (Control-click) and choose "CSS Styles→Convert Inline CSS to Rule."**

The Convert Inline CSS dialog box appears.

23. **Using the "Convert to" menu, choose "All h2 tags." In the "Create rule in" group, turn on the radio button labeled "The head of this document," and then click OK.**

Notice that all the h2 headings now look the same. The text gets a little smaller—the style you just created applies to all <h2> tags, and they now share the same font size, 20 pixels.

Next, you'll change the text's color.

24. **In CSS Designer Selectors, choose h2. Below that, in the Properties section, scroll down until you see the Text group and the color property. Replace the color currently there with *#339966*.**

You changed the color to a lighter and brighter shade of green.

25. **Under font-style, choose Italic.**

This italicizes the text and updates the h2 style you created earlier—that's why the other Heading 2 headlines are now italicized, too.

26. **Select the four paragraphs under the headline Specialties; drag from the start of the first paragraph to the end of the fourth paragraph.**

You can also drag up starting from the end of the last paragraph.

27. **In the Properties panel, click the HTML button, and then click the Unordered (bulleted) List button (see Figure 1-28).**

The paragraphs turn into a bulleted list of items, called an "unordered list" in HTML-speak. Finally, you'll highlight the Cafe's location and hours.

28. **Select the two paragraphs below the Location headline (beginning with "700 SW 5th" and ending with the phone number).**

You'll make the address bold.

29. **Make sure you have the HTML button pressed in the Properties panel, and then click the B button.**

Dreamweaver boldfaces the text, but you won't see any change in CSS Designer. Even though you find the Bold options in two places—the HTML Properties panel and the CSS Font Weight setting (Font→Font Weight→Bold)—they do different things. When you select bold in HTML mode, Dreamweaver inserts the HTML <strong> tag—used to "strongly" emphasize text. But when you choose Font→Font Weight→Bold button in CSS mode, Dreamweaver adds CSS code to the page to make the text look bold. It's a subtle but important difference—in HTML mode, you change the formatting of just the selected text, but in CSS mode, you'd create a style, and that style could change the formatting of all the text that shares the same tag, the paragraph tag (<p>) in this example. (You'll read more about this on page 104.) In this case, you want to use the HTML <strong> tag to emphasize the selected text.

30. **Repeat the previous step for the two paragraphs below the Hours headline, and then save the page.**

You'll add a few more design touches to the page, but first you should see how the page looks in a real web browser.

The Mysterious Haunted Steering Wheel

When I select a paragraph, an image...heck, anything at all, in Design view, a weird icon appears. It looks like a ship's steering wheel. What is it and how do I get rid of it?

You click this steering-wheel icon to open the Code Navigator window. That window (described on page 390) lists the CSS styles related to whatever page element you select. It's useful for people who like to skip Dreamweaver's user-friendly CSS Designer panel and create and edit CSS by hand. If you're new to CSS, this isn't a useful tool and that goofy icon, which looks like something Ahab's ghost misplaced, gets in the way. To hide it, click the icon to open the Code Navigator and turn on the "Disable indicator" checkbox in the bottom-right. If you ever want to turn the Navigator back on, choose View→Code Navigator to open the Code Navigator window, and then turn off the Disable checkbox.

Phase 5: Preview Your Work

Dreamweaver's Design view gives you a visual way to add and edit HTML, but its page presentation is frequently a long way off from that of a real web browser. Dreamweaver may display *more* information than you'd see on the Web, for example, including "invisible" objects, like table borders and those line breaks you removed earlier, or it may display *less* information (it sometimes has trouble rendering complex designs).

Furthermore, much to the eternal woe of web designers, different browsers display pages differently. Pages you view in Internet Explorer don't always look the same in other browsers, like Safari, Firefox, or Chrome. In some cases, the differences may be subtle (text may be slightly larger or smaller, for instance). In other cases, the changes are dramatic: Earlier versions of Internet Explorer, for example, can't display the text or drop shadows discussed on page 412.

If you're designing web pages for a company intranet and only have to worry about the one web browser your IT department puts on everyone's computer, you're lucky. Most people have to deal with the fact that their sites must withstand scrutiny from a wide range of browsers, so it's a good idea to preview your pages using whatever browsers you expect your visitors to use. Fortunately, Dreamweaver lets you do that using any browser you have on your computer.

NOTE With the increasing popularity of tablets and mobile phones, you can no longer just worry about how your web pages look in desktop browsers; you also have to think about how they look on the small screens of an iPhone, Android phone, or Windows phone. Chapter 12 has information on how Dreamweaver CC can help you make your websites mobile-ready.

One quick way to check a page in a web browser is to use Dreamweaver's built-in Live view, which lets you preview a page using a browser that's built into Dreamweaver.

1. **In the Document toolbar, click the Live button (circled in Figure 1-30).**

   The Live button highlights. The page doesn't look that different—for a simple page like this it won't, but Live view is great for previewing more complex CSS and for testing JavaScript interactivity (see page 573).

FIGURE 1-30

Dreamweaver's Live view (circled) lets you preview a page in a real web browser, one built into Dreamweaver.

There is one problem with Live view: It uses the page display engine that's working behind Google's Chrome browser. Chrome isn't the only browser out there, of course, so you want to test your page designs in other browsers, too. Fortunately, Dreamweaver makes it easy to jump straight to any browser installed on your computer.

2. **Click the Live button again to exit Live view.**

This is an important and easily overlooked step. When you're in Live view, you can't edit a page in Design view. Since a page in Live view can look very much like it does in Design view, it's easy to try to work on the page while you're in Live view and say "Hey, what's going on? Dreamweaver isn't working any more!" So always remember to exit Live view when it's time to work on your pages.

To preview your page in a web browser, you need to make sure Dreamweaver knows which browsers you have installed and where they are.

TIP While you can't edit a page in Design view while Live view is on, you can edit the HTML code in Code view. One common technique among HTML jockeys is to display Split view, and then turn on Live view. This opens the HTML code on the left and a live browser display on the right. They then merrily edit the HTML and view the changes in Live view. However, to see the effect of any changes you make in Code view, you need to click into the Live view area or press F5 to refresh the page.

---

3. **Choose File→Preview in Browser→Edit Browser List.**

The "Preview in Browser" preferences window opens (see Figure 1-31). When you install Dreamweaver, it detects the browsers on your computer; a list of them appears in this window. If you installed a browser *after* you installed Dreamweaver, it doesn't appear here, and you need to follow steps 4 and 5 next; otherwise, skip to step 6.

4. **Click the + button.**

The Add Browser or Select Browser window opens.

5. **Click the Browse button. Search your hard drive to find the browser you want to add to the list.**

Dreamweaver inserts the browser's default name in the Name field. To change it, select it, and then type in a new name. (But don't do this *before* you select the browser, since Dreamweaver erases anything you typed as soon as you select a browser.)

6. **In the window's Browser list, select the browser you most commonly use. Turn on the Primary Browser checkbox, and then click OK.**

You just designated this browser as your *primary* one. You can now preview your pages in this browser with a simple keyboard shortcut: F12 (Option-F12 on Macs—unfortunately, Apple assigned the F12 key to the Mac's Dashboard program, so it takes two keys to preview a web page—Option and F12 together; you can change this by creating your own keyboard shortcut, as described on page 869). If you use a Macintosh laptop, you may have to press Option-F12 *and* the function [fn] key in the lower-left corner of the keyboard.

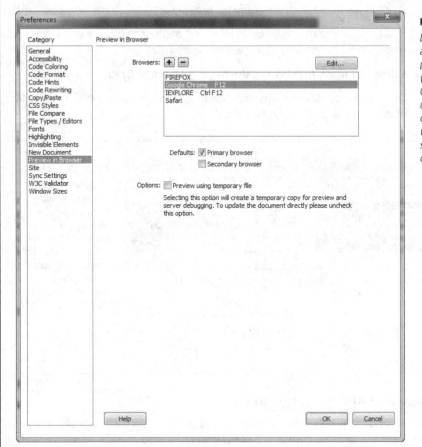

FIGURE 1-31

FIGURE 1-31

Dreamweaver can launch a web browser and load a page so you can preview your design-in-progress. One option—"Preview using temporary file"— comes in handy when you work with an external CSS style sheet, as described on page 150.

If you like, you can choose a secondary browser, which you launch by pressing Ctrl+F12 (⌘-F12).

Now you're ready to preview your document in your favorite browser.

NOTE Windows PCs don't list Google Chrome in the Program Files directory, as they do for most other programs. Depending on your version of Windows, you'll find Chrome in one of these locations:

- Windows 7: *C:\Users\Username\AppData\Local\Google*

- Vista: *C:\Users\UserName\AppDataLocal\Google\Chrome*

- XP: *C:\Documents and Settings\UserName\Local Settings\Application Data\Google\Chrome*

7. **Press F12 (Option-F12) or choose File→Preview in Browser and then, from the menu, select a browser.**

   The F12 key (Option-F12) is the most important keyboard shortcut you'll learn; it opens a web page in your primary browser so you can preview your work.

   You can also use the "Preview in Browser" menu (the globe icon) in the document window to preview a page (see Figure 1-32).

8. **When you finish previewing the page, go back to Dreamweaver.**

   Do so using your favorite way to switch programs on your computer—the taskbar in Windows or the Dock in Mac OS X.

FIGURE 1-32

The document window's "Preview in Browser" option is another way to preview a page. This menu has the added benefit of letting you select any browser on your computer, not just the ones to which you assigned keyboard shortcuts.

Phase 6: Finishing the Page

You've covered most of the steps you need to finish this web page. Now you just need to add a graphic, format the copyright notice, and provide a little more structure to the page.

1. **Scroll to the bottom of the page and select all the text in the copyright notice.**

   You can either triple-click inside the paragraph or drag from beginning to end.

2. **Click the CSS button in the Properties panel and make sure the Targeted Rule menu displays <New Inline Style>. Then, from the Size menu, choose 12.**

   You've created a new CSS style within a paragraph <p> tag. You can see the result in the CSS Designer's Selectors section. This time you want to create a reusable style that applies only to specific paragraphs of text—not every paragraph. So, you need to use what's called a *class style*.

3. **With your cursor still in the copyright text, right-click (Control-click) and then choose CSS Styles→Convert Inline CSS to Rule.**

   The Convert Inline CSS dialog box makes its appearance.

4. **Leave the "Convert to" menu set to "A new CSS class." In the text box to the right, type the word *copyright*. Click the "The head of this document" button and then click OK.**

While you won't see a change in the document's design, you've successfully created a new CSS class that you can apply to any paragraph you want. Notice in the Properties panel's CSS view that the Targeted rule now displays *.copyright.* Don't overlook the period (.) that precedes the word, as that's how browsers identify the CSS style as a class. Look in the CSS Designer's Selectors (Figure 1-33) and you see *.copyright* listed there, too. Scroll through the Properties for the *.copyright* selector and you see that it has the *font-size* property set to 12 px (pixels).

Another way to separate the copyright notice from the page's main content is to add a simple line above it. CSS lets you do that in the CSS Designer with a property called Border.

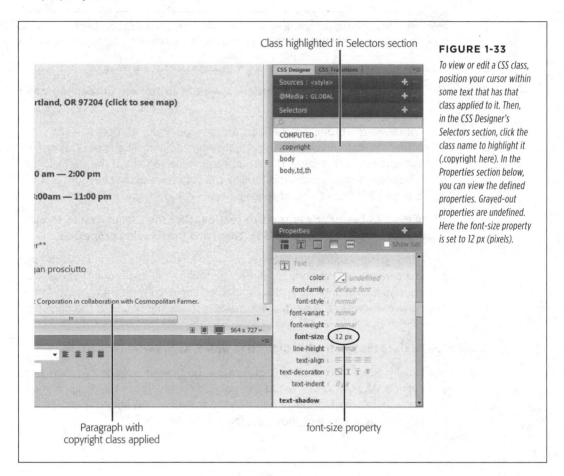

Class highlighted in Selectors section

Paragraph with
copyright class applied

font-size property

FIGURE 1-33

To view or edit a CSS class, position your cursor within some text that has that class applied to it. Then, in the CSS Designer's Selectors section, click the class name to highlight it (.copyright here). In the Properties section below, you can view the defined properties. Grayed-out properties are undefined. Here the font-size property is set to 12 px (pixels).

5. **In CSS Designer's Sources section, click <style>.**

Dreamweaver displays all the CSS selectors defined in the document's head in the Selectors section.

6. **In Selectors, click the *.copyright* class.**

You may need to scroll through the list to find it.

7. **In the Properties section of the CSS Designer, click the Border button (Figure 1-34) to scroll down to the Border group. Then, choose solid from the border-top-style menu.**

The CSS Designer panel is the command center for working with style sheets (see Figure 1-34). It lists all the styles available to the current web page and lets you edit them. You can even use CSS Designer to add new styles, as you'll learn on page 104.

> **NOTE** It takes three properties to define a border: border-style, border-width, and border-color. To add to this smorgasbord, you can place your border left, right, top, bottom, or on all sides of the selected text (see Figure 1-35).

8. **In Border properties, set border-top-width to *1px* and border-top-color to *#CC9900*.**

With all three properties defined (border-top-style, border-top-width, and border-top-color), your copyright notice has a handsome line to separate it from the rest of the page. Borderlines touch the content of the element they surround—in other words, this top line sits very close to the copyright text. It'll look better if there's a bit of space between it and the copyright notice.

9. **In the CSS Designer's Properties section, click the Layout icon to scroll to Layout properties (Figure 1-36). Then, find the Padding properties.**

Padding is the space that appears between an element's content (like the text in a paragraph or the graphic in the image tag) and its border. Dreamweaver displays its padding properties using a rectangle to represent content. As you make changes to the border properties, you see the results in the document window.

10. **Replace the *0* at the top of the box with *5*, as shown in Figure 1-36.**

Initially, the border setting is grayed out because the property hasn't been defined. After you enter a number, you see the change in the document window—there's more distance between the copyright text and the border. Next, you'll link to a map that shows the location of the cafe.

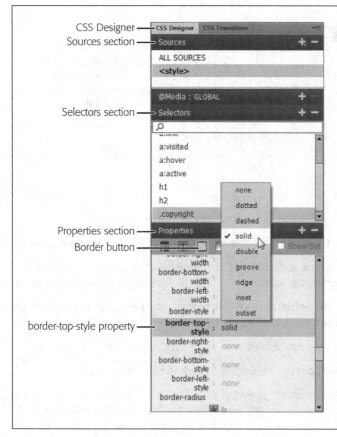

CSS Designer
Sources section
Selectors section
Properties section
Border button
border-top-style property

FIGURE 1-34

You'll often work in the CSS Designer panel from the top down, selecting from the sections Sources, Selectors, and Properties. Here, you've selected the <style> in the Sources section and the .copyright class in the Selectors section, and you're in the process of setting the border-style property.

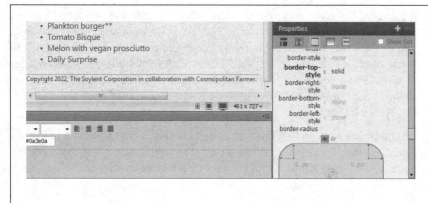

FIGURE 1-35

The CSS Border settings let you add a border around any (or all) of the four edges of any page element. In this case, you're adding a line just above the copyright notice. If, on the other hand, you were formatting a "What's new" sidebar, you might add a border around all four edges to make it stand out.

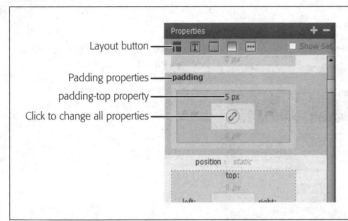

Layout button

Padding properties

padding-top property

Click to change all properties

FIGURE 1-36

Click the Layout button in CSS Designer's Properties section to see padding and margin properties. Here the padding-top property is set to 5 px. If you want to set the padding for all four sides at once, click the "link" button in the center.

11. **In the middle of the page, select the parenthetical text "click to see map."**

To create a link, you just need to tell Dreamweaver which page you want to link to. You can do this several ways. Using the Properties panel is the easiest.

12. **In the Properties panel, click the HTML button, and then click the folder icon that appears to the right of the Link field.**

The Select File dialog box appears.

13. **Click the Site Root button and double-click the file *map.html*.**

The Site Root button jumps you right to the folder containing your site. It's a convenient way to move quickly to your root folder. Double-clicking the file name tells Dreamweaver to insert the HTML needed to create a link along with the link's address.

If you save the page and then preview it in a web browser, click the link you just added. The browser jumps to another page (one already created for you). You'll notice that there's text near the bottom of the map that reads "back to home page." Since you just learned the powerful link-adding skill, open *map. html* and add a link to that page. Select the text "back to home page" and link to the *index.html* file by following steps 11 and 12, and then save the *map.html* file. We'll wait for you....

You may have noticed that the map page's content is contained in a box that's nicely centered in the middle of the screen. That would look great on your home page. You'll create a new layout element to achieve this effect.

14. **Return to the *index.html* file; click anywhere inside the page, and then choose Edit→Select All or press Ctrl+A (⌘-A).**

    You selected all the contents on the page. You'll wrap all the text and images in a <div> tag to create a kind of container for the page contents.

15. **Choose Insert→Div.**

    The Insert Div window opens (see Figure 1-37). A <div> tag simply provides a way to organize content on a page by grouping HTML—think of it as a box containing other HTML tags. For example, to create a sidebar that includes navigation links, news headlines, and Google ads, you'd wrap them all in a <div> tag. It's a very important tag for CSS-based layouts. You'll read more about it on page 428.

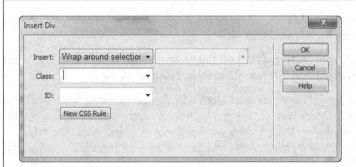

FIGURE 1-37

The Insert Div window provides an easy way to divide sections of a web page into groups of related HTML—like the elements that make up a page banner, for example (logo, navigation bar, and so on). You'll learn all the functions of this window on page 430.

Next, you need to create a style that provides the instructions that format this new <div> tag. You've already used the Properties panel to create a style, but that works only for text. To format other tags, you need to create a style in another way.

16. **Click the New CSS Rule button at the bottom of the Insert Div window.**

    The New CSS Rule window appears (a CSS style is technically called a "rule"). This window lets you specify the type of style you create, the style's name, and where Dreamweaver should store the style. You'll learn the ins and outs of this window in Chapter 3.

17. **From the top menu, choose "Class (can apply to any HTML element)," and then type *.container* in the "Choose or enter a name for your selector" field. Don't forget to include the period, and make sure you have "This document only" selected in the bottom menu. Click OK.**

    The "CSS Rule definition" window appears. (There's a lot going on in this box, but don't worry about the details at this point. You'll learn everything there is to know about creating styles later in this book. This part of the tutorial is intended to give you a taste for some of a web designer's daily page-building duties. So relax and follow along.) First, you'll add a border around the edges.

18. **From the left-hand list of categories, select Border. Leave the three "Same for all" checkboxes turned on, and choose "solid" for the style, type in *1* for the width, and then type *#336633* for the color.**

This action adds a green border around the edges of the content. Next, you'll give the <div> tag a set width and center it on the page.

19. **Click the Box category, and then, in the width field, type *760*.**

This makes the box 760 pixels wide—the same width as the banner. To make sure the text doesn't butt right up against the edge of the box, you'll add a little padding around the inside of this style.

20. **Make sure the "Same for all" checkbox is turned on, and then type *10* in the Top field under Padding.**

This adds 10 pixels of space inside the box, essentially pushing the text and the graphics away from the edges of it.

21. **Under the Margin settings, turn off the "Same for all" checkbox, and then, for both the right and left margin menus, select auto.**

The window should now look like Figure 1-38. Selecting "auto" for the left and right margins is your way of telling a browser to automatically supply values for those margins—in this case, as you'll see in a moment, it has the effect of centering the <div> element in the middle of a browser window.

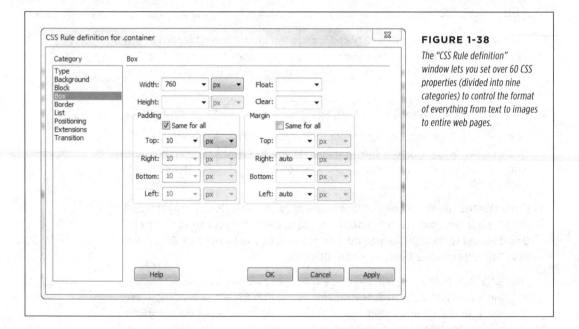

FIGURE 1-38

The "CSS Rule definition" window lets you set over 60 CSS properties (divided into nine categories) to control the format of everything from text to images to entire web pages.

22. **Click OK to complete the style.**

The Insert Tag window reappears, and the name of the style you just created—"container"—appears in a field labeled Class.

23. **In the Insert Div window, click OK.**

This inserts the new <div> tag and at the same time applies the style you just created. Now it's time to take a look at your handiwork.

24. **Choose File→Save All, and then press F12 (Option-F12) to preview your work in your browser (Figure 1-39).**

The Save All command saves the changes you made to both *index.html* and *map.html*. Test the link to make sure it works. Resize your browser and watch how the content centers itself in the middle of the window.

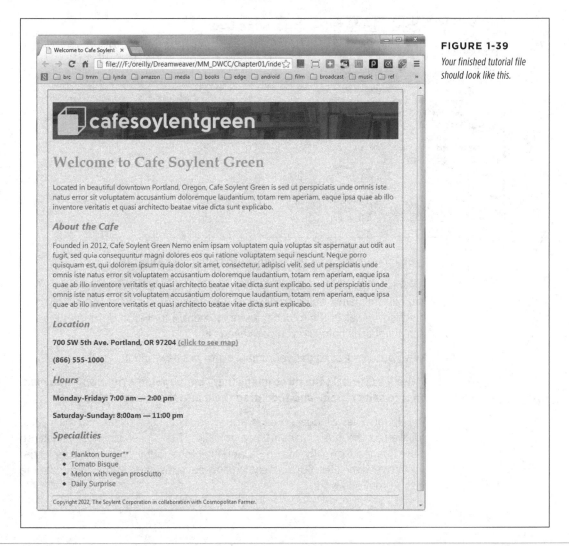

FIGURE 1-39

Your finished tutorial file should look like this.

Phase 7: Organizing Your Files

There's one last housekeeping chore to attend to. If you look at the Files panel, you'll notice that there are two web pages, three graphics (.png files), and a text file. Most web designers like to organize graphics files into folders to keep them in one place. You could create a folder in Windows Explorer or the Mac Finder, but why bother when you can do it directly in Dreamweaver?

1. **In the Files panel, right-click (Control-click) the Site folder listed under "Local view" (circled in Figure 1-40). From the drop-down menu, choose New Folder.**

   Dreamweaver adds a new "untitled" folder to the files list and highlights the name, ready for editing.

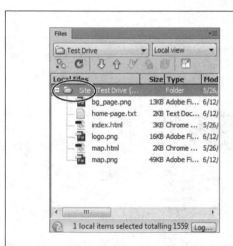

FIGURE 1-40

Dreamweaver's Files panel is more than just a way to see all the files in your site. You can use it to open a file (double-click the file name), rename a file (click the file name, pause, and then click the file name again), add folders (right-click on a file or folder and choose New Folder), and move files around (drag a file into a folder, for example).

2. **Type *images* to name the folder, and then press Enter (Return).**

   The folder might still read "untitled" if you click elsewhere in the program before you edit the name; doing so deselects the folder. If that happens, simply click "untitled" to select the folder, pause a moment, and then click "untitled" again to highlight the name so you can change it.

   Now you just need to get your images into this new folder.

3. **Ctrl-click (⌘-click) the three image files (*bg_page.png, logo.png,* and *map. png*) to select them, and then drag them into the *images* folder.**

   The Update Files window appears, letting you know that by moving these files, you'll affect the *index.html* and *map.html* files. That's because those pages use these images. Normally, moving a web file that another page uses breaks the link between the files. Fortunately, Dreamweaver's smart enough to update the links so they still work.

4. **Click Update.**

Dreamweaver quickly updates the web pages so that they now reference the new location for the three images.

5. **Choose File→Save All to save all the changes you just made.**

The Save All command is an invaluable tool. It saves any changes you've made to all open files.

Congratulations! You just built your first web page in Dreamweaver, complete with graphics, formatted text, and links. You've even used one of Dreamweaver's site-management features to create a new folder and organize your site's files without breaking them! If you want to compare your work with the finished product, go to *Chapter01_complete* in the *Tutorials* folder and load the file *index.html*.

Much of the work of building websites involves the procedures covered in this tutorial—defining a site, adding links, formatting text, placing graphics, creating styles, and inserting <div> tags. The next few chapters cover these basics in greater depth and introduce other important tools, tips, and techniques for using Dreamweaver to build great web pages.

TIP To get a full description of every Dreamweaver menu, see Appendix B, "Dreamweaver CC, Menu by Menu."

Working with Text

Nowadays, streaming video, audio, and high-quality graphics are what draw many people to websites. After all, it's exciting to hear the latest song from your favorite band, preview a yet-to-be released blockbuster, or watch the kid down the street embarrass himself in front of a billion YouTube viewers.

But while entertainment may grab the Internet spotlight, the Web is woven primarily with *words*. News, Justin Bieber gossip, and countless personal blogs about cats still drive people to the Internet. As you build web pages and sites, you'll spend a lot of time adding and formatting *text*. To get your message across effectively, you need to understand how Dreamweaver works with text. That's what this chapter is all about—it covers the not-always-simple act of getting text *into* your Dreamweaver documents. In Chapter 3, you'll learn how to format that text so it looks professionally designed.

■ Adding Text in Dreamweaver

In Design view, Dreamweaver works much like a word-processing program. When you create a new document, a blinking cursor appears at the top of the page, ready for you to begin typing. When you finish typing a paragraph, you press Enter (Return) to start a new one. Text, as well as anything else you add to a web page, starts at the top of the page and works its way to the bottom.

If you build websites for clients or as part of a team, your writers likely send their text to you as a word-processing document. You can copy text from that document (or from another source, like an email message) and paste it into Dreamweaver's Design view; you have a couple of options for doing that.

TIP If the text you want to paste comes from a Microsoft Word or Excel file, you're lucky. Dreamweaver includes special commands for pasting text from these two programs (see "Paste Special" below). If you use Windows, you can *import* Word and Excel files directly into a web page using Dreamweaver's File→Import→[Word/Excel] Document command (see page 71).

Simple Copy and Paste

For non-Microsoft-spawned documents, you can, of course, simply copy and paste text, like generations of web designers before you.

Open the document in whatever program created it—WordPad, TextEdit, your email program, whatever. Select the text you want (by dragging through it, for example), or choose Edit→Select All (Ctrl+A [⌘-A]) to highlight the text. Then choose Edit→Copy, or press Ctrl+C (⌘-C), to copy it to your virtual Clipboard. Switch to Dreamweaver and, in the Design view of the document window, click where you want the text to go, and then choose Edit→Paste (Ctrl+V [⌘-V]). This drops the text into place. Unfortunately, you lose any formatting the text had (font type, size, color, bold, italics, and so on), as shown in Figure 2-1.

Furthermore, you may find the pasted paragraphs in the resulting HTML separated by line-break characters instead of true paragraph tags, <p>. In HTML, the line-break character—the <br> tag—adds a "soft" carriage return, simply dropping the text that follows onto the next line. This means that when you paste in a series of paragraphs, Dreamweaver treats them as though they were one gargantuan paragraph, which can pose problems when you try to format what you *think* is a single paragraph. To get true paragraphs, you first have to make the line breaks visible. Choose Edit→Preferences (Dreamweaver→Preferences) or press Ctrl+U (⌘-U). Click the Invisible Elements category. Make sure you have the Line Breaks checkbox turned on. Now you see each line break as a small gold shield. (If you still don't see the line break character, choose View→Visual Aids, and make sure you have the Invisible Elements checkbox turned on.) Select the shield and then hit Enter (Return) to eliminate the break *and* create a true paragraph.

TIP If you *have* to copy and paste text from non-Microsoft programs, you do have one way to get paragraphs (and not just lines separated by the line-break character) when you paste text into Dreamweaver. Just make sure whoever's typing up the original document inserts an empty paragraph between each paragraph of text. Pressing Enter (Return) twice at the end of a paragraph does that. When you copy and paste, Dreamweaver removes the empty paragraphs *and* pastes the text as regular paragraphs.

Paste Special

Dreamweaver's Paste Special command supports four document formats, ranging from plain text to highly designed HTML. But in reality, Dreamweaver supports only two formats for *all* pasting operations—text only and text with structure (see the next page). The other two formats—text with basic formatting and text with full formatting—work only with Microsoft Word or Excel documents.

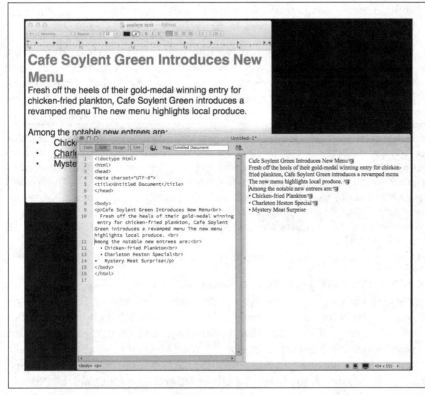

FIGURE 2-1

Usually when you copy text from a non-Microsoft program (top) and paste it into Dreamweaver (bottom), you lose all formatting, and line breaks replace paragraph breaks. The five gold shields that appear at the end of some of the lines in Design view (bottom right) represent invisible line breaks (the <br> tags you see in Code view, bottom left). Select a shield and then hit Enter (Return) to get a true paragraph.

Note that these operations work only when you paste text in Design view—if you paste a document in Code view, Dreamweaver just dumps in the plain text, without paragraphs, line breaks, or any other formatting.

Here are your Paste Special command choices:

- **Text only.** This is the most basic option of all. It pastes text without any formatting whatsoever, ignoring even paragraphs and line breaks (this is also how text appears when you paste it in Code view). You end up with one long, uninterrupted series of sentences. Though you won't want this effect often, it can come in handy when you copy a long paragraph of text from an email program that adds unnecessary line breaks at the end of each line of text.

- **Text with structure (paragraphs, lists, tables).** Here, Dreamweaver tries to preserve the structure of the text, including paragraphs, headers, bulleted lists, and so on. This option doesn't retain any formatting applied to the text, however, such as boldface or italics. You use this option with most non-Microsoft Office-copied text. In most cases, however, Dreamweaver ends up preserving only paragraphs and misses bulleted lists and headers.

- **Text with structure plus basic formatting (bold, italic).** When you paste text using this option, Dreamweaver formats the same elements as the "Text with structure" option but also preserves text formatting, such as boldface, italics, and underlines. This is the method Dreamweaver uses when you paste Microsoft Word or Excel text and numbers, as described in the next section.

- **Text with structure plus full formatting (bold, italic, styles).** This option includes everything you get with basic formatting, and it also converts Word formatted text into CSS styles, placing them in an internal style sheet in the <head> section of the web page.

> **NOTE** In most browsers, you can copy an entire page of HTML and paste it into Dreamweaver. Click inside a web page, press Ctrl+A (⌘-A) to select the entire page, and then press Ctrl+C (⌘-C) to copy the HTML. Next, switch to Dreamweaver, click inside an empty page, and press Ctrl+V (⌘-V) to paste. Results vary depending on your operating system and the browser you use. With Google Chrome, Firefox, and Internet Explorer, Dreamweaver copies the HTML (including links to graphics) from the body of the page. The text shows up with HTML tags for paragraphs and headings, but you lose CSS styles, because internal style sheets and links to external style sheets are stored in the head of HTML documents. See page 107 for more details on style sheets and page xix for the structure of HTML documents.

■ CHANGING PASTE SPECIAL'S DEFAULT BEHAVIOR

If you always work with the same type of documents, you can set Dreamweaver's behavior for the Paste Special command. Choose Edit→Paste Special to open the Paste Special window (Figure 2-2). Here, you can choose which of the four techniques you wish to use as the default. Well, sort of. You're limited to what Dreamweaver can actually paste. For non-Microsoft Office products, you get only the first two options—text and text with structure—the others are grayed out. But with text copied from Word or Excel, you can choose from any of the four options.

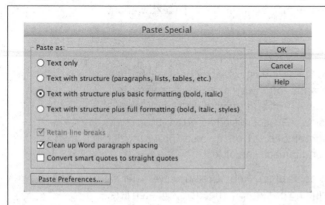

FIGURE 2-2

The Paste Special command lets you paste text copied from other programs. If you want Dreamweaver to use the same option each time you use Paste Special, click Paste Preferences. This opens the Preferences window. Select whatever settings—basic formatting, for example—you want Dreamweaver to apply each time you click Paste Special.

For text copied from most programs, it's best to use "Text with structure" and keep the "Retain line breaks" checkbox turned on. You still have to manually replace line breaks with paragraph markers, as described in the note on page 48, but without

"Retain line breaks" turned on, Dreamweaver removes single hard returns, resulting in one long paragraph of text.

In addition, when you paste text that includes traditional quotation marks (also called "curly" quotes), you can tell Dreamweaver to insert "straight" quotes by turning on the "Convert smart quotes to straight quotes" checkbox. This option forces Dreamweaver to replace opening and closing double quotes (" and ") with the " character, and single quotes (' and ') with straight single quotes ('). Only turn on this option if you really like the "Hey, I wrote this on a dumb computer that has no understanding of real typography" look, or if you're pasting HTML code from a Word document that accidentally placed all HTML properties inside curly quotes (like that happens a lot). For Word or Excel files, there are a few better options, described next.

Pasting Text from Microsoft Word: The Basic Method

While text pasted from non-Word applications doesn't retain much formatting beyond paragraphs, Dreamweaver includes both basic and advanced ways to copy and paste Word text.

Frequently, you'll just want to preserve basic formatting, like bold or italic text, headlines, and bulleted lists. You won't need (and in most cases, won't want) more extravagant formatting, like different fonts, colors, or margin settings. After all, you're the web designer, and you'll use your own design sense and CSS formatting rules to add beauty to basic text.

You paste Word text just as you would any other: Select the desired text in Word, copy it, switch to Dreamweaver, and then choose Edit→Paste to drop the text into a web page. You don't have to spend a lot of time reformatting the text since Dreamweaver preserves many basic formatting options:

- Paragraphs formatted with Word's built-in heading styles (Heading 1, Heading 2, and so on) get HTML heading tags: <h1> (for Heading 1), <h2>, <title>, and so on.

- Paragraphs remain paragraphs...most of the time. Actually, the way Dreamweaver pastes paragraphs depends on how Word formatted the paragraphs to begin with and whether you turned on the Paste Special window's "Clean up Word paragraph spacing" setting (see Figure 2-2). If you did, paragraphs you paste from Word can sometimes appear in Dreamweaver as one large paragraph, with line break characters at the end of each paragraph—not the best way to get an HTML paragraph. To get Dreamweaver to paste each paragraph *as* a paragraph, choose Edit→Paste Special, turn off the "Clean up Word paragraph spacing" checkbox, and then click OK.

NOTE If the source Word document has an empty line between each paragraph (in other words, an empty paragraph generated by pressing the Enter key twice after each real paragraph), make sure you *do* have the "Clean up Word paragraph spacing" checkbox turned on. That eliminates the empty paragraphs.

- Bold and italic text maintain their look (Dreamweaver uses the HTML <strong> tag for bolded text and the <em> tag for italicized text, as described on page 96).

- Basic text-alignment options (left, right, and center) remain intact. Justified text, on the other hand, gets pasted as left-aligned text. (You can compensate for this using the Justify option in the Properties panel, as described on page 140.)

- Numbered lists come through as numbered lists in Dreamweaver (see page 85) *if* you used Word's Automatic Numbered-List feature to create them.

NOTE Suppose you copy some HTML, maybe out of the Source view of an actual web page or from a "How to Write HTML" website. You'll notice that when you paste it into Dreamweaver's Design view, all the HTML tags appear in that view, complete with brackets (< >) and other assorted messiness. To get HTML into a page (and make it work like HTML), you have to go into Code view and paste the code directly into the page's HTML. (To see the HTML for a page, click the Code view or Split view buttons at the top of the document window.)

- If you paste text created using Word's built-in list-bulleting feature, you end up with a proper HTML bulleted list (see page 85). If you create your own bulleted list style in Word, make sure you select the "list" type when you create the style; otherwise, copying and pasting the custom list might just paste plain paragraphs of text.

- Graphics from Word documents get pasted as graphics. In fact, even if the original graphics aren't in a web-ready format (if they're BMP, TIFF, or PICT files, for example), Dreamweaver converts them to either the GIF or JPEG format, which web browsers understand. Dreamweaver even copies the files to your local site folder *and* links them correctly to the page. (Chapter 5 covers images in depth.)

NOTE Keep in mind a couple of caveats when you paste material from Word: First, you can't copy and paste more than a couple hundred KB worth of text at a time, so you have to transfer really long documents in pieces (or better yet, spread them out among multiple web pages). Second, the ability to keep basic HTML formatting in place when you paste works only with versions of Word later than Office 97 (for Windows) or Office 98 (for Macs).

Pasting Text with Word Formatting

If you simply *must* keep that three-inch-tall, crazy orange font you used in a Word document, you can turn to the Paste Special "Text with structure plus full formatting" option. After copying text from Word and returning to Dreamweaver, choose Edit→Paste Special or press Ctrl+Shift+V (⌘-Shift-V). When the Paste Special window appears, choose the full formatting option, and then click OK.

Dreamweaver pastes the text with as much formatting as possible, including margins, fonts, and text colors and sizes. Behind the scenes, Dreamweaver pastes the text *and* adds CSS formatting that attempts to approximate the look of the text as it appeared in Word.

NOTE Sometimes when you paste from Word (even using the standard Paste command), you end up with empty hyperlink (<a>) tags in your HTML. They appear as gold shields in Dreamweaver's Design view (circled in Figure 2-3). The links might look something like this: *<a name="OLE_LINK1" id="OLE_LINK1"></a>*. Feel free to delete them—they're unnecessary crud that Word adds.

Unfortunately, all this extra code increases the document's file size and download time, and can interfere with future formatting changes. What's worse, most of your visitors won't even be able to *see* some of this formatting—if you use an uncommon font, for example, that font may not be available on your visitors' computers. For these reasons, it's best to skip this feature, paste Word text using the regular Paste command, and then create your own styles to make the text look great (you'll learn how to do that in the next chapter).

Pasting Excel Spreadsheet Information

Dreamweaver also lets you paste text and numbers from Microsoft Excel. Options include a basic method—using the standard Edit→Paste command (Ctrl+V [⌘-V])—and a format-rich method, using the full formatting option of the Paste Special window: Choose Edit→Paste Special (or press Ctrl+Shift+V [⌘-Shift-V]), choose "Text with structure plus full formatting" from the Paste Special window, and then click OK.

Both methods paste spreadsheet information as an HTML table composed of cells, rows, and columns. (See Chapter 6 for more on tables.) But unlike pasting from Word, using the basic Paste command with Excel preserves *no* formatting—it doesn't even hang on to bold and italic text. The full formatting option, however, preserves advanced formatting like fonts, font sizes, text colors, and cell background colors.

Importing Word and Excel Documents (Windows)

Windows fans can import documents directly from a Word or Excel file into Dreamweaver. In Design view, position your cursor where you want to insert the text or spreadsheet, and then choose File→Import→Word Document (or Excel Document). An Open File dialog box appears; find and double-click the Word or Excel file you want.

Dreamweaver captures the information just as if you'd used Edit→Paste. That is, for Word documents, it carries over basic formatting like bold, italics, headlines, and paragraphs, and imports and converts images. The importing process doesn't create style sheets or apply advanced formatting. For Excel documents, you get just an organized table of data—no formatting.

■ Adding Special Characters

Many useful special characters—such as copyright and trademark symbols—don't appear on your keyboard, making them difficult or impossible to type. Dreamweaver's Insert toolbar's Common tab lets you use a variety of symbols and international characters simply by clicking an icon.

To open the Insert panel's Common tab:

1. **On the Insert panel or toolbar, choose the Common category.**

   If you can't see the Insert panel, choose Window→Insert to open it, or use the keyboard shortcut Ctrl+F2 (⌘-F2). As explained on page 8, the Insert panel can appear as a toolbar, a floating palette, or a panel. If you use the Compact or Expanded toolbar, you see the Insert panel shown in Figure 2-3, middle.

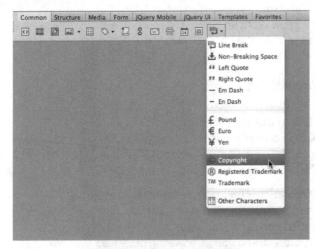

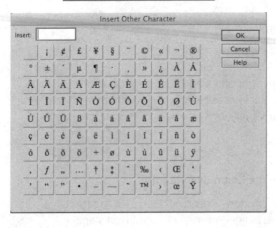

FIGURE 2-3

Top: At the end of the Insert→Common toolbar, you can open the Character menu, which displays some of the most common special characters, like the copyright mark.

Middle: The Insert panel is shown as a panel (as opposed to a toolbar) with the Common category selected. Character options are at the bottom of the menu. Click the triangle to open the menu or click Other Characters to open the Insert Other Character dialog box (bottom).

Bottom: The Insert Other Characters dialog box gives you access to many characters that are difficult or impossible to type on a keyboard.

TIP There are more characters in the Western alphabet than the Insert Other Character dialog box lists (Figure 2-3). You can find a table of these characters and their associated entity names and numbers at *http://tinyurl.com/ffl5g*.

As advertised, the Insert→Common category gives you quick access to elements you frequently pop into web pages, such as images, media, tables, and links. The last option on the Common panel or toolbar, Other Characters (Figure 2-3), offers a range of symbols and international characters. Unlike regular Western characters, such as *a* or *z*, Dreamweaver represents special characters using an HTML value or code name. For instance, the code *™* adds the trademark symbol (™); another way to write this symbol in HTML is *™*.

TIP If you like card games or just want to add a heart to a web page without using a graphic, choose the Other Characters option from the Insert panel and type *♥*. Type *♦* for a diamond, *♠* for a spade, or *♣* for a club. (Don't forget the semicolon at the end of each—that's part of the code.)

2. **From the menu at the end of the Insert panel, select the symbol you want to insert.**

   Dreamweaver inserts the appropriate HTML into your web page. (Alternatively, you can select Other Characters to bring up the wider-ranging Insert Other Character dialog box.)

NOTE If you set the encoding of your page to anything other than Western European or Unicode (UTF-8) in the Page Properties window (by choosing Modify→Page Properties, and then clicking the Title/Encoding category), you can reliably insert only line breaks and nonbreaking spaces. The other special characters available from the Character category of the Objects panel may not work (see the box on page 80 for more on encoding).

Line Breaks

Pressing Enter (Return) in Dreamweaver's Design view creates a new paragraph, just as it does in a word processor. Unfortunately, web browsers add extra space above and below paragraphs—which is a real nuisance if you want to create several single-spaced lines of text, like this:

> 702 A Street
> Boring, OR
> 97009 USA

Here, each part of the address is on its own line, but the entire address still represents just a single paragraph (and each of the lines share that paragraph's formatting, as you'll learn in the next chapter).

NOTE If you want to dispense with the space that browsers insert between paragraphs *entirely*, don't use line breaks each time. Instead, use CSS Designer to eliminate the top and bottom margins of the <p>. See page 105 for details on creating styles with CSS Designer.

To create this single-spaced effect in HTML, you need to insert a *line break* at the insertion point, using one of these techniques:

- Press Shift+Enter.

- Select Line Break from the Characters menu in the Insert→Common category.

- Choose Insert→HTML→Special Characters→Line Break.

Keyboard Shortcuts for Special Characters

Dreamweaver uses UTF-8 (also called Unicode) encoding when you create a new page (unless you specify otherwise). Without getting into the messy details, UTF-8 lets you include almost any type of character available to the languages of the world—it lets a Chinese speaker embed actual Chinese characters in a page, for example. When you use the Other Characters window, Dreamweaver inserts what's called an HTML *entity*—a code that replaces the real character. For example, the HTML entity for the © symbol is *©*. But UTF-8 lets you add the actual symbol to a page—the trick is knowing how to do that through your keyboard.

On the Mac, a handful of keyboard shortcuts let you type special characters, like curly quotes. directly into your budding web page. Here are a few of the most common characters and their shortcuts:

- Ellipsis (three periods in a row): Option+;

- Em dash (—): Option+Shift+-

- Opening single quote ('): Option+]

- Closing single quote ('): Option+Shift+]

- Opening double-quote ("): Option+[

- Closing double-quote ("): Option+Shift+[

- Copyright symbol (©): Option+G

You can also use the Mac Character Palette to insert unusual symbols. To open it, select Edit→Special Characters from the Finder.

In Windows, you have to press the Alt key, type the Unicode value using your keyboard's numeric keypad, and then release the Alt key. Note that you can't use the regular number keys for this—you must use the numeric keypad. For example, to add an ellipsis, hold down the Alt key, type *0133*, and then release the Alt key. Here are a few other codes for Windows PCs:

- Open single quote: Alt+0145

- Closing single quote: Alt+0146

- Opening double-quote: Alt+0147

- Closing double-quote: Alt+0148

In Windows, it's easier to use the character map to insert special symbols and characters. Visit *http://tinyurl.com/5blqek* to learn how.

NOTE When you insert a line break in Dreamweaver, the Design view may give you no visual hint that the break is even there; after all, a regular paragraph break and a line break both create a new line of text. This is especially likely if you copy text from programs other than Microsoft Word or Excel. You might find text from those programs—especially email programs—loaded with an infuriating number of line breaks. To add to the confusion, a line break may go unnoticed if it occurs at the end of a line of text that goes off-screen.

Your only workaround is to make line breaks visible. To do that, choose Edit→Preferences (Dreamweaver→Preferences), or press Ctrl+U (⌘-U). Click the Invisible Elements category. Make sure you have the Line Breaks checkbox turned on. Now you see each line break as a small gold shield. (If, after doing this, you still don't see the line break character, choose View→Visual Aids, and make sure you have the Invisible Elements checkbox turned on.)

You can select a line break by clicking the shield, and then delete it just as you would any other page element. Better yet, select the shield and then hit Enter (Return) to eliminate the line break *and* create a new paragraph.

Nonbreaking Spaces

Sometimes, the way a sentence breaks over two lines in your text can distort what you're trying to say, as shown in Figure 2-4. If that's the case, a *nonbreaking space* can save the day. It looks just like a regular space, but it acts as a glue that prevents the words on either side from being split apart at the end of a line. For example, adding a nonbreaking space between the words "farmer" and "says" in Figure 2-4 ensures that those words won't get split across a line break and helps clarify the presentation and meaning of this headline.

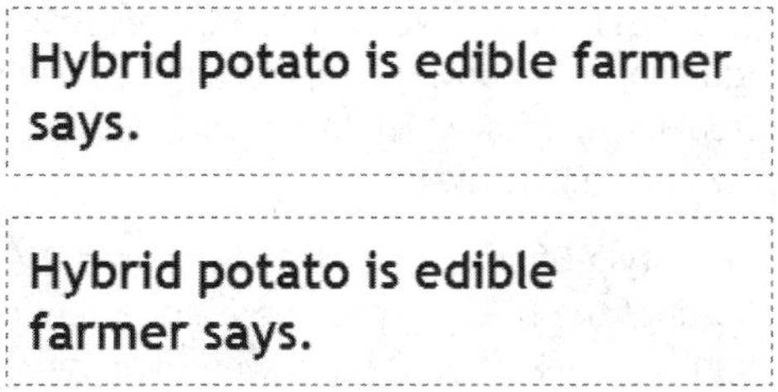

Hybrid potato is edible farmer says.

Hybrid potato is edible farmer says.

FIGURE 2-4

Headlines sometimes break between lines, leaving a single word alone on a line (top). In typography, this is known as a widow. Adding a nonbreaking space (bottom) can prevent widows and clarify a headline's meaning.

To insert a nonbreaking space between two words, delete the space already there (for example, by positioning your mouse after the space and pressing the backspace key), and then do one of the following:

- Press Ctrl+Shift+Space bar (⌘-Shift-Space bar).

- From the Characters menu in the Insert panel's Text category, select Non-Breaking Space.

- Choose Insert→HTML→Special Characters→Non-Breaking Space.

Multiple Spaces

You may have noticed that if you type more than one space in a row, Dreamweaver ignores all but the first one. This isn't a glitch in the program, it's standard HTML. Web browsers ignore any spaces following the first one.

Therefore, a line like "Beware   of   llama," with several spaces between each word, appears on a web page like this: "Beware of llama." Not only do web browsers ignore multiple spaces, they ignore any spaces that aren't *between* words. So if you hit the space bar a couple of times to indent the first line of a paragraph, you're wasting your time. A browser won't display any of those spaces (and Dreamweaver doesn't display them, either).

This feature makes good sense, because it prevents web pages from being littered with extraneous spaces that many people insert when writing HTML. (Extra spaces in a page of HTML often makes the code easier to read.)

There may be times, however, when you *want* to add more space between words. For example, consider the text navigation bar at the bottom of a web page, a common element that lists the sections of a website. Visitors can click one of the section titles to jump directly to that area of the site. For clarity, many designers like to add multiple spaces between the links, like this:

News   Classifieds   Jobs

One simple way to add space is to insert multiple nonbreaking spaces as described in the previous section. A browser *does* display every nonbreaking space it encounters, so you can add multiple nonbreaking spaces between words, letters, or even at the beginning of paragraphs. This technique has a few downsides, though: You have to type in the code for a bunch of nonbreaking spaces, which takes work, and it adds code to your web page, making it download a bit slower.

Alternatively, you can enlist Cascading Style Sheets (CSS) to add spaces. While you won't get in-depth detail on CSS until the next chapter, here are a few CSS *properties* (formatting rules) to tuck in the back of your mind when you need to add space to your text:

- To indent the first line of a paragraph, use the CSS *text indent* property (page 143).

- To add space between words in a paragraph, use the *word spacing* property (page 143).

- To increase or decrease the space between letters, use *letter spacing* (page 143).

- And, if you want to increase the space between links, as in the previous example, you can add either left and right *margins* or *padding* to each link (page 58).

NOTE If you often add multiple spaces to a line of text, Dreamweaver offers a shortcut. Choose Edit→ Preferences (Dreamweaver→Preferences) to open Dreamweaver's Preferences window. Click the General category and then turn on "Allow multiple consecutive spaces." Now, whenever you press the space bar more than once, Dreamweaver inserts *nonbreaking* spaces.

In fact, Dreamweaver is even smarter than that. It inserts a regular space if you press the space bar just once, a nonbreaking space followed by a regular space if you hit the space bar twice, and multiple nonbreaking spaces followed by a regular space if you hit the space bar repeatedly. Why does Dreamweaver automatically add the regular spaces? Since nonbreaking spaces act like glue that keeps words stuck together, the regular spaces let the lines break normally, if necessary.

Adding a Date to Your Page

The Insert panel's Common category offers an icon called Date (it looks like the page of a calendar) that inserts the current date. Clicking the icon, or choosing Insert→Date, opens the Insert Date dialog box (Figure 2-5). You can specify whether to include the day of the week and the current time along with the date.

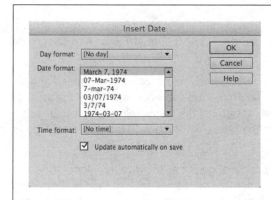

FIGURE 2-5

When you insert a Date object (a placeholder for the actual date) into a web page, you have several options: If you want to add the day of the week, choose the format you want from the "Day format" drop-down menu. You may also add the current time in hours and minutes—in either military time (22:18) or regular time (10:18 PM)—from the "Time format" drop-down menu.

Select the format you wish from the Date Format list. You have 13 configurations to choose from, such as March 7, 1974 or 3/7/74.

You may wonder why Dreamweaver includes an insert date function anyway. How hard is it to type *Thursday, July 12*?

Actually, the real value of the feature lies in the "Update automatically on save" checkbox. Turning on this option forces Dreamweaver to *update* the date each time you save the document.

You can use this feature to stamp a web page with a date that indicates when you last updated it. For example, you might type *This page was revised on:* and then choose Insert→Date, simultaneously turning on the "Update automatically on save" checkbox. Now, each time you change a page, Dreamweaver rewrites the date to reflect the last time you saved the document. You never have to worry about dating pages again.

■ Selecting Text

After you get text into your Dreamweaver document, you'll undoubtedly need to edit it. You'll delete words and paragraphs, move sentences around, add words, and fix typos.

The first step in any of these procedures is learning how to select text, which works much as it does in a word processor. You drag your cursor across text to highlight it, or click at the beginning of the selection and then hold down the Shift key as you click at the end of the selection; you'll automatically select everything in between. You can also use shortcuts like these:

- To select a word, double-click it.

- To select a paragraph, triple-click anywhere in it.

- To select a line of text, move your cursor to the left of the line until it changes from an I-beam to an arrow, signaling that you've reached the left-margin selection strip. Click once to highlight one line of text; click once and then drag vertically to select multiple lines.

- While pressing Shift, use the left and right arrow keys to select one letter at a time. Use Ctrl+Shift (⌘-Shift) and the left and right arrow keys to select one *word* at a time.

- Ctrl+A (⌘-A) selects everything in the body of a page—text, graphics, and all. (Well, this isn't 100 percent true: If you use tables or <div> tags [page 428] to organize a page, Ctrl+A may select just the text within a table cell or <div> tag; clicking the <body> tag in the Tag Selector [page 7] is the sure-fire way to select everything on a page.)

Once you select text, you can cut, copy, or delete it. To move it to another part of the web page, or even to another Dreamweaver document, use the Cut, Copy, and Paste commands in the Edit menu. You can also move text around by dragging and dropping it, as shown in Figure 2-6.

Once copied, the text remains in your Clipboard and you can place it again and again (until you copy something else to the Clipboard, of course). When you cut (or copy) and paste *within* Dreamweaver, all the code affecting that text comes along for the ride. If you copy a paragraph that includes bold text, for example, you copy the HTML tags for both creating the paragraph and for producing bold text.

To delete any selection, press Delete or choose Edit→Clear.

> **NOTE** Not *all* text formatting necessarily comes along for the ride. For example, if you format text using an external style sheet (page 107) and cut and paste that text into a web page that's not linked to the CSS file, the formatting does *not* show up in the new page. So on some occasions, you may copy text from one document, paste it into another, and find that the formatting disappears.

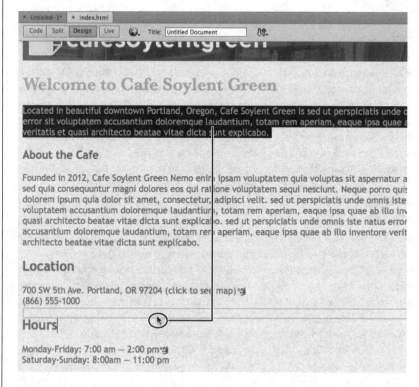

◼ HTML Formatting

Getting text onto a web page is a good start, but effective communication requires effective design. Large, bold headlines help readers scan a page's important topics. Colorful text focuses attention. Bulleted sentences crystallize and summarize ideas. Just as a monotonous, low-key voice puts a crowd to sleep, a vast desert of plain text is sure to turn visitors away from the important message of your site. In fact, text formatting could be the key to making your *Widgets Online 2014 Sale-a-Thon* a resounding success instead of an unnoticed disaster.

Formatting text is a two-step process. First you apply the appropriate HTML tag to a chunk of text, and then you create styles using CSS to make that text look great. You add HTML tags not so much to format text (though they *can* do that, with the undesired side effect that different browsers can interpret the tags differently); rather, you use them to *structure* the text into logical blocks. Once you set up those blocks, you can use CSS to format them to your liking—and not just in the current page, but across your site. That's one of the big benefits of CSS.

Decoding Encoding

In some cases, when you copy a symbol like © from Microsoft Word and then paste it into Dreamweaver, you see *©* in the HTML. Other times, you see the actual symbol (©). Which you get depends on the type of *encoding* Dreamweaver uses on your web page. Unless you work with languages other than English, encoding isn't much of an issue; you can work happily without ever worrying about how Dreamweaver encodes your HTML. But if you commonly need to type characters that don't appear on the standard English keyboard, such as Chinese, Kanji, or simply the accented letters of French or Spanish, Dreamweaver's encoding method is helpful.

Computers don't think in terms of letters or any of the other symbols we humans normally use to communicate with each other. Computers think in terms of bits and bytes. They represent every letter or symbol on a web page by a numeric code. The process of converting those letters and symbols to computer-friendly code is called *encoding*. But since the world is filled with symbols from many languages—Latin, Chinese, Arabic, Cyrillic, Hebrew, and so on—there are many *encoding schemes* used to accommodate the alphabets of the world. Versions of Dreamweaver prior to CS3 used Western Latin encoding, which handles most of the characters in English and Western European languages. But it doesn't handle all the symbols. That's why, when you copy a © symbol from Word and paste it into a web page with Western Latin encoding, you end up with *©* in your HTML instead of the copyright symbol. *©* is called an *entity*, and browsers know that when they see that particular entity, they should display the copyright symbol.

Dreamweaver uses a newer type of encoding when it creates a web page—Unicode. Unicode, which Dreamweaver refers to as *Unicode (UTF-8)*, accommodates many of the alphabets of the world, so you can mix Kanji with Cyrillic with English on a single page, and all the characters display as they should. A page encoded with Unicode also produces slightly different HTML when you paste symbols from other programs. Instead of using entities in the page, like *”* for a curly right quotation mark, you see the actual character (") in the HTML. This quality generally makes HTML much easier to read. However, if you've previously built a site using a different encoding scheme, like *Japanese (Shift JIS)*—yes, that's the actual format name—you may want to stick to that method.

You probably won't ever need to change Dreamweaver's encoding scheme, but if you update a site and want to upgrade to the new Unicode encoding (maybe so you can type © instead of *©* in your HTML), choose Modify→Page Properties, click the Title/Encoding category, and then select a method from the encoding menu. If you want to change the default encoding for all new documents (for example, if you absolutely must stick with the *Shift JIS* to match the encoding method of other pages on your site), choose Edit→Preferences (Dreamweaver→Preferences), click the New Document category, and then select an option from the Default Encoding menu.

Note that if, later on, you switch back to Unicode (UTF-8), make sure you select "C (Canonical Decomposition)" from the Normalization field, and leave the Include Unicode Signature checkbox *turned off*; otherwise the page may not display correctly.

Finally, if you use the Insert Special Character menu (page 71), Dreamweaver always inserts an HTML entity (*®*, for example) instead of the actual symbol (™), even in a UTF-8 page. You can, however, type many of these symbols on your keyboard, as described in the Power Users' Clinic on page 74.

For example, you'd use the <h1> (Heading 1) tag to indicate the most important heading on a page, and the <ol> (ordered list) tag to list a series of numbered steps. Structuring your text like this not only adds some rudimentary formatting (the resulting page has a large, boldfaced headline and a numbered list), it also structures your text so that search engines and alternative browsing devices, like screen readers for the vision-impaired, can weight the relative importance of each block of text. However, HTML's limited formatting options aren't very appealing. That's where CSS comes in. You use CSS to fine-tune the visual appeal of text by changing fonts, applying color, adjusting font size, and a lot more.

The fundamental difference between HTML and CSS is so important that Dreamweaver treats these two technologies separately by splitting the Properties panel into two tabbed areas, one for HTML, the other for CSS. That way, you always know when you're applying which type of formatting code (see Figure 2-7). In this chapter, you'll learn to use HTML tags to structure text on a page; in the next chapter, you'll create beautiful typography with CSS.

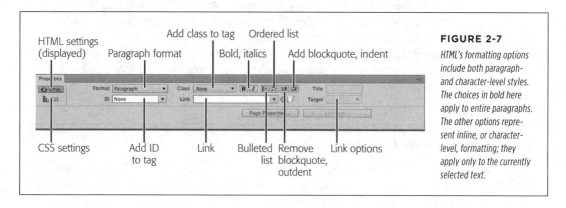

FIGURE 2-7

HTML's formatting options include both paragraph- and character-level styles. The choices in bold here apply to entire paragraphs. The other options represent inline, or character-level, formatting; they apply only to the currently selected text.

■ Paragraph Formatting

Just as you use paragraphs to help organize your thoughts into clear, well-structured units, so you organize content into blocks of information using HTML tags (see page xxi for more about tags). The most basic block of information is the simple paragraph, which you identify in HTML with a paragraph tag, like this:

```
<p>Hello. This is a paragraph on a web page.</p>
```

A web browser considers everything between the opening <p> tag and the closing </p> tag as part of the same paragraph. You can apply many Dreamweaver formatting options—headlines, lists, indentations, and alignment, for example—only to full paragraphs of text rather than to individual words. In a word processor, you call this kind of formatting *paragraph* formatting; in web design, it's called *block-level* formatting. Either way, the idea is the same: The formatting you apply affects an entire paragraph (that is, a *block* of text, whether that block consists of just a single sentence or of several sentences). On the other hand, you can apply *character-level* formatting to individual characters or words. Character-level formatting includes bold and italic letters or words. In the world of HTML, you get character-level formatting using *inline elements*, like the <strong> and the <em> tags.

Paragraphs

If you create a new document in Dreamweaver and start typing right away, the text you type has no formatting at all, as indicated by the word "None" in the Format menu at the left side of the Properties panel (see Figure 2-7). (*None* isn't an HTML tag; it just means that you aren't using *any* of the text tags this menu offers—<p>, <h1>, and so on.)

However, when you press Enter (Return), Dreamweaver transforms that text into a new paragraph, complete with opening and closing <p> tags. Still, your newly born paragraph has no *design* applied to it. When a visitor looks at the paragraph, he doesn't see text in a font and size of your choosing; rather, he sees it format-ted according to his browser's Preferences settings. For example, if a visitor sets his browser to display unformatted text as Vladimir Script, your page will look as though John Hancock wrote it. Since most people don't bother to set a default font, browsers usually use some version of the widely supported Times New Roman font for paragraphs (you'll be able to specify your own fonts using CSS, as described on page 127).

Separating Structure from Presentation

HTML isn't about good looks or fancy design, it's about architec-ture. HTML tags apply *structure* to your page, providing search engines with valuable insight into how you organize your content. In fact, most visitors to your site won't ever see, and probably don't care, which HTML tags you use. But Google, Bing, and other search engines do. They use your tags to determine which text is the most important and to understand what your page is really about.

Google, for example, puts a lot of stock in <h1> tags, seeing the text inside as defining the page's subject. That's why search engine experts recommend using only one <h1> tag per page, and suggest that you make the text descriptive: <h1>My page</h1> isn't good, but <h1>The Ultimate Chia Pet Resource</h1> is.

In general, use HTML to structure your page the same way you'd structure a report or term paper. For example, the Heading 1 tag (<h1>) indicates a headline of the highest level and, therefore, of greatest importance; the smaller Heading 2 tag (<h2>) represents a headline of slightly less importance: a subhead. You see this kind of structure in this book—each section begins with a headline and includes subheads that further divide the content into logical blocks of information.

Structure is more about organizing content than it is about making a page look pretty. Even if this book used different colors and fonts for every headline, its fundamental organiza-tion—chapter title, main headlines, subheads, bulleted lists, numbered instructions, and so on—remains the same.

HTML is also important for devices that don't read or can't display CSS. For example, people with vision impairment often rely on screen readers (programs that literally read the text on a page out loud) to surf the Web. For screen readers, good HTML structure is the only way they can understand a page—clear use of headline, paragraph, and other tags help screen readers convey the structure of a page.

You can add the paragraph tag to any block of text. Since that attribute affects all the text within the block, you don't need to select any text as a first step. Simply click anywhere inside the block of text, and then do one of the following:

- In the Properties panel, choose Paragraph from the Format drop-down menu.
- Choose Format→Paragraph Format→Paragraph.
- Press Ctrl+Shift+P (⌘-Shift-P).

> **NOTE** Much to the chagrin of web designers, web browsers display a line's worth of blank space before and after many block-level elements, like headings and paragraphs. If you find this gap distracting, you can't, unfortunately, get rid of it with regular HTML. However, many of the formatting limitations of HTML, including this one, go away when you use CSS. Using CSS Designer (page 104) you can create a style that sets the top and bottom margin for paragraphs to 0.

Headlines

Headlines announce information ("The Vote Is In!") and help organize content. HTML headings come in a variety of sizes to reflect a piece of content's importance. Headlines range in size from 1 (most important) to 6 (least important), as shown in Figure 2-8.

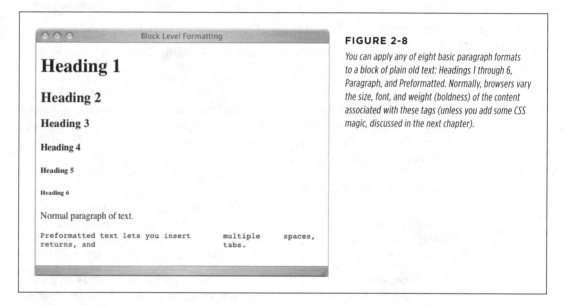

FIGURE 2-8

You can apply any of eight basic paragraph formats to a block of plain old text: Headings 1 through 6, Paragraph, and Preformatted. Normally, browsers vary the size, font, and weight (boldness) of the content associated with these tags (unless you add some CSS magic, discussed in the next chapter).

To turn a paragraph into a headline, click anywhere inside the line, or block, of text and then do one of the following:

- From the Format menu in the Properties panel, select one of the heading levels (Heading 1 through Heading 6).
- Choose Format→Paragraph Format→Heading 1 (or Heading 2, Heading 3, and so on).
- Press Ctrl+1 (⌘-1) for the Heading 1 style, Ctrl+2 (⌘-2) for Heading 2, and so on.

Preformatted Text

Web browsers normally ignore extra spaces, tabs, and other blank-space characters in HTML. However, the Preformatted paragraph format overrides this behavior. Preformatted paragraphs display *every* text character in a paragraph, including tabs, multiple spaces, and line breaks, so you don't have to resort to multiple nonbreaking characters (page 75) to insert more than one space at a time.

The original idea behind the Preformatted format was to display tabular data—like that in a spreadsheet—without the use of tables. That's why preformatted paragraphs use a *monospaced* font like Courier, where each letter of the alphabet, including *i* and *w*, have the same width, making it easy to align letters in columns. That's also why, when you use the Preformatted paragraph style, you can use tabs to align text in columns. (When you use any other paragraph format, web browsers ignore tabs.) However, using an HTML table is a much better way to display data in columns; see Chapter 6.

Nonetheless, you can still find the Preformatted format—when you want to display sample HTML or programming code, for example. You add the Preformatted format to any block of text by clicking inside the block, and taking one of these two steps:

- In the Properties panel, choose Format→Preformatted.

- Choose Format→Paragraph Format→Preformatted Text.

Keep in mind that preformatted text appears exactly as you type it. Unlike normal paragraph text, lines of preformatted text don't automatically wrap if they're wider than your visitor's display. That means that if you present your visitor with a really long line of preformatted text, she has to scroll horizontally to see all of it. To end a line of preformatted text and create another, you must press the Enter (Return) key, thus creating a manual line break.

Indented Paragraphs

Dreamweaver's Properties panel includes a button that looks like the indent buttons in word processors. However, the button doesn't really create an indent; it actually inserts the HTML blockquote tag (though the Indent button has a different function when you apply it to working with lists, as described on page 90).

The blockquote tag was designed to set apart quoted material, such as an excerpt from a book or part of a famous speech. However, since HTML indents blockquotes from the left edge of the page, some novice web designers use it to indent text. That's not a good idea for a couple of reasons. First, the tag indents text from *both* sides of a page, so it doesn't make sense as a way to indent a paragraph. In addition, you don't have any control over how *much* space a visitor's browser adds to the margins of a blockquote. Most insert about 40 pixels of blank space on the left and right sides.

As you'll see on page 439, CSS gives you precise control over indented elements using the *margin* or *padding* properties. However, if you *do* want to quote passages of text, you should use the blockquote tag. To do so, click inside a paragraph or any block-level element (like a paragraph), and do one of the following:

- In the Properties panel, click the Blockquote button (see Figure 2-7).

- Choose Format→Indent.

- Press Ctrl+Alt+] (⌘-Option-]).

If you ever want to remove the blockquote, you can use Dreamweaver to *outdent* it (yes, *outdent* is a real word—ever since Microsoft made it up).

To remove a <blockquote> tag, click inside the paragraph, and then do one of the following:

- In the Properties panel, click the Remove Blockquote button.

- Choose Format→Outdent.

- Press Ctrl+Alt+[(⌘-Option-[).

NOTE When you work with lists (as you will next), the Blockquote and Remove Blockquote buttons change their name and their behavior. They become Indent and Outdent buttons.

■ Creating and Formatting Lists

Lists organize the everyday information of our lives: to-do lists, grocery lists, least favorite celebrity lists, and so on. On web pages, lists are indispensable for presenting groups of items, such as links, company services, or sets of instructions.

HTML offers formatting options for three basic types of list (see Figure 2-9). The two most common are *bulleted* lists (called *unordered* lists in HTML) and *numbered* lists (called *ordered* lists in HTML). The third and lesser-known list type, the *definition* list, comes in handy when you want to create glossaries or dictionary entries.

Bulleted and Numbered Lists

Bulleted and numbered lists share similar formatting. Dreamweaver automatically indents list items in both cases, and automatically precedes each item with a character—a bullet, number, or letter, for example:

- Unordered, or bulleted, lists, like this one, are good for groups of items that don't necessarily follow a sequence. Browsers precede each list item with a bullet.

- Ordered lists are useful when you want to present items that follow a sequence, such as the numbered instructions in the next section. Instead of a bullet, a number or letter precedes each item in an ordered list. Dreamweaver suggests a number (1, 2, 3, and so on), but you can substitute Roman numerals, letters, and other variations.

You can create a list from scratch within Dreamweaver, or apply list formatting to text already on a page.

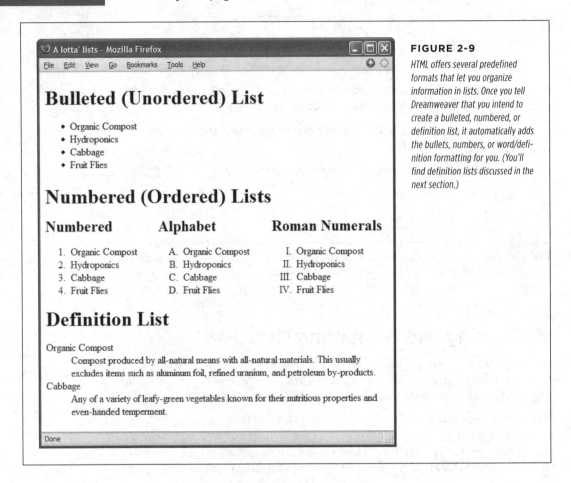

FIGURE 2-9

HTML offers several predefined formats that let you organize information in lists. Once you tell Dreamweaver that you intend to create a bulleted, numbered, or definition list, it automatically adds the bullets, numbers, or word/definition formatting for you. (You'll find definition lists discussed in the next section.)

■ CREATING A BULLETED OR NUMBERED LIST

To create a list in Dreamweaver, first choose a list format, and then type in the list items:

1. **In the document window's Design view, select the point on a page where you want to start the list.**

2. **In the Properties panel, click Ordered List or Unordered List to apply the list format (see Figure 2-7). (The Unordered option is also known as a bulleted list.)**

   Alternatively, you can choose Format→List→Unordered List or Format→List→Ordered List. Either way, the first bullet or number automatically appears in your document.

3. **Type in the first list item, and then press Enter (Return). Repeat this step until you add all the items to the list.**

The text you type appears after the bullet or number (*Organic Compost*, for example, in the list in Figure 2-9). When you press Enter (Return), a new bullet or number appears, ready for your next entry. (If you want to move to the next line *without* creating a new bullet, insert a line break by pressing Shift+Enter [Shift-Return].)

> **NOTE** You can use the Properties panel to create a numbered or bulleted list in Code view, but Dreamweaver won't automatically add a new list item each time you hit Return. To insert a new list item, you must click outside the current list item (either before an opening <li> or after a closing </li>) and choose either Insert→HTML→Text Object→List Item, or just type the HTML yourself (for example: *<li>New item</li>*). As you can see, using Design view for lists is a lot easier. The only benefit to Code view is that you can insert paragraphs, headlines, and other elements inside the <li> tags, which is perfectly valid HTML, but which Dreamweaver doesn't let you do in Design view.

4. **When you finish the list, press Enter (Return) twice.**

The double hard return ends the list and creates a new empty paragraph.

◼ FORMATTING EXISTING TEXT AS A LIST

You may have several paragraphs of text you already typed up or pasted in from another program. You can easily change any such group of paragraphs into a list:

1. **Select the text you want to turn into a list.**

The easiest way to do this is to drag from the first list item straight down to the last one. Lists are block-level elements; each paragraph, whether it's a headline or a regular block of text, becomes one bulleted or numbered item in the list.

> **NOTE** You can use the Properties panel to change existing text into a list in Code view as well.

2. **Apply the list format.**

Just as you created a list from scratch as described previously, click either the Unordered List or Ordered List button in the Properties panel, or choose from the Format→List submenu. The selected paragraphs instantly take on the list formatting, complete with bullets or numbers.

> **NOTE** You may sometimes run into this problem: You select what looks like a handful of paragraphs and apply the list format, but only one bullet (or number) appears. This glitch arises when you use the line break <br> tag to move text down one line in a paragraph. While it's true that using the <br> tag visually separates lines in a paragraph into separate blocks, the text is still part of a single paragraph, and it appears as only *one* bulleted or numbered item. The presence of multiple <br> tags can be a real problem when you paste text from other programs. See page 33 for more on the <br> tag and how to get rid of these pesky critters.

Whichever way you create your list—either by typing it in from scratch or formatting existing text—you're not stuck with the results of your early decisions. You can add onto lists, add extra spaces, and even renumber them, as described in the following section.

Reformatting Bulleted and Numbered Lists

HTML tags define lists, just as they define other web page elements. Making changes to an existing list is a matter of changing those tags, using Dreamweaver's menu commands and Properties panel.

TIP Web browsers generally display list items stacked directly one on top of the other. If you want to add a little breathing room between each item, use the CSS *margin* property to add space above or below the <li> tags, as described on page 439.

■ ADDING NEW ITEMS TO A LIST

Once you create a list, you can easily add items. To add an item at the beginning of a list, click in front of the first character of the first entry in the list (not the first bullet point or number), type the item you want to add, and then press Enter (Return). Your first item now sits beside the first bullet or number, and pressing Enter (Return) automatically generates the next bullet or number (and renumbers the other list items, if necessary).

NOTE Adding items this way works only in Design view, not in Code view.

To add an item to the middle or end of a list, click at the end of the *previous* list item, and then press Enter (Return). The insertion point appears after Dreamweaver adds a new bullet or number; type your list item on this line.

■ FORMATTING BULLETS AND NUMBERS

Bulleted and numbered lists aren't limited to just the standard round black bullet or the numbers 1, 2, and 3. You can choose from two bullet types and a handful of numbering schemes. Here's how to change these settings:

1. **Click once inside any list item.**

   Strangely enough, you can't change the properties of a list if you first select the entire list, a single list item, or several list items.

NOTE Most of the settings in the List Properties dialog box produce invalid HTML for HTML5, as well as for the strict versions of HTML 4.01 and XHTML 1.0. If you use this dialog box, stick to XHTML transitional or HTML transitional document types (see page xx for more on picking a document type).

2. **Open the List Properties dialog box (Figure 2-10).**

Either click the List Item button in the bottom half of the Properties panel or choose Format→List→Properties. (If the list is inside a table cell, your only choice is to use the Format menu, because the List Item button doesn't appear when you format text inside a table cell.)

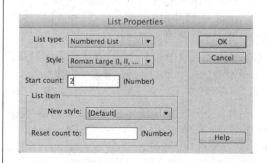

FIGURE 2-10

The List Properties dialog box lets you set the type and style of a list. For example, if you select a numbered list, you can choose from five number styles: Number (1, 2, 3); Roman Small (i, ii, iii); Roman Large (I, II, III); Alphabet Small (a, b, c); and Alphabet Large (A, B, C). While the options in the top half of this window apply to an entire list (every item within the <ol> or <ul> tag), the options in the box labeled "List Item" apply to just the single list item you clicked before opening the List Properties dialog box.

3. **Skip the "List type" drop-down menu.**

It lets you turn a numbered list into a bulleted one, and vice versa. But why bother? You can achieve the same thing by simply selecting a bulleted list and clicking the numbered list button in the Properties panel and vice versa. In addition, this menu has two other options—Directory List and Menu List—which insert obsolete HTML, so avoid it.

4. **Choose a bullet or numbering style.**

Bulleted lists can have three styles: *default*, *bullet*, or *square*. In most browsers, the default style is the same as the bullet style (a simple, solid, black circle). As you might guess, the square style uses a solid black square for the bullet character.

Numbered lists, on the other hand, offer a greater variety of style options. Dreamweaver starts you off with a simple numbering scheme (1, 2, 3, and so on), but you can choose from any of five styles for ordered lists, as explained in Figure 2-10.

TIP You can achieve the same effect as step 4 above using CSS. Not only does CSS give you more options—you can use a graphic you created as a bullet, for example—but you avoid inserting obsolete HTML. See page 144 for CSS list options.

5. **Set the starting number for the list.**

You don't have to begin a numbered list at 1, A, or the Roman numeral I. You can start it with any number you wish—a trick that can come in handy if, for example, you create a web page that explains how to rebuild a car's engine. As part of each step, say you want to include a photograph. You create a numbered list, type in the directions for step 1, hit Return, and then insert an image (as described in Chapter 5). You hit Return again, and then type in the text for step 2. Unfortunately, the photo, because it's technically an item in an ordered list, now has the number 2 next to it, and your real step 2 is listed as step 3!

If you remove the list formatting from the photo to get rid of the 2, you create one list above it and another below it. The real step 2, *below* the photo, now thinks it's the beginning of a new list—and starts over with the number 1! The solution is to make the list below the photo think it's a *new* list that begins with 2.

To start a list at something other than 1, type the starting number in the "Start count" field (Figure 2-10). You must enter a number, even if you want the list to use letters. So, to begin a list at D instead of A, type *4* in the "Start count" field.

You can even change the style of a *single* list item. For instance, you could change the third item in a numeric list from a 3 to the letter C. (Of course, just because you *can* doesn't mean you should. Dreamweaver is very thorough in supporting the almost overwhelming combination of options available in HTML, but, unless you're building a Dadaist revival site, how often do you want a list that's numbered 1, 2, C, iv, 1?)

6. **Click OK to apply the changes.**

■ NESTED LISTS

Some complex outlines require multiple *levels* of lists. Legal documents, for instance, may list major clauses with capital letters (A, B, C, and so on) and use Roman numerals (i, ii, iii, and so on) for subclauses.

You can easily create nested lists in Dreamweaver using the Properties panel's indent button; Figure 2-11 shows you the steps.

You can change the style of a nested list—for example, change the nested list in Figure 2-11, bottom, into a bulleted list—by clicking the appropriate list type in the Properties panel. Changing the nested list's type doesn't affect the parent list type (that is, the outer list); for example, changing the nested list in Figure 2-11 from a numbered list to a bulleted list doesn't change the outer list to a bulleted list.

> **TIP** You can also create a nested list by hitting the tab key to indent a list item to another level. Shift-Tab outdents the item.

Definition Lists

You use *definition lists* to create dictionary or glossary entries, or whenever you need to present a term and its definition. Each item in a definition list is composed of two parts: a word or term and its definition.

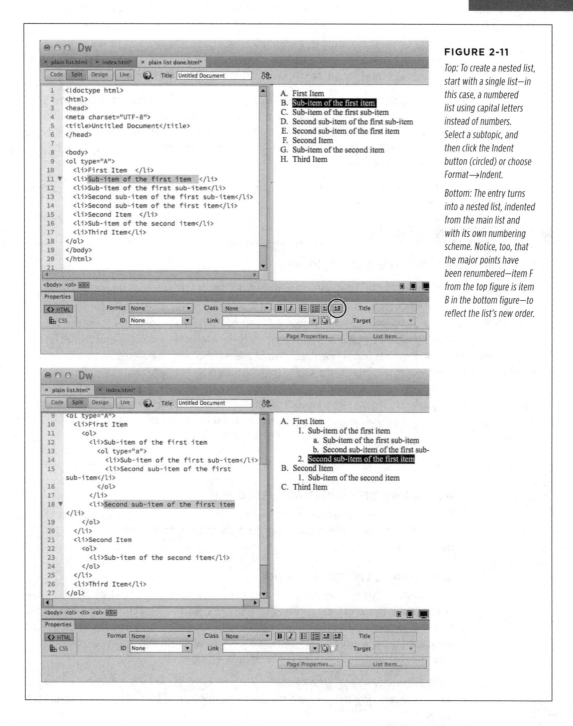

FIGURE 2-11

Top: To create a nested list, start with a single list—in this case, a numbered list using capital letters instead of numbers. Select a subtopic, and then click the Indent button (circled) or choose Format→Indent.

Bottom: The entry turns into a nested list, indented from the main list and with its own numbering scheme. Notice, too, that the major points have been renumbered—item F from the top figure is item B in the bottom figure—to reflect the list's new order.

NOTE Behind the scenes, Dreamweaver creates an entire definition list using the <dl> tag. It applies two tags to each item in the list: <dt> for the word or term you want to define, and <dd> for the definition itself.

As you can see in Figure 2-9, definition lists aren't as fancy as they sound. They present the first item in the list—the word or term—on its own line with no indent, and displays the second item—the definition—underneath, indented.

You can't create a definition list using the Properties panel. Instead, you start by creating a list of definitions and terms: Each term and definition should be in its own paragraph, and the definition should immediately follow the term. Next, highlight the paragraphs that contain the terms and definitions, and then choose Format→List→Definition List.

To turn a definition list *back* to regular paragraphs, select the list, and then choose Format→List→None, or, in the Properties panel, click the Outdent button.

FREQUENTLY ASKED QUESTION

When Not to Approach the Insert Panel

I like the convenience of the Insert panel. Should I use its Structure category to format text?

In a word, no. Unlike the way web designers use most of the other categories in the Insert panel, they use Structure mainly when working in Code view. It contains many of the same formatting options as the Properties panel; the Insert panel's h1, h2, and h3 headings, for instance, are the same as Headings 1, 2, and 3 in the Properties panel's Format drop-down menu.

However, using some of the panel's text options, such as <li>, can generate invalid HTML if you don't use it correctly.

Furthermore, despite its usual tidiness, Dreamweaver doesn't clean up the code produced this way.

In fact, some of these options, when used in Design view, actually split the document window in two, showing the HTML code on one side and Design view on the other. This arrangement is confusing if you're not accustomed to seeing—or if you're not interested in seeing—the raw HTML. All major text-formatting options are available from the Properties panel and Format menu. If you stick to these two tools, you can safely avoid the Structure category.

Removing and Deleting List Items

Dreamweaver lets you take items out of a list two ways: either by removing the list *formatting* from items (and changing them back to normal paragraphs) or by deleting their text outright.

■ REMOVING LIST FORMATTING

To remove list formatting from one or more list items (or an entire list), highlight the lines in question, and then choose Format→List→None (or, in the Properties panel, click the Outdent button). You just removed all list formatting, and the text remains on-screen, now formatted as standard paragraphs. For nested lists, you need to click the Outdent button once for each level of indent.

If you reformat an item in the middle of a list using this technique, it becomes a regular paragraph, and Dreamweaver turns the items above and below it into separate lists.

■ DELETING LIST ITEMS

You can easily delete a list or list item using the Tag Selector in the document window's status bar (see Figure 2-12). To delete an entire list, click anywhere inside it, click its tag in the Tag Selector—<ul> for a bulleted list, <ol> for a numbered list—and then press Delete. You can also, of course, drag through all the text in the list, and then press Delete.

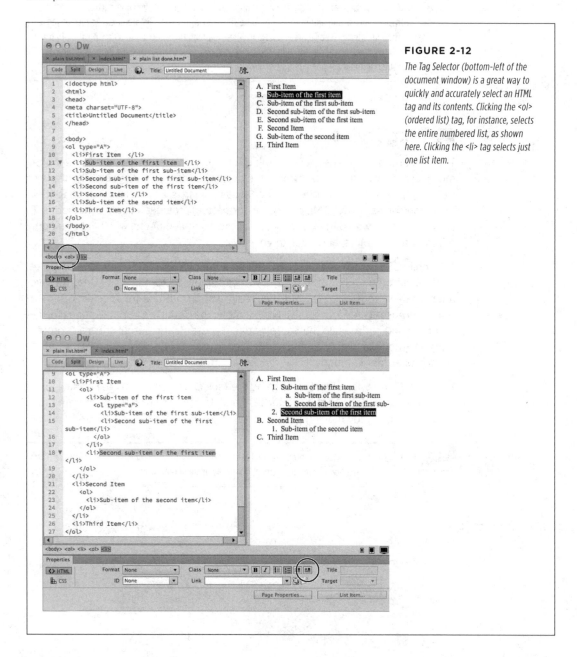

FIGURE 2-12

The Tag Selector (bottom-left of the document window) is a great way to quickly and accurately select an HTML tag and its contents. Clicking the <ol> (ordered list) tag, for instance, selects the entire numbered list, as shown here. Clicking the <li> tag selects just one list item.

To delete a single list item, click that item in the document window, click the <li> tag in the Tag Selector, and then press Delete.

TIP You can rearrange a list in Design view by dragging a list item to another position within the list. If it's an ordered list (1, 2, 3, and so on), Dreamweaver automatically renumbers it.

However, selecting a list item can be tricky. If you simply drag to select the text, you don't actually select the list item itself, with all its formatting and numbering. To be sure that you select a list item *and* its formatting, click the <li> tag in the Tag Selector (see Figure 2-12). Now, when you drag the selection to a new position in the list, the number (or bullet) goes along for the ride. You can also copy or cut the selected list item, and then paste it into another position in the list.

■ Text Styles

The formatting you can apply through HTML tags isn't much to write home about, much less to advertise on a résumé. It's pretty basic; browsers generally display a Heading 1, for instance, in black and bold using a large Times New Roman font. As mentioned on page 82, HTML paragraph formatting provides *structure*, not looks. To create standout web pages, you need Cascading Style Sheets, which let you apply different fonts, colors, and sizes to your text.

And while CSS, which you'll learn in the next chapter, is the mother lode of styles, HTML itself offers a handful of tags you can apply to format text. Dreamweaver refers to these tags as *styles*, but they really just format text for specific, often obscure, purposes (see Figure 2-13). For example, the Code and Variable styles format programming code, while the Sample style represents the output from a computer program—not exactly styles you need often in promoting, say, your *Cheeses of the World* mail-order company.

To use an HTML style, select the text, and then select a format from the Format→Style menu. (You can also use the Properties panel to apply the <strong> or <em> tags to emphasize text by making it bold or italic.)

TIP Use italics with care. While printed material uses it frequently to add *emphasis* or to reference a book title, it can be difficult to read on a computer screen, especially at small type sizes.

FIGURE 2-13

Top: While the Properties panel lets you apply bold and italic formats to text, the Format→HTML Style menu offers a larger selection of styles. Don't be confused by the term "styles," which, in this case, merely refers to different HTML tags. They're unrelated to CSS styles and are intended to customize very specific types of text, like citations from a book or magazine, or programming code.

Bottom: As you can see, the many style options usually include bold, italic, your browser's monospaced font (usually Courier), or some combination of the three. But don't worry about how they look "out of the box"—as you'll learn in the next chapter, you can make any of these tags appear any way you want by applying CSS.

Unless you intend to use HTML tags that properly format your content, like using the Code style to display computer code, for example, you're better off avoiding such styles. But if you think one of them might come in handy, you can find more about these styles in Dreamweaver's built-in HTML reference; see page 370.

TIP The teletype (<tt>) tag is truly, genuinely, absolutely, obsolete. When was the last time you used a teletype machine? The tag has been removed from HTML5, so avoid it.

When Bold and Italics Are Neither

You may be confused by the HTML Dreamweaver produces when you tell it to make text bold or italic. Instead of using the <b> tag—the original HTML code for bold—Dreamweaver uses the <strong> tag. And instead of using <i> for italic, clicking the Properties panel's I button gets you the <em> tag, the one for emphasis. That's because Adobe decided to follow industry practices rather than stick to an old tradition.

For most purposes, <strong> and <em> behave identically to <b> and <i>. The results look the same—bolded or italicized text—in most browsers. However, when screen readers (programs or equipment that read web pages aloud for the visually impaired) encounter these tags, the <strong> tag triggers a loud, strong voice. The <em> tag also brings an emphasis to the voice of screen readers, though with less strength than the <strong> tag.

Since most browsers simply treat the <strong> tag like the <b> tag and the <em> tag like the <i> tag, you'll probably never notice the difference. However, if you prefer the simple <b> and <i> tags, choose Edit→Preferences. Select the General category, and then turn off the checkbox labeled "Use <strong> and <em> in place of <b> and <i>."

HTML5 slightly redefines these tags. It rewrote the <i> tag for text in an "alternate voice," such as a foreign word, a technical term, or typographically italicized text such as a book title. You use the <b> tag just to make text look bold so that it stands out visually. Basically, imagine you're reading text out loud. If you encounter a word that you would emphasize with your voice ("For crying out loud," for example), use the <em> tag; if you'd shout the word ("Help!!!"), use the <strong> tag. If you simply want text to look a certain way, you can use the <i> or <b> tags, or, better yet, the CSS *font-weight* and *font-style* properties described on page 140. You can read more about HTML5 and the <b>, <strong>, <i>, and <em> tags at *http://tinyurl.com/yau4mze*.

■ Spell-Checking

You spend a lot of time perfecting your web pages, making sure that the images look great, the text is properly formatted, and everything aligns to make a beautiful visual presentation. But one step is often forgotten, especially given the hyper-development of web content—making sure your web text is free of typos.

Spelling mistakes look unprofessional and imply a lack of attention to detail. Who wants to hire an "illustraightor" or "web dezyner?" Dreamweaver's spell-checking feature can help.

About Dictionaries

Before you start spell-checking, make sure you have the right *dictionary* selected. Dreamweaver comes with 47 of them, ranging from Bulgarian to Turkish (including four variants of English, and four of German). When it checks your spelling, the program compares the text in your document against the list of words in one of these dictionaries.

To specify a dictionary language, choose Edit→Preferences (Dreamweaver→ Prefer-ences) or press Ctrl+U (⌘-U) to open the Preferences dialog box. Select the General category and then, from the Spelling Dictionary drop-down menu at the bottom of the window, choose a language.

Performing a Spell-Check

Once you select a dictionary, open the web page whose spelling you want to check. You can check as much or as little of the text as you like, as follows:

1. **Highlight the text you want to check (which can even be a single word).**

    If you want to check the *entire* document, make sure you have nothing selected in the document window (one good way to do this is to click in the middle of a paragraph of text).

> **NOTE** Unfortunately, Dreamweaver doesn't offer a site-wide spell-checking feature. You must check each page individually.

GEM IN THE ROUGH

Clean Up Word

From Word, you can save any document as a web page, essen-tially turning it into an HTML page—except that Word produces hideous HTML. One look at it, and you'd think that your cat fell asleep on the keyboard.

Here's what happens: To let you reopen the document as a Word file when the time comes, Word injects reams of information that adds to the file size of the page. This is a particular problem with the latest versions of Word, which add loads of XML and Cascading Style Sheet information.

Fortunately, Dreamweaver's Clean Up Word HTML command strips out most of that unnecessary code and produces leaner web pages. To use it, open the Word HTML file just as you would

any other web page, by choosing File→Open. Then choose Commands→Clean Up Word HTML.

The Clean Up Word HTML dialog box opens; Dreamweaver automatically detects whether the HTML was produced by Word 97/98 or a later version, and then applies the appropriate rules for cleaning up the HTML.

Unfortunately, Dreamweaver doesn't always catch all the junk Word throws in, so if you have the original Word document, you're better off just opening it, copying the contents, and pasting it into Dreamweaver. Then you can use Dreamweaver's tools for formatting the text so that it looks just the way you want it to, without any unnecessary code.

---

2. **Choose Commands→Check Spelling (or press Shift+F7).**

    The Check Spelling dialog box opens (see Figure 2-14). If a word isn't in Dream-weaver's dictionary, it appears in the top box, along with a list of suggested spellings.

    The first suggestion is listed in the "Change to" field.

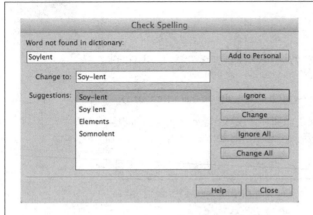

FIGURE 2-14

Dreamweaver's spell-checking feature checks only words in the document window. It can't check the spelling of comments, <alt> tags, or any text that appears in the head of the document, with the exception of the page's title. Nor can you spell check an entire website's worth of pages with a single command; you need to check each page individually.

3. **If the "Change to" field is correct, click Change.**

   If Dreamweaver correctly flags a word as misspelled but the correct spelling isn't in the "Change to" field, double-click the correct spelling in the Suggestions list below it. If the correct spelling isn't *there*, type it into the "Change to" box yourself. Then click the Change button to correct this one instance, or click Change All to replace this misspelled word everywhere in your document.

   Dreamweaver makes the change and moves on to the next questionable spelling.

4. **If the word is actually correctly spelled but not in Dreamweaver's dictionary, click Ignore, Ignore All, or Add to Personal.**

   If you want Dreamweaver to ignore this word *every* time it appears in the document, rather than just this instance of it, click Ignore All.

   On the other hand, you'll probably use some words that Dreamweaver doesn't have in its dictionaries. You may, for instance, use a client's name throughout your pages. If that name isn't in Dreamweaver's dictionary, it consistently flags the name as a spelling error.

   To teach Dreamweaver the client's name, click Add to Personal. Dreamweaver adds the word to your personal dictionary, which is a special file that Dreamweaver consults when it checks your spelling.

   After you click Ignore or Change, Dreamweaver moves on to the next word it doesn't recognize. Begin again from step 3. If you didn't start the spell check from the beginning of the document, once Dreamweaver reaches the end, it asks if you want to continue spell checking from the beginning.

5. **To finish the spell check, click Close.**

Introducing Cascading Style Sheets

What you see on a web page when you use garden-variety HTML tags like <h1>, <p>, and <ul> pales in comparison to the text and styling on display in, say, a print magazine. If web designers had only HTML to make their sites look great, the Web would forever be the ugly duckling of the media world. HTML doesn't hold a candle to the typographic and layout control you get when you create a document in even the most basic word processing program.

Fortunately for web designers, you can change the ho-hum appearance of HTML using a technology called Cascading Style Sheets (CSS). CSS gives you the tools you need to make HTML look beautiful. If you think of HTML as the basic structure of a house (the foundation, walls, and rooms), then CSS is the house's interior design (the paint, carpeting, and color, style, and placement of furniture). CSS gives you much greater control over the layout and design of your pages. Using it, you can improve the look of common web page elements like links, images, and tables. For example, you can add margins to paragraphs (just as in a word processor), colorful and stylish borders to images, and even dynamic rollover effects to text links. Dreamweaver's streamlined approach to CSS makes it fast and easy to create styles and store them in a central style sheet that controls the look of all the pages in your site.

CSS is a big topic. It's also the heart of today's cutting-edge web design. So instead of dedicating just a single chapter to it, this book provides instructions in nearly every chapter. In this chapter, you'll learn the basics of CSS and how to use Dreamweaver's powerful CSS tools—with an emphasis on the program's new CSS Designer. You'll also learn to expand your font library using new web fonts.

Once you're comfortable with the basics, you'll find in-depth information on CSS in Chapter 9. In Chapter 10, you'll learn how to harness the power of CSS to fully control the layout of a web page. And in Chapter 11, you'll learn how to troubleshoot CSS problems.

■ Cascading Style Sheet Basics

If you've formatted text in programs like Microsoft Word or Adobe InDesign, styling pages with CSS will feel familiar. A *style* is simply a rule describing how a browser should format a particular element on the page, like a heading or an image. A *style sheet* is a collection of these styles.

For example, you might create a style that formats text in the Arial font with red letters and a left margin of 50 pixels. You can also create styles specifically for images; for instance, you can create a style that aligns an image along the right edge of a web page, surrounds the image with a colorful border, and adds a 50-pixel margin between the image and the surrounding text.

Once you create a style, you can apply it to text, images, or other elements on a page. For example, you could select a paragraph and instantly change the text's size, color, and font just by applying a style.

Why Use CSS?

When designers styled web pages in the past, HTML alone provided the formatting options for text, images, tables, and other page elements. Today, professional web designers use CSS to style their pages.

> **NOTE** The World Wide Web Consortium, the organization that defines Web standards, has phased out older HTML tags that were used to format text and other page elements in favor of CSS. Following industry practice, Dreamweaver CC has made it impossible to add obsolete HTML tags, such as the <font> tag (unless you write the code yourself).

CSS has many benefits over HTML. With it, you can format paragraphs to look as fancy as those that appear in a book or newspaper (with the first line indented and no space between paragraphs, for example), and control the leading (the space between lines of type in a paragraph). When you use CSS to add a background image to a page, you get to decide how (and whether) it tiles (repeats). HTML can't even begin to do any of these things.

Style sheets also make it easier to update your site. You can collect all your styles into a single style sheet and link it to every page on your site. When it's time to change every Heading 2 tag (<h2>) to lime green, you edit the style in the style sheet, and that change ripples throughout your site, *wherever* you used that style. You can thus completely change the appearance of a site simply by editing a single style sheet.

Getting to Know (and Love) CSS

Cascading Style Sheets are an exciting—and complex—addition to your web-building toolkit, worthy of entire books and websites themselves. Here are some resources:

- For an excellent tutorial on CSS, visit W3 Schools' CSS tutorials at *http://www.w3schools.com/css/.*

- If you like video tutorials, Sitepoint's CSS Video Crash Course (*www.sitepoint.com/videos/videocss1/*) will teach you a lot about CSS in under three hours.

- If you want to get help *and* learn more about CSS, the Sitepoint CSS Forums (*http://tinyurl.com/cmeaubn*) are always busy with advice from a great community of CSS enthusiasts.

- Sitepoint also provides a great CSS reference at *http://reference.sitepoint.com/css*. It's a dictionary-like resource of all CSS properties, and includes information on which browsers support which properties.

- For the ultimate authority on CSS, turn to the World Wide Web Consortium's website at *www.w3.org/Style/CSS*. The W3C is the body responsible for many of the standards that drive the Web—including HTML and CSS. (Beware: This site reads like a college physics textbook.)

- For a great list of CSS-related sites, visit the Information and Technology Systems and Services website at the University of Minnesota, Duluth (*http://tinyurl.com/jg2fe*).

- If you just love to curl up by the fireplace with a good tech book, try *CSS3: The Missing Manual* by David McFarland (hey, that name rings a bell!). It's written in the same style as this book, with in-depth coverage of CSS and step-by-step tutorials that guide you through every facet of this complicated technology.

Internal vs. External Style Sheets

As you create new styles, you'll add them to a style sheet you store either in the web page itself (in which case it's called an *internal style sheet*), or in a separate file called an *external style sheet*.

NOTE There's actually a third place where CSS styles can appear: within the HTML code itself. These are called *inline styles*, but don't confuse them with internal style sheets. Inline styles are out of fashion because they mix page formatting (CSS) with page content (the HTML). For details, see the box on page 103.

In Dreamweaver, the most common use of inline styles is as a temporary style that you quickly convert to an internal or external style sheet, as described on page 46.

Internal style sheets appear in the <head> portion of a web page and contain styles that apply to that page only. You use internal style sheets when you want a very specific format for a single web page. For example, the marketing department might ask you to create a one-page flyer with a unique format and its own distinctive look, the perfect use of an internal style sheet.

TIP As you design a new web page, it's often easier to add styles to an internal style sheet. Then, once you're satisfied with the design, you can export the styles to an external style sheet—for use by all your site's pages. See page 381 for details.

An external style sheet, on the other hand, contains only styles—no HTML—and you can link numerous pages to it. In fact, you can link every page on your site to it, giving your site a uniform, site-wide set of styles. For instance, you can put a headline style in an external style sheet and link every page on the site to that sheet. Every headline on every page then shares the same look—instant design consistency! Even better, when the boss (or the interior decorator in you) calls up and asks you to change the color of the headlines, you only need to edit a single file—the external style sheet—to update hundreds or even thousands of web pages.

You can easily create both types of style sheet in Dreamweaver, and you aren't limited to choosing one or the other. A single web page can have both an external style sheet (for styles that apply to the whole site) and an internal style sheet (for styles that apply to just that page). You can even attach multiple external style sheets to a single page.

Types of Styles

CSS styles come in several flavors, the three most common being *class*, *ID*, and *tag* styles. Dreamweaver's CSS Designer calls these styles "selectors" because you use them to select and format specific elements on a page.

A class style is one you create, name, and attach to an HTML tag or to selected text (in other words, text you select with your cursor). Class styles work much like styles in word processing and page layout programs. To display the name of your company in bold and red wherever it appears on a web page, for example, you can create a class style named *.company* that formats text in boldface with red letters. You'd then highlight your company's name on the page and apply this style to it.

An ID style lets you format a *unique* item on a page. Use ID styles to identify an object (or an area of a page) that appears only once—like a website's logo, copyright notice, or main navigation bar. An ID style is similar to a class style in that you name the style and then apply it to a page element. But while you can apply a class to many different elements on a page, you can apply an ID to only a *single* element per page. (It's okay to use multiple IDs on a single page, so long as each ID is different.) ID styles aren't as popular as they once were—partly because you can only use the ID (and thus the style) once per page, but mostly because ID styles pose problems when your site's styles grow more complex and your style sheets longer. You'll learn the details on page 385, but for now, keep in mind that class styles can do anything ID styles can do, and you'll use class and tag styles (discussed next) more frequently than ID styles in this book.

Inline Styles vs. Internal Style Sheets

What's the difference between an inline style and an internal style sheet?

An *inline style* is attached directly to the HTML tag that it formats. Inline styles have no "style sheets"—the styles are interspersed throughout the <body> of the web page. For example, a paragraph formatted with an inline style that turns the text red would have the code:

```
<p style="color: #FF0000">This paragraph
is really, really red!</p>
```

This inline style affects that particular paragraph only. You don't need to specify a "selector" (that is, a target for the style) because you just tacked the formatting command onto the paragraph tag. With no selector (in other words, without a target for the style), you can't attach this "style" to any other paragraph.

Internal style sheets, on the other hand, are legitimate style sheets. Dreamweaver stores them in the head of a web page. Internal styles use selectors to identify elements on a web page, so you can apply a single style to multiple elements using the same selector. When a web page uses an internal style sheet, you're likely to find more than one CSS rule stored there. Here's an example of an internal style sheet that has two rules:

```
<style type="text/css">
h1 {
```

```
    color: #CC9900;
    font-family: Baskerville, "Palatino
Linotype", Palatino, "Century Schoolbook
L", "Times New Roman", serif;
}
.copyright {
    font-size: 12px;
    border-top: 1px solid #CC9900;
    padding-top: 5px;
}
</style>
```

This internal style sheet has rules for the h1 heading and a copyright class. The style sheet appears inside of <style> opening and closing tags. The entire style sheet is stored in the <head> of the web page.

The best practice these days is to separate formatting from content, so most designers don't use inline styles. If you perform all your CSS chores in CSS Designer, it's unlikely that you'll ever create an inline style. Designer doesn't create or edit inline styles. If you use the Properties panel's CSS mode, you can create inline styles, and you may occasionally create an inline style and then convert it to a class that you store in an internal or external style sheet. That process is described on page 381.

The other major type of CSS style is called a tag style, and it applies to a specific HTML tag globally, as opposed to individual paragraphs or selections. Suppose you want to display every Heading 1 in the Arial font. Instead of creating a class style and applying it to every Heading 1 on a page, you could create a tag style for the <h1> tag, in effect redefining the tag so that browsers display all h1 headlines in Arial.

The main benefit to redefining a tag this way is convenience—you don't have to go into your site's pages, find every <h1> tag, and then apply the style by hand. The h1 style you create says that *all* <h1> tags must use Arial, so a browser displays all <h1> tags in Arial. Styling HTML tags like this is the easiest way to format a page.

Nevertheless, sometimes only a class style will do, such as when you want to format just a few words in a paragraph. Simply redefining the <p> tag won't do the trick, since that would affect the entire paragraph (and every other paragraph on your site). Instead, you have to create a class style and apply it to just the words you wish to style. In addition, class styles are handy when you want to format just one instance of a tag differently from others. If you want to format the introductory paragraph on a page one way and all the other paragraphs a different way, for example, you create a class style and apply it to that first paragraph. (Another solution is a slightly more complicated, but more flexible, type of style called a *descendent selector*—you'll read about those on page 370.)

NOTE In addition to class, ID, and tag styles, other types of styles provide added control for particular situations. You'll read about these more advanced styles on page 367.

Creating Styles

Dreamweaver CC includes a shiny new tool to help you manage styles: CSS Designer, shown in Figure 3-1. Replacing an earlier patchwork of panels, palettes, and menus, CSS Designer puts everything you need to build and manage styles in one convenient, well-organized location. Learn how to use the Designer's system of *Sources*, *Selectors*, and *Properties*, and you'll master all your CSS chores. (Dreamweaver still provides some of the old tools for specific tasks and for pros reluctant to learn new ways.)

In this section, you'll tour CSS Designer and learn how to create new styles. In the next section, on page 112, you'll look at the Properties panel's CSS mode, another place you can create and modify styles.

TIP If you've used Dreamweaver before, you may groan when you hear there's a new way to create CSS rules. Why learn yet another way to work through the maze of CSS styles? The answer is that you'll probably find the new system faster and more logical. Adobe added earlier CSS tools to Dreamweaver piecemeal over the years. It designed this new system from the ground up, reflecting the way designers use CSS today. If you already have experience with CSS, it won't take long to get a handle on CSS Designer.

Creating New Styles with CSS Designer

Dreamweaver divides the CSS Designer panel into four sections: Sources, Media, Selectors, and Properties. (If you don't see the CSS Designer panel, press Shift+F11 [Windows only] or go to Window→CSS Designer.) In most of Dreamweaver's workspaces, the panel appears in the lower-right corner, sharing space with the CSS Transitions panel. The Designer's appearance changes slightly depending on the workspace you choose (Figure 3-1).

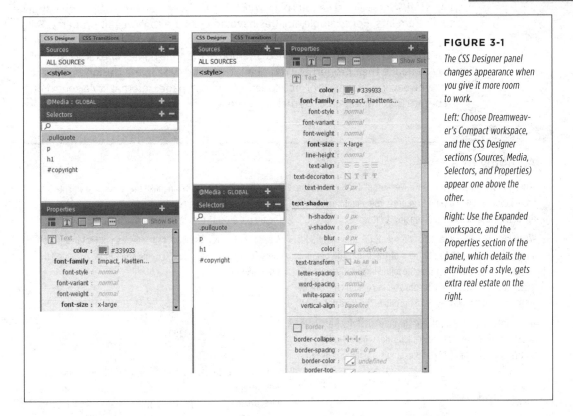

FIGURE 3-1

The CSS Designer panel changes appearance when you give it more room to work.

Left: Choose Dreamweaver's Compact workspace, and the CSS Designer sections (Sources, Media, Selectors, and Properties) appear one above the other.

Right: Use the Expanded workspace, and the Properties section of the panel, which details the attributes of a style, gets extra real estate on the right.

In most cases, creating a new style is a three-step process, all of which you accomplish in the Designer panel, moving from one section to another. Here's a rough outline of the process:

1. **Choose a Source for your style rule.** You add styles to an internal or an external style sheet, or you create a new style sheet.

2. **Choose a Selector.** The selector can be a class, an ID, or an HTML tag. You can modify existing selectors using the CSS Designer or you can create new ones.

3. **Set Properties for the Selector.** After you choose a selector in step 2, you can set or change its properties—also known as creating a rule or editing one, respectively. For example, you can set text properties by choosing a *font-family* (Arial), *font-color* (green), and *font-size* (large).

NOTE There are four sections in the CSS Designer: Sources, Media, Selectors, and Properties. This part of the book doesn't cover Media, which you use to create media queries. Media queries determine what type of device (computer, phone, or tablet) is displaying a web page. Then, CSS can be used to provide the page content in the best manner. Media queries are covered on page 506.

There are dozens of CSS properties. Using class, ID, and tag selectors, they can be applied to text, images, videos, or some arbitrary group of elements you define using HTML's versatile <div> tag (page 428). Naturally, certain properties don't apply to all elements. For example, images have no use for a font-weight property. Still, Dreamweaver's CSS Designer gives you access to all the styles and a consistent way to apply them. You don't have to memorize the style names or exactly the right way to define their properties. You point, click, and type in the Designer, and then Dreamweaver writes the correct code in your web page (internal style sheet) or a separate CSS document (external style sheet).

UP TO SPEED

Anatomy of a Style

When you style a page, Dreamweaver automatically writes the proper code. But if you want to impress your neighbors, here's the behind-the-scenes scoop on how that works.

When you create an internal style sheet, Dreamweaver adds a pair of <style> tags to the head of the page. The opening <style> tag tells a browser that the following information isn't HTML—it's CSS code. When the browser encounters the closing </style> tag, it knows that it's at the end of the style definition.

Within that <style> tag, you see one or more styles (reminder: in CSS-speak, styles are also called rules). An HTML tag style for the Heading 1 tag (<h1>), for example, might look like this:

```
h1 {
    font-size: 24px;
    color: #003399;
}
```

The first part—<h1>—is called a *selector*, and it identifies the style's target. In this case, a browser applies this style wherever it finds an <h1> (Heading 1) in a web page's code.

The information between the braces—{}—defines the formatting the browser should apply. The preceding code contains two formatting instructions for the <h1> tag. Each is called a *declaration* and is composed of a *property* and a *value*. For instance, *font-size: 24px* is one declaration, which has a property of *font-size* and a value of *24px*. In other words, this rule

tells a browser that it should make the text inside an <h1> tag 24 pixels tall. The second declaration makes a browser display the text of all <h1> tags in the color #003399.

A class style looks just like a tag style, except that instead of the selector being a tag, it's a name *you* supply, preceded by a dot, like this:

```
.company {
    font-size: 24px;
    color: #003399;
}
```

Styles in an external style sheet look exactly the same; the only difference is that external style sheets are separate files whose names end in .css, don't include the <style> tags, and must not include any HTML. You link an external style sheet to a web page using the <link> tag. For example, to link a style sheet named *styles.css* to a web page, you could add this HTML code to the page:

```
<link href="styles.css" rel="stylesheet"
type="text/css">
```

In Dreamweaver, you can easily get a look at the style definitions in an external style sheet:

Near the top of the document window, in the list of related files, just click the CSS file's name (Figure 1-3).

TIP In CSS Designer, to enlarge or reduce the size of a section, position your cursor along the top border of the section (just above the section's name) until the arrow cursor turns into a resize cursor (two parallel lines with arrows at either end), and then drag up or down.

Here's a closer look at each of the steps you take to create a new CSS style.

Choose a Style Source

When you create a style in CSS Designer (Window→CSS Designer), you have to decide where that style will reside—as part of your web page or as an external style sheet. Go to the Sources section of CSS Designer and click the + sign on the right (Figure 3-2, top). The Add CSS Source menu appears, offering three options:

- **Create A New CSS File.** This option opens a dialog box that lets you create a new, external style sheet. Style sheets contain only CSS formatting rules; they don't include any page content. You're likely to use this option when you build a website and want consistent formatting across many pages. Here's the scenario: You build pages with the usual HTML tags, like <p>, <h1>, and <h2>. Perhaps you create some classes, like .copyright or .pullquote, to handle special formatting. Then you define the style for those tags and classes in your external style sheet. A single line of code at the top of your web page identifies the relevant style sheet.

- **Attach Existing CSS File.** If you created a style sheet earlier (say in step 1 above) and you want to apply the styles you created there to the current page, select this option. You can also create a new CSS rule and store it in an attached style sheet—just keep in mind that styles you add to an existing sheet may affect other pages. You can attach more than one external CSS style sheet to a web page. For example, suppose your site includes several "glossary" pages with definitions. You might create an additional style sheet to format those pages.

- **Define in Page.** This option stores a CSS style internally, in the same page where you specify the style. This method has both limitations and advantages. On one hand, if you store styles within a page, you won't be able to apply them to other pages. On the other hand, styles defined in a page can override styles applied through an external style sheet, which can come in handy. Suppose you have a website of several pages, and it uses an external style sheet called *soylent_styles.css*. You want to change the Heading 1 style for just one of your pages, so you apply the *soylent_styles.css* to that page and then use an internal style sheet to create a new definition for the <h1> heading. Web browsers will see both <h1> definitions, but they'll use the one in the internal style sheet because internal styles take precedence over external styles.

After telling CSS Designer where to find your style, the style sheet's name appears in the Sources panel (Figure 3-2, bottom). For some projects, you may see an extensive list of sources, because a single page can use several style sheets (including internal style sheets, listed as <style> in the Sources section). The next step in creating a style is to choose the style's target, known as a Selector in CSS-speak. That's up next.

TIP If you don't see any white space below the dark gray Sources bar, the section is collapsed. You collapse and expand sections by clicking the dark gray bars.

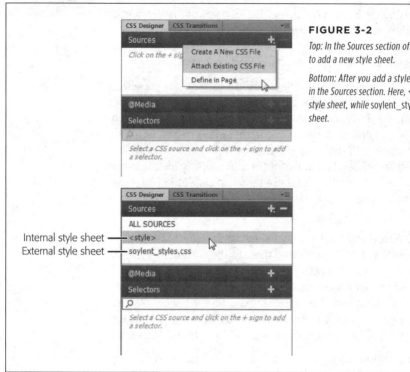

FIGURE 3-2

Top: In the Sources section of CSS Designer, click the + button to add a new style sheet.

Bottom: After you add a style sheet, Dreamweaver lists it in the Sources section. Here, <style> designates an internal style sheet, while soylent_styles.css is an external style sheet.

Choose a Selector

Selectors target specific elements in web pages. They include HTML tags like the paragraph <p> and Heading 1 <h1> tags, or you can selectively style page elements by creating class selectors. For example, you may want to create a *.copyright* class to format the copyright notice at the bottom of a page, or you may create a *.caption* class to set photo captions off from body text. Web designers use another selector, ID, less frequently these days because it's less flexible; you can only apply an ID selector to a single element on a page.

To see the selectors you identified in a set of CSS rules, click the source of those rules in (where else?) the Sources section of CSS Designer. To see all the selectors applied to a page, choose All Sources in the Sources section.

To create a brand-spanking-new selector, follow these steps:

1. **In the Sources section of CSS Designer, tell Dreamweaver where you want to put the new selector and its related styles.**

   To add a selector to an existing style sheet, whether it's an internal or external sheet, click the name of the style sheet in the Sources list (Dreamweaver lists internal style sheets as "<style>"). If the source doesn't exist, create it by following the steps on page 107.

2. **In the Selectors section, click the + sign to add a selector.**

   Dreamweaver positions your cursor in a text box at the bottom of the list of selectors. Type in a name for the selector. (If the + sign is grayed out, you probably haven't selected a valid source.)

   If you selected All Sources in step 1, the Add Source + sign isn't active because you need to identify a single, specific destination for your new style. Otherwise, CSS Designer won't know where to store the rule.

3. **Type in a name for your selector.**

   HTML tags are predefined, so you don't need to rename a selector to style tags. If you create a class selector, remember to add a period to the beginning of the class name; *.caption* and *.pullquote* are both valid class names, for example. In naming ID selectors, always precede the name with a pound sign (#); *#copyright* is a valid ID name, for instance.

   For both class and ID selectors, the character immediately following the period or pound sign must be a letter. After that, you can use any combination of letters, numbers, underscore characters, and hyphens you want. If you don't start typing a period or a pound sign when you name your selector, Dreamweaver displays a list of valid HTML tags as you type. You can continue typing or choose one of the tags.

■ **TAG HINTS**

Dreamweaver is ready to help when it comes to naming tags. In Design view, put your cursor in a block of text before you click the + sign, and Dreamweaver displays the HTML tag. It's a little confusing, though, because CSS Designer always suggests a *compound selector* as the tag. A compound selector is a selector within another selector. In this case, the compound selector targets a paragraph (<p>) within the body (<body>) of your HTML document. In other words, the <p> tag resides within the <body>. That's why Dreamweaver suggests *body p* as the selector, though you don't have to accept that. You can use *p* only (the paragraph tag) only as your selector—just delete *body* from the suggestion. Compound selectors are key to the "cascading" behavior of cascading style sheets. You'll find more details on page 384.

Set Properties for the Selector

Once you choose a selector, you need to specify the style rules the selector should follow. You do that by setting values for the selector's properties. Highlight a selector in the Selectors section, and Dreamweaver displays its properties in the Properties section. Scroll down the list to see just how extensive the properties are. You can easily read the property names, but most of their values are grayed out, which means you haven't set a value for the property yet. In other words, there's no rule defining the style for that property. To create a rule, you simply provide a value for the property. Dreamweaver does its best to make it easy—just highlight one of those grayed-out property values, and Dreamweaver displays a pop-up menu, a color picker, or some other widget that helps you set the value.

Say you want to set the color for the text in a paragraph. Before you create that rule, you need to choose a source (the place where you'll store the rule) and a selector—the class, ID, or HTML tag you're styling. In this example, you'll style a paragraph and store its rule in an external style sheet called *soylent_styles.css*:

1. **In the Sources section of CSS Designer, click the Add Source button (the + sign). Then, from the drop-down menu, select Create a New CSS Style.**

   The Create a New CSS Style dialog box appears.

2. **Type *soylent_styles.css* in the File/URL field, leave the Link radio button selected, and then click OK. (For details on the Conditional Usage field, also known as media queries, see page 506.)**

3. **In the Selectors section, click the plus sign to add a selector, and then, in the selector text box that appears, type *p*.**

   When you press *p*, Dreamweaver displays a list of matching HTML tags in case you can't remember the name of the tag name or you want to save a few keystrokes by choosing a name from the list. After you enter the tag, Dreamweaver displays a list of related properties in the Properties section.

4. **At the top of the Properties section, click the T (for "text") button.**

   Dreamweaver automatically scrolls to the list of text properties. Dreamweaver displays style rules in two parts:

   ```
   name : value
   ```

   The colon separating the name from the value is part of the rule, as you'll see when you inspect a CSS style sheet (page 379). The box on page 106 gives you more detail on CSS's two-part naming system.

   The first property Dreamweaver lists is *color*. It displays a color swatch next to the property, with a red line drawn through it and the word "undefined" beside it. Both the property and its value are grayed out because you haven't set a value for either yet.

TIP There are so many CSS properties that Dreamweaver organizes them in categories and provides relevant buttons at the top of the Properties section (see Figure 3-3). From left to right, the categories are Layout, Text, Border, Background, and Others.

---

5. **Click the color swatch and then choose a color from the color picker.**

   When the color picker opens, you dial in a color using the three sliders on the right. They control the hue, lightness/darkness, and transparency. Your selection is shown inside the ring in the large square. You can adjust the color by dragging that ring to a different spot. There are two smaller squares in the upper-left corner of the color picker. The square on the left shows the new color you're specifying; the one on the right shows the original color. If you see the exact color you want already on the web page or anywhere on your computer screen, click the eyedropper in the lower-right corner. Then, click on the color. That loads the color spec in the color picker. When you're happy with your color, press Enter. Dreamweaver closes the color picker and writes the CSS rule for your style. So, if you inspect the innards of *soylent_styles.css*, you see this as the style for paragraphs:

```
p {
    color: #336633;
}
```

You can create multiple rules for a single selector. So, in the case of the paragraph tag, you may want to continue to define the style by choosing values for font-family, font-size, and font-weight. Each time you set a property value, Dreamweaver writes the CSS in the style sheet.

The real trick to defining styles is mastering all the properties available to each style (such as borders, margins, and background colors), and *then* applying them so they work reliably in different browsers. Keep in mind that it's not necessary to define every property for a selector—just focus on the ones that are important to your page.

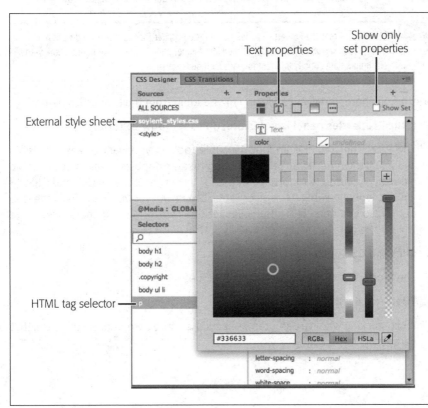

FIGURE 3-3

You're about to define a CSS style that will apply to all <p> (paragraph) tags. Dreamweaver will store the rule for the <p> tag in the external style sheet soylent_styles.css. As you define a style, you give different properties, like the text color here, different values. Dreamweaver helps you out with relevant tools. For example, when you set a color value, as above, Dreamweaver opens the color picker for you. If you want to see only properties that have their values already set (a fast way to review the styles you're using), turn on the checkbox in the upper-right corner.

TIP To move your CSS Rules from an internal style sheet to an external style sheet, switch to Code view in the document window. Then in the <head> of your page, click inside a single rule you want to move or drag to select multiple rules. (A rule includes the selector and the properties in the curly brackets.) Choose Format→CSS Styles→Move CSS Rules. In the "Move To External Style Sheet" dialog box, browse to an existing style sheet. (If you haven't created an external style sheet yet, you can click the "A new style sheet" button.) Dreamweaver includes many tools for managing your style sheets; you'll learn about them on page 107.

Creating Styles with the Properties Panel

Most of the time, you'll create new styles using CSS Designer. But you can do some of the same chores from the CSS mode of the Properties panel (Figure 3-6, bottom). (If you've used Dreamweaver in the past, the Properties panel's CSS mode and dialog boxes will be familiar, but some of the procedures, especially for creating new styles, have changed.)

Creating a new style in the Properties panel is more complex than doing so in CSS Designer because you need to wade through more dialog boxes to get the same results. But the idea is the same: First, you highlight the page element you want to style. Then you select (or create) an internal or external style sheet (the Source), choose a selector (a class, ID, or tag), and write the rule. That creates an inline style you can convert into an external CSS rule by selecting the text that has the inline rule, and then choosing Format→CSS Styles→Convert Inline CSS to Rule.

NOTE Keep in mind that the Properties *panel*, which resides under the document window, is a different beast from the Properties *section*, which is part of the CSS Designer panel. You can use both to work with CSS styles, but the techniques are entirely different for each method.

For example, here's how you style an <h1> heading from the Properties panel:

1. **If the Properties panel isn't visible, go to Window→Properties.**

    The Properties panel is an indispensable tool, so you want to keep it visible almost all the time. If you're highlighting text (as opposed to an image or table element), you see two buttons on the far left of the panel: HTML and CSS. (If you *are* working with an image or table, Dreamweaver doesn't display the CSS button, so you need to turn to CSS Designer for formatting chores; see page 104 for the details.)

2. **Click the CSS button.**

    The Properties panel changes to CSS mode.

3. **Triple-click within an <h1> heading.**

    Triple-clicking within a paragraph selects the entire paragraph; in this case, that paragraph is a heading.

4. **In the Properties panel, click the color box and then choose a dark green.**

You could format several other properties from this panel, including the font, size, or alignment of the text you selected. And you can change more than one property at a time.

Once you choose a color, the Targeted Rule field displays <inline style>. As explained on page 103, Dreamweaver doesn't store inline styles in a style sheet (internal or external), and they don't have a selector. They're formatting instructions attached to HTML tags in the body of the page.

5. **From Dreamweaver's menu commands, choose Format→CSS Styles→Convert Inline CSS to Rule.**

Dreamweaver displays the Convert Inline CSS dialog box (Figure 3-4) so you can choose a selector and a source for your new rule. It also removes the inline style from the body of your document.

6. **Choose "All h1 tags" from the "Convert to" menu.**

Since you highlighted an <h1> page element, Dreamweaver assumes you want to style <h1> tags, so it automatically suggests h1 as the selector (Figure 3-4). If you wanted to create a *class* selector, you'd choose the first option, "A new CSS class," and name the class.

7. **In the "Create rule in" section, choose "The head of this document."**

This option creates an internal style sheet within the <head> section of the current document. Choose "Style sheet" when you want to store your style as an external style sheet, and then click the Browse button to select or create the sheet.

8. **Click OK.**

When you click OK, a couple of things happen. Dreamweaver creates a style rule and writes the code that defines the style for <h1> tags.

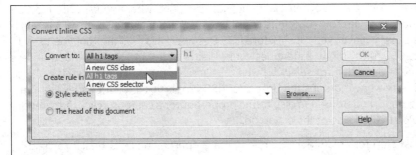

FIGURE 3-4

When you convert inline CSS formatting to a CSS rule, use this dialog box to identify the selector and source.

■ CREATING STYLES FOR NON-TEXT ELEMENTS

If you want to style non-text elements using the Properties panel, the process is a little different. When you select an object like an image or a table, Dreamweaver doesn't display the CSS button in the Properties panel. To create the style, right-click (Control-click) the selected element and choose CSS Styles→New. The New CSS Rule dialog box appears, which you use to choose a selector and identify a source. You'll see four options under the Selector Type menu, but they really are just the usual selector suspects, described back on page 108:

- Class (can apply to any HTML element)

- ID (applies to only one HTML element)

- Tag (redefines an HTML element)

- Compound (based on your selection)

A compound selector, like the <body p> selector you learned about on page 109, targets a page element that sits inside another page element. (Find out more about compound selectors on page 367.)

Under Selector name, type in a name. Precede class names with a period (.), and ID names with a pound symbol (#). Tags do not have a preceding character.

By their nature, compound selectors comprise more than one selector. For example, a compound selector for an image might be: *body p img.* In other words, you're targeting an image inside of a paragraph which is inside of the body of the document.

At the bottom of the New CSS Rule box, use the Rule Definition menu to choose a source. Your options are:

- **This document only.** Choose this to create an internal style sheet.

- **New Style Sheet File.** Choose this to create a new external style sheet.

If you previously attached a style sheet to the page, Dreamweaver displays its name in the menu, too. Choose it to store your new style in the existing sheet.

After you click OK, a second dialog box appears, one where you specify the CSS rules for the style. This "CSS Rule definition for..." dialog box (Figure 3-5) is familiar to Dreamweaver veterans. Before CSS Designer, this was the tool you used to create CSS rules. The box identifies your selector at the top of the window. It says "CSS Rule definition for *selector*," where selector is the name of your class, ID, or tag. Dreamweaver groups the dozens of CSS properties into categories like Type, Background, and Border. To display the properties for a category, click the category name on the left side of the dialog box.

The last step for creating a CSS rule in the Properties panel is similar to creating rules in CSS Designer. Use the menus, text boxes, number boxes, and color pickers to set values for properties. You can set several properties at once, and you can switch from one category's properties to another's. When you're done, click OK, and Dreamweaver writes the code and stores it in the source you identified earlier.

NOTE The CSS Rule definition dialog box displays most of the same properties as CSS Designer, but it groups those properties into different categories, with different category names. This alone may force you to choose a single tool (CSS Designer or the Properties panel) for creating styles.

■ Using Styles

If you're formatting a tag, once you create the tag style, your work is done. Browsers automatically apply that style to the appropriate tag on the page. If you create a <p> style, for example, anything in your document with the <p> tag applied to it has the style you just created.

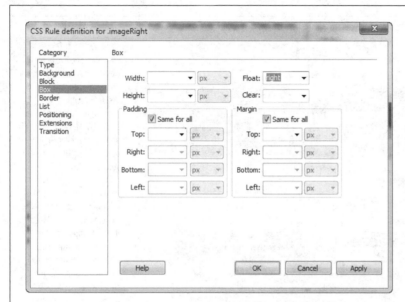

FIGURE 3-5

The CSS Rule definition window displays the same CSS property names and values as CSS Designer. Click a category name to see its properties. As you change properties, click the Apply button to see their effect on the page. When you're done, click OK to apply all the property changes and close the dialog box.

When you create styles for class or ID selectors, however, you need to take an extra step: You must assign the class or ID to the tag you want to format.

You can apply class styles to any selection in the document window, whether it's a word, an image, or an entire paragraph. In fact, you can apply a class style to *any* individual HTML tag, such as a <p>, <td> (table cell), or <body>. You can even select just a single word within a paragraph and apply a style to *it*.

■ APPLYING A CLASS STYLE TO TEXT

After you create a class and its style rules using the steps on page 108, you can assign that class (and its formatting) to elements in your document. For example, to style text using a class selector, start by selecting the words you want to format in the document window. Then, from the Properties panel, select the class you previously created—you can do this either in HTML mode, in which case you select the name from the Class drop-down menu (Figure 3-6, top), or in CSS mode, where you use the Targeted Rule menu (Figure 3-6, bottom).

To style an entire paragraph or heading, click to place your cursor within the paragraph or heading, and then use the Properties panel to select the class. When you use this method, don't inadvertently highlight a piece of text, or Dreamweaver applies the style to just that selected text, not the entire paragraph. When you style a paragraph, you're actually telling Dreamweaver to apply the style to an individual `<p>` tag. To accomplish that, Dreamweaver adds a special *class* property to the paragraph. Suppose you defined a class named *.company*. After you apply the class to the paragraph, its tag looks like this:

```
<p class="company">
```

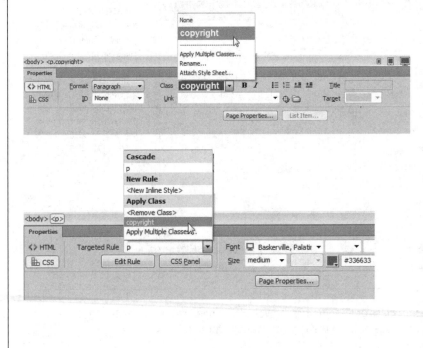

FIGURE 3-6

The easiest way to apply a class style is through the Properties panel. When you select a non-text element like an image or table, a Class menu appears in the top-right of the panel. For text, you apply class styles using the Class menu if the Properties panel is in HTML mode (top) or the Targeted Rule menu when it's in CSS mode (bottom). Dreamweaver uses only the bottom section of the Targeted Rule menu (the stuff below "Apply Class") to add or remove a class style from a selection of text. The other options here let you create new styles or view the styles that apply to the selection.

▪ APPLYING A CLASS STYLE TO OBJECTS

To apply a class style to an object (like an image or a table), start by selecting the object. As always, the Tag Selector at the bottom of the document window is a great way to select a tag. Then, at the top of the Properties panel, use the Class drop-down menu to select the style name.

NOTE You can apply any class style to any element, although doing so doesn't always make sense. If you format a graphic with a style that specifies bold, red, Courier type, the image doesn't look any different.

■ OTHER CLASS STYLING OPTIONS

You can also apply a class style by selecting whatever element you want to style, choosing Format→CSS Styles, and then, from the submenu, selecting the style. Or you can right-click (Control-click) an element in the document window and choose CSS Styles from the context menu. From there, you can assign an existing class; create a new class, ID, or tag style; or apply multiple classes (covered in the next section) to a page element. Choose the option you want from the submenu.

Finally, you can apply a class from the document window's Tag Selector, too, as shown in Figure 3-7.

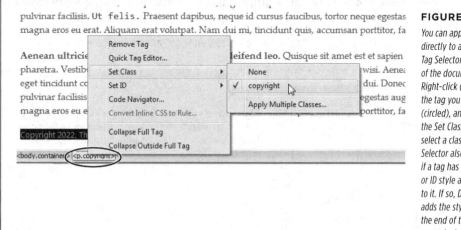

FIGURE 3-7

You can apply a class style directly to a tag using the Tag Selector at the bottom of the document window. Right-click (Control-click) the tag you want to format (circled), and then, from the Set Class submenu, select a class style. The Tag Selector also lets you know if a tag has a class style or ID style already applied to it. If so, Dreamweaver adds the style's name to the end of the tag. For example, in this figure, the body tag has a class named .container applied to it (<body.container>) and the paragraph has the class named .copyright applied to it (<p.copyright>).

Applying Multiple Classes

The rules of HTML and CSS let you apply more than one class to a single tag, which is handy when you have page elements that share some formatting but have their own style requirements as well. For example, say you want to add a border and colorful background to a set of images in a portfolio (you'll learn how to add borders and backgrounds on pages 155 and 160). You could create a class style (for example, *.portfolioImage*) with the properties you want, but you might want some photos to appear on the right side of the page and others on the left (you'll learn how to do this on page 236). In other words, you'll format the images similarly, but position them differently. To make that happen, you'd create two new class styles (say, *.imageLeft* and *.imageRight*). You apply both the *.portfolioImage* and the *.imageLeft* classes to pictures you want to have a border and align to the left, and add the *.portfolioImage* and *.imageRight* classes to flush-right images.

Using multiple classes is increasingly common in web design, but until Dreamweaver CS6, the only way to do that was to type the multiple classes in Code view. Fortunately, Dreamweaver CC provides a simple way to use the Properties panel to add more than one class to a tag:

1. **Select an element you want to style with more than one class.**

    This could be a headline, a paragraph, an image, a <div> tag (page 428), and so on.

2. **If you're in the Property panel's HTML mode, click the Class drop-down menu and select Apply Multiple Classes. If you're in CSS mode, choose Apply Multiple Classes from the Targeted Rule drop-down menu.**

    In either case, the Multiclass Selection window appears (see Figure 3-8).

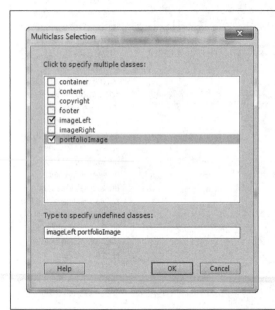

FIGURE 3-8

Dreamweaver's new Multiclass Selection window lets you apply more than one class to a page element. You can choose from a list of classes that already exist, or type the class names (separated by spaces) in the text field at the bottom.

> **NOTE** You can also apply multiple classes to a tag using the Tag Selector at the bottom of the document window. Right-click (Option-click) the tag and choose Set Class→Apply Multiple Classes (see Figure 3-7).

3. **In the Multiclass Selection window, select the classes you want to apply to the selected tag.**

    Only CSS classes you already added to a page's internal or external style sheet appear in this window, so it's best to create the styles before applying class names to HTML tags. However, you can apply the names of classes even if they don't appear in a page's style sheet. Type each class name into the text field at the bottom of the window, adding a space between each class name (and leave out the period that precedes a class name in a style sheet). For example, *portfolioImage imageLeft* is correct, but *.portfolio.imageLeft* is not.

4. **Click OK to close the Multiclass Selection window and apply the classes to the tag.**

   Under the hood, Dreamweaver simply adds the names of the classes you chose to the HTML tag, like *<img class="portfolioImage imageLeft" src="photo.jpg">*.

You can always remove or add classes by selecting a tag and choosing Apply Multiple Classes from the Properties panel's Class menu. If you deselect all the class names, Dreamweaver removes the class attribute from the tag. Alternatively, you can use the technique described next to remove all the classes from a tag.

TIP If you're a master of the mouse, you'll be happy to know you can reach the Multiclass Selection window by right-clicking (Control-clicking) selected text and then choosing CSS Styles→Apply Multiple Classes.

Removing a Class Style

You remove a class style from a page element in one of four ways:

- To remove a class style from text, select the text and then, from the Properties panel, choose None from the Class menu (in HTML mode) or <Remove Class> from the Targeted Rule menu (in CSS mode).

- To remove a class style from another object (like an image), select the object and then, from the Properties panel's Class menu, choose None.

- To remove a style from any selection (even non-text elements like images and tables), choose Format→CSS Styles→None.

- To remove a class style from a particular tag, first use Dreamweaver's Tag Selector to locate the tag. Suppose you want to remove the *.copyright* class from a paragraph. In the Tag Selector, right-click (Control-click) the <p.copyright> tag. Then, from the drop-down menu, choose Set Class→None. One advantage to this method is that the Tag Selector makes it very clear what HTML tag the class is applied to.

TIP If you applied a class style to a selection of text, you don't have to select *all* the text to remove the style. Just click anywhere inside it, and then select None from the Properties panel's Class menu or <Remove Class> from the Targeted Rule menu. Dreamweaver is smart enough to realize that you want to remove the style applied to the text. (If you applied the style to a tag, then Dreamweaver removes the Class property. If you applied the style using the <span> tag, which is used to group random elements, Dreamweaver removes the <span> tag.)

You can't, however, remove *tag* styles from HTML tags. For example, suppose you redefined the <h2> tag using the steps on page 105. If your page has three Heading 2 (<h2>) paragraphs, and you want the third heading to have a different style from the other two, you can't simply "remove" the <h2> style from the third heading. You need to create a new class style with all the formatting options you want for that heading, and then apply it directly to this particular <h2> tag. (By the magic of CSS, the class formatting options override any existing tag style options—see page 384 for more on this sleight of hand.)

Applying IDs to a Tag

As discussed on page 102, webmasters don't use ID styles as frequently as they use classes. If you're working on a site with IDs, you can style them in Dreamweaver CC. To apply an ID to text, select the text and use the ID menu in the Properties panel's HTML mode (see Figure 3-6, top). Since you can apply each ID name only once per page, the menu lists only unassigned IDs—IDs that exist in your style sheet but that you haven't applied to the current page.

For non-text elements, select the element, and then, in the Properties panel, type the ID name into the ID field. (For some elements, the ID field is unlabeled, but you can always find it on the far left of the Properties panel.)

You can also apply an ID using the Tag Selector, as outlined in Figure 3-7. Right-click (Control-click) the tag, select Set ID from the drop-down menu, and then select the ID from the submenu.

> **NOTE** The Tag Selector tells you whether you applied an ID to a tag by including the # symbol with the ID name. For example, *body#catalog* indicates that the <body> tag has an ID named *catalog* applied to it.

Whenever you apply an ID to a tag, Dreamweaver adds a bit of HTML to your page. For instance, an ID style named *#copyright* applied to a paragraph looks like this in HTML:

```
<p id="copyright">
```

This is just like the *class* property Dreamweaver adds when you use class styles, as described on page 115.

To remove an ID from a text element, select the text, and then, from the Properties panel's ID drop-down menu, select None. For non-text elements, select the element, and then, in the Properties panel's ID field, delete the ID name.

Linking to an External Style Sheet

When you create an external style sheet while working on a page, Dreamweaver automatically links the sheet to the current document. To use that document's styles on a different page, you must *attach* the style to the page.

To do so, open the page and then, in the Sources section of CSS Designer, click Add Source and choose Attach Existing CSS File (see Figure 3-2, top). (If CSS Designer isn't open, choose Window→CSS Designer or press Shift-F11.)

> **TIP** You can also use the Properties panel to attach a style sheet. Just select Attach Style Sheet from the Class menu in HTML mode (see Figure 3-6, top).

The Attach Existing Style Sheet window appears (see Figure 3-9, bottom). Click Browse. In the Select Style Sheet File dialog box, navigate to and double-click the CSS (*.css*) file you want to attach to the document. If the style sheet you select is outside the current site—if, for example, it's in another of your websites—Dreamweaver offers to copy the style sheet to your site's root folder; click Yes.

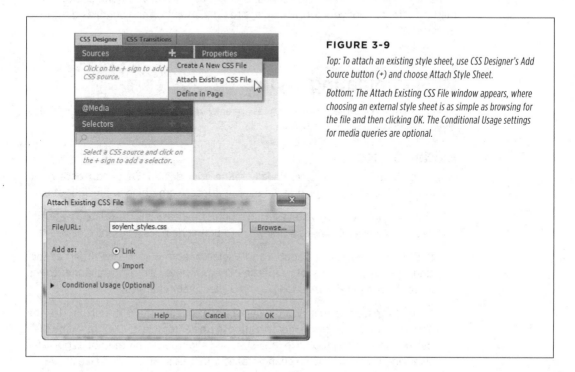

FIGURE 3-9

Top: To attach an existing style sheet, use CSS Designer's Add Source button (+) and choose Attach Style Sheet.

Bottom: The Attach Existing CSS File window appears, where choosing an external style sheet is as simple as browsing for the file and then clicking OK. The Conditional Usage settings for media queries are optional.

The Attach Existing Style Sheet window provides other options. You can choose how you want to attach the style sheet by linking to it from the current document, or by importing it into the current web page. The choices are nearly identical; they're simply two different ways of applying styles from an external style sheet to a web page. The method preferred by the pros, and Dreamweaver's suggested choice, is linking to the sheet, so go with the Link option.

You can also specify the conditions under which a page uses one style sheet over another. For example, you might use one style sheet for a page displayed on a monitor, and a second sheet for a page that you want visitors to print out, like a receipt. Browsers figure out which style sheet to use by performing a *media query*, that is, by figuring out the destination device. You'll find in-depth information on media types and how to use them on page 506. In the meantime, if you simply want to attach a style sheet to a page so that the styles always apply (when viewed on a screen *or* printed out), you can ignore the Conditional Usage options in the Attach Existing Style Sheet dialog box.

After choosing your options, click OK, and Dreamweaver adds the necessary HTML to the head of the web page and automatically formats any tags according to the style sheet's tag styles. In Design view, you see the formatting changes take place immediately.

If the style sheet contains *class* styles, on the other hand, you don't see their formatting effects until you apply the class to an element on the page, as described on page 115.

■ Manipulating Styles

As with anything in Dreamweaver, styles are easy enough to edit, delete, or duplicate; all you need is a map of the terrain.

Editing Styles

As you build a website, you continually refine your design. That chartreuse background may have looked great at 2 a.m., but it loses something in the light of day.

Fortunately, one of CSS's greatest selling point is how easy it is to update a website's styles. Dreamweaver provides many ways to edit style rules:

- In CSS Designer, select a source and a selector and then, in the Properties section, change the values for properties. Dreamweaver writes the changes to the style sheet and reformats the page to reflect your changes.

- In the Properties panel (Window→Properties), click the CSS button. Use the Targeted Rule drop-down menu to choose a selector (class, ID, or tag), and then use text formatting tools like font, size, and alignment. This method is good for tweaking text styles. Each change takes effect as soon as you make it.

- In the Properties panel, click the CSS button. Use the Targeted Rule drop-down menu to identify a style, and then click Edit Rule. The CSS Rule Definition window (Figure 3-5) opens, where you can make changes to multiple properties. Use the Category list on the left to display the types of properties, and then make your changes using the menus, checkboxes, and other widgets in the main window. When you click OK, Dreamweaver records all the changes to the style sheet and updates your page to reflect those changes.

Deleting a Style

At some point, you may find that you created a style that you don't need anymore. Maybe you redefined the HTML <code> tag and realized that you never use it. You don't need to keep it around, taking up precious space in the style sheet.

When Formatting Disappears

Sometimes when I copy text from one web page and paste it into another, all the formatting disappears. What's going on?

When you use Cascading Style Sheets, keep in mind that the actual style information is stored either in the <head> section of a web page (for internal style sheets) or in a separate CSS file (an external style sheet). If a page includes an internal style sheet, when you copy text, graphics, or other page elements, Dreamweaver copies those elements and any class or ID style definitions those elements use. When you paste the HTML into another page, Dreamweaver writes the styles into the <head> of that page. This feature can save you some time, but it doesn't solve all your woes. It doesn't, for example, copy any *tag styles* you created, nor does it carry over most advanced styles, like compound selectors (see page 367 for more on advanced styles). So, if you copy and paste, say, a styled <h1> tag, the tag and its contents end up in the page, but the style information doesn't.

In addition, if you copy and paste text from a page that uses an external style sheet, the styles themselves don't go along for the ride. So, if you copy a paragraph that has a class style applied to it and paste it into another document, the class code in the paragraph gets pasted (<p class="company"> for instance), but the actual *.company* style, with all its formatting properties, doesn't.

The best solution is to use an external style sheet that you attach to all the pages on your site. That way, when you copy and paste HTML, all the pages share the same styles and formatting. So, in the preceding example, if you copy a paragraph that includes a class style—*class="company"*—into another page that shares the same style sheet, the paragraphs look the same on both pages. Page 107 has more on creating an uber, site-wide external style sheet.

To delete a style rule for a specific selector, such as an <h1> tag or a *.copyright* class, go to CSS Designer. In the Sources section, choose the source for the style rules. It can be a single specific source, or you can click the All Sources option to see all available sources. Then, in the Selectors section, choose the selector you want to delete. In the dark gray bar at the top of the Selectors section, click the Remove Selector button, also known as the minus sign (-).

You can remove all the styles in a sheet by removing the source. In the Sources section of CSS Designer, click the style sheet you want to remove, and then click the Remove CSS Source button (the minus sign again). In the case of an external style sheet, that removes the link between your web page (HTML document) and the CSS file. It doesn't delete the actual style sheet, however. In the case of an internal style sheet, the process removes the rules from the head of your web page.

Unfortunately, deleting a class style *doesn't* delete any references to the style in your site's pages. For example, if you create a style called *.company*, apply it throughout your site, and then delete the style from the style sheet, Dreamweaver doesn't remove the <span> tags or class properties that refer to the style. Your pages will be littered with orphaned code like this, even though your text looks unstyled:

```
<span class="company">Cafe Soylent Green</span>
```

You solve this problem using Dreamweaver's powerful "Find and Replace" tool, discussed in Chapter 8.

Renaming a Class Style

You can rename any style by selecting it in CSS Designer, pausing a second, and then clicking the name again. This makes the name editable, at which point you can type a new name in its place. Of course, if you change a style named *p* to a style named *h1*, you've essentially removed the style for the <p> tag and added an <h1> style to your style sheet—in other words, all the paragraphs in your pages would lose their formatting, and all the <h1> tags would suddenly change appearance.

Another way to edit a style name is to open the style sheet in Code view, find the style name, and then edit it.

No matter which method you choose, when it comes to class styles, just changing the name doesn't do much good if you already applied the style throughout your site. The *old* class name still appears in the HTML everywhere you used it.

FREQUENTLY ASKED QUESTION

When Undo Won't Do

Sometimes when I edit a style—say, change a font color—I can undo that change. But other times, I can't undo changes I make to a style. What gives?

You can only undo changes in a currently open document. If you're working on an HTML file in either Design, Code, or Split view, you can undo any changes you make to that file. For example, say you add an internal style sheet to a document. If you edit one of those styles, Dreamweaver lets you undo those changes. Because the styles in an internal style sheet are part of the web page you're working on, choosing Edit→Undo undoes the last change you made.

However, if you're working on a web page with an external style sheet, you're actually working on *two* files at the same time—the web page you're building and the style sheet you're editing. So if you're designing a web page and edit a style in the external style sheet, you're actually making a change to the style sheet file. In this case, choosing Edit→Undo undoes only

the last change you made to the *web page*. If you want to undo a change you made to the external style sheet, you need to use Dreamweaver's related files feature. The name of the external style sheet appears in the Related Files toolbar, which appears below the title of the web page; click the filename to move to its code, and then choose Edit→Undo. Click the Source Code button to return to your web page (you'll learn more about the Related Files toolbar on page 332).

If you're in Split view with the HTML code displayed on the left and the Design view on the right, you can click the CSS file in the Related Files toolbar and see the code for that file on the left. At this point, the Undo command works on the active document—in other words, click in the CSS code on the left and Edit→Undo undoes the last change to the CSS; click in Design view on the right and Edit→Undo undoes the last change to the HTML of the page.

What you really need to do is rename the class style, and *then* perform a find-and-replace operation to change the name wherever it appears in your site. Dreamweaver includes a handy tool to simplify this process.

To rename a class style:

1. **In the Properties panel, choose Rename from the Class menu (on the HTML tab of the Properties panel).**

   The Rename Style window appears (Figure 3-10).

FIGURE 3-10

Dreamweaver's Rename Style tool is a fast and easy way to change the name of a class style even if you used the style hundreds of times on your site.

2. **From the "Rename style" drop-down menu, choose the name of the style you want to rename.**

   This menu lists all the class styles in the page's style sheets, both internal and external.

3. **In the "New name" box, type the new style name, and then click OK.**

   Follow the usual rules for naming class styles (described on page 114), but don't precede the name with a period; Dreamweaver knows you're working with classes.

   If you're changing an internal style, Dreamweaver makes the change and your job is done.

   If the style belongs to an external style sheet, Dreamweaver warns you that other pages on your site may also use this style. To successfully rename the style, you have to use Dreamweaver's Find and Replace tool to search your site and update all the references to the old style name.

4. **If you get cold feet, click Cancel to call off the name change, or click Yes to open the Find and Replace window, and then click Replace All.**

   One last warning appears, reminding you that you can't undo the find-and-replace.

NOTE If you click No in the warning box that appears after step 4, Dreamweaver still renames the style in the external style sheet, but it doesn't update your pages.

5. **Click Yes.**

   Dreamweaver goes through each page of your site, dutifully updating the name of the style everywhere it appears. When you finish with Find and Replace, it's likely that you'll still see the Search panel in your workspace. To close it, use the menu in the upper-right corner and choose Close Tab Group.

NOTE Dreamweaver doesn't supply a similar tool for renaming ID styles. While you can change the name of an ID style in the CSS styles panel—select the style, pause, and then click its name for editing—Dreamweaver doesn't automatically update the HTML that references that style. You can use Dreamweaver's Find and Replace feature (Chapter 8) for that.

Duplicating a Style

Dreamweaver makes it easy to duplicate a style, which is handy when you want to use the formatting from one style as the starting point for a new style. In the Sources section of CSS Designer, choose All Sources, or choose a specific source from the list. In the Selectors section, right-click (Control-click) the name of the style you want to duplicate, and then, from the shortcut menu, choose Duplicate (Figure 3-11, left). Dreamweaver copies the file and displays both the original and duplicate filenames in the Selectors section, with the doppelganger filename highlighted and ready for editing, as shown in Figure 3-11, right. (Sometimes the name box closes before you get a chance to rename the file. If that happens, select the filename, pause a second, and then click the name again to edit it.) As long as you have two styles with the same name, Dreamweaver won't attempt to rename the references in your web pages.

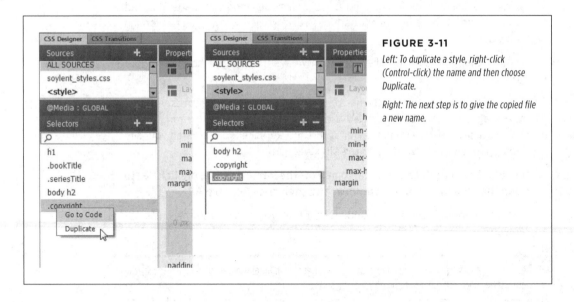

FIGURE 3-11

Left: To duplicate a style, right-click (Control-click) the name and then choose Duplicate.

Right: The next step is to give the copied file a new name.

■ Formatting Text with CSS

The early World Wide Web was not a pretty place. It was a sea of plain text, with a few changes in type size and a bit of bold and italic thrown in here and there. Of course, that's all changed. Today's websites dazzle the eye with stunning design that rivals the best printed pages. But artists have always faced a dilemma designing for the Web. When you create a design for a book, magazine, newspaper, or roadside sign, your audience sees exactly what you do. When you design a web page, however, you don't have that kind of control. One major issue is fonts. (If you're a print designer, you might call them typefaces.) In the comfort of your design cubicle, you can build your web page with any font stored on your computer. But your audience won't see that font unless they have that font on their systems, too, or unless they can seamlessly get that font from the Web. This section shows you how to make sure your audience sees all the fonts and formatting you want them to see.

One of the best uses of Cascading Style Sheets is converting the drab appearance of HTML text into lavishly designed prose. Alternatively, if you like a somber, corporate style, CSS can help with that, too. Whatever your design inclination, you can improve the look of your text using CSS.

The most commonly used properties for styling text appear in CSS Designer's Properties section, under Layout and Text. As the names imply, you use layout properties to form blocks of text and apportion the space around them, while the text properties focus on the font, size, style, color, and more of the type.

NOTE You can apply nearly every CSS property to text. For example, you can use the border property to underline text and the margin property to remove the space between paragraphs. You'll find these properties, and others not listed in the Layout or Text categories, introduced later in this book (you don't want to blow your circuits too quickly). For now, you'll learn the most type-centric properties.

Choosing a Font

You can include fonts with your web page two ways. The traditional method uses fonts installed on your visitor's computer, while a newer technique uses specially prepared typefaces called *web fonts.*

The traditional method relies on fonts already installed on a visitor's computer. For example, as you craft a web page, you can select any font on your computer, even that fancy font you just bought from a small company in Nome, Alaska. Unfortunately, when you publish that document on the Web, not all visitors see the page you created because not all visitors own the same fonts as you. Your guests can still read your pages—their computers will substitute a default font, usually some version of Times, Arial, or Courier.

You can deal with this dilemma several ways. One is to convert your text into graphics—type your copy into an image-editing program like Photoshop, and then save that document as an image file. Unfortunately that process takes time and forces your visitors to download byte-hogging images just to read your web page.

Another solution is to specify the font you'd *like* to use; if your visitor's computer has that font, that's what he'll see. You can specify secondary or tertiary fonts, too, in case your preferred font isn't available. In fact, Dreamweaver offers prepackaged lists of such "first choice, second choice, third choice" fonts, as you'll find out in the following section.

■ FORMATTING FONTS

The quickest way to specify primary and backup fonts is from the CSS mode of the Properties panel. After you click the CSS button, choose a set of fonts (which includes primary and backup fonts) from the Font menu.

You can also select font sets from CSS Designer. In the Designer's Properties section, click the big T (the Text button) or scroll down until you see the *font-family* property, and choose a font set. Either way, you're creating a new style (as described on page 104) or updating an existing one.

You'll soon discover that Dreamweaver's font menus aren't quite what you're used to. When you apply a font to text, you choose from one of the prepackaged lists just described; a typical choice is something like "Arial, Helvetica, sans-serif." In other words, you don't just choose a single font, such as Helvetica, you choose a matched set of fonts.

If the first font isn't installed on your visitor's computer, the browser looks down the list until it finds a font that is. Different operating systems use different fonts, so these lists include at least one font common on Windows PCs and another, similar-looking font that's common on Macs. Arial, for instance, is found on all Windows machines, while Macs offer the similar Helvetica.

That's it. You just selected a set of predefined fonts, and any styles on your web page will use the font you selected. For more control over the fonts your page displays, read on.

> **NOTE** Technically, you can specify any number of fallback fonts in one of these lists, not just first, second, and third choices. These days, it's common to see five or more fonts listed.

Using Adobe Edge Web Fonts

While primary and fallback fonts serve their purpose, a newer way to distribute type ensures better compatibility with your guests' computers. You no longer have to rely on serendipity to make sure your guests see the page you designed; your visitors can download the fonts you used on your pages from the Web itself. These so-called web fonts free you from restrictive font choices. Visitors pick up the fonts from either your own site or from a site that hosts fonts (Adobe and Google are examples).

Prior to Dreamweaver CC, using web fonts was a cumbersome and confusing process. You had to hunt down the fonts you wanted at sites like Google Fonts (*www.google.com/fonts/*) and FontSquirrel (*www.fontsquirrel.com/fontface*). Then you needed to make sure you could legally use the font—some companies don't want their fonts used on the Web because an unscrupulous person could download them and use them for free. Even the process of getting and using fonts varied depending on the source. And different web browsers and devices, such as iPhones and iPads, require web fonts in different file formats. Some font providers automatically provide all the formats, while others expect you to convert the fonts. Despite all these problems, it was worth the hassle to be able to use a font other than Arial and Times Roman for your web page.

Knowing Your Font Types

You can express your every written thought by choosing from among tens of thousands of fonts, from bookish, staid, classical typefaces to rounded, cartoonish squiggles.

Most fonts are divided into two categories: serif and sans-serif. Graphic designers often use serif fonts, where the letters include small decorative strokes at the extremities (the "hands" and "feet" of r's, for example)—for long passages of text, as it's widely believed that serifs gently lead the eye from letter to letter, making the text easier to read. Examples of serif fonts include Times, Times New Roman, Georgia, and Minion.

Designers often use sans-serif ("without serifs") fonts for headlines, thanks to their clean, simple appearance. Arial, Helvetica, Verdana, and Formata are all sans-serif fonts (you're reading Gotham sans-serif right now). Some people believe that you should use only sans-serif fonts on web pages because the delicate, decorative strokes of serif fonts get muddy on the coarse resolution of a computer screen. But that's an aesthetic judgment, and you should feel free to use whatever font you think looks (and reads) the best.

You can find other classes of fonts as well, like monospace and script fonts. Monospace fonts—Courier is perhaps the best known—resemble the characters a typewriter (remember those mechanical beasts?) produces—all the letters have the same width (useful for aligning text into columns). Script fonts resemble handwriting, and they're usually bold, fun, and difficult to read at small sizes. However, the different operating systems have few of these types of fonts in common, so if you do want to use a fancy-looking font, you'll have to use a web font (described next).

Enter Dreamweaver CC and Adobe Edge Web Fonts, which simplify font acquisition and give you access to hundreds of free fonts you can legally use. Adobe acquired web fonts from all kinds of sources, so if you've used web fonts in the past, you'll likely find some old friends here. Best of all, you can set up web fonts without leaving Dreamweaver, by using the Modify→Manage Fonts command.

NOTE The "Edge" in Adobe Edge Web Fonts is a brand name for a family of tools and services that Adobe provides web developers. The other products include Animate (web animation and effects [page 701]), Reflow (responsive design prototyping), Code (text/code editor), PhoneGap Build (mobile app development [page 544]), and Inspect (preview websites on mobile devices during the design process [page 500]).

■ MANAGING ADOBE EDGE WEB FONTS

Before you can use web fonts in Dreamweaver, you have to add the fonts to the program using the Manage Fonts window. This step simply registers the fonts with Dreamweaver so you can use them on any site you create:

1. **In Dreamweaver, choose Modify→Manage Fonts.**

   The Manage Fonts window appears (see Figure 3-12). It has three tabs across the top, labeled Adobe Edge Web Fonts, Local Web Fonts, and Custom Font Stacks. Use the first tab, Adobe Edge Web Fonts, to preview and choose a font. The second tab, Local Web Fonts, helps you manage fonts you downloaded from other sources. If you stick with the easier Adobe Edge web fonts, you may never use this tab. Use the third tab, Custom Font Stacks, to create font sets—lists of fonts and their fallback options, as described on page 131. Dreamweaver displays these lists in the font menus of the Properties panel and CSS Designer.

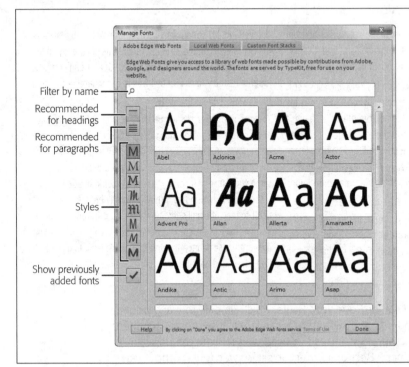

FIGURE 3-12

The Manage Fonts window lets you select web fonts for your sites. Initially, it displays the Adobe Edge Web Fonts tab, where you can choose from more than 500 free-to-use fonts. Buttons along the left side of the window help you zero in on fonts you want to preview.

Filter by name
Recommended for headings
Recommended for paragraphs
Styles
Show previously added fonts

2. **On the Adobe Edge Web Font tab, find one or more fonts you want to use.**

   Use the buttons along the left side of the window to narrow your choices (Figure 3-12). For example, using the top two buttons, you can limit the list of fonts to those suitable for headings and fonts better suited for paragraphs. (Naturally, you can use the fonts however you want.) Another group of buttons filters the list by font style: serif, sans-serif, typewriter, cursive, and so on. If you know the name of the font you want, type it in the "Filter by font name" box. You can select more than one font. For example, fonts often come in families, so you might want to add PT Sans, PT Sans Caption, and PT Serif at the same time.

3. **Click a font name to add it to your list of available fonts.**

   A checkmark appears in the upper-right corner. If you change your mind, click again to remove the checkmark. Dreamweaver only adds fonts that have checkmarks.

4. **Click Done.**

   When you click Done, the font becomes part of your Dreamweaver fonts lists. To find it, go to the Properties panel, make sure you're in CSS mode, and then use the Font drop-down menu. You'll also find your new font in CSS Designer. Go to the Properties section and find the *font-family* property. Fonts you added with the Manage Fonts window appear near the bottom of the list in the Properties panel and in CSS Designer.

If you ever decide to remove a font from Dreamweaver's fonts lists, open the Manage Fonts window (Modify→Manage Fonts), go to the Adobe Web Fonts tab, and then turn on the checkmark in the bottom-left corner. You'll see all the Adobe Edge Web Fonts you added to the program. Click to remove the checkmarks from fonts you no longer want, and then click Done.

■ CREATING A CUSTOM FONT STACK

When you use web fonts in your pages, Dreamweaver provides a code so that your visitors can get those fonts from the Web. In most cases, they'll be able to get the font you specify, but it's good practice to give your visitors some fallback options. These next steps explains how to create a custom font stack:

1. **Choose Modify→Manage Fonts.**

   The Manage Fonts window opens.

2. **Click the Custom Font Stacks tab.**

   Dreamweaver divides the Custom Font Stacks window into three panes (Figure 3-13). The first one, called "Font list," sits at the top of the screen and displays all the fonts currently available in Dreamweaver. (These are the font choices you see in the Properties panel and CSS Designer.) You use the two panes below that to build new font stacks and add them to the Dreamweaver's fonts list.

3. **Click the + button at the top-left of the Font list.**

   You'll see a message at the bottom of the fonts list that says "Add fonts in list below."

4. **Scroll through the "Available fonts" list to find a font. If you know its name, type the name in the text box below "Available fonts," and Dreamweaver scrolls through the list to display it.**

   The Adobe Edge Web Fonts you added appear at the bottom of the list of Available fonts.

5. **Double-click a font you want to use in a new custom font stack.**

   When you double-click a font, or click the << arrow, Dreamweaver adds it to the Chosen fonts on the left. To create a stack, add several fonts to the Chosen fonts list. Often, you start off with a web font you've chosen, and then add a fallback font popular on Windows PCs, and another popular on Macs. Finally, choose a generic option, like a serif or sans-serif font, for visitors who have none of your preferred fonts on their machine.

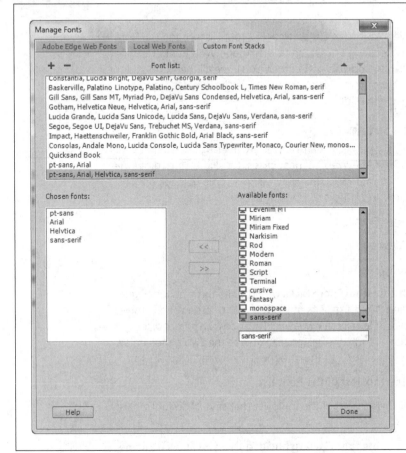

FIGURE 3-13

Use the Custom Font Stacks tab to create new lists of fonts—first choice and fallback options—to use in your styles. Click the + button (upper-left) to start a new list. Then select a font in the "Available fonts" box and click the << arrow to move the font to the "Chosen fonts" box. After you complete your list, click Done. You'll find your new font stack in the Properties panel's drop-down Fonts menu and the font-family property in CSS Designer.

TIP If you're not sure how popular a font is, consult a website like *http://cssfontstack.com/*. Mouse over the info button to see the percentage of Windows or Mac PCs that have the font installed.

6. **Click Done.**

   This closes the Manage Fonts window. Your new font stack will be available in the Properties panel's CSS mode and in CSS Designer under Properties→font-family (Figure 3-14).

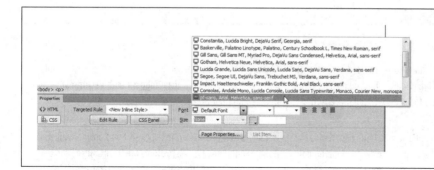

FIGURE 3-14

The font stacks you create in the Manage Fonts window show up in the Properties panel (shown here) and in CSS Designer.

■ USING ADOBE EDGE WEB FONTS

After using Dreamweaver's Manage Fonts tools to add fonts to your list of available fonts, you use them just like any other font. For example, you'll find the new fonts and custom font stacks in CSS Designer's Properties section. The *font-family* menu lists the newcomers along with all the usual suspects. You're not required to do anything special to use the new fonts—just pick them off the list. However, when you specify an Edge web font, Dreamweaver performs a few extra bits of web font magic. When visitors view your page, their browsers need to know where to find its fonts. Dreamweaver adds a line of code to the page that points to a JavaScript file that handles all your web font chores. For example, if your font specification includes the PT Sans font, this bit of code appears in the head of your page:

```
<script src="http://use.edgefonts.net/pt-sans:n4:default.js"
type="text/javascript"></script>
```

In most cases, the entire process takes place so fast your visitors won't notice the difference between using web fonts and the fonts already installed on their computer.

Changing the Font Size

Varying the size of fonts on a web page is one way to direct a viewer's attention. Large type screams "Read Me!"—excellent for attention-grabbing headlines—while small type fades into the background, perfect for necessary but unexciting legal mumbo-jumbo like copyright notices.

Unless you specifically set a type size for web page text, it appears on a visitor's monitor at the default size specified by their browser, usually 16 pixels. However, not only can people change that default size (much to the eternal frustration of web designers), but different operating systems display text at different sizes. Bottom line: You can't assume that the way text appears on your monitor is the way it'll appear on your guests' monitors.

Using Non-Adobe Edge Web Fonts

If you use web fonts other than those provided by Adobe on the Adobe Edge Web Fonts tab (Figure 3-12), you're in for some extra work and you'll need to take extra legal precautions. Here's a quick rundown of the issues.

First of all, the way you get and use web fonts depends on the source of the font. Different providers use different methods. In the case of Google Fonts, for example, you choose your fonts, copy a bit of code that Google provides, and paste it into the head of your web pages. This code tells your visitor's browsers where to find the files needed to display the fonts. In the case of Font Squirrel (*www.fontsquirrel.com*), you download font files to your computer. Initially, Font Squirrel provides OTF (Open Type Format) fonts. You use their Webfont Generator to convert OTF fonts to web font files that different browsers can use. Then you use Dreamweaver's Font Manager (Modify→Manage Fonts) to add them to the list of available fonts in the Properties panel and CSS Designer (Figure 3-15). The bottom line is that different

font providers use different methods for procuring their fonts, and you'll need to do a little digging with each provider to understand their process.

The other issue you need to consider when using third-party fonts is whether you can legally use them on the web. The Google Fonts site says "All the fonts are Open Source" and that you are "free to use them in every way you want, privately or commercially—in print, on your computer, or in your websites." Other third-party font providers aren't that emphatic. That's why Dreamweaver passes the legal responsibility to you. To use a font that you downloaded to your computer, go to Modify→Manage Fonts and then click the Local Web Fonts tab. Before you register downloaded fonts (what Dreamweaver calls local fonts) for use in Dreamweaver, you have to turn on a checkbox that says, "I have properly licensed the above font(s) for website use." Translation: It's your fault, not Adobe's, if a font designer wants to sue.

To set a font size, use either the Size menu in the Properties panel's CSS mode (Figure 3-16.) or the Properties section of CSS Designer (Figure 3-17); in the latter, look for the *font-size* property. Whichever you choose, you're either creating a new style as described on page 104 or updating an existing style (page 122).

The choices available from the Size menu break down into four groups:

- The *None* option removes any size information applied to the text. The text returns to its default size.

- The numeric choices—9 through 36—indicate how tall you wish to make the text, measured in pixels. Nine-pixel-tall text is nearly unreadable, while 36-pixel copy makes a bold statement. One benefit of specifying pixel sizes is that the resulting text appears nearly the same across different browsers and operating systems, obviating the problems mentioned above.

- The options *xx-small* through *xx-large* indicate fixed font sizes, replacing the sizes 1 through 7, used with the old HTML <font> tag. The *medium* size is usually the same as the standard browser font size of 16 pixels.

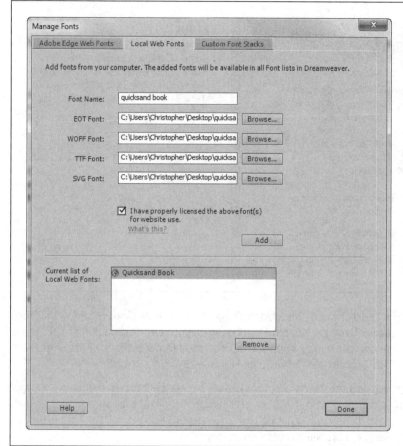

FIGURE 3-15

Use the Local Web Fonts panel to manage web fonts you've downloaded from the Web. You need to include each of the font formats (EOT, WOFF, TTF, and SVG) to cover all the formats different browsers need. If you downloaded a complete "web font kit," all the formats should be in the same folder.

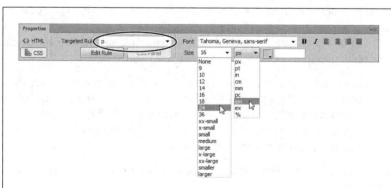

FIGURE 3-16

You can set a dizzying array of font sizes using CSS. When you use the Properties panel's CSS mode to set the size of text, you either create a new style—in which case you see <New CSS Rule> in the Targeted Rule field (circled)—or you edit an existing style, as shown here. In this case, you have the tag style <p> listed, so picking a font size edits the font size of all the paragraphs on the page.

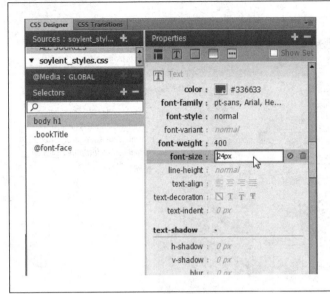

FIGURE 3-17

*While you can set some text formats from the Proper-
ties panel, CSS Designer's Properties section offers
additional options. For example, you get the ability to
control the space between lines of text (line-height),
and an option to add drop shadows (h-shadow and
v-shadow).*

- The last two choices—*smaller* and *larger*—are relative sizes, meaning that they shrink or enlarge the selected text based on your page's default text size. These choices come in handy when you define a base font size for an entire page using the Page Properties window (see Figure 1-22).

  Suppose you set the default text size for a page at 12 pixels. If you apply *larger* to a selection of text, the text gets bigger (the exact amount varies by web browser). If, later, you change the base size to 14 pixels in Page Properties, all that "larger" text will increase proportionally.

To change the size of text, select it, and then, from the Properties panel, choose a new font size or edit the appropriate CSS, as described on page 140. If you applied a pixel value, you have an additional option: You can type in any number you wish if you don't like any of the sizes listed. In fact, unlike HTML, browsers can handle humongous text—hundreds of pixels tall, if that's what you're into.

You don't have to specify the text size in pixels. You can use points, picas, ems, percentages, and exes (an *ex* is the width of the letter X in the current font). Select the unit of measure you want from the drop-down menu to the far right of the Size field. Most of these units were developed for print publishing, and may have little relevance to type sizes. Of them, the most useful are:

- *Pixels* ensure that text looks the same size across different browsers and operating systems.

- *Ems* are a relative measure, meaning that the actual font size varies. Ems are based on the size of the capital letter M.

  One em is equal to the default font size. Suppose a web browser's default size is 16 pixels. In that case, 1 em means characters are 16 pixels tall, 2 ems would be twice that (32 pixels tall), and 1.5 ems would be 24 pixels tall.

  The advantage of ems is that they let visitors control their browser's base font size to fit their needs. For example, if someone finds standard text too small, she can increase her browser's base font size. Any text measured in ems then changes according to the browser's new setting. (For a good set of instructions on how to change the starting font size in all major browsers, visit *http://tinyurl. com/7b9ndbg.*)

NOTE You don't need to use ems to let browsers resize text. All current browsers have a Zoom command that enlarges not only text, but all other page elements (pictures, navigation links, and so on), too.

You can use pixels and ems together. You could, for instance, set the base font size of your page to 16 pixels, and then use ems for other parts of the page. For example, you could set headlines to 2 ems, making them 32 pixels tall. If you later thought the overall text was too small or too large, you could change the base font size for the page, and the headlines and other text would resize proportionally.

NOTE As you get more familiar with CSS, you'll probably run into some weird problems with ems or percentage text sizes due to an advanced concept known as the *cascade*. The gruesome details begin on page 384.

- *Rems* are another relative measure, similar to ems. When Dreamweaver calculates the size of text in rems, it bases that size on the size of the root element—in other words, on the default font size. The advantage of rems over ems is that rems avoid the cascading issues mentioned in the Note above.

- *Percentages* (%) are another relative size measurement. When you apply it to text, it's functionally equivalent to ems—100% is the same as 1 em, 200% is 2 ems, and 75% is .75 ems. If you're more comfortable with the notion of percentages than the typography-inspired ems, use percentages.

There are other measurement options displayed in CSS Designer's *font-size* property, but they aren't used by many designers because don't offer advantages over pixels, ems, rems, or percentages. They include old-fashioned type measures like points (pt) and picas (pc). They also include measurements based on letter or glyph size. Ex is based on the lower case x, for example, and ch is based on the number 0.

The upshot is that you're safe using pixel values—they're easier to understand, more consistent across browsers, and compatible with the Zoom feature of all currently shipping browsers.

Picking a Font Color

To set the hue of your text, use the CSS *color* property. You can do so in the Properties panel's CSS mode or in CSS Designer's *color* property for text.

Whether for text or the background of a web page, most color formatting in Dreamweaver uses the *color picker*. When the color picker opens (Figure 3-18), you dial in a color using the three sliders on the right. They control the hue, lightness/darkness, and transparency. Your selection is shown inside the ring in the large square. You can adjust the color by dragging that ring to a different spot. There are two smaller squares in the upper-left corner of the color picker. The square on the left shows the new color you're specifying; the one on the right shows the original color. When you're happy with your color, press Enter.

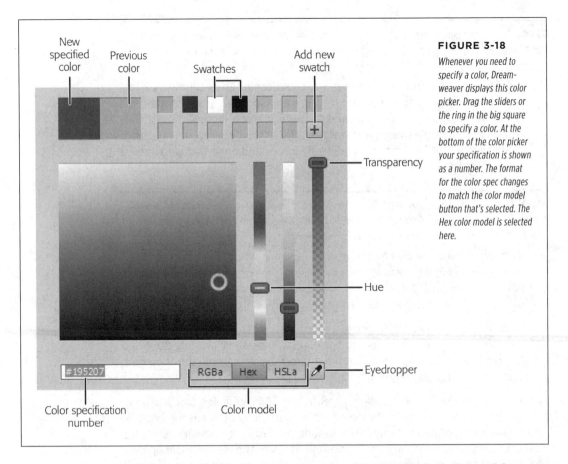

FIGURE 3-18

Whenever you need to specify a color, Dreamweaver displays this color picker. Drag the sliders or the ring in the big square to specify a color. At the bottom of the color picker your specification is shown as a number. The format for the color spec changes to match the color model button that's selected. The Hex color model is selected here.

In addition, you can use the eyedropper cursor that appears in the lower-right corner of the color picker. The eyedropper comes "empty," meaning that when you click any spot on your screen, the cursor takes on that color, passing it to the color picker. That trick comes in handy when you want to use a color from an image elsewhere in your document (to have headline text match the color in an image, for example).

This sample spot doesn't have to be from within Dreamweaver, either—you can switch to another program and click a color there, and Dreamweaver's color picker reflects that color.

Normally, Dreamweaver records the colors you select in hexadecimal notation, but Dreamweaver CC supports a much broader range of color notations than before, including RGB, HSL, RGBa, and HSLa (see the box on page 141). To use one, click one of the color model buttons in the color picker (Figure 3-18).

> **NOTE** Internet Explorer 8 and earlier support only three color formats: RGB and two hex formats. Until Internet Explorer users upgrade to IE 9 or switch to Firefox, Chrome, Safari, or Opera, you're better off sticking with RGB or hex color values for your pages.

If you decide you don't want to add a color, or you want to remove a color you already applied, click the trash can next to the color swatch in CSS Designer's Properties section. Without a color specified, web browsers use default colors for the element in question. For instance, unless you specify otherwise, text on a page is usually black.

If you know your colors—and more important, your color values—you can bypass the sliders and set a color by hand. To do so, look for the text box in the lower-left corner of the color picker (Figure 3-18). Type the color value into this box, and the color picker displays your chosen hue. This method is sometimes faster and more precise than eyeballing it with the sliders and the ring.

Adding Bold and Italic

You can make text bold or italic using HTML tags or CSS styles. In most cases, the text looks the same, but there's a geeky, subtle difference. When you use the Properties panel in HTML mode and click the B button, the selected text is wrapped in HTML <strong> tags, like this:

```
<strong>I'm feeling bold</strong>
```

Most browsers and devices boldface text when they come upon this expression, but that doesn't have to be the case. Someone could build a browser that uses red text or a different font. It just doesn't happen very often. On the other hand, when screen-reading software for the impaired sees the <strong> tags, it might increase the volume of the spoken words. In the Properties panel's HTML mode, the I button works in a similar way, but it adds <em> tags (think em for emphasis).

CSS works differently from the HTML tags. As always, CSS uses rules to style your text. These rules are less ambiguous than those for HTML. For example, in the Properties panel, if you click the CSS button to switch to CSS mode, you see two menus to the right of the Font menu. The first one (*font-style*) gives you a choice of normal or italic text—no wiggle room there. The next menu (*font-weight*) offers different values. Various fonts offer different options, so you may see numbers (like 400 or 700) or words (like normal, bold, bolder) that represent *font-weight*. When using the number system, 400 is a normal font weight, while 700 is bold.

So, how do you decide whether an HTML tag or a CSS rule should format your text? If you just want to change the appearance of text, use CSS mode. But if you actually want to emphasize text because it's important to the sentence's meaning (and therefore to the way search engines perceive the sentence), use HTML mode. For example, if you want the word "Monday" to stand out on a page, use CSS. But, for a sentence like "He *never* makes mistakes," the emphasis on "never" is important to understanding the sentence; in that case, use HTML mode. The people viewing your site might not notice the difference, but Google, other search engines, and screen readers will.

NOTE Browsers automatically display headlines in boldface, so highlighting a headline and then clicking the B button in CSS mode has no effect. But what if you want to *remove* the bolding from a headline? Clicking the B button works for normal text, but not for headlines. To remove the bold formatting from headlines, you have to use the CSS Style Definition window, and then, from the *font-weight* menu, select *normal* or *400*.

Aligning Text

The alignment buttons in the Properties panel's CSS mode set the CSS *text-align* property to either *left, right, center*, or *justify*. These same options are available in CSS Designer in the Properties section.

Text Properties in CSS Designer

In CSS Designer's Properties section, click the T (Text) button to see the properties you use to format text.

NOTE It's a little confusing, but CSS Designer and the Properties panel in CSS mode use different names for the same properties. CSS Designer uses the same property names as those in a CSS style sheet. So you see lowercase words and hyphens between two words. For example, you use *font-family* to specify a font. The labels on the Properties panel widgets are more generic, so you see a *Font* menu to specify a font. In either case, once you choose an option in CSS Designer or the Properties panel, Dreamweaver writes the same, correct code in a style sheet.

- **color.** Set the text color using Dreamweaver's color picker, as described on page 138.

- **font-family.** Choose a font or a font stack for the new CSS rule from the font menu. This menu offers both Dreamweaver's stock fonts and any web fonts you added to Dreamweaver, as discussed on page 128.

- **font-style.** Choose either normal or italic from the menu.

- **font-variant.** This drop-down menu lets you specify small-caps type, if you like—a slightly formal, fancy-looking style much favored by attorneys' offices.

- **font-weight.** Weight refers to the thickness of a font. CSS Designer's font-weight property offers 13 thicknesses. Normal and Bold are the most common, and they work in all browsers that understand CSS. See Figure 3-19 for details.

Web Colors

CSS supports several color notations: hexadecimal, RGB, HSL, RGBa, and HSLa. These formats are just different ways to specify a color, and you can get the same color using any of them.

Traditionally, you specify colors in CSS using hexadecimal notation. "Hex" represents colors using a six-digit code, like this: #fe3400. (Hexadecimal notation is a system computers use for counting. In this system, you count like this: 0, 1, 2, 3, 4, 5, 6, 7, 8, 9, a, b, c, d, e, f. The # symbol tells a computer that the following sequence is a series of hexadecimal numbers.) The best way to find a color's hex value is to choose the color you want by clicking on it in the palette and then looking at the code that Dreamweaver writes in the text box below.

Hex colors comprise three pairs of numbers. For example, the number above, #fe3400, is really fe, 34, and 00. Each pair represents a number for red, green, and blue color values, which, when combined, make up a color. You sometimes see only three numbers, like this: #f00—that's shorthand used when both numbers in a pair are the same. For example, you can shorten #ff0011 to just #f01. In the color box's "Color format" menu (see Figure 3-18.), Dreamweaver refers to these formats as "six-digit hex" and "three-digit hex."

However, CSS supports other formats for specifying color. RGB stands for "Red Green Blue" and is the format most commonly associated with computer graphics. Most graphics programs let you pick colors using RGB, and, in fact, hex colors are really just RGB values specified using hex numbers. For example, the hex color #ff0033 looks like this as an RGB value in CSS: rgb(255,0,51). Each value represents a color and uses a number from 0 to 255, so rgb(255,0,51) means 255 red, 0 green, and 51 blue. RGB color values work in all web browsers (even Internet Explorer 6), so if you're more comfortable with RGB, feel free to use it.

HSL stands for "Hue, Saturation, Lightness" and is yet another way to specify colors based on its color (hue), intensity (saturation), and lightness (how close a color is to white or black). You specify the hue using a number from 0 to 360 (representing the degrees around a color wheel with red being both 0 and 360, green 120, and blue 240), the saturation is a percentage from 0 (gray) to 100 (full intensity), and lightness is a percentage from 0 (black) to 100 (white). That hex color above, #ff0033, is written like this in HSL: hsl(348,100%,50%). Some people find HSL colors easier to understand than RGB or hex, but all three let you specify the same colors. However, HSL colors work only in Internet Explorer 9 and later. Since IE 8 and 7 still are popular, you're better off skipping HSL for now.

Finally, RGBa and HSLa colors add the dimension of transparency to color: The "a" stands for alpha transparency and refers to how transparent the color is. In other words, you can create "see-through" colors. For example, you could make the color of a headline partially transparent so that a background image on the page shows through the headline. There are many fun and creative effects possible with alpha transparency (for example, the article at *http://tinyurl.com/ydj8658* uses RGBa color). Unfortunately, Internet Explorer 8 and earlier don't understand RGBa or HSLa, so use these formats with caution. If you do want to explore them, they work just like their non-transparent counterparts, with the addition of one extra value from 0 (completely invisible) to 1 (completely opaque). So if you wanted a vivid red color that was 50 percent transparent, you'd specify an RGBa value using this notation: rgba(255,0,0,.5). In HSLa notation, that color is hsla(0,100%,50%,.5). If you use Dreamweaver's Color Format menu to select an RGBa or HSLa color, Dreamweaver always sets the transparency to 1; you can change it in the color field to anything from 0 to 1 (such as .25 to get 25 percent transparency).

- **font-size.** As described on page 136, you can choose from many standards to size text, but the most common are pixels, ems, and percentages.

- **line-height.** Line height, otherwise known as *leading* (pronounced "led-ing"), refers to the space between lines of text in a paragraph (see Figure 3-20). To set the line height, choose a unit of measure (like pixels or ems), and then type in a number. For example, to increase the amount of space between lines in a paragraph, type a number greater than the font size into the line-height property field .

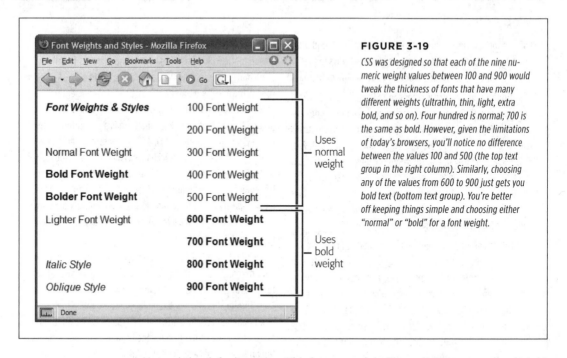

FIGURE 3-19

CSS was designed so that each of the nine numeric weight values between 100 and 900 would tweak the thickness of fonts that have many different weights (ultrathin, thin, light, extra bold, and so on). Four hundred is normal; 700 is the same as bold. However, given the limitations of today's browsers, you'll notice no difference between the values 100 and 500 (the top text group in the right column). Similarly, choosing any of the values from 600 to 900 just gets you bold text (bottom text group). You're better off keeping things simple and choosing either "normal" or "bold" for a font weight.

Normal, the default setting (third paragraph in Figure 3-20), uses a line height that's slightly larger than the height of the text. You don't get access to the drop-down menu of measurement units (pixels, points, percentage, and so on) unless you type a number in this box.

TIP A good strategy for setting line height is to type in a percentage measurement, such as *120%*, which is relative to the size of the text. So if your text were 10 pixels tall, the space from the base of one line of text to the next would be 12 pixels (120% of 10). Now, if you change the size of the text, the *relative* space between lines remains the same.

- **text-align.** This property controls the alignment of a block-level element, like a paragraph or table. You can choose from among the usual suspects—left, center, right, or even justify. (Like the text in this paragraph, justified text aligns copy on both the left and right edges.)

Use the "justify" option with care, however. Because web browsers don't have the advanced controls that page-layout software does, they usually do an awful job of justifying text on a computer screen. The results can be difficult to read—and ugly.

- **text-decoration.** These three buttons let you dress up your text, mostly in unattractive ways. Underline, overline, and line-through add horizontal lines below, above, or directly through the affected text, respectively. An option called blink, which made text flash on and off, was so universally hated and poorly supported by web browsers that it's no longer available.

- **text-indent.** This useful option lets you indent the first line of a paragraph. If you specify 15 pixels for this property, Dreamweaver gives each paragraph an attractive first-line indent, exactly as in a real word processor.

  You can also use a *negative* number, which makes the first line extend past the *left* margin of a paragraph, creating a hanging indent (or *outdent*)—a nice effect for a sentence that introduces a bulleted list or for glossary pages. If you use a negative number, it's a good idea to set the left margin for the paragraph equal to the value of the negative text indent (see page 58). That moves everything, including the outdented line, away from the edge of the browser window. Otherwise, the first line might extend too far to the left, off the screen!

- **text-shadow.** This group of properties creates a drop shadow that sets off text from a page, but only fairly new browsers know how to interpret the settings. To create an effective drop shadow, you need to set all of the *text-shadow* properties. The h-shadow and v-shadow values offset the shadow from the original line of text so that the text appears to pop off the page. The blur setting softens the shadow. Use the color setting to choose the shadow's hue. Want to experiment? Start off with these settings:

  — h-shadow : 7 px

  — v-shadow : 5 px

  — blur : 6 px

  — color : #666666

  View the results using Dreamweaver's Live view.

- **text-transform.** This menu lets you set the case for text. To capitalize the first letter of each word, choose Capitalize. The Uppercase option gives you all capital letters, while Lowercase makes all the letters lowercase. The factory setting is None, and it has no effect on the text.

- **letter-spacing.** This property governs the space between *letters*. To add space l i k e t h i s, type a value of about 5 pixels. The result can make long passages hard to read, but a little space between letters can add a dramatic flair to short headlines and movie titles.

- **word-spacing.** This property helps you clean up text by adding or removing space *between* words. The default value, Normal, leaves a normal, single space between words. If you want words in a sentence to be spaced   apart   like this, use a value of about 10 pixels (choose Value from the first drop-down menu, and the units of measure from the second). The bigger the number, the larger the gap between words. You can also *remove* space between words by using a negative number—a great choice when you want to make your pages difficult to read.

- **white-space.** This property controls how a browser displays extra white space (spaces, tabs, returns, and so on). Browsers normally ignore extra spaces in the HTML of a page, reducing them to a single-space character between words and other elements, as described on page 76. The *pre* option functions just like the HTML <pre> tag: Extra white space (like tabs, multiple spaces, and hard returns) that you put *in the HTML code* appear in the document itself. Setting the *nowrap* option prevents lines from breaking (and wrapping to the next line) when they reach the end of the browser window.

- **vertical-align.** With this property, you can change the vertical placement of an object—such as text or an image—relative to the items around it. For example, you can add a trademark character, copyright symbol, or footnote by offsetting the characters from the surrounding text using the options *super* and *sub*. If you wanted to add the trademark symbol to, say, *Chia Pet*™, you'd select the letters TM and set the vertical alignment to *super*. For more accurate placement, you can type a positive value, like 10 percent, to raise an object above its normal baseline, or a negative value (like -10% or -5 pixels) to move an object down.

  You can also vertically align images, and designers often use the options Top, Bottom, and Middle to position content within a cell.

> **NOTE** The *sub* and *super* alignment options don't change the size of the selected text. To create true subscript or superscript characters (for chemical symbols, trademark or copyright symbols, and so on), you should specify a font size for the sub or super text that's smaller than the font size used for the body of the page; 75% works great.

Other Properties

As you might guess, the Others category in CSS Designer holds properties that didn't fit nicely inside of Layout, Text, Border, or Background. For the most part, these properties help you to exercise greater control over bulleted and numbered lists (see Figure 3-21):

- **list-style-position (List-style-Position).** This property controls where the bullet appears relative to the list item's text. The "outside" option places the bullet outside the margin of the text, exactly the way bulleted lists normally look. "Inside," on the other hand, displays the bullet within the text margin, so that the left edge of the *bullet* aligns with the left margin of the text; Figure 3-21 makes the effect clear.

- **list-style-image (List-style-image).** For the ultimate control of your bullet icon, skip the boring options preprogrammed into a web browser (like disc, circle, square, or decimal) and supply your own bullets. Click the Browse button and then, from your site folder, select a graphics file. Make sure the graphic is appropriate bullet material—in other words, small.

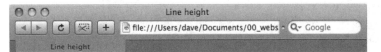

FIGURE 3-20

Control the space between lines with the line-height property in the CSS Rule Definition dialog box. In this example, each paragraph's text is set in a 16-pixel Trebuchet MS font. With CSS, you can make lines bump into each other by setting a low line-height value (top paragraph), or spread them far apart by using a larger value (bottom paragraph).

TIP The *background-image* property, which you'll learn about on page 240, is a more versatile solution to adding customized bullets to a list. The *list-style-image* property lets you specify a graphic to use as a bullet, but CSS doesn't offer any controls to position that image. On the other hand, you can accurately position a background image, so it's much easier to tweak the placement of a bullet using the *background-image* property. Here's how: Create a style for the <li> tag (or a class style that you apply to each <li> tag). Set the *list-style-type* property type to *none* (this hides the bullet), set the background image to your graphical bullet, and play with the background position values (page 265). Playing with the padding values (page 439) helps position the text relative to the image.

- **list-style-type (List-style-type).** Select the type of bullet you want in front of a list item. Some of the options included are: "disc," "circle," "square," "decimal" (1, 2, 3), "lower-roman" (i, ii, iii), "upper-roman" (I, II, III), "lower-alpha" (a, b, c), "upper-alpha" (A, B, C), and "none" (no bullet at all).

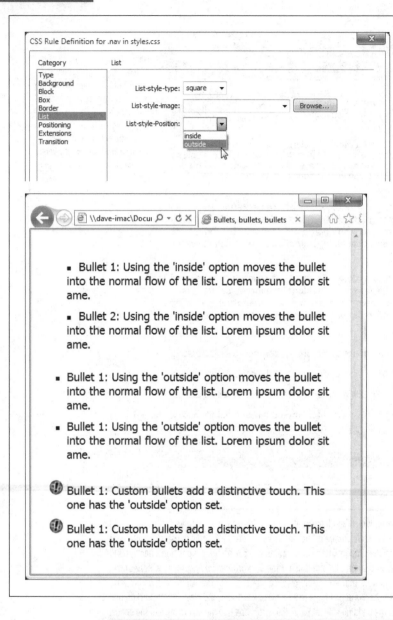

FIGURE 3-21

Top: Take control of your bulleted and numbered lists using the CSS Rule Definition window's List category. With Cascading Style Sheets, you can even supply your own graphic bullets.

Bottom: A bullet-crazed web page, for illustration purposes. Parading down the screen, you can see "inside" bullets, "out-side" bullets, and bullets made from graphics.

NOTE If you want to adjust the amount of space web browsers normally use to indent lists, set the left padding property (page 439) to *0*, and then set the left margin (see page 439) to the amount of indent you'd like. Sometimes you want no indent at all—for example, when you're creating a list of links that should look like buttons, not bulleted items—set both the left padding and left margin to *0* (and while you're at it, set the bullet type to *none*, as described previously).

■ Cascading Style Sheets Tutorial

In this tutorial, you'll practice creating and editing styles. Make sure you grasp the fundamentals covered in the following pages—you'll be building lots of style sheets in the other tutorials in this book using these methods.

In this tutorial, you'll create an external style sheet that formats pages on the Cafe Soylent Green website.

> **NOTE** Before you get started, download the tutorial files from *http://oreilly.com/missingmanuals/cds/ dreamweaverccmm13/*. See the Note on page 33 for details.

Setting Up a Site

Once you download the tutorial files and open Dreamweaver, you need to set up a site for this tutorial. You learned how to do that in the first chapter, but here's a quick recap—practice makes perfect!

1. **Choose Site→New Site.**

   The Site Setup window appears.

2. **For the Site Name, type *CSS Tutorial*.**

   Now you need to tell Dreamweaver where to find the site's files.

3. **To the right of the "Local site folder" box, click the folder icon.**

   The Choose Root Folder window appears. This is just a window into your computer's file system; navigate to the folder you want to use as your site's main folder.

4. **Navigate to and select the *Chapter03* folder located in the *MM_DWCC* folder. Click the Select button (Choose on Macs) to select this folder, and then, in the Site Setup window, click Save to complete the process of defining a site.**

   You've named your site and identified its root folder where Dreamweaver will store your web pages.

Adding Web Fonts

In this tutorial, you'll use Dreamweaver CC's new web fonts feature. The first thing you want to do is add fonts to Dreamweaver's fonts manager.

1. **Choose Modify→Manage Fonts.**

   Dreamweaver's Manage Fonts window opens (Figure 3-22). You'll add your first font.

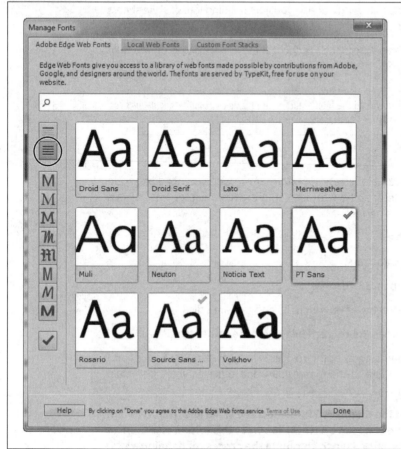

FIGURE 3-22

Dreamweaver CC's new Manage Fonts window displays free-to-use fonts on the Adobe Edge Web Fonts tab. This window makes it easy to choose attractive fonts that work well with all browsers.

2. **From the vertical set of buttons on the left, click the second one from the top, the one that says "List fonts recommended for paragraphs" when you hover over it (circled in Figure 3-22).**

   The window displays fonts suitable for body text. Use the button above for headings. The other buttons filter the fonts so you can see different typeface styles, such as sans-serif, decorative, and cursive.

3. **In the search box at the top, type a couple of the letters of *PT Sans*.**

   As you type, Dreamweaver displays fonts that match. Eventually, the only fonts you'll see are PT Sans, PT Sans Caption, and PT Sans Narrow.

4. **Click the PT Sans tile.**

Dreamweaver puts a checkmark in the upper-right corner, indicating that it added the font to its list of available fonts.

5. **Click the X at the end of the search box, and then click the "List fonts recommended for paragraphs" button once more (second from top).**

Once you clear the filters, Dreamweaver displays all the fonts.

6. **Click the checkmark button at the bottom of the left-hand column.**

With this button ("List of fonts previously added to font list") turned on, Dreamweaver displays only the Edge Web Fonts you added to its font library (which now includes PT Sans).

7. **At the top of the Manage Fonts window, click the Custom Font Stacks tab.**

You see three boxes in the resulting window. The top one, "Font list," lists your custom stacks. The box on the bottom-right lists your available fonts, and the one on the bottom-left lists your "Chosen fonts" as you build new font stacks.

8. **Click the + button (upper-right corner).**

In "Font lists," a message appears that says: Add fonts in list below. This is your prompt to move fonts from the "Available fonts" box to the "Chosen fonts" box to build a new custom font stack.

9. **In the text box below the "Available fonts" window, type *pt sans*. When Dreamweaver highlights pt sans, click the << button.**

As you type in a font name, Dreamweaver automatically scrolls the "Available fonts" list to any matches. When you click <<, Dreamweaver adds pt sans to the "Chosen fonts" list. Its position at the top of the list makes it the preferred font. Dreamweaver uses the fonts listed below that as fallback options.

10. **Repeat the previous step to add Arial, Helvetica, and sans-serif fonts to the "Chosen fonts" list.**

As you add the fonts, Dreamweaver displays them as a font stack in the "Font list" pane above (Figure 3-23). Browsers use the fonts in the order listed. In this case, browsers will use PT Sans because your site provides it. If Dreamweaver doesn't show Arial or Helvetica in the "Available fonts" box, use another sans-serif font, like Gill Sans or Verdana.

11. **Click Done.**

The Manage Fonts window closes. As you'll see below, your new font stack, including PT Sans, will be available from *font* and *font-family* menus.

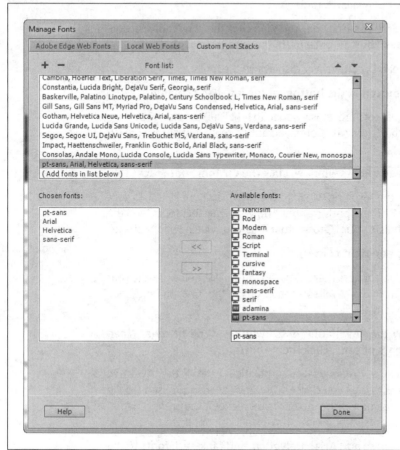

FIGURE 3-23

You use the Custom Font Stack panel to build lists of fonts starting with a preferred font, followed by fallback options. The goal is to provide fonts with a similar, suitable appearance where at least one of the options will be available to your visitors or already installed on their systems.

Creating an External Style Sheet

Now that you've got Dreamweaver ready to use web fonts, you'll create a new external style sheet and start adding styles.

1. **In the Files panel, double-click *about.html*.**

   The "About Us" web page opens in the document window. (If you don't see the Files panel, choose Window→Files to open it.)

2. **In CSS Designer's Sources section, click the + (Add CSS Source) button.**

   Dreamweaver displays a menu with three options: Create a New CSS File, Attach Existing CSS File, and Define in Page.

3. **Choose Create a New CSS File.**

   The Create a New CSS File window appears, where you can name the file and choose other options.

4. **In the File/URL box, type *soylent_styles* and leave the "Add as" radio button set to Link.**

   The name of your external style sheet will be *soylent_styles.css*, but you don't need to add the .css extension here. The Link option adds a line of code to your web page that links *soylent_styles.css* to your web page.

5. **Click OK.**

   The Create a New CSS File window closes and Dreamweaver lists *soylent_styles.css* in the Files panel (Figure 3-24). The same file name now appears in the CSS Designer's Sources section. The next step is to create a CSS style.

6. **Put your cursor in the first line of text, About Us. Then, in CSS Designer's Sources section, click *soylent_styles.css*. Finally, in the Selectors section, click the Add Selector button (+).**

   Dreamweaver adds a new selector called "body h1." This is a compound selector, and it'll apply to all the <h1> headings in the body portion of your document. Just to review, the term *h1 headings* means text that appears between HTML tags, like this:

   `<h1>About Us</h1>`

   Since all the content of your web page is inside HTML <body> tags, the selector <body h1> applies the style you're creating to all <h1> headings.

   Dreamweaver gives you the option to keep this tag or rename it. In this case, you'll keep it, so click an empty spot in Selectors to deselect the editing field.

7. **In the Selectors section, choose body h1, and then, in the Properties section, click the Text button (T).**

   The list of properties scrolls to show those related to text, like color, font-family, and font-style.

8. **To the right of font-family, click the grayed-out words "default font." Then, near the bottom of the font stack, choose "pt sans, Arial, Helvetica, sans-serif."**

   You format CSS properties with a property name and value pair, separated by a colon. In this case, font-family is the property name and "pt sans, Arial, Helvetica, sans-serif" is the value.

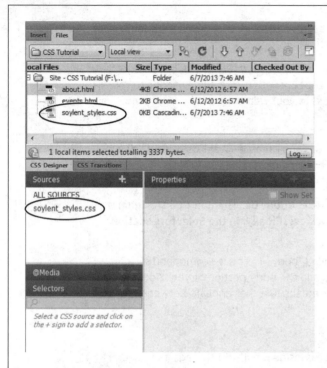

FIGURE 3-24

When you create a style sheet, Dreamweaver lists it in the Local Files panel. In this case, the style sheet (circled) sits in the site's root folder, but you can put it in any folder on your site. For example, some web developers like to reduce the clutter in the root folder by placing all their CSS files in a folder named "css." No matter where you put the style sheet, Dreamweaver lists it in the Sources panel when it's linked to the current page.

9. **In Properties, set font-weight to 700.**

    The font-weight property for pt sans can have just two values, 400 and 700, to control the thickness of the characters. The value 400 is the same as normal-weight text, while 700 is bolded text.

    You created a style that Dreamweaver applies to the <h1> headings in your document. Now it's time to see the results.

10. **In Design view, find the About Us heading, and then click the Live button.**

    You have to switch to Live view to see web fonts. The <h1> heading About Us uses a sans-serif font. When you click the Live button, it still displays a sans-serif font, but there are differences. Note the shape of the letter "b" in "About." The Live view displays the PT Sans font. However, you can't edit your document in Live view, so click Live again to exit Live view and go back to work.

NOTE Because Live view often looks just like Design view, it's easy to get caught in the frustrating situation where Dreamweaver won't let you select text or edit the web page. If this happens, take a breath, look to see if the Live button is toggled on, and then click it to turn off Live view. Dreamweaver switches to Design view, where you can edit. If you're in Split view, you can edit the HTML and leave Live view turned on. HTML pros often work this way, typing HTML tags into the code half of Split view and checking the updated display in Live view.

11. **Click the Code view button.**

    Dreamweaver displays the underlying code for your web page (Figure 3-25). Notice the line:

    `<link href="soylent_styles.css" rel="stylesheet" type="text/css">`

    This links your style sheet to your web page. After the <body> tag, you see the code for the <h1> heading:

    `<h1>About Us</h1>`

    Don't put any formatting rules in the h1 link because the CSS rules (font-family, font-weight) for the <h1> tag are in the style sheet, and Dreamweaver will apply them to all the <h1> headings in the page. The next step is to add a bit of color to your style. You can do this in CSS Designer, but for variety and practice, you'll use the Properties panel.

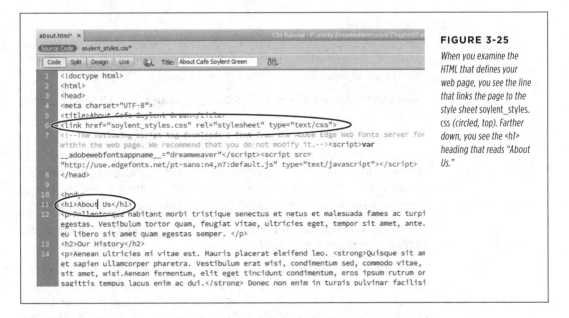

FIGURE 3-25

When you examine the HTML that defines your web page, you see the line that links the page to the style sheet soylent_styles. css *(circled, top). Farther down, you see the <h1> heading that reads "About Us."*

12. **In the Properties panel, below the document window, click the CSS button.**

    This changes the Properties panel to display CSS properties.

13. **Click to place your cursor in the About Us heading.**

The Targeted Rule in the Properties panel shows "body h1." Any changes made in the Properties CSS mode panel changes the styles applied to the "body h1" selector. Notice that the font-family and font-weight styles already reflect the changes you made in the CSS Designer.

14. **Next to the Text Color box, type *#145207* and then press Enter (Return).**

The color of the <h1> heading changes. Use the color picker to select another color if you prefer.

15. **Change font-size to 36.**

This sets the font size of your headline to 36px (pixels) as shown in Figure 3-26.

FIGURE 3-26

Choosing properties for an element that already has a style applied to it—like the body h1 selector shown here—updates that style.

Editing a Style

You won't always create the perfect style on your first try—you may make a mistake or just want to change the font, font size, or color of text. Fortunately, Dreamweaver makes it as easy to edit a style as it does to create one.

1. **Open CSS Designer (Window→CSS Designer) and select All Sources in the Sources section.**

In CSS Designer, when you click on a source in the Sources section, that list in the Selectors section changes to show all the selectors (classes, IDs, and tags) defined in that source. When you choose All Sources, you see all the selectors the style sheet uses to format the page. In this case, there's only one source (*soylent_styles.css*) and so far, you've defined only one selector (<body h1>).

2. **If the Selectors section isn't open, click the dark gray bar at the top of the section, and then click body h1.**

The Properties section now displays the CSS rules for the body h1 selector. You need to click the Text button (T) or scroll down to see body h1's properties: color, font-family, font-weight, and font-size. Even though you didn't set a value for font-style, Dreamweaver automatically set it to "normal," the default over the other option, italic. Properties with grayed-out values represent properties you haven't set yet.

3. **At the top of the Properties section, click Borders.**

The Borders button is the third from the left. After you click it, Dreamweaver displays 18 styles related to borders. Why so many? You can set options for border spacing, color, thickness, and corner radius. You can set different values for many of the border properties. For example, you can set different values for the left, right, top, and bottom borders. To see more options, expand CSS Designer by dragging the top of the panel up, as shown in Figure 3-27.

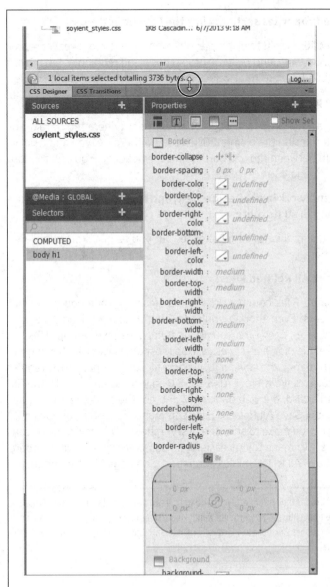

FIGURE 3-27

Drag the top edge (circled) of CSS Designer to see more of the border properties. You can set individual left, right, top, and bottom properties for many border options.

4. **Set border-top-color to #145207 and then set border-top-style to solid. Click the value next to border-top-width and choose px, and then type *2*. Use the same values for border-bottom-color, border-bottom-style, and border-bottom-width.**

   Here, you're setting the values for the top and bottom borders independently. If you want to set the values for top, bottom, left, and right all at once, use a setting like border-color or border-style, where you don't specify the border position. Next stop—layout styles.

5. **At the top of the Properties section, click the Layout button.**

   The Properties section scrolls to display layout properties. Dreamweaver represents the *margin, padding,* and *position* properties using rectangles where you can set top, bottom, left, and right values independently, or as a single value.

6. **For the padding property, set the top value to *2px*.**

   Padding is the space between the edge of an element (where the border appears) and the stuff inside the element (like text). In this case, you add 2 pixels of breathing room between the top border and the headline. You'll learn more about padding on page 439.

7. **Examine your handiwork in the Design view, and then click Live view to see your <h1> heading in all its glory.**

   Now you have a distinctive-looking headline. But you've just started building styles for this page.

8. **Choose File→Save All Related Files.**

   The Save All Related Files command can be a lifesaver when you work with external style sheets. Even though you're looking at and working on a web page (*about.html* here), each time you add a style, Dreamweaver updates the external style sheet file (*soylent_styles.css*). So most of the work you've done so far has gone into updating the *soylent_styles.css* file. Unfortunately, the regular keyboard shortcut to save a file, Ctrl+S (⌘-S), only saves changes to the file you can see—in this case, the web page only, and not the style sheet that goes along with it. Use the Save All Related Files command frequently, or you could lose all the changes you make to an external style sheet if Dreamweaver or your computer crashes. (To make things easier, you can create your own keyboard shortcut for the Save All Related Files command. See page 332 for details.)

   NOTE The File→Save All command also protects your hard work. It saves every file that has unsaved changes. Feel free to use this command frequently even if you might want to undo some of those changes—Dreamweaver's smart enough to let you undo changes you make to a file even after you save those changes (but only if you don't close the file in the meantime).

Adding Another Style

Dreamweaver lists files related to the current web page in tabs just above the document window. Below the "about.html" tab, a button says *soylent_styles.css*. Click it to see the CSS code you created to format <h1> headings.

Next on the agenda—a new look for those <h2> headings, so click the Design button and get to work.

1. **In Design view, place your cursor in the line that says "Our History." Make sure you're not in Live view. In the CSS Designer Sources section, click *soylent_styles.css*, and then, in the Selectors section, click the Add Selector button (+).**

   A new selector appears with the name "body h2."

2. **In CSS Designer's Properties section, click the Text button (T).**

   Dreamweaver scrolls to the text properties.

3. **Set the font-family property to "pt sans, Arial, Helvetica, sans-serif."**

   You'll use the same font as in Heading 1, but you'll change its size and color.

4. **Click the font-size value, choose px, and then type *24*. For the color property, click the grayed-out word "undefined," and then type *#033E00*.**

   This creates medium-sized, dark-green text. To make the headline stand out a bit, you'll make all the text uppercase. Fortunately, you don't have to hold down the caps-lock key and retype each headline to do so—a CSS property can handle that for you.

5. **Find the text-transform properties and click the AB button.**

   One problem with this page is the gap between the subheads and the paragraphs that follow. Removing this gap visually ties the two together better. To make this change, you must first remove the margin below each headline.

6. **At the top of the Properties section, click the Layout button.**

   Dreamweaver scrolls down the long list of properties until it gets to those related to layout, such as padding and margins.

7. **Click the grayed-out 0 at the bottom of the margin box and type *0*.**

   These settings remove any space that appears below the Heading 2 tags, but the space between the headlines and the paragraphs hasn't changed a bit! What gives? Paragraphs and headlines have space both above *and* below. The space you're seeing is actually the *top* margin of the paragraph tag.

   Top and bottom margins have a peculiar feature: They don't add up, like 1+1=2. In other words, a web browser doesn't add the bottom margin of Heading 2 to the top margin of the paragraph to calculate the total space between the two blocks of text. Instead, a web browser uses the margin with the *largest* value to determine the space between paragraphs (a lot of text layout programs, including word processors, share this behavior).

For example, say the <h2> tag has a bottom margin of 12 pixels, while the paragraph following it has a top margin of 10 pixels. The total space between the two isn't 22 pixels (10+12)—it's 12 pixels (the value of the larger margin). So, if you remove the bottom margin of the headline, the gap between the two blocks of text isn't gone—it's now 10 pixels, the value for the paragraph's top margin. That's the situation here: You need to modify the paragraph's top margin as well. You do that by creating another style.

8. **Click somewhere in the paragraph below Our History.**

   Make sure you don't actually select text, you just want your cursor placed in the paragraph.

9. **In CSS Designer's Sources section, click *soylent_styles.css*, and then click the Add Selector button (+).**

   A new selector appears: <body p>.

10. **In the Properties section, click the Layout button. Then, in the margin box, click the 0 at the top and type *0*.**

    It may seem like you're replacing one 0 with another, but the margin-top property was initially grayed out, meaning it was undefined and therefore using a default value. Take a look at your page and you see the desired result (Figure 3-28).

    While you're defining <p> properties, you might as well make the text look spiffy.

11. **In the Properties section, click the Text button (T), and then change font-family to "pt sans, Arial, Helvetica, sans-serif."**

    This is one of the web fonts you added earlier.

12. **Click value next to font-size, choose px, and then type *14*.**

    CSS provides a lot of control over type, including the ability to adjust the leading, or space between, lines in a paragraph.

13. **Click the grayed-out value next to line-height, choose %, and then type *150*.**

    The line-height property controls the space between lines of text. In this case, you set that space to 150 percent, which means that each line will be 150 percent (or 1.5 times) the size of the font. A setting of 150 adds more space than usual between each line of text in a paragraph—the result is more white space and a more luxurious feel.

FIGURE 3-28

Headings like Our History look better when they sit snug atop a paragraph. To create this look, you need to change both the heading's margin-bottom value and the paragraph's margin-top value. In this example, both are set to 0.

Creating a Class Style

Now you'll create a style to format the copyright notice at the bottom of the page. It's inside a regular paragraph tag (<p>), so it gets all its formatting from the <p> tag style. Here's an instance where you'd like to style a single paragraph without affecting the other paragraphs on the page. A class style is perfect for this kind of task.

1. **In CSS Designer's Sources section, click *soylent_styles.css*. Then, in the Selectors section, click the Add Selector button (+), and then type *.copyright*.**

   Don't forget the period at the beginning of "copyright." That identifies your selector as a class rather than as an HTML tag.

> **NOTE** Some beginners think that whenever you create a new style, you also need to create a new external style sheet. On the contrary, you can—and should—store more than one style in a single external style sheet. In fact, if you're creating a set of styles for an entire site, put them all in the same external style sheet.

2. **In the Selectors section, click .copyright, and then in the Properties section, click the Text button (T).**

   CSS Designer scrolls to the text properties. By now, you probably know the drill.

3. **Click font-family and choose "pt sans, Arial, Helvetica, sans-serif." For the font-size property, choose px, and then type _12_. Set the font-weight property to 700. At the top, click the color box and choose white.**

Because the text is now white (the same color as the page), you'll change the background color to make the copyright notice stand out.

4. **In the Properties section, scroll down through the border category until you see background-color.**

You'll add a background color now (background images are discussed on page 240).

5. **In the background-color box, type _#145207_.**

To allow a little breathing room around the copyright text, you'll add some padding.

6. **In the Properties section, click Layout. Then, in the padding box, click the link in the center and type _5_ in any of the number boxes.**

The link lets you set the top, bottom, left, and right padding to the same values. While margins control the space between elements (like the gap between paragraphs), _padding_ controls the space between the content and the content's border, which includes the background of the page. In other words, adding padding enlarges the background around the text (or other content) you're styling.

You'll change the copyright notice's margin settings as well.

7. **For the margin-top value, type _25_. For margin-left, type _0_.**

The window should look like the one in Figure 3-29. The 25 pixels of the top margin push the copyright notice away from the bottom of the paragraph above it. In addition, since Dreamweaver indents all the paragraphs 75 pixels from the left edge, you need to set the left margin here, in the copyright notice, to _0_. This overrides the 75-pixel margin from the <p> tag style and lets the copyright notice hug the left edge of the page.

You may have noticed that none of your .copyright styles have taken effect. That's because the line at the bottom of your page doesn't know it's a copyright. Unlike HTML tag styles, class styles don't show up anywhere until you apply them by hand.

8. **Scroll to the bottom of the page and select the last paragraph, the one with the copyright notice.**

This action sets you up for applying the style. You can also just click anywhere inside the paragraph (without selecting any text) to apply a class style to it.

9. **In the Properties panel, click the HTML button, and then, from the Class menu, choose copyright (see Figure 3-30).**

Boom—the copyright notice suddenly changes size and color. Magic.

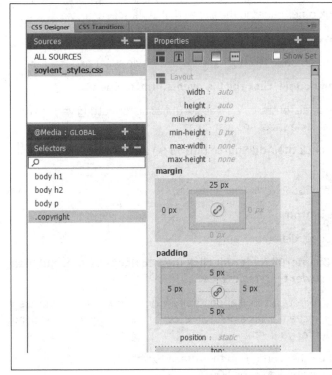

FIGURE 3-29

The difference between padding and margin settings is subtle but important. Both properties add space around content you're styling. And if you don't have a background color, image, or border, both properties pretty much act the same. However, when you do have a background color, image, or border, padding adds space between the content and the backgrounds and borders. Margins add space outside the border and background.

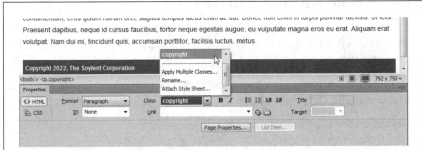

FIGURE 3-30

The Class menu in the HTML mode of the Proper-ties panel lists all class styles. It also displays the style name using the style's formatting—in this case, bold, white text with a dark green background. Notice that the menu lists only class styles; tag styles don't appear here, since you don't apply them manually. You can also apply a class using the Properties panel's CSS mode, as described on page 114.

Attaching an External Style Sheet

Now that you've created these styles, you may wonder how you can use them on other pages—after all, that's the beauty of external style sheets. Once created, it's a simple process to link other pages in the site to that style sheet.

1. **Choose File→Save All Related Files, and then close the** *about.html* **page.**

   You'll open a new web page to attach the external style sheet to it.

2. **In the Files panel, double-click the file** *events.html* **to open it.**

   This file is another page for the cafe's website. It has no formatting yet, so you'll attach the external style sheet you just created.

3. **In CSS Designer, click the Add Source button (+) and choose Attach Existing CSS File.**

   The Attach Existing CSS File window appears.

4. **Click the Browse button.**

   The Select Style Sheet dialog box appears.

5. **Navigate to the Chapter03 folder (or click the Site Root button), and then double-click the** *soylent_styles.css* **file.**

   Don't forget the Site Root button. It appears on every window in which you need to save, open, or select a file. It's a great shortcut to make sure you're working in the correct folder for your site.

   You can ignore the other settings in the Attach External Style Sheet window for now (they're described on page 509).

6. **Click OK to attach the style sheet to the page.**

   Dreamweaver instantly formats the headlines and main text of the story. Pretty cool—and very efficient. You need to apply the *.copyright* class style only to the last paragraph on the page.

7. **Scroll to the bottom of the page, and then click anywhere inside the paragraph with the copyright notice.**

   Next you'll style the paragraph.

8. **From the Class menu on the Properties panel, select copyright.**

   This page is almost done. Preview it in a web browser to see what you need to do next.

9. **Press F12 (Option-F12) to preview the page.**

Dreamweaver probably prompts you to save your files; go ahead and do that. The page opens in a browser; notice that the bulleted list doesn't use the same font as the paragraph text. You'll change that now.

10. **Return to Dreamweaver and add a style for the <ul> tag.**

In other words, place your cursor in the list. In CSS Designer' Sources section, select *soylent_styles.css*. In the Selectors section, click the Add Selector button (+). The selector name <body ul li> appears in the Selectors section. Click an empty spot in Dreamweaver to accept that name. To review, the compound name identifies a list item (<li>), within an unordered list (<ul>) within the body of the page (<body>).

11. **In the Properties section, click the T button. Set font-family to "pt sans, Arial, Helvetica, sans-serif," choose px from the font-size drop-down menu, and then type *14*.**

This matches the settings for the paragraph text. Lastly, change the bullet to a square shape.

12. **In the Properties section, click the Layout button, and then, beside margin-left, type *50*.**

This sets the list off from the left edge of the page.

13. **Click the Others button in the Properties section. Then, beside list-style-type, choose square.**

You finished the style for the bulleted list items. To see the square bullets and some of the other formatting changes, you may need to go into Live view.

14. **In the upper-right corner of the Properties section, click Show Set.**

The Properties section displays only the properties to which you've given values. The Show Set feature is helpful when you want to quickly review and update the styles for a selector.

15. **Press F12 (Option-F12) to preview the page.**

Dreamweaver prompts you to save your files; go ahead and do that. The finished page should look something like Figure 3-31. If you'd like to compare your finished product to the completed version, you'll find those pages in the tutorial's *Chapter03_complete* folder.

NOTE   You may need to hit your browser's Refresh button to see the most recent changes you made to a style sheet. This is one problem you'll encounter when you design pages with external style sheets—web browsers often *cache* them. Normally that's a good thing—it means repeat visitors have to wait only once for the CSS file to download—the first time they visit your site. But when you're in the midst of a design, frantically switching back and forth between Dreamweaver and a web browser preview, the browser might retrieve the obsolete version of the external style sheet saved in its cache rather than the newly updated file on your computer. (The Safari browser is particularly aggressive at holding onto cached files, so if you preview in that browser, make sure to reload the page when you do.)

You can work around this problem. Open the Preferences window (Edit→Preferences [Dreamweaver→Preferences]), select Preview in Browser, and then turn on the "Preview using temporary file" checkbox. Now when you preview the page, Dreamweaver makes a temporary file on your computer that incorporates both the CSS and HTML of the page. This defeats a browser's cache so that now you're seeing the very latest changes. This setting has the added benefit of stopping Dreamweaver's annoying "You must save your file before previewing" dialog box each time you preview an unsaved page.

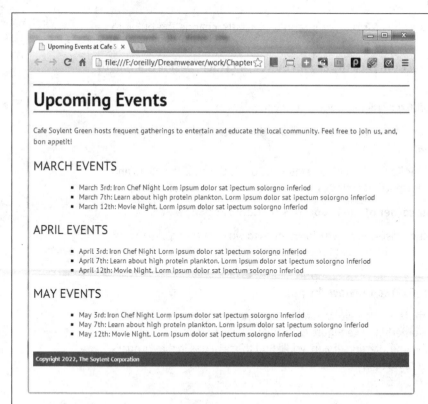

FIGURE 3-31

CSS offers a lot of design tools to produce beautiful typography for your web pages. In addition, an external style sheet lets you quickly, easily, and consistently style hundreds of pages without much extra work.

Links

The humble hyperlink may not raise eyebrows anymore, but the notion that you can navigate a whole sea of information, jumping from one island of content to another with a simple mouse click, is a powerful phenomenon. Interested in a particular band? Go to Google, type in the band's name, *click* to go to its website, *click* to see its upcoming gigs, *click* to go to the venue's website, and then *click* to buy tickets.

Although embedding links is a basic task in building web pages, and even though Dreamweaver—for the most part—shields you from the complexities of doing so, links can be tricky to understand. The first section of this chapter gives you an overview of links and explains the technical distinctions between different types of links. The rest of the chapter, with sections on formatting the appearance of your links and creating navigation menus, will help turn you into a link-crafting maestro.

> **NOTE** If you already understand links or you're eager to start using them, jump to the tutorial on page 204.

■ Understanding Links

Links are snippets of code that give web browsers directions to get from one web page to another. What makes links powerful is that the distance covered by those directions doesn't matter. A link can lead to another page on the same site just as easily as it can lead to a page on a web server halfway around the globe. Behind the scenes, a simple HTML tag called the anchor tag (<a>) makes each and every link work. Links come in three flavors: *absolute*, *document-relative*, and *root-relative*. Page 170 shows you examples of each.

Absolute Links

When people want to mail you a letter, they ask for your address. Suppose it's 123 Main St., Smithville, NY 12001, USA. No matter where in the country your friends are, if they write *123 Main St., Smithville, NY 12001, USA* on an envelope and mail it, their letters will get to you. That's because your address is unique.

Similarly, every web page has a unique address, called a *URL* (most people pronounce it "you-are-el"), or Uniform Resource Locator. If you open a web browser and type *http://www.cafesoylentgreen.com/events/index.html* into the address bar, the browser opens the events page for Cafe Soylent Green.

This URL is an *absolute link*—it's the complete, unique address for a single web page. Absolute links always begin with *http://*, and an absolute link leads to the same destination page, no matter what page you put that link on—an absolute link in a web page can call up another page within the same site or a page on another site entirely. You'll use absolute links any time you link to a web page *outside of your own site*—that's the *only* way a web browser can go from a page on your site to a page outside of your site. However, when you want to call up a page *within* your site, there's another way to write a link, described next.

The bottom line: Use absolute links when you want to link to a page on another website.

Document-Relative Links

Suppose you, the resident of 123 Main Street, drop in on a couple who just moved into a house directly across the street. After letting them know about all the great restaurants nearby, you tell them about a party you're having at your place.

When they ask you where you live, you could say, "I live at 123 Main St., Smithville, NY 12001, USA," but your neighbors would probably think you needed psychiatric help. Instead, you'd say something like, "Just walk across the street, and there you are." Of course, you can't use these instructions as your mailing address, nor would they make sense, for a neighbor who lived seven houses down. Those directions only help the neighbors directly across the street get from their house to yours.

To link from one web page to another in the same website, you use a similar shorthand, called a *document-relative link*. In essence, a document-relative link—like the directions you gave your neighbor—tells a browser where to find a page *relative* to your current location, in this case, relative to the current web page. If two pages are in the same folder, for instance, the path is as simple as the code version of "Go to that page over there"—in its entirety, the link is no more than the target filename, *index.html*, for example. You can leave off all that *http://www.your_site.com/* business, because you're already on that site and within that directory.

Document-relative links can be finicky, however, because they're completely dependent on the location of the page containing the link. If you move that page to another part of your site—filing it in a different folder, for example—the link won't work. It's as though your neighbors moved across town—they can't walk across the street to get to your house any longer. This vulnerability makes web designers reluctant to use document-relative links, even though they're ideal for linking from one page to another in the same site.

Fortunately, Dreamweaver makes working with document-relative links so easy you may forget what all the fuss is about. In Dreamweaver, whenever you save a page that has a document-relative link on it to a folder different from the page's original folder—a maneuver that would normally shatter all the links on a page—Dreamweaver quietly *rewrites* the links before it saves the file so that the links still work. Even better, using the program's site-management tools, you can cavalierly reorganize your site with impunity, moving files and folders without harming the delicate connections between your site's files. (You'll learn about Dreamweaver's site-management features in Part 4 of this book.)

Root-Relative Links

Root-relative links, also called *site root-relative links*, tell browsers how to get from one page to another within the same site, just as document-relative links do. But in this case, the link describes the path *relative to the site's root folder*—the folder that contains the home page and all your other site pages, folders, and files. (For a detailed description of the root folder and the structure of a website, see Chapter 16.)

Here's how a root-relative link works. Imagine you work in a big office building. You need to get to a coworker's office in the same building, so you call her for directions. She may not know the precise directions from your office to hers, but she *can* tell you how to get from the building's entrance to her office. Since you both know where the building's front door is, these directions work well. In fact, she can give everyone in the building the same directions and they'll be able to find her office, too (they all know where the entrance is). Think of the office building as your site, and its front door as the *root* of your site. Root-relative links always begin with a slash (/). This slash is a stand-in character for the root folder—the front door—of your site. The same root-relative link always leads to the same page, no matter where the link is on your website.

If you use Dreamweaver for all your web page development, you probably won't need root-relative links. Using document relative links, Dreamweaver does a great job of mapping the connections to all the pages and files on your site, with very little effort on your end. Still, on rare occasions, you may find it necessary to create root-relative links. For example, suppose your boss asks you to create a new page for an existing site. Your client gives you text, some graphics, and a list of the other pages on the site that this page needs to link to. The problem is, your client doesn't know where on the site the new page needs to go, and his webmaster won't return your calls.

Fortunately, you can use root-relative links to solve this dilemma. Since root-relative links work no matter where the page is on your site, you could complete the page and let the client put it wherever in her site, and the links will still work.

There's one major drawback to root-relative links: They don't work when you test them on your own computer. If you view a web page sitting on your computer's hard drive, clicking a root-relative link in your browser either doesn't work at all or produces only a "File not found" error. Root-relative links work only when their pages reside on a web server. That's because the technology behind web servers understands root-relative links, but your personal computer doesn't.

One solution to the root-relative links problem is to install a web server on your computer and put your site files inside it (see page 885). That's the approach you'll take when you build dynamic sites, discussed in Chapter 22.

UP TO SPEED

Parts of a URL

Each chunk of a URL helps a web browser locate the proper web page. Take the following URL, for instance: *http://www.cafesoylentgreen.com/events/index.html.* Many websites these days even leave off the www, and you can find them simply by their domain name, like *http://cafesoylentgreen.com.*

- **http://.** This portion of the address specifies the *protocol,* the communications technology a browser uses to interact with the web server. *HTTP* stands for *hypertext transfer protocol;* you use it to go to a web page. You use other protocols for other Web tasks, such as *ftp* when you want to transfer files to and from a server, and *mailto* when you want to send email messages to mail servers. *HTTPS* stands for hypertext transfer protocol secure, and you write it as https:// in the address bar of a browser. HTTPS requires a special server setup, and it encrypts the communications between a browser and a web server so snoops can't see the information you send and receive.

Bank websites, e-commerce sites, and other sites that deal with sensitive information use HTTPS web servers.

- **www.cafesoylentgreen.com.** This is the Web address of the computer dishing out the pages for Café Soylent Green's website—that is, it's the address of the web *server* where all the café's pages reside. The *www* part identifies a website within the *domain* cafesoylentgreen. com (*http://cafesoylentgreen.com*). You can have multiple websites in a single domain, such as *http://news. cafesoylentgreen.com, http://secret.cafesoylentgreen. com,* and so on.

- **/events/.** This is the name of a folder (also called a directory) on the web server.

- **index.html.** This is the name of the file the web browser will open—it's the filename of the web page itself, the HTML document you created in Dreamweaver.

NOTE There's one exception to the "root-relative links don't preview correctly" dilemma. Dreamweaver lets you preview a web page two ways: *with* a temporary file or *without* one. The temporary-file option has a couple of advantages: You can preview a page without having to save it first, and you can preview *on your local computer* any root-relative links on the page.

To turn this feature on, go to Edit→Preferences (Dreamweaver→Preferences), click the "Preview in Browser" category, and then turn on the Preview Using Temporary File checkbox. Behind the scenes, Dreamweaver rewrites root-relative links as *document-relative* links whenever it creates a temporary file. If you see files in your site with weird names like *TMP2zlc3mvs10.htm,* those are the temporary files Dreamweaver creates. Feel free to delete them.

Unless you have a specific reason to use root-relative links (like your IT department tells you to), avoid their pitfalls by sticking to document-relative links for your pages. But keep this discussion in mind. (Later in the book, you'll see that, behind the scenes, Dreamweaver's site management features use root-relative paths to track your site's files.)

NOTE You can run into trouble with root-relative links if the site you're working on is located in a folder inside a web server's root folder. For example, say your buddy gives you space on his web server. He says you can put your site in a folder called *my_friend*, so your URL is *http://www.my_buddy.com/my_friend/*. In this case, your web pages don't sit at the root of the site—they're in a folder *inside* the root. So a root-relative link to your home page would be */my_friend/index.html*. Dreamweaver can handle a situation like this, but only if you provide the correct URL for your site—*http://www.my_buddy.com/my_friend/*—when you set it up (see Figure 4-1).

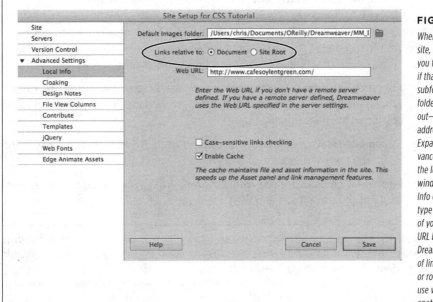

FIGURE 4-1

When you set up a new site, Dreamweaver asks you for the site's URL. Even if that address leads to a subfolder within your root folder, it's easy to figure out—it's the site's actual address on the Internet. Expand the list of Advanced Settings options on the left of the Site Setup window, click the Local Info category, and then type the full web address of your site in the Web URL box. You can also tell Dreamweaver which type of link—document-relative or root-relative—it should use when it points to another page on your site (circled). You can always return to this window to change this option. Choose Site→Manage Sites, select your site, and then click Edit.

Link Types in Action

Figure 4-2 shows a website as it appears on a hard drive: folders filled with HTML documents and graphics. Here's a closer look at some links you might find on those pages and how they might work.

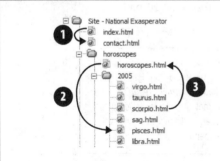

■ LINK FROM THE HOME PAGE TO THE CONTACT US PAGE (CONTACT.HTML)

Most websites use the filename *index.html* or *index.htm* for the home page. You can link from this page to the *contact.html* page—identified by the number 1 in Figure 4-2—using any of the three link types and these addresses:

- **Absolute link address: *http://www.nationalexasperator.com/contact.html*.** What it means: Go to the website at http://www.nationalexasperator.com and download the page contact.html.

- **Document-relative link address: *contact.html*.** What it means: Look in the folder the current page is in and download contact.html.

- **Root-relative link address: */contact.html*.** What it means: Go to the top-level folder of the current site and then download contact.html.

> **TIP** If you can write an absolute URL, you can easily write a root-relative URL. Simply strip off the *http://* and the web server name. In the example above, erasing the *http://www.nationalexasperator.com* in the absolute address leaves */contact.html*—the root-relative path.

■ LINK FROM THE HOROSCOPES PAGE TO THE PISCES PAGE

Now imagine you built a web page that you want to link to a page in a *subfolder* of your site. Here's how you'd use each of the three link types to do that (in this example, the subfolder's called "2005"), as identified by the number 2 in Figure 4-2:

- **Absolute link address: *http://www.nationalexasperator.com/horoscopes /2005/pisces.html*.** What it means: Go to the website *http://www.nationalex-asperator.com*, look in the Horoscopes folder, then look in the folder *2005*, and then download the page *pisces.html*.

- **Document-relative link address: *2005/pisces.html*.** What it means: From the current page, look in the folder *2005* and then download the page *pisces.html*.

- **Root-relative link address: */horoscopes/2005/pisces.html*.** What it means: Go to the top-level folder of this site, go to the Horoscopes folder, look in the folder 2005, and then download the page *pisces.html*.

■ LINK FROM THE SCORPIO PAGE TO THE HOROSCOPES PAGE

Now suppose you built a web page and stored it in a deeply nested folder, and you want to link it to a document outside of that folder, like link 3 in Figure 4-2:

- **Absolute link address: *http://www.nationalexasperator.com/horoscopes/horoscopes.html*.** What it means: Go to the website at *http://www.national-exasperator.com*, look in the Horoscopes folder, and then download the page *horoscopes.html*.

- **Document-relative link address: *../horoscopes.html*.** What it means: Go up one level—outside of the current folder—and download the page *horoscopes. html*. In website addresses, a slash (/) represents a folder or directory. The two dots (..) mean, "Go up one level," into the folder that contains the current folder. So to link to a page that's up two levels—for example, to link from *scorpio.html* to the home page (*index.html*)—you would use ../ twice, like this: *../../index.html*.

- **Root-relative link address: */horoscopes/horoscopes.html*.** What it means: Go to the top-level folder of this site, look in the folder Horoscopes, and then download the page *horoscopes.html*.

In short, use absolute URLs to link to pages *outside* your site folder, use document-relative links to link to pages *within your site*, and, unless you know what you're doing (or your IT department tells you to), avoid using root-relative links altogether.

■ Adding a Link

If all this talk of links gets you confused, don't worry. Links *are* confusing, making them one of the best reasons to use Dreamweaver. If you can navigate to a document on your own computer or anywhere on the Web, you can create a link to it in Dreamweaver.

Browsing for a File

To create a link from one page to another on your local website, use the Properties panel's "Browse for File" button (see Figure 4-3) or its keyboard shortcut Ctrl+L (⌘-L).

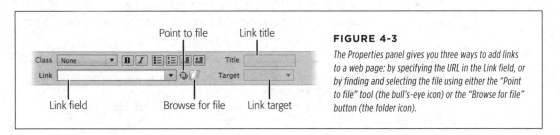

FIGURE 4-3

The Properties panel gives you three ways to add links to a web page: by specifying the URL in the Link field, or by finding and selecting the file using either the "Point to file" tool (the bull's-eye icon) or the "Browse for file" button (the folder icon).

To browse for a file in Dreamweaver, you use the same type of dialog box that you use to open or save a file, making "Browse for File" the easiest way to add a link. (To link to a page on another website, you need to type the web address into the Properties panel. Turn to page 176 for instructions.)

1. **In the document window, select the text or image you want to make a link.**

   For text links, you can select a single word, a sentence, or an entire paragraph. When you add a link to text, the selected words appear blue and underlined (depending on your visitors' web browser settings), like billions of links before them.

   You can turn a picture into a link, too—a great way to add attractive graphics-based navigation buttons. Your visitors will see the "pointing finger" icon when they mouse over the picture.

   NOTE When you add a link to an image, Internet Explorer 8 and earlier draws a blue border around the image, just like linked text has a blue underline. Fortunately, with some simple CSS, you can get rid of that blue outline by creating a CSS style for the <img> tag (see page 104 if you're unsure about creating styles). Under the Border category of the CSS Rule Definition window, set the border style to "none" (see page 238 for more information on CSS borders).

2. **In the Properties panel, click the folder icon (a.k.a. the "Browse for File" button), or choose Modify→Make Link, or press Ctrl+L (⌘-L).**

   Whichever command you use, the Select File dialog box opens (see Figure 4-4 for Windows, Figure 4-5 for Macs).

   TIP You can also use the Browse for File method when you work in Code view: Select the text and then press Ctrl+L (⌘-L).

3. **Navigate to and select the target file; that is, the file you want the link to open.**

   When you use the Browse for File technique, you can only specify a file that's part of your website—you can't "browse" to an external web page via the Browse for File dialog box, in other words—the file needs to reside in your local root folder (see the box on page 25) or in a folder therein. Why? Remember that, to a website, the root folder is like the edges of the known universe—nothing exists outside of it. If you try to link to a file *outside* the root folder—like to a file on your desktop—Dreamweaver tells you it's a problem and offers to copy the file to your root folder for you. Accept the offer.

   NOTE You can double-click the name of a file in the Select File dialog box and Dreamweaver selects the file *and* closes the Select File dialog box in one step.

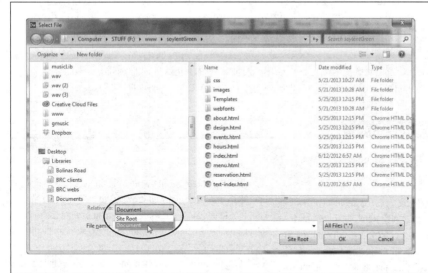

FIGURE 4-4

In Windows, use the Select File dialog box to identify a link's target file. When you initially set up a site, you can tell Dreamweaver whether to use document- or root-relative links. Later, if you find the need to temporarily switch to a different type of link (to a root-relative link if you set up your site to use document-relative links, for example), use the "Relative to" drop-down menu (circled).

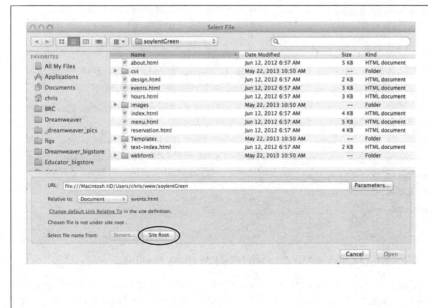

FIGURE 4-5

Every file in a website has to be somewhere inside a local root folder (see the box on page 25). This master folder holds all your site's files, including subfolders that hold yet other files. Because the site root is so central to site management, Dreamweaver includes a Site Root button (circled) in every window that requires selecting or saving a file. (This example shows a Mac window; on Windows PCs, the button's near the lower-right corner, as shown in Figure 4-4.) Click this button to jump straight to your site's root folder so you know exactly where you are on your hard drive, making it easy to navigate to the file you need.

4. **Make sure you select the correct type of link—document- or root-relative—from the "Relative to" drop-down menu.**

   As noted earlier, document-relative links are usually your best choice. Root-relative links don't work when you preview your site on your own computer. (They do, however, work once you move the pages to your web server.)

NOTE You can skip step 4; just set the type of link you want in the Site Setup window, and then forget about it. Dreamweaver always uses the link type you specify there. See Figure 4-1 for details.

The Mysterious Triple Slashes

Why do my links start with file:///?

Links that begin with *file:///* (*file:///C:/missingmanual/book_site/cafe/events.html*, for example) aren't valid links on the Web. Rather, they're temporary addresses that Dreamweaver creates as placeholders for links it will rewrite later. (A *file:/// path* tells Dreamweaver to look for the file on your computer.) You'll spot these addresses when you add document-relative links to a page you haven't saved, or when you work with files outside of your site's local root folder.

Suppose you're working on a web page that contains your company's legal mumbo-jumbo, but you haven't yet saved it. After adding a document-relative link to your home page, you notice that the Properties panel's Link field begins with *file:///*. Since you haven't saved your legal page, Dreamweaver doesn't know its folder location and can't create a relative link telling a browser where to go to get the page. So it creates a temporary link, which helps it keep track of which page to link to. Once you save the page somewhere on your site, Dreamweaver rewrites the link in proper document-relative format, and the temporary *file:///* link disappears.

Likewise, Dreamweaver can't write a "legitimate" link (a link that really *will* work in a web browser) to a file outside the local root folder. Since it considers anything beyond the root folder outside the bounds of the site, Dreamweaver can't write a link to "nowhere." So, if you save a page *outside* the local root folder, Dreamweaver writes all document-relative links on that page as file paths beginning with *file:///*. (This problem can also crop up if you use Dreamweaver without first setting up a site—that's why that simple site setup process, described on "Setting Up a Site", is so important.) To avoid this invalid link problem, always save your web pages inside the local root folder or in a folder *inside* the local root folder. (To learn more about root folders and websites, see Chapter 16.)

If you set up a site and link to a page—or add an image (Chapter 5)—that's stored outside your local root folder, Dreamweaver has the same problem. However, in this instance, Dreamweaver gives you the option of copying the out-of-bounds file to a location of your choosing within the root folder.

---

5. **Click OK (Windows) or Choose (Mac) to apply the link.**

   The text or image you made a link in step 3 now links to another web page. If you haven't yet saved the other web page in your site, Dreamweaver doesn't know how to write the document-relative link. Instead, it displays a dialog box saying that it will assign a temporary path for the link until you save the page—see the box above.

After you apply a link, the link text appears underlined and colored in Design view (using the color defined by the Page Properties window, shown in Figure 1-22). Press F12 (Option-F12 on Macs) to preview the page in your browser, where you can click the link.

Using the Point-to-File Tool

You can also create links by dragging an icon from the Properties panel to the Files panel (see Figure 4-6). If your site involves a lot of links, learning to use the Point-to-File tool will save you time and energy.

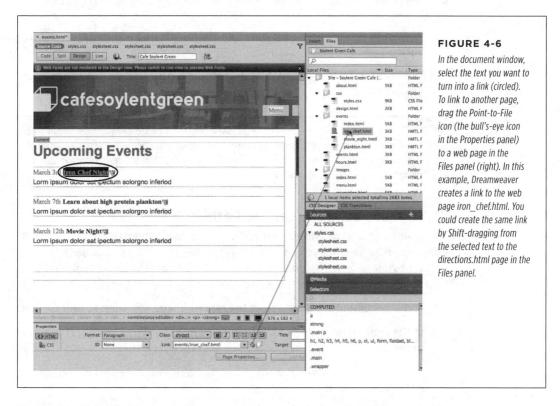

FIGURE 4-6

In the document window, select the text you want to turn into a link (circled). To link to another page, drag the Point-to-File icon (the bull's-eye icon in the Properties panel) to a web page in the Files panel (right). In this example, Dreamweaver creates a link to the web page iron_chef.html. You could create the same link by Shift-dragging from the selected text to the directions.html page in the Files panel.

To use this trick effectively, position your document window and Files panel side by side.

1. **In the document window, select the text or image you want to turn into a link.**

   Make sure you have both the Properties panel and Files panel open. To open the Properties panel, choose Window→Properties. To open the Files window, choose Window→Files. (Before using the Files window, you need to create a local site, as described on page 19.)

   NOTE The point-to-file tool works in Code view as well.

2. **Drag the Point-to-File icon from the Properties panel onto a web page in the Files window.**

Or Shift-drag the selected text or image in the document window to any web page in the Files panel, bypassing the Properties panel altogether (this method only works in Design view, however).

> **TIP** You can also drag a file from the Files panel into the Link box in the Properties panel to link to it. If you haven't selected any text, when you drag a file from the Files panel, Dreamweaver automatically adds its name as text. For example, if you drag "mysong.mp3" from the Files panel, that filename appears on the page.

3. **With your mouse hovering over the right web page, release the mouse button.**

The selected text or image in your web page now links to the file you just pointed to.

> **NOTE** Bizarre Bug Alert: If you use two monitors as you build web pages, the Point-to-File icon might not work. If your main monitor (the one with the Start menu for Windows, or the one where a program's menu bar appears on Macs) is on the right, and the second monitor is on the left, the Point-to-File icon may not work. Then again, it might! Strange, but truly infuriating.

Typing (or Pasting) a URL or Path

If you need to link to another website, or you feel comfortable working with document-relative links, you can simply type the URL to the target page into the Properties panel. Note that this technique and the hyperlink object tool discussed next are the *only* ways to add links to pages *outside* your website.

1. **In the document window, select the text or image you want to make a link.**

2. **In the Properties panel's Link field (Figure 4-3), type the URL (the path) to the file.**

If the link leads to another website, type an absolute URL—that is, a complete web address, starting with *http://*.

> **TIP** An easier approach is to copy a complete URL—including the *http://* part—from the address bar in your browser window and paste it into the Link field.

To link to a page on your own site, type a document-relative link (see page 170 for some examples). Letting Dreamweaver write the correct path using the point-to-file or browsing technique described above is a good way to avoid typos. But typing the path name can come in handy when, say, you want to create a link to a page you haven't yet created, but know its eventual URL.

3. Press Enter (Return) to apply the link.

While you don't necessarily have to hit Enter (Return)—sometimes you can just click elsewhere on the page and keep working—Dreamweaver has been known to forget the link and not apply it. This is true for most fields in the Properties panel. So if you type information directly into the Properties panel (to create a link, add a title, and so on), get into the habit of hitting the Enter (Return) key to make sure your change sticks.

NOTE If you add an absolute link to a website without specifying a web page, add a final forward slash (/) to the end of the address. For example, to link to Yahoo, type *http://www.yahoo.com/*. The final slash tells the web server that you're requesting the default page (the home page) at Yahoo.com.

Although leaving out the slash works, too (*http://www.yahoo.com*), the server has to do a little extra work to figure out which page to send back, resulting in a slight and unnecessary delay.

Also include the final slash when you link to the default page inside a folder on a site, like this: *http://oreilly.com/ missingmanuals/*. That saves the browser from first requesting a file named *missingmanuals*, and then requesting the default page inside the folder "missingmanuals."

Using the Hyperlink Object

Dreamweaver gives you yet another way to add a link. The Hyperlink object in the Common category of the Insert panel (Figure 4-7) lets you insert a link with many optional properties. Its only real benefit is that it lets you add text and a link in one step (instead of adding text to a page, selecting it, and then specifying a link address). Unfortunately, this tool only works with text (not graphics), and some of the optional properties don't work in all browsers.

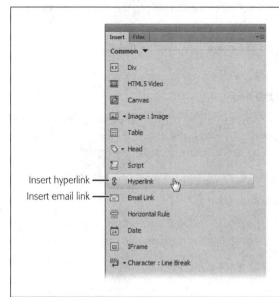

FIGURE 4-7

The Insert panel's Common category offers one-button access to creating hyperlinks and email links (to link to an email address).

Insert hyperlink

Insert email link

Here's how you add a hyperlink.

1. **Click the spot on a web page where you want to insert the hyperlink, or select a section of text (or the image) that you want to turn into a hyperlink.**

   Let your cursor sit there for a minute.

2. **Choose Insert→Hyperlink, or click the chain icon on the Insert→Common toolbar.**

   The Hyperlink dialog box opens (see Figure 4-8).

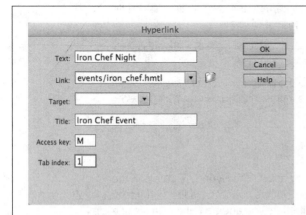

FIGURE 4-8

As an alternative to using this dialog box, you can apply all the settings you see here, except the "Access key" and "Tab index" properties (see steps 6 and 7 below), to existing text or images from the Properties panel. Also, keep in mind one somewhat special case. If you want to add an access key and tab index to an existing link, you have a couple of options: Go into Code view (as described in Chapter 7) and hand-edit the HTML.

3. **In the Text box, type the label for your link (that is, the link's text).**

   Whatever you type here is what you'll see on the page, and what your audience will click to follow the link. If you selected existing text on the page, Dreamweaver displays that text in the Text box automatically.

4. **Click the folder icon and find the page you want to link to.**

   Alternatively, type a URL in the Link box.

5. **Set the target window for the link.**

   If you want the linked page to open in the current window—as most linked pages do—don't select anything. To make the page open in a new window, select *_blank* (see the box on page 179 for more on targeting links).

   The last three options—Title, Access key, and Tab index—are more interesting.

6. **Type a title for the destination page.**

   This is optional. Most browsers display page titles in a small tooltip window when a visitor mouses over the associated link, as described in the box on page 170.

Targeting and Titling Links

What purpose do the Title box and Target menu in the Properties panel serve?

A link's *Title* property supplies additional information about a link, usually to clearly indicate where the link leads. For example, if you linked the words "Click here for more" to an article describing different types of termites, the link text doesn't explain where the link leads—"Click for more *of what?*" you might ask. In this case, you could, in the Properties panel, add the title "A complete list of termite species" to the page (see Figure 4-3). The Title property is optional, and if your link text already tells you where the link leads, don't bother setting it. In fact, you can avoid thinking about the Title property altogether if you write text that explains where the link leads: "Click here for a complete list of termite species," for example.

However, in the case of linked images (such as a logo that also acts as a link back to a site's home page), adding a title is a very good idea. Search engines like the Title property, because it lets them know the purpose of the link; people who use screen readers (programs that help those with vision problems surf the Web) also benefit, since the Title property can be read out loud and the visitor will know where the link goes. The Title property has one other unique feature: Web browsers display a drop-down tooltip with the title's text in it when a guest moves her mouse over the link.

The *Target* menu has nothing to do with the accuracy of your links, nor with shooting ranges. It deals with how a browser displays the destination page when you click a link. You can have the new page (a) replace the current page in the browser window (the way most links work); (b) open in a new browser window (choose the *_blank* option); or (c) appear in a different *frame* on the same page (an obsolete HTML feature).

_blank is pretty much the only option used these days, but be careful if your pages use the Strict forms of HTML 4.01 and XHTML 1.0; the Target attribute isn't valid code for these doctypes. However, HTML5, recognizing the usefulness of being able to open links in a new tab or window, allows the *_blank* target... and so does every browser on the planet.

7. **Type a key in the "Access key" box.**

An *access key* lets you trigger a link from your keyboard. For example, if you type *h* in the link's "Access key" box, a visitor using Google Chrome for Windows can press Alt+H to mouselessly open the link. Of course, unless your visitors are psychic, you should tell them about the access key next to the link itself, as in "Home Page (Alt+H)."

To actually use access keys requires a little computer-savvy on the part of your visitors. In addition to knowing they can use an access key, they need to know how to use an access key with their browser. The key combinations are different depending on the browser and the operating system, and in the past, browsers were all over the place as to the key combinations. It's a little more uniform with the latest batch of browsers. Here's the rundown on current Windows browsers:

- Alt+ the access key works in Google Chrome, Safari, and Opera.
- Alt+ the access key + Enter for Internet Explorer.
- Alt+Shift+ the access key works on Firefox.

Recently, Mac browsers have achieved a little consistency:

- Control+Option+ the access key for Safari (version 4+), Chrome, Firefox, and Opera.

8. **In the "Tab index" box, type a number for the tab order.**

In most browsers, you can press the Tab key to step through the links on a page (and boxes on a form). This feature not only gives you a handy way to go from link to link from your keyboard, it also lets people who can't use a mouse due to disabilities cycle through the links.

Normally when you press Tab, web browsers highlight the links in the order they appear in the page's HTML. The Tab index, by contrast, lets *you* control the order in which links light up. For example, you can give your navigation buttons priority when someone presses Tab, even if those buttons aren't the first links on the page.

For the link that you want first in the Tab order, type *1* in the "Tab index" box. Number the other links in the order you want the Tab key to trigger them. If you aren't concerned about the order of a particular link, leave this option blank or type *0*. The web browser highlights that link after the visitor tabs through all the links that *do* have a Tab index.

EXTENSION ALERT

QuickLink Is Quick Work

Dreamweaver makes it easy to add innovative commands and tools—including those written by independent, non-Adobe programmers—to the program. You can read a lot more about these add-on programs, called *extensions*, in Chapter 21.

When you work with links, one extension that really comes in handy is QuickLink (*http://tinyurl.com/3cquzkl*). Created by Dreamweaver guru Tom Muck, this extension instantly turns text into either a *mailto* or an *absolute* URL. Amazingly, even though this extension hasn't been updated since Dreamweaver MX 2004, it still works in CC.

Once you install the extension, here's how it works: Suppose you insert your cursor somewhere on a web page in Dreamweaver and type the text, "You can download the free PDF viewer at *http://www.adobe.com*." While that may look like a link, at this point is just plain text on the web page. To turn *http://www.adobe.com* into a link, you can either select the text, go to the Properties panel, and then type *http://www. adobe.com*, or—with QuickLink—simply select the text and choose Commands→QuickLink. QuickLink writes the proper code in the Properties panel, including the initial (and mandatory) *http://*, even if those characters were missing from the original text. (Note that this extension has one small bug: After you install it, the QuickLink command will appear *twice* in the Commands menu. Either one works.)

QuickLink also converts email addresses to proper *mailto* links: Just select the email address (*missing@sawmac.com*, say), apply the QuickLink command, and watch as the extension automatically inserts the correct code (mailto: *missing@ sawmac.com*) into your page.

For even faster action, create a keyboard shortcut for this command, like Shift+Ctrl+L. (See page 869 for more on keyboard shortcuts.)

■ Adding an Email Link

If you want to invite your site visitors to contact you, an *email link* is the perfect solution. When someone clicks an email link, his email program automatically launches, and a new, empty message opens with your email address already in the To field. Your guest can then just type his message and click Send.

Consider the email link *mailto:chef@cafesoylentgreen.com*. The first part of any email link, *mailto*, indicates the type of link (an email link in this case), while the second part (*chef@cafesoylentgreen.com*) specifies the email address.

NOTE Email links work only if the person who clicks the link has an email program set up and running on his computer. If someone visits your site from a computer at the public library, for example, he might not be able to send mail. Likewise, if he's using a web-based email client, like Gmail, clicking an email link won't open his Gmail page in a web browser.

You create an email link the same way you create any other Dreamweaver link: by selecting text or an image and typing the *mailto* address in the Properties panel's Link field, as shown above. Dreamweaver offers a shortcut, too:

1. **Type in or select the text you want to turn into a link.** *Email me!* or *Email the webmaster* are good options.

    You have to have something to link from, right?

2. **Under the Insert panel's Common category, click the "Email link" icon, which looks like an envelope (see Figure 4-7).**

    Alternatively, choose Insert→Email Link. The Email Link dialog box opens (see Figure 4-9).

FIGURE 4-9

The Email Link dialog box lets you specify the text for the email link label and the email address itself. You can also select text in your document and click the Email Link icon on the Objects panel. The text you selected will appear in the Text field in this dialog box.

3. **Check the Text field. The word or phrase you highlighted in step 1 should appear here.**

    You can edit the link label if you like.

4. **Type an email address in the Email field.**

This is the address that appears in your visitors' email program when they click the link. (You don't have to type *mailto*—Dreamweaver adds it automatically.)

5. **Click OK.**

Dreamweaver makes the *mailto* link active.

> **NOTE** Some people don't add email links to their websites because they're afraid of spammers' automated programs that search the web and collect email addresses. There are some tricks to fool these "spambots," but spammers have figured most of them out. The fact is, spammers can attack even "Contact Us" web forms.
>
> If you're absolutely obsessed with never being spammed, leave your email address off your site. However, many businesses rely on people contacting them for more information, and the harder you make it for a legitimate visitor to contact you, the fewer legitimate contacts you'll receive—after all, you wouldn't have much of a freelance design business if you never provided a way for someone to contact you. Your best bet is to let the spam come, but add a spam filter to your email program to separate the wheat from the chaff.

■ Linking Within a Web Page

Clicking a link usually loads a web page in a browser window, but what if you want to link to a specific *spot* on the *same* page? You see this technique used frequently on long web pages, like FAQs, where links at the top of the page let visitors jump to specific content lower on the page; see Figure 4-10. You create this type of link by adding an HTML tag to the target section of the destination page, giving it a unique ID and then linking to that ID. Although this method is newer, it works with all current web browsers.

> **NOTE** If you've been building web pages for a while, you're probably familiar with the "named anchor" technique for creating in-page links. That method uses an <a> anchor tag with a name attribute. Because the named anchor isn't used in HTML5, Dreamweaver no longer offers the Insert→Named Anchor command. Instead of named anchors, use the ID method described here.

Adding an ID to a Target Page

To link to a specific spot in a destination page, assign an ID to that spot. For example, if you want to link to a subhead way down on a page (a Heading 2, or <h2> tag, for example), you can assign an ID to that heading. For text, you add an ID by clicking anywhere inside a paragraph and, in the Properties panel's ID box, typing the ID name you want to use. (Keep in mind that you can't use spaces or punctuation marks.)

For non-text elements, like images or tables, select the tag (the Tag Selector discussed on page 7 is the best way), and type a name in the ID box on the left side of the Properties panel.

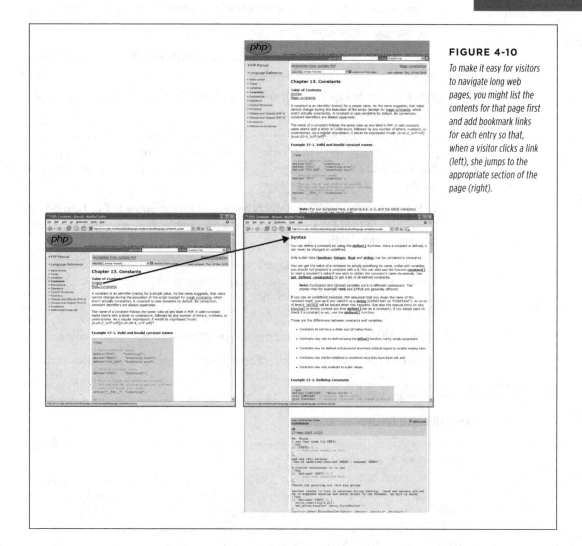

FIGURE 4-10

To make it easy for visitors to navigate long web pages, you might list the contents for that page first and add bookmark links for each entry so that, when a visitor clicks a link (left), she jumps to the appropriate section of the page (right).

You might use IDs in another context, too: to identify and style discrete sections of your page by adding an ID to a tag and then styling the page using CSS (see page 120 for more on ID styles). The good news is you can use that same ID to both identify the destination point in a target page *and* to style the tag in a style sheet.

Linking to an ID

Once you add an ID to a tag, creating a link to that ID from within the same web page or from a different page isn't all that different from linking to a web page.

To link to an ID on the same page:

1. **In the document window, select the text or image you want to turn into a link.**

   For example, drag across some text, or highlight a graphic.

2. **In the Properties panel's Link field, type #, followed by the ID name you chose.**

   The # sign indicates that the link points to an ID. So, to link to an ID named *directions*, you'd type *#directions*.

You can also link from one web page to a particular location on *another* web page. First, you need to add an ID to the destination page. Then, follow the same process you followed to link to a same-page ID, except that you have to specify not only the ID, but the path to the web page as well.

1. **In the document window, select the text or image you want to turn into a link. Then, in the Link field of the Properties panel, type or choose the URL or path to the destination page.**

   You can use any of the methods described above: browsing, point-to-file, or typing in the path name. Unfortunately, if you browse to select the destination page, Dreamweaver doesn't display any of the IDs on that page, so you need to type in the ID's name as explained in the next step.

2. **Click at the end of the URL or path. Type # followed by the ID's name.**

   In the end, the Link field should look something like this: *contact.html#directions*.

FREQUENTLY ASKED QUESTION

Where Bookmarks Fall Short

When I click a link to a bookmark, the web browser is supposed to go to the page and display the bookmark or the tag with the specified ID at the top of the browser window. But sometimes the linked-to spot appears in the middle of the browser. What's that about?

Web browsers can't scroll beyond the bottom of a web page, so if you have a bookmark ID near the bottom of a page, the browser can't pull the page all the way up to that particular point.

If one of your own web pages exhibits this problem and it really bothers you, the fix is simple: Create a style for the <body> tag and add *bottom padding* (page 58). This adds space after the last bit of content on the page, so browsers can scroll the page all the way to the bookmark.

■ Modifying a Link

At some point, you may need to change or edit a link. Perhaps the URL you were linking to has changed, or you simply no longer need that link.

Changing a Link's Destination

As you'll read in Part 4 of this book, Dreamweaver provides some amazing tools for automatically updating links on your pages so that your site keeps working, even if you move files around. But even Dreamweaver isn't smart enough to know when a page on someone *else's* website has been moved or deleted. And you may decide you simply need to change a link so that it points to a different page on your own site. In both cases, you need to edit the links by hand:

1. **Select the text or picture link.**

   The link path appears in the Properties panel's Link field.

2. **Use any of the techniques described on page 171 to specify the link's new target.**

   For example, click the "Browse for File" button in the Properties panel and locate a different web page on your site, or type a complete URL that points to a page outside your site.

Removing a Link

Sometimes, you want to stop a link from linking—when the web page you were pointing to no longer exists, for example. You want to keep the originating text or image, but remove the outdated link. In that case, select the link text or image and then use one of these tactics:

- Choose Modify→Remove Link, or press Ctrl+Shift+L (⌘-Shift-L).

- Delete the text in the Link field of the Properties panel and then press Enter (Return).

The text or image remains on your web page, but it no longer links to anything. If it's a text link, the color changes from your site's link color to the normal text color for the page.

Of course, if you're feeling particularly destructive, you can delete the link's text or image itself, which simultaneously deletes the link.

■ Styling Links

You can control the basic look of links from the Links category of the Page Properties window (Figure 4-11). To open it, choose Modify→Page Properties→Links (CSS), press Ctrl+J (⌘-J)→Links (CSS), or click the Page Properties button in the Properties panel (the button appears only when you have either nothing on the page selected or you have text selected; it doesn't appear if you have an image selected). In the Category list, click "Links (CSS)."

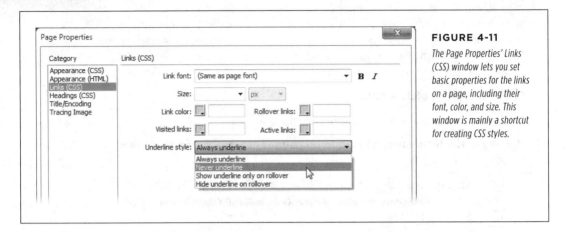

FIGURE 4-11

The Page Properties' Links (CSS) window lets you set basic properties for the links on a page, including their font, color, and size. This window is mainly a shortcut for creating CSS styles.

The top set of options—font, size, bold, italic—sets the basic format for every link on the page. The next group of options sets the color of the links under specific conditions. Web browsers keep track of how a visitor interacts with the links on a page, such as when you move your mouse over a link. Each link has four modes (called *states*): a plain, unvisited link is simply called a *link*; a link that a visitor has already clicked (determined by your guest's browser history) is called a *visited* link; a link that a guest's mouse is currently pointing to is technically called a *hover* state, though Dreamweaver refers to it as a *rollover* state; and a link in the process of being clicked (where a visitor has pressed but not released his mouse button) is known as an *active* link.

You can style each type of link individually. In most web browsers, a plain link appears blue until you visit the linked page—then the link turns purple. This helpful color-coding lets a visitor know whether to follow a link: "Hey, there's a page I haven't seen," or, "Been there, done that."

The rollover (or hover) link is useful in telling visitors they can click the link because it provides visual feedback, and it lends itself to a lot of creative potential. For example, you can change the link's color when a visitor mouses over it add a background image, or change its background color. (To get neat effects like these, you need to go beyond the Page Properties window and set styles for your links via CSS, as described next.)

Finally, an *active* link is for that fleeting moment when a visitor clicks a link but has yet to release the mouse button. It happens so fast that it's usually not worth spending too much time formatting the state.

NOTE Internet Explorer applies the active link style to any link a visitor *tabs* to (some web surfers can't, or don't want to, use a mouse, so they rely on the keyboard to navigate websites). Firefox, Safari, Opera, and Chrome use yet another link state, called *focus*, to style links that someone reaches via the Tab key. See the note on page 188 for more on a link's focus state.

The Page Properties window lets you change the color of each link state. In addition, the "Underline style" menu lets you control whether a browser underlines a link (the default), displays nothing beneath the link, displays an underline when a guest mouses over the link, or underlines the link by default but removes it once a visitor mouses over it. Since web surfers are accustomed to thinking of underlined text as a big "Click Me" sign, think twice before removing underlines from links. Without some clear indication that the text is a link, visitors may never see (or click) the links on your page.

One problem with using the Page Properties window to style links is that the settings apply only to the current page. That's because the Page Properties window saves the CSS styles to an internal style sheet in the current page. Fortunately, you don't need to set the Page Properties on every page of your site; you can export those styles or even drag them into an external style sheet. (To learn how, see page 377.) Alternatively, you can bypass the Page Properties window altogether and create CSS link styles from scratch—which you'll learn about next.

CSS and Links

Using CSS Designer to style your links gives you access to many more formatting options besides the font, color, and size options that Page Properties gives you. In fact, CSS Designer lets you apply nearly every CSS property to links. For example, you can use all the text options discussed on page 140—font size, weight, variant, letter spacing, and so on—to format a link. In addition, you can add a border (page 56) and a background color to a link to make it look like a button.

To format the look of all your links, create a tag style (page 102) for the <a> tag (the tag that creates links) using the instructions on page 104. To create a different look for a particular link (if you want that "Buy Now!" link to be bigger and bolder than other links on a page, for example), create a class style (page 102) and apply it to that link.

To control how a link looks for different states (link, visited, hover, and active), you need to dip a little deeper into the CSS pool and use what's called a *pseudo-class*. As you may remember, a selector is merely the part of a style that instructs a browser where to apply the style—*h1* is the selector for formatting every Heading 1, for example. When you work with links, it's all about the <a> tag, so you want to find and choose the *a* selector in CSS Designer's Selector section. In CSS, you distinguish pseudo classes from selectors by using a colon between the two. So in a style sheet, the four pseudo classes for the *a* link look like this: *a:link*, *a:visited*, *a:hover*, and *a:active*. It's easy to create a selector and pseudo classes in CSS Designer because a pop-up menu prompts you with valid classes as soon as you type in the colon (see Figure 4-12).

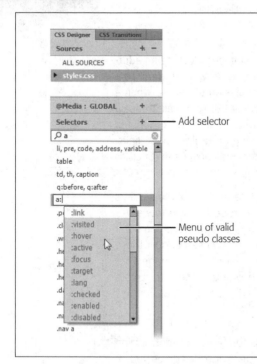

— Add selector

— Menu of valid
pseudo classes

FIGURE 4-12

Create a selector for <a> tags by clicking Add Selector (the + sign button) and then typing "a." To add a pseudo class to the selector, type a colon (:). As soon as you do, a pop-up menu appears with the names of valid pseudo classes. All you need to do is click. The first three are the most common pseudo classes used with links: link, visited, and hover.

You don't have to set all four pseudo-classes; if you're not interested in how your link looks during the nanosecond that a visitor clicks it, skip the *a:active* option. If you want to set more than one pseudo-class, you must create them in the order that they appear in the pop-up Class menu, or the styles may not display as you intend them. In CSS Designer's Selectors section, that means your pseudo-classes should be in this order, from the top: *a:link*, *a:visited*, *a:hover*, and, if you're using it, *a:active*. (A helpful mnemonic for remembering this rule is LoVe HAte—that is, *:link* comes before *:visited*, which comes before *:hover*, which comes before *:active*.) If your links are in the wrong order in Selectors, move them. Click the source in CSS Designer's Sources section, and then, in Selectors, click and drag your selectors and their pseudo classes to the proper position. This actually rearranges the code in the style sheet.

NOTE Safari, Firefox, and Chrome browsers understand an additional pseudo-class related to links: *a:focus*. This selector applies when a visitor uses the Tab key to move from one link to another on a page. Each time she jumps to a new link, the browser highlights it and gives the link "focus." All versions of IE treat *a:active* as if it were *a:focus*.

To create a style that formats a link when a visitor tabs to it (instead of mouses over it), create what's called a group style. Here's how: When you create the "highlighted" link style, choose Compound for the selector type. For the selector name, type in *a:focus, a:active*. This highlights the "tabbed to" link in all current browsers.

Using these styles, you can make your link text appear red and underscored before a visitor clicks the link, twice as large when he mouses over it, purple and boldfaced when he clicks it, and pale pink after he visits the linked site. (Granted, if you try this design, Martha Stewart may never hire you to design her site, but you get the point.)

> **NOTE** For security reasons, current browsers limit the styling you apply to a visited link to just a different color. In other words, say you create the pseudo-class style *a:visited* and change the font, font-size, background-color, underline, and set its text color to red; the only visual change the browser will make to a visited link is to change its text color to red—browsers simply ignore the font, background-color, and other settings.

Note that these link pseudo-classes have one drawback: Setting them affects *all* the links on a page. In that respect, adding pseudo-classes to the <a> tag is like creating tag styles.

To apply a style to only certain links on a page, you need to create a class and then create CSS rules to style the class and its pseudo classes, like link and hover. For example, to create a special look for the text link "Buy Now!", create a selector called *.buynow:link* in CSS Designer. The class, *.buynow*, has the pseudo class *:link* tacked onto it. To make that link look different when someone mouses over it, create a *.buynow:hover* selector. Naturally, you need to create the style rules that go along with the *.buynow* class and its pseudo classes. You can change the color, size, style, and other properties for the text to make the link stand out. To do that, follow the steps for creating a style on page 157. Once you define the style, all you need to do is apply the *.buynow* class to the text on your page. You can do that easily in the Properties panel's Class menu. Check your work in Live view and you'll see the link with the *.buynow* class applied.

> **NOTE** Descendent selectors provide a more efficient—but more complex—way to format specific links differently from all the other links on a page. You'll find this CSS concept discussed in "Descendent Selectors" on page 370.

Creating a Navigation Menu Tutorial

Every website should have navigation links that let visitors quickly jump to different sections of a site. On a shopping site, for example, those links might point to the categories of products for sale—books, DVDs, CDs, electronics, and so on. For a corporate intranet, links to human resources, office policies, company events, and each department might be important. Whatever the site, you should strive to get visitors where they want to go via the shortest route possible. Navigation menus are a good solution, because everyone using a computer is familiar with them.

Dreamweaver CC doesn't have a built-in system for building navigation menus, but with the help of some third-party tools, you can easily do so. Some menus rely on JavaScript and its jQuery plug-in, while others use only CSS to work their magic.

Most, however, use HTML unordered lists to create a hierarchy of menus, submenus, and menu items. (For details on unordered lists, see page 85.) That makes it easy to add and remove menu items over time, and keeps the structure of the menu separate from its formatting.

Getting a CSS Menu System from Adobe Exchange

The tutorial in this chapter uses a menu-builder called Advanced CSS Menu Light from Ajatix (Menu Light for short). There are a number of menu creators out there, but this one is available from Adobe Exchange, which means it's easy to get and install. Ajatix offers a few menu builders, but this one is everyone's favorite price—free.

Follow these steps to download and install Advanced CSS Menu Light from Adobe Exchange:

1. **Choose Window→Extensions→Adobe Exchange.**

   The Adobe Exchange panel opens. Four buttons at the top filter the extensions displayed. For example, you can limit the list to extensions that are free or to those that you have to pay to use.

2. **Click Free.**

   The panel displays no-cost extensions. At this point you may see Advanced CSS Menu Light in the list of extensions. If not, take the next step.

3. **In the Search box (upper-right) type *CSS Menu*, as shown in Figure 4-13.**

   Extensions related to CSS and menus appear in the list.

4. **Click Advanced CSS Menu Light.**

   Details about Advanced CSS Menu Light fill the panel. If you want more information, explore the Info, Previews, Notes, and Reviews sections.

5. **Click the blue Free button.**

   The Exchange displays a warning telling you to save your work, because Dreamweaver may need to close to install the extension. This is good advice even though downloading and installing this extension doesn't usually require a Dreamweaver restart. But you do usually need to restart Dreamweaver before you can *use* extensions.

6. **Click OK to close the warning.**

   The download and installation begins. An "Installing" message and graphic appears in the panel. When the installation is complete, a dialog box reports "Installation successful."

FIGURE 4-13

Adobe Exchange is your tool for finding and installing Dreamweaver extensions like Advanced CSS Menu Light. To browse the extensions, use the All, Paid, and Free buttons. To search for a specific one, type a couple of keywords in the Search box. Once you find an interesting candidate, click to see more details.

7. **Click OK to close the Info box. Then close the Adobe Exchange panel.**

   You've installed the extension in Dreamweaver. To double-check, see the next step.

8. **Restart Dreamweaver and then go to the Insert panel and open the Categories menu, as shown in Figure 4-14.**

   The Ajatix group appears at the bottom of the menu. In that category, you see Advanced CSS Drop Down Menu Light. The command to launch Menu Light also appears in the Insert menu (Insert→Ajatix→Advanced CSS Drop Down Menu Light), but you need to restart Dreamweaver before you can see it.

NOTE   In Adobe Exchange, the name for this extension is "Advanced CSS Menu Light," but once it is installed on your computer, the name in the Insert panel is the wordier "Advanced CSS Drop Down Menu Light." They are actually the same thing.

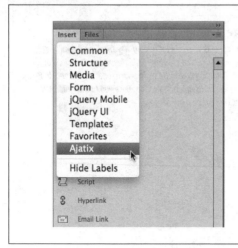

FIGURE 4-14

After you download and install Menu Light, you see Ajatix listed as one of your Insert panel categories. Click it and you'll see Advanced CSS Drop Down Menu Light, ready for your projects.

Adding a Menu with Submenus

The first step in inserting a menu is deciding where on the page to put it. A horizontal menu bar, with buttons sitting side by side, works well either at the very top of a page or below the area dedicated to a logo (often called a "banner"; see Figure 4-15). A vertical menu bar, whose buttons are stacked one on top of the other, usually sits at the left edge of a page, below the banner area.

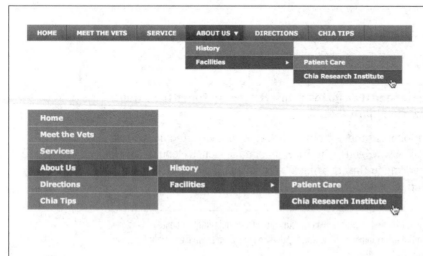

FIGURE 4-15

Menu builders like Advanced CSS Menu Light usually let you choose between a horizontal (top) or vertical (bottom) navigation bar for your website. Drop-down submenus let you cram loads of links into a small space, but be merciful to your visitors: Navigating a rat's maze to reach a link in a sub-submenu is sometimes a tiring test of patience and hand-mouse coordination.

In the next steps, you'll create a menu with submenus for the imaginary Chia Vet web site. You can follow along, or change the item names for your own nefarious purposes. These steps assume you've already downloaded and installed the menu builder described in the previous section.

Here are the steps to build a menu using Advanced CSS Menu Light:

1. **Start with a web page you've already named and saved. In the document window, click the spot where you want to insert the menu.**

   You can add a menu bar in either Design view or Code view, but it's easier to position it in Design view.

2. **In the Insert panel (Window→Insert), click the Categories menu, and then click Ajatix.**

   The Insert panel shows extensions from Ajatix that you can use in document-building. If you installed Menu Light as described on page 190, you see it listed here as Advanced CSS Drop Down Menu Light. If you have other products from the company, they appear here, too.

3. **Double-click Advanced CSS Drop Down Menu Light.**

   Menu Light opens its Start Wizard, offering two choices, "Create a new menu" and "Insert an existing menu."

4. **Choose "Create a new menu," and then click OK.**

   Menu Light replaces the Start Wizard with a Select Theme panel. The box on the left shows a number of themes of different styles. Horizontal menus top the list, while vertical menus appear near the bottom.

5. **In the left-hand box, click "Horizontal – Leaf Green," and then click Apply (lower-right corner).**

   As you click theme names on the left, Menu Light previews them on the right. Once you choose a theme that has the color, font, and styles you want, click Apply. Menu Light closes the Select Theme window and opens yet another window, the New Menu window (Figure 4-16). This window is worth getting to know because you use it to build your menu link by link. And later, when you need to make changes to an existing menu, you use a very similar control panel.

TIP If you want to insert an incomplete menu in a page to serve as a placeholder, you can do that now. Click OK, then give your menu a name and click Save. A menu bar appears in your document with a single item named Unnamed. With your placeholder menu on the page, you can come back later and build your menu by adding items, submenus, and all the trimmings, as explained on page 196.

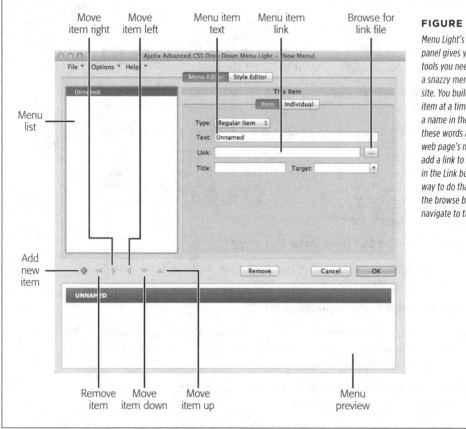

Move item right

Move item left

Menu item text

Menu item link

Browse for link file

Menu list

Add new item

Remove item

Move item down

Move item up

Menu preview

FIGURE 4-16

Menu Light's New Menu panel gives you all the tools you need to create a snazzy menu for your site. You build one menu item at a time by adding a name in the Text box; these words appear on the web page's menu. Then, add a link to another page in the Link box. The best way to do that is to click the browse button and navigate to the page.

6. **In the box labeled Text, type *Home*.**

   The words you type in the Text box are the words that will appear in the menu. For this first menu item, change the word "Unnamed" to "Home." As you type, Menu Light adds your new item to the list on the left and changes the preview at the bottom to read "Home. "

7. **In the Link box, type *index.html*.**

   You can type in any valid link. For this example, it makes sense to type *index. html* because that's the standard name for a website's home or default page. However, the best way to add most links is to click the Browse button ("...") next to the Link box and browse your way to the destination page. That creates a link with the proper path and no typos!

   At a minimum, you should provide a label and URL for your menu items. As explained in the box on page 179, you don't have to add a title or target. In fact, ignore the target option unless you want the linked page to open in a new browser window. Fill in a title for the link if you feel the need to provide a better description than the one in the Text box. Titles benefit people with screen readers and they can give you a boost with search engines. In this example, we'll add a title.

8. **In the Title box, type *Welcome to Chia Vet.***

   For most browsers, this message appears as a tooltip that pops up when someone mouses over a menu item. Screen readers read these words aloud to visitors, and some search engines read and evaluate these words when ranking a page.

9. **Click the + sign button on the left side of the panel.**

   That adds a new menu item. The functions for the other buttons on this row are pretty easy to figure out. The – sign button removes an item from the list, while the arrow buttons move items up and down, and in- and outdents them. The details are on page 194.

10. **For the new menu item, change "Unnamed" to "About Us" in the Text box. Then, type *about.html* in the Link box. In the Title box, type *More Info about Chia Vet.***

    It's just that easy to create a second menu item, complete with a link and title. In the next step, you'll add a submenu to About Us.

11. **Click the + sign button on the left side of the panel. Below the menu list, click the right arrow button (the Move Item Right button).**

    When you click the + sign button, a new Unnamed item appears below About Us. When you click the Move Item Right button, the Unnamed item shifts to the right in the list. In preview, a down arrow (triangle) appears next to About Us—a standard indication that this menu includes a submenu. If you mouse over About Us, you see the submenu with one "Unnamed item" listed.

    Using the arrows below the menu list (Figure 4-16), move items from one place to another in the list. Moving items up and down changes their position in the list. You see the results immediately in the preview at the bottom. To create a submenu or to add an item to a submenu, click the right arrow button. The left arrow button removes an item from a submenu, bumping it up a level. If it's the last item in the submenu, it removes the submenu.

12. **With "Unnamed item" selected in the list, type *History* in the Text box and then type *history.html* as the link.**

    The submenu item now has both a title and a link. Continue adding items and submenus as needed.

13. **When you're done, click OK.**

    The "Save Menu As" box appears where you name the menu.

14. **Type *NavChiaVet* and then click Save.**

You use the CSS filename *NavChiaVet.css* to add this same menu to other pages on your site. When you click Save, Menu Light creates two new files in your site's root folder. The file *NavChiaVet.css* formats the menu and its items. The file *NavChiaVet.ajm* is an Ajatix proprietary file (.ajm) that stores information about the menu you just created. Dreamweaver uses this information when you add the menu to other web pages.

You won't need to edit these files, so don't worry about them too much, but don't move or delete them, either. If you do, your menus won't work as expected.

Once you finish a menu, you'll see something like the menu shown in Figure 4-18. It may include several submenus, like the About Us and Facilities menus do here. Naturally, you'll adapt the actual menu to match your project. Page 216 explains how to add an existing CSS menu to another page. The next section explains how to make changes to your menu after you create it.

FREQUENTLY ASKED QUESTION

Who's on First: Pages or Menus?

Should I create my navigation system before I create my pages?

This is a typical chicken-and-egg question that comes up when you're developing a navigation system for a website that's still under construction. Do you build the menu before or after you create your web pages? Here's a recommended workflow:

- **Create a list of web pages for your site.** You can jot this down on the back of a napkin or work in Notepad, TextEdit, or any other app that helps you make a list. The main thing is to consider the needs of your site and to work up a list complete with the order of the pages. If your site is large, you might create sections that include groups of pages. For example, the Chia Vet site may have an About Us section. Within that section there could be a History page, a Facilities page, and a Directions page.

- **Create, name, and save empty pages.** Use File→New to create the pages and then you can immediately use File→Close to save and name the pages. At this point, you aren't worrying about the actual content of the page. The goal is simply to create placeholder files that you can point to when you build your navigation menu. If your plan calls for some files to be stored within folders, go ahead and create the folders and store those files there before you create your menu. Keep in mind, those folders need to be within the root folder of your site.

- **Create your menu and link to the site's pages.** Now that you've got pages (albeit empty pages) on your site, you can build your navigation menu (see page 190 for instructions). The advantage of having actual files in your site folder is that you can use the Browse button to find those files, and Dreamweaver automatically fills in the Link field. The menu builder creates the proper path, ensuring that your links are typo-free.

Adding, Editing, and Removing Menu Links

At some point, you're going to want to edit one of your menus—your site structure may have changed and you need to relink pages, or you may have added a section to your site that you want to appear in the menu.

To edit a menu, open a page that uses it. Go to the Insert panel (Window→Insert), click Ajatix, and then double-click Advanced CSS Drop Down Menu Light. Dreamweaver opens the panel shown in Figure 4-17. It has three choices: Create a new menu, Insert an existing menu, and Edit menu on page. Choose the last item, "Edit menu on page." A box at the bottom of the panel lists all the menus you've created for the site so far. Select the menu you want to edit and then click OK. Dreamweaver opens your menu in a window like the one in Figure 4-16.

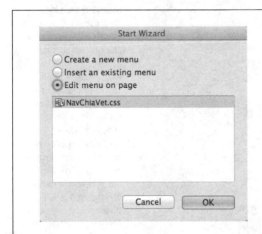

FIGURE 4-17

After you create a menu, you can reopen it to edit it or add new entries. To do that, use the Insert panel or go to Insert→Ajatix→Advanced CSS Drop Down Menu Light. If you already created and saved a menu, you can add it to the current page. If the current page already has a menu, you can edit it.

At this point, editing your menu is like creating a new one (described on page 192). Your menu panel should look like the one in Figure 4-18. Use the + and – sign buttons to add and remove menu items. Use the arrow buttons to position items in the list, or to move them back and forth between submenus. If you need to edit a link, select the menu item (that is, the link's label) from the list on the left and then use the browse button next to the Link field to select a new destination.

NOTE As you work with the Light version of Advanced CSS Drop Down Menu, you're likely to encounter features that have an asterisk and a note that says "Not available in the Light version." These features let you create and edit animated effects, highlight current items, add rounded corners to drop-down menus, and manually position submenus. Bottom line: If you need to support touch devices, assign individual colors to specific buttons, or want the most recent update to the CSS menus, you're better off ponying up the cash for the full-featured version of the program at *http://www.ajatix.com/*.

Changing the Look of the Navigation Menu

When you first create a menu with Advanced CSS Drop Down Menu Light (Menu Light for short), you choose from 18 themes. They include horizontal and vertical menus, and offer a choice of color schemes and fonts. Some themes have a rounded, three-dimensional appearance, while others appear flat. Chances are, you'll find something suitable for your site.

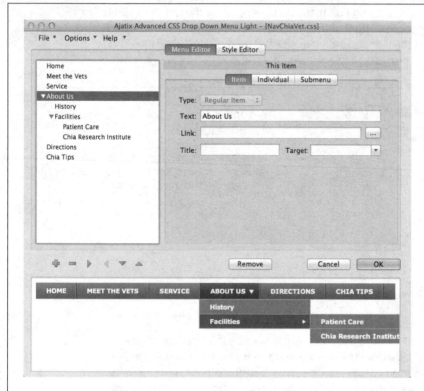

FIGURE 4-18

You'll find everything you need to change the structure of your menu under this panel's Menu Editor tab. As you make changes, Dreamweaver previews the results at the bottom of the panel. The menu actually works, so you can click submenus to open them. The structure of your menu is displayed in the list on the left. Use the buttons below to add, move, and rearrange items. You can edit the text, links, or label for any item you select in the list. Want to remove a menu from a web page? Click the Remove button.

But when it comes to making your menu "perfect" for your site, you probably have your own ideas about colors, fonts, and other styles. Menu Light formats its menus using CSS style sheets. So you could head over to CSS Designer, find the source for your menu, and start editing styles. However, Menu Light uses some pretty cryptic names for selectors, so you'd spend way too much time just identifying the selectors that control the styles you want to change. The easier way to edit your menu is with the Style Editor, found under an eponymous tab at the top of the edit window. The Style Editor (see Figure 4-19) makes it easy to identify page elements and then apply changes. As you saw in the previous section, you use the Menu Editor to create the structure of your navigation menu. You use the Style Editor to modify its appearance. These two editing tools share the same window, so you fire them up in the same manner.

Suppose you want to change the font the Chia Vet menu uses. You first open a page that has the menu in it. Then, from the Insert panel, open the Ajatix category and double-click Advanced CSS Drop Down Menu Light. In the Start Wizard that opens (Figure 4-17), choose "Edit menu on page," select the *NavChiaVet.css* menu, and then click OK.

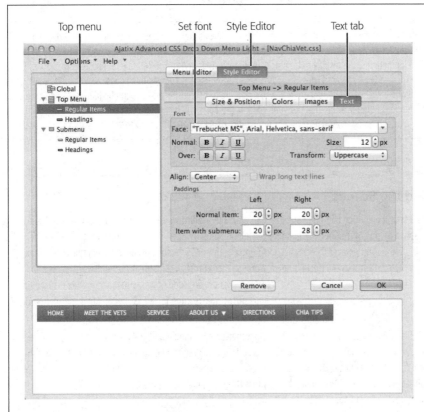

FIGURE 4-19

To change the appearance of your menus, click the Style Editor tab and then, in the lower row of tabs, choose the type of change you want to make: Size and Position, Colors, Images, or Text (selected). You make changes using the editor's buttons, boxes, and drop-down menus. Behind the scenes, it writes the CSS that creates the styles you specify.

When Dreamweaver opens the menu editor, click the Style Editor tab, shown in Figure 4-19. The style editor's layout is similar to the menu editor's, and you work with the two the same way. Use the pane on the left to select a section of your menu, the main part of the window to edit styles, and the bottom pane to preview your changes. For example, to edit the font for your menu items, you'd select that element from the list on the left.

The entries on the left—Global, Top Menu, and Submenu—identify the major sections of any menu. To see the properties for a menu item, click Regular Items under Top Menu. Dreamweaver displays the properties for top menu items in the main part of the window. An additional row of tabs (Size & Position, Colors, Images, and Text) lets you refine styles. Click Text, for example, and you see several text-related widgets, including one that lets you change fonts.

So the key to styling menus is identifying the menu item you want to format in the Style Editor list and then hunting down the property you need to tweak. The good news is that the menus all use CSS styles and the tabbed panels are fairly well organized. So if you're familiar with CSS color, text, border, background, and positioning properties, you have a head start with the Style Editor. The next few sections explain how to style different parts of your menu.

> **TIP** The preview at the bottom of the Style Editor shows you the effect of your new style. When you click OK and close the Style Editor, you should see those changes reflected in Design view, but that doesn't always happen. Sometimes, the display gets "stuck" on the previous styles. You can take a few steps to fix this. First, choose File→Save All Related Files. If you find Save All Related Files grayed out, choose Save All. This saves your website and any changes you made to it, and saves the CSS style sheets the menu builder uses. Switch to Live view and you should see the effect of your edits. If the page still looks odd, click the Refresh button (the one with two arrows going in a circle). One of those steps should update the menu to your new styles.

POWER USERS' CLINIC

CSS Menus Behind the Scenes

A CSS menu might look like a fancy navigation bar made up of colorful buttons and interactive menus, but under the hood it's just a simple list of links. Some pretty clever CSS creates the cool-looking menus complete with rollover effects, and shows or hides submenus.

The structure of the menu itself is an unordered list. In other words, the items in your menu and the tiered menus and submenus are the result of HTML code alone. You can find that HTML in the source code of your web page (right-click the page and then choose View Source from the pop-up menu)—just run a search for words that appear in the menu. For example, the first few lines for a menu that has Home and About Us buttons might look like this in your source code:

```
<ul>
  <li><a href="index.html">Home</a></li>
  <li class="tsub"><a class="ajxsub"
href="about.html">About Us</a>
```

The <ul> tag begins the unordered list. List items comprise the next two lines, as you can tell by the <li> tags. In the second line, you see a link to *index.html* and a label for the Home page link. Similarly, the third line includes a link and a label, About Us. (These CSS menus use non-breaking spaces between words so that a browser can't break up multi-word labels. HTML represents non-breaking spaces with the code * ,* so if you look at the source code for a CSS menu, you'll see plenty of * *'s where you'd normally see a space.)

The other unique thing about the third line is that you apply a class to the link tag and another class to the anchor <a> tag. These classes define the style for the navigation menus, a formatting function that's pure CSS.

If you're comfortable editing HTML code and CSS style sheets, you may want to jump in and edit your menu code by hand. You can do that, but there are consequences. If you edit the HTML by hand, Menu Light won't recognize your changes when you try to structure or style the menu. In fact, if you manually make changes and then use the Menu Editor, it overwrites your manual changes. For this reason alone, it's best to stick with Ajatix's editing tools.

■ FORMATTING TOP MENU ITEMS

In Menu Light, buttons in the Top Menu are always visible, whether you use a vertical or horizontal menu. You can style the background of the top menu bar and the menu items themselves—that is, the navigation buttons. To change the background bar, select it in the Top Menu list. Menu Light displays the top menu properties under two tabs in the main window, Layout and Style.

Use the Layout tab (Figure 4-20) to change the menu's orientation, set the width of the background bar, and align the menu on your web page.

- **Orientation.** This drop-down menu gives you two options, horizontal and vertical. Even if you initially chose a theme with a horizontal orientation, you can use this menu to change it to a vertical menu.

- **Width.** Choose *none* if you don't want to specify a width. In that case, the length of the button labels determine the width of the menu bar. Choose *Fixed* to set a specific width using pixels as the unit of measure. Choose *100%* if you want the menu bar to fill the available space. Choose *Min* to set the minimum space, in pixels, for the menu background. That way, the width of your menu bar will always be equal to or greater than the minimum value. Choose *auto* to have the background menu bar change size depending on the size of menu items, their spacing, and padding.

- **Menu align.** You can choose left, center, or right to position your menu on the page. Most people choose left.

- **Sublevel offset.** Use these settings to position submenus when they pop up. Left to the default of *0*, the submenus will touch the menu item that triggered them. To move the menu down from a triggering item, set a positive value (in pixels) in the y property. To move a submenu to the right, set a positive value in the x property. Negative values position submenus up or to the left of their triggering items.

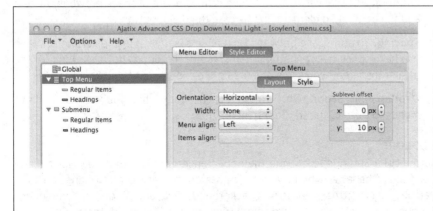

FIGURE 4-20

The Style Editor tab gives you the tools you need to change the appearance of your menus. With Top Menu selected on the left and the Layout tab selected in the main part of the window, you see the properties to orient, size, and position the top menu; that is, the part of the menu that's always visible.

Using the Style Editor's Style tab, you can change the color and images of the menu's background. Make sure you select Top Menu in the list on the left, and then set values for these properties:

- **Background color.** Click the swatch and choose a color. Use the Transparent option to make the background invisible so that Dreamweaver displays only the menu items (buttons), not the backgrounds. Menu Light uses your operating system's color picker, so the Windows tools look different from the Mac tools.

- **Border.** To add a border, turn on the checkbox and click the swatch to choose a color.

- **Background image.** You can use an image for your menu's background. Use the alignment tools to position the image horizontally and vertically. If your image is smaller than the background bar, set the Repeat menu to "Repeat." This replicates the image both horizontally and vertically. Choose repeat-x if you want to repeat the image horizontally only, or repeat-y to repeat it vertically. The repeat options are standard CSS settings, which you can learn more about on page 241.

To change the background color of a menu item (as opposed to the entire menu bar), go to the list on the left and, beneath Top Menu, choose Regular Items. The main part of the window displays the properties related to the buttons in the menu. Menu Light groups the properties under four tabs: Style & Position, Colors, Images, and Text.

■ SIZE & POSITION

- **Width.** Turn on the Width checkbox to use a fixed width, measured in pixels. Otherwise, Menu Light automatically adjusts the width to fit the text.

- **Height.** This works the same way as the width. Turn on the Height checkbox and type in a value in pixels.

- **Padding.** As usual with CSS, padding is the amount of space between the text and the edge of an element, in this case the menu button.

- **Spacing.** To add space between menu items, set a value in pixels here. When you have space between menu items, the background shows through, (if the bar's transparent, you see elements on the web page peek through).

- **Overlap child dropdown.** Turn on this checkbox when you want drop-down menus to overlap the triggering menu item.

■ COLORS

Use the color settings to change the appearance of buttons in their Normal and Over states (the latter when a mouse is positioned over them). Clicking the color swatches next to Items (the button's background), Text, and Border standard opens your operating system's standard color picker, which will look different for Windows and Macs. In either case, you specify colors by clicking them or typing in values.

■ IMAGES

Click this tab to choose background images for buttons. You can choose different images for buttons that lead to submenus and for those that don't. For even snazzier effects, choose different images for the normal and hover states.

◼ TEXT

The Text tab lets you format the "usual suspects": the font (called Face in the Font group), size (specified in pixels), style (bold, italic, or underlined), and capitalization (none, Capitalize, Uppercase, and Lowercase), known as Transform in Menu Light. Use the Align menu to position the button text left, right, or center. You can add left and right padding and specify different values for items that lead to submenus.

◼ FORMATTING ROLLOVER MENU BUTTONS

Visitors get instant feedback when they interact with menus. Moving a mouse over a menu button changes the color of the button and its text, letting visitors know "Hey, I'm a link, click me!" You set the colors when you style your menus, as described in the previous section. With the Style Editor tab selected, from the list on the left, select Top Menu→Regular Items. This displays the properties that style your Top Menu buttons. Click the Colors tab. To set the colors Dreamweaver displays when a mouse hovers over a button, change the Mouseover values.

To create rollover buttons for submenus, choose Submenu→Regular Items, and then click the Colors tab. To set the background color for a submenu item, click the Normal swatch under the Item heading, and then choose a color from your color picker. Repeat the process with the Mouseover swatch under Item, but, of course, choose a different color. In this case, you choose the background color that appears when your guest moves her mouse over the submenu item. If your color scheme calls for it, you can repeat the process to create different Normal and Mouseover colors for the submenu button's text and border.

◼ FORMATTING SUBMENU BUTTONS

Submenu buttons appear in Menu Light's drop-down menus. In fact, with Menu Light, your submenus can have submenus. But don't get carried away nesting menus or you'll try the patience of your visitors.

Using the Style Editor, format your submenus the same way you format the top menu. In fact, you use the same properties and have the same options as in the top menu. If you prefer an understated appearance, style your submenus with the same colors and rollover properties as your top menu. If you want your submenus to stand apart from the top menu, use different but complementary colors.

To format a submenu's background box, click Submenu in the list. To format the submenu's buttons, click Regular Items beneath Submenu.

NOTE   Menu Light displays an Animation tab when you choose Submenu from the list. This feature is listed, but not available, in the Light version of the menu builder. Its properties control the speed, direction, and other effects used to display the submenu. If you're interested in controlling a submenu's animation, you can get the full version of Advanced CSS Drop Down Menus from Ajatix at *http://www.ajatix.com/*.

■ Link Tutorial

In this tutorial, you'll link to other pages on your own site, link to another site on the Web, and create a great-looking CSS-powered navigation bar, complete with fancy drop-down menus. (To see the completed page, skip ahead to Figure 4-28.)

TIP You'll need to download sample files from *http://oreilly.com/missingmanuals/cds/dreamweaverccmm13/* to complete this tutorial. See the Note on page 33 for details.

Linking to Other Pages and Websites

Once you download the tutorial files and open Dreamweaver, set up a new site as described on page 19. In a nutshell, Choose Site→New Site. In the Site Setup window, type *Links Tutorial* into the Site Name field, click the folder icon next to the Local Site Folder field, navigate to and select the *Chapter04* folder inside the *MM_DWCC* folder, and then click Choose or Select. Finally, click OK.

Once again, you'll be working on a page from Cafe Soylent Green.

1. **In the files panel, double-click the file *index.html*.**

   You can also choose File→Open, select the filename, and then click OK (Select on Macs). You're looking at a basic web page, with a banner, some text, and a footer. It's all contained inside a <div> tag that's 800 pixels wide and centered on the screen (you learned how to do this in the tutorial in Chapter 1, "Finishing the Page").

   If your screen is wide enough to show both Code and Design views side-by-side, click the Split button in the top-left corner of the document window. If you can't fit both comfortably, click the Design button.

   At the end of the last paragraph on the page, in the section with the headline "All Natural Ingredients," you'll see the text "Read more about our natural ingredients." This sentence should link to another page.

2. **Select the text "Read more about our natural ingredients." In the Properties panel, to the right of the Link box, click the Browse for File button, the folder icon.**

   Dreamweaver opens the Select File window.

3. **Click the Site Root button (at the bottom-right) to go to your site's main folder. Double-click *ingredients.html*.**

   Dreamweaver closes the Select File window. That's it? Yup. You just created a link. Now, you'll learn an even faster way to do the same thing.

4. **In the last paragraph before the page's footer, select the text "Read more about our nutritional principles."**

   Make sure you have the Files panel open (Window→Files).

5. **In the Properties panel, drag the small Point-to-File icon (see Figure 4-6) beside the Link box into the Files panel, move your mouse over the file *nutrition.html*, and then release the mouse button.**

Dreamweaver adds the link to your page. (If you have the double-monitor configuration discussed in the Note on page 176, this point-to-file technique won't work. Use the method described in steps 3 and 4 to link to *nutrition.html*.)

Note that if you wanted to link the text in the examples above to a page on another website, you couldn't use either of the methods outlined here. Instead, you'd need to type an absolute URL into the Link box, as you'll see in the next two steps.

6. **Scroll to the bottom of the page. In the footer, find the phrase "in collaboration with Cosmopolitan Farmer." Select the text "Cosmopolitan Farmer."**

You want this text to link to the site's parent company.

7. **In the Properties panel's Link box, type *http://www.cosmofarmer.com/*, and then press Enter (Return).**

Now the text "Cosmopolitan Farmer" links to the CosmoFarmer.com website. Unfortunately, the blue links don't fit in with the cafe's color palette. You'll remedy that next.

Formatting Links

You can change the look of links using a little CSS.

1. **Make sure you have CSS Designer open (Window→CSS Designer). In the Sources section, choose *soylent_styles.css*.**

In the Selectors section, you see the selectors you created in *soylent_styles.css*. You haven't added a selector for links (the <a> tag) yet. (That's why the text for your link uses the link default color, blue.)

2. **In Selectors, click the + sign to add a selector. In the text box, type *a*, and then press Enter (Return) twice.**

When you type *a*, the new selector replaces the selector CSS Designer suggested. The first time you press Enter (Return), you select the <a> tag from the pop-up menu. The second time you press Enter (Return), you create a new selector for anchor tags.

3. **In the Properties section of CSS Designer, click the T (text) button. Make sure you have the "Show Set" box unchecked.**

Dreamweaver scrolls the list of properties until it gets to Text.

4. **Click the swatch next to the color property field, type *#417F2C*, and then press Enter (Return).**

   This color makes your text green. After you press Enter (Return), the links on the page change to green. You'll change one more property to remove the underline from your links.

5. **With the *a* selector still highlighted in the Selectors section of CSS Designer, find the text-decoration property in the Properties section. Click the first box—the one with the diagonal line through it (circled in Figure 4-21).**

   Setting *text-decoration* to none overrides the default value, underlined links. As a result, browsers won't underscore your links and pseudo classes like *hover* will inherit the *text-decoration* style. In fact, *hover*'s up next for some styling.

FIGURE 4-21

To remove an underline from a link, set the CSS Text-decoration property to "none." You can create a look similar to an underline (but with a lot more design choices) by turning underlining off here, and then using the CSS Border property to create a dotted, dashed, or different-color underline.

6. **In CSS Designer's Selectors section, click the + sign to add a selector, type *a:hover* in the text box, and then click Enter (Return) twice.**

   A new selector appears in the list. This time, the selector includes the pseudo class *hover*.

7. **With *a:hover* selected in Selectors, click the T (for text) in the Properties section. Then, find the *color* property, click the swatch next to it, and then type *#0A2F02*.**

   To see how this rollover style works, use Dreamweaver's Live view.

8. **In the Selectors section of CSS Designer, choose the *a* selector.**

9. **At the top of the document window, click the Live button (or choose View→Live View).**

Dreamweaver includes an embedded version of the Google Chrome browser, and Live view uses it to let you preview the look and functionality of a web page. With Live view, you can interact with JavaScript and see CSS hover effects. Move your mouse over the various links on the page, and you see the link change to dark green and the underline disappear. (Of course, to check your work thoroughly, you should also preview your pages in Safari, Internet Explorer, and Firefox. You can do that using the File→Preview in Browser command if you have those browsers installed.)

10. **Click the Live button (or choose View→Live View) a second time to leave Live view.**

You can't edit a page in Live view, so you always need to click out of it when you're ready to work on your page again.

Adding an Email Link

You'll find the Café's email address—*info@cafesoylentgreen.com*–at the bottom of the *index.html* page. Clicking it, however, doesn't do anything. Here's how you turn that address into a link that opens your visitor's email program and addresses a note to you:

1. **Select the text *info@cafesoylentgreen.com,* or place your cursor where you'd like to add the email link.**

The text you select doesn't have to be an email address—it could say "Email us" or something similar. Likewise, if you haven't selected any text, click where you'd like to insert the email link and move on to step 2.

2. **Choose Insert→Email Link (or click the Email link button under the Common category of the Insert panel, shown in Figure 4-7).**

Dreamweaver opens the Email Link window (Figure 4-22) with the link text and email address already filled in (it copies the link text from the text you selected in step 1). If you didn't select any text, the Text box is blank. The Email box displays the address for the last Email link you created. You'll find this helpful if you link to the same email address all the time, or annoying if you don't.

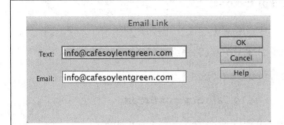

FIGURE 4-22

When you insert an email link, Dreamweaver copies any text you selected on the page into the Text field. If the text on the page is in the form of an email address, the program helpfully copies that into the Email field as well.

3. **Click OK.**

Dreamweaver adds the email link (pretty easy, huh?).

Adding a Navigation Bar

A navigation bar with rollover effects and smooth drop-down menus gives your website a professional look and feel, and it makes navigating your site easy for visitors.

These next steps use the Advanced CSS Drop Down Menu Light from Ajatix (which we'll call Menu Light for the sake of brevity). If you haven't downloaded and installed this Dreamweaver extension, do that now by following the steps on page 190. Then:

1. **Return to Dreamweaver and make sure you have the file *index.html* open; in the banner at the top of the page, click just to the right of the word "Green."**

    You'll insert a horizontal menu bar that spans most of the page's width. Placing it near the top of the page, as part of the banner, lets site visitors easily find and use it.

2. **Choose Insert→Ajatix→Advanced Drop Down Menu Light.**

    The Start Wizard dialog box opens, giving you two choices: "Create a new menu" and "Insert an existing menu."

3. **Choose "Create a new menu," and then click OK.**

    Menu Light closes the Start Wizard and opens the Select Theme window. Choose from any of the themes listed in the box on the left. Click a theme to preview it in the box on the right.

4. **Choose the "Horizontal-Dark Olive" theme and then click Apply.**

    Menu Light closes the Select Theme window and opens the New Menu window (see Figure 4-23).

5. **In the Text field where the word Unamed is displayed, type *Home*.**

The words you type here will show up as a button in your menu. As you type, you're replacing the "Unnamed" label that Menu Light automatically gave the button with your own name for the link, Home in this case. You see the change to Home in the page list on the left and in the preview window.

1. **Click inside the blank field next to Link, and then click the Browse button (the three dots) at the end of the box.**

    Menu Light opens a window displaying your website's files.

2. **Click *index.html*, and then click Open (Select on Macs).**

    A link to *index.html* appears in the Link box.

3. **In the Title box, type *Welcome to Cafe Soylent Green*.**

    You won't include a title for every link in the menu, but the text "Home" is so generic that a description will help web visitors who use screen readers.

Menu item properties

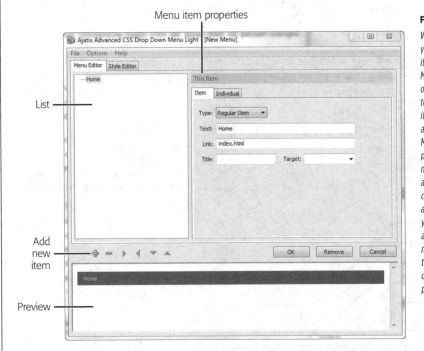

FIGURE 4-23

With Menu Light, you build your navigation menu one item at a time. You use the Menu Editor list (shown on the left in this figure) to add and organize the items in your menu. Select a menu item in the list and Menu Light displays its properties on the right, the most important of which are Text and Link. As you can see from the preview at the bottom, the words you type in the Text box appear in the navigation menu. The Link box stores the link to a specific page or to a bookmark on a page.

List

Add new item

Preview

4. **Below the list, click the + sign ("Add New Item") button.**

   Menu Light adds a new, "Unnamed" menu item to the list. Next, you'll create a drop-down menu that holds Cafe Soylent Green's breakfast, lunch, and dinner menus.

5. **In the Text box, type *Menu*. Click the Browse button next to the Link field, select the file *menu.html*, and then click Open (Select on Macs).**

   The "Menu" button ranks at the same hierarchical level as the Home button. The next three items you add—Breakfast, Lunch, and Dinner—will go in a submenu.

6. **Click the Add New Item button (the + sign) again, and then click the right-pointing triangle, a.k.a. the "Move Item Right" button.**

   After you add a new, top-level menu item, you turn it into a submenu by using the right arrow key to nest the item under an existing menu item.

7. **In the Text box, change "Unnamed" to "Breakfast." In the Link field, click the Browse button, and then select *breakfast.html*.**

   You've labeled your first button and created the first link for this menu bar.

8. **Repeat steps 6 and 7 to add Lunch and Dinner buttons to the submenu.**

No mysteries here. Use *lunch.html* and *dinner.html* for the link URLs respectively. When you finish, the New Menu window should look like the one in Figure 4-24. Time to move on to the About Us page.

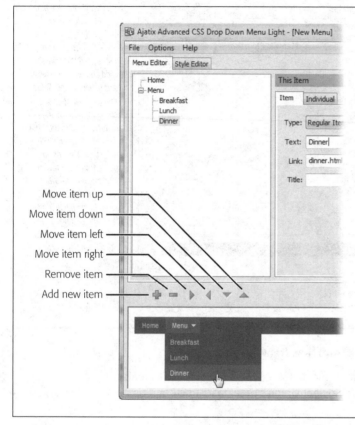

Move item up
Move item down
Move item left
Move item right
Remove item
Add new item

FIGURE 4-24

In the list pane, the structure of your menu appears in standard outline form. You can expand and collapse the submenus by clicking the + or – sign buttons in Windows (shown here) or the flippy triangle on Macs. The preview pane not only shows you what your menu looks like, it lets you try out the drop-down menus, too. Triangle icons automatically added to menu items with submenus let visitors know there are more options.

9. **Click the Add New Item button (the + sign) to add a new, unnamed menu item to the list, and then click the left arrow to move the item left and make it a top-level button. Type *About Us* in the Text field, and then, in the Link box, browse to and select *about.html*.**

The left arrow button repositions the new Unnamed item so that it's at the same level as the Home and Menu buttons. Next, you'll add two submenu items under About Us, Directions and Hours.

10. **Repeat steps 6 and 7, using the labels Directions and Hours in the respective Text boxes, and *directions.html* and *hours.html* as the two link destinations.**

As you add each button, Menu Light previews it as a submenu item under About Us.

11. **Click OK. In the File name box of the Save Menu As window, type** *soylent_ menu.* **Click Save to save your menu with a descriptive name. This is a good time to save all your work, so choose File→Save All.**

The New Menu window closes and you see your menu in Design view in all its glory. If you're eager to give it a test drive, switch to Live view. On the document toolbar's Live View Options menu, turn on the Follow Links Continuously checkbox. You haven't added your menu to the other pages in your site, so you'll need to use the "back" arrow on the document toolbar to return to the Home page. Remember to turn Live view off when you move on to the next section, where you'll style your menu.

Styling the Menu Bar

The basic look of your menu isn't too bad, but it could benefit from some style changes. For example, the text is a little small, and the menu bar has only three items, so it doesn't need to extend across the banner. Fortunately, styling your menu is almost as easy as creating it.

1. **With** *index.html* **open in Design view, choose Insert→Ajatix→Advanced Drop Down Menu Light.**

The Start Wizard opens, with the radio button "Edit menu on page" preselected and the menu you just created listed in the filename box. If your cursor is inside of your menu, when you choose the Insert→Ajatix→Advanced Drop Down Menu Light command, the Start Wizard does not appear. The menu editor opens with your menu loaded and ready for editing. In that case, you can skip the next step.

2. **Click** *soylent_menu.css,* **and then click OK.**

Menu Light's Menu/Style Editor window opens, with the name of the menu in the title bar. You used the Menu Editor in the previous exercise to build your menu. Now, you'll use the Style Editor to make it look nice.

3. **Click the Style Editor tab.**

The list on the left changes from listing the individual menu buttons you previously created like Home and About Us, to listing the generic terms Global, Top Menu, and Submenu. In the following steps you will see that the Global styles apply to the entire menu. Top Menu styles affect all Top Menu items and Submenu styles apply to all submenu items.

Initially, the Global item is selected so you see the Z-index property on the right. You see other Global properties grayed out because they're not available in the Light version of Advanced CSS Drop Down Menu.

4. **Leave the Z-index set to** *100* **and then, in the list, click Top Menu.**

The Z-index determines whether your menu appears in front of or behind other elements on the page. It's a standard CSS property covered on page 461. Here's how it works: The Z-index controls the order of stacked elements on a web page. An element with a larger Z-index (a higher number) appears in front of other elements. Menu Light automatically gives your menu a very high Z-index number: 100. In most cases, you won't need to change it. However, if your menu is hidden underneath another page element, say the banner at the top of the page, you can enter a higher number here, to fix the problem. And, if you want your menu *underneath* another element, change this to a lower number. It may take some experimenting to get the order just right.

When you click Top Menu, the window changes. Two tabs divvy up the styling chores, Layout and Style.

5. **Click the Layout tab, leave Orientation set to Horizontal, change the Width value to None, and leave "Menu align" set to Left.**

When you finish, the settings should look like those in Figure 4-25. The Width property affects the width of the bar that holds your Top Menu buttons. Set to None, Menu Light applies no specific width to the menu bar. This removes the green band (background) that extends beyond the three menu items. The "Menu align" setting—Left, Center, or Right—positions the top menu bar. The Left option works best for Cafe Soylent Green because it places the menu directly below the name of the cafe.

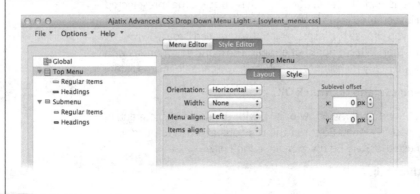

FIGURE 4-25

To change a menu from horizontal orientation to vertical or vice versa, use Menu Light's Orientation option. In this example, you set the width to None, so the menu bar can stretch and shrink to fit menu items. The Alignment option positions the menu bar to the right, left, or center of the page.

6. **Click the Top Menu's Style tab and then click the Background color swatch. In the Select Color window, choose Transparent. Turn off the Border option.**

The Top Menu *color* and *border* settings apply to the background bar that appears behind menu items. With these settings, you hide that background bar. In the following steps, you'll space out the menu buttons so you can see part of the banner behind them.

7. **In the menu list, click Regular Items under Top Menu.**

The properties here format the top-level menu buttons. Initially, the Size & Position tab is selected.

NOTE Under Top Menu and Submenu, there are options for "Headings." These aren't available in the Light version of the Advanced Drop Down Menu.

8. **Set the width to 100px, the height to 30px, and the spacing to 20px.**

   With the Width and Height boxes checked, the dimension item (the rectangle) is set to fixed dimensions. So an item with the text "lunch" will have the same size background rectangle as an item with more text, like "early breakfast." There's one case that overrides this setting. If the text overflows the width of the box, the width remains fixed, but the "height" automatically adjusts, adding more lines to accommodate the text. For this project, with a width of 100px and a height of 30px, the text in the top menu buttons has some breathing room. The Spacing setting puts some distance between each of the menu items. With the background bar hidden (step 6), you see the site's banner behind the top menu items. You can't quite see the effect at this point because the top menu items don't have any background color. You'll fix that next.

9. **Click the Colors tab and then turn on the checkboxes next to Normal and Mouseover.**

   You'll pick the colors for a menu item's normal state (when the link just sits on the page) and for the state when someone's mouse hovers over the button. For each state, you can choose colors for the button's background, text, and border.

10. **Click the color swatch for Normal/Item.**

    The process for choosing a color in Menu Light is different for Windows PCs (Figure 4-26, left) and Macs (Figure 4-26, right). For the menu portion of this tutorial, you'll specify colors as Red, Green, Blue (RGB) values.

    On Windows PCs you see the operating system's familiar color picker with swatches on the left and a spectrum square on the right. Below that, boxes let you specify color as a hex value, an HSL value, or a Red, Green, Blue (RGB) value. For this tutorial, use the RGB system.

    When you click a color swatch **on Macs**, you see familiar color picker options. Choose your color using the color bar sliders (second button from left in the Colors window). Then, from the drop-down menu, choose RGB Sliders.

11. **For the Normal menu link, set the RGB values as follows:**

    - For Items, use 70, 133, 49.

    - For text, specify 242, 229, and 194.

12. **As a finishing touch, turn on the border checkbox and set the border color to match the text (242, 229, and 194).**

    With these settings, buttons in their normal state have a green background and a dark gray border. The text is the same light color you used at the bottom of the page for the copyright background. For the menu's mouseover state, you'll swap the text and background colors.

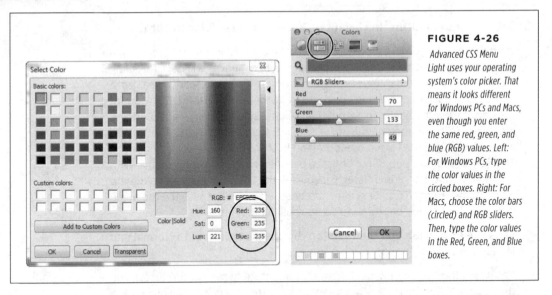

FIGURE 4-26

Advanced CSS Menu Light uses your operating system's color picker. That means it looks different for Windows PCs and Macs, even though you enter the same red, green, and blue (RGB) values. Left: For Windows PCs, type the color values in the circled boxes. Right: For Macs, choose the color bars (circled) and RGB sliders. Then, type the color values in the Red, Green, and Blue boxes.

13. **Move to the Mouseover color swatches. Set the Item color to 242, 229, 194 and the text color to 70, 133, 49.**

    Reversing colors is a good way to provide feedback for rollover items. In the next step, you increase the size of the button text.

14. **Click the Text tab and then, in the Face (think typeface) drop-down menu, choose "Verdana, Geneva, sans-serif." Turn on the B (Bold) buttons next to Normal and Over, set the size of the text to 14px, set the Transform menu to Uppercase, and then set "Align menu" to Center.**

    CSS menus don't currently recognize web fonts, so choosing "Verdana, Geneva, sans-serif" is a reasonable substitute for pt-sans. The bold and size settings make the button text easier to read. The Uppercase setting makes the text for all the items uniform in appearance. The Top Menu Text settings should now match Figure 4-27.

    You style submenu items separately from top menu items. That's next on the agenda.

15. **In the list, click Submenu and then click the Style tab. Set the background and border colors to RGB (242, 229, 194).**

    You can use dramatically different colors for submenus, but that can be distracting. In this case, you're styling the submenu to complement the colors in the Top Menu.

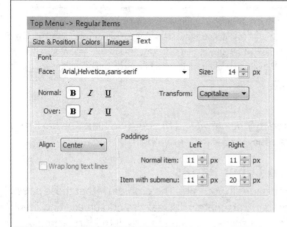

FIGURE 4-27

Use the Style Editor's Text tab to style your buttons. You style the top menu and submenu text separately, but the Property panel and widgets for the menu and submenu are the same.

16. **In the list under Submenu, click Regular Items. In the Size & Position tab, set the width to 100px, the height to 27px, and the spacing to 3px.**

    This width—100px—matches that of the top menu, while the height makes the submenus a tad shorter than the top menu. The spacing lets the submenu background show through. In effect, this creates a matching border around each of the submenu buttons.

17. **In the Colors tab, set the Normal colors to match the Normal colors in the top menu.**

    - For Items, use (70, 133, 49).

    - For text, specify (242, 229, 194).

    - For the border, use (242, 229, 194).

    Next, pick the colors for the Mouseover (hover) state.

18. **For the Mouseover state, set the Item color to "242, 229, 194" and the text and border colors to "70, 133, 49."**

    The button's background and text switch colors when a guest mouses over the item.

19. **Click the Text tab. In the group of fonts at the top of the window, set Face to "Verdana, Geneva, sans-serif," and the font size to 12. Turn on the bold setting (click the B button) for the Normal and Over states, set the Transform menu to Uppercase, and then set the Align menu to Center.**

    The text for the submenu will be a little smaller than the text for the Top Menu, but the other characteristics will match.

20. **Click OK.**

Menu Light rewrites the *soylent_menu.css* file to match your specifications.

> **NOTE** If you don't see the changes immediately in your document, it may be because Dreamweaver hasn't loaded the changes from the CSS file. If that's the case, follow these steps. Choose File→Save All Related Files. That command may not be available if you used it recently. If that's the case, choose File→Save All. Click the Live view button and then, in the document toolbar, click Refresh to reload the HTML and CSS files.

21. **Choose File→Save All.**

You save any changes made to *index.html* and to your CSS files. The next step is to add your menu to the other pages in your website.

Adding the CSS Menu to Other Pages

You've built a menu that links the pages in your site. The problem is that those pages don't have the same navigation bar. Fortunately, it's easy to add an existing menu to a web page. After all, the CSS file *soylent_menu.css* has all the formatting your menu needs, and Menu Light's definition file, *soylent_menu.ajm*, stores the menu description.

1. **Choose File→Open and select *about.html*.**

You need to have a web page open in the document window to add an existing menu.

2. **In the banner, click after the word "Green."**

This positions the cursor where you want to insert the menu.

3. **Choose Insert→Ajatix→Advanced CSS Drop Down Menu Light.**

Menu Light's Start Wizard offers two options, "Create a new menu" and "Insert an Existing menu."

4. **Click "Insert an existing menu" and then click OK.**

The dialog box closes and the Open Menu window appears, where you can select a file.

5. **Choose *soylent_menu.css* and then click Open (Select for Macs).**

The menu editor appears, where you see the Menu Editor and Style Editor tools. You don't need to make any changes at this point.

6. **Click OK.**

The menu editing window closes and Menu Light adds your menu to the page.

7. **Choose File→Close. When prompted to save your page, click Yes.**

Menu Light saves and closes your web page, complete with its shiny new menu.

8. **Repeat steps 1 through 7 for each page in your site.**

   Once all the pages have the same menu, visitors will find it a snap to jump from one to the other.

FIGURE 4-28

Adding a CSS drop-down menu may take quite a few steps, but it delivers a high-quality, dynamic navigation bar. By using a Dreamweaver extension for the menu instead of building your own from scratch, you save yourself countless hours of CSS and JavaScript programing and testing.

Images

Nobody believes that a picture is worth a thousand words more than today's web designers, as evidenced by the highly visual nature of the Internet. In fact, it's not difficult to stumble onto a home page composed almost entirely of graphics, as you can see in Figure 5-1.

Even if you don't want to go that far, understanding how to effectively use graphics on a web page is invaluable. Whether you want to plop a simple photo onto your page, cover it with clickable "hotspots," or design an interactive set of buttons that light up when a cursor passes over them, Dreamweaver makes the job easy.

Adding Images

If you were writing out the HTML instructions for your web page by hand, you'd insert an image using the image tag: <img>. For example, the HTML snippet:

```
<img src="images/george.jpg">
```

tells a browser to display a graphic file named *george.jpg*, which it can find in the Images folder. (An image tag's primary property is called the *source* [src]; it indicates the path to the graphics file.)

FIGURE 5-1

Some websites rely almost exclusively on graphics for both looks and function. The home page of the Curious George website (http://pbskids. org/curiousgeorge/), for instance, uses graphics not just for pictures of the main character, but for the page's background and navigation buttons, too.

Dreamweaver does all the necessary coding for you when you insert a picture into your fledgling page. Here are the steps you follow:

1. **Save the web page that will include the image.**

   To insert an image, Dreamweaver has to know where to find it, which could be anywhere on your hard drive. Saving the page lets Dreamweaver determine the correct path from the page you just saved to the image.

2. **In the document window, position your cursor where you want the image to appear.**

   You can choose anywhere within a paragraph, a cell in a table (see Chapter 6), or a <div> tag (see page 428). To set your graphic apart from the text on the page, you can create a new paragraph for it. Press Enter (Return) to create a blank line before the next step.

3. **Choose Insert→Image.**

   Alternatively, from the Insert panel's Common category, you can click the Image button (Figure 5-2). Or, if you're a keyboard shortcut fan, press Ctrl+Alt+I (⌘-Option-I).

The Select Image Source dialog box opens. It's nearly identical to the Select File window that appears when you add a link to a page (Figure 4-4).

4. **Browse to and then select the graphics file you want to add to the page.**

The file must be in one of the formats that work on the Web: GIF, JPEG, or PNG.

Store the file somewhere in your local site folder (see page 25) or in one of its subfolders. If you don't, Dreamweaver can't add the correct path to your web page.

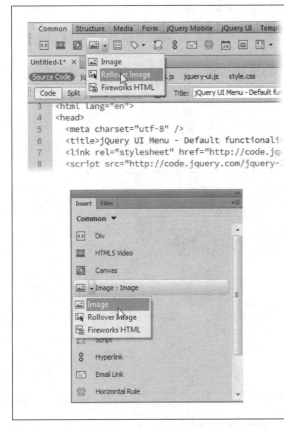

FIGURE 5-2

The Image menu in the Insert panel's Common category provides tools that let you add graphics to your pages. If you've dragged the insert panel to the top of the screen between the Document toolbar and the Application bar (top), the Insert panel is actually a toolbar near the top of your screen. The "Compact" workspace layout (bottom) displays the Insert panel grouped with other panels on the right side of the screen. See page 14 for more on Dreamweaver workspaces.

NOTE The primary file format for Fireworks, Adobe's Web-friendly image-editing program, is PNG (just as Photoshop's format is PSD). However, a native Fireworks file contains additional data the program uses to keep track of fonts, layers, and other information. That extra data significantly increases the file size and isn't needed to display a picture on your web page. So always make sure you use the Fireworks' Export command to properly compress the image into a GIF, JPEG, or PNG file without all the extra info. Fireworks CS6 changed the way it names its native files (the big ones) so that you don't confuse them with compressed images. It now adds .fw to the native filename—*logo.fw.png*, for example. If you see *.fw.png* at the end of the filename, don't use it on your web page. Instead, open the file in Fireworks and use the File→Export command to create a smaller file.

That's why, if you try to insert a graphic that's not in your site folder, Dreamweaver offers to add a *copy* of the image to that folder. If you choose yes, a Copy File As dialog box opens so you can save the file to your local root folder, renaming it if you wish. If you choose no, Dreamweaver uses a file-relative path (beginning with *file:///*) for the image's location. But clicking No is a bad idea: While you can see the graphic as you work in Dreamweaver on your computer, the graphic doesn't appear once you move the document to the Web (see the box on page 174).

NOTE Dreamweaver lets you choose a Photoshop (PSD) file from the Select Image dialog box when you insert an image, but it doesn't actually insert the PSD file. It opens a second window where you can save the image as a GIF, JPEG, or PNG file with Web-appropriate optimization settings. Page 224 has the full story.

5. **Click OK (Windows) or Choose (Macs).**

   Dreamweaver inserts the image. The Properties panel displays the properties related to the image (Figure 5-3). That includes helpful details such as the size of the image and the Alt text field where you add a brief description for any image that adds meaning to your page. For example, if you insert a graphic of your company's logo, the alternative text should be your company's name.

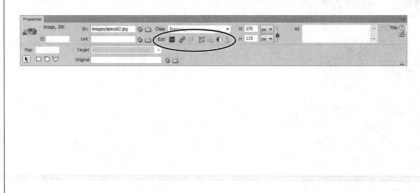

FIGURE 5-3

After you insert an image in your page, the image remains selected, and you see the properties for it in the Properties panel. Some of these properties are unique to images, such as the Edit options (circled), which you can use to crop, sharpen, and adjust the brightness and contrast of a pic.

TIP Dreamweaver offers several drag-and-drop techniques so you can quickly add images to your pages.

First, set up a site as described on page 19. Then open the Files window (press F8). You can drag any graphics file from that window right into an open Dreamweaver document. You can also drag graphics from the Assets panel, as described on page 729.

Dreamweaver even lets you drag a graphic from your desktop (including Photoshop images) onto a web page. If you do this, Dreamweaver dutifully informs you that you must copy the file into your site folder (and provides a dialog box that lets you specify *which* folder), so that the image shows up when you transfer your site files to the Web. (You can even define a default Images folder for a site, so that when you drag an image onto a page, Dreamweaver automatically copies it into the correct folder [see page 715].)

Adding an Image Placeholder

Past versions of Dreamweaver let you add a placeholder image to your document. Just as the name implies, the placeholder staked out territory on the page, waiting patiently for you to add the real image. For example, you may start building a page even before your client gives you all the necessary photos, banners, and navigation buttons. What you need is an empty object to reserve the spot—what graphic artists call an FPO (For Placement Only) holder.

In earlier versions of Dreamweaver, the Insert menu provided the tools you needed to insert a placeholder. Now, however, you're on your own. Fortunately, it's not hard to add your own placeholder.

1. **Choose any image and insert it as described on page 219.**

   Seriously, any image will do. The actual image won't stay around long.

2. **In the Properties panel, delete the text in the *src* box.**

   This breaks the reference to an actual image. As a result, your page displays a battleship gray box where the image used to be. Dreamweaver displays the dimensions of the placeholder in the box, as shown in Figure 5-4. You may not need to change the dimension of the placeholder. For one thing, if you don't have the final image, you may not know what size it will be. However, if it helps the design process at this stage, you can change the dimensions of your gray placeholder, as described in the next step.

3. **In the Properties panel, change the width (W) and height (H) properties.**

   Type in any dimension you want and the size of the gray placeholder box changes. If the proportions are different from the image you inserted in step 1, make sure you turn off the Toggle Size Constraint padlock.

You don't need to place the actual image before you style it, such as adding Alt text or using CSS to place a margin around the image.

When the real image (that prima donna) is ready to take the stage, store it with the other images on your site. Often, that's a folder named Images, but you can also put it in the root folder or some other folder, as long as it sits inside the site.

At this point, all you need to do is identify the source for the new image. There are a couple of ways to do that. You can double-click the image and then, when the Select Image Source window opens, choose the source file (described in steps 4 and 5 on pages 221 and 222). Another option is to drag the Src "Point to File" button on the Properties panel to the image in your Files panel.

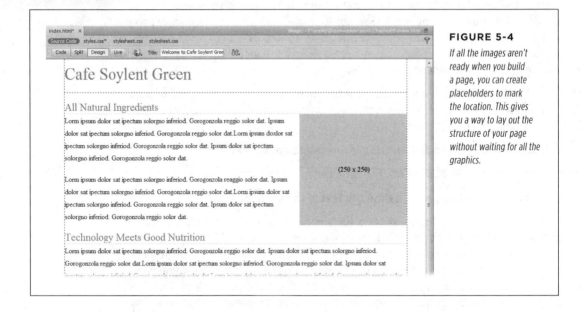

FIGURE 5-4

If all the images aren't ready when you build a page, you can create placeholders to mark the location. This gives you a way to lay out the structure of your page without waiting for all the graphics.

Inserting an Image from Photoshop

Since Adobe makes the world's most popular image-editing program, Photoshop, it only makes sense that Dreamweaver's engineers provide a streamlined process for moving images back and forth between Photoshop and Dreamweaver. You can add a Photoshop document to a web page two ways: Insert a PSD file (Photoshop's native format), or copy an image from Photoshop, and then paste it into Dreamweaver.

The first method—inserting a PSD file—supports what Adobe calls *Smart Objects*, which lets Dreamweaver keep track of whether you update the original Photoshop file, and, if so, gives you the option to update the compressed, Web-ready version of the image, too. That's great news if you're the type who constantly tweaks your artwork in Photoshop. The second method—copying and pasting from Photoshop—doesn't keep track of any changes to the original file. Both methods are explained below.

Method 1: Adding Photoshop Images

You can insert a regular Photoshop file using the same steps you use for inserting GIF, JPEG, or PNG files, described on page 219. For example, use the Image button on the Insert panel, or choose Insert→Image. You can then choose a Photoshop document (a .psd file).

NOTE You can also insert a PSD file by dragging it directly from the desktop (or any folder) and dropping it into a Dreamweaver document. If you stored the PSD file somewhere inside your local root folder, you can drag it from the Files panel and drop it onto the page.

GIFs, JPEGs, and PNGs: The Graphics of the Web

Computer graphics come in hundreds of file formats. The assorted acronyms can be mind-numbing: GIF, JPEG, PNG, TIFF, PICT, BMP, EPS, SVG, and so on.

Fortunately, the limited graphics formats the Web uses makes things simpler. All of today's web browsers support three common graphics formats, each of which provides good *compression*, which reduces a graphic's file size so it can travel more rapidly across the Internet. The graphics format you choose depends on the image you wish to add to your page.

GIF (Graphics Interchange Format) files provide good compression for images with big areas of solid color: logos, text, simple banners, and so on. GIFs also offer single-color transparency, meaning you can make one color in the graphic disappear, permitting the background of a web page to show through part of the image. In addition, you can create limited animations with GIF files (like a flashing "Buy Me" button).

GIF images support a maximum of only 256 shades of color, generally making photos look posterized (in other words, not completely realistic). That radiant sunset photo you took with your digital camera won't look so good as a GIF file.

JPEG (Joint Photographic Experts Group) graphics, on the other hand, pick up where GIFs leave off. JPEGs support millions of colors, making them ideal for photos. Not only that, they compress multicolored images much better than GIFs do, because the JPEG compression formula considers how the human eye perceives adjacent color values; when your graphics software saves a JPEG file, it runs a complex color analysis to lower the amount of data required to accurately represent the image. On the downside, JPEG compression makes any text you have in an image and large areas of solid color look blotchy, so it's not a good choice for logos or simple drawings.

Finally, the PNG (Portable Network Graphics) format includes the best features of GIFs and JPEGs, but you need to know which version of PNG to use for which situation. PNG8 is basically a replacement for GIFs. Like a GIF, it supports 256 colors and basic one-color transparency. And while PNG8 usually compresses images to a slightly smaller file size than GIF, Dreamweaver's image optimization tool does the opposite, making PNG8 files slightly larger than GIF versions of the same graphic.

PNG24 and PNG32 offer the expanded color palette of JPEG images, without any loss of quality. This means that photos saved as PNG24 or PNG32 tend to be of higher quality than JPEGs. But before you jump on the PNG bandwagon, JPEG images offer very good quality and a much smaller file size than either PNG24 or PNG32. In general, JPEG is a better choice for photos and other images that include lots of colors.

1. **Choose Insert→Image.**

   You can insert a regular Photoshop file using the steps described on page 224 for inserting GIF, JPEG, or PNG files. Alternatively, you can use the Image button on the Insert panel. Either way, the Select Image Source window appears, just as it does when you insert a standard web-ready file.

2. **Choose a Photoshop document (a .psd file), and then click OK (Choose).**

Dreamweaver places the image on the page and opens the Image Optimization window (see Figure 5-5). In the next step, you tell Dreamweaver how to convert the file from the Photoshop format to one of the standard file formats for a web page. Like the name of the dialog box, the process is called "Image Optimization."

3. **Use the Preset menu to choose one of six file format options.**

The six choices are related to the file formats GIF, JPEG, and PNG. Dreamweaver provides good hints for choosing one over the other. As always, the goal with choosing image formats and settings is to achieve the right balance between image size and quality. Image size affects how fast your web page and photos appear in a visitor's browser. Quality affects how good your images look. Here are the choices:

- **PNG24 for Photos (Sharp Details).** As advertised, this choice is good for photos. The file is compressed (making it smaller), but none of the image detail is lost. This compression technique is called "lossless."

- **JPEG for Photos (Continuous Tones).** JPEG is the most common file format for photos. Unlike PNG24, the JPEG format uses a "lossy" compression technique. When you choose this preset, the image quality is set to 100. That's the highest quality setting, which means you lose a minimal amount of detail.

- **PNG8 for Logos and Text.** This preset does not work well for photos, but it's good for images like logos or other graphics that have large swathes of solid color.

- **JPEG High for Maximum Compatibility.** This JPEG preset is a good choice for many photos. It creates smaller files than the JPEG for Photos option above by using a quality setting of 80. You lose a little more detail than you do with JPEG for Photos, but in many cases it may be a good size/quality trade off.

- **GIF for Background Images (Patterns).** GIFs are also great for images with solid colors or any graphic that displays a repeating pattern. The GIF format can compress these types of images into very small files. But don't use the GIF format for photos or graphics with gradients (one color blending into another)—the results leave a lot to be desired.

- **PNG for Background Images (Gradients).** This is the option to use if you have a logo or another colorful graphic that uses gradients.

When you select a preset from this menu, Dreamweaver updates the image on the page so you can preview the optimization setting. You also see the properties for the preset displayed at the bottom of the Image Optimization dialog box. These properties vary depending on the file format. You can make adjustments, as you'll see in the next step.

FIGURE 5-5

Dreamweaver CC lets you insert a Photoshop (.psd) file directly into Dreamweaver, and in the process choose how you want to convert that file into a Web-ready GIF, JPG, or PNG file. You can choose a graphic file type such as PNG8 and set various options that help compress the image to a smaller file size.

4. **Optional: Tweak the image settings provided by the preset in step 3.**

   In most cases, the preset file formats provide the results you need. But if you're not happy with the look and understand the ins and outs of different file formats, you can tweak the properties. At the top of the list, regardless of the preset you choose in step 3, you see a Format menu. Using this menu, you can, for example, change from a PNG to a JPEG or a GIF file format. Doing so negates any benefit you get from choosing a preset, however.

   Here's a description of the other settings you can tweak for the different presets.

   - **PNG24 for Photos (Sharp Details).** There are really no options when you choose the PNG24 preset. The only thing you can do is change the Format as described above.

   - **JPEG for Photos (Continuous Tones).** Initially, the Quality setting for JPEG for Photos is at its maximum: 100. To make the file smaller, drag the Quality slider to the left. As the quality value gets lower, the file becomes smaller file and image quality poorer. Check the preview to judge the acceptability of the image. It's unlikely that you'll be happy with values below 50.

   - **PNG8 for Logos and Text.** Set the Palette to Adaptive for color images. For black and white images, you can create smaller files by choosing GrayScale. The Color menu lets you choose the number of colors in the image. Options range from 2 to 256. Fewer colors create a coarser image. If your image has transparent areas, turn on the Transparency checkbox. The Matte option helps you minimize the jaggies that sometimes appear at the edge of images with transparency. In that case, you might want to choose a color that's closer to the background color. The background for an image with transparency isn't part of the image, it's either the page's background itself, or the background of a section of the page, such as a sidebar.

- **JPEG High for Maximum Compatibility.** The single option here is the Quality slider. Move it to the left for smaller file sizes and poorer image quality. If you move the slider up to 100, you get the same quality as the JPEG for Photos preset.

- **GIF for Background Images (Patterns).** The settings for a GIF are identical to PNG8 (above) with one exception, the Loss slider. That governs the quality of the image, but in this case, moving the slider right decreases the quality.

- **PNG for Background Images (Gradients).** With PNG for Background Images you can turn on transparency and choose a Matte color. See PNG8 above for a description.

5. **Click OK in the Image Optimization window.**

    The Save Web Image window appears.

6. **Navigate to a location in the site where you want to save the Web-ready image (for example, an Images folder in the site's root folder).**

    Click Save.

    Dreamweaver optimizes the image (converting it to GIF, JPEG, or PNG format) and saves it to the site.

> **NOTE** You can't import animated GIFs using the Image Preview window; instead, you need to first export the animated GIF from the program in which you created it (like Fireworks or Photoshop), and then import it into Dreamweaver.

When you insert a Photoshop image this way, Dreamweaver, unfortunately, ignores images you made using Photoshop's "slice" tool. This handy tool lets web designers export just bits and pieces of a complete web page design in Photoshop—for example, you could design the look of a site's home page in Photoshop and then show it to your client for feedback. Then you can export just parts of the design as separate image files, like a logo in the upper-left corner of the document, individual navigation icons along the top, or a photo in the middle of the document. So if you want to use an exported slice as a graphic on your web page, the import-from-Photoshop technique isn't the best; Dreamweaver tries to insert the entire image, not just slices of it. To get around this, you need to stick with Photoshop and its page "Save for Web" command.

■ JPEG OPTIMIZATION OPTIONS

Dreamweaver doesn't give you many choices for optimizing JPEG images. It offers two presets: JPEG for Photos (Continuous Tones) and JPEG High for Maximum

Compatibility. These presets don't really do anything besides choose JPEG as the file format and set the Quality level to 100 or 80. You're better off selecting JPEG from the Format menu and then choosing a quality setting of from 1 to 100 (see Figure 5-6).

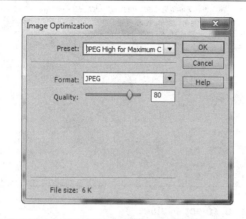

FIGURE 5-6

Move the quality slider down (for smaller files, but worse-looking images) or up (for larger files and better-looking images). Keep an eye on the file size listed at the bottom of the window. It tells you the size of the Web-ready JPEG file Dreamweaver will create.

The quality level you set affects both how good the image looks and its file size. The higher the quality, the larger the file; the worse the quality, the smaller the file. Dreamweaver's Quality setting runs from 1 (low quality/small file) to 100 (high quality/large file). Eighty is a good choice for very good quality and manageable file size; 60 works when you want to keep file size on the slim side. The best setting depends on the image, so move the Quality slider back and forth until the image preview (in Design view) looks good.

■ GIF AND PNG8 OPTIMIZATION OPTIONS

GIF and PNG8 files have nearly identical optimization settings. The number of colors an image has—the size of its *palette*, in other words—contributes most to its file size. Fewer colors mean a smaller file size. Most of the settings available for GIF and PNG8 images control the number and type of colors you can use (see Figure 5-7).

For optimal compression settings with a GIF or PNG8 image, follow these steps:

1. **From the Palette menu, select Adaptive.**

   Since both image types are limited to just 256 colors, this menu determines which colors your image will use. You have a lot of options here, but you can ignore all of them but Adaptive, which means that Dreamweaver picks the best 256 colors from the image itself. The only other option, Grayscale, converts the graphic to a black-and-white image.

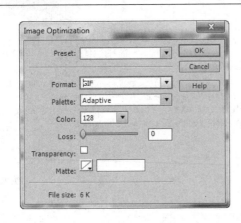

FIGURE 5-7

GIF and PNG optimization settings are nearly identical when you insert a Photoshop image in Dreamweaver. The only difference is the "loss" option—it's only available for GIFs, and it trades image quality for smaller file size.

2. **In the "Number of Colors" menu, select a value.**

You can tell Dreamweaver to use two to the maximum of 256 colors. If the original Photoshop image started out with only 64 colors, choosing 256 doesn't add colors or quality to the image. However, you can often choose a *lower* number, eliminating colors from the graphic and reducing the file size significantly without overly harming the image's quality. Again, each image is different, so trial and error is the best way to balance the minimum number of colors you need with the quality you want.

3. **Choose a value for "Loss" (available only for GIF images).**

The Loss option decreases file size at the cost of image quality. In general, increasing the "loss" setting makes an image look spotted and windswept, so unless you're going for a special effect, use a low setting or none at all.

4. **If the Photoshop image includes transparent areas, turn on the Transparency checkbox.**

Transparency lets some of the content behind an image show through. Images that include transparent areas sometimes show jagged edges where the image stops and the transparent part of the background begins. These ugly jaggies can be minimized by applying a matte color. It helps blend the colors at the edge of the image with the colors of the background. To choose a matte color for your image, pick a hue that matches (or is at least close to) the color of your background. You can do this by clicking the color picker and using the eyedropper to sample the color. This blends the semi-transparent areas of the image (like a see-through drop shadow or the edges around the visible part of the graphic) with the background color, creating a more natural-looking image.

TIP If the graphic doesn't have any transparency and you choose the GIF format, the Matte setting performs a different function: It removes a selected color from the image, making that part of the image transparent. Click the Matte color picker and use the eye dropper to pick the soon-to-be-transparent color in the image. Generally, the results don't look very good, however, so you're better off creating the transparent effect in Photoshop.

In the case of PNG8 images, you don't need to select a matte color as long as the Photoshop image has a completely transparent background. Dreamweaver is smart enough to apply an "alpha transparency" to this kind of image. Alpha transparency doesn't have the same "jaggies" issues.

TIP If you're inserting an image that has a transparent background and is a good candidate for a GIF or PNG8 (that is, large areas of solid color as described in the box on page 225), choose PNG8 and turn on the Transparency checkbox. Dreamweaver saves PNG8 images with full alpha transparency, which looks a lot better than the color transparency GIF images offer.

■ PNG OPTIMIZATION OPTIONS

If you save a file in the PNG8 format, you have the same options as you do with GIF images (see the previous section). If you choose PNG24, your choice is simple... well, actually, you don't have a choice. In the Image Preview window, just click OK, and then save the file. As mentioned in the box on page 225, PNG24 images aren't a good choice for web pages. While they provide better quality than JPEG images, they produce significantly larger file sizes.

As with PNG8 images, you can turn on the Transparency checkbox for PNG32 pics (see Figure 5-8). In fact, you'd only want to use PNG32 if an image contains an alpha transparency channel (256 levels of transparency) and the image has lots of colors: for example, a gradient that transitions from a solid color to a transparent background or a photograph whose edges fade off to a transparent background. In other words, use PNG8 with transparency if the image has 256 colors or less (like a logo), and choose PNG32 with transparency if the image has more than 256 colors and has transparent areas. (See the box on page 225 for more on choosing a graphic file format.)

■ Modifying an Image

After you insert a graphic, you can manipulate it several ways. You can attach a link to it, apply a CSS class style to it, and even create an "image map" so that different areas on the image link to different web pages. You can also use some of Dreamweaver's basic editing tools to crop, resize, optimize, sharpen, and adjust the image's contrast and brightness.

As with most objects on a web page, you set image properties using the Properties panel (see Figure 5-9).

FIGURE 5-8

Saving a Photoshop file as a PNG32 image doesn't provide a lot of choices. In fact, the only advantage to using PNG32 is the transparency option. Skip selecting a matte color for PNG32 images—you only need to turn on the Transparency checkbox to use the alpha transparency that PNG32 already provides.

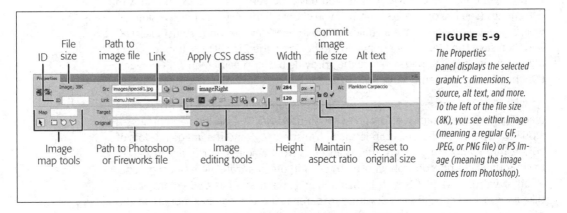

FIGURE 5-9

The Properties panel displays the selected graphic's dimensions, source, alt text, and more. To the left of the file size (8K), you see either Image (meaning a regular GIF, JPEG, or PNG file) or PS Image (meaning the image comes from Photoshop).

Adding an ID to an Image

In the Properties panel, just to the right of an image's thumbnail, you'll see a small field where you can type in an ID. The ID is JavaScript's standard way to identify an individual object on a page. Cascading Style Sheets also use IDs, as described on page 108. For example, in CSS Designer, you use IDs as selectors so you can apply unique formatting to just that element. So you might use the ID to add a border to an image.

Most of the time, you'll leave this field blank. But if you plan to add interactive effects to the image, like the rollover effect discussed on page 254 or your own JavaScript programming (see Chapter 13), you need to add an ID. Here are the rules for ID names. The first character must be a letter (upper or lowercase). Following that, you can use numbers, hyphens, underscores, colons, and periods. Spaces and other punctuation are not allowed. The purpose of an ID is to identify a single element on

the page, so IDs must be unique. If you give an image on the page the ID "logo,"
you can't use it for another element on the same page.

When you add an ID to an image in the properties panel, Dreamweaver adds the ID
attribute to the image tag, like this:

```
<img src="images/logo.jpg" alt="" width="120" height="150" id="logo"/>
```

Adding a Text Description to an Image

Not everyone who visits your website gets to see those stunning photos of your summer vacation. Some people deliberately turn off graphics when they surf, enjoying
the web without the wait, since graphics-free pages appear almost instantly. Other
people have vision impairments that prevent them from seeing the web's visual
aspects. They rely on special software that reads web page text aloud, including
any labels you give your graphics.

To assist web surfers in both situations, make a habit of setting an image's *Alt* property. Short for *alternative text*, the Alt property is text that describes an image. To
add a description to an image, type it in the Properties panel's Alt field (see Figure
5-9). If you're naming navigation buttons, for example, you could use the text that
appears on the button, such as *Home* or *Products*. For images that carry greater
meaning—such as a photo of the product itself—you might use a more detailed
description: "Photo of Sasquatch relaxing at his lodge in the Adirondacks."

NOTE In some cases, a description is more of a distraction than a help. For example, you might insert an
image of an intricate swirling line to act as a visual divider between two paragraphs. The image doesn't actually
convey any meaningful information; it's just for decoration.

Changing an Image's Size

A graphic's width and height properties do more than determine its size on-screen;
they also help web browsers load the graphic quickly and efficiently. Since the
HTML of a web page downloads before any graphics do, browsers display the text
on a page first and add images as they arrive. If you don't include width and height
attributes with an image, the browser doesn't know how much space on the page
to reserve, so it has to redraw the page after it downloads each image. As a result,
the pages appear to "stutter" with each redraw. This disconcerting behavior does
little for your reputation as a cool, competent web designer.

Fortunately, you don't have to worry about specifying a picture's dimensions yourself.
Whenever Dreamweaver inserts an image into a page, it automatically calculates
its width and height, and enters those values into the Properties panel's W and H
fields (see Figure 5-9).

You can, if you like, *shrink* a graphic by typing smaller values into the W and H fields,
but doing so doesn't do anything to speed up the page's download time. You make
the picture *appear* smaller, but a browser still has to download the entire file. To
make your graphic smaller in both appearance and file size, you have to shrink it

in an image-editing program like Fireworks or Photoshop, or use Dreamweaver's Resample Image tool, described on page 245. Not only do you get an image that's exactly the size you want, but it usually looks better and you trim a few bytes off its file size (and maybe even save a second or two of download time).

On the other hand, setting width and height values that are *larger* than the dimensions of a graphic merely distorts the image by stretching it, creating an undesirable pixelated effect. If you want a larger image without distortion or pixelation, start with a larger original image. To do so, return to your digital camera or stock photo file, or recreate the graphic at a larger size in Photoshop or Fireworks.

Dreamweaver provides some helpful tools when you resize an image. The lock icon to the right of the Width and Height boxes (Figure 5-9) maintains the aspect ratio of the image when locked. For example, say you insert an image that is 200 pixels wide by 100 pixels tall. You click in the W (width) box in the Properties panel and type *100* because you want the image to be smaller: If the lock icon is closed, the H box will change to 50 pixels, too. Dreamweaver maintains the proportions of the image when you type a value in either the W or H boxes, so long as the lock icon is closed. On the other hand, if you click the icon to unlock it, you can type values in the W and H boxes that stretch the image beyond its normal proportions. (You'll probably also stretch your client's patience when he sees what a mess you made of his company's logo.)

In addition, if you're not happy with the new dimension you typed (or you accidentally resized the image by typing in the W field instead of the H field, or you grabbed the image-resize handles discussed in the box on page 235), click the "Reset to original size" button (see Figure 5-9). That returns the image to its original dimensions. Finally, if you do change the image's size and you're happy with the new look, click the "Commit image size" button, which permanently alters the file (basically, it does the same thing as the Resample Image tool described on page 245).

> **NOTE** Dreamweaver 5.5 and earlier included an alignment menu and a border and margin settings box in the Properties panel. The Dreamweaver engineers removed those because they're better handled with CSS, as described next.

Controlling Images with CSS

Cascading Style Sheets aren't just for styling text. You can also use its design power to add borders to an image, force text to wrap around an image, and even add images to the background of other elements. For example, the CSS *background-image* property lets you place an image in the background of a web page, or add a graphical background to a link, headline, or any other HTML tag.

UP TO SPEED

Making Accessible Websites

Some people using the Web have disabilities that make reading, seeing, hearing, or using a mouse difficult. Visually impaired people, for example, may not benefit from images on the screen, even if they have software that reads a web page's text aloud.

Dreamweaver includes a number of features that make your websites more accessible. That's good news if you're building a site for the federal government or one of the many states that support Section 508 of the Workforce Investment Act, the law that requires websites built for or funded by the government to offer equal or equivalent access to everyone. Throughout this book, you'll find tips for using Dreamweaver's accessibility features.

The Alt property described on page 233 is an important first step in assisting visually impaired web surfers. For complex images,

such as a graph that plots changes in utility rates over time, you can supply a more detailed description on a separate web page. The *Longdesc* (long description) property of an image lets you specify a link to a page containing a text description of the image. Some web browsers understand this property, letting visually impaired visitors jump to that description page.

Longdesc was officially part of HTML4, but was initially left out of HTML5. As you might imagine, this led to a debate about whether *Longdesc* was the best way to provide accessibility. When this book went to press, Dreamweaver CC didn't include tools for *Longdesc*, but that may change in the future. For the most current details on the subject, go to *www.w3.org* and search on the term *longdesc*. For an overview of web accessibility and helpful tips on making accessible sites, visit *www.w3.org/WAI/gettingstarted/*.

WORD TO THE WISE

Watch Those Resize Handles!

After you insert an image in the document window, a thin black border appears around it, indicating that it's selected. Three small black squares—resize handles—appear on the right edge, bottom edge, and lower-right corner.

Dragging these handles changes the graphic's width and height—or, rather, it changes the Width and Height properties in the Properties panel. Pressing Shift while dragging the corner handle maintains the proportions of the image. The graphics file itself remains unchanged.

Dragging one of these handles to make the picture appear bigger is almost always a bad idea, resulting in distortion

and ugly pixelation. And you can far too easily accidentally grab and drag the pesky handles. In fact, sometimes you may resize a graphic and not even know it. Perhaps you accidentally dragged the left resize handle a few pixels, making the graphic wider, but not enough to notice.

Fortunately, the Properties panel lets you know when a graphic differs from its original size: If you see the "Reset to original size" button (the little circle with a slash icon pictured in Figure 5-9), you know you've resized the image. Click this button to roll the pic back to its original dimensions.

In general, you probably don't want to create a tag style (see page 105) for the <img> tag. That type of style affects *every* image on a page (or on an entire site if you use a site-wide external style sheet). And while you may want a bright-red, 10-pixel border around each thumbnail in a photo gallery, you probably don't want that border around the site's logo or the navigation buttons on the same page. You're more likely to create class styles you can manually apply to certain graphics. In the thumbnail example, you'd create a class style with the proper border setting, and then apply that class to each gallery image (you can be even more efficient and use a *descendent selector* as described on page 370).

Wrapping Text Around an Image

After you add an image to a page, you might initially find yourself staring at a bunch of empty white space around the image (see Figure 5-10, top). Not only does this waste precious screen real estate, it's usually unattractive. Fortunately, you can wrap text around images using the CSS *float* property (see Figure 5-10, bottom).

FIGURE 5-10

Placing an image on the same line as text (top) creates unsightly open space, which you can put to better use. By floating an image to the right (bottom) or left, you force content that would otherwise sit beneath the image to wrap around it.

To do so, in CSS Designer's Layout category, set the *float* property (see Figure 5-11). You can float an element *left* or *right*. If you want an image to appear on the right side of a page and have text flow around its left and bottom edges, choose "right" from the Float menu. The Float property behaves just like the right and left alignment options for images (see the Note below).

FIGURE 5-11

The Layout category contains some of the most-used CSS properties: the float property (shown near the bottom of the CSS Designer panel) to align images and other page elements to the left or right, the margin property so you can add or remove space between elements (like adding space between the edge of a right-floated image and the text that wraps around it), and the padding property to add space between the content within an element and the edges of that element.

NOTE The Float property has many uses, from positioning images on the right or left side of a page to creating thumbnail photo galleries to laying out entire web pages. You'll learn about using it for layout in Chapter 10. For an excellent introduction and set of tutorials on the Float property in general, visit *http://css.maxdesign. com.au/floatutorial*. Book lovers should pick up *CSS3: The Missing Manual* for an in-depth discussion, tutorials, and practical tips on using floats.

One thing to keep in mind with floats: The floated element must appear *before* anything you want to wrap around it. Say you have a paragraph of text you'd like to wrap around a right-floated image. You need to insert the image before the text (a good spot is before the first letter of the paragraph you want to wrap around the image). If you float an image to the right but place the image after the text, the image moves to the right, but the paragraph remains above the image.

You'll frequently use the Margin property with floats. A margin is the outermost space surrounding an element. It lets you add space between one element and another. So, for a right-floated image, it's usually a good idea to add a little *left, bottom,* and *top* margin. This creates a bit of breathing room between the image and anything that wraps around it; omitting a left margin on a right-floated image can cause text to butt right up against the image.

You can specify a margin using any unit of measure—pixels, percentages, and so on—that CSS supports.

Adding Borders

As you saw in the tutorial for Chapter 3, you can add a border to any element on a page—a paragraph or even a single word. But borders can really add impact to a photo on a page, because they give the image a polished "frame-like" appearance; in addition, borders can help unify a page full of thumbnail images.

You control the border, logically enough, from CSS Designer's Border category (see Figure 5-12). (If CSS designer isn't visible, choose Window→CSS Designer.)

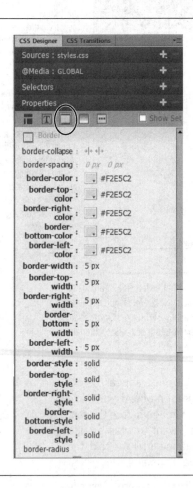

FIGURE 5-12

Click the border button (circled) to see the options for framing a page element. Add colorful and stylish borders to paragraphs, images, tables, and links with CSS border properties. Turning on only the bottom border for a paragraph is a great way to add a horizontal rule between paragraphs. While HTML's Horizontal Rule object also does this, only CSS lets you control the rule's color.

You can control the properties of each *side* of a border independently, so that each has its own color, width, and style:

- **border-color.** Use the ubiquitous color picker to set the *border-color* property for all four borders. To set border colors individually, specify values for *border-*

top-color, *border-left-color*, and so on. If you don't assign border colors but do assign border *widths*, the border color matches that of the surrounding text.

- **border-width.** Border widths work the same way. You can make all the widths the same by setting a value for *border-width* only, or you can set border widths for each side. Choose one of the preset widths—thin, medium, or thick—or choose a unit of measure from the pop-up menu and then type in a value. Again, you can choose from a range of units: pixels (the most common), percentage, inches, and so on (see page 136 for more on CSS units of measure). If you want to eliminate the border on one side, type *0* into the appropriate box, or click the Remove CSS property button (a.k.a. the trash can).

- **border-style.** This menu lets you specify the type of line web browsers draw for the border. It gives you more options than a frame shop: none (the default), dotted, dashed, solid, double, groove, ridge, inset, and outset (see Figure 5-13). Use *border-style* to set a style for all sides, or use the individual border properties to set the style for each side.

NOTE If you don't choose a border style option, or if you set it to "none," you don't see the borders even if you set their width and color properties. The same is true if you don't set a width property or have it set to 0.

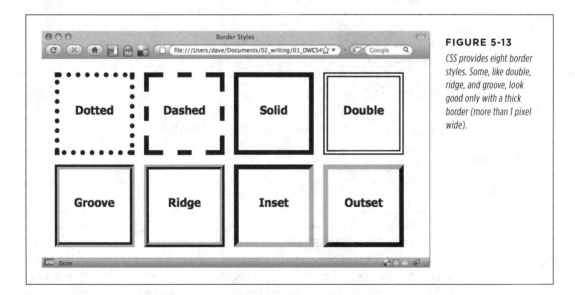

FIGURE 5-13

CSS provides eight border styles. Some, like double, ridge, and groove, look good only with a thick border (more than 1 pixel wide).

If you use borders to "frame" an image, you can use the *padding* property to add space between the image and the border—this simulates the appearance of the cardboard matte used in professionally framed photographs. Padding is the gap that separates content—such as a paragraph of text or an image—and its border.

You set the padding from CSS Designer's Layout category (see Figure 5-24). To put a 1-pixel border around an image and add 10 pixels of space between the image and the border, go to CSS Designer→Properties, and then click the Layout button. In the Padding box, click the Link ("Click To Change All Properties"). Click in one of the number boxes around the edge of the box and type *10*.

Background Images

Adding an image to a page is one way to enhance your site, but CSS also lets you add an image to the *background* of any tag. That way, you can use a graphic as the background of a page, enhance a headline with an icon, or add your own custom graphics to links.

You control background images by setting the following properties in CSS Designer's background-image property (see Figure 5-14).

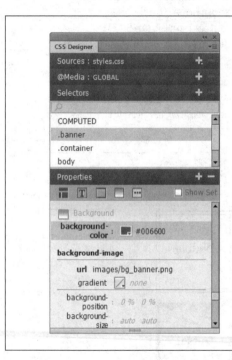

FIGURE 5-14

CSS's background properties lets you specify both a background color and background image for a given element, such as a div that makes up a sidebar. While you won't frequently apply a color and image (after all, the image would usually cover up anything behind it), it can come in handy when you use it with the Padding property (see page 439) to create a customized "matte" to surround the image.

■ BACKGROUND-IMAGE

Add a background image to a tag in CSS Designer by choosing a source (an internal or external style sheet), a selector (a tag, such as <body>, <h1>, or <div>), and then, in the Properties section, by clicking the Background button. Dreamweaver scrolls down to the background properties. Under *background-image*, you see "URL," prompting you to locate the background image file. After clicking in the value box, click the folder icon and then browse your way to the image. If you choose an image outside of your site, Dreamweaver automatically adds it to the images folder you designated when you set up your site. You can also type in an absolute URL, starting with *http://*, to use an image from the Web.

To fill the background of your entire web page with a repeating graphic, you could either redefine the <body> tag using the *background-image* property, or create a class or ID style with a *background-image* property, and then apply the class or ID to the <body> tag as described on page 115 (the tutorial from Chapter 1 uses this technique to add a background pattern to the page).

You can even control how an image tiles (repeats) and where Dreamweaver puts it on a page (see below). Furthermore, you can add background images to any *individual* element on your page: paragraphs, tables, <div>s, and so on.

Background images appear above any background color, so you can (and often will) combine the two. For example, you may want to position an interesting graphic on top of a colorful background image.

NOTE One common byte-saving technique when you use navigation buttons on a site is to create an image that has all the characteristics of a button—burnished edges and so on—except for a label. You use this generic button as the background image for navigation links on a page. The links themselves include regular text—"Home," "About Us," and so on—but the background of each link makes them look like graphical buttons. The main benefit to this technique is that you don't need to create separate graphics for each button.

■ BACKGROUND-REPEAT

When a browser displays the background for a web page, it usually *tiles* the background image. That is, it repeats the image over and over again, across and down. A small image of a carrot added to the background of a page appears as a field of carrots—one next to another, row after row. (Not all web designers use a background image for their pages; some leave the background white or set a color property, such as black, for sites that use white text.)

But with CSS, you can control *how* the background image repeats. In CSS Designer, you select from the following properties for background images:

- *repeat* tiles the image horizontally and vertically. This is how browsers normally display a background image.

- *repeat-x* and *repeat-y* display a horizontal and vertical band of images, respectively. If you want a single row of images at the top of a page, use the *repeat-x* option; it's a good way to add a graphical background to a banner. *repeat-y*, on the other hand, is great for a graphical sidebar that appears down the edge of a page.

- *no-repeat* displays the image only once (see the examples in Figure 5-15).

■ BACKGROUND-ATTACHMENT

By default, the background image on a page scrolls with the rest of the page—as you scroll down to read a long web page, the image scrolls "off the screen" along with the text.

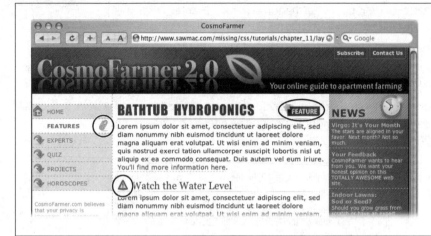

FIGURE 5-15

Background images aren't just for the body of a web page. You can apply a background image to any page element, including links, headlines, and paragraphs of text. The circled graphics in this image are just a few examples of background images that have the "no-repeat" setting.

But using CSS, you can lock the image in place by choosing *fixed* from the *background-attachment* menu. Say you add your company's logo to the background of a page and set the Repeat property (described above) to "no-repeat." The logo now appears only once in the upper-left corner of the page. If you use the "fixed" option for this property, when a visitor scrolls the page, the logo remains fixed in the upper-left corner. (Choosing "scroll" from the Attachment menu means, of course, that the background image scrolls with the page—this is a default behavior, so you don't need to choose this option.) Note that "fixed" really works out only when you apply an image to the body of a page—the image stays fixed when the rest of the content scrolls.

■ POSITIONING THE BACKGROUND IMAGE

Using the horizontal and vertical settings for *background-image*, you specify a position for the background image within a container, such as a <div> tag or the <body> tag of the page. There are two ways to apply the background-position properties. You can use general terms to define the position, like left, right, top, bottom, and center. Or you can apply number values, such as 40 px (pixels) or 10 %. For example, if you chose Center for both the horizontal and vertical background position, your image is centered inside the container. Choosing Left would position the left edge of the image at the left edge of the container.

When you choose a value and unit of measure, the top-left corner of the image is positioned relative to the top-left corner of the container. So if you set the horizontal property to 10 px and the vertical property to 45 px, the top-left corner of your image is 10 pixels to the right of the left edge of the container and 45 pixels down from the top. There's a long list of units of measure you can choose from when you apply values, but the most useful are pixels, percentages, and ems.

Keep in mind that these positioning options refer to the position of the background image *within the container*. Suppose you create a class style that includes a background image with both the horizontal and vertical positions set to *center*. Then say you apply that class style to a paragraph. The background image would appear in the center of that *paragraph*, not in the center of the web page.

And if you wanted to place an image in the exact center of a page, you'd choose the <body> tag as the selector in CSS Designer. In other words, it's the container for the image. Then, after setting the URL for your background image, you'd set the background-position properties to "center" for both the horizontal and vertical. The background-repeat property should be set to "no-repeat."

◼ Editing Graphics

Nothing's ever perfect, especially when you're building a website. Corrections are par for the course—not just to a web page, but to the pictures on it as well. Perhaps a picture is a tad too dark, or you'd like to crop out the rowdy coworker being escorted from your company's holiday party.

In the hands of less capable software, you'd face a tedious set of steps each time you wanted to edit a graphic. You'd have to open Photoshop, Fireworks, or whatever graphics program you prefer; choose File→Open; navigate to your website folder; find the graphic that needs touching up (if you can even remember its name); and then open it to make your changes.

But Dreamweaver simplifies all that. It includes tools that handle many basic graphics-editing tasks. For more complex work, like changing the text on a button from "Now Firing" to "Now Hiring," you do need to switch to a different program. But even here, Dreamweaver is considerate of your time; it lets you access your favorite graphics program with just a couple of clicks.

Dreamweaver's Built-In Editing Tools

Dreamweaver includes four tools so you can crop, resample, sharpen, and adjust the brightness and contrast of an image (see Figure 5-16). Suppose your boss emails you his portrait with instructions to put it on his "Meet the boss" page. Unfortunately, the picture's too big and too dark. Rather than launch a separate image-editing program, you can add the photo to the page and then make the corrections within Dreamweaver.

But first, a warning: All of Dreamweaver's tools change the *original* GIF, JPEG, or PNG image in your site folder. If you shrink a graphic and later change your mind, you may be out of luck. It's a good idea, therefore, to back up your images before you use these tools. In addition, if you add a Photoshop document and create a Smart Object (page 248), the tools discussed next break the link with the Photoshop file. That means that, for Smart Objects, you're better off editing the original Photoshop document as discussed on page 248. The reason? That retains the relationship between the image on your web page and Photoshop; if you edit the graphic in

Photoshop at some point and then launch Dreamweaver, Dreamweaver tells you the image has changed, and lets you update it on your site.

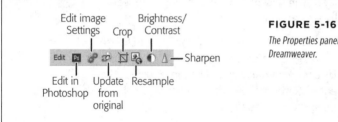

FIGURE 5-16

The Properties panel includes tools for editing images from Dreamweaver.

Furthermore, remember that if you use that same file on other pages, your modifications appear on those pages, too. For instance, if you decide to shrink your company logo on one page, you may find the smaller logo on *every* page on your site! What's worse, the image's width and height settings don't change on the other pages, so the logo looks unnaturally pixelated there. If you want to change a graphic on only one page, make a copy of it first, insert the *copy* in the page you wish to change, and then modify just that image file. That way, the rest of your site keeps the original graphic.

Of course, if you discover right away that you made a change you don't want, you can choose Edit→Undo or press Ctrl+Z (⌘-Z). Until you close the page, you can undo multiple image changes.

USELESS TRIVIA

Meet the Geeks Behind Dreamweaver

Want to see pictures of the engineers behind Dreamweaver? OK, maybe you don't, but you can. Go to the Properties panel and select an image in the document window. On the left side of the panel, Ctrl+double-click (⌘-double-click) the graphic's thumbnail. A picture of one of Dreamweaver's programmers appears, along with his or her name. Ctrl+double-click (⌘-double-click) the thumbnail repeatedly to cycle through the names and pictures of other members of the Dreamweaver team.

■ CROPPING AN IMAGE

Dreamweaver's Crop tool can remove extraneous or distracting parts of an image. You can use it to focus on a single person, or to get rid of those teenagers making faces in the corner.

To do so, select the graphic you want to crop, and then, in the Properties panel, click the Crop tool (see Figure 5-16). Alternatively, choose Modify→Image→Crop.

A rectangular box with eight resize handles on it appears inside the image; anything outside the box will be cropped out. Move this box (by dragging it) and resize it (by dragging the handles) until you've got just what you want inside the box.

When you're done, double-click inside the box, or click the Properties panel's Crop tool again. Dreamweaver crops the image, discarding the unwanted areas.

To undo a crop, press Ctrl+Z (⌘-Z). In fact, you can back out before you've used the Crop tool at all; click anywhere on the page outside the image to make the cropping box go away.

■ RESAMPLING AN IMAGE

If a photo is just too big to fit on a web page, you could select the image and use one of the resize handles to alter its dimensions. Unfortunately, graphics you shrink this way give you the worst of both worlds: They look muddier than they were before, and they download slowly because you're still grabbing the larger image.

You can, however, use this resizing technique with Dreamweaver's Image Resample tool to resize the actual graphic. You'll end up with a trimmed-down file with its appearance intact.

To use the Resample tool, select an image and then resize it using the resize handles. (Shift-drag to prevent distortion.) When you're done, click the Resample button in the Properties panel (Figure 5-16), and Dreamweaver resizes the image.

You can even make an image larger than the original using this technique. The end result isn't perfect—even Dreamweaver can't create image information that was never there—but the program does its best to prevent the image from looking pixelated. You don't want to enlarge images this way often, but in a pinch, it's a quick way to make a photo just a little bit larger.

> **TIP** When working with a Photoshop Smart Object, you can make the image on the page in Dreamweaver smaller, and then click the Update from Original button to create a smaller version without resizing the Photoshop file (see page 248).

Dreamweaver changes the actual image, altering its width and height. If you change your mind about resampling the image, your only option is the old Undo command, Ctrl+Z (⌘-Z).

■ BRIGHTNESS AND CONTRAST

If an image on a page is too light, dark, or washed-out, use Dreamweaver's Brightness/Contrast dialog box to fix it.

First, select the picture, and then click the Brightness/Contrast icon in the Properties panel. In the Brightness/Contrast dialog box (Figure 5-17), move the Brightness slider to the right to lighten the image (great for underexposed interior shots), or to the left to darken the image. The Contrast control works the same way: right to increase contrast (making dark colors darker and light colors lighter), left to decrease contrast (moving all colors toward gray).

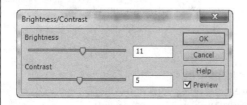

FIGURE 5-17

If you've ever used image-editing software like Fireworks or Photoshop, this dialog box should look familiar. Make sure you have the Preview checkbox turned on so you can see your changes right in the document window before you click OK.

You'll often use the Brightness and Contrast sliders together. Brightening (lightening) an image also has a fading effect. By increasing the contrast at the same time, you restore some punch to a brightened image.

As with the other image-editing controls, if you're unhappy with the changes you make, choose Edit→Undo or press Ctrl+Z (⌘-Z) to return the image to its previous glory.

■ SHARPENING IMAGES

Sometimes graphics, even those from scanners and digital cameras, can look a little fuzzy, especially if you resample the image (see page 245). Dreamweaver's Sharpen tool helps restore clarity and make such images "pop." It works like similar tools in graphics-editing programs: It increases the contrast between an image's pixels to create the illusion of sharper, more focused graphics.

To use the tool, select a graphic, and then, in the Properties panel, click the Sharpen icon (Figure 5-16). The Sharpen window appears, with a single slider. Move the slider to the right to increase the amount of sharpening, or type a number in the box (*10* is maximum sharpening; *0* is no change). You probably won't use the maximum setting unless you're going for a special effect, since it tends to highlight "noise" in the image, creating an unappealing halo effect around the pixels. Once you select a level of sharpening you like, click OK.

If you're unhappy with the results, just press Ctrl+Z (⌘-Z), or choose Edit→Undo.

Setting Up an External Editor

When you double-click an image file in the Files panel, your favorite image-editing program launches and opens the file, ready for you to edit. When you first install Dreamweaver, it tries to figure out which program to use by looking through the software installed on your computer. But if you want to use a program other than the one Dreamweaver assigns, you need to tell Dreamweaver.

1. **Choose Edit→Preferences (Dreamweaver→Preferences).**

   The Preferences dialog box opens, as shown in Figure 5-18.

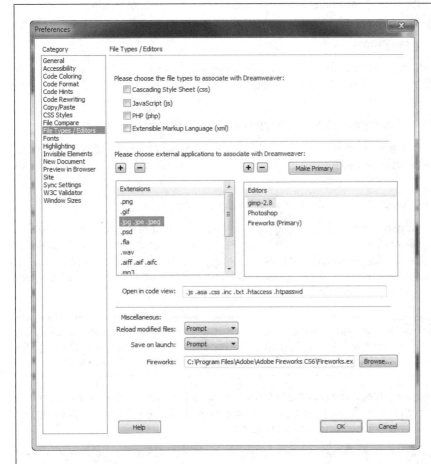

FIGURE 5-18

You can tell Dreamweaver to use certain programs for editing different types of files, such as GIF, JPEG, or PNG files. If you have .fla (Flash files), .mp3 (music files), or other types of non-HTML files on your site, you can assign programs to those file types as well—double-clicking the filename in the Files panel launches the associated editing program.

2. **In the left pane, click File Types/Editors.**

   The Preferences box displays your preferred editing programs for different types of files. Two columns appear: Extensions and Editors.

3. **From the Extensions list, select a graphics file extension.**

   The box lists several types of graphic files, including: GIFs, JPEGs, and PNGs. You can choose a different editing program for each type if you like. Add filename extensions for file types not shown by clicking the + button above the Extensions list.

4. **Click the + button above the Editors list.**

   The Select External Editor dialog box opens.

5. **On your hard drive, find the program you want to use to edit the selected type of graphics file.**

It can be Photoshop, Photoshop Elements, Fireworks, or whatever.

6. **If you wish to make this program your primary image-editing tool, click Make Primary.**

This *primary* editor is the one Dreamweaver opens when you choose to edit a graphic. (You can define other, less frequently used editors as well. See the Tip below.)

7. **Repeat steps 3–6 for each type of graphics file you work with.**

Dreamweaver treats GIFs, JPEGs, and PNGs as separate file types, so you need to assign an editor to each. Of course, most people choose the same program for all three types.

8. **Click OK to close the Preferences dialog box.**

From now on, whenever you need to touch up a graphic on your web page, just select it, and then click Edit in the Properties panel. Alternatively, in the Files panel, you can simply double-click the file, or Ctrl-double-click (⌘-double-click) the image on the page. In any case, your graphic now opens in the program you set as your primary editor.

NOTE When you insert a Photoshop image into a web page in Dreamweaver, you always convert it to a web-friendly format like JPG or PNG. Later, clicking the Properties panel's Edit button launches Photoshop and opens the original PSD file—no matter what you changed the image's file type to in Dreamweaver.

Now you can edit the graphic and save changes to it. When you return to Dreamweaver, the modified image appears on the page. (If you're a Photoshop or Fireworks fan, you're in even better shape; read on.)

NOTE You aren't limited to just one external editor for each file type. For instance, if there's a Fireworks feature you need, even though Photoshop is your primary editor, you can still jump to Fireworks directly from Dreamweaver.

The trick is to right-click (Control-click) the image you want to edit, whether it's in the document window or the Files panel. Choose the Open With menu. If you added the image editor to your preferences (Figure 5-18), the submenu lists that editor. Otherwise, from the contextual menu, select Browse, and then, in the resulting dialog box, choose the editing program you want to use. That program opens, with the graphic you clicked open and ready for your edits.

Editing Smart Objects

Since Adobe makes the ubiquitous Photoshop as well as Dreamweaver, it makes sense that the two programs work together. As you read on page 224, you can get a Photoshop image by simply inserting the PSD file, just as you would insert a regular web-ready graphic. Doing this creates a *smart object*.

Smart Objects really are a, well, smart idea. They let you preserve an original high-resolution Photoshop file as the main source of one or more web-ready graphics. Since producing web graphics often entails reducing a file's size, any edits you make to the image are best made to the highest-quality version you have. For example, if you want to change the font in your company's logo, don't edit the GIF or PNG file you used on a web page. Instead, edit the higher-quality PSD version in Photoshop. Smart Objects make that easy.

You can launch Photoshop and then open the PSD file to work on it, or, better yet, you can launch Photoshop directly from Dreamweaver—on your web page, select the Smart Object, and then click the Properties panel's "Edit in Photoshop" button (see Figure 5-19). This opens the PSD file in Photoshop, where you can make the desired edits—modify the company logo, crop the image, use creative filters, and so on. When you're done, save and close the file.

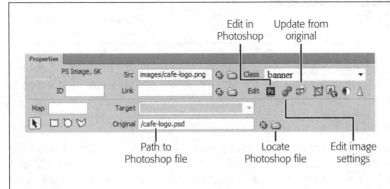

FIGURE 5-19

When you use Smart Objects on a page, the Properties panel includes an "Update from original" button, which lets you update the image on a page whenever you change the original image in Photoshop. You can also revisit the original image settings—if you decide, for example, that you want a PNG8 image instead of a GIF or if you want to change the compression settings—by clicking the Edit Image Settings button.

TIP You can also launch Photoshop to edit a Smart Object's original Photoshop document directly from the Files panel. Right-click (Control-click) the Smart Object—which is a GIF, JPEG, or PNG file in the Files panel—and then, from the contextual menu that appears, choose "Edit Original with Photoshop."

Smart objects are "smart" because they keep track of any changes you make to the original PSD file. You can recognize a Smart Object by the recycling logo that appears in the upper-left corner of the image in Dreamweaver's Design view (see Figure 5-20). Immediately after you insert a Photoshop image, the two arrows in the icon are green, meaning that the image on the page is based on the latest version of the file (Figure 5-20, top). If you update the Photoshop document in Photoshop, the bottom arrow turns red (Figure 5-20, middle). This means someone modified the original Photoshop document. To sync the web page file with the original, select the image, and then click the Update From Original button in the Properties panel. You can also right-click (Control-click) the image and select Update From Original from the contextual menu.

FIGURE 5-20

A Smart Object is a GIF, JPEG, or PNG file you import from Photoshop. In Design view, Dreamweaver displays an icon in the top-left corner of Smart Objects. Top: Green means file relationships are well and the displayed image is up to date. Middle: Red arrows mean the image on the page needs to be updated from the original. Bottom: Dreamweaver displays a warning symbol (a yellow triangle with an exclamation mark) in certain situations, described below.

When you update an image this way, Dreamweaver retains all the previous optimization settings—including the file format (GIF, JPEG, or PNG), cropping, resizing, and file name.

■ SMART OBJECT WARNINGS

Sometimes you see a warning symbol (a yellow triangle with an exclamation mark) as part of the Smart Object icon (see Figure 5-20, bottom). That means one of two things: Either Dreamweaver can't locate the original PSD file, or you resized the inserted image in Dreamweaver—probably by dragging the resize handles, as discussed on page 235.

If Dreamweaver loses track of a PSD file, simply select the Smart Object (you need to be in Design view), and then click the folder icon in the Properties panel (to the right of the Original box). This opens the Select Original File window—just a basic "pick a file on your computer" dialog box. Navigate to the PSD file, and then select it. Unfortunately, once Dreamweaver loses track of the PSD file, it also loses all the optimization information, such as the file format and the name of the web-ready file. You have to set all these options again, as described on pages 225–228.

The second instance in which you can see the yellow warning symbol is when you resize an image in Dreamweaver. If you make the image on the page *smaller* than the original PSD file (for example, by dragging the resize handles or entering smaller width and height values in the Properties panel), click the Properties panel's "Update from Original" button (see Figure 5-19). Doing so re-exports the original image (using all your optimization settings) so that it matches the new size you set on the page. (This has no affect on the original PSD image; it always remains the same.)

However, if you resize the image on the page so that it's *larger* than the original PSD file, the yellow warning icon remains, no matter what. In this case, it indicates that the PSD file doesn't have enough pixels to make the image the size you want it without affecting the image's quality. In other words, you can't make the images on your page larger than the Photoshop file they come from without getting a worse-quality image.

NOTE If you resize a Smart Object on a page, you can return it to its original size (that is, the size of the image in the original Photoshop file). In Design view, right-click (Control-click) the Smart Object, and then, from the menu that appears, choose "Reset size to original."

Optimizing an Image

You can optimize an image—compress it so it downloads faster—by clicking the "Edit image settings" button (the one with the two gears) in the Properties panel (see Figure 5-19). After clicking the button, the Image Optimization window appears. This is the same one that appears when you import a Photoshop file. Although the Optimize feature does leave you with a smaller image file, you should use it only if you're applying it to a Photoshop Smart Object. If you try to optimize a regular GIF, JPEG, or PNG, you're compressing an already compressed file. Applying additional optimization often degrades the image's quality. However, clicking the "Optimize image" button after selecting a Photoshop file lets you create a new web-ready file—GIF, JPEG, or PNG—from the original Photoshop file without any loss of quality.

If you have do have a JPEG file that you think should be a GIF (see the box on page 225 for guidelines), or you simply want to see if you can shave a few more bytes from a file by optimizing it again, it's best to return to the original file (Fireworks, Illustrator, or whatever program you used to create the graphic), if available, and use that program's export or "Save for Web" feature to generate a new GIF, JPEG, or PNG.

If you decide to ignore this warning (or you don't have the original image and really need to optimize the image further), follow the directions on pages 228–231. Once you make your changes, click OK in the Preview Image window. Dreamweaver optimizes the image again. You can choose Edit→Undo to back out of the change.

■ Image Maps

As Chapter 4 makes clear, you can easily turn a graphic into a clickable link. You can also add *multiple* links to a single image.

Suppose your company has offices all over the country and you want to provide an easy way for visitors to locate the nearest one. One approach is to list all the state names and link them to separate pages for each state, but that's boring! Instead, you could use a map of the United States—a single image—and turn each state's outline into a hotspot linked to the appropriate page, listing all the offices in that state.

The array of invisible links (called *hotspots*) responsible for this magic is called an *image map*. Image maps contain one or more hotspots, each leading somewhere else.

Here's how to create an image map:

1. **Select the graphic you want to make into an image map.**

   The Properties panel displays the image's properties and, in the lower-left corner, the image map tools (see Figure 5-21). (You see these tools only with the Properties panel fully expanded—double-click the empty gray area to show the full Properties panel.)

2. **In the Properties panel's Map field, type a name for the map.**

   The name should contain only letters and numbers, and can't begin with a number. If you don't give the map a name, Dreamweaver automatically assigns it the ingenious name *Map*. You don't really need to change the name; your visitors never see it, and a browser uses it just to find the file. If you create additional image maps, Dreamweaver calls them *Map2*, *Map3*, and so on.

3. **Select one of the image map tools.**

   Choose the rectangle, circle, or polygon tool, depending on the shape you have in mind for your hotspot. For instance, in the image in Figure 5-21, the polygon tool was used to map the state of Oregon.

4. **Draw the hotspot.**

   To use the rectangle and circle tools, click directly on your picture, and then drag diagonally to form a rectangle or circle. To make a perfect square, press Shift while you drag the rectangle tool. (The circle tool always creates a perfect circle.)

   To draw an irregularly shaped hotspot using the polygon tool, click once to define one corner of the hotspot. Continue clicking until you define each corner of the hotspot. Dreamweaver automatically joins the corners to close the shape.

   Dreamweaver fills the inside of the hotspot with a light blue tint to make it easy to see. Your visitors won't see the blue highlighting, so you don't need to draw a perfect hotspot.

   If you need to adjust the hotspot you just drew, click the Arrow button in the Properties panel. You can drag the light blue square handles to reshape or resize the hotspot, or drag inside it to move the hotspot as a whole. If you change your mind about the hotspot, press Delete to get rid of it.

   When you begin to draw, Dreamweaver reminds you to add an Alt property to the hotspot you're about to create. Each hotspot can have its own Alt description, which assists visitors using screen readers.

NOTE After you draw a hotspot, the drawing tool remains active so you can draw additional hotspots. To disengage it, click the Arrow button.

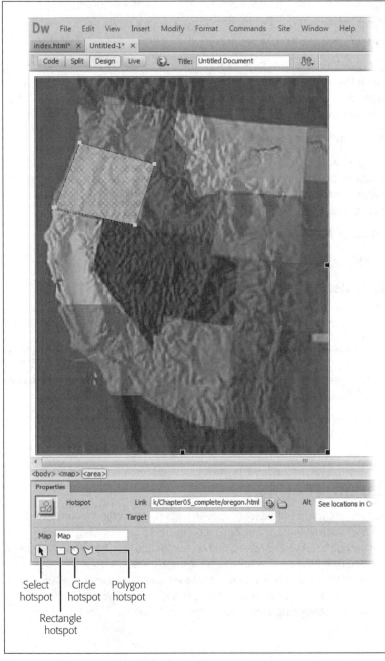

FIGURE 5-21

Each link on an image map is called a hotspot. Here, you've created a hotspot for the state of Oregon. You'll create other hotspots and links for the other states. When you select a hotspot, the Properties panel displays its Link, Target, and Alt properties. The lower half of the panel displays the name of the map, as well as tools for selecting and drawing additional hotspots.

5. **Add a link to the hotspot.**

After you draw a hotspot, that hotspot is selected; its properties appear in the Properties panel. Use any of the techniques discussed on page 171 to link this hotspot to another web page or location (ID).

6. **If necessary, set the Target property.**

Most of the options in the Target drop-down menu are useful only when you work with frames, as discussed on page 179. The "_blank" option, however, is useful any time: It forces your visitor's browser to load the linked page into a *new* browser window. The original page remains open, underneath the new window.

7. **Set the hotspot's Alt property.**

By typing a label into the Properties panel's Alt box, you provide a written name for this portion of the graphic. As noted on page 233, *alt* attributes are extremely important to people who surf the web with graphics turned off or use text-to-speech reading software.

8. **Repeat steps 2–7 for each hotspot you wish to add to an image.**

As you work, you can see the light blue hotspots filling in your image map.

Editing a Hotspot's Properties

As noted in step 4, you can change a hotspot's shape by dragging its tiny square handles. But you can also change its other properties—like which web page it links to.

To do so, click to select the image map. Click the black Arrow button—the hotspot selection tool—on the Properties panel's far left side (see Figure 5-21), and then click the hotspot you want to edit. Use the Properties panel controls to edit the Link, Target, and Alt properties.

If you're having a fit of frustration, you can also press Delete or Backspace to delete the hotspot altogether.

■ Rollover Images

Rollover images are common interactive elements on the Web. Webmasters frequently use them as navigation buttons (see Figure 5-22), but you can use them anytime you wish to dramatically swap one image for another. Say you put a photo of a product you're selling on a web page. The photo links to a page that describes the product and lets your visitor buy it. To add emphasis to the image, you could add a rollover image so that when a visitor moves his mouse over the photo, *another* image—for example, the same image but with "Buy Now!" or "Learn more" banner across it—appears.

FIGURE 5-22

Rollover graphics appear frequently in navigation bars. Here, all the top and bottom buttons have a similar appearance. When you move your cursor over a button, as with "web development" above, your browser swaps in a new image, giving the button a pushed look.

This simple change in appearance is a powerful way to inform visitors that the graphic is more than just a pretty picture—it's a button that actually does something. Rollovers usually announce that the image is a link, though you can use them for other creative effects, as described on page 254.

Behind the scenes, you create a rollover by preparing *two different* graphics—a "before" version and an "after" version. One graphic appears when the web page first loads, and the other graphic appears when your visitor mouses over the first. If your guest moves her cursor away without clicking, the original image pops back into place.

You achieve this dynamic effect using *JavaScript*, a programming language that lets you add interactivity to web pages. Dreamweaver includes many prewritten JavaScript programs, called *behaviors*, that let you add rollover images and other interactivity to your pages. (You'll find more about behaviors in Chapter 13.)

To insert a rollover image, start by using a graphics program to prepare the "before" and "after" images. Unless you're going for a bizarre distortion effect, both images should be exactly the same size. Store them somewhere in your website folder.

TIP In cases where normal and mouseover versions of a rollover are similar, it often makes sense to create both buttons in the same Photoshop or Fireworks document. Using different layers, you can export similar but slightly different images, as in the case of Figure 5-22. When you export related rollover images, it helps to give them similar names such as *button.gif* and *button_ro.gif*.

Then, in the document window, click the spot where you want to insert the image. If you're building a navigation bar, you might place several images (the buttons) side by side.

Choose Insert→Image Objects→Rollover Image (or, on the Insert panel's Common category, click the Rollover Image button). Either way, the Insert Rollover Image dialog box appears (see Figure 5-23).

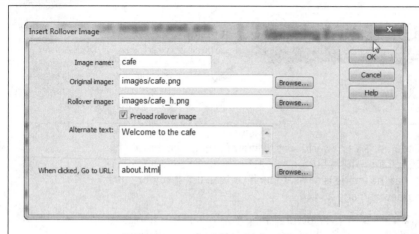

FIGURE 5-23

This box lets you specify the name, link, and image files browsers use to create a rollover effect. The option "Preload rollover image" forces the browser to download the rollover image along with the rest of the page to avoid a delay when a guest mouses over the image for the first time.

Fill in the blanks like this:

- **Image name.** Type a name for your graphic. JavaScript requires *some* name to complete the rollover effect. If you leave this field blank, Dreamweaver gives the image an unimaginative name—like *Image2*. If you plan to add additional interactive effects (Chapter 13) later, you may want to change this generic name to something more descriptive, so you can easily find the graphic later.

- **Original image.** When you click the top Browse button, a dialog box appears, prompting you to choose the graphic you want to use as the "before" button— the one that appears when the web page first loads.

- **Rollover image.** When you click the second Browse button, Dreamweaver prompts you to choose the "after" graphic—the image that appears when your visitor mouses over the original button.

- **Alternate text.** You can add a text description for a rollover button just as you can for any other graphic, as described on page 233.

- **When clicked, go to URL.** Most web pages use rollover images as navigation elements that, when clicked, take a web surfer to another page. In this box, you specify the destination page. Click the Browse button to select a page from your site, or, if you wish to link to another site, type an absolute URL (see page 170), one beginning with *http://*.

When you click OK, you return to your document window, where only the "before" button appears. You can select and modify it just as you would any other image. In fact, it's just a regular image with a link and a Dreamweaver behavior attached.

You can see the rollover effect in action right from Dreamweaver. Click the Live button near the top of the document window—this turns on Dreamweaver's embedded

WebKit browser so you can actually see the JavaScript work just as it will in a "live" browser (or as it will in Google's Chrome and Apple's Safari browsers, both of which use WebKit). When you're done, click Live again to return to editing the page. To see how the rollover effect works in other browsers, press F12 (Option-F12) or select File→Preview in Browser.

You can achieve this same rollover effect with a little more effort using Dreamweaver's Swap Image behavior, discussed on page 610. In fact, this versatile behavior lets you create multiple, simultaneous image swaps where several images change at the same time.

Tutorial: Inserting and Formatting Graphics

In this tutorial, you'll learn how to insert a photo, add a rollover image, and apply CSS to improve the look of a web page. You'll also learn how to use background images to enhance the look of headlines.

> **TIP** You'll need to download the tutorial files from *http://oreilly.com/missingmanuals/cds/dreamweavercc mm13/* to complete this tutorial. See the note on page 33 for more details.

Setting Up

Once you download the tutorial files and open Dreamweaver, set up a new site as described on page 19. You should be pretty good at this routine by now, but here's a quick recap, as well as an introduction to another setting that's helpful when you work with images.

1. **Choose Site→New Site.**

   The Site Setup window appears.

2. **For the Site Name, type *Images Tutorial*. To the right of the Local Site Folder box, click the folder icon.**

   The Choose Local Root Folder window appears. This is just a window into your computer's file system; navigate to the proper folder just as you do when you work with other programs.

3. **Navigate to the *MM_DWCC* folder, and then select *Chapter05*. Click Select (Choose) to identify this folder as the local root folder.**

   These steps are the only ones required to define a new site; however, you'll find one other setting useful when you work with images.

4. **Click Advanced Settings in the left-hand side of the window to reveal several additional categories.**

   Most of the options are related to Dreamweaver's site-management tools and the Contribute web-editing program, but the options in the Local Info category are useful for links and inserting images.

5. **Select the Local Info category. To the right of the "Default Images folder" box, click the folder icon. Inside the *Chapter05* folder, double-click the *Images* folder to select it. Click Save to complete the process of setting up the site.**

By defining a default destination for image files, certain operations, like dragging an image from the desktop or inserting a Photoshop image, go faster—Dreamweaver already knows where you want those images to go.

Adding an Image

Once again, you'll work on a page from the Cafe Soylent Green site.

1. **In the Files panel, double-click the file *index.html*.**

If you need a refresher on the Files panel, see page 28 and Figure 1-5.

2. **Click at the beginning of the paragraph, immediately following the headline "All Natural Ingredients" (before the "L" in "Lorum ipsum").**

You'll add an image here.

3. **Choose Insert Image→Image, or click the Image button on the Common tab of the Insert panel. Navigate to the *Images* folder, and then double-click the file *special1.jpg*.**

A photo of one of the cafe's dishes appears. A black outline around the image and three resize handles indicate that you've selected the image—if you don't see the handles, click the image to select it. Dreamweaver inserts the image where your cursor is, pushing the text down the page to accommodate the image height.

4. **Before you forget, type a description for the image, like Plankton Carpaccio, in the Alt text box of the Properties panel.**

The Alt text provides a verbal description of the image, as explained on page 233. Next you'll link this image to another page.

5. **In the Properties panel, to the right of the Link box, click the folder icon. Click the Site Root button to make sure you have the *Chapter05* folder (the local site folder) selected, and then double-click the *menu.html* page.**

If you need a recap on linking, check out page 171.

The image is a bit too close to the headline, and the large empty white space to the right of the graphic is distracting. Fortunately, CSS can help with both those problems.

6. **Make sure CSS Designer is open (Window→CSS Designer). In Sources, choose *soylent_styles.css*. Then, in Selectors, click the Add Selector (+) button.**

A new selector appears with the name box open for editing.

7. **Type *.imageRight* and then press Enter (Return).**

The newly named selector appears in your list of Selectors. Dreamweaver displays its attributes in the Properties section. The Layout properties appear the first on the long, scrolling list.

8. **In the margin-top property box, type *10*; in margin-bottom, type *10*; and then, for margin-left, type *15*. Leave the units set to px.**

Here, you're setting each of the margins separately. If you don't provide a value for a margin, Dreamweaver automatically sets it to zero. That's what you want for the right side, so you don't need to change a thing over there.

9. **Scroll down until you see the Float properties (see Figure 5-24). Click the "right" icon, the middle of the three options.**

Floating this image right forces the image to the right side of the page.

Next, you'll add a decorative border.

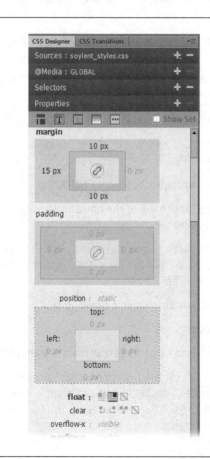

FIGURE 5-24

"Float" is one of the most commonly used CSS properties. It lets you align an element, like an image, to the left or right of a page. Content adjacent to the floated element wraps around it; when you use the Float property on <div> tags, it helps you create multicolumn page designs (which you'll learn about in Chapter 10).

10. **At the top of CSS Designer, click Border. Then, in border-color, type #F2E5C2; in border-width, type *4 px*; and then, in border-top-style, choose solid.**

11. **Select the Border category. Choose solid from the border-style menu; type *4* for the border-width property; and then type #F2E5C2 for border-color.**

    Once you make all these changes...nothing happens. You have to apply the class style.

12. **Click the image to select it. In the Properties panel's Class menu, choose imageRight.**

    Dreamweaver adds a tan border around the image, moves it to the right of the content, and scoots it down from the headline 10 pixels.

13. **Click at the beginning of the paragraph immediately following the second headline. Repeat steps 3–5 to insert the image *special2.jpg*. Select the image, type *Grilled Mozzarella* for the Alt text, and then link the pic to *menu. html*.**

    You've inserted a second graphic and link; now you'll apply the class you created earlier.

14. **Click the *special2.jpg* image to select it. In the Properties panel, from the Class menu, choose imageRight.**

    The café name at the top of the page looks a bit drab; let's replace it with the café's logo.

Inserting a Photoshop File

Dreamweaver makes it easy to insert and optimize files from Photoshop.

1. **Select the text "Cafe Soylent Green" at the top of the page and press Delete to remove it. Choose Insert Image→Image.**

   The Select Image Source window appears so you can specify the Photoshop (.psd) file. You can also drag the PSD file from the Files panel and drop it into the empty space where the text used to be.

2. **Click the Site Root button, and then double-click *cafe-logo.psd*.**

   The Image Optimization window appears.

3. **Choose PNG8 from the Format menu and turn on the transparency checkbox.**

   The Photoshop file has a transparent background—that's not so important right now since the logo is sitting on a white page, but if you add an image behind the logo (which you soon will) it's important to make sure that the transparent areas of the graphic are truly see-through.

4. **Click OK, and then, in the "Save Web Image" box, save the file as *cafe-logo. png*. Click OK once more.**

   A big photo appears on the page (see Figure 5-25). You'll notice the Smart Object logo in the top-left corner (circled in Figure 5-25), and three resize handles. The logo is a bit large, but you can resize it in Dreamweaver.

5. **In the Properties panel's Alt box, type *Café Soylent Green*.**

   This is a verbal description of the café's logo. Even though the graphic looks like type in the logo, a screen reader just sees it as another image.

FIGURE 5-25

Photoshop Smart Objects look just like regular images except for the small icon in the top-left corner (circled).

6. **Hold down the Shift key and drag the image's bottom-right resize handle up and to the left until the image is about 110 pixels tall (look in the Properties panel's H box to see the image's height).**

   If you don't see the resize handles, click the image to select it. The Shift key makes sure the image scales proportionally, which, in turn, ensures that you don't accidentally distort the image.

   Now you see a yellow warning sign in the image's upper-left corner (see Figure 5-26). This means that the dimensions of the image no longer match the width and height specified in the HTML—by resizing the image, you change the HTML but not the actual image file. As mentioned in the box on page 235, this isn't a good idea—the image doesn't look as good and the file is larger than it needs to be (meaning it will download more slowly). Fortunately, because this is a Smart Object, you can easily create a PNG file that matches the smaller dimensions you just specified while maintaining the image's original quality.

FIGURE 5-26

When you see a warning icon (the yellow triangle) on a Smart Object, it usually means you resized the image on the page. The "Update from Original" button lets you recreate the image from the original to match the dimensions you're after.

7. **In the Properties panel, click "Update from Original" (the button with the recycle icon, circled in Figure 5-26).**

   Dreamweaver re-optimizes the image based on the Photoshop file. This means that, behind the scenes, Dreamweaver creates a new PNG file—complete with all your original optimization settings (PNG8 with transparency in this case). Modifying an image using Smart Objects, aside from being very fast, is the best way to assure a high-quality web image.

   If you own Photoshop CS5 or later, launch it now (if you don't have Photoshop, just skip to the next paragraph); then, in the Chapter05 folder, open the *cafe-log.psd* file and edit it—apply a filter, add some text, whatever. Save the file, and then return to Dreamweaver. You'll see a red "out-of-sync" arrow on the image. Select it, press the Update from Original button again, and Dreamweaver creates a new image from the edited PSD file. You'll now see the new, filter-enhanced version of the image without having to make a stop at the Image Preview window. Very cool.

Using Background Images

The HTML <img> tag isn't the only way to add an image to a web page. You can also use the CSS *background-image* property to give any HTML tag a graphical backdrop. You added a background image to the body of a web page in the first tutorial. In fact, a little-known trick is adding a background image to the <html> tag and another to the <body> tag: This basically lets you overlap two different images that cover the canvas of your web page.

1. **Make sure CSS Designer is open (Window→CSS Designer). In the Sources section, in the panel's bottom-right corner, choose *soylent_styles.css*. Then, in Selectors, click the Add Selector button (the + sign icon).**

   A new selector appears in the list, ready for you to give it a name.

2. **Type *html*.**

   As you type, Dreamweaver displays matching selectors. When you see *html*, stop typing and hit Enter (Return).

   CSS Designer's Properties section displays the properties you can set for your selector.

3. **Click the Background button. Under background-image, next to URL, click the box, and then click the folder icon. Navigate to and select the file *bg_page.png*.**

   The image is a simple, textured, sand-color background. But what gives? There's no background image! Again, Dreamweaver's Design view fails us—many common CSS tricks, like adding a background image to the <html> tag, just won't appear in Design view. You'll only see the background effect when you view the page in a browser or in Dreamweaver's Live view.

4. **Click the Live button in the Document toolbar.**

   The background texture looks great! Unfortunately, the color matches the word "Soylent" in the logo. To get the logo back, you can add another background image.

5. **Click the Live button again to exit Live view.**

   You'll next add a background image to the <body> tag. The tag already has a style associated with it, so you just need to edit the style.

6. **In CSS Designer, with *soylent_styles.css* selected in Sources, locate and select the <body> tag in the Selectors section.**

   The properties for the body selector appear in the Properties section of CSS Designer. Most of the properties are grayed out, which means you haven't set any yet.

7. **In the Properties section of CSS Designer, click the Background button. Then, under background-image, click next to URL, and then click the folder icon. Browse to and select *bg_banner.png*.**

   The image is a dark-green bar that will run along the top of the page. Normally, background images tile from left to right and top to bottom, which would fill the body of the page here. If you press the Apply button, you'll see this effect in Design view...not pretty. Fortunately, you can control how a background image tiles.

8. **Scroll down until you see the background-repeat properties. Choose repeat-x.**

   CSS Designer should now look something like Figure 5-27. "Repeat-x" repeats the image horizontally, along the x-axis. Time to create a style for the list items.

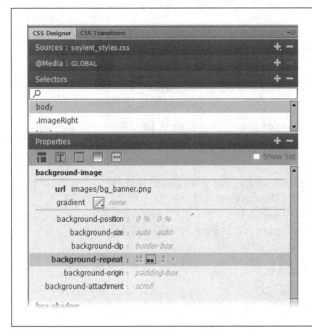

FIGURE 5-27

When you want a tiled image to repeat horizontally, choose repeat-x from the background-repeat menu; to tile the image vertically, choose repeat-y.

9. **In the Sources section of CSS Designer, select *soylent_styles.css* and then, in Selectors, click the Add Selector button (the + icon).**

   You'll create a style for the <li> element this time.

10. **In the Selector Name box, type *li*.**

    The Properties section shows properties you can set for the *li* tag.

11. **In the Properties section, click Background. Then, under background-image, click the URL property. Finally, click the folder icon and browse to and select the file *list_dignbat.png*.**

    The image is a small icon with a green box. You encounter the same problem here as you did in step 7 above; the entire unordered list (<ul>) area is filled with little green boxes.

12. **Scroll down to the background-repeat property and select no-repeat. Then, for background-position, type *1 px* in the first box (for the x position), and *4 px* in the second box (the y position).**

CSS Designer's Properties section should look like Figure 5-28. The no-repeat setting means that the background image will appear only a single time; you can control where the image appears in the background of the element with the two position settings specified above. In this case, the 1 and 4 mean "place the image 1 pixel from the left edge of a list item and 4 pixels down from the top of the element." Why those values? Trial and error! Each image and element will probably require different position values to look good.

Because you're using an image for the list item's bullet, you need to make sure web browsers don't also display the normal bullet icon.

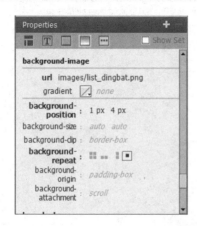

FIGURE 5-28

You can specify a horizontal and vertical position for background images. You can use pixel values (like the 1 and 4 pictured here) or choose from text values like left, center, and right for horizontal placement, or top, center, or bottom for vertical placement.

13. **Select the List category in CSS Designer's Selectors section. In the Properties section, click Others, and then, in list-style-type, choose none.**

The image is in place but doesn't look right. The text is covering it up! Whenever you use a background image as an icon like this, you need to add padding to scoot the tag's content out of the way. So you need to go back and edit the style.

14. **With the <li> tag still chosen in Selectors, click the Layout category in the Properties section. In the margin box, click the link button ("Click To Change All Properties") and then type *0* as the value for any side. On the left side of the padding box, type *20*.**

CSS Designer should look like Figure 5-29. You're done!

15. **Choose File→Save All and preview the page in a web browser (File→Preview in Browser).**

The finished page should look like the one in Figure 5-30. As you see, you can use graphics in numerous ways to enhance the look of a web page. For an added exercise, you'll find two other graphic files—*tech-icon.png* and *ingredient-icon.png*—in the Images directory. Create styles for the first two headlines on the page so that those graphics appear as icons to the left of the text. (Hint: You'll need to use class styles to achieve this.)

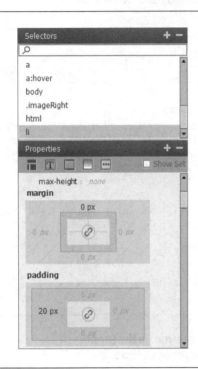

FIGURE 5-29

When inserting a background image, you'll frequently add padding to scoot text or other content away from the image. In this case, an icon appears on the left edge of a list item, so adding left padding adds space to the left of the text, making room for the icon.

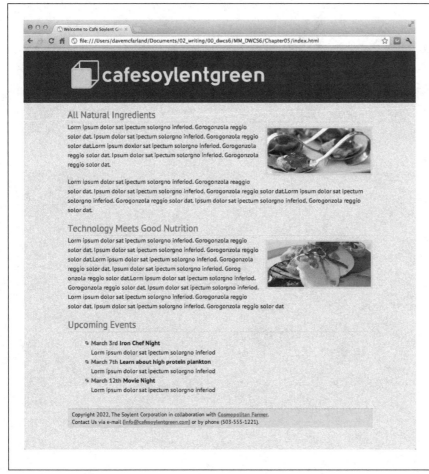

FIGURE 5-30

Photos, icons, and other graphic elements add visual interest to any web page.

Tables

The HTML <table> tag has had a somewhat infamous existence in the world of web design. It was originally intended to present scientific data in spreadsheet-like format. But as the Web grew, graphic designers got into the web design game. They wanted to recreate the types of layouts they saw in magazines, books, and newspapers (in other words, they wanted to make good-looking websites!). The most reliable tool at the time was the <table> tag, which designers used as a back-door way to create columns, sidebars, and, in general, to precisely position elements on a page.

Today, with nearly everyone on the planet using advanced browsers like Internet Explorer, Firefox, Safari, and Opera, web designers use a more facile page-styling technique—CSS-based layout. Table-based layout is an aging dinosaur that produces pages heavy with code (so they download slower), harder to update, and hostile to alternative browsers, like screen readers, mobile phones, and text-only browsers.

This chapter shows you how to use tables for their intended purpose: displaying data and other information best presented in rows and columns (Figure 6-1). If you're a long-time web designer who still uses tables for page layout, you can use Dream-weaver and the instructions in this chapter to continue that technique. However, you're better off making the switch to CSS. Dreamweaver's advanced CSS tools make building well-designed pages much simpler than table-based layout. You'll learn all about CSS layout in Chapter 10.

FIGURE 6-1
You can do all your page layout and design with CSS, and use tables for their intended purpose—displaying rows and columns of information. The list of tasty delights on this page is nestled inside a basic <table> tag, while the rest of the page—the logo, headline, and so on—is laid out using CSS.

■ Table Basics

A table is a grid of rows and columns that intersect to form *cells*, as shown in Figure 6-2. If you've used a spreadsheet before, an HTML table will feel familiar.

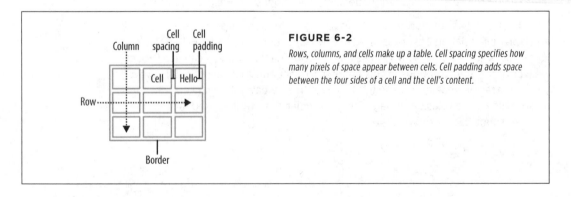

FIGURE 6-2

Rows, columns, and cells make up a table. Cell spacing specifies how many pixels of space appear between cells. Cell padding adds space between the four sides of a cell and the cell's content.

A table row usually represents a collection of data for a single item. In Figure 6-1, for example, each row holds data for one dish. A table *column* represents data of a particular type. The first column in Figure 6-1 contains the name of each dish, for example, while the second column provides a tantalizing description, and the third displays the price. A table cell, then, holds one piece of data for a particular row, like the cell that displays the price of the Soylent Green Salad.

At a minimum, you use three HTML tags to create a table (there are actually quite a few tags related to table design, as you'll read about soon, but these three are the core table tags). You set the boundaries of the table with the <table> tag. Then, within this structure, you add rows using the *table row* <tr> tag. Finally, you divide a table row into individual cells, each of which holds one piece of data.

You create a cell that holds data—$6.00, for instance—with the <td> or *table data* tag. Browsers align the text inside a <td> cell to the left edge.

A fourth tag, the <th>, or *table header*, tag also creates cells within a row, but instead of holding data, table headers tell you the *kind* of information you'll find in a row or column (like Price). Text inside a <th> tag appears centered and in boldface.

Figure 6-1, for example, contains one table (it uses one <table> tag), and 12 rows (12 <tr> tags). The top row contains one table header (<th>) that identifies the type of data in the cells below. In this example, that header is Starters. The next row contains three table headers, labeled Item, Description, and Price. The following four rows contain data, and you create them with simple <td> tags.

■ Inserting a Table

One of the main problems with HTML tables is that they require a lot of code. Not only is this one reason why CSS is a better page layout method than HTML, it's also a good reason to use Dreamweaver to create tables. If you've ever hand-coded an HTML table, you know what a tangled mess of code it requires; one typo can sink your whole page. Fortunately, Dreamweaver makes the process simple.

1. **In the document window, position your cursor where you want to insert the table.**

   You can add a table anywhere you can add a paragraph of text. You can even add a table inside *another* table, by clicking inside a table cell.

2. **Choose Insert→Table.**

   You can also click the Table button on the Insert panel (it's under the Common category). Finally, you can press Ctrl+Alt+T (⌘-Option-T). Either way, the Table dialog box opens (see Figure 6-3).

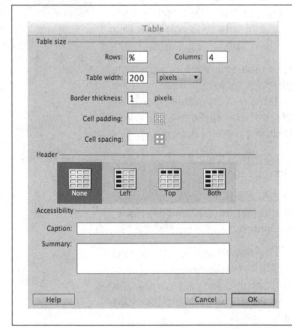

FIGURE 6-3

The Table dialog box lets you control a table's appearance. Leaving the Cell Padding and Cell Spacing fields empty isn't the same as setting them to 0. If you leave the values blank, most browsers insert 1 pixel of cell padding and 2 pixels of cell spacing. If you notice unwanted gaps between cells in a table, or between content in a cell and the cell's edges, blank settings are the likely culprit. To truly leave zero space, set Cell Padding and Cell Spacing to 0. (Dreamweaver remembers the settings you use. When you use the Insert Table dialog box again, it starts with the settings you entered previously.)

3. **Using the Rows and Columns fields, specify how many rows and columns you want in your table.**

   Don't fret too much over your estimate, because you can always add or remove rows and columns later.

4. **Type the amount of cell padding, in pixels, you want for the table.**

   Cell padding is the buffer around the content in a cell—the space from the edge of the cell to the contents inside it (see Figure 6-2). Unfortunately, this property applies to *every* cell in a table (it also applies equally to all four sides of the cell). You can't specify cell padding for individual cells, nor can you use different padding for each edge of the content (you can't, for example, specify 10 pixels of padding on the left side of a cell, and only 5 pixels at the top) unless you use the CSS *padding* property, as described on page 439. Designers often type either *0* or leave this box empty, and then use CSS to control the spacing in individual cells (via the <td> and <th> tags).

5. **Type the amount of cell spacing, in pixels, you want for the table.**

   Cell spacing specifies how many pixels of empty space separate one cell from another. Like *cell padding*, this property applies to every cell in a table. CSS provides an equivalent property, *border-spacing*, and you need to use CSS Designer to add this property to a table (see page 374). In addition, Internet

Explorer 7 and earlier ignore border spacing. So if you want space between each table cell, it's easiest to add a cell spacing value here (you can change it later). Type *0* to remove any space between cells. (Note that leaving these fields empty isn't the same as setting them to 0; see Figure 6-3.)

6. **In the Table width field, specify how wide you want the table to be (in units you specify using the field's drop-down menu).**

    You can create a table that has either a specified, fixed minimum width, or one whose width is a specified percentage of the space available on the page. To set a fixed width, choose pixels as the unit of measure, and then, in the Table width field, type in an amount. Fixed-width tables remain the same size regardless of the browser window's size.

    Percentage-width tables grow or shrink relative to the space available. If you place a 100% wide table on a blank web page, the table stretches all the way across your visitor's browser window, no matter how wide or narrow he has it set. But the percentage isn't always based on the overall browser window width. If you place a table *inside* another object—for example, within a <div> tag—and that <div> has a set width, Dreamweaver calculates the percentage based on that <div>'s set width. Say you have a sidebar on a page, and the sidebar is 300 pixels wide; if you insert an 80% wide table inside the sidebar, then the table takes up 80 percent of 300 pixels, or 240 pixels.

7. **In the "Border thickness" box, type a number, in pixels, for the border.**

    If you don't want a border, type *0*. Dreamweaver uses dotted lines in Design view to help you identify rows, columns, and cells whose border is 0. (The dotted lines won't appear on your finished page.) Again, CSS offers a much better way to add borders, so it's best to set this to *0* and use CSS for your borders (see page 56).

8. **Using the buttons in the middle of the dialog box, select a Header option.**

    The Table Header property creates the specialized cells in the top row or left-hand column of a table that identify the content in the associated cells. When you select one of the Header options here, Dreamweaver inserts the <th> tag to indicate that these cells are *headlines* that identify the kind of information in the cells below or to the right of the header. For instance, a table that displays a company's yearly sales figures broken down by region might have a top row of headers for each year (2010, 2011, 2012), while the left column would have table headers identifying each region (Northwest, West, South, and so on).

    The only visible change you see with a <th> tag is that web browsers display the text center-aligned and in bold type. However, this option also makes the table more accessible by telling screen readers (used by the visually impaired) that the cell serves as a header for the information in the related column or row. (You can always change the look of these cells using CSS; just create a style for the <th> tag.)

9. **In the bottom section of the Table dialog box, add any Accessibility notations you want.**

   In the Caption box, type in a description for the table; it appears, centered, above the table. Use the Summary box when you want to explain a particularly complex table. This information doesn't show up in a browser window; it's intended to clarify the contents of a table to search engines and screen readers. Basic data tables (simple rows and columns) don't need a summary; search engines and screen readers can understand them just fine. It's only when you create a complex table with merged cells (see page 287) and multiple levels of headers that you might want to fill out the Summary box.

   For more information on these options, and to get a complete rundown on table accessibility, visit *http://tinyurl.com/5vgvv2e*.

10. **Click OK to insert the table.**

    Once you add a table to a page, you can begin filling its cells. A cell works like a small document window; you can click inside it and add text, images, and links using the techniques you've learned so far. You can even insert a table inside a cell (a common technique in the bad old days of table-based layout).

    To move your cursor from one cell to the next, press Tab. When you reach the last cell in a row, the Tab key moves the insertion point to the first cell in the row below. And if the insertion point is in the last *cell* of the last row, pressing Tab creates a new row at the bottom of the table.

    Shift+Tab moves the cursor in the *opposite* direction—from the current cell to the previous one.

■ Selecting Parts of a Table

Tables and their cells have independent properties. For example, a table and a cell can have different alignment properties. But before you can change any of these properties, you must first *select* the table, rows, columns, and cells you want to affect.

Selecting a Table

You can select a table in the document window a number of ways:

- Click the upper-left corner of the table, or anywhere on the bottom or right edges. (Be careful using the latter technique; it's easy to accidentally *drag* the border, adding a height or width property to cells in the table.)

- Click anywhere inside the table, and then select the <table> tag in the document window's Tag Selector.

- Click anywhere inside the table, and then choose Modify→Table→Select Table.

- Right-click (Control-click) inside a table, and then, from the shortcut menu, choose Table→Select Table.

- If the insertion point is in a cell inside the table, pressing Ctrl+A (⌘-A) twice selects the table.

Once selected, the table grows a thick black border and three tiny, square resize handles—at the right edge, bottom edge, and lower-right corner.

Selecting Rows or Columns

You can select an entire row or column of cells by doing one of the following:

- Move your cursor to the left edge of a row or the top edge of a column. When it changes to a right- or down-pointing arrow, click, as explained in Figure 6-4.

- Click a cell at either end of a row, or the first or last cell of a column, and then drag across the cells in the row or column to select them.

- Click any cell in the row you want to select, and then click the <tr> tag in the Tag Selector (the <tr> tag is how HTML indicates a table row). This method doesn't work for columns.

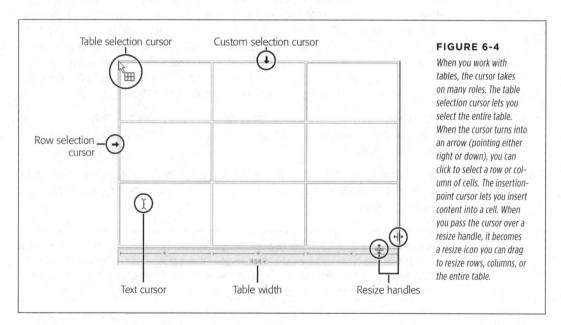

FIGURE 6-4

When you work with tables, the cursor takes on many roles. The table selection cursor lets you select the entire table. When the cursor turns into an arrow (pointing either right or down), you can click to select a row or column of cells. The insertion-point cursor lets you insert content into a cell. When you pass the cursor over a resize handle, it becomes a resize icon you can drag to resize rows, columns, or the entire table.

When you select a cell, its border turns dark. When you select multiple cells, each has a dark border.

Selecting Cells

To select one or more cells:

- Drag across adjoining cells. A solid black border appears around a cell or cells when you select them.

- To select several cells that aren't necessarily adjacent, Ctrl-click (⌘-click) them one at a time. (You can also Ctrl-click [⌘-click] an already selected cell to deselect it.)

- Click a cell, and then Shift-click another cell. Your two clicks form diagonally opposite corners of an imaginary rectangle; Dreamweaver highlights all cells within it.

- Use the Tag Selector (page 7) to select a cell. Click inside the cell you wish to select, and then click the <td> (or <th>, for table headers) tag in the Selector.

- If the insertion point is inside the cell you want to select, press Ctrl+A (⌘-A).

■ Expanded Tables Mode

If you remove all padding, cell spacing, and borders from a table, you may find it hard to select tables and individual cells. This is especially true if you nest tables within table cells (a common table-layout technique). To help you out, Dreamweaver offers Expanded Tables mode. Right-click (Control-click) inside a cell, and then choose Table→Expanded Tables mode. That adds visible borders to every table and cell, and increases on-screen cell padding. Expanded Tables mode never changes the actual HTML of your page, it merely affects how the page looks in Design view. The guideline borders and extra spacing won't appear in browsers.

If you simply use tables to display data, you'll probably never need Expanded Tables mode, but if you have to edit old web pages built with complicated table layouts, Expanded mode is a big help.

To return the table to its normal look, click the Exit link that appears in the black toolbar above the document window (this toolbar appears only when you're in Expanded Tables mode).

TIP Go to View→Visual Aids to see your options for displaying or hiding table widths and borders, as well as for other features, like the ability to have your divs outlined or to see normally invisible elements, like paragraph markers. In general, the Visual Aids are design-time tools that help you understand why your page looks like it does.

■ Formatting Tables

When you first insert a table, you set its number of rows and columns, as well as its cell padding, cell spacing, width, and borders. You're not stuck with the properties you first give a table, however; you can change any or all of the settings—and set a few additional options—using the Properties panel.

When you select a table, the Properties panel changes to reflect that table's settings (see Figure 6-5). You can adjust the table by entering different values for width, rows, columns, and so on in the appropriate fields.

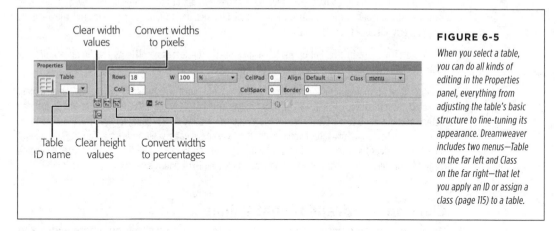

FIGURE 6-5

When you select a table, you can do all kinds of editing in the Properties panel, everything from adjusting the table's basic structure to fine-tuning its appearance. Dreamweaver includes two menus—Table on the far left and Class on the far right—that let you apply an ID or assign a class (page 115) to a table.

In addition, the Properties panel lets you set alignment options and add colors or a background image to a table, as described next.

Aligning Tables

In the normal flow of a web page, a table acts like a paragraph, header, or any other HTML block-level element. Browsers align it to the left of the page, with other elements placed either above or below it.

But you can make several useful changes to the way a table interacts with text and other page elements. After selecting the table, use one of the three alignment options in the drop-down menu on the right of the Properties panel:

- The Left and Right options align the table with the left or right page margins. Anything you then add to the page—including paragraphs, images, or other tables—wraps around the right or left side of the table. You can apply the CSS Float property to a table (just as with images) to achieve the same effect (see page 236).

- The Center option makes the table sit in the center of a page, interrupting the flow of the elements around it. Nothing wraps around the table.

NOTE Some of the properties Dreamweaver lets you adjust to make tables look better aren't technically valid for some of the different HTML document types. Dreamweaver can create HTML 4.01 Transitional, XHTML 1.0 Transitional, and several other types of HTML documents. In general, HTML 4.01 Transitional and XHTML 1.0 Transitional are commonly used document types—HTML5 is the "out of box" setting in Dreamweaver. However, the more "strict" types, like HTML 4.01 Strict and XHTML 1.0 Strict, don't support some table properties, and the *align* property, discussed above, is one of them.

HTML5 is even more restrictive. Not only is the *align* property considered obsolete, so are the *table width, cell padding,* and *cell spacing* options.

This discrepancy is more a technicality than a design nuisance; most web browsers still display the alignment you select, even when you create HTML5, HTML Strict, and XHTML Strict documents. The newer and recommended method of alignment is to use CSS properties to accomplish the same display goals; for example, using CSS to set the left and right margins of a table to *auto* center the table on the page, while applying a CSS Left Float or Right Float property does the same as the Left and Right alignment options. The CSS Width (page 438) and Padding (page 439) properties for tables are fine replacements for their HTML equivalents.

Clearing Width and Height Values

When you create complex tables, it's easy to get into a situation where width and height measurements conflict and produce unreliable results. For example, it's possible to set one cell to 300 pixels wide, and later set another cell *in the same column* to 400 pixels wide. Since a browser can't do both (how can one column be both 300 *and* 400 pixels wide?), you might not get the results you want.

In tables with many cells, these kinds of problems are tough to ferret out. That's when you'll find the following timesaving tools—located behind the obscure-looking buttons in the Properties panel's bottom half (see Figure 6-5)—handy. They let you delete the width and height measurements and start from scratch (see page 279).

- Clicking Clear Height Values removes the height properties from the table and each cell. Doing so doesn't set the heights to zero; it simply deletes the property altogether.

- Clicking Clear Width Values does the same thing with the width properties of a table and its cells.

Two additional buttons let you convert pixel-based table widths to percentage measurements and vice versa. In other words, if a table is 600 pixels wide and you click Convert Widths to Percentages, Dreamweaver assigns percentages to the table and each cell whose width you specified using pixels.

These percentages depend on how much of the document window your table takes up when you click the button. If the document window is 1,200 pixels wide, that 600-pixel-wide table changes to a 50% wide table. Because you'll rarely do this, don't waste your brain cells memorizing such tools.

NOTE Dreamweaver CC doesn't provide access to outdated table properties like *border color, background color*, and *background image* from the Properties panel. Instead, use the CSS equivalents: *border* (page 56), *background-image* (page 240), and *background-color*. You'll find examples of how to use CSS to add background images, colors, and table borders in the tutorial at the end of this chapter. In addition, you'll learn how to use the very valuable *border-collapse* property on page 304.

Resizing a Table

While you define the width of a table when you first insert it, you can always change it. To do so, select the table, and then take either of these steps:

- Type a value in the W (width) box in the Properties panel, and then choose a unit of measure, either pixels or percentages, from the drop-down menu.

- Drag one of the resize handles on the right edge. Avoid the handle in the right corner of the table—this adds a *height* property to the first cell in the bottom row. If you do add a *height* property this way, you can easily remove it using the "Clear Height Values" button in the Properties panel.

In theory, you can also convert a table from a fixed unit of measure, such as pixels, to the stretchy, percentage-style width setting—or vice versa—using the two Convert Table Width buttons at the bottom of the Properties panel (see Figure 6-5). What these buttons do depends on the size of the current document window in Dreamweaver. Suppose the document window is 700 pixels wide, and you insert a table that's 100 percent wide. Clicking Convert Table Widths to Pixels sets the table's width to around 700 pixels (the exact value depends on the margins of the page). However, if your document window were 500 pixels wide, clicking the same button would produce a fixed-width table of around 500 pixels.

NOTE The HTML <table> tag doesn't officially have a Height property. Dreamweaver, however, adds Height properties to table cells when you drag their top or bottom borders, but it won't add a Height property to the table tag, which is a good thing, since it's invalid HTML. You could add it manually—<table height="500">—since most browsers understand the Height property and would obey your wishes. But since it's not standard code, there's no guarantee that newer browsers will support it.

You have a couple of alternatives: First, you could decide not to worry about height. After all, it's difficult to control the height of a table precisely, especially if there's text in it. Since text sizes appear differently on different operating systems and browsers, the table may grow taller if your guest's text is larger than yours, no matter what height you set.

Your second option is to use the CSS *height* property (page 438) to set the table's stature.

The Convert Table Width to Percentages buttons take the opposite tack. They set the width of a table and its cells to percentages based on the amount of the document window's width and height they cover at the moment. The bigger the current document window, the smaller the percentage.

Because the effects of these buttons depend on the document window's size, you'll find yourself rarely, if ever, using them.

■ Modifying Cell and Row Properties

Cells have their own properties, separate from the properties of the table itself. So do table *rows*—but not table columns (see the box on page 282).

When you click inside a cell, the top half of the Properties panel displays the cell's text formatting properties; the bottom half shows the properties of the cell itself (see Figure 6-6).

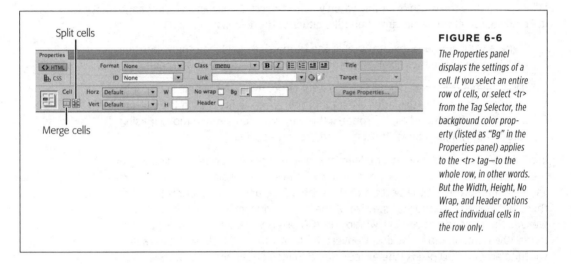

FIGURE 6-6

The Properties panel displays the settings of a cell. If you select an entire row of cells, or select <tr> from the Tag Selector, the background color property (listed as "Bg" in the Properties panel) applies to the <tr> tag—to the whole row, in other words. But the Width, Height, No Wrap, and Header options affect individual cells in the row only.

Alignment Properties

At the outset, a cell's contents hug the left wall and float halfway between the top and bottom of the cell. After selecting a row, a cell, or several cells, you can change these alignments in the Properties panel. For example, the "Horz" (horizontal) menu offers Left, Center, Right, and Default alignment. ("Default" gives you the same effect as "Left" without adding any extra HTML code.)

Note that these options are distinct from the *paragraph* alignment options discussed in Chapter 3. In fact, you can mix and match the two. Suppose you have a table cell containing four paragraphs, and you want to center-align all but the last one, which you want right-aligned. To do so, you could set the alignment of the *cell* to Center, and then select just the last paragraph and set its alignment to Right. The paragraph's alignment overrides the alignment applied by the cell.

You set the vertical alignment property the same way. Select the relevant cells, and then use one of the five options available in the Properties panel's "Vert" (vertical) menu: Default (the same as Middle), Top, Middle, Bottom, or Baseline. The Baseline option aligns the bottom of the first line of text in the cell to the baseline of text in all the other cells in the row—really only useful if you have different size type in different cells and you're an extremely picky designer (which you might be, and that's OK).

NOTE The CSS *text-align* property (in the Text category of CSS Designer) provides the same effect as horizontal cell alignment; the *vertical-align* property (also in the Text category of CSS Designer) is the CSS replacement for a cell's vertical alignment.

Table Header

The Table Header option lets you convert a <td> tag to a <th> tag, which is useful when you want to turn, say, the row at the top of a table into a header. It works just like the column or row header options available in the Table dialog box, described on page 272.

NOTE You can also turn off the Table Header box to turn a table header into a regular table cell. This is handy when you insert a table that shouldn't have headers, but you forgot to unselect the header option in the Table dialog box.

You usually use the Table Header option for tables that include tabular data (like a spreadsheet) to identify the type of data in the other cells in a row or column. For example, you may have a table containing data from different years; each cell in the top row could identify the year the data in the cells below it was compiled.

While Dreamweaver lets you change a single cell into a header, you'll most likely apply this to the top row or left column of cells.

A Property to Forget

The No Wrap option is of such little value that you'll probably go your entire web career without using it.

But for the sake of thoroughness—and in case you actually find a use for it—here's a description. The No Wrap property prevents a web browser from wrapping a line of text within a cell onto multiple lines. The browser widens the cell instead, so that it accommodates the line without breaks. The result is almost never useful or attractive. Furthermore, in some browsers, if you specify a width for the cell, the browsers ignore the No Wrap option!

Cell Decoration

Table cells needn't be drab. As with tables themselves, you can give individual cells background colors or even background graphics. But also just as with tables, you should avoid decorating cells through the options available in the Properties panel. Instead, use CSS's *background-color* property to add color to a cell, the *background-image* property (see page 240) to add a graphic to the background of a cell, and the *border* property (see page 238) to add color borders around cells.

The Dawn of Columns

As far as the standard HTML language is concerned, there really isn't any such entity as a column. You create tables with the <table> tag, rows with the <tr> tag, and cells with the <td> tag—but there's no column tag. Dreamweaver calculates the number of columns in a table based on the number of cells in a row. If you have seven rows in a table, each with four cells,

the table has four columns. In other words, the number of cells you add to a row determines the number of columns in a table.

Two tags introduced in HTML 4—the <colgroup> and <col> tags—let you control various attributes of columns in a table. Unfortunately, Dreamweaver provides no easy way to add the tags. You can find out more about them, however, from *http://tinyurl.com/3whpctc*.

Suddenly Jumbo Cells

When I add text to a cell, it suddenly gets much wider than the other cells in the row. What gives?

It isn't Dreamweaver's fault, it's how HTML works.

Web browsers (and Dreamweaver) display cells to match the content inside. For example, say you add a three-column table to a page. In the first cell of the first row, you type in two words, leave the second cell empty, and add a 125-pixel-wide image in

the third cell of that row. Since the image is the biggest item, its cell is wider than the other two. The middle cell, with nothing in it, is given the least amount of space.

Usually, you don't want a web browser making these kinds of decisions for you. By specifying a width for a cell, as explained below, you can force a browser to display a cell with the dimension you want. But keep in mind that there are exceptions to this rule; see page 283.

Setting Cell Dimensions

Specifying the width or height of a particular cell is simple: Select one or more cells, and then type a value in the Properties panel's W (width) or H (height) field. You can specify the value in either pixels or percentages. For instance, if you want a 50-pixel-wide cell, type in *50*. For a cell that you want to take up 50 percent of the total table width, type in *50%*. Read the next section for details on the tricky business of controlling cell and table dimensions.

You can also resize a column or row of cells by dragging a cell border. As your cursor approaches the cell's edge, it changes shape (to two parallel lines with arrows beside each) to indicate that you can begin dragging. Dreamweaver also provides an interactive display of cell widths (circled in Figure 6-7) when you use this method. This helpful feature lets you know the exact width of your cells at all times, so you can drag a cell to a precise width. When you resize table cells this way, Dreamweaver sets the width of the cell using the type of measure you specified for the overall table width—pixels or percentages. In other words, if you insert a table and set its width to 100%, when you drag the side wall of a cell to resize that cell, Dreamweaver sets the cell width using a percentage value (30%, for example); however, if you initially set the table to 500 pixels wide, Dreamweaver displays the cell widths as pixel values when you resize them.

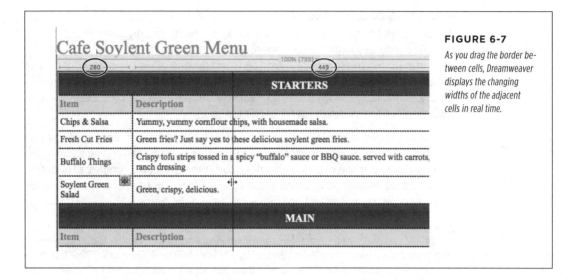

FIGURE 6-7

As you drag the border between cells, Dreamweaver displays the changing widths of the adjacent cells in real time.

Tips for Surviving Table-Making

Nothing is more confounding than trying to get your tables laid out exactly as you want them. Many beginning web designers throw their hands up in despair when working with tables, which often seem to have minds of their own. Here are a few problems that often confuse designers—and some ways to make working with them more straightforward.

■ THE CONTENTS TAKE PRIORITY

Say you create a 300-pixel-wide table and set each cell in the first row to 100 pixels wide. You insert a large graphic into the first cell, and suddenly—kablooie! Even though you set each cell to 100 pixels wide, as shown in Figure 6-8, the column with the graphic is much wider than the other two.

FIGURE 6-8

Because a web browser can't shrink an image or hide part of it, the top-left cell in the table above has to grow to fit it. That first column of cells now measures 161 pixels wide; the other two columns must shrink in order to keep the table 300 pixels wide. The numbers at the top of each cell indicate its width as set in the HTML—100—and, in parentheses, the actual width as displayed in Dreamweaver (161, 58, and 59).

That's because an individual table cell can't be smaller than the largest piece of content inside it. In this case, although you set the cell to 100 pixels wide, the image is 161 pixels wide, which forces the first column to grow—and the other columns to shrink—accordingly.

■ SETTING COLUMN WIDTHS

To set the width of a column of cells, you set the width of only *one* cell in that column. Say you have a table with three rows and three columns. You need to set only the width for the top row of cells; you can (and should) leave the cell widths for the remaining cells in the two bottom rows empty. In fact, that's what Dreamweaver does automatically—when you drag a vertical border between cells, Dreamweaver only modifies the Width property of the top cells.

This principle can save a lot of time and, because it reduces the amount of code on a web page, make your pages load (and therefore appear) faster. The same holds true for the height of a row. You only need to set the height of a single cell to define the height for its entire row. When you drag a horizontal border, Dreamweaver adds a Height property to the first cell in the row above the border.

> **TIP** You can actually set the width of a column if you use the <colgroup> and <col> tags when creating a table. Unfortunately, Dreamweaver doesn't provide any way, aside from hand coding, to add those tags. But if you're interested, you can learn more about using those tags and CSS to define the width of individual table columns at *http://tinyurl.com/5qt25f*.

■ DO THE MATH

Calculators are really useful when you build tables. Although you *could* create a 400-pixel-wide table with three 700-pixel-wide columns, the results you'd get on the screen could be unpredictable (after all, 700 plus 700 plus 700 does not equal 400).

As it turns out, web browsers' loyalty is to *table* width first, and then to column width. If the combined widths of your columns add up to the width of your table, you'll save yourself a lot of headaches.

Don't forget that you need to account for borders, cell padding, and cell spacing. For example, say you create a 500-pixel-wide table with two columns and 10 pixels of padding. If you want the first column 100 pixels wide, you'd set the width value to 80 pixels: 10 pixels of left padding plus 80 pixels of cell space plus 10 pixels of right padding equals 100 pixels total width.

The same is true when you use percentage values for tables and cell widths. Just make sure the value of the widths of the cells in a row totals 100 percent. That is, if you have three columns and you want the first to be twice as wide as the other two, you could set its width to 50% and the other two cells' widths to 25% each. This is true even if you set the initial width of the entire table to something smaller than 100%, say, 80%. That 80% table width simply means that the table will be 80% of the width of its container—the page, for example, or a <div> tag. Even though the table takes up only 80% of the browser window, all the cells together still make up 100% of the table width.

Beware the Resize Handles

Dreamweaver provides several techniques for resizing tables and cells in Design view. Unfortunately, the easiest way to resize a table—dragging a cell or table border—is also the easiest way to make a mistake. Because moving the cursor over any border turns it into the Resize tool, almost every Dreamweaver practitioner drags a border accidentally at least once, overwriting carefully calculated table and cell widths and heights.

In addition, if you grab either of the two bottom resize handles (they look like black squares) when you have a table selected,

you'll set the table's Height property. As mentioned in the note on page 279, it's actually invalid HTML to add a Height attribute to the table tag.

On occasions like these, don't forget Dreamweaver's undo feature, Ctrl+Z (⌘-Z). And if all is lost, you can always clear the widths and heights of every cell in a table (using the Properties panel's buttons) and start over by typing in new cell dimensions (see Figure 6-5).

■ Adding and Removing Cells

Even after you insert a table into a web page, you can add and subtract rows and columns. The text or images in the columns move right or down to accommodate their new next-door neighbors.

Adding One Row or Column

To add a single row to a table, use any of these approaches:

- Click inside a cell. Choose Modify→Table→Insert Row (Figure 6-9).

- Select Ctrl+M (⌘-M) to insert a new row of cells above the current row.

- Right-click (Control-click) a cell, and then, from the shortcut menu, choose Table→Insert Row.

- To add a new row at the end of a table, click inside the last cell in the table, and then press Tab.

The new row inherits properties of the row you originally clicked.

To add a single *column* of cells:

- Click inside a cell, and then choose Modify→Table→Insert Column.

- Click inside a cell, and then press Ctrl+Shift+A (⌘-Shift-A).

- Right-click (Control-click) a cell, and then, from the shortcut menu, choose Table→Insert Column.

In each case, a new column appears to the left of the current one.

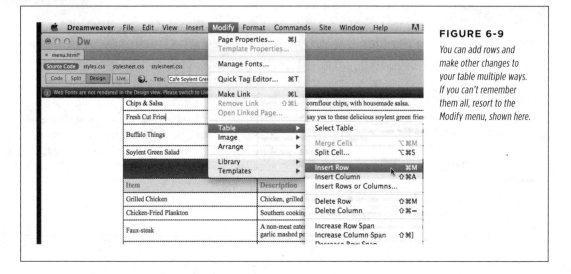

FIGURE 6-9

You can add rows and make other changes to your table multiple ways. If you can't remember them all, resort to the Modify menu, shown here.

Adding Multiple Rows or Columns

If you need to add a *lot* of rows or columns to a table, you use a special dialog box.

1. **Click inside a cell. Choose Modify→Table→Insert Rows or Columns.**

   The Insert Rows or Columns dialog box appears (see Figure 6-10).

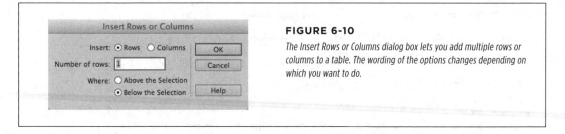

FIGURE 6-10

The Insert Rows or Columns dialog box lets you add multiple rows or columns to a table. The wording of the options changes depending on which you want to do.

2. **Turn on either the Rows or Columns radio button. Type the number of rows or columns you want to add.**

   Windows users can also click the tiny up- and down-arrow buttons next to "Number of rows" (or columns).

3. **Tell Dreamweaver where you want the new rows or columns to appear, relative to the cell you selected, by clicking Above or Below (for rows), or Before or After (for columns). Click OK to insert them.**

   Using this dialog box gives you an advantage over the single row/single column expansion described above. There, new rows always go above the current cell, and new columns always go to the left. This dialog box lets you choose whether the new row or column comes *before* or *after* the selected cell.

Deleting Rows and Columns

To delete a row from your table, use one of the following techniques:

> **NOTE** . When you remove a row or column, Dreamweaver eliminates everything inside the cells. So before you start hacking away, it's a good idea to save a copy of the page.

- Select the row (see page 275) and then press Delete to remove all the row's cells—and all the content in them.

- Click a cell. Choose Modify→Table→Delete Row, or use the keyboard shortcut Ctrl+Shift+M (⌘-Shift-M).

- Right-click (Control-click) inside a cell, and then, from the shortcut menu, choose Table→Delete Row.

Deleting a column is equally straightforward:

- Select the column, and then press Delete. You just eliminated all the selected cells and everything in them.

- Click a cell, and then choose Modify→Table→Delete Column, or use the keyboard shortcut Ctrl+Shift+Hyphen (⌘-Shift-Hyphen).

- Right-click (Control-click) inside a cell, and then choose Table→Delete Column from the shortcut menu.

> **NOTE** Dreamweaver doesn't let you delete a row if you *merged* one of its cells with a cell in another row. Nor can you delete a column if it contains a cell merged with an adjacent cell. (You'll learn about merged cells in the next section.)

Deleting a column like this is actually quite a feat. Since there's no column tag in HTML, Dreamweaver, behind the scenes, has to select individual cells in multiple rows—a task you wouldn't wish on your worst enemy if you had to do it by editing the raw HTML.

■ Merging and Splitting Cells

When you first create a table, cells are very basic creatures. All the cells in a row are the same height and all the cells in a column are the same width. That's not always the best way to express the underlying information. Sometimes you want to merge cells, as shown in Figure 6-11. This table shows you the number of subscribers to *CosmoFarmer* magazine for the years 2006 and 2007. Since the data for each year is further broken down into Men and Women subscribers, each year generates two columns' worth of information. To accurately label those columns, the cells that contain the year labels would have to span the two columns below them. The trick to making that happen is to *merge* cells—combine the area of one or more—to create a larger cell that spans multiple rows or columns.

CosmoFarmer Subscriber Information by Year

Year	2006		2007	
Gender	Men	Women	Men	Women
Number	10,000	15,000	25,000	27,000
Average Age	39	34	33	30
Avg Yearly Income	$65K	$66K	$100K	$100K

FIGURE 6-11

You can create cells that span multiple rows or columns by merging adjacent cells. When you do, you can represent multiple related rows or columns of information using a single table header.

To merge cells, select the cells you want to combine using any of the methods described on page 287. You can only merge cells that form a rectangle or square. You can't, for instance, select three cells in a column, and only one in the adjacent row, to create an L shape. Nor can you merge cells that aren't adjacent; in other words, you can't merge a cell in one corner of a table with a cell in the opposite corner.

Then, in the Properties panel, click the Merge Cells button (Figure 6-12) or choose Modify→Table→Merge Cells. Dreamweaver joins the selected cells, forming a single new super cell.

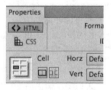

FIGURE 6-12

Dreamweaver makes the Merge Cells button active only when you select multiple cells. The Split Cells button appears only when you select a single cell or when you click inside a cell.

TIP Better yet, use this undocumented keyboard shortcut: the M key. Just select two or more cells, and then press M. It's much easier than the keyboard shortcut: Ctrl+Alt+M (⌘-Option-M).

You may also find yourself in the opposite situation: You have one cell that you want to *divide* into multiple cells. To split a cell, click or select a single cell. In the Properties panel, click Split Cells. (Once again, you can trigger the Split Cell command several ways: By choosing Modify→Table→Split Cell, or, if you prefer keyboard shortcuts, by pressing Ctrl+Alt+S [⌘-Option-S]. You can even right-click [Control-click] the selected cell, and then, from the shortcut menu, choose Table→Split Cell.)

When the Split Cell dialog box opens (Figure 6-13), click one of the buttons to indicate whether you want to split the cell into rows or columns. Then type the number of rows or columns you want to create, and click OK.

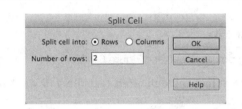

FIGURE 6-13

The Split Cell dialog box lets you divide a single cell into multiple cells. You can divide the cell into rows, with multiple cells on top of one another, or columns, with multiple cells side by side.

If you split a cell into columns, everything in the cell winds up in the left column, with the new, empty column or columns to the right. When you split a cell into rows, the current contents end up in the top row.

Tabular Data

Since tables are meant to display information, Dreamweaver provides useful tools that let you import and work with data.

Importing Data into a Table

Say your boss emails you your company's yearly sales information, which includes data on sales, profits, and expenses organized by quarter. She asks you to get this up on the Web for a board meeting she's having in half an hour.

This assignment could require a fair amount of work: building a table and then copying and pasting the correct information into each cell of the table, one piece at a time. Dreamweaver makes your task much easier, because you can create a table and import data into its rows and columns in one pass.

For this to work, the table data you want to import must begin life in *delimited* format. Most spreadsheet programs (including Excel) and database programs (such as Access or FileMaker Pro) export delimited data easily. In most programs, you do this by choosing File→Export or File→Save As, and then choose a tab-delimited or comma-separated text file format.

NOTE If you use Dreamweaver for Windows, you don't need to create a delimited-format file for Microsoft Excel data. Dreamweaver directly imports the data and converts it into a well-organized table. See page 71 for details.

In a delimited file, each line of text represents one table row. You keep the individual pieces of information in that line of text discrete using a special character called a delimiter—most often a tab, but possibly a comma or colon. Each discrete piece of data will go into a single cell in the row. In a colon-delimited file, for example, Dreamweaver would convert the line *Sales:$1,000,000:$2,000,000:$567,000:$12,500* into a row of five cells, with the first cell containing the word *Sales*.

Once you save your boss's spreadsheet as a delimited file, you're ready to import it into Dreamweaver as a table:

1. **Choose File→Import→Tabular Data.**

   The Import Tabular Data dialog box appears (see Figure 6-14).

2. **Click Browse. Navigate to and select the delimited text file you want to import.**

   The delimited file isn't a spreadsheet, it's a plain text file. Find the file name and double-click it to fill in the Data file field.

3. **From the Delimiter drop-down menu, select the delimiter you used to separate the data in the file.**

   You can select a tab, comma, colon, or semicolon as the delimiter, or you can choose your own delimiter by selecting Other. When you do the latter, an additional field appears where you type in your delimiter character.

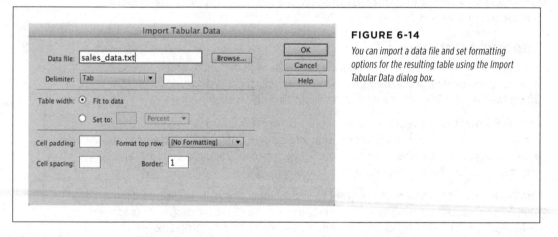

FIGURE 6-14

You can import a data file and set formatting options for the resulting table using the Import Tabular Data dialog box.

4. **Select a table width.**

   Choose "Fit to data" if you want the table to fit itself to the information you're importing—an excellent idea when you aren't completely sure how much information the file contains. (You can always modify the table after you import the data.)

   On the other hand, if your web page needs a table of a certain size, you can specify its dimensions by selecting the "Set to" button, and then typing a value in the field next to it. Finally, select Pixels or Percent (see page 273).

5. **Set values for cell padding, cell spacing, and a border, if you like.**

See page 272 for details.

6. **Select a formatting option for the top row of data.**

If the first line in the text file has column headings—1st Quarter Sales, 2nd Quarter Sales, and so on—Dreamweaver lets you choose Bold, Italic, or Bold Italic to set this row apart from the rest of the table. Unfortunately, this option doesn't turn the cells in the first row into table header (<th>) tags, which is what they should be. It's best to choose no formatting, manually select the cells, and then turn them into table header (<th>) tags as described on page 281.

7. **Click OK to import the data and create the table.**

Dreamweaver adds the table to your web page. It's a regular HTML table at this point, and you can edit the contents as you normally would, or modify the table itself (add rows and columns, for example) using any of the techniques discussed in this chapter.

Sorting Data in a Table

If you have a table that lists employee names, you probably want to present that list in alphabetical order—or alphabetically *and* by department. Dreamweaver's Sort command takes a lot of the drudgery out of that task.

1. **Select the table you want to sort.**

See page 274 for some table-selection techniques.

2. **Choose Commands→Sort Table.**

The Sort Table dialog box appears (Figure 6-15).

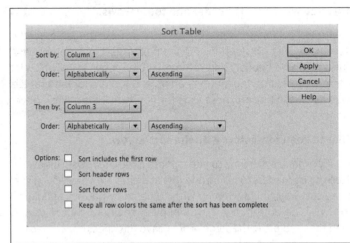

FIGURE 6-15

The Sort Table command is an excellent complement to Dreamweaver's Import Tabular Data feature. Once you import data into a table, the Sort Table command lets you organize that information. Imagine you get a text file listing all your company's employees, import the data into a table, and then realize that the names aren't in any particular order. This dialog box lets you granularly dictate the sorting scheme.

3. **Using the "Sort by" drop-down menu, choose the column by which you want to sort.**

   You can choose any column in the table. Suppose you have a table listing a bunch of products. Each row has the product name, number, and price. To see the products listed from least to most expensive, sort by the Price column.

4. **Use the next two drop-down menus to specify how you want Dreamweaver to sort the data.**

   You can sort it alphabetically or numerically. To order the products in the example above by price, choose Numerically from the Order drop-down menu. If you're sorting a Name column, choose Alphabetically.

   Use the second drop-down menu to specify whether you want an Ascending (A–Z, 1–100) or Descending (Z–A, 100–1) sort.

5. **If you like, choose an additional column to sort by, using the "Then by" drop-down menu.**

   This secondary sort can come in handy when several cells in the *first* sorting column have the same value. If several items in your product list cost $100, a sort by price would place them consecutively in the table; you could then specify a secondary sort that would place the products in alphabetical order within each price group. Doing so lists all the products from least to most expensive, *and* lists all same-priced products alphabetically within their group.

6. **If the first row of the table contains data you want to sort, turn on the "Sort includes the first row" checkbox.**

   If, however, the first row contains *headings* for the columns, leave this box turned off.

7. **Choose whether you want to sort header and footer rows.**

   The "Sort header rows" option isn't referring to cells that have the Table Header property set (see page 281). This option, and the next one, "Sort footer rows," refer to the <thead> (table header) and <tfoot> (table footer) tags, which let you turn one or more rows into repeating headers and footers for long tables. Since Dreamweaver doesn't insert these tags for you, you'll most likely never use these options.

8. **Choose whether to keep row colors with the sorted row.**

   One way to visually organize a table is to add color to alternate rows. This every-other-row pattern helps readers focus on one row at a time. However, if you sort a table formatted this way, you'd wind up with some crazy pattern of colored and uncolored rows. The bottom line: If you applied colors to your rows and you want to keep those colors in the same order, leave this checkbox turned off.

   Dreamweaver is even in step with current web design practices, which don't assign a background color to table rows using the outmoded *bgcolor* HTML property but instead use CSS. A common approach to coloring table rows is to apply a CSS class style to every *other* row in a table. That class style might have the *background-color* property set so that alternating rows are colored. When you use the Sort Table command, Dreamweaver keeps the class names in the proper order. That is, it keeps the classes applied to every other row, even when you reorganize the data in those rows. This only works if you *don't* turn on the "Keep all row colors the same" checkbox—so don't turn it on!

9. **Click Apply to see the effect of the sort without closing the dialog box.**

   If the table meets with your satisfaction, click OK to sort the table and return to the document window. (Clicking Cancel, however, doesn't undo the sort. If you want to return the table to its previous sort order, choose Edit→Undo Sort Table after closing the sort window.)

Exporting Table Data

Getting data *out* of a table in Dreamweaver is simple, too. Just select the table and then choose File→Export→Table. In the Export Table dialog box, select the type of delimiter (tab, comma, space, colon, semicolon, or Other) and the destination computer's operating system (Windows, Mac, or Unix), and then click OK. Give the file a name and save it on your computer. You can then import this delimited file into your spreadsheet or database program.

■ Tables Tutorial

In this tutorial, you'll create a menu for the café site you've been working on. In addition, you'll use some Cascading Style Sheet magic to make the table look great (skip ahead to Figure 6-26 if you want to see the finished page).

> **TIP** You need to download files from *http://oreilly.com/missingmanuals/cds/dreamweaverccmm13/* to complete this tutorial. See the note on page 33 for more details.

Once you download the tutorial files and open Dreamweaver, set up a new site as described on page 19: Name the site *Tables Tutorial*, and select the *Chapter06* folder inside the *MM_DWCC* folder. (In a nutshell, choose Site→New Site. In the Site Setup window, type *Tables Tutorial* into the Site Name field, click the folder icon next to the Local Site Folder field, navigate to and select the *Chapter06* folder, and then click Choose [Select]. Finally, click OK.)

Adding a Table

Once again, you'll be working on a page for the good people who run *Cafe Soylent Green*.

1. **Choose File→Open.**

   You'll work on a page similar to the ones you've built so far.

2. **Navigate to the Chapter06 folder and double-click the file named *menu. html*. Click in the empty space beneath the headline "Cafe Soylent Green Menu."**

You'll insert a table into this space.

3. **Choose Insert→Table.**

You can also click the Table button in the Insert panel's Common category. Either way, the Table window appears (see Figure 6-16). You need to define the table's basic characteristics.

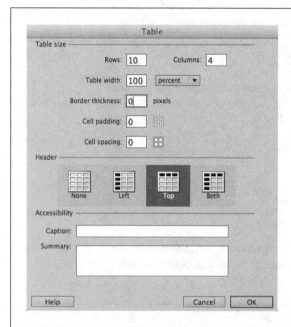

FIGURE 6-16

Inserting a table into a web page is a matter of making a few choices in the Table dialog box. Any text you type into the Summary box doesn't appear in a browser window, so you probably won't use this field much. It's intended to explain a particularly complicated table to non-visual web browsers (like search engines such as Google and Bing, or screen readers used by the visually impaired).

4. **Type *10* in the Rows box and *4* in the Columns box.**

Time to set the table's Width, Spacing, and Padding properties.

5. **Set "Table width" to 100 percent. Type *0* in the "Border thickness," "Cell padding," and "Cell spacing" boxes.**

Setting a table's width to 100 percent makes it fit the space available to it—in this case, you're about to insert this table into a <div> tag that has a set width of 800 pixels. The browser will make this table fill that space and, in effect, display an 800-pixel-wide table. Using a percentage value is a good idea, because if you decide to change the width of the main content area of the page (make it 1,000 pixels wide instead of 800 pixels, for example), the table grows to fit the new dimensions. If you use pixels for the width, you'd have to go back to the table and change its width every time you decided to change the width of the page.

Setting the other three properties here to 0 is common—you get greater control over border and cell attributes using CSS.

6. **In the window's Header section, select Top.**

The header setting indicates which cells Dreamweaver will mark as "table headers"—the cells that contain labels describing the information in the cells below (when you select Top), or in the cells of a row (when you select Left). Now that you've picked Top, the top row of cells will hold labels like Product, Cost, and Manufacturer.

You can skip the caption. It's not a requirement, and the page's title makes clear what the table is all about. The window should now look like Figure 6-16.

7. **Click OK.**

A new table appears on the page, filling the space provided by the main content <div> tag. At this point, you could begin adding content by typing in a cell. However, this book isn't about improving your typing skills, so forget about typing in the menu items and use Dreamweaver's very useful Import Tabular Data command instead.

Importing Tabular Data

While it's not difficult to type data into a table, it does take time. And, if you already have the data you want to insert in spreadsheet format, there's a better way to add data to that table. In this section of the tutorial, you'll use the Insert Tabular Data command to create and fill a table in several easy steps—but first, you need to remove the table you just added.

1. **Select the table you created in the steps above and press Delete (or select Edit→Cut).**

You can select a table several ways (see page 274). One is to click the top-left corner of the table to get the Table selection cursor (Figure 6-4). But when a table has no borders, padding, or cell spacing, that can be tricky. For a surefire method, right-click (Control-click) and then choose Table→Select Table.

Another easy way is to just click inside any cell in the table and then, in the Tag Selector (page 7) in the bottom-left of the document window, click the <table> tag to select the table and all its contents. Then press Delete to remove the table.

Now you'll import a text file.

2. **Make sure your cursor is in the empty space below the café's headline and choose File→Import→Tabular Data.**

Dreamweaver opens the Import Tabular Data window (Figure 6-17).

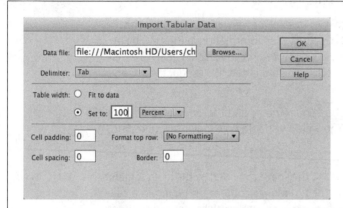

FIGURE 6-17

Dreamweaver makes it easy to import a text file's worth of data into a brand-new HTML table. Leave the "Format top row" setting on No Formatting. You're better off controlling the formatting—including the border, padding, and spacing attributes you earlier set to 0—with CSS.

3. **Click the Browse button to open a file selection window and double-click the file *menu.txt* in the Chapter06 folder.**

   This file contains tab-delimited data. That is, each line in the file represents one row in a table, and within that line, you separate the content for each cell using the Tab key. This is a common way to export information from a spreadsheet program like Microsoft Excel or Apple Numbers, or even from database programs.

4. **Make sure you have Tab selected in the Delimiter menu.**

   The option you select from the Delimiter drop-down menu depends on the delimiter used in the file you're importing. The file you just selected separates each piece of information by a tab character. Dreamweaver can use that tab to identify the data for individual cells and figure how many columns the table will need. When you export a spreadsheet, you can use other delimiting characters, including commas, semicolons, and colons, to demarcate each cell.

5. **In the "Table width" section, select "Set to," type *100*, and then choose Percent. Set the "Cell padding," "Cell spacing," and Border boxes to *0*.**

   The window should now look like the one in Figure 6-17.

6. **Click OK to import the data and create a new table.**

   Dreamweaver creates the new table, 3 columns wide by 16 rows high, and inserts all the information for the café's menu (see Figure 6-18).

   The café's menu includes three categories: Starters, Main, and Dessert. In the first row, you'll see the word "Starters" sitting in a single cell on the left. This really should span the entire table, since it's introducing this section of the menu. Fortunately, that's an easy task to accomplish.

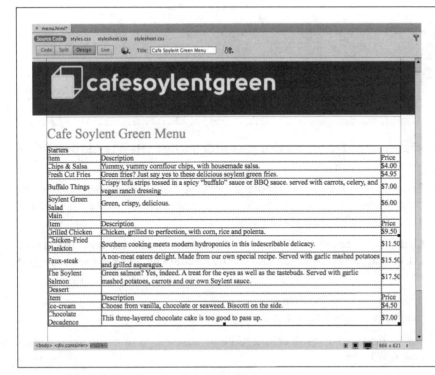

FIGURE 6-18

Dreamweaver's Import Tabular Data feature makes it easy to convert a comma- or tab-delimited file into a complex HTML table. It's certainly a lot easier than adding data to each cell individually. When you need to create an HTML table filled with data, try to get your data into a CSV (comma-separated value) file.

7. **Ctrl-click (⌘-click) the three cells in the top row. Press the M key to merge those cells.**

   The three cells turn into one big cell that spans the width of the table. You could also have selected the row using any of the methods described on page 275—for example, in Expanded Table Mode (right-click [Control-click]→Table→Expanded Tables Mode), you could click on the left edge of the first cell to select the row, or you could click in the left cell and drag to the right until you select all the cells.

   You can also merge those cells by clicking the Merge Selected Cells icon in the Properties panel (circled in Figure 6-19).

   Because this row introduces the content that follows, it's a good candidate for the table header (<th>) tag described on page 281.

8. **In the Properties panel, turn on the Header checkbox.**

   This converts a regular table cell (a <td> tag) into a table header (a <th> tag).

FIGURE 6-19

The Header checkbox (lower-right) turns the selected table cell into a table header using the <th> tag. You see the Header box only if you click inside a table and the Properties panel is completely expanded, as described on page 11. The Merge Selected Cells button (circled) combines table cells.

9. **Repeat steps 7–8 for the two rows with the text "Main" and "Dessert" in them.**

   Below these three rows is another set of cells that make good candidates for table headers: the Item, Description, and Price cells all indicate what type of information will appear in that column.

10. **Click inside each of the three Item, Description, and Price cells (that's nine cells altogether), and then turn on the Header checkbox in the Properties panel.**

    A quick way to do this is to Ctrl+click (⌘-click) all nine cells, and then turn on the Header checkbox. Just as in step 8, this turns each <td> tag into a <th> tag.

    You've discovered that a couple of items are missing from the menu, so it's time to add them.

11. **Click in the very last cell of the table, the one with the $7.00 price, and then press the Tab key.**

    Dreamweaver adds a new row to the bottom of the table.

12. **Type *Hot Fudge Sundae*, and press Tab to jump to the next cell. Type *The ultimate dessert experience*. Press Tab again, type *$5.00*, and then press Tab one last time.**

    You added a row's worth of information, and then added another blank row to the end of the table. Unfortunately, that was a mistake. You don't need that last row. What an excellent time to learn how to delete a row.

13. **Click inside the last cell in the bottom-right corner of the table. Drag to the left until you select all three empty cells, and then press Delete.**

    Dreamweaver removes the row easily. Now you need to add another row in the middle of the table. The Tab-to-add-a-row technique only works if you're in the last table cell. To add a row in the middle of a table, you need to try something else.

14. **Click in the cell with the text "The Soylent Salmon." Select Modify→Table →Insert Row.**

    Dreamweaver inserts a new, blank row above. The last step is to add another entrée to the menu.

15. **Click in the first cell of the newly inserted row. Type *Shiitake Burger*, and press Tab to jump to the next cell. Type *The best hamburger mushrooms money can buy.* Press Tab one last time and type *$12.00*.**

    The menu's complete. Now it's time to make it look good.

Formatting the Table

Tables, like everything HTML, are drab by themselves. To make data really stand out, you need to turn to the power of Cascading Style Sheets. In this section, you'll format the table's basic font attributes, make the headers stand out, and add lines around the cells.

1. **Make sure CSS Designer is open (Window→CSS Designer); in the Sources section, click *soylent_styles.css*. Then, in Selectors, click the Add Selector button (the + icon).**

   A new selector appears in the list, ready for you to give it a name. You'll create a class style for the table tag headers and store the CSS information in an already attached external style sheet—*soylent_styles.css.* (For a recap on creating style sheets called a source in CSS Designer, turn to page 107.)

2. **Type *.menu* in the Selector Name box.**

   The Properties section shows the properties you can set for the new class *.menu.* Instead of creating a style for the <table> tag, you're creating a class style. That's because, if you created a *tag* style, it would apply to every instance of that HTML tag. So if this site had other tables in it, that single <table> tag style would format *all* of the site's tables, and that might not be what you want. By using a class style, you have the flexibility to create different designs for different tables.

3. **In Properties, click the Text button. From the Font-family menu, select "pt-sans, Arial, Helvetica, sans-serif." In the Font-size box, choose px, and then type *14*.**

   You'll only see pt-sans if you completed the tutorial in Chapter 3, which added the pt-sans web fonts to Dreamweaver (see page 147).

   The table is a bit close to the bottom of the headline above it; adding a little margin to the top of the table will help.

4. **Click Layout, and in the top position of the Margin box, type *20*.**

   This class style doesn't take effect until you apply it.

5. **Click the bottom border of the table to select it (or use any of the techniques described on page 274). From the Properties panel's Class menu, choose menu.**

The menu scoots down the page a bit, and the font gets smaller. You won't see the effect of the pt-sans font, since Dreamweaver can't display web fonts in Design view; however, if you preview this page in a browser or click the Live button, you'll see the new font in action.

The table headers don't really command enough attention. You'll make them stand out by using a background graphic and increasing the space inside each cell.

6. **With *soylent_styles.css* still selected in Sources, click the Add Selector button in Selectors. For the selector name, type *.menu th*, as shown in Figure 6-20.**

Selectors with two names are called *compound selectors*, or what CSS veterans know as *descendent selectors*—a style name composed of two or more CSS selectors. You'll learn more about this setting in the next chapter, but for now, keep in mind that you want to create a style that affects only the table headers that appear inside the table on this page—<th> tags that appear inside a table that's styled with the *.menu* class, in other words.

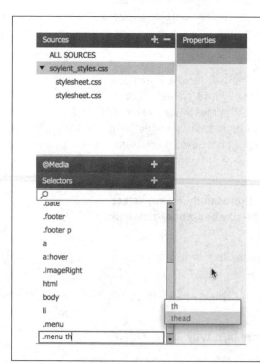

FIGURE 6-20

Dreamweaver uses the catch-all term "compound style" for any type of CSS style, including class, ID, or tag styles. More significantly, Dreamweaver uses compound styles to create one of the most important types of CSS style: descendent selectors, like the .menu th selector pictured here. This selector homes in on a very specific group of tags: <th> tags inside any other tag that has the class .menu applied to it.

7. **In the Properties section, click the Text button. For font-family, choose "pt-sans, Arial, Helvetica, sans-serif." For font-size choose 16 px. Set font-weight to 700 and color to #468531.**

This makes the text bold, green, and 16 pixels tall. Now you'll add a background color.

8. **In the Properties section, scroll down past the Background box and, beside background-color, type #F2E5C2 (a tan).**

Dreamweaver centers the column headers in their cells. To have them match the appearance of the other cells, you'll align them to the left.

9. **Click the Text button, and then, from the text-align options, choose *left*.**

You could also use the Properties panel to set the horizontal alignment of each table header to Left, but not only is that more work, it adds extra HTML to your page. The CSS method is easier and makes for faster-loading web pages.

Review your page using the Live view to see how this style is shaping up. The text is a bit cramped inside each cell. To add some breathing room between the edges of each cell and the text inside it, you'll use the CSS *padding* property.

NOTE In CSS Designer, if you accidentally drift away from the *.menu th* properties, choose *soylent_styles. css* in Sources, and then choose *.menu th* in Selectors.

---

10. **Click the Layout button. In the Padding properties box, click the link (Click To Change All Properties), and then set any of the sides to 5 px.**

The 5-pixel setting applies to all four sides of the table header. One last touch: a border separating the table headers from the rows below it.

11. **Click the Border button. Set border-bottom-color to #EC6206. Set border-bottom-width to 1 px. Set border-bottom-style to solid, as shown in Figure 6-21.**

This adds a border below each table header. In this particular table, you have two rows of different types of headers: the category headers (Starters, for example) and the headers that announce the dish, its description, and its price. Sharing the same style, the stacked header rows look a bit...well, boring. You'll create a class style to apply to each category of dish.

12. **Make sure you have *soylent_styles.css* chosen in Sources. Then, in Selectors, click the Add Selector button (+). To name the new selector, type *.menu .course*.**

This is another descendent selector. This one is composed of two class names and can be translated to mean, "Apply this style to an element with a class of *.course*, but only when it's inside another element with a class of *.menu*." In other words, you're about to create another style that includes a new class name, *.course*, which you'll apply to the first table header in each section of the menu.

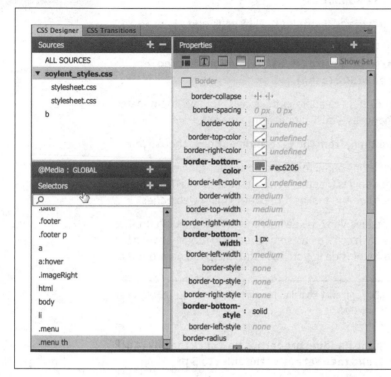

FIGURE 6-21

You can apply borders to any or all sides of an element. For example, when you set border-style to solid, you're putting a solid line around the outside of the entire table. On the other hand, you can set border-bottom-style to solid, which makes only the bottom border solid.

13. **In Properties, click the Text button. Then, set color to white (#FFFFFF), set font-size to 18 px, and then set text-transform to uppercase.**

    You may need to scroll down a little to find the text-transform property.

14. **In Properties, click the Background button. In background-color, type #0A2F02. Click in the "url" box of the background-image property, click the folder icon, and then, in the site's Images folder, select the file *bg-th. png*. For background-position, set the value on the left (X) to center. Set the value on the right (Y) to top.**

    The Properties should look like Figure 6-22. Just a few last touches and you'll be done.

15. **Click the Text button, and choose center from the text-align options.**

    This centers the text in the row. To scoot these table headers down a little, you'll add a bit of padding.

16. **Click the Layout button. In the padding box, type *13 px* in the top position.**

    Nothing happens...you need to apply the class style to the table header.

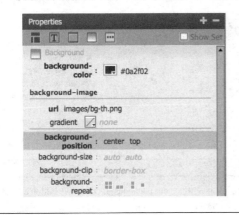

FIGURE 6-22

Why add a background color when you're already using a background image? Remember that, in the last step, you made the text white. To make sure visitors can read your text, you need a dark background (white-on-white isn't so easy to read). If, for some reason. the background graphic doesn't appear (the visitor has turned off her graphics, for example, or the image doesn't download properly), the table headers would appear as white text on a white background. By setting a dark background color in addition to a background image, you're covered—if the image doesn't download, the text is still readable—white text on a dark-green background.

17. **Click inside the table header with the text "Starters." From the Properties panel's Class menu, select course.**

    Dreamweaver centers the text, turns it white, and adds a green gradient background .

18. **Repeat step 17 for the table headers Main and Dessert.**

    Now it's time to tackle the look of the main table cells.

19. **With *soylent_styles.css* still selected in Sources, in Selectors click the Add Style button (+). Give the new style the name *.menu td*.**

    You should be getting the hang of these descendent selectors by now. This style will apply to every <td> tag (that's an individual table cell) within another tag that has the class named *.menu* applied to it. You'll add padding and border lines to clearly differentiate each cell.

20. **Click the Layout button. In the padding box, click the link (Click To Change All Properties), and then type *5 px* in any one of the fields.**

    Each cell will have 5 pixels of padding around all four sides. Time to add some borders.

21. **Click the Border button. Set border-color to white—#FFFFFF. Set border-width to 1px, and then set border-style to solid.**

    If you preview the page in a browser (press F12 [Option-F12]) or click the Live button at the top of the document window, you'll notice that, where two cells touch, the borders are a bit thick (see Figure 6-23). Because you added a border around all four sides of each cell, the border is twice as thick and looks a little chunky where two cells meet (circled in Figure 6-23). You could edit the style and add a border to only some sides of the cell (like the left and bottom sides) so that the borders don't double up, but CSS gives you an easier way.

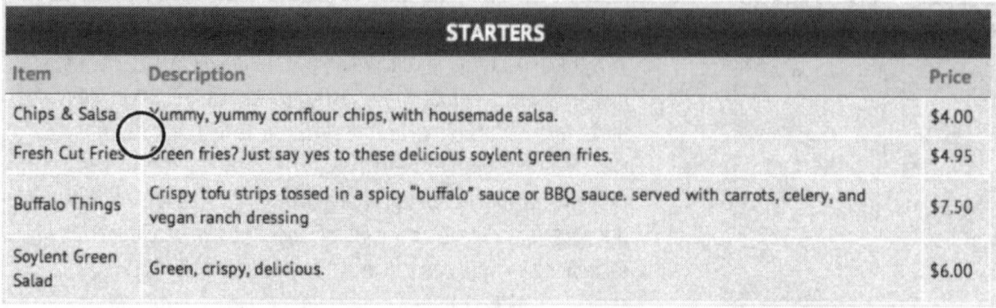

FIGURE 6-23

Adding a border to table cells creates slightly chunky double borders where cells touch. Fortunately, with a little-known CSS property, you can overcome this aesthetic nuisance.

NOTE Make sure to exit Live view when you finish viewing your page—just click the Live button a second time. If you don't leave Live view, you can't edit your page.

Final Improvements

To finish this tutorial, you'll get rid of the double-border problem and make the table rows easier to read by coloring every other row.

1. **Make sure CSS Designer is open (Window→CSS Designer) and that you have *soylent_styles.css* chosen in the Sources section.**

   When you choose *soylent_styles.css* in the Sources section, the Selectors section shows the tags, classes, and IDs for the styles.

2. **In Selectors, locate the style named *.menu*, click it, and then, in the Properties section, click the Border button.**

   The Properties pane scrolls so that the border-collapse property is the first one listed (see Figure 6-24).

3. **In the border-collapse property, choose collapse.**

   Border-collapse is a special CSS property that forces adjoining cells to "collapse" into each other. Essentially, it removes the space between cells, thus preventing the double border. You don't see the effect of this in Dreamweaver's Design view, but if you click the Live button or preview the page in a browser, you will.

   Now you'll highlight alternating table rows. This technique makes tables easier to scan. To accomplish this, you'll create an advanced CSS style.

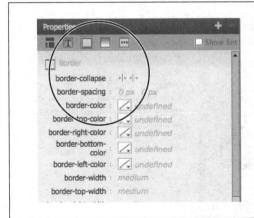

FIGURE 6-24

The border-collapse property (circled) offers you two options, represented by icons: collapse and separate. The collapse option (on the left above) resolves the double-border issue.

4. **In Selectors, with *soylent_styles.css* still chosen, click the Add Selector button (+). When the new selector appears, name it *.menu tr:nth-child(odd)*.**

   As you type a name, CSS Designer may prompt you with suggestions. This style is an advanced CSS selector. In a nutshell, it selects every odd table row inside the table with the class *.menu* applied to it. There's a similar style for every even table row: *tr:nth-of-type(even)*. All you need to do now is define a background color for the shaded rows.

5. **In CSS Designer's Properties section, click the Background button. Then, in the background-color property, click the swatch to open the color picker. Click the RGBa button (Figure 6-25). Then drag the middle slider (lightness/darkness) all the way to the top.**

   As mentioned on page 141, CSS supports several color formats; "rgba" stands for "red, green, blue, alpha," and it lets you pick a color that is partially transparent. This gives your table a neat effect since it lets colors or images below the element show through.

   You'll see *rgba(255,255,255,1.00)* in the *background-color* box. If the box can't fit all that in, either use your keyboard's arrow keys to move right until you see the 1 at the end of the value, or drag the left edge of the CSS Styles panel to make it wider. The *255,255,255* specifies the color white, while the *1* means 100% opaque—in other words, you can't see through it. Time to change that.

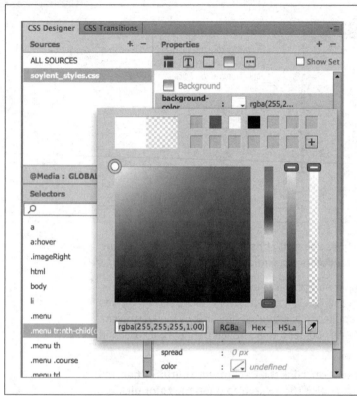

FIGURE 6-25

Dreamweaver's color picker lets you choose different color models. Here the rgba model is selected, so the color specification is displayed as rgba(255,255,255,1.00). Translation to humanese: white. Changing that last number 1.00 to a fraction will make the color semi-transparent.

6. **Change the 1 to .5 so that the color value now reads rgba(255,255,255,.5).**

   You won't see any effect in Design view, but if you preview the page in Live view or a web browser, you'll see every other table row with a slightly lighter background. One last design change and you're done. The menu items don't really stand out. Simply making them bold will help guide visitors' eyes to the tasty food the café offers.

   NOTE Neither the nth-of-type selector nor RGBA colors work in Internet Explorer 8 or earlier. While all other browsers, including IE 9 and 10, display this style correctly, if you want to add striped rows to your tables and you want it to work in Internet Explorer 8, you need to create a class style—*.odd*, for example—with a background color of your choosing (but using only hexadecimal [#FFFFFF] or RGB [for example, *rgb(255,255,255)*] colors). Then you need to manually apply the style to every other table row by selecting the row and using the Properties panel to apply the class to that row (which is a lot of work!).

7. **With *soylent_style.css* chosen as the Source, click the Add Selector button (+) in Selectors. When the new selector appears, name it *.menu td:first-child*.**

CSS Designer may prompt you with the *:first-child* option as you type. If you see those words highlighted, press Enter (Return) to complete the name. The *:first-child* style is a new type of style called a *pseudo-element*, and it selects an element that's the first child nested inside another tag. In this case, *td:first-child* means "Select the first table cell (the first <td> tag) that's nested inside its parent." To understand how it works, it helps to examine the HTML for one row from the table:

```
<tr>
    <td>Chips & Salsa</td>
    <td>Yummy, yummy cornflour chips, with housemade salsa.</td>
    <td>$4.00</td>
</tr>
```

Here, the <tr> tag wraps around all the <td> tags. In CSS-speak, the <tr> tag is called a parent, while the <td> tags that appear immediately inside it are called children. In this example, there are three <td> tags, and thus three children. The first child is the <td> tag with the menu item Chips & Salsa in it. So the new selector *.menu td:first-child* will select that <td> and every other first table cell inside a row that's also inside a table with the class *.menu* applied to it. Wow, that seems like a pretty complex selector, but you'll see in a moment how it will make formatting this table easy.

NOTE   Unlike the *:nth-of-type selector*, the *:first-child* selector works in Internet Explorer 7 and later. Only the nearly extinct IE 6 doesn't understand it, so you should feel free to use it.

---

8. **In the Properties section of CSS Designer, click the Text button (+). Then, set font-family to "pt-sans, Arial, Helvetica, sans-serif," and set the font-weight to 700. Then press F12 (Option-F12) to preview your hard work in a browser.**

The complete page should look like Figure 6-26. Notice that the name of each food item is bold, but none of the other cells in each row are. Without that *:first-child* selector, the only way to achieve this effect would be to manually select each food item and make it bold or apply a class style to it.

You'll find a completed version of this tutorial in the *Chapter06_complete* folder that accompanies the downloaded tutorial files.

FIGURE 6-26

With Dreamweaver and a little CSS, you can make elegant HTML tables.

HTML Under the Hood

Dreamweaver started life primarily as a visual web page editor, but over the years, its code-editing tools have evolved to rival those of the best text editors, including those that hard-core hand-coders use. Some people bypass Dreamweaver's Design view entirely and use only its Code view, where they edit their HTML, CSS, and JavaScript directly. In fact, you can use Dreamweaver to edit any text-based file, including XML, Java, ActionScript, and just plain text itself.

Dreamweaver's code editor includes professional features like customizable syntax highlighting, auto indenting, line numbering, and code hints; code collapse, so you can concentrate on just the code you want; and the Code view toolbar, which provides one-click access to frequently used hand-coding commands. Dreamweaver may be the only web-page creation program that hardcore code junkies ever need. In fact, Adobe aimed many of Dreamweaver CC's improvements at those who use Code view to edit pages built with HTML, CSS, JavaScript, and the server-side programming language PHP.

■ Controlling How Dreamweaver Handles HTML

Unlike many other visual HTML editors, Dreamweaver has always graciously accepted HTML written by hand (and even by other programs). This openness lets you write code the way you want, without worrying that Dreamweaver will change it. For example, suppose you format your handwritten code a particular way. Maybe you insert an extra hard return after every <td> (cell) tag, or you like to use multiple tabs to indent nested tags. In cases like these, Dreamweaver doesn't rewrite your code to fit its own style—unless you ask it to.

Auto-Fixing Your Code

That's not to say that Dreamweaver doesn't ever change your code. In fact, when you open a page created in another program, Dreamweaver can automatically fix errors, including:

- **Overlapping tags.** Take a look at this example:

  `<p><strong>Fix your tags!</p></strong>`

  This HTML is invalid, because both the opening and closing <strong> tags should appear *inside* the <p> tag. Dreamweaver rewrites this snippet correctly:

  `<p><strong>Fix your tags!</strong></p>`

- **Unclosed tags.** Tags usually come in pairs, like this:

  `<em>This text is in italic</em>.`

  But if a page is missing the ending tag (<em>*This text is in italic*), Dreamweaver adds it.

- **Extra closing tags.** If a page has an *extra* closing tag (<strong>bold text </strong> </strong>), Dreamweaver helpfully removes it.

NOTE If you use only Dreamweaver's Design view to create the HTML for your web pages, you don't have to worry about these code-rewriting options. Dreamweaver adds the HTML correctly.

This auto-fix feature comes turned *off* in Dreamweaver. If you work on a site that was hand-coded or created by a less capable web-editing program, it's wise to turn this feature on, since all those errors are improper HTML that can cause problems for browsers. (Once upon a time, for example, some web developers deliberately omitted closing tags to save a few kilobytes in file size. Although most browsers can still interpret this kind of sloppy code, it's poor practice.)

You can activate auto-fixing in the Code Rewriting category of Dreamweaver's Preferences window (see Figure 7-1); turn on the checkboxes next to "Fix invalidly nested and unclosed tags" and "Remove extra closing tags." If you leave these options turned off, Dreamweaver doesn't fix the HTML, and there's no command you can run to correct the tags. Instead, Dreamweaver highlights the mistakes in Design and Code views (skip ahead to Figure 7-5 to get a glimpse of that).

NOTE The "Warn when fixing or removing tags" option doesn't really warn you so much as report code that Dreamweaver went ahead and fixed on its own. You can't undo these auto-changes, but you can close the file without saving it to retain the old (improperly written) HTML.

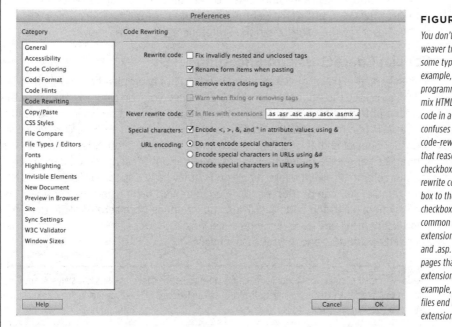

FIGURE 7-1

You don't want Dreamweaver trying to "fix" some types of code. For example, many server-side programming languages mix HTML and server-side code in a way that confuses Dreamweaver's code-rewriting tool. For that reason, turn on the checkbox next to "Never rewrite code." The text box to the right of that checkbox lists the most common server-side file extensions, such as .php and .asp. If you write pages that end in an extension not listed—for example, Ruby on Rails files end in .rb—add the extension to this box.

Dreamweaver can also change the capitalization (case) of HTML tags and properties if you want. For example, you might prefer lowercase letters for tags and properties, like this:

```
<a href="nextpage.html">Click here</a>
```

Dreamweaver can convert uppercase tags (<A HREF="next.html">) to lowercase (and vice versa) when it finds them in pages created by other programs. You can turn on this feature in the Code Format section of the Preferences menu (Edit→Preferences [Dreamweaver→Preferences]), as described in "Line breaks" on page 33.

Server-Side Web Pages

Dreamweaver can leave pages with certain file extensions—pages created with a server-side programming language like PHP, Cold Fusion, C#, or Ruby—untouched. (Server-side programming lets web pages talk to databases, process HTML forms, and send email.) Server-side programming relies on code within the HTML of a page—code that Dreamweaver might "fix," mistakenly interpreting it as error-prone HTML.

Unless you change its settings, Dreamweaver doesn't rewrite the code in files whose names end in .asp (active server pages that run on Microsoft's IIS Web Server), .aspx (Microsoft's .NET technology), .cfm and .cfml (ColdFusion markup language pages that run on Adobe's ColdFusion server), .jsp (JavaServer pages that run on any Java

Server), or php files (PHP pages), among others. Nor does it rewrite code inside an external JavaScript file (a .js file), since it's common practice to write JavaScript that creates HTML on the fly—many times this means JavaScript coders add HTML fragments (incomplete tags and code) to their files. If you edit other types of files with Dreamweaver and don't want it interfering with them, add their extensions to the "Never rewrite code" list in the Preferences window, as shown in Figure 7-1.

Special Characters and Encoding

Some characters have special meaning in HTML. For example, the "less than" symbol (<) indicates the beginning of an HTML tag, so you can't, for example, use the filename *bob<zero.html* in, say, a link. If you typed this in, a browser would read it as the start of a new HTML tag (called *zero*). The solution is to have Dreamweaver "encode" special characters, like <, >, &, and " whenever you enter them into the Properties panel or a dialog box. It uses a code to represent the character, since the character itself, like the less-than sign (<), may have a special meaning in HTML. For example, you can produce a space on your web page using the code *%20*, or the < symbol using the code *<*. Thus, the infamous *bob<zero.html* file becomes *bob<zero.html*, and your link works just fine. Other characters, like ™ or ©, get encoded as *™* and *©* respectively.

> **TIP** Whenever possible, avoid strange characters when you name pages, graphics, CSS styles, or any other object in your site. Stick to letters, numbers, hyphens, and underscores (_) because they're the only characters that web servers can universally read.

To set up encoding, choose Edit→Preferences (Dreamweaver→Preferences on Macs) and select Code Rewriting from the category list. Your options are as follows:

- **Special characters.** Turn on this checkbox to have Dreamweaver convert the <, >, &, and * characters to the specially encoded format mentioned above. (This doesn't apply to code you type in Code view, nor to text you type into the document window in Design view.)

- **Do not encode special characters.** Select this option, the first of three under "URL encoding," to tell Dreamweaver not to touch any web addresses you enter (in the Properties panel's Link box, say). (Again, selecting this option has no effect on links you add in Code view.)

- **"Encode special characters in URLs using &#."** This is the best of the three "URL encoding" options. Unlike the option above, this option gives you encoding help when you need it (and the option below applies to browsers so old you'll never use it). This option is especially helpful if you use a language that has a non-Latin alphabet. If you name your files using Japanese characters, for example, choosing this option translates them into code that successfully transmits over the Internet.

- **"Encode special characters in URLs using %" is intended for use with older browsers** (and we're talking *old*, as in pre-Internet Explorer 4), so unless you've got a time machine and plan on going back to 1998 to build websites, skip this option.

> **NOTE** Encoding Preferences don't apply to special characters you type in Code view or in the document window in Design view. Dreamweaver always encodes special characters you type directly into a page in Design view; conversely, it never encodes special characters in Code view.

■ Code View

Dreamweaver provides several ways to view a page's HTML:

- **Code view (View→Code).** In Code view, Dreamweaver displays your page's raw code, just as any text editor would.

- **Split view (View→Code and Design).** This view displays both the HTML and the visual design of a web page (Design view) side-by-side: code on the left, design on the right (Figure 7-2). You can reverse this order (View→Design View on Left) or stack one view on top of the other by turning off View→Split Vertically. In addition, if the page has an external style sheet, you can use Dreamweaver's Related Files feature (page 332) to display the CSS code in one half of the document window and the visual Design view in the other half.

- **Split Code view (View→Split Code).** This option is for serious coding junkies. It lets you view the code *twice*, so you can work on two sections of a page at once. That's useful for pages with lots of HTML and can come in handy when you want to edit the CSS in the <head> region of a page while crafting HTML in the <body> section. It also works with Dreamweaver's Related Files feature (page 332); in Split Code view, you can check the HTML for a web page in one half of the document window and the CSS for an external style sheet in the other half (or the JavaScript from an external JavaScript file for that matter).

- **Code Inspector.** The Code Inspector displays your HTML in a floating window so you see your working pages in their full glory in the document window, rather than have them cut in half in Split view. To open the Code Inspector, choose Window→Code Inspector, or press F10 (Option-F10). If you have multiple monitors, the Code Inspector is especially handy, because you can display your HTML code on one monitor and the document window on the other. Multitasking code warriors can also use the Code Inspector to look at one area of code while using the main document window to work on another area of code (though the Split Code view works well for this, too).

The rest of this chapter assumes that you're using Code view to edit your HTML.

Dreamweaver gives you two ways to select a view. From the View menu, choose Code, Split Code, Design, or Code and Design (a.k.a. Split) view; you can also click one of the buttons in the document window's toolbar.

Code/Design

Code   Design   Live view

FIGURE 7-2

In Split view, you can display raw code right beside the visual Design view. In Split view, when you select an object in the visual half (like the selected "About Us" headline on the right above), Dreamweaver selects the corresponding HTML in the code half (the highlighted <h1> tag in Code view)—a great way to identify an object in your HTML. As you work in one half of Split view, Dreamweaver updates the other half. Use the buttons (labeled) in the document window's toolbar to jump between the different views. (Notice that the Tag Selector at the bottom of the document window also identifies the tag you selected [circled].)

TIP You can quickly jump between Code and Design views by pressing Control+` (on both Windows and Macs). In Split view, this shortcut jumps between the two views, so you can insert an image in the design half of Split view, and then press Control+` to jump right into the HTML for that image in the code half of the window. (If you have the Code Inspector open, this keyboard shortcut jumps between the Code Inspector and the document window.)

Code view functions much like a text editor (only better, as you'll soon see). You can click anywhere inside the window and start typing in HTML, JavaScript, CSS, or any other programming code you want (such as PHP or ColdFusion).

You don't have to type out *everything* by hand; the Insert panel, Insert menu, and Properties panel also function in Code view. Use these sources of canned HTML to combine hands-on coding with convenient, easy-to-use Dreamweaver objects. This trick can be a real timesaver when you need to add a table, which would otherwise be a multiline exercise in typing accuracy.

You can also select a tag (like a photo's <img> tag) in Code view and use the Properties panel to modify it.

NOTE When you add HTML in Code view, Dreamweaver doesn't automatically update Design view, which can be disconcerting when you work in Split view (after all, how would Dreamweaver display a half-finished tag like this: *<img src="?*). In the Properties panel, click the Refresh button (see Figure 7-3) or press F5 to update the visual display.

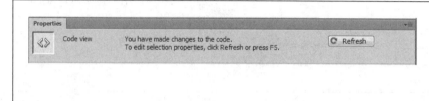

FIGURE 7-3

After you change the HTML on the code side of Split view, click the Refresh button in the Properties panel to update the Design view.

To help navigate your code, Code view provides several visual cues. They include:

- **Syntax coloring.** Dreamweaver displays different elements in different colors. Comments, for example, are gray, while text is black; most HTML tags appear in blue, though web page form tags (like the <input> tag) are orange. Image tags are purple, and links are green. You can change any of these colors, and even specify unique colors for different types of tags, using the Preferences window (see Figure 7-4).

  To really make a tag stand out, you can underline, boldface, or italicize it, and even give it a background color. Dreamweaver offers separate color schemes for 25 types of documents, such as CSS, ASP, and XML files. (But do you really need different colors for HTML forms in JavaScript files, HTML pages, and PHP pages? You be the judge.)

- **Bad code highlighting.** When you type incorrect code (say an opening tag without a closing tag, or improperly nested tags), Dreamweaver highlights it in yellow (circled in Figure 7-5), but only if you turn on the Highlight Invalid Code option (View→Code View Options→Highlight Invalid Code) or click the Highlight Invalid Code button in the Coding toolbar (see Figure 7-6).

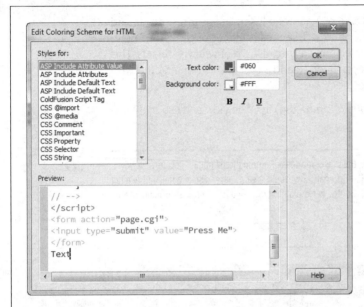

FIGURE 7-4

From Dreamweaver's Preferences window (Edit→Preferences in Windows, Dreamweaver→Preferences on Macs), you can control the hue Dreamweaver uses to color-code your web page's HTML, CSS, and script in Code view. Select the Code Coloring category, select the type of document you're working on—HTML, CSS, PHP, or whatever— and then click Edit Coloring Scheme. In the Edit Coloring Scheme window, shown here, select a page element whose color you want to change—like CSS Property values or HTML Form Tags, for example—and set a text and/ or background color using the color boxes. You can also make the code bold, italic, or underlined using the appropriate formatting buttons.

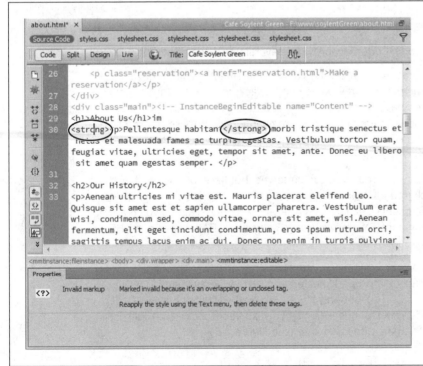

FIGURE 7-5

Dreamweaver highlights incorrect HTML in bright yellow in Code view (like the <strong> tags circled here). If you click the yellow area, the Properties panel reveals your mistake. In this case, you improperly nested a tag—part of it lies outside the surrounding <p> tag. (In Design view, on the other hand, Dreamweaver indicates mistakes by showing the HTML tag— </strong> for example—in front of a bright yellow background.)

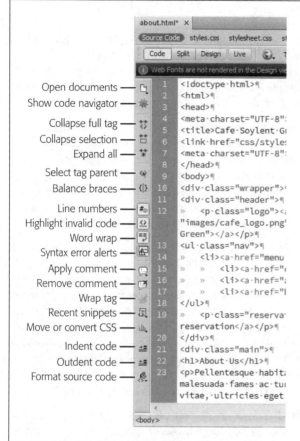

Open documents
Show code navigator
Collapse full tag
Collapse selection
Expand all
Select tag parent
Balance braces
Line numbers
Highlight invalid code
Word wrap
Syntax error alerts
Apply comment
Remove comment
Wrap tag
Recent snippets
Move or convert CSS
Indent code
Outdent code
Format source code

FIGURE 7-6

In Code view, you get easy access to common code-writing commands in the Coding toolbar (left edge). Using the toolbar, it's easy to wrap a selection of HTML in an HTML comment, hide code you don't want to see or edit, and turn on or off Code view options like line numbering and highlighting invalid code.

- **Non-editable highlighting in templates.** You'll learn about templates in detail in Chapter 20, but for now, templates include both editable and non-editable regions. Dreamweaver displays non-editable regions in light gray. This is a little confusing because Dreamweaver displays HTML comments in gray, too, and you *can* edit those. You can change either color, however, as shown in Figure 7-4.

- **Browser compatibility highlighting.** Much to the anguish of web designers, browsers sometimes react differently to CSS formatting. What looks great in Firefox may crumble in Internet Explorer 6. Dreamweaver's Browser Compatibility Checker alerts you to possible cross-browser CSS problems. When you see a squiggly line underneath code, Dreamweaver is telling you there's a potential issue.

- **Library item highlighting.** Code from Library items (Chapter 19) has a light yellow background.

You can also control the following Code view display options from the View→Code View Options submenu:

- **Word Wrap.** This option makes long lines of code wrap (at the window's edge) to the next line, so you don't have to scroll horizontally to see the entire line. This option affects only how Dreamweaver *displays* the line; it doesn't actually change your code by introducing line breaks. Dreamweaver turns this option on by default; if it got turned off, go to View→Code View Options→Word Wrap.

- **Line Numbers.** Automatic line-numbering can come in handy when you encounter an error in a page containing JavaScript or server-side code (such as PHP, described in Chapter 22). In Code view, you can click a line number to select the entire line, which is a great way to delete or cut a line of code. Normally, Dreamweaver displays line numbers, but if you don't see them in Code view, click the "Show line numbers" button in the Coding toolbar (Figure 7-6) or choose View→Code View Options→Line Numbers to turn them on.

- **Hidden Characters.** Some characters you type on a keyboard don't show up on-screen: the end of a line, created by hitting the Enter or Return key, for example. Occasionally, these hidden characters can cause big trouble. When you work with dynamic, server-side web pages, for example, you might find some cool code on the Web and copy it to your own page. Sometimes copying and pasting code from a web page introduces hidden characters that prevent the code from working. Turning on the Hidden Characters option (View→Code View Options→Hidden Characters) helps ferret out problem characters so you can eliminate them. Spaces appear as dots, paragraph breaks as paragraph symbols, and tabs as a set of double arrows (see the code in Figure 7-6).

- **Highlight Invalid Code.** This option is the on/off switch for highlighting bad HTML in Code view (see Figure 7-5). Dreamweaver normally turns this option off, but it's a good idea to turn it on: Go to View→Code View Options→Highlight Invalid Code.

- **Syntax Coloring.** This option turns tags, comments, and text into colorful (and informative) text (see Figure 7-4). Dreamweaver turns this option on by default.

- **Auto Indent.** When you work with nested HTML tags, it's often helpful to press Tab to indent each level of nested tag, making it easier to identify large blocks of HTML (such as a table and all its contents). The Auto Indent option left-aligns the indent for multiple lines of content each time you hit Enter (Return).

  Suppose you hit the Tab key twice, type a line of code, and then hit Enter (Return). Dreamweaver puts the insertion point on the next line, indenting it two tabs. To outdent, press the Backspace key. Dreamweaver normally turns this option on.

- **Syntax Error Alerts in Info Bar.** This feature benefits JavaScript and PHP programmers. When you turn it on, Dreamweaver highlights potential syntax errors in both languages (meaning it signals typos or improper code) and displays a yellow info bar at the top of the document window. You can also turn this feature off and on from the Coding toolbar (Figure 7-6).

Coding Toolbar

Dreamweaver includes a handy toolbar on the left edge of the document window in Code view that makes many basic hand-coding tasks go much more quickly. If you don't see it, turn it on by choosing View→Toolbars→Coding or by right-clicking (Control-clicking) on another toolbar, such as the Standard or Document toolbar, and then, in the drop-down menu, selecting the Coding option. Use the same technique to close the toolbar if you don't use it.

The toolbar's buttons duplicate tasks and preference settings from other parts of Dreamweaver. Here's a quick rundown, with brief explanations of what the buttons in Figure 7-6 do and, when applicable, a cross-reference to a more detailed description of the tool or action:

- **Open Documents.** This pull-down menu displays all your open documents so you can switch among them. Since it's actually easier to click a document's tab at the top of the document window, you probably won't use this button much.

- **Show Code Navigator.** Dreamweaver's Code Navigator lets you see which CSS styles affect the currently selected HTML. If you have no HTML selected, the Navigator displays the HTML tag in effect at the cursor location. It also lets you jump quickly to the code in a style sheet so you can edit the CSS. Read more about this feature on page 390.

- **Collapse Full Tag/Collapse Selection/Expand All.** These three buttons work with Dreamweaver's Code Collapse feature described on page 326. They let you collapse (and expand) multiple lines of code, essentially hiding those lines on-screen so you can concentrate on another piece of code.

- **Select Parent Tag.** This handy feature lets you quickly select the tag that surrounds your current selection. Say you select the text inside a link tag (<a>), or just click inside that tag, and your cursor is blinking happily. Click this button, and Dreamweaver selects the entire <a> tag and all its contents. Click it again, and you select that link's parent tag. If you really want to be productive, the keyboard shortcut Ctrl+[(⌘-[) is quicker.

- **Balance Braces.** If you do a lot of programming in JavaScript or a server language like PHP, .NET, ColdFusion, or Java Server Pages, this button helps you find the matching brace ({ or }) in a chunk of program code—actually this tool selects *all* the code between an opening and closing brace, but doing so lets you identify where the braces begin and end. Just click to the right of an opening brace ({), and then click this button to find the closing brace. To find a closing brace's mate, click to the left of the brace, and then click this button. You can also find matching parentheses this way. The keyboard shortcut Ctrl+' (⌘-') is even faster.

- **Apply/Remove Comments.** Comments let you include helpful notes in your code, which don't appear when a browser displays the page. For example, you may want to leave explanatory notes to help future generations of web developers. Or you might put a comment before a <div> tag that explains what should go inside it—"Put corporate logo and navigation bar here." People frequently use comments to mark the end of a page section—"End of navigation bar," for example. These buttons let you add or remove comments in HTML, CSS, JavaScript, PHP, and VBScript code, as demonstrated in Figure 7-7.

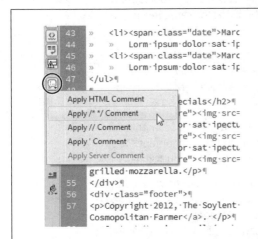

FIGURE 7-7

Dreamweaver's Coding toolbar lets you wrap HTML, CSS, JavaScript, and other program code within comment characters. Select the code you want to turn into a comment, click the Apply Comment button (circled), and then select the type of comment you want to add: Use the HTML comment option to "comment out" (hide) HTML code; the /* */ option to hide multiple lines of CSS, JavaScript, or PHP; the // option to hide each line of JavaScript or PHP code; and the ' option to hide VBScript code. The last option, Apply Server Comment, hides server-side code; use it to comment both HTML and server-side programming code in one step. To remove a comment, select all the code (including the comment markers), and then click the Remove Comment button (hidden in this figure; it's just below the Apply Comment button).

TIP You can easily turn style properties on and off in Cascading Style Sheets by taking advantage of "comment" behavior. Open a CSS file, select a property inside a style, and stick a pair of comment tags around it (/* at the beginning and */ at the end). When you preview a page that uses the style, you see the style minus the property you "commented out," as programmers call it. This maneuver lets you add a new style and preview it, temporarily hiding the effect of one or more other styles without permanently deleting them. It's also a great help in debugging problematic styles. In fact, it's so useful, the CSS Styles panel provides a button that makes it easy to turn style properties on and off (see Figure 7-6).

- **Wrap Tag.** Works the same way as the Quick Tag editor described on page 339.

- **Recent Snippets.** This drop-down menu lists all the snippets (pieces of reusable code; see page 807) you recently used. Select an item and Dreamweaver inserts it into your web page.

- **Move or Convert CSS.** This drop-down menu lets you move an inline CSS style to either an internal or external style sheet, or lets you move a rule from an internal to an external style sheet. You'll find more details on page 377.

- **Indent/Outdent.** These buttons indent or outdent lines of selected code, using the settings you defined in the Indent box of the Code Format preferences window (see page 329).

- **Format Source Code.** This button lets you enforce a consistent style for your code by applying specific formatting to an entire web page or to just a section of code. It uses the code-formatting options you set up in the Code Format preferences window (see page 329) and the rules defined in the type-A-uber-geek-what-a-lot-of-work Tag Library described in the box on page 334. In other words, if you want to make your HTML easier to read (by making Dreamweaver write every opening <tr> tag and closing </tr> tag separately on their own lines, for example), you can.

Code Hints

Typing code can be a chore, which is why even longtime hand-coders take advantage of anything that speeds up the process. A perfect example is Dreamweaver's Code Hints feature (shown in Figure 7-8). It lets you select tags, attributes, and even Cascading Style Sheet styles from a drop-down menu as you type.

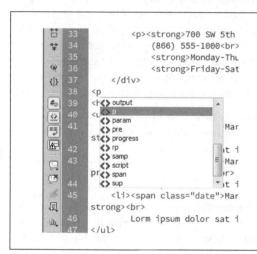

FIGURE 7-8

Dreamweaver's Code Hints feature saves your tired fingers from typing tags and tag properties. As soon as you type <, the program launches a list of tags. Select the one you want, and Dreamweaver types it in for you. Dreamweaver's even thoughtful enough to show you all the available CSS styles when you insert a class attribute in a tag.

NOTE Code Hints work with other tags as well as scripting languages like JavaScript, PHP, ASP.NET, and ColdFusion. In addition, Dreamweaver includes CSS code hints, so if you write your style sheets by hand, you can take advantage of the auto-complete feature of Code Hints to quickly type out CSS style properties.

Here's how it works. When you begin a new tag by typing an opening bracket (<), a menu pops up, listing all the available HTML tags. Use your mouse or arrow keys to select a tag, or type in the first few letters of it, and Dreamweaver finds the closest match. When you press Enter (Return), Dreamweaver automatically fills in the tag name. Even better, a second menu pops up, listing all the properties of that tag.

TIP You can also open the Code Hints menu by pressing Ctrl+space bar (in both Windows and on Macs). This shortcut's really useful when you're editing code and want to add a property or edit the property of a tag you already created. For example, you could click inside the name of a class style applied to a tag—inside the word "copyright" in the code *class="copyright"*, for instance, and then press Ctrl+space bar. This action not only selects the name so you can change it, it also opens a menu listing all the classes available to the page. Then you can use the up and down arrow keys (or even your mouse) to select a different CSS style.

If Code Hints annoy you, you can turn off the feature completely, rein it in by setting a delay (so that lists don't appear immediately), or turn it off for selected types of elements (such as tag properties). To make any of these adjustments, open Dreamweaver's Preferences window (Ctrl+U [⌘-U]), and then select Code Hints. Make your desired changes, and then click OK.

Dreamweaver also simplifies writing closing tags: As soon as you type </ (the first two characters for any closing tag), Dreamweaver automatically finishes your thought by closing the tag for you. For example, after you type an opening <p> tag and add the paragraph's content, Dreamweaver finishes the closing tag—</p>—the moment you type </. For a longer tag, like </address>, this feature saves your fingers a lot of work. You can change this behavior to make Dreamweaver automatically insert the closing tag immediately after you finish typing the opening tag, or, if you just can't stand the feature, turn off "Enable code hints" in the Code Hints preferences window.

NOTE If you like Code Hints, you'll love the Snippets panel, which makes reusing code a snap. See Chapter 19 for details.

■ HTML5 CODE HINTS

While Dreamweaver CC doesn't provide any visual tools for working with HTML5 (for example, you won't find any objects in the Insert panel for inserting HTML5 tags), you'll find HTML5 code hints in Dreamweaver, which work just like code hints for regular HTML. In other words, if you type *<he* in Code view, the code hint window pops up, listing not only HTML4 tags like <head> or <thead>, but also the HTML5 tag <header>.

■ JAVASCRIPT CODE HINTS

JavaScript programmers also have access to a wide array of code-hint features that make programming go faster. In general, JavaScript code hints work just like HTML hints. As you type in JavaScript, Dreamweaver pops up a box of suggestions that match what you're typing. But JavaScript code hints go much further than simple lists of JavaScript keywords. Dreamweaver provides hints for basic JavaScript objects like arrays, dates, numbers, and strings. For example, say you create an array (gentle reader, if you have no idea what a JavaScript array is, feel free to skip this section). If you then write the array's name in your code, a hint box pops up listing all the methods and properties of JavaScript array objects.

In addition, Dreamweaver keeps track of JavaScript functions *you* create and provides code hints using your own function names, as well as custom-created classes. Even better, Dreamweaver is aware of document object model (DOM) properties and provides hints for all the properties and methods of DOM objects. Finally, if you use either the Spry or Prototype JavaScript library, Dreamweaver has built-in code hints for those as well.

■ JQUERY CODE HINTS

jQuery is a popular JavaScript library used on millions of websites, from one-person blogs to ESPN, NBC, and even Microsoft. jQuery lets web designers jump into JavaScript programming by simplifying many common JavaScript programming tasks. It's so popular that Dreamweaver CC adds detailed code hints for jQuery. If you've no idea what jQuery is, skip this section, or better yet, pick up a copy of *JavaScript & jQuery: The Missing Manual*, which covers eponymous programming in detail.

Dreamweaver's jQuery code hint feature is very sophisticated. Not only does Dreamweaver provide hints for all of jQuery's built-in functions, it also provides hints for all class and ID selectors on a page, along with tooltips for functions that have multiple properties (see Figure 7-9.)

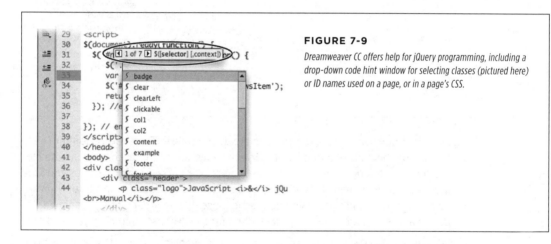

FIGURE 7-9

Dreamweaver CC offers help for jQuery programming, including a drop-down code hint window for selecting classes (pictured here) or ID names used on a page, or in a page's CSS.

Dreamweaver CC adds a kind of built-in jQuery cheat sheet as well. When you type in a jQuery function, a yellow box appears above the code (circled in Figure 7-9). It displays the function's name as well as which *arguments* it accepts (in programming, an argument is a piece of information that you can hand off to a command, and it affects how that command works). In some cases, a built-in jQuery function might work in several ways, each requiring a different kind of argument. In the example in Figure 7-9, a programmer has begun typing jQuery's $() function. The yellow pop-up box indicates that there are seven ways she can use that function. Clicking the left or right arrow keys steps her through examples of the methods, indicating the number and type of arguments she'd need to provide in each case.

■ PHP CODE HINTS

Dreamweaver includes advanced code-hinting for the server-side programming language PHP, too (but not for other server-side technologies like .NET, ColdFusion, Ruby on Rails, or Java Server Pages). Not only does Dreamweaver support code-hinting for built-in PHP functions, it also makes note of variables, functions, and classes you create (see Figure 7-10).

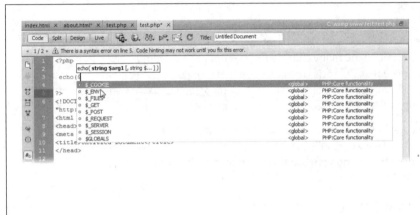

FIGURE 7-10

Dreamweaver is pretty unforgiving of syntax errors (typos or missing punctuation) in PHP code. Most of the time, you start typing PHP code and Dreamweaver displays a yellow "there is a syntax error" bar along with a red mark at the point it thinks you made an error. Don't worry, this happens a lot as you program. The important thing is that, once you finish, you have no remaining syntax errors. If there are, you probably left off a closing), }, ', or ".

Since it's common for programmers to create multiple PHP files and add them all to (or include them all in) a master file, Dreamweaver CC searches through all the files the current working file references and analyzes (or *parses*) them. Then, as you type more PHP code, Dreamweaver displays code hints based on the names of the variables, functions, and classes you defined in those files. In other words, Dreamweaver personalizes its code hints for your site and for the PHP programming you add to it.

In addition, since many PHP frameworks, like CakePHP and Zend, and many PHP-based content management systems (CMSes), like Drupal, Joomla, and WordPress rely on many separate PHP files, Dreamweaver includes something called site-specific code hints. This is only available for PHP-based websites (you'll learn how to set up a site for PHP in Part 6 of this book), and it's intended to let you identify which folders Dreamweaver scans to create its code hints for your site.

Dreamweaver's site-specific code hints have a few benefits. First, if you often include PHP files outside your root folder (for example, the Zend framework keeps its Include files outside the web-accessible root folder), you can tell Dreamweaver to scan the folder above the current local root folder. Second, many CMS systems and PHP frameworks use tons of files with tons of variables, functions, and class names.

Sites like these use the files internally, in the programming that drives the systems. You, as a programmer, don't ever need to see most of them, and you certainly don't want their elements cluttering up your code hint window.

With your PHP page open, you can turn site-specific code hints on by choosing Site→Site-Specific Code Hints. This opens a new window (see Figure 7-11). If you're using either Drupal, Joomla, or WordPress, you can select your environment from the top Structure menu, and Dreamweaver automatically identifies the proper folders, files, and paths. Click OK, and you're done.

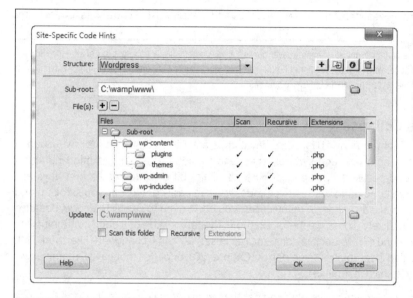

FIGURE 7-11

To add the function names, class names, and variable names you use in your site's PHP code to Dreamweaver's Code Hint feature, choose Site→Site-Specific Code Hints and tell Dreamweaver which files and folders to scan.

If, however, you're using a PHP framework or some other PHP CMS, you need to tell Dreamweaver which folders to analyze by following these steps:

1. **Click the folder icon and navigate to the folder containing your site and all the PHP files you want Dreamweaver to scan.**

   If you don't have any PHP files outside your local root folder, you can skip this step because Dreamweaver automatically selects the local root folder. However, you may have PHP files one level up from the local root folder. In this case, click the folder icon and select the folder one level up that contains both the PHP files and your local site root.

2. **Click the + button.**

   The Add File/Folder window opens. You can click another icon to select either one particular PHP file or a folder's worth of PHP files. If you pick a folder, turn on the checkbox labeled Recursive if you want Dreamweaver to scan the files in subfolders within this main folder. You can ensure that Dreamweaver searches only .php files by clicking the + button to the right of the Extensions label, and then typing in *.php*. Dreamweaver won't look through any other files and, as a result, it displays code hints faster. But if you do use other extensions for your PHP files, such as .inc, make sure to add them as well.

You can prevent Dreamweaver from scanning a folder you added from the main Site-Specific Code Hints window, too. Select the folder from the Files list, and then turn off the "Scan this folder" checkbox. You can also turn off recursive scanning and change the file extensions from this window.

3. **Click OK to finish.**

Dreamweaver scans the selected files and creates a list of code hints for your site.

> **NOTE** You may find that Dreamweaver doesn't always automatically pop up a box of site-specific code hints as it does when you use regular PHP functions. You may need to coax Dreamweaver into displaying them by using the keyboard shortcut Ctrl-space bar.

Code Collapse

One problem with raw HTML, CSS, JavaScript, and PHP is that, well, it's raw—a bunch of letters, numbers, and symbols that tend to blend together in a mind-numbing sea of code. This can make locating a particular bit of code needle-in-a-haystack tough. On large pages with lots of code, you can easily get lost as you scroll up and down to make a change. In many cases, you don't need to see all the code, because you're not likely to change it—for example, the top portion of a page containing the doctype and *HTML* declarations—or because you can't change it—like the HTML embedded in template-based pages (Chapter 20), or pages that have Dreamweaver Library items (Chapter 19).

Fortunately, Dreamweaver lets you get that code out of your face. Its Code Collapse feature condenses multiple lines of code into a single highlighted box of 10 characters. The basic process is simple: Select the code you want to collapse—like all the code above the <body> tag—and then click one of the icons that appears just to the left of both the first and last line you wish to collapse. In Windows, this icon is a small box with a minus sign (-) in it (Figure 7-12 top, circled); on Macs, it's a down-pointing arrow at the beginning of the selection and an up-pointing arrow at the end. The code collapses into a gray box. To expand it, select the condensed code and then click the "expand" icon (a plus sign [+] in Windows, a flippy triangle on Macs).

> **TIP** To quickly select multiple lines of HTML (or any code, for that matter), click in the line-number area to the left of the code at the beginning of your selection, and then drag to the end of your selection. (If you don't see any line numbers, turn them on using the Coding toolbar or by clicking View→Code View Options→Line Numbers.)

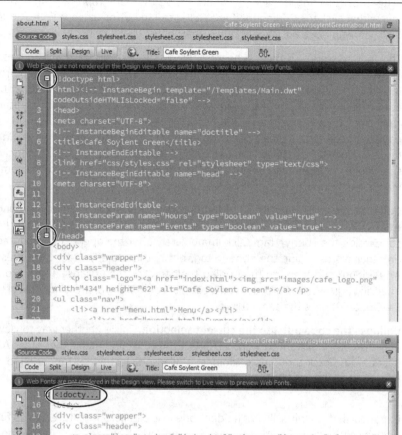

FIGURE 7-12

Now you see it, now you don't. You can collapse multiple lines of code (top) into a compact little gray box (circled, bottom) by clicking one of the Code Collapse icons (circled, top). The collapsed code is still there in your page—you haven't deleted it—but now it's conveniently tucked out of sight. If you need a reminder of what the code is, move your mouse over the gray box and a tooltip displays the hidden code.

Dreamweaver includes a few more nuanced ways to collapse code. You can:

- **Collapse an individual tag.** Say you want to hide a long paragraph of text. Instead of selecting it, click anywhere inside the paragraph tag (<p>), and then either click the Coding toolbar's Collapse Tag button, choose Edit→Code Collapse→Collapse Full Tag, or press Ctrl+Shift+J (⌘-Shift-J).

  This feature works on the tag nearest the cursor. Say you have a paragraph of text and, inside it, a link. If you click inside the <a> tag and use this feature, the <a> tag collapses. But if you click anywhere else inside the paragraph (but not inside any other tag), the paragraph itself collapses. This behavior is a little confusing, but it can be really useful. Say you want to hide everything inside a page's <head> tags. Instead of having to select all the lines inside the <head> tag, click anywhere between the beginning and ending <head> tags (but make sure you're not inside *another* tag, like the <title> tag), and use any of the commands mentioned in the previous paragraph.

- **Collapse the code outside an individual tag.** This lets you hide everything *except* the code you want to work on. Suppose you want to see only the code inside the <body> tag. Click immediately after the opening <body> tag (in other words, inside the <body> tag, but not inside any other tag), press Alt (Option) and then, on the Coding toolbar, click the Collapse Tag button. Choosing Edit→Code Collapse→Collapse Outside Full Tag or pressing Ctrl+Alt+J (⌘-Option-J) does the same thing.

- **Collapse the code outside the current selection.** This is another way to view only the code you want to work on. Select the code, and then either press Alt (Option) and click the Coding toolbar's Collapse Selection button, or choose Edit→Code Collapse→Collapse Outside Selection, or press Ctrl+Alt+C (⌘-Option-C).

- **Expand All.** If you miss all that hidden code, you can quickly restore it to its full glory by clicking the Coding toolbar's Expand All button, choosing Edit→Code Collapse→Expand All, or pressing Ctrl+Alt+E (⌘-Option-E).

NOTE You can only use the Collapse Full Tag and Collapse Outside Full Tag commands when you work with HTML. They have no effect on CSS, JavaScript, or PHP pages.

You can hide any number of code regions in a page—for example, the top portion of a page, a navigation sidebar that never gets edited, or the copyright notice at the bottom of a page—so you can easily identify the code you really want to work on. Dreamweaver even remembers the state of these sections, so if you collapse a code section and then close the document, the collapsed section remains hidden when you reopen the file.

Setting Code Formats

As you work away building your web page in the document window, Dreamweaver writes the relevant HTML code behind the scenes. Web browsers read that code and display your page. As long as you write the code properly, web browsers don't care how the code looks in writing. For example, here's a chunk of code from the menu of the Soylent Cafe site:

```
<table width="100%" border="0" cellpadding="0" cellspacing="0"
class="menu"><tr><th colspan="3" class="course">Starters</th></
tr><tr><th>Item</th><th>Description</th><th>Price</th></tr>
```

Browsers don't care if there's any white space in the lines of code; they just read what's there and display the elements defined by the code.

You, on the other hand, may care a lot if you're trying to troubleshoot your HTML. White space like line breaks and indents can detangle your code. Here's the same chunk of code as above, but with a little white space added:

```
<tr>
    <th colspan="3" class="course">Starters</th>
</tr>
<tr>
    <th>Item</th>
    <th>Description</th>
    <th>Price</th>
</tr>
```

Here, it's easier to see that there are two table rows, the first of which spans three columns. It's also easier to identify the text that appears inside the table header (<th>) tags: Starters in the first row, then Item, Description, and Price in the second row.

Out of the box, Dreamweaver adds white space, like line breaks and indents, to your code automatically. And while these standard settings work fine, you can tweak them in the Preferences window (Edit→Preferences [Dreamweaver→Preferences for Macs]). For example, you might want to change the size of the indent, or automatically have Dreamweaver write all tags in lowercase. Click the Code Format category on the left to see your options (Figure 7-13).

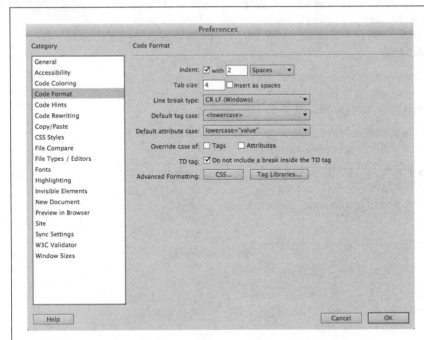

FIGURE 7-13

To control the way Dream-weaver writes HTML, go to the Code Format category of the Preferences window. For most people, this degree of control is over-kill, but if the way HTML appears on a page matters to you, go wild. (These settings don't affect how the page looks in a web browser, only how the code appears when you view it in Dreamweaver's Code view, another text editor, or when you look at the page's source code in a browser.)

■ INDENTS

To make your code easier to read, it helps to indent nested tags and other block-level elements. But if you prefer that Dreamweaver quit auto-indenting such elements, turn off the Indent checkbox. This is also your opportunity to tell Dreamweaver whether you want to indent code using spaces or tabs, and to set the amount of indentation:

- If you select **Spaces** in the Indent menu, type in the number of spaces you want Dreamweaver to move the code over in the Indent field. The default setting is 2, meaning that Dreamweaver will indent your code two spaces in from the edge of the preceding code.

- If you select **Tabs** in the Indent menu, the number in the "Tab size" field indicates the size of each tab, measured in spaces. (The size you specify here affects only the display in Code view. In the code itself, Dreamweaver simply inserts a plain tab character.)

NOTE If you choose to indent using tabs, you can save yourself a few bits of file size. Since Dreamweaver defaults to two-space characters for each tab, switching to tabs saves you one character (that is, your document will use just one tab instead of two spaces for each indent).

▪ LINE BREAKS

The Windows, Mac, and Unix operating systems each look for a different invisible character at the end of each line of code. This can cause problems if you create a page under one operating system and your remote server uses another. Fortunately, Dreamweaver fixes the problem when it transfers files to your server.

If you plan to use another text editor to edit Dreamweaver-built pages you copy from a server, select that server's operating system from the "Line break type" drop-down menu. Doing so assures that the program on the receiving end will properly read the line breaks in your Dreamweaver-produced pages.

▪ CHARACTER CASE FOR TAGS AND ATTRIBUTES

In standard HTML, you can write tag and property names using either uppercase letters (<B>bold</B>) or lowercase letters (bold); browsers don't care. However, *you* may care how they appear in Code view. Choose your preference from the two "case" drop-down menus, "Default tag case" and "Default attribute case." Most web developers write tags in lowercase, so if you share your pages with colleagues, you're best off selecting lowercase (see the Note below).

NOTE HTML may treat upper- and lowercase tags identically, but XML does not. Both it and the hybrid language *XHTML* require all-lowercase tag and property names. That's why many web developers now strictly use lowercase characters, even in their HTML. And that's why, if you select the XHTML option when you create a new page, Dreamweaver ignores any uppercase preferences you set—even if you turn on the "Override case of" checkboxes.

If you turn on the "Override case of" checkboxes, Dreamweaver scans tags and properties when it opens a page someone else (or some other program) created. If the case doesn't match your preference, Dreamweaver rewrites the code so that it does.

▪ THE <TD> TAG

Adding a line break after an opening <td> (table cell) tag may look good in Code view, but in some browsers it adds an unwanted extra space character in the table cell. The extra space can wreak havoc on your design, so make sure you always turn this box on.

▪ ADVANCED FORMATTING OPTIONS

For real format sticklers, two Advanced formatting buttons (Figure 7-13) let you control the way every aspect of your HTML and CSS code looks. The CSS button opens the CSS Source Format Options window, which lets you dictate how Dreamweaver writes your CSS—whether it indents properties, whether it uses separate lines for each property, where it puts the opening brace in CSS rules, and whether it inserts a blank line between rules to make your CSS more readable. All these options are matters of personal preference and don't affect the performance of your web page or CSS.

The Tag Libraries button opens the same-named dialog window, discussed in the box on page 334.

If you find yourself wading through lots of HTML and CSS, you might want to experiment with these settings to make the code Dreamweaver produces more readable. Both the Tag and CSS format windows preview your customized HTML and CSS.

Keep in mind that these settings don't affect how *you* write code. But if you do find that your own HTML or CSS hand-coding doesn't look as elegant as Dreamweaver's, you can turn to the Apply Source Formatting command (Commands→Apply Source Formatting) to make Dreamweaver clean up your code. That command changes a page's code—adds indents, line breaks, and so on—based on the instructions defined in the Tag and CSS options.

> **NOTE** Another set of preference settings affects how Dreamweaver creates CSS code. The Preferences window's CSS Styles category tells Dreamweaver whether or not to use CSS shorthand properties (see page 377).

Related Files

With external style sheets, JavaScript libraries, and server-side programming becoming more and more a part of the average web designer's toolbox, Dreamweaver includes a feature that makes it easier for code jockeys to jump around the vast collection of files required to make a single web page work. The Related Files toolbar lists all the files a current web page uses (see Figure 7-14). (Can't find the toolbar? See the Note below.) This includes external style sheets, external JavaScript files (like those jQueryUI uses), and server-side files such as *server-side includes*. Web developers use server-side includes like building blocks for web pages. For example, if you use the same header on every page of your site, you can store that HTML header code in a single file on your web server. Then, using a server-side include, you can automatically attach the header to every page on your site as the server dishes it out.

The first item in the toolbar—Source Code—refers to the web page you're currently editing. The other items represent linked files. For example, the web page you're building in Figure 7-14 has 10 related files—eight external style sheets (including web fonts) and two JavaScript files (related to jQueryUI).

> **NOTE** If you don't see the Related Files toolbar, it may have gotten turned off. To turn it back on, choose Edit→Preferences (Dreamweaver→Preferences), click the General category, and then make sure you turn on the Enable Related Files checkbox. A dialog box explains that you need to restart Dreamweaver to see the change.

When you click the name of a related file in the toolbar, Dreamweaver displays that file's code. If you're in Design view, Dreamweaver switches to Split view and displays the web page in the Design window and the code for the related file in the other pane. If you're in Code view, Dreamweaver simply switches from the HTML of the web page to the CSS, JavaScript, or server-side code of the related file.

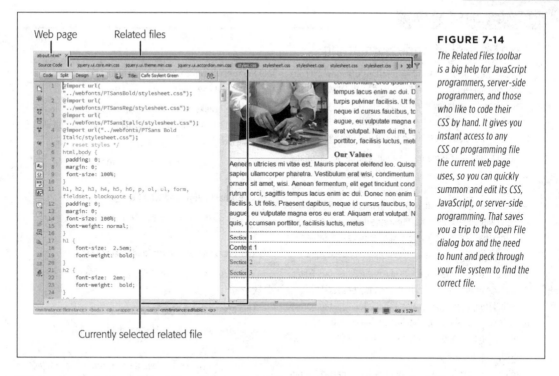

Web page   Related files

FIGURE 7-14

The Related Files toolbar is a big help for JavaScript programmers, server-side programmers, and those who like to code their CSS by hand. It gives you instant access to any CSS or programming file the current web page uses, so you can quickly summon and edit its CSS, JavaScript, or server-side programming. That saves you a trip to the Open File dialog box and the need to hunt and peck through your file system to find the correct file.

Currently selected related file

When you work on a related file, all the normal file operations apply only to that file. For example, if you select a CSS file from the Related Files toolbar and edit and save it, Dreamweaver saves only the CSS file when you choose File→Save; it doesn't record any changes you made to the web page's code or to any other related files (see the tip below). Likewise, if you choose Site→Put to move a file to your web server (see page 779), that CSS file gets whisked off to the server, but the web page itself stays put. This sequence gets a little confusing when you work on related files in Split view, because the web page appears on one half of the screen while the code for a different file appears in the other half.

Note, however, that when you work on a web page in the Design view half of Split view, Dreamweaver applies all your file operations to that web page document.

TIP   When you work with the Related Files feature, you may be editing multiple files (for instance, the web page, the CSS, and the JavaScript code) at the same time. To make sure you save the changes to *all* the files, use the File→Save All Related Files command, which saves the current web page and all its helper files. Better yet, create a keyboard shortcut (see page 869) for this useful command.

Take Control of Code Formatting

For ultimate control over tag formatting, Dreamweaver includes the Tag Library Editor. Not only does it let you control *exactly* how Dreamweaver formats every HTML tag it inserts into a page, it lets you dictate the formatting for nine other tag libraries, such as those for PHP, ASP, JSP, and ColdFusion.

Even if you're using some new bleeding-edge tag language unfamiliar to Dreamweaver, you're not out of luck. You can create additional tag libraries and even import custom ASP, .NET, and JSP tags, as well as DTD Schemas for XML. You can also add additional tags to any library; so if the HTML standard suddenly changes, you can add new or remove obsolete tags.

To control the way Dreamweaver formats tags in a library, choose Edit→Tag Libraries, which opens the Tag Library Editor. Dreamweaver displays a list of all the tag libraries. Click the + symbol (flippy triangle on Macs) to the left of a tag library name to see a list of tags for that library. Select a tag, and then, from the Tag Format area in the bottom half of the window, select formatting options.

Here's a shortcut for quickly reformatting a particular tag already present on a page: Select the tag in the Tag Selector and then choose Edit→Tag Libraries; Dreamweaver preselects

that tag. You can control where a line breaks in relation to the tag through four settings:

- **No line breaks at all**. If you applied this option to the `<a>` tag example above, for instance, you'd end up with code like this:

  ```
  <p>Here is a <a href="home.html">link</
  a></p>
  ```

- **Line breaks before and after the tag**:

  ```
  <p>Here is a</p><a href="home.html">link</
  a>
  ```

- **Line breaks before, inside, and after the tag**:

  ```
  <p>Here is a <a href="home.html">link</
  a></p>
  ```

- **Line break after the tag only**:

  ```
  <p>Here is a <a href="home.html">link</
  a></p>
  ```

In addition, you can choose whether Dreamweaver applies formatting rules to the contents of a tag, and choose the case—upper, lower, or mixed—that Dreamweaver uses when it adds the tag to your code.

The Related Files feature works hand in hand with the Code Navigator. As described on page 390, the Code Navigator (the small ship steering wheel floating above page elements) displays a drop-down list of all the CSS styles applied to the page element under your cursor. If you click one of the styles and it happens to be in an external style sheet, Dreamweaver switches to Split view, opens the CSS file, and positions your cursor on the appropriate style so you can edit it. (That said, you might find the other methods of editing CSS, described on pages 122 and 374, easier and more error-free.)

■ FINDING NESTED PHP FILES

When programmers write code in the server-side language PHP, it's common to include several levels of programming files by using server-side includes. For example, the popular blogging system WordPress uses a single file, *index.php*, to control an entire blog—this one file manages every one of the blog's pages, from the home page, to a category page, to a single blog post.

To do this, the *index.php* file includes tons (really, we mean a *lot*) of other PHP files. If you wanted to edit your WordPress site using a text editor other than Dreamweaver, the only way to work on your files would be to open each one manually. But with Dreamweaver, you simply open the *index.html* file and let Dreamweaver "discover" all the related PHP files. Follow these steps:

1. **Set up a staging server.**

   A staging server (also called a "testing server") is basically a server you set up (frequently on your own computer or a networked computer in your office) so you can test your PHP files before moving them to the Internet for all the world to see.

   It's not hard to set up a testing server on your own computer (page 885). Windows users can learn how at *http://uptospeedguides.com/wamp* and Mac fans can learn how at *http://uptospeedguides.com/mamp.*

   After you set up a testing server, you need to edit the Site Definition settings (Site→Manage Sites) to let Dreamweaver know about it. You can review that process on page 19.

2. **Open a PHP file.**

   When you open a PHP file, you won't see the familiar HTML tags; you'll see PHP code (see Figure 7-15). PHP code often uses multiple server-side includes to build a page. There are a couple of ways to "include" a PHP file in another PHP file. Dreamweaver has a command that lets you add basic Includes: Insert→Server-Side Include (see page 892). When you insert an Include using this command, Dreamweaver automatically recognizes the PHP files and displays them in the Related Files toolbar with no further effort on your part. But you might also include PHP files within *other* Include files. In cases like these, you need to tell Dreamweaver to "discover" them.

3. **Click the "Discover" link in the Document toolbar above the document window (see top image in Figure 7-15).**

   Dreamweaver displays a warning box saying that it will execute the scripts on this page. That's not a problem, so turn on the "Don't warn me again" checkbox to skip this window in the future. Dreamweaver finds all the PHP files the currently open dynamic page uses. This may be just a few files, or, in the case of a complex PHP application like WordPress, quite a few. For example, in the bottom image of Figure 7-15, you can see that the Related Files toolbar is chock-full of file names.

4. **Select a related file to work on.**

   Once Dreamweaver discovers all the related PHP files, you can use the Related Files toolbar as you normally would to open a file. If there are a lot of files, as in the case of a WordPress site, navigate through the list by clicking the left- and right-arrow buttons, or click Show More to see a drop-down menu of all the related files. Select a name from that list to open the file in Code view.

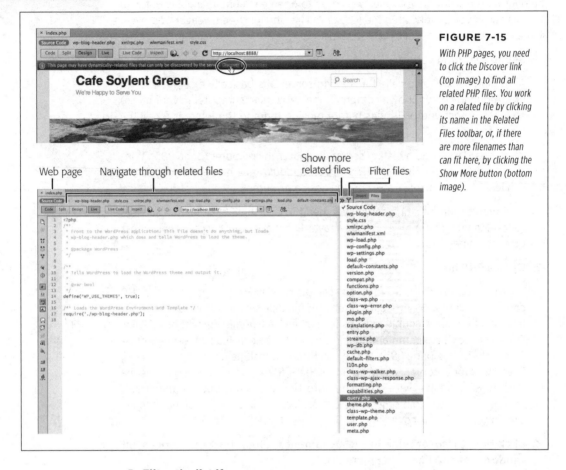

FIGURE 7-15

With PHP pages, you need to click the Discover link (top image) to find all related PHP files. You work on a related file by clicking its name in the Related Files toolbar, or, if there are more filenames than can fit here, by clicking the Show More button (bottom image).

5. **Filter the list if necessary.**

You may not want to see or work on some of the files in the Related Files toolbar. For example, in the case of WordPress, you'll see many PHP files listed, most of which you never want to touch since they're part of the core WordPress program and editing them might break your blog.

Fortunately, you can filter the list of related files so you see just the ones you want. The Filter button in the top-right corner of the Related Files toolbar lets you do two things. First, clicking it pops up a menu that lets you filter by file type—meaning you can show or hide CSS, PHP, or JavaScript files, or any other file type that your web page references. By default, Dreamweaver displays all file types, so to hide one, click the Filter button and then click the extension (.css, .php, .js, and so on) for the file type you want to hide. To show those file types later, select them again from the same menu.

You can create a custom filter, too. Click the Filter button, and then choose Custom Filter to bring up a dialog box. Type in the filenames and/or file types you want to see. For example, with WordPress, you may want to edit the PHP theme files—the ones WordPress uses to create your blog's look. To have Dreamweaver display the relevant files, enter their filenames separated by a semicolon, like this: *index.php; footer.php; header.php,* and so on. You can also filter by file type. To show all JavaScript files plus *index.php, footer.php,* and *header.php,* type this in the Related Files toolbar: *index.php; footer.php; header.php;.js.* Don't include spaces after the semicolons or you'll get an "invalid filter" error message.

When you're done, click OK to close the Custom Filter. Dreamweaver displays only the files you specified in the Related Files toolbar.

NOTE Custom Filters are useful but, unfortunately, Dreamweaver doesn't save them, so once you close a file, that filter is lost and you have to recreate it the next time you open the file. In addition, you can't filter by folder—all PHP files within a particular folder only, for example—although that would be helpful when you work with certain CMS systems, like WordPress, which keep files related to the design of the site in a dedicated folder. Maybe next time.

■ Live Code

When you see animated effects on a page, like photo slideshows or moving elements, there's usually a script (a chunk of programming code, like JavaScript) behind the scenes rewriting the HTML and CSS of your page to make those effects happen. The same thing is true with interactive pages that display additional text or images when you click a button or check a box in a form. Scripting tools like JavaScript and PHP literally rewrite the HTML or CSS of a page before a browser displays it. So, as a web developer, how do you troubleshoot pages like these, written on the fly? The answer is Live Code.

Back on page 51, you learned that Dreamweaver's Live view lets you see what an in-progress web page looks like in a real browser, right from within Dreamweaver. You may have noticed that, when you click the Live view button, another button shows up in the document toolbar: Live Code (Figure 7-16 middle, circled). Live Code works in conjunction with Live view to give you an option you don't get with Live view alone: the ability to see the HTML code as it changes in response to programming. That means you can see how the page's components—its HTML, CSS, JavaScript, and so on—work together in real time to create a web page (or not, if you've got programming problems).

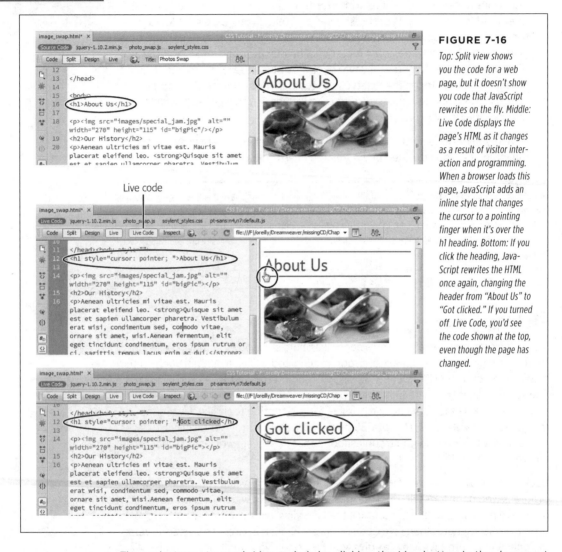

FIGURE 7-16

Top: Split view shows you the code for a web page, but it doesn't show you code that JavaScript rewrites on the fly. Middle: Live Code displays the page's HTML as it changes as a result of visitor interaction and programming. When a browser loads this page, JavaScript adds an inline style that changes the cursor to a pointing finger when it's over the h1 heading. Bottom: If you click the heading, Java-Script rewrites the HTML once again, changing the header from "About Us" to "Got clicked." If you turned off Live Code, you'd see the code shown at the top, even though the page has changed.

The easiest way to reach Live code is by clicking the Live button in the document window, and then clicking the Live Code button. If you're a fan of menus, you can choose View→Live Code. Either way, Dreamweaver displays the page's Live view in one half of the document window and the underlying HTML in the other half. Live Code displays the HTML with a yellow background, a not-so-subtle reminder that you can't edit code in this view. Click on an interactive element in Live view, and Dreamweaver highlights the relevant HTML in pink to help you zero in on the code responsible for dynamically created pages.

Here's an example: Figure 7-16 shows three views of the same page. At the top, you see the page in Dreamweaver's Split view with the HTML on the left and the page displayed in Live view on the right. The h1 heading (circled) is programmed to change when a visitor interacts with it, but you can't tell that from this view. In the middle view, you have Live Code turned on, and you see that the <h1> tag has an inline style:

```
style="cursor: pointer; "
```

When a browser loads this page, it also runs a JavaScript program that rewrites parts of the page's HTML. In this case, that script adds the inline style to the h1 heading, and changes the cursor to a pointing finger whenever you hover over the h1 heading. You can see the rewritten code in Live Code (Figure 7-16, middle), and see the cursor change in Live view when you move it over the heading. When you actually *click* the heading (instead of just hovering over it), JavaScript rewrites your HTML again. In this case, it changes the heading to read "Got clicked."

This is a simple example, but the ability to rewrite HTML and CSS on the fly is extremely powerful. You can change the color, size, position, and appearance of any element on a page through inline styles or by assigning classes and IDs to page elements on the fly. PHP scripts rewrite pages, too. They'll often use server-side includes (page 892), where your web server builds just-in-time pages by adding code blocks stored in separate files. Using Live Code, you can see the actual code that web browsers use to display the page to your visitors. Without being able to see that final HTML, it's difficult to troubleshoot a problem.

And if you're not a JavaScript programmer? You still might have an interest in Live Code. It's useful if you're using someone else's JavaScript code or a program you found online, like one of the many marvelous jQuery plug-ins for web pages (*http://plugins.jquery.com*). Using Live Code, you can see the HTML and the class and ID names it generates. Looking at JavaScript-generated HTML, it's pretty easy to figure out some of the CSS that formats the page, such as class styles (page 115) if JavaScript adds class names to tags, ID styles (page 120) if it adds ID names to tags, or descendent selectors (page 370) that match the HTML.

> **TIP** The F6 key freezes any currently running JavaScript, so you can make a drop-down menu "stick" in place when you mouse over it. It's like freezing the entire page, and it's great for working with Live Code, since you can freeze a dynamic rollover effect and see how the JavaScript programming affects the HTML of the page.

■ Quick Tag Editor

Code view is great when you really need (or want) to jump into the trenches and fine-tune your HTML. But if you're aesthetically oriented, you probably spend most of your time in Design view, enjoying the pleasures of its visual authoring environment.

Occasionally, however, you want to dip into the HTML pond, especially when you need to use some HTML that's unavailable from the Insert panel. You might wish you could type out a quick HTML tag on the spot, right there in Design view, for example, without having to make the mental and visual shift to Code view.

That's what Dreamweaver's Quick Tag Editor is all about—it lets you tweak the underlying HTML code while remaining in Design view. To access the Quick Tag Editor, in Design view press Ctrl+T (⌘-T)—or, if you're feeling especially mouse-driven, in the Properties panel, click the Quick Tag Editor button (circled in Figure 7-17).

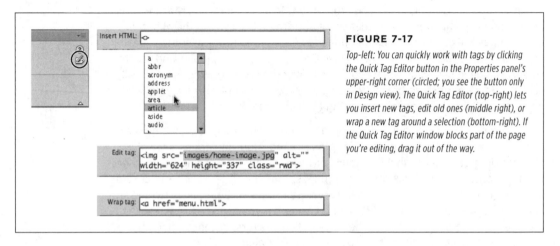

FIGURE 7-17

Top-left: You can quickly work with tags by clicking the Quick Tag Editor button in the Properties panel's upper-right corner (circled; you see the button only in Design view). The Quick Tag Editor (top-right) lets you insert new tags, edit old ones (middle right), or wrap a new tag around a selection (bottom-right). If the Quick Tag Editor window blocks part of the page you're editing, drag it out of the way.

Depending on what you select in the document window, the Quick Tag Editor opens in one of the following three modes:

- **Insert HTML.** Inserts a new tag on the page. You get this mode if you haven't selected anything in your document window.

- **Edit tag.** Lets you edit the tag of whatever element you select in the document window (a graphic, for example). You can also edit all of that element's properties.

- **Wrap tag.** If you select a swath of text or other object (like two images), the editor opens in this mode, which lets you easily wrap a new tag around your selection.

> **TIP** You can cycle through Quick Tag modes by repeatedly pressing Ctrl+T (⌘-T).

Using the Quick Tag Editor

You can type tag names, properties, and property values directly into the Quick Tag Editor. If you're editing a selected tag, you can change any of the properties listed, and even add new ones. When you're done, press Enter (Return). The Quick Tag Editor closes, and the changes take effect.

To make all this even easier, the Quick Tag Editor sports a helpful list—called *tag hints*—of HTML tags and properties for your selection pleasure. It's much like Code view's Code Hints (in fact, in the Preferences window, the Code Hints category also controls tag hints). When you're in Insert HTML mode, for example, a menu of available tags appears (top-right in Figure 7-17). Use the up and down arrow keys or the scroll bar to move through the list, or type in the first few letters of a tag or property, and Dreamweaver jumps to the nearest match.

To choose the highlighted tag name, press Enter (Return). Dreamweaver adds that tag or property name to the Quick Tag Editor. If you select a tag property, Dreamweaver adds the proper punctuation (*href=" "*, for example), and the cursor appears between the quotation marks, waiting for you to type in the property's value.

TIP When you edit an existing tag in the Quick Tag Editor, press Tab to select the next property or property value. Shift+Tab selects the *previous* property or value.

Comparing Versions of a Web Page

Sometimes you make a change to a page, save it, preview it, close it, and move along to the next assignment for the day. Only later, when you take a second look at your day's changes before moving pages to your web server, do you see that one of them has a problem you didn't notice at first. Perhaps the left sidebar is suddenly wider than it was before. Since you already closed the file, you can't use the Undo command to reverse whatever pesky mistake you made. You could, of course, retrieve the current version of the page from the server, thus overwriting your changes. But what if you did a lot of good work on the page—added text, graphics, and links—that you don't want to lose? Ideally, you'd like to see all the changes you made to the page, and selectively undo the mistake you accidentally introduced.

Enter the Compare File command. With it, you can compare two files and identify lines of code that differ between them. This tool is a perfect solution for problems like the unintentionally botched sidebar mentioned above. Compare the local file (the one with the messed-up sidebar) with the remote file (the live version of the website page that works, but is missing your most recent edits). You can then identify any changes you made and smoke out your mistake. Before you can tackle that, you need to download and install a file-comparison program, and then you need to tell Dreamweaver where to find the tool. Fortunately, you only have to do the installation and setup once.

Downloading and Setting Up "Diff" Tools

Dreamweaver doesn't actually have a built-in file-comparison program. Instead, it passes the files to a separate file-comparison utility (often called a "diff" tool, since it identifies *differences* between files). Before you can use Dreamweaver to compare files, you need to download one of these utilities, and you have a lot to choose from. Fortunately, several of them are free for both Windows PCs and Macs (see the following boxes for suggested programs).

After you download and install the file-comparison utility, you need to tell Dreamweaver where to find it:

1. **Open Dreamweaver's Preferences panel, by choosing Edit→Preferences (Dreamweaver→Preferences) or pressing Ctrl+U (⌘-U), and then click the File Compare category.**

   There's not much to this Preferences category, just a single box and a Browse button.

2. **Click Browse, and then navigate to and select the file-comparison utility.**

   For example, on Windows you might find your utility at *C:\Program Files\WinMerge\WinMergeU.exe*.

WINDOWS ONLY

Getting Your Hands on the Goodies

You can find lots of file-comparison tools for Windows. One commercial product, Beyond Compare from Scooter Software (*www.scootersoftware.com*), costs $30 and offers a range of comparison options.

But for a free alternative that provides all the basics you need, check out WinMerge (*http://winmerge.org*). Go to *http://winmerge.org* and click Download Now. At this point you're asked to save the file to your computer. Of course, if you're using Internet Explorer, one of those yellow "Warning, warning, enemy attack" banners appears—you need to click that,

and then choose "Download File" to actually download the file to your computer.

Once you download the program, the process of installing it is like most other Windows programs. Double-click the filename to launch an installer, and follow the step-by-step instructions. You have several options along the way, but accept the suggested settings and you'll be fine.

Once you install WinMerge, you're ready to proceed as described below.

On Macs, the process is slightly different. Instead of selecting the text-editing program TextWrangler or BBEdit in Dreamweaver, you need to specify the proper "diff" tool, which is stored in a special location on your computer. Navigate to the */usr/local/bin* folder—*Macintosh HD:usr:local:bin* for most Macs—and select the correct file. For TextWrangler, it's *twdiff*; for BBEdit, it's *bbdiff*; and for FileMerge, it's *opendiff*.

3. **Click OK to close the Preferences window.**

   Dreamweaver's been notified of the utility's location, so you're ready to compare files.

MACS ONLY

What Difference Does It Make?

The Mac version of Dreamweaver supports only three file-comparison tools: File Merge (which is a Mac developer program that comes with the XCode tools on your Mac OS X installation disc), BBEdit (the powerful, $125 commercial text editor), and TextWrangler (the free little brother of BBEdit). Bare Bones Software (*www.barebones.com*) produces both BBEdit and TextWrangler, but since TextWrangler is free, it's the best place to begin.

Point your Web browser to *http://tinyurl.com/ctwmby* and click any of the download links to save the program to your computer. As with many Mac applications, this download opens a disk image—just like a folder—with the program inside it. Just drag it to your Applications folder to install it.

Comparing Files from the Files Panel

The most common use of a diff tool is to see how a local file (one stored on your computer) differs from a file on your web server. You can start the process from the Files panel. For example, to compare a local file called *about.html*, with a file of the same name on the remote server, follow these steps:

1. **In the Files panel, choose "Local view."**

   The Files panel displays files stored on your computer.

2. **In the Files panel, right-click (Control-click) *about.html*. Then, from the pop-up menu, select "Compare with Remote Server," as shown in Figure 7-18.**

   Dreamweaver does a little behind-the-scenes trickery before passing your files off to the file-comparison program. First, it creates a folder (if it doesn't already exist) named *_compareTemp* in the local root folder. It then creates a temporary copy of the remote file and stores that in the new folder. As you can see, you're not actually comparing the live web page on your server with the local web page (the one on your computer); you're comparing a *copy* of the local file with a *copy* of the remote file.

   Then your selected file-comparison program—for example, WinMerge or TextWrangler—starts up and compares the two files. If it finds no differences—if they're *exactly* the same—you'll most likely get a message saying something like "The Selected Files are Identical." Your work is done. If there *is* a difference, the file-comparison program displays the two files and identifies the code that differs between them (see Figure 7-19 and Figure 7-20).

FIGURE 7-18

Start the file-comparison process by choosing a location from the Files panel, such as "Local view" (top circle), and then right-clicking (Control-clicking) a filename. From the menu that pops up, choose "Compare with Remote Server" (bottom circle). The steps for the rest of the comparison process vary depending on the diff tool you're using.

3. **Evaluate the differences, and incorporate any changes into your local file.**

   All file-comparison programs work the same way. As they compare two files, you see the code for each side by side. In addition, they highlight the differences in the code in some way. You can then review the differences and merge the changes into one file or the other. For example, say you accidentally delete a table from your local file; a comparison of this file with the remote file shows the table intact in the remote file, but missing from the local file. You can copy the table code from the remote file into the local file. If, however, you deleted the table purposefully (making the pages the same), then do nothing, and move on to evaluate the next difference.

   You want to move changes in only one direction—from the temporary server file to your local file. That's because any changes you make to the temporary file have no effect on the live file on your web server. So how do you update the remote file? Make changes to your local file, save it, return to Dreamweaver, and upload the local file to your remote site folder. Then pour yourself a cup of tea and be thankful you don't have to do *that* very often.

4. **Save any changes to the local file, return to Dreamweaver, and then move your newly updated local file to your web server.**

The exact process varies from program to program, but see the next sections for details about using WinMerge and TextWrangler.

It's easy to get confused as you compare files, make changes to those files, and then move the files between your computer and your live website. To introduce as little worry into the process as possible, it helps to compare the files the same way each time. The steps above explain how to compare a local file to one on a server, save changes to the local file, and then upload those changes to the server. This is a good work path that helps prevent mistakes from going live on your website. But you don't have to follow this path. You can, instead, start with a file on the remote server (by choosing "Remote server" in step 1 above). Then you can save changes to the file on your web server. It works, but it's a bit riskier.

TIP You can compare two files on your local hard drive (the home page of the site you're working on with a backup of the page you made last week, for example) if the two files are in the same site (perhaps you have a backup folder in your local root folder). Ctrl-click (⌘-click) to select the two in the Files panel. Then, right-click and choose Compare Local Files from the pop-up menu.

Comparing Files with WinMerge

Since Dreamweaver doesn't have its own diff tool, you have to get one from a third party. Several manufacturers make diff tools, so, each works a little differently. But you always start comparing files by identifying them in Dreamweaver's Files panel, and then using the "Compare..." command as described above.

Once your diff tool launches, the steps for comparing files and saving changes varies by program. WinMerge is a popular diff tool for Windows PCs, in large part because it's free. Here's how it works.

WinMerge compares files side by side, as shown in Figure 7-19. It displays the first file you select (in this case, the file on the local server) on the right. It shows the file you're comparing it to on the left. In this example, the latter file came from the remote server. The Location Pane (far left) displays two bars that graphically represent the two files. A gold band in one of the bars indicates content that's missing from the other file. A gray band indicates where in the other file that content is missing.

If you want to check every difference between the two files, start at the top of the diff report and choose Merge→Next Difference to work your way down through all the differences. Even better, use the "next diff," "previous diff," "first diff," and "last diff" buttons on the toolbar to navigate between the differences. As you check through the differences, the two versions of your document scroll to the spot where those differences occur. WinMerge highlights the currently displayed difference in red and shows the nature of the difference in the Diff Pane below the files. You can now figure out which code you want to keep.

Once you zero in on a spot where the two versions differ, you can copy changes from the left file to the right or vice versa. For example, Figure 7-19 shows a table in the remote version of a file (left) that isn't in the local version (right). Choose Merge→Copy to Right, or just click the toolbar button as shown in the figure, to copy the table to the local file.

The next step is to save the changes you made using the File→Save command. You leave WinMerge and go back to Dreamweaver, which displays the warning, "This file has been modified outside of Dreamweaver. Do you want to reload it?" Click Yes to accept the changes you just made.

Now you have a single file with all the elements you want in it. You just need to upload it to your web server. You do that in the Files panel by selecting the file and clicking the "Put file to remote server button." (See page 776, for all the details on moving files to your web server.)

NOTE WinMerge is a standalone program, so you can fire it up and run it like any other program on your Windows computer. That means you can use it to compare *any* two files on your computer. You can even use it to compare the contents of two folders.

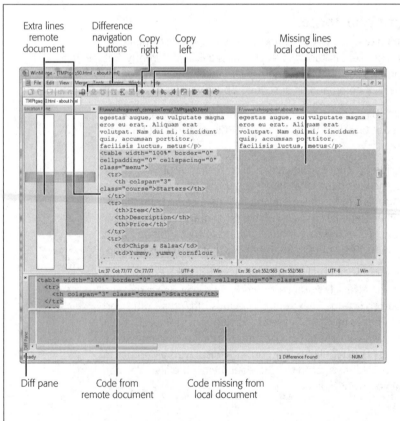

Extra lines remote document

Difference navigation buttons

Copy right

Copy left

Missing lines local document

Diff pane

Code from remote document

Code missing from local document

FIGURE 7-19

WinMerge includes a kind of bird's-eye view of code differences in the far-left Location Pane. Here, the gold band marks a table that's present in the remote file, while the gray band marks the location in the local file where that table is missing. One click of the Copy Right button and you'll copy the missing table over to the locally stored file.

Comparing Files with TextWrangler

TextWrangler is a standalone diff program for Macs. You can download and install it as described in the box on page 42.

NOTE The popular program, BBEdit, is a more powerful version of TextWrangler, so this description works for that commercial program as well.

You start comparing files as usual, in Dreamweaver's Files panel. Choose a location, right-click (or Control-click) the file you want to check, and then choose the "Compare..." command from the pop-up menu. For example, you might set the location menu to "Local view," right-click *about.html*, and then choose "Compare with Remote Server." At this point, TextWrangler's diff tool starts up. It displays the first file you selected (in this example, the local file) on the right and the temporary file copied from the remote server on the left. It displays the differences between the two files and breaks out the problematic code in the Differences panel below the two pages (see Figure 7-20).

TextWrangler tells you how the lines differ: For example, "Nonmatching lines" means the lines are similar (some of the code is the same) but not identical, while "Extra lines before line 678" means that one file uses a line of code that's completely different from the line of code in the other file.

In the Differences panel, double-click the anomaly you want to inspect. TextWrangler scrolls to the point of difference in both files. To make sure you catch all the differences, start at the top of the differences report and work your way down. If the code from the server file looks correct, click the Apply button to transfer the code from the remote file to your local file.

After you make changes to the local version of your file, choose File→Save. Then, choose File→Quit to leave TextWrangler and return to Dreamweaver. Once back in the comfortable environs of Dreamweaver, you see a message that says: "This file has been modified outside of Dreamweaver. Do you want to reload it?" Click Yes to accept your changes.

At this point, the "perfect" copy is your local file. It has all the correct code from the remote file, and all the correct code originally in the local file. If you don't have any other changes to make, you can upload the local file to your web server. You do that in the Files panel by selecting the file and clicking the "Put file to remote server" button. See page 776 for the details.

Remote temporary file · Local file

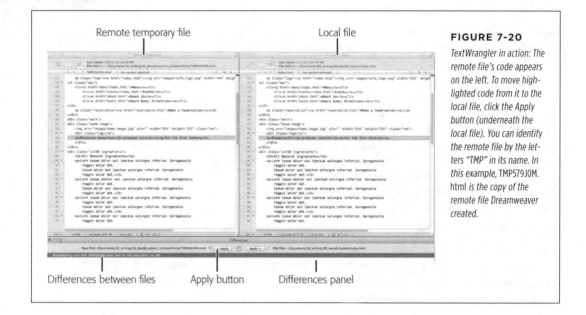

FIGURE 7-20

TextWrangler in action: The remote file's code appears on the left. To move highlighted code from it to the local file, click the Apply button (underneath the local file). You can identify the remote file by the letters "TMP" in its name. In this example, TMP579J0M.html is the copy of the remote file Dreamweaver created.

Differences between files · Apply button · Differences panel

■ Finding References

When it comes to building websites, there's a lot to know. After all, HTML, Cascading Style Sheets, and JavaScript are filled with cryptic terms and subtle nuances. Dreamweaver used to provide a Reference panel to make your search for knowledge a little bit easier. Unfortunately, the references became outdated. As a result, the Help→Reference option has been removed from Dreamweaver CC.

But you can still find great references on the Web. Here are a few resources to get you started:

- For CSS help, SitePoint.com's free, online reference to CSS is great: *http://reference.sitepoint.com/css*.

- For JavaScript, W3Schools.com provides an in-depth reference: *www.w3schools.com/jsref/default.asp*. For in-depth coverage in book format, check out *JavaScript & jQuery: The Missing Manual*.

- For PHP, you can't beat the Source. The official PHP site has excellent documentation on every aspect of PHP: *www.php.net/manual/en*.

Find and Replace

You've probably encountered find-and-replace tools in word processing programs. As its name implies, the command *finds* a piece of text ("webmaster," for example) and *replaces* it with another piece of text ("webmistress"). Like Microsoft Word, Dreamweaver can search and replace text in the body of your web pages, but it also offers options that enhance your ability to search-and-replace within the tag-based world of HTML.

Dreamweaver lets you find and replace text on *every* page of your site simultaneously, not just the current, open document. In addition, you can *remove* every appearance of a particular HTML tag, or search and replace text that matches very specific criteria. For example, you can find every instance of the word "Aardvark" that appears within a paragraph styled with the class name *animal*. These advanced find-and-replace maneuvers are some of the most powerful—and under-appreciated—tools in Dreamweaver. If you learn how to use them, you can make changes to your pages in a fraction of the time it would take otherwise.

> **TIP** You can use Find and Replace to search an entire site's worth of files. This is powerful, but it can also be slow, especially if some folders hold files you don't want to search—old archive files, for example. Fortunately, you can hide files from Find and Replace using Dreamweaver's Cloaking feature (see page 782 for details).

■ Find and Replace Basics

To start a search, press Ctrl+F (⌘-F), or choose Edit→Find and Replace. The Find and Replace window opens (see Figure 8-1). Now all you have to do is fill in the blanks and set your options.

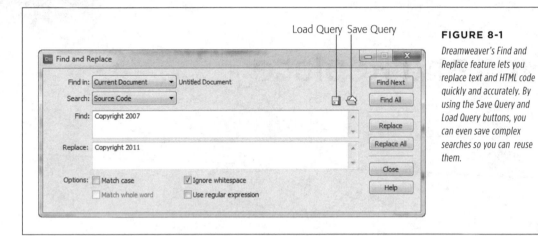

Load Query   Save Query

FIGURE 8-1

Dreamweaver's Find and Replace feature lets you replace text and HTML code quickly and accurately. By using the Save Query and Load Query buttons, you can even save complex searches so you can reuse them.

Whether you perform a simple text search or a complex, tag-based search-and-replace, you use the Find and Replace feature the same way. First, you need to tell Dreamweaver *where* to search (within highlighted text on a page, for example, or in a file, a folder, or across your website). Next, tell it *what* to search for (text, HTML, or a particular tag with a specific attribute). Finally, you dictate the replacement item. (This last step is optional; you can use Find and Replace simply as a way to locate an item on a page or on your site, without changing the found term to anything.)

TIP   After you enter the Find and Replace criteria, click the Save Query button (see Figure 8-1). A Save dialog box appears; you can type in a name for your query, which Dreamweaver saves as a .dwr ("Dreamweaver replace") query) file. If it's a query you'll use for a particular site, you might want to save it with that site's files. To reuse a query, click the Load Query button in the Find and Replace window and locate the .dwr file. After the search-and-replace criteria load, click any of the four action buttons—Find Next, Find All, Replace, or Replace All.

■ Basic Text and HTML Searches

Dreamweaver can search all the source code in a page or focus on just the text in the document window. Here's the difference:

- Source code searches let you find and replace any code on a page, including words, letters, and symbols. This means *anything* you see in Code view, such as HTML, CSS, or the server-side programming used to create dynamic database-driven sites described in Part Six of this book. Code searches are the only type of search Dreamweaver allows on non-web page files, such as external JavaScript files or external CSS files.

- Text searches are more refined. They only look for text that appears within the <body> element of a page. That is, Dreamweaver ignores HTML tags, properties, and comments when it executes a text search—in short, it ignores anything that doesn't appear as actual words in the document window. By using a text search when you want to change the word "table" to "elegant wood table," for example, you won't accidentally change the very useful HTML <table> tag into a browser-choking <elegant wood table> tag.

If you've used the Find and Replace feature in other programs, the process will seem familiar. The degree to which you can refine a search is unique to Dreamweaver, however.

Phase 1: Determine the Scope of Your Search

Using the "Find in" drop-down menu (see Figure 8-2), choose any of these search options:

- **Selected Text.** Searches only the highlighted section of the page you're working on. You might find this useful if you're working in Code view and you want to search the code in just a certain section of the page, like the head of the document. But it also comes in handy if you have a large HTML table full of data, and you want to search and replace just the content inside that table— you'd select the table (for example, click <table> in the Tag Selector [see page 7] or use any of the techniques described on page 275), and then choose the Selected Text option.

- **Current Document.** Searches the web page you're working on.

- **Open Documents.** Searches all currently open Dreamweaver documents, handy if you're working on a bunch of pages at once and you realize you made the same typo on each.

- **Folder.** Searches all the web pages in a particular folder. Dreamweaver also searches web pages in all folders *within* the selected folder. You can use this option to search pages that aren't part of the current site.

- **Selected Files in Site.** To use this option, open the Files panel and select the files you want to search in the Local Files list (see page 746 for details).

- **Entire Current Local Site.** Searches every web page in the current site folder, including pages in folders *inside* the site folder. This option is invaluable when you need to change a basic piece of information throughout your site. If your company hires a new boss, for instance, you can replace every instance of "Mark Jones" with "Joe Smith."

NOTE Using the Find and Replace command is one of the best ways to quickly make changes to an entire site, but it's also one of the easiest ways to wreck a site's worth of web pages. Dreamweaver *can't* undo Find and Replace changes to files that aren't open when you execute the command. So be careful. If you plan to make extensive changes, make a backup copy of your files first!

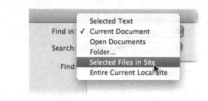

FIGURE 8-2
The search the Find and Replace command executes isn't limited to the current document. You can also search multiple web pages, or even an entire site.

Phase 2: Specify What to Search For

For your next trick, you'll tell Dreamweaver what you want to search for. Use the Search pop-up menu to choose one of these two options:

- **Text.** This makes Dreamweaver search for a certain word or phrase that appears in the *body* of the documents you specify. Type the text you want to find into the Search field. To search for text using wildcard characters, enter a *regular expression* here and turn on the "Use regular expression" checkbox. (See the box on page 359 to learn about regular expressions.)

- **Source Code.** Basic text searches are useful, but they're limited to text that appears in the body of a page (what you see in the document window). If you want to search and replace *code*, you need the Source Code option.

  Source code searches work identically to text searches, except that Dreamweaver searches *everything* within a file—text, HTML, JavaScript, CSS, and so on—and replaces any part of the file. Using this option, you could search for any instance of the tag <img src="mark_jones_photo.jpg">, for example, and replace it with <img src="joe_smith_photo.jpg">. (If you're in Code view, Dreamweaver automatically selects the Source Code option.)

  As you fill in the Find box, be aware that some plain-English words are also special words in HTML, JavaScript, or CSS. If you replace *table* with *desk* using a source-code Find and Replace command, for instance, you'll destroy any <table> tags on the page.

  Just as you can with text, you can search for patterns in your source code, too (see the box on page 359).

Phase 3: Provide the Replacement Text

To change the text that Dreamweaver finds, type the replacement text into the Replace box. It may be the word or words you want to swap in (for a text search), or actual HTML code (for a source-code search).

TIP Dreamweaver won't let you create a new line in the Search or Replace boxes—you can't, for example, replace one line of HTML with two lines of HTML, at least not in the normal way. That's because, when you hit the Enter key to add the second line, Dreamweaver executes the search instead. To add another line, use Shift-Enter (Shift-Return).

If you just want to find text without replacing it, skip this step and perform a replace operation, described in Phase 5.

Phase 4: Choose the Search Settings

Dreamweaver gives you three options to govern its search and replace, some quite complex:

- The **Match Case** option limits the Find command to text that exactly matches the case (capitalization and lowercase) of the text in the Search field. If you search for the text *The End* with the Match Case checkbox turned on, Dreamweaver finds a match in "The End is near," but not in "You're almost at the end." Use this trick to find every instance of *Web* and replace it with *web*, for example.

- **Match Whole Word** searches for an entire word—not a portion of a larger word. With this option turned on, a search for *Rob*, for example, matches only "Rob," and not any parts of "Robert," "robbery," or "problem." If you don't select this option, Dreamweaver stops on all four instances of "rob." This could cause serious problems if you also *replace* "Rob" with something like "Bob" (unless, of course, you've come up with a new word for thefts committed by people named Bob: Bobbery). Note that if you selected the Match Case option here, Dreamweaver matches *Rob* in "Rob" and "Robert," but *not* in "robbery" and "problem," since they don't include a capital R.

- The **Ignore Whitespace** option treats multiple spaces, tabs, non-breaking spaces, and carriage returns as single spaces during a search. For instance, if you search for *the dog* with this option turned on, Dreamweaver matches "the dog" as well as "the   dog"—even if the multiple spaces are actually the HTML non-breaking space character * * (see page 75).

NOTE Note to Mac users: Unfortunately, in the Mac version of Dreamweaver, the Find and Replace function doesn't treat non-breaking space characters as spaces, so if you have *the dog* in your HTML and search for *the dog* with the Ignore Whitespace box checked, Dreamweaver will report no matches.

Unless you have a good reason, always leave this option turned on. The HTML of a page can contain lots of extra spaces, line breaks, and tabs that don't appear in a web browser or in Dreamweaver's document window. For example, in the HTML of a document, it's possible to have two lines of code that look like this:

```
<p>This sentence will appear on one
line in a Web browser</p>
```

Even though this text would appear on a single line in the document window, a search for "one line" *without* the Ignore Whitespace box turned on would find no match—the carriage return after "one" is not an exact match for the space character in "one line."

NOTE You can't turn on the Ignore Whitespace option when you have the Use Regular Expression checkbox turned on.

- The **Use Regular Expression** option uses wildcard characters to match text. For a discussion of this advanced technique, see the box on page 359.

Phase 5: Take Action

Finally, you're ready to set the search in motion by clicking one of four buttons in the Find and Replace window (see Figure 8-1):

- **Find Next** locates the next instance of your search term. If you're searching the current document, Dreamweaver highlights the matching text. If you're searching an entire website or a folder of pages, Dreamweaver opens the file *and* highlights the match. You can cycle through each instance of the search term by clicking this button repeatedly.

TIP As in other programs (notably Microsoft Word), you can press Enter to repeat the Find Next function (Windows only). If you click in the document window—or even close the Find window—you can press F3 (⌘-G) to repeat the Find Next function.

- **Find All** locates every instance of the search term, and lists them under the Search tab of the Results panel (Figure 8-3). The name and location of each file (if you searched multiple files) appear to the left, and the matched text appears to the right. Dreamweaver displays part of the sentence in which the matched word or words appear, and it underlines the exact match with a squiggly red line, so you can see the search in context.

  Unlike the Find Next action, Find All doesn't automatically open any of the web pages containing matches. To open a matched page and highlight the matches, double-click its filename in the results list.

- **Replace** locates the next instance of the search term *and* replaces it with the text in the Replace field, leaving the replaced text highlighted for your inspection.

  You can use this button in combination with Find Next to selectively replace text. First, click Find Next. Dreamweaver locates and highlights the next match. To replace the text, click Replace. Otherwise, click Find Next to search for the next match, and repeat the cycle. This cautious approach lets you supervise the replacement process and avoid making changes you didn't intend.

- **Replace All** is the ultimate power tool. It finds every instance of the search term and replaces it with the text in the Replace field. Coupled with the "Find in Entire

Local Site" option, you can quickly make site-wide changes (and mistakes—so back up all your files before you Replace All!).

When you click this button, Dreamweaver warns you that it can't undo this operation on any closed files. You can erase mistakes you make with Find and Replace in *open* documents by choosing Edit→Undo in each document, but Dreamweaver *permanently* alters closed files that you search and replace. So be careful! (On the other hand, changes to open documents aren't permanent until you close those files.)

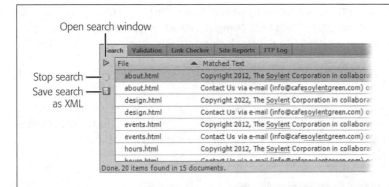

Open search window

Stop search
Save search
as XML

File	▲ Matched Text
about.html	Copyright 2012, The Soylent Corporation in collabora
about.html	Contact Us via e-mail (info@cafesoylentgreen.com) o
design.html	Copyright 2022, The Soylent Corporation in collabora
design.html	Contact Us via e-mail (info@cafesoylentgreen.com) o
events.html	Copyright 2012, The Soylent Corporation in collabora
events.html	Contact Us via e-mail (info@cafesoylentgreen.com) o
hours.html	Copyright 2012, The Soylent Corporation in collabora

Done. 20 items found in 15 documents.

FIGURE 8-3

The green-arrow button reopens the Find and Replace window. Click the red Stop button to abort the current search (when you inadvertently search for "the" in a 10,000-page website, for example). You can also save a rather useless XML file that reports the results of the search (remember the old adage: Just because you can, doesn't mean you should).

TIP Before you take the plunge and click Replace All, it's a good precautionary step to click Find All first and then preview the results in the Results panel (Figure 8-3). That way, you can be sure that you're going to change exactly what you *want* to change.

If you use the Find All or Replace All commands, the Find and Replace window closes, and the results of your search appear in the Search tab (see Figure 8-3). You can reopen the window—with all your previous search criteria still in place—by clicking the green arrow (called the Find and Replace button), but only if you haven't selected anything else first—like text on a page.

■ Advanced Text Searches

For greater control over a text search, use the Find and Replace command's *advanced* text search option, which lets you hunt down text either inside or outside a specific tag.

For example, when Dreamweaver creates a new blank document, it sets the page's Title property to *Untitled Document*. Unfortunately, if you forget to change the name, your site will quickly fill up with untitled web pages. A basic text search doesn't identify this problem, because it searches only the <body> portion of a page, and titles appear in the <head> section. And a source-code search for *Untitled Document* would turn up the words "untitled document" *wherever* they appeared in the page, not just inside the <title> tag.

In cases like this, an advanced text search is your best choice. You set the Find and Replace command to search for *Untitled Document* whenever it appears within the <title> tag. To search using this technique, follow the routine described above, but before you click one of the action buttons, you need to change a few more things in the dialog box. See below.

Limiting a Search by Tag

To see Find and Replace's expanded controls, choose Text (Advanced) from the Search pop-up menu (see Figure 8-4). Now, from the menu next to the + and – sign buttons, choose either Inside Tag or Not Inside Tag. For example, consider this line of code:

```
Stupid is as <strong>stupid</strong> does.
```

The first instance of "stupid" sits outside the <strong> tag, but the second instance is inside it. Depending on your choice on the Inside Tag/Not Inside Tag menu, Dreamweaver will highlight one of these words when you search for "stupid."

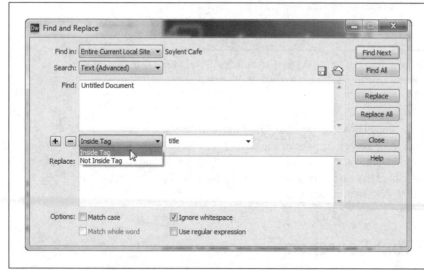

FIGURE 8-4

Use an advanced text search to limit your search to text that appears within a particular HTML tag. Conversely, you can use it to search for text that doesn't appear within a tag.

> **NOTE** A more descriptive name for Inside Tag option is *"Enclosed by* Tag." Dreamweaver executes tag searches by examining the text between opening and closing tags. In fact, a text search using the Inside Tag option doesn't literally identify text inside the brackets of a single tag, it searches the text between opening and closing tags. For example, searching for "Aliens" inside an <img> tag—<img src="ufo.jpg" alt="Aliens live among us.">—won't work. Dreamweaver doesn't search inside the angle brackets of a single tag, so it won't find the Alt text. But a search for "Aliens" between opening and closing <strong> tags—<strong>Aliens live among us.</strong>—would work. In the first example, *Aliens* appears as part of the <img> tag, while in the second, *Aliens* is enclosed by the opening and closing <strong> tags.

Once you specify whether you're looking for text inside or outside a tag, you can choose that tag from the Inside Tag/Not Inside Tag drop-down menu (Figure 8-4). The menu lists all HTML tags, not just those with both an opening and a closing tag. So the image tag (<img>) appears here, even though Dreamweaver won't search for text inside it.

TIP A great way to search for text in both the title and the body of a web page is to choose the Inside Tag option and then select *html* from the Tag drop-down menu. That way, you can search for any text between the opening and closing <html> tags of the page—which, since those tags start and end any web document, is *all* the text on a page. This trick is handy when you want to change text that might appear in the body *and* in the title of a page (for example, to change a company name).

Limiting a Search by Attribute

To limit your search further, click the + sign button (see Figure 8-5) to launch the Tag Modifier menu. It offers another six options for your search:

- **With Attribute/Without Attribute.** To limit your search, you can specify that a tag either must have a specific property (With Attribute) or must not have that property (Without Attribute).

  For example, say the following lines of code appear throughout a site:

  ```
  <p>For assistance, please email<a href="mailto:mail@chia-vet.com">
  Chia Vet.</a></p>
  ```

  For the sake of argument, say you need to change that line to read "For assistance, please email Customer Service." A basic find-and-replace search would incorrectly change the words "Chia Vet" to "Customer Service" *everywhere* on the site.

  However, an advanced text search using the With Attribute option lets you find the text "Chia Vet" wherever it appears inside an <a> tag whose *href* attribute is set to *mailto:mail@chia-vet.com*. That way, you tell Dreamweaver to replace "Chia Vet" with "Customer Service" in this case only, leaving all other instances of "Chia Vet" alone. (For tips on where to find more HTML references, see page 348.)

  After you choose With Attribute, use the menu on the right to select *which* of the tag's properties you want to find. (Dreamweaver automatically lists properties appropriate for the tag you specify.) For example, if you search inside a <table> tag, Dreamweaver lists properties such as *align*, *background*, and *bgcolor*.

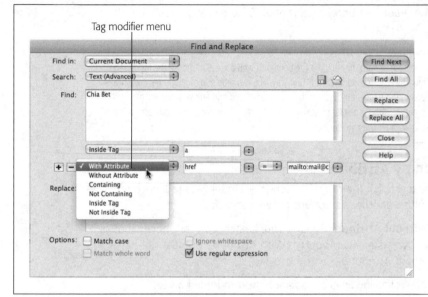

Tag modifier menu

FIGURE 8-5

When you click the + sign button in the Find and Replace window, Dreamweaver displays a new set of fields. Use these options to carefully hone your Find and Replace command.

Advance to the next drop-down menu to tell Dreamweaver how to compare your search term with what it finds on the page. Choose equal to (=), not equal to (!=), greater than (>), or less than (<). You'll only use the less than or greater than options when a property's value is a number, such as the *width* property of a table cell. For example, you could locate all the table cells wider than 100 pixels using the width > 100 parameter. You can only compare values expressed as numbers, not values expressed as words. So the Find and Replace command has no effect on *center* in this code example:

```
<td align="center">
```

Finally, type the value of the property in the last field. If you were searching for a black-colored background, for example, you'd type *#000000* (the hex value for black).

You can also click the menu and choose "[any value]"—a useful option when you want to find tags that have a certain property, but you're not interested in the property's value. For example, if you want to find all <table> tags with a background color (no matter whether the color's #336699, #000000, or #FFFFFF), choose the *bgcolor* attribute and "[any value]."

- **Containing/Not Containing.** These options let you specify whether a tag contains or doesn't contain specific text or a particular secondary tag.

When you choose this option, Dreamweaver displays a new set of fields. Choose either Text or Specific Tag from the menu to the right, and then, in the last field in the row, either enter text or select a tag. For example, another (less error-proof) solution to the find-and-replace problem above would be to search for the text "Chia Vet" wherever it appears inside a <p> (paragraph) tag that *also* contains the text "please email."

- **Inside Tag/Not Inside Tag.** These last two choices are identical to those described in "Limiting a Search by Tag" above. They let you specify whether a search term is inside—or not inside—a specific tag. For example, you can use these options to limit a search to text that appears within a <span> tag that itself is *inside* an <h1> tag.

If you like, you can add even more restrictions to your search by clicking the + sign button and repeating the steps. If you're really on a roll, you can add so many modifiers that the Find and Replace window grows past the bottom of your monitor. To remove a modifier, click the - sign button.

POWER USERS' CLINIC

Turbocharge Your Searches

If you want to find the phone number 555-123-5473 on your site, no problem: Just type *555-123-5473* into Find and Replace's Search field. But what if you want to find *every* phone number—555-987-0938, 555-102-8870, and so on—on a web page or across your site?

In such a case, you need to use *regular expressions*, the geeky name for a delightfully flexible search language that lets you use wildcard characters to search for *patterns* of text instead of actual letters or numbers. Each phone number above follows a simple pattern: three numbers, a dash, three more numbers, another dash, and four more numbers.

To search for a pattern, you use a variety of symbols combined with regular text characters to tell Dreamweaver what to find. For example, in the world of regular expressions, "\d" stands for "any number." To find three numbers in a row, you could search for \d\d\d, which would find 555, 747, 007, and so on. There's even shorthand for this: \d{3}. The number between the braces ({}) indicates how many times in a row the preceding character must appear to match. To search for phone numbers, then, you could use a regular expression like this:

    \d{3}-\d{3}-\d{4}

The \d{3} finds three numbers, while the hyphen (-) following it is just the hyphen in the phone number, and \d{4} finds four numbers.

Here are some of the other symbols you'll encounter when using regular expressions:

- . (period) stands for any character, letter, number, space, and so on.

- \w stands for any letter or number (but not spaces, tabs, nonbreaking spaces, or line breaks).

- * (asterisk) represents the preceding character zero or more times (and is always used after another character). For example, the regular expression colou*r matches both "colour" and "color"—the * following the u indicates that the u is optional (it can appear zero times). This search term would also match "colouuuuur" (handy for those times when you've fallen asleep on the keyboard).

To see a complete list of regular-expression characters Dreamweaver understands, as well as a brief tutorial on regular expressions, visit *http://tinyurl.com/3zw4oj6*. For a quick reference, there's a great cheat sheet for regular expressions at *http://www.visibone.com/regular-expressions/*. A full-length discussion of regular expressions could—and does—fill a book of its own. Check out *Mastering Regular Expressions*, Third Edition (O'Reilly, 2006) by Jeffrey E. F. Friedl (*http://oreilly.com/catalog/9780596528126*) or, for made-to-order regular expressions, visit the Regular Expression Library at *http://regexlib.com*. For an example of using regular expressions in Dreamweaver, see the box on page 359.

Advanced Tag Searches

If you find the number of options an advanced text search offers overwhelming, you haven't seen anything yet. Dreamweaver's tag search adds even more choices to help you quickly search for, and modify, HTML tags. You can use a tag search to strip out unwanted HTML tags (for example, if you're migrating a very old site to CSS, you could remove the obsolete <font> tag), transform one tag into another (you could turn the old-style *bold* [<b>] tag into the more widely accepted *strong* [<strong>] tag), and perform a host of other powerful actions.

In its basic outline, a tag search is much like the regular text search described on page 350. But this time, you choose the Specific Tag option from the Search menu. Now a Tag menu appears next to the Search menu, and the dialog box expands to display a new set of fields (see Figure 8-6). Some of them are the same as the controls you see with an advanced text search (page 355), such as the Tag Modifier menu and the + sign button that lets you add additional restrictions to the search.

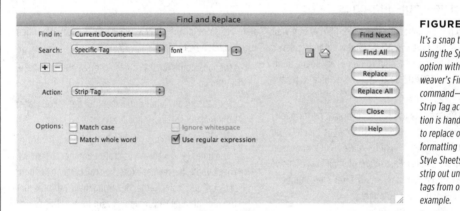

FIGURE 8-6

It's a snap to remove tags using the Specific Tag option with Dreamweaver's Find and Replace command—just select the Strip Tag action. This option is handy if you want to replace old-style text formatting with Cascading Style Sheets. Use it to strip out unwanted <font> tags from old sites, for example.

But a key difference here is the Action drop-down menu (Figure 8-7), which lets you specify the action Dreamweaver takes on tags that match the search criteria when you click Replace or Replace All. If you intend to search, but not replace, these options don't apply:

- **Replace Tag & Contents.** Replaces the tag and anything enclosed by the tag (including other tags) with whatever you put in the With box to the right of this menu. You can either type or paste text or HTML here.

- **Replace Contents.** Replaces everything enclosed by the tag with the text or HTML you specify. The tag itself remains untouched.

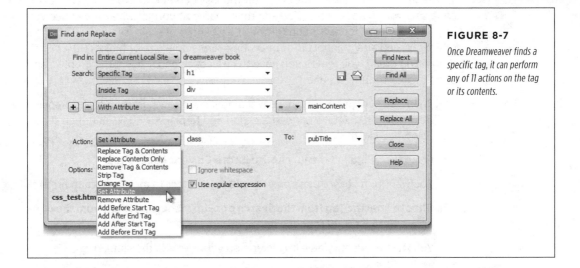

FIGURE 8-7

*Once Dreamweaver finds a
specific tag, it can perform
any of 11 actions on the tag
or its contents.*

NOTE Dreamweaver doesn't offer Find and Replace options for all HTML tags. For example, the <img> tag has
just an opening tag (<img>), not the opening and closing tags of, say, a paragraph (<p> and </p>, respectively).
In cases like this, Dreamweaver doesn't offer the option to let you change the content between opening and
closing tags because there are no tag pairs.

- **Remove Tag & Contents.** Deletes the opening and closing tags and *everything*
  inside them.

- **Strip Tag.** Deletes the tag from the page, but leaves anything enclosed by it
  untouched. The outmoded <font> tag is a perfect candidate for this action.

- **Set Attribute.** Adds an attribute to the tag. For example, you could use this
  command to set the *alt* property of an image (see the example on page 362).

- **Remove Attribute.** Removes an attribute from a tag. You could remove the
  not-at-all-useful *lowsrc* attribute from all image tags on your pages, for example.
  (Since you're dying to know, in the olden days of slow web connections, the
  lowsrc attribute provided faster-loading, low-resolution versions of images.)

- **Add Before (After) Start (End) Tag.** The last four actions in the menu offer
  variations on the same theme. Each lets you place content in a web page just
  before or after the tag for which you're searching.

To understand how this works, remember that most HTML tags come in pairs.
The paragraph tag, for example, has an opening tag (<p>) and a closing tag
(</p>). Say you search for a paragraph tag; you could add text or HTML *before*
or *after* the start tag (<p>), or *before* or *after* the end tag (</p>). To see when
you might use this feature, see the box on page 364.

■ A Powerful Example: Adding Alt Text Fast

You've just put the finishing touches on the last page of your brand-new, 1,000-page site. You sit back and smile—and then snap bolt upright when you notice you forgot to add an Alt description for the site's banner graphic (see page 233). This graphic, called *site_banner.gif*, appears on every single one of those 1,000 pages. With rising dread, you realize you have to open each page, select the graphic, and add the *alt* attribute by hand.

And then you remember Dreamweaver's advanced tag-based Find and Replace feature. Press Ctrl+F (⌘-F) to open the Find and Replace window, and then set up the dialog box like this:

1. **From the "Find in" menu, choose Entire Current Local Site.**

   You want to fix *every* page on your site (remember to make a backup first!).

2. **Choose Specific Tag from the Search pop-up menu, and then, from the pop-up menu to its right, choose img.**

   You start by identifying every image on your site (via the <img> tag).

3. **In the next row, use the three pop-up menus to choose With Attribute, src, and the equal to sign (=).**

   This tells Dreamweaver to look for specific images—in this case, images with a *src* attribute (the path that tells a browser where to find the image) that has a specific value.

4. **Type .*site_banner\.gif in the box next to the = sign.**

   For this exercise, assume you stored the graphics file in a folder called *images* located in the root folder of your site. The filename *site_banner.gif* is the name of the image file. The .* is the magic "wildcard" that matches any text, and you'll see how it works in a moment (ditto the backslash hanging out before the second period).

5. **Click the + sign button.**

   Dreamweaver displays another row of Tag Modifier menus.

6. **From this new row of menus, choose Without Attribute and alt.**

   You've further limited Dreamweaver's search to only those images that don't already have an *alt* attribute. (After all, why bother setting the *alt* property on an image that already has it?)

7. **From the Action menu, choose Set Attribute, and then, from the drop-down menu, choose alt.**

   You just told Dreamweaver to add an *alt* attribute if it finds an *alt*-less <img> tag that matches your search criteria.

In this example, you might type *Chia Vet* in the To field to specify the *alt* text you want Dreamweaver to add to the image.

8. **Turn on the "Use regular expressions" checkbox.**

   Regular expressions, described on page 359, let you search for patterns of characters and, in this case, help you accurately identify the banner graphic everywhere it appears.

   You know you're looking for the file *site_banner.gif* wherever it appears on your site. Unfortunately, if you just type *site_banner.gif* as the value of the *src* property in step 3, Dreamweaver can't find the file. That's because the *src* attribute—the part of the <img> tag that includes the location of the file—varies from page to page. Depending on where a page is relative to the graphic, the src path might be *site_banner.gif*, *images/site_banner.gif*, or even *../../../images/site_banner.gif*. What you need is a way to find every *src* attribute that ends in *site_banner.gif*.

   A simple regular expression, *.*site_banner\.gif*, does the trick. The period stands for *any* character (6, g, or even %, for example), while the asterisk means "zero or more times." When you prepend these codes to the graphic filename, you instruct Dreamweaver to find every *src* value that ends in *site_banner.gif*.

   In other words, *.** matches *images/*, *../../images/*, and so on. It even matches nothing at all, such as when the page actually sits inside the *images* folder; in that case, the *src* property is just *site_banner.gif*.

   Note the backslash before the last period: \.gif. In the world of regular expressions, a period means "any character," so simply using *site_banner.gif* would not only match *site_banner.gif*, but also *site_banner1gif*, *site_bannerZgif*, and so on—in other words, any character that sits between *site_banner* and *gif*. The backslash tells Dreamweaver to treat the next character literally; it's just a period with no special regular-expression power.

   The Find and Replace dialog box should look like the one in Figure 8-8 now.

9. **Click Replace All and sit back.**

   In a matter of moments, Dreamweaver updates all 1,000 pages of your site.

   To test this out, you might try a more cautious approach first: Click the Find Next button to locate the first instance of the missing *alt* attribute, verify that it's correct by looking in the Search box (see Figure 8-8), and then click Replace to add the proper *alt* value. Double-check the newly updated page to make sure everything worked as planned. You can continue updating pages one at a time this way, or, once you're sure the search works correctly, press Replace All.

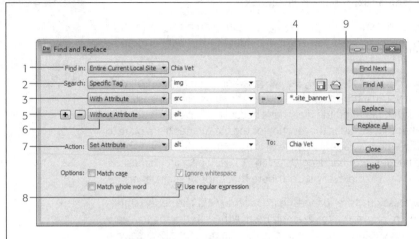

FIGURE 8-8

The numbers shown here correspond to the steps in this example, in which you want to add an alt attribute to every occurrence of the banner logo for the benefit of people who can't, or don't want to, see graphics in their browsers.

FREQUENTLY ASKED QUESTION

Convenient Copyright Notices

I want to add a copyright notice to the bottom of each page in my website. Is there a way to automate this process so I don't have to edit every page by hand?

You bet. Use Dreamweaver's Find and Replace command to add text or HTML to the bottom of any web page. The trick is knowing how to use the command's Specific Tag option.

First, choose Edit→Find and Replace to open the Find and Replace window. Next, choose Entire Current Local Site from the "Find in" menu, and then choose Specific Tag from the Search menu. Choose "body" from the Tag menu. Remember, the <body> tag in HTML encloses everything that appears inside a browser window—it's equivalent to what you see in the document window.

From the Action menu, choose Add Before End Tag. The end tag in this case is </body>. Since </body> marks the end of any content in a web page, whatever appears directly before

this closing tag will appear at the bottom of the page (you can probably see where this is going).

In the text field next to the Action menu, type (or paste) the copyright notice you want on each page. (You may want to first design the copyright message using Dreamweaver, and then copy and paste the HTML into this field.)

Now, click Replace All. Dreamweaver handles the rest.

You may not want to put the copyright notice at the *very end* of a page's HTML, as in this example. You might want it to go inside a particular <div> tag that's already on the page. Say that that div has an ID of *footer*. You'd search for a <div> tag from the Tag menu and then select "With attribute" ID equal to "footer." Then you use either the Add Before End Tag or Add After Start Tag options to place the copyright notice either at the end or the beginning of that div.

TIP To get a full description of every Dreamweaver menu, see Appendix B, "Dreamweaver CC, Menu by Menu."

Building a Better Web Page

Advanced CSS

Chapter 3 introduced you to the basics of Cascading Style Sheets. In other chapters, you learned how to use CSS to style links, navigation bars, text, and tables. You can go a long way in web design with just those techniques (and many people do). However, to really become a web design expert, you should become familiar with a handful of advanced CSS concepts. Fortunately, Dreamweaver includes tools to help you with these concepts so you can work more efficiently and avoid those head-scratching "Why the heck does my design look like that?!" moments. In addition, Dreamweaver CC includes a few approaches for adding shiny, new CSS3 properties and a fun tool for adding basic CSS animations. (Even if you're not ready for some of the advanced CSS concepts discussed in this chapter, don't skip the section on CSS Transitions [page 397] because they're fun and easy to create.)

> **NOTE** This chapter will help you on your journey from CSS novice to master. But keep in mind that it's the rare mortal who understands everything about CSS from reading a single chapter. If you really want to know the ins and outs of CSS, check out *CSS3: The Missing Manual.*

■ Compound Selectors

It's pretty easy to learn how to use class, ID, and tag styles. Technically, however, these aren't really styles at all. In CSS lingo, they're *selectors*, instructions that tell a browser *what* page element to look for so it can then apply CSS formatting rules. For example, a tag selector (not to be mistaken with Dreamweaver's time-saving selection tool, *the* Tag Selector) tells a browser to apply formatting to *any* instance of a particular tag on a page. Thus, browsers apply *h1* tag styles to *all* <h1> tags on a page. They apply class selector styles, on the other hand, only when they encounter an element with the right class name attached to it. Similarly, browsers apply ID selector styles to a tag with a matching ID name, like *<body id="home">*. (Flip back to page 108 for a review of key differences between class and ID selectors.)

> **NOTE** For a detailed discussion of selectors, visit *http://tinyurl.com/29dnb4*.

But class, ID, and tag selectors are just the tip of the selector iceberg. CSS offers many other types of selector, and they let you format even the smallest page element. In the past, Dreamweaver lumped these laser-focused selectors under the term *compound selectors* (a Dreamweaver term, not an official CSS term, so don't go using it at your weekly web designer get-togethers). Dreamweaver used the term to describe advanced selectors, such as the "pseudo-class" styles you use to format different link states (*a:link, a:visited, a:hover,* and *a:active*), as described on page 187, or the descendent selectors used with some JavaScript widgets, like JavaScript/jQuery menu bars (page 573). With its new CSS Designer (Window→CSS Designer), Dreamweaver is moving away from the term compound selector.

The CSS arsenal includes a variety of advanced selectors—you'll find a few of the most common and useful ones mentioned below—but in Dreamweaver, you write all of them using the same three-step process:

1. **Choose or create a source for the CSS rule.**

   The source is where your CSS rules live. If you were adding a style to your web pages, you might add that style to an existing style sheet. In that case, the existing style sheet is the source.

   Web browsers look up formatting rules in the source document. Your source can be internal (like the internal style sheet that goes in the head section of a web page) or external (such as a separate .css file). If you're working on a page in progress, you may already have defined one or more sources. To add a source, click the + button in CSS Designer's Sources section. That gives you three options: to create a new style sheet, attach an existing one, or define the style in your web page (in the head section to create an internal style sheet). For a complete explanation of these choices, turn to page 107.

2. **Choose or create a Selector.**

   Selectors can be classes, IDs, or tags. When you combine two or more selectors, you create a "compound" selector. For example, Figure 9-1 shows a selector that defines an anchor <a> tag. But the rules apply only when that anchor is inside of a list <li> tag that's inside an unordered list <ul> tag that's inside the body <body> of the page. You can create a tag like this by simply clicking the add selector icon (+) and typing the names in the Selector text box. If you don't remember the exact names for each tag, in Design view, put your cursor inside of the text you want to define. If you're creating a selector for an image or other media, select the image in Design view. Then, after you choose a source, click the + button. Dreamweaver will suggest a compound selector for the text with the cursor in it. You can edit Dreamweaver's suggested selector however you want.

3. **Set values for the CSS properties.**

Highlight your selector in the Selectors section of CSS Designer, and Dreamweaver displays the selector's properties in the Properties section. When you turn on the Show Only Set Properties checkbox, you see only properties that have already been defined for that selector. To see *all* the properties available to a selector, leave this box unchecked. The result is a very long, scrolling list. Use the buttons at the top of the Properties section to jump to the properties for a page's layout, text, borders, background, and more. After a page or two, you'll become familiar with the location of the properties you use most often and you'll zip right to them.

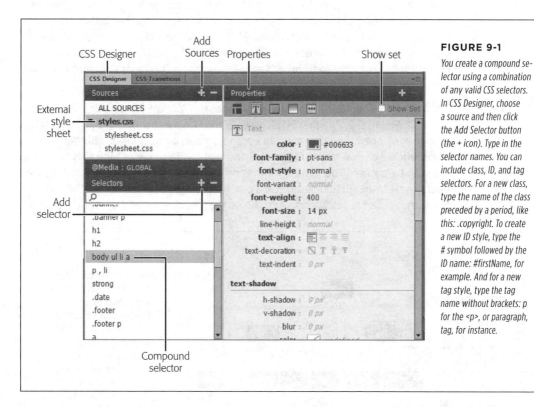

FIGURE 9-1

You create a compound selector using a combination of any valid CSS selectors. In CSS Designer, choose a source and then click the Add Selector button (the + icon). Type in the selector names. You can include class, ID, and tag selectors. For a new class, type the name of the class preceded by a period, like this: .copyright. To create a new ID style, type the # symbol followed by the ID name: #firstName, for example. And for a new tag style, type the tag name without brackets: p for the <p>, or paragraph, tag, for instance.

As described in the following sections, you use a different naming convention for each type of selector. The rest of the process for creating an advanced style works just like creating a class or tag style, and the process of editing or deleting the styles is also identical.

Descendent Selectors

Tag styles have their drawbacks. A tag style for the <p> tag, for example, makes simple work of formatting every paragraph on a page, but it's also indiscriminate. You may not *want* every paragraph to look the same.

Suppose you want to divide your web page into sections—a sidebar and a main content area, say—and use smaller text in the sidebar. You *could* create two class styles—such as *.sidebarText* and *.mainText*—and then apply them to the appropriate paragraphs (<p class="sidebarText"> for sidebar paragraphs, and <p class="mainText"> for body text), but who has that kind of time?

What you really need is a "smart" tag style, one that adapts to its surroundings, like a chameleon does, and applies the appropriate format depending on where it finds the element on the page. Enter *descendent selectors*.

You use descendent selectors to format every instance of a particular tag (the same way tag selectors do)—but only when those tags appear in a particular part of a web page. In effect, it's like saying, "Hey, you <a> tags in the navigation bar, listen up. I've got some formatting for you. All you other <a> tags, move along, there's nothing to see here." In other words, a descendent selector lets you format a tag based on its *relationship* to other tags. To understand how descendent selectors work, you need to delve a little more deeply into HTML.

Think of the HTML that forms any web page as a kind of family tree, like the one shown in Figure 9-2. The first HTML tag you use on a page—the <html> tag—is the grandpappy of all the other tags. In essence, when a tag is *inside* another tag, it's a *descendent* of that tag. In Figure 9-2, the text "wide range of topics" is bolded in the long paragraph. You get that format by applying a <strong> tag to that phrase. Because that bolded text sits inside a paragraph (inside a <p> tag, in other words), the <strong> tag is a descendent of the <p> tag—a descendent of that paragraph.

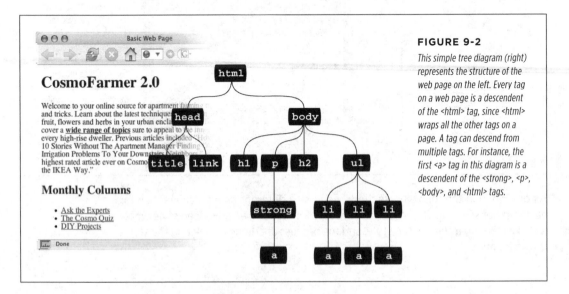

FIGURE 9-2

This simple tree diagram (right) represents the structure of the web page on the left. Every tag on a web page is a descendent of the <html> tag, since <html> wraps all the other tags on a page. A tag can descend from multiple tags. For instance, the first <a> tag in this diagram is a descendent of the <strong>, <p>, <body>, and <html> tags.

Descendent selectors let you take advantage of the HTML family tree by formatting tags differently when they appear inside certain other tags. For example, say you have an <h1> tag on your page, and you want to emphasize a word within that heading. One option is to select the word and press the B button on the Properties panel—that applies the <strong> tag to that word. The trouble is, most browsers boldface the words in headings anyway, so your visitors won't see any difference between the emphasized word and the other words in the headline. Creating a tag selector to change the <strong> tag's color and make it stand out from the headline isn't much of a solution: You end up changing the color of *every* <strong> tag on the page, even those inside paragraphs or bulleted lists. A descendent selector lets you do what you really want: Change the color of the <strong> tag *only when* it appears inside of an <h1> tag.

Creating descendent selectors isn't much more difficult than creating any other type of style. You follow the same one-two-three CSS Designer process described on page 104. After you choose a source for your styles, click the Add Selector button (+) and then type in a name for your selector. Figuring out how to name the selector is the tricky part, but Dreamweaver can help with that, too. In Design view, put your cursor inside the text you want to define as a selector. Say you click inside a <strong> tag that's inside an <h1> tag. In this case, when you click Add Selector (+), Dreamweaver suggests the name "h1 strong."

NOTE After you click the Add Selector button and start typing, Dreamweaver prompts you with HTML tags. So, after you press "b" you see *base, basefont, bgo, bgsound.* If you continue to type, adding "o," you see *body* and *tbody.* If you select body, add a space, and then start typing another tag name, you'll see more prompts related to the letters you type. Want to see a list of the classes already defined for your page? Press period (.) and then begin typing. For a list of IDs, enter the pound character (#) first.

You name a descendent selector by tacking together the series of parent selectors (separated by spaces) that identify the location in the family tree of the element you want to style. The most distant ancestor is on the far left and the element you wish to style is on the far right. Consider the example of the bolded word inside the headline discussed above. To style that bolded text (but leave any other bold text as it is), the descendent selector is *h1 strong*. You read this from right to left, so <strong> is the actual tag you're formatting, but only when it's inside an <h1> tag.

Figure 9-2 shows another example of descendent selectors. There are four links (<a> tags) on the page. Three of them appear inside bulleted list items (that's the <li> tag). To create a style that applies only to those three links, leaving the fourth untouched, you'd create a *li a* descendent selector. Again, the actual tag you want to format—the <a> link here—appears on the far right, while the tag that wraps around the link—the <li> tag—appears to the left.

You can have descendent selectors with more than just two elements. The following are all valid selectors for the <a> tags inside the bulleted list in Figure 9-2:

- li a

- ul li a

- body li a

- html li a

- html body ul li a

These five selectors—all of which do the same thing—demonstrate that you don't have to describe the entire lineage of the tag you want to format. For instance, in the third example—*body li a*—you don't need the ul found in the previous selector. This selector works as long as there's an <a> tag that's a descendent (somewhere along the lineage) of an <li> tag (which itself is a descendent of the <body> tag). This selector can just as easily apply to an <a> tag inside an <em> tag inside a <strong> tag that's inside an <li> tag, and so on.

NOTE One reason you might make a descendent selector longer by tacking on additional selectors is if you've written several rules that simultaneously format a tag. The more selectors that appear in a style name, the more powerful that style is and the more likely it is to override any conflicts with other styles. (More on this concept on page 384.) However, it's best to keep your selectors as short as possible to get the job done. In the above example, all five selectors work, but *li a* is the shortest, and therefore the best one to use.

When you click that Add Selector button in CSS Designer, Dreamweaver suggests a descendent selector based on the position of the cursor in your page, or what you currently have selected on the page. For example, say you had the page in Figure 9-2 open in Dreamweaver. If you select the link with the text "Ask the Experts," choose a source, and then click the Add Selector button, you'd see something like Figure 9-1. Having Dreamweaver compose the selector for you is, as you can imagine, a brain-cell saver. In this case, Dreamweaver suggests *body ul li a*—a descendent selector that formats every link (<a>) inside a list item (<li>) that's part of an unordered list (<ul>) that is itself inside the body of the page (<body>).

That's a pretty long-winded style name and, as mentioned above, you don't have to have all that information to accurately target an element on a page. For example, a simpler name, *li a*, would get the job done. Dreamweaver generally suggests the most complete descendent selector, meaning the tag you want to format and every ancestor tag (every tag that wraps around the selected element). In most cases, you won't need such complicated descendent selector names. You can replace Dreamweaver's suggestion with a simpler one; just delete what Dreamweaver provides and type in another. Often, you can dispense with the tags on the left side, because those are the most general. For example, everything in your page is likely to be within the <body> tag.

■ DESCENDENT SELECTORS WITH CLASS AND ID STYLES

You're not limited to using tag selectors in your descendent selector names, either. You can build complex descendent selectors by combining different types of selectors. Suppose you want links to appear in yellow in introductory paragraphs (which you designate with a class style named *.intro*). The following selector does the trick: *.intro a*. This descendent selector formats any link (<a> tag) inside any other tag that has the *.intro* class applied to it.

Web designers frequently format the same tag differently, depending on where the tag appears in a layout. For instance, you'll often want paragraphs in the main area of your page to look different from paragraphs in sidebars (you might use a different font and a smaller font size, for example). You'll usually wrap each section of a page inside <div> tags that have a class applied to them. For example, you might wrap the main content area in a <div> tag and apply the class name *.content* to it. To format just the paragraphs inside that <div> tag, you'd use the descendent selector *.content p* (don't leave out the period). You'll use this technique frequently when you work with CSS layouts like those discussed in the next chapter.

You can apply either class or ID names to <div> tags to create sections within a web page. While web designers used to use IDs with <div>s to identify unique page-layout elements, such as banners (for example, *<div id="banner">*), classes work just as well (*<div class="banner">*, for example). In either case, you might want to target specific tags inside those <div>s. The process is the same whether you use class or ID names, so if you want to define the look of bulleted lists wherever they appear inside a tag with an ID named *#banner*, you'd type *#banner ul* in the Selector Name box; if the tag had the class *.banner*, then the selector for a bulleted list inside that <div> would be *.banner ul*.

TIP   When you work with descendent selectors, it helps to read the selector name *backwards, from right to left*. Take, for example, the selector *#content .nav li*. The *li* means "This style applies to the <li> tag." The *.nav* means, "But only when it's inside a tag with a class of *.nav* applied to it." And *#content* means, "And only when that tag is inside another tag that has the ID *#content* applied to it."

To review, after you choose (or create) the source of a style and use the Add Selector command to name a descendent selector, you're ready to start adding the CSS properties that define the style you want to apply to the selector. That's simply a matter of finding properties in the Properties section of CSS Designer and using the available widgets to set their values (see page 104 for a refresher).

Styling Groups of Tags

Sometimes you want to several page elements to share the same formatting. Say you'd like all the headers on a page to share a certain color and font. Creating a separate style for each type of header—*h1, h2, h3, h4, h5, h6*—is way too much work. In addition, if you later want to change the color of all the headers, you have to update all six styles. A more streamlined approach is a *group* selector, which lets you apply a style to multiple selectors at the same time.

As always in CSS Designer, choose your source first. Then, in the Selectors section, click Add Selector (+). In the Selector Name box, type a list of selectors separated by commas. To style all heading tags with the same style, for example, you'd create the following selector: *h1, h2, h3, h4, h5, h6*. For a similar example, see Figure 9-3.

FIGURE 9-3

To style more than a single tag at a time, use a group selector. You can use any valid selector (or combination of selectors) as the group selector. For example, the selector circled here applies to the <h1> tag, the <p> tag, any tag styled with the .copyright class, and any links inside a tag that has the class .nav.

TIP At times, you may want a bunch of page elements to share *some*—but not all—formatting properties. Suppose you want to use the same font for several tags, but apply different font colors to each of those tags. You can create a single style using a group selector with the shared formatting options, and separate styles with unique formatting for the individual tags. That's a perfectly valid (and common) approach. Web browsers just "tally up" all the different CSS properties applied to a tag to create a kind of uber style, as described on page 391.

■ Fast Style Editing with CSS Designer

The CSS Rule Definition window can be a rather tedious way to edit CSS properties. Just getting to the window takes several steps. In Design view, click in the text you want to format or select an image or other piece of content. Then, in the Properties panel just below the document window, make sure you have CSS selected, and then click Edit Rule.

Opening this Rule Definition window and jumping around the categories and menus may slow down experienced CSS jockeys. Fortunately, CSS Designer streamlines the process so you can edit styles in a jiffy (Figure 9-4). After you select the page element you want to format, CSS Designer (Window→CSS Designer) displays the selectors that trigger the style for that element. Click on a selector, and Dreamweaver displays the properties for that element in the Properties section of Designer. If you're adjusting an already defined property, turn on the Show Set checkbox so you see only properties where you've already set the value—in other words, you see the style's old rules. This makes it easier to find the exact property you want to tweak. When you make changes, Dreamweaver rewrites the rule for that selector in the style sheet. Keep in mind that the changes you make may affect other elements on your page. If the rule is in an external Style sheet shared by multiple pages, you may be changing more than one page. How do you know which style sheet holds the rule definition? That's easy. When you choose a selector, CSS Designer highlights the style source in the Sources section.

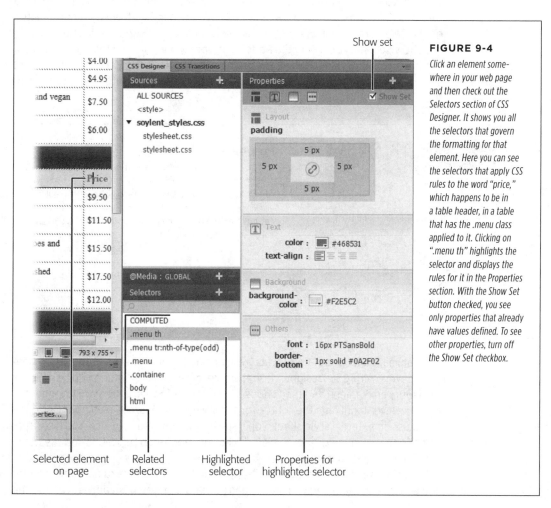

FIGURE 9-4

Click an element somewhere in your web page and then check out the Selectors section of CSS Designer. It shows you all the selectors that govern the formatting for that element. Here you can see the selectors that apply CSS rules to the word "price," which happens to be in a table header, in a table that has the .menu class applied to it. Clicking on ".menu th" highlights the selector and displays the rules for it in the Properties section. With the Show Set button checked, you see only properties that already have values defined. To see other properties, turn off the Show Set checkbox.

Using Designer's Show Set option, it's easy to edit property values. To increase the size of a page's text, for example, find *font-size* in CSS Designer's Properties section, and then bump it up to a larger size.

For many properties, CSS designer displays the name of the property on the left and a value box on the right. You can type in a value or click the value box and drag to scrub in a value. You see the number change as you drag. Drag left to decrease the value; drag right to increase it. Menus and other widgets help you provide values in the proper format, using the proper units of measure. Some properties, such as colors, border-radius, margins, and padding give you more visual tools for setting the value. If you don't see the property you want to change, make sure you have the Show Set checkbox turned off.

Sometimes, you'll want to remove a property from a rule. For example, you may have set your <h1> headings to have 5px of padding all the way around and decided that wasn't the right choice after all. To remove the padding from the <h1> selector, go the Selectors section of Designer and select h1. In the Properties section, turn on the Show Set checkbox. Find the Padding property and then, on the right side, click the trash can icon to delete it from the h1 rule (Figure 9-5). To preview the effect this will have before you make the change, click the disable button (the circle with the diagonal line through it).

FIGURE 9-5

Click the trash can icon to remove a property and its rule from a selector. Use the Disable button to the left of the trash can to see the effect the rule has on your layout. It works like a toggle, so you can disable and then enable specific rules. Remember to do all this in Live view, so Dreamweaver renders the style in a real browser. Otherwise, you may not get the complete picture.

You can learn a lot about CSS styles by watching Dreamweaver edit the style sheet as you work with CSS Designer. For example, after you click inside your web page to identify an element, and then choose a selector in CSS Designer, you'll notice that Dreamweaver highlights the source for the style in the Sources section of Designer. If you use an external style sheet, you'll see a filename ending in .css. You'll see that same file name in the group of related files above the web page. Click on the name and Dreamweaver automatically switches to Split view, showing the style sheet on the left side. Your blinking cursor will appear in the code in the rule for the selector you chose in Designer. As you make changes, you can watch Dreamweaver edit the style sheet.

If your styles are in an internal style sheet, the process is slightly different. When you choose a selector in CSS Designer, the highlighted style sheet is "<style>." In that case, click the Source Code button to the left of the related files tabs. Scroll through the <head> of your document until you see the CSS rules. The code for your styles appears between two tags. The first will read:

```
<style type="text/css">
```

The closing tag is:

```
</style>
```

After you zero in on the CSS rules in the head of your document, you can watch Dreamweaver edit the code as you work in CSS Designer.

TIP Another quick way to find the code for a specific selector is to right-click the selector in CSS Designer, and then choose Go to Code from the pop-up menu. Dreamweaver launches Split view, displays the CSS code in the left pane, and places your cursor in the rule for the selector so you can edit it.

FREQUENTLY ASKED QUESTION

CSS Shorthand

In CSS Designer's Properties section, I'll sometimes see all the font properties grouped into a single property named font; *other times, font properties are listed individually, like* font-family, font-size, *and so on. Why is that?*

Some CSS properties seem to go together: font properties, background properties (like *background-color, background-image, background-repeat*, and so on), margin, border, padding, and *list-style* properties. CSS supports a shorthand that combines related properties into a single property name. For example, it can combine the properties *font-family, font-size, font-weight, font-style*, and *line-height* into a single property it calls *font*. This shorthand makes writing CSS by hand faster. Instead of typing all the above font properties—one line of CSS code per property—you can combine them into a single line like this:

```
font: italic  bold 16px/150% Tahoma, Ver-
dana, Arial, Helvetica, sans-serif;
```

Dreamweaver uses either the shorthand or longhand method depending on your Preferences settings. Choose Edit→Preferences (Dreamweaver→Preferences) or use the keyboard shortcut Ctrl+U [⌘-U]); click the CSS Styles category to view the settings Dreamweaver uses when it writes CSS code. The top group of checkboxes lets you turn on and off shorthand mode for specific categories. The second group of buttons and boxes controls how and when you can use shorthand. Initially, Dreamweaver uses shorthand for borders and transitions. That's a good setting when you're still getting used to all the mysteries of CSS.

If you hand-edit your CSS, you might want to turn on other shorthand checkboxes. If Dreamweaver writes all your CSS, its best to turn off these boxes. Unless you know your CSS well, shorthand versions of CSS properties can be harder to edit—it's very easy to mistype something.

Moving and Managing Styles

In the old days, when CSS support in web browsers was new, site designers would create just a handful of styles to format headlines and text. Keeping track of a site's styles back then wasn't too hard. Today, with great support for CSS and CSS-based layouts the norm, you can easily create a style sheet with hundreds of styles.

You might want to take a really long, complicated style sheet and split it into several smaller, easier-to-read external style sheets, however. One common design practice is to store styles that serve related functions in separate style sheets—for example, all the styles related to web forms would be in one style sheet, styles for text in another, and styles for page layout in yet another. You can then link each of the style sheets to your site's pages as described on page 107.

Or you might find yourself in the opposite situation: You have too many style sheets and want to combine them into a single one to cut down on the number of files a web browser needs to download from your web server.

NOTE For really busy websites, the conventional wisdom is to use only a single external style sheet. That's because each request for a new file takes time and server power, so the more requests a browser makes for files, the slower the server performs. But unless your site is as busy as Yahoo, Google, or Amazon, your visitors won't notice if you use one or five external style sheets.

Even if you're not worried about creating new external style sheets (or cutting down on the number you already have), it's still useful to organize the styles *within* a style sheet. Web designers frequently use this strategy. For example, they keep all the styles for basic layout in one section of a style sheet, basic tag selectors in another section, and styles for text, images, and other content grouped according to where on the site they use them (sidebars, banners, and so on). By grouping related styles, it's a lot easier to find a particular style when it comes time to edit it.

Fortunately, you don't need to venture into Code view to move styles around in your style sheets. Dreamweaver provides a simple and logical way to do so (and to move styles from one style sheet to another, too).

- To move a style from one place to another in the same style sheet, drag the style's selector in CSS Designer (see Figure 9-6, left). Dreamweaver lists styles in the order in which they appear in the actual style sheet—so when you drag one style below another, for example, Dreamweaver repositions the CSS code in the style sheet. (Order can be important in CSS for reasons you'll learn on page 384, but in a nutshell, CSS gives styles listed lower in a style sheet greater priority if that style conflicts with other styles higher up.) You can select and move more than one style at a time by Ctrl-clicking (⌘-clicking) each style and then dragging the highlighted group (Ctrl-click [⌘-click] a selected style to deselect it). Select a range of styles by clicking one style and then Shift-clicking another style: That highlights every style between the two mouse clicks.

- To move one or more styles *between* two style sheets, drag the selectors from the Selectors section of CSS Designer onto the name of the style sheet in the Sources section. Dreamweaver will remove the selector and its related CSS rules from one style sheet and add them to the other. Using this method, you can move CSS rules from internal style sheets to external sheets and vice versa. (Internal style sheets are represented in CSS Designer as <style>, while external style sheets are identified by a filename ending in .css.)

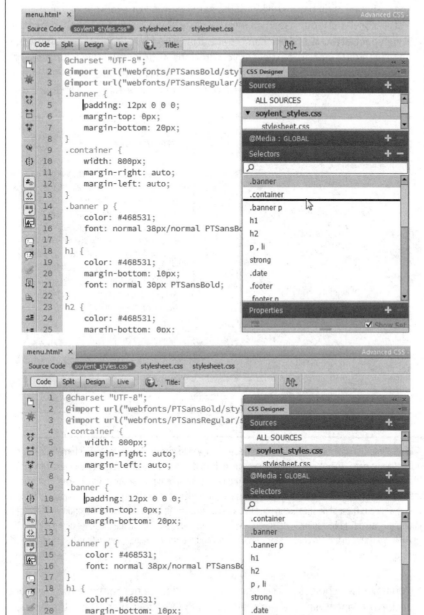

FIGURE 9-6

In CSS Designer, you can drag selectors to different locations within a style sheet (left). In this case, dragging the .banner class below the .container class groups all the banner selectors together, as shown at right.

• To copy one or more CSS rules to another style sheet without deleting the originals, hold the Alt (Option) key down when you drag.

You need to give Dreamweaver a little help if you drag a style into another style sheet that already has a style with the same name. For example, say you define a style for the <body> tag in an internal style sheet, and you've got an external style sheet attached to the same page that also has a <body> tag style (perhaps with different properties). If you drag the <body> tag style from one style sheet onto another, Dreamweaver thinks you're trying to add the same-named style a second time and informs you of the potential problem (see Figure 9-7).

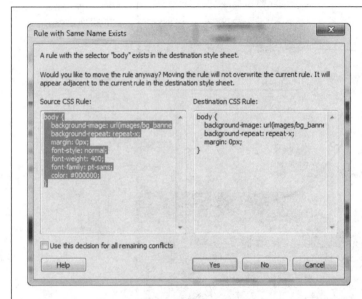

FIGURE 9-7

When you drag a style from one style sheet to another and a style by the same name exists in the destination sheet, this dialog box appears, letting you either cancel the move or move the style anyway. To help you figure out what to do, Dreamweaver lists the properties in both the style you're trying to move (left) and the one already present (right). You can use this information to determine which of the two styles you wish to keep, or to figure out which properties from each style are most important.

NOTE Unfortunately, Dreamweaver doesn't give you a way to reorder the sequence of internal and external style sheets on a page. They're attached to the page in the order in which you added them. For example, if you attach an external style sheet to a web page and then create an internal style sheet, the internal style sheet's code appears *after* the link to the external style sheet. The order of style sheets dictates the order in which a browser downloads those style sheets and can affect how a browser applies styles that have conflicting properties (thanks to the cascade in Cascading Style Sheets, described on page 384). To change the order of the style sheets in the HTML, you have to go into Code view (View→Code) and reorder the <link> tags in the <head> of the HTML document.

You have two choices at this point. You can decide not to move the style and click No (Cancel has the same effect), and Dreamweaver closes the window without moving the style. Or you can click Yes and Dreamweaver moves the style to the style sheet. It doesn't replace the old style, nor does it merge the properties of the two styles. It simply adds the new style to the destination style sheet—in other words, you end up with a style sheet that has two separate styles, each with the same name. Even though this is perfectly valid CSS, it's confusing. Delete one of the styles, and, if necessary, edit the remaining one to add any properties you wanted from the deleted style.

NOTE Dreamweaver says that it will place the rule "adjacent" to the rule with the same name when it moves like-named rules, but it doesn't. It positions the rule at the end of the list.

- You can also move one or more styles to an external style sheet that's not attached to the current page. As discussed on page 101, external style sheets are the most efficient way to style a website's collection of pages. But it's often easier to use an internal style sheet when you first start a design. That's because, as you tweak your CSS, you only have to edit one file (the web page with the internal style sheet in it) instead of two (the web page *and* the external CSS file). But once you finish your design, it's best to move your styles from an internal sheet to an external one. This process can be done from within the Source Code.

TIP If you are most comfortable working within CSS Designer, you can add a source to the Source section. Use Shift-click or Ctrl-click (⌘-click) to highlight selectors and then Alt-drag to move styles to the new source.

To find your styles in the Source Code, it's easiest to start in CSS Designer. Right-click (⌘-click) a selector that has <style> as the source. From the pop-up menu, choose Go to Code. Dreamweaver changes to Split view if you aren't already there and displays the CSS code that's in the <head> section of your page. To move all your code, select everything between *<style type="text/css">* and *</style>*, but don't select the tags themselves. Right-click (⌘-click) on the selection and choose CSS Styles→Move CSS Rules (see Figure 9-8, top). The Move to External Style Sheet window opens (Figure 9-8, bottom). You can then either add the rules to an existing external style sheet by clicking the Browse button and navigating to the CSS file, or turn on the "A new style sheet" radio button to create a new CSS file and move the styles there. When you click OK, Dreamweaver either moves the styles to an existing style sheet, or it displays a dialog box letting you name and save the new style sheet. Either way, Dreamweaver removes the styles from the internal style sheet and places them in the external sheet. (That's the style sheet you found with the "Browse" command or a new style sheet, if you chose "A new style sheet.") Even better, if the external CSS file isn't already attached to the current page, Dreamweaver attaches it for you, which saves you from doing so manually.

NOTE If you move all the styles from an internal style sheet to an external one, Dreamweaver still leaves some useless <style> tags in your web page. To remove them, in CSS Designer's Sources section, select *<style>* from the list and then click the Remove CSS Source button (the minus-sign icon, -). You can also edit the HTML Source Code for your web page, by clicking the Source Code button in the document window. To remove the style tags, delete the starting tag <style type="text/css"> and the closing tag </style>. If you've moved all the CSS Rules to an external style sheet, there shouldn't be anything between the two tags.

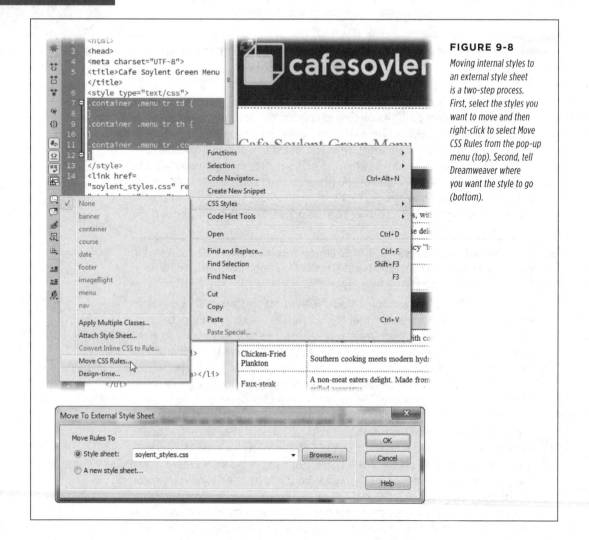

FIGURE 9-8

Moving internal styles to an external style sheet is a two-step process. First, select the styles you want to move and then right-click to select Move CSS Rules from the pop-up menu (top). Second, tell Dreamweaver where you want the style to go (bottom).

Resolving CSS Conflicts

As you begin to pile more and more styles into your pages, you may notice that a page might not look exactly as you expect. A paragraph of text might be green even though you didn't create a style for a green paragraph. Or you may have styled a paragraph to appear with green text, but it refuses to change color. Most of the time, peculiar behaviors like these occur when styles collide. The rules governing these interactions can be complex, but they boil down to two main concepts: *inheritance* and *the cascade*.

Inheritance

Imagine you create a new style by redefining the paragraph tag (<p>). The style specifies red text displayed in the Arial font at a height of 24 pixels. Then you select a single word in a paragraph and apply bold formatting to it. When you use the Properties panel's bold button to do this, Dreamweaver wraps that word in a pair of <strong> tags.

When a browser loads the page, it formats all the paragraphs in red Arial text with a font size of 24 pixels, because that's how you defined the <p> tag. But what happens when the browser encounters the paragraph with the <strong> tag in it? Since you didn't redefine the <strong> tag in red, Arial, 24 pixels, the browser scratches its little silicon head and asks, "Should I resort to my *default* font, text size, and color when I get to the <strong> tag, ignoring your style rules?"

And you can answer, "Of course not!" The bolded word should look just like the rest of the paragraph: red, Arial, 24 pixels high—and now boldfaced to boot. And indeed, that's how CSS works: The <strong> tag *inherits* the formatting of the surrounding <p> tag.

Just as human babies inherit traits like eye color from their parents, nested HTML tags inherit the properties of tags that surround them. In fact, a tag nested inside another tag—such as that <strong> tag inside the <p> tag above—is called a *child*, while the enclosing tag is called the *parent*.

> **NOTE** As you read on page 370, a tag inside another tag is also called a *descendent* tag, while a tag that surrounds another tag is called its *ancestor*.

Inheritance passes from parent to child and ancestor to descendent. So in this example, the <p> tag (the parent) passes on the red text, Arial font, and 24-pixel size to the <strong> tag (the child). But just as children have their own unique qualities, the <strong> tag adds its own quality—boldness—to the properties it inherits from its parent.

> **NOTE** Inheritance applies to all styles, not just tag styles. For example, if you apply a class style to the <body> tag, then all the tags inside the <body> tag—paragraphs, images, and so on—inherit the properties of the class style.

Inheritance comes in quite handy at times. Say you want to display *all* the text on a page (paragraphs, headings, unordered lists, and links) in the Verdana font. You could dedicate yourself to a lengthy tagging extravaganza and redefine *every* HTML tag used to format text—<h1>, <h2>, <p>, <a>, <ul>, and so on—or create a class style and then manually apply it to all the text on the page.

But there's a better and faster technique, and it takes advantage of inheritance. Every web page contains a <body> tag, which contains *all* the elements of your page. The <body> tag, therefore, is an ancestor to *all* the HTML you see on a page—images, paragraphs, headings, and so on. To quickly format all the page's text, you can create a style for the <body> tag and set the font to Verdana, or create a class style using that font and apply it to the <body> tag. Every bit of text inside the body—all children—will inherit the Verdana font property.

> **NOTE** Actually, tags don't inherit *all* CSS properties. For the most part, the exclusions are logical. For example, say you create a border around an unordered list to visually set it off in its own box. If the border property were inherited, all the elements *inside* the unordered list—like list items, links, or bolded words—would each have their own box around them as well. Padding and margin are two other common properties that tags don't inherit.

The Cascade

At times, styles can conflict. Say you redefine the <h1> tag in an external style sheet, so that all <h1> headings show up in red in the Arial font. Then you attach this external style sheet to a web page that has an *internal* style sheet where you set the <h1> tag style to the Times font at 24 pixels high.

Now, when a browser tries to display an <h1> heading, it runs into a little dilemma. The page specifies two styles—two sets of formatting rules—for the *same tag*. To make matters even more confusing, suppose one <h1> tag has a class named *.highlight* applied to it. The *.highlight* class style sets the font family to Trebuchet MS and makes all the text uppercase. So which style does the browser choose: the style from the internal style sheet, the style from the external style sheet, or the class style?

The answer is "All of them." The browser adopts elements of the three styles according to these hierarchical rules (hence the term "cascading" in "Cascading Style Sheets"):

- Properties that don't conflict are applied as usual. In the previous example, the red color property exists only in the external style sheet, while the internal style sheet is the only one to specify a font *size*. And the class is the only style to specify uppercase text. So far, the browser knows that, for this page, text inside <h1> tags should be red, 24 pixels tall, and uppercase.

- When properties *do* conflict, the browser uses the property from the style with the greatest specificity. *Specificity* is just CSS jargon that means "the style with the most authority." The type of selector you use on a page is one way to affect specificity: ID styles are considered more specific than class styles, which are more specific than tag styles. In general, this means that properties from an ID style override properties from a class style, and properties from a class style override conflicts with a tag style.

> **NOTE** For an amusing—but accurate—description of specificity, read the article *CSS: Specificity Wars* (*http://tinyurl.com/7ogaq*). Make sure you print out the accompanying *Star Wars*-themed chart (*http://tinyurl.com/dz9cf*), which visually explains specificity by equating class selectors with Darth Vader and IDs with the Dark Emperor himself. May the force be with you. (If you're more an aquatic-type, there's also a CSS "Specifishity" chart at *http://tinyurl.com/89bafl2*.)

- If two styles with the same specificity conflict—like the *h1* style in the external style sheet and the *h1* style in the internal style sheet in this example—the browser chooses the properties from the styles that were added to the page last. Say you first create an internal style sheet (at which point Dreamweaver inserts the appropriate HTML and CSS into the web page) and *then* attach an external style sheet. That means the link to the external style sheet appears *after* the internal style sheet in the web page. In this case, a style from the external style sheet with the same name as a style from the internal style sheet wins out. Similarly, if you attach the external style sheet first and then create the internal style sheet, the internal style sheet wins.

To summarize, then: Once the browser sorts things out, it determines that the text inside the <h1> tag on this web page should be Trebuchet MS and uppercase (from the *.highlight* class style), red (from the *h1* style in the external style sheet), and 24 pixels high (from the *h1* style in the internal style sheet).

NOTE Descendent selectors, which include combinations of class, ID, and tag names, such as *.main p*, *#banner h1*, or *h1 strong*, have even more authority than a tag or class style by themselves, since Dreamweaver calculates specificity by combining all the selectors listed. Say you create a <p> tag style that produces bright-red text, and a descendent selector, *.sidebar p*, with purple text. Any paragraphs inside another element (like a <div> tag) that use the *.sidebar* style are purple—*not* red. Fortunately, Dreamweaver provides several ways to decipher this confusing jumble of conflicting styles (described in the next section).

Inherited properties, however, have no specificity, so when child elements inherit properties from parent elements (as described on page 383), any style applied directly to the child element overrules properties inherited from the parent element—no matter the specificity of the parent tag's style. Suppose you create an ID style named *#homepage* with the following properties: purple text and the Arial font. If you apply the *#homepage* ID to the <body> tag, the child elements (anything within the <body> tag) inherit those properties. If you then redefine the paragraph tag so that it displays text as green, the paragraph text inherits the Arial font from the <body> tag, but ignores the purple color in favor of the green. Even though an ID style like *#homepage* has greater authority than a simple <p> tag selector, the properties applied to the paragraph through the <p> tag style overrule the properties inherited from the ID selector.

TIP Because ID selectors are so powerful (they have greater specificity than either class or tag selectors), many web designers steer clear of them. For example, when you create a descendent selector like *#main p*, you can't override that style unless you create an even more powerful selector like *#main .special*. This can lead to some really long descendent selectors. If you stick with class and tag selectors, you won't need to work so hard to overcome conflicts the cascade causes.

To learn more than you probably ever wanted to know about the cascade, visit *www. w3.org/TR/css3-cascade/*.

NOTE   In *CSS3: The Missing Manual*, you'll find chapters dedicated to both inheritance and the cascade.

CSS Sleuthing with Computed Properties

If you haven't yet put this book down in hopes that the swelling in your brain will subside, you've probably absorbed the notion that using multiple style properties can get complex. With all this inheritance and cascading going on, it's easy for styles to collide in hard-to-predict ways. To help you discern how styles interact and to ferret out possible conflicts, Dreamweaver has some useful tools starting with the Computed feature in CSS Designer, which tells you how a web browser formats a selected item—such as an image, paragraph, table, or <div> tag—*once it takes into account inheritance and the cascade*. That's pretty cool.

The Computed feature, found in the Selectors section of CSS Designer, is an invaluable tool for diagnosing weird CSS behavior associated with inheritance and the cascade. But like any incredible tool, it requires a good user's manual to learn how it works. First of all, even though that word Computed appears in the Selectors section, it's not really a selector. It's better to think of it as a tool.

As usual, your first step is to click some text, select a picture, or highlight some other media on your web page. CSS Designer displays the selectors that govern that element's formatting. The all-caps word COMPUTED also appears at the top of that list. Click Computed and it shows a blue highlight to indicate it is selected. A different set of properties appear in the Properties section: the *computed properties*. The Computed tool automatically displays the post-inheritance and post-cascade properties and values that format the element that you first selected in the document window. The different properties CSS Designer displays when you click on Computed may be associated with different selectors. For example, the font-family may be defined by a style attached to a div. The color of the text may be defined by a style attached to a heading. In other words, different selectors produce the end result, but by clicking Computed, you see all the properties in the Properties section at one time. You can go ahead and make changes to the values for the properties while viewing the effect those changes have on your page (remember to render the page in Live view). When you click the name or value widget for a property in CSS Designer's Properties section, the related selector appears bold in the Selectors section. That way, you know which CSS rule you're editing. This is important because your changes will affect other elements on the page, or even other elements on other web pages, that use the same CSS rule.

So, how does the Computed value help you in the real world? Suppose you have a headline that's orange but you never created an <h1> tag that specified orange text. You can find out which selector passed the hideous orange on to the heading by clicking inside the headline. Then, in CSS Designer's Selectors section click the word Computed. At that point, the Properties section displays the headline's computed properties (see Figure 9-9), one of which is *color*. You'll see an orange swatch next to it. Click either the color property name or value. One of the selectors in the Selectors section now appears in bold type. That is the selector with the CSS rule that sets the color for the headline. Perhaps your <h1> is inside a <div> tag that has the .uglyOrange class applied to it. In your page's HTML, that would look like this:

```
<div class="uglyOrange">
```

When you select the Color property in the Properties section of CSS Designer, the program displays ".uglyOrange" in bold type in the Selectors section. Now you know which selector defines that ugly orange color. You can change the color value for the selector .uglyOrange, which will likely affect other elements styled the .uglyOrange class. To fix the problem, you could create a color rule specifically for your <h1> tag. That rule would override the .uglyOrange class, but it will affect other <h1> elements. A third option is to create a new class, say .notOrange, where you set a color value and then apply that class to your <h1> heading. You need to specifically set a color value for this new class, or the style sheet will have no color rule, and so it won't override .notOrange.

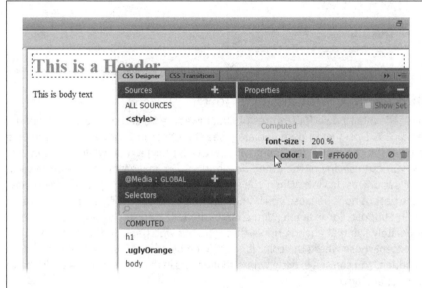

FIGURE 9-9

Here, the Computed selector displays all the rules that affect the <h1> header in the sample document. Clicking the Color property highlights the .uglyOrange class in Selectors, telling you which selector defined the color.

When you finish, click inside your <h1> heading again to check out the Computed properties and values. Notice that the *color* property displays your new shade. Select *color* or its assigned value and you'll see the selector that now governs the <h1> tag is something other than that .uglyOrange class.

You may be surprised to notice that you can still find the .uglyOrange class listed in the Selectors section. That's because you're still applying the class to a "parent" of your <h1> header. The .uglyOrange class may even have other rules that still affect your heading. Now, if you click .uglyOrange in Selectors and find the text color property (Figure 9-10), you see the property name with a strikethrough line. Pause with your cursor over the property and a message appears that says, "Color does not apply to your selection because it has been overridden by the rule .notOrange."

If you changed the color for <h1> tags, Dreamweaver would cite that rule instead of *.notOrange*.

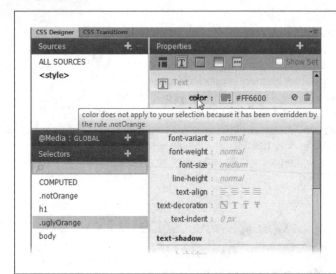

CSS Sleuthing with Inspect View

One of the most powerful features of Dreamweaver CC is that you can tweak the rules in CSS Designer and immediately see the effect in Live view (click the Live button at the top of the document window). Don't forget that, while you're in Live view, you can use any of the other view options Dreamweaver offers—Code view, Split view, or Design view. When you work with CSS Designer, Split or Design view are the best options because you immediately see the effect of the rules you create or edit. Suppose, for example, you change the text color for the <body> tag. You immediately see that change ripple through your web page. It affects every bit of text, except those where the color is overridden by another rule. And if your rule is overridden, you can see exactly where that occurs in the context of the entire page using Inspect view.

When you're in Live view, you see two additional buttons to the right of the Live button: Live Code and Inspect. When you click Inspect or press Alt+Shift+F11 (Option-Shift-F11), the behavior of your cursor changes. Now if you hover over a page element, CSS Designer shows you that element's computed properties. You also see colorful highlights around the element; blocks of text appear in cyan (blue-green), margins in yellow, and padding in purple. This visual representation of CSS properties is extremely helpful as you make design decisions. You can use CSS Designer to change or disable values momentarily to understand their effect on your page.

If you're not sure exactly which page element is under the Inspect microscope, check the bottom of the document window, where Dreamweaver displays the current selection's class, ID, and tag names. In Figure 9-11, for example, you can see an

Inspected element and its entire hierarchy of tags and classes. You can see that the <img> tag is highlighted, indicating that it's currently under inspection.

As you check out page elements in Inspect view, CSS Designer displays the elements' computed properties and their values. You can position your cursor on a value and edit it as you normally would.

FIGURE 9-11

With the Inspect view turned on, Dreamweaver highlights elements on the page as you mouse over them. Here, you're inspecting an image and you can see the padding around the image (the purple border). At the bottom of the document window you see the entire family of tags and classes. The highlighted <img> tag tells you that it's the focus of the inspection. Use your left and right arrow keys to move the focus to different tags. Throughout the process, CSS Designer displays the associated selectors and properties.

TIP Sometimes, when you're sleuthing through your CSS rules, you may need more room for CSS Designer. Switching from the Compact workspace to the Expanded (page 9) provides more room for the Properties section. You can click and drag any of the gray bars (vertical or horizontal) between the sections to adjust the spacing. In some cases, it may help to drag the CSS Designer tab away from the dock to create a floating palette. For more workspace details, see page 14.

Analyzing the Cascade

When CSS Designer displays computed selectors and properties, it's showing you the cascade of CSS rules. In the Selectors section of CSS Designer, the rules that have the most precedence are at the top of the list. You can click each of the selectors to see their contribution to the formatting of the currently selected element. If you see a property name with a strikethrough, the rule doesn't apply to the current selection. To learn which selector governs that property, move your cursor over the property name and a tooltip pops up with the name.

You can also see the cascade of rules listed in the Properties panel. Select the text you want to analyze, click the CSS button in the Properties panel, and then select the Targeted Rule menu—the top group of items in the menu lists the cascade. In this case, the cascade is shown in reverse order. The rules with the least precedence are at the top, while the most powerful selectors are at the bottom.

> **TIP** One way to make a style more "powerful"—so that its properties override properties from conflicting styles—is to use a descendent selector. For example, a *body p* descendent selector has more authority than just a plain <p> tag style, even though both styles target the exact same tags. Likewise, a *.content p* style is more powerful than a *body p* style since it applies a class selector (which is more powerful than a tag selector) and one tag selector. You can quickly rename a style or create a more long-winded and powerful descendent selector using CSS Designer. Just select a target element on the page, choose a source for the CSS code in Designer's Sources section, and then click Add Select (+). CSS Designer then suggests a verbose selector, which you're free to edit.

■ Using the Code Navigator

Dreamweaver includes yet another valuable CSS tool, this one aimed at CSS pros who like to use Code view when they write and edit CSS. The Code Navigator gives you a quick way to see all the CSS styles applied to any element you select. It's kind of like CSS Designer's Computed feature, but the CSS styles appear in a pop-up window instead of in CSS Designer (see Figure 9-12).

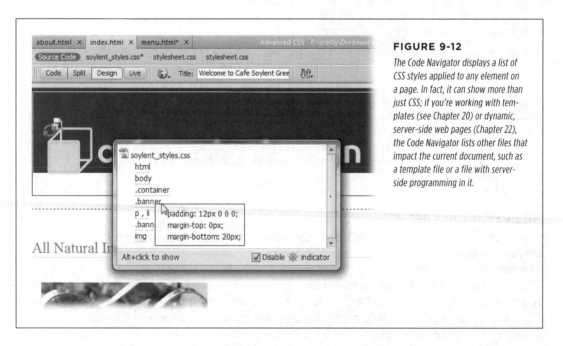

FIGURE 9-12

The Code Navigator displays a list of CSS styles applied to any element on a page. In fact, it can show more than just CSS; if you're working with templates (see Chapter 20) or dynamic, server-side web pages (Chapter 22), the Code Navigator lists other files that impact the current document, such as a template file or a file with server-side programming in it.

To launch the Code Navigator, hold down the Alt key and click an element on the page (Mac owners need to press ⌘-Option and click). You can click any element whose CSS you wish to examine: an image, a heading, a paragraph, a table, and so on. For example, in Figure 9-12, Alt-clicking (⌘-Option) the café's logo opened the Code Navigator, which lists the styles that apply to that headline.

You can launch the Code Navigator several other ways:

- Click the Code Navigator icon (the ship steering wheel, circled in Figure 9-13). This icon appears next to an element you select on a page (or above an element when you put your cursor on it). It usually takes a second or so to appear, so you may want to stick with the keyboard shortcut (Alt-click or ⌘-Option-click).

- Right-click any item on the page, and choose Code Navigator from the pop-up menu.

- Select an item on a page and choose View→Code Navigator, or press Ctrl-Alt-N (Windows) or ⌘-Option-N (Macs).

FIGURE 9-13

If the Code Navigator's ever-present steering wheel icon bothers you, get rid of it by turning on the Disable checkbox in the Code Navigator window (see Figure 9-11). From that point on, you open the Code Navigator using the keyboard shortcut or one of the other methods discussed above.

Once the Code Navigator window opens, you see all the styles that affect the current item. In Figure 9-12, for example, the Navigator lists seven styles that format the logo. If you move your mouse over one of them, you'll see a list of that style's CSS properties. In Figure 9-12, hovering over the *.banner* style lists that style's properties: padding of 12px; margin-top of 0px; and a margin-bottom of 20px. Although this is a quick way to view styles and their properties, it isn't as useful as CSS Designer's Computed feature, which shows you exactly which *properties* (not just which styles) apply to the current selection. In addition, the Code Navigator window doesn't always accurately display the CSS cascade (page 384)—it does list the styles in order of specificity, but it splits up the list of styles by style sheet, so if a page has more than one style sheet, you may not get a clear picture of the cascade. CSS Designer's Computed feature (page 386), on the other hand, shows a complete list of styles from least to most specific, regardless of how many style sheets you use.

If you're a code jockey who prefers to type CSS code instead of relying on Dreamweaver's windows and panels, the Code Navigator lets you jump immediately to a style sheet. Open it and click any style listed. Dreamweaver jumps into Split view and displays the CSS for the selected style. Of course, you need to know how to write CSS for this to be useful. If you're not comfortable with that, you should stick with CSS Designer and the methods for editing styles, discussed on page 122.

■ Styling for Print

You may be surprised to see a section on print design in a book dedicated to creating beautiful on-screen presentations. However, it's common for people to print out web pages—directions to a concert, a list of product names and ratings, or a long-winded treatise that's easier to read on paper while reclining in a favorite chair.

Unfortunately, some web pages just don't print well. Sometimes the banner's too big to fit on one sheet of paper, so it spans two printed pages, or the heavy use of ads wastes ink. And some CSS-based layouts simply print as jumbled messes. Fortunately, CSS has an answer: *printer style sheets*. The creators of CSS realized that people might use web pages in different ways, such as printing them out. In fact, they went so far as to define a large group of potential "media types" so web designers could customize pages for different output devices, including Teletype machines, Braille readers, and so on.

Basically, by specifying a media type, you attach an external style sheet that Dreamweaver applies *only* when someone sends the page to a particular device. For instance, you could have a style sheet that comes into play only when someone looks at a web page on a monitor, and another that applies only when they print the page. You can tweak a page's styles so it looks good when you print it out without affecting its appearance on-screen. Figure 9-14 shows the concept in action.

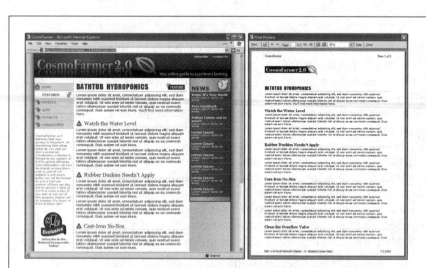

FIGURE 9-14

When you print a web page (left), you really don't need its navigation links or information unrelated to the topic at hand (left). Create a print style sheet to eliminate unnecessary content and format the page so it looks nice on paper (right).

The basic process involves creating an external style sheet that contains styles suited to a particular media type (like a printer or monitor), and then attaching the style sheet to a web page and identifying the destination device. The Sources section of CSS Designer automates the process for you. Simply click the Add CSS Source button (+) and choose either Create a New CSS File or Attach Existing CSS File.

That opens a window like the one in Figure 9-15, where you name the CSS file. Next to "Add as," choose Link. To specify a style sheet for print, expand the Conditional Usage panel by clicking the right-pointing arrow (lower-left). Set the first menu to "media" and the second to "print," and then click OK.

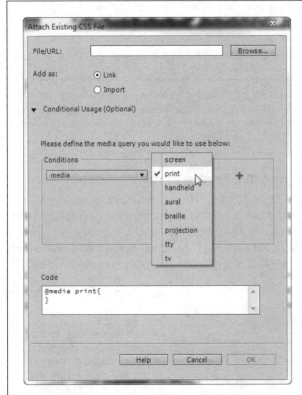

FIGURE 9-15

When you attach an external style sheet to a web page, you can assign it to a specific output device, such as a printer ("print") or monitor ("screen"). If you don't specify one or the other, the browser uses the style sheet for all output devices. By clicking the + button, you can continue to add conditions like max-width or min-color. You use them to specify styles used only when a browser encounters certain conditions (like a screen that's no wider than 480 pixels). Most of these options aren't that useful, but some are great for creating different designs for mobile phones. You'll learn about these other "media queries" on page 506.

Say you name your style sheet *print.css*. When you follow the steps above, you add a line to the <head> section of your web page that looks like this:

```
<link href="print.css" rel="stylesheet" type="text/css" media="print">
```

The key feature of this line is the last bit, media="print", which tells Dreamweaver you'll be sending this page to a printer.

NOTE If you attach an external style sheet and select a media type, Dreamweaver displays the media type on the CSS Styles panel. For example, if you attach an external style sheet named *print.css* and specify the "print" media type, Dreamweaver displays "*print.css* [print]" in CSS Designer's Sources section.

Although Dreamweaver lists many media types, there are only three related to crafting printer style sheets: *print, screen*, and *all*. "Print" specifies that the styles apply only when someone prints the page; "screen" indicates a style sheet that takes effect only when the page appears on a display; and "all" is the same as not selecting anything—the style sheet applies when you print the page, view it on a monitor, feel it on a Braille reader, and so on. The "all" option comes in handy when you want to create a style sheet that defines the basic look of your website—such as its font, line height, and text alignment—no matter whether someone prints it or views it on-screen. You can create two additional style sheets from this basic one, one specifically designed for print, the other for monitors.

NOTE When you use CSS Designer to add a style sheet to the Sources section and to set a media type, Dreamweaver doesn't give you "all" as an option, because it's the same as not specifying a media type. However, if you write the code by hand in Source Code view, you'll see a code hint listing "all" as well as a ream of other media options.

Previewing Media Styles in Dreamweaver

Web designers use Dreamweaver mainly to create pages that people view on-screen. Because of that, the program displays formatted pages only when you either haven't selected a media type at all or when you specify the "all" or "screen" type. So how can you see what a printed version of the page will look like when you design a print style sheet? Use the View→Style Rendering→Design Time options shown in Figure 9-16.

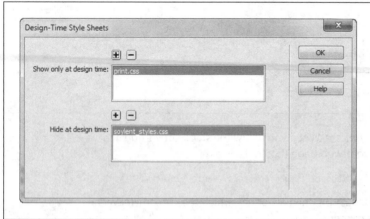

FIGURE 9-16

The Design-Time Style Sheets dialog box lets you pick and choose which styles Dreamweaver should apply as you work. This gives you a way to view your "print" media styles and turn off the "screen" styles that format your page for a computer monitor.

NOTE If you're in Live view, the Style Rendering toolbar has no effect. In Live view, Dreamweaver only displays what the page will look like in a web browser.

To see the effect your print style sheet has on your document, you want to use its styles. At the same time, you want to turn off the styles used to display the document on-screen. That's exactly what you can do in the Design-Time Style Sheets box (Figure 9-16). Click the + button above "Show only at design time," and then navigate to your print style sheet. To temporarily hide the screen styles, add the name of that style sheet to the "Hide at design time" list. After you click OK, you'll see the formatting as advertised. Keep in mind that you can add as many style sheets as necessary to the show and hide lists. For example, if your web page uses more than one style sheet for the screen, you'll want to hide them all to see the printed view. For more details on the uses of Design Time Style Sheets, see the box on page 397.

NOTE If your CSS styles don't seem to have any effect on a page, you might have turned them off. Make sure that you turn on the View→Style Rendering→Display Styles checkbox or you won't see any CSS styling.

Tips for Printer Style Sheets

A printer style sheet can redefine the look of any element on a page when you print that page. You can change fonts, adjust type size, increase the leading (space) between lines of text, and so on. You can use any CSS property you want, and modify any style to your liking, but there are a few common tasks that most printer style sheets perform.

- **Override properties from another style sheet.** If you attach an external style sheet with the "all" media type or you didn't specify any media type at all, the printed page uses styles from that style sheet. When you create the print style sheet, you may need to override some of the settings in the web page's style sheet. The best way to do this is to simply create styles with names that match the styles you wish to override. For example, if a style sheet attached to a page has a *p* tag style that specifies a font size of 12 pixels, you can create another *p* tag style in the print style sheet that changes the font size to 12 points. (Due to the rules of the cascade [page 384], the printer style sheet needs to be attached *last* to the web page for its styles to overrule similarly named styles in another sheet.)

  Another solution is to simply create two style sheets—one for print and one for monitors—and attach each with its respective media type. This way, there won't be any overlap between styles in the two sheets.

- **Text size and color.** You size text that appears on-screen using pixels, ems, or percentages (see page 136). Unfortunately, these units of measure don't make a lot of sense to an inkjet printer. If you've ever used Microsoft Word, you know the measurement of choice for printed text is points. If you don't like the size of type when you print a page, redefine font sizes using a printer-friendly size.

In addition, while bright yellow type on a black background may look cool on-screen, black type on white paper is the easiest to read. If you colored your text, it may print out as a shade of gray on a black-and-white printer. Setting text to black in a print style sheet can help your visitors' weary eyes.

- **Hide unnecessary page elements.** Guests don't really need to (and often times don't want to) print some parts of a web page (a navigation menu or a sidebar of links, for example). After all, you can't click them! Fortunately, CSS provides a property that lets you hide unwanted page elements on printed pages. Just create a style that applies to the part of the page you want to hide—for instance, with CSS-based layouts, you typically divide a page into sections using <div> tags, each with its own unique ID. Say you have the site's navigation bar inside a tag that has a class named *.navbar* attached to it. To hide the nav bar when someone prints the page, create another class style named *.navbar* in your print style sheet. In the CSS Rule Definition window, click the Block category and then choose None from the Display property menu. (In Figure 9-14, right, for example, the banner and both sidebars don't appear in the printed version of the page.)

- **Adjust margins and widths.** To make a website look more elegant, you might increase the margins around the edges of a page. But this extra space only wastes paper when printed. In the print style sheet, remove any margins you applied to the body tag. In addition, if you hide parts of a page when you print it, the remaining page elements may not fill the printed page. In that case, add a style to the style sheet that changes the widths of the printed elements. For example, if you have a two-column design—a sidebar with links and other site-specific info, and a main column filled with all the useful info that should appear on a printed page—and you hide one column (the sidebar), you'd then set the width of the remaining column to 100% and remove any margins on its left and right sides. That way, the printed information fills the width of the page.

- **Take advantage of *!important*.** Sometimes the print style sheet needs to over-ride certain CSS properties from another style sheet. Thanks to the cascade (page 384), a style must have greater "specificity" to overrule another style. If you're trying to override, say, the font color used for a descendent selector named *body #wrapper #maincontent p*, you have to add the same long-winded style name to your print style sheet. Fortunately, CSS provides a simpler method: the *!important* directive. Adding *!important* to a property in a CSS style lets that property overrule any conflicting property values from other styles, even if those other styles are more specific.

Unfortunately, Dreamweaver doesn't give you a way to easily add this option. You have to manually edit the style sheet in Code view. Say you want the text of all paragraph tags to print black. Create a *p* tag style in the print style sheet and set the *color* property to black. Then open the print style sheet in Code view and add *!important* after the color value and before the semicolon. Here's what that would look like in Code view:

```
p {
    color: #000000 !important;
}
```

When you print the page, this style overrides any color settings for any paragraph tags in a competing style sheet—even a much more specific style.

A Time to Design

A Dreamweaver feature called *Design Time style sheets* lets you quickly try different CSS style sheets as you develop web pages. With it, you can hide external style sheets you've attached to a web page and substitute new ones.

Design Time style sheets come in handy when you work on HTML that, later on, you intend to make part of a complete web page. Dreamweaver Library items are a good example; this feature (discussed in Chapter 19) lets you create a chunk of HTML that any number of pages on your site can use. When you update the Library item, Dreamweaver updates every page that uses it. A timesaving feature, for sure, but since a Library item is only *part* of a page, it doesn't include the <head> portion needed to either store styles or attach an external style sheet. So when you design a Library item, you're working in the dark (or at least without any style). By using Design Time style sheets, you can access all the styles in an external style sheet and even preview the effects directly in Design view.

You can apply a Design Time style sheet by clicking the Design Time style sheet button in the Style Rendering toolbar (see Figure 9-16) or by choosing Format→CSS Styles→Design-Time.

The Design Time Style Sheets window appears. Click the top + button to select an external style sheet. Note that clicking this button doesn't attach the style sheet to the page,; it merely lets you access the properties of a .css file as you work on a page.

To properly view your page with this new style sheet, you may need to get an attached external style sheet out of the way. To do that, use the bottom + button to add it to the Hide list.

You can only use Design Time style sheets when you work in Dreamweaver. They have no effect on how a page looks in a web browser. That's both the good news and the bad news. Although Dreamweaver lets you apply class styles from a Design Time style sheet to your web page, it doesn't actually attach the sheet to the page. For example, if you use a Design Time style sheet to design a Library item, Dreamweaver doesn't guarantee that the web page using the item has the style sheet you're using attached to it. You have to attach the sheet yourself, or your visitors will never see your intended result.

■ CSS Transitions

In Chapter 4 you learned about the *:hover* pseudo-class, which lets you change the style of a link as a visitor mouses over it. For example, the background color of a link in a navigation bar might be deep blue, but when you mouse over the link, the background changes to bright orange. That change, from blue to orange, occurs instantaneously, but it might feel a bit abrupt to some. What if you could animate the change so that the link starts out blue and then morphs, moving through a range of colors on the way to turning solid orange. When you take your mouse off the link, the color would go from orange to blue. Now *that* would be cool...and, thanks to CSS3's new CSS Transitions property, it's easy to achieve.

In a nutshell, a CSS transition is an animation between one or more CSS properties to another set of CSS properties. Web browsers handle the animation. You only need to supply the starting point (the blue background of a link, for instance) and the ending point (the orange background). You also need to add the CSS Transition property, which, unfortunately, requires a fair amount of code. However, Dreamweaver CC provides a simple, straightforward tool for creating that code: the new CSS Transitions panel. Here's how you use it:

> **NOTE** CSS transitions are fun and look great, but they're relatively new, so not all browsers support them. While Safari, Firefox, and Chrome understand CSS transitions, only version 10+ of Internet Explorer does. That means that about half of the web-surfing world won't be able to enjoy your finely crafted CSS transitions...yet. But since CSS transitions are really just eye candy anyway, visitors coming to your site with IE 7, 8, or 9 won't know what they're missing.

1. **Create a style for an element on your page.**

   That element can be a class, ID, or tag, or any CSS selector style. The element's style represents the beginning of the animation, and you can set the style using a wide range of CSS properties, including *background-color; background-position* (page 242); *border-color* and *border-width* (page 56); *color* (page 138); *font-size* (page 141); *font-weight* (page 140); *margins* (page 439); *padding* (page 439); *width* and *height* (page 438); the left, top, bottom and right position settings (page 457); *word-spacing* (page 143); and more. (You can find a complete list of valid, animate-able properties at *http://tinyurl.com/dxjbdhd*, though not all browsers support all the properties.)

   If you're creating a style for a navigation button, for example, you could start with a simple class (*.nav*) that you apply to each link you want to animate. Or, if all the nav buttons are together inside a single <div> tag or unordered list, you could add a class name to the <div> or list tag (<ul class="nav">, for example), then use a descendent selector (discussed on page 370) like *.nav a* to style all the links.

2. **Choose Window→CSS Transitions to open the CSS Transitions panel (see Figure 9-17).**

   The CSS Transitions panel lists any CSS transitions already applied to the page. You can use the panel to add new transitions or edit or delete existing ones.

> **TIP** If you use either the Compact or Expanded workspace, you'll find CSS Transitions sharing space with CSS Designer.

3. **Click the New Transition button (the + icon).**

   The New Transition window opens (see Figure 9-18).

Create new transition

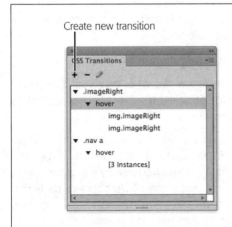

FIGURE 9-17

The CSS Transitions panel lets you add, edit, and delete animations between CSS properties. It lists all the CSS transitions defined in the style sheet(s) for the currently open web page.

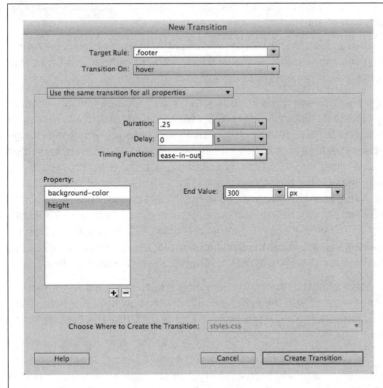

FIGURE 9-18

The New Transition window looks a bit overwhelming at first, but it's really an easy way to create a CSS transition: Identify a page element you want to animate using the Target Rule drop-down menu, specify a trigger for the animation (the "Transition on" option), choose a CSS property you want to animate, and then set some timing options.

4. From the Target Rule menu, select the style you created in step 1.

This menu lists all the styles in the page's style sheet, including class, ID, and tag styles. It also lists any IDs applied to page elements, even if you never created an accompanying ID style, which comes in handy if you simply want to animate an element without first creating an ID style for it.

5. From the Transition On menu, select the animation's trigger.

Unfortunately, you can't just animate an element whenever you like—you're limited to a handful of events related to CSS selectors. The *:hover* pseudo-class is the most well-known, but there are others you can tap into:

- *active* refers to the moment you click a link. It's the same as the *:active* pseudo-class discussed on page 187. Browsers also apply an active state any time you click an element and hold the mouse button down. In other words, you could create a CSS animation so that when a visitor clicks a particular <div> element and holds his mouse button down, that <div>'s background color changes, its width increases, and its font size grows.

- *checked* applies to checkboxes (page 637) and radio buttons. However, there aren't a lot of CSS properties that apply to checkboxes and radio buttons that are worth animating.

- *disabled* and *enabled* apply to form elements visitors can't select or change. Since you can't disable or enable a form element without JavaScript, you probably won't ever need to use either of these settings.

- *focus* refers to text fields in web forms. When a visitor either clicks into or tabs to a text field, that field receives what's called "focus." You can apply a separate set of styles to a field when it's focused and animate the change between the look of the field as it normally appears and as it appears when a guest clicks into it to type. For example, you could set the height of a multi-line text field (also called a *textarea*, as described on page 632) to 100 pixels, and then create a CSS transition that changes the field's height to 500 pixels. When a visitor clicks into that text box, it grows to 500 pixels high, and when she tabs or clicks out of the box, it shrinks back to 100 pixels. Likewise, you could set the background color of a text field to white, but when a visitor clicks into it, the background slowly changes to bright yellow.

- *hover* is the most commonly used option. It applies when a visitor mouses over an element. While you'll commonly use the hover transition with links, you can apply it to any page element: paragraphs, div tags, headlines, and so on.

- You probably won't ever use the *indeterminate* setting. It applies only to checkboxes and radio buttons, and refers to a checkbox or radio button that is neither turned on or off. Sounds very Zen, but it's also very useless. You can only specify the *indeterminate* setting using JavaScript, and since you probably won't ever need to use the state, there's no need to create an animation for it, either.

- *target* applies to named anchors, described on page 179, and it applies when a visitor clicks a link that jumps to that anchor. For example, say you add a link at the top of a page that jumps down the page to a named anchor. You could add a background color and a CSS transition to that named anchor so that when a visitor clicks the link and jumps to that spot on the page, the color fades into view.

NOTE For some ideas on what you can do with the CSS *:target* pseudo-class, check out *http://tinyurl.com/6mxqbz7* and *http://css-tricks.com/on-target/*.

6. **Choose either "Use the same transition for all properties" or "Use a different transition for each property."**

   As you'll see in steps 7–9, you can set a duration for the animation (how long it takes), a delay (how long before it begins), and a "timing function" (the rate of change during the animation). You can apply the same settings to all CSS properties or set different timings for each property. For example, if, when a visitor mouses over a navigation button, you want that button to change from blue to orange, have its text grow from 16 to 25 pixels, and enlarge its border from 1 pixel to 10 pixels in width, you have a choice. You can have all three animations occur at the same rate, or set different rates for each. For example, you could have the background color change quickly, make the border change more slowly, and wait for a second before the text increases in size. To create these transitions, you'd choose "Use a different transition for each property."

   Depending on which selection you make, the next steps will vary. If you selected the "Use the same transition" option, continue to the next step. If you selected "Use a different transition," skip to steps 10 and 11 to add a CSS property to animate, and then jump back to steps 7–9 to set the duration, delay, and timing function for that property.

7. **Type a number in the Duration box and select either "s" (for seconds) or "ms" (for milliseconds) from the menu to the right.**

   The duration specifies how long the animation takes. While it may seem cool to slowly change the background color over the course of 10 seconds, most web surfers are impatient and don't want to wait to savor your carefully choreographed animation. A good value is .25 seconds (250 milliseconds)—that speed is fast enough for anxious visitors, but slow enough so they can see it. However, you may want to try .5 seconds (500 milliseconds) or longer to see how the effect looks.

   As mentioned in step 6, you can set different timings for each property, so you might want one animation to happen really quickly (like a change in the text size), but another (like a change in background color) to happen more slowly.

NOTE Don't leave the Duration box blank. Otherwise, the transition takes place immediately, with no animation.

8. **Type a number in the Delay box and select either "s" (for seconds) or "ms" (for milliseconds) from the menu to the right.**

   The delay value indicates how long the browser should wait before starting the animation. In general, it's best to type 0, since waiting for any significant amount of time before starting the animation might confuse visitors. In addition, an animated transition reverses itself the moment the "trigger" stops: In other words, if a visitor mouses over a link, the animation begins, but when he moves the mouse off the link, the animation stops (even if the animation hasn't ended) and goes back to the original CSS property. If you add a long delay, your visitors may never see the animation.

9. **Choose an animation speed from the Timing Function drop-down menu.**

   While the duration setting indicates how long the animation takes from start to finish, the timing function (also known as an "easing" function) controls the rate of change in an animation. Normally, a CSS transition doesn't progress at the same speed for the entire animation. That is, if you're changing the background of a link from blue to orange, the background color will start moving toward orange slowly at first; more quickly in the middle, reaching a more orangish color rapidly; and then slowly turning solid orange at the end. Different timing functions specify different rates of change. You can get some interesting and more "natural"-looking animations with different options:

   • The cubic Bezier setting is the most complex. It requires four numbers that plot four "control points" along a line. Each point is a number from 0 to 1. In reality, all the timing functions follow what's called a Bezier curve that plots the amount of visual change over time (if you've worked with a drawing program like Photoshop Elements, you've probably used Bezier "handles" to add curves to lines). The math isn't worth explaining (that's just our way of saying it's too confusing even for us), so you're better off using an online tool to create and test different settings. The "CSS cubic-bezier Builder" tool at *http://tinyurl.com/bljzsxl* is particularly good. It lets you drag the control handles around and test how the animation changes over time. Once you find a curve you like, note the four numbers listed beside "cubic-bezier" (for example, "cubic-bezier(.17, 1, .78, .42)") and then type them into the Timing Function box.

   • The Ease option is the normal way a transition animates: slowly at first, rapidly in the middle, and then slowly at the end.

   • The Ease-In setting begins slowly at first, then picks up speed to finish the animation rapidly.

   • The Ease-In-Out option begins very slowly, proceeds very rapidly in the middle, and ends very slowly.

- The Ease-Out option begins very quickly, and then ends slowly.

- The Linear option provides a smooth animation, where every step in the show represents the same amount of progress. There's a reason that this setting isn't the default for animations...it's just boring.

> **TIP** The best way to pick a timing function is to simply experiment. Try different settings and see which you like best. You can always go back and edit the setting, as described in Figure 9-19.

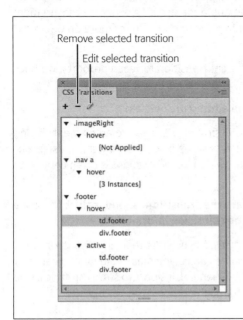

Remove selected transition

Edit selected transition

FIGURE 9-19

To edit a transition, select the triggering event (hover, active, and so on) in the CSS Transitions panel, and then click the edit button. Deleting a transition is a bit more complicated, as explained next.

10. **From the Property menu (Figure 9-18) pick the CSS Property you want to animate.**

While the list is very long, there are a few properties that work particularly well. Any property that uses color, like the *background-color, border-color*, and *color*, are good candidates; positioning properties like *left, right, top,* and *bottom* (used with absolutely positioned elements, described in Chapter 9) also look great when animated, as do the *width* and *height* properties. Some animated properties don't look very good or don't work at all in most browsers. For example, while Chrome can animate a change in *background-image*, no other browser can, and animating *font-weight* (from normal to bold, for example) doesn't work in any browser.

You should select a CSS property you specified in the original selector, the property you chose for step 4. For example, if you want to animate the background color of an element, make sure you first give the element a background color before you add a CSS transition to it. While it's possible to animate a property without first adding that property to the beginning style (the Target selector), it sometimes produces weird results.

11. **Set the value for the property in the End Value box.**

What you add to this box depends on what property you selected in the previous step. If you picked *background-color*, for example, Dreamweaver displays a color picker box; either select a color from it or type a color value into the box (see page 138 for more on CSS colors). If you picked a property that requires a numeric value, like *width, height, margin-left*, and so on, Dreamweaver displays two options: a box to enter a value and a menu for selecting a measurement unit, like pixels (px), ems, or percentages (see page 136 for more on CSS measurement units).

If, in step 6, you chose to set a different transition for each property, go back to steps 7–9 to set the timing options for this particular property.

12. **Repeat steps 10 and 11 to continue adding properties.**

You don't need to animate every CSS property applied to an element. Trying to add too many visual changes not only slows down the browser, it also probably distracts your audience. One or two animated changes is often enough to capture people's attention.

13. **From the "Choose Where to Create the Transition" menu, select the style sheet to which you want to add the transition information.**

CSS transitions are really just CSS styles, so you store them in either an internal or external style sheet. This is the same choice you make when you create any CSS style, as described on page 107. In general, it's best to store the style in the same external style sheet you use for all the other styles in your site.

14. **Click Create Transition.**

Dreamweaver closes the New Transition window, adds the required CSS to the page's style sheet, and lists the animation in the CSS Transitions panel (see Figure 9-19).

> **NOTE** If you choose to create a CSS transition using a class style as the target (step 4 on page 400), Dreamweaver adds the class name to the HTML element currently selected (or where your cursor is currently positioned). This can be a bit disorienting since, if you aren't paying attention and simply create a CSS transition, Dreamweaver will apply that class to the current element, possibly significantly altering the look of that tag. The solution is to remove the unwanted class from the tag (see page 119). That doesn't remove the CSS transition, so it will still work for the elements you intended.

Understanding the CSS Transitions Panel

Dreamweaver's CSS Transitions panel isn't really intuitive. You have to specify three components for each transition you want to animate: the target selector, the triggering event, and a list of matched elements. On the far left are the CSS selectors—they represent the selectors the transition targets, and they're the same as the targets you selected in step 4 on page 400, when you created the transition. For example, in Figure 9-19 you can see *.imageRight, .nav a,* and *.footer.* Those represent three selectors: two class selectors and a descendent selector (*.nav a*), which targets links inside another element that has the class *.nav* applied to it.

Next, the action that triggers the transition appears indented underneath each selector. For example, the *.imageRight* class has a hover transition, as do all the links inside another page element that have the class *.nav* applied to it.

You can have more than one trigger listed for a target. For example, you could create one transition that appears when a visitor mouses over an element, say a link, and a different transition when he clicks the link (or makes it active): That's the case for the *.footer* element in Figure 9-19.

Dreamweaver lists (and indents) the elements that match the target selector below the trigger event. While the list of target selectors and triggers are defined in the style sheet the page uses, the elements list is specific to each page. For example, in Figure 9-19, Dreamweaver lists the hover transition for the *.imageRight* class selector as "[Not Applied]." That means that Dreamweaver won't apply the transition to any element on the page because no HTML tag has the *.imageRight* class applied to it; there may be a tag with that class on another page that uses the same style sheet, but not on this page.

The same transition may also apply to more than one element on a page. This is common when you apply a CSS transition to each button in a navigation bar. In Figure 9-19, for example, the panel states that there are "[3 instances]" of the button transition on the page, meaning three links on this page use the same transition. Likewise, you see *td.footer* and *div.footer* listed under both the active and hover triggers of the *.footer* selector. That means there's one <td> tag and one <div> tag with the *.footer* class applied to it, and both of these elements have a CSS transition for hover and active states. If you apply the *.footer* class to additional elements on the page, Dreamweaver lists those as well.

Deleting a CSS Transition

Deleting a CSS transition is more complicated than you might think. As discussed in the box on page 408, Dreamweaver acts on two styles each time you add a transition: the initial target selector (the style before the animation begins) and the finished state (a pseudo-class like *:hover* or *:active* [see page 187]). So when you delete a CSS transition, Dreamweaver can immediately tell which styles you wish to edit.

To remove a CSS transition:

1. **Select the target selector (for example, *.imageRight, .nav a,* or *.footer*) and click the minus-sign icon (a.k.a. the Remove Transition button).**

   Dreamweaver opens the Remove Transition window (Figure 9-20).

   If you have more than one trigger event (like hover and active triggers) on the same element, you can select the trigger to remove just that transition (the one for the element's active state, for instance), and leave the other one alone (the hover transition, for example). If there are two trigger events and you choose the target selector, you can delete all the transitions for that selector.

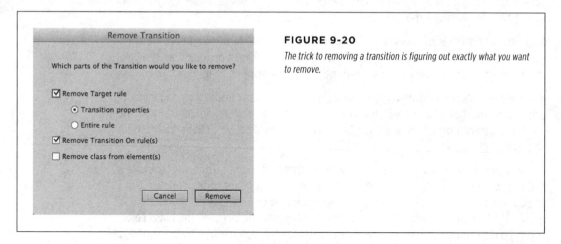

FIGURE 9-20

The trick to removing a transition is figuring out exactly what you want to remove.

2. **In the Remove Transition window, turn on the checkboxes that tell Dreamweaver what you'd like to remove.**

   Here's the confusing part about deleting a transition. Dreamweaver gives you several options, which have different effects.

   • The Remove Target rule option relates to the style that controls the appearance of the target element—that is, the style that defines the look of the element before the transition begins. As mentioned in the box on page 408, that initial style also contains the CSS transition property—the CSS property that tells a web browser that you want to animate a change in the CSS.

   • Choose the "Transition properties" radio button if you simply want to remove the CSS transition property but leave the rest of the style untouched. You'll usually select this option, since the style will also contain properties you'd like to preserve, like the *font, font-size, background-color, margin,* and *padding* properties. But if you *really* want to remove a style, formatting and all, turn on the "Entire rule" radio button. Just keep in mind that this removes all the formatting applied by that style to the target element.

   • Turn on the Remove Transition On rule(s) checkbox to delete the pseudo-class style (*:hover, :active,* and so on) that Dreamweaver added to your style sheet. This removes the end result of the animation—the style that formats the element when a visitor interacts with it (by hovering over the element, for example). Leave this checkbox turned off if you simply want to remove the animation. For example, you may find that you like the abrupt change in background when a visitor mouses over a link and you prefer to not have that change animated. If that's the case, turn on the "Remove Target rule" checkbox, and select the "Transition properties" button, but leave the

"Remove Transition On rule(s)" and the "Remove class from element(s)" checkboxes turned off.

- The "Remove class from element(s)" checkbox appears only if you apply a transition to a class selector (*.imageRight*, for example). Turning on this checkbox simply removes the class from any HTML tag on the page, so use this checkbox when you want to completely remove all traces of a transition, including the styles and classes used in it. However, if you're keeping the initial class style and its formatting (but not its transition properties), don't turn on this checkbox—that way, you'll leave the class on the HTML tag, and the remaining styling information will still apply to that element.

So, in a nutshell, if all you want to do is remove an animation, turn on the "Remove Target rule" checkbox, turn on the "Transition properties" radio button, and leave all the other checkboxes turned off. If you want to erase everything Dreamweaver added, turn on the "Remove Target rule" checkbox, select the "Transition properties" button, and turn on the "Remove Transition On rule(s)" checkbox.

3. **Click Remove.**

The Remove Transition window closes and Dreamweaver makes the requested changes, altering styles and the HTML where needed. Because Dreamweaver might make several changes at this point, you can't simply choose Edit→Undo to reverse the Remove Transition action, so be careful when you delete a transition.

Another Way to Create CSS Transitions

Dreamweaver CC offers yet another way to create CSS transitions, though this method requires that you know how CSS transitions really work (to find out, read the box on page 408). To animate CSS transitions, you use the CSS3 Transition property. Dreamweaver CC lets you add that property when you create a style using the CSS Rule Definition window (see Figure 9-21).

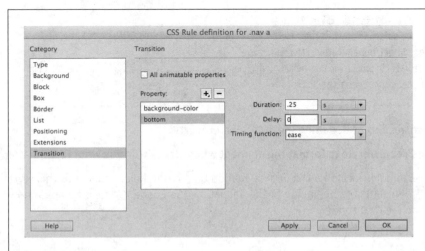

FIGURE 9-21

You can use the CSS Rule Definition window to add a CSS transition property to any element. You'll also need to create another style that triggers the transition, like a :hover pseudo-class style.

Behind the Scenes of CSS Transitions

Dreamweaver CC's CSS Transitions panel makes it easy to create complex animated transitions. Behind the scenes, however, Dreamweaver generates quite a bit of CSS. As you've read, a CSS transition is an animation between changes in CSS properties. You define those properties in two separate styles. The first defines the beginning of the animation, and the second specifies the final set of properties at the end of the animation. For example, creating a style for the <a> tag sets the style for links on a page, while an *a:hover* style sets the appearance of links when a visitor mouses over them.

When you create a CSS transition and set the Transition On property to "hover" (see step 5 on page 400), Dreamweaver creates a new style with the *:hover* pseudo-class for whatever selector you chose in step 4 on page 400. For example, say you had an image on the page with the class *.imgBorder* applied to it. You want to add a cool animation that changes the image's border color when a visitor mouses over the pic. By following the steps on page 398, you add a new CSS transition. Dreamweaver creates a new style named *.imgBorder:hover* with the new border color you specified. The CSS for that would look something like this:

```
.imgBorder:hover {
    border-color: #457348;
}
```

By itself, this new rule doesn't have any special CSS transition magic. It simply changes the border color when someone mouses over that image. To get the animation effect, Dreamweaver has to add another CSS property to the original style—in this example, to the *.imgBorder* class style. That's

how CSS transitions work: You add the transition property to the starting point for the animation; that is, to the style that formats the element when the page first loads. That way, a web browser knows that it needs to animate the changes from this style to the *:hover* style.

Unfortunately, because the transition property hasn't yet been finalized by the W3C (the group that determines how CSS works), each browser requires its own special version of the transition property, which Dreamweaver precedes with a special prefix: -ms for Internet Explorer, -webkit (Safari and Chrome), -moz (Firefox), and -o (Opera). That means that to add a CSS transition, Dreamweaver actually has to write five lines of CSS, not just one:

```
.imgBorder {
    border: 10px solid #758837;
    -webkit-transition: border-color .5s
ease-out;
    -moz-transition: border-color .5s ease-
out;
    -ms-transition: border-color .5s ease-
out;
    -o-transition: border-color .5s ease-
out;
    transition: border-color .5s ease-out;
}
```

Thankfully, Dreamweaver takes care of all this coding for you.

To create a transition using the Transition property:

1. **Create a style to format the element whose transition you want to animate.**

   Examples include a link in a navigation bar, a form field, and so on. This style represents the beginning of the animation. (See page 104 for a recap on how to create a style.)

2. **Open the Rule Definition window for that style by choosing, from the Properties panel below the document window, CSS→Edit Rule. Then, click the Transition category.**

   The Transition category is at the bottom of the list of categories on the left side of the Rule Definition window.

3. **Choose which property you want to animate by turning off the "All animatable properties" checkbox, clicking the + button, and then selecting a CSS property (like *background-color* or *height*).**

   Of course, instead of picking a property to animate, you can leave the "All animatable properties" checkbox turned on. This tells a browser to animate any changes in style properties. This may be what you're after, but in many cases you'll only want to change one property. For example, say you have a link with a background color, a font color, and a 1-pixel border. You then create a *:hover* pseudo-class style that sets different background and font colors and a different size border. If you want the browser to animate both color and border changes, you'd leave the "All animatable properties" box turned on. But if you want to animate only the background color, you'd turn off the "All animatable" checkbox, click the + button, and then select *background-color* from the menu.

4. **Type a duration and delay amount, and then pick a timing function.**

   These settings are described in steps 7–9 on pages 401–402.

5. **Repeat steps 3–4 above to add more CSS properties, and then click OK to complete the style.**

   Dreamweaver writes the necessary CSS code to add a transition to the style—but you're not done yet. Dreamweaver won't animate anything until you also add a style that defines the formatting for the end of the transition. Dreamweaver's New Transition window (Figure 9-18) handles this part automatically, but when you create a transition using the Rule Definition window, you need to define this style yourself.

6. **Click the New CSS Rule button on the CSS Styles panel.**

   The New CSS Rule window opens, ready for you to create a second style.

7. **In the New CSS Rule window, choose Compound from the Selector Type menu, and type a name with a pseudo-class in the Selector Name box.**

   Since CSS transitions only animate a change in styling, you must use one of the handful of CSS pseudo-classes that dynamically change an element. These include the same options mentioned in step 5 on page 400: *hover, active, focus, target, checked, disabled, enabled,* and *indeterminate. Hover* is the most common.

   The name of the selector should match the one for the style you created in step 1 above. Say, for example, the original style is for a descendent selector that targets all the links inside an element that has the class *.nav* applied to it. That style would be named *.nav a*. To create a style to format those links when the mouse hovers over them, you'd create a style named *.nav a:hover*. (Note that there's no space between the "a" and the ":hover.") To create a style for the active state of those same links, you'd name it *.nav a:active*.

8. **Add the properties you want using the Rule Definition window, and then click OK to complete the style.**

    Now you have two styles—the starting style that has the CSS transition property, and the hover (or active or focus, and so on) style. You're done!

Using CSS3

The Web continually evolves—not only do new websites appear (Facebook, YouTube, Twitter), but the fundamental technologies used to build websites change and grow. Web designers who used to use HTML tables to lay out pages, for instance, now use CSS. The web design world today is abuzz with the next incarnation of the CSS standard: CSS3. CSS3 offers amazing new design effects for websites, such as drop shadows for text or page elements, animated effects, rounded corners on images, gradient backgrounds, and more (see a list of the most popular CSS3 properties on page 412).

But there are drawbacks to CSS3. First, it's a work in progress; the W3C is still hammering out the list of CSS3 properties and how they work. As a result, browser support for CSS3 varies significantly. Internet Explorer 6 was created long before CSS3, and even Internet Explorer 9 doesn't understand many aspects of the standard. Some browsers don't support any of the properties proposed in CSS3. In addition, to get some CSS3 properties to work in the browsers that *do* support them, you have to use special "browser vendor prefixes." For example, here's the HTML to add a drop shadow to page elements (like a sidebar, div, or headline):

```
box-shadow: 2px 3px 4px #000;
```

But to get that box shadow in Safari and Chrome browsers, you have to write that same code like this:

```
-webkit-box-shadow: 2px 3px 4px #000;
```

And for Firefox, you'd write it like this:

```
-moz-box-shadow: 2px 3px 4px #000;
```

In other words, to add a drop shadow to an element, you have to write three lines of code, and even then it won't work in Internet Explorer 8 or earlier!

Because the CSS3 standard isn't complete and doesn't work universally across browsers, Dreamweaver doesn't support it in the same way that it supports the W3C-sanctioned CSS 2.1 standard. CSS 2.1 has wide support among browsers—even Internet Explorer 6 understands most of its properties—and Dreamweaver's CSS Rule Definition window reflects this. You can find most of the CSS 2.1 properties in that window, but you won't find many of the new CSS3 properties there. On the other hand, you'll find a slew of CSS3 properties in the new CSS Designer and, of course, in the CSS Transitions window. Web fonts covered back on page 128 are also part of CSS3.

TIP If you want to know which browsers support which CSS properties, visit the "When can I use…" website at *http://caniuse.com/*. It's an invaluable resource for web designers.

Code Hinting

Dreamweaver also includes CSS3 code hints. You read about code-hinting in Chapter 7, but in a nutshell, it's a helpful aid for designers who like to type their HTML, CSS, and JavaScript by hand. As you add CSS properties to a style sheet, Dreamweaver lists properties that match as you type away. For example, type *co* and Dreamweaver lists *color, column-count*, and other CSS properties that begin with *co*. In Figure 9-22, for instance, after typing *-webkit-*, Dreamweaver lists all WebKit-specific CSS3 properties. You can hit Return to accept Dreamweaver's suggestion, move to and select the property with your mouse, or use the up and down arrows on your keyboard to select the desired property. Unfortunately, code-hinting is really a power user's tool: You need to know how the CSS3 property works to correctly fill out the required value.

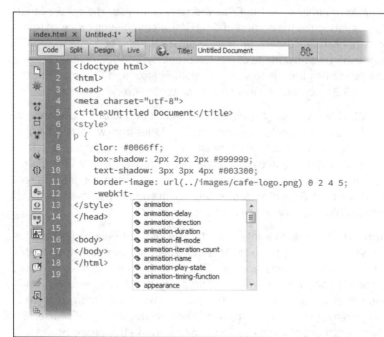

FIGURE 9-22

Dreamweaver's code-hinting feature is a time- and finger-saver. As you type a few letters of a CSS property, Dreamweaver opens a window that lists matching properties. You can select a property from the list and let Dreamweaver type the rest. This feature works with HTML tags and JavaScript programming as well.

Common CSS3 Properties

Although CSS3 is still in development, a range of browsers support a limited set of its properties. Many web designers have begun testing the CSS3 waters and include judicious amounts of CSS3 in their pages. Some of the most exciting (and supported) properties are:

- **Text-shadow.** Adds a drop shadow to headlines or any other text. Unfortunately, Internet Explorer before version 10 don't support this property, but it works in Safari, Firefox, Chrome, and Opera without a special vendor-specific prefix (like -webkit or -moz). You can use CSS Designer to add *text-shadow* to a style (see page 143). For more on the *text-shadow* property and a useful tool for previewing its effect, visit *http://tinyurl.com/cxxhavg*.

- **Box-shadow.** Adds a drop shadow to any HTML element, like a sidebar, banner, or any box on a page. You can even add a rectangular shadow around headlines and paragraphs of text. All major browsers (except IE 8 and earlier) support this property. Unfortunately, like many CSS3 properties, you'll need to use special prefixes to make this work in some browsers (for example, you need to specify *-webkit-box-shadow* instead of *box-shadow* for version 5 of Safari and early versions of Safari for iOS). Visit this useful tool for previewing box-shadow effects: *http://tinyurl.com/c2h2rrv*.

- **Border-radius.** If you've ever struggled trying to create rounded corners using multiple background images, this CSS3 property is for you. The *border-radius* property lets you round the corners of any HTML element—you can even round just one, two, or three corners, or provide different radii for each. Again, IE 8 and earlier can't take advantage of this fun property, and you need to provide additional properties for this to work in Safari, Firefox, and Chrome. Visit the Hands-On CSS Border Radius Generator at *http://tinyurl.com/bpkamka*.

- **Gradient.** CSS3 lets you add a gradient to the background of any element, so you could, for example, create a background that fades from white to dark gray without using graphics. You can create either linear (top to bottom or left to right) or radial gradients (circular from the center outward). Internet Explorer doesn't support this property, and the other major browsers require different property names for it. For a great tool to help you preview and write the required CSS, visit *http://www.colorzilla.com/gradient-editor/*.

- **Transforms.** Have you ever wanted to rotate an element on a page—perhaps make a <div> tag look like a piece of paper that's been set down askew on a table top? Well, even if you haven't, you can! Thanks to CSS3 you can rotate, skew, and scale an element with the Transform property. You'll need vendor-specific prefixes for Internet Explorer 9 (-ms-transform), Safari and Chrome (-webkit-transform), Firefox (-moz-transform), and Opera (-o-transform). Of course, IE 8 and earlier are left out of the party. To learn how to use this property and test it out, visit *http://tinyurl.com/d8dle98*.

■ Advanced CSS Tutorial

In this tutorial, you'll create a descendent selector, and use Dreamweaver CC's new CSS Transitions tool.

TIP You need to download files from *http://oreilly.com/missingmanuals/cds/dreamweaverccmm13/* to complete this tutorial. See the note on page 33 for details.

Once you download the tutorial files and open Dreamweaver, set up a new site as described on page 19. In a nutshell, choose Site→New Site. In the Site Setup window, type *Adv CSS Tutorial* into the Site Name field. Click the folder icon next to the Local Site Folder field, navigate to and select the Chapter09 folder inside the MM_DWCC folder, and then click Choose (Select). Finally, click OK.

Creating a Descendent Selector

Once again, you'll be working on a page for the good people who run *Cafe Soylent Green*.

1. **Choose File→Open.**

   You'll work on a page similar to the ones you built in Chapter 5.

2. **Navigate to the *Chapter09* folder and double-click the file *index.html*.**

   You can also double-click the *index.html* file in the Files panel to open it. You'll notice a simple navigation bar in the upper-right corner of the page. These links would look a lot better as buttons, so you'll add a style to make that happen.

3. **Make sure you have CSS Designer open (Window→CSS Designer). In the Sources section, click *soylent_style.css* and then, in the Selectors section, click the Add Selector button (the plus sign icon).**

   Dreamweaver creates a new selector and positions your cursor in the name text field. It also suggests a name, depending on where you had your cursor on the web page (see Figure 9-23).

   You follow the same process you do to create any style (see page 104 if you need a recap). You want to style these links (navigation links in this example), but creating an <a> tag style would affect every link on the page (in this case, the links at the bottom of the page, and those associated with the two images). A better option is a descendent selector that targets just the navigation links (About Us, Menu, and Home). In this case, the links are actually bulleted list items that have a bit of styling already. The outer <ul> tag has a class applied to it: *<ul class="nav">*. This class name is all you need to create a style that affects just the links inside the bulleted list.

FIGURE 9-23

You can create any type of CSS selector, like the descendent selector .nav a pictured here, by clicking Add Selector and then typing a selector name. You use the same technique to create basic tag, class, and ID styles.

4. **In the name field for the new selector, type .nav a. The New CSS Rule window should look like the one in Figure 9-23.**

The selector you just typed—*.nav a*—is a descendent selector. The element on the far right of the selector, "a", is the target. The selector to the left, *.nav*, is an element that wraps around the <a> tag. Time to create the style.

5. **In CSS Designer's Properties section, make sure you have the Show Set box unchecked.**

If you have the Show Set box checked, Dreamweaver displays only the Properties whose values you've already set. In that case, if there are no rules for a property, you won't see it listed.

6. **With *soylent_styles.css* selected in the Sources section and *.nav a* selected in Selectors, in Properties, click the T button to display text properties. Then, next to the field for font-family name, choose pt-sans. Set font-weight to 700.**

   If you don't see pt-sans, you may not have installed it yet. This is a web font introduced in the Chapter 3 tutorial. You can either go back to page 147 and follow the instructions to install pt-sans, or select another font from the font-family list.

7. **In Properties, click the Background button, and then, beside background-color, click the value box to the right of the color swatch. Type in the hex color value #0A2F02.**

   The pound sign (#) tells Dreamweaver that the value is in hexadecimal format.

8. **Click the Layout button and scroll down to the display property. Using the drop-down menu, set the value to "inline-block."**

   The inline-block setting is useful if you want to add margins and padding to an inline element.

9. **Click the Border category button. Set border-style to solid. In border-width, choose px as the unit of measure and then type *1* in the value box. For border-color, type in #1C6300.**

   By choosing simply border-style and not specifying individual top, bottom, left, and right borders, CSS uses the border-style value for all the edges. This is true with the color and width, too. When you're done, you have a green border around all four sides of each link, creating a button-like box effect. Because the border lines will come very close to the link text, you'll add some padding to push the border away from the text.

10. **Click the Layout category, and then in Padding, type *3px* for the top and bottom values. Type *10px* for the left and right values. If you don't choose a unit of measure, CSS Designer automatically uses pixels (px).**

    The window should look like Figure 9-24. You're all done with this style.

11. **Click OK to complete the style and close the window.**

    Because the unordered list already had a *.nav* class applied to it, the styling you just created immediately appears on the links at the top of the page. Now it's time to add a CSS transition.

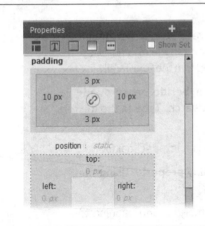

FIGURE 9-24

Whenever you add a border around an element that has text in it, it's usually a good idea to add some padding as well. Padding pushes the border away from the text so the text doesn't look cramped.

Adding a CSS Transition

CSS transitions are simple animations between two sets of CSS rules. Dreamweaver CC makes it easy to add these fun CSS3 effects.

1. **Choose Window→CSS Transitions.**

   Dreamweaver displays the CSS Transitions panel, which is probably sharing space with CSS Designer. If you want, you can drag it by its tab to create a floating panel or dock it someplace else in your workspace.

2. **Click the + icon (the Create New Transition button).**

   The New Transition window launches. You'll specify what element you wish to animate.

3. **From the Target Rule menu, select *.nav a*.**

   This menu lists all the CSS styles available to the page, as well as any IDs used in the page's HTML. In this case, you chose the descendent selector you just created since you want to add a transition to the navigation links.

4. **From the Transition On menu, select "hover."**

   While Dreamweaver gives you other options, many aren't useful. Hover is by far the most common option, as it animates an element's appearance when a visitor mouses over it.

5. **Make sure you have "Use the same transition for all properties" selected from the drop-down menu. Type *.25* in the Duration box, *0* in the Delay box, and choose ease-in-out from the Timing Function menu.**

This creates an animation that takes .25 seconds from start to finish, has no delay, and starts slowly, then changes rapidly, and then slows down as the .25 seconds comes to an end.

6. **Click the + button below the Property box, and choose background-color from the pop-up menu. Type *#E1EBEB* in the End Value box.**

   The window should now look like Figure 9-25. You're done.

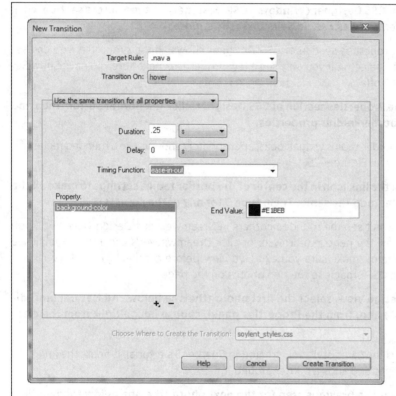

FIGURE 9-25

It's possible to animate each CSS property differently (choose "Use a different transitions for each property"). However, animating each property at a different rate, with a different delay and a different timing function, can result in a confusing animation.

7. **Click Create Transition to close the window and complete the transition.**

   Behind the scenes, Dreamweaver adds a new style, *.nav a:hover*, and the proper CSS transition code to the *.nav a* style. Time to check your work.

8. **Click the Live button in the Document toolbar to preview the transition. Mouse over the various links.**

   The background color gently fades into view when you mouse over a link, and fades out when you move your mouse out. If you don't see this effect, you may have accidentally selected a different transition trigger (like "active" or "focus" instead of "hover"). If that's the case, select the transition in the CSS Transitions panel and then click the minus-sign button to delete it.

9. **Click the Live button again to exit Live view.**

   Now you'll add a CSS3 property to the links.

Adding CSS3 Properties

You can add CSS3 properties to your web page using CSS Designer. But, keep in mind that you won't find many CSS3 properties in the Rule Definition window you access from the Properties panel's CSS mode.

1. **Open CSS Designer (Window→CSS Designer). In the Sources section, click *soylent_styles.css*. In Selectors, click *.nav a*.**

   The Properties section of CSS Designer shows all the properties you can set for the selector. If you only see a few properties, make sure you have Show Set turned off.

2. **In the Properties section of CSS Designer, click the Border button, then find the border-radius properties.**

   The border-radius widget looks, appropriately enough, like a rounded rectangle, as shown Figure 9-26.

3. **Click the link icon in the center of the border radius settings to make all the border radii the same. Then, type *3* for any of the corners.**

   You won't see the rounded corners in Dreamweaver's Design view, but if you preview the page in a browser or click Dreamweaver's Live button, you'll see the effect (make sure you exit Live view before continuing). Next, you'll add some CSS3 magic to the two photos on the page.

4. **In Design view, select the first photo (the one below "All Natural Ingredients") and, from the Properties panel, choose imageRight from the class menu.**

   This is the same style you created in Chapter 5's tutorial. It floats the image to the right and adds a border around it.

5. **Repeat the previous step for the next photo (the one below the headline "Technology Meets Good Nutrition").**

   Now you'll add another CSS3 property.

6. **In the Sources section of CSS Designer, click either *soylent_styles.css* or All Sources. Then, in the Selectors section, click .imageRight (it's near the bottom of the list). In Properties, scroll down until you see "opacity," and then type *.75* in the box to the right.**

   The opacity property controls the transparency of an element. You can use a value of between 0 and 1. Zero makes the element completely invisible, while 1 makes it completely opaque. A value in between, like the .75 here, lets a little bit of the background show through while still displaying the element. Why would you want to do this? So you could animate it with a CSS transition, of course!

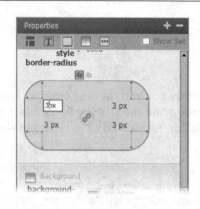

FIGURE 9-26

The CSS border-radius property adds rounded corners to elements. You can give all four corners the same radius (as in this case) by clicking the center link button before you set a value. If you want to create a completely rounded "box," use 50% for all four corners.

NOTE As with the *border-radius* property, you can't see the effect of the opacity property in Dreamweaver's Design view.

Adding One Last Transition

1. **Click to select one of the two images.**

   When you create a CSS transition from a class selector (the *.imageRight* style you applied in the previous step), Dreamweaver has the unfortunate habit of adding that class to whatever element is currently selected on the page. If you don't select one of the images, Dreamweaver ends up adding the *.imageRight* class to another element on the page, causing unwanted animation when someone mouses over that element.

2. **Open the CSS Transitions window (Window→CSS Transitions), and then click the New Transition button (the + icon).**

   You'll specify what element you want to animate.

3. **From the Target Rule menu, select .imageRight.**

   This is the class style where you just added the opacity property.

4. **From the Transition On menu, select "hover."**

   This time, you'll set different timings for two different CSS properties.

5. **Choose "Use a different transition for each property."**

   The window changes.

6. **Click the + button below the Property box, and choose "border-color" from the pop-up menu. Type *1* in the Duration box and *0* in the Delay box. Choose "ease-in-out" from the Timing function menu, and then type *#0A2F02* in the End Value box.**

This creates an animation that lasts 1 second (pretty long), gradually changing the border color around the image to dark green.

Now you'll add the opacity property.

7. **Click the + button below the Property box and choose "opacity" from the pop-up menu. Type *.5* in the Duration box and *0* in the Delay box. Choose "ease-out" from the Timing function menu, and then type *1* in the End Value box.**

The window should look like Figure 9-27. This animation makes the images appear vibrant and colorful when a mouse moves over them. Since it only takes half a second to complete, it will happen more quickly than the changing border color.

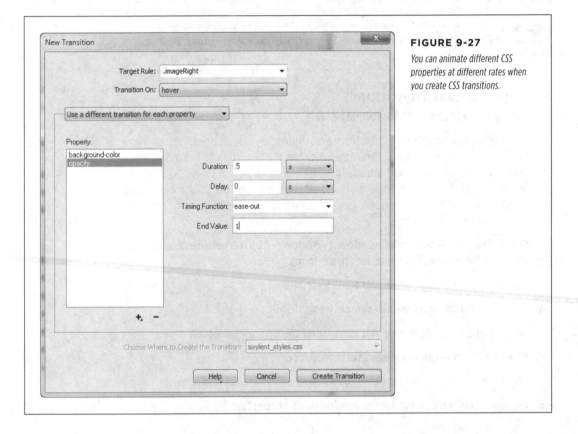

FIGURE 9-27

You can animate different CSS properties at different rates when you create CSS transitions.

8. **Click Create Transition to close the window and complete the transition.**

   Behind the scenes, Dreamweaver adds a new style, *.imageRight:hover*, and the proper CSS transition to the *.imageRight* style. Time to check out your work.

9. **Click the Live button in the Document toolbar. Mouse over the two photos.**

   The photos should pop vibrantly from the page, while the border will more slowly change to dark green (see Figure 9-28). You can find a completed version of this tutorial in the *Chapter09_complete* folder that accompanies the downloaded tutorial files.

FIGURE 9-28

You can enliven any web page by adding CSS transitions to links, navigation bars, and even images. In this example, a "soft" image becomes vibrant and its border slowly turns dark green when a visitor mouses over the picture. There's no need for JavaScript—just a little CSS3 magic. (Unfortunately, you'll find that these effects won't work in Internet Explorer 9 or earlier.)

Page Layout

Web design, unfortunately, isn't like most other forms of graphic composition. For magazine and book projects, software like InDesign lets you place text and images anywhere you want—and even rotate and overlap them. But web designers are stuck with the basic technology of HTML, which wants to flow from the top of a browser window to the bottom, in one long column. To place elements around the page and create multiple columns of content, you need to resort to some fancy footwork, and that's where this chapter comes in.

For much of the Web's short life, designers have used the HTML <table> tag to control the position of elements on a page—to create columns, sidebars, banners, and so on. But the <table> tag was intended to display information in a spreadsheet-like format, and bending it to a web designer's vision often resulted in complex HTML that downloaded slowly, displayed sluggishly, and challenged coders.

Now that CSS-friendly web browsers like Internet Explorer, Safari, Firefox, Chrome, and Opera rule the Web, designers can safely rely on a much better (though sometimes frustrating) method of page layout: Cascading Style Sheets. That's right, not only is CSS great for formatting text, navigation bars, images, and other bits of a web page, it also has all the tools you need to create sophisticated designs, like the ones shown in Figure 10-1.

CSS provides a couple of ways to control the placement of elements on a page. The most common is to create multiple-column layouts using the CSS Float property (the same property you used in Chapter 5 to position an image to the left or right of a page).

FIGURE 10-1

CSS Zen Garden (www.csszengarden.com) is the original showcase for CSS layout. Although the designs haven't been updated in a while, in its day it caused many a web designer to bow down and proclaim, "I'm not worthy, I'm not worthy." The site not only demonstrates great design, it shows you the power of CSS-based layout. Each page includes the same content and the same HTML. The only difference is their external style sheets and graphics. CSS lets you redesign sites without rewriting any HTML.

Dreamweaver includes a starter set of CSS layouts that use this float-based approach. These stock pages cover the most commonly used layouts—designs with two or three columns of content, a header for a logo and banner, and a footer for a copyright notice, for example. These files aren't complete page designs so much as basic web page building blocks you can modify to match your sensibility.

CSS also includes a Position property, which lets you place elements "absolutely"— that is, at a pixel-specific position on the page. While this might sound like the answer to page layout, absolute positioning has its own problems, and web designers usually don't use it for full page layout. Instead, they use it to accurately place small elements in a precise position on a page, or in conjunction with JavaScript to make elements pop onto the page above other page components—a menu bar (page 192), for example, may use absolute positioning to display the bar's drop-down menus over the page's underlying content.

NOTE CSS layout is one of those complex topics that is sometimes better learned by doing instead of reading. To get a taste of how CSS layout works, try the tutorial on page 470, then flip back to the beginning of this chapter for all the messy details.

This chapter introduces the basic concepts behind float-based layouts—what they are, how they work, and how to create one; it also provides instructions for modifying Dreamweaver's CSS designs. In addition, you'll learn about absolute positioning, and how to use it to place select elements where you want them.

This chapter introduces the basic concepts behind float-based layouts—what they are, how they work, and how you create them. It also shows you how to modify Dreamweaver's canned CSS Layouts, and how to absolutely position page elements so you can place them just where you want them.

■ Types of Web Page Layouts

Being a web designer means dealing with the unknown. What kind of browsers do your visitors use, will your design work in all of them, and so on. But perhaps the biggest challenge designers face is creating attractive designs that work across different size screens. Monitors vary in size and resolution, from petite 15-inch 640 x 480 pixel displays to 30-inch monstrosities displaying, oh, about 5 million x 4.3 million pixels. In addition, designers have to cope with the very small displays found on millions of cell phones and other mobile devices. (Chapter 12 has information on how to use CSS to create sites for tablets and smartphones.)

NOTE A new approach to web layout, called Responsive Web Design, uses a liquid layout and some fancy CSS to completely change a page's design at different screen sizes. That is, you can create one design for a phone, a different design for a tablet, and a third layout for desktop browsers. You'll learn about this technique, as well as the tools in Dreamweaver that let you build these kinds of layouts, in Chapter 12.

Float-based layouts offer two approaches to this problem: *fixed-width* and *liquid layouts* (the latter is also called *fluid layouts*). A fixed-width layout gives you the most control over your design but can inconvenience some of your visitors. Folks with really small monitors have to scroll to the right to see everything, and those with large monitors see wasted space that could display more of your excellent content. Liquid layouts make designing pages more challenging, but they also make the most of your guests' screen sizes.

- **Fixed-width layout.** Many designers prefer the consistency of a set width, like the page shown in Figure 10-2, top. Regardless of how wide a browser window is, the page content's width remains the same. In some cases, the design clings to the left edge of the browser window. More often, the content is centered. With the fixed-width approach, you don't have to worry about what happens to your design on a very wide (or very small) monitor.

  Fixed-width designs can range anywhere from 760 pixels wide to 1,000 pixels or more wide. These days, however, the screens on even tiny 10-inch netbooks or Apple iPads are at least 1,024 pixels wide, and all desktop computers support at least 1024 x 768 pixels, so most new sites use much bigger dimensions—960 pixels wide is now a common baseline for fixed-width designs, but you'll also see 1,000 pixels and even a bit more on some sites.

- **Liquid layout.** Sometimes, it's easier to roll with the tide instead of fighting it. A liquid design adjusts a page's dimensions to fit a browser's width—whatever that may be. Your page gets wider or narrower as your visitor resizes his browser window (Figure 10-2, bottom). While liquid design makes the best use of browser real estate, you have to do more work to make sure your design looks good at different window sizes. On very large monitors, these types of designs can look ridiculously wide.

  Fixed-width designs are probably the most common type of layout on the Web, since they provide a consistent display and make it much easier for designers to work with.

■ Float Layout Basics

Float-based layouts take advantage of the CSS *float* property to position elements side by side and create columns on a page. As you read on page 236, you can float an image to make text wrap around a photograph. But it's also a powerful layout tool that lets you move a bunch of related page elements (like a list of links you want to appear in a left-hand column) to one side of the page or the other. In essence, the *float* property moves a page element to the left or the right. Any HTML that appears *after* the floated element moves up on the page and hugs the side of the float.

Float is a CSS property, available when you create a CSS style (see page 104 for instructions on creating styles). You'll find it in CSS Designer's Layout category (see Figure 10-3). Choose the *left* option, and the styled element floats to the left; choose the *right* option, and the element moves to the right.

FIGURE 10-2

CSS gives you several ways to deal with the uncertain widths of browser windows and browser font sizes. You could simply ignore the fact that your site's visitors have different resolution monitors and force a single, unchanging width on them, as the Target.com website does. As you can see in the top two images, resizing the browser window doesn't change the page—it remains the same width (but centered in the browser window) when you make the browser window wider. Many websites take this approach. Alternatively, you could create a liquid design whose content flows to fill whatever width window your visitor uses. That's how Amazon's site works (bottom two images).

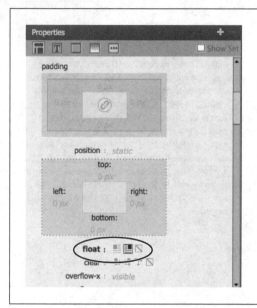

FIGURE 10-3

You have just three options when you float an element: left, right, and none. You might never need "none"—it simply positions the element as though it were a normal, unfloated element. Since this is the regular behavior of any element, you need this option only if you want to turn off a float applied by another style (see page 384 for more on how multiple styles can affect the same element).

The Mighty <div> Tag

Whatever layout method you use, web page design involves putting chunks of content into different regions of a page. With CSS, the most common way to organize content is with the <div> tag. The <div> tag is an HTML element that has no inherent formatting properties (besides the fact that browsers treat it as a block element, with a line break before and after it); you use the <div> tag to define a logical grouping of elements (a *division*) on a page, a chunk of HTML that belongs together.

For example, the elements comprising the logo and navigation bar in Figure 10-4 occupy the top of the page, so it makes sense to wrap a <div> tag around them (labeled "banner div" in the figure). At the very least, you would include <div> tags for all the major regions of your page, such as the banner, main content area, sidebar, footer, and so on. But it's also possible to wrap a <div> tag around one or more *other* divs. People often wrap all the HTML inside the <body> tag in a <div> tag. This tag, therefore, wraps around all the other divs on the page, and you can set some basic page properties by applying CSS to this *wrapper* div. For example, you can style a div to set the overall width for the page, set left and right margins, or center all the page's content in the middle of the screen.

Once you've got your <div> tags in place, you add either a class or ID style to each one so you can style each div separately. For the basic building blocks of a page, designers usually apply either an ID or a class selector (page 108) to the div. For example, the <div> tag for a page's banner area might be *<div id="banner">* or *<div class="banner">*.

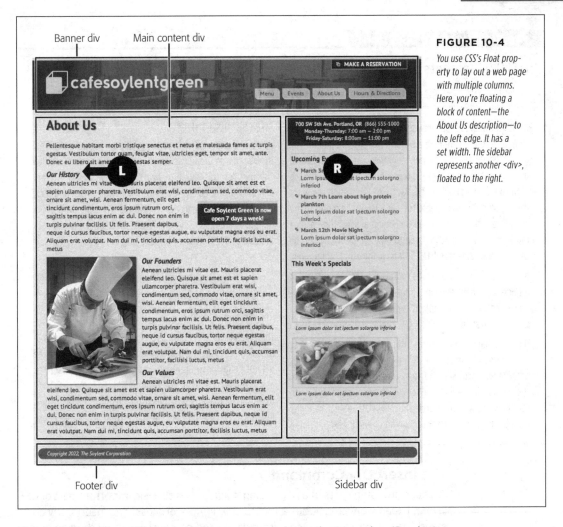

FIGURE 10-4

*You use CSS's Float prop-
erty to lay out a web page
with multiple columns.
Here, you're floating a
block of content—the
About Us description—to
the left edge. It has a
set width. The sidebar
represents another <div>,
floated to the right.*

There are only a few differences between using a class selector and an ID selector
to identify a region of a page. Recall that you can use an ID only once per page,
so if you have an element that appears multiple times, use a class selector instead.
For example, if you have several divs that position photos and their captions, you'd
add a class to each div rather than an ID, like this: *<div class="photoBox">*. Another
difference is that, in the case of a style conflict, ID selectors in CSS take precedence
over class selectors. For example, if you apply both an ID and a class selector to
the same <div> tag and then you create class and ID styles, any properties in the
ID style that conflict with those in the class style would win out. This is one of the
basic rules of the CSS cascade, described on page 384.

FREQUENTLY ASKED QUESTION

HTML5 Elements

I hear that HTML5 has lots of new elements that replace the <div> tag. Is the <div> tag still relevant?

HTML5 introduces many new tags to help organize web page content. These "sectioning elements" are intended to let you group specific types of content together. For example, you'd use the <header> tag to group content that appears at the top of the page (like a banner). The <section> tag sets off—wait for it—a "section" of your page. The <article> tag is for grouping all the tags that make up an individual article. The <aside> tag is for content that's related to other content and can be used to create sidebars. HTML5 offers many other tags as well.

Basically, you use these tags to group common sections of a page, and they're meant to take the place of the humble <div> tag for all the content types listed above (headers, articles, and so on).

However, the <div> tag works just as well as all those tags. In fact, there's nothing inherently different in how the new tags act in a web browser, and from a site visitor's perspective, there's no difference whatsoever. You can style divs with CSS the same way you'd style the new HTML5 tags. Then why the new tags? The HTML5 sectioning elements are intended

to help *computers* understand a page's structure better. For example, Google might look for an <article> tag in a page to better identify key content.

Internet Explorer 8 and earlier don't understand the new HTML5 tags, so Dreamweaver uses a standard solution called "html5shiv." This chunk of JavaScript code makes Internet Explorer 8 and earlier play well with the new <header>, <footer>, <article>, <section>, and <aside> tags. Dreamweaver's templates automatically add a line in the header of web pages to get the code necessary for IE to play well with HTML5:

```
<!--[if lt IE 9]>
<script src="http://html5shiv.googlecode.
com/svn/trunk/html5.js"></script>
<![endif]-->
```

That line tells the older browsers to get the JavaScript code from the googlecode archive. It works as long as JavaScript is on (the default behavior for Internet Explorer) and the browser has access to the Internet. If you want to add the same capability to web pages that aren't created from Dreamweaver templates, just copy that code into the <head> portion of the web page.

The Insert Div Command

Because grouping parts of a page using <div> tags is such an important part of CSS layout, Dreamweaver includes a tool to simplify the process. The Insert→Div command lets you wrap a <div> tag around selected content, or simply drop an empty div onto a page that you can fill with images, links, paragraphs of text, or whatever. In other words, the single command creates both the opening and closing tags for a Div element. They look like this:

```
<div>  </div>
```

To use this tool, either select the content you want to wrap (for example, click at the beginning of the selection and drag to the end of it) or click in the page where you wish to insert an empty div tags. Then choose Insert→Div, or better yet, use the Insert panel—the Div option appears at the top of both the Common and Structure categories (see Figure 10-5).

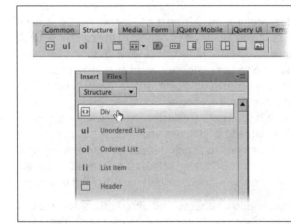

FIGURE 10-5

The Common and Structure category of the Insert panel includes a button that adds both the opening and closing <div> tags. In this figure, the top image shows the Insert bar displayed as a toolbar (learn how to do this on page 8), and the bottom image shows the Insert panel as Dreamweaver displays it by default.

In any case, the Insert Div window appears (Figure 10-6).

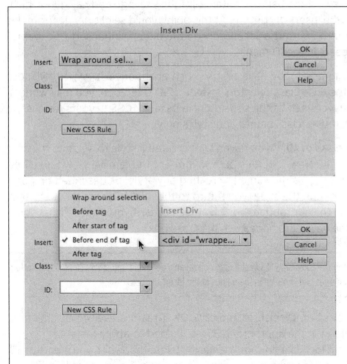

FIGURE 10-6

The Insert field of the Insert Div window (top) lets you tell Dreamweaver where to put a <div> tag in relation to other tags on a page (bottom). The Insert drop-down menu to the right of that lets you tell Dreamweaver where to put the <div>. That menu lists tags that have an ID applied to them, or, if you chose "After start of tag" or "Before end of tag," it lists the <body> tag. Suppose, for example, you want to insert a <div> tag to display a footer at the bottom of a page. Because you know the footer will go last on the page, you click the Insert Div button, select "Before end of tag" from the left menu, and then <body> from the right menu. Dreamweaver puts the <div> at the very end of the page's content, just before the closing </body> tag.

If you click OK, Dreamweaver wraps any content you selected in a <div> tag, or, if you didn't select anything on the page, it drops a new <div> tag onto the page with the text "Content for New Div Tag Goes Here" (of course, you'll replace that with your own content). But usually, you'll take an additional step, applying either a class or ID selector to the div. You do this a couple of ways:

- **Choose a class from the Class menu or an ID from the ID menu.** The Class menu on the Insert Div window lists all the class styles available to the current page. A class selector is the way to go if you want to format several divs the same way. For example, you might use a <div> tag to position an image and a caption on a page, or to create a pull-quote in the middle of an article. If you had multiple instances of photos with captions, you could create a class style (like *.figure*) to format each photo-caption pair. You could then select a photo and caption on the page, use the Insert Div command, and then select the class name (*.figure* in this example) from the Class menu. You could repeat this process multiple times on a single page. But you can also apply a class to a div even if you use that div for a unique set of elements—such as the banner at the top of a page.

  The ID menu on the Insert Div window behaves a bit differently. Since you can only use an ID once per page (see page 102 for the reason), the ID menu lists only those IDs that exist in your style sheet, and to which you haven't yet applied any tags. Say you create an ID style named *#banner* that you plan to apply to a <div> tag. You select the banner content (like the site logo and navigation bar), and then click the Insert Div button. At this point, you'd select *banner* from the ID menu. If you then insert a second div on the page using Insert Div, *banner* no longer appears in the ID menu.

  Since web designers today have pretty much abandoned ID styles for most uses (that is, they use class selectors instead of ID selectors), you may wonder how Dreamweaver itself handles selectors in its stock CSS Layouts (discussed on page 447). It uses class names and styles only.

- **Create a new class or ID.** If you haven't yet created a style to apply to the new <div> tag, click the New CSS Rule button. It opens the familiar New Style Rule window. The process is the same as creating any style, as described on page 104. Once you define the style, you return to the Insert Div window, and that style appears in the appropriate box (in other words, if you create a class style, the name of the new class appears in the Class box).

> **TIP** If you're more comfortable using CSS Designer, by all means, go ahead and create class or ID selectors there. Once you do, their names will show up in the menus in the Insert Div box.

After you apply a class or ID selector and click OK, Dreamweaver inserts the new <div> tag, complete with the appropriate HTML needed to apply the style. For example, that tag might look like *<div id="banner">*. (Note that when you create an ID style, you add a # sign—for example, *#banner*—but when Dreamweaver inserts the HTML for the ID name, it omits the # sign.) The same applies to class names: *<div class="photo">* is correct; *<div class=".photo">* is not. In addition, Dreamweaver applies any styling you create for the class or ID to the div. In the case of a CSS layout, that could mean sizing the div and positioning it on the page, as well as adding a background color, changing the size of the text, or any other CSS formatting. You can add new content inside the div, edit what's there, or delete the div completely.

NOTE CSS-based layout is a big topic, worthy of a book or two by itself. For more in-depth coverage, including solutions to common float problems, pick up a copy of *CSS3: The Missing Manual*.

A Simple Example

To get a better idea of how divs help with page layout, look at the layouts in Figure 10-7. This design has a banner (a logo and navigation bar), sidebar, and the main story. Figure 10-7 left, shows the order in which the HTML appears on the page: The banner elements come first, the sidebar second, and the main story (headlines, paragraphs, photo, and so on) last. (Remember, what you're seeing demonstrates the power and beauty of the HTML/CSS tango: Your HTML file contains your structured chunks of content, while your CSS controls how a browser displays that content.) Viewed in a web browser, without any CSS styling, these different HTML sections would all appear stacked one on top of the other.

NOTE You don't have to create and name divs to get started laying out your pages with CSS. Dreamweaver ships with 18 premade CSS-based layouts called, shockingly enough, CSS Layouts. You can read about them on page 447.

To create a two-column design, follow these steps:

1. **Select the page's banner.**

   For example, click before the logo image and drag until you select the navigation bar. With this HTML selected, you can wrap it in a <div> tag.

2. **In the Structure category of the Insert panel, click the Insert Div button.**

   This launches the Insert Div window so you can wrap the selected content in a <div> tag. In the Class box, type in a class name (or an ID name, if you prefer).

   You can name the style several ways, depending on whether you want to create the style immediately, whether you've already created the style, or whether you want to create the style later on.

   - To create a class or ID style, click the New CSS Rule button. The process at this point is the same as that for creating any new style, as described on page 102. In this case, you might name the class style *.banner* (or the ID style *#banner*). You can set any CSS properties you want for the banner: Add a border around all four sides, color the background, or even specify a width.

   - Select a class name from the Class menu, or an ID name from the ID menu. The web page may already have an external style sheet attached, which contains all the necessary styles for the layout. Just select the class name for the div you're inserting (for example, *.banner*).

- Type a name in the Class (or ID) box. If you don't want to create a style, you could just type *banner* in the Class or ID box, and create style rules later.

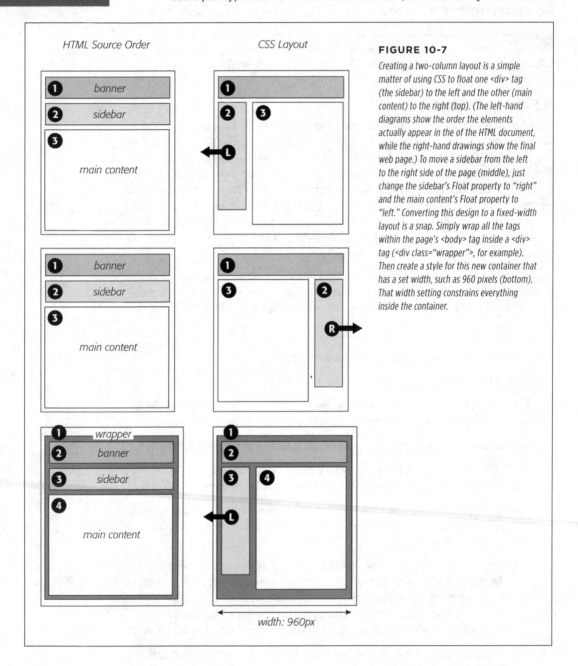

HTML Source Order

CSS Layout

FIGURE 10-7

Creating a two-column layout is a simple matter of using CSS to float one <div> tag (the sidebar) to the left and the other (main content) to the right (top). (The left-hand diagrams show the order the elements actually appear in the of the HTML document, while the right-hand drawings show the final web page.) To move a sidebar from the left to the right side of the page (middle), just change the sidebar's Float property to "right" and the main content's Float property to "left." Converting this design to a fixed-width layout is a snap. Simply wrap all the tags within the page's <body> tag inside a <div> tag (<div class="wrapper">, for example). Then create a style for this new container that has a set width, such as 960 pixels (bottom). That width setting constrains everything inside the container.

NOTE When you create a class style using the New CSS Rule box, you have to start the class name with a period, like this: *.banner.* However, when you type the class name in the Insert Div window, you omit the period; you just type *banner* (or select banner from the Class menu). The same applies to ID styles—use a # when you create a style in the New CSS Rule box (*#banner*, for example), but omit it in the Insert Div window.

3. **Click OK to close the Insert Div window.**

    Dreamweaver wraps the selected HTML with a <div> tag, and, if you created a new style, formats the banner.

4. **Select the contents of the sidebar, and then, from the Insert toolbar, click the Insert Div button. Click the New CSS Rule button and create another class (or ID) style. Name it whatever you like, such as *.sidebar* or *.section-Nav,* and then click OK.**

    This style formats and positions the left sidebar. You're finally getting to the "float" part of this design.

5. **In the New CSS Rule window, click the Box category, and then, from the Float menu, select "left" (see Figure 10-8).**

    When you work with floats, the source order (the order in which you add HTML to a file) is important. The HTML for the floated element must appear *before* the HTML for the element that wraps around it.

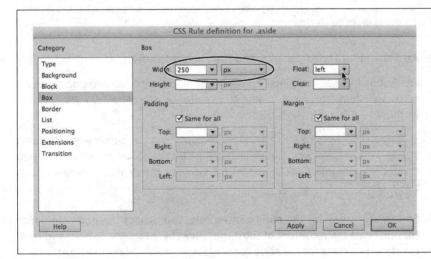

FIGURE 10-8

Whenever you float an element (other than an image), always set a width. It constrains the floated element so that a browser can wrap other content around it.

Figure 10-7 shows three two-column layouts. The diagrams on the left show the page's HTML source order: a <div> for the banner, followed by a <div> for the sidebar and, lastly, a <div> for the main content. On the right, you see the actual page layout. The sidebar comes *before* the main content in the HTML, so it can float either left (top, bottom) or right (middle). The main text area then moves up the page and wraps around the floated element.

6. **Type a value in the Width box (circled in Figure 10-8).**

   Unless you're floating an image with a predefined width, you should always give your floats a width. That way, you create a set size for the floated element, allowing the browser to wrap other content around it.

   You can use a fixed width, say *250px*, or you can specify a percentage for a flexible design based on the width of the browser window (see page 426 for more on set versus variable dimensions). If you set the sidebar to 20% of the width of the browser window and the window is 700 pixels wide, the sidebar will be 140 pixels wide. But if your visitor stretches her window to 1,000 pixels wide, the sidebar grows to 200 pixels. Fixed-width sidebars make page design easier, since you don't have to fret over differently sized browser windows.

   NOTE If you set a fixed width for your overall design (by wrapping all the page contents in a <div> tag with its width property set), percentage width values for the sidebar are based on the containing element, not on the window size, and that percentage doesn't change when someone changes the size of their browser window. This is true of any element whose width you specify using a percentage value. The percentage is based on the width of the tag that surrounds the element.

7. **Add any other styles you like, and then insert the div.**

   At this point you can continue to style the sidebar. You could add a background color, set a font family that, thanks to inheritance (see page 382), will apply to all the text inside the div, and so on.

   When you're done, click OK in the Style Definition window. Dreamweaver returns you to the Insert Div window, which has the Class box filled in with your freshly created style's name. Click OK to insert the div, and then watch the sidebar float.

   Now it's time to style the main column.

8. **Follow steps 4–7 for the main content div, too: Select the page elements that form the main content of the page, click the Insert Div button, and then create a new class (or ID) style for the page's main content region.**

   In this instance, you don't need to float anything. You merely have to add a left margin to the main content div so that the content won't wrap *below* the end of the sidebar. If the sidebar is shorter than the other content on the page, the text from the main column wraps underneath the sidebar, much as the main text interacts with the right-floated photo in Figure 10-4. If the main content wrapped underneath the sidebar, the integrity of two side-by-side columns would be ruined. Adding a left margin that's equal to or greater than the width of the sidebar indents the main content of the page, creating the illusion of a second column.

By the way, it's usually a good idea to make the left margin a little bigger than the width of the sidebar: That creates some empty space—a gutter—between the two elements. So if the sidebar is 170 pixels wide, adding a left margin of 185 pixels for the main content div adds an extra 15 pixels of space. If you use percentages to set the width of the sidebar, use a slightly larger percentage value for the left margin.

In addition, avoid setting a width for the main content div. It's not necessary, since browsers simply expand the width of the content to fit the available space. Even if you want a fixed-width design, you don't need to set a width for the main content div, as explained in Figure 10-7.

Expanding the two-column design to one of three columns isn't difficult either (see Figure 10-9). First, add another <div> *between* the two columns and float it to the right. Then add a right margin to the middle column, so that if the text in the middle column runs longer than the new right sidebar, it won't wrap underneath the sidebar.

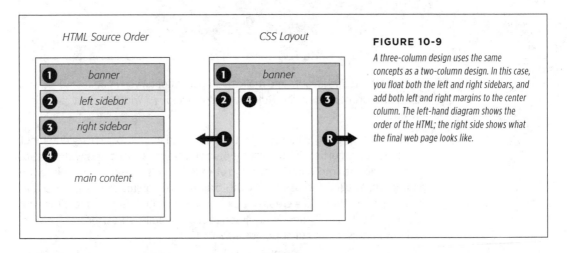

FIGURE 10-9

A three-column design uses the same concepts as a two-column design. In this case, you float both the left and right sidebars, and add both left and right margins to the center column. The left-hand diagram shows the order of the HTML; the right side shows what the final web page looks like.

TIP If you're concerned about displaying your HTML in a specific order—for example, you'd like the main content region to appear before a sidebar—you can do that simply by floating the main content and the sidebar boxes. You'll see an example of this in the tutorial at the end of this chapter.

Understanding the Box Model

It's no coincidence that you find the Float property in the Box category of the CSS Rule Definition window (Figure 10-10) and in the Layout category of CSS Designer. Float is fundamental to the "box model" that website developers use for page layout.

The box model concept states that all page elements (text, pictures, and so on) are boxes. Starting on the inside and moving out, those boxes are made up of content, padding, a border, and a margin. A page element may not always have all those features. For example, a picture may not have a border. Margins and padding can be set to *0*. In any case, the size of a page element is the sum of those features: content, padding, border, and margin. When you build your page, you're arranging the boxes.

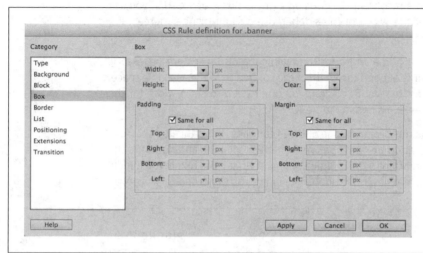

FIGURE 10-10

Use the Box category to define the dimensions of a style, to position an object on the page, and to add space between the styled object and the objects around it.

To fully understand CSS layouts and make the most of floats, you need to understand the other CSS properties in the Rule Definition window: width, height, padding, margin, and clear.

- **Width and height.** You can specify the width and height for any styled object using these properties. If you want a paragraph that's 100 pixels wide, create a class style with the Width property set to 100 pixels, and then apply it to the paragraph. You'll often use the Width property in conjunction with the Float property to do things like create a box with a set width that floats to either the left or right side of the page—a common format for pull-quotes, message boxes, and sidebars (see the bullet point below).

  Be careful with the Height property. Many designers use it for precise control over page elements. Unfortunately, height is tricky to control. If you set a height for a sidebar that contains text and you later add more text, you can end up with text spilling outside the sidebar—the same thing can happen if a visitor increases the text size in his browser. In other words, set the height of an object only if you're *sure* the content inside will never get taller—for example, if the content is an image.

- **Float.** To force an object to the left or right side of a page and have other content wrap around it, use the Float property. Of course, that's been most of the point of this chapter, so you probably understand this property by now. However, there's one important point to keep in mind: Floating an object doesn't necessarily move it to the side of a page or browser window. A floated object merely goes to the left or right edge of what's called its "containing block." If you float a div to the left of a page to create a sidebar, and then insert an image into the sidebar and float that image to the right, the image goes to the right edge of the sidebar, *not* to the right edge of the page. In addition, if you float multiple elements, they can often end up sitting beside each other—you use this technique to create four-column layouts, where each column floats next to the other.

- **Clear.** Clear *prevents* an element from wrapping around any object with a right or left Float property. This property comes in handy when you want to force an element to appear *below* a floated object instead of wrapping around it. The classic example is a page's footer (the area at the bottom of a page that usually contains contact information and a copyright notice). If a page has a left-floated sidebar that's longer than the main content, the footer could move up the page and wrap around the sidebar, not what you want. In this case, the bottom of the sidebar is at the bottom of the page, and the footer is now somewhere in the middle of the page. To fix this problem, set the footer's Clear property to *both*. That forces the footer to drop below both left- and right-floated elements. (If you merely want something to drop below a left-floated element but still wrap around anything floated right, choose the *left* option; to clear a right-floated element, choose *right*.) In other words, if you ever see page content next to a floated element instead of underneath it, use the *clear* property to properly position that content.

- **Padding.** Padding is the gap that separates the content of a page element—like a paragraph of text or an image—and its border. If you put a 1-pixel border around an image and want to add 10 pixels of space between the image itself and that border, type *10* into the Top padding box, and then choose "pixels" from the drop-down menu. To set the padding around each edge separately, turn off the "Same for all" checkbox and then type values into each of the four boxes.

- **Margin.** Margin is the amount of space *surrounding* an element. It surrounds the border and padding properties of the style, and lets you add space between elements. Use any of the values—pixels, percentages, and so on—that CSS supports.

Padding, margins, borders, and the content inside a styled tag make up what web designers call the CSS Box Model, seen in Figure 10-11. Margins and padding are invisible. They also have similar effects: 5 pixels of left padding adds 5 pixels of space to the left edge of a style; the same happens when you add a 5-pixel left margin. Most people use margins to put space between elements (for example, between the right edge of one column and left edge of an adjacent column) and padding to add space between an element's border and its content (like a column of text and its surrounding borderline). Because you can't see padding or margins (just the empty space they occupy), it's often difficult to know if the gap between, say, the banner at the top of your page and the main content area results from the banner's style or the main area's style.

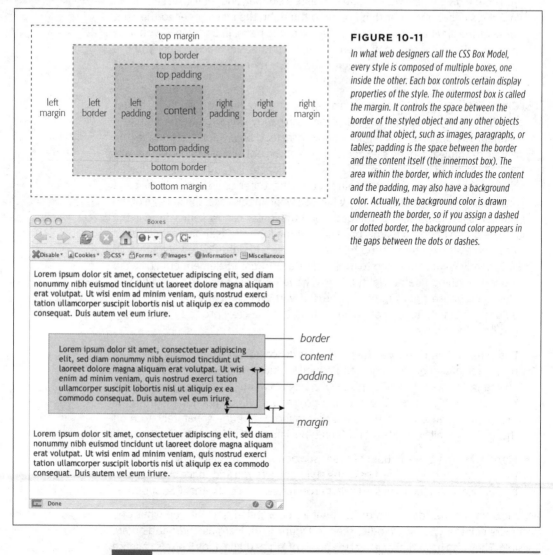

FIGURE 10-11

In what web designers call the CSS Box Model, every style is composed of multiple boxes, one inside the other. Each box controls certain display properties of the style. The outermost box is called the margin. It controls the space between the border of the styled object and any other objects around that object, such as images, paragraphs, or tables; padding is the space between the border and the content itself (the innermost box). The area within the border, which includes the content and the padding, may also have a background color. Actually, the background color is drawn underneath the border, so if you assign a dashed or dotted border, the background color appears in the gaps between the dots or dashes.

NOTE Dreamweaver includes a tool to help you visualize the margins and padding of elements. To learn how to use Inspect mode, see page 487.

You also can't always tell if the extra space comes from the padding or the margin setting. Dreamweaver includes a helpful diagnostic tool (View→Visual Aids→CSS Layout Box Model) that lets you see these invisible properties (see Figure 10-12).

When you select a <div> tag that has its margin or padding properties set, Dreamweaver draws a box around the div and adds slanting lines to indicate the space the margins and padding occupy.

Margins, the space between a piece of content and its border, appear outside of padding, and Dreamweaver represents margins with lines that slant *downward* from left to right. Padding appears inside of margins, and Dreamweaver indicates it with lines that go *upward* from left to right. When you select a <div> tag (the Tag Selector discussed on page 7 is a great way to do so), Dreamweaver highlights the margins and padding values defined in that ID style.

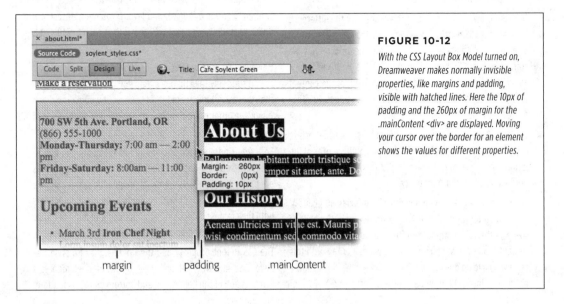

FIGURE 10-12

With the CSS Layout Box Model turned on, Dreamweaver makes normally invisible properties, like margins and padding, visible with hatched lines. Here the 10px of padding and the 260px of margin for the .mainContent <div> are displayed. Moving your cursor over the border for an element shows the values for different properties.

If you find these visual aids confusing, turn them off by choosing View→Visual Aids →Layout Box Model. These same steps turn the margin and padding visual aids back on.

■ Dreamweaver's CSS Layouts

You'll contend with many details as you build CSS-based layouts. For example, you need to understand the intricacies of the CSS Box Model, as well as the sometimes-bizarre behavior of floats. In addition, different browsers handle some CSS properties differently, which sometimes means a design that looks great in Firefox completely falls apart in Internet Explorer 6. (Remember, even though much of the Windows-loving world has upgraded to IE 8 and IE 9, there are still plenty of folks cruising around the Web in IE 6 jalopies.) Fortunately, Dreamweaver is ready to give you a helping hand with predesigned CSS Layouts.

When Width Doesn't Equal Width

In my style sheet, the CSS Width property of one of my styles is 150 pixels. But when I preview the page in a web browser, the <div> tag I applied the style to is much wider than 150 pixels. Is there a bug in my browser?

No, your browser is fine. The problem lies with the difference between the CSS *width* property and the final calculated width of an element on-screen. The width you see on-screen is the sum of several CSS properties, not just the Width property. The Width property merely defines the width of the content area of the style—the place where the text, images, or other nested tags sit.

The actual width—that is, the amount of screen real estate assigned by the web browser—is the *total* of the widths of the left and right margins, left and right padding, left and right borders, *and* the Width property.

Say you create a style with a width of 100 pixels, 10 pixels of padding on all four sides, a 2-pixel border, and 20 pixels of space in the left margin. While the space dedicated to the content inside the style is 100 pixels wide, any tag with this style will have an on-screen width of 144 pixels: 100 (width) + 10 (left padding) + 10 (right padding) + 2 (left border) + 2 (right border) + 20 (left margin).

This can cause problems if you're not careful. For example, in a fixed-width layout, you might create a div that wraps around all other page elements. Its width is 960 pixels, so everything inside that div must fit in that 960-pixel-wide space. If you wanted to create a four-column layout, you might insert four divs and create styles that set the width of each to 240 pixels (960 divided by 4).

However, if you added even a 1-pixel border to one of the divs, they'd suddenly take up more than 960 pixels, and you'd find that the last column wouldn't fit—in fact, it would drop down *below* the other three columns, creating a very weird-looking layout.

So if you find yourself floating lots of elements and one of them drops below another when it should sit beside it, odds are pretty good that the elements are just too wide to sit side by side. So decrease the width, margins, padding, or borders until the elements fit (breaking out a calculator and adding up the margins, padding, borders, and widths helps).

The CSS Height property and the final height of a style behave the same way. The on-screen height of an element is a combination of the height, top and bottom margins, padding, and borders.

Dreamweaver's CSS Layouts aren't finished web page designs. They don't have graphics, fancy text, drop-down menus, or any whiz-bang features. They're intended to lay the foundation for *your* design talents. Each layout is a simple HTML file and style sheet, each works with all current browsers, and each design's handcrafted CSS irons out the many wrinkles in troublesome browsers (most notably Internet Explorer 6). In other words, instead of spending a day stretching and sizing your own canvas, a Dreamweaver CSS layout is like going to the art store and buying a ready-made and primed canvas so you can get busy painting.

NOTE If you used previous versions of Dreamweaver, you may be surprised at how few templates there are in Dreamweaver CC. Adobe has been trimming the ranks of templates for the last few versions. One reason, Adobe says, is that they found that most people used the same two- or three-column templates and were confused by the other options. Another reason is the move toward mobile web surfing and the need for responsive designs to accommodate smartphones and tablets. To meet that need, Adobe developed the fluid grid layouts discussed in Chapter 12. If you miss one of the old templates or you're looking for more options, head over to the Adobe Exchange (Help→Dreamweaver Exchange). Use the Filter menu to limit your search to shareware, open source, or commercially licensed options. For details on using templates, see Chapter 20.

Creating a new CSS layout page takes just a few steps:

1. **Choose File→New.**

   This is the same first step you take when you create any new web page. Dreamweaver launches the New Document window (Figure 10-13). You can also use the Ctrl+N (⌘-N) keyboard shortcut to open this window (however, it's possible to disable this keyboard shortcut, as described on page 26, and you might want to do that if you'd rather skip this clunky window when you just want a new, blank web page).

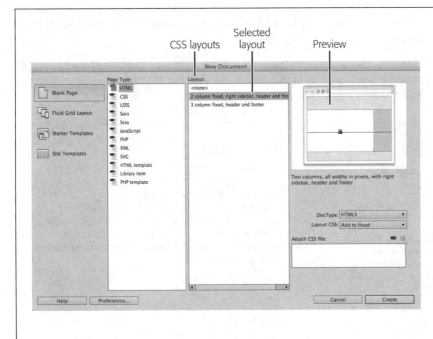

FIGURE 10-13

This New Document dialog box for a blank web page lists Dreamweaver's ready-made CSS layouts. For example, "2 column fixed, right sidebar, header and footer" indicates a design with two columns: the main content column on the left, and a thinner sidebar (for supplementary info like links) on the right. The design also sports a fixed width and has header and footer divs. A preview of the selected layout appears in the top-right of the window; a brief description below the preview provides more detail on how the layout works.

2. **Choose Blank Page from the left column, and the type of page—HTML, PHP, and so on—you wish to create in the Page Type column.**

Usually, you'll select HTML from the Page Type category, since most of the time you'll create regular web pages. However, if you're creating a page that uses a server-side language like PHP, you'd select PHP from the list.

> **TIP** You can choose from four layout categories on the left side of the New Document window (Figure 10-13). Blank Page includes empty templates. Fluid Grid holds templates for smartphones and tablets. Starter Templates get you going with jQuery Mobile pages. And the last category, Site Templates, holds templates you created for your existing websites.

3. **From the Layout column, select a page layout.**

This is where the fun begins. As you read before, choose *<none>* to create an empty web page. The other options let you choose one of Dreamweaver's prefab CSS-based layouts. For example, with the two layouts shown in the HTML category, you choose whether you want a two- or three-column fixed-width layout.

A fixed-width design maintains a constant page width no matter the width of a visitor's browser window. The fluid grid layouts let the overall width of the page change with the size of a browser window and device. (See page 447 for more on these types of layout.)

Dreamweaver previews each design in the top-right corner of the New Document window. See Figure 10-14 to decipher the visual codes that help you understand how the layouts behave.

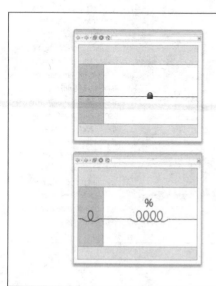

FIGURE 10-14

The layout previewed in the Blank Page New Document window visually identifies the type of CSS layout you select. A small lock icon indicates a fixed-width design (top); the layout sets the width of each column using pixel values, and the widths don't change when a guest resizes her browser window. The % symbol indicates a liquid design (bottom). It defines column widths using percentage values that change based on the width of the browser window; a wider browser window means wider columns.

4. **Choose a doctype from the DocType menu.**

Here's where you decide which type of HTML/XHTML you want to use for the page. It's the same option you face when you create a new, blank web page, as described on page xx. You're safe going with the default option of HTML5.

5. **From the Layout CSS menu, select where you want to store the layout's CSS code.**

Each Dreamweaver CSS layout requires its own style sheet, which includes all the styles that make the layout work. When you create a new page from a CSS layout, you can store that style sheet several places. The "Add to Head" option creates an internal style sheet in the HTML file Dreamweaver creates. Most of the time, you don't want this option, since external style sheets are more efficient (see page 107 for an explanation).

You can also store the CSS layout styles in a new, external style sheet. Choose Create New File to do so. You choose this option when you first use one of Dreamweaver's CSS layouts to create a new page. This creates a separate file with all the CSS necessary to control the page's layout. To add another page to your site using a layout you've already used (for example, a two-column fixed design with a header and footer), read on.

The "Link to Existing File" option sidesteps the entire process of creating new CSS styles. It assumes you have the appropriate styles defined in another external style sheet. If you previously created a web page using the same type of CSS layout, choose this option.

Say you create a two-column fixed layout using a Dreamweaver CSS layout. You saved the necessary styles for that layout in an external style sheet and saved the sheet to your site. Now you can create a *new* two-column fixed-layout page using the same external style sheet. Choose "Link to Existing File," and then proceed to step 6 to link the external style sheet to the new page.

Keep in mind, however, that each CSS layout has its *own* style sheet. So if you create a two-column fixed-layout page and then want to create a page with three columns and a liquid layout, you can't link to the style sheet Dreamweaver created for the two-column layout. In other words, whenever you create a new *type* of CSS layout (two-column fixed, three-column liquid, and so on), choose the Create New File option so Dreamweaver creates the appropriate CSS file in a new, external style sheet.

TIP   You don't need to go through these steps each time you create a page using a CSS layout you've used before. Suppose you want to build a 40-page site with two-column, fixed-layout pages. Instead of going through the New Document dialog box (and the steps listed here) 40 times, use the New Document dialog box to create the initial page, and then choose File→Save As to save a copy of that design for the next two-column page you want to create. Better yet, use Dreamweaver's Template tool described in Chapter 20 to manage pages that have the same layout.

---

6. **Click the Attach Style Sheet button to attach an external style sheet to the page (see Figure 10-15).**

   This is an optional step, but if you already have an external style sheet you want to use to format your site, now's the time to link to it. In addition, if you chose "Link to Existing File" in the previous step, you have to link to an external style sheet to create a particular layout type. The process of linking to external style sheets is the same as with any other web page, as described on page 120.

   NOTE   If, when you create a new web page, you link to an external style sheet as described in step 6, Dreamweaver may pop up a warning message that says something about needing to save your web page in order to correctly attach the style sheet. You can safely ignore this message. In fact, turn on the "Don't show me this message again" checkbox so you don't see this annoying message in the future.

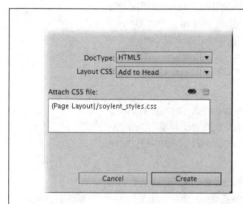

FIGURE 10-15

You can attach more than one external style sheet when you create a CSS-based layout. One sheet might define the basic look of headlines, text, images, and other elements, for example, while another controls column layout, and a third handles "printer" styles that dictate how the page will look when printed (see page 392).

7. **Click the Create button to bring your new web page to life.**

   If you selected the Create New File option in step 5, Dreamweaver asks you to name the new style sheet and select where you want to save it (just like when you create any new external style sheet, as described on page 107). Dreamweaver suggests names for the CSS files for each of its layouts—such as *HTML5_twoColFixRtHdr.css* for an HTML5, two-column, fixed-width design with a right sidebar and a header and footer. You can change the name if you like, but the name Dreamweaver suggests is descriptive.

   After all of that, you end up with a page that has a basic structure and some tutorial text telling you how CSS formats the different areas of the page (see Figure 10-16). Don't forget to save and title the page.

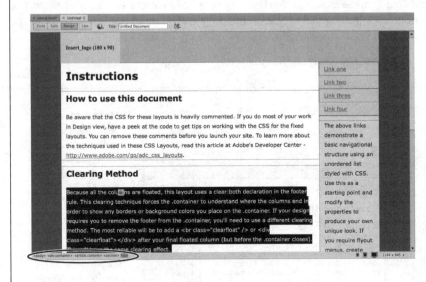

FIGURE 10-16

It doesn't look like much, but a CSS layout page has the basic scaffolding of a bona fide web page in place: <div> tags to organize the page and CSS styles to position those divs. Click inside any area of the page, and the Tag Selector (circled) shows you the structure of the HTML at that point. In this case, if you click inside a paragraph in the main column, the Tag Selector shows you which tags wrap around that paragraph. You read this info from right (the se-lected <p> tag) to left (the <body> tag that contains everything you see inside the document window). For this two-column design, the <p> tag is inside a section, which is inside of an article with a class of .content (that's what the <article.content> means), which is itself inside a <div> with a class of .container. Finally, the <body> tag encloses all the other tags.

The Structure of Dreamweaver's CSS Layouts

Dreamweaver's CSS Layouts are made up of a handful of page elements that suggest their intended use. As explained in the box on page 430, Dreamweaver templates use HTML5's new descriptive tags, like <header>, <article>, and <section>, to architect a new page. It also adds some JavaScript to the page so that these new-fangled tags work with older browsers. When you examine the structure of Dreamweaver's templates, you'll see descriptive tags used in the same way that <div> tags have been used in the past. They stake out territory on a web page-in-progress for the header, footer, sidebars, and main article of the page, as shown in Figure 10-17. In some cases, these descriptive HTML tags will have classes assigned to them. For example, click in the main article on the page, and then in the Tag Selector at the bottom of the document window, you're likely to see something like:

```
<body><div.container><article.content><section><p>
```

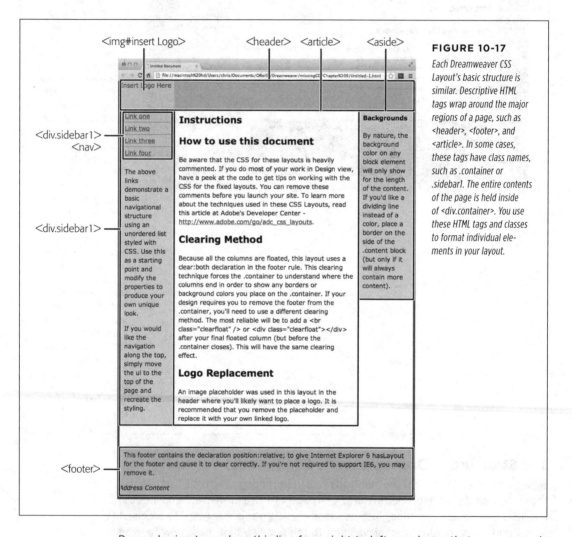

FIGURE 10-17

Each Dreamweaver CSS Layout's basic structure is similar. Descriptive HTML tags wrap around the major regions of a page, such as <header>, <footer>, and <article>. In some cases, these tags have class names, such as .container or .sidebar1. The entire contents of the page is held inside of <div.container>. You use these HTML tags and classes to format individual elements in your layout.

Remembering to analyze this line from right to left, you know that your cursor is inside of a paragraph's <p> tags, which happens to be inside of <section> tags. That section, in turn, appears inside the <article> tag, which has the *.content* class applied to it. Then, there's a <div> tag with the *.container* class applied to it (*<div. container>*). As explained previously, this tag usually represents the page's outer container, and you use that container to position all the content of the web page. For example, you can center the page by centering the div. Just outside of *<div. container>* are the <body> tags for the web page.

The good news is that once you get a handle on one of Dreamweaver's pre-designed layouts, you can apply that knowledge to the other layouts you use. Whether you structure page elements with descriptive HTML tags or <div> tags and classes, you format and position them the same way, through CSS.

You may wonder that if all of Dreamweaver's CSS Layouts share the same name for their divs, how do you end up with different types of designs? Each page has its own style sheet. When you create a new CSS Layout page and save those styles in an external style sheet (as described in step 5 on page 445), Dreamweaver suggests a name such as *HTML5_thrColFixHdr.css* (for a three-column, fixed design with a header and footer), or *HTML5_twoColFixRtHdr.css* (for a two-column, fixed design with a right sidebar). Each style sheet has different rules for its container, content, sidebar, header, and footer styles. This means that if you plan on using more than one CSS Layout page, you need to keep separate style sheets for each one—in other words, if you attach *twoColLiqRt.css* to a three-column, fixed design, you end up with some weird results.

So what do you do if you want to, say, have the same design for all the paragraphs inside the main content div (*<div class="content">*) when you use two different CSS Layouts? Create a third style sheet, named something like *global.css* or *site. css*, attach it to both types of pages, and create a descendent selector (page 370) like this: *.content p*. This formats just the paragraphs that live inside a tag that has the class *.content* applied to it, and since it's in a style sheet shared by both pages, it works in both designs.

Modifying Dreamweaver's CSS Layouts

The basic look of a freshly minted Dreamweaver CSS Layout doesn't have much to recommend it. For example, the fixed-width layouts have a green and tan color scheme. One of the first things you want to do with a CSS Layout is remove any Dreamweaver formatting that doesn't fit with your design ideas. In addition, you might want to tweak some of the basic layout properties, like the width of a fixed-width design or the width of sidebars and main columns.

Making General Changes to a CSS Layout

Unless you really like Dreamweaver's green and tan color scheme (and if you do, your job is a lot easier), one of your first tasks should be to remove (or change) the background colors for the sidebar and other page elements of a CSS Layout. This generally means editing the CSS in the Dreamweaver-supplied style sheet. You already know the basics for creating a CSS rule: Choose the source of the style, choose the selector that triggers the style, and then set the values for the properties in the rules. These steps are covered in detail on page 104. Editing an existing style rule is similar, but you may be able to take some shortcuts when it comes to zeroing in on the property you want to tweak.

Suppose you want to change the format of the main part of your web page—you may want to change the font or adjust the size of the margins. Here's how to find the CSS rule you need to change:

1. **Click inside a paragraph in the main part of your web page.**

   Clicking inside of a paragraph selects that element of the web page. If you're working with a photo or video clip, click it to select it. In either case, you can examine the tags that define the element in the Tag Selector at the bottom of the document window (Figure 10-18, left). You can also Alt-click (Option-click) to bring up the CSS Navigator.

2. **In CSS Designer's Sources section, examine the Computed properties.**

   When Dreamweaver highlights "Computed" in the Selectors section of CSS Designer, it displays the rules that style the selected tag in the Properties section (Figure 10-18, bottom). Dreamweaver may store these CSS rules (property/value pairs) in different sources. For example, one source may be the template's external CSS style sheet *HTML5_twoColFixRtHdr.css*, and another could be a style sheet like *soylent_styles.css*, where you create styles to format specific page elements.

3. **If you don't see the property that you want to edit in the list of Computed properties, go to the Tag Selector (Figure 10-18 left, circled) and click on another tag. Start reading from the right side and move to the left.**

   If you don't see the property you want to change in the list of Computed properties, a page element a little higher on the food chain probably governs it. For example, a rule that positions a sidebar isn't going to be in the paragraph <p> selector. It's more likely to be in the <div> that has the *.sidebar1* class applied to it. So look in the Tag Selector for the <div> with a *.sidebar* class. As you click on different tags in the Tag Selector, Dreamweaver displays different properties in CSS Designer's Properties section. Usually, it only takes a couple of clicks to find the property and CSS rule you need.

4. **When you see the property (rule) you want to edit, click the property/value pair to identify the selector and source.**

   The selector and source that define the CSS rule appear in bold type in the Selectors and Source sections of CSS Designer.

   In many cases, you can tweak a value—that is, edit a CSS rule—just by changing the value in CSS Designer's Properties section. However, it's always best to understand exactly which *selector* you're changing and which *source* style sheet holds the rule. After all, you may use that same CSS rule elsewhere on the current page, or on some other page in your website. Often, instead of changing the rule, you may just want to create a new overriding rule for a particular element on the page.

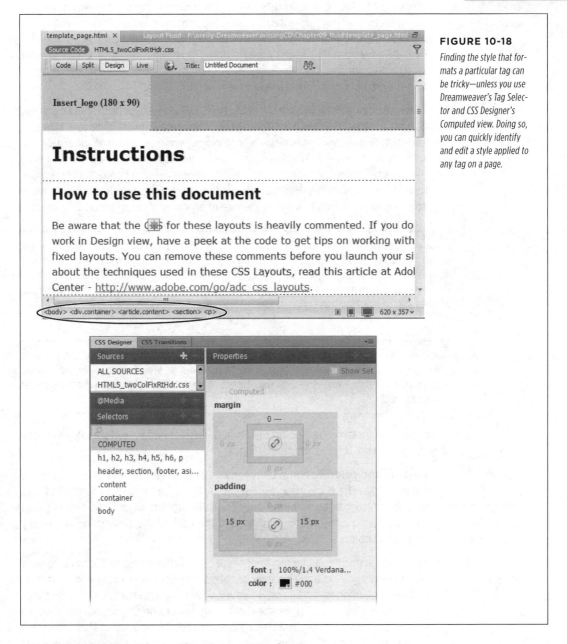

FIGURE 10-18

Finding the style that formats a particular tag can be tricky—unless you use Dreamweaver's Tag Selector and CSS Designer's Computed view. Doing so, you can quickly identify and edit a style applied to any tag on a page.

5. **Set values for the properties you want to change.**

   At this point, you can change the property values in CSS Designer's Properties section. Suppose you want to change the background color of a sidebar that has the selector *.sidebar1*. You'd go to the Tag Selector and click *<div.sidebar1>*. CSS Designer then goes to the Properties section and calls up the Background-color property for the sidebar. You see the *background-color* swatch with the color you want to change highlighted. Clicking the property name (*background-color*) highlights the source file *HTML5_twoColFixRtHdr.css* and the selector *.sidebar1*. Dreamweaver displays both names in bold. To change the color, click the color swatch and choose a new color or enter a number for it. You can also remove the rule entirely by clicking the trash can icon.

To override an existing rule in *HTML5_twoColFixRtHdr.css* (rather than change it), you do the CSS Designer three-step: Choose a source, choose a selector, and then tweak the properties. You can place your new rule in an external style sheet or in the <head> portion of the web page. Just make sure that the link to the external style sheet or code for the internal style sheet comes after the link to *HTML5_twoColFixRtHdr.css* in the <head> section of your page. If the link comes before, it won't override the rule in an internal or external style sheet.

NOTE The styles for Dreamweaver CSS Layouts use what's called CSS "shorthand properties." For example, you can combine the values for *background-color* and *background-image* into a single property named *background*, while you can specify all four margins of an element (top, right, bottom, and left) with just one property: *margin*. This makes for more compact styles, but it also means that, to edit a shorthand property in the Properties section, you need to know how to write the values yourself.

NOTE Dreamweaver doesn't provide a color box, link button, or any other of the helpful tools it provides when you set the values of a "longhand" property like *background-color*. In other words, unless you know CSS well, to change one of the layout's styles, you should use CSS Designer to select a source and selector, and to set property values.

Once you select a layout region on the page (header, sidebar, and so on), you probably want to make a few common changes:

- **Background color.** To completely remove a div's background color, delete the value next to the *background-color* property in the Properties section of CSS Designer. You can also double-click the style's name in the CSS Styles panel to open the Rule Definition window, and then select the Background category to edit the color.

- **Text formatting.** You can modify the text and other content of a page to your heart's content. This book's earlier chapters show you how to format headlines, paragraphs, images, and links. However, when you create styles for these elements, use an external style sheet other than the one Dreamweaver supplies for the layout. You can store these types of styles in a generic style sheet like *styles.css*, instead of the layout-specific style sheet, such as *twoColFixLtHdr.css*. See step 5 on page 445 for the reason.

Paying Attention to Conditionals

I've noticed that when I create a page using Dreamweaver's fluid grid layout, the page has some weird-looking code just above the ending </head> tag. What's that about?

If you go into the Code view of any of Dreamweaver's fluid grid layout, you'll notice some grayed-out HTML that begins with *<!—[if lt IE 7]>* and ends with *<![endif]—>*. It's grayed out because Dreamweaver treats this code as an HTML comment. People who hand-code their pages use HTML comments to leave notes about their page—like why they added a chunk of HTML, or to identify which div a particular closing </div> tag belongs to. Dreamweaver and browsers ignore HTML comments.

However, this particular HTML comment, while ignored by every other browser, has special significance for Internet Explorer. HTML comments that begin like this *<!—[if IE]>* are actually secret messages, called *conditional comments*, intended just for Internet Explorer. Conditional comments let you send HTML, CSS, and JavaScript to Internet Explorer only; you can even send special HTML to particular versions of Internet Explorer. For example, *<!—[if lt IE 7]>* sends HTML to versions 6 and earlier

of Internet Explorer (the "lt" part stands for "less than," so it addresses Internet Explorer 6 and earlier).

You'll encounter comments in the fluid grid layout that link to the JavaScript code for *html5shiv.googlecode.com/svn/trunk/html5.js* described on page 430. It makes older versions of Internet Explorer play well with new HTML5 features. In fluid grid layouts, you'll also find conditional comments that identify different versions of Internet Explorer and then apply a class (like *ie6 oldie* or *ie7 oldie*) to the <html> tag. The template code uses these classes to handle special problems with each version of Internet Explorer.

Fortunately for web developers everywhere, IE 6 is nearly gone (see the box on page 495), and IE 7 is following close behind it. Odds are that soon you won't need to worry about either of these browsers and, depending on how tech-savvy your audience is, you might be able to stop supporting IE 7 now.

For a brief tutorial on conditional comments, visit *http://tinyurl.com/commentsforexplorer.*

Modifying Fixed Layouts

Dreamweaver's fixed CSS Layouts are 960 pixels wide, a common page width. It fits 1,024-pixel-wide screens (that is, most netbooks, laptops, tablets, and desktop computers). However, that width may be too wide or too narrow for your tastes. If you're designing for the cinema-screen audience, you might want a page that takes advantage of a wider screen, so you might bump the width to 1,100 pixels or more. In addition, you may want to change the widths of columns on a page. Here's how you make a few key layout changes like these:

- **Page width.** Dreamweaver fixes the area of the page that includes the header, sidebars, and main content at 960 pixels. It defines this width in the *container* div. Select the div and change 960 to whatever width you want.

NOTE Nine hundred and sixty pixels is way too wide for mobile phones. Fortunately, Dreamweaver CC includes support for a CSS technique called "media queries" which lets you adjust a page's layout based on the screen dimensions of the destination device. In other words, you can design both a 960-pixel-wide layout for desktop computers and a 320-pixel-wide layout for phones. See Chapter 12 to learn how to use media queries.

- **Column width.** In its two-column layouts, Dreamweaver makes its sidebar columns 180 pixels wide, and the main content region 780 pixels wide. For three-column designs, it makes the main content area 600 pixels wide. Select the sidebar you wish to make wider or narrower, and then adjust its Width property.

Unfortunately, you often have to do a little math if you want the three columns to sit side by side. Since the container has a set width (960 pixels by default), the width of all three columns should also add up to 960 pixels. If their total is bigger, the content area's width actually becomes smaller than the width of the two sidebars. So if you increase the size of one sidebar, you need to decrease the width of the main content area (the *.content* style) by the same amount. For example, in a two-column fixed design, if you increase the sidebar to 200 pixels wide (20 pixels more than it starts out with), you need to subtract 20 pixels from the width of the *<article.content>* selector. In other words, in the Tag Selector, click *<article.content>*. Then, in CSS Designer's Selectors section, click *.content*. Finally, in the Properties section, change the width to 760 px.

Things get even trickier if you add margins, padding, or a border to the left or right of any column. As discussed in the box on page 442, the actual horizontal space of any element is the sum of its width, left and right margins, left and right padding, and left and right border. If you add a 1-pixel right border to a sidebar, you increase the total width of all the columns to 961 pixels (1 pixel more than the container's 960-pixel width). The result? The main content area drops below the sidebar. Ay carumba! In other words, if you make a change to a sidebar, or the main content area, and the *article.content* div suddenly drops down on the page, check your math!

> **TIP** If you use Dreamweaver CSS Layouts often, you may frequently make the same adjustments over and over again. For example, you might always remove the padding and background color, and adjust the column widths. Instead of repeatedly doing that, edit the default HTML and CSS files Dreamweaver uses when it creates a new blank CSS Layout page. In Windows, you find them in C:\Program Files\Adobe\Adobe Dreamweaver CC\Configuration\BuiltIn\Layouts. On the Mac, they're in the Applications→Adobe Dreamweaver CC→Configuration→BuiltIn→Layouts folder.
>
> You can clean up the Layout folder by deleting designs you don't use. Just make sure you back up the folder before you do anything to the files inside. And then, back up your new designs so that if you ever have to reinstall Dreamweaver, you have a backup of your modified templates.

Creating and Modifying Liquid Layouts

Liquid layouts adjust to the width of a browser window. Columns grow wider as visitors widen their browser window, and shrink when they narrow it. For example, you can create a layout where Dreamweaver displays all the content in 80% of the space allowed by the browser window. Then you can divvy up that space between one or more sidebars and a main article. You designate these regions using <div> tags with classes, or by using HTML5's new descriptive tags, like <article> and <aside>.

For example, to quickly whip up a liquid layout, you might create a class called .container that you'd apply to a <div> tag. You plan to place all the elements of your web page inside this <div>, and then apply formatting. So you create CSS rules for .container, setting the width to 80% and margin-left and margin-right to auto. Dreamweaver centers any content you place inside that <div> and it occupies 80% of the available space. That leaves 10% empty space on the left and right sides of the main content area. You can add borders, color, or an image to the background as well as any other formatting that's appropriate for your container. To create a sidebar, use the HTML5 <aside> tag. You can then create styles for major regions of the page, such as a header, footer, sidebar, and article.

Here are some of the properties you can use to format your page:

- **Page width.** In a liquid layout, the page content adjusts its width. So, if the width is set to 80%, there is empty space on one or both sides of the page. If you center the page, Dreamweaver leaves 10%, on both sides. To remove this space to make the page fill the entire width of the browser window, edit the .container style: Just delete the width entirely—don't set the width to 100 percent because that'll make the page appear a little *wider* than the browser window, forcing visitors to scroll right to see all of a page's content. See the box on page 442 for an explanation.

NOTE You can provide built-in limits for the width of a container div using Dreamweaver's *max-width* and *min-width* properties. *Max-width* defines the maximum width of the div and keeps it from becoming unreadably wide on extremely large screens. So, for example, a value of 1260 px would be appropriate for many web pages. The *min-width* property, by contrast, keeps the div from shrinking past the point of readability. A value of 780 pixels is common. To change or delete these values, go to the Layout category of CSS Designer's Properties section (see the tip on page 110).

- **Column width.** As with fixed-width layouts, you can set the sidebar and main content widths using CSS's Width property. The only difference for liquid layouts is that you use percentages, with the combined width of the sidebars and the content div at 100%. Just as with fixed layouts, if you change the width of one div, you need to adjust the width of another. So in a three-column liquid design, to make the left sidebar, say, 25% instead of the usual 20%, you need to remove 5% from the .content div, the right sidebar, or split that between the two: For example, change the .content style to a width of 57% (from its normal 60%) and the .sidebar2 style to 18%.

Other Styles to Change

Here are a few other styles you might want to modify or delete.

- **Text spacing.** It's common for web designers to add some empty space between the edge of a column and the content inside it. This "white space" makes the text feel less cramped and more readable. You can add padding to the div that creates the column—for example, to the *<div class="content">* element that CSS Layouts uses to create the main content region. However, as mentioned above, adding padding to that div increases its overall width, potentially making the column too wide to fit next to other columns. So, instead of adding padding to the sidebars or main content styles, Dreamweaver uses a group style ("h1, h2, h3, h4, h5, h6, p") that includes left and right padding. Because it applies the padding to tags *inside* the column and not the column itself, the overall width of each column remains the same. You get the same visual result—added white space on either side of each column—without having to futz with width settings.

The only downside to this approach is that it will apply to *every* header and paragraph on the page. What if you want a little less white space inside the left sidebar and a little more inside the main content area? The answer is descendent selectors (see page 370). For example, to create a style that affects the padding of just the headings and paragraphs in the first sidebar, you'd create this (long-winded) group style:

.sidebar1 h1, .sidebar1 h2, .sidebar1 h3, .sidebar1 h4, .sidebar1 h5, .sidebar1 h6, .sidebar1 p

Then, any left and right padding you add to the *.sidebar* style applies only to the headings and paragraphs *inside* the sidebar (see page 373 for instructions on creating a group style).

You'll also find styles named *.content ui* and *.content ol*, which Dreamweaver uses to add white space around bulleted and numbered lists inside the main content area. You may want to adjust or delete these styles as well.

- **Links.** Dreamweaver's CSS Layouts also include styles for the link states discussed on page 187 (*a:link, a:visited*, and so on). You may not like these styles, so feel free to change or delete them. And if the pages in your site use different CSS Layouts (two-column fixed and three-column fixed pages, for example), you're better off creating a shared, external style sheet (*site.css* or *styles.css*, for instance), putting your link styles there, and then linking the external style sheet to all your pages (see page 120 to learn how to do that, and page 377 to learn how to move styles between style sheets). That way, all your pages, even the ones with different layouts, will have consistent link styles.

- **Navigation bar.** Some of Dreamweaver's layouts include a simple navigation bar in a sidebar. If you like the basic style, you can change its appearance by editing the various styles that begin with *ul.nav* in the layout's style sheet. They control the appearance of the list and the links inside. If you don't plan on using the navigation bars, feel free to delete the styles entirely.

NOTE The style sheets Dreamweaver supplies with CSS Layouts are chock-full of CSS comments. This is a good thing when you're getting started, because they're like a mini-lesson in CSS layout. Read through the comments in at least one of the style sheets and you're sure to learn a few things. However, when it's time to put your site on the Web, all those comments are unnecessary bloat that slow page downloads. You can delete them by hand (CSS comments are gray in Code view and begin with /* and end with */) or you can use Dreamweaver's Find and Replace tool to quickly remove them all.

For a little help, download Dreamweaver expert David Powers' Stored Query to Remove CSS Comments (basically, a saved find-and-replace command) from *http://tinyurl.com/4ywjk42*. You can read about Dreamweaver's powerful Find and Replace tool in Chapter 8.

■ Absolute Positioning

Beyond float-based layouts, CSS's other main technique for placing elements on a page, *absolute positioning*, lets you specify the exact position on a page for any element. But before you start thinking you've found page-layout heaven, keep in mind that the Web is a fluid environment that's difficult to control with pixel-level precision. If a visitor increases the font size in her browser, the enlarged text may spill out of your carefully crafted layout. In addition, it's nearly impossible to force a footer to the bottom of a page laid out using absolute positioning (a trivial task with float-based layouts). That's why most of Dreamweaver's CSS Layouts use floats and the techniques discussed at the beginning of this chapter.

That's not to say you shouldn't use absolute positioning. It's great for moving small elements, like a logo, image, or short set of links, to a specific position on a page. And it's the only way to have one element overlap another (see Figure 10-19). As long as you don't try to dictate the exact width, height, and position of every page element, you'll find absolute positioning powerful and helpful.

FIGURE 10-19

One unique aspect of absolute positioning is its ability to place an element on top of other page content. That lets the drop-down menu pictured here overlap the page content below it.

The CSS Positioning Properties

Several CSS properties position elements on-screen. You'll find them under the Layout category of the CSS Designer window (Figure 10-20).

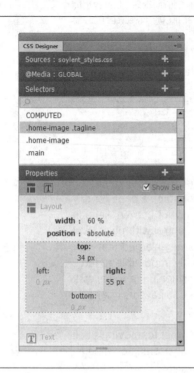

■ POSITIONING TYPE

Normally, browsers position elements on the screen in the order they appear in the HTML. The first element tagged in the HTML appears at the top of the browser window, while elements at the end of web-page files appear at the bottom of the browser window. In Figure 10-21, the top-left image shows a headline, followed by a paragraph of text, followed by a headline, an image, and another paragraph. This is the order in which the elements appear in the HTML, top to bottom.

The CSS Position property, however, lets you alter the order of a styled element on-screen by assigning one of four available position types: *absolute*, *relative*, *static*, and *fixed*.

- **Absolute** is the most common option. It lets you place a tag anywhere on a page, regardless of the tag's position in the page's HTML. The top-right image in Figure 10-21 displays a graphic of a sticky note. Even though the image falls after the headline Malorum Gipsum in the page's HTML, it appears at the top of the page (and even a little bit above the top) because it's absolutely positioned. The space the graphic used to occupy (top-left image) is now filled by the paragraph of text beneath the second headline.

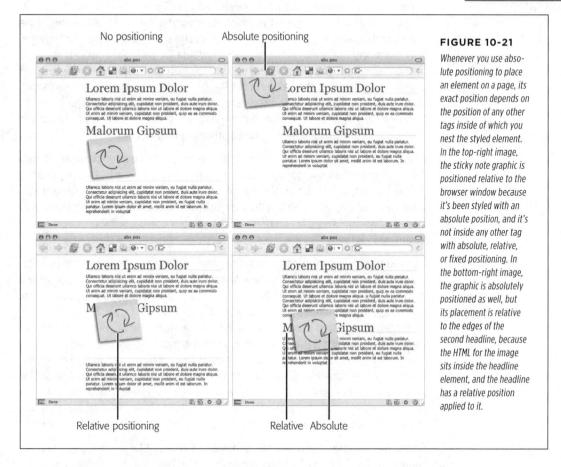

FIGURE 10-21

Whenever you use absolute positioning to place an element on a page, its exact position depends on the position of any other tags inside of which you nest the styled element. In the top-right image, the sticky note graphic is positioned relative to the browser window because it's been styled with an absolute position, and it's not inside any other tag with absolute, relative, or fixed positioning. In the bottom-right image, the graphic is absolutely positioned as well, but its placement is relative to the edges of the second headline, because the HTML for the image sits inside the headline element, and the headline has a relative position applied to it.

In other words, with absolute positioning, HTML code can go *anywhere* inside a <body> tag and still appear *anywhere* on a page—its location in the code has nothing to do with its location on-screen. In addition, absolutely positioned elements are removed from the normal flow of a page—other tags on the page aren't even "aware" that the absolutely positioned (AP) element exists.

After you select the Absolute option, use the Placement properties to specify a position (see page 463 for details).

Browsers, however, don't always put absolutely positioned elements in relation to the page itself. If you create a style to position an element inside another element that's either positioned relatively (see the next bullet point) or absolutely, the browser positions the first element *in relation to the latter element*, not in relation to the page itself. The next bullet point clarifies this confusing concept.

- The **Relative** option lets you position a tag relative to its position in the HTML. When you choose this option, the positioned element appears relative to where it appears in the HTML. The bottom-left image in Figure 10-21 shows the same sticky note positioned using the Relative property. Although it has the same top and left placement values (page 463) as the top-right image, the browser now positions the sticky note relative to where its tag sits in the HTML—just below the Malorum Gipsum line. Even so, the note sits in the top-left position of that line, reflecting the values in the Relative property. Another side effect of relative positioning is that the space formerly taken up by the image (top-left in Figure 10-21) remains. Notice that the last paragraph doesn't try to fill up the space where the graphic was—there's still a big empty area.

    At first glance, the Relative option might seem less than useful. After all, what's the point of positioning something on a page, just to leave a big empty space? In many cases, you don't actually apply relative positioning to an *element* you want to position, you apply it to a *tag* that wraps *around* the element you want to position in order to create a new set of coordinates for an absolutely positioned element.

    Say you put an image inside a headline, and you want the image to appear on the left edge of that headline. If you simply position the image in an exact spot in the browser window on the left edge of the headline tag, you're taking your chances. If the headline moves (say you add some new body text above it), the absolutely positioned image stays glued to its assigned spot. Instead, what you want to do is position the image *relative* to the headline tag, so that when the headline moves, so does the image. Look at the bottom-right image of Figure 10-21. The headline Malorum Gipsum is relatively positioned, and the sticky note is absolutely positioned, but it's absolutely positioned *inside the headline tag*. Even when, later on, you add a little more text above the header (thereby forcing the headline to move down), the sticky note travels along for the ride.

- **Static** positioning is the normal behavior of HTML. Static simply means the content follows the normal top-down flow of HTML. Why would you want to assign an element static positioning? The short answer: You probably never will.

- **Fixed** positioning is similar to the *fixed* value of the CSS Attachment property used to lock a background image in place (see page 241). This option "fixes" an element in place in a browser window. When you scroll down the page, the AP element doesn't move—it remains in a precise spot in the browser window. It's a cool option with exciting possibilities. For example, you could create a navigation bar that sticks to the top of the browser window. When visitors scroll down the page, the navigation bar stays in place. Internet Explorer 6 ignores the fixed option, but since that browser is nearly extinct, it's worth experimenting with this property.

■ WIDTH AND HEIGHT

These properties, logically enough, set the width and height of an element. You can use any of the available CSS units of measure, like pixels, ems, or percentages. In most cases, when you want precise control over the dimensions of your tags—that is, a page element that's *exactly* 200 pixels wide and won't change even if a visitor changes the size of his browser window—use pixels. If, however, you want the element to resize as the visitor resizes his browser, use percentages. That way, you can specify a style that's 50% the width of the browser window, no matter the size of the window. Width and height are at the top of the Properties list in the Layout category of CSS Designer.

NOTE The Width and Height properties available under the Positioning category of the CSS Rule Definition window are identical to the options of the same name under the Box category (see Figure 10-10) in the same window. Also note that CSS calculates the total width of a style as the width value *plus* any borders, margins, or padding (see the box on page 442 for more). The same is true for the height of an element.

■ VISIBILITY

Left to its own devices, a web browser makes the contents of all tags visible on the page, so you'll usually leave this property blank. After all, if you put something on your page, it's usually because you want people to see it. But there are situations in which you may want to make a certain tag (and its contents) invisible to your visitors.

For example, you might want a page element to appear when a visitor clicks a button or mouses over another element (that's how tooltips work). However, most web designers use the Display property (page 396) for this, not the Visibility property. Why? Because when you hide an element using the visibility property, the element is still there taking up space. When you hide an element by setting display to none, poof! It's as if it isn't there at all. To make an element disappear, set the display property to *none*; to make it visible, set the display property to *block* (for block-level elements like headlines, paragraphs, and divs) or *inline* (for inline elements like images, links, and <span> tags).

In other words, skip the Visibility property.

■ Z-INDEX

Welcome to the third dimension. Absolutely positioned tags are unique in the world of web elements because they "float" above (or even behind) a web page and can overlap each other, completely or partially.

If you were awake in high school geometry, you may remember the graphing system in which the x-axis specified where a point was in space from left to right and the y-axis specified where the point was from top to bottom. And if you were awake *and* paying attention, you may remember that the z-axis denotes a point's position in *front-to-back* space. When you draw a three-dimensional object on this type of graph, you need to use all three axes: x, y, and z.

The Z-Index of an absolutely positioned element doesn't make your web page *appear* three-dimensional; it simply specifies the "front-to-backness" of overlapping AP elements. In other words, the Z-Index, represented by a number in the Z-Index field, controls the stacking order of AP elements on a page.

The page itself lies behind all AP elements, and the AP elements stack up from there. In other words, the higher the Z-Index number, the higher above the page the AP element sits, so an AP element with a Z-Index of 4 appears *behind* an overlapping AP element with a Z-Index of, say, 7.

Z-Index numbers have no relation to the actual number of absolutely positioned items on a page. You can have three AP elements with Z-Indexes of, say, 2, 499, and 2000 if you choose. You'd still have just three AP elements, one on top of the other in ascending order. Spacing your Z-Index numbers in this somewhat arbitrary manner is helpful, since it lets you insert divs between already positioned divs as you develop your page, without having to renumber the Z-Indexes of all your AP elements.

■ OVERFLOW

Suppose you create a square div that's 100 x 100 pixels. Then you fill it with a graphic that's 150 x 162 pixels—that is, larger than the div itself.

You've already seen how a table cell reacts to this situation: It simply grows to fit the content inside. Divs (and other elements), however, are more (or less) flexible, depending on your choice of Overflow settings in the Properties panel. The following options let you decide how browsers handle the excess part of the image:

- **Visible** will display any content that doesn't fit inside the element. The element doesn't expand to fit the content (something you'll notice if you apply a background or borders to the element); it lets the graphic "pop out" of the box.

- **Hidden** chops off the excess content. In the example above, you'd only see the top-left 100 x 100 pixels of the image.

- **Scroll** adds scroll bars to the element, so that visitors can scroll to see all of the element's contents. It's like having a miniature browser window embedded in the page. This feature offers an interesting way to add a small, scrollable window within a web page. Imagine a small "Latest Company News" box that visitors can scroll through to read the text inside without disturbing anything else on the page.

- **Auto** adds scroll bars to an element *only* if necessary to accommodate oversize contents.

In Design view, you see the complete element, overflow and all. Switch to the Live view and the overflow reflects the *hidden*, *scroll*, or *auto* properties. If you select any option besides Visible, you see the div's set dimensions—for example, 100 pixels by 100 pixels. Dreamweaver doesn't display any content outside that area.

> **NOTE** You can use the Overflow property on any element, not just absolutely positioned divs. For example, if you want to create a 100-pixel-tall div with scrollbars and lots of content inside that visitors can scroll through, just create a style with a 100-pixel height and the Overflow property set to *Scroll*, and apply that style to the div, no positioning required.

■ PLACEMENT

Dreamweaver's Placement properties let you specify an absolutely positioned element's position, which is, after all, the whole point of AP elements. The four Placement properties control where each of the four edges of the AP element begin. Setting the Top box to 200 pixels positions the top of the element 200 pixels down the screen, whereas the Bottom option identifies where the bottom of the element starts. Similarly, the Left and Right properties set the beginning of the left edge and right edge of the AP element.

You'll frequently use a combination of the Width property (page 438) and the Top and Left or Right properties to position AP elements. To place a 150-pixel-wide sidebar 200 pixels from the top of a page and 15 pixels in from the left, you'd set the Width property to 150 pixels, the Top property to 200, and the Left property to 15 pixels.

You'll also find the Right property handy. Say you want to put a 200-pixel-wide sidebar on the right side of a page. Since you don't know the exact width of a visitor's browser—580 pixels, 1,200 pixels?—you can't know ahead of time how far the AP element needs to be from the left edge of the window. So you can set the Right property to 0—if you want the sidebar to touch the right edge of the page. If you want to indent the AP element 20 pixels from the right edge of the window, type *20*.

In addition, you can skip setting a width by assigning both Left and Right positioning simultaneously—say, placing an AP element 50 pixels from the left edge and 20 from the right. You can do the same with Top and Bottom settings as well—don't set the height of an element, just set its Top and Bottom values.

> **TIP** Here's a cool trick: Absolutely position a div and set its top, left, bottom, and right positions to 0. You'll have a div that fills the browser window—even when someone resizes the window.

Positioning isn't quite as straightforward as it may seem. The exact location of a positioned div is a combination of not only these position values, but also of what type of placement you choose for the positioned element—absolute or relative. As noted earlier, with relative positioning, the numbers you type for Top or Left, for instance, are calculated based on where the AP element already appears in the HTML and on the screen. So setting the Top property to 100 pixels doesn't place the AP element 100 pixels from the top of the browser window, it places it 100 pixels from where it would appear on the screen based on the HTML.

Absolute positioning, however, lets you place an AP element at an exact spot on a page. So setting the Top and Left properties for an absolutely positioned element to 100 and 150 pixels *will* place that AP element 100 pixels from the top of the browser window and 150 pixels from the left edge.

NOTE There's one additional wrinkle to absolute positioning: For a div nested inside another div that has either a Relative or an Absolute position setting, the browser calculates position values based on the position of the *parent* div. If you have one AP element 300 pixels from the top of a page, and an absolutely positioned AP element nested inside *that* AP element with a Top position of 20, it doesn't appear 20 pixels from the top of the page. It appears 20 pixels from the top of the parent AP element; in this case, 320 pixels from the top of the page.

■ CLIP

The Clip property can hide all but a rectangular piece of an AP element. In most cases, you should avoid this property, since it's rarely useful except for animated special effects.

Suppose you put a large graphic into an AP element but you want to display only one small area. You *could* use the Clip property, but a browser still has to download the *entire* graphic, not just the clipped area. You're much better off preparing the smaller graphic at the right size to begin with. The kilobytes you save may be your own.

You can use JavaScript to *move* the clipping area, creating an effect like a spotlight traveling across the AP element. Although that may be a more useful purpose for the Clip property, Dreamweaver doesn't support it, unfortunately. Those effects are frequently created using a program such as Edge Animate.

The four Clip settings—top, right, bottom, and left—specify the positions of the clipping box's four edges. In other words, these indicate the borders of the visible area of the AP element.

■ Adding an AP Element to Your Page

In most cases, the <div> tags you position will include a variety of HTML elements—images, paragraphs, headlines, and so on. For example, to place a series of links at the top of a page, you could use the Insert Div command (page 428) to wrap the links in a <div> tag. Then you'd position the div so that it sits atop the page.

Start out by selecting existing content, or click in the spot where you want to add a new absolutely positioned div. Next, create a class or ID style (with the positioning properties discussed above), and then select that style from the Class or ID menu of the Insert Div window. Alternatively, you can create the class or ID style by clicking the New CSS Rule button in the Insert Div window (see Figure 10-6).

But absolute positioning isn't just for <div> tags; you can absolutely position any HTML tag—forms, paragraphs, headlines, and images. You just need to create a style and set the Position property to Absolute (page 458), and voila, you have an absolutely positioned element.

Unless you add a background color or border to your AP element, it's difficult to identify its boundaries. To make working with AP elements easier, Dreamweaver provides visual cues in Design view, as shown in Figure 10-22, and explained below:

- **AP element marker.** The gold shield with the letter C (huh?) represents where in the underlying HTML the code for the AP element actually appears. (Actually, the shield appears for any tag with either absolute or relative positioning.)

Dreamweaver doesn't display these markers by default. To see them, you have to turn them on in the Preferences window: Press Ctrl+U (⌘-U) to open the window, click the Invisible Elements category, and then turn on the "Anchor points for AP elements" checkbox.

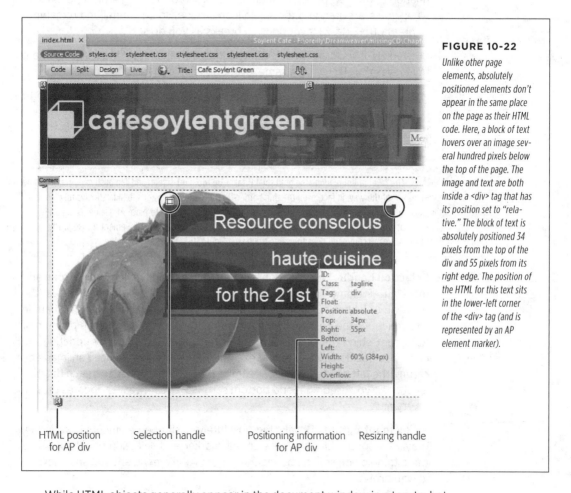

FIGURE 10-22

Unlike other page elements, absolutely positioned elements don't appear in the same place on the page as their HTML code. Here, a block of text hovers over an image several hundred pixels below the top of the page. The image and text are both inside a <div> tag that has its position set to "relative." The block of text is absolutely positioned 34 pixels from the top of the div and 55 pixels from its right edge. The position of the HTML for this text sits in the lower-left corner of the <div> tag (and is represented by an AP element marker).

HTML position for AP div   Selection handle   Positioning information for AP div   Resizing handle

While HTML objects generally appear in the document window in a top-to-bottom sequence that mirrors their order in the HTML, the position of AP elements *doesn't* depend on where the AP code appears in the page's HTML. In other words, you can have an AP element in the first line in the HTML of a page, while the element itself actually appears near the bottom of the final line on the page.

To move the HTML of an AP element, drag the shield icon. You can place the icon (and therefore the code) at the beginning, end, or anywhere else in your

HTML, but you need to be careful. As discussed on page 458, when you position an element absolutely, its exact location depends on whether its parent element has either a relative or absolute position. If the parent element is itself absolutely positioned and you drag the element outside its parent, its top, left, bottom, and right coordinates will change—a browser may now position that element in relation to the browser window. Likewise, if you drag the shield inside another absolutely positioned element, the browser displays that element in relation to the new parent element. In other words, it can get pretty confusing when you start dragging the shield icon around, so be careful and remember to press Ctrl+Z (⌘-Z) if your design breaks as you do so.

Conversely, if you drag the selection handle of an element, it moves the element but leaves the HTML in the same location (described next).

That distinction often confuses Dreamweaver users. For instance, if you want to reposition an AP element, don't drag the AP element's marker—the gold shield that represents the HTML code—that simply moves the HTML to another spot inside the code. It doesn't reposition the element on-screen.

> **NOTE** The AP element marker (the gold shield) takes up room on-screen and can push text, graphics, and other items out of the way. In fact, even the thin borders that Dreamweaver adds to indicate divs take up space in the document window, and the space they occupy may make it difficult to place AP elements precisely. The keyboard shortcut Ctrl+Shift+I (⌘-Shift-I) hides or shows invisible items like AP element markers. The Visual Aids→Hide All menu command does the same thing (see Figure 10-23).

- **Selection handle.** The selection handle provides a convenient way to grab and move an AP element around a page. The handle appears when you select the element, or when you click inside the element to add material to it. The handle lets you move the position of the AP element without changing the position of its code. Behind the scenes, Dreamweaver updates the CSS by updating the element's positioning values. For example, if you originally placed an image by setting the left and top values, Dreamweaver changes those to match the new location. If you used right and bottom settings, Dreamweaver updates those... pretty nifty.

- **AP element outline.** Unselected absolutely positioned elements have a thin, gray, 3-D border. Like the AP element marker and selection handle, it's only there to help you see the boundaries of the AP element, and doesn't show up in web browsers.

- **AP element positioning summary.** If you select an AP element and hover your mouse over that div, Dreamweaver pops up a box with information about that AP element (see Figure 10-22), including the name of the class or ID, what type of positioning you used, the AP element's dimensions, and so on. This gives you a bird's-eye view of the CSS properties defining the AP element's placement on the page.

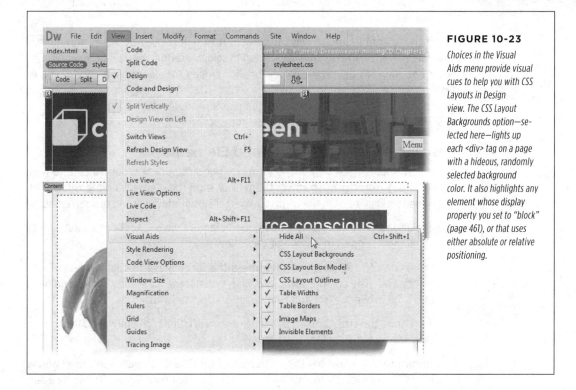

FIGURE 10-23

Choices in the Visual Aids menu provide visual cues to help you with CSS Layouts in Design view. The CSS Layout Backgrounds option—selected here—lights up each <div> tag on a page with a hideous, randomly selected background color. It also highlights any element whose display property you set to "block" (page 461), or that uses either absolute or relative positioning.

NOTE If one AP element overlaps another, the top AP element—the one with the higher Z-Index, as described on page 461—has a solid outline; the lower element appears as a dashed line where the top AP element overlaps it.

Modifying AP Element Properties

Once you add an AP element, you don't need to go back to CSS Designer to edit many of its positioning properties. Using the Properties panel, you can rename, resize, move, and align the div with other AP elements, and set many other properties.

But first, you have to select the AP element using one of these methods:

- Click the AP element's selection handle (see Figure 10-22).

- Click the AP element's border. The border turns red when you move your mouse into the proper position.

- Click the AP element marker (the gold shield) that indicates where the HTML for the absolutely positioned item resides. (Out of the box, Dreamweaver hides these markers, since they can get in the way of your design work. To show them, select Ctrl+U (⌘-U) to open Dreamweaver's Preferences window, click the Invisible Elements category, and then turn on the "Anchor points for AP elements" checkbox.)

And if those aren't enough ways to select an AP element—Adobe's programmers never sleep—you can also Shift-click them to select multiple AP elements simultaneously, and then set the properties of (or align) many AP elements at once. If you're working with an AP element or have one selected, Shift-clicking another AP element selects them both. (Shift-click a selected element to deselect it.) You can continue to Shift-click to select additional AP elements.

Resizing Absolutely Positioned Elements

When you select an AP element, eight resize handles appear around its edges (see Figure 10-22). You can drag any of them to change the element's dimensions. The corner handles resize both the width and height simultaneously and proportionately.

You can also resize an absolutely positioned element via the keyboard. First, select the AP element, and then do one of the following:

- Press the Ctrl (⌘) key, and then press the arrow keys to change the AP element's size. The up and down arrow keys adjust the element's height one pixel at a time, while the left and right arrows affect its width.

- To change the size *10* pixels at a time, press Ctrl+Shift (⌘-Shift), and then press the arrow keys.

For better precision, use the Properties panel (or CSS Designer) and the W and H boxes to set an exact width and height for the element (see Figure 10-24). You can specify any unit of measure that CSS understands: px (pixels), pc (picas), pt (points), in (inches), mm (millimeters), cm (centimeters), em (height of the current font), ex (height of the current font's x character), or % (percentage)—see page 136. To pick your measurement unit, type its abbreviation *immediately* after you type in the size value. For example, type *100px* into the W box to make the AP element 100 pixels wide. Don't include a space, and don't leave out the measurement unit—px, em, or %, for example—or browsers won't display the correct dimensions of the AP element.

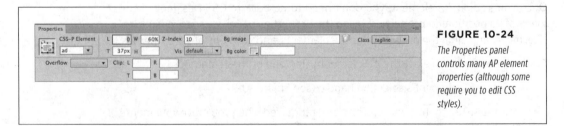

FIGURE 10-24

The Properties panel controls many AP element properties (although some require you to edit CSS styles).

Another benefit to using the Properties panel to resize elements is that Dreamweaver lets you change multiple elements at once. Shift-click two or more elements to select them, and then type new widths and heights. Dreamweaver sets all the selected AP elements to these dimensions.

Moving AP Elements

Moving an absolutely positioned element is just as simple as resizing it—drag any border of the element, or the element's selection handle. Avoid the eight resize handles, however, because they'll change the size of the element when you drag them.

For less speed but greater precision, you can use the keyboard. First, select the element and then do one of the following:

- To move an AP element one pixel at a time, press the corresponding keyboard arrow key.

- Press Shift while using an arrow key to move the element 10 pixels at a time.

Placing AP Elements

As you'd guess, you can also control an AP element's placement using the Properties panel or CSS Designer. Dreamweaver measures an AP element's position relative to the left and top edges of a page (or, for nested AP elements, from the left and top edges of a parent div when you set the Position property to either absolute or relative). The Properties panel provides two boxes for these values: L specifies the distance from the left edge of the page to the left edge of the selected AP element, and T specifies the distance from the top of the page to the top of the selected AP element. In CSS Designer's Properties section, go to the Layout category's Position box and then set the top, bottom, left, and right values.

> **NOTE** You can't edit an AP element's Right or Bottom positioning properties from the Properties panel. For these properties, use CSS Designer.

To position an AP element using the Properties panel, select the div (for example, by clicking the div's border or by selecting its name in the AP Elements panel), and then type distances in the L and T boxes. You can use any of the units of measure mentioned previously. You can even use negative values to move part or all of an AP element off the page entirely (offstage, you might say), which you might want to do if you intended a subsequent animation to bring it *onstage*, into the document window using JavaScript.

If you draw a 100-pixel-tall by 50-pixel-wide AP element, you can move it to the very top-left corner of the page by selecting it, and then typing *0* in both the L and T boxes. To position that same AP element so that it's just off the left edge of the page, type *-50px* in the L box.

Aligning AP Elements

At times, you may want to align several AP elements so that their left, top, bottom, or right edges line up with each other. Dreamweaver's Align command does just that. It can even make the width and height of selected AP elements the same.

To use this feature, select two or more AP elements (by Shift-clicking them), choose Modify→Arrange, and then select one of the following options from the submenu:

- Align Left aligns the left edges of all the selected AP elements. In other words, it gives each AP element the same L property.

- Align Right aligns the right edges.

- Align Top aligns the top edges, so that all the T properties are the same.

- Align Bottom aligns the bottom edges of the AP elements.

- Make Same Width sets the same width for all the selected AP elements (in the W box in the Properties panel). Make Same Height does the same for the height of the AP elements.

The AP element you select *last* dictates how Dreamweaver aligns the AP elements. Say you have three AP elements—A, B, and C—and you select them in order from A to C. You then set their Align property to *Left*. Dreamweaver uses the left edge of AP element C (the last one you selected) as the value for the other AP elements.

Background Image and Color

To add a background image to an AP element, click the folder icon next to the "Bg image" field, and then select an image from your site folder. As usual, Dreamweaver tiles the image, if necessary, to fill the entire element's area with repeating copies of the graphic. (To adjust how or whether the image tiles, you need to edit the AP element's style using the standard CSS style-editing techniques, described on page 122.)

Setting a background color is even easier. Just use the "Bg color" box to select a color or to sample one from your screen.

■ CSS Layout Tutorial

In this tutorial, you'll create a two-column web page using CSS floats. You'll also use absolute positioning to control the placement of navigation elements (skip ahead to Figure 10-33 to see the final page). You can achieve a design like this many ways. You could, for example, use Dreamweaver's CSS Layouts (page 447), add divs, position them using CSS, and then add content. In this exercise, though, you'll start with an already created web page: It contains basic HTML, but no divs to organize the content, or style sheets to format the page.

> **NOTE** You need to download the tutorial files from *http://oreilly.com/missingmanuals/cds/dreamweaver ccmm13/* to complete this tutorial. See the note on page 33 for more details.

Once you download the tutorial files and open Dreamweaver, set up a new site as described on page 19. Name the site *CSS Layout*, and then select the *Chapter10* folder (inside the *MM_DWCC* folder). (In a nutshell: choose Site→New Site. In the

Site Setup window's Site Name field, type *CSS Layout*, click the folder icon next to the Local Site Folder field, navigate to and select the *Chapter10* folder, and then click Choose or Select. Finally, click Save.)

1. **In the Files panel, double-click the file *about.html*.**

   Alternatively, choose File→Open and double-click *about.html*. Dreamweaver opens a web page with a little content and basic HTML formatting. You'll start by grouping the banner content—the logo, nav bar, and "Make a reservation" link.

2. **Click to the right of "Make a reservation" and drag up until you select the link, navigation bar, and logo at the top of the page.**

   You'll wrap all this in a <div> tag.

3. **Choose Insert→Div or click the Insert Div button under the Common or Structure tabs of the Insert panel.**

   Either way, Dreamweaver opens the Insert Div window. You want to create a CSS style to format this div.

4. **Click the New CSS Rule button, and in the New CSS Rule Window, choose Class from the Selector Type menu, type *.header* in the Selector Name field, and choose New Style Sheet File in the Rule Definition menu.**

   The window should look like Figure 10-25.

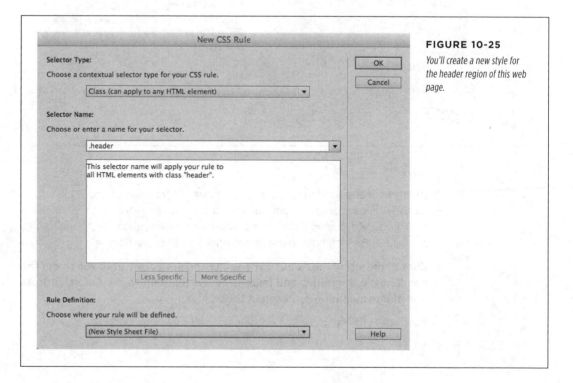

FIGURE 10-25

You'll create a new style for the header region of this web page.

5. **Click OK and save this style sheet file as *soylent_styles.css* in the CSS folder of the site.**

   Dreamweaver launches the CSS Rule Definition window. You're creating a style for the page's banner, and, as you can see in Figure 10-4, it's just a box that stretches across the page. You don't need to float or absolutely position it, but you'll add a background image and a few other properties.

6. **Select the Background category from the Rule Definition window.**

   Click the Browse button to the right of the Background-image property and select the file *bg_banner.jpg* from the Images folder.

   This box holds only a bit of content—the logo and navigation elements—so you'll set a height for it to match the final design.

7. **Select the Box category and then type *140* in the Height box.**

   Turn off the margin setting's "Same for all" checkbox and type *20* in the Bottom margin box. Click OK.

   Dreamweaver returns to the Insert Div window. Notice that header (the style you just created) appears in the Class box (see Figure 10-26).

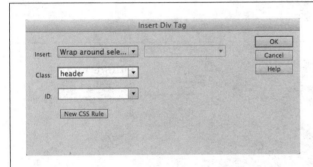

FIGURE 10-26

The Insert Div window not only inserts a <div> tag, it lets you create a new CSS style and apply a class or ID (or both) to the tag.

8. **Click OK.**

   Dreamweaver adds the div tag to the page. There's something a bit wrong with it—the navigation bar and the link to the "Make a reservation" page don't fit. That's OK for now. Later in this tutorial, you'll use absolute positioning to relocate these elements to the upper-right corner of the banner.

9. **Click to the left of the About Us headline and drag down until you select the headlines, paragraphs, and images—everything up to the Cafe's address and phone number—don't select those.**

   This area is the main content of the page and should be in its own div.

10. **Choose Insert→Div.**

    Dreamweaver opens the Insert Div window. You want to create a CSS style to format this div, too.

11. **Click the New CSS Rule button, and in the New CSS Rule window, choose Class from the Selector Type menu; type *.main* in the Selector Name field. Select *soylent_styles.css* from the bottom Rule Definition menu, and then click OK.**

    These are the same steps you followed for the previous div.

12. **Select the Box category, type *64* in the Width box, and then select % from the drop-down menu to the right. Choose left from the Float menu, turn off the margin setting's "Same for all" checkbox, and then type *25* in the Bottom margin box.**

    The CSS Rule Definition window should look like Figure 10-27. Here, you're using a percentage width, so the main column will change its width as a guest changes the width of his browser window. The "left" float places this column on the left side of the browser window.

13. **Click OK to return to the Insert Div window, and click OK again to close the window and insert the new <div> tag.**

    The main content's text floats to the left of the page, and the content that was previously below it wraps around the right side, creating two columns (see Figure 10-28).

    You'll also float the sidebar column.

14. **Click to the left of the address (700 SW 5th Ave), and then drag down to select everything up to the copyright notice (the black-highlighted area in Figure 10-28).**

    This area is the sidebar and you'll add a div to it as well.

15. **Choose Insert→Div Tag to open the Insert Div window.**

    Click the New CSS Rule button, and in the New CSS Rule window, choose Class from the Selector Type menu, type *.sidebar* in the Selector Name field, and then click OK.

    These are the same steps you followed for the previous div.

16. **Select the Background category and, in the Background-color box, type *#E7EBE0*.**

    This adds a greenish background to the sidebar. You'll add a border next.

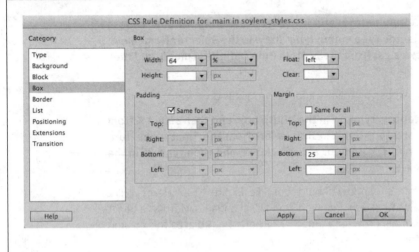

FIGURE 10-27

Percentage-width values means that an element will change size based on the width of its parent element. For example, a 64% wide box placed inside the body of a web page makes that box 64% of the browser window's width. As a visitor resizes the window, the box changes width. However, if you place that box inside another div with a pixel-value width—say 1,000 pixels wide—that box will now be a fixed width (64% of the 1,000-pixel-wide container, or 640 pixels).

17. **Select the Border category.**

    Select "solid" from the Style menu, type *1* in the Width box, and then type *#E5E5E5* in the color box.

    You added a gray border to the box. Time to position it.

18. **Select the Box category, type *33%* in the Width box, choose "right" from the Float menu, turn off the margin setting's "Same for all" checkbox, and then type *25* in the Bottom margin box.**

    You'll float this div to the right of the window. Notice that the width of this column (33%) and the main column (64%) don't add up to an even 100%. There's a couple of reasons for that. First, since the two columns are floated in opposite directions, the remaining space (3%) will appear as a bit of white space (a "gutter") between the two columns, giving the content some breathing room. Second, when using percentage widths, you need to be careful when you add padding, margins, or borders. As you read in the box on page 442, the actual width of an element is a combination of the border, padding, and width values.

    Because you added a border to the sidebar, its screen width will be slightly wider than the 33% you specified. If you set the two columns' width values to equal 100%, they wouldn't fit side by side, since 100% width plus 2 pixels of left and right borders would total greater than 100%. The sidebar would end up dropping below the main column of content.

19. **Click OK to return to the Insert Div window, and then click OK again to close the window and insert the new <div> tag.**

Dreamweaver adds the tag to the page. The sidebar column appears with a light green background. You'll add a couple of CSS3 properties next.

FIGURE 10-28

A simple left float and a set width is the easiest way to get multiple columns to sit side by side.

Adding CSS3 Properties

Dreamweaver CC's CSS Designer makes it easy to add CSS3 properties—it's your best bet when you're working with the latest, greatest CSS features

1. **In CSS Designer's Sources section, click *soylent_styles.css*, and then, in Selectors, click .sidebar.**

Properties for the *.sidebar* class appear in the Properties section of CSS Designer. Turn on the Show Set checkbox if you want to examine the properties that are already part of the CSS rule for *.sidebar*, but make sure you turn off the checkbox before moving on to the next step.

2. **In the Properties section, click the Border and scroll down until you see the border-radius box.**

The border-radius box looks like a rounded rectangle and has value boxes at each corner. There's a link in the middle labeled "Click To Change All Properties."

3. **Click the link to change all the properties to the same value. Then, click Value for any of the corners and type *5*, as shown in Figure 10-29.**

   This adds rounded corners to the sidebar. The *border-radius* property works only in modern browsers (that excludes IE 8 and earlier). Next, you'll add a drop shadow.

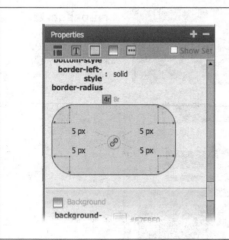

FIGURE 10-29

The CSS3 Border-radius property lets you add rounded corners to one, two, three, or all four corners of an element. Make sure you add either a background color or border to the element—otherwise, you won't be able to see the rounded corners!

4. **Scroll down in the Properties section until you see the Box-shadow properties.**

   You style a box shadow by setting six properties: h-shadow, v-shadow, blur, spread, color, and inset.

5. **Type *2* in the h-shadow, v-shadow, and blur boxes. Type *#999999* in the color box (see Figure 10-30).**

   Press Enter (Return) to close the settings box.

   This adds a drop shadow to the sidebar, but you won't see anything in Dreamweaver's Design view. You need to use Live view or preview the page in a browser.

   You're almost done with the layout. If you look at the page, you'll notice that the copyright notice appears below the sidebar and to the right of the main column of content. It should drop below both columns.

6. **Select the paragraph with the copyright notice ("Copyright 2022, The Soylent Corporation").**

   You're going to wrap this in a new div. You should be having a sense of déjà vu at this point.

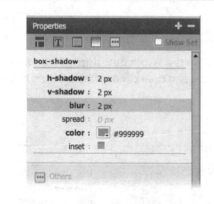

FIGURE 10-30

The CSS3 Border-radius property lets you add drop shadows to any element. You can learn more about this property at http://css-tricks. com/snippets/css/css-box-shadow/.

7. **Choose Insert→Div to open the Insert Div window.**

   Click the New CSS Rule button, and in the New CSS Rule window, choose Class from the Selector Type menu; type *.footer* in the Selector Name field, and then click OK.

   These are the same steps you followed for the previous div.

8. **Select the Box category and, from the Clear menu, select "both."**

   The Clear property prevents an element from wrapping around a floated element. The "both" setting prevents the footer from wrapping around either left- or right-floated elements.

9. **Click OK to return to the Insert Div window, and then click OK again to close the window and insert the new div tag.**

   The page's basic structure is in place. You have a two-column layout with a header and footer. If you preview the page in a browser, you'll see that the design uses a liquid layout—that is, it grows wider or becomes narrower as the browser window's width changes. That's because you used percentage widths for the columns. However, you can easily turn this design into a fixed-width layout.

Creating a Fixed-Width Design

To turn the current liquid layout into a fixed-width layout, you simply wrap the contents of the page in a <div> tag with a set pixel width.

1. **In the Tag Selector at the bottom left of the document window, click <body>.**

   You just selected the entire body of the web page. (The Tag Selector, discussed on page 7, is the best way to select a tag.)

2. **Choose Insert→Div to open the Insert Div window.**

Click the New CSS Rule button and, in the New CSS Rule window, choose Class from the Selector Type menu, type *.container* in the Selector Name field, and then click OK.

Now you'll set the width for this tag, and position it in the middle of the screen.

3. **Select the Box category, type *1000* in the Width box, turn off the "Same for all" checkbox in the Margin settings, and then choose "auto" from both the Left and Right margin boxes.**

The window should look like Figure 10-31.

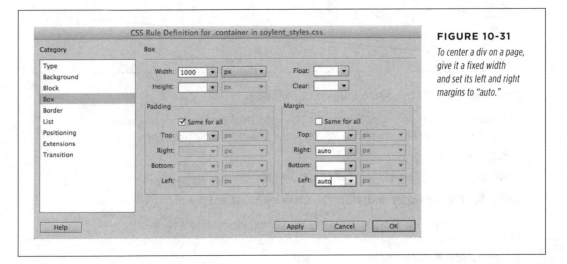

FIGURE 10-31

To center a div on a page, give it a fixed width and set its left and right margins to "auto."

4. **Click OK to return to the Insert Div window, and then click OK again to close the window and insert the new <div> tag.**

The new div wraps around all the other content on the page. By giving this container <div> a set width, browsers constrain all the contents inside to that width.

Adding Styles and Using Absolute Positioning

At this point, you could create new styles to format this page using the techniques you read about earlier in this book—change the font and font sizes, add underlines to headlines, rejigger the look of links, and so on. For the sake of keeping this book shorter than *War and Peace* (actually, this edition is just about 50 pages shy of that), we assume you already have those skills under your belt, so you'll attach a style sheet with some ready-made styles.

1. **In the Sources section of CSS Designer, click the Add CSS Source button (the + sign in the upper-right corner). Then choose Attach Existing CSS File from the menu.**

The Attach Existing CSS File window opens.

2. **Click the Browse button, navigate to the css folder, double-click the filename *final.css*, and then click OK.**

Dreamweaver links the style sheet to the page, and styles the page's content. The new styles really change the look of the page, but there's nothing about them that you haven't already seen. For example, the picture of the chef is simply aligned to the left using the Float property, the text is set to different sizes and colors with CSS, and so on.

One thing that does need some changing is the banner. The navigation bar and the reservation link are crowded together, and there's too much empty space on the right. You'll use absolute positioning to move these elements into place.

3. **In CSS Designer's Sources section, click *final.css* and then, in the Selectors section, click .nav.**

A list of properties appears in the Properties section.

4. **In Properties, click the Layout button, scroll down until you see the Position properties, and then choose absolute.**

Type *0 px* in the Right box and *32 px* in the Bottom box (see Figure 10-32).

Where did the navigation bar go? If you preview the page in a browser (or click the Live button), you'll find it at the bottom and right edge of the document window. Normally if you absolutely position an element on a page, the coordinates you use (top, left, right, and bottom) are set in relation to the browser window. But that's not what you want here. You want to position the navigation bar in relation to the bottom and right edges of the header div. To do that, you just need to give the header div a position of "relative."

FIGURE 10-32

When absolutely positioning an element, you only need to type a value for one of the horizontal (left or right) and one of the vertical (top or bottom) settings.

5. **In the Sources section of CSS Designer, click *soylent_styles.css* and then, in Selectors, click .header.**

Dreamweaver displays the properties for the *.header* class in the Properties section.

6. **In Properties, click the Layout button, and then scroll down to the Position property, and set the value to relative.**

The navigation bar pops into placed inside the header (you may need to click in the document window to see the change). Now you'll position the reservation link.

7. **In CSS Designer's Sources section, click *soylent_styles.css* and then, in Selectors, click the + sign to add a selector, and then type *.reservations* as the class name for the new selector.**

A new class style named *.reservations* appears in the Selectors section.

8. **In the Properties section, go to the Position property, set the value to absolute, set its top position to *8* and its right position to *0*, and then click OK to complete the style.**

These absolutely positioned properties position the reservations button above the navigation bar.

9. **Press F12 (Option-F12) to preview your hard work in a browser.**

The complete page should look like Figure 10-33.

You'll find a completed version of this tutorial in the *Chapter10_complete* folder that accompanies the downloaded tutorial files.

NOTE To get a full description of every Dreamweaver menu, see Appendix B, "Dreamweaver CC, Menu by Menu."

FIGURE 10-33

It doesn't take much CSS to create a multi-column layout, or to accurately place elements, like a navigation bar.

Troubleshooting CSS

Cascading Style Sheets are the most important technology in a web designer's toolkit. Unfortunately, they're also the source of many frustrations. As you pile style upon style to transform drab HTML into beautiful web pages, you increasingly run the risk that those styles will interact in ways you don't expect. As discussed in Chapter 9, the CSS concepts of inheritance and the cascade dictate how styles interact on a page, and those concepts have their own complicated rules. Adding to the confusion, different browsers can display CSS differently—and that's especially true with older versions of Internet Explorer. Even newer browsers exhibit some frustrating inconsistencies in how they display CSS.

In this chapter, you'll look at Dreamweaver's tools for diagnosing CSS problems, as well as solutions to common problems you'll encounter as you build the kinds of CSS layouts discussed in the previous chapter.

■ Analyzing CSS with Dreamweaver

Dreamweaver's CSS tools are as good as they come—you can use them to build complex designs without ever dipping your toe into code. You can manage complex style sheets easily, and quickly add external style sheets to your pages. But building and managing styles is only one part of the CSS puzzle. You also need to analyze what the CSS is doing to the tags on your page—to see why text, for example, is purple instead of the green you specified.

As described on page 104, CSS Designer gives you different ways to explore the CSS rules that format your pages. When you're building a web page, CSS Designer's Properties section can display just about every CSS property known to mankind.

When you're troubleshooting, you can use the Show Set checkbox to limit the list of CSS properties to those that have set values in your HTML. In other words, you can see the CSS rules that have already been established. If you're not sure which class, ID, or tag selector the page uses for formatting, or you're not sure where the rule is stored, you'll be grateful for CSS Designer's Computed feature (see Figure 11-1). It displays the CSS properties for a selected element and helps you zero in on the selector and source.

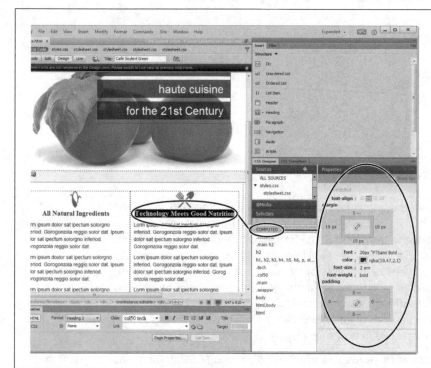

FIGURE 11-1

CSS Designer's Computed feature is a great tool for learning why a section of your web page looks the way it does. After you click an element on the page (like the headline selected here), CSS Designer highlights the Computed entry in the Selectors section with a gray background, and displays all the properties that format your selection in the Properties section. Even though you may have applied CSS rules to different selectors and stored the rules in different style sheets, Computed performs the handy task of gathering them all in one spot.

The Computed view is the place to start analyzing styles and their effect on your page. As you read on page 382, tags can inherit properties (like color and font) from tags that wrap around them. If, for example, you create a style for the <body> tag style that has a color property of *#F00*, a browser displays the text inside the <body> tag (and even the text inside tags within the <body> tag, such as <p>, <h1>, and <li>) as red. In other words, the styling of any one tag may be the result of a combination of properties from multiple styles. The ultimate set of properties that format a tag is the result of the complex interaction of styles governed by the rules of CSS inheritance (page 382) and the cascade (page 384).

You can view this combined, "computed" style by clicking an element in Design view. CSS Designer highlights Computed in its Selectors section. That's its way of saying, "I'm displaying the results of multiple selectors." Then CSS Designer displays style properties and their values in the Properties section. In Figure 11-1, for example, the

Properties section shows rules for *text-align, margins, padding, font family, size, color,* and *weight.* If you hover your mouse over one of the property names or values, a tooltip appears explaining the property or the values Dreamweaver applies.

Editing CSS Properties

There are lots of ways to change CSS styles in Dreamweaver. To quickly format an element, use the CSS settings in the Properties panel below the document window. For more complete control, turn to CSS Designer. In CSS Designer's Properties section, with the Show Set box unchecked, you see a complete list of properties. That's great for creating new rules. Using the Category buttons at the top of the Properties section, you can zero in on Layout, Text, Border, Background, and List properties. If you want to fine-tune an already created style, turn on the Show Set checkbox (in the upper-right corner of the Properties section) to see the properties whose values you've already set. Want to bump up the size of the type or adjust a color? Go ahead, click the value assigned to a property and change it.

These techniques are all well and good if you know which style you need to edit, but if you have a really long list of styles or you're working on a site for the first time in a while, you may not know which style you're after or where Dreamweaver stores the CSS rule. Is it in an internal style sheet? External? What class, ID, or tag is the selector? In a case like this, use the Computed view to home in on just the properties you want to change. Here's a step-by-step guide to that process:

1. **In the document window, select the element whose style you want to change.**

   For example, if a paragraph has green text and you want to make it blue, select that paragraph using one of the many techniques Dreamweaver offers: Triple-click to select the paragraph, click once in the paragraph and then click the tag's name in the Tag Selector at the bottom of the document window, or just drag to highlight the whole paragraph.

TIP These same selection techniques work in Code view as well.

---

2. **Examine the Computed properties in CSS Designer.**

   When you select a page element in Design view, CSS Designer displays the sources, selectors, and properties for that element. In the Selectors section of the Designer, Dreamweaver highlights "Computed" with a gray background and lists, but doesn't highlight, other selectors. In the Sources section of Designer, you see one or more style sheets, though none are highlighted. The Properties section displays a seemingly random bunch of properties. They may derive from different categories in the Properties section, like Layout, Text, Border, or Background. No matter their origin, these are all properties that format the element you selected in Design view.

3. **Click one of the property names.**

   When you click either a property name or its value, CSS Designer shows you both the Source and the Selector for that CSS rule. They appear in bold type. This is important because you need to know if the changes you make to a rule will affect other elements on your page or another page on your website.

   If CSS Designer lists more than one source, it's worth noting the order. For example, if you see an external style sheet (*styles.css*) listed before an internal style sheet (<styles>), the external style sheet link appears before the internal styles in your page's HTML. Style sheets listed earlier in your page's HTML have less precedence than those listed later.

   The order of selectors is also worth noting. Those at the top of the list are the most specific to the selected element, making them "more powerful" when it comes time for a browser to format the selection. If there's a conflict, the tags and classes at the top of the list win out.

   Occasionally, in CSS Designer's Properties section, you'll see a property name with a line through it. This strikethrough means there's a rule for that property, but it's not in effect, because another rule is overriding it. To learn more about the conflict, hold your cursor over the property name. Dreamweaver displays a tooltip explaining why it isn't applying the style, and names the selector that won the formatting battle.

4. **To edit a property's value in Computed view, click the Value widget and make the change.**

   CSS Designer sports a variety of widgets to help set the value for properties in the proper format. If there's a choice for the unit of measure, you'll see a menu. For example, *font-size* gives you a choice of 17 units of measure, from pixels to ems to percentages!

Sometimes you won't find the property you expect to see in a list of Computed properties. If that's the case, head over to the Tag Selector at the bottom of the document window. Start from the right and click the next tag to the left. If you still don't see the property, click the next tag to the left. You're moving from the most specific tags to those that are less specific, but one of them may have that *font-color* property you need.

As you can see, you can go a long way in tweaking a site's styles simply by selecting elements in the document window and using CSS Designer to quickly locate and edit the properties you want to change.

TIP Even if you're not as interested in editing an existing property as you are in *adding* new properties, CSS Designer is a big help. Select the element you want to embellish with a new property—the font for the copyright notice, for example. You can examine all the CSS rules that apply to that paragraph. If you see a selector that specifically targets the paragraph (like a class selector named *.copyright* or a descendent selector like *.footer p*), you can click it and set a value for the *font-family* property. Or, if you find there isn't a selector that formats the copyright notice's font, you can create one.

Analyzing CSS in JavaScript and Server-Side Pages

CSS Designer is great at locating and editing styles that affect the elements on a page, but what about the HTML you don't normally see in the document window? These days, lots of sites use fancy JavaScript effects to display content—tooltips, form validation notices, and menu bars display certain page elements only when someone interacts with the page, for example. Likewise, when you create server-side-driven pages, like PHP pages that retrieve information from a database, you see the completed page and all its elements only *after* a web server processes the server-side programming and sends a completed web page back to your browser.

> **NOTE** You can't change a page in Live view—that is, you can't click inside a paragraph and add new text, for example. However, you *can* edit the HTML, CSS, and JavaScript in Split view (page 313), and Live view will reflect those changes. You can also edit the CSS of a page in Live view using CSS Designer. To exit Live view, click the Live button in the Document toolbar or choose View→Live View. You can also use the keyboard shortcut Alt-F11 (Option-F11) to toggle Live view off and on.

So how do you make sure pages that require real-time interaction with a web browser look and act the way you want? Easy: Dreamweaver includes a Live view feature called Inspect mode. Once in Live view, click the Inspect button (circled in Figure 11-2) to mouse around a page and analyze its CSS. You can even interact with JavaScript-driven effects like drop-down menus, and analyze the CSS of page elements that aren't normally visible in Design view.

A few things happen when you're in Inspect mode:

- **Dreamweaver highlights a tag's box, padding, and margins.** As you mouse around the page, Dreamweaver highlights the box model of each tag you mouse over. As you may remember from page 79, every block-level tag (like a headline, div, or paragraph) is basically a box with a width, height, margins, padding, and borders. When you mouse over a tag in Inspect mode, the underlying "box" turns blue to reveal its dimensions; padding appears in light purple, and margins show up in light yellow. Not every element has all these properties, so you may see some but not others. In fact, since you can set padding and margin values individually for each side of a tag, you might see padding or a margin on only one side of an element.

- **The Tag Selector displays the HTML structure.** When you mouse over page elements, such as images, paragraphs, <div> tags, and so on, the Tag Selector at the bottom of the document window identifies the tag you're over, as well as the tags that wrap around the current one. For example, in Figure 11-2, the Tag Selector's highlighting *<article>*, meaning your mouse is over an <article> tag (<article> is a new HTML5 tag). The page's HTML encloses that tag in several other tags—in this case, a bunch of divs.

Element
(blue)

Padding
(purple)

Margin
(yellow)

FIGURE 11-2

Dreamweaver's Inspect mode is a great way to see which CSS styles affect which elements on a page. It's especially useful for pages with a lot of JavaScript-created elements (like drop-down menus and tooltips), or pages that include server-side programming, like PHP files. This figure shows a blog post made with the popular WordPress blogging system. In WordPress and other "content management systems" like Joomla and Drupal, web "pages" aren't individual files like the ones you've been building in this book, they're dynamically created screens that pull information from a database and construct the HTML for the page on the fly. Live view lets you see what a page created with server-side programming looks like in a browser; Inspect mode lets you analyze the CSS that formats the different parts of a page, like the blog posting shown here.

- **CSS Designer updates.** When you use Live view and its Inspect mode, CSS Designer displays the Computed properties for a selected element in the Properties section, and updates the Source and Selectors lists. In other words, Inspect mode gives you a birds-eye view of the page's CSS. In Figure 11-2, for example, you can see this level of detail. The mouse sits over an article, and in the Selectors section, you see the classes, IDs, and tags used to format the article. In the Properties section, you see the specific styles that Dreamweaver applies.

If you decide to edit the styles for a particular element, click the element while you're in Inspect mode; this selects the element and displays its CSS Computed rules in

CSS Designer. You can then edit the styles in the Properties section, as described on page 109.

Once you click an element, Dreamweaver exits Inspect mode (although it stays in Live view). To re-enter Inspect mode, press the Inspect button again (or use the keyboard shortcut Shift-Alt-F11 [Shift-Option-F11]).

TIP In Inspect mode, it's sometimes hard to select the exact tag you want to analyze in CSS Designer. For example, when you mouse over a div nested inside another div, Dreamweaver highlights the innermost div, and selecting the outer, parent div may not be easy. The solution? While you mouse over an element in Inspect mode, press the left arrow key to highlight the next-nearest parent element (the tag wrapped around the currently highlighted tag). You can keep pressing the left arrow key to move up the nest of HTML tags. (Press the right arrow key to move back down to the original element.) Finally, when the tag you're interested in gets highlighted, click the mouse button to select it. Dreamweaver displays all its CSS rules in CSS Designer's Properties section.

■ FOLLOWING LINKS IN SERVER-SIDE PAGES

Dreamweaver CC includes a Browse function in Live view. That is, you can actually click links in Live view to jump to different pages within your site. The linked page then appears in the document window. This is kind of cool, but not that useful for links that call up other pages on the Web—you can't edit those live pages. It's not even that useful for regular web pages within your own site—after all, you can just open those pages from the Files panel to edit them.

NOTE The information in this section applies to server-side-driven pages, such as pages written in the PHP programming language. You need to have a web server set up on your computer, as explained on page 885. Chapter 22 discusses server-side programming.

To follow links on a page, you need to:

1. **Enter Live view.**

   Click the Live button in the Document toolbar, choose View→Live View, or press Alt+F11 (Option-F11). In Live view, Dreamweaver displays the navigation toolbar seen in Figure 11-3. It's made up of buttons, text boxes, and menus that function like the tools in your web browser.

2. **Ctrl-click (⌘-click) a link.**

   This loads a linked page into Dreamweaver's Live view. In the case of some dynamic pages, like WordPress, Dreamweaver doesn't actually load a new page, it sends a request to the web server and the *index.php* file, which does a bunch of behind-the-scenes magic to generate a new chunk of HTML and display a newly minted page on the fly.

   When you're in Live view, you have to Ctrl+Click (⌘-Click) links to follow them. But you can fine-tune your Dreamweaver browsing experience. To the right of the navigation toolbar, click the Live view options menu, shown in Figure 11-3. To make the links respond as usual; that is, with just a click of your mouse, select Follow Links Continuously.

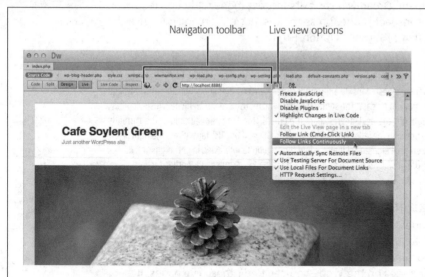

Navigation toolbar   Live view options

FIGURE 11-3

The Browser Navigation toolbar acts like the toolbar you see in web browsers. You can refresh a page, go backward or forward through the links you've visited, and even type a URL in the address bar. The toolbar only appears when you're in Live view, and it's most useful when you work with server-side pages.

Overcoming Common CSS Problems

As you get more adventurous with CSS, you'll probably encounter—as many web designers before you have—some of the weird intricacies of working with floated elements ("floats"). This section describes a few common problems and their solutions. (And if you ever stumble on a problem not listed here, you can always take it to one of the online forums listed in Appendix A on page 909.)

Clearing and Containing Floats

As you learned in the last chapter, the CSS *float* property is a powerful design tool. It's the only way to get content to wrap around other content. Floating a photo lets text below it move up and wrap around the image. When you create float-based column designs, though, sometimes you *don't* want content to move up and next to a floated element. For example, you probably want to keep copyright notices, contact information, and other housekeeping details at the bottom of your web page, below all the other content. The last thing you want is for any of these elements to move up the page and wrap around core page content.

In the CSS layouts discussed in the last chapter, you saw that if the main column of content is shorter than either of the floated sidebar columns, the footer moved up and around the left-floated column (Figure 11-4, left, circled). To make the footer stay below the sidebars, you use the *clear* property (page 439), which prevents an element from wrapping around floats (Figure 11-4, right, circled).

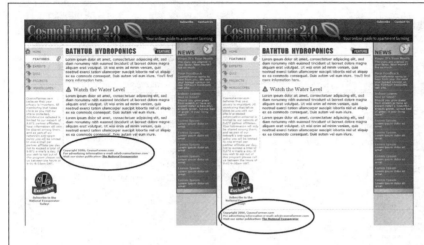

FIGURE 11-4

You don't always want an item to wrap around a floated element (left). Copyright notices and other housekeeping info that belong at the bottom of a page usually need to clear any floats they encounter. The Clear property forces the copyright notice to the bottom of the page, below any floated elements (right).

Add the *clear* property to the style for any tag you want to prevent from wrapping around a floated element (you find the property in the Layout category of CSS Designer and in the Box category of the CSS Rule Definition window). You can make an element drop below a left-floated object by selecting "left" in the Clear drop-down menu, or below a right-floated object by selecting "right." For footers and other items that need to appear at the bottom of the page, select "both" to drop below left- and right-floated elements.

Another problem occurs when you float one or more elements inside a non-floated containing tag, like a <div>. When the floated element is taller than the content inside the div, it sticks out of the bottom of the enclosing element. This snafu is especially noticeable if that tag has a background or border. The top image in Figure 11-5 shows a <div> tag that has an <h1> tag and two columns created by floating two divs. The enclosing div's style applies background and border properties to the entire box, but they appear only around the <h1> tag. That's because the floated columns are bigger than their container. So, instead of expanding the borders of the box, the columns pop out of the bottom of it. What you really want is something like the bottom image in Figure 11-5.

You see a similar problem with the three boxes that contain photos in Figure 11-5, top. In this case, the style floats each image left inside a containing div that has a border. Because the images are taller than their boxes, they pop out of the bottom. Unfortunately, this problem is even worse than the previous one, because each image causes the image below it to wrap to the right, creating an ugly staggered effect.

You can tackle the problem of renegade floats many ways. You'll learn several of the most common techniques in the bullet points below. They use Figure 11-5 as an example, but the solutions apply to all dropped floats.

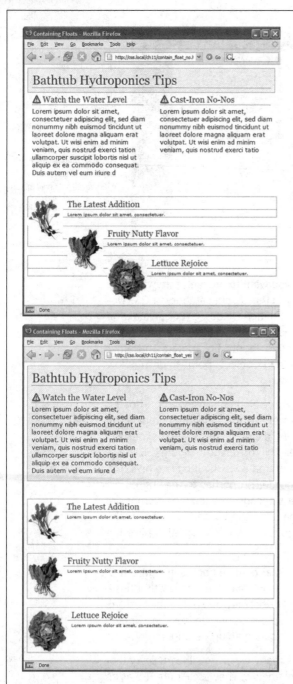

FIGURE 11-5

A floated element can escape its containing div if it's taller than the container. If the containing tag includes a background or border, the escaping elements can look like they're not even part of the container, as you can see in the top image—the bathtub tips should have the same tinted background as the headline does (bottom image), but they're popping out of their container (the tinted box with the headline in it). In addition, a floated element can bump into other elements—including other floats, thereby creating a "stair-step" effect, like the one you see in the three boxed elements in the top image. You really want the nicely stacked boxes you see in the bottom image.

- **Add a clearing element at the bottom of the containing div.** This solution's the most straightforward. Simply add a tag—like a line break or horizontal rule—as the last item in the <div> containing the floated element (that is, right before the closing </div> tag). Then use the *clear* property to force that extra tag below the float. This trick makes the enclosing div expand, revealing its background and border. For example, add a line break
 before the closing </div> tag and then add a class to it: *<br class="clearfloat">*. The quickest way to do this is to manually type this in Code view. Then, in CSS Designer's Selectors section, you'll need to create a CSS class (*.clearfloat*). Finally, in Properties, set the "clear" property to *both* (see below).

- **Float the containing element.** An easier solution is to float the div that contains the floated elements. A floated container div expands to fully include the floated elements inside it. In Figure 11-5, top, for example, the *float* property's been added to the div containing the heading and the two floated columns. In the process, the div's entire box—right down to its background and borders—expands to fit everything inside it, including the floated elements. Strange, but true (Figure 11-5, bottom).

  If you go this route, make sure you add a *clear* property to whatever element follows the floated container so that the following element drops below the container.

- **Use overflow:hidden.** Another common technique is to add the *overflow* property (page 462) to the tag that wraps around the floated elements. In CSS Designer's Properties Section, set the overflow property to hidden.

  The *overflow:hidden* property is just another one of those weird CSS things: It forces the containing block to expand and contain the floated elements.

  In general, this technique works very well. However, if you have any absolutely positioned elements (see page 458) inside the container, they may not show up. Because the CSS hides the "overflow," it hides the stuff that appears outside the container, such as an element absolutely positioned outside it. You'll experience this if you have a drop-down menu inside another tag and the drop-downs, when they appear, should be outside the container element. If that's the case, use one of the float-taming methods described above.

Avoiding Float Drops

Say you call up your website-in-progress and find that one of your page's columns simply drops down below the others (see Figure 11-6). You've got the dreaded "float drop," a symptom of there being too little room to fit the float. "But," you say, "it looks like there's plenty of room for all the columns to exist side by side." It looks that way, but there's a problem with your math.

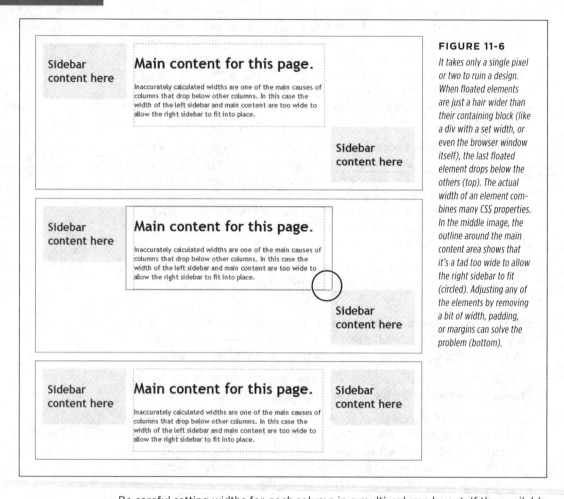

FIGURE 11-6

It takes only a single pixel or two to ruin a design. When floated elements are just a hair wider than their containing block (like a div with a set width, or even the browser window itself), the last floated element drops below the others (top). The actual width of an element combines many CSS properties. In the middle image, the outline around the main content area shows that it's a tad too wide to allow the right sidebar to fit (circled). Adjusting any of the elements by removing a bit of width, padding, or margins can solve the problem (bottom).

Be careful setting widths for *each* column in a multi-column layout. If the available space in a browser window (or in a div containing the columns in a fixed-width design) is less than the *total* widths of the columns, you're asking for a float drop. You need to check your arithmetic. If you're using one of Dreamweaver's fixed-width layouts, a <div> tag with the ID *.container* wraps around the other tags on the page. Dreamweaver's stock style sheet sets the div to a width of 960 pixels. In a two-column design, you'll find two other divs, one for the main content and the other for a sidebar. If the combined widths of these two divs is greater than 960 pixels, the main content div drops below the sidebar.

Also, keep the CSS box model in mind: As discussed in the box on page 442, the width of an element displayed in a browser window isn't the same as its *width property*. The displayed width of any element combines the element's width, left and right border sizes, left and right padding, and left and right margins. For columns to fit side by side, the browser window (or containing div) must accommodate the total of all these widths.

While miscalculated column widths are the most common cause of dropped floats, they can also result from rounding errors if you use percentage widths. Browsers sometimes make mistakes when calculating the actual number of pixels needed to display something on the screen. That is, they can round numbers up, making elements slightly too large for the available space. So be careful when you set widths in percentages—err on the side of caution and make your percentage widths total slightly less than 100 percent.

Bottom line: The only reason you'll see a float drop is because there's not enough room to hold all of a page's columns side by side. Rather than strive to use every last pixel of screen space, give your elements a little wiggle room. Get in the habit of making the overall column widths a bit smaller than the max, and you'll spend less time troubleshooting float drops.

FREQUENTLY ASKED QUESTION

Should I Care About IE 6?

I keep hearing that Internet Explorer 6 is dead and we don't need to worry about it anymore. Is this true?

If you're a web designer, you've probably got the latest version of Internet Explorer, Safari, Firefox, Chrome, or Opera on your computer. Previous versions of this book talked quite a bit about Internet Explorer 6 and even provided a section on how to deal with IE 6 bugs. You won't find that section in this edition because IE 6 is rapidly disappearing.

If you're building sites with a US audience in mind, less than 0.2 percent of web surfers use that outdated browser; in the UK, it's 0.5 percent. The exact figure varies depending on whom you ask and where the web audience is. For example, when this was written, the website Internet Explorer 6 Countdown (*http://www.IE6countdown.com*) says that worldwide usage is 6.3 percent. In China, however, IE 6 is still widely used.

Even statistics that include the geographic region of your site's audience don't truly reflect which browsers your visitors use. If you build a site aimed at tech-savvy web designers, odds are that IE 6 hasn't tapped your site in a long time. But if your site is aimed at people in China, you may need to contend with IE 6.

The best way to find out how much of your traffic comes via IE 6 is to look at your web server's log files or sign up for Google Analytics (*http://www.google.com/analytics*) so you can track your visitors' browsers (among many other things).

For the great majority of web design projects, IE 6 is effectively gone. Hooray!

Designing Websites for Mobile Devices

Web designers used to build web pages for the 800 x 600 pixel resolution of 15-inch monitors. Then, as large LCD screens became popular, most web wizards designed pages for monitors that measured 1,024 pixels wide and larger. Today, the explosive growth of smartphones, like the iPhone and Android models, make it clear that designers need to craft sites for much smaller screens, too. A majestic, panoramic web page that looks beautiful on a 27-inch monitor may turn into a tiny, unreadable postage stamp on an iPhone.

You can accommodate the multitude of mobile browsing devices several ways. Some designers build separate, mobile versions of their sites (see Figure 12-1). Using server-side programming, these sites detect the type of device you have and deliver a web page customized for that device. An iPhone web surfer, for example, will see the mobile version of a site, which provides a greatly simplified experience: a single-column design with most of the navigation elements removed, but with a prominent search box added.

Of course, not all of us have the time to create two versions of a website, or the technical skills to program a server to detect a visitor's browser. Fortunately, Dreamweaver CC includes several tools that tackle the problem of mobile site design. The most straightforward of them uses CSS; CSS3 offers a feature called *media queries* that lets you check the resolution of a device (how many pixels wide a screen is) and supply styles for just that resolution. For example, if a screen is 320 pixels wide (typical for phones held vertically, in "portrait" mode), you can apply styles that format the page for that dimension. In other words, instead of sending out different versions of the site to different-size devices, you distribute the same site, but use different style sheets to format the HTML.

FIGURE 12-1

Many large companies, like Amazon.com and Target.com (pictured), create mobile versions of their sites, optimized for display on handheld devices like the iPhone.

Dreamweaver CC also provides tools for building pages using jQuery Mobile, a JavaScript library that helps you build websites specifically tailored to mobile devices. With some simple HTML, some fancy CSS, and some complex JavaScript programming, jQuery Mobile lets you create the navigation elements commonly found on smartphones. You can create a website that really feels like a phone application, or you can use HTML, CSS, and jQuery Mobile to actually *create* a phone application that you can install on Android devices or upload to Apple's App Store for use on iPads, iPhones, and iPod Touches. Dreamweaver CS5.5 introduced this jQuery tool, and CC enhances it, adding a "swatches" panel that lets you quickly apply different designs to a jQuery mobile-powered web page, for example.

Dreamweaver CC has also improved on a feature called *fluid grid layouts*. It combines the results of a media query with a fancy grid-based layout tool to create pages designed for the destination device (that's called "responsive Web design" in Internet argot). Based on media query results, the site changes to a layout based on one of three basic browser widths—mobile, tablet, and desktop—and then uses percentage widths to scale the layout for a specific device—after all, not all mobile phones have screens that are 320 pixels wide, and not all tablet screens are 760 pixels wide. Using this flexible layout, you can create designs that scale to a range of widths and adapt for the myriad screen sizes on mobile and tablet devices.

■ Previewing Pages at Different Resolutions

Testing web pages in different browsers has always been a chore for webmasters, and that's especially true for mobile design. As smartphone and tablet makers battle for market share, they change screen sizes and pixel density (number of pixels per inch). That means web designers are left to cope with new challenges. In the past, to preview a web page on a phone, you had to store the page on your server and use your mobile phone to connect to the website to see how it looks. Now, Dreamweaver jockeys have more resources for envisioning their layouts on the wide variety of screens. You can use the built-in Window Size feature in Design view. If you have an Apple or Android phone or tablet, you can use Adobe Edge Inspect to examine your Dreamweaver pages on that device. In addition, there are a few resources out on the web to help you. This section explores all these options.

Previewing Different Screen Sizes in Dreamweaver

Dreamweaver CC simulates different mobile devices' screen sizes right within Design view. Down in the lower-right corner of the document window are the Window Size controls. Three icons of different sizes look suspiciously like smartphone, tablet, and desktop displays (Figure 12-2). Next to those icons is a drop-down menu that displays the dimensions of the Design window's current view. For example, you may see 1000 x 620, which means the view is set to 1,000 pixels wide by 620 pixels tall.

For a quick look at your page layout in phone, tablet, or desktop form, click one of the three icons at the bottom of the page. For all but the shortest of web pages, you'll see a scroll bar on the right side to help you view all your content. As you click on the device icons, you may notice that the window size numbers change. The phone, tablet, and desktop buttons use preset dimensions, but you're not limited to those.

A click on the Window Size numbers opens a menu with close to a dozen window size options. Each indicates a screen size and a type of device. For example, one option is "768 x 1024 Tablet," which are the dimensions of the original iPad. Want to see that tablet screen in landscape mode? Choose Orientation Landscape from the menu.

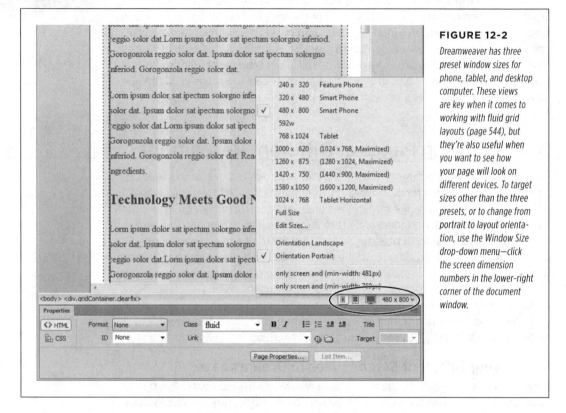

FIGURE 12-2

Dreamweaver has three preset window sizes for phone, tablet, and desktop computer. These views are key when it comes to working with fluid grid layouts (page 544), but they're also useful when you want to see how your page will look on different devices. To target sizes other than the three presets, or to change from portrait to layout orientation, use the Window Size drop-down menu—click the screen dimension numbers in the lower-right corner of the document window.

What if you don't see the size you need? Perhaps it's important that you know what your design looks like on an 800 x 600 screen. You can create a new window size option. Click Edit Sizes from the Window Sizes menu and Dreamweaver's Preferences window opens with the Window Sizes category already selected (Figure 12-3).

Previewing Your Layout with Edge Inspect

Simulating screen sizes is all well and good, but there's nothing like viewing the web page you're designing on an actual device. You get to see how your page looks in the real world, and you discover any quirks that pop up on mobile touchscreens. If you own an iPhone, iPad, or Android phone or tablet, Adobe has a tool that can help. Adobe Edge Inspect works through your wireless network. Your desktop computer uses the Google Chrome browser with a special Inspect plug-in. Your mobile device uses a free app you download from the app store. Once you set everything up, your desktop computer can literally beam a web page you're looking at in Chrome on your desktop straight to your phone or tablet. In fact, you can send a page to all your iOS or Android devices simultaneously. So, after you make changes to a page in Dreamweaver, you can use File→Preview in Browser to view the page in Chrome.

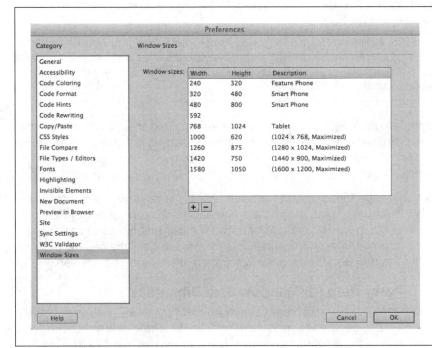

FIGURE 12-3

You can add options to Dreamweaver's Window Sizes list by going to Preferences→Windows Sizes. Click the + button to add a new size, and then enter a width, height, and name for your new window size. For example, you can create a 800 x 600 window and dub it "Old Monitor."

To use Inspect, you need a Creative Cloud account and you have to download and install the desktop application through the Creative Cloud panel. On your mobile device, download the free Edge Inspect app from your app store (Apple or Android). If you don't have Google Chrome, you should get a copy for cross-browser testing, even if you don't want to use Inspect. You can download Chrome for free at *http://www.google.com/chrome*.

NOTE One significant drawback with Inspect is that you need to set up a local testing server to view the pages you're designing in Dreamweaver. See page 885 to learn how to install a testing server for Windows (WAMP) or the Mac (MAMP).

After you install the desktop and mobile apps, you need to fire them up on your computer, phones, and tablets. The first time you run Inspect on your desktop, you'll be asked to install the Edge Inspect plug-in for Google Chrome. This is a one-time chore.

Once you have Inspect running on your desktop and mobile devices, you need to establish a connection between the two. Your mobile app will request the name of your local network or the IP (Internet Protocol) address of your desktop computer (see the Tip below on how to find an IP address). After you type in the info, you get a six-number code to type into the Google Chrome plug-in. Fortunately, you only have to do this once.

TIP   To find the IP address for a Windows computer, press the Windows key and type *cmd* in the search box. This opens a primitive DOS-like window, where you can type in commands. Type *ipconfig* and then press Enter. Several details about your network connection appear. The line "IPv4 address" displays the number you need. It'll be in a form like this: 192.168.1.104.

To find the local IP address for a Mac, click the Apple icon. Choose "About This Mac." In the About This Mac window, click More Info. In the next window, click System Report. In the report that appears, click Network in the left-hand column of categories. At the top of the page you'll see a line that says AirPort. To the far right of that is the IP address—four numbers separated by periods.

The process is simpler the next time you use Inspect. Start the apps on your desktop and mobile devices, turn on Inspect in Chrome (as shown in Figure 12-4), and then, in your mobile app, click the name of the desktop device you want to connect to (Figure 12-4, bottom).

When your page shows up on the mobile device, you can take screenshots of the display. That way, you can show a client how a page looks on a phone or table. You get a screen grab two ways: through controls within the mobile app, or by requesting one through the desktop program. As icing on the cake, the desktop program includes a button to easily open the folder where the snapshots are stored.

Third-Party Help for Window Size Dilemmas

You're not alone in trying to figure out how your web pages will work on the variety of devices out there, so you may as well learn from those who have gone before you. In fact, some of those folks have created tools that can give you a hand.

For example, if you go to *www.websitedimensions.com*, you find helpful explanations about devices, their pixel count, and the actual space available to web pages (Dreamweaver calculates this usable space by subtracting the area taken up by toolbars and scrollbars). The two most interesting features on the site are the "Live pixel checker" and the "Does your site fit" tool. The "Live pixel checker" displays the resolution of your browser window. So if you connect to the site with your smartphone, you'll see a grid that measures the height and width of the screen in pixels, as shown in Figure 12-5.

The "Does your site fit" tool simulates what a site would look like on iPhones, iPads, and desktop computers. Feed the tool a web page address, and you see how it squeezes into the browser windows of the devices with different orientations. Everything is displayed on a single web page, so the view is similar to the Multiscreen Preview tool in Dreamweaver CS6, but removed from Dreamweaver CC. The downside to the tool is that the page you're checking needs to be live on the Internet to be tested.

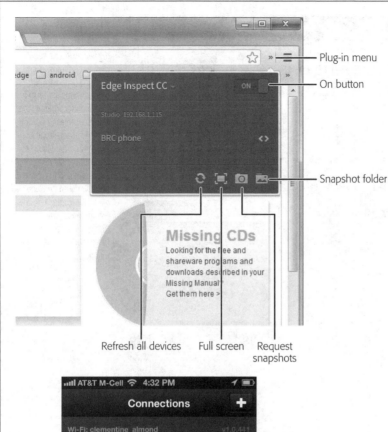

Plug-in menu

On button

Snapshot folder

Refresh all devices   Full screen   Request snapshots

FIGURE 12-4

Top: In Google Chrome on your desktop, launch the Inspect plug-in from the plug-in menu and then click the On button. Once you make a connection with a mobile device, using Inspect is pretty easy. Generally, when you click links and go from one page to another in a desktop browser, you see the results in the connected mobile devices. If necessary, you can force a refresh with the button shown here. Click the camera icon to request snapshots from each of the connected devices. Click the folder icon to open the folder where snapshots are stored.

Bottom: Inspect mobile apps remember connections they've made, so after your first session, reconnecting is a matter of clicking a name like Studio or Gravenstein shown here.

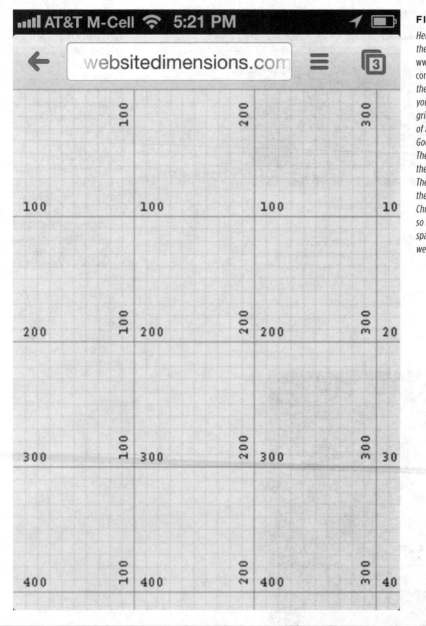

FIGURE 12-5

Here's the display from the live pixel-checker at www.websitedimensions. com. The grid marks off the screen resolution of your browser window. This grid measures the window of an iPhone 4s using Google's Chrome browser. The width is 320 pixels and the height is 415 pixels. The grid doesn't include the area occupied by Chrome's navigation bar, so the space you see is the space that's available to a web page.

Another site, Screenfly (*http://quirktools.com/screenfly/*), provides a similar tool for viewing live web pages. After you type in a web address, Screenfly displays your page below the program's toolbar (Figure 12-6). You can then use Screenfly's tools to see what your site looks like on different devices, in landscape or portrait orientation, and with or without scrollbars. Many tools like this focus only on iPhones and iPads; Screenfly is noteworthy because it includes mock-ups for many other devices, like the Kindle Fire.

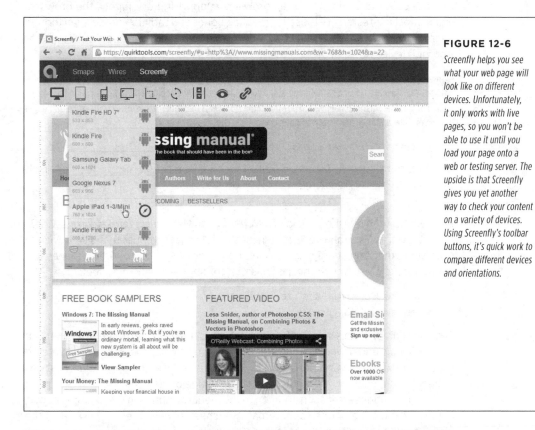

FIGURE 12-6

Screenfly helps you see what your web page will look like on different devices. Unfortunately, it only works with live pages, so you won't be able to use it until you load your page onto a web or testing server. The upside is that Screenfly gives you yet another way to check your content on a variety of devices. Using Screenfly's toolbar buttons, it's quick work to compare different devices and orientations.

When you're feeling particular geeky, you may want to head over to CSS-Tricks (*http://css-tricks.com*). Check out some of the lively forums, where you'll find questions and answers on all sorts of CSS, JavaScript, and PHP topics ("Why doesn't this slider work?" "Can I use JavaScript to delete a row in a table on the fly?"). The CSS-Combat forum is a good place to learn more about CSS and strategies for different window sizes. The Snippets section provides examples of working code. So, for example, this page (*http://css-tricks.com/snippets/css/retina-display-media-query/*) shows you how to fashion a media-query that specifically targets Apple devices equipped with high-resolution Retina displays. Not sure what a media query is? Read on.

■ Media Queries

As mentioned at the beginning of this chapter, CSS3 includes a concept called *media queries*, which lets you assign styles to a page based on the width and height of the destination browser. So you can create custom styles for mobile phones, tablets, and desktop browsers, and, in turn, customize your site's presentation so that it looks its best on each type of device. Because media queries are part of the yet-to-be-finished CSS3 standard, not all browsers support it. Fortunately, the browsers you're most interested in—those for mobile phones and tablets—do, so even though Internet Explorer 8 doesn't know what a media query is, your good old iPhone or Android device does.

> **TIP**   You can make IE 8 and earlier understand your media queries by adding a bit of JavaScript to the <head> section of your document. You'll need to download the *respond.js* file from *http://tinyurl.com/7w49a6z*. Put the file on your site, and then link it to your page using the <script> tag. For example:
>
> ```
> <script src="respond.min.js"></script>
> ```
>
> This little maneuver forces IE 6, 7, and 8 to understand media queries. In fact, Dreamweaver CC's new fluid grid layout automatically adds this JavaScript to your pages (see page 544).

A "query" is just a question asked of a web browser: "Is your screen 320 pixels wide?" If the answer is Yes, the browser launches a style sheet for just that size device (a style sheet that you supply, as explained on page 104). The code that makes this happen looks pretty much the same as that for any external style sheet:

```
<link href="css/phone.css" rel="stylesheet" type="text/css" media="only
screen and (width:320px)">
```

The one addition to this standard style sheet link is the *media* attribute, which sets up the conditions under which Dreamweaver uses a particular sheet. You encountered the media attribute in Chapter 9, where you told a browser to apply different styles depending on whether you want to print out a page or view it on-screen (see page 392). Media queries are just an addition to the media attribute. In the example above, a browser loads the *phone.css* external style sheet when someone views your site with a browser whose width measures 320 pixels.

Because 320 pixels is very precise—what if there's a phone with a slightly smaller screen, say one that's just 300 pixels wide—it's best to use a range of values in your media query. For example, you might want to apply a particular style for screens that are less than or equal to 480 pixels wide:

```
<link href="css/phone.css" rel="stylesheet" type="text/css" media="only
screen and (max-width:480px)">
```

The notation "max-width:480px" is the same as saying "for screens that are at most 480 pixels wide." So the <body> tag style would apply to screens that are 480px wide, 320 pixels wide, and 200 pixels wide, for example.

Likewise, there's a min-width option that determines whether a browser is at least a certain width. This is useful when you target a device that's bigger than a mobile phone or tablet. For example, you could write this link to apply styles to screens wider than the 768 pixels of many tablets:

```
<link href="css/desktop.css" rel="stylesheet" type="text/css" media="only
screen and (min-width:769px)">
```

To use this style sheet, a browser window must be at least 769 pixels wide—that's 1 pixel wider than a tablet.

And finally, you can set both Max Widths and Min Widths to target devices that fall between phones and desktop browsers. For example, you could use this CSS code to create styles for a tablet that's 768 pixels wide,:

```
<link href="css/tablet.css" rel="stylesheet" type="text/css" media="only
screen and (min-width:481px) and (max-width:768px)
```

In other words, the browser's screen must be at least 481 pixels wide, but not more than 768 pixels wide. The style sheet listed above wouldn't apply to a 320-pixel-wide smartphone, nor would it apply to a desktop browser with a screen width of 1,024 pixels.

In the discussion about media queries, you may notice a lot of emphasis on browser window width. There's a reason for that. The biggest problem with viewing most websites on a phone is that their pages are just too wide, forcing you to either zoom in and scroll left and right to read the page, or squint and try to make out the tiny-tiny type of a three-column web page displayed at 320 pixels. Most web pages are already too tall to fit inside a browser window without scrolling anyway, so worrying about a browser's height doesn't make much sense.

Fortunately, Dreamweaver doesn't require you to know how to write media queries. CSS Designer give you the tools you need to create them for desktop, phone, and tablet browsers. When you click the Add Sources button (the + sign) in CSS Designer's Sources section, you use Conditional Usage options to define a media query. Below the Sources section, you'll see the Media section, which you use to insert media queries into existing files. The media query retrieves the dimensions of the web browser window, and then tells the browser which CSS rules to use.

With CSS Designer, you can create a media query and Dreamweaver writes the necessary code. Used in conjunction with the window size previews discussed above, you can build media queries and preview their effects directly in Dreamweaver. Read on to learn how.

CSS3 media queries can do more than just check the width of a browser. The current media queries standard states that you can check for height, orientation (whether a phone is held upright in portrait mode, or sideways in landscape mode), and even whether a device uses a color or monochrome screen. There are a few other browser characteristics you can check with media queries, but not all browsers support them. You can learn more at the W3C website, *www.w3.org/TR/css3-mediaqueries.*

Two Approaches to Media Queries

Dreamweaver provides the tools you need to attach separate external style sheets for each screen size you target: a phone style sheet, a tablet style sheet, a desktop style sheet, and so on. You can have as many style sheets as you want, each for a different screen resolution.

You can either attach those style sheets directly to a web page (see Figure 12-7, top) or to an intermediary style sheet—called a site-wide media queries file—that is, in turn, attached to the web page (Figure 12-7, bottom). The benefit of the site-wide file is that you need only one line of code to attach a style sheet to the page, instead of one line of code for each style sheet you create (for example, three lines of code that load phone, tablet, and desktop style sheets).

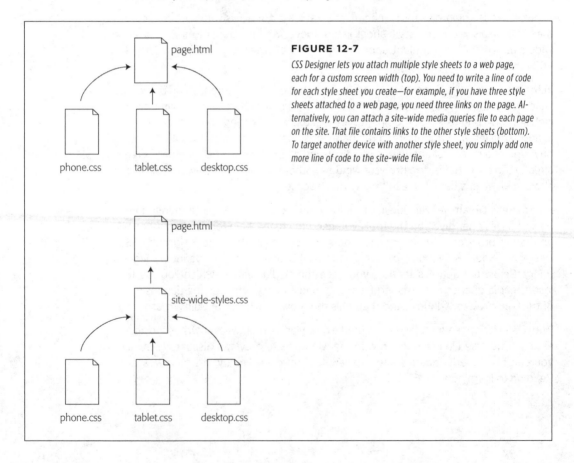

FIGURE 12-7

CSS Designer lets you attach multiple style sheets to a web page, each for a custom screen width (top). You need to write a line of code for each style sheet you create—for example, if you have three style sheets attached to a web page, you need three links on the page. Alternatively, you can attach a site-wide media queries file to each page on the site. That file contains links to the other style sheets (bottom). To target another device with another style sheet, you simply add one more line of code to the site-wide file.

In addition, by using the site-wide media queries file, it's easier to add or remove style sheets for different devices. For example, say you start off with three style sheets, one for smartphones, one for tablets, and a third for desktop browsers, and you attached those sheets to each page on your site. If you later decide you only need style sheets for phones and desktop browsers, you need to edit every page on your site to remove the link to the tablet style sheet. If, however, you use a site-wide media queries file, you only need to edit the site-wide file to remove the tablet style sheet. Since each page on your site links to the site-wide file, Dreamweaver automatically applies any changes you make to that file to every page.

NOTE If you use a site-wide file, you need to create a link to that file using the regular <link> tag—the same way you attach any external style sheet (see page 120). However, the site-wide media queries file itself won't have the CSS styles; instead, it uses a rule called *@import* in conjunction with a media query to attach device-specific style sheets:

```
@import url("phone.css") only screen and (max-width:320px);
```

Creating Media Queries with CSS Designer

In CSS Designer, Sources are locations where Dreamweaver stores CSS rules. When you identify a source, Dreamweaver lets you create a media query at the same time. Here, for example, are the steps to create an external style sheet named *phone.css* and a media query that links that style sheet to a web page if the screen width is less than 480 pixels.

1. **In CSS Designer, with your web page open in the document window, go to the Sources section, click the + icon to add a CSS source), and then choose "Create a New CSS File."**

   The Create a New CSS File window opens.

2. **In the File/URL box, type *phone.css*. Leave "Add as" set to Link.**

   Dreamweaver names your external style sheet *phone.css* and links it to this web page using code in the head portion of the HTML. Naturally, you give your external style sheets any name you want, as long as it ends in .css. Usually, something short and descriptive works best, so *phone.css*, *tablet.css*, and *desktop.css* are good choices.

3. **Click the flippy triangle next to Conditional Usage.**

   The window expands to show a box named Conditions and a text box named Code. As you add conditions, you can see Dreamweaver write the code for your media query. The Conditions box includes two menus. Initially, the menu on the left displays the word "media" and the one on the right shows "screen." This is exactly what you want when you create a media query for screen properties. In effect, you're saying that the first condition for this media query is that the *media* must be a *screen*. That's just the beginning, as you'll go on to add more conditions.

4. To the right of the two menus, click the + sign button ("Add condition").

Two more menus appear beneath the others. You'll use them to add another condition to the query. The word AND appears after the first condition. This logical AND operator is Dreamweaver's way of telling you that you must meet both conditions before Dreamweaver will link the style sheet.

5. Click the left menu and choose max-width.

When you open the menu, you see all the conditions Dreamweaver supports (Figure 12-8)—screen orientation, screen size, resolution, aspect ratio, and device size. After you choose, *max-width* the value portion of the condition changes to help you provide the value in the proper format. There's a text box where you enter the value and a drop-down menu with units of measure (like px (pixels), pt (points), and % (percentage).

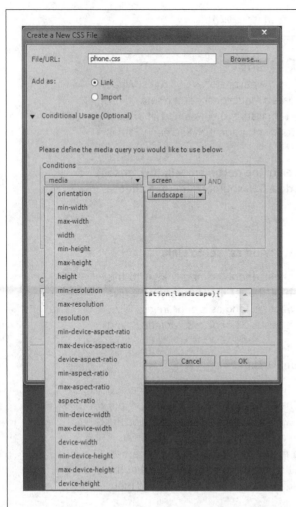

FIGURE 12-8

Using the Conditional Usage option in the Create a New CSS File window, you can develop media queries while you link an external style sheet to your page. You build your query by adding conditions. Here, the first condition is "screen" for the target media. The menu for the next condition is open, showing the variety of media queries that Dreamweaver supports.

6. **In the box between max-width and px, type *480*.**

The max-width property accepts a value and a unit of measure. When you're done, the Create a New CSS File window should look like Figure 12-9.

7. **Click OK.**

The Create a New CSS File window closes. The external style sheet *phone.css* appears in Sources, with an description of the media query appearing in brackets like this: [screen and (max-width:480px)]. Behind the scenes, CSS Designer has added the code for the media query to the <head> section of your web page. Check the Code view and you see a line that looks like this:

```
<link href="phone.css" rel="stylesheet" type="text/css" media="screen and
(max-width:480px)">
```

The first part is a normal "link" to an external style sheet. The last part following the word "media" is the conditional. In effect it says, "Use the phone.css style sheet for screens that are 480 pixels or less."

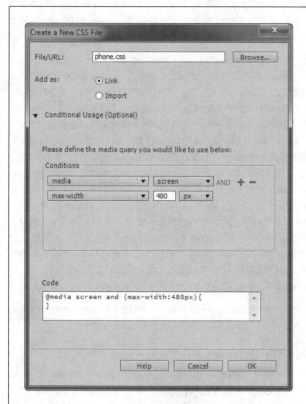

FIGURE 12-9

The conditions for the media query are set to check a device to see if the screen has a width of 480 pixels or less. That's a good test for identifying smartphone screens. The Code box shows the code for the query. Keep an eye on the box as you add queries and before you know it, you'll be able to hand-code media queries.

The media query described above has a single condition, but it could have more. For example, you could have added "orientation portrait" as another condition. In that case, when both conditions are met (the screen is 480 pixels wide *and* it's positioned in portrait mode), the query will link the *phone.css* style sheet to your web page.

■ MEDIA QUERIES FOR DESKTOP AND TABLET BROWSERS

After you create a media query for phone-sized screens, you'll want to create CSS style sheets (Sources) and media queries for the other screen sizes you want to target. For example, you might create style sheets named *desktop.css* and *tablet.css* and then link those to your pages with media queries. In general, you follow the same steps described on page 509 to build your media queries, but you identify different screen sizes and link the different style sheets.

To create a media query for desktop browsers, use min-width instead of max-width in your conditional statement (max-width targets phone screens). By using min-width, you're saying, "The browser window must be at least this wide." For example, if you set min-width to 769px, only browsers at least 769 pixels wide will load the style sheet. It also applies to wider browser windows (1,024 pixels wide, 2,000 pixels wide, and so on), but not to narrower windows—768 pixels, 480 pixels, and so on.

To create a media query for the desktop, follow the steps on page 509, but create or attach the file *desktop.css* (step 2), choose min-width as a condition (step 5), and then set the value to 769 pixels (step 6).

Creating media queries for tablets requires some strategic thinking. Tablets come in a variety of dimensions. The Kindle Fire measures 600 pixels by 1024 pixels, for example, as does the Samsung Galaxy Tab 2. The iPad is 768 pixels by 1024 pixels wide. Of course, if you hold any of these tablets in landscape mode, they'll measure 1024 pixels wide. Since 1024 pixels is wide enough to fit most web pages, there's really no reason to create a separate style sheet for these tablets when held in landscape mode, but you might want to tighten up the design for tablets held in portrait mode—for example, you might take a three-column design for the desktop and convert it to a two-column design for tablets. To do this, you create a media query that handles screens larger than your phone's (480 pixels), but smaller than your desktop's browser window (769 pixels). So, you create a media query for tablets the same way you create one for phones and desktop browsers—you create or attach a tablet style sheet, include a min-width condition of 481 pixels, and then add another condition (see Step 4, on page 509), one that sets the max-width to 768 pixels. These conditions target screen sizes between those for phones and those for desktops.

At this point, your style sheets have no CSS rules. You need to add selectors and set property values for the styles you want to apply to the various screens.

Using a Site-Wide Media Queries File

A site-wide media query is a single, external style sheet that points to other style sheets, depending on your target device. Each page in your site links to the site-wide file, which in turn loads the appropriate style sheet for the target device. As mentioned on page 508, this approach means you add just one line of HTML to your page (for the site-wide file), and makes it easy to add or remove a media query from your site because you only have to edit one site-wide file. In addition, as you'll see next, it's faster to add the site-wide file to a web page using Dreamweaver. Because of these advantages, it's generally a good idea to use a side-wide media query.

NOTE The one downside to site-wide media queries is that they require one additional request of the web server—the receiving browser has to download the site-wide file *and* the style sheet for your visitor's device. Downloading that additional file results in a slight performance hit, but unless you get huge amounts of traffic, no one will notice.

The steps for setting up a site-wide media query file include:

- Create an external style sheet to hold the media queries—this is your site-wide media queries file.

- Add links to web pages that point to the site-wide file.

- In the site-wide file, create media query import rules for the separate style sheets that handle phones, tablets, and desktop browsers.

- Develop CSS rules for different screens and store those in the separate style sheet for phones, tablets, and desktop browsers.

In CSS Designer, it's easy to create a new external CSS file and link it to a web page at the same time. So, you can tackle the first two tasks at once. Here's the process:

1. **With a web page open in the document window, in CSS Designer's Sources section, click the + sign (Add CSS Source), and then choose Create a New CSS File.**

   The Create a New CSS File window opens.

2. **In the File/URL box, type *sitewide.css*. Leave "Add as" set to Link.**

   You can use any name that seems appropriate for the external CSS file. As always, something short and descriptive works best.

3. **Click OK.**

   Dreamweaver creates the file *sitewide.css* and adds a link to the currently open page. There's nothing special about the link that attaches the CSS file to your page; it looks like any other link you'd create:

   ```
   <link href="sitewide.css" rel="stylesheet" type="text/css">
   ```

   You want to add this line of code to the other pages in your site that use the media queries in *sitewide.css*.

After you create the *sitewide.css* file, you can add the link to your pages in a couple of ways. You can use CSS Designer's "Add CSS Source" button (the + icon) described in step 1 above. Instead of choosing "Create a New CSS File," choose "Attach Existing CSS File." When the Attach Existing CSS File window opens, use the Browse button to identify your style sheet (*sitewide.css*). If you're comfortable in Code view, an even quicker method is to simple copy and paste the line of code (step 3) from one web page to another. Just make sure to paste the code into the <head> section of the new pages.

At this point, your site-wide queries file is empty, so the next step is to add queries to *sitewide.css.* If you plan on having separate CSS files to handle phone, tablet, and desktop browsers, you create three media queries. It doesn't require much code, so the easiest method is to just open the *sitewide.css* file in Dreamweaver's Code view and type in the rules (see Figure 12-10). For example, a media query to import *phone.css* might look like this:

```
@import url("phone.css") only screen and (max-width:480px);
```

The instruction to import the file is "@import." The "url()" portion defines which file you want to import. In this case, that's *phone.css,* so type that into the URL field, putting the filename in quotation marks.

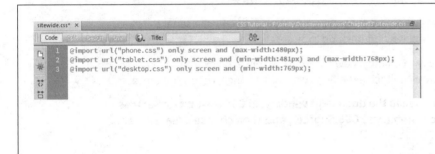

FIGURE 12-10

The site-wide media queries file named sitewide.css is open in Code view for editing. Three lines of code identify the external CSS files that apply different formatting depending on the width of the destination screen.

The word "only" in the code sample above is meant for older browsers, those that don't handle media queries. Those browsers ignore the media query when they see the word "only."

The last portion of the media query file ("max-width:480px") should look familiar. It's the conditional statement used to target phones with screens that are 480 pixels wide or less. When Dreamweaver imports the file, it's as if it copied the CSS rules from *phone.css* to the *sitewide.css* file at the point of the import instruction. The position is important because the usual CSS rules of inheritance (page 382) and the cascade (page 384) apply. That can become an issue if you combine media queries with global CSS styles, as described on page 517.

To query tablets and desktop browsers, you can edit the line of code above so that it calls up the relevant external style sheets and uses different conditions:

```
@import url("desktop.css") only screen and (min-width:769px);
```

```
@import url("tablet.css") only screen and (min-width:481px) and (max-
width:768px);
```

The last step in developing a site-wide queries file is to add CSS rules to your *phone. css*, *tablet.css*, and *desktop.css* files. You do that from within CSS Designer, as described on page 104. What is a little *different* from the normal site-wide query file are the strategies behind the rules you create when you develop styles for phones, tablets, and desktop browsers. For those details, see page 518.

NOTE There's an issue you need to be aware of when you develop media queries that target desktop browsers. The still-popular Internet Explorer 8 doesn't understand media queries. Without some help, it fails to load the CSS styles used in the query. The best solution to add a bit of JavaScript code to the <head> of your document, as described in the Tip on page 430.

Using @Media to Add Queries to Internal Style Sheets

As usual with Dreamweaver and with CSS, there's more than one way to get the job done. On page 509, you saw how to use a media query to use styles you saved in an external style sheet. On page 512, you saw how to create a site-wide queries file that imports external style sheets. But you can also use media queries in an internal style sheet. That style sheet may include other styles, too, styles that Dreamweaver applies globally, for example, as explained on page 517.

Suppose you want to create a single rule that sets the font size for h1 headings to "large." You want to apply this rule to devices with screen widths of 480 pixels or less. You can create a media query for that rule and place it in the <head> section of your web page, along with any other styles you want to store internally.

1. **With your web page open in Design view, in the Sources section of CSS Designer, click the + sign (Add CSS Source) and then choose Define in Page.**

   If you already have an internal style sheet for the page, you can simply select <style> from the Sources section.

2. **With <style> selected in the Sources section of CSS Designer, go to the Media section and then click the + sign (Add Media Query).**

   The Define Media Query window opens. It looks like the Conditional Usage section of the Create a New CSS File window (Figure 12-9). The only difference is that the media query doesn't include tools to identify a file because you're going to put the query in the currently open page.

3. **For the first condition, set the left menu to media and the right menu to screen. Then, click the + sign to add a condition.**

   A new row appears where you can define a second condition. As always, you can add multiple conditions to the media query.

4. **For the second condition, set the left menu to max-width and then type *480* in the box next to px.**

   The code in the Code box looks like this:

   ```
   @media screen and (max-width:480px){

   }
   ```

   That is your media query. As you'll see next, Dreamweaver applies any CSS rules that appear between the curly braces ({}) when the media query's conditions are met.

5. **Click OK.**

   A new media query appears in the Media section of CSS Designer. As you can see in Figure 12-11, its name actually describes the query.

6. **With the media query, "screen and (max-width:480px)" selected in Media, click the + button (Add Selector) in the Selectors section.**

   A text box opens in the Selectors list, where you can name your selector. If you don't see the media query in Media, you probably don't have <style> selected in Sources. The media query will only appear when you select <style> or All Sources.

7. **In the selector name box, type *h1*.**

   The h1 selector targets h1 headings.

8. **In the Properties section of CSS Designer, click the T button to see Text properties. Click to the right of the font-size property, and then choose large from the menu.**

   You created a style rule for the h1 headings that sets the font-size property to "large." CSS Designer has placed that rule inside the curly brackets ({}) of the media query in the page's internal style sheet. In the document window, click Source Code to see the code Dreamweaver inserts into your HTML. It looks like this:

   ```
   @media screen and (max-width:480px){
   h1 {
       font-size: large;
   }
   }
   ```

   The CSS rule for the heading is comprised of the second, third, and fourth lines.

At this point, you can continue to add CSS rules to your media query. You do that by clicking the + sign (a.k.a. the Add Media Query button) in the Media section of CSS Designer (Figure 12-11). Then you add selectors and set property values. Dreamweaver puts all the rules you create inside the curly braces of your media query. You can create additional queries for other screen sizes and store them in your internal sheet. Just follow the steps above and provide different conditions for the query. You can also create CSS rules in the internal style sheet that don't use media queries. For details, see the next section.

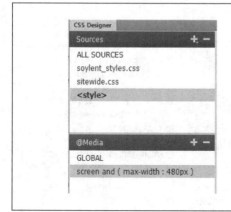

FIGURE 12-11

With the internal style sheet <style> selected in the Sources section of CSS Designer, you see the media queries Designer uses in the Media section. In this example, the Media section shows that you have a media query called "screen and (max-width:480px)." If there were other media queries in <style>, Dreamweaver would list them here, too. If you select a source and don't see any media queries in the Media section, that means there are no media queries in that source.

Using Media Queries and Global CSS Styles

As the previous sections explain, you can include media queries in external or internal style sheets, just as you would any old CSS rule. No matter where Dreamweaver stores media queries, it's not unusual for web pages to use styles that result from media queries and those that apply globally to all the pages on your site (in other words, rules that aren't governed by media queries). For example, you might have a set of styles that apply to all devices: page background color, font-family, and font-color. In addition, you may have other styles specific to phone, tablet, or desktops browser windows. These device-specific styles might change the font-size, image size, layout widths, and the float arrangement of columns.

So, after you create a combination of styles that use media queries and styles that don't, how can you tell the difference within CSS Designer? If Dreamweaver stores your media query and its rules in an internal style sheet, that style sheet's name appears in CSS Designer's Media panel. If your media query is a link to an external style sheet, the filename appears in the Sources section, with a description of the query in brackets. If you created a site-wide media queries file, with multiple media queries inside it, you'll see the name of the site-wide queries file listed in the Sources section with a flippy triangle next to its name. Click the triangle to display all the media queries in the file (see Figure 12-12). When you click a specific query in CSS Designer, the Selectors section shows you the selectors the query governs, while the Properties section displays related properties. Turn on the Show Set checkbox to see only properties with established rules. To see styles that are ungoverned by media queries, click a source or select All Sources in the Sources section. Then, click Global in the Media section. When you do, Dreamweaver displays only those selectors independent of media queries. In other words, you see only styles that Dreamweaver applies globally. With Show Set turned on, the Properties section of CSS Designer shows only the properties that have values set. Show Set hides properties that don't have defined values.

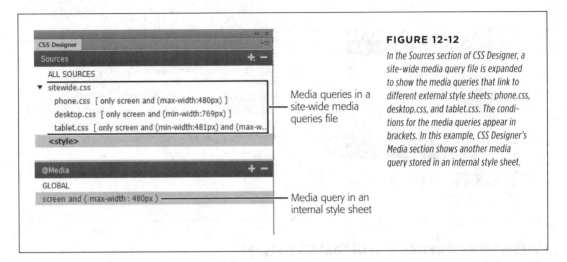

FIGURE 12-12

In the Sources section of CSS Designer, a site-wide media query file is expanded to show the media queries that link to different external style sheets: phone.css, desktop.css, and tablet.css. The conditions for the media queries appear in brackets. In this example, CSS Designer's Media section shows another media query stored in an internal style sheet.

Sometimes, you'll want to approach the issue of style ancestry from the style end. Say you have a green h2 heading. Is the rule that triggers green text a global style or one governed by a media query? Here's how you figure it out. In Design view, click the h2 heading, then look in the Selectors section of CSS Designer. Dreamweaver highlights the word Computed, indicating that the displayed properties may come from more than one source. In the Properties section, click the Color property—that's the one making your text green. Now, look in the Sources and Media sections of Designer. Dreamweaver displays the source for the color property in bold. You may see that it's an external style sheet loaded with a media query. In that case, you see the query's filename with the query in brackets.

If you see a source displayed in bold without brackets or a media query, that means your style isn't controlled by a media query.

On the other hand, you may see a query in Designer's Media section that's bold. In that case, a media query stored in an internal style sheet governs your CSS rule. If Dreamweaver highlights <style> in the Sources section and Global in the Media section, that means the program stores your style in an internal style sheet, but one that's independent of any media queries.

■ Strategies for Using Media Queries

Now that you know how to add media queries to a page, what's the best way to use them to make your site mobile-friendly? Most site pages are just too wide to look good on a mobile phone. Phone browsers typically zoom out to give you a bird's-eye view of the page. If the page has multiple columns and was designed at a width of 960 pixels, it's impossible to read on a phone without zooming in and dragging the page around.

Web designers use a few techniques when they design for mobile devices:

- **Remove columns.** Multiple side-by-side columns look great on a big monitor (and even on a tablet in landscape mode), but not so much on a phone. Remove the floats (see page 426) to stack a page's content divs one on top of the other.

- **Remove widths.** If you use a fixed-width design, your pages won't look good on a phone. A 960-pixel-wide page is just too much for the 320 or 480 pixels of a cellphone. A better approach is setting the widths of your content divs to *Auto* or *100%*. This converts your page from a fixed-width design to a liquid, or flexible, design. In other words, no matter how wide a phone's screen, the divs will fit 100 percent of it. If a person holding an iPhone in portrait mode (so that the screen width is 320 pixels) suddenly turns the phone horizontally (changing the screen width to 480 pixels), divs set to Auto or 100% simply resize to fit the new space.

- **Tighten up white space.** Ample space between headlines, graphics, and other page elements adds breathing room to a design on a 23-inch monitor, but creates a scattered layout and wastes space on a phone's small screen. Shrinking *margin* (page 439) and *padding* (page 439) values lets you fit more onto those small screens.

- **Shrink fonts.** Large fonts look good on large screens, but take up too much room on handheld devices. Change the fonts on your page so they're smaller but still readable.

- **Hide content.** Many designers strip away content from mobile versions of sites. While it's easy to scan several columns and hundreds of lines of text on a desktop monitor, too much information on a phone can be overwhelming. You can use CSS to simply hide content that you think is superfluous for mobile users by setting the CSS display property to "none" (page 396).

- **Use background images.** If you put a 960-pixel banner on a page, no phone will display it without zooming out. One approach is to make sure your images are small enough to fit inside a phone's screen; another is to use CSS background images instead (see page 240). For example, you could create a div and add a class to it like this: *<div class="logo">*. Then, in the style sheet for the desktop browser, set the div's width and height to match the size of the large logo, using the Background-image property to insert the image into the background. For example:

```
.logo {
    width: 960px;
    height: 120px;
    background-image: url(images/large_logo.png)
}
```

You could then put another style inside the style sheet used for mobile phones that resizes the logo div, using a smaller background image:

```
.logo {
    width: 320px;
    height: 60px;
    background-image: url(images/small_logo.png)
}
```

TIP Web designer Ethan Marcotte suggests another way to deal with images in mobile design. His "fluid images" technique is described at *http://tinyurl.com/ch9e43*. It's a lengthy but amusing explanation that shows how to use an image's max-width property to resize images on the fly. It includes a workaround to accommodate Internet Explorer. Fluid images are part of what make up responsive Web design, used in Dreamweaver's new Fluid Grid Layouts tool, and described on page 544. If you follow the link above, be forewarned: geeky waters ahead.

Organizing Your Style Sheets for Media Queries

So how do you actually resize your site based on screen resolution? You can take several approaches:

- **Create separate style sheets for each device.** In other words, create a phone style sheet, a tablet style sheet (if you're concerned about those), and a desktop style sheet, and then use Dreamweaver's media queries tool to attach each sheet to its respective page. However, since Internet Explorer 8 and earlier don't understand media queries, attaching a desktop style sheet using a media query in IE 8 and earlier won't work. One way around this is to use JavaScript (see the tip on page 506) to make IE 8 understand media queries. Another approach is to use an IE conditional comment (see the box on page 430) to attach the desktop style sheet. To do this, add the following code after the media queries on your page:

```
<!--[if lt IE 9]>
<link href="desktop.css" media="screen" rel="stylesheet">
<![endif]-->
```

You need to change the *href* value above to specify the path to your desktop CSS file. Dreamweaver can't insert this code for you, and its link management tools don't know how to locate and track it, so if you move the CSS file, you need to change the *href* value to point to the new location.

The other downside to this approach is that you need to specify all the styles in *each* style sheet. If you want to use the same font for an <h1> tag, for instance, and you use three style sheets (one for phones, tablets, and desktop browsers), you need to add the h1 style to each sheet.

- **Use a master style sheet and then individual style sheets for each device.** This method is similar to the one described for print style sheets on page 392. Basically, you start by creating a style sheet for the desktop version of the site, just as you'd normally do. Then you use CSS Designer and media queries to attach style sheets for other devices: one for phones, for example. In this second style sheet, you add styles that override the styles in the master sheet.

For example, say the main style sheet (the one attached without a media query) has a style for a div with the class *content*. You name the style *.content*, and float it to the right, with a fixed width of 564 pixels. In the phone style sheet, add another style named *.content*, but set its *float* property to *none* and its *width* to *auto*. Because of the rules of the cascade (see page 384), and because the phone style sheet appears second in the HTML, its *.content* style overrules the style with the same name in the master style sheet. You can continue adding styles to the phone style sheet that override those in the master sheet.

The phone style sheet doesn't have to override *all* the styles from the master sheet—that's one of the benefits of this approach. So if you don't create a style with the same name as one in the master sheet, the style from the master sheet prevails. Because of this, you only need to create a single style (in the master style sheet) for any site-wide formatting you want to see in phone, tablet, and desktop browsers (like fonts, page colors, and so on). Having the desktop styles in the main style sheet also avoids the need to use the IE conditional comment mentioned above.

Adding Styles to Media Query Style Sheets

As noted earlier, after you use CSS Designer to create a style source that has a media query, you still need to define the styles within the style sheets. In other words, media queries merely control when a browser uses a specific style sheet—the actual style sheet (*phone.css*, *tablet.css*, *desktop.css*) is otherwise the same as any other external style sheet. You use the same CSS Designer tools and techniques described elsewhere in this book to add, edit, delete, and manage the styles in those sheets. For example, follow the steps on page 104 to add a style, page 122 to edit a style, and page 122 to delete a style.

■ jQuery Mobile

Media queries and Dreamweaver's Fluid Grid Layouts (page 544) let you take one website and give it different designs for different devices, but what if you just want to create a mobile site from the get-go? Perhaps you want to design a "mobile-only" version of your site, one optimized to look and perform like a native phone application (see Figure 12-13). Dreamweaver lets you do just that with its support for jQuery Mobile.

FIGURE 12-13

Unlike a regular website, a jQuery Mobile site, like this one for the educational site Khan Academy (www.khanacademy.com), replicates the screen elements found in phone applications.

jQuery Mobile is a "mobile development framework," which means that it provides the tools you need to build web pages that act more like mobile applications than traditional web pages. A page built with jQuery Mobile includes screen transitions (one web page slides into view as the old one slides out), a more phone-like interface (large, rounded-corner buttons and smooth color gradients), and support for non-mouse-like interactions (like screen taps and swipes).

jQuery Mobile (*http://jquerymobile.com*) is a project of the enormously popular JavaScript framework jQuery (*http://jquery.com*), which simplifies the process of writing JavaScript. jQuery solves cross-browser problems and makes normally complicated JavaScript programming a lot easier. It provides JavaScript programming specific to phones, as well as the CSS that formats the HTML so your site mimics the screens you see in iPhone and Android apps.

So how do you use jQuery Mobile? In a nutshell, you construct a page using the basic building blocks of HTML—divs, images, paragraphs, and headers—and jQuery Mobile transforms them, through the power of JavaScript and some fancy CSS, into something that looks and feels a lot different from a regular web page. For example, the Khan Academy website, pictured in Figure 12-13, uses basic HTML transformed into a phone-like presentation by jQuery Mobile.

If you have a smartphone, now's a good time to whip it out and visit a few sites that use jQuery Mobile—it's more informative to experience it rather than read about it. Here are a few mobile sites worth trying: True Value Paint (*http://truevaluepaint. com/*), Macworld (*www.macworld.com*), and Moulin Rouge (*http://m.moulinrouge. fr*).

You can build a basic, mobile-only web page with just HTML and Dreamweaver CC, as you'll see next.

NOTE To get the most out of jQuery Mobile, you need to be a pretty proficient JavaScript programmer. In fact, with some programming chops (and some patience), you can build true, native phone applications that work in iPhones, Android devices, Blackberries, Symbian phones, and more (see the box on page 544).

Creating a Basic jQuery Mobile Page

Fortunately, while there's a lot of complex programming behind a jQuery Mobile web page, actually adding content and building a page uses techniques you already learned in this book: inserting divs (page 428), typing in text, and adding images.

1. **Choose File→New.**

   The familiar New Document window opens—the same one you use to create a blank, new HTML file (Figure 12-14).

2. **Select the Starter Templates category from the left-hand list of options (circled in Figure 12-14), and then click the Mobile Starters folder from the Sample Folder column.**

   You'll see three options listed in the Sample Page category. The three options specify three different ways to include the required jQuery mobile files.

3. **Select either "jQuery Mobile (CDN)," "jQuery Mobile (Local)," or "jQuery Mobile with theme (Local)."**

   The first option, CDN, refers to a "content delivery network," which simply means you don't keep the required external files on your computer. Instead, jQuery's web server stores the files for you. When someone visits your site, her browser downloads your page from your server, but downloads the JavaScript, CSS, and graphic files from jQuery.com. This has some benefits: jQuery.com manages those files, so you save your web server the effort and expense. However, the

CDN option won't work without an Internet connection, and you're dependent on the jQuery.com servers—if they break down, your site won't work. (Also, if you're not connected to the Internet when you use Dreamweaver to build your jQuery Mobile site, you won't be able to preview your page to see if it works.) In addition, since the CSS file sits on jQuery's server, you can't edit it, so customizing the look of the site is difficult.

The second option, jQuery Mobile (Local), puts all the required files in your site folder. This gives you everything you need to work with jQuery Mobile, as well as a style sheet you can modify to make the site look the way you wish.

The most flexible option, however, is the last: jQuery Mobile with theme (Local). Like the second option, Dreamweaver deposits all necessary files in your local site folder. However, Dreamweaver breaks the CSS file into two external files. The first style sheet, *jquery.mobile.structure-1.0.min.css* provides all the CSS required for the basic functions and layout of a jQuery Mobile site. In other words, the CSS in that file is crucial to the working of jQuery Mobile, and you shouldn't edit it. The second file—*jquery.mobile.theme-1.0.min.css*—contains styles that affect the basic look of a jQuery Mobile site, including its fonts, colors, drop-shadows, and so on. This option is particularly useful because it works with jQuery Mobile's ThemeRoller website, which lets you visually customize the look of jQuery Mobile elements and then download a new, mobile theme CSS file. In short, choose "jQuery Mobile with theme (Local)" when you create a new jQuery Mobile page because it gives you the easiest way to customize the look of your mobile site (see page 521 for more on styling jQuery Mobile sites).

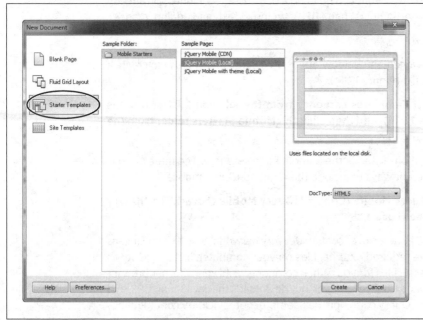

FIGURE 12-14

When you create a sample jQuery Mobile page, make sure you leave the HTML5 doctype selected. If you select another doctype, like HTML 4.01 Transitional, some of jQuery Mobile's features won't work.

4. **Click Create.**

Dreamweaver creates a new, simple-looking web page with some sample content (see Figure 12-15). If you chose either of the Local options in the previous step and then saved the page, Dreamweaver saves the additional files mentioned in the previous step to your computer and places them in a *jquery-mobile* folder on your site.

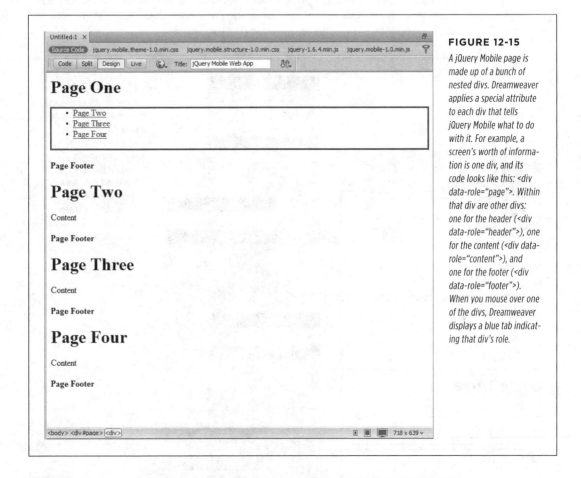

FIGURE 12-15

A jQuery Mobile page is made up of a bunch of nested divs. Dreamweaver applies a special attribute to each div that tells jQuery Mobile what to do with it. For example, a screen's worth of information is one div, and its code looks like this: <div data-role="page">. Within that div are other divs: one for the header (<div data-role="header">), one for the content (<div data-role="content">), and one for the footer (<div data-role="footer">). When you mouse over one of the divs, Dreamweaver displays a blue tab indicating that div's role.

NOTE At the time of this writing, jQuery Mobile is at version 1.1.0. Dreamweaver CC ships with jQuery Mobile version 1.0. To upgrade, go to the jQuery Mobile site (*http://jquerymobile.com*) and download the latest version. Replace the files in the *jquery-mobile* folder that Dreamweaver created. You also need to remove the links to the old files from the <head> of the page and attach the new style sheet (see page 120 for a refresher on attaching external style sheets) and the two JavaScript files (see the tip on page 506 for an example that shows how to attach a JavaScript file to a web page).

Anatomy of a jQuery Mobile Page

One peculiar feature of a jQuery Mobile site is that it's just a single file. When a guest visits the site, his browser downloads a single HTML file, but only displays a *portion* of the HTML at a time. For example, the left image in Figure 12-16 represents Dreamweaver's stock jQuery Mobile page: one page with multiple div tags. However, when you look at the page in a browser, the browser converts that HTML into separate "pages." The top-right image in Figure 12-16 represents the "home page." It lists three links: Page Two, Page Three, and Page Four. Clicking the Page Four link loads that page's <div> and its contents (bottom, right).

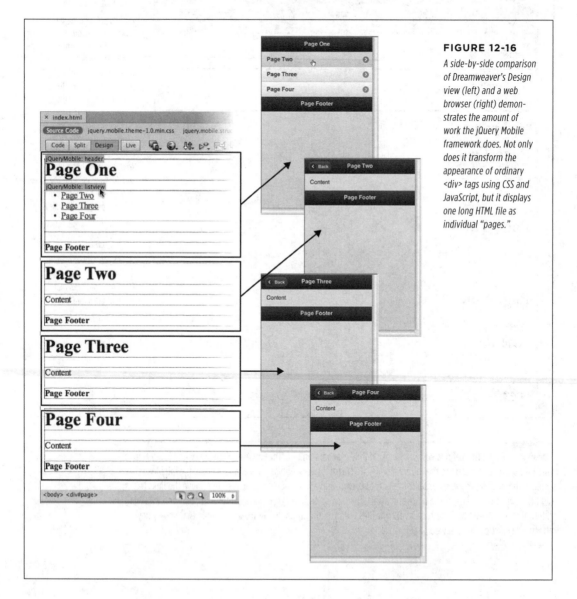

FIGURE 12-16

A side-by-side comparison of Dreamweaver's Design view (left) and a web browser (right) demonstrates the amount of work the jQuery Mobile framework does. Not only does it transform the appearance of ordinary <div> tags using CSS and JavaScript, but it displays one long HTML file as individual "pages."

TIP Dreamweaver's Live View (page 51) and Window Size menu (Figure 12-2) provide a great combination for previewing a jQuery Mobile site. Choose the "320 x 480 Smart Phone" option and then click the Live View button on the Document toolbar. It's like having a smartphone built right into Dreamweaver (minus the roaming charges).

jQuery Mobile's programming converts those divs into separate screens, and applies the CSS that formats the page elements. But how does jQuery Mobile know which div is a page, and how does it make the other elements, such as a link, look like a button? The secret is a creative use of HTML attributes applied to HTML tags. The jQuery Mobile programming reads the attributes you apply to a tag and then formats that tag based on those attributes. For example, the basic structure of Dreamweaver's stock mobile page looks like this:

```
<div data-role="page" id="page2">
    <div data-role="header">
        <h1>Page Two</h1>
    </div>
    <div data-role="content">
        Content
    </div>
    <div data-role="footer">
        <h4>Page Footer</h4>
    </div>
</div>
```

As you can see, the "page" is a div tag with data-role="page" added to it. When the page loads in a browser, the jQuery Mobile programming kicks in and transforms the div into a "page." Dreamweaver usually includes three other divs within that "page": one for a header, one for the content, and the third for a footer. Thanks to their respective "data-role" values, each div looks different. jQuery Mobile formats the header and footer as dark stripes with light text, while it gives the content area a light background with dark text.

jQuery Mobile also applies special attributes to other HTML tags. For example, it creates the list of links in the top-right image in Figure 12-16 (called a "list-view" in jQuery Mobile) using a simple unordered list:

```
<ul data-role="listview" data-inset="true">
    <li><a href="#page2">Page Two</a></li>
    <li><a href="#page3">Page Three</a>
    <li><a href="#page4">Page Four</a></li>
</ul>
```

By adding data-role="listview" to a <ul> tag, you can change the list from a basic bulleted set to a special, mobile-enhanced list. jQuery Mobile provides other, similar mobile elements, as described in the next section.

NOTE Although Dreamweaver CC's starter file puts all the site's "pages" into a single file, you can create a mobile site with true multiple pages.

Adding Content to a jQuery Mobile Page

As you can see in Figure 12-15, a jQuery Mobile page is just some very basic HTML: divs, unordered lists, and links. To add content, select the dummy text Dreamweaver provides and change it. For example, to change the "Page One" headline that appears on the first page, highlight the text and type in your own headline: "My Great Web App," for example. Likewise, you can change the footer text—"Page Footer"—by selecting it inside the footer div and typing in something new.

NOTE If you type a long sentence in either the header or footer and then preview the page in a phone, you'll notice that jQuery Mobile keeps the text to a single line and simply cuts off anything that doesn't fit. Because of that, keep your header and footer text short.

The central div in each page is where you add the main content. Dreamweaver places the word "content" inside that div, but you can delete it and add HTML as you normally would: headlines, paragraphs, bulleted lists, and images. In addition, you can insert special jQuery Mobile items—list views, layout grids, collapsible blocks, and link buttons—as well as additional "pages" using the Insert panel (see Figure 12-17).

■ ADDING LISTS

jQuery Mobile includes its own "widgets"—elements for links, layout, and content display. The page, header, and footer divs are widgets, for example. You can also insert a list of links that lets guests navigate from page to page on your mobile site. Dreamweaver's stock mobile "home page" includes a list of links to Page Two, Page Three, and Page Four, for example (Figure 12-16, top right). Dreamweaver calls a list like this the "list view," and jQuery Mobile supplies several variations (see Figure 12-18).

To add a list:

1. **Click inside the content div of a "page" div and click the List View button on the Insert panel (Figure 12-17).**

    Alternatively, choose Insert→jQuery Mobile→List View. Either way, the jQuery Mobile List View window opens (Figure 12-19).

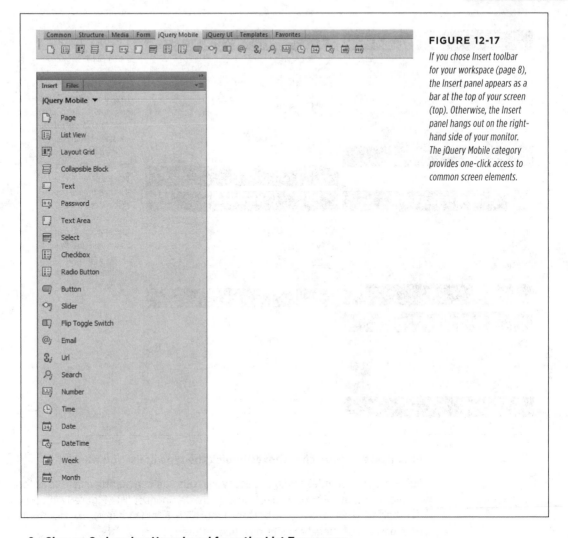

FIGURE 12-17

If you chose Insert toolbar for your workspace (page 8), the Insert panel appears as a bar at the top of your screen (top). Otherwise, the Insert panel hangs out on the right-hand side of your monitor. The jQuery Mobile category provides one-click access to common screen elements.

2. **Choose Ordered or Unordered from the List Type menu.**

   Ordered lists include numbers on the left side of each item. Use ordered lists for "Top 10" items, or to indicate the specific order of steps in a process, like baking a soufflé. If the order isn't important, use an unordered list.

3. **Choose the number of list items from the Items menu.**

   You can choose from 1 to 10 items; however, since a List View is simply an HTML list, you can use the technique described on page 88 to add as many items as you want.

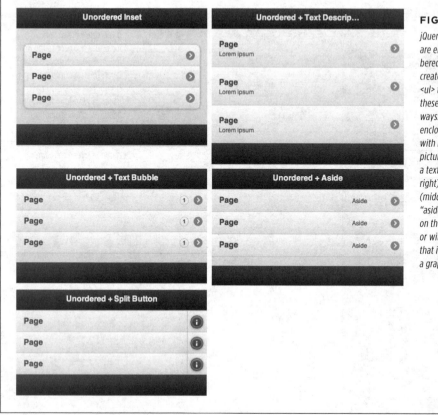

FIGURE 12-18

jQuery Mobile List views are either ordered (numbered) or unordered lists, created using the <ol> and <ul> tags. You can display these two types of list five ways: inset (with the list enclosed in its own box with rounded corners, as pictured at top left), with a text description (top right), with a text bubble (middle left), with an "aside" or small bit of text on the right (middle right), or with a "split button" that includes both text and a graphic (bottom left).

4. **Turn on one or more checkboxes to pick the type of list you want.**

   jQuery Mobile provides five basic list types, but you can combine list types to vary your options. For example, you can create an inset list (Figure 12-18, top left) that also includes a split button (Figure 12-18, bottom left). Try different combinations of checkboxes to produce different types of lists.

5. **If you select the Split Button option, choose an icon from the Split Button Icon menu.**

   NOTE A Split Button list type inserts both text and an icon in a button, and each provides a link that can point to separate pages. For example, the text portion might lead to a page of detailed information, but the icon might link to a short page of supplementary information.

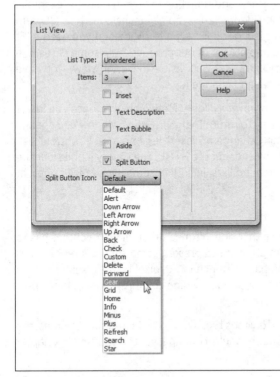

FIGURE 12-19

jQuery Mobile lets you pick from a range of list types. In addition, if you select the Split Button option, which lets you include both text and a graphic in the same button, you can choose from one of 19 icons for the graphic.

6. **Click OK to insert the new list view.**

   Depending on the list type you select, Dreamweaver inserts either an HTML unordered list (<ul> tag) or a numbered (ordered) list (<ol> tag). You can edit these list items as you would any other list (see page 88).

   TIP   If you add data-rel="dialog" to a link (an <a> tag) on a jQuery Mobile page, the linked page pops into view like a dialog box, complete with a close button.

   ---

7. **Change the label and link for each list item.**

   Each list item includes the text "Page" with an empty link (# appears in the Properties panel's link box). You can select the text and type in whatever you wish. Then link that text to another page. If you link to another website, just type a complete, absolute URL beginning with *http://*. If you link to another HTML file on your site, you can use any of the techniques described on page 171.

   If you use Dreamweaver's suggested approach to mobile site development—one HTML file with multiple "page" divs inside it—you link to another "page" just as you would to a named anchor, as described on page 182. For example, if you want to link to a "page" div with an ID of "page8," you type *#page8* in the Properties panel's link box.

Some of the list view types include additional text you can edit. For example, the "Text Description" option (Figure 12-18, top right) includes text ("Lorem ipsum") you can change. This is a good list type to pick when you need a bit of explanatory text ("See a complete list of our products"). In some cases, like the Text Bubble list type, the extra text isn't visible in Design view—you have to look in the HTML code to see and change it.

Unfortunately, as with all of Dreamweaver's jQuery Mobile objects, once you insert a list view into a page, there's no way to return to the List View window and change its settings. For example, you can't change an insert list into a "split button" list. You can, however, go into Code view and edit the HTML. The jQuery Mobile website provides helpful information on creating lists, including some even fancier ones, at *http://tinyurl.com/d8sjfhz*.

■ ADDING A LAYOUT GRID

Although phone screens are small, that doesn't mean that all your content has to sit inside one long column. You might want to present some small content in rows and columns. For example, if you have a bunch of 30-pixel by 30-pixel thumbnail images, you can arrange them in several side-by-side columns. jQuery Mobile provides "layout grids" for just that purpose.

A layout grid is basically a series of div tags that jQuery floats to create columns, the same technique you used to create the multi-column layouts described in Chapter 10. To insert a layout grid:

1. **Click inside the content div of a "page" div and then click the Layout Grid button on the Insert panel (Figure 12-17).**

   Alternatively, choose Insert→jQuery Mobile→Layout Grid. Either way, the jQuery Mobile Layout Grid window opens (top image in Figure 12-20).

2. **Choose the number of rows and columns you want.**

   There's not too much to this step, but keep in mind the limitations of a phone's screen. Choosing five columns and trying to put a lot of text into each column in one row will probably make the page wider than a phone's screen can handle.

3. **Click OK.**

   Dreamweaver inserts a number of <div> tags into the page. They don't look like much in Design view, but you can add any content you like (just make sure it isn't too big for a phone's screen).

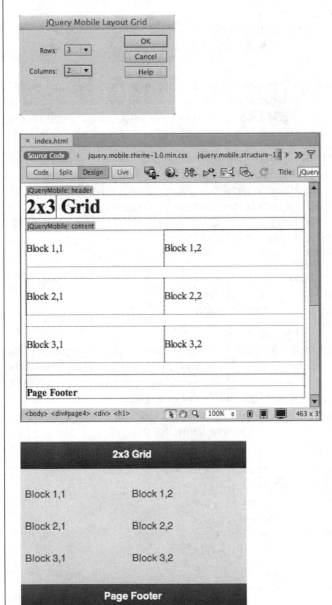

FIGURE 12-20

The layout grid in Dreamweaver's Design view (middle image) looks decidedly less glamorous than what it looks like in a web browser (bottom image).

You can't revisit the Layout Grid window, so if you want to change a three-column grid to two columns, you have to dip into the HTML. Fortunately, it's not so difficult. Here's the HTML for a one-row, two-column grid:

```
<div class="ui-grid-a">
    <div class="ui-block-a">Block 1,1</div>
    <div class="ui-block-b">Block 1,2</div>
</div>
```

jQuery Mobile uses a <div> tag to define layout grids. In the above example, that's <div class="ui-grid-a">. The letter in the class name determines the grid's number of columns: For example, *ui-grid-a* is a two-column grid, *ui-grid-b* gives you a three-column grid, *ui-grid-c* results in a four-column grid, and *ui-grid-d* is a five-column grid.

jQuery Mobile includes additional divs within this tag that define each block of content. So the above example includes two div tags. The class on those tags determines into which column jQuery Mobile inserts the content. For example, ui-block-a is the first column in a row. Say you want to turn the above two-column, one-row grid into a three-column, one-row design. You simply change the class name on the grid's div and then add a div for the new block, like this:

```
<div class="ui-grid-b">
    <div class="ui-block-a">Block 1,1</div>
    <div class="ui-block-b">Block 1,2</div>
    <div class="ui-block-c">Block 1,3</div>
</div>
```

In other words, you change <div class="ui-grid-a"> to <div class="ui-grid-b"> and add another block: <div class="ui-block-c">. You just have to be sure you keep the block's class names in order—a, b, c, and so on—and that you have the proper number of blocks for the type of grid you specify. For example, since the ui-grid-b class defines a three-column layout, you need three div tags per row. To add an additional row, duplicate the div tags from the previous row, like this:

```
<div class="ui-grid-b">
    <div class="ui-block-a">Block 1,1</div>
    <div class="ui-block-b">Block 1,2</div>
    <div class="ui-block-c">Block 1,3</div>
    <div class="ui-block-a">Block 2,1</div>
    <div class="ui-block-b">Block 2,2</div>
    <div class="ui-block-c">Block 2,3</div>
</div>
```

You can read more about jQuery Mobile grids at *http://tinyurl.com/cdwdlk7*.

■ **ADDING A COLLAPSIBLE BLOCK**

A collapsible block is a combination of a header and a hidden chunk of content. Click the header and the content reveals itself (bottom image in Figure 12-21). It's a good way to keep your page simple and short for phone-viewing—content only appears when a guest clicks a headline, and it disappears when he clicks the headline a second time.

To insert a collapsible block in Dreamweaver:

1. **Click inside the content div of a "page" div and click the Collapsible Block button in the Insert panel (Figure 12-17).**

   Alternatively, choose Insert→jQuery Mobile→Collapsible Block. Unlike other jQuery Mobile objects, there's no dialog box for this: Dreamweaver just drops a series of div tags into the page (Figure 12-21, top).

2. **Edit the headline and the content.**

   Select the dummy "Header" text and type in your own headline. Remember to keep it short, however, since jQuery Mobile limits the header to a single line. You can change the dummy content Dreamweaver inserts—a simple <p> tag with the text "Content" inside it—to anything you want. You can even insert multiple paragraphs, lists, and images.

Dreamweaver inserts four div tags when you add a collapsible block to a page. The HTML looks like this:

```
<div data-role="collapsible-set">
    <div data-role="collapsible">
        <h3>Header</h3>
        <p>Content</p>
    </div>
    <div data-role="collapsible" data-collapsed="true">
        <h3>Header</h3>
        <p>Content</p>
    </div>
    <div data-role="collapsible" data-collapsed="true">
        <h3>Header</h3>
        <p>Content</p>
    </div>
</div>
```

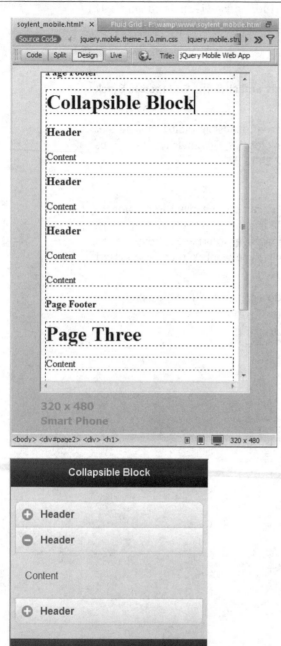

FIGURE 12-21

Collapsible blocks are a good way to keep a page's appearance simple, because the blocks hide content until a visitor wants to read it.

The outer div—<div data-role="collapsible-set">—indicates that the div tags inside are part of a group (a "block") of collapsible elements. Each collapsible element—a header/content pair—sits inside another div, <div data-role="collapsible">. If you wish to have only two collapsible elements, delete one of the divs Dreamweaver inserts. If you want more, copy the div (including the header and content) and paste it before that last closing </div> for the set.

By default, all collapsible blocks start life closed. You can make sure that a collapsible block's content is visible by adding data-collapsed="false" to the <div> tag for a header/content pair. The first header/content pair in a collapsible block starts off hidden:

```
<div data-role="collapsible">
        <h3>Header</h3>
        <p>Content</p>
</div>
```

But you can show the content when the page first loads by adding an attribute to the div for that block:

```
<div data-role="collapsible" data-collapsed="false">
        <h3>Header</h3>
        <p>Content</p>
</div>
```

You can read more about collapsible blocks at *http://tinyurl.com/cd63jv2*.

■ ADDING FORM ELEMENTS

The jQuery Mobile category of the Insert panel includes many form elements—text fields, password fields, checkboxes, radio buttons, and so on. However, these fields don't work like traditional form fields (which you'll learn about in the next chapter). In fact, they don't work at all unless you add JavaScript programming. And, unfortunately, Dreamweaver CC doesn't provide any tools to do so. In other words, to use any of these form elements effectively, you need to learn JavaScript and jQuery programming.

However, the button element isn't restricted to forms page; you can use it anywhere to insert links that *look* like buttons, too.

To insert button links:

1. **Click inside a div in one of the "pages" in the jQuery Mobile file.**

   For example, in the "content," "header," or "footer" divs described on page 526.

2. **Click the Button button on the Insert panel (Figure 12-17).**

   Alternatively you can choose Insert→jQuery Mobile→Button. Either way, the jQuery Mobile Button window appears (Figure 12-22).

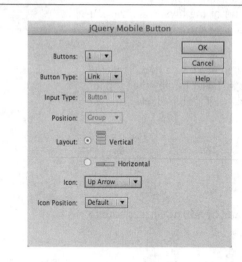

FIGURE 12-22

Unless you know how to write JavaScript, select only "Link" from the Button Type menu. This lets you insert regular page links that look like attractive buttons. The Input Type menu is only available when you select "Input" from the Button Type menu, and it lets you select one of the HTML form buttons discussed on page 645—but again, this is only an option if you're comfortable programming the buttons yourself to make them do something.

3. **Select the number of buttons you want on the page.**

   You can choose between 1 and 10 buttons, but remember you're designing for a small phone screen, so 10 buttons won't sit side-by-side.

4. **Choose Link from the Button Type menu.**

   The two other options (Button and Input) insert buttons in a form (like a "Submit" button); they require custom programming to work.

5. **Choose either Inline or Group from the Position menu.**

   The Inline option creates separate lozenge-shaped boxes for each button, while the Group option treats the buttons as a homogenous group (see the two bottom examples in Figure 12-23).

6. **Choose a Vertical or Horizontal layout.**

   These options are only available when you select "Group" in the previous step, and they affect how the grouped buttons appear on a page, either stacked one on top of the other ("Vertical") or side-by-side ("Horizontal"), as pictured in Figure 12-23. Keep in mind that if you place too many buttons side-by-side, some will drop down to the next space on the page and turn into stacked rows of buttons.

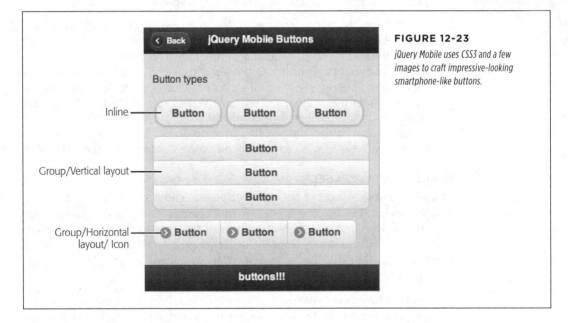

FIGURE 12-23

jQuery Mobile uses CSS3 and a few images to craft impressive-looking smartphone-like buttons.

7. **Choose an option from the Icon menu.**

   This step is optional, but it adds a neat graphical touch to each button. jQuery gives you 18 graphics to choose from (Right Arrow, Gear, Star, and so on), and if you don't want any of them, choose None. (In Figure 12-23, the bottom row of buttons have a right arrow icon applied to them.) You can see all 18 icons in action at *http://tinyurl.com/c2z6hyu*.

8. **If you selected an icon in the previous step, place it using the Icon Position menu.**

   You can choose Left or Right to put the icon at either the left or right edge of the button, and Top or Bottom to place the icon either above or below the button's text. Choose No Text to display only the icon.

9. **Click OK to insert the button(s).**

   Dreamweaver inserts as many buttons as you selected in step 3. In Design view, they don't look like much—just the word "button" repeated once for each one you added. Select that text to change it to something better. In addition, the text has a regular HTML link attached to it, just like the ones you learned about in Chapter 4. You can change the link using the Properties panel, just as you would for a regular link.

   If you plan to link to another "page" within the jQuery file, use the # symbol followed by the ID you apply to the <div> tag for that "page." For example, to link to "page2" in the sample jQuery Mobile file Dreamweaver supplies, you type #page2 in the Properties panel's Link field. This is the same as linking to a named anchor within a page, as described on page 182.

Unfortunately, once you insert one or more buttons, you can't revisit the jQuery Mobile Button window (Figure 12-22) to edit them—in other words, you can't change the buttons' icons, grouping, or positioning once you insert them. Well, you can, but you have to go into Code view and change the attributes applied to the buttons. For example, to change a button's icon, go into Code view, locate the <a> tag for that button, and change the *data-icon* attribute to the proper value. For instance, changing data-icon="arrow-r" to data-icon="gear" changes a button's icon from a right-pointing arrow to a gear. The web page for jQuery Mobile buttons is an invaluable aid in this process: *http://tinyurl.com/d78s8pt.*

■ ADDING NEW "PAGES"

As you read above, you can put multiple "pages" into a single HTML file. jQuery Mobile then hides all but one "page" when a browser loads the file. As you click links, the browser displays different portions of the page as if they were separate web pages (thanks to jQuery Mobile's JavaScript programming). A "page" is really just a div tag with an ID and a special HTML attribute—for example, <div data-role="page" id="page4">.

The stock mobile page Dreamweaver supplies has four "pages" but you can add more. It's important to make sure, however, that you don't insert a page inside another page's div. The best way to ensure this is to use the Tag Selector page 7). For example, say you want to insert another page after the last page in a mobile file:

1. **Click inside the div for the last "page."**

   For example, inside the header, footer, or content div.

2. **In the Tag Selector, click the div for that page (see Figure 12-24).**

   You'll see something like <div#page4> in the Tag Selector.

3. **Press the right arrow key to move the cursor outside of the div.**

   The right arrow key moves the cursor below the div, so you can insert a new page after the currently selected one. To insert a page *before* the currently selected one, press the left arrow key.

4. **Click the Page button from the jQuery Mobile category of the Insert panel.**

   Alternatively, choose Insert→Query Mobile→Page. Either way, the jQuery Mobile Page window opens (Figure 12-25).

5. **Type an ID for the page, and then select whether you want a header and footer.**

   The ID can be anything you like. For example, if the page contains information about your company, you might name it "about." The ID you provide is important for links—you use that ID when you create a link that points to this new page, as described on page 528. Normally, pages include a header and footer; if you don't want them, turn off their checkboxes.

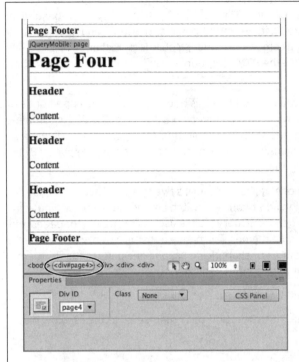

FIGURE 12-24

The Tag Selector is the most accurate way to select and navigate among HTML tags.

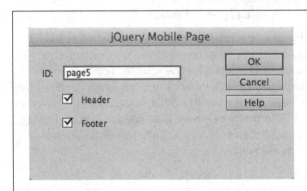

FIGURE 12-25

jQuery Mobile "pages" are just a series of divs—one for the header, one for content, and one for a footer. You can choose to leave out either the header or footer (or both).

6. **Click OK.**

   Dreamweaver inserts the <div> tags needed to add a page to the file, as described on page 526. You can add content to this new page following the instructions on page 528.

Formatting a jQuery Mobile Page

When viewed in Dreamweaver's Design view, a jQuery Mobile Page is pretty unimpressive (Figure 12-16, left). However, the browser view of the same HTML is astonishingly different (Figure 12-16, right). The formerly ho-hum HTML turns into a slick, mobile page with subtle gradients, rounded corners, shadows, and sophisticated icons. Where does this design come from? jQuery Mobile is more than JavaScript—it's also complex CSS that makes the HTML for mobile devices look like an application for a smartphone.

You can use the CSS skills you picked up in this book to change the appearance of your jQuery Mobile site, but you're in for a lot of work if you do. The CSS is complex, and there are literally hundreds of styles required to make jQuery Mobile work. If you want to give it a try, Dreamweaver's Inspect mode (described in page 487) is your best bet at deciphering the CSS.

Another approach is to use one of jQuery Mobile's five themes. That's right, jQuery Mobile has five built-in designs that you can switch among simply by adding attributes to the HTML tags. By default, jQuery Mobile uses its "a" theme for pages, but you can choose its b, c, d, and e themes. To change a theme, specify a data-theme for a jQuery Mobile-specific tag. For example, to change one page to the "b" theme, add data-theme="b" to that page's <div> tag like this:

```
<div data-role="page" id="page" data-theme="b">
```

To change a List View to the "e" theme, add *data-theme="e"* to the list view div:

```
<ul data-role="listview" data-theme="e">
```

Fortunately, you don't need to add that theme data by hand. Dreamweaver CC includes a handy, context-sensitive jQuery Mobile Swatches panel (see Figure 12-26). You open it by choosing Window→jQuery Mobile Swatches.

You apply a swatch simply by clicking into a jQuery mobile element. The Swatches panel displays the formatting options for the current element. For example, in Figure 12-26, Dreamweaver displays the options for the selected link (circled) inside a jQuery mobile list view (page 528). In this instance, you could apply one of five swatches (labeled a to e) to the list itself, as well as other swatches for the different types of available lists. Clicking into another element, like a page header, updates the Swatches panel to list just the swatches available for page headers. Click a swatch to apply it to the selected page element.

If you want to create your own look for a jQuery Mobile site, visit the jQuery Mobile ThemeRoller website (*http://jquerymobile.com/themeroller/*). There, you can try different fonts, colors, borders, and shadows, and see a live, interactive rendering of your design choices. Once you're satisfied, click the Download button. You'll end up with a CSS file containing your design, as well as an Images folder containing the icons for the design. Simply move those files into the *jquery-mobile* folder in your site (replacing the original files). Change the link from the CSS file Dreamweaver supplies (*jquery.mobile.theme-1.0.min.css*) to your new theme file, and you're done. In fact, Dreamweaver is smart enough to realize you're using a new theme, and displays it in the jQuery Mobile Swatches panel.

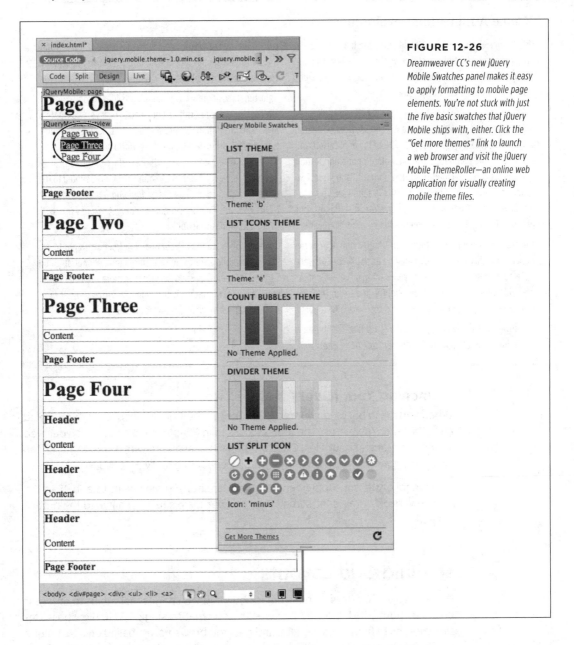

FIGURE 12-26

Dreamweaver CC's new jQuery Mobile Swatches panel makes it easy to apply formatting to mobile page elements. You're not stuck with just the five basic swatches that jQuery Mobile ships with, either. Click the "Get more themes" link to launch a web browser and visit the jQuery Mobile ThemeRoller—an online web application for visually creating mobile theme files.

Mobile Application Development

Using jQuery Mobile, you can build a website that looks great on mobile phones, but it's still a website: A visitor uses the browser in her phone to go to the site and clicks through pages just as she would on any other site.

However, you can also use jQuery Mobile to build an application for the iPhone, Android phones, and other devices. Although you use HTML, CSS, and JavaScript to build the application, you can turn it—or "compile" it—into a native phone application that guests can download from that phone's "app store." So instead of viewing the jQuery Mobile site in a browser, you actually download it from the phone's app store, install it on your phone, and launch it just as you would any other application.

The real trick lies in converting the HTML to a native application. Usually this involves downloading an "SDK," or Software Development Kit, for each phone you want to target—iPhones, Android phones, Windows Phone, WebOS, and so on. This step is fraught with peril for all but diehard software developers.

Dreamweaver CC, however, provides a direct line to something called the "PhoneGap Build Service" (*http://build.phonegap.*

com/). This site can ingest your HTML, JavaScript, and CSS and, through some magic on their end, turn out native applications you can install on a phone.

Unfortunately, Dreamweaver doesn't provide the tools for actually creating the application; you need to be a very competent JavaScript programmer to get your app to actually do anything. Mobile application development is a world unto itself, and this book can't even begin to scratch the surface of the intricacies involved. However, there are a couple of books devoted to the subject, both by Jonathan Stark: *Building iPhone Apps with HTML, CSS, and JavaScript*, and *Building Android Apps with HTML, CSS, and JavaScript*.

However, once you build your app, you can go straight to the PhoneGap build service by selecting Site→PhoneGap Build Service→PhoneGap Build Service. For more information on how this works, check out the videos at *http://tinyurl.com/d34aw4k* and *http://tinyurl.com/cunv958*.

Launching Your jQuery Mobile Site

When you finish building your mobile website, put it on the web just as you would any other site. You can use the tools discussed in Chapter 18 to connect to your web server and transfer your files. Once on the web, any phone with a web browser can visit the page and see its awesome mobile-enabled beauty.

If the mobile site is a supplement to a regular site, you may want to add "See the mobile version of this site" somewhere on your main site, with a link to the mobile version.

■ Fluid Grid Layouts

Dreamweaver CC offers a great tool for building web pages that adapt to different browser widths. Its Fluid Grid Layouts let you create a single HTML file whose design morphs to fit phones, tablets, and desktop browsers. It's based on a technique called Responsive Web Design, which includes CSS media queries, flexible column layout (where columns adjust their widths to match a browser width), and fluid images (see Figure 12-27).

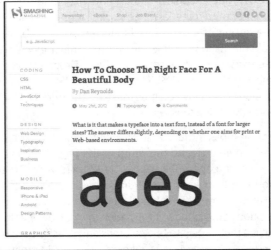

FIGURE 12-27

The web design site Smashing Magazine (http://smashingmagazine. com), uses responsive Web design to customize the site's layout for phones (top left), tablets (top right), and desktop browsers (bottom). Each device receives the same HTML file, but CSS media queries direct different CSS to each device, creating unique layouts appropriate to each device.

NOTE Responsive Web design (RWD) is a term coined by the web designer Ethan Marcotte. You can learn more about it from the article that kicked off the RWD movement: *www.alistapart.com/articles/responsive-web-design/*.

Understanding Fluid Grid Layouts

Dreamweaver's Fluid Grid Layouts combine lots of concepts, and to use them correctly you need to understand a few key ideas:

- **Grid layout.** Graphic designers have used grids to design books, brochures, and other printed material for centuries. A grid is an invisible pattern that underlies the design of a page (see Figure 12-28). In web design, a grid is a pattern of columns used to define the width of major elements placed on a page. Those elements are often <div> tags, but Dreamweaver's Fluid Grid Layouts also support the new HTML5 tags like <article>, <aside>, <header>, and <nav>. You decide how many columns make up the grid. That layout then determines how wide the <div> tags will be.

  For example, the layout grid in Figure 12-28 has 12 columns. Think of each column as a single unit, and the width of the page is 12 units. A header div that spans the entire page, then, would be 12 units wide. To add side-by-side columns, you simply divide those 12 units among the number of columns you want. For example, say you want to place the page's main content in a wide column and include some sidebar information in a narrower column to the right. You might divide that page into two columns and specify a main content column of 8 units, and a sidebar of 4 units. Likewise, you could create two equal-width columns of 6 units each, or three side-by-side columns of 4 units apiece.

  Finally, as you'll read on page 548, when you set up a new Fluid Grid Layout page, you get to define the underlying grid yourself. For example, you may not like 12 columns as an organizing principle; maybe you like more or fewer columns. Dreamweaver lets you pick your grid—anywhere from 2 to 24 columns wide. In fact, you'll specify three grids—one for mobile phones, one for tablets, and one for desktop browsers.

- **Fluid layout.** The width of each unit in the grid can vary. That is, there's no fixed width of, say, 100 pixels for a unit. Each unit represents a part of the overall grid's width, and that unit's width can vary depending on the destination device and that device's browser width. That's the "fluid" part of fluid layout. When you add columns to a fluid layout, Dreamweaver uses percentage values to size those columns. That means that the columns resize to fit the available space in the browser window.

- **Breakpoints.** The CSS media queries you read about above make it possible to apply different styles for different destination devices. For example, you can send one style sheet to a mobile browser whose screen is 480 pixels wide, and another to a browser that's at least 789 pixels wide. The dimension at which a browser applies a different style sheet is referred to as its "breakpoint." And while Dreamweaver's Media Query tool (page 506) lets you set any number of breakpoints (and apply any number of style sheets) to a page, Dreamweaver's Fluid Grid Layouts put the brakes on that idea—it offers only three breakpoints: one for mobile devices, one for tablets, and one for desktop browsers.

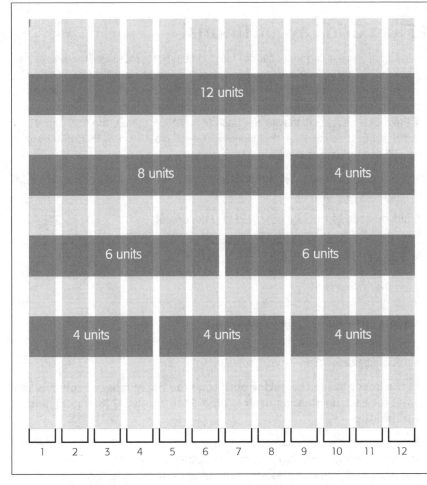

FIGURE 12-28

A layout is simply a grid of columns that gives a page structure. In this example, the layout comprises 12 columns. The page's designer distributes those columns among any number of page elements. For example, a <div> tag that houses the page's header would fill the entire page, taking up all 12 columns (or units).

Dreamweaver applies styles to mobile devices when their width is 480 pixels or less. Tablet layouts kick in when pages are between 481 and 768 pixels wide, and desktop layouts take over for pages between 769 and 1,232 pixels wide. These numbers are hard-wired into Dreamweaver's fluid grid system, and you can't change them without breaking the fluid grid tools.

- **Flexible media.** Another key feature of Responsive Web Design is "flexible media," or images that resize based on the width of their containers. In Responsive Web Design, if a column containing an image gets thinner, the image gets narrower, too. So an image that's, say, 600 pixels wide when you look at it in a desktop browser automatically scales down to fit the limited space of a mobile phone. This happens thanks to some clever CSS (in fact, you don't need to do anything to get this feature, just insert images as you normally would, as explained on page 219).

■ Fluid Grid Layout Tutorial

In this tutorial, you use Dreamweaver's Fluid Grid Layout tools to create a layout that adapts to mobile, tablet, and desktop browsers. Dreamweaver CC's Fluid Grid Layout pages use some special CSS, media queries, a bit of JavaScript, and a dedicated visual tool to get the job done. Because of this, you can't "turn" a regular web page into a Fluid Grid Layout page with the push of a button. In fact, the CSS and HTML for a grid layout is so complex that the only way to create a new fluid grid page is to use a Fluid Grid Layout template.

In this tutorial, you'll build a fluid grid document from scratch and add content from a text file and an images folder.

But first, you need to create a new fluid grid document.

> **NOTE**   You can find the files for this tutorial on this book's Missing CD page at *http://oreilly.com/missing-manuals/cds/dreamweaverccmm13/*. The working files are in the folder *Chapter12*, and the completed project is in the folder *Chapter12_complete*.

1. **Choose File→New→Fluid Grid Layout.**

    Dreamweaver opens the New Document window with the Fluid Grid Layout category selected (see Figure 12-29).

2. **In the boxes inside the device outlines, type the number of columns you want for each destination device. Type *5* for Mobile, *12* for Tablet, and *12* for Desktop.**

    Here, you're not saying how many columns you'll insert into the web page, you're letting Dreamweaver know how many columns to draw on the screen to form the page grid. You use these columns as units of measure when you specify how much room you want a page element to use. What you type here really depends on the design you're after. Here are a few guidelines:

    - For mobile design, web designers often use just a single column for content (see the top-left image in Figure 12-27). Because smartphones have narrow screens (480 or fewer pixels wide), placing more than one column in a row makes the design look squished. However, Dreamweaver won't let you type *1* in the Mobile column box, so you need to type *2* or a larger number. If you're going to simply stack the content blocks one on top of the other (as many web designers do), it doesn't matter what you type here. If you *do* plan to place columns side by side (and you should probably stick with two columns as the maximum for mobile designs), the number you type here determines the ratio of one column to the next. Type *2* if you want two equally sized columns sitting side by side. If you want columns of different proportions, type a larger number here to set up the ratio you want. For example, if you type 3, you can make one column 2 units wide and the second column 1 unit wide.

- For tablet design, type a number large enough to accommodate the different combinations of columns you envision for the device. If you think that you might want two equally sized columns, make sure you enter an even number; if you want three equally sized columns, you need a number divisible by 3. Twelve is a good number to use since it's divisible by both 2 and 3, so you can create two columns that are each 6 units wide, or three columns that are each 4 units wide. In short, 12 units gives you lots of combinations of column number and browser widths. Keep in mind that this number only applies to devices whose width is between Mobile (greater than 480 pixels) and 768 pixels. In other words, this would apply to an iPad in portrait orientation (768 pixels wide), but not to an iPad you hold in landscape mode (1,024 pixels wide). Nor would this apply to a Kindle Fire or Samsung Galaxy Tab 2, no matter which way you hold it, since the screens on those tablets measure 1024 by 800 pixels. In those cases, the tablet's browser would use the desktop design.

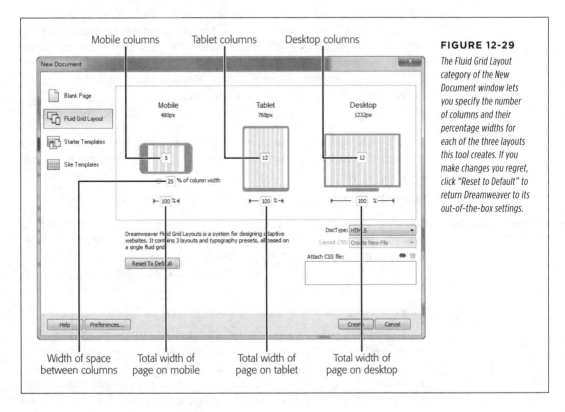

FIGURE 12-29

The Fluid Grid Layout category of the New Document window lets you specify the number of columns and their percentage widths for each of the three layouts this tool creates. If you make changes you regret, click "Reset to Default" to return Dreamweaver to its out-of-the-box settings.

- For desktop design, use the same logic you applied to tablets: how many columns do you want, and what proportion do you want for them? Twelve is a good value here, too, since it gives you many unit combinations for a wide number of columns, but Dreamweaver will accept a value of up to 24.

3. **In the "% of column width" box, type *20* for the space between columns.**

A good value is between 20% and 30%, though you might want to create a couple of pages with different values and test them out before you commit to one and build an entire site. The space that separates columns (called the "gutter" in graphic design) is defined as a percentage of an individual column width. You can't set different values for each type of layout: the mobile, tablet, and desktop layouts all share the same percentage of column widths (see Figure 12-29). However, since you can set different numbers of columns for each layout, the actual width of the gutter will vary. Unfortunately, once you set the "% of column width" and close this window, there's no way to return to this screen to change the percentage. Dreamweaver uses this value to make some complex calculations concerning the columns you insert, so even trying to change it by editing the CSS code is a bad idea.

4. **Type *100* as a percentage width for each layout.**

The content for a fluid grid page sits inside a container div. You can set a width for that div to control how much of the browser window your design will fill. The normal values are 91%, 93%, and 90%. Why? We don't know. It seems weird that you'd choose not to use the entire width of a mobile phone's already thin screen. In fact, it seems weird that you wouldn't use all of the horizontal space allowed. So set the value to 100% for each layout.

5. **Click Create.**

Dreamweaver opens the Save Style Sheet File As dialog box. You're about to save an external style sheet that contains all the styles necessary to control the layout of the page.

6. **Type a style sheet name—*layout.css*—and then click Save.**

Dreamweaver saves the style sheet to your site and displays the page in Split view with the Design half of the screen showing the Mobile size. You can examine the code if you want, but it's pretty cryptic at this point. You'll notice some directives embedded in the comments at the top of the page to deal with Internet Explorer issues.

7. **Click the Design button to switch to Design view.**

In Design view, you see the tall, thin Mobile layout (see Figure 12-30). You can switch to other views (Tablet and Desktop) using the buttons in the lower-right corner of document window. However, to get started with Fluid Grid Layouts, it makes sense to begin with the mobile layout because it's usually the simplest to build. When you first create a fluid grid layout page, Dreamweaver inserts a single div at the top of the page.

Fluid grid layout div

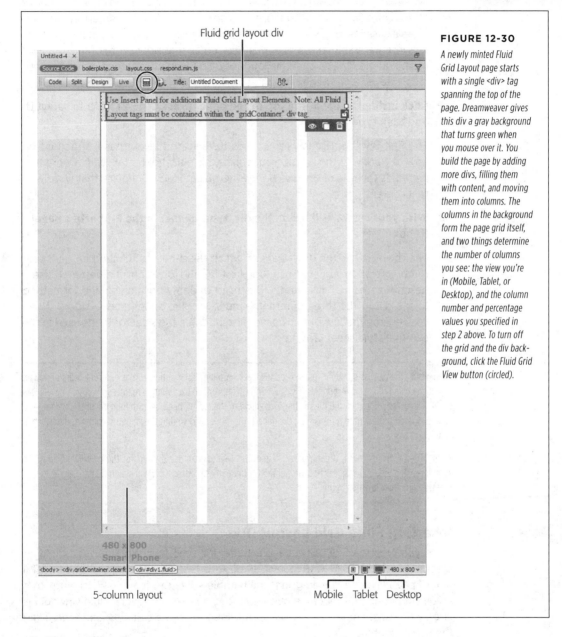

5-column layout

Mobile Tablet Desktop

FIGURE 12-30

A newly minted Fluid Grid Layout page starts with a single <div> tag spanning the top of the page. Dreamweaver gives this div a gray background that turns green when you mouse over it. You build the page by adding more divs, filling them with content, and moving them into columns. The columns in the background form the page grid itself, and two things determine the number of columns you see: the view you're in (Mobile, Tablet, or Desktop), and the column number and percentage values you specified in step 2 above. To turn off the grid and the div background, click the Fluid Grid View button (circled).

8. **Choose File→Save.**

   Type a filename, like *Soylent Green Fluid*, and then click Save to store the HTML page on your site. When you see a follow-up dialog box that mentions dependent files, click OK.

Dreamweaver saves the web page and opens a dialog box informing you that it needs to save two files, *boilerplate.css* and *respond.min.js*, to your site. *Boilerplate.css* is an external style sheet based on the HTML5 boilerplate template (*http://html5boilerplate.com/*); it sets up many basic CSS properties and provides a baseline for displaying various HTML tags. The *respond.min.js* file targets just Internet Explorer 8 and earlier and forces that browser to understand the media queries the fluid grid layout uses. You won't be altering either of these files—they just work their magic behind the scenes.

9. **Click inside the div at the top of the page, press Ctrl+A (⌘-A) to select it, and then type *Banner*.**

   The first div that Dreamweaver adds to fluid grid layout has instructions on how to work with the layout. You replace this placeholder text with a word that identifies the role of the div (*Banner* here). Later, you'll replace that word with real content.

10. **With your cursor still inside the div, type *banner* in the Properties panel's ID box.**

   The div now has the ID of *banner*, which describes its function in the layout (Figure 12-31). You could use IDs like Div1 and Div2, but it's better to use a descriptive name. This unique ID is used to apply positioning and formatting to the div in the three different layouts: mobile, tablet, and desktop. When you rename the div, Dreamweaver also updates the selector that's used in the external style sheet layout.css.

NOTE The discussion about IDs and classes, back on page 102, mentioned that in recent years designers have been using classes and shunning IDs. Fluid Grid Layouts are an exception to that trend. Adobe's developers use IDs to identify the fluid grid divs as they are added to the layout, because each fluid div grid is unique. You should stick with that strategy, renaming the generic IDs (div1, div2) so that they have meaning, as described in step 10.

As mentioned on page 430, Dreamweaver's Fluid Grid Layouts can use div tags or the new HTML5 tags like <header>, <footer>, and <aside>. This tutorial will continue to use div tags and will assign IDs and classes to tags that describe their function in the layout.

Inserting Fluid Grid Layout Divs

Once you create a Fluid Grid Layout page, it's time to insert the basic building blocks of the design. As with many CSS designs (see Chapter 10), the fundamental unit of page layout in a fluid grid is the humble <div> tag (page 428), the box that holds your content. Creating a page layout using Dreamweaver's Fluid Grid tool is largely a process of inserting divs, sizing them to create columns, and then filling them with content.

You use the usual tools (the Insert panel or menu) to add new divs, so it may seem that there's nothing unusual about them. Like a regular web page, when you insert a div, Dreamweaver adds an HTML <div> tag to the page. You place your content (images, headlines, paragraphs, and so on) inside the div. Every device—phone, tablet, and desktop browser—downloads the same HTML file with the same <div> tags and content. However, unlike a regular web page, these divs can look different on each device, thanks to the power of CSS media queries. That is, on a phone, the divs might stack one piece of content on top of another to form a single column. On a tablet, some divs might sit side by side to form a two-column layout, while the wide screen of a desktop browser lets you organize the same divs into a four-column design.

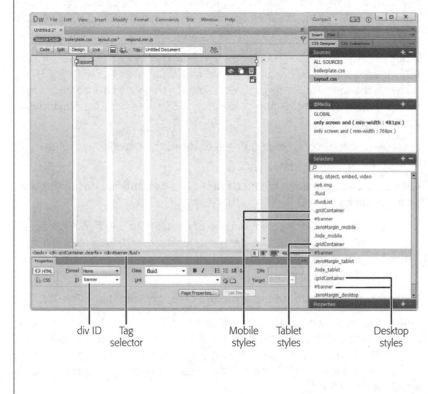

FIGURE 12-31

Unlike the media queries you read about on page 506, Fluid Grid Layout pages put media queries (and their accompanying styles) in a single external style sheet. In this example, that sheet is layout.css. As you can see in CSS Designer's Selectors section (right), a style sheet associated with a Fluid Grid Layout has triplicate selector names. In fact, there are three sets of styles for each layout div. In this case (a page with a single layout div), you see the ID style #banner listed three times. In addition, since Dreamweaver wraps all Fluid Grid Layouts in a div with a class of gridContainer, the .gridContainer class style is also listed three times. From top to bottom in the Selectors section, you see that the first instance of duplicate styles is associated with the Mobile layout, the second with the Tablet layout, and the third with the Desktop layout. See page 550 for more on Fluid Grid Layout style sheets.

div ID Tag selector Mobile styles Tablet styles Desktop styles

Before you start inserting divs, keep in mind a couple of rules:

- You must place your divs (or HTML5 tags like <article>, <header >, and so on) inside the container div, which has the class *gridContainer* applied to it. You can tell if your cursor is inside the container by looking for <div class="gridContainer"> in the Tag Selector at the bottom-left of the document window (see Figure 12-31).

- For major sections of your page, put new divs either before or after existing divs. For example, you don't want to place your main article div inside the page's header—your design won't work. It may take a little practice to make sure you don't accidentally nest divs. The surefire way to avoid that is to use the Duplicate DIV button that appears when you click inside an existing div (see Figure 12-32, bottom). Otherwise, just make sure that you click outside an existing div—that is, to the left or right of the div's bounding box. Then you can use Insert→Div or one of the Insert Div buttons in the Insert panel.

- When you insert a div in one of the device views—Desktop, for example—Dreamweaver adds that same div to the Phone and Tablet views as well. The HTML is always the same for the three devices, though the page's appearance might differ because the browser applies different CSS styles based on the browser window width.

Once you place the cursor where you want to insert the new div, you're ready to add a new Fluid Grid Layout div:

1. **Click between right edge of the banner div's box and the document window's scroll bar.**

   The object is to place the cursor outside of the existing div. If you're successful, you won't see dark border or the Hide, Duplicate, and other tools shown in Figure 12-32, bottom. In the Tag Selector, the item furthest to the right should be <div.gridContain.clearfix>.

2. **In the Insert panel, choose the Structure category, and then click Div.**

   This is the same command you used to insert divs into other web layouts. However, when you work with fluid grids, a special Insert Div window opens (Figure 12-32, top). Dreamweaver knows you're working on a fluid grid layout, so the box "Insert as Fluid Element" is checked. You're prompted provide either a class or ID for the div.

> **NOTE** If you use HTML5 tags, you'll see a similar panel that includes the option to insert those tags as fluid elements. Once you do, they'll work just like the divs described here.

3. **Click ID, type in the descriptive name *story1*, and then click OK.**

   Dreamweaver uses this name as the ID for the div—*<div id="story1">*. It adds three copies of the ID selector to the page's style sheet *layout.css*. Dreamweaver puts the selectors within the fluid grid system of media queries. They dictate the width and placement of the div for mobile, tablet, and desktop browsers.

4. Click OK

Your new div appears in the layout on its own row. It's up to you to resize and position it for mobile, tablet, and desktop layouts.

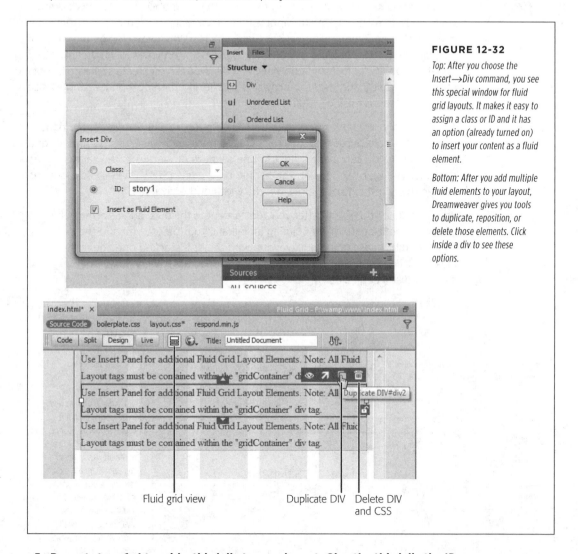

FIGURE 12-32

Top: After you choose the Insert→Div command, you see this special window for fluid grid layouts. It makes it easy to assign a class or ID and it has an option (already turned on) to insert your content as a fluid element.

Bottom: After you add multiple fluid elements to your layout, Dreamweaver gives you tools to duplicate, reposition, or delete those elements. Click inside a div to see these options.

Fluid grid view   Duplicate DIV   Delete DIV
                                         and CSS

5. Repeat steps 1-4 to add a third div to your layout. Give the third div the ID *story2*.

When you insert divs into your project, Dreamweaver includes placeholder text, like "This is the content for Layout Div tag Story1." This helps you identify the different divs in the layout. You can simplify these labels even further by changing the text to something simple, like Banner, Story1, and Story2. Eventually, you'll replace these words with real content.

Formatting Fluid Grid Layout Divs

Once you insert divs into a Fluid Grid Layout page, you can organize them into a layout. Dreamweaver's tools make it easy. But first you need to understand that Dreamweaver creates a unique view for each device—mobile, tablet, and desktop—which you control by clicking the appropriate window size button in the bottom-right corner of the document window (see Figure 12-33). When you change the width of a div or turn it into a column that sits next to one or more other divs, Dreamweaver updates the CSS for just that one view. In other words, you create separate layouts for mobile, tablet, and desktop browsers by clicking the appropriate window size button, and then resizing the divs for that view.

To resize a div, simply click inside it and use the Resize Div handle (to the right of the div). The sole purpose of this handle is to make a div a certain number of grid units wide so you can place it next to one or more other divs in the same row. As explained in Figure 12-33, skip the handle on the left (Shift Div)—it increases the margin to the left side of the div, not the width of the div itself.

You can adjust your layout after you add content to the divs, but it's often helpful to get your layout bearings by building an initial layout before you add the clutter of content. In this case, the Mobile layout, with the divs stacked one above the other, looks just fine. However, when you switch to the Tablet view, it will look better if *story1* and *story2* sit side by side.

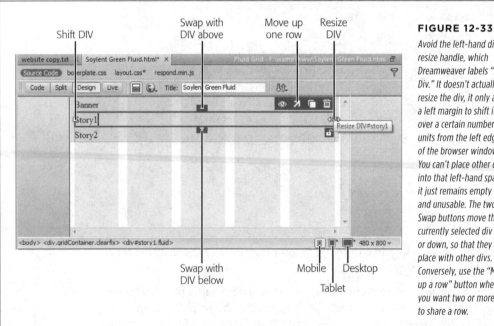

FIGURE 12-33

Avoid the left-hand div resize handle, which Dreamweaver labels "Shift Div." It doesn't actually resize the div, it only adds a left margin to shift it over a certain number of units from the left edge of the browser window. You can't place other divs into that left-hand space; it just remains empty and unusable. The two Swap buttons move the currently selected div up or down, so that they swap place with other divs. Conversely, use the "Move up a row" button when you want two or more divs to share a row.

Follow these steps to make that happen:

1. **In the lower-right corner of the document window, click the Tablet button.**

   You see the Tablet view with its grid of 12 columns.

2. **Click inside story1, grab its right resize handle, and then drag to the left, until the tooltip identifies the width as 6 columns. See Figure 12-34, top.**

   The underlying grid you selected in step 2 on page 548 dictates the possible widths for the div. Dreamweaver will snap the div to the nearest grid column. For example, in the page pictured at the top in Figure 12-34, the underlying grid is 12 columns wide. Dragging the story1 div's resize handle to match up with Column 6 (top image) sets that column's width to 6 grid units.

   NOTE Dreamweaver snaps the div's width to the nearest grid column, so you don't need to be super-accurate when you resize the width of a Fluid Grid Layout div.

3. **Grab the right resize handle for story2 and drag it to set its width to 6 column units as well (Figure 12-34, middle).**

   For this div to sit next to the one you just set up, its width must be equal to or less than the remaining column units for the row. In this example, you set both story1 and story2 to 6 column units, so they share the available space equally, as shown in Figure 12-34, bottom. It's important to note, though, that the widths don't have to be equal. You could just as easily have made story1 8 columns wide and story2 4 columns wide. So long as the total doesn't exceed the grid's total of 12 columns, divs can share a row.

   NOTE When you resize a div that you want to move up and to the right of another div, it's tempting to grab the handles on the left side of the div. Don't!!! See Figure 12-33 for an explanation.

4. **Move story2 up by clicking the "Move up a row" button (Figure 12-34, middle).**

   Dreamweaver moves story2 up to share a row with story1 (as long as there's enough space for it to fit). This is probably a good time to see if fluid grids are really working their magic.

5. **Choose File→Save All Related Files**

   Dreamweaver saves the HTML file and the changes to *layout.css*. It's best to use the Save All Related Files command when working with fluid grid layouts—if Dreamweaver doesn't update all the files related to a page, you're likely to see unexpected results when you preview the page.

6. **Press F12 or go to File→Preview in Browser.**

   Your web browser opens and displays the fluid grid layout (Figure 12-35).

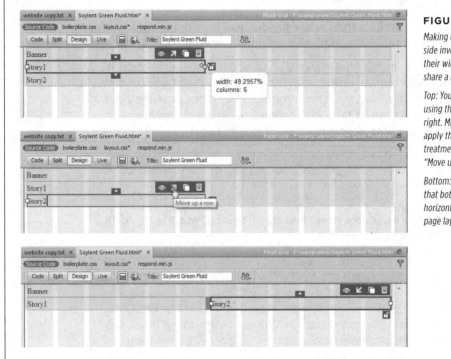

FIGURE 12-34

Making divs sit side by side involves changing their width so they can share a row.

Top: You resized story1 using the handle on the right. Middle: After you apply the same resizing treatment to story2, click "Move up a row."

Bottom: The end result is that both divs share the horizontal space in the page layout.

7. **Change the width of the browser window.**

   When the width of the browser window is Tablet sized (481 to 768 pixels), story1 and story2 appear side by side. Otherwise (that is, in Mobile and Desktop widths), the two stories are still stacked vertically. If things don't look as expected, see the box on page 559.

■ ADDING MORE DIVS TO YOUR LAYOUT

At this point, you have three divs and you've tweaked the layout for Tablet view. In the next steps, you add a div for a sidebar and a div to hold the copyright notice at the bottom of the page. Then you'll head over to the Design view and work on the layout.

1. **Click to the right of the story2 div and then choose Insert→Div. In the Insert Div window, click the ID button and then type *sidebar*.**

   A sidebar div appears at the bottom of the page, taking up an entire row. You may want to change the placeholder text to read "Sidebar."

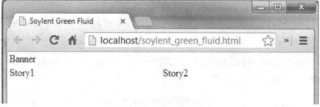

FIGURE 12-35

You can preview your fluid grid layout in your web browser.

Top: Resize the browser window to a mobile phone width and all three divs stack vertically.

Bottom: Change the width of the content div to the target size for tablets, and you see story1 and story2 sit side by side.

2. **With your cursor inside the sidebar, click the Duplicate Div button.**

    The Duplicate Div command is simply another way to add a new div to your project. The new div has the same content as the old one. Dreamweaver gives the new div the generic ID div1. It's up to you to give it a meaningful one.

UP TO SPEED

Troubleshooting Fluid Grid Layouts

Sometimes, you'll preview your fluid grid layout and it won't look the way you think it should. That's one reason it's important to follow the rule "Save early and save often." Previewing your work is another task you should do early and often. It's easier to catch and fix problems if you work incrementally. For example, after you set up a new row of divs, save your work and preview it. Then, after you add content to your divs, save and preview once more. And when you save the file, use the Save All Related Files command. Dreamweaver transforms your work of arranging different layouts for mobile, tablet, and desktop devices into CSS code. If you don't save that CSS file before previewing your work, you won't see any changes.

If your layout doesn't look as expected, the first thing to do is use the Save All Related Files command again, just to make sure you saved the associated CSS file. When you preview the page in your browser, press F5 to reload the page and the CSS formatting. Sometimes, even this doesn't solve the problem. To be honest, fluid grid layouts are a bit fragile. If you put a div inside another div when it shouldn't be there, or if you record a CSS style in the wrong media query, or if you leave out a bracket in the layout CSS file—bad things happen. Fixing issues like this after the fact may not work, so sometimes the best (and quickest) solution is to start over. To do that for this tutorial, you would start by closing all the documents. Then, in the Files panel, delete all the files except for *website copy. txt* and the images folder.

3. **Click inside the new div. Press Ctrl-A (⌘-A), and then type *Copyright.* In the Properties panel, change the ID to *copyright.***

   The new div now has new placeholder text and an ID that indicates its role in the layout (Figure 12-36).

4. **In the lower-right corner of the document window, click the Desktop and then the Mobile layout buttons.**

   At this point, all the views—mobile, tablet, and desktop—are identical, with their divs stacked vertically. But you've only been working in Tablet view, so how did the other two views get their divs? That showcases one of the beauties of mobile design in Dreamweaver: If you add a div in any of the views, it shows up in the other two. Conversely, if you move and position divs in a particular view, it affects that view only.

   Up to this point, however, you haven't made any changes to any of the views. You'll do that now.

5. **Click the Desktop layout view, and then change the width of story1, story2, and the sidebar to 4 column units.**

   All three divs are now the same size (4 column units) and will fit in a single row (which is 12 column units wide).

6. **Click inside story2, and then click the "Move up a row" button. Repeat the process for the sidebar.**

   The Desktop layout for your page is now different from the Mobile and Tablet layouts. You can see the difference if you change views in the document window. You'll also see the difference if you preview your project in a browser.

   Now, it's time to add content to these divs!

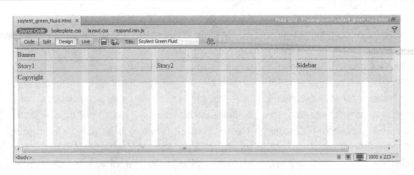

FIGURE 12-36

After adding two more divs—a sidebar and a copyright notice—and making changes in the Desktop layout, your project looks like this. Each of the other views now sports a different layout, thanks to the magic of media queries and CSS.

Adding Content to Fluid Grid Layout Pages

Adding content to a Fluid Grid Layout page is no different from adding content to any other web page. You insert images and text inside the layout divs just as you'd insert HTML content into a web page. In this example, you'll copy and paste text from a file called *website_copy.txt* and insert images using the Insert→Image command or the Insert Image tools in Dreamweaver's Insert panel.

NOTE When you insert an image into Fluid Grid Layout page, Dreamweaver doesn't assign a width or height to the image as it does for other types of web pages (see page 233). Instead, it leaves those values blank and uses some tricky CSS to make the image "fluid"—that is, to make the image itself shrink in size as the div gets smaller. (To learn how this works, read the original article on this technique by Ethan Marcotte at *www.alistapart. com/articles/fluid-images/*.)

1. **In the lower-right corner of the document window, click the Mobile button.**

   You see the mobile layout with the divs stacked vertically.

2. **In the Files panel, double-click *website_copy.txt*.**

   The text file opens in the document window. You'll copy and paste text from this file into the divs in your fluid grid layout.

3. **Select the headline "All Natural Ingredients" and the three paragraphs below it, and then press Ctrl+C (⌘-C).**

   Dreamweaver copies the text into the Clipboard.

4. **At the top of the document window, click the tab for *soylent_green_fluid. html*, click inside the story1 div, press Ctrl+A (⌘-A) to select all the place-holder text, and then press Ctrl+V (⌘-V) to insert the copied text from the Clipboard.**

   The copied headline and three paragraphs of text appear inside the story1 div. If you find it difficult to select all the placeholder text in a div, the Select All command (Ctrl+A [⌘-A for Mac]) comes in handy.

5. **Repeat this process to copy the next headline and its three paragraphs from *website_copy.txt* and paste the contents into the story2 div.**

   In Mobile view, the two stories appear stacked. If you switch to Tablet or Desktop view, you see the content side by side.

6. **In the same file, copy the next four lines of text into the sidebar div, and then copy the following two lines into the copyright div.**

   You've swapped out the placeholder text with some actual Soylent Green content. Still, things are looking pretty dull. Time to add some pics.

7. **Click inside of the banner div, press Ctrl+A (⌘-a), and then press Delete.**

   This selects and then deletes the banner text. You'll replace it with a banner image.

8. **Choose Insert→Image→Image, select *café_logo.png*, and then press OK.**

The image file appears in the banner div. The colors are so light it's hard to see. You'll fix that later by adding a background to the div. You can use the Insert menu, the Insert panel, or the keyboard shortcut Ctrl+Alt+I (⌘-Option-I) to add images to your layout. Dreamweaver adds the image and CSS adjusts its size to suit the mobile, tablet, or desktop layouts.

9. **In the sidebar div, click before the words "Soylent green fluid" and then insert the *special1.jpg* image. Press the right-arrow on your keyboard to move the cursor between the image and the captions, then press Ctrl+Enter (⌘-Return) to add a line break that forces the text to the next line.**

You now have an image and text caption in the sidebar div. You'll add two more images to the sidebar.

10. **Repeat step 9 to add the next two "special" pics.**

At this point, your sidebar div has a heading, three pictures, and three text captions below the pictures. It should look like Figure 12-37.

Styling Fluid Grid Layout Pages

Dreamweaver CC's Fluid Grid Layout tools control just the layout of divs—they don't do anything to help style the look of the content you place *inside* those divs. For that, you turn to the regular CSS tools.

The first step in styling raw text is to add HTML tags to it. Then you create CSS rules for those tags and use IDs as selectors to target the major sections of your layout: banner, story1, sidebar, and so on.

When you first get started with fluid grid layouts, keep things simple by creating just a few global styles and storing them in a new external style sheet. Remember, you just want to set style rules here, not lay out the page—that's the work of the fluid grid's layout CSS. So avoid specifying sizes, widths, and heights for page elements in this style sheet.

Suppose, for example, that you want all the copyright divs to have a green background and white text in the pt-sans font. In your external style sheet, you create a rule for the *copyright* class selector that applies that formatting. In the web page's HTML, you link to this style sheet after you link to the fluid grid layout style sheet, so that this style sheet's rules override those in the fluid grid layout.

One advantage of this technique is that it separates your global typographic and background formatting from the complex CSS in the fluid grid layout that handles different-sized page elements. In short, with this method, you're less likely to foul up the fluid grid layout. Also, when you work with global rules in a separate, external sheet, you don't have to worry as much about where you place the rule within the media query hierarchy. (See the bullet points on page 107 for details.) Best of all, there's an easy solution if your styles don't work. Suppose you accidentally override a style you shouldn't have with a global rule. You can fix it by editing the rule or removing a selector from your typographic style sheet. If more drastic measures are needed, you can click the – sign button (the Remove CSS Source button) to completely disconnect your global styles from the web page. At that point, only the fluid grid style sheet governs your page.

FIGURE 12-37

You can add content to your web page by copying and pasting text and by inserting images and other media using the standard Insert commands. The fluid divs can contain multiple paragraphs and images, as shown here in the sidebar div. Fluid grid layouts like this let you organize page contents to fit different screen sizes.

Here's how you create a style sheet that specifies fonts and colors for your page. You start by applying basic HTML tags to your headlines:

1. **In the story1 div, put your cursor inside the line "All Natural Ingredients," and then, in the Properties panel's Format menu, choose Heading 1.**

   That changes the HTML <p> tag to an <h1> tag. It doesn't change the style sheet, even though it changes the appearance of the text. In addition, since all the layouts share the same HTML and style sheet, your tag change affects all the fluid layouts: mobile, tablet, and desktop.

2. **Use the same technique from step 1 to create an h1 heading in the story2 div and an h2 heading in the sidebar div.**

Both articles now have HTML headings. Now it's time to add some style using CSS. First, you need to create a new external style sheet.

3. **In the Sources section of CSS Designer, click the + sign ("Add CSS Source"), and then choose "Create A New CSS File" from the menu. In the dialog box that pops up, type *soylent_styles.css* in the File/URL box, and then click OK.**

Dreamweaver lists your new external style sheet in the Sources section, along with the fluid grid style sheets *boilerplate.css* and *layout.css*. You'll leave those sources alone, while you add new rules to *soylent_styles.css*.

4. **In Sources, click *soylent_styles.css* and then, in the Selectors section, click the + sign to add a selector. Type *body* in the box for the selector name.**

Dreamweaver adds *body* to the list of selectors. You can format the tag and those styles will apply to any text between the beginning and ending <body> tags. In addition, Dreamweaver applies the rules to all three fluid layouts; it sticks to global rules, ones that specify fonts and maybe colors, but not font-sizes or other styles related to text size or positioning.

5. **In the Properties section of CSS Designer, with "body" still highlighted in the Selectors section, make sure you have the Show Set checkbox turned off, click the T button to see the text styles available, and then set the font-family to "pt-sans, Arial, Helvetica, sans-serif."**

This global style sets the basic font for your layout to sans-serif. (If you haven't added the pt-sans web font as explained on page 147, use a sans-serif alternative.) All the text in your layout will use this font unless you change it for a specific selector (and you'll do that in the step 7).

6. **Click the Background button, and then set the URL for background-image URL to *images/bg_page.png*.**

The background image provides a textured, colored background (as long as the browser supports background images, of course).

7. **With *soylent_styles.css* still selected in Sources, in the Selectors section, click the + sign button. In the name box for the selector, type *h1*. In Properties, set the text color to #006600 (a dark green), and then set the font-family to pt-serif or another typeface with serifs.**

Your h1 headings reflect these changes. In some cases, you may not see the specified typeface until you preview your page in a browser.

8. **Use the technique from step 7 to create an h2 selector, and then set the text color to #FFFFFF (white), the font-family to pt-serif, the font-variant to small-caps, and text-align to center.**

This creates a unique look for the h2 heading in the sidebar.

9. **Click the Background button and set the background color to #006600 (dark green).**

Your sidebar now sports a green bar for the title.

10. **With *soylent_styles.css* still selected in Sources, click the + sign and then, in the name box, type *#banner, #copyright*.**

This shortcut makes it easy to apply the same style to more than one selector at a time. Just make sure you put a comma between the two selector names. CSS Designer prompts you with valid IDs after you type the pound symbol (#).

11. **Click the #banner, #copyright selector, and then, in Properties, click the Background button and set the background color to #006600 (a dark green).**

The background for the banner and copyright divs is now green. At last you can see your logo!

12. **Click the Layout button and then, in the padding box, click the link to change all the properties at once. Then set the value of one of the padding boxes to 7px, and the text color to #FFFFFF (white).**

The padding provides a little breathing room around the contents of the divs. The text in the copyright inherits its san-serif font-family from the body style rule (steps 4 and 5) and its color from the *#banner, #copyright* rule (step 12). This is probably a good time to save and preview your work.

13. **Choose File→Save All Related Files, and then press F12 to preview your page in your browser. Resize the browser window (by dragging the left edge, for example) to see the layout at different breakpoints for mobile, tablet, and desktop design.**

At the mobile screen width, Dreamweaver stacks everything vertically, but the way you formatted the heading and body text gives the layout an attractive appearance. At the Tablet screen width, the main stories appear in side-by-side columns. The sidebar appears, a little awkwardly, in a vertical orientation below them (you'll fix this in the last part of the tutorial, on page 566). At the Desktop screen width, the page has three equal columns, two for the two main stories, and one for the sidebar. In addition, the sidebar's green bar sets it off from the two stories.

You can continue to add to or tweak the global styles; just be sure to follow a few straightforward rules:

- Make sure you edit the *soylent_styles.css* source, not one of the other style sheets.

- Keep in mind that you want to apply these styles *after* you apply the fluid layout styles, so in the source code for your web page, make sure the link to *soylent_styles.css* comes after the link to *layout.css*.

- Avoid making changes to width, height, or other size or position properties that might override the fluid grid layout's hard work.

- Be cautious about applying margins and padding.

- Double-check the results after you create a rule. If you override the wrong property, it may disturb the fluid grid layout.

If you run into problems, try deleting specific rules (property/values or selectors) in *soylent_styles.css*. If that doesn't work, try detaching *soylent_styles.css* using the Remove CSS Source button (the - sign) in CSS Designer's Sources section.

Next, you'll learn how to nest fluid divs inside each other, a technique you'll use to fix the sidebar in the Tablet layout.

Nesting Fluid Grid DIVs

When you lay out the major sections of your page, identifying the banner, stories, and sidebars that make it up, you try to avoid putting one fluid grid div inside of another. However, there are times where you might want to nest some "lesser" fluid divs inside a major section. Consider a sidebar with pictures and captions, like the one in this tutorial. The sidebar looks fine in Mobile and Desktop views, but not so good in Tablet view. It would be great if those pictures and captions could float into a horizontal layout on tablets. You can make that happen by placing each picture and its caption in a fluid div. You'll contain those divs, in turn, in a sidebar div.

> **NOTE** In the earlier versions of Fluid Grid Layouts, you couldn't nest one fluid grid div inside another. This feature is new to Dreamweaver CC.

Continuing with the Soylent Green tutorial, follow these steps:

1. **In the lower-right corner of the document window, click the Mobile size button.**

   You can add new divs in any of the views, but it's usually easier to work in the Mobile layout with the divs stacked one on top of the other.

2. **Click to place the cursor after the last word in the sidebar div, mozarello. Then use the Insert panel to add a new div.**

   You insert a div a couple of ways, like using the Insert→Div command or the Insert panel (Common→Div). Either way, the Insert Div window opens, where you can name a class or ID div.

Creating CSS Rules for Specific Screen Sizes

If your fluid grid layout project demands more complex formatting than what you can get from a global style sheet, you may want to create individual style rules for different screen sizes. For example, you may want to add a background color or background image to a sidebar in the desktop view, but not in the other two views.

To create this kind of rule, you need to understand how Dreamweaver organizes the media queries and rules in a single, external style sheet for Fluid Grid Layout pages. If you create a CSS rule specifically for desktop screens, you need to make sure you place that rule in the right spot in the style sheet. You can create or edit rules by writing the code yourself or by letting CSS Designer do the work. You get a good understanding of the structure of the fluid grid CSS file if you open it up and take a look, so consider the hand-coding option first.

To hand-code a new CSS style, open the fluid grid style sheet in Code view. (In the tutorial, that style sheet is *layout.css*.) Within the CSS rules, you see comments (gray text) explaining where to place your code. For example, about a quarter of the way into the code, there's a comment that explains:

```
/* Mobile Layout: 480px and below. */
```

If you want your rule to apply to phone size screens, place it between this comment and the next one (for tablets). The styles in this section apply to mobile screens, but they apply to the other screen sizes too, unless you override a rule appearing later in the style sheet. Move down through the code and you see another comment:

```
/* Tablet Layout: 481px to 768px. Inherits
   styles from: Mobile Layout. */
```

Thanks to the CSS cascade, discussed on page 384, these styles override the same-named selectors used for mobile devices. It's kind of like the style sheet saying "Hey browser, here's some styles to use...oh, wait a minute, I see that you're wider than 480 pixels, so why don't you use these styles instead."

The last screen size comment in the fluid grid CSS code is for desktops:

```
/* Desktop Layout: 769px to a max of
   1232px.  Inherits styles from: Mobile Lay-
   out and Tablet Layout. */
```

So, if you want to add background color to the sidebar for desktops without changing the background for mobile and tablet devices, place that rule after the comment for the desktop layout. In that case, your rule for the sidebar might look like this:

```
#sidebar {
    width: 32.2033%;
    margin-left: 1.6949%;
    clear: none;
    background-color: #FAFFCD;
}
```

You use the same principles when you add device-specific styles using CSS Designer. Instead of manually editing the code, you use the media queries in CSS Designer's Media section. By choosing the correct media query, CSS Designer places your rules in the proper location in the CSS file.

To add a device-specific style, first select the fluid grid style sheet—that's *layout.css* in this example. Then the Media section displays three media queries (Figure 12-38): *Global*, *only screen and (min-width: 481px)*, and *only screen and (min-width: 769px)*. They correspond to the screen size comments in the CSS file.

By choosing one of the media queries before you edit or add a style, you can target specific screen sizes. So, for example, to add a background color to a sidebar when it's viewed on a desktop screen, you'd follow these steps.

In CSS Designer's Sources section, click the name of the fluid grid CSS file (for example, *layout.css*). In the Media section, click *only screen and (min-width: 769px)*. In the Selectors section, click *#sidebar* (the ID you applied to the sidebar div). Finally, in the Properties section, go to the background properties and set the *background-color* to a specific value.

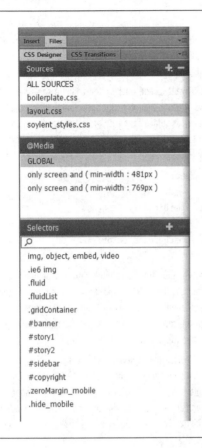

FIGURE 12-38

Layout.css is the source file for this fluid grid layout. In the Media section of CSS Designer, you've selected Global, so in the Selectors section, you see the selectors for styles that Dreamweaver applies globally (unless a media query below Global overrides those styles). For example, to create a rule that applies to tablet screens, you select the media query "only screen and (min-width: 481px)." Styles you edit or create with this media query selected won't apply to smaller screens. Want to target desktops? Use the "only screen and (min-width: 769px)" media query.

3. **Type** *special* **in the Class box. Leave the "Insert as Fluid Element" checkbox turned on and then click OK.**

   This div will hold the picture and caption for a Soylent Green Café special. You need two more divs to cover all three café specials.

4. **Click inside the new div and then click the Duplicate Div button twice.**

   You should have three divs, nested inside the sidebar div. It's time to fill them with content. You'll cut the images and captions out of the main part of the sidebar and paste them inside the divs you just added to the sidebar.

5. **In the sidebar div, select the first picture and caption. Press Ctrl+X (⌘-X) to cut the selection, click inside the first "special" div, press Ctrl+A (⌘-A) to select its contents, and then press Ctrl+V (⌘-V) to paste the image and caption into the div.**

   The image and caption replace the placeholder text.

6. **Repeat step 6 to add pictures and captions to the other two special divs.**

   When you're done, there's a gap between the special divs and the sidebar title. These are empty paragraph tags. Clean them up using the Delete key.

7. **In the lower-right corner of the document window, click the Tablet size button.**

   Your special divs use as much space as the sidebar provides. Each one is 12 column units wide.

8. **Drag the top special div's right handle to the left until the tooltip indicates it is 4 columns wide. Then use the "Move up a row" arrow to position the special divs so that they are all on one line.**

   In Tablet view, the nested special divs sit side by side in the sidebar div. In the other views, the nested divs are stacked, as shown in Figure 12-39.

FIGURE 12-39

The sidebar "This Week's Specials" is a garland of fluid grid elements: a fluid grid element holds each of the photo-caption pairs, and they appear inside the sidebar, which is itself a fluid grid element.

Top right: On an iPhone, the nested elements are stacked vertically.

Top left: On an early model iPad, the photos and captions appear side by side.

Bottom: On an Android tablet, which has higher resolution than the early iPad, the pictures and captions are stacked in the sidebar, the same way they are in the desktop version of the site.

Bringing Your Pages to Life

Adding Interactivity with jQuery

J avaScript has grown from the simple language behind pop-up windows and image rollovers to a full-blown programming tool that can change the content on a web page even as you look at it. It's the key to interactivity on the Web today. It can even download new data behind the scenes and update a page (that's why you can scroll to new sections of a Google map without loading new pages—your browser's already downloaded the rest of the map). JavaScript is the key to today's interactive websites.

Dreamweaver, which always tries to provide features that meet web designers' needs, includes a set of JavaScript tools that let you add interactive elements, like content sections that expand and collapse, tabbed panels, and pop-up calendars, to a page. That's what this chapter is all about.

The first section discusses the relationship between JavaScript, jQuery, and the jQuery UI library of widgets. The sections that follow describe the features of the other jQuery UI widgets along with tips on how to use them effectively. At the end of the chapter, you learn about Dreamweaver behaviors. Behaviors have been part of Dreamweaver for some time, but with Dreamweaver CC, Adobe trimmed those that were out of date. You're likely to find uses for the ones that remain.

■ JavaScript, jQuery, and jQuery UI

JavaScript is a programming language (technically, it's a "scripting" language because it doesn't create standalone applications.) When a browser opens a web page that has a program (a script) embedded in it, it reads the script and performs the indicated actions. JavaScript isn't part of HTML, but you use it to *manipulate* the

HTML elements that make up a web page. For example, webcrafters often use Java-Script to show or hide parts of a web page—it's the magic behind the accordion and tab widgets in Figure 13-1. You can also use JavaScript to rewrite your page's code. Consider a web page photo gallery, with one main picture and several thumbnails. When you click a thumbnail, its image replaces the main picture. Behind the scenes, JavaScript rewrites the URL of the source file for the main picture.

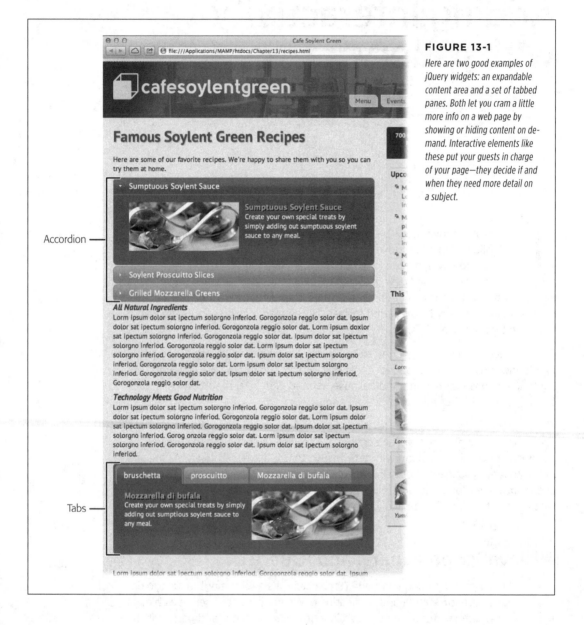

FIGURE 13-1

Here are two good examples of jQuery widgets: an expandable content area and a set of tabbed panes. Both let you cram a little more info on a web page by showing or hiding content on demand. Interactive elements like these put your guests in charge of your page—they decide if and when they need more detail on a subject.

Think of JavaScript as a general-purpose language you can use to do just about anything when it comes to web pages.

Doing something from scratch in JavaScript, like building an expanding and collapsing accordion section for a web page, takes a lot of time and work. So helpful and industrious JavaScript coders have developed libraries of scripts that perform specific tasks. These libraries make it easy to add widgets and many other feats of magic to a page.

The most popular JavaScript library is *jQuery*. jQuery makes it easy to identify elements on a web page and it works seamlessly with CSS. Combining the capabilities of jQuery and CSS gives you a ton of programming power. In fact, jQuery is so popular, developers created libraries for this library (see Figure 13-2). Adobe included two of them with Dreamweaver: jQuery UI (for "user interface") and jQuery Mobile. You add these libraries' widgets to your web pages using Dreamweaver's Insert panel (Window→Insert).

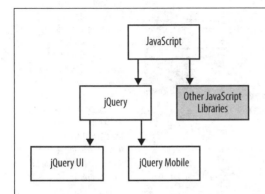

FIGURE 13-2

You can think of jQuery UI as the third generation of a scripting family. First there was JavaScript, the general-purpose scripting tool, which begat jQuery. jQuery made it easier to select elements on a page and work with CSS. Then, jQuery begat jQuery UI and its sibling jQuery Mobile (discussed on page 521). Each helps with even more specific site development chores.

When you add a jQuery widget to a page, Dreamweaver writes the necessary code and grabs to the library source files. The first time you save a page that uses jQuery UI widgets, Dreamweaver creates a jQueryAssets folder and stores the needed files in that folder.

NOTE   Want to know more about these interactive languages? A complete review of JavaScript and jQuery can be found in *JavaScript and jQuery: The Missing Manual* by David Sawyer McFarland (O'Reilly). You can also find information at *www.w3schools.com/js* or *https://developer.mozilla.org/en/JavaScript*. (At this point, you might want to know that if you have experience with any programming language, you'll have a head start with JavaScript because it shares many programming concepts with other languages.)

Versions of Dreamweaver prior to CC included the Spry framework, a library of tools and widgets similar to those in jQuery UI. Those tools fell out of date, and Adobe dropped them from Dreamweaver. If you're interested, you can still download them. Go to Adobe's blog at *http://tinyurl.com/ly4zhr8* to see why they no longer include Spry, and to download the Spry framework.

■ Adding an Accordion

No, you don't have to study music theory to use the jQuery UI accordion. Even more surprising, you don't have to study JavaScript or jQuery. All you need to do is pick a spot in your web page and head over to the Insert panel (Window→Insert). Choose the jQuery UI category and then click Accordion. Voila! You added a set of collapsible sections to your web page. Your accordion doesn't look very impressive in Design view, so click the Live button. You can see that your accordion has three sections (Figure 13-3), imaginatively named Section 1, Section 2, and Section 3. To the left of each section header is a flippy triangle that tells guests they can expand (or collapse) that part of the page. Initially, the first panel is expanded, but if you click Section 2, the second section expands while Section 1 collapses.

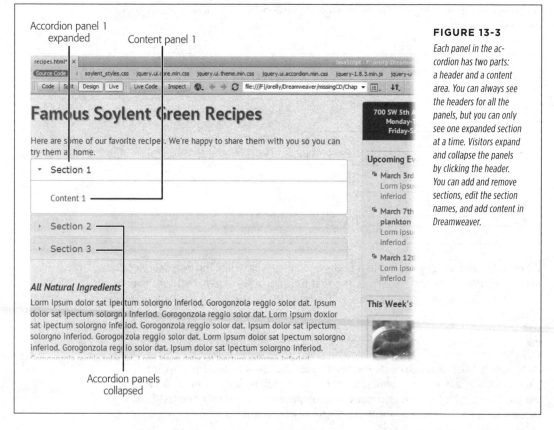

FIGURE 13-3

Each panel in the accordion has two parts: a header and a content area. You can always see the headers for all the panels, but you can only see one expanded section at a time. Visitors expand and collapse the panels by clicking the header. You can add and remove sections, edit the section names, and add content in Dreamweaver.

The accordion lets you stuff a lot of information into a little screen real estate. You don't want to overwhelm your web guests with information that they aren't ready to digest. An accordion widget lets you hide details until your guest wants them.

Suppose your web page sells digital cameras. Along with the usual product pictures and sales pitch, you add an accordion full of details. The first panel is open when the page loads, so you fill it with an overview of the camera's features. The second panel is collapsed at first, but the heading "Specifications" lets visitors know that there are some geeky details available. A third panel describes the items that come with the camera: a detachable lens, a battery, and a case. The fourth panel sells optional accessories: lenses, tripods, and memory cards. The last panel quotes the glowing reviews the camera got from the media. Using an accordion, you put all these details on a single page. The panel headings tell visitors what info's underneath. As any good salesperson knows, once customers start interacting with the details, you're on your way to a sale.

To add a jQuery accordion:

1. **Click the location on your web page where you want to insert the accordion widget.**

   Here are some design issues to keep in mind when choosing a location: The shape and size of an accordion widget can vary. Initially, the width fills the page or the div that holds the accordion. Depending on the options you set, the sections can grow to accommodate large chunks of content, or they can remain a single, fixed size.

2. **On the Insert panel (Window→Insert), select jQuery UI from the drop-down menu, (Figure 13-4).**

   The jQuery UI library offers several user interface widgets, such as a date-picker, buttons, and a slider. The accordion tops the list.

FIGURE 13-4

The Insert panel's jQuery UI category holds 11 widgets from this popular library. When you choose one, Dreamweaver adds the necessary code to your web page.

3. **Click Accordion.**

When you do, Dreamweaver inserts a three-panel accordion in your web page and adds several lines of code to the <head> section of your document. This code links to the JavaScript and jQuery files needed to display and format the accordion. Some of the lines of code are temporary—they disappear the first time you save the page with the jQuery widget in it.

4. **Click inside the accordion, and then click the blue tab at the top.**

Unselected, your accordion looks a little like an HTML table (page 269). When you click anywhere inside it, though, a blue line marks its boundaries and a tab at the top identifies it as "jQuery Accordion: Accordion1" (Figure 13-5). (The portion after the colon is the widget's ID.) Clicking the tab selects the accordion and displays its properties in the Properties panel.

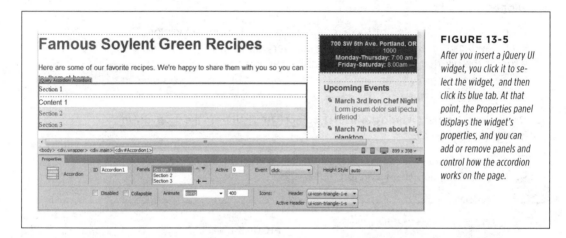

FIGURE 13-5

After you insert a jQuery UI widget, you click it to se-lect the widget, and then click its blue tab. At that point, the Properties panel displays the widget's properties, and you can add or remove panels and control how the accordion works on the page.

5. **In the Properties panel, give your accordion a new ID, such as *acc-recipes*.**

If your page has lots of elements, it may be helpful to add a prefix like "acc" to the ID to remind you that it is an accordion. This ID works like any other ID in Dreamweaver; you use it in conjunction with CSS to format your content. For example, if you want to change the width of the accordion, you do that in CSS Designer by choosing a source (an internal or external style sheet), adding the accordion ID as a selector, and then setting a value for the Width property.

Of course, adding an accordion to the page is only half the battle. You'll always want to change the section headers and add content to the expandable panels. Most of the time, you'll also want to tweak the widget's properties.

TIP You may be tempted to save the page as soon as you add a widget, but hold off if you plan to add more than one, see page 580.

Adding Content to an Accordion

For the most part, you edit an accordion's panel headers and content just as you would any other element on the page. To change "Section 1," for example, select the text and then type in a new heading. The words "Content 1" identify the collapsible portion of Section 1. You can add images, tables, or any other element you'd use on a web page. Keep in mind, however, that accordions change shape depending on their content and the options you set in the Properties panel. The JavaScript/ CSS code combo give the element the organization and formatting it needs to look good (Figure 13-6).

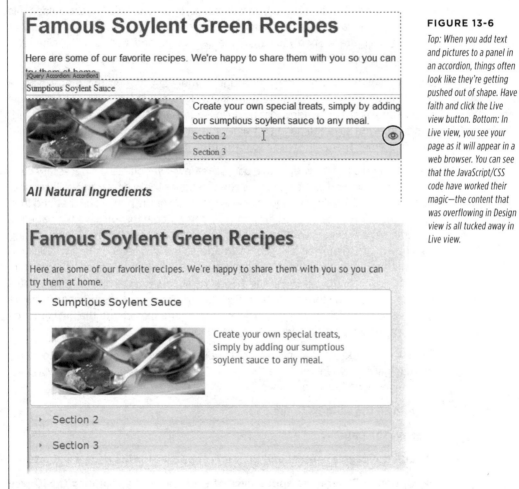

FIGURE 13-6

Top: When you add text and pictures to a panel in an accordion, things often look like they're getting pushed out of shape. Have faith and click the Live view button. Bottom: In Live view, you see your page as it will appear in a web browser. You can see that the JavaScript/CSS code have worked their magic—the content that was overflowing in Design view is all tucked away in Live view.

There is one trick you need to know about adding content to an accordion. In Design view, if a panel is collapsed and the content is hidden, you can expand it by moving your cursor over the section header bar. When the eye icon appears (Figure 13-6, circled top). Click the eye to show the content for that panel.

NOTE Formatting jQuery UI widgets gets pretty complex. You'll see more details on page 583, but for now, it's worth noting that some attributes for fonts, position, and color come from jQuery UI style sheets. You'll see how to add your own CSS rules to change the formatting on page 587. For example, at the bottom of Figure 13-6, you see a picture floated to the left. The CSS rule positioning that picture is in the web page's main style sheet—not in the jQuery UI code.

Saving Your Widget Web Page

When savvy site developers work on web pages, they usually follow the golden rule "Save early and save often." It's good practice to name and save a page almost as soon as you create it. Then you can hit the Save command, Ctrl+S (⌘-S), whenever you pause for a second.

But when you work with jQuery UI widgets, you want to alter this practice just a bit. If your page will include more than one widget, say an accordion of collapsible content and a tabbed window, as shown in Figure 13-1, it's best to add all your widgets *before* you save the page that first time. Why? It has to do with the CSS files and the themes (page 583) used to format the page.

When you add a jQuery widget to a page, Dreamweaver places the necessary code in the <body> section of the page (this code identifies the widget), and it places links to scripts and CSS style sheets in the <head> section of the page. It fetches and then temporarily stores the needed files on your computer, until you save the page the first time. When you do, you see a dialog box like the one in Figure 13-7 left, letting you know that Dreamweaver is about to add a slew of files to your site. Click OK and a number of things happen. Dreamweaver creates a folder called jQueryAssets and places JavaScript files (.js) and CSS style sheets (.css) inside. It also creates an Images folder to store a bunch of PNG (.png) graphics with odd names like *ui-bg_glass_55_fbf9ee_1x400.png*. These small image files create the backgrounds and icons for the jQuery UI widgets you added to your page.

If you want to add just a single widget to your web page, you don't need to worry too much about when you save the page. But if you're adding multiple widgets, here's a good workflow to follow:

1. **Add all the widgets to the page.**

2. **Save the page.**

3. **Edit the page's content and then set properties for the page's widgets.**

4. **Optional: Change the appearance of your widget by changing the jQuery UI theme (see page 583).**

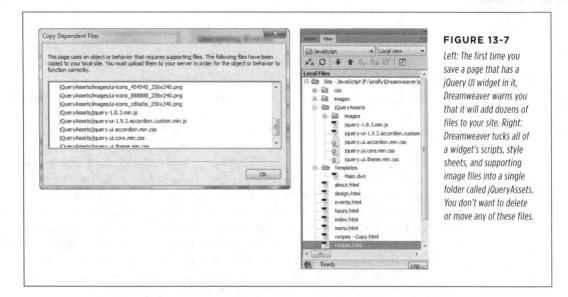

FIGURE 13-7

Left: The first time you save a page that has a jQuery UI widget in it, Dreamweaver warns you that it will add dozens of files to your site. Right: Dreamweaver tucks all of a widget's scripts, style sheets, and supporting image files into a single folder called jQueryAssets. You don't want to delete or move any of these files.

5. **Optional: Change the widget's look using CSS Designer. You can, for example, choose a different font or type size for the widget's headings. One note of caution: If you follow this step, you may override some of the CSS rules that define the widget's theme.**

Changing an Accordion's Properties

The great thing about accordions is that they're flexible. (Sorry, bad pun couldn't be helped.) After you add an accordion to a page, chances are you'll want to add or remove sections, and change the way the widget opens and operates. You can do all those things in the Properties panel. First, click somewhere inside the accordion, and then click the blue tab at the top-left. At that point, the Properties panel displays the accordion's attributes. Many jQuery UI widgets use these same properties. Here's what they do:

- **ID.** Dreamweaver needs to keep track of each widget on a page, so it uses IDs to uniquely identify them. As usual, to tweak the formatting, you use the ID as a CSS selector and then create style rules to position or size the element on the page.

- **Panels.** Use the Panels property to add, remove, and position accordion panels. Click the + sign button to add a new panel or the – sign button to remove one. Each panel you add includes a header and a content section. To change the vertical position of an accordion panel, select its name in the Panels box, and then use the up and down arrows to move it.

- **Active.** You can choose which accordion panel is expanded when the web page loads, just keep in mind that computers like to number things starting with 0.

So the top panel of an accordion is 0 and the panel *second* from the top is 1. Why do they always do that?

- **Event.** This menu specifies which action expands an accordion panel. Initially, it's set to "click," so a visitor has to click on a heading in the accordion to expand the panel beneath it. If you think that requires too much effort on the part of your guests, choose "mouseover" as the event. That way, visitors only have to mouse over the header to expose the content underneath.

- **Height Style.** Initially, a widget's Height Style menu is set to Auto. In most cases, that's the right choice, because the widget will set the height of *all* its collapsible panels equal to the height of the tallest one. The advantage is that if the accordion sits in a block text or other page elements, it won't be constantly pushing other elements up and down the page as guests take a look at the panels. The "content" option changes the height of *each* collapsible panel to accommodate its content. In this case, the height of the entire accordion widget may change as your guest clicks different headers. This means elements below the accordion will move up or down the page. The "fill" option is supposed to change the height according to the "parent" element—for example, a div that holds the widget on the page. In some cases, this creates an accordion panel with scrollbars. The fill option can be temperamental in other ways, so if you decide to use it, double-check the results in different browsers.

- **Disabled.** You can disable an accordion, but that pretty much defeats its purpose. With Disabled selected, a browser displays the accordion, but guests can't open the collapsed sections (unless you apply some JavaScript code to open it later—but again, the whole point of a collapsible section is being able to open and close it at will).

- **Collapsible.** Choose this option to let your visitors collapse all of an accordion's collapsible content panels at once. If a visitor clicks the header of an open panel, that panel closes, leaving all the other panels closed, too. Consider this option the ultimate space-saver for accordions.

- **Animate.** Accordion panels don't open instantly—they slide open over time, using a little animation for entertainment. The widget's Animate property lets you change the timing and the motion of the animation using a property known as "easing." See the box on page 583 for details about easing. The number box determines how long the entire action takes. The number is specified in milliseconds, so 1000 is a second and 400 (the default value) is four tenths of a second.

- **Icons.** There are two menus that determine the appearance of the "expand" and "collapse" icons on the accordion's header bar. At first, both are set to display the "flippy" triangles that are familiar to Mac users. You can change these to up and down arrows or plus and minus signs. Go crazy. You can even mix and match, but it will be darn confusing to visitors.

Easing into Animation

What's "easing" and why do I care?

Web designers often use jQuery to animate elements—moving headlines, sliding menus, bouncing graphics—on a page. In animation terms, "easing" smooths those motions, so they act like they would in real life. Think about how a car moves. It doesn't travel at the same speed for its entire journey. It starts off slowly, gains speed, and then slows down again before it comes to a stop. Likewise, a ball falling to the ground probably bounces once or twice before it comes to a stop. By applying easing to an animation, you create more realistic, or at least amusing, motion to elements.

Give it a try with an accordion panel. Set the Animate menu to "EaseOutBounce" and then set the time to *1000* (1 second).

Switch to Live view or Preview in Browser and click some of the accordion headers. The panels bounce into place, taking a second to complete the action.

There are a number of standard jQuery easing options with names like easeOutSine and easeInCubic. They work with many types of jQuery widgets, not just accordion panels. If you're a math whiz, these names may give you a clue as to how they work, but if you're a mere mortal who forgot everything you learned in trig, try different easing options and choose the one that looks best. For visual examples of the different easing effects head over to *http://easings.net/*.

Changing the Look of the Accordion Widgets

When you add an accordion or any other widget to your web page, it comes styled, thanks to a Cascading Style Sheet (CSS) that comes with the widget. The smart folks who wrote the code for jQuery UI followed best practices and separated the widget's content from its formatting. So you can change a widget's colors, background images, and text styles by creating a different style sheet, or editing the one that came with the widget. jQuery UI refers to this combination of style sheets (.css) and graphic files (.png) as *themes*.

When you first insert a widget, Dreamweaver gives it a somewhat generic look, known as the Smooth theme. With its light gray colors and standard text formatting, the greatest virtue of Smooth (Figure 13-6, bottom) is that it won't look out of place on most pages. But it won't make anyone say "Wow!", either.

When this book went to press, Dreamweaver provided no easy way to change a widget's theme. But if you're up for a visit to the jQuery UI website (*http://jqueryui.com/*) and game for a little file-swapping, you can change your widget's theme. This gives your widget a dramatically different appearance. (If that sounds too risky, skip ahead to page 587, where you learn how to make minor changes using CSS Designer.)

After you add a widget and save the page, Dreamweaver creates a folder called jQueryAssets. Inside it, you'll find a file named *jquery.ui.theme.min.css* (Figure 13-7, right). That file formats your widget. It has style rules that specify the font family, font size, and font style. It also specifies the header bars' background colors and images (Dreamweaver stores the latter in an images folder it created inside the jQueryAssets folder). So, to change the look of a widget, you replace the *jquery.ui.theme.min.css* file and add new graphics. You can think of this process as swapping themes.

■ CHOOSE A THEME

The first step in the process is to find a theme you like. Head to the website jQuery User Interface (*http://jqueryui.com/*) and then, on the navigation bar at the top of the page, click Themes. That launches a page called ThemeRoller, where you "roll your own" (as the site says) custom theme. Using the panel on the left, choose the fonts, colors, and background images you want for your accordion, and then check out the results on the sample widget in the main part of the page.

You don't have to create a theme to replace one, however. You can use one of the themes offered in the ThemeRoller gallery. Click Gallery at the top of the left-hand panel and check out the thumbnail themes. Click an example to see the sample widget take on the look.

■ DOWNLOAD ALL JQUERY UI GALLERY THEMES

Theme files are small so that the associated widget can respond quickly to guest interaction. So, if you're going to use any ThemeRoller theme, it makes sense to download all the themes (go to *http://jqueryui.com/download/*) so you have the widest choice possible.

ThemeRoller is designed for web developers working outside of Dreamweaver, and as such it lets them download packages that combine the widget and its themes (Figure 13-8). Obviously, you need just the themes, so you want to click the link labeled Themes to download only those files (*jquery-ui-themes-1.9.2.zip*). When this was written, ThemeRoller offered two versions of each theme, "Stable (Themes)" and "Legacy (Themes)." Use the Legacy option and click Themes. If you click the word Stable or Legacy, you'll download both the widget and the theme.

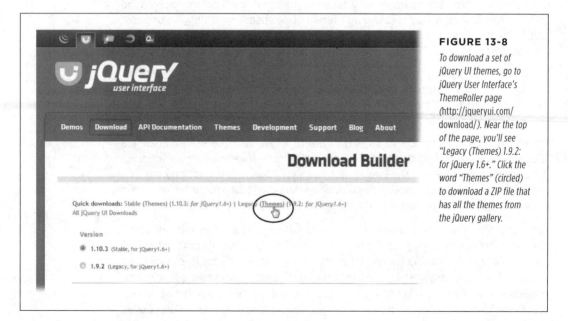

FIGURE 13-8

To download a set of jQuery UI themes, go to jQuery User Interface's ThemeRoller page (http://jqueryui.com/download/). Near the top of the page, you'll see "Legacy (Themes) 1.9.2: for jQuery 1.6+." Click the word "Themes" (circled) to download a ZIP file that has all the themes from the jQuery gallery.

NOTE When this book went to press, only the Legacy version of themes (version 1.9.2; for jQuery: 1.6+) worked with Dreamweaver. To make sure you download the right version of a theme (besides being sure to click the Legacy button, of course), or to see if a widget you already added to a page is the right version, compare the version number in the theme's filename to the Legacy version number (1.9.2). They should match. For example, when you add the accordion widget to a page, its version number (1.9.2) matches the one in the accordion widget's filename (*jquery-ui-1.9.2.accordion.custom.min.js*).

Keep in mind that Dreamweaver may use a different version number by the time you read this. That's OK, because in finding the right theme, the version number is the critical issue. Your theme's filenames should include the version number of the theme you added.

■ SWAPPING JQUERY UI THEMES

Once you download the gallery of themes as described above, a file named *jquery-ui-themes-1.9.2.zip* sits on your computer. It's an archive file that compresses several files into one and stores them as a single, small file. You need to expand this .zip file before you can get at the files inside. Once there, you'll choose the CSS file and images folder you want to copy to your site so you can refresh your widget's theme.

1. **Uncompress *jquery-ui-themes-1.9.2.zip* by double-clicking it.**

   This creates a folder of the same name. You'll find a few text files in that folder, along with a "themes" folder like the one in Figure 13-9.

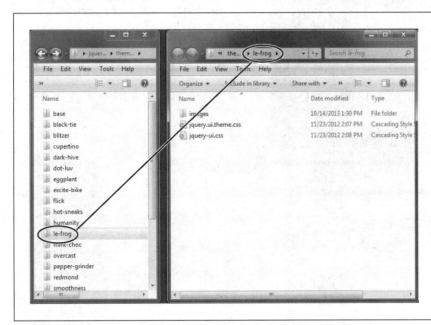

FIGURE 13-9

You'll see over a dozen subfolders inside the jquery-ui-themes-1.9.2 folder. They have names like dark-hive, eggplant, and le-frog. Each holds one theme. If you can't guess what a theme looks like from its name, see "Choose a theme" on page 583. To change a widget's theme, copy the jquery.ui.theme.css file and the images folder to your website.

2. **Double-click a theme folder.**

   If you double-click "le-frog," for example, the folder opens to reveal a file named *jquery.ui.theme.css* and a folder called *images*. In step 4, you'll copy this file and folder to your Dreamweaver site, but before you do that, you need to rename a file.

3. **In Dreamweaver's Folders panel, find the file *jquery.ui.theme.min.css*. Change its name to *jquery.ui.theme.css* by deleting ".min". When Dreamweaver asks if you want to update your web pages, click Update.**

The name Dreamweaver gives the CSS file it writes when you add a widget to a page differs slightly from the name of the file you downloaded from Theme-Roller. In this step, you change the filename to match the one Dreamweaver gave your widget. That way, Dreamweaver will automatically update the links in your pages. In the next step, you'll replace the widget's original theme file with the one you downloaded.

4. **Drag *jquery.ui.theme.css* and the *images* folder from Dreamweaver's Files panel to your jQueryAssets folder as shown in Figure 13-10.**

A warning box appears, asking if you want to overwrite the files on your website.

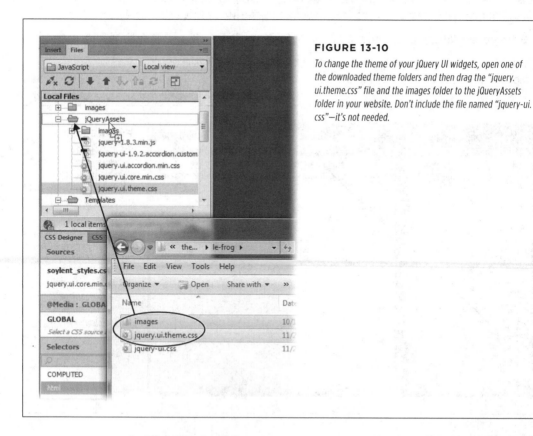

FIGURE 13-10

To change the theme of your jQuery UI widgets, open one of the downloaded theme folders and then drag the "jquery. ui.theme.css" file and the images folder to the jQueryAssets folder in your website. Don't include the file named "jquery-ui. css"—it's not needed.

5. **Click "Yes to all."**

Dreamweaver copies the new theme files to your site. The CSS file replaces the style sheet Dreamweaver added when you first inserted your widget. The images folder has PNG graphics; most of these have different names from the ones that Dreamweaver added, so these files are added to the PNG files already in the folder.

6. **Click the Live view button and then click Refresh.**

   If you copied the le-frog theme to your jQueryAssets folder as described in step 2, your accordion should now have a greenish hue (Figure 13-1). If you don't see the expected changes, you may need to press F5 or click Refresh at the top of the document window.

Formatting Widgets with CSS Designer

When you change the theme of a widget, you dramatically change its look in one fell swoop. But you can make minor changes, too, that have a subtle but less stark effect. You can, for example, use a different font for headings and paragraphs, or float images to the left or right. You do that by creating new style rules in CSS Designer and by overriding the styles defined in the theme. Figure 13-1 shows two widgets, for example: an accordion and a tabbed content window. Both have headings formatted using CSS Designer. Style rules also govern the position of the images. In the accordion, the picture floats to the left, while in the tabs, it floats to the right. CSS Designer handled all these changes.

Here are the steps to change the look of the text in the accordion header bars. Accordion headers have two states: selected and not selected. You'll change the text color for both starting with the selected headers.

1. **In Design view, one accordion panel always displays content. Click inside the text of the header bar for the panel whose content you can see.**

   When your cursor's in header, the Tag Selector displays a long string of tags related to the accordion. On the right side of those tags you see *<div#Accordion1><h3><a>*. (If you've given your accordion a different ID, you'll see that ID instead of *#Accordion1*.)

2. **Go to CSS Designer (Window→CSS Designer).**

   In the Sources section of CSS Designer, the name of the CSS file *jquery.ui.theme. css* is bold. That's the filename of the external style sheet for the jQuery UI theme. In Selectors, Dreamweaver highlights a very, very long selector. In fact, you can probably only see part of it, and that's okay. This selector defines the several properties it'll apply to h3 heading when a guest selects one.

3. **In CSS Designer's Properties section, click the Show Set button.**

   You see the Properties for the selector that have set values. One of those values is *color*. There's a color swatch next to it showing the current color.

4. **Click the swatch and choose a new color.**

   The color of the header text changes. You'll see the change in Design view, but to get the full effect, click the Live button. Just don't forget to turn Live view off before the next step, where you change the text color for "not selected" headers.

5. **Click one of the headers where the accordion content is hidden.**

   Again, you see *jquery.ui.theme.css* highlighted in CSS Designer's Sources section. In Selectors, a different, but equally long and equally cryptic selector is highlighted.

6. **In CSS Designer's Properties section, make sure the Show Set box is still checked.**

   You see the properties for accordion headers that are unselected. One of those properties is Color.

7. **Click the color swatch and choose a new color.**

   The color for unselected headers changes.

You can continue to make changes to the styles for headers as long as your cursor is inside the header in the document window and its selector is highlighted in CSS Designer's Selectors section. To add new style rules, turn off the Show Set box in the Properties section. Then find the property you want to define. For example, to create a drop shadow for the text, set *h-shadow* and *v-shadow* to a value like 3 pixels. Then, set *text-shadow* color to *black*.

Formatting the text inside an accordion's collapsible panel is similar to formatting any other text on your page. You use the same HTML tags to define blocks of text: <p> for paragraphs, <a> for links, and header tags for headers. The accordion uses <h3> tags for the headers that you click to show and hide panels, so, to avoid conflict, it's best to use <h4> or some other tag when you create a heading inside the collapsible panel. At that point, you can use CSS Designer to create a rule for headers inside an accordion. See Figure 13-11.

Accordion collapsible panels can hold just about any type of HTML element, including images. In Figure 13-1, you see an image inside a panel, with the image "floated" to the left. You create that look using a class attribute and the CSS Float property. Here are the steps to create and apply the class.

1. **In CSS Designer's Sources section, choose a source (style sheet) for your "float left" rule.**

   If you already have an external style sheet, choose that sheet in Sources. Otherwise, click the + sign button and choose Create a New CSS Style and then name the new sheet.

2. **In the Selectors section, click Add Selector (the + sign button). In the selector name field, type *.float-left*.**

   Don't forget the period in front. You've just create a class called *float-left*.

3. **In the Properties section, click Layout and then scroll down to the Float property. Set its value to left.**

   You're new float-left class has a single rule that tells elements on the page to float left.

4. **In Design view, click on an image in your accordion. Then, in the Properties panel below the document window, set the class menu to float-left.**

The image in the accordion collapsible panel floats to the left, while any text in the panel shifts to the right of the image.

FIGURE 13-11
Here, you've selected the style sheet soylent_styles.css in the Sources section of CSS Designer, and, in the Selectors section, created a selector named accordion1 h4. You'll use that selector to format the h4 headings in the accordion widget. You can set properties for the font color and text-shadow to format the accordion's text.

■ Tabs

In many ways, jQuery tabs are similar to accordions. They both conserve space on a web page by hiding and showing content, most guests are familiar with using them, and they share many of the same jQuery properties.

So if you're familiar with the accordion widget described on page 576, you have a jump start on using tabs.

Here are the basics for inserting a set of tabs and changing the tab and content text.

1. **Click on the page where you want to insert tabs.**

2. **Go to the Insert panel (Window→Insert) and choose the jQuery UI category from the drop-down menu.**

Tabs are second on the list of jQuery UI widgets, right under Accordion.

3. **Click Tabs.**

Dreamweaver inserts a set of tabs in your page. You see Tab 1, Tab 2, and Tab 3 at the top. The content portion of the tab widget shows *Content 1*. That's the content that visitors see when they click Tab 1.

4. **In the document window, click the Live button to preview your tabs.**

Tab panels have two parts: the Tab with a heading at the top and the content area below. To see them in action, switch to Live view by clicking the Live button at the top of the document window. When you click on a tab such as Tab 2, the content area changes to display Content 2.

5. **Click the Live button again to turn off Live view.**

You can't edit the text in Tabs in Live view.

6. **Click Tab 1, then press Ctrl+A (⌘-A). Type *bruschetta*.**

The text at the top of Tab 1 changes to bruschetta.

7. **Repeat step 6 for Tab 2 and Tab 3. Change Tab 2 to *prosciutto* and change tab 3 to *mozzarella di bufala*.**

If you use a longer name for the tab header, it may look odd in Design view, but it will look better in a browser or in Live view. The tab changes width to accommodate the longer name. Still, it's best to keep those tabs short and sweet because there is limited horizontal space after you add a few tabs.

8. **At the bottom of the tab panel, click "Content 1," then press Ctrl+A (⌘-A). Type *Soylent bruschetta is a delicacy that brings back memories of summer feasts al fresco.***

Your text will appear when you select the "bruschetta" tab.

9. **Move your cursor over the second tab (prosciutto). Click the eyeball icon on the tab. Replace "Content 2" with your own text.**

The content area below the tab changes to show "Content 2." This content is displayed when visitors click the "prosciutto" tab.

10. **Repeat Step 9 to change the text for the third tab (mozzarella di bufala).**

In addition to adding plain text, you can insert other HTML elements inside the content area of your tabs. For instance, you can add pictures or tables. You can even add headings. It's best to use the h4 heading, because the actual tab (the top part) uses h3 headings. If you use h4 for headings in the content area, you can style the two types of headings separately.

Setting Properties for Tabs

Use the Properties panel below the document window to change the way the jQuery UI tabs look and operate. To display the tabs properties, click inside one of the tabs on your web page. A blue line appears around the tabs and a blue tab appears at the top that says "jQuery Tabs: Tabs1." Click that blue tab to display the widget's properties (Figure 13-12). With only a couple of exceptions, the properties for tabs are identical to those for accordions.

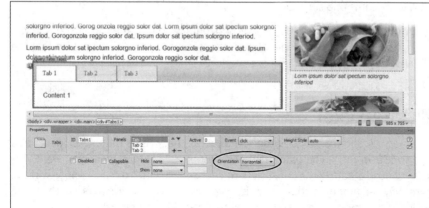

FIGURE 13-12

The jQuery UI accordion and tabbed panels widgets perform similar jobs, so it's not surprising to see similar properties for both. One place they do differ is the Orientation property (circled), where you choose whether your tabs align horizontally or vertically on the page. Here, you see the horizontal orientation, which has the tabs at the top. The vertical orientation puts the tabs on the left side of the screen.

- **ID.** jQuery UI widgets use ID selectors so that each widget has a unique name. You can use the ID as a selector in CSS Designer to apply style rules to the widget.

- **Panels.** Use the Panels property to add, remove, and position the tab panels. Click the + sign button to add a new panel or the – sign button to remove one.

- **Active.** Choose which tab panel a browser displays when it loads the page. The tab on the left is *0*, the second from the left is *1*, and so on.

- **Event.** This menu controls which action opens the tabbed panel. Choices include *click* and *mouseover*.

- **Height Style.** You have three options here: Auto, Content, and Fill. *Auto* sets all the tabbed panels to the height of the tallest one. So if the accordion sits in a block of text or other page elements, it won't be constantly push those elements up and down the page as it displays new panels. The *content* option changes the height of the panel to accommodate its content. The *fill* option changes the panel's height according to the "parent" element—for example, a div on the web page.

- **Disabled.** When you turn on the Disabled checkbox, the widget appears on the page, but clicking the tabs has no effect. If you're a JavaScript/jQuery programmer, you can control this property through a script.

- **Collapsible.** When you turn on this option, clicking an open panel's tab hides the content panel, leaving only the tabs at the top visible.

- **Hide** and **Show.** The Hide and Show properties change the animated effect used to display the tabs. Your choices include options like bounce and slide. The number boxes next to Hide and Show specify how long the animation takes. The unit of measure is milliseconds, so *1000* equals 1 second and *400* (the default) is four-tenths of a second.

- **Orientation.** Usually, tabs appear horizontally so that they sit at the top of a section of content. You have the option to change that to vertical, so that the tabs roost on the left side of the section.

◼ Datepicker

The jQuery UI datepicker does the same job as the HTML5 datepicker described on page 635. In short, you plop the datepicker down in a form when you want visitors to choose a date. Your guest gets to choose the date from a calendar widget, where they see months and days of the week. When your visitor submits the form, it includes a complete date in the proper format. The jQuery UI datepicker has a different look from its HTML counterpart (see Figure 13-13).

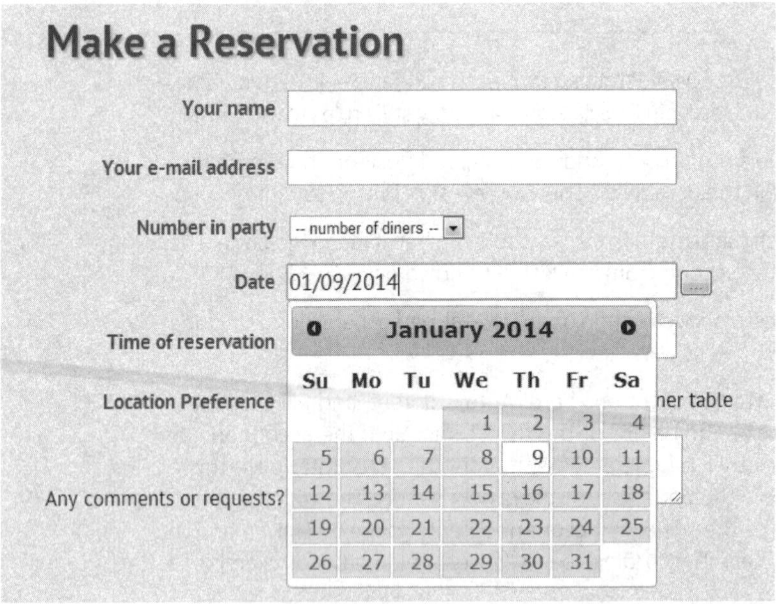

FIGURE 13-13

The jQuery UI datepicker feels right at home in a form, where guests specify a date. Initially, the datepicker looks like an ordinary text-input box, but the calendar appears as soon someone clicks in it. Turn on the datepicker's Button property to display a button to the right of the text box, as shown here.

As with all the jQuery UI widgets, you fine-tune your datepicker in the Properties panel (Window→Properties). Other than the ID (which all widgets have), the properties you use with the date picker are unique to the job it performs. Here's a description:

- **ID.** As usual with jQuery UI widgets, you can use an ID to name your datepicker, and then use that ID as a selector to format the datepicker.

- **Date Format.** This menu changes the way the widget displays the date. Initially, it appears as mm/dd/yy and, when a visitor chooses a date from the calendar, the box displays it like this: 01/09/2014. However, you can choose an alternative date format, like Thursday, 9 January 2014.

- **Locale.** Choose a country and the datepicker provides the month and days of the week in the appropriate language.

- **Button Image.** The datepicker opens to display a calendar as soon as someone clicks in the text box. This option lets you add a button to the right side of the text box to emphasize the fact that this widget has extra talents (a pop-up calendar in this case). The default button has ellipses (...) , but you can change that by specifying an image file in the box under Button Image.

- **Change Month**, **Change Year.** The datepicker displays forward and back arrows at the top of the calendar so visitors can move through time. Turn on these options to display month and year drop-down menus.

- **In line.** This option displays the datepicker as a calendar instead of a text box when the page opens.

- **Show Button Panel.** Turn on this option to add a panel of buttons to the bottom of the datepicker's calendar. The buttons perform different functions; Today, for example, jumps to the current date in the calendar, and Done closes the datepicker.

- **Min Date** and **Max Date.** If you want guests to choose a date within a certain range, supply a Min Date and Max Date.

- **Number of Months.** Normally, the datepicker displays a single month at a time, but you can display multiple months by putting a number in this box.

■ Dialog

When you need to display a pop-up message, turn to the jQuery UI dialog widget. You've probably visited enough websites to know that some pop-up dialogs are useful. For example, you might see a dialog box warning you that you're about to send your credit card information on an unencrypted form. In other cases, however, pop-ups are just annoying. Consider pop-up advertisements.

It's up to you to decide whether you use the dialog widget for good or evil. Lots of them are small, with just a few words, but they certainly aren't limited in size. You can add images, forms, and any other element you want to your dialog box and, as you'll see, still control its size.

You insert the dialog widget by clicking somewhere on the page and selecting Insert→jQuery UI→Dialog. The truth is, it doesn't matter where you click on the page because the dialog box, by design, floats independent of it.

In the Properties panel, give your widget an ID. Fill in the Title box with a message that'll get the attention of your visitors—something like Breaking News! or Buy Now! These words appear at the top of the dialog widget (see Figure 13-14). You position the box's on-screen location by choosing *center, left, right, top,* or *bottom* from the Position menu.

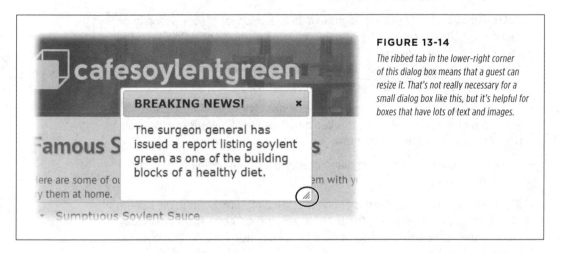

FIGURE 13-14

The ribbed tab in the lower-right corner of this dialog box means that a guest can resize it. That's not really necessary for a small dialog box like this, but it's helpful for boxes that have lots of text and images.

A few settings in the Properties panel deal with the dialog box's dimensions. Its default width is 300 pixels and its default Height is set to *Auto.* That works well for brief messages. With the Height set to *auto,* the box grows to accommodate the content. If your message is bigger than can comfortably fit, increase the Width value. (There is no *auto* setting for Width.) When the height is set to a specific value, instead of auto, there's always a chance the text won't fit in the box. In that case, the dialog automatically adds scroll bars. The dialog also has Min Width, Min Height, Max Width, and Max Height properties, which you can set to limit the amount of fun your visitors have resizing the box. If you really want to restrict their box-resizing activities, turn off the Resizable checkbox. While you're at it, you can turn off the Draggable checkbox so they can't reposition the box.

Here are some of the other properties that govern the way your dialog box works:

- **Auto Open.** Check this box to have the dialog box appear when the page loads. If you don't use Auto Open, you need to provide some other way to trigger the dialog box. As you'll see below, you can use a stock trigger or, if you're a JavaScript/jQuery programmer, you can write some code to do the job.

- **Close on Escape.** With this option turned on, your guests can close the dialog box by pressing the Esc key.

- **Modal.** This options makes the dialog box a bit more demanding. On display, it dims the rest of the screen and prevents your visitor from selecting anything on it, except the button that dismisses the dialog box.

- **Hide** and **Show.** These options control the animation that makes the dialog box appear and disappear. You have a number of choices. You can, for example, make the dialog box appear with a shake and then disappear in a puff. Use the number box to specify how long the animation lasts. As with the other jQuery UI time settings, the unit of measure is milliseconds, so *1000* milliseconds gets you 1 second of animation.

- **Trigger Button.** If you don't want your dialog box to appear the instant the page loads, turn off the Auto Open option. You can use a jQuery UI button to act as the trigger for the dialog box. (To add a button, see page 596.) After you add the button, its ID appears in the Trigger Button menu. Choose it and you've got your button/dialog action going.

- **Trigger Event.** This property works hand-in-hand with the trigger button. Initially, the trigger event is set to *click*. That's what most visitors expect to do with a button, but it's not your only option. You can choose *dblclick* or *mouseover*, which work as expected. Two other options may seem curious at first. They are *keydown* and *keypress*. The two options are almost identical. They trigger an event when a visitor presses a key on their keyboard. The main difference is that *keydown* triggers the event when you press almost any key on the keyboard, including non-printing keys like Shift or Esc. The *keypress* option only works with letters, numbers, and other characters that display on the screen. They work when someone uses the Tab key to move from one page element to the next. When they tab to the triggering button, giving it focus, the button highlights on the page, and pressing any keyboard key opens the dialog box. Unfortunately, you can only choose one option in Dreamweaver, so you can't use both the *click* and *keypress* options.

jQuery UI Widgets for Programmers

Some of the jQuery UI widgets on Dreamweaver's Insert panel are only useful if you're able to write JavaScript/jQuery code. Widgets like the progressbar and the slider can carry a "value" property, but you need to write a script to do something useful with that value. Other widgets, like buttons, are natural triggers to initiate an action. In most cases, the action is defined in a script. The next few sections describe what these programmable widgets do, but you need to turn to a book like *jQuery UI* by Eric Sarrion (O'Reilly Media, Inc.) to learn how to write code to use them.

Progressbar

The purpose of a progressbar is to let your visitors know something is going on behind the scenes. They may have to wait for a moment...just this much longer. For example, it's typical for a website to display a progressbar while it downloads a particularly large file. For a progressbar to show how much of a download is complete and how much is left, it needs two pieces of information: the size of the file being downloaded and how much of the file has already been downloaded. With these two values, a progressbar can create an image like the one in Figure 13-15.

> **TIP** Usually, the code behind the progressbar widget displays an instant-by-instant report on the status of the download. But there are times when you might want to use a "static" progressbar. Suppose you develop a quiz that has 10 questions, each on its own page. You could place a progressbar at the top of each page, setting different values for the length of the bar on each page at design time. None of the progressbars would be animated, but each would let the student know how far he'd progressed in the quiz.

Your file is being downloaded...

FIGURE 13-15

A progressbar reassures the impatient. It shows you how much of a process has been completed. Ideally, a progressbar updates periodically, but that requires a bit of JavaScript/jQuery know-how.

Autocomplete

The jQuery UI Autocomplete widget looks like a mild-mannered textbox, but its purpose is to provide hints and help visitors fill in text fields with the appropriate options. To work its magic, Autocomplete needs a list (also known as an array of values). You can provide that list as an external JavaScript file or you can create a script on the page to do so.

Slider

The slider is similar to the progressbar, but instead of passing a value to the widget, the widget passes a value to you. With the progressbar widget, for example, the code communicated a value to your visitor that said, in essence, "Your download is 35% done." The slider, on the other hand, lets you *get* a value from your guests. Moving the knob on the slider, your visitor selects a specific value, one the widget can use in its calculations and then act upon. As with the other widgets in this section, you need some knowledge of JavaScript and jQuery to use the slider.

jQuery Buttons and More Buttons

The jQuery UI Insert panel gives you several types of buttons: a single button, a "buttonset," checkbox buttons, and radio buttons. The Properties panel provides very few tools for you to work with the buttons, so in most cases, you need to write the code to place them in a form or otherwise use them. For example, with the help of some code, you can program the single button to trigger an event, such as opening a new browser window. The Buttonset option groups multiple push-buttons together. You can name, add, and remove buttons from the Buttonset in the Properties panel. The Checkbox Buttons work as expected—they let visitors choose several options at once. For example, if you sell magazine subscriptions online, you could put a checkbox button next to a picture of each magazine and let your visitors select the ones they want to receive. On the other hand, radio buttons give visitors several choices, but they can only choose one. The Soylent Green Cafe's reservation form (page 658) uses HTML5 radio buttons to let guests select where they want to sit (anywhere, at the bar, or at a corner table).

If you're prepared to write some scripts, you may be interested in the jQuery UI buttons. Otherwise, their usefulness is limited.

■ Dreamweaver Behaviors

Dreamweaver behaviors are prepackaged JavaScript programs that let you add interactivity to your pages, even if you don't know the first thing about JavaScript. While the behaviors were once revolutionary—JavaScript programming without any programming!—Adobe hasn't updated them in years. Many of the behaviors aren't very useful these days—you can get some of the same results with CSS, for example, and jQuery widgets have supplanted other behaviors. On top of that, some of the behaviors just didn't work as advertised. That said, a few are still worth discussing.

Behavior Basics

To use a behavior, you need three elements: an HTML tag, an action, and an event:

- First, you select an HTML tag to apply the behavior to.

- Next, pick an action. The action is whatever the behavior is supposed to *do*—such as open a new browser window or hide an element on a page.

- Finally, you assign an event to the behavior. The event *triggers* the action, which usually involves a visitor interacting with your site, like clicking a Submit button, mousing over a link, or even simply loading the web page into the browser.

For instance, say that, when a visitor clicks a link, instead of just sending him to another page, you want a new browser window to open and load that linked page. In this case, the HTML tag is the link itself—an <a> tag; the *action* is opening another browser window and loading a web page in it; and the *event* takes place when your visitor clicks the link—his browser opens a new window and loads the new page. Voilà—interactivity!

■ Applying Dreamweaver Behaviors

Dreamweaver makes adding behaviors as easy as selecting a tag and choosing an action from a drop-down menu in the Behaviors panel.

The Behaviors Panel

The Behaviors panel is the control center for Dreamweaver's behaviors (Figure 13-16). On it, you can see the behaviors applied to a tag, add more behaviors, and edit the behaviors you already applied.

FIGURE 13-16

Dreamweaver's Behaviors panel lists all the behaviors applied to the currently selected HTML tag. Because the same event can trigger multiple actions, Dreamweaver groups the actions by event. In this example, the onClick event for an <a> tag (a link) triggers one action. When a visitor clicks this link, a page element appears or fades away (the Fade effect) and a new browser window opens. The order in which the behaviors occur is determined by their order in this panel. For instance, when a visitor clicks the link in this example, she sees the Fade effect first, and then a browser window opens. To change the order of these events, use the up and down arrows. To change the type of event, click the event name and select a different event from the drop-down menu. If a unique event triggers each action, the order in which the events appear in the panel is irrelevant.

To open the Behaviors panel, choose Window→Behaviors. Dreamweaver shows you the currently selected tag at the top of the panel; a list of the behaviors applied to that tag, if any, appears below that. The panel breaks down each behavior into two parts: events and actions.

You can choose from two views in the Behaviors panel; switch between them using the buttons at the upper-left corner:

- "Show set events" gets down to the specifics: which behaviors you applied to a tag and which events trigger them. When you work on a web page, this view moves extraneous information out of your way.

- "Show all events" lists all the events *available* to a particular tag. This view isn't that useful, since you see a complete list of events for that tag when you select the tag and add an action.

Applying Behaviors, Step by Step

Open the Behaviors panel and proceed as follows:

1. **Select the object or tag to which you want to assign a behavior.**

   You have to attach a behavior to an HTML tag, such as a link (an <a> tag) or the page's body (the <body> tag). Take care, however; because it's easy to accidentally apply a behavior to the wrong tag. Form elements, like checkboxes and text fields, are easy to target—just click one to select it. For other kinds of tags, consider using the Tag Selector, as described on page 7, for more precision.

2. **In the Behaviors panel, add an action.**

Click the + sign button in the Behaviors panel and, from the "Add behavior" menu, select the action you wish to add (see Figure 13-17). You'll find a list of these behaviors and what they do beginning on page 602.

The menu dims some actions because your web page doesn't include an element that the action can affect. If your page lacks a form, for instance, you won't be able to select the Validate Form behavior. Other behaviors are grayed out because you have to apply them to a particular page element. For example, Jump Menu is off-limits until you add a select menu (Insert→Form→Select) to the page and highlight it.

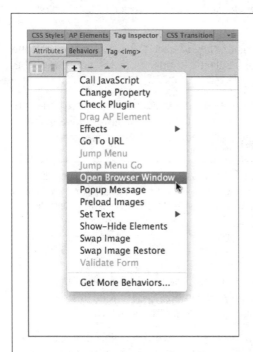

FIGURE 13-17

Dreamweaver grays out behaviors you can't apply to a currently selected tag. The reason? Your page is either missing a necessary object, or you selected an object that can't exhibit that behavior. For example, you can't apply the Show-Hide Elements behavior if your page doesn't have at least one tag with an ID applied to it.

3. **In the dialog box that opens, set options for that action.**

Each action has properties specific to it, and you set them in the dialog box. For instance, when you choose the Go To URL action, Dreamweaver asks what web page you want to load. (You'll find these actions described beginning on page 602.)

4. **Click OK to apply the action.**

At this point, Dreamweaver adds the HTML and JavaScript required for the behavior to your page's underlying code. The behavior's action appears in the Behaviors panel.

Unlike HTML objects, behaviors usually add JavaScript code in two places in a document: to the head of the document itself *and* to the HTML tag of the target behavior in the body of the page.

5. **Change the event, if desired.**

When your newly created action shows up in the Behaviors panel, Dreamweaver displays a default event (a trigger) in the Events column for the selected tag and action. For example, if you add an Open Browser Window behavior to a link, Dreamweaver suggests the *onClick* event.

However, this default event may not be the only one available. Links, for instance, can handle many events. An action could begin when your visitor's cursor moves *over* the link (the *onMouseOver* event), *clicks* the link (the *onClick* event), and so on.

To change the event for a particular behavior, click the event's name, and the Events drop-down menu appears. Select a trigger from the list of available events for that tag.

When you're done, you can leave the Behaviors panel open to add more behaviors to the current tag, or to add behaviors to other tags. For the latter, select another tag using the document window or the Tag Selector, and then repeat steps 2–5.

> **NOTE** Dreamweaver sometimes displays a yellow warning bar above a document after you insert a behavior. It does so when it believes there's a mistake in a JavaScript program, and it tells you that the code was written incorrectly. In fact, this yellow bar often appears even if there is no JavaScript error. Close and re-open the page and the error bar goes away.

Editing Behaviors

Once you apply a behavior, you can edit it any time. Double-click the behavior in the Behaviors panel to reopen the Settings dialog box as described in step 3 of the previous instructions. Make any changes you like, and then click OK.

To remove a behavior from your web page, select it in the Behaviors panel, and then click the - sign button or press Delete. (If you *accidentally* delete a behavior, choose Edit→Undo Remove Behavior.)

A Quick Example

The brief example shows you the behavior-creation process. In it, you'll use a behavior that makes an important message appear when a web page opens.

1. **Choose File→New to create a new, untitled document.**

You'll start with a new page.

2. **Choose File→Save and save the file to your computer.**

It doesn't matter where you save the page since you won't include any graphics or links to other pages.

You start the process of adding a behavior by selecting a tag—in this case, the page's <body> tag.

3. **In the Tag Selector, click <body>.**

   Once you select a tag, you can apply one or more behaviors to it. But first, make sure you have the Behaviors panel open. If you don't see it, press Shift+F4 or choose Window→Behaviors.

4. **Click the + sign button on the Behaviors panel. From the "Add behavior" menu, choose Popup Message.**

   The Popup Message dialog box appears.

5. **In the message box, type "Visit our store for great gifts!", and then click OK.**

   Dreamweaver adds the required JavaScript code to the page. Notice that the Behaviors panel lists the *action* called Popup Message next to the *event* called *onLoad*. The *onLoad* event triggers an action *after* a page and everything on it—graphics and so on—loads.

   To see the page in action, click the Live view button at the top of the document window or preview the page in a web browser by pressing F12 (Option-F12).

> **NOTE** Dreamweaver behaviors rely on little JavaScript programs that run inside web browsers. For security reasons, Internet Explorer doesn't always like running JavaScript programs from your own computer. If the JavaScript you add to a page doesn't work when you preview it in IE, look for a warning at the bottom of the browser. (Older versions of IE display a similar warning at the top of the window.) Click the "Allow blocked content" button to see the pop-up message. This fussy behavior only happens when you view a page that's sitting on your computer; once you move the page to the Web, Internet Explorer eases its security precautions and runs JavaScript without the warning.

■ Events

Events are at the heart of interactive web pages. They trigger behaviors based on your visitors' actions, like clicking a link, mousing over an image, or simply loading a page. But not all events work with all tags. For example, the *onLoad* event works only with web pages and images, not paragraphs, divs, or any other page element. The Event menu in the Behaviors panel can help; it lists only those events available for the tag you're targeting.

Current browsers—Internet Explorer 9 and newer, Safari, Firefox, and Chrome—support events for many HTML tags. Many events work with other tags as well, such as headline, paragraph, and <div> tags. But don't go crazy. Making an alert message appear when someone double-clicks a paragraph is more likely to win your site the Hard-To-Use Website of the Month award than a loyal group of visitors.

A Sampler of Actions, One by One

While events get the ball rolling, actions are, yes, where the action is. Whether it's opening a 200- x 200-pixel browser window or slowly fading in a photograph, you'll find an action for almost every type of interactivity you need. After you complete the steps required to set up an action as described on page 598, the new action appears in the Behaviors panel, and your web page is ready to test. At this point, you can click the event's name in the panel, where you can use the drop-down menu to change the event that triggers the action, as shown in Figure 13-16.

Effects

Dreamweaver CC gives you a bundle of visual effects to apply to the elements on your page. In the Behaviors panel, when you click the add behaviors button (the + sign), a menu of actions appears. Mouse over the Effects item on the menu to see a submenu of visual effects. These effects can do things like highlight elements on a page, make a photo fade in, or shake an entire sidebar of information as though it were in an earthquake. They're mostly eye candy and work well when you want to draw attention to an element or create a dramatic introduction. It's easy to abuse these effects, however. If every part of your page blinks, shrinks, shakes, and flashes, most visitors will quickly grow tired of the nonstop action.

In some cases, you'll add an effect to the "Current Element." For example, you could make a picture fade away when someone clicks it. In other cases, you'll want to target a specific element on the page. Perhaps you want to click some text to make that picture fade away. To do that, you first have to apply an ID to the "target" element—the part of the page you want to affect.

You usually think of IDs as a way to format a unique element on a page using Cascading Style Sheets. But IDs are also handy when you want to add interactivity to a page. In fact, you can add an ID to HTML without ever creating a CSS style for it.

Recall that the HTML ID attribute marks a tag with a unique name. Because that name targets a specific area of your page, you can control that area using JavaScript. How you apply an ID to a tag depends on the tag, but here are the most common techniques:

- **Div tags.** Assign an ID to a div using the Property Inspector. Just select the <div> tag and then use the ID field to give it a unique name. In addition, you can wrap any collection of HTML tags (or even a single element, like an image) inside a <div> tag and apply an ID at the same time, using the Insert Div Tag tool (see page 428).

- **Images.** When you select an image in the document window, you can type an ID for that image in the Property Inspector's ID box.

- **Forms.** Select the form and type an ID in the ID field on the left edge of the Property Inspector.

- **Form fields.** When you insert a form field, you can set the field's ID in the Input Tag Accessibility Options window. You can later set or change a field's ID by selecting it and then using the ID field on the left edge of the Property Inspector.

- **Other elements.** To add an ID to paragraphs, headlines, bulleted lists, and other tags, select the tag in the Property Inspector and then type a name in the ID field.

After you apply an ID to the target, you add a behavior to the tag that triggers the effect. For example, say you want the site's banner image to emerge on the page after the page loads. The target is the banner image, but you apply the effect to the <body> tag using the *onLoad* event.

■ FADE

To make an element fade in or out, use the Fade effect. To add a dramatic introduction to your site, you can fade in a large photograph on your home page after the page loads. Or you can have an "Important Announcement" box disappear when a visitor clicks it.

To use this effect:

1. **Select the tag that you want to trigger the fade in or out.**

   For example, a link such as an image inside a <div> tag could trigger the effect, or you could use the <body> tag coupled with the *onLoad* event.

2. **From the Actions list on the Behaviors panel, choose Effects→Fade.**

   The Fade window opens (see Figure 13-18).

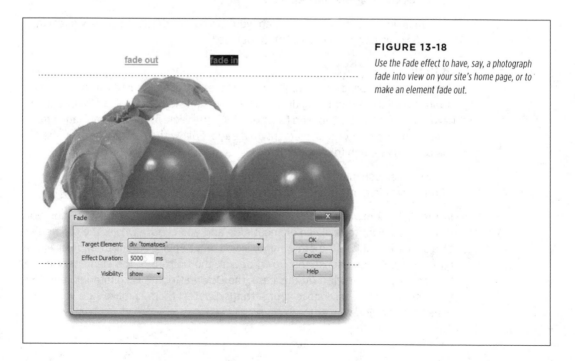

FIGURE 13-18

Use the Fade effect to have, say, a photograph fade into view on your site's home page, or to make an element fade out.

3. Select a target element from the first menu.

Here's where you specify which page element should appear or fade away. The menu lists every tag on the page that has an ID applied to it. In addition, you may see <Current Selection> listed, which refers to the tag you selected in step 1. Choose this option if you want to apply the behavior to any <div> tag that contains some kind of message—like "We'll be closed February 2nd to celebrate Groundhog Day!" When a visitor clicks the message, it fades away.

4. Type an amount in the "Effect duration" field.

This setting controls how long the fade in or out lasts. You set the duration in milliseconds, so typing *1000* gets you 1 second. If you want the target element to appear or disappear immediately, enter *0*.

5. Set the Visibility attribute of effect. Your choices are Show, Hide, or Toggle.

Choose Show to make the element fade in or Hide to make it fade out. Use Toggle to go back and forth—if the element is visible, the toggle action hides it and vice versa. If you want the target element to fade into view, you have to hide it to begin with. Otherwise the fade-in effect looks really weird: First you see the photo, then you don't, and *then* it fades in. To make the element invisible, add (or edit) a style for the target element, and then set the CSS *display* property (page 396) to *none*. Of course, if you go this route, you can't use the hidden element you selected in step 1 as the trigger; after all, you can't click or mouse over an element that's invisible.

6. Click OK to apply the behavior.

Once you add the effect to a tag, you can edit or delete it just as you can any other behavior; see page 600 for details.

■ BLIND

Don't worry: The Blind effect won't hurt your eyes. It's actually just a way of simulating a window blind—either being drawn closed over an element to hide it or opened to reveal it. The basic concept and functionality is the same as the Appear/Fade effect: It lets you hide or reveal an element on a page. Follow the basic steps described in the previous section for Appear/Fade.

Once you select Blind from the Effects menu in the Behaviors panel, you can control all the basic elements of the effect from the Blind dialog box (Figure 13-19).

In the dialog box, use the Direction pull-down menu to choose the motion you want. If you want to make an element hide and you choose Down, the top begins to disappear first. On the other hand, if you want your element to appear with a bit of flair and you choose the Down option, the bottom of the element appears first and it grows upward (in this case, the Down attribute is counterintuitive). So the watchword here is, choose your settings, but test them to make sure your blind works the way you want it to.

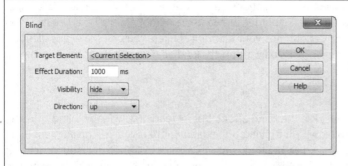

FIGURE 13-19

The Blind effect dialog is similar to Fade. You choose a target element, set the duration for the effect, and to show, hide, or toggle the element's visibility. The attribute specific to the Blind effect is the direction of the animation. The choices are Up, Down, Left, Right, Vertical, and Horizontal.

■ HIGHLIGHT

Adding a background color to a paragraph, headline, or div is one way to create visual contrast and make an important piece of information stand out. A red box with white type will draw the eye quicker than a sea of black type on a white page. But if you really want to draw someone's attention, use the Highlight effect. Highlighting an element lets you add a flash of bright background color to it. For instance, on a form, you may have an important instruction for a particular form field ("Your password must be 10 characters long and not have !, #, or $ in it"). You could add the Highlight effect to the form field so that when a visitor clicks in the field, the instruction's background color quickly flashes, ensuring that the visitor sees the important information.

As with other effects, you use the Behaviors panel to apply the Highlight effect to some triggering element (like a form field you click in, or a link you mouse over). Then use the Highlight window (Figure 13-20) to set the target element (any tag with an ID), the duration of the effect, the visibility, and the color. To choose a color, click the swatch to choose from the standard Adobe color picker. The hex color specification (page 141) is shown in the box. If you have a color specification in number form, you can enter it in the color picker. For details on coloring by number, see page 141.

FIGURE 13-20

Use the Highlight effect (sparingly) to draw attention to elements on the page for a moment. The Effect Duration property shown here determines just how long that moment lasts. Set the Visibility to Show unless you're turning off a highlight. Click the color swatch to use Adobe's standard color picker to choose a color for the highlight.

■ SHAKE

The Shake effect is like adding an earthquake to a web page. The target element shakes violently left to right for a second or so. And that's all there is to it. When you apply this behavior, you can choose the duration and the direction: left, right, up, or down. To make a quake bigger, increase the number in the Distance box. You can also set the number of times your element shakes. You can shake any element with an ID—a div or even just a paragraph. It's kind of a fun effect...once...and maybe just for kids.

■ SLIDE

The Slide effect is just like the Blind effect, but instead of a "window blind" moving over an element to hide it (or moving off an element to reveal it), the element itself moves. Say you have a <div> tag that contains a gallery of photos. If you target that div with a "slide up" effect, the images all move upward and disappear at the top edge of the div. Think of the div as a kind of window looking out onto the photos. When the photos move up past the "window," you can't see them any longer.

Suppose you want to make an image slide up and out of view when your visitors clicks it. The motion should last 2 seconds. In the Slide dialog box (Figure 13-21), make these changes. Set the Target Element to Current Selection. That's always the choice to use when you want the trigger to serve as the target, too. Set the Duration to 2000 because you want the animation to last for 2 seconds. Set the visibility to hide. (If you leave it set to show and the element is already visible, you won't notice any effect at all.) Choose Up as the direction. In the Distance box, enter the number of pixels you want the image to move before it disappears. For example, if you leave this option set to 20, the image moves up 20 pixels and then fades away. However, if the image is 320 pixels tall, it may look a little funny. To make the image appear to slide away entirely, set the Distance to 320.

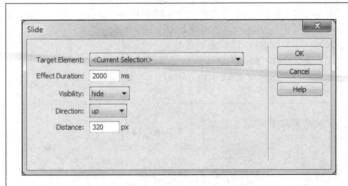

FIGURE 13-21

The Slide effect works just like the Blind effect described on page 604. The only difference is that the element itself moves and disappears (as opposed to a "blind" being drawn over the element).

Open Browser Window

Sometimes, when a visitor action opens a new browser window, you want to dictate the size of that window. If you have a link to a "Sign up for our newsletter form," for example, you may want to open the sign-up page in a window that matches the exact width and height of the form. Or, when a visitor clicks on a thumbnail image, you may want to open a new window whose dimensions match that of the full-size photo—and prevent that window from displaying all the distracting browser "chrome," like the location bar, status bar, toolbar, and so on.

Enter Dreamweaver's Open Browser Window action (Figure 13-22). Use it to tell your visitor's browser to open a new window to a height and width *you* desire. In fact, you can even dictate what *elements* the browser window includes. Don't want the toolbar, location bar, or status bar? No problem; this action lets you include or exclude the frills.

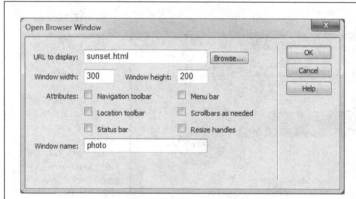

FIGURE 13-22

Here, you can define the properties of the new window, including what web page loads into it, its dimensions, and so on. If you leave the "Window width" and "Window height" properties blank, you'll get different results in different browsers. In Firefox, Chrome, and Opera, you won't get a new window—the page opens up a new tab. In Internet Explorer and Safari, you get a new window, but it's the same size as the window that spawned it.

To open a new browser window, you start, as always, by selecting the tag to which you want to attach the behavior. You can attach it to any HTML tag, but you usually want to add it to a link with an *onClick* event, or to the <body> tag with the *onLoad* event.

> **NOTE** Most browsers have pop-up blockers. This nifty feature prevents a browser from opening a new browser window unless the visitor initiates the request. In other words, you probably won't be able to open a new browser window when a page loads in the current window, but you can open a new browser window based on a visitor's action—like clicking a link.

Once you select this action from the Add Behavior menu (the + sign) in the Behaviors panel, you see the dialog box shown in Figure 13-22.

Specify the following options:

- **URL to display.** In this box, type the URL or path to the page you want to load, or click Browse and find the page on your computer (the latter is a near-foolproof way to ensure functional links). If you want to load a web page that's on somebody else's site, don't forget to type in an *absolute* URL, one beginning with *http://*.

- **Window width, Window height.** Next, define the width and height of the new window. Specify these values in pixels; most browsers require a minimum window size of 100 x 100 pixels. Also, if the width and height you specify are larger than the available space on your visitor's monitor, the window fills the monitor (but won't ever generate a wider or taller window).

- **Attributes.** Turn on the checkboxes for the elements you want the new window to include. Figure 13-23 shows the different pieces of a standard browser window. Note that in most browsers, you can't really get rid of the resize handle, so even if you leave that option turned off, it still appears and a visitor will still be able to resize the window.

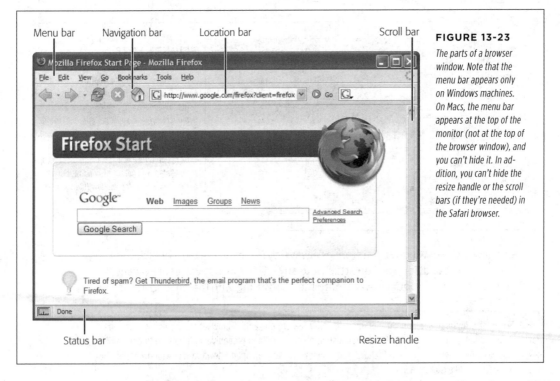

Menu bar   Navigation bar   Location bar   Scroll bar

Status bar   Resize handle

FIGURE 13-23

The parts of a browser window. Note that the menu bar appears only on Windows machines. On Macs, the menu bar appears at the top of the monitor (not at the top of the browser window), and you can't hide it. In addition, you can't hide the resize handle or the scroll bars (if they're needed) in the Safari browser.

- **Window name.** Give the new window a name (using letters and numbers only). If you include spaces or other symbols, Dreamweaver displays an error message and lets you correct the mistake. The name won't actually appear on your web page, but it's useful for targeting links or actions from the original window.

Once you set up the Open Browser Window action, you can load web pages into the new window from the original page; simply use the name of the new window as the link's target. For example, you could add the Open Browser Window behavior to a link labeled "Open photo gallery" that, when clicked, opens a small window showcasing a photo. You could include additional links on the main page that load additional photos into that small window.

If you use more than one Open Browser Window behavior on a single page, make sure you give each new window a unique name. If you use the same name, your page might retain the first new window's settings and you might not get the width, height, or other settings you want in the new window.

When you click OK, your newly created behavior appears in the Actions list in the Behaviors panel.

Image Actions

Images make web pages stand out, but using Dreamweaver behaviors with images can make them come to life.

■ PRELOAD IMAGES

It takes time for images to load over the Internet. A 64 KB image, for instance, takes about 1 second to download over a DSL modem. Add 10 images of this size to a page, and it can take a while to actually load the page. However, once a browser loads an image, it stores that image in its *cache* so if the page requires that same graphic again, it loads extremely quickly. The Preload Images action takes advantage of this concept by downloading images and storing them in your browser's cache *before* the page actually needs them.

Preloading is especially important when you use mouse rollover effects on a page. When a visitor moves her mouse over a button, it may, for example, appear to light up. If the rollover image weren't preloaded, the light-up graphic wouldn't appear when your visitor rolled over the button; in fact, it wouldn't even begin to download until she rolled her cursor over the button. The resulting delay would make your button feel less like a rollover and more like a layover.

If you use the Insert Rollover Image command (see page 254), you don't need to apply the Preload Images action by hand because Dreamweaver adds it automatically. But there are exceptions. For example, when you use the CSS *background* property (page 240) to add an image to the hover state of a link (see page 187), a new background image appears when a visitor mouses over the link. But the browser loads that image only when a visitor triggers the hover state, not before. In a case like this, you want to add the Preload Images action to the event.

To do so, select the <body> tag. You can apply the Preload Images behavior to any tag, but it really only makes sense to attach it to the <body> tag using an *onLoad* event, so that when the web page first loads, the browser begins downloading the images.

If you add rollover images to your page, Dreamweaver may have already applied this behavior to the <body> tag. If that's the case, just select the tag (click <body> in the Tag Selector) and then double-click the Preload Images action that should be listed in the Behaviors panel. If it isn't, choose Preload Images from the Add Behaviors menu (the + sign) in the Behaviors panel. Either way, Dreamweaver displays the Preload Images dialog box.

Click Browse and navigate to the graphics file you want to preload, or type in the path and (if the graphic is on the Web) the absolute URL. Dreamweaver adds the image to the Preload Images list. To preload another image, click the + sign button and repeat the process. Continue until you add all the images you want to preload.

You can remove an image from the preload list by selecting it and then clicking the – sign button. (Be careful not to delete any images required for a rollover effect you already created—the Undo command doesn't work here.)

When you click OK, you return to your document and your new action appears in the Behaviors panel. You can edit it, if you like, by changing the event that triggers it. But unless you're trying to achieve some special effect, you usually use the *onLoad* event on the <body> tag. That's all there is to it. When your page loads in a browser, the browser continues to load and store the graphics you specified quietly in the background. They'll appear almost instantly when they're called by a rollover action or even by a shift to another page that incorporates the graphics.

■ SWAP IMAGE

The Swap Image action exchanges one image on your page for another (see Figure 13-24). (See the end of this section for detail on Swap Image's sibling behavior, Swap Image Restore.)

Simple as that process may sound, swapping images is one of the most visually exciting things you can do on a web page. It works something like rollover images, except that you don't have to trigger the swap with a mouse click or mouse pass. You can use *any* tag-and-event combination. For instance, you can create a mini slideshow by listing the names of pictures down the left side of a web page and inserting an image in the middle of the page. Add a Swap Image action to each slide name, and the appropriate picture replaces the center image when a visitor clicks on a new name.

To make this behavior work, your page has to include a *starter image*, and the images you want to swap in have to match the width and height of that starter graphic. If they don't, the browser resizes and distorts the swapped pictures to fit the "frame" dictated by the original image.

To add the Swap Image behavior, first identify the starter image (choose Insert→Image, or use any of the other techniques described in Chapter 5). Give your image an ID in the Property Inspector so JavaScript knows which image to swap out. (JavaScript doesn't really care about the original graphic itself, but rather about the space that it occupies on the page.)

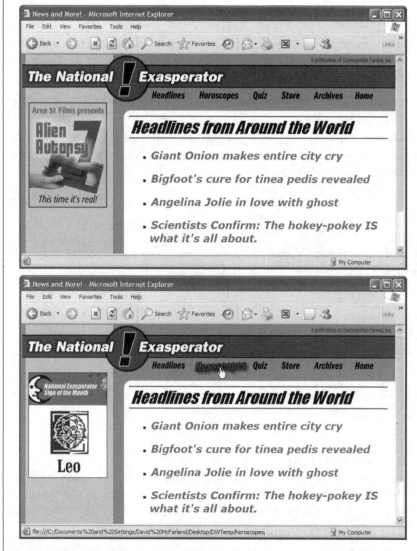

FIGURE 13-24

You can use the Swap Image behavior to simultaneously change multiple graphics with a single mouseover. A humble web page (top) comes to life when a visitor moves her mouse over the Horoscopes button (bottom). Not only does the graphic for the button change, so does the ad in the left sidebar; it now offers a tantalizing look at the Sign of the Month. The Swap Image action lets you easily get this type of effect, sometimes called a disjoint rollover.

TIP You can swap more than one image at a time with a single Swap Image behavior. Using this trick, not only can a button change to another graphic when you mouse over it, but any number of other graphics on the page can change at the same time. An asterisk (*) next to the name of an image in the Swap Image dialog box (Figure 13-25) indicates that the behavior will swap in a new image for that particular graphic. In the example in Figure 13-24 you can see that two images—*horoscope* and *ad*, both marked by asterisks—swap as a result of a single action.

Now select the tag you want to associate with the Swap Image behavior—you can choose a link, a paragraph, another image, or even the starter image itself. When you choose this action's name from the Behaviors panel, the Swap Image dialog box appears, as shown in Figure 13-25.

- **Images.** From the list, click the name of the starter image.

- **Set source to.** Here's where you specify the *image* file you want to swap in. If it's a graphics file in your site folder, click Browse to find and open it. You can also specify a path or an absolute URL to another website, as described on page 170.

- **Preload images.** Preloading ensures that image downloads don't slow down the swap-in.

- **Restore images onMouseOut.** You get this option only when you apply the Swap Image behavior to a link. When you turn on this checkbox, the previous image reappears when a visitor moves *off* the link.

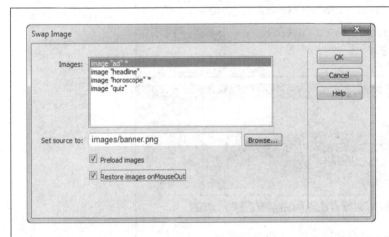

FIGURE 13-25

Some actions, like Swap Image, can automatically add behaviors to a web page. In this case, the "Preload images" and "Restore images onMouseOut" options actually add a Swap Image Restore action to the onMouseOut event of the currently selected tag and a Preload Images action to the onLoad event of the <body> tag.

■ SWAP IMAGE RESTORE

The Swap Image Restore action returns the last set of swapped images to its original state. Most designers use it in conjunction with a rollover button so that the button returns to its original appearance when the visitor moves his cursor off the button.

You'll probably never find a need to add this behavior yourself; Dreamweaver automatically adds it when you insert a rollover image and choose the "Restore images onMouseOut" option when you set up a regular Swap Image behavior. (The Swap Image Restore dialog box offers no options.)

Popup Message

Use the Popup Message behavior to send important messages to your visitors, as shown in Figure 13-26. Your visitor must click OK to close the dialog box. But because a pop-up message demands immediate attention, reserve this behavior for important announcements.

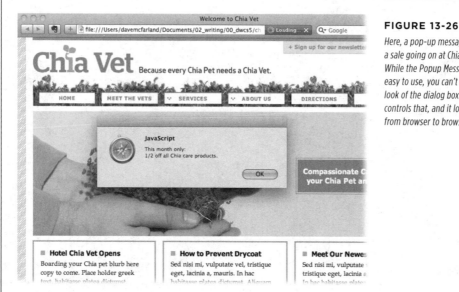

FIGURE 13-26

Here, a pop-up message indicates a sale going on at Chia-Vet.com. While the Popup Message behavior is easy to use, you can't customize the look of the dialog box. The browser controls that, and it looks different from browser to browser.

To create a pop-up message, select the tag that you want to trigger the behavior. For example, adding this action to the <body> tag with an *onLoad* event makes the message appear when a visitor first loads the page; adding the same behavior to a link with an *onClick* event makes the message appear when your visitor clicks the link.

From the Add Action menu (the + sign button) in the Behaviors panel, choose Popup Message. In the Popup Message dialog box, type the message you want to appear, and then click OK.

TIP JavaScript programmers, your message can also include any valid JavaScript expression. To embed JavaScript code in a message, place it inside braces ({ }). If you want to include the current date and time in a message, for example, add {*new Date()*}. If you just want to display a brace in the message, add a backslash, like this: \{. The backslash lets Dreamweaver know that you *really* do want a { character—and not just a bunch of JavaScript—to appear in the dialog box.

Forms

A website is a great way to brand your company, announce a new product, post late-breaking news, or rant about the state of the world. But all that's *one-way* communication, and you may want to interact with your audience more directly—to get feedback on your product or company, for example, or you may want to build your business by gathering vital statistics from customers.

If you want to *receive* information as well as deliver it, it's time to add *forms* to your website design repertoire (see Figure 14-1 for a simple example). Say you want your site visitors to sign up for your email newsletter. You'd build a form to collect their name and email address. Accepting lunch reservations for Cafe Soylent Green? Create a form to get the details of date, time, and number of guests. Whatever type of information you need to collect on your site, Dreamweaver's *form objects* make the task easy.

■ Form Basics

A form begins and ends with the HTML <form> tag. The opening tag (<form>) indicates the beginning of a form and sets its properties; the closing tag (</form>), of course, marks the form's end.

You put form elements that your visitors interact with between those two tags—radio buttons, text fields, and pull-down menus are just a few options you can choose from. It's perfectly OK to include other HTML elements inside a form, too. In fact, your visitors would be lost if you didn't add (and format) text that explains each element's purpose. And if you don't use a table or Cascading Style Sheets to lay out your form in an organized way, it can quickly become an unreadable mess (see the box on page 643).

FIGURE 14-1

A form can be as simple as a single empty text box (called a field) and a button, or as complex as a 100-question survey of fill-in-the-blank and multiple-choice questions.

Every form element, whether it's a text field or a checkbox, has a *name* and a *value*. You supply the name, which should reflect the information you're trying to collect. For example, if you want a visitor to type his email address into a text field, you might name that field *email*. The value, on the other hand, is what your *visitor* types in—the text he enters into a text field, for example, or the selections he makes from a pull-down menu.

After a visitor fills out a form and clicks the Submit button, his browser sends each form element as a name/value pair, like this: *email=bob@bobville.com*. You need to provide a name/value pair for each form element. After all, without a name, a value of "39" doesn't mean much (39 what? Potatoes, steps, days until Christmas?). The name/value pair (*age=39*) provides context for your visitor's input.

The Code Backstage

Creating a form is just the first step in collecting information. You also need to *transmit* that information to a program that actually *does* something with it. That program may simply email the data from the form to you. But it could also do something as complex as contacting a bank, processing a credit card payment, creating an invoice, or notifying the shipping department to deliver a poster of Justin Bieber to someone in Nova Scotia.

A form is pretty useless if you don't have a form-processing program on the other end of things, running on your web server. These information-crunching programs come in a variety of languages—Perl, C, C#, Visual Basic, VBScript, Java, ColdFusion Markup Language, PHP, Ruby—and may be part of a dedicated application server, like Adobe's ColdFusion Server or Microsoft's .NET technology.

While writing the necessary behind-the-scenes forms software can be complex, the concepts behind the forms themselves are straightforward:

1. First, someone fills out a form on your website and clicks the Submit button (or the Search, Buy, or whatever button you actually label the button that transmits information).

2. Next, the browser transmits the form data over the Internet to a processing program on your web server.

3. The form-processing program collects the data and takes action, doing whatever you decide it should do. It could, for example, send data off as an email to you, search a vast database of information, or store the information in a database.

4. Finally, the server returns a page to the browser, which your visitor sees. It may be a standard web page with a message like "Thanks for the info," or a page the program generates on the fly that includes information like a detailed invoice or the results of a search.

So how do you create the processing half of the forms equation if you're not a programmer? Your web hosting company may offer free form-processing programs as part of their services. Contact them and ask; most companies provide basic instructions on how to use these programs. If you're part of a company's web development team, you may already have programmers on staff who can create the processing program. You can also find Dreamweaver Extensions that can help with a variety of form-processing tasks (see the boxes on pages 646 and 649).

If you feel adventurous, many form-processing programs are available free on the Web. For a thorough sampling, see the CGI Resource Index at *http://cgi.resourceindex.com*. Using these free programs can be tricky, however, because you need to download a program and install it on your web server—something not every web host allows.

Lastly, you can use a form-processing service like Wufoo (*http://wufoo.com*), which handles all the complicated parts of collecting and storing information from forms and provides tools for retrieving that information in a variety of formats.

◼ Creating a Form

In Dreamweaver, you can build forms with one-click ease using the Insert panel's Forms category (see Figure 14-2).

FIGURE 14-2

Dreamweaver's Insert panel has a category devoted to form objects, complete with icons that make it easy to identify each object's purpose.

You may want to keep a palette of form objects open as you build forms—just drag the Insert panel by the tab and position it within easy reach.

To begin, you need to insert a <form> tag in your web page to indicate the boundaries of the form:

1. **In Design view, click the location in the document window where you want to insert the form.**

   You might decide to place it after a paragraph of introductory text, for example, or into a <div> tag that holds the page's main content.

NOTE If you plan to use an HTML table to organize a form's fields (see page 643), insert the form first, and then insert the table inside the <form> tag.

---

2. **On the Insert panel, select the Forms category.**

   The tab reveals 30 form-building tools.

3. **Click the Form icon (the very first icon in the list).**

   If you're a menu-driven person, choose Insert→Form→Form.

NOTE What you see when you insert an object using the Insert panel depends on whether you position your cursor in Design view or Code view. These instructions assume you're inserting form elements in Design view. In Code view, Dreamweaver inserts the tag for the selected element, but the underlying code is sometimes different. For example, in Design view the Insert→Text command adds a text box and a label to your page along with an ID and other helpful HTML code. In Code view, the Insert→Text command adds just a single, stripped-down tag <input type="text">. So, unless you consider hand-coding forms a recreational activity, you're better off working in Design view.

   Either way, a rectangle with a red line appears in the document window, indicating the form's boundaries. The line is dashed on Windows PCs, and solid on Macs. (If you don't see it, choose View→Visual Aids→Invisible Elements.) The top line represents the opening <form> tag; the bottom represents the closing tag. It's best to insert form objects, like buttons and menus, *inside* these lines. With HTML5, you can associate elements in any location to a specific form, but not all browsers support this feature.

   Since you can place so many other HTML elements inside a form, you'll often find it easier to insert the form first, and then add tables, graphics, text, and form objects later.

4. **If it isn't already selected, click the red line to select the form.**

   This step not only selects the form, it highlights everything inside the red lines, too. The Properties panel displays the Form ID ("reservation" here) in the upper-left corner, as shown in Figure 14-3.

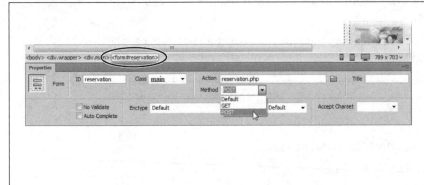

FIGURE 14-3

If you find selecting a form by its thin red line hard, click inside the form and then, in the Tag Selector, click the form tag (circled). Unless you're creating a search form, you'll want to send data to a processing server using use the Post method of transmission; step 7 has the details.

5. **Type a name for your form into the Form ID field.**

   This step is optional. Dreamweaver supplies a generic ID, *form1*. The name doesn't appear anywhere on the page, so you can leave the default name if you wish. However, a descriptive name is useful if you need to identify the form later, and you might want to add one to your CSS or JavaScript code. For example, if you have two forms on a page, a descriptive name makes it easier to remember the differences between the forms.

   > **TIP** The "Title" attribute is another optional naming device. In most browsers, text you enter in the Title box appears as a pop-up tool tooltip when a visitor mouses over the form.

6. **In the Action field, type a URL, or select a file by clicking the tiny folder icon.**

   Your mission here is to specify the location of the program that processes the form. If someone else is responsible for the programming, ask that person what to enter here. It's a standard web address—either an absolute URL (one that begins with *http://*) or the path to the server's form-processing program (see page 170 for more on these different kinds of links).

   Either way, the filename you add to the Action field *doesn't* end in *.html*. The path might be, for example, *../scripts/mail-form.php*. In this case, the .php extension indicates a program written in the PHP programming language. Other common file extensions for web programs include .cfm (for ColdFusion Markup Language), .aspx (.NET pages), .jsp (Java Server Pages), or .cgi (CGI programs).

7. **Using the Method pop-up menu, specify how you want a browser to transmit the form data to the processing program (see Figure 14-3).**

Basically, browsers can transmit form data to a web server two ways. You'll use the more common method, called Post, most often. It sends form data in two steps. First, the browser contacts the form-processing program at the URL you specified in step 6, and then it sends that data to the server. This method gives your data a bit more security, and it can easily handle forms with lots of information.

The Get method, on the other hand, adds the form data to the destination URL, like this: *http://search.yahoo.com/search?p=dogs.* (Even though the Get method *sends* data, it's named Get because its purpose in life is to *receive* information—such as the results of a search.) The characters following the *?* in the address represent the form data. This code submits a single form field named *p*, with the value *dogs*, to the server. If a form has lots of fields and accepts lots of user input, a Get URL can become extremely long. Some servers can't handle very long URLs, so don't use the Get method if your forms collect a lot of data.

NOTE The Get method has one big benefit: You can *bookmark* it, which is great if you want to save and reuse a Google search, for example, or you want to send someone Google Maps driving directions, or a list of Dreamweaver books you searched for on Amazon. The reusability of bookmarks is the reason search engines use the Get method for form submissions.

8. **If you're using frames, select a Target option.**

You'll most likely skip this menu. Frames are *so* 1998 web design that they pose serious problems for web designers and search engines. But even if you don't use frames, you can choose the "_blank" option to display the results in a new browser window. (See page 179 for more on the Target property.)

9. **Select an encoding type, if you like.**

You usually don't have to select anything from the Enctype menu. Leaving the encoding type set to Default is almost always correct, and it's the same as selecting the much more long-winded "application/x-www-form-urlencoded" option.

But if you use the File field button (see page 622) to let visitors upload files to your site, you should use the "multipart/form-data" option. In fact, Dreamweaver automatically selects this option when you add a File Field to a form. See the box below for more info on potential problems with File Field forms.

You've laid the foundation for your form. Now you're ready to add the controls—menus, checkboxes, and so on, described next.

FREQUENTLY ASKED QUESTION

Using a Form to Upload Files

I want to let visitors upload photos to my site, but when I include a File Field button in one of my forms, I get an error message from the server when I try to submit the form. Why?

To upload files from a web page, you need to do two things: Change the encoding method (see step 9 above) to "multipart/form-data" and set up your server to receive files. Dreamweaver automatically takes care of the first part: Whenever you insert a file field, it changes the form's encoding method to "multipart/form-data."

The second part is up to you (or your web hosting company). Many web servers have this option turned off for security reasons. Check to see if your web host lets you use forms to upload files to your server. If it doesn't, find a hosting company that does.

In addition, you have to program the form-processing script to accept data in the "multipart/form-data" format. Since this task is challenging, you might want to enlist some help. The box on page 646 provides several resources for commercial Dreamweaver extensions.

If you decide that's too much trouble and you delete the File Field button, you're still in trouble. Dreamweaver doesn't reset the encoding method to the original "application/xwww-form-urlencoded," so when visitors try to submit the form (even without the File Field), they get a nasty error message from the server. You must remedy the situation manually, by selecting the form, and then using the Properties panel to change the encoding method back to "application/x-www-form-urlencoded."

■ Adding Form Elements

Unless you've never used a computer before, the fields for HTML forms should look familiar (Figure 14-4): text fields where people can type in information (names, addresses, phone numbers, and so on); checkboxes for making multiple-choice selections; and menus for picking items from a list. The Insert panel's Forms category lets you create all these elements and more.

The elements you insert into a form have many things in common. The example below uses a basic text box—the second item in the Form category of the Insert panel—to walk you through the common features.

> **TIP** As an alternative to using the Insert panel, you can use the Insert→Form submenu (for example, Insert→Form→Text Field). It lets you tap the same form elements that are on the Insert panel. However, the order of the elements differs between the two, so it's a good idea to choose one method and stick with it.

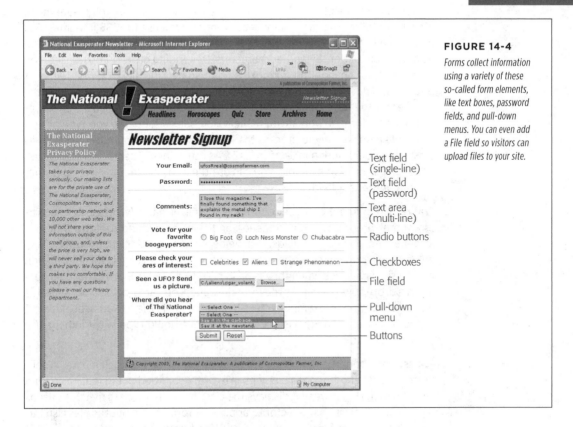

FIGURE 14-4

Forms collect information using a variety of these so-called form elements, like text boxes, password fields, and pull-down menus. You can even add a File field so visitors can upload files to your site.

What All Form Input Elements Have in Common

No matter the specific type of element, adding form elements to your document always involves the same steps:

1. **In Design view, insert a form (Insert→Form→Form).**

    If the page already has a form, click inside its red border..

2. **In the Insert panel's Forms category, click Text (see Figure 14-2).**

    One click adds two elements to the form on your web page: the text field (the blank box) and a label that displays the words "Text Field" followed by a colon. The text field remains selected after you add it into the form, so you see its properties in the Properties panel (Figure 14-5). Those include Name, Value, Class, Title, Form, and Tab Index. You'll find these properties for many (but not all) of the elements you insert through the Form category. It's worth taking a little closer look at the function of each:

- **Name.** When you first add a form element, Dreamweaver gives it a generic name, like *textfield*. Add a second element and you end up with *textfield2*. That's not very helpful, so you'll want to rename elements as you create them. Be sure to follow the same naming conventions you use for CSS ID names: Begin with a letter; use only numbers, letters, hyphens, or underscores; and skip spaces, punctuation, and other characters. Depending on its purpose in life, you might want to change the *textbox* name to something like *city*, *first-name*, or *search_words*. The name you give an element serves two purposes. It's both the "name" for the form element and it's also the element's ID. When a web server processes a form, it works with name/value pairs. The name you type here is available later, when you process the form. For example, *numberGuests=24* is easier to understand than *textfield2=24*. As usual, the ID identifies a unique element on a page. For example, you can use the ID as a selector in CSS Designer to format the text field.

- **Value.** The primary purpose of forms is to deliver name/value pairs to a program that processes the information and does something useful with it, like order airline tickets. Text fields, URL fields, password fields, radio buttons, and most other form elements have a value property. The value is the information your visitor provides when they type in text, click a button, or choose an item from a drop-down menu. As the form designer, you can provide an initial value for an element. For example, a text field labeled "My favorite baseball team" could be set to "San Francisco Giants." Visitors would type in something else if they disagree.

- **Class.** The Properties panel also displays a class for many elements. If your form is inside another page element, like a <div> or <body> tag that has a class applied to it, Dreamweaver displays the class name in the class menu. As usual, you'll use the class as a selector to apply CSS formatting, but the class isn't as vital to the form's function as the ID is. With forms, it is important to identify the values assigned to unique page elements so Dreamweaver can apply form functions to IDs rather than to classes.

- **Title.** In most browsers, text you enter in the Title box appears as a pop-up tool tooltip when a visitor mouses over the form element. Screen readers audibly say these words for web visitors when the focus is on the element.

- **Form.** This is a newer HTML5 property that connects a form element with a particular form. Using this property, you can put a form element outside of the form's red border, but still associate it with the form. Browser support for this feature is still hit or miss, so it's best to stick with the old ways. Put your form elements into a form.

- **Tab Index.** When visitors enter data in a form, their hands are on the keyboard much of the time. Most savvy computerists know they can hit the Tab key to move from one field to the next. As a web designer, you can control the order of that journey using Tab Index numbers. Suppose your form has street, city, state, and postal code text boxes. Assign tab index numbers like this:

Street, 3

City, 4

State, 5

Postal code, 6

Each press of the Tab key takes your web visitors to the next logical input box. That said, you may not need to manually type in a value for each form element. Even if you don't provide a Tab Index value, web browsers still move the focus from one element to the next. If you arrange your form elements in a fairly logical left-to-right, top-to-bottom order, most browsers handle it well. So, it makes sense to build your form and add its elements at the same time. Then, test Tab key navigation with a few browsers. If you're not happy with the results, it's time to set the Tab Index property for each element.

FIGURE 14-5

When you select a form element, the Properties panel displays its attributes. Many elements have Name, Value, Class, Title, Form, and Tab Index properties. It's not necessary to set properties for every little box in the panel, but it's always a good idea to change their names to something descriptive. For accessibility purposes, you should add a title in the Title box of the Properties panel.

3. **In the Name field of the Properties panel, type *first-name*.**

   This name appears in the name/value pair that goes to your web server for processing. The ID is also set to first-name.

4. **In Design view, select the label's text (Text Field:) and change it to describe the form element. For example, type *First Name:*.**

   The label's text appears on your web page, telling visitors what type of information they should type in. Depending on the tone and style of your site, you can be long-winded and folksy, or terse and businesslike. Editing the label is no different from editing any text on your web page. Labels differ from ordinary text in that you associate labels with a particular form element. The Text field label is associated with the first-name text box. If you click the "First Name" text and then click <label> in the Tag Selector at the bottom of the document window, you see the "For" property in the Properties panel, with the menu set to "first-name." When you first inserted your text field, it was named "textfield" and the label's *For* property was set to *textfield*. When you renamed the text field, Dreamweaver cleverly updated the label's *For* property to *first-name*.

Click the Source Code button, and you see that the underlying code for your label and text field looks like this:

```
<label for="first-name">First Name:</label>
<input name="first-name" type="text" id="first-name">
```

The label comes before the input (text) field, as it appears on the page. Both elements are independent, the only link between them being the attribute in the label tag: *for="first-name"*. Both the name and ID of the input tag are set to "first-name." (For a closer look at the HTML underlying form elements, see the box on page 628.) So if labels are just text on a page, what's the big fuss about associating a label with a specific form element? One good reason is that screen readers can audibly identify form elements whose labels use the For property.

> **NOTE** Sometimes you don't need or want a label. In those cases, Dreamweaver doesn't automatically create them. HTML's buttons, like Submit or Reset, are an example—the name you gave it also serves as the label.

5. **In the Properties panel's Title box, type an explanatory message, like "Please type in your first name."**

The words in this box appear as a pop-up tooltip when someone mouses over the form element. Screen readers say these words aloud to web visitors.

6. **Optionally, in the Properties panel's Tab Index box, type a number.**

The Tab Index lets you number each field in your form and, in the process, sets the focus order for the fields as a visitor presses the Tab key.

7. **Optionally, set the Properties panel's "Form" menu to identify a specific form on the page.**

Using this feature, you can place form elements outside of a form's border. However, as explained in the "Form" bullet point on page 624, this feature is still a gem in the rough because not all the major web browsers support it.

Each form element has different properties, suited for its specific function, as you can see in Figure 14-6. The good news is that you can always use the Properties panel as command central to set up the form elements to retrieve just the information you need from your web visitors. The next sections focus on the specific details for different form elements.

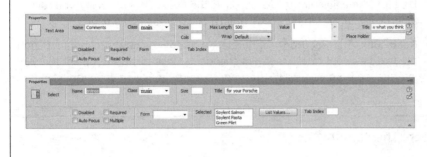

FIGURE 14-6

The Properties panel looks slightly different depending on the type of form element you choose. The Text Area form element (top) handles large amounts of text, like comments or (gasp!) complaints. When you place the Select form element (bottom) on a page, visitors choose from a set of pre-defined menu options.

Many elements have other properties in common, and you can see that in the four identical checkboxes in the lower-left corner of the Properties panel. Here's how each option works:

- **Disabled.** This grays out the text field and prevents visitors from clicking into it, or even selecting any text that's already there (from the Value property discussed above). In addition, when you disable a field, a browser doesn't submit that field's data when it submits the completed form itself. So, you may ask, why have an unusable field that doesn't provide information when the form is processed? JavaScript turns this property on and off based on what your visitor does. For example, you might have a spouse's name field disabled until someone checks the "married" box.

- **Required**. Turn on the Required property to make sure someone provides information in a text field. If you require a field and the guest doesn't provide the information for it, the form data will not be sent to your web server. Instead your visitor sees a prompt asking him to complete the form. Sadly, browser support for this helpful property is mixed. It doesn't work in Safari or Internet Explorer 9 and earlier.

- **Auto Complete.** We all get tired of entering the same information over and over into forms. Auto Complete helps alleviate this annoyance. When you turn Auto Complete on for a field, the web browser anticipates the input. For example, if you name the field "Email," the browser prompts the visitor with a list of email addresses that they've entered into similar boxes.

- **Auto Focus.** Nope, this doesn't have anything to do with camera lenses. In form-speak, the term *focus* means a page element is selected in the browser and ready for input. So, if your guest's cursor is blinking in the Last Name field, the Last Name field has the focus. Using the Auto Focus property, you can give a particular form element focus when a browser loads the page.

- **Read-only**. The Read-only option lets a visitor select and copy anything in the text field, but doesn't let him change it. Since forms are meant to collect information from visitors, it's best not to taunt them with uneditable fields.

UP TO SPEED

Form's Chameleon: The <input> Tag

Form elements have many properties in common, as explained in this chapter. Most form elements have another, somewhat surprising feature in common: the HTML <input> tag. Text fields, checkboxes, radio buttons, select menus, and even the Submit button are all created in your web page using the <input> tag. So why do they all look so different? That's the job of the "type" attribute in a form field—it lets you select different versions of the same "type" of field, such as the text field. For example, a text field's input tag might look like this:

```
<input type="text" name="first-name"
id="first-name">
```

While the input tag for a radio button looks like this:

```
<input type="radio" name="delivery"
id="delivery" value="UPS">
```

As the examples show, there are no closing input tags. Everything input elements need is between the opening and closing angle brackets. Simply changing the type attribute gives a form element an entirely different look and way of functioning. The first 16 form elements in the Insert panel's Form category are

text fields at their core. By using different types, such as *email*, *url*, *color*, or *date*, they may look different in your guest's web browser. For example, when a visitor needs to select a color, Chrome displays a swatch and color picker, and it displays a calendar when a visitor needs to type in a date. Less savvy web browsers simply show a text box where the guest has to manually type in a value.

The File form field uses the input tag (type="file") and the Image button is similar (type="image"). Both of these form elements use the <input> tag, but with different type attributes. All three "buttons" in the Form category of the Insert panel use the input tag, but they all have different type attributes: *button*, *submit*, and *reset*.

While the majority of the form elements share the input tag, there are some exceptions. The Text Area element, used to handle large quantities of text, has its own tag, <textarea>. The label field doesn't store data for processing, so it's not considered an input element. It has one attribute (for="formelement"), used to associate the label with a specific form element.

Providing Options with a "Datalist"

Another property that many form elements have in common is the *datalist*. Just as the name implies, a datalist stores several pieces of information. HTML gives you several ways to provide pre-defined options in your forms. You've seen checklists (page 641), radio buttons (page 640), and menus (page 641). HTML5 adds one more tool for the text field and many of the new form elements. It's called List in the Properties panel, but it's also known as a datalist because it uses the <datalist> tag. Suppose you want your guests to type in the name of their favorite sport. Normally, you'd just give them an empty text field to fill in, where they'd type *football*, *biking*, or *fly fishing*. By using a datalist, you can save them some typing and offer suggestions at the same time. The datalist works with a variety of form elements, including Text, Number, Range, and Color. You need to follow two steps when you use a datalist with a form element. First, you need to build the list. Then, you tell the element the name of the list you want it to use. You can use the same list with more than one element in a form. That's something you might do if you sold football caps, jerseys, and jackets with team names. You would create one datalist with the team names and use it for each of the products.

Right now, the only way to build a list in Dreamweaver CC is by writing the code in Code view. Fortunately, it's a pretty simple process. You begin your list with an opening tag that includes an ID *<datalist id="sportlist">*. The ID is important because it associates list entries and form elements. You close your list with a typical closing tag *</datalist>*. In between the datalist tags, you provide your options, like this:

```
<option value="Fly Fishing">
```

The value in quotes is what actually appears in the list on your form. A complete datalist looks like this:

```
<datalist id="sportlist">
    <option value="Fly Fishing">
    <option value="Baseball">
    <option value="Biking">
    <option value="Football">
    <option value="Soccer">
</datalist>
```

Once you write the code for your datalist, you can use it with a form element. Select an element like a text field and check out its properties in the Properties panel. In the lower-right corner, click the drop-down List menu shown in Figure 14-7. Dreamweaver displays the names of any datalists you coded in the web page. Select the name of the list you want to use. Your datalist work is done.

To test the list, choose File→Preview in Browser. Recent versions of Chrome, Firefox, and Opera support datalists. Safari and older browsers don't, so they treat form elements that use a datalist as an ordinary text field.

FIGURE 14-7

After you create a datalist, you can use it with form elements like text fields. Here, you've selected an element in Design view. Open the drop-down List menu in the lower-right corner, and Dreamweaver displays all the datalists you've stored on this web page.

Text Fields

To collect a specific piece of information, like a person's name, city, or brand of tooth paste, use a text field (shown in Figure 14-4). Text fields accept typed responses, and they're great for open-ended questions. Text fields take up just a single line on a form, and they give rise to a variety of form elements that collect information, like a phone number, URL, generic number, or date (see page 635). You can also choose the Password form element, which hides your keystrokes from snooping eyes as you type in your passcode. And if you want visitors to supply a lengthy, multi-line response, use the Text Area form element (page 632).

All these examples are just variations on the text field theme. You'll learn more about text fields at the end of this section.

Once you insert a text field, you can adjust the following settings in the Properties panel:

- **Size.** Dreamweaver measures the width of a text field (the box) in characters, so if you type *20* for the size setting, the program creates a box that holds 20 typed letters. If someone enters more than 20 characters, they won't see them all. Be aware, however, that the *physical* width of the field (how many inches or pixels wide it is) can vary from browser to browser. (You can use Cascading Style Sheets to set an exact width using the *width* property, as described on page 438.)

- **Max Length.** This setting lets you limit the number of characters a field accepts. It's a good way to ensure that guests type in the right information in the right place. For instance, if you use a field to collect a visitor's age, odds are you don't need to allot more than three characters; very few 1,000-year-olds surf the Web these days (and those who do don't like to reveal their ages).

- **Place Holder.** Use this option to prompt people filling out your form. The words initially appear in the text box, but disappear when someone clicks in the box and starts typing. If your visitors don't enter any new information, your server doesn't consider the placeholder text a value when it processes the form.

- **Pattern.** Use the Pattern option to validate the input text when your server processes the form. In other words, if you want a response that has only letters in it and no numbers, you can specify that in the Pattern property. The challenge of this property is that it requires regular expressions, a geeky shorthand used to describe strings of text, numbers, and other characters. For example, here's a pattern attribute that has a regular expression inside the quotes:

  ```
  pattern="[A-Za-z]{2}"
  ```

  The letters in the brackets specify that your visitor must type upper- or lowercase letters. The number in the curly brackets specifies that the field will accept up to two characters.

  That's a simple example, but regular expressions get complicated pretty quickly. Entire books explain how to use regular expressions. If you're looking for a good reference, get hold of *Mastering Regular Expressions*, Third Edition (O'Reilly,

2006), by Jeffrey E. F. Friedl (*http://oreilly.com/catalog/9780596528126*). To see a complete list of regular-expression characters that Dreamweaver understands, as well as a short tutorial on regular expressions, visit *http://tinyurl. com/3zw4oj6*. For an online reference, check out the Regular Expression Library at *http://regexlib.com*.

Label

As explained on page 625, the <label> tag lets you associate a label with a particular form element, like a checkbox or text field. Labels don't store information, so web servers don't process them. When you add form elements from the Insert panel, Dreamweaver includes a label and automatically associates the label with the form element. Of course, you can always place plain text next to a form element. But because Dreamweaver "attaches" a <label> tag to a particular form element, the label is more helpful in explaining the function and layout of your form to people who use assistive technologies, like screen-reading software for the blind.

> **NOTE** Labels also make forms more usable. By adding a <label> tag to a checkbox, for example, a visitor can click both the checkbox and the label text to check the box, extending the "clickable" region. Likewise, clicking a label on a text field places the cursor inside the text box so a visitor can start typing.

In the case of text fields, the label precedes the text field. In other cases, like checkboxes and radio buttons, the element comes first. Either way, you can select a label and move it to a different position. You won't break the connection between the label and the form element, because the For property handles that.

In most cases, you won't need to change the For property for a label because Dreamweaver automatically sets up the association as you add form elements. Dreamweaver even edits the label's For property when you change the name of a form element. Even so, for those rare moments when you need to change the For property, here's how: Select a label and find the For property in the Properties panel. In Design view, the easiest way to select a label is to click on its text, and then use the Tag Selector at the bottom of the document window. In the Properties panel, click the For menu and you see a list of the names and IDs for all the form elements. Choose one from the list. In your source code, a label with its For property looks like this:

```
<label for="sport">What's your favorite sport?</label>
```

Labels have opening and closing tags. The text that appears on the web page lies in between. In this example, the text is *What's your favorite sport?* The duties of associating the label with a particular form element is handled by the attribute *for="sport"*.

Password

The password form element is similar to the text field, but it conceals text as a guest types it in, usually displaying big dots instead characters. The purpose is to keep the other folks at your favorite cafe from learning how to log into your bank account. As a form designer, you can set the size (width) and the maximum length of the field when you create a password form element. The password form element is a single line, like the text field. You can set the width of the box displayed on the page by typing a value in the Size property. So, with Size set to *20*, the box can show 20 characters. To set the number of characters your visitors can type into a password box, type a number in the Max Length property.

Text Area

Like text fields, the text area element accepts text your guests enter. The difference is that the text area element is designed to accommodate large amounts of text. Use it when you ask visitors to submit a short story or explain why they're returning an item. The text area box handles multiple lines of copy, and automatically sprouts a scroll bar when necessary. In many browsers, your visitor can drag the lower-right corner of the text box to resize it on the screen, making it easier to type in their rant.

Use the Max Length box to limit the number of characters someone can enter, as you do with other Text style elements. Beyond that, the Text Area element has some unique properties:

- **Rows and Cols.** When you design your form, you set the size of the text area box using the Rows and Cols properties. You aren't creating rows and columns as you would in a spreadsheet, you're just specifying the height (Rows) and width (Cols) of the box, using characters as the unit of measure. So, a modest size box might be 10 Rows high and 50 Cols wide.

- **Wrap.** This property determines whether the form stores text as a single string of characters or whether it breaks up the text using line breaks (a.k.a. *newline characters*). Most of the time, you want to leave the Wrap menu set to the Default value, which is the same as the property's Soft option. That means that the form stores the text as one long line of characters. When your server processes that text or opens it in a program like Word, that program decides how to display multi-line text. The other option, Hard, inserts newline characters to format the text to fit the input box. Usually, that's not how you want it on the processing end.

Email, Number, Date, and Other Special Input Types

It's not surprising that forms on many sites ask for the same type of information: phone numbers, email addresses, website addresses, and more. HTML5 has a slew of text fields specifically designed to collect certain types of information. Sure, you could use a plain, old-fashioned text field to collect this type of information, but these new input-specific form elements have advantages for guests and for you.

Your guests benefit because browsers can prompt your visitors for the right information. For example, when Google Chrome finds the "date" form element on a web page, it displays a calendar so visitors can just click on a date rather than type it in. The guest can move through the months of the year and select a specific date. Choosing the date is a pleasant visual—no need for anyone to remember the 24th is a Tuesday. There are some great tools for the other form elements too, when it comes to choosing numbers, times, and colors. Input-specific form elements provide benefits to guests using their phones or tablets, too. When you use the *email* or *url* input type in your forms, visitors on iPhones see extra, helpful keys like @ and *.com* on their screen-based keyboards.

The advantage to you as a web developer is that you receive the data you want in usable form. Web browsers that recognize input-specific elements check your visitor's entries when he clicks the Submit button. If he hasn't provided information in the proper format, your web server won't process the form. It stays on-screen, usually with a message explaining the problem.

Unfortunately, there are still lots of browsers that don't support many input-specific form elements. When a browser doesn't recognize an element, like the Time element for example, it displays a simple text box, ready for input. That's just the way browsers work. For example, if a browser sees this in your code:

```
<input type="mysterious" id="dunno">
```

It automatically becomes a text field. You can draw two conclusions from this. First, there's no downside to using input-specific form elements. Some of your guests will see and use the data-collecting widgets, while others will see a text field where they supply info the old-fashioned way—by typing it in. Second, you need to do everything you can to make it clear what information you want from your guests. The tools for doing that include labels, explanatory text, titles, and placeholders. For example, if you want visitors to format the date a certain way, like January 1, 2014, you should provide an example in the label's text and the date element's placeholder property.

Here's a rundown on the different input types available in Dreamweaver:

- **Email.** Surprise! This input element is designed for email addresses like *sol@ soylentgreencafe.com*. For the convenience of your visitors, turn on the Auto Complete box. Then, when they begin to type the email address they always use to answer this question, they'll be prompted with the full address as soon as they type a few letters. As with all input-specific elements, you don't have to turn on validation. Browsers that recognize the form element will check a visitor's input when she presses Submit. They won't actually check to see if the email address exists, but they will check details. For example, email addresses should have an @ symbol and a period, and should be absent spaces or strange characters. Browsers won't send the form to your web server until the email address passes format muster. Instead, a message like the one in Figure 14-8 appears.

- **URL.** The form element for URL's works a lot like the one for email. It checks to make sure the address entered looks like a web address, complete with *http://* at the front.

- **Tel.** The Tel tag is intended to validate telephone numbers. If you've ever made a phone call outside your own country, you're probably aware that they vary a lot. So it may come as no surprise that none of the major browsers support this input-specific option. Still, it doesn't hurt to use this element in your pages. Browsers will treat it as a text field until the day they begin to validate phone numbers.

FIGURE 14-8

Firefox, Chrome, and Internet Explorer pop up a message like this if someone enters something other than an email address in an email input field. Web browsers that don't recognize the email input field simply treat it as a text input box.

- **Search.** Add a Search element to your page instead of a simple text box for your search term, and Chrome and Safari display an input box that looks like the operating system's search tool. You even get an "x" button on the right end to clear the box for a new entry. Don't get too excited, though. If you want to provide true search features, you or your programmer need to provide the form-processing functions for it. It's likely that as time goes on more browsers will recognize the search element, so this is a form element to keep your eye on. Search is such a basic function on the web that, in the future, there will be more ways to tie this element into Google and other search engines.

- **Number.** The number form element gives you the tools necessary to get just the number you need from your guests. In the Properties panel, you can set a minimum, maximum, and step value. Suppose, for example, that you sell LED lightbulbs at 5, 10, 15, 20, 25, and 30 watt options. Set *Min* to *5*, *Max* to *30*, and *Step* to *5*. Visitors use the number tool on your site, a box with up and down arrows in it called *spinarrows*, to select one of the values. They will be able to type in other values; but number-savvy browsers will display an error message when guests submit the form. Most recent browsers except Firefox support the number form element, so it's well worth using on your web pages starting today.

- **Range.** The range element appears as a slider in the browsers that support it. Sliders are great, as they give people a visual way to adjust a value. The biggest problem with the HTML5 range tool is that it doesn't automatically display the value. You use the same properties you used with the number element: Min, Max, and Step. That's great for a slider. But when your visitor adjusts the slider, web browsers don't automatically display the resulting value. This makes the range element not very useful for most jobs, unless you're willing to roll up your JavaScript/jQuery programming sleeves and head over to Code view. Before you make that journey, however, head over to the CSS-Tricks site (*http://tinyurl.com/3ta7ejw*), where there's an article by Chris Coyier that has working examples of the range element and the necessary jQuery code.

- **Color.** If you're selling iPhones or Porsches, your customers need to choose the color they want. The color form element can help. Sadly, as this book went to press, only recent versions of Chrome and Opera recognize the color form element. In other browsers, your visitors see a simple text field. So, until more browsers catch up with the color element, you may be better off using radio buttons (described on page 640) to provide color options. In the browsers that support color input, visitors see a color swatch like the one at the top of Figure 14-9. You should provide a label that prompts them to select a color with something like, "Click the swatch to choose a color." You'll also want to set a color in the Value property; otherwise, the swatch is black.

When your guest clicks the swatch, the browser opens the operating system's color picker. So, both Windows and Mac users see a familiar color-picking tool. One of the best things about the color element is that it works well with the datalist option mentioned on page 628. If you're selling Porsches in a limited number of colors, you can provide color swatches by creating a datalist.

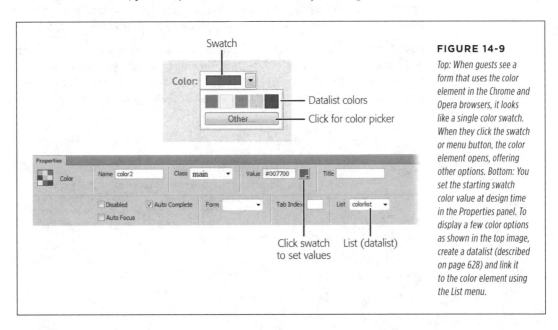

FIGURE 14-9

Top: When guests see a form that uses the color element in the Chrome and Opera browsers, it looks like a single color swatch. When they click the swatch or menu button, the color element opens, offering other options. Bottom: You set the starting swatch color value at design time in the Properties panel. To display a few color options as shown in the top image, create a datalist (described on page 628) and link it to the color element using the List menu.

- **Date.** The date element works well in browsers that support it. Pop it into a page, and Chrome, for example, displays a text box with a prompt that looks like this: mm/dd/yyyy (see Figure 14-10). That lets visitors know the format you expect for a date. It gets better. Chrome displays spinner arrows on the right side of the box. So, for example, when your guest wants to type in a month, he can use the spinner to choose a number between 1 and 12. The spinner only shows valid numbers, and it gracefully rolls over from the maximum value to the minimum value and vice versa. But as the infomercial folks say: Wait! There's more! Click the arrow at the very end of the field to open a date picker calendar, where it's easy to browse from one month to another and choose a specific date. Current versions of Chrome, Safari, and Opera support the Date element. They also support the elements for Month and Week (see below).

- **Month.** The Month element works like the Date element above, except that it limits your guest's selection to an entire month rather than an individual day.

- **Week.** Selecting a week is probably a lot less common than choosing a specific day or month. But, when you need it, the tool for the job is on your trusty Insert panel.

- **Time.** Need the time? Put the time element in your form and visitors can dial up a specific time before they submit the form. On the web page, the time is displayed as hours, minutes, and AM or PM. In the Properties panel, Dreamweaver lets you set Min, Max, and Step values. So, for example, if you're creating a form for a dentist's office, you can choose hours between 8:00 am and 6:00 pm and make sure the time entered is in hourly increments. If you want to give your visitors a choice of specific times and they don't fall neatly into regular intervals, the "step" option won't work. In that case, create a datalist as described on page 628. Then, in the Properties panel, set the List property to the name of the datalist.

- **Date Time.** The Date Time element simply combines the functions of the Date and Time elements into one. The Date Time element lets your guest provide a time zone, such as Pacific or Rocky Mountain. Your browser sends the date/time value to the server as a single name/value element. Current versions of Safari and Opera support this element.

FIGURE 14-10

If your website is in the business of making appointments, your guests will love the Date element for web forms. To specify a date, they just point-and-choose from a pop-up calendar. The Date element ensures that, when your guest submits a date-containing form, the date is in a format that web servers understand.

- **Date Time Local.** This element works like Date Time except that it doesn't include the time zone in the value. So Date Time Local works well if you and your guest are in the same general neighborhood. Current versions of Chrome, Safari, and Opera support this element.

Using the Password Field for Credit Card Numbers

Can I use the Password field for credit card numbers and other sensitive information?

Yes, but it doesn't give the information any extra security.

The Password field does one thing: It hides what people type into it. Someone looking over your guest's shoulder can't read what he's typing—it looks like a bunch of dots—but once a browser submits that information over the Internet, it's unprotected.

To provide real security for form information, you need an encrypted connection between your web server and your visitor's computer. Most website creators use SSL (Secure Socket Layer) technology for this purpose. You can identify a site using SSL by its URL: It begins with *https://*. The "s" stands for "secure," and browsers usually indicate a secure connection by displaying a padlock icon at the top or bottom of the browser window.

Web browsers understand SSL, but your web server must be specially configured to work in this mode. Contact your web host to see if their servers support SSL (the answer is usually yes). If so, they can tell you where to put your files and how to access them from a web browser. You don't have to make any special changes to your web pages, and once the server is set up, you transfer your web pages to it just as you would for a non-secure website (Chapter 17 covers moving your files onto the Web).

Checkboxes and Checkbox Groups

Checkboxes (see Figure 14-4) are simple and to the point; a guest either checks them or not. They can come solo or in groups. For example, you'll often see a single checkbox used when you register with a website—"By checking this box you agree to our terms and conditions." But you can also find checkboxes grouped together for questions that can have more than one answer. Suppose you offer visitors their choice of three email newsletters. In your form, you might include some text—"Check the boxes for the newsletters you want to receive"—and three corresponding checkboxes with labels that indicate the name of each newsletter.

Once you add a checkbox to a form, you can set up its options in the Properties panel (see Figure 14-11):

- **Checked.** If you like, you can have a checkbox already filled in when your web page first loads. You've probably seen this if you've ever signed up for something on a commercial site. There's usually a checkbox—already checked—near the bottom of the form with fine print like this: "Check here if you want to get daily, unsolicited email from our marketing department."

- **Value.** This is the information a browser sends to your form-processing program when a visitor selects the checkbox. Since visitors never actually see this information, it doesn't have to match the checkbox's label; it could transmit a coded response.

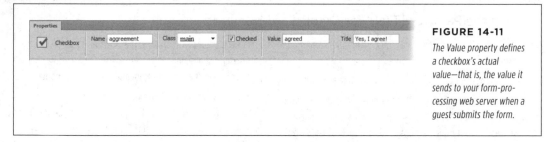

FIGURE 14-11

The Value property defines a checkbox's actual value—that is, the value it sends to your form-processing web server when a guest submits the form.

Checkboxes don't have to come in groups, but they often do. Dreamweaver includes a tool to make inserting multiple checkboxes easier, as discussed next.

■ CHECKBOX GROUPS

Checkboxes can travel in groups if you ask a question with more than one possible answer, like "What activities do you like? Check all that apply." Here's how you set up a checkbox group.

1. **On the Insert panel, click the Checkbox Group button near the bottom of the list of form elements.**

   The Checkbox Group window opens (see Figure 14-12).

2. **In the Name field, type a name.**

   This name applies to all the checkboxes in the group, saving you the trouble of typing in the name for each checkbox. The name you type is the name the browser submits to your web server, so follow the formatting rules for naming form fields: letters and numbers only, no spaces or funny characters except underscores and hyphens. (To see how Dreamweaver differentiates checkboxes when they all have the same name, see the box on page 640.) Although each checkbox shares the same name, Dreamweaver treats them individually—if someone selects multiple checkboxes, the browser sends the data from *all* the checked boxes to the server.

3. **In the Label column, click Checkbox and then type in a label for the first box.**

   For example, if you add a set of checkboxes so visitors can sign up for one or more newsletters, you might type the name of the newsletter here—"Design Newsletter," for example. This label will appear next to the checkbox.

> **NOTE** If you use the Checkbox Group tool, Dreamweaver places the form element inside the label's beginning and ending tags. (See the code in the box on page 640.) This is valid HTML, but it's difficult for screen readers to decipher. So you may want to skip the Checkbox Group tool and just insert checkboxes one at a time.

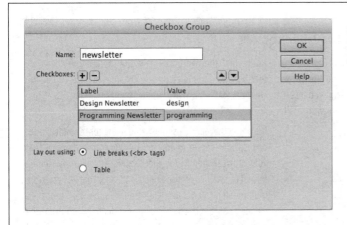

FIGURE 14-12

The Checkbox Group dialog box lets you quickly add multiple checkboxes to a page.

4. **Hit the Tab key to jump to the Value column for that checkbox, and then type in a value.**

   This is the value the browser passes to the web server when somebody selects the checkbox and submits the form—for example, the value for the Design Newsletter might be "design."

5. **Repeat steps 3–4 for the second checkbox in the group.**

   You can create additional checkboxes by clicking the + sign button. Follow steps 3 and 4 for each checkbox you add.

6. **Select a layout for the group.**

   Dreamweaver puts each checkbox on its own line. You can choose whether you want Dreamweaver to do that using a line break (<br>) or by creating a table with one checkbox per row. Don't care for either option? Pick the "Line breaks" option—it's easier to modify—and read the Note below.

NOTE If you want a group of checkboxes to appear side by side instead of stacked one on top of the other, choose the "Line breaks" option in the Checkbox Group dialog box. Then, with Dreamweaver set to display the invisible line break character (see page 33), click the line break's gold shield in Design view, and hit Backspace or Delete to move the checkbox on the line below onto the same line as the current checkbox.

7. **Click OK to add the group of checkboxes to your page.**

   The checkboxes and their labels are essentially text on the screen. You can move the checkboxes around, change their labels, and, in the Properties panel, alter each checkbox's properties.

How Dreamweaver Uniquely IDs Checkboxes

When you insert checkboxes using the Checkbox Group tool, Dreamweaver inserts all the checkboxes using the same name, but gives each a unique ID. For example, if you insert two checkboxes with this tool, you might end up with HTML that looks like this:

```
<label><input type="checkbox"
name="newsletter"
value="design" id="newsletter_0" />
Design newsletter</label>
<br />
<label><input type="checkbox"
name="newsletter" value="programming"
id="newsletter_1" />Programming newsletter
</label>
```

Notice that the two boxes have the same name—newsletter—but, since you need unique ID names to differentiate the checkboxes, Dreamweaver creates them by tacking _0, _1, and so on onto the end of each ID.

It's perfectly valid to use the same name for multiple checkboxes, but keep in mind (and tell your programmer) that your browser submits the checkbox data as an *array*—a data format common to programming languages that lets you store multiple items under a single name. So a browser sends the values of all the checked boxes as a single group using the name you supplied in step 2, but also using the unique ID that Dreamweaver added.

Radio Buttons and Radio Groups

Radio buttons, like checkboxes, are simple page elements (see Figure 14-4); they appear either selected (represented by a solid circle) or not (an empty circle).

Unlike checkboxes, radio buttons require your visitor to make a single choice from a group, just like the radio buttons on a car or the buttons on a blender. Radio buttons are ideal for multiple-choice questions that require a single answer, like "What is your income: A. $10,000–35,000, B. $35,001–70,000, C. $70,001–100,000, D. None of your business." Of course, you'd replace the letter choices here with a radio button.

In the Properties panel, set the following options for a radio button (Figure 14-13):

- **Name.** Dreamweaver supplies the generic name *radio* (or *radio2, radio3*, and so on) when you insert a radio button. Make sure you change the name to something more descriptive, and, when you insert a group of related radio buttons, give them all the *same name*. Your visitors should be able to select only one button in the group. To make sure that's the case, every button in the group needs to share the same name. On the other hand, each radio button should have a different value (see the bullet point below), because that's the information sent to the program that processed the form. So, if you're selling cars, the name of a radio button group might be "color" and the individual value buttons could be: "burgundy," "slate," and "forest." (They'd never be just red, gray, and green.)

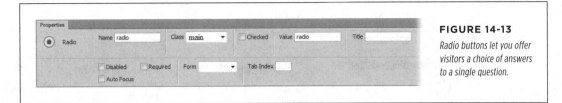

FIGURE 14-13

Radio buttons let you offer visitors a choice of answers to a single question.

If, when you test your page, you notice that you can select more than one radio button at a time, you must have given them different names. (Consider using Dreamweaver's Radio Group object, described in the next section. It acts like a wizard, simplifying the process of creating group radio buttons.)

- **Checked.** When you create a radio-button form, you can have one of the buttons pre-checked when the page loads. To do your visitors this timesaving courtesy, turn on the Checked checkbox for the button that holds the default value—the one they'll choose most often.

  Of course, if making a choice here is optional, leave all the buttons unselected by setting their initial state to Unchecked. However, once somebody *does* select a radio button, only the Reset button (if you add one) can unselect them *all* again (see page 647 to learn how to create a Reset button).

- **Value.** This is the information a browser submits to the server if your visitor selects this button. Once again, the info doesn't have to match the button's on-screen label. If you filled out the Accessibility window's ID box, Dreamweaver uses the ID you supplied as the checked value. If you don't like it, change it here.

Finally, you should add a text description for the entire group. For example, if you use radio buttons to let visitors choose a method of payment, your introductory text might say, "How would you like to pay for your item(s)?" There isn't any special HTML for creating a label for an entire group of buttons, so you just type the descriptive text next to the group of radio buttons.

■ RADIO GROUP

Although you can easily create a group of radio buttons using the Radio Button object, Dreamweaver makes it even simpler with the Radio *Group* object, a single dialog box that creates a group of radio buttons and their labels in one fell swoop. It works the same way as the Checkbox Group tool discussed on page 637, except that Dreamweaver inserts radio buttons instead of checkboxes.

Select Menus and Lists

While checkboxes and radio buttons let you ask multiple-choice questions, use them when your questions offer relatively few answer choices. Otherwise, your form can quickly become overcrowded with buttons and boxes. And therein lies the beauty of *Select menus*—they offer many choices without taking up a lot of screen space (Figure 14-14 shows an example).

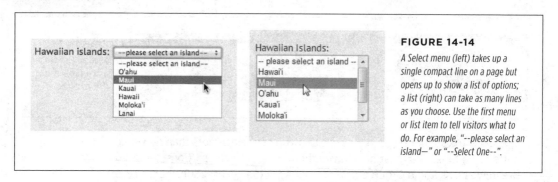

FIGURE 14-14

A Select menu (left) takes up a single compact line on a page but opens up to show a list of options; a list (right) can take as many lines as you choose. Use the first menu or list item to tell visitors what to do. For example, "--please select an island—" or "--Select One--".

Once you insert a menu or list object into your document, adjust its settings in the Properties panel.

- **List Values.** This is the most important button, because it opens a dialog box where you type in the items that make up your menu or list. You specify two pieces of information for each item: a *label* (the text that appears on the menu or a list on the web page) and a *value* (the information your form submits to the web server, which isn't necessarily the same thing as the label). To use this dialog box, type in an item label. Press Tab (or click in the Value column), and then type a value, if you like. Values are optional; if you don't specify one, the form submits the item's label *as* the value. Still, you'll often find a separate value useful. Imagine you design a pull-down menu on an e-commerce site so your visitors can select their credit cards' expiration month. Figure 14-15 shows what the items might look like. It displays the names of the months, but the form actually transmits the *number* of the month to your form-processing program—when a visitor selects "April," the form submits 4.

  Computer programs often work more easily with numbers than with names, while humans do the opposite. So when you offer visitors a pop-up menu of products, the label might use the human-friendly name of the product ("Blue Wool Cap"), while the value sent to the server reflects a model number that your form-processing program readily understands (XSD1278, say).

  As with other form elements, you can, and probably should, add some explanatory text alongside the menu or list in the document window. As shown in Figure 14-15, it's common to use one line in the list to explain what you want visitors to do. In that example, the item reads, "Please select an island."

- **Selected.** The Selected box displays your list items . You can pick one of them to appear selected in the list when a browser loads the page.

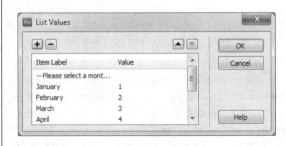

FIGURE 14-15

Using the + sign button, you can add items to the end of a list. When you click inside the last item's Value column, pressing Tab creates a new list item. To delete an item, select it, and then click the - sign button. You can move an item higher or lower in the list by selecting it and then clicking the up- or down-arrow buttons. Like radio buttons, pop-up menu items and list items always flock together—nobody ever creates a set of options with just one entry.

Two properties change the look of your select menu and turn it into a scrolling list. Enter a value in the Size box or check the Multiple box and your menu turns into a scrolling list like the one on the right of Figure 14-14.

- **Size.** You might not guess it from the name "size," but when you place a value in this box, it changes the height of the box. Here, type in the number of lines you want the list to take up on the page. That can vary from a single line (in which case you might as well use a menu) to many lines (displaying a number of choices at once). If you specify a height that's smaller than the number of items in the list, Dreamweaver adds a vertical scroll bar.

- **Multiple.** Here's a key difference between menus and lists: If you turn on the "Allow multiple" option for your list, a visitor can simultaneously select more than one item from the list by pressing the Ctrl (⌘) key while clicking items. (If you choose this option, be sure your instructions tell visitors they can select multiple items.)

WORKAROUND WORKSHOP

Giving Order to Your Forms

If you're not careful, creating forms can quickly lead to visual chaos. The different shapes and sizes of text boxes, radio buttons, and other form objects don't naturally align well with text. One solution: Use tables to control your forms' appearance.

If you simply place form labels and fields line after line, you end up with an ungainly zigzag pattern created by the differing lengths of label text and form fields. The result is not only ugly, but hard to read.

To better organize a form, you can insert the <form> tag, then insert an HTML table made of two columns and as many rows as

you have form fields; one column holds the label, the other the text box (or other form field). Align the text in the first column to the right, and you'll create a clean edge that effectively mirrors the edge created by the form fields.

To make this table-based solution work most effectively, set each text field to the same width using the *Size* property (page 632) or the CSS Width property (page 438).

You can also use CSS to lay out a form. You'll use this technique in the tutorial starting on page 649.

File Field

Receiving responses to checkboxes, radio buttons, and pull-down menus is all well and good, but what if you want your visitors to submit something a little meatier—like an entire file? Imagine a bulletin board system that lets guests post .jpg images of themselves, or upload word processing documents to share with others. Dreamweaver's File Field form object (see Figure 14-4) can help (but not without a little magic from your web server).

Before you get carried away with the possibilities the file field offers, you need to do a little research to see whether you can use it on your site. Although Dreamweaver lets you easily *add* a field so guests can upload images, text files, and other documents, you need to check with your web host to see if they permit anonymous file uploads (some don't for fear of receiving viruses or performance-choking large files). Then, of course, you have to ensure that the program that processes the form actually *does* something with the incoming file—stores it on the server, for instance. Dreamweaver doesn't have any built-in functions that help with this back-end work, but you can enlist some third-party solutions, as described in the box on page 649.

When you click the File button on the Insert panel's Forms category (or choose Insert→Form→File), Dreamweaver inserts a text field *and* a Browse button; together, they constitute a single file field. When you click either one, you highlight both.

NOTE Browsers display file fields in different ways. For example, in Firefox and Internet Explorer, a file field looks like a text field with a button next to it. In Chrome and Safari, the field is simply a button with the text "Choose File" on it and, to the right of the button, either the text "No file chosen" (when the page first loads) or the name of the file (after a visitor selects a file from their computer).

The Browse button opens the standard Windows or Macintosh Open File dialog box, letting your visitor navigate to and select the file she wants to upload.

The Properties panel offers few settings, as shown in Figure 14-16. At the very least, you want to give your file element a name. You haven't finished the file field until you add instructions or a label in the document window, something like "Click the Browse button to select a file to upload."

Hidden Field

Most form elements are designed to accept input from your guests: the value of a selected radio button, the text from a text field, or the choice from a menu of choices, for example. But visitors don't even know about, and don't ever see, one kind of form field: the *hidden* field.

NOTE Hidden fields aren't exactly hidden—it's true that visitors don't see them in a browser, but they (and their data) are visible if a visitor checks the page's HTML (using the browser's View→View Source or View Page Source command). In other words, despite their name, don't put anything into a hidden field that you wouldn't want someone to see.

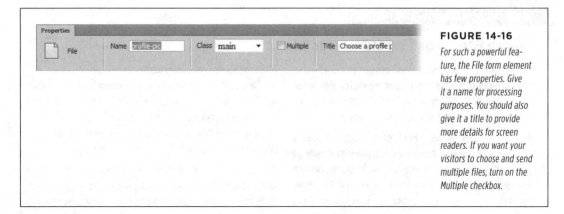

FIGURE 14-16

For such a powerful feature, the File form element has few properties. Give it a name for processing purposes. You should also give it a title to provide more details for screen readers. If you want your visitors to choose and send multiple files, turn on the Multiple checkbox.

Why, you're probably asking, would you need to submit a value you already know? Because hidden fields supply information to the programs that process forms—information that the program has no other way of knowing. Many web hosting services, for example, offer a generic form-processing program that collects information submitted with a form and emails it to the site's administrator. But how does the program know where to email the data? After all, it's a *generic* program that many other people use. The solution: A hidden field that stores the information required for the program to properly process the form—like *email=me@mydomain.com*.

To insert a hidden field, click the Insert panel's Hidden button (under the Forms category), or choose Insert→Form→Hidden. A gold shield appears on the page (this is Dreamweaver's symbol for HTML you can't see in web browsers). Use the Properties panel to give the field a name and a *value*—that is, the value you want the browser to submit to your form-processing program (in the example above, that value would be your email address).

NOTE Gold shields indicating hidden fields appear only if, in the Preferences window's Invisible Elements category, you turn on the Hidden Form Fields checkbox (see the note on page 75) and, in the View menu, you turn on Invisible Elements (View→Visual Aids→Invisible Elements).

Buttons

No form is complete without a Submit button so your visitors can register their choices (see Figure 14-4). Only when guests click this button do their responses set out on their way to your form-processing application. People sometimes add a Reset button, which visitors can click if they make an error; it clears all their form entries, and resets all the form fields to their original values. Dreamweaver provides a third button, a generic one that's essentially a blank canvas—it's up to you to tell it how to behave.

Adding File-Upload Ability to Your Site

Imagine adding a "Job Application" page to your site, where applicants can upload their resumes for review. Or a web-based way for your clients to submit graphics files and word processing documents they want included in the pages you're building.

Dreamweaver lets you add a File Field to a form, but doesn't provide the tools you need to make this useful feature work on your site. To compensate for that glaring omission, you can turn to extensions that add this power to Dreamweaver. But before you shell out any hard-earned cash for the extensions listed next, make sure your web hosting company allows anonymous file uploads from a web form—some don't.

DMXZone (*www.dmxzone.com/index?3/1019*) offers three fee-based extensions for the programming tools ASP, ASP. NET, and PHP. The Pure Upload extension offers many different settings to manage the process of uploading files to a site, including the ability to rename duplicate files and to add file information to databases.

WebAssist (one of the big players in the Dreamweaver extensions market) offers a commercial product, Universal Email, for uploading *and* downloading files from a server (*http:// tinyurl.com/68dj2lt*). As its name indicates, this extension also handles sending the contents of a form as an email message. This extension works for PHP.

You find all three buttons on the Insert panel's Forms category. Click any of them to insert it in your form. Dreamweaver doesn't include a separate label when it inserts a button, since the button itself has "Submit," "Reset," or whatever text you wish emblazoned across its face.

> **NOTE** Like other form elements, buttons appear in your source code as <input> elements (see page 628). It's the type attribute that dictates their function *and* their appearance. For example, the Submit button has the attribute *type="submit"*. For the Reset button, the type is "reset." The generic button's type is "button."

The Properties panel's controls (Figure 14-17) for a freshly inserted button differ depending on the button's function. The Submit button sends information to a web server, for example, so it requires properties that the Reset or generic buttons don't. All the buttons have name and value properties:

- **Name.** The button's name provides the first half of the name/value pair that a browser sends to your server (see page 615).

- **Value.** The value is the button's label. Dreamweaver proposes *Submit*, but you're free to substitute *Buy Now, Make It So*, or *Send my data on its merry way*.

What your visitors see printed on the button—Click Me, for example—is the value a browser transmits (along with the button's name) when a guest submits the form. This characteristic opens up some interesting possibilities. You could, for example, include *several* Submit buttons, each with a different label. If you create a form that works with a database, one button might say Delete, while another says Edit. Depending on which button your visitor clicks, the program processing the form either deletes the record from the database or modifies it.

FIGURE 14-17

The Submit button has more properties than the Reset or even the generic button, but most of the time, the only thing you need to change is the Value. The words you put in the Value field are displayed on the button.

The Submit button has the same properties as the Form element, but you don't need to set these properties for the Submit button if you set them for the form, as described on page 620. Form Action is the URL where the form is processed. Form Method lets you choose between using the Get or Put methods to communicate data. Form Enc Type lets you choose how to encode the data when a browser sends it.

■ THE RESET BUTTON

The "Reset form" button resets all the fields to their original values. (The fields, checkboxes, or menu items aren't left blank or unselected, they return to their *initial* state, which you specified when you created the control. For example, if you set the initial state of a checkbox to Checked and your visitor unchecks it and then clicks the Reset button, the box becomes checked once again.)

The Reset button used to appear on nearly every form on the Web; these days it's much less frequent, mainly because it's unlikely that anyone would want to *completely* erase *everything* she's typed into a form. In addition, its presence offers the unfortunate possibility that a visitor, after painstakingly filling out a form, will mistake the Reset button for the Submit button, and click it—erasing everything she's typed. So if you include a Reset button, it's probably best not to put it right next to the Submit button.

> **NOTE** While Reset buttons aren't common on forms used to collect new information—"Sign up for our newsletter"—they do come in handy on a page intended to *update* information. An update form contains previously recorded information (like the shipping address for your Amazon.com account). In this case, a Reset button lets you erase any mistakes you make when you update your account information. Click the Reset button and the form goes back to displaying the original information, like your original shipping address.

■ THE GENERIC BUTTON

The generic button that you get by clicking Button in the Form category of the Insert panel has no effect on the *form*. "Gee *that's* useful," you're probably thinking. But while the button doesn't trigger an action related to the form, you *can* use it to trigger one of Dreamweaver's built-in behaviors (see Chapter 13), like popping a message up on the screen. That way, you get a single, common user interface—the button—that can trigger many different actions, like opening a new browser window. If you're a JavaScript programmer, you can also use this button to launch your own programs.

> **NOTE** You can use a graphic as a Submit button, too, thus freeing you to be more creative with the look of the button. That's thanks to something called an Image Field. On the Insert panel, click the Image Field button or choose Insert→Form→Image Button to select the graphic you want to use. When a visitor clicks the image, it submits the form and all its data. (Image Fields do only one thing: Submit form data. You can't use them as a Reset button, for example.)

The <fieldset> Tag

The <fieldset> tag is a form-organization tool that lets you group related form fields together. To add a fieldset, go to the Form category on the Insert panel and choose Fieldset. That creates opening and closing <fieldset> tags in your page's code. You can think of Fieldset as a box that holds other form elements. For example, if you create an online order form, you can organize all the "ship to" information—address, city, state, Zip code, and so on—as a self-contained component of the form. You'd put the form elements for these details between the opening and closing <fieldset> tags. Again, this arrangement can help those using assistive technology to understand the organization and intent of a form.

The <fieldset> tag also has a visual benefit: Browsers display a border around fieldsets. If you prefer, you can use CSS Designer to create a custom border (page 56) or background color (page 160). In addition, the <legend> tag (which Dreamweaver automatically adds whenever you insert a fieldset) lets you add a description of the fields that make up a fieldset. Dreamweaver displays the legend at the top of the fieldset.

To use this tag, in the document window, click to select the form fields you want to add to the fieldset. You have to position fieldset form fields next to each other on-screen, and you can organize them within other HTML elements, like a table. Then, on the Insert panel's Forms category, click the Fieldset button. In the Label window that appears, type a label (called, somewhat dramatically, a legend) for the fieldset, and then click OK.

In addition to displaying the label you type, Dreamweaver creates a simple border around the group of fields you select. Because different browsers display this border differently, make sure you preview the page (F12 [Option-F12 on a Mac]) in a recent version of Internet Explorer, Firefox, Chrome, Safari, and Opera (page 739) to see how the label and surrounding border look in different browsers.

Emailing Form Results

I don't want to store form submissions in a database or anything fancy like that. I just want to get an email message that includes the information a guest submits. How do I do that?

This common function—available on countless websites—may seem like an easy task, but Dreamweaver doesn't supply a tool to automate the process. Basically, you need a program to collect the data and send it off in an email message. Most web hosting companies provide just such a program. They generally work like this: You build a form, set the form's Action property (see page 620) to point to the URL of the server's form-emailing program, and then add one or more hidden fields. The hidden fields contain information that the program uses—your email address, for example, and the URL of the page the browser should load after it submits the form. Since this form-emailing

program varies from server to server, you need to contact your hosting company for details.

Many commercial Dreamweaver extensions can help you, too. Here are two extensions that in addition to form handling offer much more advanced emailing features, including the ability to mass-mail newsletters to email addresses stored in a database:

- WA Universal Email ($99) from WebAssist (*http://tinyurl.com/5uhm4g4*) works for PHP pages and also supports file uploads.

- DMXZone sells both an ASP (*www.dmxzone.com/go?5578*) and a PHP (*www.dmxzone.com/go?5628*) version of its Smart Mailer extension ($49).

For all these extensions, however, your server has to support the appropriate programming language (ASP or PHP)—Part 6 of this book has more on server-side programming.

■ Forms Tutorial

In this tutorial, you'll build a simple reservation form for Cafe Soylent Green's website (skip ahead to Figure 14-29 if you want to see the final result). To make sure the folks at the Cafe get all the information they need to book a reservation, you'll use HTML5's new form elements.

NOTE To complete this tutorial, you need to download the practice files from *http://oreilly.com/missing-manuals/cds/dreamweaverccmm13/*. See the note on page 33 for details.

Once you download the tutorial files, open Dreamweaver and define a new site as described on page 19. Name the site *Forms*, and then select the *Chapter14* folder (inside the *MM_DWCC* folder). (In a nutshell: Choose Site→New Site. In the Site Definition window, type *Forms* into the Site Name field, click the folder icon next to the Local Site Folder field, navigate to and select the *Chapter14* folder, and then click Choose or Select. Finally, click OK.)

Insert a Form

The first step in building a form is inserting a <form> tag. This tag encloses all the fields within a form, and indicates where the form begins and ends. As noted earlier in this chapter, you can insert other HTML elements into the form, like text elements and <div> tags.

1. **Choose File→Open. Double-click the file *reservation.html* in the Chapter14 folder to open it.**

   If you have the Files panel open (Window→Files), just double-click *reservation. html*. The page is partly designed, with a banner, sidebar, and footer.

2. **Click the empty white space directly below the headline "Make a Reservation."**

   You're going to stake out the place on the page where you'll insert the form.

3. **On the Insert panel, select the Forms category from the drop-down menu (see Figure 14-2) and then click Form at the top of the list.**

   A red rectangle appears in the document window, indicating the boundaries of the form. (The red rectangle's line is dashed in Windows and solid on Macs.) In later steps, you'll insert form elements inside the form's border. First, though, you'll set the properties for the form itself.

4. **If necessary, select the form (click inside it), and then, at the bottom of the document window, use the Tag Selector to locate the <form#form1> tag. When you do, click it.**

   When you first insert a form on your web page, Dreamweaver automatically selects it. If you click elsewhere, you deselect the form. You can select it again by clicking its red border, but that takes a bit of mouse marksmanship. The surefire way to select a form is to click inside its red border, and then choose the form using the Tag Selector. Once you select your form, Dreamweaver displays its properties in the Properties panel.

5. **In the Properties panel's Form ID field, type *reservation* (see Figure 14-18).**

   You just added an ID to your form.

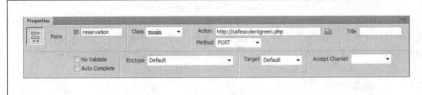

FIGURE 14-18

The Action property of a form is simply a URL pointing to the program that processes the form.

6. **In the Action field, type *http://cafesoylentgreen.com/reserve.php*.**

   Leave off the period after the URL in the sentence above (we added it to make our copyeditors happy).

A form's Action property identifies the Internet address of the program that processes the form. In this case, you've been spared the effort of writing (or hiring a programmer to write) the required form-processing software. That program already exists on the website whose address you just typed in, and it's waiting to process the form you're about to design.

7. **In the Method field, make sure you see Post selected. Leave the Target and Enctype fields set to *Default*.**

   The Method specifies how a form sends information to a form-processing program, and the Post option is the most common way (see page 620).

The form has properties that help a web server process it, but it relies on other form elements to collect information.

Add a Text and Email Field

Your guests type text in boxes, click buttons, and perform other form-filling tasks to communicate with you. In the next steps, you'll add two form elements that get information *from* your visitors: a Text field and an Email field.

1. **In the document window, click inside the form—anywhere within the red dashed lines. On the Insert panel, click the Text button or choose Insert→ Form→Text.**

   Dreamweaver inserts two elements, one beside the other: a label and then, to the right of that, a text field. The label reads Text Field, and the text field itself looks like a blank box.

2. **Click inside the text field box.**

   There are three clues that you've selected the text field: A dotted line appears around the text field, you see <input#textfield> as the last tag in the Tag Selector, and the properties for the text field appear in the Properties panel.

3. **In the Name field, type *diner*.**

   Dreamweaver adds "diner" to both the *name* and *ID* properties of the field's HTML. The form-processing program uses the *name* property to connect an ID with the value a visitor types in; in this case, his name. When a guest clicks Submit, the form-processing program receives information in what's called a name/value pair—*diner=Bob*, for instance (see page 624 for details).

   The ID uniquely identifies the form element. If you want, you can create an ID style to format this particular form field—for example, to assign it a width or background color.

   Next, you'll change the label's text.

4. **With the diner field still selected, turn on the checkboxes in the lower-left corner for Required, Auto Complete, and Auto Focus.**

   The people at the café aren't really picky about what their visitor types in the diner field—for example, they'll allow names like Jenny Stadler and Omicron 9 from *@^$(&!(%^. However, they do require at least *some* name for the day of the reservation—"Omicron 9, your table is ready!" When browsers see that a form element is *required*, they check to see if that element has a value before they send the form to a web server. If the element has no value, the browser doesn't submit the form. Instead, your guest sees the form still in place, with a message asking him to fill in the field. *Auto Complete* helps your guest fill in form details. Chances are if a guest has entered their name over and over in text boxes like this (and haven't we all?), the browser will prompt the visitor by name here. *Auto Focus* places the cursor in the diner box when the page first loads.

5. **In the Properties panel, find the Title box and then type** *Please enter your name.* **In the Place Holder box, type** *name required.*

   The Title and Place Holder properties are options, but they let your guest know what you want in the fields, so why not use them? Title text appears as a tooltip when your guest mouses over the text field. The Place Holder text appears inside the text box, but disappears once your guest enters her name since it isn't considered a value for the text box.

6. **In the document window, select the text "Text Field," and then type** *Your name.*

   After you change the label's text, the document window should now look like Figure 14-19. Next you'll add another text field.

FIGURE 14-19

After you insert a form into your web page (indicated by the red dotted line here), you add form elements one at a time. Here you see a Label form element ("Your name," which you changed from the default "Text Field") and the first Text field (the rectangle beside the label). When you insert a text field, Dreamweaver automatically includes a label for it. As explained on page 631, Dreamweaver associates the label with the text field through the text field's For attribute.

7. **Click to the right of the rectangular text box you just added and hit Enter (Return) to create a new line. In the Insert panel's Form category, click Email.**

   As in step 1, Dreamweaver inserts two elements, a label and a text box. In this case, the Type attribute for the box is "email." It doesn't look much different from the text field you set up in step 1. But when a browser goes to submit your form, it checks to make sure the text your visitor typed in the email box is valid. In other words, the email address should include the @ symbol and a period, and it shouldn't have any spaces or strange characters.

8. **While you have the Email element selected, turn on the checkboxes for Required and Auto Complete in the lower-left corner.**

Now you have two text boxes. You need to fill in both before you submit the form to a web server and its processing program. When the page first loads in a browser, the cursor appears in the diner text field, ready for your guests to enter their names. Both fields try to help your guests by suggesting a name or email address they've used in the past. The email field checks the validity of the email addresses when your visitor submits the form.

9. **Choose File→Save.**

Dreamweaver saves the page and its form. You feel good, knowing that if the power goes out or some other disaster strikes, you won't have to repeat all your work.

NOTE As mentioned in other parts of this chapter, not all browsers support the new HTML5 Form features. For example, a browser that doesn't recognize the *email* field will treat it as any old text field. In that case, it won't validate the text before submitting the form. The same holds true for other HTML5 input types and attributes. Using HTML5 features won't break your form if someone has an old browser—your forms still work, for example—but you and your guest lose some of HTML5's benefits.

Adding (and Removing) a Number Field

The Number field makes it easy for your guests to tell you how many diners to expect. You could simply provide a text box and ask for the number, but if you use the Number field, you'll minimize the hassle of receiving something that isn't a number. For the sake of learning, you'll add the number form element and then learn how to remove it and other form elements.

1. **Click to the right of the email address field and press Enter (Return) to create a new, empty paragraph.**

You'll use the paragraph for your next input element. Both the previous text fields were placed inside paragraph <p> tags, and you'll place this text field inside a paragraph, too.

2. **In the Insert panel's Form category, click Number.**

Dreamweaver displays the label "Number" beside a text box. Just to make sure there's a difference between this text box and the other text boxes you've worked on (for email addresses and regular text, for example), you'll check out the Number box in Live view.

3. **In the document window, click the Live button. Click the spinner arrows to call up a number and make sure the number box works, and then set a value. When you're done, click the Live button to turn off Live view.**

In Live view, you see your form as it appears in the Google Chrome browser. Click the spinner arrows to change the value in the number box.

Say you've decided to offer visitors the choices 1 through 7 in the number box, with a final option of "8+," for visitors bringing in eight or more diners. That won't work with the number field, because 8+ isn't a number. So you decide to use a Select menu instead, because it displays both numbers and text. Time to remove an element from your form, the number box.

4. **Click inside the number box and look at the Tag Selector.**

   The right-most tag reads <input#number>. That's the number input field. To the left of it is a <p> tag, meaning that this number field resides inside a paragraph.

5. **Click inside the label "Number" and check out at the Tag Selector.**

   The right-most tag, <label>, sits next to a <p> tag, so both the label and number field live inside the same paragraph.

6. **In the Tag Selector, click the <p> tag next to the <label> tag and then press Delete.**

   Choosing the <p> tag selects the paragraph, the label, and the number field. Pressing Delete removes all three elements from the page.

You can use the same technique to delete any form element(s) inside a paragraph. To delete form elements or labels from elements other than paragraphs, select the appropriate tag in the Tag Selector and press Delete.

Adding a Select Menu

Select menus let you predefine values for fields. Your guest's response is limited to the options you provide. That's perfect for the "number in party" field of the reservation form.

1. **Click to the right of the email address field, and then press Enter (Return) to create a new, empty paragraph.**

   You just replaced the paragraph you removed in the previous section.

2. **Using the Insert panel's Form category, click Select.**

   The Select input element is toward the bottom of the list. When you click the Select input element (toward the bottom of the list), Dreamweaver adds a label and an empty Select menu to the page. The properties for the Select menu appear in the Properties panel.

3. **Type *diners* in the Name field of the Properties panel. Type *Number of diners* in the Title field.**

   You named your Select menu "diners." When a browser submits this form, it connects the name "diners" with the number value that defines the how many people will be eating. "Diners" is also the ID for the Name field. The words "Number of diners" will appear in a tooltip when a guest mouses over the field, and screen readers will read the words aloud.

4. In the Properties panel, click List Values.

The List Values box appears (Figure 14-20), where you add labels and values for your Select menu. Dreamweaver highlights the first menu option, ready for your text.

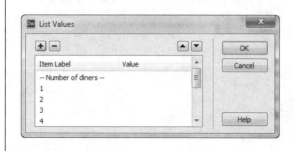

FIGURE 14-20

When you work with Select menus, you build their lists in the List Values box. Under Item Label, add the text you want to appear on the menu. In this case, the item label ("--Number of diners--") can serve as the value, too, so there's no need to add one. A browser passes this label as the value in the name/value pair it sends to a web server for processing.

5. Type – *Number of diners -- .*

The first label in the Select menu prompt your guests for *their* number of guests.

6. Click the + sign button. Under "Item Label," type the number *1*. Repeat that step to add the numbers *2* through *7* as labels. Then, instead of typing the number *8*, type *8+*.

If you don't provide a value, the menu uses the label as the value. That shortcut works fine for the reservation form.

7. Click OK.

Your label appears in the form. Dreamweaver displays the item (--Number of diners--) at the top of the list. That's great for this list. To display a different item from the list, select it in the Selected box next to the List Values button.

8. With the Select menu still selected, click Required in the lower-left corner of the Properties panel.

You want to make this field required so you know how many diners to expect.

9. Replace the label text "Select" with the words: *Number in party*.

Your Select menu has everything it needs to function. This is a good time to save your work and check out Live view.

10. Choose File→Save and then click the Live button in the document window. After you enjoy the view, click the Live button again. There's more work to be done.

At this point, the form elements look like those in Figure 14-21. In Live view, you can exercise the Select menu, but you can't edit your page.

Make a Reservation

Your name

Email

Number in party -- Number of diners -- ▾

-- Number of diners --

1

2

3

4

5

6

7

8+

After making your re... ...ou via e-mail wi...
before your reservati... ...bles longer tha...

FIGURE 14-21

The Select menu offers several predefined options via a drop-down menu, but it only takes up a little space on a form. It's helpful to provide text at the top of the menu that prompts your visitors to action.

Adding Date and Time Fields

Next, you'll add Date and Time fields. Some of your visitors will see these fields as date pickers, others will see text fields. That means it's important that you provide labels that describe the information you want. Web browsers that don't recognize HTML5 Date and Time fields treat them as ordinary text fields. You can save yourself aggravation by including good descriptive text for everyone, no matter what browser they use.

1. **Click to the right of the "Number in party" field and press Enter (Return).**

   A new line appears, ready for the next form element.

2. **Click *Date* in the Form category of the Insert panel.**

   Dreamweaver displays the Date field in the form, along with the label "Date."

3. **In the Title box, add the text: *Please enter a date (mm/dd/yyyy).***

   Dreamweaver inserts the date field with the perfectly suitable name "date," so there's no need to change it. Adding placeholder text gives you an opportunity to describe how you want visitors to format the date. You'll change the label to show the date format.

4. **With the date field selected, type _2013 12 01_ in the Min box and _2015 12 31_ in the Max box, and then turn on the Required checkbox.**

You can restrict the dates the date field accepts by setting minimum and maximum values in the Properties panel (Figure 14-22, circled). If you bought this book at a yard sale 20 years from the publication date, you may use more appropriate dates here.

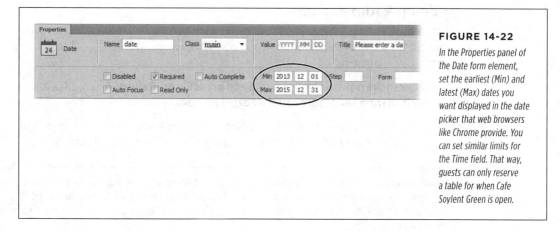

FIGURE 14-22

In the Properties panel of the Date form element, set the earliest (Min) and latest (Max) dates you want displayed in the date picker that web browsers like Chrome provide. You can set similar limits for the Time field. That way, guests can only reserve a table for when Cafe Soylent Green is open.

5. **In the document window, select the label "Date" and then type: _Date (mm/dd/yyyy)._**

The label provides another opportunity to show guests how you want the date formatted.

6. **Click to the right of the Date field, and then press Enter (Return). On the Insert panel, click _Time._**

Dreamweaver displays the Time field and its label on a new line in the form, with the time field selected and its properties displayed in the Properties panel. The Time field arrives with the perfectly suitable name "time," so you don't need to change it.

7. **In the Title box, type _Please enter the time (hh:mm:pm)_ and then turn on the _Required_ checkbox.**

Again, you use the title and its tooltip to signal the format you want for the time value. The Required setting means that visitors can't submit the form without providing a value in this field.

8. **In the Min box, type _07 00 00_, and then, in the Max box, type _23 00 00_.**

The Soylent Green Cafe staff puts in long hours to serve the public. They'll take reservations from 7 am to 11 pm. Yes, the Min and Max properties use military time to distinguish AM from PM.

9. **Change the label text from "time" to *Time (hh:mm:pm)*.**

   The label shows the format you expect for the time.

10. **Choose File→Save, and then click Live to preview your form.**

    In Live view, you see the date and time widgets in all their glory, just as it will look in the Chrome browser.

Adding Radio Buttons

When you want a visitor to select one option among many, as with a multiple-choice question, a group of radio buttons is the perfect solution. You'll add a set to handle seating arrangements.

1. **Click to the right of the Time field and press Enter (Return). Then, click Radio Button from the Insert panel's Form category.**

   A radio button and its associated label appear in a new line on the form. You need two more radio buttons, and you want them all to sit on the same line.

TIP Instead of inserting three individual radio buttons, it's tempting to use the radio button group. But, as explained on page 640, the group option wraps the radio button element inside its label. That makes it hard for screen readers to do their job. To accommodate all potential diners, Soylent Green Cafe opts to add radio buttons one at a time.

---

2. **Click to the right of the radio button's label. Then, on the Insert panel, click Radio Button again. Repeat this step to add a third radio button.**

   Two more radio buttons with labels appear on the same line. If you select each button and look at the Name properties, you see that Dreamweaver's named the buttons *radio*, *radio2*, and *radio3*. That would be fine for most form elements, but for the radio buttons to operate as a group, they all need to have the same name. Your guests should only be able to choose one of the options provided by the radio button.

3. **Select the first radio button. Change its name from "radio" to *location*. Repeat the process for the other two radio buttons.**

   Now the three buttons operate as a single form element named "location." When a browser processes the form, it sends a single value for "location." It's time to start identifying the role of each button. Rewording the labels is a good start.

4. **In the document window, select the label's text for the first radio button. Change it from "Radio Button" to *Anywhere is fine*. Select the label text for the second button and then type *At the bar*. Finally, set the text for the last label to *Corner table*.**

   The labels provide a good description for each option, but the entire group needs a description.

5. **Click to the left of the first button. Then, from the Insert panel's Form category, choose Label. Type *Location preference*. Press the spacebar and then click the Design view button.**

When you insert the label, Dreamweaver automatically switches from Design view to Split view and puts your cursor inside the label tags in Code view. The text you type becomes the text that the label displays on the page. When you click Design, the code window closes.

6. **Click the first radio button, turn on the Checked checkbox in the Properties panel, type *anywhere* in the Value box, and then type *Any seating location is fine* in the Title box.**

When a browser submits the form with this option selected, it sends the name "location" and the value "anywhere" to the server that processes the information. The cafe's maître d' hopes all guests choose Anywhere, so make it the default by turning on the Checked property (Figure 14-23).

7. **Select the second button. Change the value to *bar*. In the Title box, type *Seat us at the bar*. Select the third button, set the value to *corner*, and then, in the Title box, type *Give us a corner table*.**

You've now given all the radio buttons a value and a descriptive title. The first option, "Any seating location is fine," will be selected when the page loads.

8. **Choose File→Save. Click Live view, and give the radio buttons a test drive.**

You can choose a menu option by clicking its button or the button's label. You can only select one button at a time. If your page doesn't work that way, make sure all the buttons have the same name, "location."

FIGURE 14-23

Selecting the Checked option for a radio button ensures that a browser preselects that button. In other words, if you want to make one button in a group of buttons as the default, set its initial state to Checked. The same setting works for checkboxes.

Adding a Multiline Text Box and Submit Button

To retrieve more than a single line of text—a lengthy comment, complaint, recommendation, or movie review, for example—turn to the Text Area field.

1. **Click to the right of the "Corner table" label for the last radio button. Hit Enter (Return) to create a new paragraph, and then, from the Insert panel's Form category, click Text Area.**

   The Text area box, complete with a scroll bar, appears in the form. To the left of the box is its label, Text Area.

2. **Select the Text Area box, type *comments* for the Name field, and *Let us know of any comments or special requests* for the Title field. Type *300* in the Max Length box, and for the Place Holder box, type *Please type no more than 300 characters.***

   The Max Length box limits the number of characters a visitor can type in the text area field. After all, you don't want those special requests to get out of hand. The placeholder text delivers its message in gray, but disappears as soon as your guest enters a comment. On a similar note, you don't need to make this field required.

3. **In the document window, change the Text Area label to read *Any comments or requests?***

   You've got all your form elements in place, now you just need to add a Submit button.

4. **Put the cursor after the Text Area and press Enter (Return) to add a new line to the form. Then, on the Insert panel, click Submit.**

   Dreamweaver adds a Submit button to the form. The Properties panel displays its attributes.

5. **Change the Submit button's Value property to *Make Reservation*. For the Title, enter *Click to make a reservation.***

   The value appears on the button as its label. The words in the title appear as a tooltip. You don't need to make any other changes to the Submit button.

6. **Select File→Save and then click the Live view button for another look.**

   If you have different browsers installed on your computer, this is a good time to see how the form elements look and function in each. Figure 14-24 shows the form in Google Chrome. Figure 14-25 shows the form in Firefox.

Styling Labels

At this point, you have a functioning form, but it doesn't look very good (Figure 14-24). The form fields create a jagged line that's neither easy to read nor attractive. You'll improve this form by adding some style to the text and positioning the fields so their left edges align (Figure 14-29). To do this, you'll actually create and apply a style to the labels—in essence, you'll float (page 426) the labels to the left and give them a set width. That makes them behave much like the floating columns you created in the chapter on page layout (Chapter 10).

FIGURE 14-24

*Your form is complete—
well, sort of. All the fields
are there, but the labels
and text boxes are stag-
gered all over the page,
makes it hard to read and
click from one field to the
next. It's time for a CSS
makeover.*

1. **Choose Window→CSS Designer and then, in the upper-right corner of the Dreamweaver menu bar, choose the Expanded workspace.**

   In the Expanded workspace, CSS Designer's Properties section sits to the right of the other sections, giving you plenty of room to work with CSS properties.

2. **In CSS Designer, go to the Sources section and then click *soylent_styles.css*.**

   Soylent_styles.css is the external style sheet for the page. When you select it in Sources, the Selectors section shows the names of the classes, IDs, and tags defined in the style sheet. (If you need a refresher on this whole CSS styles thing, turn to page 104.)

3. **Click the + sign button in the light-gray Selectors bar.**

   Clicking the + sign button adds a new selector to the list. Dreamweaver opens the selector's Name box, ready for editing (Figure 14-26) so you can name the selector.

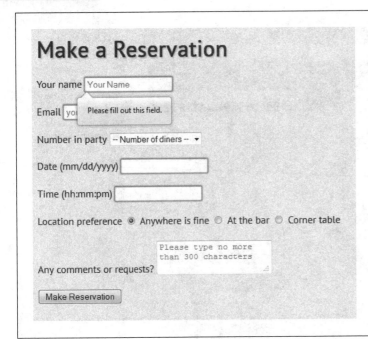

FIGURE 14-25

This figure shows just the form-containing part of your web page (so you don't see the banner, sidebar, and footer). In Firefox, if you click Make Reservation without filling in the blanks, the view looks like this. The browser helpfully marks required fields left empty in red, and error messages explain what's missing.

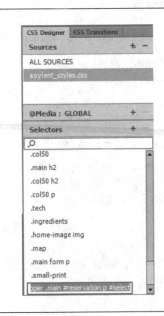

FIGURE 14-26

When you add a new selector in CSS Designer, it always suggests a name based on the location of the cursor in the document window. See the highlighted Selector name Dreamweaver suggests at the bottom of the list? Often, that's not the name you want, so type in the new one over the highlight. In this case, type ".label" to create a new class called label.

4. **Replace the suggested name with _.label_.**

   You created a new class called _label_. Next, you'll style that class.

5. **With _soylent_styles.css_ still selected in the Sources section of CSS designer and your new .label class selected in the Selectors section, go to the Properties section and click the T (text) button.**

   Dreamweaver scrolls the list of properties to display those related to text. Your labels inherit the "pt-sans, Arial, Helvetica, sans-serif" font-family property from the _.main p_ selector because they live inside paragraphs that live inside a <div> tag that has the "main" class applied to it. So, as long as your labels remain within paragraphs, you don't need to change the font-family property. You can spruce things up by changing the labels _color_ and _font-weight_ properties, however.

6. **In the Properties section of CSS Designer, make sure you have the Show Set box turned off. Change the text's Color property to #205B0A (or use the color box to select a dark-green). Click the value for font-weight and choose 700.**

   Your _.label_ class now has a rule that changes the color of the text. The font-weight of 700 makes the text bold. The way CSS Designer organizes its Properties section, it makes sense to set all the text properties first, and then move on to another category.

   Next, you'll change the alignment of the labels so they line up next to the form fields.

7. **Below the font-weight property, set the text-align property to right.**

   Setting the text-align property to right forces Dreamweaver to line up the text's right edge with the right edge of its box—in other words, you want to move the label to the right. Next, you'll use the Float property to position the label.

8. **At the top of the Properties section, click the Layout button category. Set width to 30%. Scroll down to the float property and choose left, and then, below that, choose left for the clear property. Go to the Padding settings and set the Right value (circled in Figure 14-27) to 10px.**

   Your _label_ class now styles the text and the layout. It's time to apply the class to the labels (but _not_ to the entire paragraph, which includes both the label and the form element). You can't apply the class to labels in the Properties panel, so you need to switch to Split view, where you can see your source code.

NOTE You might wonder why you didn't just create a style for the <label> tag instead of creating a class style that you had to manually apply. Good question. In some cases you can, but if you add checkboxes or radio buttons and their labels to a form, _all_ the form's labels will have the same style, and that might not be what you want. Creating a class style—_.label_—lets you pick and choose which labels get the CSS formatting.

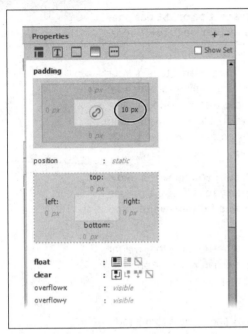

FIGURE 14-27

When you float a form label to the left, it's a good idea to set the Clear property (page 490) to "left" at the same time. That tells the label to always appear below other floated labels, preventing the label from wrapping around the right side of a cousin.

9. **In the document window, click the Split view button. In Design view, click anywhere inside the label "Your name." In the Tag Selector, click <label> to select the label tag.**

When you click <label>, Dreamweaver highlights the entire label (opening tag, closing tag, and the text in between). You'll insert the class attribute at the end of the opening tag.

> **TIP** If you're using the Expanded workspace, switch back over to Compact. This gives you more room to work with both the Code and the Design windows while you're in Split view.

10. **Click to the left of the closing bracket (>) in the opening label tag, and then type *class="label"*.**

Code view will prompt you with suggestions as you type. You can type in all the text, or choose "class" and "label" from the prompts. When you're done, the opening tag for the label looks like this:

```
<label for="diner" class="label">
```

11. **Select the text class="label", including the space before the letter "c," and then press Ctrl+C (⌘-C) to copy it.**

To save time and typing, you're going to paste this text into other labels.

12. **In Design view, click inside the label text "Email." In the Tag Selector, click `<label>`. In the Code window, click to the left of the closing bracket in the opening email label tag. Press Ctrl+V (⌘-V).**

At the end of this operation, the email label has the *.label* class applied to it, just as the diner label does. As you apply the class to the labels, they begin to fall into line, as shown in Figure 14-28.

13. **Repeat the previous step to assign the .label class to the rest of the form's labels.**

Wow! You're really getting some practice in the finer details of obsessive-compulsive web design. No time to wash hands—we need to move on to our next task, indenting the Submit button.

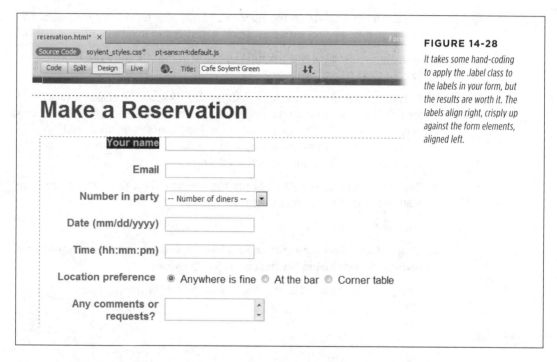

FIGURE 14-28

It takes some hand-coding to apply the .label class to the labels in your form, but the results are worth it. The labels align right, crisply up against the form elements, aligned left.

14. **In CSS Designer, with *soylent_sources.css* still selected, go to the Selectors section and click the Add Selector (the + sign) button. Name the new selector .submit.**

You're creating a special class that you can then apply to the paragraph containing the Submit button. By now, you're probably familiar with this drill.

15. **With .submit selected in the Selectors section, click the Layout button in the Properties section. In the margin box, set the left margin to 32%.**

Nothing happens yet. Because you created a class style, you need to apply it to the paragraph containing the button.

16. **In Design view, click the line containing the Submit button (either to the left or right of the button) and then choose "submit" from the Properties panel's Class menu.**

The button indents to line up with the form fields. You're almost done styling the form. Your last task is to set a width for the form's text fields. As you read on page 643, you can use the Size property, but if you use a class to do the job, it's easier to edit your layout in the future. For example, if you later need to resize all the text boxes, you only need to change the width property for a single class.

17. **In CSS Designer, with *soylent_sources.css* still selected, go to the Selectors section and click the Add Selector (the + sign) button. Name the new selector .textbox, and then, at the very top of the list in the Properties section, set Width to 50%.**

Next, you need to assign the *textbox* class to your form input elements. You can do that in the Properties panel; no mucking about in the code necessary.

18. **In Design view, click the box next to "Your name." In the Properties panel, set the class to textbox.**

The box for the "diner" text field changes size. Its actual size takes into account the way Dreamweaver nests different page elements inside each other. The text field's width is half the width of the form. The form is contained inside a <div> tag with the class *main* applied to it. The width property for that class is 64%, so it takes up 64% of the browser window.

19. **Repeat the previous step to apply the textbox class to all the other form elements except the radio buttons.**

Your form is complete.

20. **Choose File→Save, and then choose File→Preview in Browser. Choose your favorite browser from the list and enjoy the view!**

Your form should look like the one in Figure 14-29 when you're done.

FIGURE 14-29

Thanks to CSS and the careful application of classes to labels and form elements, your reservation form looks pretty stylish. Everyone's going to want to make a reservation at Cafe Soylent Green.

Adding Sound, Video, and Animation

A s you learned in previous chapters, you can bring your website to life with interactive and animated pages using Cascading Style Sheets (Chapter 3), JavaScript widgets, Dreamweaver effects and behaviors (Chapter 13), and images (Chapter 5). But as you've probably seen by now, today's web pages go even further—they blink, sing, and dance with sound, videos, and display interactive animations. That's the subject of this chapter.

You'll start off learning how to use the new HTML5 tags to add audio and video to your web pages. Along the way, you'll learn about the file formats (also known as containers) that today's web browsers work with.

For years, Adobe's Flash program dominated the web universe as the primary way to display complex multimedia presentations, such as slick animations, interactive games, and video tutorials. Flash isn't the only game in town these days, but it's still widely used, and you'll learn how to add Flash animations and video to your site. The heir apparent to Flash is Adobe's Edge Animate, and you'll learn how to add Animate creations to your web pages.

■ Adding Sound to Your Page

There are plenty of reasons to add sound to your web page. Perhaps you have a band to promote and you want to put some of your original songs online. Maybe you run a corporate website and want to include an audio message from the CEO. (He's not photogenic, so an audio works best.) Or, maybe you're the Cornell Lab of Ornithology (*http://macaulaylibrary.org/*) and you post bird sounds, as shown in Figure 15-1.

FIGURE 15-1

These days, you find audio used all over the Web. One great example is Cornell University's Macaulay Library of Natural Sounds (http://macaulaylibrary.org/), where visitors can pause, rewind, and play audio and video clips of sounds like bird calls.

In the past, webmasters had to turn to browser plug-ins like Adobe Flash to add sound clips. (See page 686 for more on Flash.) Thanks to HTML5 and its new <audio> tag, that's no longer the case. So, why isn't it as easy to add your song to a web page as it is to add a photo? It's the same old culprit making things difficult—browser incompatibility.

Modern browsers are designed to understand the audio tag and they can play audio files—you don't need any add-ons or plug-ins. That's the good news. The bad news is that each of the big five browsers—Internet Explorer, Chrome, Firefox, Safari, and Opera—play some, but not all, audio formats. The bottom line is that you can't choose a single audio format (like MP3) and be sure that your audience will hear your song. If you want to reach a wide audience, you need to provide the audio clip in at least two formats. As you'll see, your good friend Dreamweaver helps you do that. As a result, each web browser gets to play the sound clip that it understands.

There are two things you have to do to use audio on your website. First, you produce the audio files—some basic tips follow in the next section. Second, you add code to include the audio files as part of your web page. Dreamweaver handles the second task; you handle the first.

NOTE You can't put just any old song you got from iTunes on your web page because there are copyright issues to consider. You don't want Metallica showing up on your doorstep demanding royalties.

Producing Audio Files in Browser-Friendly Formats

Before you can add an audio clip to a web page, you need to record it and then convert it to the file formats you plan to offer. Your original recording may come from a handheld audio recorder, or it may have been recorded on the same computer you're using to build your website. In any case, the process involves capturing sound with a mic, converting that sound to bits and bytes, and storing it in a computer file. There are dozens of audio formats, just like there are different formats for storing photos. Original recordings are often saved in high quality formats (such as WAV or AIFF) that result in very big files. You almost always want to convert your recording to a smaller file, even at the expense of some audio fidelity. The smaller file will take up less room on your server, and more importantly, it will download faster when a guest visits your page.

Web browsers can play three audio formats. The first two, MP3 and Ogg, are the most common for web pages:

- **MP3.** This is the most popular file format, and the one most people think of when it comes to music. Internet Explorer, Chrome, and Safari all support MP3 files, which can be relatively small and yet provide pretty good sound quality. They perform this feat by compressing the audio signal, losing some sound quality along the way. So why don't all browsers support the MP3 standard? It comes down to patents and money.

- **Ogg.** This audio file format was developed as an open source, patent-free alternative to MP3. It's pretty common on Linux computers—less so with Windows PCs and Macs. Chrome, Firefox, and Opera support Ogg (sometimes called Ogg/Vorbis).

- **WAV.** Sometimes called Audio for Windows, Microsoft and IBM developed the WAV file format back when computers could barely beep. Unlike the other two formats, WAV files usually contain "uncompressed" audio. That means the sound quality is great, but the files are huge. You most likely won't use WAV files on your website because they take a long time to travel over the Internet. However, if you need to provide uncompressed audio for the best quality sound, Chrome, Firefox, Safari, and Opera support this format. (Yes, that's every browser except Microsoft's Internet Explorer. Wasn't that the company that developed the audio format in the first place?)

If you're responsible for converting audio files to browser-friendly formats, you'll need to use a program like Adobe's Audition or the open source program Audacity. If you have a subscription to Adobe Creative Cloud, you probably have access to Audition. You can download Audacity from *http://audacity.sourceforge.net/*. There are versions for Windows, Macs, and Linux computers, and best of all, it's free. These power-user audio programs do much more than convert files from one format to another. They can mix sound and take the audio from an entire orchestra and turn it all into a commercial-quality CD. You don't need all that power to convert files to web formats. In fact, the entire process is almost as easy as opening a word processing file and saving it in a different format.

Here are the basic steps for converting an audio file:

1. **In your audio program, choose File→Open to open your original audio clip. (The command is the same for Audition and Audactiy.)**

   Use the original recording or the best quality audio file you can get your hands on. That way, you'll get the best possible sound from the conversion. Initially, audio programs display the sound in waveform—a visual representation of sound. You'd work on this waveform if you were editing the sound file, but fortunately, you just want to convert it, so you can use the File menu.

2. **If you're using Audition, choose File→Export→File. For Audacity, choose File→Export (Figure 15-2).**

   This command opens a window where you can name the audio file you're creating and choose the audio file format.

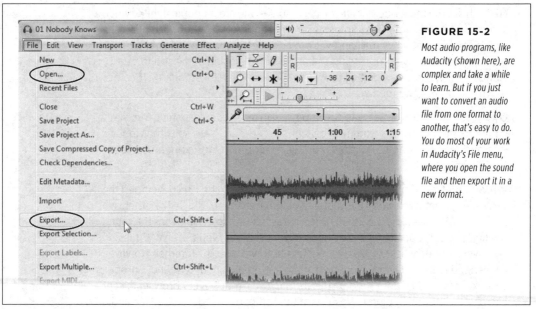

FIGURE 15-2

Most audio programs, like Audacity (shown here), are complex and take a while to learn. But if you just want to convert an audio file from one format to another, that's easy to do. You do most of your work in Audacity's File menu, where you open the sound file and then export it in a new format.

3. **Save the audio in an MP3 file. In Audition, set the format menu to MP3 Audio. In Audacity set "Save as type" to MP3 Files. Click OK (Audition) or Save (Audacity).**

   Your audio program creates a file with the *.mp3* extension. The format menus give you an idea of the variety of audio files. The important ones for web developers are MP3, Ogg, and WAV. In most cases, you want to offer your web visitors an MP3 and an Ogg audio file. Next, you create the Ogg file.

TIP When you export a file in your audio program, it uses the original file name and adds an extension like *.mp3* or *.Ogg*. You need to keep those extensions, but you can change the rest of the name. However, as you'll see in the next section, you save yourself some work when your audio clips use the same name to the left of the extension. For example, you could create *ceo_message.mp3* and *ceo_message.Ogg*.

4. **Save the audio in an Ogg file. In Audition, set the format menu to Xiph Ogg Container. In Audacity, set "Save as type" to Ogg Vorbis Files. Click OK or Save.**

   Your audio program creates a file with the *.Ogg* extension.

In most cases, you won't create a WAV file for your web page because the files are usually too big. It might be appropriate if you need top-notch audio quality or if the sound clips themselves are just a couple of seconds long. In any case, if you decide to produce a WAV file, choose the format (as in Step 4) and then save the file.

Adding Audio to Web Pages

As explained in the previous section, when you put a sound file on your website, you should offer both an MP3 file and an Ogg file. Using those two file formats, you can reach just about everyone with a modern browser. Once you have an audio clip, you need to store it with your other website files and create links in your web pages to it. You use the Insert panel to add the <audio> tag to your web page, and you use the Properties panel to manage the technical details. For example, you use the Properties panel to identify the audio source files and to choose whether or not you provide playback controls.

Here are the steps for adding an audio clip to a web page. Your first task is to add your audio files to your website:

1. **In Dreamweaver, make sure you have the Files panel open (Window→File), and then click the Files tab.**

2. **Drag your audio clips (MP3 and Ogg) from Windows Explorer or the Mac Finder to the Files panel.**

   Dragging the audio files into the Files panel is the easiest way to add them to your website. If your root folder is cluttered, you can create a separate folder for your sound or other media files.

3. **In the Files panel, double-click the web page that will provide the audio. Then click the spot on the page where you want to insert the audio file and its playback controls.**

   The playback controls are the only visual indicator that there's an audio clip there. You might also want to identify the clip with a label or other visual element. Say the boss asks you to post a message on the company intranet. You could create a heading like "A Message from Our CEO" and then place the audio in a paragraph under it.

4. **Open the Insert panel (Window→Insert) and then, using the menu at the top, choose the Media category.**

The Insert panel's Media category provides options for audio, video, Flash, and Edge Animate files.

5. **Click HTML5 Audio.**

Dreamweaver displays a rectangular placeholder with a speaker in the middle of it on your web page (Figure 15-3), indicating the presence of the <audio> tag in your page's HTML code. Now you need to identify the source of the audio.

> **NOTE** Don't just drag your audio clip from the Files menu onto a web page. That creates a link to the sound file, but it doesn't insert the <audio> tag that browsers need to actually play the clip.

6. **Click the folder icon in the Properties panel (next to the Source box), and then browse to the MP3 file.**

The file has the .mp3 extension. This is one of two file formats you're providing for your visitors. If your files share the same name but different extensions (such as *ceo_message.mp3* and *ceo_message.ogg*), Dreamweaver automatically fills in the Alt Source 1 box with the second audio file. If the two files have different names, you need to fill in the Alt Source box manually. (If the Properties panel doesn't show the same properties as those in Figure 15-3, you need to select the audio placeholder on your web page.)

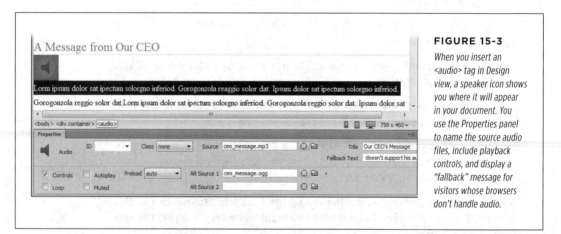

FIGURE 15-3

When you insert an <audio> tag in Design view, a speaker icon shows you where it will appear in your document. You use the Properties panel to name the source audio files, include playback controls, and display a "fallback" message for visitors whose browsers don't handle audio.

7. **In the Title box, give your audio clip a short descriptive name.**

This message appears in a tooltip whenever a visitor hovers over the audio controls.

8. **In the Fallback Text box, type something like *Sorry, your browser doesn't support this audio clip.***

If your visitor's browser doesn't support any of your audio clip formats, she'll see this message.

9. **Set the Preload menu to Auto—and then change it back to None. (Why the odd menu two-step? See the None option below.)**

As the name implies, the "preload" attribute determines whether your visitor's browser starts downloading the audio file while it downloads text, photos, and other parts of the web page. Audio files can be large, so you might not want automatic preloading. Here's what the different options do:

- **None.** Tells the browser not to preload the audio. This is the option to use if your audio file is particularly large (over a minute long) or when some of your visitors are unlikely to play the audio. You may reasonably ask why go through the rigmarole of changing the menu from none to something else and then back again. When you first insert an audio clip, Dreamweaver displays the word None in Preload menu, but it doesn't actually write the *preload="none"* code in your web page. To have Dreamweaver do that, you need to change the preload option to something other than None first, and then change it back to None. Switch to Split view to double-check the code if you're in doubt.

- **Auto.** Tells web browsers to automatically download the audio file while the page loads. Use this option if the main purpose of the page is to play the audio file, and you're sure nearly everyone will want to listen. Depending on the size of the audio file, this choice may make the entire page load slowly.

- **Metadata.** This option tells browsers to download information about the audio, such as its track list and duration. This is a good option for audio clips several minutes long.

10. **Make sure you have the Controls checkbox turned on.**

It's almost always best to give your audience audio controls. They let visitors start and stop playback and adjust the volume. Controls also provide information about the length of the audio clip.

11. **Leave the Autoplay, Loop, and Muted checkboxes turned off.**

There may be cases where it's appropriate to turn these controls on, but too often they're just plain annoying. Here's what they do:

- **Autoplay.** The audio clip starts playing as soon as it loads. But what if your web visitor is in the library or a quiet office?

- **Loop.** As advertised, this makes your clip play over and over and over and over.... Few things are more annoying than a short clip that loops. This is especially true if you haven't given your audience controls to stop it, as described in step 10.

- **Muted.** This turns off your audio clip's sound, which may be confusing to less savvy web visitors. Also, if you don't provide audio controls, guests have no way of turning the sound on.

When you finish adding audio to your page, test it on different browsers and devices (Figure 15-4). You can test drive your audio in Live view, too—you'll see and hear how it works for visitors using the Chrome browser. If you have other browsers on your computer, you can use File→Preview in Browser to check your page.

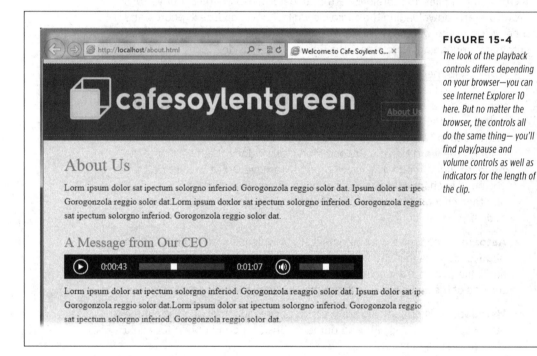

FIGURE 15-4

The look of the playback controls differs depending on your browser—you can see Internet Explorer 10 here. But no matter the browser, the controls all do the same thing— you'll find play/pause and volume controls as well as indicators for the length of the clip.

Using HTML5 Video

Video on the web isn't the novelty it used to be. Everyone's familiar with YouTube by now, and they've all seen video clips on web pages. Web video makes it possible to see your favorite band in action, to catch up on a missed episode of Downton Abbey, and to learn how to cast with a fly fishing rod. As a web designer, you should use video when still pictures and text can't adequately handle the job. At Cafe Soylent Green, you might produce a walk-through video that shows the dining room and a friendly welcome from the maître d'.

Videos have great instructional value, too. For example, if your website sells doors, you could create a video that shows how easy it is for a homeowner to install their own door.

With HTML5, the steps for adding video to your pages are similar to those for adding audio (described on page 673). It wasn't always that easy, though. In the past, web builders used the Adobe Flash plug-in to provide video (see page 696). Another popular option was to post video on YouTube and then place links on the web page.

Those options still work, but HTML5 gives you a shiny new <video> tag that you use to place video files in web pages. Modern browsers play video files without needing plug-ins like Flash. That all sounds good, but the fly in the ointment, yet again, is browser compatibility. The five major browsers play video files, but they support different file formats. To reach a wide audience, you need to supply clips in more than one format. For video, you reach the widest audience by providing three file formats: MP4, WebM, and Ogg. Fortunately, Dreamweaver does the hard work of writing the HTML that offers up a source video file and two alternatives. For tips on producing video clips in the needed file formats, read the next section. If you already have your web-friendly clips in hand, jump ahead to the "Adding Video to Your Page" on page 680.

Converting Video Files to Browser-Friendly Formats

To attract as many visitors as possible, you need to convert your video to formats that web browsers can play: MP4, WebM, and Ogg. Video-editing programs like Premiere Pro or Final Cut Pro can open video files and then save them in a different format, but they may not export to all the formats you need, and they are complicated to use. A simpler tool for the job is Miro Video Converter (*http://www.mirovideoconverter. com/*). You'll find versions for Windows, Macs, and Linux computers. The icing on the cake is that Miro is free and easy to use.

Fire up Miro Video Converter and you see a window with five menus and one big Convert Now button, as shown in Figure 15-5. Drag the files you want to showcase from Windows Explorer or the Mac's Finder onto the top part of the window. Converting video files can take some time. For example, a three-minute video takes three minutes or longer to convert. The actual processing time depends on the content and how hard the encoder has to work to compress the files. So it's a boon that Miro lets you batch-convert files. That way, you can set up a bunch of files for conversion and head off for a coffee break.

Here are the steps for converting video files to web-friendly formats with Miro Video Converter:

1. **Start up Miro Video Converter.**

   Initially, the menus and buttons are grayed out and inactive. The only thing you can do is add the video clips you want to convert. This is Miro's gentle way of guiding you through the process. Menus and buttons become active only when it's time to use them. So if you're wondering why you can't do something, you probably missed a step.

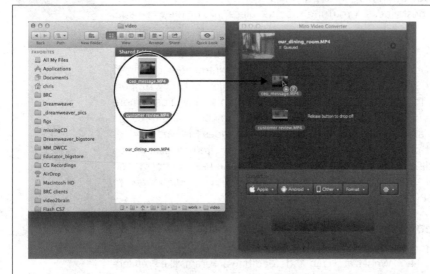

FIGURE 15-5

Drag the video files you want to convert to Miro Video Converter's main window. Once you do, use the menus at the bottom of the screen to choose a video format. In addition to creating videos for the web, the converter can produce videos for Apple and Android mobile devices. Miro keeps the big Convert button faded out until you choose a video format.

2. **Drag the video clip you want to convert to the top portion of the converter window, as shown in Figure 15-5.**

   As usual, you want to use an original recording or the best quality uncompressed video that's available. After you add the video, Miro activates the "Convert to" buttons at the bottom of the window. Their text turns white, and when you click them, they open to display options for the conversion. If you want to convert more than one file, drag the additional clips onto the converter now. Miro lists the videos in the conversion queue, one above the other.

3. **Click the Format menu (Figure 15-6), choose Video, and then choose one of the format options: WebM (HD or SD), MP4, or Ogg Theora.**

   Ideally, you want to provide clips in all three formats, so you'll repeat these steps for each format (see below for file format descriptions). If you've heard the term "codec" thrown around by video or sound pros and wonder how that relates to file formats, see the box on page 680:

   - **MP4** (.mp4). This file format is sometimes referred to as MPEG-4. That name comes from the Motion Picture Experts Group that developed the standard. Apple has championed this format for several years and Internet Explorer, Chrome, Safari, and Firefox version 21 on Windows 7 and 8 support it. iPhones and iPads use the same format. Bottom line: You'll reach a lot of browsers with this video format.

   - **WebM** HD or SD (.webm). The WebM video file format was developed specifically for web video and it's royalty-free. So, naturally all browsers support it, right? Well, not quite. Chrome, Firefox, and Opera play WebM files. Miro offers you a choice of HD (high definition, larger file) or SD (standard definition, smaller file) with the WebM format.

- **Ogg Theora** (.ogv). Theora is similar to WebM in that it's free and open source. Ogg file sizes are often larger than the file sizes of other formats. This format works with Firefox, Chrome, and Opera.

4. **Click the Convert button.**

After you choose a format, the text on the big Convert button changes so you might see something like "Convert to WebM SD" or "Convert to MP4." When you click the button, Miro makes a new copy of the video in the file format you specified. The process takes some time. If you added more than one video to the queue, Miro processes them one at a time, and automatically puts the converted file in its output folder. You're stuck with that destination (Miro doesn't let you specify a different folder), but you can easily get to that folder by clicking the Show File link under the name of the video post-conversion. You can also get to the output folder by clicking the "gear" menu and then clicking "Show output folder" link.

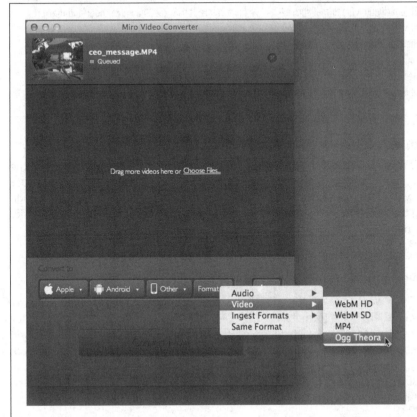

FIGURE 15-6

To create web-friendly videos, click Miro's drop-down Format menu, choose Video, and then choose a video file format. Ideally, your web page will offer video in three formats: MP4, WebM, and Ogg Theora. As a result, you'll need to go through the conversion process three times to create each format.

As explained in step 2, you can queue several videos and convert them all at once, but you can only choose one output file format. That means that, if you load several videos to the conversion queue and then choose WebM as the file format, Miro converts all those videos to WebM. It would be handier for web developers if you could add one original file and output to the three web-friendly formats, but sadly that's not the case. You need to repeat the process for each file format.

FREQUENTLY ASKED QUESTION

Video Containers and Video Codecs

Is a video file the same things as a codec?

Video pros refer to video files, like those with the extensions MP4 or WebM, as "containers." They store both video and audio data as well as other information. When you create a video, you "encode" that information in the resulting file. When you want to watch the video, that information gets decoded for playback.

The tools that perform this feat are called "codecs," short for coder/decoder. As usual in the world of computers, there are a slew of different codecs out there that provide different levels of image quality and file size. Specifying a file format such as MP4 isn't the same thing as specifying a codec, though you usually don't need to know the difference—as a web developer, you only need to worry about the file format. For example, when you use the Miro Video Converter described on page 677, you only need to choose a video *container*. The converter

automatically chooses the codecs that work with web browsers. But if you want to know all the technical details, here are the video containers and the codecs that today's web browsers use:

- MP4 video containers (.mp4) use the H264 video codec and the AAC audio codec. Apple championed this combination—it produces good quality video in a relative small file size.

- Google developed the WebM video container (.webm) as an open, royalty-free alternative to the existing video file formats. It uses the VP8 video codec and the Vorbis audio codec.

- Ogg video containers (.ogv) use the Theora video codec and Vorbis audio codec. As with the Ogg audio file format, it is popular on Linux computers.

Adding Video to Your Page

If you followed the steps to add an audio file to your web page on page 673, the procedure for adding web video will seem familiar. The first thing to do is place your three video files on your website's server. Then you add the <video> tag to your page using the Insert panel. To finish things off, you use the Properties panel to identify the video files and to provide playback controls.

Here are the steps for adding a video clip to your web page:

1. **Drag your video files into Dreamweaver's Files panel.**

   If you want to reach the widest audience, provide your video clip in all three web-friendly file formats: MP4, WebM, and Ogg Theora. That means that for every video on your web page, you'll have three video files on your web server. Each browser automatically uses the file format it supports. With this method, guests can play your videos in all the most recent desktop browsers and on all smartphones and tablets. (See the box on page 700 for adding a Flash video fallback for older desktop browsers.)

2. **Open the page where you want to display the video and then click where you want the playback window to appear.**

Placing a video on a page is similar to placing a photo. If the video is important (like a message from your CEO), you may want to center it at the top of the page all by itself. If your video is more of a side story, you can float it right or left and wrap text around it. In short, once your video is in place, you format it using the same CSS techniques you used to format a photo, as described on page 234.

3. **Go to the Insert panel's Media category and click HTML5 video, as shown in Figure 15-7.**

A rectangular placeholder with a piece of film is inserted into your web page to represent the video clip in Design view.

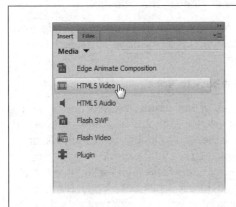

FIGURE 15-7

Use the commands on the Insert panel (shown here) to add video to your web pages. If you just drag a clip from the Files panel to your web page, Dreamweaver creates a standard link to the file (using the anchor tag, <a>); it doesn't insert the <video> tag. But when you use the Insert panel to add video, Dreamweaver does indeed add the <video> tag that browsers require to play movies.

4. **Select the "film" icon on your web page to display the video properties in the Properties panel.**

When you select the film icon, the Properties panel displays fields for additional info, like Source, Alt Source 1, and Alt Source 2.

5. **Tell Dreamweaver where to find the source video (Figure 15-8) using either the folder icon next to the Source field or by dragging the bulls-eye icon (beside the folder icon) to the MP4 video file.**

You can choose any of the file formats as your Source, but your MP4 video clip is a good choice because so many browsers and devices support it. If a browser can't play the MP4 video clip, it will try the Alt Source option, described in the next step. If all your video files have the same name but different extensions (such as *ceo_message.mp4*, *ceo_message.webm*, and *ceo_message.ogv*) you can skip the next step. Dreamweaver will automatically identify the Alt Source files in the Properties panel.

6. Set the WebM file as Alt Source 1 and the Ogg file as Alt Source 2.

Browsers will work their way through the options and play the first video file they can. If they can't play any of the options, the browser displays the fallback text described next.

TIP If it's important that visitors with older browsers can view your video, provide a Flash video fallback. See the details on page 700.

7. In the Fallback Text field, provide a message for visitors whose browsers don't support video.

For example, you can say "Sorry, your web browser can't play this video."

8. Type a short descriptive title for your video in the Title box.

This appears as a tooltip when a visitor hovers over the video link. Screen readers use the Title property to read aloud what's on the page, and search engines use it to improve their search results.

9. Set Preload to Auto, and then set it back to None.

The Preload attribute determines whether your visitor's browser downloads the video file at the same time as it downloads text, photos, and other parts of your web page. Since video files can be large, you probably don't want visitors to wait until the video downloads before they see your page. The Preload option works the same way here as it does for audio files—if you select it, a browser downloads all of a page's elements before it displays the page. But because video files are so large, the preloading issue becomes more critical with video. Here are the options for preloading video, and the situations where you'd choose preloading over not preloading.

- **None.** Tells the browser not to preload the video. This is the option to use if your video file is particularly large (more than a minute or two long) or if your visitors are unlikely to play the video. When you first insert a video clip, the preload menu in the Properties panel is set to None, but Dreamweaver hasn't actually written the *preload="none"* in the code. To actually produce the code in the HTML, you need to change the Preload option to one of the other values and then change it back to None. Switch to Split view to double-check the code if you're in doubt.

- **Auto.** Tells web browsers to automatically download the video file while the page loads. Use this option if the main purpose of the page is to play the video and you're sure nearly everyone will want to. Depending on the size of the video file, this choice may make the entire page load slowly.

- **Metadata.** This option tells browsers to download information about the video, such as its dimensions, the first few frames of video, its track list, and its duration. This is a good middle-of-the-road option for video clips several minutes long. It gives browsers enough information to size the video playback window and display an image. The rest of the video will load when your guest hits the play button.

> **NOTE** The preload behavior of different browsers and different devices varies. Surprising, isn't it? Given that, your preload settings serve more as suggestions than the law of the Web. For example, phones and tablets tend not to preload video even if there is an instruction to do so, and the amount of data that desktop browsers download with the Auto and Metadata options varies from browser to browser.

10. **In the lower-left corner of the Properties panel, make sure you have the Controls checkbox turned on, so that your audience can play, pause, and adjust the video's volume.**

    As you can see in the next step, you can control how and when your video plays. In most cases, its best to give the power to the people. Let them start and stop the video and control the audio volume.

11. **Leave the Autoplay, Loop, and Muted checkboxes turned off.**

    There may be cases where it's appropriate to turn these controls on, but too often they're just plain annoying. Here's what they do:

    - **Autoplay.** The video starts playing as soon as the page loads. (Most mobile devices ignore the Autoplay option.)

    - **Loop.** When your video reaches the end, it starts playing again from the beginning.

    - **Muted.** This turns off the sound for your video clip. If you provided playback controls as explained in the previous step, visitors can use the volume control to turn the sound on. But how will they know that?

12. **Optional: In the Properties panel, set the width of the video playback window.**

    You can set the size of the video window using the width (W) and/or height (H) values. If you don't provide a value, browsers display your video at its original size. If you want to make the video window smaller, set W (width) to a smaller size. If you try to make it bigger than the original clip, the image gets fuzzy. You don't need to set both the W and H values. Set one and leave the other empty. That way, your video keeps its original proportions. If you set both the width and height and they aren't in the same proportion as the original clip, you may get a distorted image.

13. **Optional: In the Properties panel, choose a file for the Poster property.**

    The Poster property displays a placeholder image when your video's not playing. Usually, you create the image by capturing a frame of the video and saving it as a JPG, GIF, or PNG file. However, you can use any image you want as the poster. If you don't specify a poster, most browsers display the first frame of the video clip.

After you finish adding video to your web page, you can preview the results using Dreamweaver's Live view. You'll see how your video looks when a guest plays it using the Google Chrome browser. If you have other browsers installed on your computer, you can use the File→Preview in Browser command to play the video there.

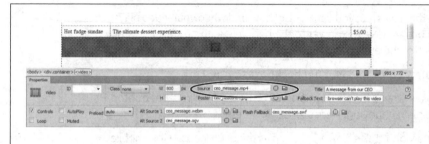

FIGURE 15-8

Use the Properties panel's Source attribute (circled) to tell Dreamweaver where to find your video file. You should provide alternative file formats in the Alt Source 1 and Alt Source 2 boxes, too.

Adding Video Through YouTube

When it first appeared on the web scene, YouTube seemed to be just a place to stash your home videos, blooper reels, and illegally copied TV shows. Now, it's more and more a place where businesses offer product demos, instructional videos, and other videos promoting their companies. In addition to showcasing the video on your site, you make it possible for a few of the billions of eyeballs that visit YouTube each month to stumble across your video and learn about your product or business—you can't beat free marketing.

There are a few other reasons why YouTube is a good video-hosting option. Video takes a lot of bandwidth and server processing power. Putting video on your own server can easily slow down your site and cost you money once you hit your web host's monthly bandwidth allotment. In addition, YouTube does all the hard work of making your video ready for pretty much any browser or device—Internet Explorer 6, Firefox, iPad, iPhone, Android—and not just the newer video-ready browsers. So you can also use YouTube as the ultimate fallback option for browsers that don't support the <video> tag. For example, you could provide a message that says, "Can't see the video in your browser? Try the YouTube version." Then, you can link the message to a page that has the YouTube video embedded in it, as explained below.

Here's how to put video on YouTube.com and include it in a web page on your site:

1. **Get a video.**

   Obviously, you'll need to create a video, have one already made, or get one from your client or boss. YouTube accepts these video formats: QuickTime .mov, Windows .avi, .mpg files, Flash Video (.flv), and even the new Google-owned WebM format. You can even record a video directly from a webcam. You don't have to worry too much about the video's resolution. YouTube handles every file from a tiny 426 x 240 pixel phone-sized video to the 1920 x 1080 pixel video you'd see on your big screen TV. The playback window is in the standard 16:9 aspect ratio of modern widescreen TVs. If your video has a different aspect ratio, your browser adds black bars at the edges to achieve the right proportion when it plays the video.

   NOTE In some cases, you can upload really long videos—up to 12 hours long—to YouTube. If you really want to upload your "My sleeping habits in real time" long-form video, visit *http://support.google.com/youtube/bin/answer.py?hl=en&answer=71673*.

2. **Get an account at *www.youtube.com*.**

   If you don't already have an account, you need to go to YouTube and sign up. It's free and easy.

3. **Upload a video.**

   Once you have an account and log in to YouTube, click Upload at the top of the home page. Then click "Select files to upload," select a video from your computer, and then click Open. The video begins to upload, and you'll see a page that lets you set its properties.

4. **Go to the YouTube page that hosts your video.**

   When your video finishes uploading, you see the message, "Your video will be live at…" followed by a link to the page. Click the link to see the YouTube page with your video on it.

5. **Right-click (Control-click) the video's image and a menu appears. Choose "Copy embed code" as shown in Figure 15-9.**

   The embed code is a snippet of HTML that lets you put the video on any page of your site. You can use the same technique to find the embed code for any video on YouTube. So if you want to embed a video you didn't create, but that you found while surfing YouTube, you can: Right-click (Control-click) the video to get the embed code.

   NOTE On some pages, the menu option reads "Copy embed HTML" instead of "Copy embed code." Don't let it throw you—they both give the code you need to embed a video in your web page.

6. Return to Dreamweaver and add the code to your page.

You copied a snippet of raw HTML, and now you need to add it in Code view. The easiest way to do that is to click where you want to add the video in Design view, and then click the Code view button; Dreamweaver positions the cursor in the right place, and you simply choose Edit→Paste to add the code.

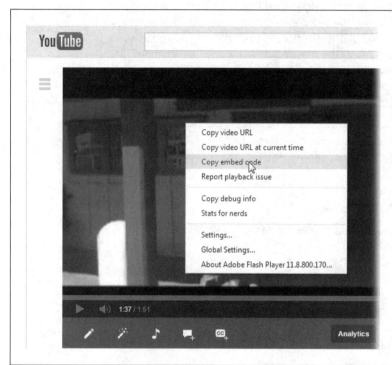

FIGURE 15-9

Right-click (Control-click) any video on YouTube and you see this menu. Choose "Copy embed code" to get the code you need to add the video to your web page. If you just want to share the video with a friend, choose the first option, "Copy video URL" to get the address of the web page—you can then paste it into an email or instant message.

■ Flash: An Introduction

A few years ago, if you wanted to add smooth animation, video, slideshows, or any other high-quality interactive effects to a web page, Flash was the only game in town. Thanks to the Flash plug-in (available for almost all browsers), web developers could use the Flash authoring program to make "videos" that played inside a browser and add programming logic so that those videos responded to visitor feedback—mouse movement, clicks, and keyboard input. However, the JavaScript programming language and the speedy JavaScript engines in today's browsers provide an alternative to many simple forms of animation and interactivity. Edge Animate compositions (page 701) are good examples of the interactive effects JavaScript offers.

But for really high-quality animation, games, and interactivity, Flash is still a viable option. For example, the games on the website *www.addictinggames.com* (Figure 15-10) were created in Flash and use the Flash plug-in to provide quick, responsive gameplay. JavaScript and its companion library jQuery are still playing catch-up when it comes to this kind of animation. You'll also find many entertainment company websites (especially those for video companies) and consumer-oriented product sites still turn to Flash to create an immersive, interactive experience (see *http://marvel.com/avengers_movie/*, for example).

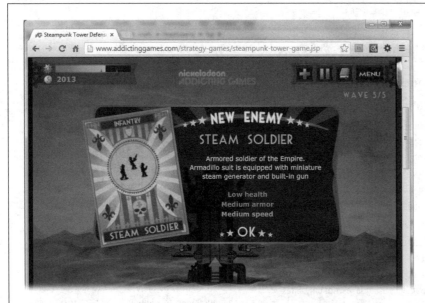

FIGURE 15-10

Some websites, like Addicting Games, use Flash because it facilitates interactivity, animation, and video playback. You create the page in HTML and then add your Flash file using the <object> tag. Web browsers need to have the Flash player plug-in installed for playback, but that's usually not an issue because 90 percent of browsers do.

Flash provides other benefits as well. It plays third-party audio and video files, and its advanced programming features let you add a level of sound, video, and interactivity that makes plain HTML pages look dull by comparison.

In addition, Flash videos look and work exactly the same way in every browser, whether you use a Windows, Mac, or even Linux PC. That kind of cross-platform compatibility is rare. And finally, the ubiquity of Flash on the web means that nearly every desktop browser—in fact, 90 percent of them—have a Flash player installed.

However, that 90 percent figure covers desktop computers only. Two of the most popular devices for surfing the Web, the iPhone and the iPad, don't support Flash at all. So if you think you'll have visitors using their iPhones or iPads to search for your business's hours, street address, and phone number, make sure you at least provide your most crucial information in HTML format. Said another way: Don't make your site's home page one big Flash video (as some sites do). Otherwise, iPhone/iPad guests will be staring at a blank page.

Of course, all this power comes at a price. You need Adobe Flash or a similar program, like Swish (*www.swishzone.com*), Toon Boom (*www.toonboom.com*), or Anime Studio (*http://anime.smithmicro.com*) to produce full-fledged videos. And although these programs aren't necessarily difficult to get started with, they represent one more expense and one more technology you have to learn.

> **NOTE** Creating external videos, animations, and applications is an art (and a book or two) unto itself. This chapter is a guide to *inserting* these goodies into your web page and assumes that a cheerful programmer near you has already *created* them. For the full scoop on creating Flash files, pick up a copy of *Flash CS6: The Missing Manual* by Chris Grover.

FREQUENTLY ASKED QUESTION

Is Flash Still Important?

I hear that Flash is dead. Is that true?

When Apple famously announced that it wouldn't ever support Flash on the iPhone or iPad, many people believed that was the beginning of the end for Flash. In many ways, it was. While Adobe still promotes Flash, they've developed a new tool, Adobe Edge Animate, to create animations using HTML5, CSS, and JavaScript. See page 701 for details on using Animate compositions in your web pages.

As explained at the beginning of this chapter, the latest browsers can play audio and video without the assistance of the Flash plug-in. Likewise, faster computers and browsers now make it possible to create slick animations using JavaScript only. Sites like Google's HTML5 Rocks (*www.html5rocks.com*) demonstrate the kinds of highly interactive experiences available in the latest crop of browsers.

And while a Flash-less future may be here one day, right now Flash is still useful in some cases. HTML5's <video> and <audio> tags are exciting, but Microsoft's still-popular Internet Explorer 8 browser doesn't understand them, and thus can't play video or audio files embedded that way. In addition, different browsers support different video formats, so while you can use the high-quality H.264 video format in Safari, Chrome, and Internet Explorer 9 and above, you need to use a different format for Firefox and Opera. In other words, using the <video> tags means you need to create three versions of your video for it to work in common browsers.

In a nutshell, it may not be the best time to take on a career as a Flash programmer. In addition, if you need to build sites that are accessible on mobile devices (including the popular iPhone and iPad), you probably want to stay away from Flash. However, in some cases, including video, Flash still has a role to play...for now.

Insert a Flash Animation

To add a Flash animation to a page, position your cursor where you want the animation to appear and then choose Insert→Media→Flash SWF (.swf is the file extension for Flash animations) or, in the Media category of the Insert panel, choose Flash SWF from the Media menu (Figure 15-11). Either way, you'll see the Select File dialog box. Navigate to the Flash file you want to embed (look for the .swf extension) and double-click it. Dreamweaver automatically recognizes the width and height of the animation and generates the appropriate HTML to embed it in your page. You'll see a gray rectangular placeholder with the Flash logo in the center; you can adjust the animation's settings as described in the next section.

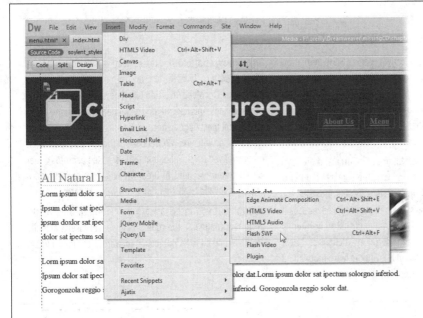

FIGURE 15-11

*You can use either the
Insert menu (pictured)
or the Insert panel to
add media to your web
page. When you use
the Insert menu, go to
Insert→Media→Flash
SWF to add a Flash
animation; go to
Insert→Media→Flash
Video to add a video and
playback controls (see
page 697).*

TIP You can also drag a Flash animation from the Files panel into the document window. Dreamweaver automatically adds the correct code.

When you insert a Flash animation, an Object Tag Accessibility Options window opens. It lets you set options intended to make accessing Flash content easier, but they don't really work in most browsers. If you don't want to set these options, just click Cancel, and Dreamweaver still inserts the Flash animation. To permanently turn off this window, open the Preferences window (Edit→Preferences [Dreamweaver→Preferences]), click the Accessibility category, and then turn off the Media checkbox.

When you save a web page after inserting a Flash animation, Dreamweaver pops up a dialog box informing you that it needs to save two files on your site—*expressInstall.swf* and *swfobject_modified.js*. These files make it possible to notify Flash-less visitors (and those with older versions of the program) that they need to download the current Flash plug-in (see page 695 for details).

Change Animation Properties

You'll rarely have to change the default properties Dreamweaver assigns Flash animations. But if you do—say you resize an animation and want to change it back to its original size, or you want to swap in a different animation altogether—the Properties panel is the place to go.

The Two Lives of the <object> Tag

If you choose View→Code after you insert a Flash animation, you may be surprised by the amount of HTML Dreamweaver deposits in your page. You may also encounter some HTML tags you've never heard of, including <object> and <param>. These tags provide browsers with the information they need to launch the Flash player and play a Flash animation.

Due to differences between Internet Explorer and all other browsers, Dreamweaver has to insert the <object> tag twice: once for IE (with all the proper settings for that browser) and once for the other browsers. To do this, Dreamweaver uses IE conditional statements—HTML comments that only Internet Explorer understands—to send special instructions to just IE (and even to specific versions of IE). You can learn more about conditional comments at *http://tinyurl.com/9osegt*.

Dreamweaver started using the <object> tag like this in Dreamweaver CS4. It replaces the old way of embedding Flash animations, which involved inserting two tags, the <object> and the <embed> tags. This new method is standards-compliant, which means that most pages where you use Dreamweaver CC to add an animation will pass W3C validation (the same validator that Dreamweaver's W3C Validation tool uses; see page 753). That wasn't true in versions of Dreamweaver prior to CS4, which produced invalid HTML that failed the W3C validator.

Ironically, if you insert a Flash animation into an HTML5 document (page xx), the code Dreamweaver inserts actually produces invalid HTML5! One step forward, two steps back.

■ PLAY YOUR ANIMATION

On Windows computers you can play your Flash animation right within Design view. In the Properties panel, click the Play button to start the animation (at which point the Play button becomes a Stop button). Once you have the video playing, the page's interactive features, like buttons, will operate. Of course, you can also check out your page's Flash animation in Live view or by using the "File→Preview in browser" command. On Macs, you need to use File→Preview in Browser to view your Flash animation. Naturally, you'll also need to have a browser with the Flash Player plug-in installed.

■ RENAME YOUR ANIMATION

Just as JavaScript can control images and buttons, so it can control Flash animations. Dreamweaver assigns a generic name to each animation you embed—*FlashID, FlashID2, FlashID3*, and so on. This act of naming your animation is important—the auto-install option discussed on page 695 requires a name—but the exact name isn't critical. If you want, you can change it in the Name field, the box directly below "SWF" at the top-left of the Properties panel (see Figure 15-12). But there's no real need to since no one visiting the page will ever see it.

■ REPLACE YOUR ANIMATION

The File field specifies your animation's location on your hard drive. To swap out the current animation, type a new path into the File field or click the nearby folder icon and browse to the new animation.

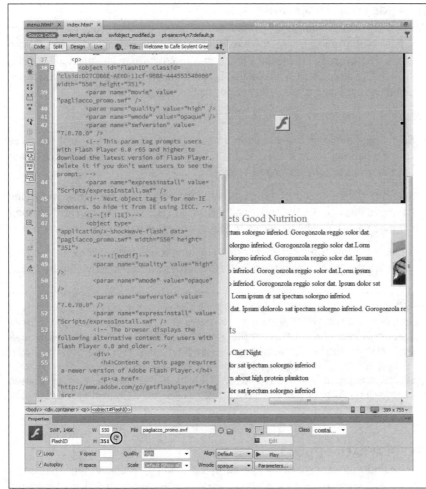

FIGURE 15-12

*Use the Properties panel
to set the display and
playback controls for a
Flash animation. Avoid the
V space, H space, and Align
settings because you'll use
CSS to handle those same
formatting options. The
Reset size button (circled)
can get you out of a jam;
see below.*

■ SET THE SRC PROPERTY

The Src field indicates the location of your original Flash file (the one with the .fla extension). When you first insert a Flash animation, the Src box is blank. If you think you'll want to edit the original Flash file, tell Dreamweaver where to find it.

To do that, click the Edit button in the Properties panel. Dreamweaver asks you to locate the original file, the one with the .fla extension. Double-click it and Dreamweaver launches the Flash program and opens the file for editing. Make any changes you wish (or not) and, in Flash, click Done. Flash exports the updated .swf file to your site, replacing the previous version of the animation. In addition, the Src property box now points to your original .fla file. That way, if you need to work on the animation in the future, you just press the Edit button. Dreamweaver launches Flash, and it opens your original animation for editing.

■ CHANGE YOUR ANIMATION'S SIZE

Enlarging GIF or JPEG images by dragging their edges usually results in a pixellated mess, but if you use Flash's vector-based tools to create your animation, you can scale it nicely. However, if the Flash animation contains bitmap images, such as GIFs, PNGs, JPEGs, or embedded video, leave the animation at its original size. If you resize an animation that has bitmaps, the images distort and pixellate.

To resize an animation, do one of the following:

- Select the animation in the document window and then drag one of the three resizing handles at its edges. To maintain the animation's proportions, press Shift as you drag the lower-right corner.

- Select the animation in the document window and then type new width and height values into the Properties panel's W and H boxes. You can also use percentage values, in which case your animation scales to fit the browser window.

If you make a complete mess of your page by resizing your animation beyond recognition, just click the Reset Size button in the Properties panel (circled in Figure 15-12).

NOTE If you want to insert a Flash animation that fills 100% of a browser window, you first need to set the animation's height and width to 100%. Then you need to create a few CSS styles. First, create a tag style for the <body> tag with the *padding* (page 161) and *margin* (page 161) values set to *0*, and the *height* and *width* (page 438) values set to 100%. Next, create a style for the <html> tag with the same settings as the <body> tag (a group selector—discussed on page xxii—makes the process of creating the styles more efficient). If the Flash animation is nested within other tags, like a <div> or a <p> tag, you need to remove the padding and margin for those tags and set their heights and widths to 100% as well. Finally, choose an appropriate Scaling setting for the animation, as discussed on the next page.

■ SET PLAYBACK OPTIONS

The Loop and Autoplay checkboxes control animation playback. When you turn on Loop, the animation plays over and over endlessly, an approach advertisers often use in animated banner ads. The Autoplay option starts playback as soon as the page loads in a browser.

However, neither of these options overrides any programming instructions you embed in the Flash animation. So if you added a Stop command to the final frame of your animation, the animation stops at that frame regardless of the Loop setting.

■ LEAVE MARGINS UNSPECIFIED

Skip the V space and H space settings in the Properties panel. They're intended to add space to the top and bottom (V) and the left and right (H) edges of your animation, but they produce invalid code for the HTML 4.01 strict and HTML5 document types (see page xx for more on doctypes). In addition, you can't control each of the four margins individually.

Instead, use Cascading Style Sheets and the CSS *margin* property (discussed on page 439) to add space around your animation. You can create an ID style (page 102) using the animation's name. For example, you might create an ID style named *#FlashID*.

■ SELECT A QUALITY SETTING

If your Flash animation requires a lot of processing muscle—if it's heavy on animation and action, for example—it may overwhelm older computers, making playback slow and choppy. Not every computer has a 3-gigahertz processor and 16 gigabytes of memory (not yet, anyway). Until that day, you may need to adjust the quality settings of your Flash animation so it looks good on all computers.

By default, Dreamweaver sets the animation quality to High, but you can choose any of the following four settings from the Quality menu in the Properties panel:

- **High** provides the best quality, but the animation may run slower on older computers.

- **Low** looks terrible. This setting sacrifices quality by eliminating all *antialiasing* (edge-smoothing) in an animation, leaving harsh, jaggy lines on the edges of every image. Animations set to low quality look bad on *all* computers, so pass it by.

- **Auto Low** forces the animation to start in low-quality mode, but switches automatically to high-quality playback if the visitor's computer is fast enough.

- **Auto High** makes the animation switch to low-quality mode only if the visitor's computer requires it. This way, you can deliver a high-quality image to most visitors, while still letting those with slow computers view the animation. This mode is the best choice if you want to provide a high-quality image but still make your animation play back at reasonable speed for those with older computers.

■ ADJUST YOUR ANIMATION'S SCALE

Scaling only becomes an issue when you specify *relative* dimensions for your animation, setting its size to, say, 90% of the width of a browser window. That's because the animation grows or shrinks as your visitor's browser grows or shrinks, and you have no control over what your visitors does with her browser—one person may prefer a small horizontal browser at the bottom of her screen, while another may use a tall, narrow window.

Enter Dreamweaver's Scale property. It lets you determine *how* Flash scales your animation. For example, in Figure 15-13, the top animation's original size is 334 pixels high by 113 pixels wide. If you resize the animation using the W and H attributes so that it's *350* pixels high and 113 pixels wide, one of three things will happen, depending on your Scale setting:

- **Show All.** This setting, the default, maintains the original aspect ratio (proportions) of your animation (second from top in Figure 15-13). In other words, although the overall *size* of the animation may change as a visitor fusses with his browser, its width-to-height ratio won't. Show All keeps your animation from distorting (but it may also cause white borders on the top, bottom, or either side of your animation; to hide the borders, make the animation's background color the same color as your web page).

- **No Border.** This setting resizes an animation according to your specifications *and* maintains its aspect ratio, but it may also crop the sides of the animation. Notice how the top and bottom of the Chia Vet logo are chopped off in Figure 15-13, third image from the top.

- **Exact Fit.** This option may stretch your animation's picture either horizontally or vertically. In Figure 15-13, bottom, "Chia Vet" is stretched wider than normal.

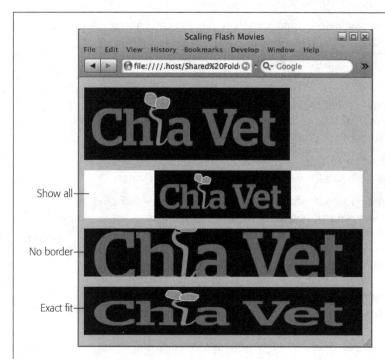

Show all—

No border—

Exact fit—

FIGURE 15-13

This browser window shows the results of choosing different settings in the Properties panel's Scale menu. A Flash animation's Scale property specifies how an animation resizes when you set its width and height properties to something different from the original. If you resize an animation, press F12 (Option-F12) to see how it looks in a web browser, and then, if necessary, choose a different setting from the Scale drop-down menu.

■ ALIGN YOUR ANIMATION

You can align Flash animations relative to the paragraphs around them just as you can align images relative to the surrounding text. In fact, the Properties panel's animation alignment options work exactly the same way as its text alignment properties. For example, when you choose Right from the Align menu, Dreamweaver positions the animation at the right edge of the screen and wraps text around its left side. (If the animation is inside a cell, Align→Right moves the animation to the right edge of the cell.) However, for strict document types and HTML5, the Align property is invalid. As with the margin settings discussed above, you're better off using CSS properties, such as the *float* property described on page 426.

■ BACKGROUND COLOR

To set a background color for a Flash animation, use the Bg Color box in the Properties panel. This color overrides any background color set in the animation itself, and becomes the animation's placeholder color when a page has loaded but the animation hasn't.

■ WMODE

Wmode stands for "Window mode" and it controls how your animation interacts with other HTML elements on the page. The standard setting, *opaque*, is useful when you include HTML that needs to appear on top of an animation—the classic example is a drop-down menu like the ones you learned about on page 190. The opaque setting ensures that the drop-down menu appears on top of the Flash animation. The *transparent* option lets HTML appear above an animation, too, but it also lets any HTML *underneath* the animation—like a page's background color—show through any transparent areas of the animation.

Finally, the *window* option is the exact opposite of the opaque option: It makes sure a Flash animation always appears above any HTML element on a page—even above a drop-down navigation menu that would normally appear over the animation.

■ Automate the Flash Download

Even though the Flash plug-in is nearly universal, you can't be sure that every visitor's browser has it. In addition, you may have created a Flash animation or video that runs only in the latest version of the plug-in, so a visitor might have the Flash plug-in, but not the correct *version* of it. The result? A video that either doesn't play back at all or doesn't play back as it should. Guests who fall into this category have to choose from three equally unpalatable options: Go to a different website to download the plug-in, skip the multimedia show (if you've built a second, plug-in-free version of your site), or skip your website entirely.

Fortunately, Dreamweaver provides a built-in solution for the playback scenarios mentioned above. When you embed a video in a web page, Dreamweaver includes code that detects your visitor's browser plug-ins. If a visitor either doesn't have the Flash plug-in or doesn't have the right version of it, the page displays a message alerting the visitor (see Figure 15-14) and offering a button (labeled "Get Adobe Flash Player") that takes guests to the plug-in download. If your visitor has at least version 6 of the plug-in, she can take advantage of its "express install" feature, which lets her upgrade to the latest version with just a mouse click.

You won't see the "missing Flash file" message in Design view; Dreamweaver keeps it hidden. But you can see and edit it by clicking the eye icon (circled in Figure 15-14).

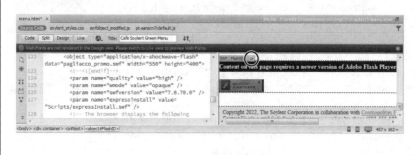

FIGURE 15-14

Here's the message a web browser displays if a visitor doesn't have the Flash player installed, has an old version of it, or is viewing the page on a device that doesn't support Flash (like an iPhone or an iPad). You can customize this message, but it's a good idea to leave the Flash player icon in place—it includes a link to Adobe.com, where your visitor can download the player.

NOTE Make sure you edit the message that appears when the Adobe plug-in isn't available. It assumes that you can download and install the Flash player. Mobile devices that don't support Flash (like the iPhone and iPad) will display this same message, and telling visitors to download software that won't run on their device is just rude. Instead, change the message to something like "Your browser either doesn't support the Flash plug-in or you need to download a newer version of it to see this content."

To make all this happen, Dreamweaver adds two files to your website, both of them inside a folder named Scripts: *expressInstall.swf* and *swfobject_modified.js*. When you move your finished web pages and Flash video to your web server (see Chapter 18), be sure to move the Scripts folder as well.

■ Add Flash Videos

In addition to playing back animations and hosting games, the Flash player plays back videos, too. In fact, *Flash Video*, as this feature is called, is still probably the most common way to play video on the Web. If you've visited a little site called YouTube, you've seen Flash Video in action. High among this format's advantages—compared to competing standards like QuickTime and Windows Media Video—is that you can reasonably count on every visitor having the new Flash browser plug-in to view your videos.

Dreamweaver makes it a snap to embed videos. Unfortunately, Flash can't play back videos in just any old format, like MPEG or AVI, without a little help. And Dreamweaver can't transform videos in these formats to the Flash Video format (which has the extension .flv). Instead, you need to use the Adobe Media Encoder, which you get when you install Flash CC, Premiere CC, or After Effects CC. If you have an older, 32-bit Windows computer, you may not see any of these programs listed in your Creative Cloud panel, because they won't run on your computer. You need to use the older Adobe Media Encoder CS6, which you can download from Adobe at *http://tinyurl. com/m29nv3u.*

NOTE For a quick intro to creating Flash videos, visit *http://tinyurl.com/63lkad9.* Adobe also dedicates an entire section of their site to Flash video: *www.adobe.com/devnet/video.*

Fortunately, creating the .flv file is the hard part. Dreamweaver makes the rest easy. Follow these few simple steps to inserts a Flash video into your page, complete with DVD-like playback controls.

1. **Click the place on the page where you want to insert the video.**

   Like other Flash videos, you'll want an open area of your page.

2. **Choose Insert→Media→Flash Video.**

   Or, from the Common category of the Insert panel, select FLV from the Media menu, and the Insert FLV window appears (see Figure 15-15). You can also just drag the .flv file from the Files panel onto the document window.

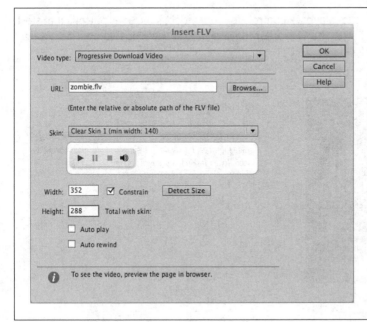

FIGURE 15-15

The Insert FLV window makes it easy to add video to your website. To play the video, all your visitors need is the Flash player, which in many cases comes preinstalled with their browser.

3. **Select Progressive Download Video from the "Video type" menu.**

   Dreamweaver provides two download options, the one above and Streaming Video. The latter requires you to have some expensive software (a Flash server) or a Flash video-streaming service, which can run you anywhere from $10 a month to a couple of hundred dollars a month. Streaming video is usually reserved for live events or to handle very large numbers of viewers. That's why websites for TV networks like ABC.com use streaming servers—it's an efficient way to distribute video when thousands of people watch the same video at the same time.

   If you choose Progressive Download, your video doesn't have to download completely before it begins playing back, so viewers don't have to wait, say, 30 minutes while your 40 MB video downloads. Instead, the video starts as soon as the first section of the file arrives on their machine, and plays back as the rest of the video downloads. That's how YouTube videos work.

4. **Click the Browse button and select the Flash video file (.flv) you want to add to the page.**

   Due to differences in how operating systems work, you're best off putting your Flash video file in the same folder as your web page. If you want to put it elsewhere (in a dedicated Flash video folder, for instance, or even on a different web server), use absolute links (see page 170).

5. **Select a skin.**

   A *skin* is a set of playback controls for your video; it includes buttons that start, pause, and stop the video; a progress bar; and various volume-adjustment controls (see Figure 15-16).

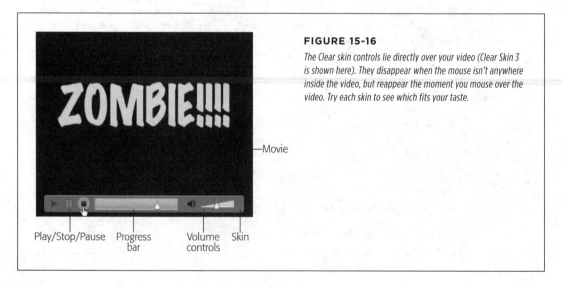

FIGURE 15-16

The Clear skin controls lie directly over your video (Clear Skin 3 is shown here). They disappear when the mouse isn't anywhere inside the video, but reappear the moment you mouse over the video. Try each skin to see which fits your taste.

Movie

Play/Stop/Pause   Progress bar   Volume controls   Skin

Dreamweaver adds the controls to your video, and offers nine styles—actually, three types of controllers, each with three different graphical styles.

6. **Click the Detect Size button.**

Flash videos contain *metadata*—information embedded inside the file that describes its features, like its dimensions, file size, and so on. The Flash video encoder adds this metadata when you create a video. Clicking the Detect Size button extracts the video's width and height measurements, adds the width and height of the playback controls, and then automatically fills in the width and height boxes in the Insert FLV window (see Figure 15-16).

If, for whatever reason, your file doesn't include metadata, you have to enter the width and height values yourself—these settings specify how much space the video occupies on your page. Note that entering these dimensions won't actually distort your video—making it really, really thin or really, really wide, for example. No matter what size you enter, Dreamweaver preserves the original aspect ratio of your video, and adds extra, empty space to fill any area not occupied by it. For example, say your video is 352 pixels wide and 288 pixels tall. If you enter a dimension of 100 x 288, respectively, the video won't stretch like you're watching it in a fun-house mirror. Instead, the video appears 100 pixels wide and 82 pixels tall, with 53 pixels of blank space above and below it.

7. **If you want, turn on the Autoplay checkbox.**

Doing so makes the video play as soon as enough video data's been downloaded from the Web. Otherwise, a visitor has to press the play button to begin the video.

8. **If you want, turn on the "Auto rewind" checkbox.**

After playback, your video automatically "rewinds" to the first frame if you turn on this checkbox. But you may not always want to abide by the old video-store credo "Be Kind, Rewind." If your video ends with a dramatic message—"Stay tuned for the next exciting installment of Blind Mole Rats from Mars!"—you might prefer to leave the video on its last frame when it's complete.

9. **Click OK to add the Flash video to your page.**

This step installs the necessary code not only for the video, but for detecting the Flash plug-in as well (described on page 695). You can check out the newly inserted video by pressing F12 (Option-F12) to preview the page in a browser.

> **NOTE** When you upload your web page and Flash video to your site (see Chapter 18), you need to upload four additional files that Dreamweaver secretly adds: the two files (and the *Scripts* folder) discussed on page 696, the file *FLVPlayer_progressive.swf* and the .swf (Flash video) file for the skin you selected. That last file is named after the skin you chose—for example, *Clear_Skin_1.swf*. Save yourself some work: When uploading your Flash-filled web page (uploading details are on page 776), choose to include "dependent files;" that way, Dreamweaver grabs these three files for you.

Using Flash as an HTML5 Video Fallback Option

Someday everyone will be using web browsers that know how to play video without the help of a plug-in like Flash. Sadly, that day is not quite here. In the meantime, web developers need to make decisions about how to support visitors who still use older web browsers. The first question to ask is, Who is my audience? If the subject of your site is cutting-edge technology and gadgets, your visitors are likely to have up-to-date browsers. You may not need to worry about supporting older ones. However, if you have a site that discusses the virtues of reverse mortgages, you may be catering to an older audience, and maybe you need to accommodate older versions of Internet Explorer.

First here's a list of the browsers that can play HTML5 video, and therefore don't need a Flash fallback option:

- Internet Explorer 9 +
- Firefox 3.5 +
- Safari 4 +
- Opera 10.5 +
- Chrome

Your HTML5 video will also play well with most smartphones and tablets. That said, the biggest concern may be web visitors who still use Internet Explorer 8. (According to StatCounter, about 11% of U.S. web traffic used IE8 in the 12-month period from October 2012 through September 2013.)

To accommodate the older browsers on desktop computers, you can provide a Flash video fallback. The browsers need to have the Flash plug-in installed, but that's the case with over 90% of desktop browsers. Produce your Flash video and publish it to a SWF file. Copy the SWF and FLV files to your website's Files panel. Follow the steps on page 680 for adding HTML5 video. When you reach Step 6, where you add Alt Source 1 and Alt Source 2 video clips, you can add one more option. In the Properties panel's Flash Fallback box, identify the SWF file for the Flash video. You can use the folder button to browse to the file or you can use the file picker tool that looks like a gun site (see Figure 15-17).

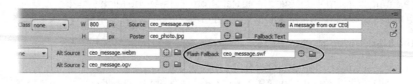

FIGURE 15-17

If you think your web visitors may be using older browsers that don't support HTML5 video, you can use Flash Video as a fallback option. In the Properties panel, after you insert the video using the Insert panel's HTML5 option, name the Flash fallback file (.swf) for your clip. Older desktop browsers will play the Flash file as long as you have the Flash plug-in installed.

■ Adding Adobe Edge Animate Animations

When Apple decided not to support Flash on its extremely popular iPhones and iPads, it created ripples throughout the Web world, but it created a tsunami over at Adobe. The writing was on the wall—HTML5 was poised to take over at least a portion of the interactive duties that Flash used to handle. As the earlier sections of this chapter explained, HTML5's new <audio> and <video> tags make it easy to add sound and video to your pages, no Flash plug-in or downloads needed for those with up-to-date browsers. But what about Flash's other area of Web dominance—animation? Apple's response was that non-proprietary technologies like HTML, CSS, JavaScript, and jQuery can create moving text and graphics. That's true, but just about everyone, except Apple, agrees that the animation capabilities of JavaScript and jQuery don't quite match the snappy response you get with Flash. However, Adobe didn't simply argue the merits of Flash. It created a tool for developing animation using HTML, CSS, JavaScript, and jQuery. The result is Adobe Edge Animate.

If you're a jQuery and CSS whiz, you can animate elements on the page by writing code. That's a lot of work and it's not much help for most designers—they're more comfortable with the kind of tools you find in Photoshop, Illustrator, Dreamweaver, and Flash. That's where Animate comes in. Using familiar tools for drawing, adding text, and specifying colors, designers can put their ideas in motion (Figure 15-18). Animate uses a Properties panel similar to the one in Dreamweaver and a timeline similar to the one in After Effects, Premiere, and Flash to work. In short, you arrange text, photos, and other graphics on an Edge Animate "stage." Change the elements over the course of time and the program rewrites the HTML, CSS, and JavaScript. (Part of the Adobe's Creative Cloud, Animate gets regular updates, adding features and making it easier to use.)

So, what does all this mean for web developers using Dreamweaver? First of all, if you're interested in web animation, you may want to dip your toe in the Edge Animate waters. Secondly, Dreamweaver streamlines the process of adding animations to your pages. An Animate animation comprises several files that arrive in a single file with the *.oam* extension. These project files are sort of like ZIP files—Animate compresses several files and then packaged them into a single file to make it easy to move them from one computer to another. When you add an Animate project file to your web page, Dreamweaver automatically opens the project file, extracts the individual files that make up the animation, and stores them in a folder on your site. It's actually easier than adding a Flash file to your project. Here are the individual steps:

1. **Click a spot on your page where you want to add the Edge Animate animation.**

    Placing an animation on a page is like placing a still image or a video. You want to consider the element's importance to the subject matter. After you add the animation, you can use CSS to add margins, padding, and to position it in relation to text and other page elements.

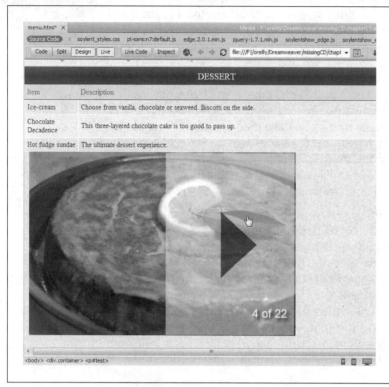

FIGURE 15-18

Edge Animate created this interactive slideshow. It uses HTML, CSS, and JavaScript/jQuery to work its magic. Animate can handle many of the interactive chores that were the exclusive domain of Flash.

2. **Open the Insert panel by clicking its tab or choosing Window→Insert. At the top of the Insert panel, choose the Media category.**

   When Dreamweaver displays the Media category in the Insert panel, you find Edge Animate Composition at the top of the list (Animate calls its projects "compositions"—how high-falutin!).

3. **Click Edge Animate Composition, browse to find the Animate project file you want, and then click OK (Open).**

   Animate project files have the .oam extension. You don't need to store the file in your website folder, because Dreamweaver extracts the files it needs, creates a folder in your website, and puts all the needed files inside. In fact, you may be surprised at the number of files that make up an Animate composition. See Figure 15-19.

4. **Click the Live view button in the document window to view your animation on the page.**

   You can see Edge Animate projects in Live view because they're made up entirely of HTML, CSS, and JavaScript code. The Live view display engine uses the same technology as Google Chrome, so it has no problem showing you Animate compositions on the page.

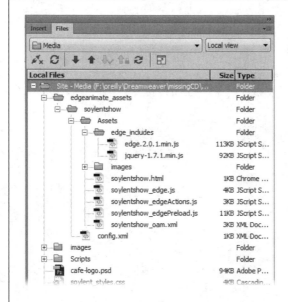

FIGURE 15-19

When you use the Insert panel to add an Edge animation to your page, you identify a single, compressed "project" file (with the .oam extension) that includes all the files the animation requires. Dreamweaver unpacks the file, putting the contents in an edge-animate_assets folder on your website. You'll find files and folders like the ones shown here inside that file. They include JavaScript, jQuery, and HTML files, as well as any other resources the project needs, such as the .jpg files used in this slideshow.

Once you embed the animation in your web page, you see just a few properties in the Properties panel: ID, Class, W (width), and H (Height). All of them work as you'd expect. For example, Animate gives your project the ID "EdgeID." You can change that to something more meaningful if you want. You can also use the ID as a selector in CSS Designer to create styles and to format the project and position it on the page. The same is true of the project's class property. (See page 108 for details on using CSS and classes.) The W and H properties let you change the width and height of the animation, but keep in mind that it's possible to distort the image using these properties.

When you add an Animate project to your website, Dreamweaver creates an *edge-animate_assets* folder. You'll find other folders and files inside of it. For example, if you added a project file called *soylentshow.oam* in step 3 above, Animate creates a *soylentshow* folder in the *edgeanimate_assets* folder. Within that, you'll find HTML and JavaScript files, an *images* folder, and an *edge_includes* folder. You don't need to do anything to these folders or files—but don't move or delete them, either. If you do, your animation won't work. When it comes time to move files to your web server, Dreamweaver takes care of moving the necessary files over.

NOTE Interested in learning more about Edge Animate? Check out *Adobe Edge Animate: The Missing Manual* by Chris Grover. Why does that name sound familiar?

Managing a Website

Introducing Site Management

A s the dull-sounding name *site management* implies, organizing and tracking your website's files is one of the least glamorous, most time-consuming, error-prone aspects of being a web designer. On the Web, your site may look beautiful, run smoothly, and appear as a gloriously unified whole, but behind the scenes, it's nothing more than a collection of various files—HTML pages, images, Cascading Style Sheets, JavaScript code, Flash movies, and so on—that must all work together. The more files you have to keep track of, the more apt you are to misplace one. And a single broken link or missing graphic can interfere with the operation of your entire site, causing personal—even professional—embarrassment.

Fortunately, computers excel at tedious organizational tasks. Dreamweaver's site management features take care of the complexities of dealing with a website's many files, freeing you to concentrate on the creative aspects of the site. In fact, even if you're a hand-coding HTML junkie and you turn your nose up at all visual web page editors, you may find Dreamweaver worth its weight in gold just for the features described in this and the next two chapters.

The first three parts of this book described how to create, lay out, and embellish your site. This part offers a bird's-eye view of the production process as you see your site through to completion and, ultimately, put it up on the Internet.

To get the most out of Dreamweaver's site management features, you need to be familiar with some basic principles for organizing web files.

◾ The Structure of a Website

When you build a website, you probably spend hours adding carefully planned links, helpful labels, and clear, informative navigation tools. You want your *site architecture*—the structure of your site—to make it easy for visitors to understand where they are, where they can go, and how to return to where they just came from (see Figure 16-1). Behind the scenes, it's equally important to organize your site files with just as much clarity and care, so you can find *your* way around when you want to update or modify the site. And, just as on your computer, a website's main organizational tool is the humble *folder*.

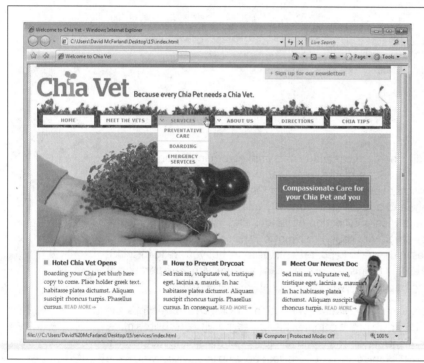

FIGURE 16-1

A good site (even a made-up one) has an easy-to-understand structure. It divides content into logical sections, and includes a prominent navigation bar—the row of buttons below the Chia Vet logo in this image—to give visitors quick access to that content. When you build a site, its "architecture" provides a useful model for creating and naming the behind-the-scenes folders that hold the site's files.

You probably organize files on your computer every day, creating, say, a folder called Personal, within which are folders called Financial Planning and Vacation Pictures. Inside the Vacation Pictures folder, you might have separate folders for memories of Maui, Yosemite, and the Mall of America.

The same principle applies to the folders that make up a website: All websites have one primary folder—the *root folder*—and that folder usually contains additional folders where you further subdivide and organize your site's files. Collectively, the root folder and its subfolders hold all of a site's web pages, graphics, and other files.

A sensible structure (see Figure 16-2) makes it easy to maintain your site because it's logically organized—it gives you quick access to whatever graphic, style sheet, or movie you're looking for. But don't fall into the trap of becoming so obsessed with bins that you put every graphic or web page in its own folder; adding structure to your site should make your job easier, not harder.

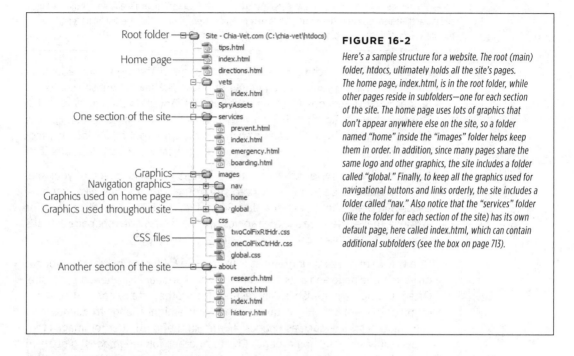

FIGURE 16-2

Here's a sample structure for a website. The root (main) folder, htdocs, ultimately holds all the site's pages. The home page, index.html, is in the root folder, while other pages reside in subfolders—one for each section of the site. The home page uses lots of graphics that don't appear anywhere else on the site, so a folder named "home" inside the "images" folder helps keep them in order. In addition, since many pages share the same logo and other graphics, the site includes a folder called "global." Finally, to keep all the graphics used for navigational buttons and links orderly, the site includes a folder called "nav." Also notice that the "services" folder (like the folder for each section of the site) has its own default page, here called index.html, which can contain additional subfolders (see the box on page 713).

NOTE If you already have a website that suffers from lack of organization, it's not too late. Dreamweaver can help you reorganize your files quickly and accurately. Take the following rules to heart and then turn to "Managing Files and Folders" on page 28.

Here, then, are some guidelines for effective site organization:

- **Plan for future growth.** Like ever-spreading grapevines, websites grow. Today you may have only enough words and pictures for 10 pages, but tomorrow you'll put the finishing touches on your new 1,000-page online catalog. It may seem like overkill to create a lot of folders for a small site, but better to start with a solid structure today than find yourself knee-deep in files tomorrow.

  For instance, it's useful to create separate folders for graphics that appear within each section of the site. If a section of your site is dedicated to promoting your company's products, for example, create a folder called *products* for your product web pages. Create an additional subfolder called *images* to store the pictures of those products. Then, when you add more products or images, you know right where to put them.

NOTE While you can start with no organizational plan and later use Dreamweaver to bring your site into shape (see page 28), you may run into unforeseen problems if your site has been up and running for a while. That's because search engines may have already indexed your site, and other websites may have linked to your pages. If you suddenly rearrange your site, people who try to access your site from a search engine may be foiled, and those cherished links from the outside world may no longer work. If that's the case, you're better off leaving the site as it is, and begin the organization process with new files only.

- **Follow the site's architecture.** Take advantage of the work you've already done in organizing your site's content. For instance, the Chia Vet site content is divided into five sections: Meet the Vets, Services, About Us, Directions, and Chia Tips, as shown in Figure 16-1. Following this structure, it makes sense to create folders—*vets, services, about*, and so on—in the site's root folder for each section's respective web pages. If one section is particularly large, add subfolders.

- **Organize files by type.** After you create folders for each section of your site, you'll probably need to add folders to store other types of files, like graphics, Cascading Style Sheets, external JavaScript files, and PDF files. Most sites, for instance, make extensive use of graphics, with several images per page. If that's the case for you, file those images neatly and efficiently.

  One way to organize your graphics is to create a folder for images that appear on your home page and another for images that appear elsewhere on your site. Often, the home page is visually distinct from other site pages and contains graphics that are not only unique to it, but which might change frequently. You can create a folder—such as *images_home*—in the root folder for images that appear only on your home page. Create another folder—*images_global*—to store graphics that appear on all or most of the other pages, like the company logo, navigation buttons, and other frequently used icons. When you add these images to other pages on your site, you'll know to look for them in this folder. Alternatively, you could create an *images* folder in the root of your site and add subfolders such as *home, global*, and *nav* (see Figure 16-2). The choice of an organizational system is yours; just make sure you have one.

- **Use understandable names.** While file names like *1a.gif, zDS.html*, and *f.css* are compact, they aren't very obvious. Make sure your file names mean something. Clear, descriptive names like *site_logo.gif* or *directions.html* make it a lot easier to locate files and update pages.

  This principle is especially important if you work as part of a team. If you're constantly explaining to coworkers that *345g.gif* is the banner for the home page, changing the file name to *home_banner.gif* could save you some aggravation. There's a tradeoff here, however, as long file names can waste precious bytes, bloating your pages and slowing down load time. For instance, a site full of file names like *this_is_the_image_that_goes_in_the_upper_right_corner_of_the_home_page.gif* is probably not a good idea.

NOTE Dreamweaver employs the industry-standard .html extension for web pages—as in *index.html*. Another common extension is .htm (a holdover from the days when Windows could handle only three-letter extensions). It doesn't really matter which you use, and if you're used to .htm, you can easily change the extension Dreamweaver uses. Just choose Edit→Preferences (Dreamweaver→Preferences) to open the Preferences window, select the New Document category, and then type *.htm* in the default extension box.

It's also helpful to add a prefix to related files. For example, use *nav_* at the beginning of a graphic name to indicate that it's a navigation button. This way, you can quickly identify *nav_projects.png*, *nav_quiz.png*, and *nav_horoscopes. png* as graphics used in a page's navigation bar, or *bg_body.png* and *bg_column.png* as graphics used as backgrounds. As a bonus, when you view the files on your computer or in Dreamweaver's Files panel (see Figure 16-3), they appear neatly sorted by name; in other words, all the *nav_* files cluster together in the file list. Likewise, if you have rollover versions of your navigation graphics, give them names like *nav_projects_hover.gif* or *nav_horoscopes_h.gif* to indicate that they're the highlighted (or rollover) state of the navigation button. (If you use Fireworks, its button-creation tools automatically use names like *nav_projects_f1.gif* and *nav_projects_f2.gif* to indicate two different versions of the same button.)

And, as mentioned in "Naming Your Files and Folders" on page 28, to make sure your files work on any web server, stick to letters, numbers, hyphens (-), and the underscore (_) character in file and folder names.

- **Be consistent.** Once you come up with an organization that works for you, follow it. Always. If you name one folder *images*, for instance, don't name another *graphics* and a third *pretty_pictures*. And certainly don't put web pages in a folder named *images* or JavaScript files in a folder named *style_sheets*.

  In fact, if you work on more than one website, you may want to use a single naming convention and folder structure for all your sites, so that switching from one project to another goes more smoothly. If you name all your graphics folders *images*, then no matter what site you're working on, you know where to look for GIFs, PNGs, and JPEGs.

NOTE It's usually best to put only files that make up your website in the root folder and its subfolders. Keep your source files—the original Photoshop, Fireworks, Flash, or Word documents—stored elsewhere on your computer. That way, you're much less likely to accidentally transfer a 14.5 MB Photoshop file to your web server (a move that would *not* gain you friends in the IT department). That said, if you do like keeping all your files together, check out Dreamweaver's *cloaking* feature (described on page 782). Using it, you can prevent Dreamweaver from transferring certain file types to your web server when you use the program's FTP feature.

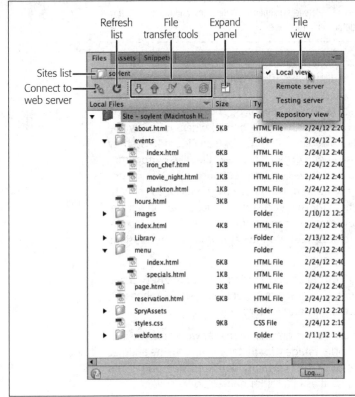

Refresh
list

File
transfer tools

Expand
panel

File
view

FIGURE 16-3

Dreamweaver's Files panel, logically enough, lists files in the currently active website. A list of all the websites you defined in Dreamweaver appears on the Sites drop-down menu. To work on a different site, select its name from the list (but be aware that you could inadvertently select files on your local drive, potentially tripping up Dreamweaver's site management tools—see the box on page 33 for details). You can use the Files panel to connect to a web server and transfer files back and forth between your local and remote sites, as described on page 776. In addition, you can tell whether you're looking at the files on your computer, the web server, the testing server, or a Subversion repository (page 788) by looking at the name that appears at the top of the file column. In this figure, for example, you're looking at files on your computer, since "Local Files" appears at the top of the Files column.

Setting Up a Site (in Depth)

Organizing and maintaining a website—creating new folders and web pages; moving, renaming, and deleting files and folders; and transferring pages to a web server—can require going back and forth between a couple of programs. With Dreamweaver's site management features, however, you can perform all those tasks from within the program. But to take advantage of this simplicity, you must first make Dreamweaver aware of your site; in other words, you need to give Dreamweaver some basic information about it.

Setting up a site in Dreamweaver involves showing the program which folder contains your website files (the *root folder*) and setting a few other options. You already know the very basics of setting up a site using Dreamweaver's Site Setup window (page 19). Here, you'll get a detailed explanation of the options available in there.

All Those Index Pages

Why are so many web pages named index.html *(or* index.htm*)?*

If you type a URL like *www.missingmanuals.com* into a web browser, the Missing Manuals home page opens on your screen. But how did the web server know which of the site's pages to send to your browser? After all, you didn't ask for a particular page, like *www.missingmanuals.com/index.html*.

When a web server gets a request that doesn't specify a page, it looks for a default web page—often named *index.html* or *index.htm*. It does the same thing even when the URL you type specifies (with a slash) a folder inside the site root, like this: *www.missingmanuals.com/cds/*. In this case, the server looks for a file called *index.html* inside the "cds" folder, and, if it finds the file, sends it to your browser.

If the server doesn't find an *index.html* file, two things can happen, both undesirable: The browser can display either an ugly error message or a listing of all the files inside the folder. Neither result helps your visitors.

While your site still functions if you don't give the main page inside each folder a default page name, it's good form to name that file *index.html*. This avoids the "404 File Not Found error" when someone requests just a folder name and not a specific file inside that folder.

Web servers can use different names for these default pages—*default.html*, for example—although *index.html* works on most web servers. In fact, you can specify any page as a default, so long as you set up your web server to look for that default page. When working with a server-side programming language, like PHP, ASP, or .NET, the index page will end with a file extension appropriate to that language, like *index.php*, *index.asp*, or *index.aspx*. Most web servers already predefine multiple default page names, so if it doesn't find a file named *index.html*, it may automatically look for one called *index.php*.

Start by choosing Site→New Site. That opens the Site Setup window (see Figure 16-4). It includes four categories of options where you specify the details of your site—Dreamweaver labels the categories Site, Servers, Version Control, and Advanced Settings.

You've encountered the Site category several times already (page 19, for example): It's where you tell Dreamweaver where on your computer it can find your website files. The Servers and Version Control settings help Dreamweaver work with your remote server; you'll learn about them in Chapter 18 (see page 776).

You'll find the Advanced Settings options (Figure 16-4, bottom) useful for different situations, later in this chapter. You'll learn about the "Local info" options next, the Cloaking options on page 782, the Design Notes category on page 795, the Templates option in Chapter 20, and the Web Fonts option on page 128. The settings are called "Advanced" for a reason, and you may not ever feel the need to visit or change them.

The most important category in the Site Setup window is the first: Site (Figure 16-4, top). Filling out the following two options are all you need to get started using Dreamweaver effectively.

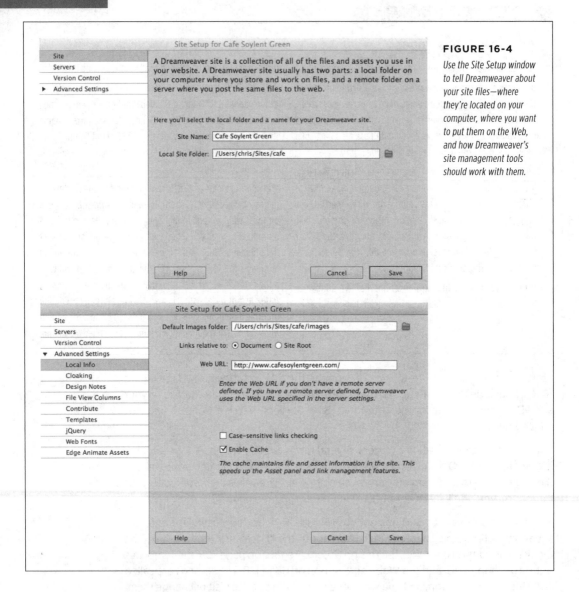

FIGURE 16-4

Use the Site Setup window to tell Dreamweaver about your site files—where they're located on your computer, where you want to put them on the Web, and how Dreamweaver's site management tools should work with them.

Site Name

In the "Site Name" field, type a name that briefly identifies the site for you—and Dreamweaver. This is the name that appears in, among other places, the File panel's Sites list drop-down menu (see Figure 16-3 for a glimpse of that), so you can tell what site you're working on. It's just for identifying your site while you work in Dreamweaver—it doesn't appear on your actual site pages.

Local Site Folder

Identify your site's local folder—the folder on your hard drive that contains all the site's files. (This is also known as a local root folder.) Click the folder icon to the right of "Local Site Folder" to browse for the folder. See the box on page 720 for more on local site folders.

> **NOTE** If you're confused about which folder is your local site folder, ask yourself this: "Which folder on my computer will contain (or contains) my site's home page?" That's your local site folder. All your site's other files and folders should go inside this one.

The Dreamweaver tools that manage your sites' files rely on the local site folder. Once you set up a site, you see all its files listed in the Files panel. In the Advanced Settings area, the "Local info" tab tells Dreamweaver how to work with the files on your computer.

The "Local info" category under the Advanced Settings menu (Figure 16-4), bottom) has some other useful settings that can help Dreamweaver work with your site's files, as described below.

Default Images Folder

When you want to display a graphic on a web page, you tell the page where to find the image by pointing to its file location. That location has to be inside the local root folder or one of its subfolders. In other words, if you link to a graphic that's sitting *outside* the root folder on your hard drive, a web browser will never find it.

Dreamweaver offers a feature that puts images in the right place even if you forget to. When you add a stray graphics file to a page on your site, Dreamweaver automatically copies the file into your default images folder. In fact, even if you drag a graphic from your desktop onto a web page-in-progress, Dreamweaver copies the file to the default images folder without missing a beat.

You identify the default images folder the same way you select the local site folder: Click the folder icon and locate the folder on your local drive. If you haven't set up the folder yet, click New Folder to create it on the spot. (For example, you might add a folder to your local root folder and name it *images*.)

Links Relative To

As discussed on page 170, you can set up links in your web pages in a variety of ways. When you link from one page to another on your site, Dreamweaver lets you create either a *document-relative* link or a *root-relative* link. As explained on page 166, document-relative links are often the easiest way to go, but Dreamweaver gives you the flexibility to choose. Click either the Document or Site Root radio button. Then, whenever you embed a link in your pages, Dreamweaver creates the link using that setting.

NOTE You can override this setting and use whichever type of link you wish—document-relative or site root-relative—when you create the link, as described in step 4 on page 174.

FREQUENTLY ASKED QUESTION

Bringing Your Own Website

I already have a website. Will Dreamweaver work with it?

Yes. In fact, Dreamweaver's site management features are an invaluable aid in organizing the files of an existing site. As you can read in "Managing Files and Folders" on page 28, you can use Dreamweaver to rearrange, rename, and reorganize files—tasks that are extremely difficult and time-consuming to do by hand.

Furthermore, Dreamweaver lets you clean up and reorganize a site without breaking links. So it's just as useful for working with a completed site as it is for creating one from scratch.

To work on an existing site, make sure it has its own root folder—in other words, that its home page, graphics, CSS files, other web pages, and any subfolders all reside in one main site folder. Then set up a new site in Dreamweaver as described above, and choose this folder as the local site folder.

Web URL

This option serves two functions: First, if you use absolute URLs to link to pages within your site (see page 166), you must fill out the Web URL field for Dreamweaver's link-management features to work (page 171). Type in your site's full URL, beginning with *http://*. Dreamweaver uses this address to check for broken links within your site and correctly rewrite them if you move pages around. For example, say your webmaster told you to link a form to *http://www.yourdomain.com/cgi/formscript. php* instead of using a document-relative link. In this case, you'd type *http://www. yourdomain.com/* in the Web URL box. Now, if you move or rename the *formscript. php* page from within Dreamweaver, the program is smart enough to update the absolute link in the form.

This setting is also incredibly valuable in one particular situation: if you use site root-relative links, but the site you're working on isn't actually located in the site root on the web server. For example, say you run the marketing department at International ToolCo. You manage just the web pages for the marketing department, and they're located in a folder called *marketing* on the web server. In essence, you manage a sub-site, which acts as an independent site within the larger International ToolCo site. Maybe your webmaster demands that you use site root-relative links—man, is that guy bossy.

NOTE If you set up Dreamweaver to upload and download files from your web server as described on page 776, you've already told Dreamweaver your website's URL (see step 10 on page 769). If that's the case, the Web URL option in the "Local info" box will be grayed out.

This is a potentially tricky situation. Here's why: Site root-relative links always begin with a forward slash (/), indicating the root folder on the web server (for a refresher on this concept, see page 170). Normally, if you add a root-relative link to, say, the main page in a folder named *personnel* located inside the local root folder, Dreamweaver would write the link like this: */personnel/index.html*. But in this case, that wouldn't work. The *personnel* folder is actually located inside the *marketing* folder on the web server. So the link should be */marketing/personnel/index.html*. In other words, Dreamweaver normally thinks that your local root folder maps exactly to the web server's root folder.

You can solve this dilemma by adding a URL that points to the "sub-site" in the Site Definition window's Web URL box. In this example, you'd type *http://www.intltoolco.com/marketing/* in the box. Then, whenever you add a root-relative link, Dreamweaver begins it with */marketing/* and then adds the rest of the path. In summary, *if* you use site root-relative links *and* you're working solely on pages located inside a subdirectory on the actual server, *then* fill out the absolute URL to that subdirectory. Finally, add this whole rigmarole to the list of reasons why document-relative links are easier to manage in Dreamweaver.

> **NOTE** Strangely, the first use of the Web URL box mentioned above—that is, managing absolute URLs pointing to files in your site—doesn't work with the second option—sub-sites. For example, if you specify a subdirectory like *http://www.intltoolco.com/marketing/* in the Web URL box, Dreamweaver isn't able to keep track of absolute links within this site. So if you had to use the URL *www.intltoolco.com/marketing/cgi/form.php* to point to a form page within your site, and then you move that form page, Dreamweaver won't update the page that uses that absolute link.

Case-Sensitive Links

Some web servers (namely, those that use the Unix and Linux operating systems) are sensitive to the case you use in filenames. For example, both consider *INDEX.html* and *index.html* different files. If your server uses either OS, turn on the "Use case-sensitive link checking" checkbox to make sure Dreamweaver doesn't mistake one file for another when it checks links. Say you link to a file named *INDEX.html*, but change the name of another file named *index.html* to *contact.html*. Without this option turned on, Dreamweaver may mistakenly update links to *INDEX.html* because it considers that file the same as *index.html*.

In real-world use, you probably won't need this option. First, it's not possible to have two files with the same name but different combinations of upper- and lowercase letters in the same folder on a Windows or Mac machine. So if your local root folder is on a Windows or Mac computer, you'll never be able to get into this situation. In addition, it's confusing (and just plain weird) to use the same name but different cases for your files.

■ CACHE

The cache is a small database of information about the files in your site. It helps Dreamweaver's site management features work more efficiently. In almost all cases, you want to keep this checkbox turned on. However, if you have a really large site, composed of tens of thousands of web pages, Dreamweaver might act pretty sluggishly when you perform basic tasks like moving files around within the site or checking for broken links.

Once you provide the local information for your site, click Save to close the Site Definition window and begin working.

Managing Dreamweaver Sites

When you work with Dreamweaver, keep in mind that you'll have a set of files on your computer for each site you work on as well as a "site" that you've set up in Dreamweaver. The files on your computer will always be there (until you or your mischievous cat delete them); they exist even without Dreamweaver. However, when you use Dreamweaver, you'll also have a list of all the sites you've set up within the program using the process described on page 712. These Dreamweaver "sites" are nothing more than the information Dreamweaver needs to locate and work with your web files and to connect to your web server. You can edit and delete a Dreamweaver "site" without doing any harm to the actual site files on your computer.

Editing or Removing Sites

Sometimes you need to edit the information associated with a site. Perhaps you want to rename the site, or you reorganized your hard drive and moved the local root folder, so you want to let Dreamweaver know the new location.

To edit a site, open the Manage Sites dialog box (choose Site→Manage Sites or, in the Files panel, choose Manage Sites from the bottom of the Site drop-down menu) and then double-click the name of the site you want to edit. The Site Setup window opens (Figure 16-4, top). Now you can type a new name in the Site Name box, choose a new local root folder, or make any other changes you want. Click OK to close the dialog box when you're done.

TIP If you want to edit the current site's information, there's a shortcut. In the Files panel (Figure 16-3), double-click the name of the site in the Sites menu. (Mac owners need to click once to select the name in the menu, and then click again to open the Site Definition window.)

Once you finish designing a site, you may want to remove it from Dreamweaver's list of sites. Open the Manage Sites dialog box (see Figure 16-5) as described above, click to select the site you wish to delete, and then click the – sign button (that's the Delete Site button).

A warning appears telling you that you can't undo this action. Don't worry; deleting the site here doesn't actually *delete* the site's web pages, images, or other files from your computer. It merely removes the site from Dreamweaver's list of sites. (You can always go back and set up the site again by following the steps on page 712.) Click Done to close the Manage Sites window.

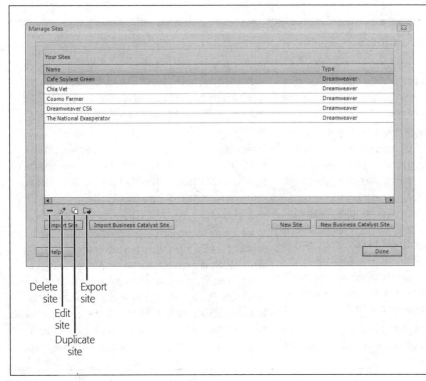

FIGURE 16-5

The Manage Sites window is the control center for managing your sites. Add new sites, edit old ones, duplicate a site definition, and even export site definitions for use on another computer, or as a precautionary backup. Adobe revamped this window recently, adding support for its web hosting service, Business Catalyst (see the box on page 722).

Delete site | Export site | Edit site | Duplicate site

NOTE If you do, in fact, want to delete the actual web pages, graphics, and other site components, you can either switch to the desktop (Windows Explorer or the Mac Finder, for example) and delete them manually, or delete them from within Dreamweaver's Files panel, as described on page 31.

Exporting and Importing Sites

When you set up a site, Dreamweaver stores that site's information in its own private files. If you want to work on your site using a different computer, therefore, you must re-set up the site for *that* copy of Dreamweaver. In a design firm where several people work on many different sites, that's a lot of extra setup. In fact, even if there's just one of you working on two computers, duplicating your efforts takes extra work.

Dreamweaver lets you import and export site setups so you can put your time to better use. For example, you can back up your site set-up files in case you have to reinstall Dreamweaver, and you can export a site setup for others to use.

Local vs. Live Site Folders

A site folder (also called a *root* folder) is a site's main, hold-everything bin. It contains every component that makes up your website: all web page documents, graphics, CSS style sheets, JavaScript files, and so on.

The word "site" in the name "site folder" implies that this folder holds your entire site. It's the master, outer, main folder, in other words, the folder in which you may have plenty of subfolders. Remember that, in most cases, your website exists in two locations: on your computer as you work on it and on the Internet where people can enjoy the fruits of your labor. In fact, most websites in the universe live in two places at once—one copy on the Internet and the original on some web designer's hard drive. (In some cases, you'll also have what's called a "testing server," often used so you can test dynamic, database-driven websites before publishing them to the Internet—you'll learn about them in Chapter 22.)

The copy on your own computer is called the *local site*. Think of it as a sort of development area, where you build your site,

test it, and modify it. (With database-driven sites, you do your testing on a testing server, and use the local site to store the files as you work on them. As you'll read on page 885, it's common for the files on your local site and testing server to be one and the same.)

Because the local site isn't on a web server, the public can't see it, and you can freely edit and add to it without affecting the pages your visitors see. The folder for the version of the site you keep on your computer, therefore, is called the *local site folder*.

After you add or update a file, you move it from the local site to the *remote server*. The site on the remote server mirrors your local site. Because you create a remote site by uploading your local site to a server, it has the same folder structure as your local site and contains the same polished, fully functional web pages. The local site also includes all the half-finished, typo-ridden drafts you're working on. Chapter 18 explains how to use Dreamweaver's FTP features to upload only your ready-for-prime-time local site and how to work with a remote server.

NOTE Exporting a site in Dreamweaver doesn't actually export your site files—all of the web pages, folders, and so on—it just exports the setup options you used when you set up the site. In other words, you just export and import the information that lets Dreamweaver work with your site's files, not the files themselves.

To export a site setup:

1. **Choose Site→Manage Sites.**

   The Manage Sites window appears, listing all the sites you defined (Figure 16-5).

2. **Select a site from the list, and then click the "Export site" button (the folder with an arrow on it).**

   If you haven't told Dreamweaver about your remote server, skip to step 4.

3. **Select either "Back up my settings" or "Share settings with other users" and then click OK.**

   If the site setup includes remote server information (so Dreamweaver can connect to your web server and move files onto it, as described on page 776), you'll see a dialog box called "Exporting site" (Figure 16-6). If you simply want to make a backup of your site definition because you need to reinstall Dreamweaver, select the "Back up my settings" radio button.

The other option, "Share settings," isn't all that useful. It's intended to let you share your site settings with a person working on another copy of the same site on their own computer. When you elect to share settings, Dreamweaver doesn't include the username and password you use to connect to the remote (web) server, a good thing. But it also excludes the site-file paths you defined because, presumably, the person you're sharing the settings with has her site files in a different location on her computer from your paths. For that reason, it's just as easy for that person to simply create her own site setup following the instructions on "Setting Up a Site (in Depth)" on page 712.

The Export Site panel appears.

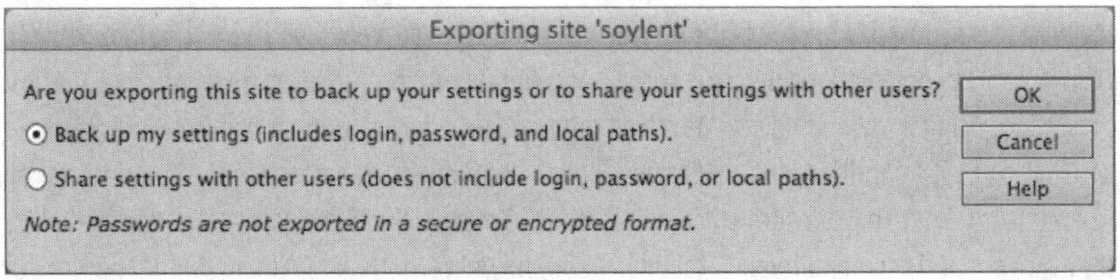

FIGURE 16-6

This dialog box lets you back up your site settings or share them (minus your login information) with other people.

4. **In the Export Site panel, specify where you want to save the file and give it a name.**

   If you're making a backup, save the file outside the local root folder (for example, with the Photoshop, Fireworks, and Word source files for your site). Because the export file can potentially contain the username and password you use to move files to your remote site, you don't want to keep the file anywhere in your local root folder—you might mistakenly upload it to the web server, where someone might find it and wreak havoc with your site.

   Dreamweaver uses the extension .ste for site definition files.

TIP You can export multiple sites in a single step. Select all the sites you want to export (Ctrl-click [⌘-click] the names of the sites), and then click Export. You won't however, be able to name each export file in this step—just the first one. In addition, Dreamweaver saves all the site definitions you export this way in the same folder. You can, of course, move and rename the files. Just make sure to keep the .ste file extension at the end of each filename.

Once you create a site setup file, you can import it into Dreamweaver as follows:

1. **Choose Site→Manage Sites.**

   The Manage Sites panel appears.

2. **Click the "Import site" button (see Figure 16-5).**

   The Import Site panel appears. Navigate to the set-up file—look for a file ending in .ste. Select it, and then click OK.

If you import the site setup options to a computer other than the one you used to export it, you may need to perform a few more steps. If Dreamweaver can't find the location of the local site folder in the site setup file, it asks you to select a local site folder on the new computer, as well as a new default Images folder.

Business Catalyst

Dreamweaver CC includes the ability to create or import Business Catalyst websites. Business Catalyst is Adobe's commercial web hosting company. However, it's more than just a place to park your web files. It offers many tools to supercharge your (or your client's) online presence. It includes a content management system (CMS) so you can edit pages using a web browser and without any knowledge of HTML or CSS, as well as web analytics so you can track how many visitors come to your site, where they come from, what they click on, and how long they stay. And that's just for the basic $6.59-per-month package.

For a higher fee (ranging from $12.21 to $38.88 per month), you can add complete e-commerce functionality (including credit-card processing), a blog, email marketing, a "customer relationship management" system for collecting and analyzing guest information, and even database-based web applications.

However, creating a Business Catalyst site isn't like building the types of web pages you've been reading about in this book. Business Catalyst is a "system" that has a lot of functionality right out of the box. In other words you don't start by creating regular web pages: You start by creating a Business Catalyst site, and downloading all the specially created Business Catalyst web files to your computer. You can then add various modules to the site—photo galleries, product catalogs, web forms, and so on, from the Business Catalyst panel (Windows→Business Catalyst). And you can customize the CSS and HTML of Business Catalyst template files (similar to Dreamweaver templates discussed in Chapter 20) from within Dreamweaver.

To learn more about Business Catalyst, visit *http://www.businesscatalyst.com*. The site also includes training videos to learn how Business Catalyst works (*www.businesscatalyst.com/training*) and information on using Dreamweaver with Business Catalyst (*http://www.businesscatalyst.com/support/dw*). For even more information on Business Catalyst, visit Adobe TV's "Learn Business Catalyst" show at *http://tv.adobe.com/show/learn-business-catalyst/*.

Viewing Files in the Files Panel

Once you set up your local site, you can use Dreamweaver's Files panel as command central for organizing your files, creating folders, and adding new web pages. To open the Files panel, choose Window→Files, or press F8.

In its most basic incarnation, the Files panel lists the files in the current site's local root folder. This list looks and acts very much like Windows Explorer or the Mac's Finder; you see names, file sizes, and folders. You can view the files inside a folder by clicking the + sign (flippy triangle on Macs) next to the folder (or simply by double-clicking the folder name). Double-click a web page to open it in Dreamweaver. You can also see the size of a file, the type of file it is, and the last time you modified it. That's a lot of information to fit in that space, so if you find this new view a little too cramped, hide any columns you don't like—see page 798.

NOTE You can open certain types of files in an outside program of your choice by defining an external editor for that file type. For example, you can tell Dreamweaver to open GIF files in Fireworks, Photoshop, or another image editor. See page 246 for more.

You can view your site's files four ways, using the View drop-down menu (shown in Figure 16-3):

- **Local view** lists the files in your local root folder. Dreamweaver displays folders in this view as green.

- **Remote server** displays the files in your remote site folder; in other words, the files on your web server (see the box on page 25). Of course, before you post your site to the Web, this list is empty. Dreamweaver adds files to this folder only after you set up a connection to the remote server and upload files to it. Dreamweaver displays folders in this view as yellow on Windows PCs and blue on Macs.

- **Testing server view** is useful when you create the dynamic, database-driven sites discussed in Chapter 22. No files appear in this view until you set up a testing server (see page 885) and connect Dreamweaver to it. When you do, Dreamweaver displays folders in this view in red.

- **Repository view** gives you a peek inside a file-versioning system called Subversion. You'll learn about this advanced file-management tool on page 788.

You can view any combination of these two views side by side—for example, you can see a list of your local files next to a list of the files on your web server—by clicking the Expand Panel button (see Figure 16-3). This undocks the Files panel from the side of the screen, turning it into a floating window (see Figure 16-7). You'll find this most useful when you want to compare files on your local computer with those on your web server or testing server.

TIP If you've got a small monitor, the Files panel (and other panel groups) might take up too much space to let you comfortably work on a web page. You can hide (and show) all panels, including the Properties panel and Insert bar, by pressing F4.

Modifying the Files Panel View

Dreamweaver stocks the Files panel with loads of information on its inhabitants: the file name, the size of the file, the type of file (web page, graphic, and so on), and the date you last modified it. That's all useful to know, but if you have a relatively small monitor, you may not be able display everything without having to scroll left and right. What's worse, the filenames you want front and center often get clipped by other columns of information.

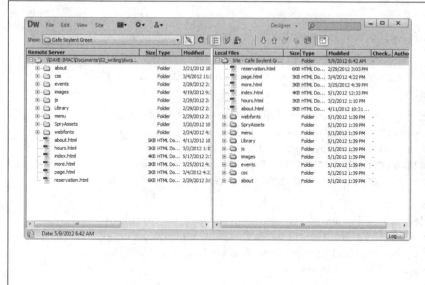

FIGURE 16-7

Click the Expand/Collapse button shown in Figure 16-3 to maximize the Files panel and display two views simultaneously. This way, you can view both your remote site and local site at the same time. Local files normally appear on the right, but might be on the left, depending on the preference you set under the Site category of the Preferences window. (If you want to change this, press Ctrl+U [⌘-U] to open Preferences and then click the Site category.) The view that appears opposite the local files view—Remote Server, Testing, or Repository—depends on which view you selected before clicking the Expand button. To change views, click a different view button.

There are a couple of ways to fix this. First, you can resize the width of each column by dragging one of the dividers that separates the column names (for example, the vertical line between the "Local Files" and "Size" columns in Figure 16-3). Using this technique, you can at least display the full name of each file.

If you don't like the number of columns Dreamweaver displays, you can hide any or all of them. After all, how useful is listing the type of each file? The folder icon clearly indicates when you're looking at a folder and each filename's extension—for example, .html for a web page or .jpg for a JPEG graphic—clearly indicates the file's type. For most folks, that's enough.

Unfortunately, there's no program-wide setting to control which columns appear. You have to define the visible columns on a site-by-site basis:

1. **Choose Site→Manage Sites and double-click the name of the site whose Files panel you want to modify.**

   The Site Setup window opens.

2. **Click the Advanced Settings category to display the list of options, and then select File View Columns (see Figure 16-8, top).**

   Dreamweaver lists all the columns the Files panel can display and indicates which it currently displays ("Show") or hides ("Hide"). Under the Type heading, all the files initially say "Built In" to indicate columns that Dreamweaver displays by default. As you'll read on page 799, you can add your own customized columns to this list.

3. **Double-click the row that holds the column you want to change.**

   For example, double-clicking the Type row displays the options you see in Figure 16-8, bottom: Column Name, "Associate with Design Notes," and "Share with all users of this site." Most of the options are dimmed out because they only apply to custom-created columns, described on page 799.

4. **Change the alignment of the column (Left, Right, or Center) from the Align menu, and turn on or off the Show checkbox to show or hide a column.**

   For example, to hide the Size column, turn off the Show checkbox in the Size column's options window.

5. **Click the Save button to close that column's settings.**

   Repeat steps 3–5 for any other columns you wish to edit, and when you're done, click the Save button on the Site Setup window.

You can change the order of the columns, too—perhaps a file's Modified date is more important to you than its size. Select a column and click the up or down arrow. The up arrow moves the column to the left in the Files panel, while the down arrow scoots a column over to the right.

Site Assets

Web pages integrate lots of page elements: PNGs, GIFs, JPEGs, links, colors, JavaScript files, and Flash movies, to name just a few. On a large site with lots of files, it's a challenge to locate a particular image or remember an exact color.

To simplify the process, Dreamweaver provides the Assets panel. For want of a better generic term, Dreamweaver defines the term *asset* to mean any element you use on a web page, such as a JPEG, a link, or even an individual color.

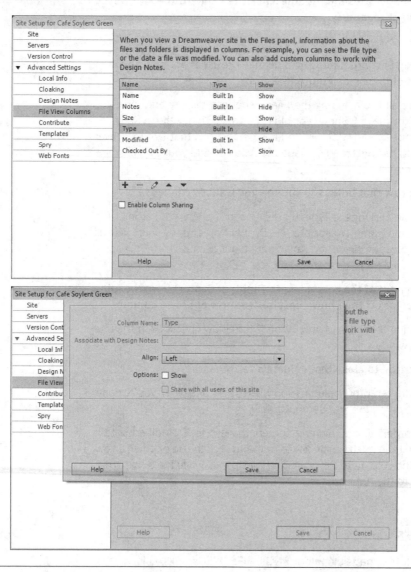

FIGURE 16-8

Use the File View Columns category to show or hide columns in the Files panel. You can rearrange the columns by selecting one and clicking the up or down arrow (top image). The up arrow moves the column to the left in the Files panel, while the down arrow moves it to the right. You can also use the File View Columns category to work with Dreamweaver's collaborative note-sharing feature called Design Notes (bottom). Instructions on using Design Notes start on page 795.

POWER USERS' CLINIC

Changing the New-Page Default

Whenever you create a new web page—by choosing File→New or by right-clicking (Control-clicking) an existing file in the Files panel—Dreamweaver gives you a blank document. But what if you always want your pages to have special HTML comments indicating that your company created the page, or you always want to include a link to the same external style sheet?

Every new web page you create is actually an untitled copy of a default template document called *Default.html*. You can find this file in Dreamweaver's configuration folder. On Windows 64-bit computers, it's in *C:\Program Files (x86)\Adobe\Adobe Dreamweaver CC\configuration\DocumentTypes\NewDocuments*. If you have a 32-bit Windows computer, it will be *C:\Program Files\Adobe\Adobe Dreamweaver CC\configuration\DocumentTypes\NewDocuments*. On a Mac, you can find it in the *Applications→Adobe Dreamweaver CC→Configuration→DocumentTypes→New-Documents* folder. Save a copy of this folder so you can always return to the original, Dreamweaver-supplied file. In Windows XP, use the folder name *C:\Documents and Settings\[your user name]\Application Data\Adobe\Dreamweaver CC\en_US\Configuration*. In Windows Vista, use *C:\Users\[your user name]\AppData\Roaming\Adobe*

Dreamweaver CC\en_US\Configuration. On a Mac, try *Volume Name→Applications→Adobe Dreamweaver CC→Configuration→DocumentTypes→New Documents*.

You can then open a file from the NewDocument folder in your personal configuration folder and edit it however you like: Change or add HTML comments, meta tags, pre-canned links to a style sheet, or whatever, so that all subsequent new pages inherit these settings. Also, make sure you don't touch an HTML fragment that may look incorrect, namely, the *charset="* snippet, which appears at the end of the <meta> tag. This fragment of HTML is indeed incomplete, but when you create a new page, Dreamweaver correctly completes the code according to the alphabet (a.k.a. character set) your page uses—Chinese, Korean, Western European, or UTF-8, for example.

You'll notice lots of other files in this folder. Since Dreamweaver can create lots of different file types—Cascading Style Sheets, Active Server Pages, and so on—you'll find a default blank file for each. You can edit any of these—but don't, unless you know what you're doing. You can easily damage some of the more complex file types, especially those that involve dynamic websites.

Viewing the Assets Panel

Dreamweaver lists your site's assets on the eight category "pages" of the Assets panel (Figure 16-9). To open the panel, choose Window→Assets.

Select an asset by clicking its name. Dreamweaver previews the asset above the Assets list. To preview a movie, click the arrow that appears in the upper-right corner of the preview pane.

Dreamweaver divides your site's assets into eight categories, represented by icons on the left side of the Assets panel. To view the assets in a particular category, click its icon:

- **The Images category lists all the GIF, JPEG, and PNG files in your site.** Dreamweaver lists the dimensions of each image next to its name so you can quickly identify whether *logo1.gif* or *logo2.gif* is your 728 x 90 pixel banner logo. You can also see the images' sizes, types, and locations (you may need to scroll to the right to see all this).

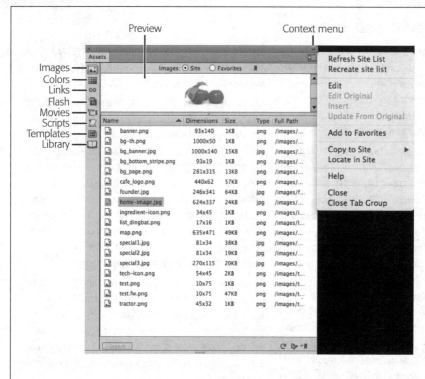

Preview   Context menu

FIGURE 16-9

Dreamweaver duplicates most of the Assets panel's drop-down menu commands in this static Assets panel, but three options appear only on the drop-down menu (upper-right corner). "Recreate site list" comes in handy if you add or delete files without Dreamweaver's help, using Windows Explorer or the Mac Finder. It rebuilds the site cache and updates the site's list of assets. "Copy to Site" copies the selected asset to another site. "Locate in Site" switches to the Files panel and selects the file. You can also open the contextual menu by right-clicking (Control-clicking) any asset in the list.

- **The Colors category shows you all the colors specified in your site's pages and style sheets.** These include link colors, background colors, and text colors.

- **The Links category lists all external links—and not just standard *http://* links, but also email links, FTP addresses, and JavaScript links.**

- **The two multimedia categories—SWF (meaning Flash movies) and Movies (meaning Flash video or QuickTime movies)—are roughly equivalent.** They each display movie files with their corresponding extensions: .swf (Flash), .flv (Flash video), and .mov or .mpg (QuickTime and MPEG). Unfortunately, the Movies category hasn't kept up with the times: Thanks to HTML5 video (see page 676), there are other movie formats to think about, such as MPEG4 (.mp4), Ogg Vorbis (.ogv), and WebM (.webm). Unfortunately, Dreamweaver doesn't support these video formats.

- **The Scripts category lists JavaScript files.** It includes only external script files your web pages link to. Dreamweaver doesn't include scripts embedded *in* a web page, like Dreamweaver behaviors.

- **The last two categories—Templates and Library—are advanced assets that streamline website production.** You'll find them discussed in Chapters 19 and 20.

You can switch between two views for most asset categories—Site and Favorites—by clicking the radio buttons near the top of the Assets panel. (There are no Favorites in the Templates and Library categories.) The Site option lists all the assets in your site for the chosen category. Favorites lets you create a select list of your most important and frequently used assets (see page 730).

If you add assets as you work on a site—for example, if you create a GIF image in Fireworks and import it into your site—you need to update the Assets panel. To do so, click the Refresh Site List button (see Figure 16-9).

Inserting Assets

The Assets panel's prime mission is to make it easy for you to add elements to your site by dragging the asset from the panel into your document window. For example, you can add graphics, colors, and links with a simple drag-and-drop operation. Note that most of the categories on the panel refer to external files you commonly find on web pages: images, Flash files, movies, and scripts.

You can drop an asset anywhere on a page where you'd normally insert an object—in a table cell, a <div> tag, at the beginning or end of a page, or within a paragraph. You can also add script assets to the head of a page (see Figure 16-10). (If you're billing by the hour, you may prefer the long way: Click in the document window to plant the insertion point, click the asset's name, and then click Insert at the bottom of the Assets panel.)

■ ADDING COLOR AND LINK ASSETS

Color and link assets work a bit differently from other asset files. Instead of standing on their own, they *add* color to any text selection in the document window or *link* to text or images selected in the document window. This makes it easy to quickly add a frequently used link—the URL to download the Adobe Reader, for example.

To do so, start by highlighting the text whose color you want to change, or by highlighting the words or an image that you want to turn into a link. In the Assets panel, click the appropriate category button—Colors or Links. Click the color or link you want, and then click Apply. Alternatively, you can drag the color or link asset from the panel to the selected text or image.

In the case of links, Dreamweaver simply adds <a> tags to the selection, along with the proper external link. For color, Dreamweaver pops up the New CSS Rule window and asks you to create a new CSS style—you then need to go through the whole rigmarole described on page 138. Unfortunately, Dreamweaver's not smart enough to update the text color of any style already applied to the selected text. In other words, applying colors with the Assets panel is more trouble than it's worth.

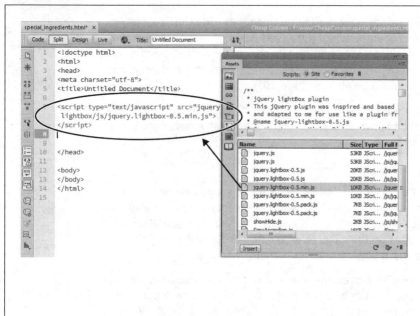

FIGURE 16-10

Although you'll insert most assets into the body of a web page, you can (and usually should) place script files at the head of the page. To do this, choose View the page in Code or Split view, and then drag the script from the Assets panel into the head portion of the page (after the <head> tag and before </head>, as shown here). (Adding a script asset doesn't copy the JavaScript code into the web page. Instead, just as with external style sheets, Dreamweaver links to the script file so that when a browser loads the page, it looks for and then loads the JavaScript file from the website.)

However, there is one way to use the color assets effectively, sort of. As you'll recall (or not) from page 138, the Dreamweaver color picker lets you sample colors that appear on your monitor. So if you want to use a color from the Assets panel, make sure you have the Assets panel open and the color assets visible. Then, when you want to select a color (for example, to add a color to text in the CSS Rule Definition window), click the color box (the cursor changes to an eye dropper), and then click a color in the Assets panel.

Favorite Assets

On a large site, you may have thousands of images, movies, colors, and external links. Because scrolling through long lists of assets is a chore, Dreamweaver lets you create a compact list of your favorite, frequently used assets.

For example, you might come up with five main colors that define your site's color scheme, which you'll use much more often than the miscellaneous colors on the Assets list. Add them to your list of favorite colors. Likewise, adding graphics you use over and over—logos, for example—to a list of favorites makes it easy to locate and insert those files into your pages. (You can also use Dreamweaver's Library and template features for this function. They're similar but more powerful tools to keep frequently used items at the ready. Turn to Chapters 19 and 20 for the details.)

■ IDENTIFYING YOUR FAVORITES

If the color, graphic, or other element you want to add to your Favorites list already appears on your Assets panel, highlight it in the list and then click Add to Favorites (see Figure 16-9).

Even quicker, you can add favorites as you go, snagging them right from your web page. If you're working on your site's home page, for example, and you insert a company logo, that's a perfect time to make the logo a favorite. Simply right-click (Control-click) the image. From the shortcut menu, choose Add Image to Favorites. Dreamweaver instantly adds the graphic to your list of favorites *within that asset category*—meaning that you'll see the file when you're in the Favorites view *and* you have the Image category selected. You can use the same shortcut for colors, links, and for script, Flash, or movie files.

When it comes to colors and links, you can turn them into favorites another way: In the Assets panel, select the Color or URLs category, click the Favorites radio button, and then click the New Asset button (see Figure 16-11).

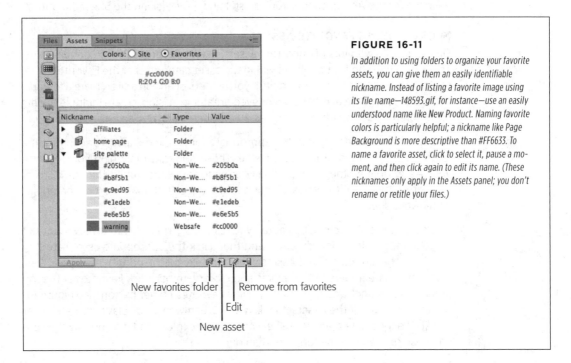

FIGURE 16-11

In addition to using folders to organize your favorite assets, you can give them an easily identifiable nickname. Instead of listing a favorite image using its file name—148593.gif, for instance—use an easily understood name like New Product. Naming favorite colors is particularly helpful; a nickname like Page Background is more descriptive than #FF6633. To name a favorite asset, click to select it, pause a moment, and then click again to edit its name. (These nicknames only apply in the Assets panel; you don't rename or retitle your files.)

New favorites folder | Remove from favorites

Edit

New asset

Then:

- If you're adding a favorite color, the Dreamweaver color box appears. Select a color using the eyedropper (see page 138).

- If you're adding a favorite link, the Add URL window opens. Type either an absolute URL (a web address starting with *http://*) in the first field or an email address (for instance, mailto:*info@cafesoylentgreen.com*). Next, type a name for the link—such as *Acrobat Download* or *Info Email*—in the Nickname field and then click OK.

Your new color or link appears in your Favorites list.

■ USING FAVORITES

You insert assets from your Favorites list into web pages just as you would any other asset. For example, for an image or other media, just drag it from the Assets panel onto your page.

■ REMOVING FAVORITES

Removing an asset from your Favorites list is just as straightforward as adding one: Select it in the Favorites list and then press Delete. The "Remove from Favorites" button on the Assets panel does the same thing (see Figure 16-11). Yet another approach is to use the contextual menu (Figure 16-10).

Don't worry; removing an asset from your Favorites list *doesn't* delete that asset from your site (or the Assets panel). You can still find it by clicking the Site radio button.

■ ORGANIZING FAVORITE ASSETS

On a large site with lots of important assets, even a Favorites list can get unwieldy. That's why you can set up folders within the asset categories of the Favorites panel to organize your assets. For example, if you use lots of ads on a site, create a folder in the Image category called Ads or, for even greater precision, create multiple folders for different types of ads: Banner Ads, Half Banner Ads, and so on.

You can then drag assets into the appropriate folders and expand or contract the folder to show or hide the assets inside. These folders simply help you organize your Assets panel; they don't actually appear anywhere within the structure of your site. Moving a Favorite asset into a folder doesn't change the location of files within your site.

To create a Favorites folder, make sure you're in Design view (Dreamweaver doesn't let you create folders in Site view), and then click the appropriate asset category button on the left edge of the Assets panel (any except the bottom two, since, alas, you can't create folders for templates and Library items). Click Favorites at the top of the Assets panel, and then click the New Favorites Folder button (see Figure 16-11) at the bottom of the Assets panel. When Dreamweaver displays the new folder with its placeholder name, type a new name for the folder and then press Enter (but don't use the same name for more than one folder).

To put an asset into a folder, just drag it there from the list. And if you're really obsessive, you can even create subfolders by dragging one folder onto another.

GEM IN THE ROUGH

Nothing Could Be Kuler

Adobe's Kuler web tool (*http://kuler.adobe.com*) is an online gallery of color palettes. It lets you build your own sets of colors and offers tools based on the science of color theory to create harmonious color combinations for your site. Even better, you can see thousands of palettes created by *other* web designers, showcasing everything from cool and subtle schemes to loud and vibrant color mixes. It's a great site if you're eager for a little color inspiration.

To make it even easier for you to use this site, the extension developer WebAssist has a free Dreamweaver extension named PalettePicker. This simple add-on is essentially a floating palette within Dreamweaver that lets you browse or search Kuler's large collection of color palettes. When you find colors you like, you can use Dreamweaver's color box and eyedropper tool to sample a color from the PalettePicker palette just as you'd sample a color from a picture on a web page. You can find the extension at *http://tinyurl.com/njzwnyg*. It is part of a WebAssist's Free Tools package. To learn how to use and install extensions, turn to page 874.

Testing Your Site

As you no doubt realize by now, building a website involves quite a few steps. At any point in the process, you can easily introduce errors that affect the performance of your pages. Mistakes both small (like typos) and site-shattering (think broken links) occur frequently in the web development cycle.

Unfortunately, web designers often neglect to develop a set of best practices for testing their sites. This chapter offers helpful techniques for testing your site, and shows you how Dreamweaver's wide array of site-testing tools can help.

■ Site Launch Checklist

Don't wait until you finish your site before you develop a thorough strategy for regular testing. If you do, serious design errors may have so completely infested your pages that you have to start over, or at least spend many hours fixing problems you could have prevented early on. These guidelines help you avoid such a predicament:

- **Preview early and often.** The single best way to make sure a page looks and functions the way you want it to is to preview it in as many browsers as possible. For a quick test, click the Live button in Dreamweaver's Document toolbar (page 51). This is a great way to quickly check JavaScript components, web fonts, and the way a browser displays pages with complex CSS. You see pages as your web visitors will see them in the Google Chrome web browser, because Live view uses the same rendering engine. Your page will look similar in Safari and many mobile browsers.

- Chrome is a fast, modern browser that adheres to Web standards, so it makes sense that Adobe chose it for Live view. In short, it doesn't muck up the works inside Dreamweaver. Unfortunately, you can't stop testing once you finish with Chrome, because people will visit your site using other browsers, some not so well-behaved. So you need to check your pages in other popular browsers, like Internet Explorer, Firefox, and Opera.

To see how your layouts, CSS, and JavaScript features hold up in other browsers, use Dreamweaver's Preview command (File→Preview in Browser) to test your pages in every browser you can get your hands on (Dreamweaver lists your installed browsers when you click Preview, and you select one from the list). Make sure the graphics look right, your layout remains intact, and Cascading Style Sheets and Dreamweaver behaviors work as you intend.

For a thorough evaluation, however, you should preview your pages using every combination of browser *and* operating system you think your site's visitors may use. How do you know what browser your visitors use? StatCounter (*http:// gs.statcounter.com/*) is a good place to start your research. At this free-to-use website, you can learn which browsers are popular in different countries and regions of the world. You should also examine the stats on browser versions, because all Internet Explorers were *not* created equal. As you can see in Figure 17-1, the StatCounter window is pretty intuitive. Make a few choices from the drop-down menus and StatCounter provides information—on browser use, visitor's country of origin, and so on—in graph or map form. For example, when this book went to press, browser stats indicate that for the past 12 months, Internet Explorer 9, 8, and 10 (in that order) were the most popular browsers in the United States. Combined, the IEs account for 38% of Web traffic. Other versions of Internet Explorer account for less than one-half a percent. Looking at the stats, Google Chrome usage is significant at 28%, followed by Firefox (17%) and Safari (14%). So, if you're designing a site focused on the U.S., you should test your pages in Internet Explorer 8, 9, and 10, and Chrome, Firefox, and Safari. That way, you know your pages will look good on 97% of the browsers out there. If you're designing pages for a site in another country or region, you should study the statistics for your target audience. For example, in China during the same period, Internet Explorer 6 accounted for over 5% of Web traffic. If a significant part of your audience is in China, consider testing earlier versions of Internet Explorer, too.

> **TIP** If you already have a site up and running, you can find useful browser information in your site's *log files*. They track information about visits to your site, including which browsers and platforms your visitors use.

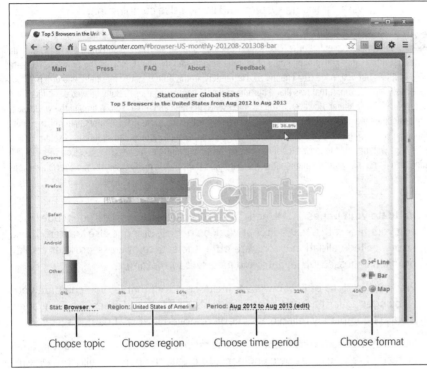

Choose topic   Choose region   Choose time period   Choose format

FIGURE 17-1

StatCounter (http:// gs.statcounter.com/) is a valuable research tool for web developers. Dial in a topic you want to research, such as browsers, browser versions, screen resolution (size), or operating system, and then choose a country or region and a time period. StatCounter displays the information it's collected from web logs as line charts, bar charts (shown here), or maps. This display shows overall browser stats. By choosing Browser Version as the topic, you can see which versions of a browser are popular.

NOTE Most web hosting companies provide access to these files and the software that analyzes the confusing code inside them. You can use this information to see, for example, whether *anyone* who visits your site still uses Internet Explorer 6. If no one does, that's one less browser you have to design for. And if you don't have access to your log files, you can use Google Analytics (*www.google.com/analytics/*), a free service that tracks guests who visit your site. You just need to sign up for a free Google Analytics account and add a little snippet of JavaScript to each page of your site.

Unfortunately, you'll discover that what works for one browser/operating system combination may not work for another. That's why you should preview your designs *early* in the process of constructing your site. If you design a page that doesn't work well in Internet Explorer 8 on Windows, for example, it's better to catch and fix that problem immediately than to discover it after you build 100 pages based on that design. In other words, once you create a page design you like, don't plow ahead and continue building your site! Check that page in multiple browser/operating system combos, fix any problems, and then, Grasshopper, begin to build.

To test your site, enroll your friends and family so you can check your pages on as many setups as possible. You may even need to turn to websites like BrowserStack (*http://www.browserstack.com/*), where you can explore even more browser, operating system, and screen size combinations.

> **NOTE** Internet Explorer 6 is often where most web pages fall apart. This old and crotchety browser is full of bugs that often cause hair-pulling bouts of hysteria among web designers. Most of the problems relate to the CSS that lays out your page (see Chapter 9). Fortunately, in the United States, Internet Explorer 6 is all but dead—most statistics report that less than 1 percent of the US population uses it. Many US web designers don't even test for IE 6 any longer. However, it still has a presence in China and other nations around the world, so if you're designing for a global audience, you may still need to test your designs in IE 6. Professional web designers recommend previewing your page using Dreamweaver's Live view and Firefox, Safari, or Internet Explorer 9 first. Get the page working right in those browsers, and then preview it in IE 6 to fix bugs. If you design with just IE 6 in mind, you'll find that your site might not work in Firefox, Safari, and, in many cases, the more recent versions of IE.

- **Validate your pages.** HTML and CSS errors can easily slip into your code if you edit your files with a text editor or work on pages someone else created. These errors, called validation errors, are often the source of cross-browser display problems, messed-up layouts, and incorrect formatting.

  Previous versions of Dreamweaver included a tool that let you compare your web pages against agreed-upon standards for HTML and other web languages. It wasn't completely reliable, so Adobe removed it from Dreamweaver CS5.

  However, in Dreamweaver CS5.5, Adobe resurrected the validator! But this time, instead of relying on its own engineers to create the perfect validator, Dreamweaver CS5.5 and later use the industry-standard W3C validator. The W3C, or World Wide Web Consortium, develops most of the technologies web designers rely on, like HTML and CSS, and they've always provided a very good validator. It resides online, but Dreamweaver CC makes the testing process simple by connecting to it from within the program. You'll learn how to use it on page 752.

While you do the bulk of your checking during page development, you should do some troubleshooting at the end of the process, too, just before you move a page (or an entire site) to your web server:

- **Check your spelling.** Amazingly, people often overlook this simple step. As a result, you can easily find otherwise professional-looking pages undermined by sloppy spelling. To use Dreamweaver's built-in spell-checker, see page 96.

- **Check your links.** A website can be a complex and twisted collection of inter-connected files. Web pages, graphics, videos, and other types of files all have to work together. Unfortunately, if you move or delete a file, problems can ripple through your entire site. Use Dreamweaver's Check Links command to identify and fix broken links (see page 745).

- **Run site reports.** It's always the little things. When you build a website, small errors inevitably creep into your pages. While not necessarily life-threatening, forgetting to title a page or add an Alt property to an image does diminish the quality and professionalism of a site. Use Dreamweaver's site-reporting feature to quickly identify these problems (see page 758).

Testing Web Pages with BrowserStack

Web browsers are free, so you can download and install several of them on your computer. But you'd soon find it unwieldy to install every version of every browser available, and then test all your pages in each one. And if the browser issue weren't enough, you need to consider the different operating systems and different devices (tablets, smartphones) out there. In the past, you could test pages using Adobe's BrowserLab service, which let you see your web pages in a variety of browsers and operating systems. Adobe stopped offering the service in March 2013, and now recommends third-party services like BrowserStack. As the box on page 744 explains, there are plenty of options.

NOTE BrowserStack costs $19 a month, but you can sign up for a free 30 minutes of testing time. If you're organized, that's actually enough time to check out a moderately-sized website. You can sign in and sign out of BrowserStack as often as you like, so you don't need to check all your pages in one session. If you sign up for BrowserStack through Microsoft's modern.IE website (*http://www.modern.ie*), you can get a three-month trial with time restrictions on certain features. The Microsoft site also provides web testing tools, with an emphasis on the most recent versions of IE.

BrowserStack uses a "virtual machine"—a computer that loads and runs the operating system/browser combo you chose— to preview the web pages you want to see. You choose an operating system and a specific version of a web browser—for example, Safari 5.1. You also specify the page you want to preview. BrowserStack runs that operating system and browser, opens the page you want to preview, and sends a "live" copy to your computer. You can click buttons, operate menus, and browse your way to other pages on your site or on the Web. In short, you experience your website just as a visitor will when they use that operating system/browser combo. There's a slight delay, because BrowserStack plays interference between you and the web pages you request, but you can trust the results.

Here's how you sign up with BrowserStack and then view a page on the Web.

1. **Go to *http://www.browserstack.com* and click the Free Trial button.**

   It's in the upper-right corner. After you click, BrowserStack displays a simple form.

2. **Fill in your email address, password, and name. Check the "Remember me" box and then click the Sign Up button.**

   You know the drill. You don't need to provide a credit card for the free trial. A new page appears when you click the Sign Up button. It displays two tabs: "Test a public URL" and "Test an internal URL" (see Figure 17-2).

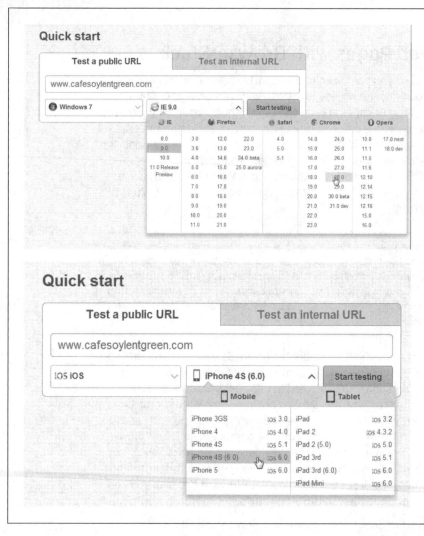

FIGURE 17-2

BrowserStack lets you preview web pages and entire sites. You can choose the operating system and a specific version of a browser simply by choosing options off a menu. Top: Here are the browser options available when you choose the Windows 7 operating system. Bottom: There are fewer options when you choose the mobile iOS operating system, but your choices include several versions of tablets and phones.

3. **Click the "Test a public URL" tab and then fill in the address of the website you want to preview.**

   Initially, BrowserStack displays the "public" option and automatically fills in the URL text field with the website cited in your email address, but you can change it to any one you want, so long as it's publically accessible on the Web.

4. **Below the web address, use the menu on the left to choose an operating system.**

   There are options for Windows, Macs, and mobile devices.

5. **Use the menu on the right to choose a browser.**

Your choice of operating system determines your browser options. You can choose a specific browser and version.

6. **Click "Start testing."**

BrowserStack entertains you with the play-by-play shown in Figure 17-3 while it sets up a virtual machine with the combination operating system and browser you specified. Once that's done, you see the test results on your computer.

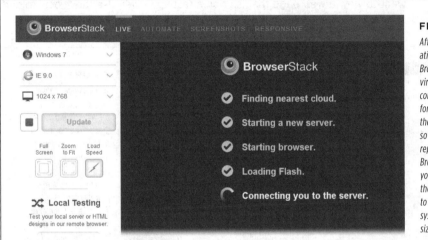

FIGURE 17-3

After you choose an operating system and browser, BrowserStack creates a virtual machine on its computers. It takes time for BrowserStack to run the necessary software, so you see this progress report in the interim. Once BrowserStack previews your page, you can use the controls on the right to test a new operating system, browser, or screen size.

Previewing Pages with BrowserStack

Ideally, you want to preview your web pages before you send them off to a web server where everyone in the world can see them. BrowserStack has a pretty ingenious way of handling that, too. The process is called "tunneling." Here's how it works: You create a connection between your computer and the BrowserStack computer (the tunnel). The BrowserStack computer runs a version of the operating system and browser you specify, and then it loads the web page from your computer. The results appear on your computer screen as if the operating system and browser were installed on your computer. It requires a few extra steps and means that you have to give BrowserStack permission to look at the files on your computer. After all, BrowserStack can't display files without reading them.

Here are the steps to set up a "tunnel."

1. **Click the "Test an internal URL" tab.**

The tab has two buttons, Web Tunnel and Command Line. Web tunnel is the easier one to use, because you don't have to type in cryptic Java commands in a terminal window.

2. Click "Web Tunnel."

BrowserStack displays a page telling you that it takes a few seconds to set up a web tunnel. Depending on your computer's operating system and security settings, you probably need to provide permission to run the Java applet (program) that creates the tunnel between you and BrowserStack. Figure 17-4 shows the message and permission buttons for Windows 7. After you let the applet run, BrowserStack displays a panel with two options: "Local server" and "Local folder." Use the "Local server" option if you have a testing server running on your computer. (See page 885 for details on setting up a testing server.) If you want to view a web page that isn't on a testing server, use the "Local folder" option, as explained next.

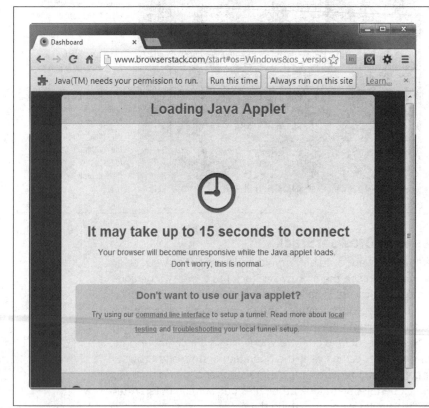

FIGURE 17-4

To view pages on your local computer but not on the web, Browser-Stack creates a "tunnel" between your computer and theirs. You probably need to provide permission to complete the process. Here, Windows 7 asks permission to run the Java program that creates the tunnel. If you have a different operating system and security settings, you'll see different warnings and permission requests.

3. **Choose "Local folder." Use the Browse button to identify a folder.**

    When you click Browse, BrowserStack displays a window so you can choose a folder on your computer. Then BrowserStack returns you to the "Setup a local tunnel" page, where you see the Finish button.

4. **Click Finish to create the tunnel, and then click Finish again to view the results.**

    The first time you click Finish, BrowserStack lets you know that it's creating the "local connection." Once it does, it tells you that you can access your local folder. You need to click the Finish button again to actually view the contents of the folder. Since you only provided the name of a folder, BrowserStack still needs to know what file to display.

5. **Click the HTML file that you want to preview as a web page.**

    BrowserStack displays the web page, as shown in Figure 17-5.

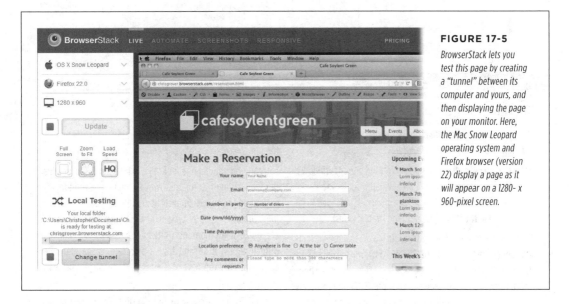

FIGURE 17-5

BrowserStack lets you test this page by creating a "tunnel" between its computer and yours, and then displaying the page on your monitor. Here, the Mac Snow Leopard operating system and Firefox browser (version 22) display a page as it will appear on a 1280- x 960-pixel screen.

Changing Settings in BrowserStack

Fortunately, you don't have to go through all those steps just to see your web page in a different browser. Once you view your first page, you can change the operating system and browser settings using the controls on the left side of the page (Figure 17-6). One of the great things about BrowserStack is the number of options available. Don't forget to preview your pages in using the iOS and Android operating systems.

FIGURE 17-6

The controls on the left side of the BrowserStack page let you change the operating system, browser, and screen size on the fly. Choose your options from the top three menus. The square red button stops the virtual machine (handy if you're trying to squeeze every second out of your 30-day free trial). Click Update to display the page using the new settings.

Testing Your Sites in Multiple Browsers

How can I test my website if I have only a couple of the most common browsers on my computer?

If you don't have every browser ever created on your Windows, Mac, and Linux machines (you *do* have all three, don't you?), you can use the BrowserStack service discussed on page 739 (at least to tackle the Windows, Mac, and mobile sides).

However, there are other options, such as CrossBrowserTesting.com (*http://CrossBrowserTesting.com*), which costs $30 a month (ouch) for 150 minutes of use and offers an added benefit: interactive testing. You see your page running remotely on a PC under your control, so you can test features that a screenshot can't capture, like Flash movie playback, animation, and JavaScript interactions.

Browsershots (*www.browsershots.org*) is a free alternative, which provides screenshots for a wide range of browsers that run on Windows and Linux systems.

Windows users can try out a program named IETester (*www.my-debugbar.com/wiki/IETester/HomePage*). It lets you see how your pages look in multiple versions of IE, including 6, 7, 8, 9, and 10. Microsoft also offers a browser testing program

called modern.IE (*http://www.modern.ie*), which focuses on the more recent versions of Internet Explorer.

You can see what a page looks like in Internet Explorer 5.5 all the way through 10 for free with NetRenderer, though your pages need to be on a publicly accessible website. Visit *http://ipinfo.info/netrenderer*, type in the URL of the page you want to see, and in a few moments NetRenderer displays a screenshot. Unfortunately, it doesn't take a picture of a complete web page—just the top part of it—if it's a long page, you won't see the bottom.

If you're a Mac person with an Intel chip at the heart of your system, you can install Windows on your machine using Apple's Bootcamp program (*www.apple.com/support/bootcamp/*) or use third-party "virtualization" software that runs Windows and Mac OS X simultaneously on the same computer (and believe it or not, the universe does *not* implode). VMWare Fusion for Macs (*www.vmware.com/products/fusion*) and Parallels Desktop (*www.parallels.com/products/desktop*) let you run multiple versions of Windows (XP, Vista, and Windows 7), as well as Mac OS X.

■ Find and Fix Broken Links

Broken links are inevitable. If you delete a file from your site, move a page or a graphic outside of Dreamweaver, or simply type an incorrect path name to a file, you may end up with broken links and missing graphics. In the B.D. era (Before Dreamweaver), you could fix such problems only by methodically examining every link on every page in your site. Fortunately, Dreamweaver's link-checking features automate the process.

> **NOTE** In this context, a link doesn't mean just a hyperlink connecting one page to another. Dreamweaver checks links to external files, such as PNGs, GIFs, and JPEGs that reside in different folders, external CSS style sheets, and JavaScript files. For example, if a graphic is missing or isn't in the place your page specifies, Dreamweaver reports a broken link.

Finding Broken Links

Dreamweaver's Check Links Sitewide command scans an entire site's worth of files and reports all the links and paths that don't lead to a file. (It's one of Dreamweaver's site management features, meaning that you have to set up a local site before you can use this command; see page 712 for instructions.) Note that Dreamweaver checks only links and paths *within* the local site folder; it doesn't check links that lead to other people's sites (see the note at the bottom of this page for a tool that helps with *that* annoying chore).

> **TIP** If your local site contains a lot of pages, you may not want to check links in one or more folders whose pages *you know* have no broken links. You can exclude files from the Check Links Sitewide operation using the Cloaking feature described on page 782. Doing so also makes the link-checking operation go faster.

■ CHECKING JUST ONE PAGE

To check links on an open page, save it in your local site folder and choose Window→Results→Link Checker. Dreamweaver scans the page and opens the Link Checker window, which lists any broken links (see Figure 17-7). If Dreamweaver doesn't find any—you HTML god, you—the window comes up empty.

> **NOTE** Although Dreamweaver can't check links to the outside world, a free tool from the W3C, called the Link Checker (*http://validator.w3.org/checklink*), can. It checks both internal links (to pages on the same site) and external links (to pages on other sites). The only possible downside: The pages you check must already be on the Web. Likewise, Webmaster Toolkit (*http://bit.ly/hcik3*) and 1-hit.com (*http://bit.ly/4v8wwi*) provide free online link-checking services.

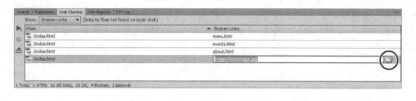

FIGURE 17-7

In addition to checking internal links, the Check Links Sitewide command generates a list of all external links and orphan files (files with no links to them). To see these details, use the Show menu. If you wish, click the Save button (the hard drive with a down arrow) to store all this information in a tab-delimited text file. You can fix a broken internal link directly inside this panel using the "Browse for File" button (circled).

■ CHECKING SPECIFIC PAGES

You can check links on specific pages of your site using the Link Checker panel:

1. **Choose Window→Results→Link Checker.**

   The Link Checker panel opens.

2. **Use the Files panel to select the site you want to check.**

   If you're already working on the site, skip this step.

3. **In the Files panel, select the files you want to check.**

   To learn all the ways you can select files and folders in the Files panel, see the box below.

   NOTE Selecting a folder in the Files panel makes Dreamweaver scan all the files in that folder.

4. **In the Link Checker, click the gray arrow on the left. From the menu that opens, choose "Check Links for Selected Files in Site."**

   Alternatively, you can right-click (Control-click) the selected files, and then, from the shortcut menu, choose Check Links→Selected Files.

   Either way, Dreamweaver scans the pages and displays any broken links (Figure 17-7).

Selection Shortcuts for the Files Panel

You'll often want to use the link-checking tools in Dreamweaver's Results panel on more than one page in your website. Fortunately, the link checker can work on multiple pages in the Files panel.

To select several consecutively listed files at once, click the first filename, scroll if necessary, and then Shift-click the last filename. Dreamweaver highlights all the files between your first and final clicks.

To select nonconsecutive files, click each one while pressing the Ctrl (⌘) key.

Once you select one or more files, you can deselect any single one by Ctrl-clicking (⌘-clicking) it once again.

Dreamweaver also includes a snazzy command that selects recently modified files in the Files panel. Suppose you want to select all the files you created or changed today (to see if the links work or to upload them to your web server). To do so, click the panel's drop-down menu button in the upper-right corner of the Files panel. From the menu that appears, select Edit→Select Recently Modified.

The Select Recently Modified window appears. You can either specify a range of dates (for files you created or changed between July 1, 2012, and July 7, 2012, for example) or a number of days (to specify all the files you modified in, say, the last 30 days). (The last option—Modified By—works only with Adobe's Contribute program.) Select the options, click OK, and then Dreamweaver selects the appropriate files in the Files panel.

■ **CHECKING AN ENTIRE WEBSITE**

You can check all the links on all the pages in your site in any of three ways. For all three techniques, you have to have your website selected in the Files panel (press F8 [Shift-⌘-F] to open the Files panel, and then use the panel's menu to select your site).

- Choose Site→Check Links Sitewide or use the keyboard shortcut Ctrl+F8 (⌘-F8).

- Open the Files panel and then right-click (Control-click) any file. From the shortcut menu, choose Check Links→Entire Local Site.

- Open the Link Checker panel (Window→Results→Link Checker), click the arrow on the upper-left side of the panel, and then, from its menu, choose "Check Links for Entire Current Local Site."

Once again, Dreamweaver scans your site and lists broken links in the Link Checker panel.

Fixing Broken Links

Of course, simply finding broken links is only half the battle. You also need to *fix* them. The Link Checker provides a quick and easy way to do that.

1. **In the Link Checker panel, click a filename in the Broken Links column.**

   Dreamweaver highlights the file's path, and displays a tiny folder icon to the right (Figure 17-7, circled).

TIP The Link Checker shows you which pages *contain* broken links, but doesn't show you the text or images for the link itself, which can make it difficult to figure out how to fix it ("Was that a button that links to the home page?"). In cases like that, *double-click* the file name in the Link Checker panel's left column. Dreamweaver opens the relevant web page and, even better, highlights the link on the page.

Once you determine where the link should lead ("Oh yeah, that's the button to the haggis buffet menu."), you can fix the link right on the page or go back to the Link Checker and make the change as described in the next step.

2. **Click the tiny folder icon on the right.**

   The Select File dialog box opens. From here, you can navigate to the correct page—the one that the link *should* have opened.

   If you prefer, you can type the correct path directly in the Link Checker. But that's usually not a good idea, since it's difficult to understand the path from one page to another just by looking at the Link Checker. Searching for the proper page using the Select File dialog box is a much more accurate and trouble-free method.

3. **Double-click the filename of the correct web page.**

   The Select File dialog box disappears, and Dreamweaver fixes the link.

   If your site contains other links that point to the same missing file, Dreamweaver asks if you'd like to fix those links, too—an amazing timesaver that can quickly repair broken links on dozens of pages.

NOTE Dreamweaver's behavior is a bit odd when it comes to fixing the same broken link, however. Once you fix one link, it remains selected in the Link Checker panel. You must click another broken link, or one of the buttons in the window, before Dreamweaver asks if you'd like to fix that same broken link on other pages.

4. **Continue to fix broken links, following steps 1–3.**

   Once you repair all the broken links, you can close the Results panel by double-clicking anywhere along the top row of tabs (for example, double-click the Link Checker tab). Double-clicking any tab reopens the Results panel.

Listing External Links

Although Dreamweaver doesn't verify links to external websites on your pages, it can list those links after you run the link checker. To see the list, choose External Links from the Link Checker's Show menu (see Figure 17-8). The list includes absolute URLs leading to other sites (like *http://www.yahoo.com*) as well as email links (like *mailto:reservations@cafesoylentgreen.com*).

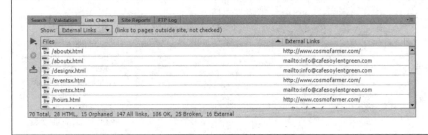

FIGURE 17-8

Although Dreamweaver can't check external links, you can use this window to change the URL of one.

This window is especially useful if you include a link to a certain external website several times throughout your site and decide to change it. For example, if you discover through testing (or through the W3C Link Checker) that an external link you peppered throughout your site no longer works:

1. **Choose Site→Check Links Sitewide (or press Ctrl+F8 [⌘-F8]).**

   Dreamweaver scans your site, and then opens the Link Checker panel.

2. **From the Show drop-down menu, choose External Links.**

   The window lists links you created to sites outside your own.

3. **Click the external link you want to change.**

   Dreamweaver highlights the link, indicating that you can now edit it.

4. **Type in the new URL, and then press Enter (Return).**

   If other pages contain the old URL, Dreamweaver asks if you want to fix them as well. If so, click Yes and the deed is done.

Orphaned Files

The Link Checker also provides a list of files that aren't used by *any* of your site's pages—*orphaned files*, as they're called. You wind up with an orphaned file when, for example, you save a GIF to your site folder but then never use it on a web page. Or you might delete the only link to a page you don't need anymore, making the page an orphaned file. Unless you think you may link to that file in the future, delete it to clean up unnecessary clutter.

In fact, that's the primary purpose of the Orphaned Files list: to identify old and unused files so you can delete them. Here's how it works:

1. **Choose Site→Check Links Sitewide, or press Ctrl+F8 (⌘-F8).**

   Dreamweaver opens the Link Checker panel.

2. **From the Show menu, choose Orphaned Files.**

   The list of orphaned files appears (see Figure 17-9).

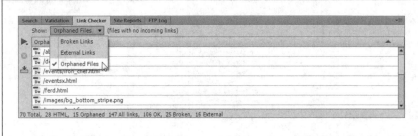

FIGURE 17-9

Identify (and delete) unused files with Dreamweaver's Orphaned Files option in the Link Checker panel. This panel can also list external links and broken links; use the Show menu to choose a set.

3. **Select the files you want to delete.**

   Ctrl-click (⌘-clicking) files to select them.

4. **Press Delete.**

   Dreamweaver asks if you really want to delete the files. Click OK if you do, or Cancel if you suddenly get cold feet.

Before you get spring-cleaning fever and delete all orphaned files in your site, however, keep a few pointers in mind:

- Just because your site doesn't *currently* use a file doesn't mean you won't need it again later. For example, say you have an employee-of-the-month page. In March, you included a photo of Robin Albert, your best salesperson. In April, someone else got the award, so you removed Robin's photo from the page. The photos still resides on your computer; it's just that no web page currently uses it, making it an orphan. But next month you may need the photo again, when Robin develops a spurt of motivation. So make sure a file really is useless before deleting it.

- More important, Dreamweaver may flag files your site actually *needs* as orphaned. For example, some sites include what's called a *splash page*: an introductory page that first appears when someone comes to the site. It can be a page with a bold graphic and the text "Click here to enter the site," or it may be a fancy Flash movie intended to make a big impact on your visitors. Usually, this page is nothing more than a welcome mat that leads to the *real* home page. Since it's simply an introductory page, no other page in the site links to it. Unfortunately, that's precisely what Dreamweaver considers an orphaned file.

- If you write your own JavaScript, you may reference graphic files and web pages. Dreamweaver doesn't keep track of references in your JavaScript code, and identifies those files as orphans (unless you insert or link to them elsewhere in the page or on your site).

On the other hand, Dreamweaver is somewhat smarter when it comes to Dreamweaver behaviors. It can track files referenced as part of its own JavaScript programs—for example, graphics files you use in a rollover effect—and doesn't list them as orphaned.

The bottom line is that while this report can be useful, use it cautiously when you delete files.

Changing a Link Site-Wide

Suppose you create a page to teach your visitors the basics of HTML. You think this page would be really, really helpful, so you create links to it from every page on your site. After a while, you realize that you just don't have the time to keep the page up to date, but you still want to help your visitors get this information. Why not change the link so that it points to a more current and informative source? Using Dreamweaver's Change Link Sitewide command, you can do just that. The process differs depending on whether you want to change a link that points to the outside world or one that points to another page on your site.

1. **Choose Site→Change Link Sitewide.**

   The Change Link Sitewide dialog box opens (see Figure 17-10), revealing two text fields, labeled "Change all links to" and "Into links to." Understanding what you're supposed to do at this point is easier if you imagine that the first label actually says "Change all links that *currently* point to." In other words, you first indicate where those links point to now, and then you indicate where they *should* point. To change links that point outside your site, go to step 2; to change links that lead within your site, see step 3.

FIGURE 17-10

Dreamweaver uses a root-relative link to specify the page whose URL you want to change, as indicated by the slash (/). Don't worry, this doesn't mean that Dreamweaver makes the link root-relative. It's just how Dreamweaver identifies the location of the page in the site. See page 171 for more on root-relative links.

2. **For links to a page outside your site, type the old web address in the "Change all links to" field.**

   For example, if your aim is to round up every link that now points to Yahoo and redirect it to Google, type *http://www.yahoo.com* here. Then, in the "Into links to" field, type the URL of the new web address, *http://www.google.com* here. The links on your site that used to lead to Yahoo will now to point to Google. Skip to step 4.

TIP   As a shortcut to following steps 1, 2, and 3, you can select a file in the Files panel and *then* choose Site→Change Link Sitewide. Dreamweaver automatically adds the selected file's path to the "Change all links to" field.

3. **To change links to a page *within* your site, click the folder icon to the right of the "Change all links to" field.**

   This brings up the "Select Link to Change" dialog box. Browse to the old link, the one you want to change throughout your site, and then click OK (Open).

   Next, specify the file that the link should point to *now*. Click the folder icon beside "Into links to" to open the "Select Link to Change" dialog box again. Select a file in the local site folder, and then click OK (Open).

   Your new link can point to graphics, Cascading Style Sheets, or any other file you can include in a web page. You'll get unpredictable results, however, if you change a link that points to a graphic file into, say, a link that points to a web page, or vice versa. Make sure the "before" and "after" links share the same file type, whether that's a web page, style sheet, or graphic.

TIP   For another way to change one external link into another, see Figure 17-8.

4. **Click OK in the Change Link Sitewide box to make the change.**

   The same Update Files dialog box you encountered in the last chapter appears now, listing every page Dreamweaver will change.

5. **Click Update to update the pages.**

   Dreamweaver scans your site and updates the pages.

◼ Validating Web Pages

The Web is a far-flung collection of technologies, programming languages, and people, all working together. When you think about it, it's pretty amazing that an 11-year-old in Fargo, North Dakota, can create a website millions of people around the world can view, and that dozens of different browsers, from Internet Explorer to smartphones, can browse the same site. This kind of global communication owes its success in large part to the World Wide Web Consortium (the W3C), an organization composed of representatives from universities, research institutions, corporations, and government agencies dedicated to creating standards for different Internet-related technologies.

The W3C developed standards for HTML5, CSS, XML, and other Web languages, and continues to create new standards as technologies evolve. Thanks to these standards, companies have a guide to follow when they create new websites or new web browsers.

It sure would be great if all companies followed the W3C's standards when building web browsers, and all web designers followed the standards when building web pages. Then anyone with any web browser could view any web page. What a wonderful world *that* would be—you'd never have to test your pages in different browsers!

Of course, this kind of utopian thinking hasn't always been applied by the major browser makers. As a result, web developers have been forced to come up with techniques to deal with the way different browsers display HTML. Dreamweaver CS4 and earlier included a built-in web page validator, but it wasn't always accurate and frequently came up with results that were different from the definitive online validator offered by the W3C (*http://validator.w3.org*). Because of that, Dreamweaver CS5 dropped its home-grown validator. But validation is so important that Adobe added the validator back into Dreamweaver CS5.5—but this time, rather than using its own tool, Adobe decided to use the online validator offered by the W3C.

NOTE Because Dreamweaver CC uses the W3C's online validator, you have to have an Internet connection to use this feature.

Steps for Validating Web Pages

Dreamweaver's validation tool works on only one page at a time, and only with a page you've opened in the document window. To validate an open page:

1. **Choose File→Validate→Validate Current Document (W3C).**

   If it's not already open, the W3C Validation tab opens in the results panel at the bottom of screen.

NOTE There's another choice under the File→Validate menu: Validate Live Document (W3C). You can select this option when you use Dreamweaver's Live View (page 51). For a plain HTML file, the Validate Live Document option isn't any different from the Validate Current Document command, but it's handy when working with some types of server-side pages, like the PHP pages discussed in Chapter 22, or a page created by a content management system like WordPress, Joomla, or Drupal.

NOTE In content management systems, what looks like a single web page from a visitor's perspective is usually many different files pieced together using information from a database to create a single HTML file. This means you can't just open a file in a WordPress site in Dreamweaver and validate it—instead, you need to view a WordPress page in Live View to see the finished HTML page and then choose File→Validate→Validate Live Document (W3C).

2. **Review the results.**

   Dreamweaver displays the results in the Validation panel (Figure 17-11) and divides each message into four columns: The first includes an icon that indicates the severity of the error, the second lists the file name, the third lists the line of code the message applies to, and the fourth describes the validation error or message.

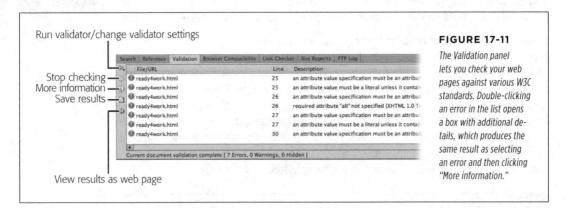

Run validator/change validator settings

Stop checking
More information
Save results

View results as web page

FIGURE 17-11

The Validation panel lets you check your web pages against various W3C standards. Double-clicking an error in the list opens a box with additional details, which produces the same result as selecting an error and then clicking "More information."

The icon at the beginning of the message helps you determine which errors are important. A red stop sign identifies a violation of the page's doctype (HTML 4.01 Transitional, XTHML 1.0 Transitional, HTML5, and so on).

In some cases, this warning can indicate that a mandatory tag (like the <body> tag) is missing—a serious problem.

Other stop-sign errors aren't necessarily fatal. For example, some JavaScript widgets may use tag attributes that are technically invalid, but won't cause problems on the page. Less serious problems are flagged with little message balloons. These may inform you that the page has *no* problems, or point out optional fixes.

NOTE Dreamweaver's validation feature doesn't help with CSS files. To make sure your CSS files are valid, you can use the W3C's CSS Validator (*http://jigsaw.w3.org/css-validator*), which lets you either point to a file out on the web, upload a CSS file (or an HTML file with an internal CSS style sheet), or simply paste a CSS style sheet into an online form. The CSS Validator then checks your style sheet to make sure you didn't make any mistakes in writing your CSS.

3. **Fix the errors.**

Alas, Dreamweaver can't fix all validation errors. It does fix errors related to improperly written code, as described on page 310. But for other errors, you need to go into the code and use your knowledge of HTML to fix the problems. For help with HTML code, see Chapter 7 (page 348).

To get started, double-click one of the errors listed in the Validation results panel. If you start in Design view, Dreamweaver switches you to Split view and puts your cursor next to the invalid HTML. You can then delete or modify the offending code. Keep in mind, though, that the code Dreamweaver produces is the result of many thousands of hours of engineering and testing. Unless you're sure you know how to fix a problem, you may just want to trust the code Dreamweaver produces.

Cleaning Up HTML (and XHTML)

You've been reading about what great HTML Dreamweaver writes, and how, no matter what doctype you pick (XHTML 1, HTML 4.01, or HTML5, for example), Dreamweaver adds the correct tags in the correct order. But there are exceptions to every rule. In the process of formatting text, deleting elements, and—in general—building a web page, it's quite possible to end up with less-than-optimal HTML. While Dreamweaver usually catches potentially sloppy code, you may nonetheless run across instances of empty tags, redundant tags, and nested tags in your Dreamweaver pages.

For example, in the normal course of adding, editing, and deleting content on a page (either by hand or even in Dreamweaver's Design view), you can occasionally end up with code like this:

```
<div> </div>
```

This empty tag doesn't serve any purpose, it just adds unnecessary HTML to your page. Remember, the less code your page uses, the faster it loads. Eliminating redundant tags can improve your site's download speed.

Another possible source of errors is you. When you type HTML in Code view or open pages created by another (perhaps inferior) program, you may introduce errors you need to clean up later.

Aware of its own limitations (and yours), Dreamweaver provides a command designed to streamline the code in your pages: Clean Up HTML (if you're using Dreamweaver's XHTML mode, the command is called Clean Up XHTML). This command not only improves the HTML in your page, it also strips out nonessential code like comments and special Dreamweaver markup code, and it can delete HTML tags you specify.

NOTE The Clean Up HTML command doesn't fix really bad errors, like missing closing tags or improperly nested tags. You can have Dreamweaver automatically fix mistakes like these when it opens a file by turning on the code-rewriting features in Dreamweaver's preferences. Choose Edit→Preferences and then, in the list on the left, click Code Rewriting. Turn on "Fix invalidly nested and unclosed tags" and "Remove extra closing tags."

To clean up your HTML:

1. **Open the web page you want to clean up.**

   Unfortunately, this great feature works on only one page at a time—no cleaning up a site's worth of pages in one fell swoop! Accordingly, it's best to first use the Site Reports feature (see page 758) to identify problem pages, and then open them in Dreamweaver and run this command.

2. **Choose Commands→Clean Up HTML (or Clean Up XHTML).**

   The Clean Up HTML/XHTML window appears (see Figure 17-12).

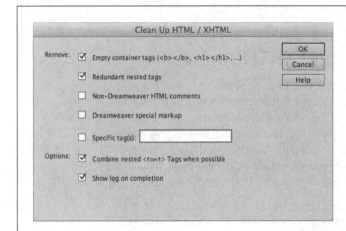

FIGURE 17-12

The Clean Up HTML/XHTML command lets you strip out redundant and useless code. You can even use it to delete unnecessary tags by targeting them in the "Specific tag(s)" field (although the "Find and Replace" command provides a much more powerful way to identify and remove HTML tags; see Chapter 8).

> **TIP** The Clean Up HTML command is extremely useful. Once you try it a few times, you'll probably want to use it on all your pages. Unfortunately, it doesn't come with a keyboard shortcut. This is a classic example of where Dreamweaver's keyboard-shortcut editor is just the white knight you need; using it, you can add a keystroke combination to trigger this command from the keyboard. See page 869 for details.

3. **Turn on the checkboxes for the options you want.**

   Here's a rundown:

   - **Empty container tags** deletes tags that don't actually contain anything. For example, you may have deleted text you set in boldface, leaving behind opening and closing bold tags without any text in between: *<strong> </strong>*. Or you may have deleted an image within a link, leaving behind a useless pair of <a> tags. It's always a good idea to turn on this option.

   - **Redundant nested tags** deletes tags that appear within other tags of the same type, like this:

     `<strong>You can't get any <strong>bolder</strong> than bold</strong>`

The inner set of bold tags does no good, so choosing this option produces this HTML:

```
<strong> You can't get any bolder than bold</strong>
```

This option is extremely useful, so turn it on.

- **Non-Dreamweaver HTML comments** deletes any comments *not* inserted by Dreamweaver as part of its site management tools. For example, the Dreamweaver Template tool (Chapter 20) inserts HTML comments to help you identify different parts of a template. But web designers also place notes within their code as instructions or to explain parts of the code. (These comments are invisible in a browser, by the way. They appear only in Code view, or in Dreamweaver's document window as a gold comment icon.) If you've finished with the page and doubt you'll need the information the comments contain, you can decrease the page's file size a little bit by using this option.

> **NOTE** Dreamweaver's Clean Up HTML command doesn't strip out CSS comments. If you use Dreamweaver's CSS Layouts, you'll find the style sheets loaded with CSS comments. To remove them, visit *http://tinyurl.com/6kcmq4g*. There, you can download a "stored query" (a reusable search) to use with Dreamweaver's "Find and Replace" tool.

- **Dreamweaver special markup** deletes any special code Dreamweaver inserted in your pages. Dreamweaver relies on special programming code to make some of its features, including tracing images, libraries (Chapter 19), and templates (Chapter 20), work. Choosing this option eliminates that special code, so use it with care. (Since the template feature can add a fair amount of this specialized code, Dreamweaver includes a Template Export command that lets you export an entire site with all the template code removed; see page 857.)

- **Specific tag(s)** deletes HTML tags you specify. Type the name of the tag (without brackets) in the field like this: *font*. To remove multiple tags at once, separate each tag name by a comma, like this: *font, blink*.

  Be careful with this option. Since it lets you remove *any* tag from a page, you could easily delete an important and necessary tag (like the <body> tag) from your page by accident. Furthermore, Dreamweaver's "Find and Replace" command provides a much more powerful tool for doing this kind of surgery (see Chapter 8).

- **Combine nested <font> tags when possible** combines multiple *font* properties into a single tag. Hopefully, you've moved to CSS for all your text formatting needs, so you don't use the <font> tag in your HTML, nor do you need this option.

- To see a report of all the changes Dreamweaver makes to a page, turn on the "**Show log on completion**" checkbox.

4. Click OK to clean up the page.

If you turned on the "Show Log on completion" checkbox, Dreamweaver displays a dialog box listing the types and number of changes it made to the page.

NOTE When running this command on an XHTML page, Dreamweaver also checks to make sure the syntax of the page matches that of an XHTML document. Among other concerns, all tags in XHTML must be lowercase, and you have to correctly terminate any empty tags—
 for the line break tag, for example. Dreamweaver fixes such problems.

As long as you keep the page open, you can undo the changes Dreamweaver makes. Suppose you asked Dreamweaver to remove comments, and then you suddenly realized you really did need them. Ctrl+Z (⌘-Z) is your savior.

TIP While Dreamweaver generally does a good job of avoiding extra, and unnecessary, HTML tags, you'll still find pages that have empty paragraphs with just a single nonbreaking space (page 75) in them, like this:

```
<p>  </p>
```

Dreamweaver inserts these paragraphs whenever you're in Design view and hit the Enter (Return) key. It fills the <p> tag with whatever you type; if you don't type anything, Dreamweaver leaves the <p> tag empty. Well, it's not quite empty since it holds a nonbreaking space, so the Clean Up HTML command's "Empty container tags" option won't help here since the container's not empty. Instead, turn to Dreamweaver's "Find and Replace" tool (Chapter 8), and search the source code for *<p> </p>*; leave the Replace value blank, and Dreamweaver strips these almost-empty <p> tags from your page (or site).

■ Site Reporting

The Clean Up HTML command is a great way to make sure you have lean code, but what if you forget about it until after you build all 500 pages of your site? Do you have to open each page and run the command, whether there's a problem or not?

Fortunately, no. Dreamweaver's Site Reports feature makes identifying problems throughout a site a snap. Dreamweaver not only locates problems that the Clean Up HTML command can fix, it checks your pages for other problems, such as missing titles, empty Alt properties for images, and other issues that can make your site less accessible to disabled web surfers.

TIP To save time when running a report, you can exclude selected folders from a site report using the Cloaking feature described on page 782.

After you run a report, Dreamweaver lists pages with problems. Unfortunately, the Site Reports feature only *finds* problems, it doesn't fix them. You have to open and fix each page individually.

To run a report on one or more web pages:

1. **Choose Site→Reports.**

    The Reports window opens (see Figure 17-13).

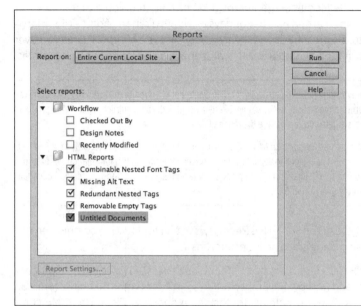

FIGURE 17-13

Dreamweaver's Site Reports feature makes quick work of finding common page errors. You won't use all these options, but at the very least, make sure you check for missing Alt text (page 233) and any untitled documents before you put a new website up on the Internet.

2. **From the "Report on" menu, select the files you want to analyze.**

    Dreamweaver can report on a single web page, on multiple pages, or on an entire site. Choose Current Document to check the web page you have open at the moment. Select Entire Current Local Site to check every web page in the local site folder, including folders within the site folder. This option is great when you want to check your entire site prior to uploading it to a web server and making it "live" (more on that in the next chapter).

    Choosing "Selected Files in Site" checks only the files you choose in the Files panel. You need to open the Files panel and then select the files from the local file list for this option to work. (See the box on page 747 for ways to select files.) Choose this option when you modify pages on, or add pages to, a site and you're ready to move them to your server.

    Select the Folder option to check all web pages in a selected folder. After you choose it, Dreamweaver displays an empty field and a folder icon. Click the folder icon to open a dialog box where you locate and select the folder you want to check; Dreamweaver automatically checks folders within your selected folder. You can also use this option to check pages that aren't actually part of the current site.

3. Select the types of report you want Dreamweaver to generate.

Dreamweaver displays two kinds of report in the Reports window. The first set, Workflow Reports, deals mostly with collaboration features that facilitate team work environments (see the following chapter). The last option in this group—Recently Modified—generates a list of files that you either created or modified within a certain number of days or within a range of dates (February 1 of last year to the present, say). When you run this type of report, Dreamweaver lists the files in the Site Reports panel *and* opens a web page listing those files.

NOTE The Recently Modified site report looks for files created or changed in the last seven days, but you can adjust that timeframe. In the Reports window, select Recently Modified, and then click Report Settings (Figure 17-13). A window appears where you can change the range of dates.

In fact, you'll find the technique described on page 747 more useful. It not only identifies recently modified files, it also selects them in the Files panel, giving you many more options for acting on this information. For example, with your recently modified files selected, you can upload them to your server, run find-and-replace operations on just those files, or apply many other tools.

The second type of report, HTML Reports, is useful for locating common errors, such as missing page titles or Alt properties.

Three of the HTML Reports options—Combinable Nested Font Tags, Redundant Nested Tags, and Removable Empty Tags—search for pages that have common code mistakes. These problems are the same ones the Clean Up HTML command fixes (see page 755).

Turn on the Missing Alt Text checkbox to search for images that lack a text description (see page 233).

Finally, turn on the Untitled Documents checkbox to identify pages that are either missing a title or that still have Dreamweaver's default title.

NOTE The Site Report command doesn't identify XHTML syntax errors like those fixed by the Clean Up XHTML command (see page 755).

4. Click Run.

Dreamweaver analyzes the pages you specified and produces a report based on the settings you specified in step 3 (see Figure 17-14). Each line in the Results window displays the name of the file, the line number where the error occurs, and a description of the error.

5. In the Results panel, double-click the filename.

Dreamweaver opens the file and highlights the offending code.

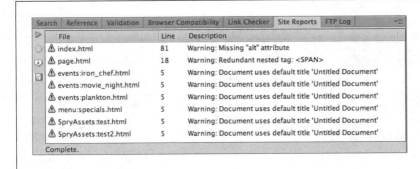

FIGURE 17-14

If you decide that Dream-weaver's taking too long to generate the error report, you can always stop the operation. In the Results panel's left-hand toolbar, click the icon that looks like a stop sign with an X through it (the icon is normally grayed out, but it's bold when Dreamweaver is busy generating a site report).

6. **Fix the problem according to its type.**

   For a page containing Combinable Nested Font Tags, Redundant Nested Tags, or Removable Empty Tags errors, use the Clean Up HTML command as described on page 755.

   For pages missing a title, add one by opening the page and typing a title in the document window's Title box as described on page 7.

   You can add missing Alt properties using the Properties panel, as described on page 233, but, if the same image is missing its Alt property on several pages, you may find it faster to use Dreamweaver's powerful "Find and Replace" command (see Chapter 8).

7. **Continue opening files from the Results window and fixing them until you correct each mistake.**

   Unfortunately, Dreamweaver doesn't provide a quick, one-step method to fix most of these problems. Except for missing Alt text, which you can universally add using the "Find and Replace" command, you must open and fix each page individually.

If you want to save the results of your report, click Save Report. Dreamweaver opens a Save As dialog box, and lets you save the report as an XML file (so you can file it in the "Files I don't really need" folder on your desktop).

Moving Your Site to the Internet

Building web pages on your computer is a big accomplishment, but it's not the whole job. Your beautifully designed and informative site will languish in obscurity unless you move it from your hard drive to a web server.

Fortunately, once your site is ready for prime time, you can put it on a server without ever leaving the comfort of Dreamweaver. The program includes simple commands for transferring files back and forth between the server and your desktop. All you need to do is provide Dreamweaver with the information it needs to connect to your server.

> **NOTE** Dreamweaver CC includes many enhancements to its file transfer abilities. It's now a lot faster, and it allows multiple, simultaneous connections to a server. In other words, the old Dreamweaver transferred files one at a time, but the new one can send multiple files at once.

■ Adding a Remote Server

As you work on your website on your computer—whether you build the site from scratch or add and modify existing pages—you keep your files in a *local root folder* (see page 25), often called a *local site* for short. You can think of a local site as a work-in-progress; you'll routinely have partially finished documents sitting on your computer.

After you perfect and test your pages using the techniques described in Chapter 17, you're ready to transfer those pages to a server that's connected to the Internet; this server stores copies of your site files so it can dispense them to visitors.

Dreamweaver calls this server the *remote server*, and you can transfer your local site files to it several ways:

- **FTP.** By far, the most common method is *FTP*, or File Transfer Protocol. Just as HTTP is the process by which web pages are transferred from servers to web browsers, so FTP is the traditional way to transfer files from one drive to another over the Internet. If your site resides at a web hosting company or your Internet Service Provider (ISP), you'll use this option or, even better, the SFTP option discussed next. One downside of FTP is that none of the information you transfer using it—including your user name and password—is encrypted. It's possible, therefore (though very unlikely), for someone monitoring the flow of data over the Internet to spot your user name and password and log into your web server and wreak havoc on your site.

- **SFTP** stands for *Secure* FTP. This transfer method encrypts *all* your data, including your user name and password, so information you transfer this way is unintelligible to Internet snoops. It's the ideal way to connect to a web server, and in many cases, it's also faster. Unfortunately, not all web hosting companies offer this advanced option, so you may be stuck with regular FTP. If you're not sure if you can use SFTP, try it—Dreamweaver will tell you if it's unable to transfer files that way. Should that be the case, switch to FTP.

- **FTP over SSL/TSL,** also called FTPS, provides security that regular FTP lacks. It encrypts your login information, and, optionally, all the data—web pages, images, and so on—that you transfer as well. Because your user name and password are secure, SFTP is a better choice for file transfers, but if your server runs Windows, SFTP isn't available. If that's the case, you can try a couple of other options. FTP over SSL/TSL comes in two flavors, Implicit (an older and less-well-supported method) and Explicit (the newer, now-standard form of FTPS). If your web server runs Windows, try connecting to it in this order: FTP over SSL/TSL (Explicit encryption); if that doesn't work, try Implicit encryption, and, finally, if that fails, use plain old FTP.

- **Local/network.** If you work on an intranet, or if your company's web server is connected to the company network, you may also be able to transfer files just as you would any other file on your office network (using the Network Neighborhood, My Network Places, or "Connect to Server" command, depending on your operating system).

- The last two options—**WebDAV and RDS**—are file-management systems for collaborative web development. They're not very common, so you're unlikely to ever use them, but you'll learn about them on pages 773 and 774.

Beyond Dreamweaver

Do I have to use Dreamweaver to move my files to the Web?

No. If you use another program to transfer files, like FileZilla (Windows, Mac, and Linux), Cyberduck (Windows and Mac), CuteFTP (Windows), or RBrowser (Mac), you can continue to use it and ignore Dreamweaver's Remote Site feature.

But if you've never used Dreamweaver to move files, you may want to at least try it because it simplifies the process. For example, to move a file from your computer to a web server using a regular FTP program, you must first browse for the file on your local machine and then navigate to the proper folder on your server. Dreamweaver saves you both steps; when you select the file in the Files panel and click the Put button (see page 776), Dreamweaver automatically locates the file on your computer and transfers it to the correct folder on your server.

Setting Up a Remote Server with FTP or SFTP

You can set up a remote server only if you first set up a *local* site on your computer, as described on page 885. If you built your site in Dreamweaver, you should already have a local site set up. Once you do, you need to tell Dreamweaver how to connect to the remote server so it can transfer your local site files to your server:

1. **Choose Site→Manage Sites.**

   The Manage Sites dialog box opens, listing all the sites you've defined so far. You're about to tell Dreamweaver how to connect to a web server so you can create a living, Internet-based *copy* of one of these hard drive-based local sites.

   NOTE Even if all you want to do is copy a live website from the Internet to your computer, you need a local site on your computer, and you want to point Dreamweaver to a folder within that local site—even if it's just an empty folder—so it has a place to store the files you download.

2. **Click the name of the site you want to put on the Internet, and then click the "Edit the currently selected site" button, also known as the pencil icon in the lower-left corner of the Manage Sites window.**

   Alternatively, just double-click the site name in the list. The Site Setup window appears for the selected site, as shown in Figure 18-1.

   NOTE You can set up your local site and remote server simultaneously, when you first begin creating your site, as described on page 19. Even then, however, Dreamweaver requires that you first give the site a name and choose a local site folder. At that point, you can rejoin the steps described here.

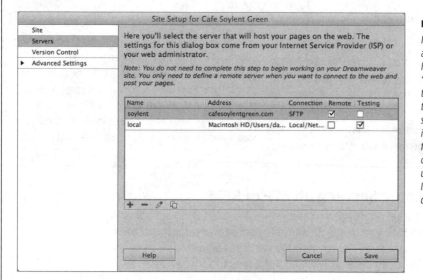

FIGURE 18-1

In addition to setting up a local site, Dreamweaver lets you set up both a "remote" server (meaning the web server on the Internet where people go to see your site) and a "testing" server (a server—frequently running on your own computer—usually used to test dynamic sites, like the PHP-driven pages described in Chapter 22).

3. **Click the Servers option.**

   This is where Dreamweaver lists your remote and testing servers. The remote server contains the site the world can see, while the testing server acts as a test bed, usually for dynamic, database-driven sites. If you're building a site without using PHP, ASP, ColdFusion, or some other server-side programming language, you don't need to set up a testing server.

   Initially, the Servers category is empty: You need to add a remote server.

   NOTE Dreamweaver lets you define as many remote and testing servers as you want, but you probably won't ever have a need for "infinity" servers. However, you may need to upload the same site to two different servers—perhaps you have a high-traffic website and put the site on several servers to balance the load. In that case, you can define a second, third, and even a fourth server. Note, though, that you can only "turn on" one remote server at a time. In other words, you can only upload and download to and from the server that has the Remote checkbox selected.

4. **Click the + sign button.**

   A new pane pops up (see Figure 18-2). Here, you supply the information Dreamweaver needs to connect to the server.

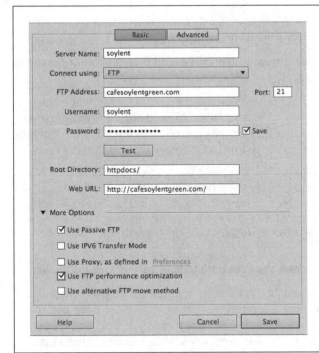

FIGURE 18-2

To connect to a server, you need to know its Web address, the FTP user name and password, and the name of the folder where the server stores your files. You get all this information when you sign up with a web hosting company. You usually don't need to change the "More Options" settings when you transfer files using FTP, though they can help if you're having connectivity problems (see the box on page 770). (If you use SFTP, the "More Options" menu doesn't appear.)

5. **Type a name in the Server Name field.**

   Dreamweaver only uses this name internally. It's not something anyone else will see, so name it anything you like, such as "My Server" or "Hosting Company."

6. **From the "Connect using" drop-down menu, choose either FTP or SFTP.**

   Ideally, you'll use SFTP—it's more secure and usually faster—but your web hosting company may not offer it, in which case you'll have to choose FTP.

   NOTE If you're not sure whether your server supports SFTP, try it out. Follow these set-up instructions using SFTP as the "Connect using" option, and then click the Test button. If Dreamweaver can't connect, try FTPS (discussed next). If you still can't tap the server, try regular FTP. And if Dreamweaver *still* can't connect, you probably typed the wrong user name, password, or FTP address.

7. **Fill in the "FTP address" field.**

   This is the address of your web server. It's usually something like *www.cafesoylentgreen.com*. It never includes directories, folders, or slashes (like *www.cafesoylentgreen.com/menu*); never includes codes for the FTP protocol (*ftp://ftp.cafesoylentgreen.com*) or HTTP protocol (*http://www.cafesoylentgreen.com*); and it may simply be a domain name, such as *cafesoylentgreen.com*. It can also be an IP address, like *64.226.43.116*. In most cases, it's the address you type in a web browser's address window (minus the *http://*) to get to your site's home page.

If you don't know the address, there's only one way to find out: Call or email your web hosting company or ISP, or check its website.

8. **In the Username field, type your user name, and then type your password in the Password field.**

Dreamweaver uses bullets (••••) to display your password so that office evil-doers can't see what you type. If you want Dreamweaver to remember your password each time you use the program, turn on the Save checkbox. That way, you won't have to type your password each time you connect to the server.

> **NOTE**   For security reasons, don't turn on the Save box if you access the Web using computers at, say, your local library, community college, or anywhere else where people you don't trust can use the machine. Otherwise, you might awaken one morning to find the following splattered across your home page: "Hi there! Welcome to Jack's house of illegally acquired and unlawfully distributed music, featuring Justin Bieber's greatest hits."

9. **In the Root Directory box, type the path to your server's root directory.**

Here, you specify the path to the *folder* on the web server that contains your web page files. This folder, known as the root folder, is the counterpart to the folder on your hard drive that holds your site files as you work on them. Common names for this folder include *docs, www, htdocs, public_html, httpdocs*, and *virtual_html*.

When you connect to your server using FTP, you rarely connect to that root folder itself. You often connect *outside* that folder, sometimes to an administrative folder for your web account, which the web host fills with site traffic reports and other housekeeping files.

The path you type in the Root Directory box depends on where on the server Dreamweaver's FTP tool connects—and that all depends on how your web host set up the server, so the only way to know what to type into this box is to contact your web host.

In many cases, you only have to type the name of the root folder followed by a slash, like this: *htdocs/.* You're specifying the path from the folder that Dreamweaver initially connects to via FTP—the web hosting company's administrative folder—to your site's root folder. In this example, Dreamweaver connects to a folder that contains the root folder, so you simply say, "Hey Dreamweaver, you're in the wrong place. Go inside the htdocs folder to find my site."

Sometimes, however, you need to use a much longer path, one that includes lots of folders, like this: */var/www/mysite.com/htdocs/.*

This type of path includes the entire path from the top level of the server's hard drive through several folders and, finally, to your root folder (htdocs) on the server. Again, there's no real way to determine the path without asking your web hosting company.

10. **Type your site's web address in the Web URL box.**

This is simply what you'd type in your web browser's address line to get to your site: *www.cafesoylentgreen.com/*, for example. Sometimes, though, you might work on files in a subdirectory of the site's root folder. For example, if you work in corporate web design, you might oversee a self-contained site for the marketing department, which means the URL to reach the files you work on might be at *www.mycompany.com/marketing*. If that's the case, you should also include the subdirectory's name in the URL, as in *www.cafesoylentgreen. com/marketing*.

NOTE What you type into the Web URL box when you set up a remote server can affect how Dreamweaver checks and updates links. See the box on page 716 for details.

---

11. **Click the Test button.**

Dreamweaver attempts to connect to your server. If it succeeds, you'll see a box that says, "Dreamweaver connected to your Web server successfully." If it didn't succeed, you'll get an error message. See the box on page 770 for the most common problems and solutions.

NOTE When Dreamweaver can't connect to a server, one of the first things you should try (after double-checking your user name and password) is turning on the "Use passive FTP" checkbox. See the box on page 770 for more.

---

12. **Click Save to save these settings.**

Dreamweaver returns to the Servers category of the Site Setup window (Figure 18-1).

13. **Click Save once again to return to the Manage Sites window, and then click Done.**

At this point, you're ready to connect to your web server and transfer files. If you're the only person working on the site, Dreamweaver's Get and Put commands will do the trick (page 776). If, however, you're part of a development team, you can use Dreamweaver's Check In/Check Out feature, described on page 785, to make sure a co-worker doesn't accidentally erase your hard work (or, ah, you theirs).

More Remote Server Options for FTP

The steps discussed above will be probably be all you ever need to transfer your files by FTP, but Dreamweaver offers a few more options, as well as some advanced settings that apply to all types of connections (see "Advanced Remote Server Settings" on page 775).

To see the additional options for FTP connections, click the More Options arrow from the Basic server setup window (see Figure 18-2). Most of these checkboxes should remain turned off, but here's what they do:

- **Use Passive FTP**. Select this setting if you can't make an FTP connection and you know you typed your FTP address, user name, password, and root directory name correctly (see steps 7–9 on page 767). You can use this option to address firewall lockout—that's when hardware- or software-based gateways that control incoming and outgoing traffic through a network prevent you from connecting. Firewalls protect your company's network or your personal computer from hackers, but they also limit how computers inside the network—behind the firewall—connect to the outside world.

FREQUENTLY ASKED QUESTION

When Your Remote Site Is Too Remote

Help! I can't connect to my web server. What should I do?

Things don't always go smoothly when you try to connect to the outside world. That's doubly true when you try to connect to a web server, since you depend on a variety of things—your Internet connection, the networks connecting you to the server, the server itself, and the FTP software that runs the show—working together in harmony. Dreamweaver presents an error message if you can't successfully establish an FTP connection with your server. The error box frequently contains useful information that can help you diagnose the problem. Here are some of the most common messages and their meaning:

- **"Remote host cannot be found"** usually means that you typed in an incorrect FTP host address (step 7 on page 767).

- **"Cannot open server folder"** usually means you mistyped the name of the root directory, or you've got the wrong name for it (see step 9 on page 768).

Unfortunately, there are lots of reasons why Dreamweaver may not be able to connect to a server, so sometimes the error message isn't particularly helpful—you'll often get a really large dialog box listing all those reasons. Even if you simply got your login or password incorrect, Dreamweaver spits out a long list of possible problems.

The first thing to do is double- (and triple-) check your username and password. Here are a few other suggestions: Make sure you're connected to the Internet (open a web browser and see if you can visit a site); return to the Site Setup window for the site, open the Servers pane, and turn on the "Use passive FTP" option under More Options (sometimes this just makes things work). In the same window, turn off the "Use FTP performance optimization" checkbox, and if you have another FTP program, like FileZilla or Cyberduck, see if you can connect using the same settings you gave Dreamweaver. If all these steps fail, visit the Adobe website at *http://tinyurl. com/2crmqey* for more troubleshooting tips.

- **Use IPV6 Transfer Mode**. You probably won't need to turn on this checkbox, but the day has finally arrived when the IP addresses we've all used for years—like 192.16.16.62—have all been used up. The new standard—called IPV6—contains many, many, many more possible addresses (340,282,366,920,938,463,463,374, 607,431,768,211,456, to be precise), so we shouldn't be running out any time soon. If your web server uses an IPV6 address (which looks something like 1A23:120B :0000:0000:0000:7634:AD01:004D), your web hosting company will tell you.

- **Use Proxy.** If you can't connect to your remote server and your company's system administrator confirms that you have a firewall, turn on the Use Proxy checkbox (also found in Site Setup→Servers→More Options), and click the Preferences link to open the Site category of the Preferences window. Enter the name of the computer hosting the firewall, along with its port number. Your firewall configuration may also require that you transfer files using passive FTP. Check with your administrator to see if this is the case, and, if so, head back to the More Options section and turn on the checkbox next to "Use passive FTP."

- **Use FTP performance optimization.** Dreamweaver normally turns on this checkbox because it helps speed up file transfers between your computer and your web server. However, it can also be a source of connection problems. If you can't connect to your server, try turning off this checkbox.

- **Use alternative FTP move method.** If everything's okay when you connect to your server but you're getting errors when you move files there, turn on this option. It's slower than FTP, but more reliable. It's also handy if you use Adobe's Contribute program for editing web pages, and take advantage of its "rollback" feature (to learn more about Contribute, visit *www.adobe.com/contribute/*).

NOTE When you set up a remote server, you'll see an Advanced button, which lets you set additional options. You can usually skip these settings, but turn to page 775 if you want to know what they do.

Setting Up a Remote Server Using FTP over SSL/TLS

As mentioned earlier, FTP isn't the safest way to transfer files: It transmits your username and password over the airwaves, and some nefarious hacker could grab that information and use it to log into your web server, wreck your site, and ruin your reputation. That's pretty unlikely, but still possible. SFTP is a much better option, but it's not available on Windows servers, so if your web host uses a server running Windows (as opposed to Linux/Unix, the more common web server operating system), try to use "FTP over SSL/TLS."

FTP over SSL/TLS (also known as FTPS or FTPSE) comes in two flavors, Implicit encryption and Explicit encryption. Use Explicit encryption since it's newer, has more features, and is an agreed-upon standard. Implicit encryption is only offered to support older servers, which don't offer Explicit encryption.

Most of the settings for FTP over SSL/TLS are the same as those for regular FTP, so you can follow steps 1–10 on page 765, but instead of choosing FTP from the "Connect using" menu, choose "FTP over SSL/TLS." The main difference between regular FTP and FTP over SSL/TLS is the use of a "server certificate" to "authenticate" the web server. That just means that the web server has a special file on it (kind of like an identification card) that "proves" it is the web server it says it is, so you know that you're really connecting to your server and not some evil server pretending to be yours (jeez, these web guys are paranoid).

Basically, if your server is set up for FTPS, you choose either None or Trusted Server from the Authentication menu (see Figure 18-3). You'll need to contact whoever is in charge of your server (your web host or your company's IT department) to determine which option you need. Once you make a selection, click Test to see if Dreamweaver can connect to your server. If not, see the troubleshooting advice in the box on page 770.

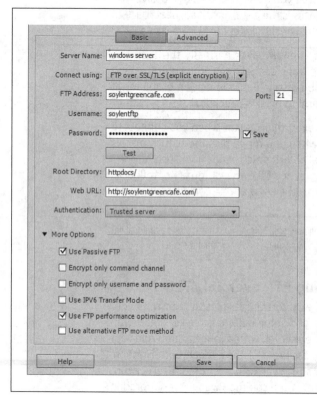

FIGURE 18-3

If you use "FTP over SSL/TLS" to connect to your web server, you'll find a few additional options under "More Options." "Encrypt only command channel" obscures only your login information and the commands you send to the server. The actual data, like web pages and images, goes out uncloaked. This translates to faster uploads and downloads. The "Encrypt only username and password" option hides just your login information (not your commands), and is a fine choice unless you're uploading particularly sensitive information that you don't want the rest of the world to see.

Setting Up a Remote Server over a Local Network

If you work on an intranet, or if your company's web server is connected to the company network, you may be able to transfer site files just as you'd move any files from machine to machine. Dreamweaver provides the same file-transfer functions as FTP, but the setup is simpler.

Follow steps 1–5 from the previous instructions (page 765), but in step 6, choose Local/Network from the "Connect using" menu. That brings up fields that collect your connection information (see Figure 18-4).

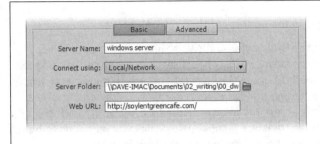

FIGURE 18-4

If your company keeps its web server in your office, the "remote site" might not be that remote. In such a case, choose a folder on your local network as the "remote" folder.

Click the folder icon next to "Remote folder," and then navigate to and select your site's remote site folder. On a local network, this folder isn't *truly* remote, because your company's web server is still within the walls of your building, but you get the idea.

Wrap up with steps 10, 12, and 13 of the previous instructions. At this point, you're ready to connect to the "remote" server and transfer files as described on page 776.

Setting Up a Remote Server with WebDAV

Dreamweaver also allows access to a remote site using *WebDAV*, short for Web-based Distributed Authoring and Versioning. Like FTP, it's a standard, or *protocol*, for transferring files. Like SFTP, it uses a secure connection (called SSL, or Secure Socket Layer) that encrypts all your data as it passes back and forth between your computer and your web server. But unlike both of those technologies, WebDAV addresses the kinds of problems you encounter when you collaborate on website development with other people.

For instance, all kinds of havoc can result if two people edit a page simultaneously; whoever uploads the page to the server *second* winds up wiping out the changes made by the first person. WebDAV supports a check-in and check-out system that works similarly to Dreamweaver's Check In and Check Out tools (see page 785) to make sure only one person works on a file at a time, and that no one tramples on anyone else's files. In fact, Dreamweaver's Check In/Check Out feature works seamlessly with WebDAV.

Both Microsoft Internet Information Server (IIS) and Apache Web Server work with WebDAV. Colleges and universities commonly use WebDAV, but that's not the case with web hosting companies, so it's pretty unlikely that you'll find commercial web hosts that offer it. To find out if your server can handle WebDAV (and to find out the necessary connection information), consult your web server's administrator (for example, call or email your web hosting company).

Setting up WebDAV access to a remote site is similar to setting up FTP access. Follow steps 1–5 on page 765, and then:

1. **Choose WebDAV from the "Connect using" menu.**

   The Site Definition window displays the WebDAV settings, which require just four pieces of information.

2. **In the URL box, type in the address of the WebDAV server.**

   In most cases, that's the URL of your website, so it begins with either *http://* or *https://*. The "s" in *https* means you'll connect securely to the server using SSL. The normal *http://* method doesn't use encryption, which means that, just as with regular FTP, your computer sends your username, password, and data "in the open" as it travels across the Internet. Note that just adding an "s" won't suddenly make your file transfers secure; the receiving server needs to be set up to accept *https* connections (a technically challenging task).

3. **In the Username and Password fields, type in your credentials.**

   Turn on the Save checkbox so you don't have to type in your password each time you move files to your server (but heed the note on page 768).

4. **Click the Test button to see if your connection works.**

   If Dreamweaver succeeds, it proudly tells you. Unfortunately, if it fails, you'll get an error message that isn't exactly helpful. WebDAV isn't nearly as finicky as FTP, so if there's an error, you most likely just typed the URL, password, or login info incorrectly, or WebDAV just isn't available for the server.

> **NOTE** Due to the different possible server configurations for WebDAV, Dreamweaver may not be able to connect even if your server has WebDAV turned on. If that's the case, you'll need to use FTP or another method to connect to your server.

The rest of the process is identical to the FTP setup process, so follow steps 10, 12, and 13 starting on page 769. At that point, you're ready to connect to your server and transfer files, as described on page 776.

Setting Up a Remote Server with RDS

RDS (Remote Development Services) is a feature of Adobe's ColdFusion Server. It lets designers work on web files and databases in conjunction with a ColdFusion application server. If you're using something other than a ColdFusion server, you don't need to worry about this option.

To create a remote site in Dreamweaver that works with RDS, follow steps 1–5 on page 765. In step 6, choose RDS from the "Connect using" drop-down menu.

The Site Definition window displays a version number, a short description, and a Settings button. Click Settings to open the Configure RDS Server window. Fill in the dialog box as directed by your server administrator or help desk.

Advanced Remote Server Settings

No matter which connection method you use (FTP, Local/Network, and so on), each remote server has a set of advanced options that you access by clicking the Advanced tab (see Figure 18-5):

- **If you don't want to synchronize files, turn off the "Maintain synchronization information" box.** Dreamweaver's synchronization feature keeps all the files in your site up to date. It helps you maintain the most recent versions of your files on the remote server by keeping track of when you change a file on your computer.

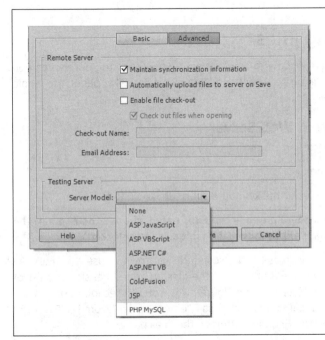

FIGURE 18-5

If you use Dreamweaver's Check In/Check Out feature and you work on your site in several locations (for example, from home and from your office), use a different check-out name for each location (BobAtHome and BobAtWork, for example). That way, you know which files you checked out to your home computer and which to your computer at work.

When you synchronize a site, Dreamweaver moves your most recent site files to your server (you'll learn about this feature in detail on page 791). If you don't want Dreamweaver to do this, turn off this checkbox. When it's on, Dreamweaver inserts little files named *dwsync.xml* throughout your site in folders named *_notes*. These files hold synchronization information about each site file, but don't clutter up your site with them if you don't synchronize. In addition, Dreamweaver spends time determining the synch status of each file, so your file transfers go more quickly with this turned off.

- **Leave "Automatically upload files to server on Save" turned off.** Not only will this slow things down—Dreamweaver has to connect and move the saved file to the server every time you press Ctrl+S (⌘-S)—it also means you may save half-finished pages on your remote server.

• **If you work with a team of developers, you may want to use Dreamweaver's Check In/Check Out tools discussed on page 785.** If you do, turn on "Enable file check in and check out." Then fill in the corresponding options as explained in Figure 18-5. If you do wind up using the Check Out feature (see page 786), you can save yourself some clicks by turning on "Check out files when opening." (Fill in your name and email address, too.) Now you can check out a file from the remote server just by double-clicking its name in the Site Files list. If you work on your own, *do not* turn on this setting, since it slows down the process of moving files to and from the server and adds unnecessary files (used to determine who has what file checked out) to both your server and your own computer.

◼ Transferring Files

Once you tell Dreamweaver *how* to send off your web pages to your server, you can set about actually *doing* so. Thanks to Dreamweaver's Files panel, the whole process takes only a few steps.

Moving Files to Your Web Server

To transfer files to your server:

1. **Open the Files panel.**

   Choose Window→Files or the keyboard shortcut F8 (Shift-⌘-F).

2. **From the drop-down Site menu in the Files panel, choose the name of the site whose files you want to move (if it isn't already selected).**

   The Files panel displays files for the selected site. You can use the File View drop-down menu to see either a list of the files on your local site or a list of the files on your remote server (see Figure 18-6). You can see local and remote server files side by side if you first choose "Remote server" from the File View menu and then click the Expand button on the Files panel.

3. **From the list in the Files panel, select the files you want to upload to the server.**

   To move a folder and every file inside it, just select the folder. (In other words, you can transfer your *entire* website to the server by simply selecting the local site folder—the folder listed at the very top of the Local Files list.) If you change only a few files on your site, you can selectively upload those files (or folders of changed files) using any of the techniques described in this section.

NOTE If you don't see the files you want to upload in the Files list, you may have selected "Remote server." Select "Local view" to see only those files on your computer, and then click the Refresh button on the Files panel (Figure 18-6).

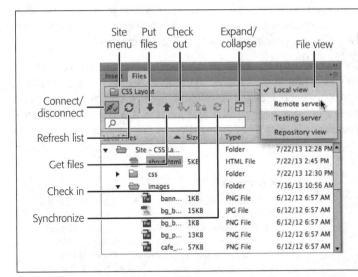

FIGURE 18-6

The Files panel offers toolbar buttons for uploading and downloading your web files to and from the web server that actually dishes them out to your site's adoring public. (See Chapter 18 for much more on this important window.)

When you use do-it-yourself FTP programs like FileZilla or Cyberduck, you have to specify a folder location for every file you transfer to the web server. Here's one of the great advantages of letting Dreamweaver do your file shuffling; it already *knows* where your files should go on the remote server. The local and remote sites are, after all, mirror images, so Dreamweaver simply puts your local files in the corresponding folders on the remote server.

For example, suppose you select the file *mayo.html*, which is in a folder called Condiments, which itself is in the local root folder. When you transfer *mayo. html*, Dreamweaver automatically puts it in the Condiments folder in the root folder on the remote server. In fact, if the Condiments folder doesn't exist on the remote server, Dreamweaver creates it for you and *then* puts the file into it. Now that's service!

You're now ready to go live with your web page.

4. **Click the "Put files" button—the up-arrow icon in the Files panel.**

   Alternatively, you can use the keyboard shortcut Ctrl+Shift+U (⌘-Shift-U).

   Several things happen when you do this. First, if you're connecting via FTP, Dreamweaver attempts to hook into your server. As you can see from the status window that opens, it may take a moment or so to establish the connection; once that happens, the Connect button (see Figure 18-6) displays that pushed-in look that means you're connected.

   Next, if any of the files you're transferring are currently open and have unsaved changes, Dreamweaver asks if you want to save the files before it transfers them.

Click Yes; if you have multiple unsaved files, click Yes To All. Dreamweaver then begins the transfer.

In addition, as Dreamweaver transfers your pages, it asks if you want to transfer any *dependent files* (see Figure 18-7). That includes graphics, external CSS files, or movies that a browser needs to display your pages properly.

The dependent files feature can save you considerable time and hassle because you don't have to hunt for and upload each graphic file or external style sheet yourself. On the other hand, if all the dependent files are *already* on the server, having Dreamweaver transfer the same files again is a waste of time. Fortunately, Dreamweaver prevents this wasted effort as described in the next step.

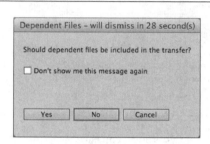

FIGURE 18-7

The File Transfer command's Dependent Files feature makes sure that Dreamweaver copies to the server all the files a browser needs to display your web pages—graphics, external style sheets, videos, and so on. The feature also includes a time limit—you'll see a "will dismiss in 30 seconds" message. If you don't click a button within 30 seconds, Dreamweaver assumes you mean "No" to whether you want to upload dependent files and it uploads just the files you selected.

NOTE If you turn on the "Don't show me this message again" checkbox in the Dependent Files dialog box and then click Yes, from that moment forward, Dreamweaver copies dependent files without asking you. On the other hand, if you turn on the "Don't show me this message again" box and then click No, Dreamweaver *never* copies dependent files.

If you turn off the Dependent Files dialog box and change your mind later, hold down the Alt (Option) key when you transfer a file (using any method except a keyboard shortcut). Or choose Edit→Preferences→Site Category (Dreamweaver→Preferences→Site Category) to turn this feature on or off.

5. **Click Yes to transfer dependent files, or No to transfer only the files you selected.**

   Dreamweaver copies the files to the server. If you copy a file that's inside a folder that doesn't exist on the remote server, Dreamweaver creates an eponymous server-side folder in the same step. In fact, Dreamweaver creates as many subfolders as necessary to make sure it transfers every local file to a mirror folder on the remote site. (Try doing *that* with a regular FTP program.)

   If you choose to transfer dependent files, Dreamweaver streamlines the process if you left the "Maintain Synchronization Information" checkbox turned on when you defined your remote site (see page 791). It determines whether the dependent file already exists on the server and, if it does, whether your local copy is newer. If the dependent file doesn't exist on the server, or if your local copy is newer (meaning you made changes to it locally but haven't yet moved it to the Web), Dreamweaver sends it when you tell it to transfer dependent files.

However, if Dreamweaver thinks that it's the same file, or that the copy of the file on the server is newer, it won't make the transfer. This behavior is a huge time-saver, since you won't have to repeatedly upload the same 50 navigation buttons each time you say "Yes" to transferring dependent files. But best of all, Dreamweaver still transfers dependent files that really *are* new.

> **NOTE** Dreamweaver's ability to correctly determine whether a dependent file on your computer is the same as a file on the server depends on its Site Synchronization feature, described on page 791.
>
> Dreamweaver's accuracy with this tool is good, but it has been known to get it wrong. If Dreamweaver isn't moving a dependent file, you can select that file and upload it manually (by selecting it in the Files panel and then clicking the Put button). Dreamweaver always obeys a direct order to move a selected file.

6. **Continue using the Put button to transfer all the files in your website to the remote site.**

    Depending on the number of files you transfer, this operation can take some time. Transferring files over the Internet using FTP isn't nearly as fast as copying files from one hard drive to another (see Figure 18-8).

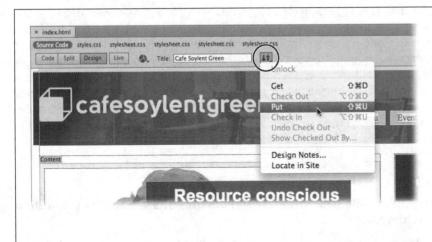

FIGURE 18-8

Click the File Status button (circled) and choose Put to quickly move a file to your server. You can also use this menu to retrieve a copy of a file from the server (Get), use Check In and Check Out tools (page 785), or review Design Notes (page 795) for the page. Note that Check In and Check Out are only available if you turned on the Check In/Check Out tool as described on page 785. To highlight this file in the Files panel, choose "Locate in Site."

■ OTHER WAYS TO MOVE FILES TO YOUR WEB SERVER

To copy a current document to server without using the Files panel at all, you can go directly to the Put command. Say you finish building or modifying a page and want to immediately move it to the Web. Just choose Site→Put, or press Ctrl+Shift+U

(⌘-Shift-U), or use the toolbar shortcut shown in Figure 18-8; Dreamweaver automatically copies the fresh page to the proper folder online.

A Little More Background on File Transfers

Dreamweaver lets you keep working as it dutifully transfers files in the background. You can edit a web page, create a new style sheet, and so on. However, there are some things you *can't* do while Dreamweaver moves files. For example, you can't edit the site definition (since that could affect how you connect to the remote server). Dreamweaver lets you know if you try to take a forbidden action while it's working with the server.

If you find Dreamweaver's background activity window a nuisance, click the Hide button and it temporarily disappears. In addition, if you accidentally start uploading a 10,000-page website, you probably don't want to wait until Dreamweaver's done; click the Cancel button to stop the transfer.

When Dreamweaver finishes moving files around, you can see a record of its actions by clicking the Log button in the bottom-right corner of the Files panel. This log differs from the raw FTP log discussed in the box on page 782. This plain-language report lets you know what Dreamweaver did—"Put successful," "Get successful," and so on. If you see a "Not transferred" message, Dreamweaver tried to Get or Put a file, but both the local and remote server copies were identical, so it didn't do anything. See the previous Note for more.

Getting Files from Your Web Server

So far, this chapter has described getting your hard drive-based pages *to* the Internet. Sometimes, however, you want to download one or more files *from* your server. Perhaps you made a horrible (and irreversible) mistake on the local copy of a file and you want to retrieve the unblemished version from the Web, effectively using the remote server as a last-ditch backup system. Maybe you've taken over a design job for a client, and the only files they have are on the server, so you need to copy the entire site to your desktop computer. Or perhaps someone uploaded files to the site and you want to download a copy to your own computer (although the Synchronize feature described on page 791 would also work).

To get files from your remote site to your local drive, open the Files panel (press F8 [Shift-⌘-F]) and proceed as follows:

1. **From the Site pull-down menu, choose the site whose files you wish to retrieve.**

    As with all of Dreamweaver's site-management features, downloading files from a web server depends on first defining a site.

2. **From the Files panel's View menu, choose "Remote server."**

    Dreamweaver tells you that it's attempting to connect to the web server. Once it makes the connection, it lists the files and folders on the server, and turns on the Connect button—it looks pushed in. (Dreamweaver automatically disconnects after 30 minutes of inactivity, at which point the Connect button pops back out.)

NOTE To change the disconnect time limit, press Ctrl+U (⌘-U) to open the Preferences window. Click the Site category and change the number listed in the Minutes Idle box. Be aware, however, that some web servers have their own settings and may disconnect you sooner than you specify.

3. **From the Remote Server file list, select the files you want to download.**

   The Shift-click and Ctrl(⌘)-click techniques for selecting files work, as explained on page 747. To download a folder and every file inside it, just click the folder. This technique also lets you get your *entire* website from the server; just select the remote server's root folder, which appears at the very top of the Remote Server file list.

TROUBLESHOOTING MOMENT

Don't Replace the Wrong File

One strange feature of the Files panel's Get and Put commands may get you in trouble. Suppose, having just added new information to your home page (*index.html*), you want to transfer that page to your server. You select it in the Local Folder list—but then you accidentally click Get instead of Put.

Not knowing your true intention, Dreamweaver dutifully prepares to retrieve the file from the server, which, of course, will replace (wipe out) the newly updated home page on your computer.

Fortunately, before causing such damage, Dreamweaver also displays a warning message asking if you really want to overwrite the local file. Click No or Cancel to save your hard work.

There may be times when you *do* want to wipe out your local copy—if, for example, your cat walks across your keyboard,

types illegible code, presses Ctrl+S to save the ruined page, and Ctrl+Q to quit Dreamweaver (keeping you from using Undo to fix the mistakes). In this common situation, you'll want to replace your local copy with the remote server copy. To do so, press Yes when Dreamweaver warns you and you'll rectify your cat's errors. Oh yeah, this is also a useful trick if *you* ever make a mistake on a page you can't fix and want to return to the working copy on your server.

Dreamweaver also includes a useful Compare button to help you sort out the differences between a local and a remote file. Clicking this button compares the two so you can identify which changes you made. This way, you can salvage changes you made to the local copy and discard errors you (or your cat) may have introduced to the page. You can learn more about this feature on page 341.

---

4. **Click the "Get files" button (the down arrow).**

   Alternatively, click Ctrl+Shift+D (⌘-Shift-D).

   If, as you retrieve a file from your server, you have the *local* version of that file open with unsaved changes in it, Dreamweaver warns you that you'll lose those changes. (No surprise there; copying a file from the remote server automatically replaces the same file on the local site, whether it's open or not.) Dreamweaver also warns you if you're about to replace a local file that's *newer* than the remote one. And finally, Dreamweaver offers to transfer any dependent files, as described in Figure 18-7.

5. **Click Yes to transfer dependent files, or No to transfer only the files you selected.**

Dreamweaver copies the files to your local site folder, creating any folders necessary to replicate the structure of the remote site.

POWER USERS' CLINIC

Troubleshoot Using the FTP Log

If you have problems moving files using Dreamweaver's FTP command, you may be able to find some clues to the problem in the records Dreamweaver keeps when it transfers files. If you've used other FTP programs, you may have seen little messages that the web server and FTP program send back and forth, like this:

```
< 200 PORT command successful
>LIST< 150 Opening ASCII mode data connec-
tion for file list
```

Dreamweaver sends and receives this information, too, but it keeps it hidden. To see the FTP log, choose Window→Results,

and then click the FTP Log tab. Any errors Dreamweaver encounters appear here.

For example, if you come across a "cannot put file" error, it may mean that you're out of space on your web server. Contact your ISP or your server administrator for help. WebDAV connections also produce a log of file-transfer activity, but it's not very easy to decipher.

And Secure FTP (SFTP) produces no log in Dreamweaver—hush, hush, it's a secret.

Cloaking Files

You may not want *all* your files transferred to and from your remote site. For example, as part of its Library and Template tools, Dreamweaver creates folders inside your local root folder. These folders don't do you any good on the web server; their sole purpose is to help you build your site locally. Likewise, you may have Photoshop (.psd), Flash (.fla), Illustrator (.ai), or Fireworks CS6 (.fw.png) files in your local site folder. They're inaccessible from a web browser and can take up a lot of disk space, so you shouldn't transfer them to your server when you move your site online.

NOTE If you work on a website with other people, you probably *will* want to have the Library and Templates folders on the server. That way, your colleagues can get at those files as well.

To meet such challenges, Dreamweaver includes a feature called *cloaking*. It lets you hide folders and specific file types from many file-transfer operations, including Get/Put, the Check In/Check Out feature (page 785), and site synchronization (page 791). In fact, you can even hide files from many sitewide Dreamweaver actions, including site reports (see page 758), search-and-replace functions (Chapter 8), the ability to check and change links sitewide (page 751), and the Assets panel (page 727). There's one exception: Files linked to library items (see Chapter 19) or templates (Chapter 20) can still "see" items even if they're in cloaked Library and Templates folders.

Dreamweaver lets you cloak folders and file types (those that end with a specific extension, such as .fla or .psd). It even lets you cloak a single file anywhere on your site. Implementing each type of cloak requires a different technique.

To hide specific types of files:

1. **Choose Site→Manage Sites.**

    The Manage Sites window opens, listing all the sites you defined in Dreamweaver.

2. **Double-click the site of interest to open it for editing.**

    Alternatively, select the site, and then click the Edit button (the pencil icon) in the lower-right corner of the Manage Sites window. Either way, that site's Site Setup window opens.

3. **Click the arrow next to Advanced Settings to expand that list of options. Click the Cloaking category.**

    The cloaking settings appear (see Figure 18-9). The factory setting is On for every site you define. (If you want to turn cloaking off, turn off the "Enable cloaking" checkbox.)

> **TIP** You can quickly turn cloaking on and off by right-clicking (Control-clicking) any file or folder in the Files panel and then selecting Cloaking→Enable Cloaking from the shortcut menu. A checkmark next to Enable Cloaking means that cloaking is turned on.

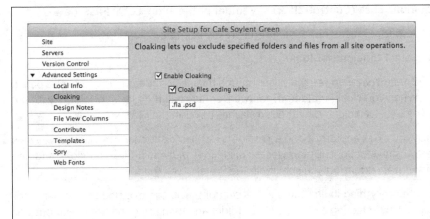

FIGURE 18-9

The Cloaking category of the Site Definition window lets you turn on or off cloaking, a feature that lets you hide folders, specific file types, and individual files from sitewide operations, like transferring files to the web server or searching and replacing text. In this window, you can specify which types of files to hide by listing their extensions (.psd for Photoshop files, for example).

4. **Turn on the "Cloak files ending with" checkbox.**

Dreamweaver identifies file types by their extensions—.fla for Flash files, for example. If you use Fireworks, which uses the extension .png, don't add the .png extension to this box. If you're using Fireworks CS6, add .fw.png to the list (the latest version of Fireworks adds .fw to its older .png file extension so as not to confuse the byte-heavy Fireworks file with the lean, compact PNG file format).

> **NOTE** Mac programs don't always add these filename suffixes, but without them, Dreamweaver can't cloak, so if you use a Mac, make sure you add an extension when you save a file. Some programs have a "Hide File Extension" checkbox that appears when you save a file—make sure you have this *turned off*.

5. **In the text box, type the extensions of the files you want to cloak.**

Each extension should start with a period followed by three or four letters. Fireworks CS6 is an exception: for those files, type *.fw.png*. To specify multiple extensions, separate them with a space.

6. **Click Save and then Done to close this and the Manage Sites window.**

In the Files panel, cloaked files will have a red slash through them.

You can also cloak a single folder or file using the Files panel, like this:

1. **Open the Files panel by pressing F8 (Shift-⌘-F).**

Alternatively, choose Window→Files.

2. **Right-click (Control-click) any folder or file in the Local Files view.**

A shortcut menu appears, offering many site-related options.

3. **Select Cloaking→Cloak.**

Dreamweaver adds a red slash through the file or folder's icon in the Files panel. When you cloak a folder, Dreamweaver hides all the files and folders *within it* as well, as indicated by the red slashes through their icons.

Once you cloak a folder, it and any folders inside it disappear from Dreamweaver's file-transfer functions. Dreamweaver also hides individual files you cloak and any files with an extension you specify in the Preferences window.

As with everything in life, there are exceptions. You can override the cloaking, for example, by selecting a cloaked file or folder and then using the Get or Put buttons as described on page 776. Dreamweaver assumes that, since you specifically selected that file or folder, you want to override the cloaking feature.

Dreamweaver also ignores cloaking if you answer Yes in the Dependent Files message box when you Put or Get files. In that case, Dreamweaver transfers all dependent files, even if you cloaked them (this applies when you try to Put or Get library and template files as well).

■ Check In and Check Out

If you're the sole developer for a website, the Files panel's Put and Get buttons are fine for transferring files. But if you're on a team of developers, those simple tools can get you in trouble.

Suppose your boss emails you an important announcement that she wants posted on your site's home page immediately. So you download the home page from the web server and start to edit it. At the same time, your co-worker Bob notices a typo on the page. He downloads it, too.

You're a much faster worker than Bob, so you add the critical news to the home page and move it back to the server. But then Bob transfers *his* corrected home page, *overwriting* your edits and eliminating that urgent notice you just added. (An hour later, your phone rings. It's the boss.)

Without some kind of system to monitor who has what file and to prevent people from overwriting each other's work, collaborative web development is a chaotic mess. Fortunately, Dreamweaver's Check In and Check Out system provides a civilized answer to the problem, specifically designed for group web development. It works like your local public library: When you check out a file, no one else can have it. When you're finished with the file, you check it back in, releasing control of it, and allowing someone else on the team to check it out and work on it.

To use the Check In/Check Out feature, you first need to turn it on. You'll find that setting under the Advanced options when you set up your remote server (as described in "Advanced Remote Server Settings" on page 775 and pictured in Figure 18-5). In addition, you must keep a few things in mind:

- When you develop a website solo, your local site usually contains the most recent versions of your files. You make any modifications or additions to the pages on your computer and *then* transfer the edited pages to your web server.

  In a collaborative environment, where many people work on the site at once, the files on your hard drive may not be the latest ones. After all, your co-workers, like you, have been updating pages and transferring them to the server. The home page sitting in your local site folder may be several days older than the file on the remote site, which is why checking out a file from the *remote server*, rather than editing the copy on your computer, is so important. It guarantees that you have the latest version of the file. (Dreamweaver can automatically check out a file whenever you open it from the list of local files. See page 785 for details.)

- In a collaborative environment, nobody should post files to the server using any method except Dreamweaver's Check In/Check Out system.

  The reason is technical, but worth slogging through: When Dreamweaver checks out a file, it doesn't actually *lock* the file. Instead, it places a small, invisible text file (with the three-letter suffix .lck) on both the remote server and in your local site folder. This file indicates who has checked out the website file. When

Dreamweaver connects to the remote server, it uses these text files to determine which web files are in use by others.

And that's why your site-development team needs to use Dreamweaver exclusively to transfer files: Only Dreamweaver understands the .lck files. Other FTP programs, like WS_FTP (Windows) and Fetch (Mac), gladly ignore those who-has-dibs files and can easily overwrite checked-out files. This risk also applies when you simply copy files back and forth over the office network.

NOTE Adobe's word processor-like web-page editing program Contribute also takes advantage of the Check In/Check Out feature, so you can use the two programs on the same site.

- All Dreamweaver-using team members must configure their remote site to use Check In and Check Out. If just one person doesn't do it, you risk overwritten files.

NOTE WebDAV people are free from the constraints of Dreamweaver's Check In/Check Out system. As long as everyone working on the site uses programs that support the WebDAV protocol, they can work seamlessly with people using Dreamweaver, and vice versa.

Checking Out Files

When you work collaboratively and want to work on a file, you check it out from the web server. Doing so makes sure that *you* have the latest version of the file, and that nobody else can make changes to it.

NOTE Dreamweaver's Check In/Check Out feature only works if everyone on the team uses it. Everyone needs to use Dreamweaver and everyone needs to turn on the Check In/Check Out feature, as described on page 785. If even a single person doesn't use Dreamweaver and this system, you'll probably run into problems.

If you're used to creating sites by yourself, this Check In/Check Out business may feel a little strange; after all, when it's just you working on a site, the local site (the files on your computer) contains the latest version of all your files. But when you work with a group, you need to consider the *remote server*—the drive that everyone can access, edit, and add new pages to—the master repository of your site's files.

NOTE There's nothing to check out when you create a new page. Since the only version of that file in the universe lies on your computer, have no fear that someone else may work on it at the same time as you. In this case, you only need to check the file *into* the site when you finish with it.

You check out a file using the Files panel; if it's not open, press F8 (Shift-⌘-F) or choose Window→Files. Then select the site you want to work on from the Site drop-down menu (shown at the top of Figure 18-10).

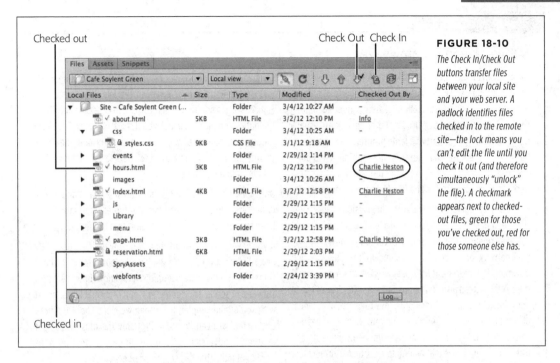

Checked out   Check Out   Check In

FIGURE 18-10

The Check In/Check Out buttons transfer files between your local site and your web server. A padlock identifies files checked in to the remote site—the lock means you can't edit the file until you check it out (and therefore simultaneously "unlock" the file). A checkmark appears next to checked-out files, green for those you've checked out, red for those someone else has.

Checked in

Now you're ready to begin. From the Local Files list in the Files panel, select the files you want to check out from the server—or, to check out an entire folder and every file inside it, select the folder itself.

TIP If, when you set up your remote server (see page 763), you select the "Check Out File when Opening" option, you can also check out (and open) a file by double-clicking it in the Files panel. This is a quick way to open a page you want to edit while still using Dreamweaver's Check Out feature.

In some instances, you may want to select a file from the "Remote server" list as well. For example, you might need to modify a page you didn't create and which you've never checked out before. In such a case, the file isn't *in* your local site, so you have to get it from the remote server. Select "Remote server" from the Files panel (see Figure 18-6); Dreamweaver connects to and then displays the remote server files. Select the ones you want to check out.

In any case, now just click the Check Out button in the Files panel, or use the keyboard shortcut Ctrl+Alt+Shift+D (⌘-Option-Shift-D). (Not enough fingers? See page 869 to learn how to change Dreamweaver's shortcuts.)

Subversion in Dreamweaver

Dreamweaver includes support for one popular version control system—software that tracks the lifecycle of a document—called *Subversion*. Well, at least it's popular among coders. Subversion is a free program that developers usually use to manage files as part of a large programming project. It has powerful features to make sure that multiple users don't overwrite each others' changes, and to make it easy to "roll back" to previous versions of a file if something goes wrong.

To take advantage of Dreamweaver's Subversion support, you first need to set up a *Subversion server*—a separate piece of software running on either your own computer, on a server on your network, or even on a server somewhere on the Internet. Download the software at *http://subversion.apache.org/packages.html*. You can also find companies that offer free or cheap Subversion hosting (in other words, they take care of the mess of setting up a Subversion server for you). Next, you need to create what's called a Subversion *repository*—an online storage locker for a set of files that belong to a particular project. For example, you would probably set up each web project you take on as its own repository. You can learn more about how to set up Subversion at *http://svnbook.red-bean.com*.

For Dreamweaver users, it's important to keep in mind that a Subversion repository is independent of the website running on your web server. In other words, you'll have a Subversion repository, local files on your computer, and another set of files out on the Web (that is, on your remote server).

You can set up Subversion support for a site in Dreamweaver by choosing Site→Manage Sites and then choosing a site to edit. In the Site Definition window, select the Version Control category and choose Subversion from the Access menu. Then fill out the other settings, such as the server address, repository path, your user name, and password.

Once you do, Dreamweaver connects to the repository when you choose Repository View from the File View menu (see Figure 18-6). In addition, when you use the Check In and Check Out buttons on the Files panel, you'll check files in and out from the Subversion repository. Dreamweaver CC includes the ability to copy, move, delete, and revert (go back to a previous version of) files in the repository.

Unfortunately, if you want to perform sitewide changes, like updating templates or changing the footer information, you need to check out the *entire* website from the repository.

If you develop websites on your own, Subversion is definitely overkill. Even if you toil in a small workgroup, unless you have someone with the system administrator know-how to set up a Subversion server and repository, you're probably better off with something simpler, like Dreamweaver's Check In/Check Out system or even WebDAV. Probably the most important feature of Subversion is its ability to go back to a previous version of a file that has somehow been wrecked.

If you're not going to use Subversion, it's definitely worth investing in some basic backup software like Retrospect Remote or Apple's Time Machine. Even most simple backup software lets you keep hourly, daily, weekly, or monthly file backups, and lets you go back in time to retrieve older versions of files. Or, take the low-tech approach: Just back up your site every day and store the copied files in a folder named something like *June_10_2012*. That way, you'll have a daily backup you can turn to if you need to recover a lost file.

However, if your company or organization does use Subversion, you can get in-depth information on using Dreamweaver with it at *http://tinyurl.com/3kxo5wu*.

Dreamweaver asks if you want to check out dependent files, too. Click Yes if you think the page you're checking out uses files you haven't downloaded. Dreamweaver then copies the dependent files to your computer, so the page you check out displays its current images, CSS style sheets, and any other linked files. It doesn't *check out* a dependent file, however, so if you do want to *edit* the dependent file—if, for example, you need to edit the styles in a linked external style sheet—you must also check out that dependent file, by selecting it from the Files list and clicking Check Out.

> **NOTE** When you edit a web page you check out, you may run into a weird problem if the page uses an external style sheet and you didn't check out the style sheet: You won't be able to edit any styles on the page. Instead, you'll get a message saying that the styles file is locked and Dreamweaver will ask if you want to check it out. Click the Check Out button and Dreamweaver tries to obey. If it informs you that someone else has checked out the file, click Cancel and wait until the other person checks the style sheet back in. Then check it out and make your changes. Bottom line: Check out your site's external style sheets if you want to edit the CSS in your pages.

When you check out files, Dreamweaver copies them to your computer and marks them as checked out so others can't change them. Like uploading and downloading files, checking out files can take time, depending on the speed of your Internet connection.

After you check out a file, Dreamweaver displays a green "checked-out" checkmark in the Files panel next to its name (see Figure 18-10). You can now open and edit the file, and, when you're done, check the file back in.

If you attempt to check out a file that someone has already checked out, Dreamweaver tells you as much. It also gives you the option to override the person's checkout—but unless you're the boss, resist the temptation, for two reasons. First, your colleague may have made some important changes to the page, which you'll wipe out with your shenanigans. Second, because you so rudely stole the file, they may stop bringing you donuts in the morning.

A better way to work with someone who's checked out a file that you need is to use Dreamweaver's email feature. You can see who checked out the file by consulting Dreamweaver's Checked Out By column (see Figure 18-10, circled). Even better, if you click the name, Dreamweaver opens your email program and addresses a message to that person, so you can say, "Hey Bob, you've had the home page checked out for two days! I need to work on it, so check it back in!"

The name and email address Dreamweaver uses depends on the information your co-workers provide when they configured their computers for remote site use (you provided the same information when you configured your computer). See the Advanced options on page 775 for more.

Checking In Files

When you're ready to move a page you've been editing back onto the server, you check it in. (You also check in *new* files you create.)

To check in files, open the Files panel (press F8 [Shift-⌘-F]), choose the relevant site from the Site drop-down menu, and then, using the Local Folder file list in the Files panel, select the files you want to check in to your server. As always, you can click a folder to check *it* in, too, along with every file inside it.

The files you check in should be files you checked out, or brand-new files that have never been on the server. If you attempt to check in a file that someone else has checked out, Dreamweaver warns you with a message box. Click Cancel to stop the check-in so you don't overwrite the checked-out file. Dreamweaver also warns you if you try to check in a file that's older than the copy on the server. Again, unless you're sure this is what you want to do, click Cancel.

POWER USERS' CLINIC

Manual Check Out Override

Occasionally, you may want to erase the checked-out status of a file. Suppose, for example, someone who's checked out a lot of files suddenly catches the plague and can't continue working on the site. To free those files so others can work on them, you have to undo his check-out (and quarantine his cubicle).

To do the former, make sure you have the Files panel in Remote Server view (this trick won't work with the local files displayed). Then, right-click (Control-click) the checked-out file and select Undo Checkout from the menu that appears.

Dreamweaver warns you that whoever checked out the file won't be able to check it back in. (This is, in fact, false. That

person can still check in the file, overwriting whatever's on the web server. So you can see why you should override the checked-out file only when the person who checked it out is very unlikely to check it back in—stranded on a deserted island, perhaps.)

When the operation's complete, a padlock icon appears next to the filename.

You can use this technique on a file *you've* checked out, too, if, for example, after you check out a file, you make a horrible mistake on the page and want to revert to the copy on the server.

NOTE If you want to check in the page you're currently working on, use the toolbar in the document window (see page 779).

You can check in the selected files in any of the usual ways:

- Click the Check In button on the Files panel (see Figure 18-6).

- Use the keyboard shortcut Ctrl+Alt+Shift+U (⌘-Option-Shift-U). (See page 869 to learn how to change any Dreamweaver shortcut to something less cumbersome.)

Dreamweaver asks if you want to check in any dependent files at the same time. You should transfer dependent files only if you first checked them out, or if the dependent files are new and have never been uploaded to the server. If you attempt to check in a dependent file that someone else has checked out, Dreamweaver warns you with a message box—click the No button in this box so you don't overwrite someone's checked-out file.

After you click through all the message boxes, Dreamweaver copies the files to your remote server. Once you check in a file, Dreamweaver locks your local copy—you'll see a padlock icon next to its name in the Local Files list of the Files panel (see Figure 18-10)—that's so you don't accidentally change the local version of the file. If you wish to modify the file in some way, check it out from the server.

NOTE Dreamweaver's Site Report feature (page 758) lets you see which files are checked out and by whom. Skip it. On a large site, the report can take a long time to run, it isn't always accurate, and you can't do the things you're most likely to do with checked-out files (like checking them back in).

FREQUENTLY ASKED QUESTION

Get and Put, In and Out

I'm using Dreamweaver's Check In and Check Out buttons to transfer my files. What do the Get and Put buttons do if I use the Check In/Check Out feature?

If you use Check In and Check Out, the Get and Put commands function slightly differently than described on page 776. *Get*, in this case, copies the selected file or files to your local site. However, Dreamweaver adds a small lock icon next to each of the "gotten" files in your "Local files" list. The files are locked, and you shouldn't edit them. Remember, checking out a file is the only way to prevent others from working on it simultaneously. If you edit a locked file on your computer, nothing stops someone else from checking out the page, editing it, and checking it back in.

But you may still find the Get command useful in such a situation. For example, suppose someone just updated the site's external style sheet. The pages you're editing use this style sheet, so you want to get the latest version. You don't want to edit the style sheet itself, so you don't need to check it out. If you use Get instead of checking out the pages, you can keep a

reference copy on your computer without locking anyone else out of the file and without having to check it back in.

Put, on the other hand, simply—and blindly—transfers the file on your local site to the remote site. If you use the Check In/Check Out feature and you haven't also checked out the file, using Put is a bad idea. The remote site should be your reference copy; several rounds of revisions may have been made to a file since you last checked it out. Your local copy will be hopelessly out of date, and moving it to the server destroys the most recent version of the file.

However, if you *do* have the file checked out, you can use Put to transfer your local copy to the server so your site's visitors see it. For example, say you're updating the home page with 20 new news items. To keep your site up-to-the-minute fresh, you can Put the home page on your server as you add each news item. Then the whole world will see each item as soon as possible. When you completely finish editing the home page, check it in.

■ Synchronizing Site Files

As you may suspect, when you keep two sets of files—on your local site and remote server—it's easy to lose track of which files are the most recent. For example, say you finish working on your website and move all the files to the server. The next day, you notice mistakes on a bunch of pages, so you make corrections on the copies in your local site. But in your rush to fix the pages, you didn't keep track of which ones you corrected. So although you're ready to move the corrected pages to the server, you're not sure *which* ones you need to transfer.

When you use the Check In/Check Out feature, you avoid this problem altogether. Using this system, the version on the server is *always* considered the latest and most definitive copy—*unless* you or someone else has checked out that file. In that case, whoever checked out the file has the most recent version.

But if you're operating solo and don't use the Check In/Check Out feature, you may get good mileage from Dreamweaver's Synchronize command, which lets you compare the remote and local sites and transfer only the newer files in either direction. (In fact, since the Synchronize command uses Get and Put to transfer files, you may not get the results you expect if you synchronize your site while also using Check In and Check Out, as described in the box on page 785.)

To synchronize your sites:

1. **Make sure you turn on the "Maintain synchronization information" checkbox when you set the server options (see the Advanced options mentioned on page 775).**

    Dreamweaver automatically turns this option on when you set up a server (see Figure 18-5).

2. **Choose Site→Synchronize Sitewide.**

    Alternatively, you can right-click anywhere inside the Files panel. From the shortcut menu that appears, select Synchronize. In either case, the Synchronize with Remote Server dialog box appears (see Figure 18-11).

FIGURE 18-11

Using the Synchronization command, you can copy newer files from your computer to your web server or get newer files from your remote site.

3. **Using the Synchronize drop-down menu, specify the files you want to update.**

    You can either synchronize all the files in the current site, or just the files you select from the "Local site" list. This last option is good when you have a really big site and want to limit this operation to just a single section of the site—one folder, for example.

4. **Using the Direction drop-down menu, choose the destination for newer files.**

    You have three choices. "Put newer files to remote" updates the web server with any newer files in your local site folder. It also copies any *newly created* files on the local site to the remote server. Use this option when you've heavily edited your local site and you want to move all the new or modified pages to your server.

    "Get newer files from remote" does the reverse: It updates your local site folder with any newer (or new) files from the remote site. Here's one instance where the Synchronize feature comes in handy in team-design situations. If you've been out of the office for a while, click this option to download copies of the latest site files. (Note that this doesn't check out any files; it merely makes sure you have copies of the latest files on your computer. This is one example where synchronization works well with Check In/Check Out, since it refreshes your local copy of the site with the latest files, including graphics and external style sheets, that any pages you do check out may depend on.)

"Get and put newer files" is a two-way synchronization. Dreamweaver transfers any new files on the local site to the remote site and vice versa. For example, if you update a page on your computer, Dreamweaver moves that file to the web server; if someone has made changes to a file on the server that is more recent than the copy on your computer, Dreamweaver downloads that file to your hard drive. The result is that both "sides" contain the latest files.

5. **Turn on the Delete checkbox, if desired.**

The way Dreamweaver words this option reflects the option you selected in the previous step. If you move newer files to the remote site, it says, "Delete remote files not on local drive." It's a useful option when, for example, you spend the afternoon cleaning up the local copy of your site, deleting old, orphaned graphics files and web pages, and you want Dreamweaver to update the web server to match.

If you chose to transfer newer files *from* the remote site, Dreamweaver lets you "Delete local files not on remote server." Use this feature when your local site is hopelessly out of date with the remote site. Perhaps you work on the site with a team, but you've been on vacation for two months (this is, of course, a hypothetical example). The site may have changed so significantly that you want to get your local copy in line with the website.

> **NOTE** Of course, you should proceed with caution when using *any* command that automatically deletes files. There's no Undo for these delete operations, and you don't want to accidentally delete the only copy of a particular page, graphic, or external Cascading Style Sheet.

If you chose the "Get and put newer files" option in step 4, Dreamweaver dims and makes unavailable the Delete checkbox. This option truly synchronizes the two; Dreamweaver copies newer files on the remote site (including files that exist on the server but not on your computer) to your local site, and vice versa.

6. **Click Preview to begin the synchronization process.**

Dreamweaver connects to the remote site and compares the two sets of files—if your site is large, this takes a long time. When Dreamweaver finishes, it opens the Synchronize preview window (Figure 18-12), listing which files it will delete and which it'll transfer, and providing an additional set of options for working with the listed files.

NOTE Synchronization is a slow process. Dreamweaver needs to connect to the remote server and then compare the remote server files with your local files. On a site with even a dozen or so pages and lots of graphics, synchronizing files can take minutes. This is one reason why, if you only need to synchronize files in one folder, you should first select that folder in the Files panel, and then, in step 3 above, choose "Selected files only." Also, make sure to take advantage of the cloaking feature described on page 782 so Dreamweaver doesn't waste time trying to synchronize files that you don't want on your server to begin with.

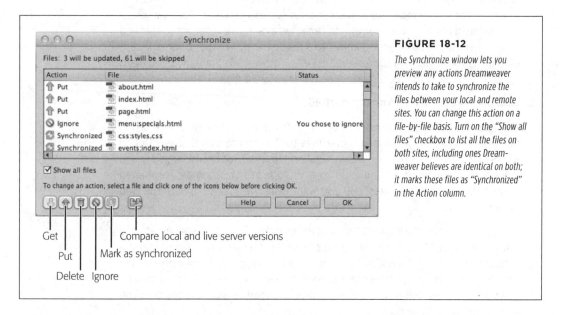

FIGURE 18-12

The Synchronize window lets you preview any actions Dreamweaver intends to take to synchronize the files between your local and remote sites. You can change this action on a file-by-file basis. Turn on the "Show all files" checkbox to list all the files on both sites, including ones Dreamweaver believes are identical on both; it marks these files as "Synchronized" in the Action column.

7. **Change the action Dreamweaver takes on the listed files.**

The preview box tells you what Dreamweaver plans to do with a file—Get it, Put it, or delete it. You can override these actions by selecting a file from the list and clicking one of the action buttons at the bottom of the window. For example, if you realize that Dreamweaver is going to delete a file that you *know* you need, select the file in the list and click the "Ignore file" button (the circle with a line through it).

Most of these options are useful only if you know Dreamweaver made a mistake—for example, when the program says you should Get a file, but you know your local copy is identical to the server's copy. In that case, you could select the file and click the "Mark as synchronized" button to tell Dreamweaver that they're identical. However, if you knew exactly which files were identical and which ones needed updating, you wouldn't need to use the Synchronize feature in the first place, right?

One option can come in quite handy. The "Compare local and remote versions" button lets you compare the code in the local file to the code in the remote file so you can identify exactly what differs between the two. You can use this feature to, for example, see exactly what changes were made to the remote copy of a file. You'll learn about this feature in detail in "Comparing Versions of a Web Page" on page 343.

8. **Click OK to proceed, or Cancel to stop the synchronization.**

   If you click OK, Dreamweaver commences copying and deleting the chosen files. If you want to stop the process, click Cancel in the Background File Activity window.

9. **Click Close.**

TIP If you just want to *identify* newer files on the local site without synchronizing them (to run a report on them, for example), click the contextual menu in the top-right corner of the Files panel and then choose Edit→Select Newer Local. Dreamweaver connects to the remote server and compares the files, and then, in the Files panel's "Local view" list, highlights files on the local site that are newer than their remote counterparts.

You can also identify newer files on the remote server: Choose Edit→"Select Newer on Remote server" from the Files panel's contextual menu.

Finally, you can identify files on your computer you either created or modified within a given date range, using the Select Recently Modified command described in the box on page 747.

◼ Communicating with Design Notes

Lots of questions arise when a team works on a website: Has this page been proof-read? Who authored this page? Where did that graphic come from? Usually, you must rely on a flurry of emails to ferret out the answers.

But Dreamweaver's Design Notes dialog box (Figure 18-13) eliminates much of that hassle by letting you attach information, such as a web page's status or author, to a file.

You can open these notes from the Files panel, from a currently open document, or automatically; edit them; and even share them with others. That makes it easy to leave your collaborators a note, like, "Hey Bob, can you make sure that this is the most recent photo of Kim and Kanye?" You can even add notes to files other than web pages, including folders, images, and external Cascading Style Sheets—any-thing, in fact, that appears in the Files panel. (As noted in the caption for Figure 18-13, however, Dreamweaver can't automatically open files, like images, that it can't open and edit on its own. That's true even if you select the "Show when file is open" option in the Design Notes dialog box.)

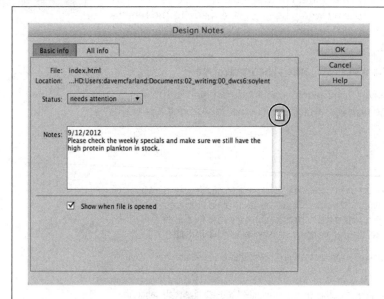

FIGURE 18-13

If you want the Design Notes window to open whenever someone opens a page, turn on the "Show when file is opened" checkbox. That ensures that no one misses important information about a page. (This option has no effect when you add notes to images [GIFs, JPEGs, PNGs] or anything other than a file that Dreamweaver can open and edit, such as a web page or an external style sheet.)

Setting Up Design Notes

You can't use Design Notes unless you turn the feature on. To find out if it is, open the Site Setup dialog box by double-clicking the site's name in the Manage Sites dialog box (choose Manage Sites from the Site menu or the drop-down menu in the Files panel). In the Advanced Setting window, click Design Notes. As you can see in Figure 18-14, two checkboxes pertain to the Notes feature:

- **Maintain Design Notes.** Turning on this checkbox lets you create and read notes using Dreamweaver's File→Design Notes command (see "Viewing Design Notes" on page 798).

- **Enable Upload Design Notes for sharing.** If you use Design Notes as part of a team, turn on this checkbox—it makes Dreamweaver upload design notes to the remote site so your fellow team members can read them.

> **NOTE** Design Notes are especially useful for keeping track of pages built and maintained by a team of web developers. But if you're a solo operator and still want to use them—maybe you're the type with a hundred Post-it notes taped to the edges of your monitor—then turn off the "Upload Design Notes for sharing" checkbox. You'll save time and server space by preventing Dreamweaver from transferring the note files to your server.

Click OK to close the Site Definition dialog box. You can double-click another site in the Manage Sites dialog box to turn on its Design Notes feature, or click Done.

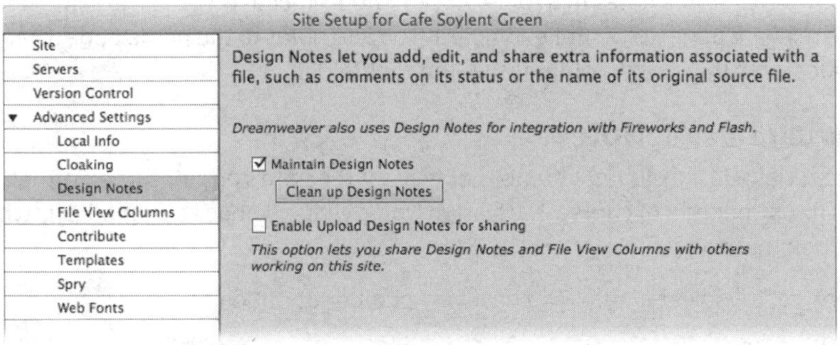

FIGURE 18-14

The Clean Up button deletes orphan notes— those that were attached to now-deleted files. (To avoid stray notes files in the first place, always delete pages in Dreamweaver's Files panel, as opposed to Windows Explorer or the Mac's Finder.) If you turn off the Maintain Design Notes checkbox, clicking Clean Up removes all Design Notes files from the site.

To add a Design Note to a document you're working on, choose your favorite method:

- Choose File→Design Notes.

- From the File Status menu in the Document toolbar (see Figure 18-8), choose Design Notes.

- Right-click (Control-click) a file in the Files panel (or an external object, such as a graphic or movie, in the document window), and choose Design Notes from the shortcut menu.

In any case, the Design Notes window opens (Figure 18-13). If you like, you can use the Status drop-down menu to let your team members know where the file stands. For example, is it ready to move to the server? Is it just a draft version? Or is there something wrong with it that requires attention? Dreamweaver provides eight options: "draft," "revision1," "revision2," "revision3," "alpha," "beta," "final," and "needs attention."

The note itself, which you type into the Note box, could be a simple question for the page's author ("Are you sure 'Kings of Leon: Defining a New Musical Language for the Modern Age' is an appropriate title for this article?") or it could offer more information about the status of the page ("Still need studio shot for high-energy plankton milkshake").

TIP   Click the calendar icon (circled in Figure 18-13) to pop the date into your note—a great way to keep a running tally of notes and the dates they were written.

When you click OK, Dreamweaver creates a file with all the note information in it. This file ends with the extension .mno and begins with the name of the file; for the file *index.html*, for example, Dreamweaver would name the note *index.html.mno*.

Dreamweaver stores notes in a folder called *_notes* that it keeps in the same folder as the relevant page or file. For example, if you add notes to the home page, Dreamweaver stores the *_notes* folder inside the root folder.

Viewing Design Notes

You can view Design Notes a number of ways. If the note's author turned on "Show when file is opened," of course, the Design Notes window opens automatically when you open that page.

Otherwise, to look at a note, you have any number of options:

- Choose File→Design Notes.

- Choose Design Notes from the File Status drop-down menu in the document window's toolbar.

- Double-click the small yellow balloon icon in the Notes column of the Files panel. (You'll only see this column if you turned on this option in the Site Definition window, as described below.)

- Right-click (Control-click) an embedded object, like a graphic or Flash movie, right in the document window, and choose Design Notes from the shortcut menu.

- Right-click (Control-click) a file in the Files panel and choose Design Notes from the shortcut menu.

Organizing the Columns in the Files Panel

Columns in the Files panel identify a file's name, size, modification date, type, and so on.

This may be more information than you're interested in—or it may not be enough. So remember that Dreamweaver lets you show or hide columns, change their order, and even create new ones with information it retrieves from a file's Design Notes.

NOTE You can adjust the relative width of these columns by dragging the dividing line between the column names. You can also sort all the pages listed in this window by clicking the relevant column's name. Click "Modified," for example, to sort the files so the newest ones appear first. Click a second time to reverse the sort, placing oldest files first.

When you set up a website in the Site Definition window, you can view the column setup by clicking the File View Columns category (Figure 18-15).

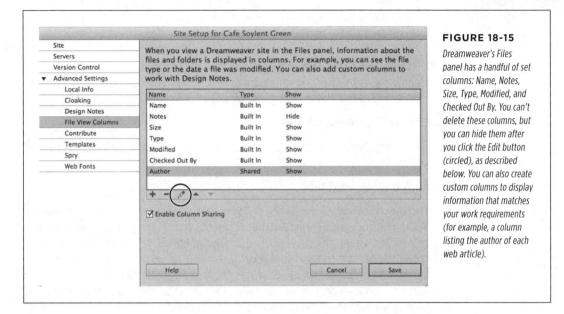

FIGURE 18-15

Dreamweaver's Files panel has a handful of set columns: Name, Notes, Size, Type, Modified, and Checked Out By. You can't delete these columns, but you can hide them after you click the Edit button (circled), as described below. You can also create custom columns to display information that matches your work requirements (for example, a column listing the author of each web article).

Once you see the screen shown in Figure 18-15, you can perform any of these stunts:

- **Reorder columns.** Click a column name in the Site Definition window to select it. Then click the up and down arrow buttons to move the column one spot to the left or right, respectively, in the Files panel.

- **Deleting columns.** Click the column name, and then click the - sign button to delete the column. (Dreamweaver doesn't let you delete the built-in columns Name, Notes, Type, Modified, and so on.)

- **Adding Columns.** You can add columns of your own, as described next.

To hide a column (or show a hidden column), select the column in the File View Options category of the Site Setup window, and then click the Edit button (circled in Figure 18-15). In the window that opens, hide the column by turning off the Show checkbox, and display a hidden column by turning on the checkbox. You can also change how Dreamweaver aligns the text in the column (left, right, or center) using the Align menu. It's a good idea to hide columns you don't need, since they take up space in the Files panel, often hiding parts of filenames.

Creating Custom Columns

Your Files panel offers columns for all the usual information: Name, Checked Out, and so on. But you may someday wish there were a column that showed each page's status, so that your Files panel could show you which files need proofreading, who wrote each article, or which pages are being held until a certain blackout date.

You can add columns of your own design, although the process isn't streamlined by any means. It involves two broad efforts: First, using an offshoot of the Design Notes feature described earlier, you set up the new columns you want to display. Then, using the column-manipulation dialog box shown in Figure 18-15, you make the new columns visible in the Files panel.

■ PHASE 1: DEFINING THE NEW INFORMATION TYPES

You create new kinds of informational flags—primarily for use as new columns in the Files panel—using the Design Notes dialog box. Here's the rundown:

1. **Choose File→Design Notes.**

   The Design Notes window opens. (You can summon it in various other ways, as described on page 795.)

2. **Click the "All info" tab.**

   This peculiar window shows the programmery underbelly of the Dreamweaver Notes feature (see Figure 18-16). It turns out that it stores every kind of note as a name/value pair. If you used the main Notes screen (Figure 18-13) to choose Beta from the Status drop-down menu, for example, you'll see a notation that says "status=beta". *Status* is the info nugget's description; *beta* is its value. If you turn on the option called "Show when file is opened," you'll see "showOnOpen=true". And if you typed *Badly needs updating* as the note itself, you'll see "notes=Badly needs updating" on this screen.

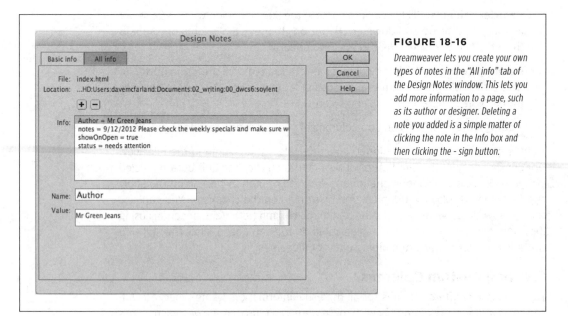

FIGURE 18-16

Dreamweaver lets you create your own types of notes in the "All info" tab of the Design Notes window. This lets you add more information to a page, such as its author or designer. Deleting a note you added is a simple matter of clicking the note in the Info box and then clicking the - sign button.

But those are just the built-in info types; you're free to create your own.

3. **Click the + button.**

You may wonder why you'd add a custom column; after all, you can type a lot of information in the Notes box itself, under the Basic Info tab. The primary benefit is that you can display the information in this new column in the Files panel.

4. **Label the new note in the Name field.**

You may choose *Author* as a label, for example, so you can note who wrote the text of each page. Or it could be *Artist*, if you wish to add a note to each image specifying who created it. Maybe you need a column called *Hold Until*, which reminds you when certain information is OK to publish online.

5. **Press Tab to jump to the Value field, and then type the contents of the note.**

You can enter the actual name of the author or artist—Jennifer Jones, for example—or the actual "Hold Until" date.

Repeat steps 3–5 to add more notes.

NOTE Keep the value short—one or two words. Otherwise, the narrow Files panel column chops off the latter part of it. If you've got enough screen real estate, you can resize the columns by dragging the divider bars between column names.

6. **Click OK.**

The dialog box closes.

◼ PHASE 2: ADDING THE COLUMN TO THE FILES PANEL

Just creating a new note type gets you halfway home; now you have to tell Dreamweaver to display that information in the Files panel.

To add a column to the Files panel:

1. **Open the Site Setup window for the particular site and select the File View Columns category under the Advanced Setting options.**

To edit a site, choose Site→Manage Sites, and then double-click the name of the site from the Manage Sites window. Expand the Advanced Settings category on the left side of the window and the File View Columns options appear.

2. **Click the + sign button.**

A pane appears (Figure 18-17) for adding the information to the new column.

3. **In the Column Name box, type the column heading you want to appear in the Files panel.**

Make it short and descriptive. If possible, it should match the note type (*Author, Artist, Hold Until*, or whatever).

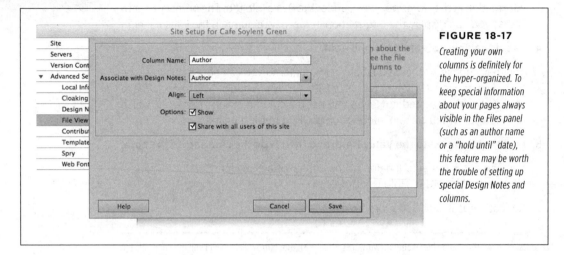

FIGURE 18-17

Creating your own columns is definitely for the hyper-organized. To keep special information about your pages always visible in the Files panel (such as an author name or a "hold until" date), this feature may be worth the trouble of setting up special Design Notes and columns.

4. **Press Tab. Type the name of the Design Note you wish to use for this column.**

This is the name part of the name/value pair described in step 4 of the previous instructions. For example, if you add a note named Author to a file, you would type *Author* here. Capitalization matters; so if you named the Design Note *Author*, type it with a capital A.

There's a drop-down menu here, too, but it always lists the same four options: Status, Assigned, Due, and Priority. If you choose Status, you'll get a column that reflects your choice from the Status drop-down menu in the Design Notes window (see step 2 on page 800). The other three options do nothing *unless* you create a matching note type in step 4 of the previous instructions. (It would be nice if this drop-down menu listed *all* the notes you created, so you didn't have to remember their names.)

Before you wrap up the column-adding procedure, you can, if you wish, choose an alignment option for the text in the column (left, right, or center). Check to make sure that the Show checkbox is turned on; otherwise, your new column won't appear, and you've just defeated the purpose of this whole exercise. Finally, turn on the "Share with all users of this site" checkbox if you like.

The Share feature works like this: The next time you connect to your remote server, Dreamweaver uploads a file containing your newly defined column information. The next time another member of the team connects to the remote site, *his* copy of Dreamweaver downloads this file, so that his Files panel shows the same columns yours does.

NOTE The column-sharing feature can be very handy; it lets everyone working on a site share the same information. But it works properly only if everyone on the team has the "Enable column sharing" checkbox turned on (see Figure 18-15).

5. **Click Save.**

You should now see the new column in your Files panel. (You may need to widen the panel to see all the columns. You can also click the Expand Files Panel button [Figure 18-6] to expand the Panel.)

Dreamweaver CC Power

Snippets and Libraries

O
K, so you finished the design for your company's new website. It looks great and your boss is ecstatic. But you've really only just begun. You have to build hundreds of pages before you launch the site. And once the site's online, you need to make endless updates to keep it fresh and inviting.

That's where Dreamweaver's Snippets and Library features come in, streamlining the sometimes tedious work of building and updating site pages.

As you create more and more web pages (and more and more websites), you may find yourself crafting the same page elements over and over again. Many of your pages may share common elements that always stay the same: a copyright notice, a navigation bar, or a logo, for example. And you may find yourself frequently using complex components, such as a pull-down menu that lists all the countries you ship products to or a particular design for photos and their captions.

Recreating the same components time after time is tiresome and—thanks to Dreamweaver—unnecessary. Dreamweaver provides two subtly different tools for reusing common page elements: *Snippets* and *Library items*.

Snippets Basics

Snippets aren't fancy or complex, but they sure save time. A snippet is simply a chunk of code you store away and then plunk into your web pages as necessary. Snippets can be as simple as boilerplate legal text, or as complex as HTML, CSS, or JavaScript code (or code from any other programming language you encounter). For example, say you always use the same table design to list product specifications in your company's catalog. Each time you want to create a similar table, you could go through all the same steps to build it—or you could turn that table into a snippet, and then, with a simple double-click, add it to page after page of your site. Or say you use the popular jQuery JavaScript library on each site you build, and have to include the code to link to jQuery's JavaScript file—rather than type that code each time, just have Dreamweaver drop the pre-typed code into the page for you.

You keep these code chunks in Dreamweaver's Snippets panel (see Figure 19-1), and summon them in a couple of ways:

- Choose Window→Snippets.

- Windows people can press Shift-F9. (There's no Mac keyboard shortcut for the Snippets panel, but you can create your own, as described on page 869.)

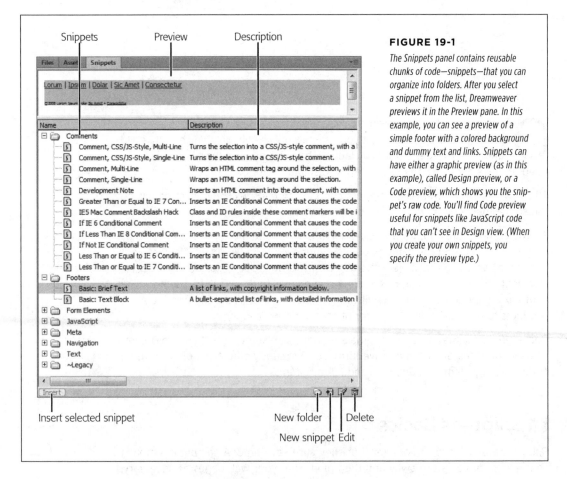

FIGURE 19-1

The Snippets panel contains reusable chunks of code—snippets—that you can organize into folders. After you select a snippet from the list, Dreamweaver previews it in the Preview pane. In this example, you can see a preview of a simple footer with a colored background and dummy text and links. Snippets can have either a graphic preview (as in this example), called Design preview, or a Code preview, which shows you the snippet's raw code. You'll find Code preview useful for snippets like JavaScript code that you can't see in Design view. (When you create your own snippets, you specify the preview type.)

Once you open the Snippets panel, you'll see a set of stock Dreamweaver snippets, but above and beyond those, you can quickly build your own.

■ Using Snippets

Snippets come in two varieties: those that are simple blocks of code, and those that wrap around a currently selected element in a document. For example, in the Snippets panel's Text folder, you'll find a snippet called Service Mark. Adding this snippet to a page instantly inserts the code *^{sm}*, creating a superscript service mark (sm) symbol.

But on occasion, you'll want to wrap code around something you've already typed. You may, for example, want to add an HTML comment to your page (a message that won't appear in web browsers, but that helps you or other web designers decipher the page). The "Comment, multi-line" snippet (in the Comments folder of the Snippets panel) helps you quickly add such a note. It wraps whatever you select with opening (<!--) and closing HTML comment markers (-->). Adding an HTML comment is as easy as typing the comment in your page, selecting it, and then double-clicking this snippet. This may sound a lot like the Apply Comment button in the Coding toolbar described in Figure 7-7, but the cool thing about this snippet is that it works in Design view, too, not just in Code view.

NOTE Unfortunately, unless the snippet's description (which you find in the Snippets panel's Description column) specifies that the snippet wraps, you can't tell whether it will or not. You either have to try out the snippet or open it in Editing mode to see. (And while you have the snippet open, you can add a note to its description indicating its ability, or inability, to wrap.)

To add a snippet to a web page, click in the document where you want the item to go, or select the object you wish to wrap with a snippet. Then do one of the following:

- On the Snippets panel, double-click the name of the snippet.

- On the Snippets panel, select the snippet, and then click the panel's Insert button.

- Drag the snippet from the panel into the document window. (If the snippet is supposed to wrap around a selection, drag the snippet *onto* the selected object.)

While you can work with snippets in either Design or Code view, some snippets make sense only in Code view. For example, you typically have to insert the JavaScript snippets that come bundled with Dreamweaver in the <head> section of a page, inside <script> tags. To use these snippets, you have to switch to Code view, insert the <script> tags, and then put the snippets inside.

TIP To quickly insert a snippet you recently used, select the snippet's name from Insert→Recent Snippets. Better yet, create a keyboard shortcut for your favorite snippets, and then insert them with a keystroke, as described on page 869.

Snippets simply dump their contents into a document—essentially copying the snippet code and pasting it into your web page. Dreamweaver doesn't step in to make sure that you're adding the code correctly. Unless you're careful—and have some knowledge of HTML—you may end up adding snippets that make your web page impossible to view. (For advice on how to avoid such pitfalls, see the box on page 814.)

Creating Snippets

Dreamweaver comes with a lot of snippets, and you may find many of them irrelevant to what you want to do. No problem—you can easily create your own. Here's how:

1. **Create and select the content you wish to turn into a snippet.**

   You could, for instance, select a table in Design view, or select the opening and closing <table> tags (as well as all the code between them) in Code view. Or, if you want to save a form's Select menu (see page 641) that took you half an hour to build, then, in Design view, just click the menu.

   If you want to make a snippet out of code that isn't visible in Design view, such as a JavaScript program or content that appears in the <head> section of a page, you need to switch to Code view first.

2. **In the Snippets panel, click the New Snippet button, a.k.a. the + sign button.**

   The Snippet window appears (Figure 19-2), displaying the code you selected in step 1 in the Insert field.

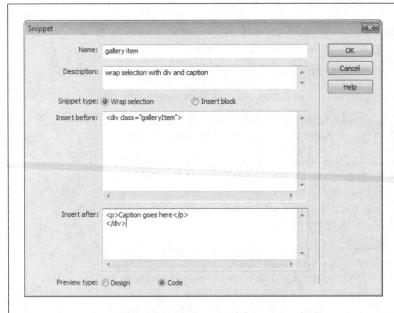

FIGURE 19-2

The Snippet window lets you create reusable chunks of HTML called snippets. For snippets that wrap around a currently selected object—for example, a snippet that adds a link to any selected text or graphic—you put code in the two Insert boxes. The code that appears before the selected object goes in the top box, and the code that goes after the object appears in the bottom box. In this example, the snippet wraps the current selection in a <div> tag with a predefined class applied to it.

> **NOTE** If you skip step 1 and just click the New Snippet button, you can either type the code or, in the Insert box, paste a previously copied selection (see step 6).

3. **Title the snippet.**

   The name you type in the Name field appears in the Snippets panel. Make sure to give your snippet a name that clearly describes what it does.

4. **In the Description field, type identifying details.**

   This step is optional, but useful. Use this field to describe when and how to use the snippet, and whether or not the snippet wraps a selection.

5. **Select a snippet type.**

   "Wrap selection" makes the code wrap around a selection when you use the snippet. The "Insert block" option is for a snippet that's a single block of code you want to insert into a document, like a copyright notice or a form menu.

6. **If necessary, add the code for the snippet.**

   If you initially selected code in the document window, it automatically appears in the "Insert before" field for a snippet that wraps around other code. For snippets that are just a single block of code, the code appears in the "Insert code" box.

   If you create a wrapping snippet, you need to add some code in the "before" field and some in the "after" field. For example, say you create a lot of photo galleries, and you want to wrap each photo in its own <div> tag with some room for a caption. Instead of adding that HTML manually over and over again, you can create a snippet that wraps the image with the appropriate HTML. For example, the code that goes before the image might include an opening <div> tag with a class applied to it, and the code that goes after the image can include the HTML for the caption and the closing </div> tag. In this case, in the "Insert before" field, you might type *<div class="galleryItem">*, and in the "Insert after" field, type the HTML that goes after the image, maybe something like *<p>Caption goes here</p></div>*.

7. **Select a "Preview type."**

   The preview type determines how the snippet appears in the Snippets panel's Preview pane. *Design* means the snippet looks as it would in Design view—a table snippet appears as a table, for instance. *Code* means the code itself appears in the Preview pane, so a snippet for a horizontal rule would preview like this: <hr>. Use Code preview for snippets, like JavaScript code, that aren't visible in Design view.

8. **Click OK.**

   Dreamweaver adds the snippet to the Snippets panel; you can then drop it in your web pages using any of the techniques described on page 809.

If you need to go back and edit a snippet—change the code, snippet type, description, or name—in the Snippets panel, select the snippet, and then click the Edit Snippet button ⬚. You can also right-click (Control-click) the snippet name, and then, from the shortcut menu, select Edit.

Whichever method you choose, the Snippet window opens. Make your changes, and then click OK.

Organizing Snippets

To keep your snippets organized, create folders and store them by category. To add a folder to the Snippets panel, click ⬜ (see Figure 19-1). An untitled folder appears; type in a name for it. If you select a folder before clicking ⬜, Dreamweaver creates the new folder *inside* that folder. You can move folders around by dragging them into and out of other folders. However, folders are always listed in alphabetical order, so you can't re-order folders by dragging them in the Snippets panel.

> **TIP**   To drag a folder or snippet outside a folder to the top level of the Snippets list, you have to drag it all the way to the *bottom* of the Snippets panel, below any other folders. If you try to drag it to the top, Dreamweaver puts the folder or snippet inside the list's top folder.

To move a snippet into or out of its folder, simply drag it. If you drag a snippet over a closed folder without releasing the mouse, that folder expands to reveal the folders and snippets inside, if any.

To delete a snippet, select it in the Snippets panel, and then click the Delete Snippet button (the trash can). Quicker yet, press Delete.

> **NOTE**   Storing lots of snippets slows down the Snippets panel. You'll probably never use many of the snippets that come with Dreamweaver, so it's best to remove the ones you don't use. An excellent candidate is the Legacy folder listed at the bottom of the panel. This folder, which really should be called the Old Garbage folder, is full of out-of-date, you-really-shouldn't-use-them snippets that Adobe added to much earlier versions of Dreamweaver. If you don't want to permanently delete these snippets, you can move them out of the Snippets folder in the main Adobe Dreamweaver CC Configuration folder and store them in a separate folder on your hard drive. (For more on the Configuration folder and how to find it, see the box on page 880.)

■ Built-In Snippets

Most of Dreamweaver's stock snippets offer solutions to problems you may never encounter, like a page footer with two lists of links and a copyright notice in it. In addition, many Dreamweaver snippets use older design techniques (like tables to lay out content) that are best avoided. However, most web developers find at least a few built-in snippets worth using. Here are some highlights:

- **Close Window Button.** When you create a pop-up window (page 607), this snippet lets you add a Close button to let people dismiss the window. The Close Window Button snippet (in the Form Elements folder) places a form button with the words "Close Window" on it, complete with the JavaScript necessary to close the window when your visitor clicks the button.

- **Dropdown Menus.** If you create a lot of forms for your sites (see Chapter 14), you'll find some other useful snippets in the Form Elements folder, especially in the Dropdown Menus subfolder. For example, the "Numbers 1-12" snippet inserts a menu with the numbers 1 to 12 already coded into it—great for capturing credit card expiration dates on an e-commerce site. (To create an even more useful drop-down snippet, see the tutorial at the end of this chapter.)

- **HTML Comments.** You can use the Comment Multi-Line snippet (in the Comments folder) to "comment-out," or hide, HTML. And this works in Design view, so just select the element you want to hide and apply this comment. This is a good way to temporarily hide some HTML—for example, to test what a page looks like with and without different chunks of HTML. To make the HTML visible again, go into Code view, because the Coding toolbar has a handy tool for quickly un-commenting HTML (see Figure 7-6).

- **IE Conditional Comments.** Sometimes older versions of Internet Explorer just don't get things right. This is frequently the case with CSS. To overcome browser differences, you sometimes need to provide IE with CSS code (or HTML or JavaScript code) that differs from the code you send to other browsers. You can insert special code (in the form of so-called conditional comments) that only IE understands. Dreamweaver provides a handful of code snippets (the last five listed in the Snippets panel's Comments folder) that create the necessary code for adding IE-oriented conditional comments. (For a good tutorial with lots of examples on how and why to use IE conditional comments, visit *http://bit.ly/H9m6UT*.)

■ Library Basics

Imagine this situation: You manage a relatively large website consisting of thousands of pages. At the bottom of each one sits a simple copyright notice: "Copyright My-BigCompany. We reserve all rights—national, international, commercial, noncommercial, and mineral—to the content contained on these pages."

Each time you add another page to your site, you *could* retype the copyright message, but that invites both typographic errors and carpal tunnel syndrome. And if you must *format* this text, too, you're in for even more work.

Fortunately, Dreamweaver's Library feature can turn anything you select in the document window (a paragraph, an image, a table) into a reusable chunk of HTML that you can easily drop into any Dreamweaver document. The Library, in other words, is a great place to store copyright notices, navigation bars, announcements, or any other chunks of frequently used HTML.

A Snippet of Caution

Snippets aren't as smart as other features in Dreamweaver. While the program usually warns you before you make a mistake, it doesn't make a peep if you incorrectly add a snippet.

For instance, when you use one of Dreamweaver's Form snippets to add, say, a text field to a page, it doesn't check to see if you're really putting the snippet into a form. Therefore, it doesn't let you know if you're missing the required <form> tag, and it certainly doesn't add the tag itself. Furthermore, if you're working in Code view, Dreamweaver lets you add snippets to the <head> section of a page (or even outside the <html> tags altogether), which is useful for creating dynamic web pages that include server-side programming, but creates messy and invalid HTML in normal web pages.

Furthermore, snippets don't take advantage of Dreamweaver's site-management features to keep track of links or paths to images. Suppose you create a snippet that includes an image. If you insert that snippet into another page, the image may not show up correctly. If you create a snippet that includes a document-relative link (page 170) from one page to another page on your site, that link may not work when you add the snippet to yet another page.

So it's best to create snippets that don't involve images or links—but there are workarounds. For instance, you can create snippets with fake links—you could use nothing but the # symbol for the link, for example—and update the link after you insert the snippet into the page. For images, you can use a placeholder object to simulate a graphic in a snippet, something as simple as a GIF or JPG file with the words "place holder" in it. After you add the snippet to the page, update the placeholder with the details (location, size, and so on) for the real image file.

If you want to create reusable content that can keep track of links and images, see "Creating and Using Library Items" on page 815.

So far, Library items sound pretty much like the snippets described in the previous section. But Library items have added power: When you add HTML to a web page using a Library item, that code remains linked to the original Library item, the one Dreamweaver created and stored in your site. Thanks to this link, whenever you update the *original* Library item, you get a chance to update every page that uses that item, too.

Suppose your company is bought, and the legal department orders you to change the copyright notice to "Copyright MyBigCompany, a subsidiary of MuchBigger-Company" on each of the website's *10,000 pages*. If you had cleverly inserted the original copyright notice as a Library item, you could take care of this task in the blink of an eye. Just open the item in the Library, make the required changes, save it, and let Dreamweaver update all the pages for you (see Figure 19-3).

NOTE You can achieve a similar effect to Dreamweaver Library items using Server-Side Includes. This option, discussed on page 892, is a bit more technical but provides even faster site updates than Library items.

Compared to snippets, Library items are smart. They possess the unique ability to update the same material on an entire site's worth of files in seconds, and can successfully deal with links and images. Unlike snippets, however, Dreamweaver's Library feature is site-specific: Each site you set up in Dreamweaver has its own Library, and Dreamweaver stores that Library's files along with all the site's other files. If you need to use a Library item from one site on a different site, you need to copy it to the new site. To do that, in the original site's Assets panel, right-click the Library item, then choose Copy to Site and choose the new site from the pop-up menu.

FIGURE 19-3

Library items are great for small chunks of HTML you use frequently. Here, on an old version of The Museum of Modern Art's home page, many of the navigation options on the page (circled) are Library items. If the Museum needed to add or remove a navigation link, they could simply update the Library item to change every page on the site in one step. In fact, since a Library item is a chunk of HTML, you could replace the left-hand navigation bar with plain-text links (instead of graphics), or any other valid HTML code.

■ Creating and Using Library Items

To create a Library item, start by opening the Library window. Click the Assets tab (to the right of the Files tab) or choose Window→Assets, and then click the Library items button (it looks like an open book, circled in Figure 19-4) to reveal the Library category.

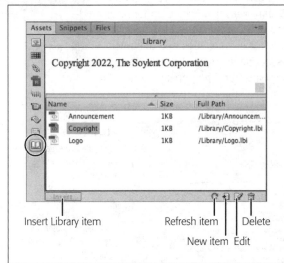

FIGURE 19-4

The Assets panel's Library category lists the name, file size, and location of each Library item in the currently open site. When you select an item from the list, Dreamweaver previews it. In this example, the Library item "Copyright" is, shockingly, a copyright notice.

NOTE Keep in mind that Library items can contain only page elements that appear in the document window—in other words, only HTML from the <body> section of a web page. You can't include anything that appears in the <head> of a page, like Cascading Style Sheets, JavaScript widgets (Chapter 13), or meta tags. This means you can't store Dreamweaver behaviors or JavaScript widgets in your Library (but you *can* include them with a Dreamweaver template, discussed in the next chapter). Furthermore, Library items must include a complete set of HTML tags—both an opening and a closing tag—as well as all the tags necessary to complete the original object. For example, Dreamweaver doesn't let you turn just a single cell, row, or column of a table into a Library item. If you try, Dreamweaver will add the *entire* table to the Library.

Now select the part of your document you want to save as a Library item: a blob of text, a graphic, whatever. This might be just a few words, or an entire paragraph or headline. You can even select a <div> tag (page 428) containing other tags.

TIP Use the Tag Selector (see page 7) to make sure you choose the precise tag you want. Sometimes, though, you want the content *inside* a tag. To select the contents inside a table cell, for example, click at the beginning of the content, and then drag until you select everything in the cell, or click in the cell and then choose Edit→Select All.

Next, add the selection to the Library. As you may expect, Dreamweaver provides several ways to do this:

- Drag the highlighted selection into the list of Library items.

- Click the New Item button (the + sign button; see Figure 19-4).

- Choose Modify→Library→Add Object to Library.

The new item appears in the Assets panel, bearing the jaunty name "Untitled." Type in a more useful name, such as *Copyright notice* or *Logo*. Your new Library item is now ready to use.

NOTE Even though you can't turn a CSS style into a Library item, you *can* turn HTML that you've styled with CSS into a Library item. For example, you can add to the Library a paragraph that has a CSS class style applied to it. When you attempt to add this paragraph to the Library, Dreamweaver warns you that the item may not look the same when you place it in other documents—because the style sheet information doesn't come along for the ride. To make sure the Library item appears correctly, make sure you attach the same style sheet to any page where you use that item. External style sheets (see page 107) make that easy.

Adding Library Items to a Page

To add a Library item to a web page, drag it out of the Assets panel's Library items list and onto your page. (The long way: Click to plant your insertion point on the page, click the Library item you want in the Assets panel, and then, in the Assets panel, click the Insert button, shown in Figure 19-4.)

When you insert a Library item into a page (or turn a selected item *into* a Library item), it sprouts a light yellow background. The highlighting indicates that Dreamweaver intends to treat the item as a single object, even though it may include many different HTML elements. You can select it or drag it around, but you can't edit it. (Unfortunately, if you turn a nontransparent graphic—like a logo, for example—into a Library item, Dreamweaver doesn't give you the helpful yellow background.)

Remember, too, that the placed Library item links to the original item in the Library. The copy in your document automatically changes to reflect any changes you make to the original version in the Library, using the technique described next.

TIP At some point, you may want to sever the connection between the Library and a Library item you placed on a page—to modify a copyright notice on just a single page, for example. Select the item on the page, and then, in the Properties panel, click "Detach from original" (Figure 19-5). Dreamweaver removes the comment tags (see the box on page 820), thus breaking the link to the Library.

You can also insert the HTML of a Library item *without* maintaining a link to the Library by pressing the Ctrl (Option) key as you add the item to your document. This treats the HTML more like a snippet, since Dreamweaver doesn't update the HTML on this page if you change the original Library file.

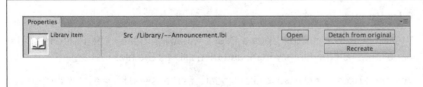

FIGURE 19-5

The selected Library item (an .lbi file) is in the site's Library folder. (The path appears after the word "Src.")

■ Editing Library Items

You'll appreciate the real power of Library items when it's time to make a change. When you update the original file in the Library, all the pages graced with that linked item update, too.

Start by opening the Library, as described on page 815. Then:

1. **Open the Library item you want to edit.**

   Double-click the Library item in the Assets panel, highlight it in the Library item list, and then click the Edit button (Figure 19-4), or highlight it on a web page and then, in the Properties panel, click Open (Figure 19-5). (You can also open the Library item—an .lbi file—in the Library folder of your site's root by double-clicking it in the Files panel.)

   Dreamweaver opens what looks like a normal web page, but it contains only the text, graphics, or other elements of the Library file.

2. **Edit away.**

   A Library item is only a selection of HTML, it's not a complete web page. That means you must not add *page* properties, like a title or background color, or one of the behaviors discussed in Chapter 13, to it. (Dreamweaver actually lets you do this, but that adds invalid HTML to the Library item as well as to every page that uses the Library item.) Also, you can insert Library items only in the body of a web page, so stick with objects that would normally appear in the document window, such as links, images, tables, and text. Don't add any code that appears in the head of a web page, such as Cascading Style Sheets, meta tags, behaviors, or JavaScript widgets.

   Since Library items can't contain style sheets, if the HTML in your Library item relies on a style, you'll have trouble previewing it correctly. Dreamweaver's Design-Time Style Sheet tool comes in handy here. It lets you temporarily "add" a style sheet while you design a page, without actually adding the CSS code to the page. For more on this useful feature, turn to page 397.

3. **Choose File→Save.**

   Dreamweaver checks to see if any pages use the Library item and, if they do, it opens the Update Library Items window. A list of the pages that use that item appears.

4. **Click Update.**

   Dreamweaver opens the Update Pages window, updates the HTML in all the pages that use the Library item, and then lists all the files it changed.

   You don't necessarily have to click Update. Perhaps you have a lot of changes to make to the Library item, and you just want to save the work you've done so far.

You're not done editing it yet, so you don't want to waste time updating pages you'll just have to update again later. You can always update them another time (see the box on page 841); to do that, click Don't Update. (Once you finish making changes and save the file for the final time, *then* you can update your site.)

5. **Click Done.**

   As you can see, the Library is an incredible timesaver that greatly simplifies the process of changing common page elements.

Renaming Library Elements

To rename something in your Library, click its name in the Assets panel. Pause briefly, click again, and Dreamweaver highlights the name, ready for your edit. Type the new name, and then press Enter (Return).

If you already added the item to your web pages, Dreamweaver prompts you to update those pages. Click Update. Otherwise, the link between those pages and the Library breaks.

NOTE If you accidentally click Don't Update, don't panic. Simply change the Library item back to its original name, and then *re*-rename it. And don't forget to click Update this time!

Deleting Library Elements

You can delete unnecessary elements from your Library any time, but use caution. When you delete something from the Library, Dreamweaver leaves behind every copy of it you placed on your pages—complete with links to the now-deleted Library item. Unfortunately, you can't edit the copies embedded in your web pages until you break those links. Unfortunately, you have to do that manually on each page where the Library item appears by selecting the item and then clicking the "Detach from original" button (see Figure 19-5). Ugh.

Now that you've been warned, here are the instructions to get rid of a Library item. In the Assets panel, click the item, and then do one of the following:

- Click 🗑.

- Press Delete.

- Right-click (Control-click) the item's name, and then, from the shortcut menu, choose Delete.

TIP If you ever accidentally delete an item from the Library, you can re-create it, provided you used it on one of the web pages in your site. Open the page containing the Library item, and then click the item to select it. In the Properties panel, click Recreate (Figure 19-5) to make the item anew. A new item appears in the Library, using the same name and HTML as the item you selected.

■ Snippets and Library Tutorial

In this tutorial, you'll do two things: First, create some useful snippets for common form elements, and second, turn an announcement on the Café Soylent Green site into a reusable Library item and add it to several pages.

> **NOTE** You need to download the tutorial files from *http://oreilly.com/missingmanuals/cds/dreamweaver ccmm13/* to complete this tutorial. See the note on page 33.

Once you download the tutorial files and open Dreamweaver, set up a new site as described on page 19: Name the site *Snippets and Library*, and then select the *Chapter19* folder (it's inside the *MM_DWCC* folder). In a nutshell, choose Site→New Site. In the Site Setup window, type *Snippets and Library* in the Site Name field, click the folder icon next to the Local Site Folder field, navigate to and select the *Chapter19* folder, and then click Select (Choose). Finally, click Save.

Creating a Snippet

1. **With your site freshly defined, make sure you have the Files panel open.**

   If it isn't, press the F8 key (Shift-⌘-F) or choose Window→Files.

2. **In the Files panel, double-click *snippet.html.***

   A page with several form pull-down menus opens. The page includes menus for the months of the year, the names of US states, and the numbers 1 to 31. You can use menus like these on your web pages for a variety of jobs: to let readers specify task to-do dates, for example, or to select a destination state for a product shipment. Dreamweaver's own snippets don't include these useful menus, but, fortunately, you can add them yourself.

3. **In Design view, click the first form menu at the top of the page, the one to the right of the words "Months of year."**

   You've selected the menu and its underlying HTML code. To add this as a snippet, you need to open the Snippets panel.

4. **Choose Window→Snippets.**

   The Snippets panel is your control center for adding, editing, and deleting snippets.

5. **At the bottom of the panel, click the + sign, the New Snippet button (Figure 19-1).**

   The Snippets window opens. Dreamweaver automatically copies the code for the menu into the "Insert before" window. You just need to name the snippet, and add a few more details.

6. **Type *Month Menu* in the Name box, and then *A list of month names, with numeric values*, in the Description box. The Snippets window should look like the one in Figure 19-6.**

   Once you create this snippet (by clicking OK in step 9 below), Dreamweaver displays its name and description in the Snippets panel. In this case, the description you wrote identifies what appears in the menu (a list of month names) and what type of value the snippet applies when a visitor selects a month from the list—a "numeric value." In other words, your description identifies the name/value pair for this form field. (See Chapter 14 for more information on how forms work.)

7. **Turn on the "Insert block" radio button.**

   Clicking this button identifies the snippet as a chunk of standalone HTML, and Dreamweaver changes the code's directive from "Insert before" to "Insert code." You can simply plop down standalone code like this anywhere on a page.

   If you want a snippet to wrap around a selected graphic or text, like a link or table cell, turn on the "Wrap selection" radio button and include the closing code in the "Insert after" box.

8. **At the bottom of the window, turn on the Design radio button.**

   You just told Dreamweaver to preview the snippet in your pages-in-progress. In other words, Dreamweaver displays the rendered snippet in your pages, not just a bunch of code.

9. **The window should now look like the one in Figure 19-6. Click OK to create your new snippet.**

   The snippet should now appear in the Snippets panel, ready for you to insert it into a page.

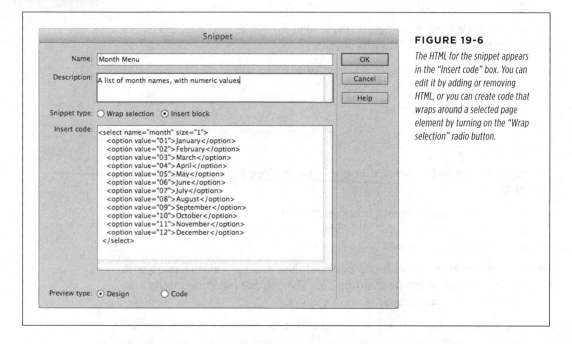

FIGURE 19-6

The HTML for the snippet appears in the "Insert code" box. You can edit it by adding or removing HTML, or you can create code that wraps around a selected page element by turning on the "Wrap selection" radio button.

NOTE   If you select a folder (or a file inside a folder) in the Snippets panel when you create a snippet, Dreamweaver stores the new snippet in that folder. To move it out of the folder and up to the top-level list of the Snippets panel, drag the snippet—Month Menu here—to the very bottom of the panel. Or, to move the snippet to another folder in the Snippets panel, just drag the snippet to that folder—in this case, the Form Elements folder would be appropriate.

10. **Select the Files panel by clicking the Files tab or by pressing the F8 key (Shift-⌘-F), and then double-click the file *reservation.html*.**

    Café Soylent Green's reservation form opens. You'll insert your new snippet here.

11. **Return to the Snippets panel once again by clicking the Snippets tab or by choosing Window→Snippets.**

    Now for the moment of truth.

12. **Drag your new snippet—Month Menu—from the Snippets panel to the right of the label "Month" (below the "number of diners" drop-down menu).**

    Ta-da! Dreamweaver adds the new menu. Now, whenever you need to add a menu that lists the months of the year, don't bother creating it from scratch; instead, just use this snippet!

13. **At the top of the document window, click the *snippet.html* tab. Click the third menu (the one with days of the month), and then repeat steps 5–12.**

Name this new snippet *Days of month* and then type *numerical days of the month* in the Description box. Insert this new snippet to the right of the label "Day" (below the menu you just added to the form) on *reservation.html*. You can close the *snippet.html* file when you finish.

Creating a Library Item

Now you'll see one way in which Dreamweaver's powerful site-management tools can help you create and update your websites more effectively:

1. **Open the file *about.html*.**

Double-click its name in the Files panel or choose File→Open and then select the *about.html* file in the site's root folder.

In the column of content near the middle of the page, a green box says, "Café Soylent Green is now open 7 days a week!" This box is a simple <span> element with some text in it. The cafe uses it for important announcements, and it appears on various pages of the site. Since you need to keep these announcements up to date, creating an easily updated Library item is an efficient tactic.

2. **Click anywhere inside the box (in the text, for example), and then, in the Tag Selector, click <span.announcement> (Figure 19-7).**

You can use this selected <span> as the basis for a new Library item.

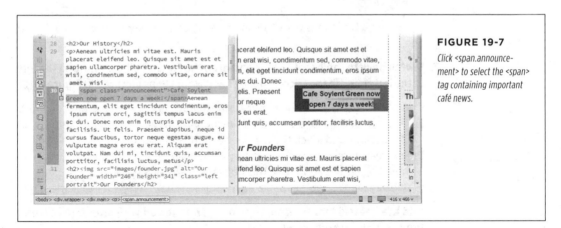

FIGURE 19-7

Click <span.announce-ment> to select the <span> tag containing important café news.

3. **Choose Window→Assets, and then click the Library button.**

The Assets panel opens, and displays the Library category.

4. **On the Assets panel, click the New Library Item button (Figure 19-4).**

A warning message appears, saying that the Library item may not look the same in other pages. Dreamweaver's telling you that Library items can contain only

HTML from the body of a web page—they can't include Cascading Style Sheets. (You can still include HTML that has a style applied to it, just as this <div> tag does, so long as you make sure that any *pages* to which you add the Library item have the appropriate style sheets attached.)

The text in this example *is* formatted using a style sheet, so, sure enough, it won't look the same in pages that don't have the same style sheet applied to them. In this exercise, however, that's not a problem, since all the pages on the site share the same linked external style sheet.

Click OK to dismiss the warning (and feel free to turn on the "Don't warn me again" checkbox while you're at it). The announcement item appears in the Library list, with the "Untitled" name highlighted for editing.

5. **Type *news* to name the new item in the Assets panel, and then press Enter (Return).**

You just checked this standard blob of text into your Library. It's ready to use anywhere else on your site. Notice that the span's background has changed to yellow in the document window—that's Dreamweaver's way of letting you know that this is a Library item.

6. **In the Files panel, double-click the filename *hours.html*.**

You'll frequently jump between the Files panel and the Assets panel, so the keyboard shortcut to open the Files panel comes in handy: F8 (Shift-⌘-F). The Assets panel lacks a keyboard shortcut, but you can create one as described on page 869.

The Hours & Directions page doesn't have an announcement box, so you'll add one.

7. **Switch back to the Assets panel and drag the "news" Library item to the left of the letter "H" in the second headline—"Hours"—as pictured in Figure 19-8.**

If you accidentally drop the Library item somewhere else on the page, choose Edit→Undo and try again. You can recognize the newly inserted item by its yellow background. Click the text in the item, and notice that you can't edit it; Dreamweaver treats the item—really a mixture of HTML, CSS, and JavaScript—as a single object. The source for this object is in the Assets panel. When you add the Library item to another page, as you do in the next step, it will look the same.

8. **Add the "news" Library item to two other pages on your site: *ingredients.html* and *philosophy.html*.**

Open each page (by double-clicking its name in the Files window), and then repeat step 7. Insert the Library item anywhere you want on these pages.

(You can close and save the pages as you go, or leave them open. Here, leave at least one open and go on to step 9.)

9. **Save the pages you added the Library item to by selecting File→Save All.**

10. **This just in!**

    New things are happening at the Café all the time, so it's time to update this announcement. Fortunately, you used a Library item, so it's easy to make the change.

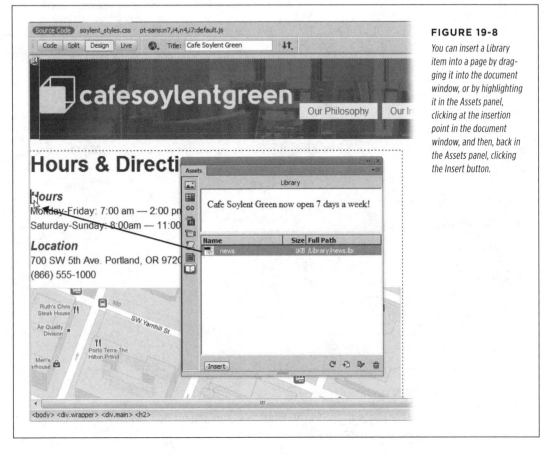

FIGURE 19-8

You can insert a Library item into a page by dragging it into the document window, or by highlighting it in the Assets panel, clicking at the insertion point in the document window, and then, back in the Assets panel, clicking the Insert button.

11. **From the list of Library items in the Assets panel, double-click the "news" item.**

    The Library item opens in the document window, ready for editing. Notice that it doesn't have any of the formatting you saw on the web page—that's because there's no CSS file attached to the item, so you see only the plain HTML version of the announcement box.

12. **Select all the text in the document window and type *Cafe temporarily (we hope) closed due to health inspection. We are sorry for the inconvenience.* Choose File→Save.**

    The Update Library Items dialog box appears (Figure 19-9), listing the four pages in the site that use this announcement box.

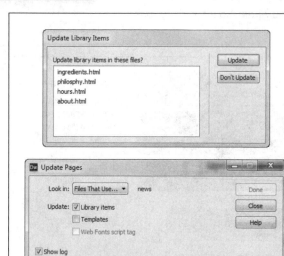

FIGURE 19-9

Top: The Update Library Items dialog box appears whenever you update a Library item. Bottom: After you click Update, the Update Pages box appears. If you turn on the "Show log" checkbox, Dreamweaver displays all the files it changed, including the names of the pages it updated and the total number of pages affected. This window also appears when you update template files, as discussed in the next chapter.

13. **Click Update.**

    Dreamweaver opens the Update Pages dialog box, and then updates all the pages that use the "news" item.

14. **Click Close to close the Update Pages dialog box.**

    Now, if you open *about.html*, *hours.html*, *philosophy.html*, or *ingredients.html*, you'll see that Dreamweaver updated the announcement box.

    Now imagine that you just used this auto-update feature on a 10,000-page site. Sit back and smile.

> **TIP** If you use a particular Library item on some pages of your site but not all, you'll want to know which pages you changed so you can move just those pages up to your server—you don't want to upload your entire website when you change just a handful of pages. Dreamweaver's Select Recently Modified command can help (see the box on page 747). You can also use Dreamweaver's Synchronization feature to make sure you get the most recent pages from your computer to your server (see page 791).

Templates

Some web designers handcraft their sites with loving care, changing layouts, colors, fonts, and banners page by page. But that approach isn't always practical—or desirable.

Consistency from one page to another is a good thing. Web pages that look and act similarly reassure visitors; they can concentrate on each page's unique content when the navigation bar and left sidebar stay the same. But even more important, a handcrafted approach to web design is often unrealistic when you need to crank out content on a deadline.

That's where Dreamweaver *templates* come in. Frequently, the underlying design of many website pages is identical. An employee directory at a company site, for instance, may consist of individual pages dedicated to each employee. Each page has the same navigation bar, banner, footer, and layout. Only a few particulars change from page to page, like the employee's name, photograph, and contact information. This is a perfect case for templates.

This chapter shows you how templates can make quick work of building web pages where most, if not all, of the pages use repetitive elements.

■ Template Basics

Templates let you build pages that share a similar structure and graphic identity, quickly and without having to worry about accidentally deleting or changing elements. Templates come in handy when you design a site where other, less Dreamweaver-savvy individuals will build individual pages. By using a template, you, the godlike Dreamweaver guru, can limit the areas that these underlings can modify on each page.

A new page based on a template—also called a *template instance*, or a *child page*—looks just like the template, except that you can only edit designated areas of the page, called, logically enough, *editable regions*. In Figure 20-1, you can see that the question-and-answer text is an editable region; the rest of the page remains consistent (and is, in fact, locked).

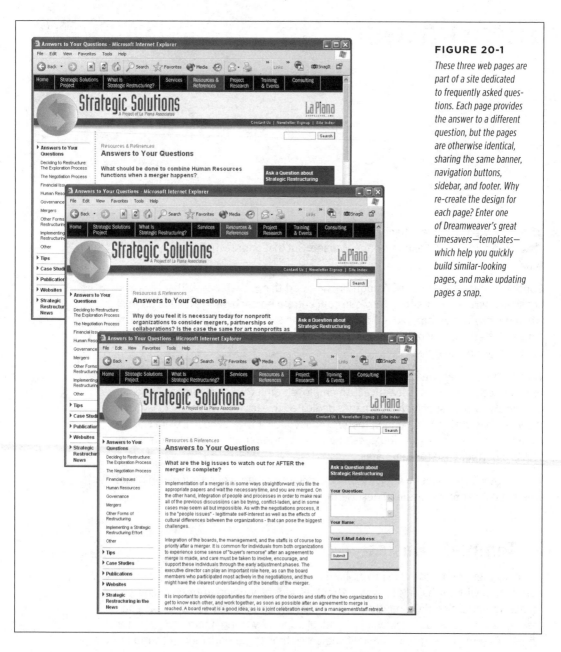

FIGURE 20-1

These three web pages are part of a site dedicated to frequently asked questions. Each page provides the answer to a different question, but the pages are otherwise identical, sharing the same banner, navigation buttons, sidebar, and footer. Why re-create the design for each page? Enter one of Dreamweaver's great timesavers—templates—which help you quickly build similar-looking pages, and make updating pages a snap.

A Dreamweaver template can be very basic, consisting of nothing more than one or more areas that a page author can change (the editable regions), along with other areas that he can't edit (the *locked regions*). At the same time, you can build templates that give page authors an impressive amount of flexibility. Here's an overview of the features you can tap when you create and use templates:

- **Editable regions.** These are the basic building blocks of a template. An editable region is that part of a page—a paragraph, the contents of a <div> tag, or a headline, for example—that page authors can change as they build template-based pages. Templates can include multiple editable regions—a sidebar and the main content of a page, for example.

- **Editable tag attributes.** There may be times when you want to make a particular tag *property* editable. For example, say you have a banner ad at the top of a page—the banner ad is just a basic image file, and each page should have a different ad. You want to make sure that no one can delete the image (after all, those ads are paying for your site), but you do want someone to be able to swap in a new image. In other words, no one should mess with the <img> tag; they should only be able to change the <img> tag's *src* attribute. To keep someone from deleting the image, but still allow them to change pictures, you'd make just the *src* property editable. (You could also make the image's *alt* property editable, and if the *width* and *height* properties vary from image to image, you can make those editable as well.)

  Or you might want a unique headline design for each section of your site. To get that, when you build the site template, assign a class to the <body> tag and make the class name editable. Then, when you create pages for different sections of the site, you add a class name specific to each section. For example, for a site's About Us page, you could set the body's class to *.about*. Once you do, you can use a descendent selector (like *.about h1*) to create a custom style for all the headlines on just that page. On template-based pages showcasing your company's products, change the class to *.products*, and then add a descendent selector style *.products h1* to your style sheet and you'll have a unique look for all the <h1> tags on product pages.

- **Repeating regions and repeating tables.** Some web pages, like those that showcase the products a company sells, include *lists* of items. For pages like these, Dreamweaver lets you define *repeatable regions* in your template. For example, your design for a page of product listings might include each product's picture, name, and price, organized in a table with multiple rows (Chapter 6). As the template builder, you may not know in advance how many products the page will eventually list, so you can't fully design the page. You can, however, use Dreamweaver to define a row—or any selection of HTML—as a repeating region, so that page authors can add new rows of product information as needed.

- **Optional regions and editable optional regions.** *Optional regions* make templates even more flexible. They let you show or hide content—from a single paragraph to an entire <div> tag full of other tags—on a page-by-page basis.

Suppose you create a template that showcases your company's products. Some products go on sale while others remain full price, so you add an *optional region* to the product descriptions that displays a big "On Sale" logo. When you create a new product page, you could *show* the optional region for products that are on sale and keep it *hidden* for the others.

Editable optional regions are similar, but have the added benefit of being editable. Maybe you're creating a template for an employee directory, giving each employee his or her own page with contact information. Some employees want their picture displayed on the page, while others don't (you know the type). Solution: Add an editable optional region that includes space for a photo. You add a different photo for each page, except for the shyer types; for them, you simply hide the photo area.

Facilitating page creation is only one benefit of templates. You'll also find that they greatly simplify the process of updating a website's design. Like Library items (Chapter 19), pages based on templates retain a reference to the original template file. Dreamweaver passes any changes you make to that template to all the pages you created from it, which can save you hours of time and trouble when it comes time to update your site's look or structure. Imagine how much time you'll save when your boss asks you to add "just one more" button to a site's navigation bar. Instead of updating thousands of pages by hand, you need to update only a single template file.

■ Creating a Template

The first step in creating a template is to build a basic web page and tell Dreamweaver that you'd like to use it as a template. You do that two ways: Build a regular, plain old web page and turn it into a template, or create a blank, empty template file and add sections for text, graphics, tables, and other content.

Turning a Web Page into a Template

The easiest way to create a template is to base it on a web page in your current site folder. Although you can create templates based on web pages that *aren't* part of your current site, you may run into problems with links and paths to images, as described in a moment.

Once you open the page, choose File→Save As Template or, on the Insert panel (Figure 20-2), choose the Templates category from the drop-down menu and then click Make Template. The Save As Template window (Figure 20-3) includes the name of the current local site in the Site drop-down menu; meanwhile, all templates for that site show up in the Existing Templates box.

FIGURE 20-2

The Insert panel's Template category gives you all the tools you need to create templates and add a variety of template components, like a table that keeps growing until it runs out of data.

NOTE At this point, you could theoretically use the Site drop-down menu to save a template in any local site folder you set up (see Chapter 16 for a discussion of local sites), but be careful with this option. If your page contains images, external style sheets, and links and you save it as a template for another local site, Dreamweaver doesn't copy the images or style sheets from the first site folder to the second one. As a result, the paths to the image files and links don't work correctly, and the page won't show any styling.

If you must use a page from one site as a template for another, copy the web page, graphics, and style sheets into the new site's root folder, open the page there, and then create the template as described here.

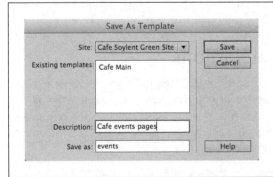

FIGURE 20-3

The Save As Template dialog box lets you store your template in any of the local site folders you've defined. Stick to your current local site to avoid broken links, missing images, and disappearing style sheets.

Dreamweaver includes a Description field where you can add a brief note characterizing the template. The description appears when you select a template as the basis for new pages. It's useful when *other* people build a site using your templates and they're not sure whether *templateA1, templateA2,* or *templateA3* is the correct choice; a simple note that says "Use this template for all FAQ pages" makes it clear.

Finally, in the "Save as" box, type a name for the new template, and then click Save. Choose Yes when Dreamweaver asks if you want to update links on the page. If you choose No, all page-relative links break, styles from external style sheets won't work, and all the images on the page appear as broken-image icons.

Dreamweaver saves the page in the Templates folder of your local site root folder. It adds the extension .dwt to indicate that it's a Dreamweaver template. (For dynamic web pages, Dreamweaver adds the .dwt *before* the file's extension. For example, a PHP template may have a name like *maintemplate.dwt.php*.)

NOTE Don't get carried away building too many templates for a site. It doesn't make any sense to create 20 templates for a 20-page site. You should only need a handful of templates to cover the different types of pages you have on a site. In fact, you might just need a single template to dictate the look of all your site's pages.

Building a Template from Scratch

It's easiest to create a web page first and then save it as a template, but you can also build a template from scratch. Open the Asset panel's Templates category by choosing Window→Assets and then clicking 🖻 (see Figure 20-4). Then click the New Template button at the bottom of the Assets panel. Once Dreamweaver adds a new, untitled template to the list, give it a new name. Something descriptive like "Press release" or "Employee page" helps you keep track of your templates.

After you create a blank template, open it by double-clicking its name in the Assets panel (or by selecting its name and then clicking the Edit button at the bottom of the Assets panel). It opens just like any other web page, so you can get busy designing it with the unchanging elements of your site—logo, navigation bar, and so on. You'll learn how to add editable regions next.

■ Defining Editable Regions

Your next task is to specify which parts of your template you want locked and which you want editable. By default, *everything* on a page is locked. After all, the main reason to use a template is to maintain a consistent, unchanging design and structure among pages. To make a template usable, you have to define the area or areas that page authors *can* change.

To add an editable region to a template, start by selecting the part of the page you want to make changeable. You can designate as editable anything in the document window (that is, any HTML between the <body> tags).

NOTE You can always add Cascading Style Sheets, JavaScript, and metatags to the <head> of a template-based page. Any <head> content in the original template files stays put in the page you create from it, however. For example, you can't remove an external style sheet applied to a template from a page based on that template.

Preview

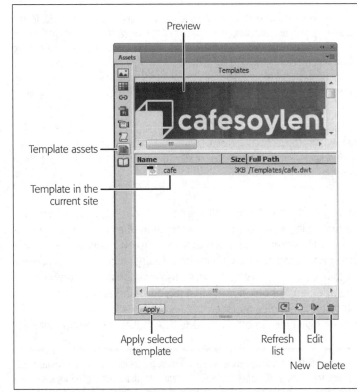

Template assets

Template in the
current site

Apply selected
template

Refresh
list

Edit

New Delete

FIGURE 20-4

*The Templates category of the Assets panel lists
the name, file size, and location of each template in the current local site. The Apply button
assigns a template to the currently open web
page. The Refresh Site List button updates the
list of templates—if you just created a template
and don't see it listed, click this button. The New
Template button creates a new, blank template
in the Templates folder. Select a template from
the list and click Edit Template to open and
change the template.*

For templates you create from scratch, place your cursor where you want to insert
an editable region. For templates you build from an existing page, drag across your
page to select the elements you want to make editable, or, for greater precision, use
the Tag Selector (see page 7) to select the exact HTML you want.

Now tell Dreamweaver that you want to make the selected elements editable. You
can use any of these techniques:

- In the Template category of the Insert panel (Figure 20-2), select Editable
  Region.

- Choose Insert→Template→Editable Region.

- Press Ctrl+Alt+V (⌘-Option-V).

- Right-click (Control-click) the selection and then, from the shortcut menu,
  choose Templates→New Editable Region.

When the New Editable Region dialog box appears, type a name for the region (you
can't use the same name twice) and then click OK. You return to your template,

where the name you gave the editable region appears in a small blue tab above the region, outlined in blue.

NOTE When you use CSS to lay out a page, you usually create separate <div> tags (see page 428) for the different areas of a page. For example, you might wrap the main content in one div, the banner in another, and the footer in yet another. For divs you use to structure the layout of a page, you want to make them editable by selecting just the *contents* of the <div> tag, not the tag itself. Here's one instance where you want to *avoid* the Tag Selector (page 7), which selects the entire div element, tags and all. If you turned the <div> tag into an editable region, someone modifying the page could delete the tag entirely, which could wreak untold havoc on your CSS-based layout.

Fortunately, Dreamweaver has a handy shortcut for selecting just the contents of a <div> tag. Click anywhere inside the <div> tag and then press Ctrl+A (⌘-A) or choose Edit→Select All. Then turn this selection into an editable region (Insert→Template→Editable Region), and the <div> tags will remain *outside* that region, so no one can inadvertently delete them.

You may find that a single editable region is all you need—for example, when you put a product review in just a single place on a page (a section of a page enclosed by a <div> tag, for example). However, if you need to be able to edit *multiple* areas of a page, just add more editable regions to the template. For instance, when you create a template for an employee page, you can create editable regions for the employee's name, telephone number, and photo. If you change your mind and want to lock a region later, select the editable region and then choose Modify→Templates→Remove Template Markup. Dreamweaver removes the code that makes the region editable.

NOTE You can rename an editable region by clicking the blue tab on the template page and typing a new name in the Properties panel. But if you built pages based on the template, that's not a good idea. Because template-based pages identify regions by their name, Dreamweaver can lose track of where content should go when you rename a region. Skip ahead to Figure 20-18 for a workaround.

Once you add at least one editable region to a template, you're ready to start adding pages to your site and filling them up with content. (Of course, you may need some of the more advanced template features—you'll learn how to add them to a template starting on page 841.)

■ Building Pages Based on a Template

Building a template is the prelude to the actual work of building your site. Once you finish your template, it's time to produce pages.

To create a new document based on a template, choose File→New to open the New Document window (see Figure 20-5). Click the "Site Templates" button, and then, from the Site list, select the site you're working on. All the templates for that site appear in the right-hand column. Select the template you wish to use, and then click Create.

FREQUENTLY ASKED QUESTION

When Save Won't Behave

I keep getting an error message when I save my template. What's going on?

If you add an editable region *inside* certain block-level elements, like a paragraph or a heading, Dreamweaver pops up a warning message when you save the template, explaining that you can't create additional paragraphs or headings inside this region on any pages you build from this template. This just means that you selected the *contents* of a paragraph or heading (not the actual paragraph or heading tag itself) when you made the region editable. Dreamweaver considers anything outside the editable region locked, so you can't change those tags. Since it's improper HTML to have a paragraph, heading, or other block-level elements inside *another* paragraph or heading, Dreamweaver won't let you add a paragraph, heading, bulleted list, or any other block-level element inside the editable contents of the locked paragraph or heading.

This characteristic may not be such a bad thing, however. Imagine you create a template for other people to use as they build a website. You have a Heading 1 with a style applied to it, and you want to make sure it looks the same on every page.

You wouldn't want anyone changing the heading tag, and possibly erasing the style. In addition, you don't want them to change the Heading 1 to a Heading 2 or a Heading 3; nor do you want them to completely erase the <h1> tag and display paragraph after paragraph of random thoughts. You just want them to type in new text for the page title. Selecting just the text inside the heading (as opposed to the <h1> tag *and* the text) and turning it into an editable region does just that. Viva micro-management!

If this is, in fact, what you want to do, you can save yourself the bother of having to constantly see the "You placed an editable region inside a block tag" warning box each time you save the template by simply turning on the "Don't show me this message again" checkbox. However, if you made a mistake and *do* want to let people change the heading or add more headings and paragraphs in this region, you need to do two things: First, unlock the editable region you created (see above), and then select the text *and* the tag (the Tag Selector [page 7] is the best way to make sure you select a tag), and turn that selection into an editable region.

NOTE If you don't want your new web page linked to a template (so that future changes to the template won't affect this page), turn off the "Update page when template changes" checkbox. The result is a new page that looks just like the template, but has no locked regions; you can edit the entire page. This is a useful technique when you want to create a new template starting with the general design and structure of an existing one. (Be aware that Dreamweaver remembers this choice the next time you create a new template-based page, so pages you create from a template in the future will *also* be unlinked—unless you remember to turn the "Update page" checkbox back on.)

A new web page opens, based on the template, and bearing a tab in the upper-right corner labeled with the underlying template's name. Dreamweaver outlines any editable regions in blue; a small blue tab displays each region's name (Figure 20-6).

Dreamweaver makes it obvious which areas of a page are off-limits; your cursor changes to a "forbidden" symbol (a circle with a line through it) when you venture into a locked area.

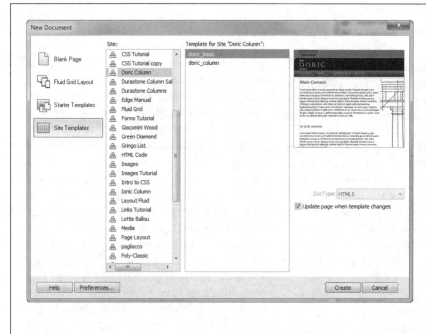

FIGURE 20-5

The Site Templates category of the New Document window lets you build new pages based on a template. Be careful of the middle "Site" column. It lets you pick any site that you've set up in Dreamweaver and open a new page based on a template from that site. It's a bad idea to pick a site other than the one you're working on. In fact, if you do, Dreamweaver doesn't bring along any of the assets that template uses (for example, style sheets, images, linked-to pages, and so on) so you'll end up with a broken template-based page. Why, Adobe, why?

To add content to an editable region, click anywhere inside the region. You can type inside it, add graphics, or add any other object or HTML you can normally add to a document. You can also change the document's title and add a JavaScript widget (Chapter 13), Cascading Style Sheet (see Chapter 3), and meta tags (items that go in the <head> of an HTML document).

Once you finish adding content, save the file and close it. You can create additional pages based on the same template by following the steps above (choose File→New to open the New Document window, click the Site Templates button, select the template, and so on). If you need to make a site-wide change to template-based pages (to add a navigation button, for example), you edit the template as described on page 839.

You might also find that the basic editable region doesn't provide the control you need. Fortunately, Dreamweaver's advanced template regions—described on page 841—might help.

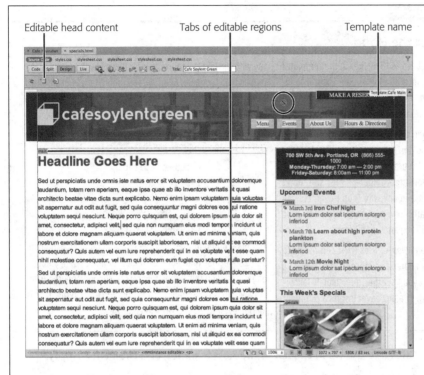

Editable head content   Tabs of editable regions   Template name

FIGURE 20-6

This page is based on a template called "Cafe main," as you can tell from the little tab in the document window's upper-right corner. You can modify this page's editable regions, which Dreamweaver labels with small tabs. In this example, one editable region, called "main," fills the main section of the page, while two additional editable regions ("events" and "specials") appear within the right sidebar. You can edit the title of any page created from a template. All other parts of the page are locked (circled); you can only change these sections in the original template file.

Applying Templates to Existing Pages

What happens if you create a web page, and *then* decide you want it to share the look of a template? No problem. Dreamweaver lets you apply a template to any web page in your site. You can even swap one template for another.

To apply a template to a page you already created:

1. **Choose File→Open to open the page you want to alter.**

   The page opens.

2. **Choose Window→Assets, and then click the Assets panel's Templates button (see Figure 20-4).**

   The Assets panel appears and reveals a list of your site's templates.

> **NOTE**   You can also apply a template to a page by choosing Modify→Templates→Apply Template to Page. Select the name of the template from the window that appears and then skip to step 5.

Templates Under the Hood

Dreamweaver saves templates as HTML files in the Templates folder inside your current local site folder (see Chapter 16 for more on local sites). Each template bears the file extension .dwt to distinguish template pages from regular web pages.

Dreamweaver treats files in the Templates folder differently from normal web pages, so don't save anything but .dwt files there. In addition, since Dreamweaver expects to find the Templates folder in the local root folder of your site, don't move it or change its name in any way (don't even change the capital "T" in "Templates," even if you're a low-key type of person). If you do, your templates won't work.

As with Library items, Dreamweaver uses HTML comments to indicate the name of a template. If you inspect the HTML of a template-based document, you'll see that, immediately following the opening <html> tag, Dreamweaver inserts a comment

tag with the text "InstanceBegin" followed by the location and name of the template. Additional comment tags indicate areas of the page you can modify and special template features, like template parameters used for optional regions. For instance, the title of a page based on a template is always editable; its comment tag might look like this:

```
<!-- InstanceBeginEditable
name="doctitle" -->
<title>My New Page</title>
<!-- InstanceEndEditable -->
```

The first comment indicates the editable region's beginning and also includes the editable region's name. When you edit pages based on this template, you can change only the HTML between these comment tags. Everything else on the page is locked, even when you work in Code view.

3. **Click a template in the list in the Assets panel, and then click Apply.**

   The Inconsistent Region Names dialog box opens (Figure 20-7).

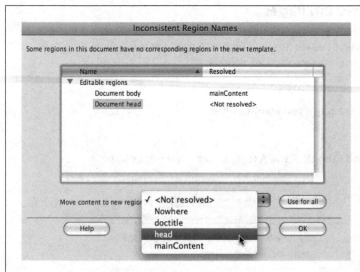

FIGURE 20-7

When you apply a template to an existing page, you must tell Dreamweaver what to do with the elements already on the page by assigning them to one of the template's editable regions from a pop-up menu, which takes charge of all editable regions in the page you're converting.

4. **Under "Editable regions" in the list, choose "Document body."**

In the Resolved column to the right, you see "<Not resolved>." This is Dream-weaver's way of saying it doesn't know what to do with the elements of the current page. You need to copy those elements to one of the template's edit-able regions.

5. **From the "Move content to new region" menu, select an editable region.**

If you want to keep the material, select the name of an editable region from the list—that'll copy the content there. Otherwise, choose Nowhere, which, in effect, creates a new blank page based on the template.

Unfortunately, you only get a single editable region in which to stuff page ele-ments. If the original page had several editable regions, Dreamweaver pushes them all into that single editable region.

6. **If "Document head" also appears in the window, select it and choose "head" from the "Move content to new region" menu.**

This step preserves any special information you added to the head of your page, like Cascading Style Sheets, meta tags, and custom JavaScript programs. Unfortunately, Dreamweaver always replaces the title of your original page with the default title of the template. You have to re-enter the title after you apply the template.

7. **Click OK.**

Your new page opens.

Updating a Template

Templates aren't useful just for building pages quickly; they also make fast work of site updates. Template-based pages maintain a link to their original template; Dreamweaver automatically passes changes you make to the original template along to every page built from it. If you used templates to build your site, you probably won't cry on your keyboard when the boss asks you to add an additional button and a link to the navigation bar. Instead of editing every page, you can simply open the template file, update the navigation bar, and let Dreamweaver apply the update to all your pages.

You update a template (and all the pages based on it) like this:

1. **Choose Window→Assets.**

The Assets panel appears.

2. **Click the Templates button.**

A list of the site's templates appears.

3. **Double-click the template's name to open it.**

   Alternatively, you can select the template in the Assets panel, and then click Edit to open the original template (.dwt) file.

   > **TIP** You can also open a template by double-clicking the appropriate filename (with the extension .dwt) in the Templates folder of the Files panel.

4. **Edit the template as you would any web page.**

   Since this is the original template file, you can edit any of the HTML in the document, including Cascading Style Sheets, meta tags, and layers. You can also add or remove editable regions.

   Take care, however, to edit *only* the areas that you did *not* mark as editable regions. The reason: When you update your pages, any region marked as editable in a template file isn't passed on to pages based on that template. After all, the template dictates only the design of those pages' *non*-editable regions. In other words, if you make a change to an editable region in a template, Dreamweaver won't pass that change on to any existing template-based pages.

   > **NOTE** Be careful when you remove editable regions from a template. If you already built pages based on that template, Dreamweaver warns you when you save the newly configured version. As described below, you can either *delete* the content that was originally in the region you removed, or you can move that content to another editable region of the page.

5. **Choose File→Save.**

   If you already created pages based on this template, Dreamweaver opens the Update Template Files dialog box. It lists all the files that use the template.

6. **Click Update to update all the files based on the template.**

   Dreamweaver automatically applies the changes you made to the template-based pages. Then it opens the Update Pages dialog box. If you want to see a list of all the files Dreamweaver changed, turn on the "Show log" checkbox.

   On a large site, this automatic update feature can be an incredible time-saver, but you may *not* want to click Update, at least not right now. Perhaps you're just saving some of your hard work on the template but aren't quite finished perfecting it—why waste time updating all those pages more than once? In such a scenario, click the Don't Update button. Remember, you can always update the pages later (see the box below).

7. **Click Close.**

   The Update Pages dialog box closes.

Remember that you need to update all your files, even if you make a simple change to the template, like changing its name.

Wait to Update

Whenever you modify and save a template, Dreamweaver gives you the option of updating any child pages on the site. The same holds true for Library items; if you change a Library item, Dreamweaver asks if you want to pass that change on to all the pages that have that item. Very often, you'll say yes.

But there are times when you want to wait to update your site. If you're making a lot of changes to templates or multiple Library items, you may wish to wait until you finish all your edits before you let the changes ripple through your pages. After all, it can take some time to update large sites.

Dreamweaver lets you update pages that use templates and Library items any time. Just choose Modify→Templates→Update Pages or Modify→Library→Update Pages.

Both menu options open the same window, the Update Pages dialog box.

At this point, you can update pages that use a specific template or Library item by going to the "Look in" menu, choosing "Files that Use," and then selecting the appropriate name from the drop-down menu. If you want to update all the pages in a site, choose Entire Site, and then, from the drop-down menu, select the name of the local site. Turn on both the Templates and "Library items" checkboxes to update all pages.

To see the results of Dreamweaver's work, turn on the "Show log" checkbox, which displays all the files Dreamweaver updated.

Unlinking a Page from a Template

If you're confident that you won't make any further changes to a page's template and you want to edit a page's locked regions, you can break the link between the page and its template by choosing Modify→Templates→Detach from Template.

You can now edit all the HTML in the page, just as you can on a regular web page—which is, in fact, what you have now. You removed all references to the original template, so any changes to the template no longer affect this page.

> **NOTE**   If you unlink a nested template from its master template, Dreamweaver removes only the code provided by the original master template. Any editable regions you added to the nested template remain.

■ Using Repeating Regions

The humble editable region is the heart of all templates—after all, the whole point of a template is to provide an easy way to create new pages. You may find that templates with editable regions are all you ever need for your site. But Dreamweaver provides several other template features that might come in handy.

Some web pages have types of content that repeat over and over. For example, a catalog page may display row after row of the same product information—picture, name, price, and description. An index of Frequently Asked Questions may list questions and the dates visitors posted them. Dreamweaver provides a couple of ways to turn content like this into an editable region in a template.

You could, of course, make the entire area where the repeating content appears editable. For example, you could use one of Dreamweaver's CSS layouts (see Chapter 10) to build a template for a FAQ page. The list of questions and answers go inside the page's main <div> tag. You can turn this div into an editable region. The downside to this approach is that you won't have any ability to enforce (or easily update) the HTML used to lay out the questions and answers, since another designer could edit or delete everything in the div.

Fortunately, Dreamweaver provides a pair of template tools to address the problem: *repeating regions* and *repeating tables*. Both let you create areas of a page that include editable and uneditable regions that you can repeat any number of times (see Figure 20-8).

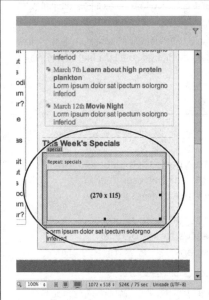
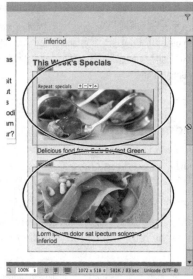

FIGURE 20-8

A repeating region lets page authors add multiple instances of information. Left: In this template, you see a repeating region labeled "specials" (circled). Right: A complete page based on this template includes two repeating editable regions (circled). If another page requires more cafe specials, you can easily add one to each list by clicking the + button at the top of the repeating region in the template-based page (right). Even though you can dictate how many repeating regions appear on a page, the master template still controls the page's editable and uneditable regions. That means page authors can't change the box that surrounds the specials, nor the headline "This Week's Specials."

Adding a Repeating Region

You add a repeating region the same way you add an editable region. Select the area of the template where you want to repeat information; it usually contains at least one element you've made editable. It could be a single list item (the <li> tag), a table row (the <tr> tag), or even an entire <div> tag.

NOTE You can make a repeating region that *doesn't* include an editable region. For example, a template for a movie review web page could include a repeating region that's simply a graphic of a star. A page author adding a new movie review could repeat the star graphic to match the movie's rating—four stars, for example. (There's just one caveat—see the Tip on page 845.)

Next, tell Dreamweaver that the elements you selected represent a repeating region. You can use any of these techniques:

- In the Templates category of the Insert panel, select Repeating Region.

- Choose Insert→Template→Repeating Region.

- Right-click (Control-click) the selection and choose Templates→New Repeating Region from the shortcut menu.

When the New Repeating Region dialog box appears, type a name for the region and then click OK. You return to your template, where the name you gave the region appears in a small blue tab above it (see Figure 20-8).

NOTE Dreamweaver lets you name a repeating region even if that name is already in use by an editable region. But don't repeat names—multiple template areas with the same name make Dreamweaver act unpredictably.

FREQUENTLY ASKED QUESTION

Hindered by Highlighting

I'm distracted by the tabs and background colors that Dreamweaver uses to indicate templates and Library items. How do I get rid of them?

When you use templates or Library items, you see blue tabs and yellow backgrounds to indicate, respectively, editable regions and Library items. Although these visual cues don't appear in a web browser, they can get in your way and even alter a page's layout while you work in Dreamweaver. Fortunately, you can change the background color of these items and even turn highlighting off altogether.

Choose Edit→Preferences or press Ctrl+U (⌘-U). In the Preferences Category list, click Highlighting. To change

the background color of editable regions, locked regions, and Library items, use the color box (see page 138) or type in a hexadecimal color value (see page 141). To remove the highlighting, turn off the Show checkbox next to the appropriate item.

Often, it's useful to keep highlighting on to help you keep track of editable regions and Library items. So if you want to turn off highlighting temporarily, simply choose View→Visual Aids→Invisible Elements or use the keyboard shortcut Ctrl+Shift+I (⌘-Shift-I) to toggle these visual cues off and on. This technique has the added benefit of hiding table borders, layer borders, image maps, and other invisible elements.

Adding a Repeating Table

Dreamweaver's *repeating table* tool is essentially a shortcut for creating a table with repeating rows. If you had time on your hands, you could achieve the same effect by adding a table to the page, selecting one or more rows, and applying a repeating region to the selection.

To use the repeating table tool:

1. **In the template page, click where you want to insert the table.**

   You can't insert a repeating table into an editable, repeating, or optional region, as you'll see on page 841. You must be in an empty, locked area of the template.

2. **In the Common category of the Insert panel, select Repeating Table from the Templates menu.**

   Alternatively, you can choose Insert→Template→Repeating Table. Either way, the Insert Repeating Table window opens (Figure 20-9).

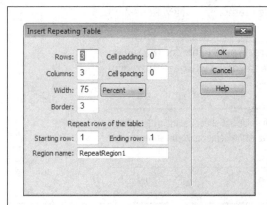

FIGURE 20-9

The Insert Repeating Table dialog box lets you kill three birds with one stone: It adds a table to a page, turns one or more rows into a repeating region, and adds editable regions in each table cell inside the repeating region.

3. **Fill out the basic properties of the table.**

   The top part of the window lets you set up the basic structure of the table: rows, columns, cell padding, cell spacing, width, and border. Basically, it's the same information you provide when you create any table, as described on page 271. You usually start a repeating table with two rows—one for a heading, another to contain the information you want to repeat.

4. **In the "Starting row" box, type the number of the row where the repeating region should begin.**

   Often you'll have just one repeating row: a row of product information, for example. You may want to use the top row to label the information contained in the rows below. If that's the case, enter *2* at this step, leaving the first row as an uneditable part of the template.

   It's conceivable, however, that you may want each entry to take up *two* rows. The first would list Product Name and Description; the second would contain a cell for a photo and a cell for the price. You set up this effect in this step and the next.

5. **In the "Ending row" box, type the number of the last repeating row.**

If you want to repeat only a single row, enter the same number you provided in step 4. If you want to create a double repeating row, add 1 to the number you provided in step 4. For example, if you need three rows for each repeating entry, add 2 to the number you entered in step 4.

6. **Type a name for this repeating region.**

Don't use the same name as another template region. You'll run the risk of unpredictable results on template-based pages.

7. **Click OK.**

Dreamweaver inserts the table into the page. A blue tab with the name of the repeating region appears, as do blue tabs in each cell of each repeated row. These tabs indicate new editable regions—one per cell.

Since these new editable regions have uninformative names like *EditRegion4*, you may want to rename them. Click the blue tab and type a new name in the Properties panel. (But do so *before* you create any pages based on the template—see the note on page 843.)

To remove a repeating region, select it by clicking the blue Repeat tab, and then choose Modify→Templates→Remove Template Markup. A more accurate way to select a repeating region is to click anywhere inside the region and then click <mmtemplate: repeat> in the Tag Selector (see page 7). Note that removing a repeating region doesn't remove any editable regions you added inside the repeating region.

If you want to rename a repeating region, heed the note on page 843.

Working with Repeating Regions

Repeating regions work a bit differently from editable regions. In most cases, a repeating region includes one or more editable regions (which you can edit using the instructions above). However, Dreamweaver provides special controls to let you add, remove, and rearrange repeating entries (see Figure 20-10).

These regions let page editors add repeating page elements—like rows of product information in a list of products. To add a repeating entry, click the + button to the right of the Repeat region's blue tab. You can then edit any editable regions within the entry. Click inside an editable region inside a repeating entry and click + again to add a new entry *after* it.

Deleting a repeating entry is just as easy; click inside an editable region within the entry you want to delete, and then click the – sign button.

TIP You can create repeating regions that don't have any editable regions—for example, you can create a repeating region with a star in it, and repeat the region several times to indicate the rating for a product. Although you can use the + button to repeat such regions, you can't delete those regions using the - button (-). In other words, you're stuck with any extra stars you add. The only workaround is to add an editable region to the repeating region—then Dreamweaver lets you remove the repeating regions.

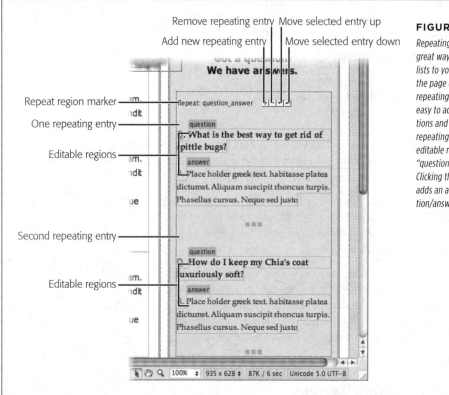

Remove repeating entry Move selected entry up

Add new repeating entry Move selected entry down

Repeat region marker

One repeating entry

Editable regions

Second repeating entry

Editable regions

FIGURE 20-10

Repeating regions are a great way to quickly add lists to your web pages. On the page displayed here, repeating regions make it easy to add sets of questions and answers. Each repeating entry has two editable regions, labeled "question" and "answer." Clicking the + sign button adds an additional question/answer pair.

To rearrange entries in a repeated-region list, click inside an entry's editable region, and then click the up or down arrows to move the entry up or down in the list (to alphabetize it, for example).

Using Editable Tag Attributes

An editable region lets you—or, more likely, page-author jockeys—edit the underlying HTML, like a paragraph, image, or an entire table, on new pages they create from your template. But when you create a template for others to use, you may want to limit the authors' editing abilities. For example, you may want to allow budding web designers to change the source of the image used in a banner ad without letting them change the width, height, or class applied to it. Or you might want to use templates but let others assign a class to the <body> tag—a move normally forbidden on template-based pages. You can use Dreamweaver's Editable Tag Attribute to specify which tag properties your successors can change.

Editable Regions, Repeating Regions, and Errors

When I try to insert an editable region inside a repeating region, I get the following error: "The selection is already in an editable, repeating, or optional region." What's that about?

This message essentially means you're trying to add a template region where it doesn't belong. It appears most often when you attempt to put a repeating or optional region inside an editable region. That kind of nesting is a no-no; page authors can change anything inside an editable region on template-based pages, and as such, Dreamweaver can't touch it.

However, you may get this error message seemingly by mistake. For instance, it's perfectly OK to add an editable region inside a repeating region, and it's even OK to add a repeating region inside an optional region, and vice versa.

But say one day you select text inside a repeating region and try to turn it into an editable region—boom, you get an error message. What probably happened was, when you selected the text, Dreamweaver actually selected part of the hidden code used to define a template region (see the box on page 838) and thought you were trying to put an editable region inside it. To avoid confusion, use the Tag Selector to select the page element you want to turn into an editable region. There, click <p> to select the paragraph inside the repeating region. Alternatively, go into Code view (see page 4), and then select whatever part of the code inside the repeating region you want to make editable.

NOTE Before you make a tag attribute editable, first set that property to a default value in the template. For example, add a class to the <body> tag if you want to make the class editable. Doing so inserts a default value and makes the attribute appear in the Editable Tag Attribute window (see steps 3 and 7 in the following instructions).

Making an Attribute Editable

To make a tag attribute editable:

1. **Select the tag whose property you want to make editable.**

   Using the Tag Selector (see page 7) is the most accurate way.

2. **Choose Modify→Templates→Make Attribute Editable.**

   The Editable Tag Attributes window opens (Figure 20-11).

3. **Select an attribute from the menu or add a new attribute with the Add button.**

   The Attribute menu displays only those properties you already set for the selected tag. In other words, if you select an image, you probably see the *src*, *width*, and *height* properties listed. But unless you set the image's alternative text, the *alt* property won't appear.

   To add a property, click the Add button. In the window that appears, type in the appropriate property name. For example, to make the *alt* (alternate text) attribute of a graphic editable, you'd type *alt* in here.

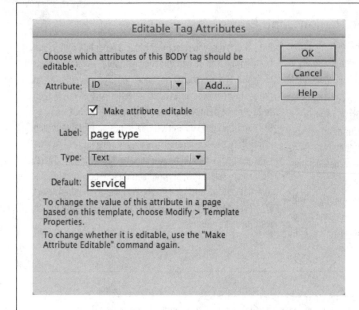

FIGURE 20-11

Dreamweaver gives you detailed control over template pages. To make just a single property of a single tag editable on pages based on your template, turn on the "Make attribute editable" checkbox. In this case, you've made the class attribute of the middle paragraph tag editable, allowing page designers the freedom to apply different CSS styles to that paragraph. Because designers can edit the CSS file, they can create entirely new styles for the paragraph with the editable attribute.

> **NOTE** If you want page editors to be able to change a CSS class or ID applied to the <body> tag on template-based pages—to apply different fonts, background colors, or any CSS formatting option to each page—you *have* to make the Class or ID attribute editable. (See page 102 for more on CSS classes and IDs.)

4. **Make sure you turn on the "Make attribute editable" checkbox.**

   If you decide at some point that you no longer want people to be able to edit this property, you can return to this dialog box and turn off editing, as described in a moment.

5. **Type a name in the Label field.**

   What you type here should be a simple description of the editable tag and property, which helps page authors correctly identify editable properties. For example, you could use *Product Image* if you make a particular image's *src* property editable.

6. **Choose a value type from the menu.**

   Your choices are:

   - **Text.** Use this option when a property's value is a word. For example, you can change the image tag's *Align* property to *top, middle, baseline*, and so on. Or, when using Cascading Style Sheets, you could make a tag's *Class* property editable to allow page authors to apply a custom style to the tag—*content, footer,* and *URL*. The text option lets page authors edit the path to a file, like an image's *src* property or a link's *href* property. That way, using its site management tools, Dreamweaver keeps track of these paths and updates them whenever you move pages around your site.

   - **Color.** If the property requires a web color, like a background hue, select this option. It makes Dreamweaver's color box available to people who build pages from the template.

   - **True/False.** You shouldn't use this option. It's intended for Dreamweaver's Optional Regions feature (discussed below), and doesn't apply to *HTML* properties.

   - **Number.** Use this choice for properties that require a numeric value, like an image's Height and Width properties.

7. **Type a default value into the Default field.**

   This step is optional. The default value defines the initial value for this property, when people first create a page based on the template. They can then modify this value for that particular page. If you already set this property in the template, its value automatically appears in this box.

8. **Click OK to close the window.**

   Dreamweaver adds code to the template page that allows page authors control of the attribute. To set this attribute on pages created from the template, see the instructions on the next page.

If you later decide that you *don't* want a particular tag property to be editable, Dreamweaver can help. Open the template file, select the tag with the editable attribute, and choose Modify→Templates→Make Attribute Editable. In the window that appears, turn off the "Make attribute editable" checkbox (Figure 20-11). Unfortunately, doing so doesn't remove *all* of the template code Dreamweaver adds. Even after you turn off editing for an attribute, Dreamweaver leaves behind the parameter used to control the tag's property. To eliminate *this* extra code, see the box on page 856.

Changing Properties of Editable Tag Attributes

Unlike editable or repeating regions, you can't readily see an editable tag attribute on template-based pages. Dreamweaver doesn't identify them with a blue tab, as it does with editable regions; in fact, nothing appears in Design view to indicate that there are *any* editable tag properties on the page. The only way to find out is to choose Modify→Template Properties to open the Template Properties dialog box (see Figure 20-12).

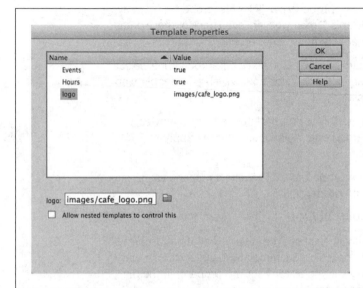

FIGURE 20-12

The Template Properties window lets you control editable tag attributes and other settings for a template's optional regions. Depending on which parameter you select, the options at the bottom of the window change. In this case, you made the src property of an image tag editable. To change the image tag's src property, click Dreamweaver's familiar "Browse for File" button and select a new graphic.

Dreamweaver displays all the editable tag attributes for this page in this window. In addition, it displays all the parameters defined for this page, including optional regions, as discussed in the box on page 852.

To change the value of a template property—in other words, to edit the property of an editable tag—select its name from the list and set its options at the bottom of the window. For example, in the case of color properties, use the color box to pick a color. If the property is a path (like a link's URL or an image's *src* property), click the folder icon to browse for the file.

When you finish , click OK.

FREQUENTLY ASKED QUESTION

The Broken-Link Blues

Why aren't the links in my template working?

When you created the link in the template file, you probably typed a path into the Properties panel's Link field—a recipe for heartbreak. Instead, always select the target page for a link by clicking the folder icon in the Properties panel, or by pressing Ctrl+L (⌘-L). In other words, when you add links to a template, always link to pages within the site by *browsing* to the desired file.

Dreamweaver saves templates in the Templates folder inside the local root folder; all document-relative links need to be relative to this location. (Absolute links, like those to other websites, aren't a problem. Neither are root-relative links; see page 170 to learn the difference.) The reason you should browse to, rather than type in, your links is so that Dreamweaver can create a proper relative link.

Imagine this situation: You create a template for all the classified ads that appear on your site. You store all the ads for April

2013 inside a series of folders like this: classifieds→2013→april, as shown in the site diagram here.

A link from a page in the April folder to the home page would follow the path marked 1 here. So, when you add that link to your template, you'd type the path *../../../index.html*. That makes sense if you're thinking about the page you'll create from the template—but it won't work.

Dreamweaver stores templates in the Templates folder, so the correct path would be path 2, or *../index.html*. When you create a new page based on the template and save it in the April folder, Dreamweaver, in its wisdom, automatically rewrites all the paths in the page so that the links work correctly.

The beauty of Dreamweaver is that you don't have to understand how all this works. Just remember to use document-relative links in your templates and create them by clicking the folder icon in the Properties panel.

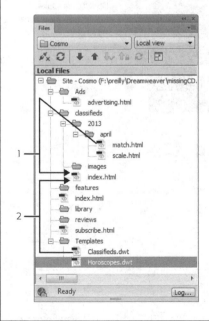

Using Optional Regions

Templates provide consistent design. While consistency is generally a good thing, it can also get boring. Furthermore, there may be times when you want the flexibility to include information on some template-based pages but not on others.

Dreamweaver provides a template tool aimed at letting you vary a page's design while still maintaining page-to-page consistency: *optional regions*. An optional region is simply part of a template you can hide or display on each template-based page (see Figure 20-13). When a page author creates a new page based on the template, she can turn the region on or off.

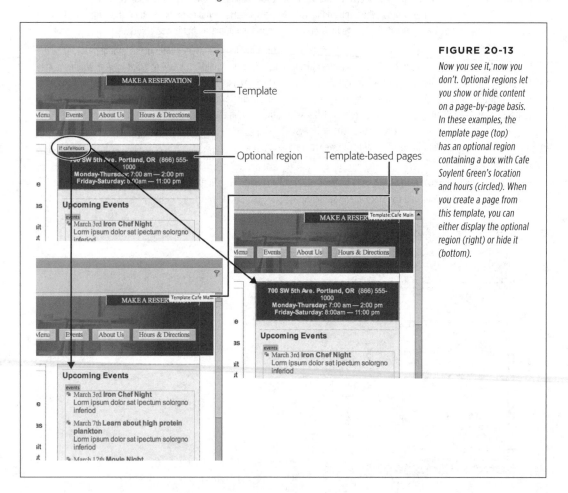

FIGURE 20-13

Now you see it,' now you don't. Optional regions let you show or hide content on a page-by-page basis. In these examples, the template page (top) has an optional region containing a box with Cafe Soylent Green's location and hours (circled). When you create a page from this template, you can either display the optional region (right) or hide it (bottom).

Adding an Optional Region

Creating an optional region is a snap. Just select the HTML you want to make optional and do one of the following:

- In the Template category of the Insert panel, select Optional Region.

- Choose Insert→Template→Optional Region.

- Right-click (Control-click) the selection and choose Templates→New Optional Region from the shortcut menu.

In the New Optional Region window, type a name (see Figure 20-14). Make sure you don't use the same name as any other region on the page, and—although Dreamweaver lets you—don't use spaces or other punctuation marks. (Following the rules for naming files as described on page 27 ensures that the optional region works properly.) Click OK to close the window and create the new optional region. Dreamweaver adds a light blue tab with the word "If," followed by the name you gave the region (Figure 20-13).

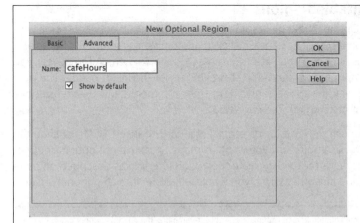

FIGURE 20-14

The Optional Regions feature lets you show or hide content on template-based pages. Turning on the "Show by default" checkbox tells Dreamweaver to display the region when you first create a template-based page. That's a good idea if you want most of your pages to display the content—you'll save yourself the effort of turning on the optional region each time you create a template-based page.

A FEATURE TO AVOID

Nested Templates

Dreamweaver includes yet another template feature called *nested templates*. Nested templates let you create a template with a very basic design so you can create new templates based on that original one, refining the design as you go along. This way, you can have a single template that dictates your core layout, and then create specialized templates for particular types of pages or sections of your site.

This might sound like a great way to provide templates that both maintain your site's basic layout via a master template

and let you create pages designed for different purposes. However, in execution, nested templates are confusing, don't always work, and aren't that necessary. With the flexibility that the optional regions discussed in this chapter give you, you can customize individual template-based pages while using only a single template file.

When it comes to nested templates, our advice is stay away.

Locking Optional Regions

An optional region can include editable regions, repeating regions, *and* locked regions. For example, if you want to allow a page editor to turn on or off a graphic

("This item on sale!"), insert the graphic outside an editable region, and then make it an optional region as described above. Since anything not inside an editable region is locked, a page editor can't change the graphic or ruin its formatting—he can only make it visible or hidden.

Repeating Optional Regions

An optional region can also include repeating regions. For example, suppose you create a repeating region (see page 841) that lets a page editor add row after row of links to a list of related articles. You could then turn this repeating region into an optional region, as described above, so that if a particular page had no related articles, the page editor could simply hide the entire "related articles" section of the page.

Optional Editable Regions

Dreamweaver's Optional Editable Region command inserts an optional region with an editable region *inside* of it. To use it, click in the template where you'd like to add it, and then choose Insert→Template→Editable Optional Region. (Alternatively, you can choose this option from the Templates category of the Insert panel.) The New Optional Region window appears; give it a name, and then follow the steps above for adding an optional region (see page 853).

This technique doesn't offer a lot of control; it's hard to insert HTML *outside* the editable region, for example. So if you want an image or table that's optional but *not* editable, it's usually better to just create the editable region as described on page 832 and turn it (and any other HTML you want to include) into an optional region.

NOTE The Optional Editable Region command doesn't let you name the editable region; it automatically assigns a generic name like *EditRegion7*. You can select the editable region and change its name in the Properties panel, but do so *before* you build any pages based on this template (see the note on page 834).

Advanced Optional Regions

A basic optional region is a rather simple affair: It either appears or it doesn't. But Dreamweaver offers more complex logic for controlling them. For example, you may want several different areas of a page to be either hidden or visible at the same time—perhaps an "On Sale Now!" icon at the top of a page *and* a "Call 1-800-SHIZZLE to order" message at the bottom of the page. When one appears, so does the other.

Because these objects sit in different areas of the page, you have to create two optional regions. Fortunately, using Dreamweaver's advanced settings for optional regions, you can easily have a *single* region control the display of one or more additional areas of a page. Here's how:

1. **Create the first optional region by following the steps on page 852.**

   Give the region a name using the Basic tab of the New Optional Region window (Figure 20-16).

2. **Select the part of the page—an image, paragraph, or table—you want to turn into a second optional region.**

In this case, you want to make the display of this region dependent on the optional region added in step 1. If the first region is visible on the page, this region should also show.

3. **Choose Optional Region from the Templates menu in the Common category of the Insert panel.**

The New Optional Region window opens.

4. **Click the Advanced tab.**

The optional region's advanced options appear (Figure 20-15). You want the first optional region to control the display of this new region. So instead of giving this region its own name, you simply select the name of the first optional region in the next step.

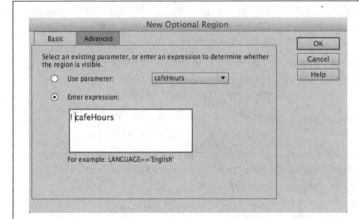

FIGURE 20-15

The Advanced section of the New Optional Region dialog box lets you more precisely control the display of optional content. You can make the region appear only when another region is visible, or use Dreamweaver's template expression language to create a more complex behavior. In this case, the selected region appears only when another region—named "kittyHead"—isn't visible (the ! is the programming equivalent of "is not").

5. **Turn on the "Use parameter" radio button and then select the name of the first optional region from the drop-down menu.**

This is what makes the first optional region control the second. If a browser displays the first region, it also displays the second region.

6. **Click OK to close the window and create the new optional region.**

You can continue adding optional regions this way, with the end result being that the first optional region controls the display of many other areas of the page.

Editing and Removing Optional Regions

After you insert an optional region, you can always return to the New Optional Region dialog box to change the region's name or settings. To edit an optional region, select it using one of these techniques:

- Click the region's blue tab in the document window.

- Click anywhere inside the optional region in the document window and then click the <mmtemplate:if> tag in the Tag Selector (see page 7 for details on the Tag Selector).

When you select an optional region, Dreamweaver displays an Edit button in the Properties panel. Click it to reopen the New Optional Region window. You can then change the region's properties.

To remove an optional region, select it and then choose Modify→Templates→Remove Template Markup. Dreamweaver removes most of the code associated with the optional region (but see the box below).

POWER USERS' CLINIC

Understanding Template Parameters

When you insert an optional region, Dreamweaver adds special code to the head of the web page. Called a *template parameter*, this code is responsible for showing or hiding an optional region.

In fact, Dreamweaver uses parameters when you make a tag attribute editable, too. A typical parameter for an optional region might look like this:

```
<!-- TemplateParam name="SaleBug"

type="boolean" value="true" -->
```

The <!-- and --> are HTML comment markers that hide this code from web browsers. *TemplateParam* tells Dreamweaver that the comment is actually part of the program's template features—specifically, a template parameter.

A parameter has three parts: name, type, and value. The name is the name you give the editable region, like SaleBug. The type—"Boolean" above—indicates that this parameter can have a value of only true or false. In this example, the value is "true," which simply means that the optional region called SaleBug is visible. (Don't worry; you don't have to actually edit this code by hand to turn optional regions on and off, as you'll see next.)

In programming jargon, a template parameter is known as a *variable*. In simpler terms, it's just a way to store information that can change. Dreamweaver reacts differently depending on the parameter's value: Show the region if the parameter's true, hide it if the parameter's false.

Editable tag attributes also use parameters to store the values you enter for tag attributes. For example:

```
<!-- TemplateParam name="PageColor"

type="color" value="#FFFFFF" -->
```

On template-based pages, you can change the value of an editable tag's parameter using the Modify→Template Parameters menu (see page 850).

Unfortunately, when you delete an optional region from a template, or remove the ability to edit a tag attribute, Dreamweaver always leaves these parameter tags hanging around in the head of the template document. Keeping in mind that Dreamweaver adds these parameter tags directly before the closing </head> tag, you can find and remove them in Code view.

Hiding and Showing Optional Regions

When working with template-based pages, you can hide or show optional region. As with Editable Tag Attributes, you use the Template Properties window to control the display. On template-based pages, you show or hide an optional region by choosing Modify→Template Properties to open the Template Properties dialog box (see Figure

20-16). Next, select the name of the optional region. To make all the page elements in the region visible, turn on the "Show" checkbox at the bottom of the window. To hide all the optional regions, turn off the checkbox.

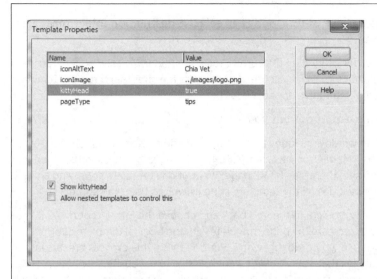

FIGURE 20-16

The Template Properties window displays a page's optional regions as well as its editable tag attributes. Template properties for optional regions—in this example, "kittyHead"—have a value of either true or false. "True" lets people see the contents of the region, while "false" hides it. (You use the "Allow nested templates to control this" option with nested templates—see the box on page 853.)

Exporting a Template-Based Site

The good news about Dreamweaver's sophisticated template features is that it lets you build complex web pages that are easy to create and update. The not-so-good news is that you need some behind-the-scenes code to achieve this ease of use. Dreamweaver's template features rely on HTML comment tags to identify editable, optional, and repeating page regions, as well as nested templates and editable tag attributes (see the box on page 838).

Although this code is only for Dreamweaver's use and has no effect on how a web browser displays the page, it does increase, by a small amount, the size of your pages. That's probably why Dreamweaver includes a feature that lets you export an entire site into a new folder on your computer *without* any template markup code—to give you the leanest HTML possible. The following steps show you how to do that.

NOTE While it's certainly possible to perform this file-slimming procedure, truth be told, it's not really necessary—the code Dreamweaver adds is minimal, so it won't have much effect on the download speed of your site.

1. **Choose Modify→Templates→Export Without Markup.**

   Dreamweaver uses the currently active site, so make sure you select the site you want to export in the Files panel. The Export Site Without Template Markup window appears, offering just three options.

2. **Click the Browse button, and then select a destination folder for the exported site.**

   Select a folder *other* than the current local site folder. You always want to keep the original files in the local folder, since they're the ones that retain the template markup, making future updates possible.

3. **Turn on the export options you want.**

   The Export window includes two options. The first, "Keep template data files," creates an XML file for each template-based page. In other words, when you export the site, there's an HTML page (without any template code) and an XML file (which includes all the template code as well as the page contents).

   Theoretically, you could then go back and choose the File→Import→XML into Template to recreate the page, complete with the original template information. But in practice, you probably won't. For one thing, this process creates lots of additional files that you wouldn't want to move to a website. In addition, when you want to edit and update the site, you should use the original files in the site's local folder, since they have the useful template code in them.

   The "Extract only changed files" option speeds up the process of exporting a large, template-based site by spitting out only those pages you changed since the last export. Unfortunately, it doesn't tell you *which* files it exports until after the fact. So, to make sure you get all those newly exported files to your server, you need to keep track of the files you change by hand.

4. **Click OK to export the site.**

   Dreamweaver goes through each page of the site, stripping out the template code and exporting it to the folder you specified.

   You can use Dreamweaver's FTP feature to upload the files to your server (see page 765), but you need to create a new site and define the folder with the *exported* files as a local root folder.

   Whenever you need to add or update template-based pages, use the original site files, and then export the changed files. You can then switch to the site containing the exported files and transfer the new or updated files to your server. If that sounds like a lot of work, it is. Every change you make means exporting the site again. You're better off just leaving the template code in your pages, or use this command only if you're absolutely sure that you're done using templates for your site.

■ Template Tutorial

In this tutorial, you'll create a template for the Cafe Soylent Green website. Then you'll build a page based on that template and enjoy an easy site-wide update courtesy of Dreamweaver's templates feature.

> **NOTE** You need to download the tutorial files from *http://oreilly.com/missingmanuals/cds/dreamweaver ccmm13/* to complete this tutorial. See the note on page 33 for more details.

Once you download the tutorial files and open Dreamweaver, set up a new site as described on page 19. In a nutshell, choose Site→New Site. In the Site Setup window, type *Templates* into the Site Name field, click the folder icon next to the Local Site Folder field, navigate to and select the *Chapter20* folder inside the *MM_DWCC* folder, and then click Choose (Select). Finally, click OK.)

Creating a Template

1. **Open the Files panel by pressing F8 (Shift-⌘-F).**

   Of course, if it was already open, you just closed it. Press F8 (Shift-⌘-F) again.

2. **In the Files panel, find and double-click the page *design.html*.**

   It's usually easier to create a template from an existing web page rather than from scratch. For the purpose of getting to bed before midnight tonight, pretend that you just designed this beautiful page.

3. **Choose File→Save As Template.**

   The Save As Template dialog box opens (see Figure 20-17).

FIGURE 20-17

The first step in creating a template from a regular web page is to choose File→Save As Template. You only need to provide a name for the new template, but a brief description can help when you have lots of templates in a site; the description appears in the New Document window when you create a new template-based page.

4. **In the description field, type "main cafe template."**

   This description appears in the New Template window when you create a page based on this template.

5. **In the "Save as" box, name the template *Main*, and then click Save. In the Update Links window, click Yes.**

   Behind the scenes, Dreamweaver creates a new folder—Templates—in the site's root folder, and saves the file as *Main.dwt* inside it. A new template is born. You can see it in the newly created Templates folder in the Files panel and in the Templates page of the Assets panel (see the Note below).

   The template is a model for other pages. And although those other pages will be *based* on this page, they won't be identical. The next step is to identify the areas of the design you want to change from page to page—the editable regions, in other words.

   NOTE Templates don't always immediately show up in the Templates category of the Assets panel (Window→Assets). Sometimes you need to click the Refresh Site List button (the circular arrow in the bottom-right of the Assets panel) to see a newly added template.

   ---

6. **Click inside the word "Headline" and choose Edit→Select All.**

   The headline and paragraph of text below it live inside a <div> tag on this page. Choosing Select All with the cursor inside a div selects everything inside the div, but not the <div> tag itself. In this case, you want to put content inside this div when you create new pages based on this template, so you'll turn the current selection into an editable region.

7. **Choose Insert→Template→Editable Region.**

   Here, as in the following steps, you can also, from the Insert panel's Common category, go to the Templates menu and choose Editable Region, or just press Ctrl+Alt+V (⌘-Option-V).

   The New Editable Region dialog box appears.

8. **Type *Content*, and then click OK.**

   A small blue tab, labeled *Content*, appears above the headline (see Figure 20-18). You just added one editable region—the most basic type of template region. You'll add other types of template regions later, but build a few template-based pages first.

9. **Choose File→Save, and then File→Close.**

   Congratulations! You just created your first template.

Creating a Page Based on a Template

Now it's time to get down to business and build some web pages:

1. **Choose File→New.**

   The New Document window opens.

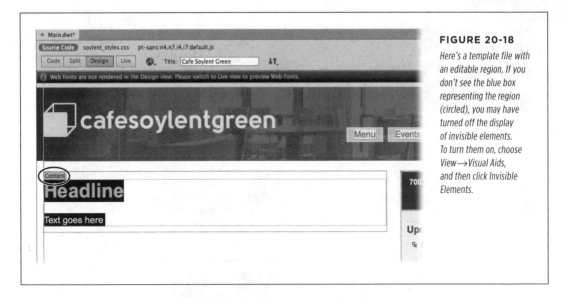

FIGURE 20-18

Here's a template file with an editable region. If you don't see the blue box representing the region (circled), you may have turned off the display of invisible elements. To turn them on, choose View→Visual Aids, and then click Invisible Elements.

2. **On the window's far left side, click Site Templates.**

   A list of the sites you've defined appears in the column labeled "Sites."

3. **Make sure you have the site you set up for this tutorial (Templates) selected in the Sites column. From the list of templates to the right, select Main, and make sure you have the "Update page when template changes" checkbox (in the right of the window) turned on.**

   If you don't turn on the "Update page" checkbox, the new page doesn't link to the template, and therefore won't update when you make changes to the template.

4. **Click Create.**

   Lo, a new web page appears—one that looks (almost) exactly like the template (Figure 20-19).

5. **Choose File→Save. Click the Site Root button and save the file as *index. html* in the root folder. In the Document toolbar's Title field (at the top of the document window), type *Welcome to Cafe Soylent Green*.**

   To indicate that it's your template's offspring, the document window has a yellow tab in the upper-right corner that reads "Template:Main." Dreamweaver indicates your editable region with a blue tab. Now it's time to add some content.

FIGURE 20-19

In template-based pages, blue tabs identify editable areas, and the yellow tab at the top-right lists the template's name (circled).

6. **Choose File→Open. In the Open file window, click the Site Root button, and then double-click the file *text-index.html*.**

   You can also open this file by double-clicking its name in the Files panel. The *text-index.html* page contains the content for the site's home page. It's just a matter of copying and pasting the text from one page to the other.

7. **Click the <body> tag in the Tag Selector (bottom-left of the document window) to select all the page contents, and then choose Edit→Copy.**

   Clicking the <body> tag in the Tag Selector is the best way to select an entire page's worth of content. As you read on step 6 above, just clicking into a page and choosing Edit→Select All doesn't necessarily select everything on the page; if the cursor were inside a <div> tag, for example, then you'd select only the contents inside that div.

8. **At the top of the document window, click the *index.html* tab to switch to the template-based page. Click the blue tab labeled "Content" (just above the headline).**

   Remember that you can add content only to an editable region. If you move your mouse over the banner, navigation buttons, or footer areas of the page, you see a black "forbidden" symbol. You can't insert the cursor anywhere but inside an editable region. Clicking the blue tab selects everything inside that region. Since it's just placeholder text anyway, you'll replace it with the content you just copied.

9. **Choose Edit→Paste.**

Dreamweaver replaces the dummy text with the new content. Thanks to the power of CSS, Dreamweaver instantly formats the plain-look HTML you just pasted (if only web design were so simple!). Of course, on your own site, you'd probably copy and paste text from an email message or Word document. Then you'd use Dreamweaver's tools to create headlines, paragraphs, links, and bulleted lists, and then add CSS to style the page.

You're done with this page!

10. **Save and close the file.**

Time to create another page...well actually four more pages! You could repeat steps 1–9 above to create the new pages, but if you're starting off with a simple HTML page that you'd like to apply a template to, there's a better way.

11. **Open the file *about.html*. Choose Modify→Templates→Apply Template to Page.**

The Select Template window appears. Since there's only a single template for this site, the choice isn't hard.

12. **Choose Main and then press Select.**

The Inconsistent Region Names window appears (see Figure 20-20). Since you're starting with an HTML file, you need to tell Dreamweaver where on the template-based page to move this existing content. In general, you simply tell Dreamweaver to place the <body> tag contents of the existing page into an editable region of the template-based page, and, if necessary, the <head> tag contents of the existing page (which includes its title, if any) into the head of the gestating page.

13. **Select "Document body" and then choose "Content" from the "Move content to new region" menu.**

This will place the page's content into the editable "Content" region from the template.

14. **Type *About Cafe Soylent Green* for the title.**

You need to do the same thing for your other site pages.

15. **Repeat steps 11–13 for the *events.html*, *menu.html*, *hours.html*, and *reservation.html* files. Add appropriate titles to each page. Choose File→Save All to save all the new pages, and then choose File→Close All to close all the open files.**

Now you'll turn to an advanced template feature, optional regions.

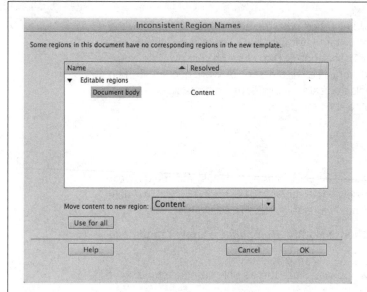

FIGURE 20-20

The oddly named Inconsistent Region Names dialog box lets you tell Dreamweaver where to put existing elements on your page within the templates' defined regions. You do that by matching the template regions (on the left) with the existing page elements (on the right).

Creating and Using Optional Regions

You may have noticed that two of the pages you just created—*hours.html* and *events.html*—have the same content in the right sidebar. While it's useful to display the hours and location on other pages, it's a bit weird to duplicate that information on the *hours.html* page. The same is true for the *events.html* page and the events listing in the sidebar. Fortunately, using optional regions, you can hide or show that information on a page-by-page basis.

1. **Return to Dreamweaver. In the Assets panel (Window→Assets), click the Templates button, and then double-click the Main template to open it.**

   The original template, *Main.dwt*, opens. You can also open the template by double-clicking its name inside the Templates folder in the Files panel.

   You'll turn the box with the location and hours in it into an optional region.

2. **Click inside the dark-green box in the sidebar on the right. In the Tag Selector in the bottom-left of the document window, click <div.hours> to select the entire <div> tag.**

   Alternatively, you could click inside that div and choose Edit→Select All twice; the first time selects the contents of the div, while the second selects the <div> tag itself.

3. **Choose Insert→Template→Optional Region.**

You can also use the Template menu on the Insert panel. Either way, the New Optional Region window opens.

4. **Type *Hours* in the Name field and then click OK.**

You'll turn the events listing into an optional region as well.

5. **Click at the beginning of the "Upcoming Events" headline and then drag down until you select the headline and all three bulleted items.**

The events listings aren't contained in their own <div> tag; they're just made up of a headline followed by a bulleted list.

6. **Choose Insert→Template→Optional Region. In the New Optional Region window, type *Events* in the Name field, and then click OK.**

The Template file should look like Figure 20-21.

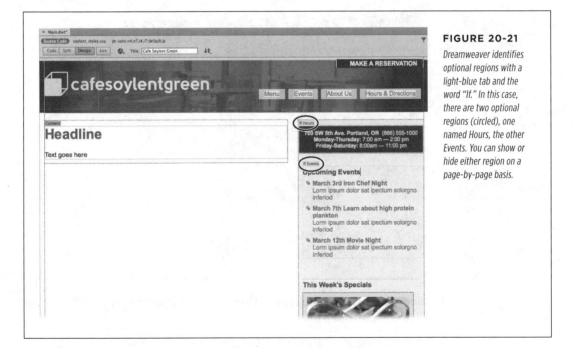

FIGURE 20-21

Dreamweaver identifies optional regions with a light-blue tab and the word "If." In this case, there are two optional regions (circled), one named Hours, the other Events. You can show or hide either region on a page-by-page basis.

7. **Choose File→Save.**

The Update Template Files window appears. Whenever you update a template, Dreamweaver updates any template-based pages built using that template.

8. **Click the Update button, and when Dreamweaver completes the update, click Close.**

Now you'll hide the hours box on the *hours.html* page.

9. **Open the file *hours.html*. Choose Modify→Template Properties.**

The Template Properties window appears (Figure 20-22).

10. **Select Hours and then turn off the Show Hours checkbox at the bottom of the window. Click OK.**

The Template Properties window closes and the hours/location box in the sidebar disappears. You bring the box back by opening the Template Properties window again, selecting Hours, and then turning on the Show Hours checkbox.

11. **Open the file *events.html*. Choose Modify→Template Properties. Select Events and then turn off the Show Events checkbox at the bottom of the window. Click OK.**

The Template Properties window closes and the events listing in the sidebar disappears.

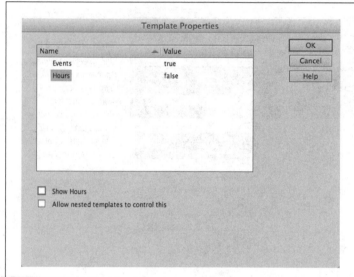

FIGURE 20-22

The Template Properties window does double duty. It lets you hide or show optional regions, and it lets you set values for editable tag attributes. The "Allow nested templates to control this box" option applies only to nested templates, which, as mentioned in the box on page 853, you should avoid.

12. **Choose File→Save All to save all the new pages, and then choose File→Close All to close all open files.**

Now you'll see the real power of Dreamweaver templates.

Updating a Template

Remember, the pages you just created maintain a reference to the original template. In this final phase of the tutorial, you're going to make a few changes to that template.

1. **Return to Dreamweaver. In the Assets panel, click the Templates button, and then double-click *Main.dwt*. (You can also open the file by double-clicking its name inside the Templates folder in the Files panel.)**

The original template, *Main.dwt*, opens. You need to change a couple of things. First, you should update the copyright notice.

2. **In the footer, locate "Copyright 2022" and change it to the current year.**

   Change the year to 2013 or whatever the current year happens to be. You'll also add a link here.

3. **On the same line in the footer, select the text "Cosmopolitan Farmer." In the Properties panel's Link field, type *http://www.cosmofarmer.com*.**

   There's a new food special that should be in the sidebar.

4. **In the sidebar, click at the end of the last paragraph and then press Enter (Return).**

   You want to add an image and some text.

5. **Choose Insert→Image→Image. In the Select Image Source window, navigate to the *images* folder and double-click *special3.jpg* to insert the image.**

   The image appears in your page.

6. **Type *Grilled Mozzarella* in the "Alternate text" box and then click OK. Press the right arrow key to deselect the image and move the cursor to the right; type *Yummy grilled mozzarella*.**

   You could add more specials, update the events listing, and change the banner and navigation bar. In short, Dreamweaver will pass on any changes you make to the non-editable areas of the template to the pages you built based on that template. Time to see the magic happen.

7. **Choose File→Save.**

   Dreamweaver displays the Update Template Files window. This is the moment of truth.

8. **Click Update.**

   Dreamweaver opens the Update Pages dialog box and updates the appropriate web pages, correcting the copyright year and adding the link and the new cafe special. In addition to making the changes, Dreamweaver displays a list so you know which pages have changed.

NOTE If, after you update pages based on a template, you don't see the number of updated pages listed in the Update Pages window, turn on the Show Log checkbox in the lower-left corner of the Update Pages.

---

9. **Click Close to close the Update Pages dialog box. Finally, open the template-based files you just created (*index.html, about.html, and so on*).**

   Notice that Dreamweaver updated the copyright notice and sidebar on all those pages (see Figure 20-23). That happened because you changed the template on which all those page were genetically linked. Ah, the power!

FIGURE 20-23

Here's the finished tutorial page, complete with a useful Chia tip, a box with a link to a related web page, and a helpful question and answer.

Customizing Dreamweaver

Whether you're a hard-core HTML jockey who prefers to be knee-deep in Code view, or a visually oriented, drag-and-drop type who never strays from Design view, Dreamweaver lets you work the way you want.

By now you're probably using the Favorites tab on the Insert panel to store your most frequently used objects, as discussed on page 10. But don't stop there. Dreamweaver lets you add, customize, and share keyboard shortcuts, too, giving you a simple way to tailor the program to your needs. And if that's not a big enough efficiency boost, you can add features that even Adobe's engineers never imagined, from simple productivity add-ons like QuickLink (page 180) to advanced server behaviors that help power complete e-commerce sites. Dreamweaver's design lets amateur and professional programmers alike write new features and functions using HTML, JavaScript, and XML (Extensible Markup Language). You can explore hundreds of these extras, called *extensions*, right from within Dreamweaver. And best of all, you can try many of them for free.

■ Keyboard Shortcuts

As you use Dreamweaver, you'll use the same keyboard shortcuts and travel to the same palettes and menus time and again. Perhaps you have a lot of HTML5 videos on your site, and you constantly use keyboard shortcuts to insert them. You may find that, after the thousandth time, Ctrl+Alt+Shift+V (⌘-Option-Shift-V) hurts your pinkie and uses too many keys to be truly efficient. On the other hand, the things you do all the time—like adding rollover images or inserting text fields into forms—have no shortcuts at all, so you have no choice but to go to a menu.

To speed up your work and save your tendons, you can define or redefine shortcuts for most Dreamweaver commands using the program's keyboard-shortcut editor.

Dreamweaver's Stock Shortcuts

Dreamweaver includes three sets of shortcuts with the program. It's easy to switch among them—a useful feature when you share your computer with someone who likes different keystrokes.

If you opt for Dreamweaver's shortcuts, you'll most likely never need to switch from the standard set, but here are your options:

- **Dreamweaver Standard.** When you first fire up Dreamweaver, the program turns on this set of shortcuts. It's the one available since Dreamweaver 8.

- **Dreamweaver MX 2004.** Some shortcuts have changed since Dreamweaver MX 2004—for example, Shift+F5 now opens the tag editor, whereas Ctrl+F5 did so in MX 2004. But the changes are so minor that you don't really need to use this set.

- **HomeSite.** Likewise, if you're adept at the Windows HTML text editor HomeSite, you may want to use its keyboard shortcuts. Don't remember HomeSite? That's because it hasn't been available for years, so you probably won't ever need this.

You access Dreamweaver's shortcuts from the Keyboard Shortcuts dialog box. Choose Edit→Keyboard Shortcuts (Dreamweaver→Keyboard Shortcuts). Be patient—the sets can take some time to load. Once the dialog box appears (see Figure 21-1), you can switch sets by choosing a new one from the Current Set drop-down menu.

Make Your Own Shortcut Set

But what if you want a set of shortcuts that *combines* Dreamweaver timesavers with those from BBEdit? Or you're a radical individualist who wants to remap *every* command to keys of your liking? No problem, you can create your own set of shortcuts. Since Dreamweaver doesn't let you change any of its three standard shortcut sets, you should make a copy of one of them to use as the basis for your own set.

Choose Edit→Keyboard Shortcuts (Dreamweaver→Keyboard Shortcuts). In the Keyboard Shortcuts window, use the Current Set drop-down menu to choose the set you want to copy, and then click the Duplicate Set button, ⊞. Dreamweaver asks you to name the new set; do so, and then click OK.

You can delete or rename any set you create—once you figure out that ⊙ is the Rename Set button. The 🗑 button, of course, lets you delete a set.

> **NOTE** Dreamweaver lets you delete the three main keyboard shortcut sets. If you want one of them back, don't worry, the file's not gone, you just need to edit a file called *mm_deleted_files.xml* in your Dreamweaver configuration folder. Remove the line that lists the shortcut set you want to get back and save the file. Then quit and restart Dreamweaver. (Note that each Dreamweaver account holder has his/her own configuration folder. See the box on page 880 for more.)

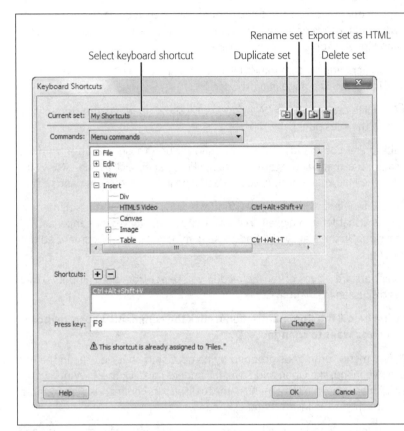

FIGURE 21-1

The Keyboard Shortcuts window lets you select or duplicate a set of shortcuts, as well as add or remove your own shortcuts, for every menu item in Dreamweaver. (You can also create keyboard shortcuts for snippets; see Chapter 19.) If you try to create a shortcut that another command already uses, Dreamweaver warns you. If you wish, you can ignore the warning and reassign the keys to the new command.

Changing Keyboard Shortcuts

Once you duplicate a set of shortcuts, you can select any command in the set and edit its shortcut. Start by choosing Edit→Keyboard Shortcuts (Dreamweaver→Keyboard Shortcuts) to open the Shortcuts window, and then:

1. **From the Commands drop-down menu, choose the command type.**

   Dreamweaver organizes shortcuts into seven (Windows) or four (Macintosh) categories (menu commands, code editing commands, and so on), which doesn't always make sense. For example, the Copy and Paste commands appear in the Code editing category, even though you use them at least as frequently in Design view. In addition, quite a few commands appear in multiple categories (though you only need to change a keyboard shortcut once to change it across all categories).

   Browse the types of commands to see which have (or could have) keyboard shortcuts:

- Menu commands, such as Insert→HTML5 Video, are those that appear in Dreamweaver's menus.

- You might use the Code editing commands when you edit HTML. However, you could just as easily use them in Design view—they include Cut, Paste, and Move to Top of Page, to name a few.

- Document editing commands let you select text and objects on a page, as well as preview a page in a browser.

- The Files panel options (Windows only) show up when you right-click a file in the Files panel.

- Site panel commands (Windows only) include those available from the contextual menu at the top-right of the Files panel, such as Site→New Site. (On the Mac, many of these commands are in the Menu commands set.)

- The Site window commands (Windows only) are an odd assortment of actions that let you close a window, quit Dreamweaver, or cancel an FTP session. On the Mac, you'll find these commands in the Document editing group.

- Snippets are pieces of reusable code you select from the Snippets panel, as discussed in Chapter 19.

2. **In the list below the Commands menu, click the command whose keyboard shortcut you want to change.**

You'll find menu commands grouped by name: Commands you see in the File drop-down menu, like Open and Save, fall under File. Click the + (Windows) or flippy triangle (Mac) next to a menu name to display its commands. For example, Figure 21-1 shows the Insert menu expanded.

If the command already has a keyboard shortcut, it appears in the right-hand column. If it doesn't, you see an empty space.

3. **Click inside the "Press key" field, and then press the shortcut keys.**

Unless you assign the shortcut to an F-key or the Esc key, you must begin your shortcut with the Ctrl key (⌘-key). For example, you can assign a shortcut to the F8 key, but not to the letter R; you'd have to press Ctrl+R (⌘-R) instead.

NOTE Your operating system may use some of its own keyboard shortcuts, and you can't assign any of your OS shortcuts to Dreamweaver. For example, in Windows, Ctrl+Esc opens Windows' Start menu, while on Macs, F12 gets you Dreamweaver's dashboard. If you try to assign an operating system shortcut to Dreamweaver, your computer won't let you.

Of course, many commands already have shortcuts. If you choose an already assigned key combination, Dreamweaver tells you which command has dibs. You can pick a different key combination, or click the Change button to reassign the shortcut to your command, leaving the original without a shortcut.

4. Click the Change button.

Dreamweaver saves the new shortcut in your custom set.

Repeat the steps above to assign other keystrokes. When you finish, click OK.

FREQUENTLY ASKED QUESTION

Sharing Shortcuts

How do I share my keyboard shortcuts with other people?

If you work on two computers—for example, a desktop in your office and a laptop at home—you can synchronize your keyboard shortcuts so that they are the same for both computers. That's done through the Creative Cloud. You set things up in your Preferences window. Choose Edit->Preferences (Dreamweaver->Preferences), then click Sync Settings. In the Settings to Sync section, turn on Keyboard Shortcuts. When you open Dreamweaver on a different computer, but with the same user account, click the Sync Setttings gear in the upper right corner. Sharing your Keyboard shortcuts with someone else takes a little more work, as explained next.

Dreamweaver stores your keyboard shortcuts as XML files, but finding them can be tricky. They're in different locations depending on your operating system. Each keyboard set's file name ends with the extension .xml. For example, if you create a new set of keyboard shortcuts named My Shortcuts, the XML file name is *My Shortcuts.xml*.

Windows stores your keyboard shortcuts in *C:\Users\[User Name]\AppData\Roaming\Adobe\Dreamweaver CC\en_US\Configuration\Menus\Custom Sets*. Note that Windows normally hides these files from you; see the Note on page 874 to get around this little problem.

Mac OS X squirrels these files away in *[User Name]→Library→Application Support→Adobe→Dreamweaver CC→en_US→Configuration→Menus→Custom Sets*. Mac OS X Lion [version 10.7] and Mountain Lion [version 10.8] normally hide your Library folder from view, but see the Note on page 875 to flush it out.

Depending on your language choice in Dreamweaver, you might see something other than "en_US" (which stands for English) in the path name, such as "de_DE" for German, or "ja_JP" for Japanese.

You can copy these files and place them in the Custom Sets folder on other computers. Once you do, Dreamweaver users on those machines can use the Keyboard Shortcuts window (Edit→Keyboard Shortcuts or, on the Mac, Dreamweaver→Keyboard Shortcuts) to select the new set, just as though you created it in that copy of Dreamweaver.

What if a command you use often doesn't have a shortcut at all? No problem, you can create one. As a matter of fact, Dreamweaver lets you assign *two* keyboard shortcuts to every command—say, one for you, and one for your left-handed spouse.

To give a command a first or additional shortcut:

1. Choose the command.

Follow the first two steps of the preceding instructions.

2. Click the + button next to the word "Shortcuts."

Your cursor automatically pops into the "Press key" field.

3. Press the keys for the shortcut, and then click Change again.

Repeat these steps to assign another set of keystrokes; when you finish, click OK.

Deleting shortcuts is just as easy. Simply click the command in the list, and then click the minus sign (–) next to Shortcuts.

Create a Shortcut Cheat Sheet

Unless your brain is equipped with a 2-terabyte hard drive, you'll probably find it hard to remember all of Dreamweaver's keyboard shortcuts.

Fortunately, you can print out a cheat sheet. Find the handy "Export Set as HTML" button at the top of the Shortcuts window (labeled with the odd icon 📄; see Figure 21-1). Click it to name and save a simple HTML page listing all the commands and keyboard shortcuts for the currently selected command set. Once you save the file, print it out or use it as an online reference—it's a great way to keep a record of your shortcuts for yourself or a team of designers.

> **NOTE** Windows normally hides certain files, such as important system files, from sight. This includes the configuration folder discussed on page 880 and the Menus folder discussed on page 873. To access these folders, you need to make hidden files visible. Windows 8 users should follow the steps at *http://tinyurl.com/win8hiddenfiles*, and Windows 7 users should do so at *http://tinyurl.com/win7hiddenfiles*.

■ Dreamweaver Extensions

While keyboard shortcuts give you an easy way to use common commands, they're not much help if the command you want doesn't exist. Suppose, for example, you use Dreamweaver's Open Browser Window behavior (page 607) to load a new web page into a window that measures exactly 200 x 300 pixels. What if you want to center the window in the middle of your visitor's monitor? Dreamweaver's Open Browser Window behavior doesn't do that, so what's a web designer to do? You could go to the Adobe site and request the new feature (*http://tinyurl.com/jbmlm*) in hopes that the bustling team of programmers will add it to the next version of the program. But you'd have to wait—and there's no guarantee that it'll be there.

Instead, legions of hard-core Dreamweaver fans have taken this wish-list feature into their own hands. As it turns out, amateur (and pro) programmers can enhance Dreamweaver relatively easily by writing new feature modules using the basic languages of the Web: HTML, JavaScript, and XML. (In fact, HTML forms, JavaScript programs, and XML documents constitute much of Dreamweaver's code. The objects in the Insert panel, for example, are actually HTML pages stored within Dreamweaver's configuration folder, and Adobe wrote all of Dreamweaver's menus as an XML file.)

Because of this "open architecture," you can add new functions and commands—called *extensions*—to Dreamweaver by downloading and installing the work of one of these programmers.

Extensions take many forms, and they change how Dreamweaver works in a variety of ways. You can add an icon to the Insert panel, for example, a behavior to the Behaviors panel, or a command in the Commands menu. You might even add an entirely new floating window, like the Properties panel, to alter some aspect of your pages.

Best of all, while you might need some programming ability to *create* extensions, you don't need any to *use* them. You can download and install hundreds of extensions, many for free. In addition, you can find many sophisticated extensions, like those for creating e-commerce sites, commercially available.

> **NOTE** If you're a Mac OS X Lion owner, some versions of the operating system let you view application preferences, plug-ins, and data in your Library folder. But OS X Lion (version 10.7) and Mountain Lion (version 10.8) hide the Library folder from you. Here's how you uncover it: In the Finder, click Go to see a list of destinations (Documents, Desktop, and so on). Hold down the Option key and the Library folder pops up in the list. Then click Library→Application Support→Adobe→Dreamweaver CC→en_US→Configuration.

Browse the Exchange

The Adobe Exchange hosts the largest collection of free and commercial Dreamweaver extensions available. Although some come from Adobe itself, an army of talented Dreamweaver fans write the vast majority of them.

Note that in Dreamweaver CC, Adobe changed the way the Exchange works. Previously, you'd go to the Exchange to find and download extensions. Now, you use the Adobe Exchange panel within Dreamweaver itself:

1. **In Dreamweaver, choose Window→Extensions→Adobe Exchange.**

   The Exchange panel opens (see Figure 21-2). Initially, the window is narrow and compact; to switch to a more capacious view, click 🔲 in the lower-right corner.

2. **Browse the extensions.**

   Click the All button near the top of the panel to see the entire extension library. Likewise, click Paid or Free to narrow the list to just those types of extension. If you know the name of the extension you want, type it in the Search field in the top-right corner.

> **NOTE** Extensions have been around for much of Dreamweaver's life. Unfortunately, each new version of the program adds a few more challenges for extension developers, so not all extensions work with all versions of Dreamweaver CC. In fact, the latest version of the Extension Manager only supports Adobe's newer .zxp extension format, not the older .mxp format. So if you have an old extension, or you find one in the .mxp format that you want to use, you may be out of luck—Dreamweaver CC's Extension Manager won't install it. There's one glimmer of hope if you have Dreamweaver CS5.5 or Dreamweaver CS6. The Extension Manager in those versions has a command to convert old extensions to the new format (Tools→Convert MXP Extension to ZXP).

3. **Select an extension to learn more about it (Figure 21-2, bottom-left).**

   Once you do, Dreamweaver displays four buttons: Info, Previews, Notes, and Reviews. The Info tab describes the extension in detail; the Previews tab shows you the visual effect the extension has on a web page (Figure 21-2, bottom-right);

the Notes tab contains additional information (and is frequently left blank by the developer); and the Reviews tab shows you what other people think of the program. Finally, a star rating appears below the name of the extension, giving you a quick take on others' opinions.

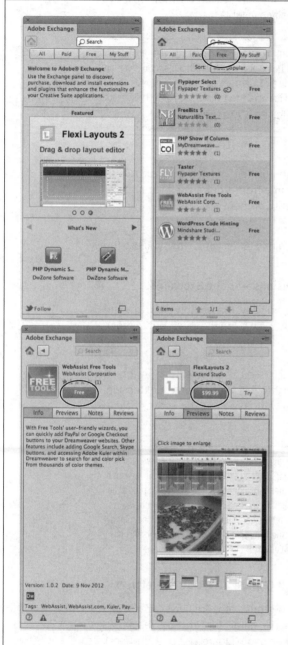

FIGURE 21-2

When the Adobe Exchange panel first opens (top-left), you see a featured extension and, below that, a carousel of new extensions. Click the Free category (top-right, circled) to see all the free programs. Click an extension and Dreamweaver launches a panel (bottom-left) that has tabs for Info, Previews, Notes, and Reviews. When you're in the Preview tab (bottom-right), click the thumbnails at the bottom of the panel for different views of the program.

4. **Click either the Free (Figure 21-2, top-right) or price button (bottom-right).**

    If the extension is free, Dreamweaver downloads it and launches the Extension Manager, which then installs the extension. If it's a paid extension, the Adobe Exchange asks for your credit card number or PayPal account. After you pay, Dreamweaver downloads the extension, and the Extension Manager installs it. Some extensions offer a free trial version; if one's available, a Try button appears beside the price (Figure 21-2, bottom-right).

5. **Accept the extension's end-user agreement.**

    The agreement is between you and the extension developer, so its wording is likely to vary from one extension to another.

6. **Quit Dreamweaver and restart it.**

    Most extensions won't work until you quit and then restart Dreamweaver. You find out how to use the extension in the Extension Manager (Figure 21-3) or on the extension developer's website (a link for which you'll find in the Extension Manager.)

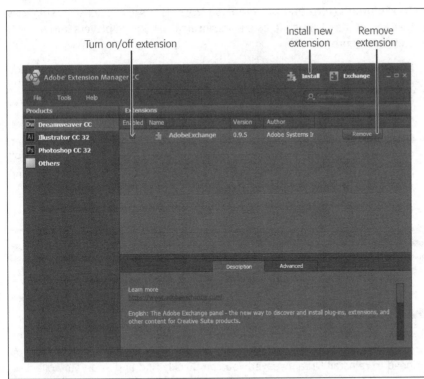

FIGURE 21-3

The Extension Manager lists each extension you've installed, along with its version number and author. Select an extension to see its description in the bottom half of the window. Skip the "Exchange" link, since it does nothing more than send you to a website that tells you to download the Adobe Exchange panel—which you've already installed!

Other Extension Sources

Unfortunately, the glory days of free extensions are mostly over. While you can still find plenty of them, many developers realized they couldn't survive by giving away their work. The upside is that there are now more excellent, polished, well-documented commercial extensions than ever—and many even offer customer support. Here's a sampling of sources:

- **WebAssist** (*www.webassist.com*) is one of the largest and most professional extension-development companies for Dreamweaver. It offers a variety of high-quality extensions, including a few for free.

- **Project Seven** (*www.projectseven.com*) offers both free and excellent commercial extensions that let you create animated HTML and CSS menus, scrolling areas of text, CSS-based page layouts, photo galleries, and more.

- **Trent Pastrana** (*www.fourlevel.com*) sells extensions that build photo galleries, display whiz-bang effects (like menus that slide onto a page), and move text up and down (or left and right) across a page. He also provides several free extensions.

- **Trio Solutions** (*http://tinyurl.com/6k8q2zg*) sells lots of inexpensive extensions that let you add CSS-style calendars, insert Flash music players into a page, and much more.

- **Hot Dreamweaver** (*www.hotdreamweaver.com*) sells extensions for server-side needs, like sending form submissions as emails, adding Captcha (those little hard-to-read pictures of letters and numbers you have to type into a form to prove you're a human), and uploading files to a web server.

- **DMXzone** (*www.dmxzone.com/index?3*) offers a range of extensions, including those that let you build a Facebook fan page for your business, embed an MP3 player on a page so visitors can listen to audio, and add extensions for PHP and ASP server-side programming. They even have a bunch of free extensions, like YouTubizer, which makes it easy to embed YouTube videos on a page.

NOTE When this book went to press, some of the sites mentioned above still offered extensions in the older—and no longer compatible—MXP format. Hopefully, these developers will update the best and most useful extensions for Dreamweaver CC.

Download and Install Extensions

Once you find a great extension, download it. You can save the file anywhere on your computer, but you may want to create a special folder for it. That way, if you ever need to reinstall Dreamweaver, you can quickly find and add your collection of extensions.

Extension file names end with .zxp (the Extension Manager no longer supports .mxp files). This special file format works with Adobe's Extension Manager—the helper program that actually installs the extension.

The Extension Manager

To add or remove a Dreamweaver extension, use the Extension Manager, a standalone program that handles add-ons for many Adobe programs, including Dreamweaver. It lets you install extensions, turn them on and off, and remove them (Figure 21-3). It's also handy if you use Adobe's Photoshop, Illustrator, Flash, or Fireworks programs—you get a single place to manage all your extensions.

You launch the Extension Manager from within Dreamweaver by choosing Window→ Manage Extensions.

To install an extension:

1. **Find and download an extension (a .zxp file).**

   If you use the Adobe Exchange panel, you don't need to follow these instructions—once you select an extension, the Exchange panel launches the Extension Manager and installs the program for you.

2. **In Dreamweaver, choose Window→Manage Extensions.**

   Dreamweaver launches the Extension Manager, which lists all the extensions you've installed.

3. **Choose Dreamweaver CC from the left-hand list of Adobe products.**

   Since the Extension Manager handles several products, you need to specify your program.

4. **Choose Install.**

   Or click File→Install Extension. The Select Extension to Install window appears, listing all the folders on your hard drive.

5. **Navigate to and select the extension you want to add.**

   A disclaimer appears with a lot of legal text. In brief, it frees Adobe from liability if your computer melts down as a result of installing the extension.

6. **Click Accept in the Disclaimer window.**

   A message may appear that asks you to quit and restart Dreamweaver. If so, follow the directions.

> **TIP** A faster way to install an extension is to simply double-click the .zxp file after you download it. This automatically launches the Extension Manager and installs the extension.

To remove an extension, select it from the list and choose File→Remove Extension, or click Remove.

If you install a lot of extensions, Dreamweaver may take longer than usual to load; it needs to process every extension file as it starts up. If you want to temporarily turn off an extension (as opposed to deleting it), open the Extension Manager and turn off the Enable checkbox next to the extension's name. To turn it back on, simply turn on the checkbox again. You may need to restart Dreamweaver to make the extension available again.

Make Your Own Extensions

The Exchange is a great resource for helper programs, but what if you can't find one that suits your needs? One option is to create your own extension.

Writing extensions requires in-depth knowledge of HTML and JavaScript, and it's beyond the scope of this book. But when you create a command that lets you complete a weekly task in a fraction of the time it previously took, the effort may just be worth it. For details on writing your own extensions, visit the Dreamweaver Exchange Producer Portal at *https://www.adobeexchange.com/producer*.

POWER USERS' CLINIC

The Secret Life of Extensions

Where does Dreamweaver store your extensions? The basic answer is inside its configuration folder. But Dreamweaver actually supplies you with more than one configuration folder: It gives you a main folder in the program folder itself, and an account-specific folder for each Dreamweaver user registered on a computer. (Windows PCs and Macs let multiple users each have an account on a single computer—one for you, one for your spouse, and one for your pet ferret, say.) Of course, you may be the only one using your computer, so there'd be only one configuration folder for your account and one in the main application folder.

On a Windows machine, you find the main configuration folder in *C:\Program Files\Adobe\Adobe Dreamweaver CC\configuration*, assuming C is your main drive and you're on an x86 (32-bit) Windows system—if you use a 64-bit version of Windows, the configuration folder is in *C:\Program Files (x86)\Adobe\Adobe Dreamweaver CC\configuration*. If you use a Mac, the configuration folder is in *Applications→Adobe Dreamweaver CC→Configuration*.

The individual account configuration folders are located in folders dedicated to each user. In Windows, look for *C:\Users\[User Name]\AppData\Roaming\Adobe\Dreamweaver CC\en_US\Configuration*. (Normally the AppData folder is hidden, so you may need to make it visible as described in the Note on page 874.)

On a Mac, try *[Volume Name]→Users→[User Name]→Library→Application Support→Adobe→Dreamweaver CC→en_US→Configuration*. (Mac OS X 10.7 [Lion] and 10.8 [Mountain Lion] owners won't usually see their Library folder—see the Note on page 875 to make it visible.)

As mentioned in the box on page 873, "en_US" means English. If you installed Dreamweaver using a different language, this folder will be named something else, such as "de_DE" for German.

Dreamweaver records your program options in your personal configuration folder. This info includes any extensions you added, keyboard shortcut sets you deleted (page 869), and workspace layouts you saved (see page 14).

The main configuration folder holds many of the files that control the way Dreamweaver looks and works. For instance, Dreamweaver describes its entire menu structure, including menu items and submenus, in a file called *menus.xml*. When you launch Dreamweaver, it uses the information in this file to draw the menus on the screen.

The configuration folder holds many subfolders, too, each with a special purpose. For example, the Objects subfolder contains files that tell Dreamweaver which icons appear on the Insert bar and how each one works.

Depending on the type of extension you download—command, object, behavior, and so on—the Extension Manager stores the required file (or files) in one or more folders inside the configuration folder. Because all the files in the configuration folder are crucial to the way Dreamweaver works, don't delete it or any of the files inside it. In fact, because the Extension Manager automatically makes any required changes to the configuration folder, there's no reason to even look inside it. (The exception is when you want to copy your keyboard shortcut set to another computer [see page 873].)

Working with Server-Side Programming

So far in this book, you've learned to build and maintain websites using Dreamweaver's powerful design, coding, and site-management tools. The pages you've created use straightforward HTML, and you can immediately preview them in a web browser. The web cognoscenti often call these kinds of pages *static*, because they don't change once you finish building them (unless you edit them, of course). For many websites, especially those where you carefully handcraft the design and content on a page-by-page basis, static web pages are the way to go.

But imagine landing a contract to build an online catalog of 10,000 products. After the initial excitement disappears (along with your plans for that trip to Hawaii), you realize that, even using Dreamweaver's Template tool (Chapter 20), building 10,000 pages is a lot of work!

For jobs like that, most developers use a database to store information about the many products the company sells, along with a kind of page template that's programmed to serve up just-in-time product-info pages. These dynamically created pages work their magic using a server-side programming language like PHP, ASP, ColdFusion, Java, or Ruby. When a visitor clicks a link to learn more about a product, he's actually requesting this template file, which talks to the database, retrieves information for a product, and then returns a fully-formed web page—one that looks just like a page you'd create by hand.

All major e-commerce sites work this way. Visit *www.amazon.com*, for example, and you'll find more books than you could read in a lifetime. In fact, you'll find more products—DVDs, CDs, even outdoor lawn furniture—than could fit inside a Wal-Mart. In just an hour, you could browse through hundreds of products, each with its own web page. Do you really think Amazon hired an army of web developers to create a web page for each product it sells? Not a chance.

Instead, when you search for a book on Amazon.com, you trigger a computer program running on what's called an *application server* that searches Amazon's large database of products. When the program finds products that match your search criteria, it merges information about that product with HTML page elements (a banner, navigation buttons, a copyright notice, and so on) to stitch together a web page on the fly and send it to your browser. You see a page that's been created, perhaps for the first time ever (Figure 22-1).

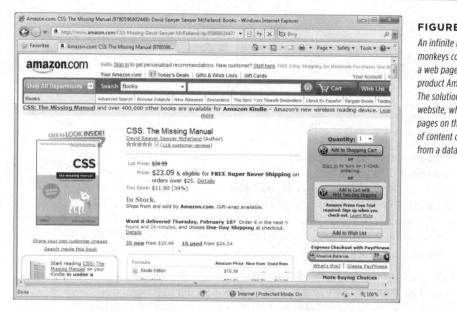

FIGURE 22-1

An infinite number of monkeys couldn't create a web page for each product Amazon.com sells. The solution? A dynamic website, which creates pages on the fly, made up of content chunks pulled from a database.

NOTE Luckily, you're not limited to *either* "static" *or* "dynamic" pages. Websites frequently use both—static pages for custom designs and handcrafted content and dynamic pages for mass-produced catalog pages, for example.

Dynamic websites are generally the realm of professional programmers. If you're reading this chapter, you're either already programming these types of pages using PHP, ColdFusion, Ruby on Rails, C#, or some other programming language...or you're interested in learning how to do so.

NOTE This chapter won't teach you how to program; its sole purpose is to show you how to set up Dreamweaver to work with dynamic websites. If you're interested in getting started with server-side programming, PHP is a very popular first step. Facebook and the popular blogging system WordPress use PHP. A good place to start learning the language is with *PHP Solutions: Dynamic Web Design Made Easy* (friendsofED) by David Powers or *Head First PHP & MySQL* (O'Reilly Media) by Lynn Beighley and Michael Morrison.

FREQUENTLY ASKED QUESTION

What Happened to Dreamweaver's Server-Side Tools?

I own a previous version of this book, which included tutorials for building database-driven websites with Dreamweaver. Where did they go?

It's true that Dreamweaver used to provide tools for connecting to a database, adding and retrieving information from that database, password-protecting pages, and a lot more. Unfortunately, those tools, called "server behaviors," were left stagnant for several versions of the program. Adobe didn't update them and the code the program produced was

just plain unprofessional. As of Dreamweaver CC, Adobe has finally removed the server behaviors altogether.

Even if that weren't the case, it's been best to steer clear of Dreamweaver's antiquated server behaviors for quite some time now and either learn how to program yourself, or use a pre-programmed content management system like WordPress, Joomla, or Drupal to handle your database needs. Alternatively, you can jump to a third-party solution like WebAssist.com (*http://WebAssist.com*), which sells its own set of PHP server behaviors.

■ Pieces of the Puzzle

Dynamic websites are more complex than simple static sites. Static sites require only the computer you use to build your pages and a web server to dish them out. In fact, as you can see by previewing your site with a browser on your own computer, you don't even need a web server to effectively view a static website.

Dynamic web pages, by contrast, require more horsepower and a mix of technologies (see Figure 22-2). Not only is there a web server that handles requests for web pages, but you need two other types of servers, an *application server* and a *database server*.

You'll still use a lot of HTML (and CSS) in building a dynamic site—for example, to provide the page layout, add banner graphics, and display navigation bars. But you'll augment that mix with some form of programming code. The application server processes that code, often retrieving information from the database server, and then it sends a completed HTML page to the web server, which, in turn, sends that page to your site's visitor.

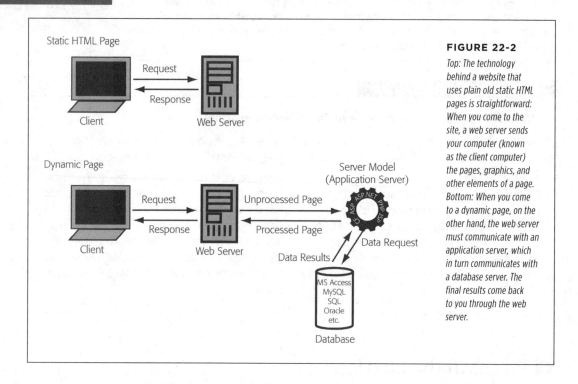

FIGURE 22-2

Top: The technology behind a website that uses plain old static HTML pages is straightforward: When you come to the site, a web server sends your computer (known as the client computer) the pages, graphics, and other elements of a page. Bottom: When you come to a dynamic page, on the other hand, the web server must communicate with an application server, which in turn communicates with a database server. The final results come back to you through the web server.

NOTE When you talk about websites, a *server* refers to the software that dishes out particular types of information—web pages, database results, or a program's output. It doesn't necessarily mean a separate computer; web hosting firms can (and frequently do) have web, database, and application servers all running happily together on a single machine.

Because dynamic websites always coordinate the work of these servers, you can't just open dynamic site pages in your browser as you build them, as you can with a regular web page. You have to view dynamic pages through a web server that has an appropriate application server running. You may also have to set up a database, and connect that database to your application server.

Although this arrangement can be quite complex, it's not difficult to set up a basic web server, application server, and database on your own computer so you can build and test database-driven web pages. It's also easy to connect to remote computers that are already configured to serve up dynamic, database-driven pages.

NOTE The term *web application* refers to web pages that work together to complete a task. All the various pages that make up an online shopping site—pages that let you search a database of products, view individual product pages, and add products to a shopping cart, for example—are collectively considered a web application.

■ Dynamic Websites: The Setup

Now that your head is spinning and you're considering some noble career alternative like farmer, firefighter, or carpenter, it's time to set up Dreamweaver to work with an application server and database.

You can configure your setup several ways. One involves using what Dreamweaver calls a *testing server*. Remember how you can create a website on your own computer (called a *local site*) before posting it online for all to see (the *remote site*)? Here, the concept is similar. When you build web applications, it's a good idea to keep all your work-in-progress pages on your own computer, just as you did when you created static pages. After all, you don't want to fill up an online database with test data, or put half-finished product pages on the Internet. But because dynamic websites require an application server and database to work, you need to set up a *testing server* to store and preview your dynamic pages—a real web server, an application server, and a database, in other words—all running on the same machine, your own computer.

Then, when you finish building your site, you transfer those pages to your remote site using Dreamweaver's built-in FTP feature (see Chapter 18). If you work in a group setting with other web developers, you can set up the testing server on a machine that's part of your group's local network. Each developer can then connect to the testing server and retrieve files to work on. (Dreamweaver's Check In/Check Out feature, described on page 785, is ideal for this type of environment.)

> **NOTE** You can always use your remote site as a testing server. If you go this route, you should have a fast Internet connection. Otherwise, testing your dynamic pages may just test your patience, as you constantly upload pages to the server for testing.
>
> Finally, whenever you work on dynamic files directly on a remote server, be aware that mistakes you make along the way may affect a database that *other* dynamic pages use. If, while hurriedly trying to complete your website, you accidentally create a page that deletes records from your database, important information may no longer be available on your site. So whenever possible, keep your testing server separate from the server that stores your finished and perfected site.

Setting Up a Testing Server

If you want to set up your own local testing server and are new to server-side programming, start with AMP, which stands for Apache, MySQL, and PHP. This is the most common trio of web server, database server, and application server; you'll find AMP at almost all hosting companies, and it's a great foundation for server-side programming. Even better, it's easy to set up on both Windows and Mac PCs.

■ WINDOWS

For Windows, WAMP is a simple installer that puts Apache, MySQL, and PHP on your computer. It's free and works with Windows 7 and 8, Windows Vista, and Windows XP. You can find it at *www.wampserver.com/en*. Because the software changes somewhat frequently, you'll find instructions that match changes to the WAMP installer at *www.uptospeedguides.com/wamp*.

■ MACS

For the Mac, MAMP provides a simple way to get Apache, MySQL, and PHP up and running. MAMP is free and available from *www.mamp.info*. The MAMP software changes (as does its website) frequently, so make sure you get the most up-to-date directions at *www.uptospeedguides.com/mamp*.

If you plan to follow along with the tutorials in this section of the book, download and install WAMP or MAMP now.

Localhost and the Local Site Root Folder

If you followed the previous instructions and installed a testing server on your computer, you've already visited a web page at either *http://localhost/* or *http://localhost/MAMP* (the home pages for WAMP and MAMP, respectively). You may be wondering, what's this *localhost* thing? For a computer, "localhost" is just another way of saying "me." When you instruct a browser to go to *http://localhost*, you're merely telling it to look for a web server that's running on the same computer as it is. Normally, when you visit a website, you type a web address like *http://www.google.com*. That sends your browser out over the Internet looking for a web page located on some computer identified as *www.google.com*. When you set up a web server on your own computer and you want to view the web pages you created there, your browser need look no further than your own system and *its* web server, a.k.a. that testing server you set up earlier.

But once the browser asks your local testing server for a web page, where does the server find that page on your computer? When you work with static web pages (like the ones you built earlier in this book), you can keep your website files pretty much anywhere you want: on your desktop, in your Documents folder, on an external hard drive, and so on.

Dynamic pages, on the other hand, work only with the help of a web server and its companions, the application and database servers. Because it has to coordinate the work of these machines, the web server expects files for a website to reside in a particular location on your computer. That folder is called the *site root* folder (you may also hear it referred to as the *document root* folder). The exact name and location of the site root folder varies from web hosting company to web hosting company, which might name the folder *htdocs, webdocs,* or *public_html*. WAMP uses a folder named *www* as the site root (*C:\WAMP\www*, for example), while MAMP uses a folder called *htdocs*; head over to Applications→MAMP→htdocs.

In the case of WAMP, if you type *http://localhost/my_page.html* into your browser, the browser requests a file named *my_page.html* from the web server running on your computer. The server then looks inside *C:\Program Files\WAMP\www* for a file named *my_page.html*; if it finds it, the server sends the file back to the browser. On a Mac running MAMP, the web server looks in Applications→MAMP→htdocs for the file *my_page.html*.

NOTE If you don't specify a particular file—for example, if you just surf to http://localhost/—the web server looks for a "default file," usually named *index.html* or *index.php*.

Remember, when you work on a dynamic, database-driven site, you need to keep your website files inside the site root folder of your testing server.

NOTE You can also put your site files in a folder *inside* the site root folder. If you placed a folder named *store* in the *www (WAMP)* or *htdocs (MAMP)* folder, you could visit a web page named *products.php* inside that folder by browsing to *http://localhost/store/products.php*.

In addition, as you build more and more dynamic sites, you might want to have separate folder names for each one. For example, you could put the site files for clientX in a folder named *clientX* inside the *www* or *htdocs* folder. Then you could test that client's web pages by typing *http://localhost/clientX/* into a browser.

More elegantly, you could have separate local sites for each client. That way, you can type a URL as simple as *http://clientX* into a web browser and your local server would find the files just for that one client. MAMP users can do with MAMP Pro ($59 and worth every penny), which easily lets you create and manage separate websites on the same server.

Setting Up Dreamweaver

After you set up a testing server on your computer, the next step (as with any site you work on in Dreamweaver) is setting up a website on your machine. The process of setting up a dynamic site, however, is slightly different from that for a static site:

1. **Start Dreamweaver, and then choose Site→New Site.**

   The Site Setup window opens (see Figure 22-3). You need to give this new site a name and tell Dreamweaver where to find the site files.

2. **Name the site in the Site Name box.**

   Use any name you like, it only shows up in Dreamweaver's Files panel. (This is the same step as described on page 19.)

3. **In the next box, click the folder icon on the far right, and then navigate to and select the folder where you'll store your local files.**

   Again, this is the same step you used to set up a static website; however, if you've set up a local testing environment using a program like MAMP or WAMP (page 885), this folder should match the name of the local root folder associated with the testing server. In the case of WAMP, you'll find that root folder at *C:\WAMP\www*; MAMP puts it in Applications→MAMP→htdocs. (If you installed Apache yourself, or used a program other than WAMP or MAMP, your local root folder will be elsewhere on your system; refer to the program's website to see where it creates local root folders.)

   You just told Dreamweaver the name you want to use for the new site and selected the local site's folder.

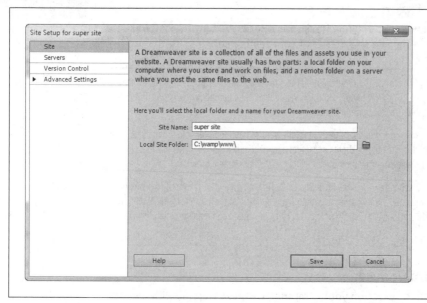

FIGURE 22-3

Setting up a dynamic site starts the same way as setting up a regular, plain old HTML site: Name the site and tell Dreamweaver where to find its files.

4. **Click Servers in the left-hand list of categories (see Figure 22-4).**

You use this screen to set up both the remote and the testing servers for your dynamic site. In other words, you use this screen to add FTP information so you can upload your site files to your live web server (as described on page 776), *and* you use this screen to tell Dreamweaver where your local testing server resides.

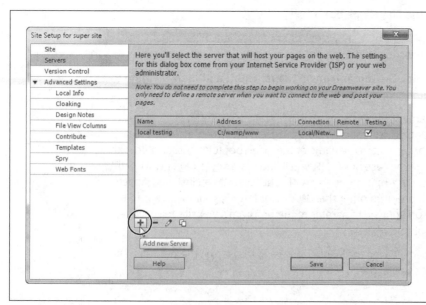

FIGURE 22-4

Dreamweaver lets you add more than one server to a site, crucial if you're building a dynamic site. Dynamic sites, just like static websites, need a regular old web server on the Internet, and you have to tell Dreamweaver how to connect to it via FTP (discussed in Chapter 18). In addition to that, dynamic sites need a testing server, and you have to give Dreamweaver the connection details for that as well.

5. **Click the Add New Server button (the + sign button, circled in Figure 22-4).**

The Basic server settings window appears (see Figure 22-5). Here, you tell Dreamweaver how to connect to your testing server and where it can find the files for your site.

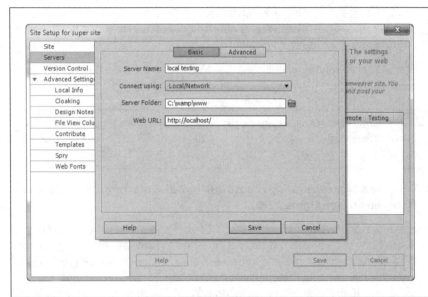

FIGURE 22-5

You want to test your dynamic site locally (on your own computer) before you upload your files to a live server on the Web. To do that, you need to tell Dreamweaver where to find the local testing server. Your setup window should look like this when you're done.

6. **In the Server Name box, type *local testing*.**

It doesn't really matter what you type here—the name just helps you identify your server in the Servers window (Figure 22-4). In this case, use *local testing* since that denotes both a testing server and the fact that it's "local" (on your own computer).

The next step tells Dreamweaver how to connect to that server.

7. **Choose Local/Network from the "Connect using" drop-down menu.**

This is the same window you used to set up connections to both local and remote servers, so even though you're setting up a local site, you'll see options like FTP, SFTP, FTP over SSL/TLS, WebDAV, and RDS here (see page 763 for more on these). Because you're setting up a local testing server, choose Local/Network.

8. **Click the folder icon and select your local site folder (basically the same as step 2).**

If you're using WAMP, the *root* folder is at *C:\WAMP\www*; if you're using MAMP, select Applications→MAMP→htdocs. Next, you need to provide a web address so you can connect to your testing server.

9. **Type *http://localhost/* in the Web URL box.**

Although Dreamweaver asks for a "Web" URL, don't type in the address for your site out on the Web. Dynamic pages only work when you have a web server, and you just set one up, called a testing server, on your own computer. Therefore, you have to tell Dreamweaver to direct a web browser to your own, local, testing server. That way, when you use Dreamweaver's File→Preview in Browser command, Dreamweaver opens a browser and tells it to find the page on the web server at *http://localhost/*.

The Site Setup window should now look like the one in Figure 22-5. Lastly, you'll tell Dreamweaver that you want to create PHP pages.

NOTE If you run MAMP and can't change the port Apache uses as described in the MAMP setup instructions at *www.uptospeedguides.com/mamp/*, you need to add the port number 8888 to the URL, like this: *http://localhost:8888/*.

---

10. **Click the Advanced tab and choose PHP MySQL from the drop-down Server Model menu (see Figure 22-6).**

This lets Dreamweaver know the type of web pages you'll create. (This step doesn't do much else, but it does ensure that Dreamweaver adds the proper file extension when you create a new file. For example, if you select PHP MySQL from this list, Dreamweaver appends ".php" to new-page filenames. If you're using a language that Dreamweaver doesn't list, like Ruby on Rails, you can still use Dreamweaver to edit those files; Live view still displays the site, and you can still preview it by using a web browser to launch it from your local testing server.

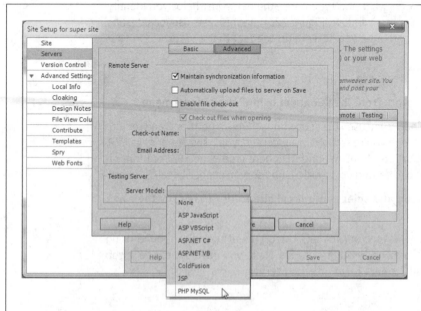

FIGURE 22-6

The Advanced server settings in the Site Setup window let you choose options related to your live web server (they're listed under "Remote server"), and pick the server model you'll use when you build your web pages. These options only come into play when you build a new, blank web page— Dreamweaver creates a file with the correct file extension (.aspx or .jsp, for example), but that's about it.

11. **Click the Save button. In the Site Setup window, turn off the Remote check-box and then turn on the Testing checkbox (see Figure 22-4).**

The last step identifies this as your testing server. When Dreamweaver previews your pages in a browser, it loads the pages from this server. You're just about done.

NOTE If you forget to turn on the Testing checkbox as described in step 11, Dreamweaver pops up an error message when you try to use the Preview in Browser command with a PHP page. It tells you that you need to set up a testing server first and gives you the option to go to the Site Setup window. If you see this message, click Yes, and then just turn on the Testing checkbox for the appropriate server.

---

12. **Click Save to save the new site.**

Whew! That took a few steps, but you've successfully set up a local site so you can build and view dynamic pages. You're now ready to start *creating* those pages.

■ Creating a Dynamic Page

Once you set up an application server and a database server, you're ready to connect to a database, retrieve information, and display it on a web page.

You already know how to handle the first step: Design an HTML page to display the database information (Chapter 10). Dynamic pages differ from regular HTML pages in a couple of ways. For starters, the name of a dynamic file doesn't end with .html. Depending on which server model you use, dynamic pages end in .php (for PHP pages), .asp (ASP), .aspx (.NET), or .cfm or cfml (ColdFusion). The file extension you use is important: A web server uses it to identify the type of page you're requesting. If a server gets a request for an .html file, it simply finds it and sends it to the web browser. But if it gets a request for a page that ends in, say, .php, it sends the page to the application server to sort out all the messy programming.

The good news is that the basic process of creating a new, blank, dynamic page is the same as creating your standard HTML page:

- Choose File→New to open the New Document window. Select the Blank Page category; from the Page Type list, choose a dynamic page type (PHP, for example). From the Layout list, choose a layout (or *<none>* if you wish to start with a fresh, blank page), and then click the Create button.

  When you save the file, Dreamweaver automatically adds the proper extension: .asp for ASP pages, .cfm for ColdFusion, or .php for PHP pages.

NOTE When you create a new page from the New Document window, Dreamweaver lets you select many different types of dynamic pages, including JSP, ASP.NET, and ASP JavaScript.

- Or, more simply, right-click (Control-click) in the Site panel and choose New File from the shortcut menu. Dreamweaver creates a file in the correct server model format, with the proper extension.

NOTE For ASP pages, just renaming a file in the Site panel (from *about.html* to *about.asp*, for example) does *not* give the file the code necessary to apply the correct server model to the page. However, PHP and ColdFusion pages don't start life with any special code in them, so you could start with an .html page, change the extension to .php, and then add PHP programming.

Once you create a blank page, you can use any of the page-building tools described in this book—Cascading Style Sheets, JavaScript, Library items, and so on—to design it. Even though the file is officially a PHP page (or an ASP or ColdFusion page), it still contains lots of HTML. Unlike a plain-vanilla HTML page, though, this one can also contain server-side programming that lets the page communicate with a database.

Finally, you can edit your newly created page in Design view, Split view, or Code view, but to add server-side programming, you need to switch to Code view.

■ Using Server-Side Includes

Even if you don't want to dive into the weird (but wonderful) world of server-side programming, you can take advantage of one timesaving featured that dynamic web pages offer: server-side includes (SSIs). SSIs are like the Dreamweaver Library items discussed in Chapter 19; they're individual files with code that you can reuse on pages throughout a site. They're great for banners, footers, copyright notices, sidebars, and other chunks of HTML. For example, you might use the same banner (logo, navigation bar, search box, and so on) at the top of each page. Instead of replicating that HTML over and over again, you can store it in a single file and "include" that file on your site's pages.

The advantage to this approach is that if you need to change anything on the banner, you open its file, make the change, save it, upload it to your web server, and voilà, your entire site is updated. Server-side includes actually make site updates easier than Library items. As you can read on page 893, when you make a change to a Library item, Dreamweaver has to update all the relevant pages on your site: Granted, that process is fast and automated, but it still requires that you upload all the changed files to your web server—and if the Library item appears on 10,000 pages, you have to update and upload 10,000 pages! That takes time.

Web servers incorporate server-side includes into a web page on the fly, when a visitor requests the page. That means that you can update your entire site just by changing and uploading the Include file: Now that's fast and efficient!

With SSIs, the web server acts like an automated copy-and-paste machine. Say your home page includes an SSI that holds the HTML for the page's banner. When someone requests that page, the web server opens the file (*index.php*, for example), sees the SSI for the banner, opens the banner file (*banner.php*, for example), copies its code, pastes it into the home page, and then sends the just-constructed page to your visitor. If the guest goes to another page on the site, the server again copies the banner code and pastes it into the newly requested page. While all this repeated copying and pasting might sound inefficient, servers are fast—so fast that the use of server-side includes are extremely common on the Web.

Creating a Server-Side Include

SSIs are simply text files that contain programming code, HTML, or both. They can be as simple as a paragraph of text with a copyright notice, or as complex as the programming required to retrieve information from a database with no HTML at all. Generally, SSI filenames end in the extension of the programming language you're using (.php, for example). In addition, since the SSI gets added to a web page, it shouldn't include the elements of a complete HTML file. In other words, just like a Dreamweaver Library item, the SSI should contain no doctype, <head> tag, or style sheet: It's just a text file that's empty, save for the content you wish to appear on a page.

Here's a simple way to create an SSI:

1. **Choose File→New.**

   Dreamweaver opens the New Document window.

2. **Click Blank Page in the left-hand list of categories, choose a page type that matches your programming language (PHP, for example), and then click Create.**

   Dreamweaver creates a new blank page. However, it's full of the usual scaffolding that web pages require, including a doctype and <html>, <head>, and <body> tags. You don't need (or want) any of that for the small snippet of HTML you'll add to the Include.

3. **Click the Code or Split view button in the Document toolbar, position your cursor in Code view, and then select and delete all the text.**

   For example, choose Edit→Select All, and then Edit→Cut. Now that you have a truly empty page, you can save it.

4. **Choose File→Save, and use the extension that matches your programming language.**

   For example, save the file as *banner.php*.

TIP One common practice among web developers is to include both .inc *and* the programming-language extension in the file name: for example, *banner.inc.php*. The .inc in the middle makes it clear that the file is an Include.

---

5. Add content to the Server-Side Include.

You can switch to Design view for this task and use tools you're already familiar with, such as the Insert bar, to add HTML. Note, however, that you can't add styles to the Include file—the SSI is just *part* of a complete web page, so you need to add any styles you want to the page itself. However, if you use Dreamweaver's Design Time Style Sheet feature (page 397), you can overcome this limitation; it "tricks" Dreamweaver into thinking that the SSI actually does have a style sheet attached to it, and you can edit the styles.

NOTE When you add links or images to an SSI, always use root-relative paths (see page 170). An SSI is simply copied and pasted by the server into other files on your site. If the server pastes the SSI into a file that's within a folder or subfolder of your site, a document-relative path probably won't work when the SSI gets pasted into the page.

Adding a Server-Side Include to a Web Page

Once you create an SSI, you can add it to any dynamic page on your site; that is, any page that ends in .php or another server-side programming extension.

1. Open the page you wish to add the SSI to.

This page must end in .php (or .asp or .cfm). They have to be dynamic pages, because you're about to add some "call-and-response" code to them.

2. Click the spot in the page where you want to insert the SSI.

While you can do this in Design view, it's usually less error-prone to do it in Code view. For example, it's easy in Design view to add an SSI within a page's <p> tag, and if the SSI includes divs, headers, or other block-level HTML, you'll generate invalid HTML.

Say you create an SSI banner for your site. To add it to a page, you'd go into Code view and place the cursor just after the opening <body> tag. Alternatively, if you want to insert a footer SSI (like a copyright notice or contact information), click just before the closing </body> tag.

3. Choose Insert→PHP→Include. (ASP command: ASP→Insert→Include. Cold-fusion command: Insert→Coldfusion→CFINCLUDE.)

If you aren't already in Code view, Dreamweaver changes to Split view. It writes the code for a Server-Side Include, positioning your cursor between quotation marks—the spot where you need to identify the Include file. For example, the PHP code looks like this:

```
<?php include(""); ?>
```

4. Type in the name of the file you want to include.

Dreamweaver adds the necessary code to attach the SSI. For example, in PHP it will look something like this:

```
<?php include("banner.php"); ?>
```

If the SSI contains any HTML, Dreamweaver displays it in Design view so you can see your full-fledged page. (You won't, however, see the results that any server-side programming should produce, such as fulfilling a database request.)

You can continue to use the SSI on additional pages on your site. You can even use it in Dreamweaver templates (Chapter 20), thereby combining two time-saving features.

NOTE When you add a Server-Side Include to a page, make sure you use a document-relative path (see page 170).

■ Working with Related PHP Files

As discussed on page 332, Dreamweaver provides a special toolbar for identifying files associated with a web page, such as an external style sheet or a JavaScript file. This Related Files toolbar not only shows you which files have been added to a page, but, with just a click of the mouse, it lets you jump directly to the code for that file. Dreamweaver considers Server-Side Includes "related files" too, so you can easily edit an SSI by clicking its name in the toolbar.

In fact, server-side programming often involves adding lots of files to a page: files for connecting to a database server, for running a database query, for sending email, and more. For example, the popular blogging system WordPress uses a single file, *index.php*, to control an entire blog—this one file manages every one of the blog's pages, from the home page to a category page to a single blog post. To do this, the *index.php* file includes tons (really, a *lot*) of other PHP files. If you're using a program other than Dreamweaver, the only way to edit a WordPress site is to open each file individually. Dreamweaver, however, can "discover" related PHP files and display them in the Related Files toolbar for easy access. To take advantage of this important feature, you need to follow a few steps:

1. **Open a PHP file.**

   If you used the Insert Server-Side Include command discussed previously, Dreamweaver automatically sees these PHP files and displays them in the Related Files toolbar with no further effort on your part. But you might also include PHP files within *other* Include files. In cases like that, you need to tell Dreamweaver to "discover" them.

2. **Click the Discover link in the information toolbar in the document window (see Figure 22-7, top).**

   Dreamweaver finds all the PHP files the currently open dynamic page uses. That may be just a few files or, in the case of complex PHP applications like WordPress, quite a few. For example, you can see that the Related Files toolbar in the bottom image in Figure 22-7 is chock-full of filenames.

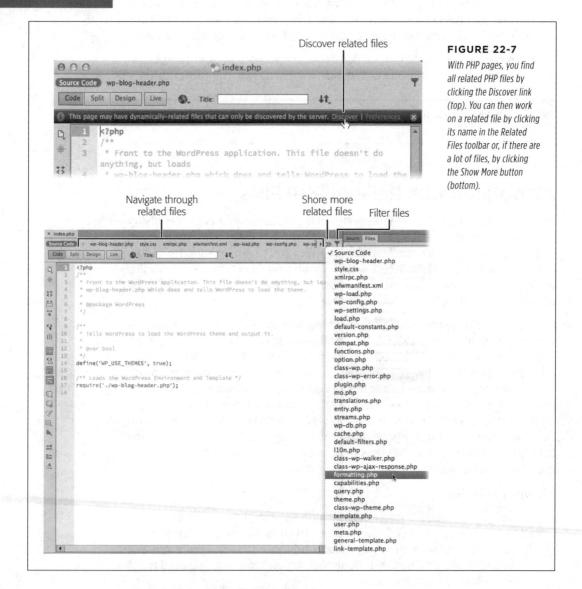

FIGURE 22-7

With PHP pages, you find all related PHP files by clicking the Discover link (top). You can then work on a related file by clicking its name in the Related Files toolbar or, if there are a lot of files, by clicking the Show More button (bottom).

3. **Select a related file to work on.**

   Once Dreamweaver discovers all related PHP files, you can use the Related Files toolbar as you normally would to open a file. If there are a lot of files, as is the case with WordPress, navigate through the list by clicking the left and right arrow buttons, or click the Show More button to see a drop-down menu of all the files. Select a name from that list to open the file in Code view.

4. **Filter the list if necessary.**

   You may not want to see or work on some of the files Dreamweaver discovers. For example, in the case of WordPress, you won't want to touch most of the discovered files because they're part of the core WordPress program and editing them might break your blog.

   Fortunately, you can see just the files you want. The Filter button in the top-right corner of the Related Files toolbar lets you filter files a couple of ways: First, you can filter by file type, meaning you can show or hide JavaScript, CSS, or PHP files, along with any other file type your web page references. By default, Dreamweaver selects all the file types, so to hide one, click the Filter button, and then click the relevant extension (.cuss, .php, .js, and so on). To show those file types later, select them again from the Filter menu.

   You can also create a custom filter. Click the Filter button, choose Custom Filter, and Dreamweaver displays a dialog box. Type in the filenames and/or file types you want to see. For example, with WordPress, you're interested in editing the PHP theme files—the ones WordPress uses to create your blog's look. To show the relevant files, enter their names separated by a semicolon, like this: *index. php*; *footer.php*; *header.php*, and so on. You can also filter by file type. To show all JavaScript files plus *index.php*, *footer.php*, and *header.php*, type this in the Related Files toolbar: *index.php; footer.php; header.php; .js*.

   When you're done, click OK to close the Custom Filter window. Now, in the Related Files toolbar, Dreamweaver displays only the files you specified.

> **NOTE** Custom filters are useful but, unfortunately, Dreamweaver doesn't remember a custom filter, so once you close a file, that filter is lost and you have to recreate it the next time you want to use it. In addition, you can't filter by folder—you can filter all PHP files within a particular folder only—although that would be really helpful when you work with certain CMS systems, like WordPress, which keep files related to the design of the site in one particular folder. Maybe next time.

■ PHP Code Hints

Dreamweaver includes advanced code hints for the PHP language, but not for other server-side technologies, like .NET, ColdFusion, Java Server Pages, and Ruby on Rails. Not only does Dreamweaver support code-hinting for built-in PHP functions, it also makes note of variables, functions, and classes you create (see Figure 22-8).

Since it's common for programmers to create multiple PHP files and then add them all to (or include them all in) a master file, Dreamweaver CC searches all the files referenced in the current working file and analyzes them. Then, as you type more PHP code, Dreamweaver displays code hints based on the names of the variables, functions, and classes you defined in those files. In other words, Dreamweaver personalizes its code hints for your site and for the PHP programming you added to it. Pretty nice.

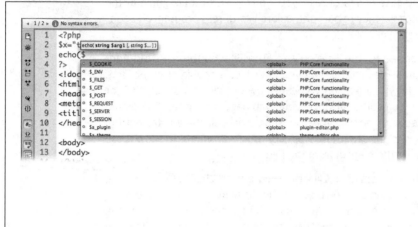

FIGURE 22-8

Dreamweaver is pretty unforgiving of syntax errors (typos or missing punctuation) in PHP code. Most of the time, you start typing PHP code and Dreamweaver displays a yellow "there is a syntax error" bar along with a red mark at the point it thinks you made an error. Don't worry, this happens a lot as you program; the important thing is that, once you finish, there're no syntax error messages left. If there are, you probably left off a closing), },', or ".

In addition, since many PHP frameworks, like CakePHP and Zend; and many PHP-based content management systems (CMSes), like WordPress, Joomla, and Drupal; rely on many separate PHP files, Dreamweaver includes something called site-specific code hints. It lets you identify which folders Dreamweaver scans to create its code hints for your site, but, alas, it comes with a hitch: It offers hints for PHP-based sites only.

Dreamweaver's site-specific code hints have a few benefits. First, if you often include PHP files outside the root folder (for example, the Zend framework keeps its include files outside the web-accessible root folder), you can tell Dreamweaver to scan the folder above the current local root folder. Second, many CMS systems and PHP frameworks use tons of files with tons of variables, functions, and class names. Sites like these use the files internally, in the programming that drives the systems. You, as a programmer, don't ever need to see most of them, and you certainly don't want their elements cluttering up your code-hint window. By specifying a scan folder, you pare down that number.

You can turn site-specific code hints on by choosing Site→Site-Specific Code Hints. This opens a new window (see Figure 22-9). If you're using either WordPress, Joomla, or Drupal, you can select your environment from the top Structure menu, and Dreamweaver automatically identifies the proper folders, files, and paths. Click OK and you're done.

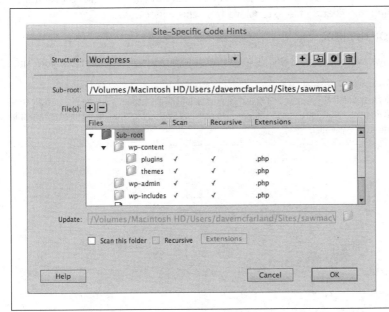

FIGURE 22-9

To add to Dreamweaver's Code Hint feature the function names, class names, and variable names you use in your site's PHP, choose Site→Site-Specific Code Hints and then tell Dreamweaver which files and folders to scan.

If, however, you're using a PHP framework or some other PHP CMS, you need to tell Dreamweaver which folders to analyze by following these steps:

1. **Identify the folder that has your site and all the PHP files you want Dreamweaver to scan by clicking the folder icon and selecting a folder.**

   If you don't have any PHP files outside your local root folder, you can skip this step because Dreamweaver automatically selects the local root folder. However, you may have PHP files one level up from the local folder. In this case, click the folder icon and then select the folder one level up that contains both the PHP files you want to scan and your local site root.

2. **Click the + sign button.**

   The Add File/Folder window appears. You can click another icon to select either one particular PHP file or to select a folder's worth of PHP files. If you pick a folder, turn on the checkbox labeled Recursive if you want Dreamweaver to scan the files in subfolders within this main folder. You can ensure that Dreamweaver searches only .php files by clicking the + sign button to the right of the Extensions label and then typing in *.php*. Dreamweaver won't look through any other file types and, as a result, it displays code hints faster. However, if you do use other extensions for your PHP files, such as .inc, make sure to add those extensions as well. To add another extension, click the + sign button next to the word Extension. A new line appears in the extension pane where you type in the extension.

You can prevent Dreamweaver from scanning a folder you added from the main Site-Specific Code Hints window, too. Select the folder from the Files list and then turn off the "Scan this folder" checkbox. You can also turn off recursive scanning and change file extensions from this window.

3. **Click OK to finish.**

Dreamweaver scans the selected files and creates a list of code hints for your site.

NOTE You may find that Dreamweaver doesn't always automatically pop up a box for site-specific code hints as it does for regular PHP functions. You may need to coax Dreamweaver into displaying them by using the keyboard shortcut Ctrl + Spacebar.

Appendixes

Getting Help

H ard as it may be to believe, even a book as voluminous as this one may not answer all your questions about Dreamweaver. Fortunately, a range of other resources awaits you when a feature's giving you trouble.

■ Getting Online Help

Adobe puts all its resources for Dreamweaver help on its support site, so you need an Internet connection to use it. Articles, videos, tutorials, and discussions abound, so Adobe gives you several ways to navigate its help system, depending on what you're looking for.

You can get to all these resources right from Dreamweaver's Help command (Dreamweaver menu bar→Help), and, in some cases, from the Welcome Screen (page 35). In fact, you may have seen some of them already.

Dreamweaver Help

The Dreamweaver support page links you to all of Adobe's help and account management tools. You can search a vast database of technical notes (short articles on specific Dreamweaver problems) that just may hold the answer you seek, find tutorials on getting started with Dreamweaver, see a list of top Dreamweaver issues (and their solutions), and review a list of the most recent Dreamweaver technical notes. You can get to this page three ways:

- On the Welcome Screen, click Resources in the lower-left corner.

- Choose Help→Dreamweaver Support Center (the *second* option under the Help menu).

- Go to *www.adobe.com/support/dreamweaver.*

NOTE The first Help menu option (Help→Dreamweaver Help), takes you to a page with detailed help articles.

All these roads lead to the web page shown in Figure A-1. It looks like a rather boring page full of links, so the trick is to know what you're looking for.

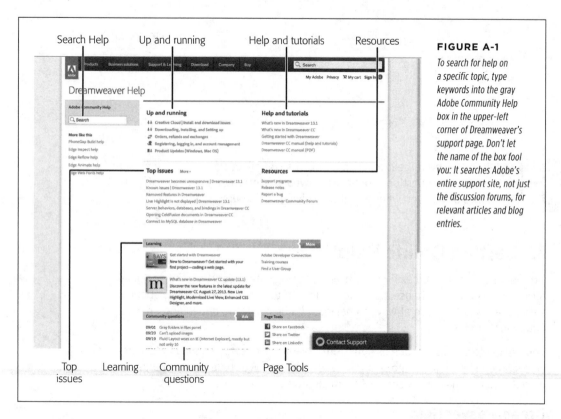

FIGURE A-1

To search for help on a specific topic, type keywords into the gray Adobe Community Help box in the upper-left corner of Dreamweaver's support page. Don't let the name of the box fool you: It searches Adobe's entire support site, not just the discussion forums, for relevant articles and blog entries.

- **Up and running.** The links in this section handle housekeeping chores. They don't help you *use* Dreamweaver, but they let you track product orders, get installation instructions, and manage your Adobe account. You can also check for the latest software updates and fixes.

- **Help and tutorials.** These innocent-looking links take you to pages packed with Dreamweaver savvy. If you need information and need it fast, look here first.

— **What's new in Dreamweaver 13.1.** A quick list of features added in the most recent incremental update to the program. If something looks different since the last time you updated (page xviii), check here to see what's up.

— **What's new in Dreamweaver CC.** This page gives you an illustrated tour of the *major* Dreamweaver features added since the previous version of the program (Dreamweaver CS6 in this case). (The previous link cited *incremental* changes to Dreamweaver.)

— **Getting started with Dreamweaver.** Opens the Beginners Cookbook, a set of articles on how to set up and begin using Dreamweaver. (This is the same page you come to when you click the Getting Started link at the bottom of Dreamweaver's Welcome Screen.)

— **Dreamweaver CC manual (help and tutorials).** Now things get interesting, and it's a bit of mystery why this important link is buried so deeply. It takes you to Dreamweaver's main tutorial page—Help and Tutorials—described in detail in the next section.

— **Dreamweaver CC manual (PDF).** As the name says, this link gives you a PDF copy of the Dreamweaver tutorials described on page 904. Depending on your setup, the PDF may open in your browser window or download and launch itself directly on your computer. You can read it on-screen or print it out to create your own 700-page guidebook!

• **Top issues.** These links cover specific Dreamweaver issues—and their solutions—covered in Adobe's Dreamweaver knowledge base. The More link reveals a full list of the most common problems.

• **Resources.** This list includes a few resources not covered in the help sections above—Adobe's for-pay support plans, a bug report form, and a link to the discussion boards.

■ LEARNING

The primary links in this section—Get Started with Dreamweaver and What's New in Dreamweaver CC Update (13.1)—are actually portholes to Adobe TV (page 908), where Dreamweaver experts walk you step-by-step through projects like starting a new web page, creating a navigation bar, and so on.

The Adobe Developer Connection link takes you to a website called Dreamweaver Developer Center, which offers similar tutorials.

TIP The "Find a User Group" link leads to *http://groups.adobe.com*, which lists Adobe-hosted online communities of folks interested in learning more about Dreamweaver and other Adobe products.

■ **COMMUNITY QUESTIONS**

This section lists some of the hottest discussions going on in the Adobe community forums (page 909). To go directly to the Forums intro page, where you can type a new question, click the Ask button at right.

■ **PAGE TOOLS**

You can bookmark, print, or share this page on social media. (Hey, not *every* Facebook post should be a picture of your cute cat.)

■ **CONTACT SUPPORT**

If you can't find what you need from the copious set of links above, Adobe gives you one more route to help on all its support pages—the Contact Support button in the lower-right corner. Click it and a little box pops up, full of housekeeping links to pages for subscription information, account management, software downloads, and product manuals. Click the How-To's button here and then choose a program (Dreamweaver is one of many options), and you get a list of links to general help pages like FAQs, the program's catalog page, and so on.

You also get a set of three buttons along the bottom of the Contact Support box, labeled Ask an Expert, Chat, and Phone (Figure A-2). The first button connects you to the Adobe forums. The Chat button prompts you for a description of your problem and then wrangles a support agent to help you. Clicking Phone brings up the same prompts as the Chat button, with the suggestion that you start your search for help by describing the problem. Do that in a sentence or two, click Submit, and you get a case number and a toll-free contact number for a support agent. The call is free if you need help with a product order or installing the program, but if you need to ask a technical question, Adobe charges $39 per call, so check out the free online resources described in this appendix first.

> **NOTE** Adobe no longer offers the for-pay service plans it offered with the Creative Suite set of programs (they had names like Gold and Platinum). If you have an existing plan, it may still be in force, but you can no longer buy these kinds of plans.

Dreamweaver Help and Tutorials (Online Manual)

The Help and Tutorials page is the place to go when you need help with a specific Dreamweaver issue. As with all Help options, you can get there in more than one way:

- Choose Help→Dreamweaver Help.

- Press F1.

- Go to *https://helpx.adobe.com/dreamweaver/topics.html*.

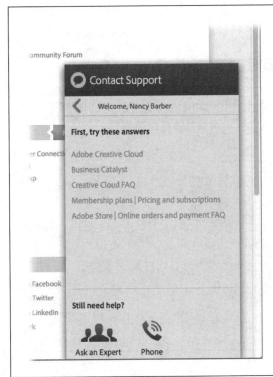

FIGURE A-2

If you prefer person-to-person contact to browsing web pages, the key lies in this unassuming little box. You need to register your copy of Dreamweaver to access the Chat and Phone options, and you may be charged for calls other than order or installation queries.

The top section of this page acts as a table of contents for the rest of the page (see Figure A-3). For example, click "Dreamweaver getting started tutorials" and you scroll down to that section of the page. The links in this section, not surprisingly, go to the Beginners Cookbook resources discussed below (page 908), like a step-by-step tutorial on creating a new web page.

But don't stop at the beginner stuff. This page is your ticket to the critical bits of information you need when you're deep into web-page construction. Click Coding, for example, and you can find out how to debug your HTML or format CSS.

> **TIP** Another option under Dreamweaver's Help menu is Dreamweaver Exchange. Described on page 875, this command launches the Dreamweaver Exchange Classic site, where you can download Dreamweaver extensions, widgets, and other add-ons.

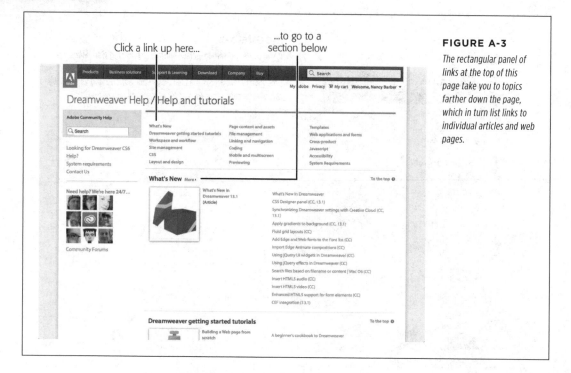

Click a link up here...

...to go to a
section below

FIGURE A-3

*The rectangular panel of
links at the top of this
page take you to topics
farther down the page,
which in turn list links to
individual articles and web
pages.*

Beginner's Cookbook

When you click the Getting Started link at the bottom of Dreamweaver's Welcome Screen, you go to a page called "A beginners cookbook to Dreamweaver." (This is the same page you come to when you click the "Getting started with Dreamweaver" link on the main Help page, described at the beginning of this Appendix.) It offers all sorts of basic help on setting up and using Dreamweaver.

To be honest, if you read the Introduction and Chapter 1 of this book, you won't learn anything new here, but the list of tutorials (Figure A-4), may be worth a peek.

Adobe TV

Why read the book when you can wait for the movie? That's the sort of thinking behind Adobe TV. You may have encountered these videos before—a bunch of them are listed on the Welcome Screen under "Top Features (videos)"—Building Mobile Apps, for example. To see the full assortment of Dreamweaver videos (Figure A-5):

- On the Welcome Screen, click More at the bottom of the "Top Features (videos)" list.

- Go to the Adobe TV page (*http://tv.adobe.com*), click the Products tab in the top bar, and then choose Dreamweaver.

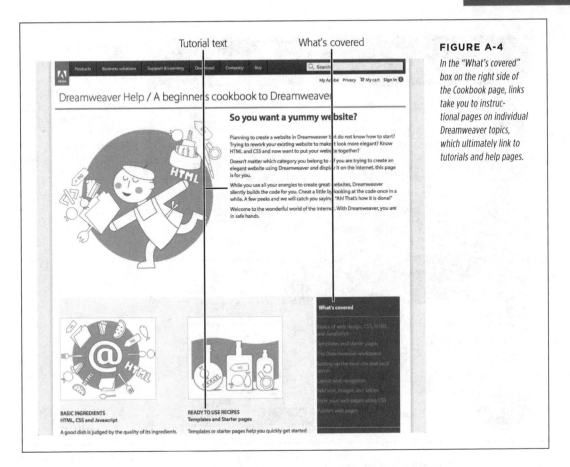

FIGURE A-4

In the "What's covered" box on the right side of the Cookbook page, links take you to instructional pages on individual Dreamweaver topics, which ultimately link to tutorials and help pages.

Some introductory videos are just a couple of minutes long, while in-depth lessons can run 10 minutes or so. And hey, they were made using Adobe tools, so you can count on clear visuals and professional production quality.

Getting Help from Other Dreamweaver Fans

Adobe provides online community forums that offer the free exchange of advice among many helpful souls. Knowledgeable souls, too, including MVPs—Most Valuable Participants. These forum mavens have been recognized by Adobe for their expertise and skill in sorting out Dreamweaver difficulties. In addition, according to Adobe, about 1,000 company employees comb the forums and answer questions.

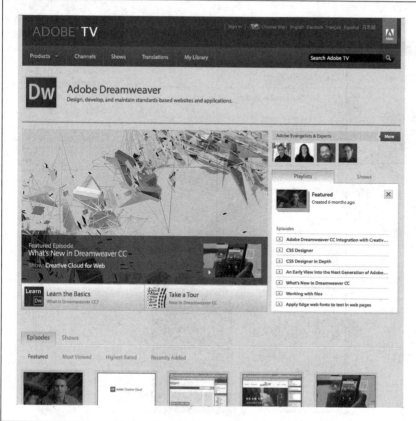

To get to the forums:

- Choose Help→Adobe Online Forums.

- Go to *http://forums.adobe.com/community/dreamweaver.*

The forums are a terrific source of information, offering almost real-time answers on Dreamweaver and related web-design techniques. You can start with the list of Frequently Asked Questions in the middle of the page (Figure A-6), or type a word or two into the "Ask a Question" box at the top of the page or in the Search Community Help box in the far-right column. Both boxes search all the discussions in the Dreamweaver forums.

You can start a new discussion if you have a unique question, but Adobe makes it a bit difficult—they prefer you search existing discussions first. In the gray column on the right, look for the heading Actions and then click "Start a discussion" underneath it.

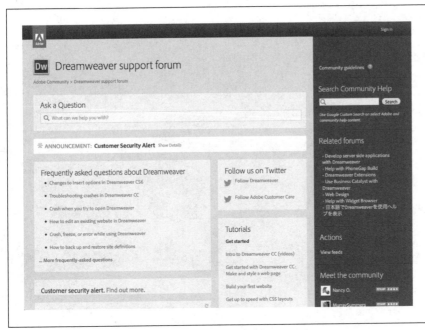

FIGURE A-6

Important announce-ments, like the security alert shown here, appear near the top of the support forum page. Signing in (top-right) gives you more options under Actions, like "Start a new discussion."

Make sure you're signed in to see this option. Click the "Sign in" link at the top-right of the page and then enter your Adobe ID (page 13) and password. If this is your first time logging in, you're asked to create a username to represent your online identity in the forums.

TIP In your travels through Adobe's labyrinth of online help, you may stumble on a page called Adobe Communities (*www.adobe.com/communities*). This catch-all page contains links to the forums and user groups mentioned in this appendix, along with other resources for contacting Dreamweaver experts—or becoming one.

Dreamweaver CC, Menu by Menu

D*reamweaver CC: The Missing Manual* is quite complete; in its pages, you'll find descriptions of every major Dreamweaver function (and most minor ones). In the interest of completeness, however, here's a quick reference to every command in every menu—and the answer to the occasional "What does that mean?" mystery.

■ File Menu

The commands in Dreamweaver's File menu include basic functions like saving and closing files, and controlling an open Dreamweaver document:

- **New.** Opens the New Document window, which lets you create various types of new Dreamweaver files. On the left side, four document categories are listed:

  — **Blank Page.** Creates an empty Dreamweaver document using any of several types of web page, from basic HTML and CSS pages to dynamic pages built on JavaScript and PHP.

  — **Fluid Grid Layout.** This option provides a basic framework for creating a site that works in mobile, tablet, and desktop browsers. Using some pre-packaged CSS and JavaScript, as well as a fancy user interface, you can basically "draw" three layouts—one for smartphones, one for tablets, and one for desktop computers—that use the same content.

  — **Starter Templates.** These templates help you set up web pages destined for mobile devices.

  — **Site Templates.** If you've created your own templates, they show up here.

- **Open.** Launches the standard Open File dialog box so you can navigate to and open a Dreamweaver document. You can set the Enable drop-down menu to display only specific types of documents—just HTML pages or style sheets, for example.

- **Open Recent.** Displays a submenu that lists the 10 most recently opened documents. Selecting a document from the list opens it. The last option in this menu, "Reopen Documents on Startup," is kind of cool. If you quit Dreamweaver with documents still open and have this option turned on, Dreamweaver automatically reopens those documents the next time you launch the program.

- **Close.** Closes the currently open Dreamweaver document. If you have unsaved changes, Dreamweaver gives you the opportunity to save them. This action also closes the files in the Related Files toolbar (see page 332).

- **Close All.** Closes *all* the currently open documents. If you have unsaved changes in any of them, Dreamweaver gives you the opportunity to save them.

- **Save.** Saves any changes you made to your document. Dreamweaver dims the Save command if you haven't made any changes to the document since the last time you saved it.

- **Save As.** As with most other programs, this command saves a copy of the current document under a new name.

- **Save All.** Saves changes to all your open documents, including other web pages, external CSS and JavaScript files, and any files listed in the Related Files toolbar (see page 332). This handy command makes sure all your changes are saved to every document you edited since opening Dreamweaver.

- **Save All Related Files.** Saves changes to the document you're currently editing, as well as files that the current document uses, such as external CSS and Java-Script files, and server-side programs such as PHP Includes. This is a good way to make sure you save every edit that affects the current file, whether you made the change in a CSS file, the HTML source code, or an external JavaScript file.

- **Save as Template.** Saves the current document as a Dreamweaver template with the extension .dwt. The "Save as Template" dialog box appears so you can specify the template's file name, and indicate which site it belongs to. Dreamweaver automatically saves all template documents in a Templates subfolder in the selected site's folder. You'll find templates discussed in Chapter 20.

- **Revert.** Undoes any changes you made to a document since the last time you saved it. Edit→Undo is often a better choice; it takes a few more steps to undo all the changes you made, but it can actually undo changes *past* your last save. So if you're one of those gotta-save-it-every-5-seconds types, the Undo command is for you.

- **Import.** Lets you import data from other sources into your Dreamweaver document. For example, you can import XML data into a template, or tabular data from a CSV (comma separated value) file into an HTML file. Windows users can also import text from a Microsoft Word document or tabular data from an Excel spreadsheet.

- **Export.** Extracts tabular data or template data in XML format from your Dreamweaver document, for use in other applications.

- **Preview in Browser.** Opens the current document in your web browser. By selecting Edit Browser List, you can add new browsers to, or delete browsers from, your browser list, or specify a preferred browser.

- **Validate.** Lets you check XML files to make sure they conform to XML standards and document type definitions. In other words, it checks to make sure your XML is correct. In addition, you can check an HTML file using the W3C's online validator—right from within Dreamweaver. Select the "Validate current document" option and Dreamweaver connects to the Web, contacts the W3C validator, and checks your page's HTML. If it finds errors, it lists them in the W3C validation pane below the Property Inspector. If you're working on a server-side page (like a WordPress page), choose the Validate Live Document option—it first processes a page through a web server and then contacts the W3C site. That way, you're actually checking the finished HTML (after the server has completed all its server-side antics and produced a real HTML file).

- **Compare with Remote/Compare with Testing.** Lets you use a third-party code-comparison tool to see how the local copy of a page differs from either the remote copy (the one on your web server) or the copy on your testing server. It identifies all code differences. You can learn more about this feature on page 343.

- **Design Notes.** Opens the Design Notes window (Chapter 18) to add information about an open document, set its status, and choose to have the Design Note appear whenever you open the document.

NOTE To use Design Notes, make sure you select the Maintain Design Notes option in the Site Definition window's "Design notes" section; see page 795.

- **Exit (Windows only).** Exits Dreamweaver. If any of your open Dreamweaver documents have unsaved changes, the program prompts you to save them before quitting. (Mac users will find a "Quit Dreamweaver" option under the Dreamweaver menu.)

■ Edit Menu

The Edit menu lets you make common changes to your documents, like copying and pasting text:

- **Undo.** Undoes the most recent change you made to your document. Choose this command repeatedly to step progressively backwards through your changes, even *after* you save the document. You can take 50 steps back in time, unless you change Dreamweaver's default in Preferences→General.

- **Redo (Repeat).** Restores whatever changes you just made using the Undo command. Selecting Redo multiple times moves you progressively forward through the changes you made. If you just used a command other than Undo, Repeat appears instead of Redo. This property lets you repeat the last action. For example, if you just pressed Delete, the Repeat command presses it again.

- **Cut.** Deletes the selected text or objects from a document, and copies them to the invisible Windows or Macintosh Clipboard so you can paste them elsewhere. (The Clipboard holds only one selection at a time.)

- **Copy.** Copies the selected text or object to the Clipboard so you paste it elsewhere, without disturbing the original.

- **Paste.** Places the most recent selection from the Clipboard into your document at the insertion point.

- **Paste Special.** Opens the Paste Special window, which lets you choose how to paste a Clipboard item into your document. Options range from Text Only for just plain text to increasingly more elaborate options, which force Dreamweaver to attempt to preserve various kinds of formatting, such as styles, bold text, italic text, bulleted lists, and so on. See page 66.

- **Clear.** Deletes the selected text or object from a document without placing it in the Clipboard.

- **Select All.** Selects everything in a document so you can make document-wide changes in one fell swoop. If you have the cursor inside a table cell or <div> tag, however, Select All selects just the contents of that cell or div.

- **Select Parent Tag.** Broadens the current selection to include everything within its *parent tag*, including the content. For example, if you have a table cell selected, this command increases the selection to include the entire table *row*. Choose the command a second time and you increase the selection to include the entire table. In short, this command ensures that any changes you make apply to the entire tag.

- **Select Child.** Narrows the current selection to include everything within the *child tag*, including its contents. If you select a table row, choosing this command decreases that selection to include only the first table *cell* and its contents.

- **Find and Replace.** Lets you search a document—or an entire site—for a specific word, tag, or piece of source code, and replace it with something different (see Chapter 8). This command lets you make these changes either en masse or one instance at a time.

- **Find Selection.** This command lets you find another instance of the current selection. Say you select the word "mothball" on a page. This command searches the page for another instance of "mothball."

- **Find Again.** Uses the most recent search setting from the Find and Replace window to search the current document, highlighting the next instance of the search item.

- **Live Search (Mac only).** Unlike Find and Replace, this tool works both inside and outside of Design view. It uses OS X's Spotlight search tool to look for text throughout a site. Instead of the Find and Replace dialog box, you type your search terms into a box in the Files panel.

- **Go to Line.** Opens the Go to Line dialog box. Type in a number, and Dreamweaver positions the cursor at the beginning of the specified line of code (available only in Code view).

- **Show Code Hints.** Immediately displays any code hints (overriding the delay set in the Preferences window) available for the current tag. Code hints, described in Chapter 7, provide a drop-down menu of properties appropriate for the current tag (available only in Code view, and only when you use the Insert Tag command Ctrl+T [⌘-T]).

- **Refresh Code Hints.** Doesn't seem to do much of anything.

- **Code Hint Tools.** When you work in Code view, this command lets you access Dreamweaver's color picker, its "Browse for File" button, and its list of fonts so you don't have to type in things like *#FF6633, ../../images/dog.gif*, or *Arial, Helvetica, sans-serif* every time you use a color, link to a file, or want to use a font. In addition, you can display a pop-up menu of all the ID, class, and element names on a page, which you'll find useful for JavaScript programming.

- **Indent Code.** Adds one indent before the selected line of code (available only in Code view).

- **Outdent Code.** Removes one indent from the selected line of code (available only in Code view).

- **Balance Braces.** When you edit a script in Code view, this command helps you check for unbalanced braces (that is, an introductory "{" without a closing "}") by highlighting the matching tags enclosing the selected code. It doesn't do anything for plain HTML, but if you're writing a JavaScript program or using a dynamic programming language like PHP or ASP, it helps identify missing braces—a common source of programming errors. Works with opening and closing parentheses and brackets ([and]) as well.

- **Repeating Entries.** Lets you cut, copy, paste, and delete repeating regions in templates. You can learn about repeating regions in Chapter 20.

- **Code Collapse.** Hides a selection of code in Code view so you see only the code you want to work on. You'll find this feature discussed on page 319, and since the same options are available more directly from the coding toolbar, you can skip this command.

- **Edit with External Editor (Windows).** If you haven't already specified an external HTML code editor, such as BBEdit or Notepad, this command opens the Preferences window and selects the File Types/Editors category so you can find and specify a text editor on your hard drive. Once you do, this command opens the current document in that editor. You can change the editor by going to Edit→Preferences (Dreamweaver→Preferences).

- **Tag Libraries.** Lets you modify the way Dreamweaver writes code for various types of tags, such as those for HTML, PHP, ASP, and ColdFusion. You can create new tag libraries for other types of tag-based languages, or modify the ones that ship with Dreamweaver.

- **Keyboard Shortcuts (Windows).** Opens the Keyboard Shortcuts window, and shows you all of Dreamweaver's current keyboard shortcuts. You can create a new set of shortcuts for specific sites or programs, or export the settings to HTML so you can share your settings with others. (You must duplicate the factory settings before you add or delete your own shortcuts, however.) You'll find details on page 869. (On the Mac, this option appears under the Dreamweaver menu.)

- **Preferences (Windows).** Opens the Preferences window, which is full of options that customize the way Dreamweaver works. You can choose from 19 categories of preferences, including those that let you edit the color and format of HTML tags, create shorthand versions of CSS styles, and change the order in which Dreamweaver's info panels appear on-screen. (On the Mac, this option appears under the Dreamweaver menu.)

■ View Menu

The View menu controls the document window's appearance. A checkmark in the menu lets you know which view you're in:

- **Code.** Displays the file's source code.

- **Split Code.** Displays the file's source code in split view, side by side. You use this feature to edit both the HTML near the top of a page (on one side of the document window), and the HTML elsewhere on the page (on the other side of the Document window.) But it's most useful when you use it in conjunction with Dreamweaver's Related Files feature (page 332). In Split Code view, you can view the HTML of the page in one pane, and the CSS of an external style sheet in the other.

- **Design.** Displays the file's visual design.

- **Code and Design.** Splits the document window into two panes: source code on the left (or top), visual design on the right (or bottom). You can adjust how much of each pane you see by dragging the center divider left or right or up or down.

- **Split Vertically.** When you're in Code and Design view, you see the page's code and its design side by side...great for really wide monitors. Unselecting this option displays the Code and Design views one on top of the other—unless you have an unusually tall monitor, this option doesn't let you see much of either.

- **Design View on Left/Top.** When you're in Code and Design view, this option dictates where Dreamweaver puts the Design view pane relative to the Code view pane. If you select Split Vertically, you can display the Design view either to the right or left of the Code view; when you stack Code and Design views on top of each other, you can place the Design view either above or below the Code view.

- **Switch Views.** Switches your cursor position between Code and Design views... of course, so does just clicking into the code in Code view, or clicking into the design in Design view!

- **Refresh Design View.** Updates the Design view to reflect changes you make directly to the source code in either Code view or Split view.

- **Refresh Styles.** Who knows? You can only select it when viewing a page in Live View, and even then it doesn't seem to do anything.

- **Live View.** Displays a web page as it would appear in a web browser (actually, as it would appear in Apple's Safari or Google's Chrome browser). You can preview JavaScript, Flash movies, and other interactive page features in this view.

- **Live View Options.** Lets you control the display of Live View. You can pause JavaScript—a useful way to see the HTML that JavaScript creates on the fly—disable JavaScript, turn off plug-ins, and control settings that affect how Dreamweaver displays the page in Live View.

- **Live Code.** In Live View, choose this option to display the HTML as it appears to a web browser—useful for pages that include JavaScript that can dynamically change the HTML of a page by adding classes to tags and even inserting or removing entire chunks of HTML. This feature is a good way to make sure the JavaScript code you write does what you want it to do to the HTML of a page. This feature is also good for server-side pages composed of multiple server-side includes (page 892) so you can see, for example, what the HTML looks like for a site using the WordPress content management system (see page 324).

- **Inspect.** This option lets you inspect the CSS of page elements in Live View. Discussed on page 487, this feature is a great way to inspect page styles in dynamically generated server-side pages (such as PHP pages), which you often can't see in Design view.

- **Visual Aids.** Lets you summon on-screen symbols that represent typically invisible page elements, like image maps, anchors, the borders of a <div> tag, and the grid used in the new Fluid Grid Layouts.

- **Style Rendering.** Lets you hide or show the effects of all style sheets on a page.

- **Code View Options.** Lets you adjust the way your HTML appears in Code view. You can turn on (or off) options that wrap lines of text to fit in the document window, add line numbers, highlight invalid HTML, turn on syntax coloring, and indent lines of code.

- **Window Size.** Lets you change the size of the page that Dreamweaver displays in the document window. Best used in conjunction with media queries (Chapter 13) to see how a page looks on different-size screens, such as the 320- x 480-pixel screen of a smartphone.

- **Magnification.** Lets you zoom in, zoom out, and generally magnify your view of the document window. It has no effect on the HTML or how a page displays in a web browser; it merely zooms in to get a close-up view of the page or zooms out to get a bird's eye view.

- **Rulers.** When you choose Show, Dreamweaver displays rulers along the top and left sides of the document window. Using the options you find here, you can choose your ruler units: pixels, inches, or centimeters. You can also reset the orientation of the two rulers so that both start from zero in the screen's upper-left corner.

- **Grid.** Places a grid of vertical and horizontal lines over the document window that you use as a guide to build your layouts. Selecting Edit Grid opens the Grid Settings dialog box, where you can adjust the grid's colors, spacing, behaviors, and line appearance.

- **Guides.** Shows, hides, locks, and erases guidelines you drag from a ruler onto the current page. Also controls options for guides, and displays guidelines that mark the visible area of a browser window for monitors of different resolutions.

- **Tracing Image.** Adjusts the document's background tracing image (page 757). You can load a new tracing image, make a current one visible, or adjust its position.

- **Display External Files.** You can insert images and other files into a page from your own or other websites on the Internet. When you insert an image from another site, you can type in or paste an absolute URL. Dreamweaver even displays the image in Design view, but only if you check this option. Because this feature requires an Internet connection, pages with links to external files may take longer to display in Dreamweaver (since it has to get the images and files from the Web). If you have lots of external images and files and your pages open sluggishly in Dreamweaver, uncheck this option.

- **Hide Panels (Show Panels).** Hides all open panels. If you've already hidden the panels, the command says Show Panels instead; it restores the panels to their original positions.

- **Toolbars.** Displays toolbars for use with Dreamweaver. Select Document from the submenu to display the Document toolbar at the top of the document window. It displays the current page's title and offers common commands, like display options, file-management options, code-navigation options, and browser previews. The Standard toolbar displays buttons for common commands for opening files, closing files, and cutting, copying, and pasting content. The Coding toolbar appears along the left edge of Code view and provides options for working with HTML, JavaScript, CSS, and PHP, such as wrapping the code in comments, indenting the code, and so on.

- **Related Files.** Lists all external CSS, JavaScript, and server-side programming files the current page uses. Select one and you'll see the code for that file. Better yet, use the Related Files toolbar that appears in the document window—it's much faster.

- **Related Files Options.** Lets you filter the files displayed in the Related Files toolbar (page 332). For example, you can hide all Server-Side Includes, display just external CSS files, or create a custom filter to show files that match a certain pattern (like all PHP files that include *DB* in the file name). You'll find filters most useful for really complicated server-side programs (like WordPress, Joomla, or Drupal) that often overwhelm the Related Files toolbar with dozens of included PHP files.

- **Code Navigator.** Pops open the Code Navigator window so you can scan all CSS rules that apply to the current HTML element (see page 390).

■ Insert Menu

The Insert menu adds selected page elements to a document at the cursor's current position. The commands listed here correspond to the buttons on the Objects panel:

- **Div.** Opens the Insert Div dialog box, which lets you easily create a new <div> container, either around something you selected or anywhere on the page. This box helps you remember to give the div a class or ID, or to go ahead and create a new CSS rule.

- **HTML5 video.** Adds the <video controls></video> tags to your page's code so you can place a video at that point (see page 676).

- **Canvas.** Adds the tags for an empty canvas, with an ID of "canvas," to your page. The Canvas Properties panel opens, so you can size the new canvas.

- **Image.** Inserts an image file (such as a JPG, PNG, or GIF), a rollover image, or a Fireworks HTML file into the current document. The Select Image Source window appears so you can navigate to the file on your hard drive. You can choose to make the URL for the file relative to either the document or to the site root folder. For a rollover image, you need to choose two image files.

- **Table.** Inserts a new table into a document. The Table dialog box appears and lets you format the table by specifying the number of rows and columns; the table width; measurements for cell padding, cell spacing, and the table border; and whether (and where) to include table headers.

- **Head.** Lets you choose from four dialog boxes—Meta, Keywords, Description, and Viewport—that help you add the appropriate tags and content to the head section of your page. You type in the dialog box; Dreamweaver creates the code.

- **Script.** Lets you insert programming code.

- **Hyperlink.** Inserts a link. The Hyperlink dialog box lets you specify the label for the link, the link's address, as well as many other link options, such as the target window and tab index.

- **Email Link.** Creates a new email link at the insertion point. The Email Link dialog box appears; you specify both the email address and the link's label (such as "Click to email me").

- **Horizontal Rule.** Places an <hr> tag at the insertion point. This is a tricky one, especially in Code view, since there's no dialog box and no chance to click OK to confirm what you've just done. In Design view, a simple black line appears across the page, and the Properties panel opens so you can style the rule.

- **Date.** Inserts the current date into a document. The Insert Date dialog box lets you format the appearance of the day of the week, the date, and the time. You can also automatically update the date each time you save the document.

- **IFrame.** Creates an empty IFrame—an inline frame—at the insertion point. A frame is a self-contained HTML document inside your HTML document. You can use an IFrame to embed an ad, a Google map, or other content on your page.

- **Character.** This handy little submenu lets you insert common symbols, like ©, £, and even ". Also handles line breaks and non-breaking spaces.

- **Structure.** HTML forms the structure of a web page, and so the Structure submenu gives you a quick way to place various HTML elements—divs, lists, paragraphs, and so on—on your page.

- **Media.** Inserts media files including Edge Animate compositions, HTML5 video, HTML5 audio, Flash, Flash Video, and plug-ins. In most cases, the standard Select File window appears, which you can use to navigate to the desired file.

- **Form.** Inserts Form Objects—the <form> tag, text fields, buttons, checkboxes, or lists—into a document. (If you don't insert the <form> tag when you insert a form object, Dreamweaver prompts you to do so.)

- **jQuery Mobile.** Lets you insert code needed to build mobile applications using the jQuery Mobile JavaScript library. For example, you can embed specialized user interface elements, like a toggle switch. See page 521.

- **jQuery UI.** Offers a direct route to interactive objects from the jQuery user interface (UI) library, like buttons users can click or date pickers they can use to enter dates in a form.

- **Template.** When you work on template files, this menu lets you insert many of Dreamweaver's template features, such as Optional, Editable, and Repeating regions.

- **Favorites.** Opens the Customize Favorite Objects dialog box, where you can pick the items you use most often—divs, canvases, Flash videos, or most other items that appear the Insert menus. From then on, these items are just a click away in the Favorites section of the Insert panel.

- **Recent Snippets.** Lists the snippets you most recently inserted. Select a snippet from the list and Dreamweaver inserts it into the document. You'll see snippets discussed in Chapter 19.

■ Modify Menu

Commands in the Modify menu adjust the properties of common document objects, like links, tables, and layers:

- **Page Properties.** Opens the Page Properties window, where you can specify document-wide attributes—such as a page's title, background and link colors, margins, and background image—or select a tracing image to use as a reference for designing the page (page 757).

- **Template Properties.** Opens the Template Properties window, where you can modify settings for template features, like the visibility of optional regions, the properties of editable attributes, and the values of any template expressions you create. Available only when you work on template-based pages, as described in Chapter 20.

- **Manage Fonts.** Opens a dialog box of the same name, where you can choose the fonts you want to use on your websites. You can choose from the new-in-Creative-Cloud Adobe Edge Web Fonts, fonts stored on your computer, or custom font stacks (sets of fonts that work in most browsers). Once you choose a font in Manage Fonts, it will appear on the Font menu in the CSS properties panel so you can add it to a style. See page 127 for more about working with fonts.

- **Quick Tag Editor.** Lets you edit an HTML tag without leaving Design view. If you don't have anything selected on a page, the Quick Tag editor prompts you to enter a new HTML tag at the insertion point (by choosing from an alphabetical list). If you have text or an object already selected, the window displays the selection's tags so you can edit them.

- **Make Link.** Turns a highlighted page element (graphic or text) into a link. The standard Select File dialog box appears; choose the document you want a browser to open when someone clicks the link.

- **Remove Link.** This command is available only when you select a link or have the cursor positioned inside a link. Remove Link deletes hyperlinks by removing the <a> tag from the selected text or image.

- **Open Linked Page**. Opens the linked page in a new document window. This command is available only when you have a link selected or have the cursor positioned inside a link. (You can, however, hold down the Ctrl key [⌘] and double-click a link to open the linked page.)

- **Table**. Opens a list of options to modify a selected table. You can adjust the number of rows and columns, add row or column spans, or completely clear cells' defined heights and widths (see Chapter 6).

- **Image**. Opens a list of options to modify a selected image, including optimizing it in Fireworks or editing it with one of Dreamweaver's built-in image-editing features, such as the Crop, Resample, and Sharpen tools. See page 231 for more.

- **Arrange**. Lets you change the Z-index (the front-to-back order) of overlapping page elements. You can send one absolutely positioned element in front of another, send it to the back, and so on. You can also tell Dreamweaver to disallow overlapping elements altogether. If you select two or more absolutely positioned elements, you can choose from one of this menu's alignment options to align the components, like the tops of the two elements. See Chapter 10 for more on absolutely positioned elements.

- **Library**. Lets you add selected document objects to a site's Library folder (Chapter 19). You can also update the current document, or multiple documents, to reflect any changes you make to a Library object.

- **Templates**. These commands work with Dreamweaver's—or your own—templates (see Chapter 20). Using them, you can apply a preexisting template to the current page, separate the page from its template, or update the page to reflect changes you made to its template. If you have a template file open, you can create or delete editable regions (remove the template markup, in other words) and update all site files based on that template. You can also add repeating template regions and editable tag attributes.

Format Menu

The commands in this menu let you format and modify a document's text:

- **Indent**. In the case of bulleted or numbered lists, this option indents the selected list items to create a nested (indented) list (see page 85). For other HTML tags, this option wraps the element in a <blockquote> tag (an HTML tag used to represent a quotation). In cases where it's against the rules of HTML to wrap the selected tag in a <blockquote> tag—an HTML table, for example—this option simply inserts an empty <blockquote> tag (really, though, a better approach to indenting text is to use the CSS Margin property, as described on page 439).

- **Outdent**. Turns selected bulleted or numbered list items into paragraph tags; for nested list items, it removes the indent. If your cursor's within a <blockquote> tag, this option removes the blockquote.

- **Paragraph Format**. Applies a paragraph format, such as Heading 1, Heading 2, or preformatted text, to all the text in the current block-level element. You can also go to this menu's submenu and choose "None" to remove the paragraph formatting.

- **Align**. Aligns text in the selected paragraph to the left margin, center, or right margin of a document. If the paragraph sits inside a table cell or layer, Dreamweaver aligns it with the left, center, or right of that cell or layer. (The CSS text-align property [page 142] is a better option.)

- **List**. Turns the selected paragraph into an ordered, unordered, or definition list. You can edit the list's format by selecting the submenu's Properties option.

- **HTML Style**. Applies predefined text styles—such as bold, italic, or strikethrough—to the selected text.

- **CSS Styles**. Lets you apply CSS styles to selected text (Chapter 3). You can also choose to attach an existing style sheet to the current document, or use a Design-time style sheet (page 397).

■ Commands Menu

Use the Commands menu to apply advanced features to your Dreamweaver document. Some menu items, like the Record command, eliminate repetitive tasks; others, such as the Clean Up HTML command, fix common problems in a single sweep:

- **Start/Stop Recording**. Records a series of actions that you can apply to other parts of a document with a click of your mouse. When you select the Start Recording command, Dreamweaver records each of your actions until you choose Stop Recording. Note that Dreamweaver retains only one recorded command at a time.

- **Play Recorded Command**. Reapplies the most recently recorded command.

- **Edit Command List**. Opens a list of all custom commands. You can rename the commands, or delete them permanently.

- **Check Spelling**. Checks the current document for spelling errors (see page 97).

- **Apply Source Formatting**. Lets you apply Dreamweaver's formatting preferences to existing HTML and CSS documents. (Normally, changes you make to Dreamweaver's HTML source formatting, defined in the Preferences window and the *SourceFormat.txt* file, apply only to newly created documents.)

- **Apply Source Formatting to Selection**. Same as the previous command, Apply Source Formatting, but applies only to selected content. This command lets you selectively apply source formatting so you can, for example, make sure that Dreamweaver nicely formats a <table> element but leaves the rest of your finely crafted HTML alone. Works with CSS as well.

- **Clean Up HTML**. Opens a list of options to correct common HTML problems, such as empty tags or redundant nested tags. Once you select what you want to fix, Dreamweaver applies those changes to the current document, and, if requested, provides a log of the number and type of changes it made (see Chapter 17).

- **Clean Up Word HTML**. If you import HTML generated by Microsoft Word, you often end up with unnecessary or cluttered HTML tags that can affect your site's performance. This command opens a list of options that corrects common formatting problems in Word's HTML. Dreamweaver applies the selected changes to the document and, if requested, displays a log of the number and type of changes it made.

- **Clean Up Web Fonts Script Tag (Current Page)**. When you use the new Adobe Edge Web Fonts, Dreamweaver adds a bit of JavaScript to your page code. That JavaScript grabs the font from the Adobe server and delivers it to the browser. If you find that the font isn't working, this command attempts to fix the link to the server.

- **Externalize JavaScript**. Lets you take all the JavaScript code in a web page and dump it into an external JavaScript file. External files can make web pages download more quickly and let you reuse common JavaScript programs throughout your site.

- **Remove FLV Detection**. If you used Dreamweaver CS3 to add a Flash Movie and you then delete that movie, this command removes the JavaScript code left behind. Again, this only applies if you have old Flash video pages you created way back when, with Dreamweaver CS3.

- **Optimize Image**. Opens the selected image in the Image Preview window so you can experiment with different compression settings to find the best balance between file size and image quality. See page 251.

- **Sort Table**. Sorts the information in a selected table alphabetically or numerically, in ascending or descending order. You can't apply this command to tables that include *rowspans* or *colspans*.

■ Site Menu

As its name suggests, the commands in this menu apply to your entire website rather than single documents. These commands help keep your site organized and promote collaboration between large workgroups:

- **New Site**. Opens the Site Setup window, where you can set up a site to start working in Dreamweaver.

- **New Business Catalyst Site**. This command lets you set up a site to work with Adobe's Business Catalyst service (*www.businesscatalyst.com*). Business Catalyst is Adobe's web hosting company for businesses; it lets you build websites that support e-commerce, blogs, a customer management system, email newsletters, and so on.

- **Manage Sites**. Opens the Manage Sites panel where you can create, delete, or edit site definitions. See Chapter 16.

> **NOTE** The next five menu commands let you transfer files between your computer (the *local* site) and a web server (the *remote* site). These commands, in other words, don't work unless you first define a local and remote site in the Site Definition window. In addition, you have to download the files you want to work on by *selecting* them in the Site window (see below).

- **Get**. Copies files (those you select in the Site window) from the remote server to your local site folder so you can edit them. Note that if you have Dreamweaver's file Check In and Check Out feature active (see Check In and Check Out below), you can't edit the downloaded files if someone downloaded a copy before you did.

- **Check Out**. Copies files (those you select in the Site window) from the remote server to your local site, and marks them on the remote server as *checked out*. No one else can make changes to the document until you upload it back onto the remote server to check it back in.

- **Put**. Uploads files (those you select in the Site window) from your local site to the remote site. The uploaded files replace the previous version of the document.

- **Check In**. Uploads files you've checked out and copied to your local site back up to your remote site, and makes them available for others to edit. Once you check a file in, the version on your local site becomes read-only (you can open it, but you can't edit it).

- **Undo Check Out**. Removes the checked-out status of selected files. Dreamweaver doesn't upload the file back to the remote server, so any changes you made to the file locally aren't transmitted to the server. In addition, your local copy of the file becomes read-only.

- **Show Checked Out By**. Lets you see who's checked out a file.

- **Locate in Site**. When you select this option while working on a document, it opens the Site window and highlights that document's filename in the site's local folder.

> **NOTE** See Chapter 16 for the full scoop on local sites, remote sites, and checking files in and out.

- **Reports**. Opens the Reports window, and lists options for generating new reports (see Chapter 17). Reports can monitor pages (such as their Design Notes and check-out status) and highlight common HTML problems (such as missing Alt text, empty tags, and untitled documents). You can generate a report on an open document, multiple documents, or your entire site.

- **Site-Specific Code Hints**. This option, available only for PHP websites, lets you specify how code hints (the tooltips that pop up as you type code) work. This advanced feature is for serious PHP programmers.

- **Synchronize Sitewide**. Opens the Synchronization window, which lets you compare all your local files with the files on your web server. Use it to make sure you transfer all the files you update locally to your web server, or that you transfer all the site files on the server to your local site.

- **Check Links Sitewide**. Analyzes the current site for broken links, external links, and orphaned pages, and then generates a report of the problems it found. You can fix problematic links directly in the Report window—or click the filename to open the errant file in a new document window, with the link highlighted and ready to repair.

- **Change Link Sitewide**. Replaces a broken link throughout your site in one step. In the Change Link dialog box, you specify the incorrect link; below it, you enter the correct link. Dreamweaver searches your site, replacing every instance of the old link.

- **Advanced**. Provides access to advanced site options, such as the FTP Log—a record of all FTP file transfers; Recreate Site Cache, which forces Dreamweaver to rescan the site's files and update its cache to reflect any changes to the files or links in the site; and Remove Connection Scripts to remove the script files Dreamweaver creates to work with dynamic, database-driven websites.

- **PhoneGap Build Service**. PhoneGap is a free tool that makes creating mobile apps using HTML, CSS, and JavaScript easier. PhoneGap is an online service that can build apps for iOS, Android, WebOS, Blackberry, and other mobile devices (see the box on page 544 for more information).

■ Window Menu

This menu controls which panels and windows Dreamweaver displays or hides at the moment. A checkmark in the menu denotes open panels:

- **Insert**. Opens the Insert panel, from which you can insert various types of objects (such as images, layers, or forms) into your document. You get all of the same options as in the Insert menu (page 8).

- **Properties**. Opens the Property Inspector, where you can edit the properties for a selected object. The options in the Property Inspector depend on the page element you select.

- **CSS Designer**. Opens the CSS Designer panel, from which you can define and edit CSS styles and selectors, or apply existing styles to selected text.

- **CSS Transitions**. Opens the CSS Transitions panel, which lets you add, edit, and remove animated transitions between two different CSS styles. You can read about this window on page 397. Click the + sign in the panel to create a new transition.

- **Business Catalyst**. Opens the Business Catalyst panel. You need to sign up for Adobe's business web hosting service (*www.businesscatalyst.com*) for this panel to work. It lets you add code so you can work with sites that this commercial ($$$) web-hosting company manages.

- **Files**. Opens the Files panel. From this window, you can open any file, and transfer files between your computer and your remote server.

- **Assets**. Opens the Assets panel, which conveniently groups and lists all the assets (such as colors, links, scripts, graphics, library items, and templates) you use in your site.

- **Snippets**. Opens the Snippets panel, which contains reusable snippets of HTML, JavaScript, and other types of code. You can create your own snippets to save your fingers from retyping code you use often on a site.

- **jQuery Mobile Swatches**. Opens the jQuery Mobile Swatches window, which lets you apply different "themes" to jQuery Mobile page elements. This option works only with the jQuery mobile pages discussed on page 521.

- **Behaviors**. Opens the Behaviors panel, which lets you associate *behaviors* (such as swapping images on a mouse rollover or checking for necessary plug-ins) to selected page elements (see Chapter 13).

- **History**. Displays the History panel, a record of all the actions you took in working on the current document.

- **Code Inspector**. Opens a pop-up window that displays the HTML for the current document. It's different from plain Code view, since the code sits in a pop-up window. While you can edit the code directly in this window, it's often easier just to use Dreamweaver's Code view or Code and Design view (View→Code and Design).

- **Results**. Lets you open Dreamweaver's many site-wide tools, such as the Find and Replace, Link Checker, and Reports commands. Pick the operation of choice from the submenu.

- **Extensions.** This command gives you one sub-option—Adobe Exchange. It opens the Adobe Exchange window, where you can find and install miniprograms that add bells and whistles to Dreamweaver, as described on page 874. If you've never used it before, the window instructs you to launch the Creative Cloud application (you must be connected to the Internet) and update Dreamweaver.

- **Manage Extensions**. Opens the Extension Manager, a program that lets you manage extensions you download from Adobe Exchange. The Extension Manager helps you install, delete, and selectively disable extensions.

- **Workspace Layout**. Lets you choose preset layouts of panels and windows. You can also use this menu to save the position and size of Dreamweaver's current panels and windows setup. This command is your ticket to customizing your Dreamweaver work environment.

- **Hide Panels**. Closes all currently open panels. Choosing Show Panels reopens only those panels displayed before you selected Hide Panels.

- **Application Frame (Macs only)**. The Application Frame treats all of Dreamweaver's panels and windows as one big window (or frame). Grabbing the bottom right corner of the frame (usually the bottom-right corner of the Files panel) lets you resize the frame. Some people like this unified feel, others don't. If you don't like it, uncheck this option. When you do, all the windows and panels act as individual units you can resize independently of each other.

- **Application Bar (Macs only)**. Opens and closes the Application bar at the top of the screen. Generally the Application bar isn't that useful, as it takes up vertical space and offers shortcuts, like switching between Code view and Design view or setting up a new site, that are just as easy to do using other commands. On Macs, you can only turn off the Application bar if you also turn off the Application Frame.

- **Cascade**. This and the next two options let you "undock" the current documents so you have all open documents floating and resizable within the document area. (Normally, when you have multiple documents open, you switch from page to page by clicking tabs at the top of the document window.) The Cascade option resizes each open document and places them one on top of the other. Windows folks can re-dock pages by clicking the Maximize button on any currently open document. Mac people can select the Combine As Tabs option.

> **NOTE** If the Cascade command is grayed out, choose Window→Application Frame to free up the open documents. You can also unlock a document by dragging its tab out of the document window. You can then use the Cascade command to organize the windows.

- **Tile Horizontally** (Windows only). Places all open documents one on top of the other. The documents don't float on top of each other; rather, they fill the available document area as row upon row of thin, horizontal windows. With more than a few documents open, you see so little of each page that it's difficult to work on any one.

- **Tile Vertically** (Windows only). Just like the previous command, except that Dreamweaver positions the documents vertically, like stripes going down the screen.

- **Tile** (Mac Only). Has the same effect as Tile Vertically above.

- **Combine As Tabs** (Mac only). Returns either tiled or cascaded documents to the single, unified tab interface in the document window.

- **Next Document, Previous Document** (Mac only). This pair of commands let you step through all your open documents, bringing each one front-and-center in turn so you can edit it.

- **List of Currently Open Documents**. Lists all the documents currently open at the bottom of this menu. Selecting one brings it to the front so you can edit it. But with the document tabs atop the document window, why bother?

Help Menu

The Help menu offers useful links and reference documents that give you more information about using, troubleshooting, and extending Dreamweaver. For a full tour of Help resources, see Appendix A.

NOTE On a Mac, the topmost command on the Help menu is a Search field. But beware: This field searches only Mac help, not Dreamweaver help. To search Adobe's online help system, choose one of the following two commands and then type into the Search field on the right side of the web page.

- **Dreamweaver Help**. Launches the Dreamweaver Help and Tutorials page (page 905) in your desktop browser. You also arrive at this page when you click the "Dreamweaver CC manual (help and tutorials)" link in the "Help and tutorials" list at the upper-right of the Dreamweaver Help page (described next).

- **Dreamweaver Support Center**. Opens the main Dreamweaver Help page (page 904), which provides access to tutorials, videos, and troubleshooting tips. You can also get to this page by clicking the Resources link at the bottom of the Welcome screen.

- **Dreamweaver Exchange**. Launches your desktop browser and loads a page called Dreamweaver Exchange Classic on Adobe.com, where you can find extensions—add-on features—that add new capabilities to Dreamweaver. (See Chapter 21 for details on extensions).

NOTE Adobe has been updating its Exchange system. The Window→Extensions→Adobe Exchange command (page 874) launches the new system, where you can download extensions right from Dreamweaver's Adobe Exchange panel. At this writing, if you prefer, you can still gain access to the Dreamweaver CS6-style Exchange website in the Help menu.

- **Adobe Online Forums**. Opens an index of forums on Adobe's website. You can interact with other Adobe customers, post questions, share techniques, or answer questions posted by others. Requires Internet access and a newsgroup reader.

- **Complete/Update Adobe ID Profile**. Ever since Dreamweaver CS6, Adobe has required owners of the software to create an Adobe ID. This menu option lets you update your profile (if you want to change your email address or password, for example).

- **Sign Out**. Logs you out of your Adobe account under the email address shown. With some licenses, you can only use Dreamweaver CC on one computer at a time, and you must sign out of your current computer before you can launch the program on another one.

- **Updates**. Launches the Adobe updater. It finds updates for Dreamweaver (and every other Adobe product on your computer).

- **Adobe Product Improvement Program**. Opens a window that lets you participate in this Adobe project, which collects information about your use of Dreamweaver. According to Adobe, all the information is anonymous.

- **About Dreamweaver** (Windows only). Opens an About Dreamweaver window, showing your software's version number. (On the Mac, you'll find this command in the Dreamweaver menu.)

Index

Dreamweaver CC

THE MISSING CD

There's no CD with this book; you just saved $5.00.

Instead, every single Web address, practice file, and piece of downloadable software mentioned in this book is available at *missingmanuals.com* (click the Missing CD icon). There you'll find a tidy list of links, organized by chapter.

Don't miss a thing!
Sign up for the free Missing Manual email announcement list at missingmanuals.com. We'll let you know when we release new titles, make free sample chapters available, and update the features and articles on the Missing Manual website.